CENTRAL COMM COLL-HASTINGS CAMPUS
3 6508 02007 830

S0-CUQ-762

ENCYCLOPEDIA OF THE WORLD'S NATIONS

VOLUME I
(AFGHANISTAN TO GERMANY)

Editor

George Thomas Kurian

Contributors

Jakob Basista
John Baxter
Carol Ann Carroll
Robert Castle
Robert Clark
Kay Margaret Cronk
Jerilyn Famighetti
Slavic Gajevic
Steven Greenfield
Richard Hantula
Tseggai Isaac
Tom Lansford
Charles Mitchell
Solomon Nkiwane
Robert Quinlan
Anne Sanow
Jeffrey Schultz
Martin Schultz
Jim Talibi
Keti Vashakidze

ENCYCLOPEDIA OF THE WORLD'S NATIONS

VOLUME I
(AFGHANISTAN TO GERMANY)

GEORGE THOMAS KURIAN

Facts On File, Inc.

Encyclopedia of the World's Nations

Facts On File, Inc.
132 West 31st Street
New York NY 10001

Library of Congress Cataloging-in-Publication Data

Kurian, George Thomas.
The encyclopedia of the World's nations / George Thomas Kurian.
p. cm.
Contents: v. 1. Afghanistan to Germany—v. 2 Ghana to Pakistan—v. 3 Palau to Zimbabwe.
Includes bibliographical references (p.).
ISBN 0-8160-4139-3 (v. 1-3) ISBN 0-8160-5187-9 (v. 1)
1. Geography—Encyclopedias. 2. History—Encyclopedias. 3. Economics—Encyclopedias. 4. Political science—Encyclopedias. I. Title.
G63 K874 2001
903—dc21 2001040162

Facts On File books are available at special discounts when purchased in bulk quantities for businesses, associations, institutions, or sales promotions. Please call our Special Sales Department in New York at (212) 967-8800 or (800) 322-8755.

You can find Facts On File on the World Wide Web at http://www.factsonfile.com

Text design by Joan M. Toro

Cover design by Cathy Rincon

Illustrations by Jeremy Eagle, © Facts On File, Inc.

Printed in the United States of America

VB TB 10 9 8 7 6 5 4 3 2 1

This book is printed on acid-free paper.

Contents

Acknowledgments

I wish to thank the book's contributors, who are listed on another page. A special acknowledgment is due to Jeffrey D. Schultz, a dear friend and colleague, who has been the principal collaborator in this work. He has contributed 101 chapters to this book, and these chapters reflect his finely honed skills, his expertise in international affairs and editorial judgment. Jeff is the editor of five encyclopedias. The *Encyclopedia of the World's Nations* owes much to the dedicated work of the team at Facts On File. This is my 17th book with Facts On File, and I wish to both applaud their commitment to fine reference books and acknowledge the consistent support I have received over the years from them. Above all, I am grateful to my beloved wife, Annie, for her unfailing devotion and encouragement.

George Thomas Kurian

Introduction

Encyclopedia of the World's Nations is at once a new publication and an old one. It is descended from, incorporates, and continues the traditions of three major encyclopedias developed by George Thomas Kurian and published by Facts On File in the 1970s and 1980s: *The Encyclopedia of the Third World* (3 volumes), which went through four editions from 1978 to 1991; the *Encyclopedia of the First World* (2 volumes); and the *Encyclopedia of the Second World*, both published in the early 1990s. At the same time, it has been entirely rewritten (while retaining some of the more useful features of its progenitors) to reflect the emerging world in the new millennium. The original encyclopedias were published at a time when the divisions between the three worlds as they emerged after World War II were clearly demarcated and seemed set in concrete. The old divisions have not been abolished; there is still a developed or "first world," the "second" or Communist world (or at least its detritus), and, above all, a "third world" of poor and developing nations. But globalization is making these divisions less of a permanent divide than it was 20 years ago. More countries today are democratic than they were at any time in the past, and dictators are becoming an endangered species. National economies as well as societies are becoming more intertwined and interdependent so that it is difficult to describe one without reference to all. It was therefore necessary to combine all the three encyclopedias into one and also recalibrate the scope and reach of the new encyclopedia to capture the *Zeitgeist*, the spirit of the age. This effort makes the *Encyclopedia of the World's Nations* an entirely new work designed for the 21st century. It surveys 190 countries of the world, providing a broad range of information based on a standard classification system, accompanied by an equally broad array of statistical data. It was a difficult undertaking. The amount of information available on the 190 countries is so immense that it would take at least 15 volumes to treat each one fully. It was therefore necessary to condense the information to achieve a brevity that in the words of Lytton Strachey "excludes everything redundant and nothing that is significant." It was also difficult because despite globalization, every country has a separate and distinct identity that is sometimes lost when adopting a common template of information. Smaller countries, especially, sometimes get lost in the welter of details that have significance only for the larger ones.

The *Encyclopedia of the Third World*, the *Encyclopedia of the First World* and the *Encyclopedia of the Second World* together covered about 168 countries. The *Encyclopedia of the World's Nations* covers 190. The difference in numbers illustrates the dramatic increase in the roster of nations following the collapse of the Soviet Union and the breakup Yugoslavia. During the same period, two countries lost their separate existence when East and West Germany and South and North Yemen merged. Nevertheless, there are more countries today than at any time in human history. In fact, more countries were born in the 20th century than in any prior century. In 1901 there were only 47 sovereign nations in the world, and at the time the United Nations was founded in 1945, it had only less than 50 members. There is always the possibility that the number of nations will continue to grow, as a result of ethnic fissures and separatist forces, given the pattern of the 20th century. In any event, the world will continue to be buffeted and transformed in the 21st century by the collision of national interests and cultures. Such upheavals make it tempting to view the world as a moving target with shifting players and outcomes. But however dramatic the changes, there are always enduring themes and issues: geography, population, ethnic groups, religion, language, politics and government, economy, defense, education, law, and foreign policy. These constitute the focus of this book.

Encyclopedia of the World's Nations provides a compact, balanced, and objective description of the dominant political, economic, and social systems of 190 sovereign countries. It identifies and describes all major components and sectors of national life and presents them within a clearly defined hierarchical structure and in a consistent sequence. In this sense, the structure of the encyclopedia is as important as its contents. The most onerous task in the work was to achieve a reasonable degree of uniformity in the treatment, despite vast disparities in the amount and nature of the available information about each country. Every effort has been made in all sections to avoid subjective interpretations, whether partisan or analytical; evaluations of people or events are deliberately avoided or made only when absolutely necessary for an understanding of the data presented.

Notes and Information Classification System

Cutoff Date

The cutoff date for this edition is June 1, 2001, although more recent significant events, such as election results, are often included. Every attempt has been made to make the encyclopedia current as of that date. However, statistical data of earlier vintage are often used when such data are the only ones available. See the caveat on statistics below. Readers should be aware that addresses of websites change frequently; those listed in the encyclopedia were current as of press time.

Frequency of Publication

Encyclopedia of the World's Nations is planned as a triennial. Each edition of the encyclopedia will focus on the immediately preceding triennial period, but will also provide significant continuity in treatment of earlier information.

Dates

All years are calendar years unless noted as fiscal years, in which case a slash or virgule appears between the years. Inclusive years are noted with a hyphen, signifying the full period of the calendar years noted.

Spelling and Geographical Usage

Proper names and place-names are based on the style of *Webster's Geographical Dictionary* as well as recommendations of the United Nations and U.S. State Department.

Statistics

All statistics in the encyclopedia are derived from publications issued by principal international agencies, such as the United Nations, World Bank, the International Monetary Fund, and so on. The time lag between collection of data by these agencies and their eventual publication is reflected in the tables. This time lag may be as long as three years. Further, there are a number of countries where internal civil strife or external wars may make the collection of data impossible, and these countries are ignored by the collection agencies. As a result there are discontinuities in the publication of data and other breaks in time series. Further, there is the problem of incomparability between data published by different agencies that use different definitions, techniques of collection, and tools of analysis. Statistical data are therefore subject to numerous qualifications and are only intended to be used *cy pres*, or as approximations and estimates. They are, however, valid within limits and may be safely used as indicators of trends.

INFORMATION CLASSIFICATION

Information on each country has been arranged according to a standard, but not rigid, pattern. This classification system is central to this work and has been adhered to throughout except where the need for clarity of presentation or the nature or absence of information required modification in the scheme. The classification system has been devised not only for ease of consultation but also to provide a framework of comparison essential in international studies.

Each country chapter has 29 sections preceded by a Basic Data Sheet that encapsulates the most important data. Some sections have both text and tables; some have only text; and some have only tables.

1. Geographical Features	Text and Tables
2. Climate and Weather	Text and Table
3. Population	Tables Only
4. Ethnic Composition	Text Only
5. Languages	Text and Table
6. Religions	Text and Table
7. Historical Background	Text for All Countries from Earliest Historical Times
8. Constitution	Text and Organization Chart
9. Local Government	Text and Table
10. Parliament	Text
11. Political Parties	Text and List for Major Countries; List Only for Others
12. Legal System	Text
13. Law Enforcement	Table Only
14. Human Rights	Text
15. Foreign Policy	Text
16. Defense	Text and Table for Major Countries; Table Only for Others
17. Economy	Text and Tables
18. Education	Text and Table
19. Science and Technology	Table Only
20. Media	Text and Table
21. Culture	Table Only
22. Status of Women	Text and Table
23. Health, Food, and Nutrition	Tables Only
24. Environment	Text and Table
25. Chronology	
26. Bibliography	
27. Official Publications	
28. Contact Information	
29. Internet Resources	

Abbreviations

ADB African Development Bank
ADB Asian Development Bank
AID Agency for International Development
AIDS acquired immunodeficiency syndrome
AMF Arab Monetary Fund
ANCOM Andean Common Market
ASEAN Association of South East Asian Nations
b/d barrels per day
BIS Bank for International Settlements
BTN Brussels Tariff Nomenclature
CACM Central American Common Market
CARICOM Caribbean Community and Common Market
CFA Communauté Financière Africaine
CIS Commonwealth of Independent States
CPLAN Colombo Plan
DF Distrito Federal
DM Deutsche mark
EC European Community
ECA Economic Commission for Africa
ECE Economic Commission for Europe
ECLAC Economic Commission for Latin America and the Caribbean
ECOSOC Economic and Social Council (United Nations)
ECU European currency unit
ESCAP Economic and Social Commission for Asia and the Pacific
ESCWA Economic and Social Council for Western Asia
EU European Union
FAO Food and Agriculture Organization
Fr franc
GATT General Agreement on Tariffs and Trade
GDP Gross domestic product
GNP Gross national product
GRT Gross registered ton
ha hectare
IADB Inter-American Development Bank
IAEA International Atomic Energy Agency
IBE International Bureau of Education
IBRD International Bank for Reconstruction and Development (World Bank)
ICAO International Civil Aviation Organization
ICC International Chamber of Commerce
ICJ International Court of Justice
IDB Inter-Development Bank

IEA International Energy Agency
ILO International Labor Organization
IMCO Inter-Governmental Maritime Consultative Organization
IMF International Monetary Fund
INTELSAT International Telecommunications Satellite Organization
INTERPOL International Criminal Police Organization
Is Island(s)
ISIC International Standard Classification System
kg kilogram
km kilometer(s)
kWh kilowatt-hour
LAFTA Latin American Free Trade Organization
LDC least developed country
LNG liquefied natural gas
LPG liquefied petroleum gas
m meter(s)
MP Member of Parliament
MSA most seriously affected (country)
MU Metropolitan Units
NATO North Atlantic Treaty Organization
NMP net material product
OAPEC Organization of Arab Oil Exporting Countries
OAS Organization of American States
OAU Organization of African Unity
OCAM Organisation Commune Africaine et Mauricienne
OECD Organization for Economic Cooperation and Development
OPEC Organization of Petroleum Exporting Countries
PLO Palestine Liberation Organization
PRC People's Republic of China
ROK Republic of Korea
SDR special drawing rights
Sen. Senator
SPC South Pacific Commission
SUNFED Special United Nations Fund for Economic Development
TV television
UAE United Arab Emirates
UK United Kingdom
UN United Nations
UNCTAD United Nations Conference on Trade and Development
UNDP United Nations Development Program
UNEP United Nations Environment Program
UNESCO United Nations Economic, Scientific and Cultural Organization
UNFPA United Nations Fund for Population Activities
UNHCR United Nations High Commissioner for Refugees
UNHHSF United Nations Habitats and Human Settlements Foundation
UNICEF United Nations International Children's Emergency Fund
UNIDO United Nations Industrial Development Organization
UNITAR United Nations Institute for Training and Research
UPU Universal Postal Union
USA United States of America
VAT value added tax
WCC World Council of Churches
WFP World Food Program
WFTU World Federation of Trade Unions
WHO World Health Organization

ENCYCLOPEDIA OF THE WORLD'S NATIONS

VOLUME I
(AFGHANISTAN TO GERMANY)

AFGHANISTAN

BASIC FACT SHEET

OFFICIAL NAME:
Islamic State of Afghanistan (Dowlat-e-Eslami-ye Afghanestan)

ABBREVIATION:
AF

CAPITAL:
Kabul

HEAD OF STATE:

HEAD OF GOVERNMENT:
Interim Chairman Hamid Karzai (2001)

NATURE OF GOVERNMENT:
Unelected provisional government set up by Bonn Conference; includes representative leaders of various anti-Taliban warlords and ethnic factions.

POPULATION:
25,825,000 (1999)

AREA:
647,500 sq km (250,000 sq mi)

ETHNIC MAJORITY:
Pushtun

LANGUAGES:
Pushtu and Dari

RELIGION:
Sunni Islam

UNIT OF CURRENCY:
Afghani (Af.)

NATIONAL FLAG:
Three equal horizontal bands of (from top) green, white, and black with the national emblem centered on the three bands.

NATIONAL EMBLEM:
The emblem features a temple-like structure with Islamic inscriptions above and below, encircled by a wreath on the left and right and by a bolder Islamic inscription above, all of which are encircled by two crossed scimitars.

NATIONAL ANTHEM:
"So Long As There Is the Earth and the Heavens"

NATIONAL HOLIDAYS:
July 17 (National Day, Republic Day); May 27 (Independence Day); August 23–25 (Days of Jashn); August 31 (Pashtunistan Day); September 9 (National Assembly Foundation Day); October 15 (Ruz-e-Nejat); also variable Islamic festivals: Muharram, Muhammad's birthday, first day of Ramadan, Id-ul-Fitr

DATE OF INDEPENDENCE:
May 27, 1919

DATE OF CONSTITUTION:
None

GEOGRAPHICAL FEATURES

Afghanistan is a landlocked nation in Central Asia that covers an area of 647,500 sq km (250,000 sq mi), about the size of Texas. Afghanistan shares its total international frontier of 5,770 km (3,585 mi) with six neighbors: China (71 km; 44 mi), Pakistan (2,466 km; 1,532 mi), Iran (850 km; 528 mi), Tajikistan (1206 km; 749 mi), Turkmenistan (744 km; 462 mi), and Uzbekistan (137 km; 85 mi). The border with Pakistan, named the Durand Line, has been contested by Afghanistan since 1893, when it was drawn by the British Indian government. There are no other border disputes.

The capital is Kabul, with a 1993 estimated population of 700,000. The other major urban centers are Kandahar (237,500), Herat (186,800), and Mazar-i-Sharif (127,800).

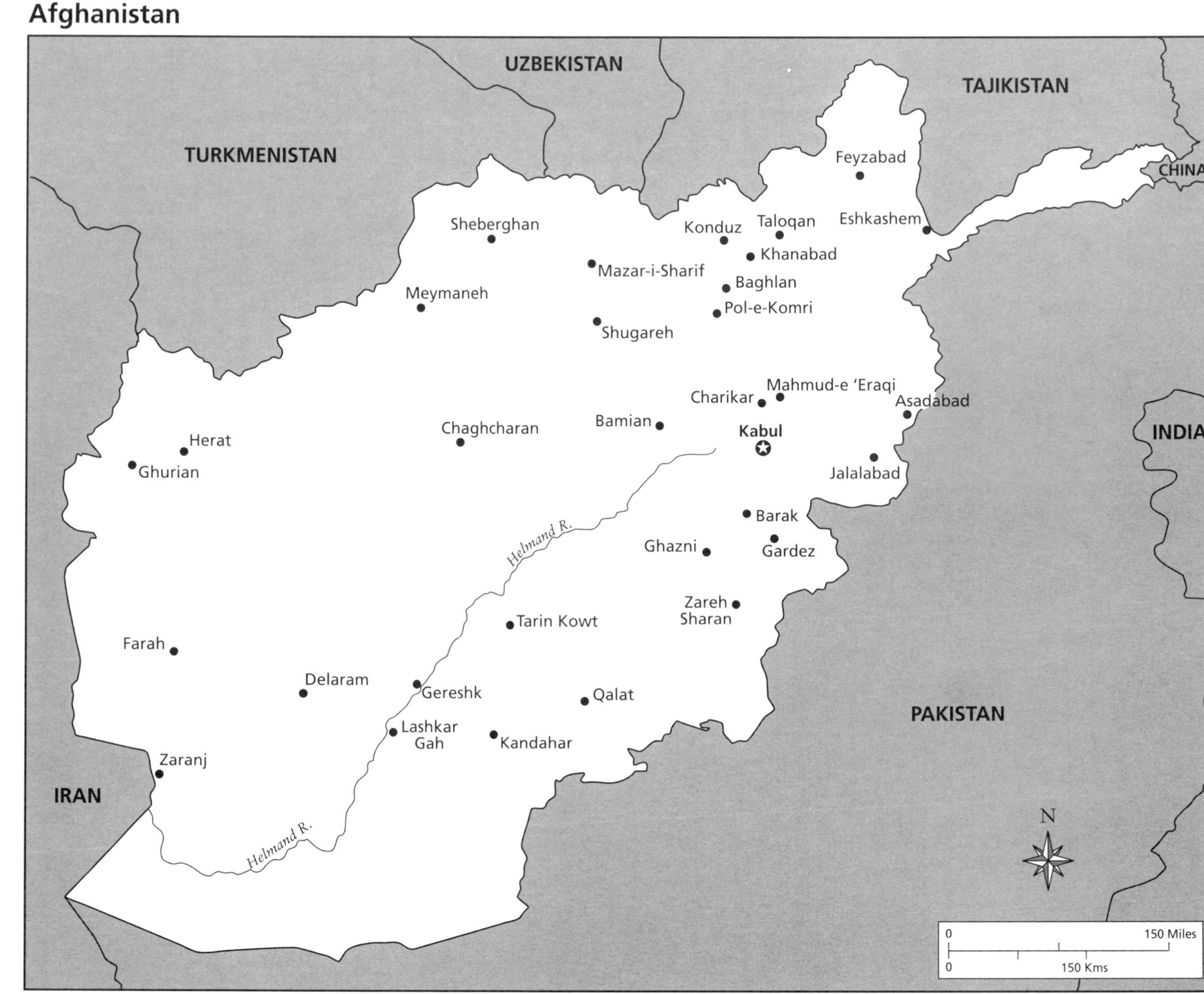
Afghanistan
UZBEKISTAN
TAJIKISTAN
TURKMENISTAN
CHINA
INDIA
PAKISTAN
IRAN
Feyzabad
Eshkashem
Konduz
Taloqan
Khanabad
Sheberghan
Mazar-i-Sharif
Baghlan
Pol-e-Komri
Meymaneh
Shugareh
Charikar
Mahmud-e 'Eraqi
Asadabad
Chaghcharan
Bamian
Kabul
Jalalabad
Herat
Ghurian
Helmand R.
Barak
Ghazni
Gardez
Zareh Sharan
Tarin Kowt
Farah
Delaram
Gereshk
Qalat
Lashkar Gah
Kandahar
Zaranj
N
0
150 Miles
0
150 Kms

There are three main geographic regions. The central highlands, parts of the Himalayan chain and that total approximately 416,398 sq km (160,771 sq mi), fan out from the Pamir Knot. Peaks on the main ridge, the Hindu Kush, rise above 6,400 m (21,000 ft), with passes up to about 4,600 m (15,000 ft). The northern plains, approximately 103,600 sq km (40,000 sq mi) in area with elevations of about 600 m (2,000 ft), are fertile and populous. The southwestern plateau is an arid zone of approximately 155,399 sq km (60,000 sq mi) with an altitude of about 900 m (3,000 ft). Three-fourths of the country's land area is covered by mountain ranges.

The principal rivers are the Amu Darya (1,250 km; 777 mi), which rises in the Hindu Kush and flows northwestward into the Sea of Aral; the largely unnavigable Kabul River (611 km; 380 mi), which joins the Indus at Attock in Pakistan; and the Helmand River (1,126 km; 700 mi), which flows into Hamun, an inland lake.

Geography

Area sq km: 647,500; sq mi 250,000
World Rank: 41st
Land Boundaries; km: China 76; Iran 936; Pakistan 2,430; Tajikistan 1,206; Turkmenistan 744; Uzbekistan 137
Coastline, km: 0
Elevation Extremes meters
- Lowest: Amu Darya 258
- Highest: Nuoshak 7,485

Land Use % Arable Land: 12
- Permanent Crops: 0
- Permanent Pastures: 46
- Forest and Woodland: 3
- Other: 39

Population of Principal Cities (early 1990s est.)

Herat	186,800
Kabul	700,000
Kandahar (Qandahar)	237,500
Mazar-i-Sharif	127,800

CLIMATE AND WEATHER

Afghanistan has a typical continental dry climate with seasonal extremes, marked differences between day and night temperatures, and rapid transition from one season to the next. The mean temperatures are 0.0°C (32°F) in January, 20°C (68°F) in May, 22°C (72°F) in July, and 10.6°C (51°F) in November. In the plains of Jallalabad summer temperatures of −26.1°C (−15°F) have been recorded in the higher plateau areas. The country suffers from the "Wind of 120 Days," which blows from June to September at velocities exceeding 177 kph (110 mph). Rainfall is scanty, nowhere more than 380 mm (15 in) annually. The rainy season extends from October to April.

Climate and Weather

Mean Temperature January 32°F
- May 68°F
- July 72°F
- November 51°F

Average Rainfall: 15 in

POPULATION

Population Indicators

Total Population: 1999 25,825,000
World Rank: 38th
Density per sq mi: 102.6 per sq km 39.6
% of annual growth (1994–99): 4.8
Male %: 51.4
Female %: 48.6
Urban %: 15.1
Age Distribution: % 0–14: 44.5
- 15–29: 26.9
- 30–44: 15.8
- 45–59: 8.6
- 60–74: 3.6
- 75 and over: 0.6

Population 2020: 43,050,000
Birth Rate per 1,000: 43.0
Death Rate per 1,000: 18.0
Population Doubling Time (years): 28
Infant Mortality Rate per 1,000 Live Births: 146.7
Rate of Natural Increase per 1,000: 25.0
Total Fertility Rate: 6.1
Expectation of Life (years): Males 46.4
- Females 45.2

Marriage Rate per 1,000: 6.2
Divorce Rate per 1,000: —
Total Number of Households: 2,110,000
Average Size of Households: 6.2
% of Illegitimate Children: —
Induced Abortions: —
- Rate per 100 live births: —

ETHNIC COMPOSITION

The Pushtuns, who are described as true Afghans, are the dominant ethnic group. The Pushtuns are divided into two major subtribes: the Durranis and the Ghilzais, who together make up 40 percent of the population. Most Pushtuns are Sunni Muslims. The Tajiks compose 30 percent of the population and live in northern Afghanistan. The mountain Tajiks are Shia, and the Plain Tajiks, or Farsiwans, are Sunni. The Hazara Mongols, who constitute the third-largest distinct ethnic group, live in the Bamyan region. They are believed to be descendants of the hordes of Genghis Khan and number nearly 1 million. The smaller ethnic groups include 800,000 Aimaks belonging to the Firuzkuhis, Taimanis, Jamshedis, and Taimuris tribes; 100,000 Baluchis; 200,000 Brahuis in the southwest; 200,000 Turkomans; 1,000,000 Uzbeks; 100,000 Nuristanis, formerly known as Kafirs; and 200,000 Qisilbashes, or Redheads. Among ethnic aliens are more than 20,000 Hindus and Sikhs and 10,000 Jews, most of whom are merchants or traders. Westerners are mostly transients.

LANGUAGES

The official national language is Pashtu, which is spoken by more than 13 million people. Dari (Farsi; Persian) is a second national language, spoken by the Tajiks and the Hazaras. It is the principal language of the administrative elite. More than 18 other languages and dialects are spoken in Afghanistan. Many of these languages are speech islands, reflecting Afghanistan's history and ethnic composition. They include Balochi, Nuristani, Kati, and three Turkic languages, South Turkic, Uzbek, and Kirghiz.

Both English and French are taught in Afghan schools as second languages.

Principal Languages and Their Speakers

Indo-Aryan languages	
Pashai	160,000
Iranian languages	
Balochi	240,000
Dari (Persian)	
Chahar Aimak	730,000
Hazāra	2,280,000
Tajik	5,270,000
Nuristani group	200,000
Pamir group	160,000
Pashto	13,530,000
Turkic languages	
Turkmen	500,000
Uzbek	2,280,000
Other	490,000

RELIGIONS

The religion of Afghanistan is Islam. About 84 percent of the Pushtuns, Tajiks, Uzbeks, and Turkomans belong to the Hanafite rite of the Sunni sect of Islam, 15 percent belong to the Shia sect, and 2 percent belong to the Ismaili sect.

Religious minorities include small communities of Hindus, Sikhs, Parsis, and Jews.

Non-Muslims are subject to legal and unwritten restrictions, and proselytizing by non-Muslims and even by the Muslim heretical sect of Ahmadiyas is prohibited. The Taliban regime is very intolerant of all religions other than Islam. This intolerance is expressed in a number of ways, such as the wanton destruction of historic statues of the Buddha in 2000 and the law requiring Hindus to wear distinguishing dress as a mark of humiliation.

Religious Affiliations

Sunni Muslim	21,690,000
Shia Muslim	3,870,000
Other	260,000

HISTORICAL BACKGROUND

The oldest elements of the present day Afghan population are the Tajiks, Pushtuns, and Nuristanis who came to the land during the eastward Aryan migrations in the second and first millennia B.C.E. The people who lived in the area before them were the Dravidians, as were most of the early inhabitants of the Indian subcontinent. About 600 B.C.E. the Aryan conquerors settled in the area around the city of Balkh in the north-central province of Mazar-i-Sharif. Northern Afghanistan, later known as Aryana or Bactria, first entered recorded history around 550 B.C.E. when it was incorporated into the Achaemenid Empire by its founder, Cyrus the Great. In 331 B.C.E. this empire fell to Alexander the Great. In the north, Hellenic cultural influences left behind by Alexander lasted for centuries, but in the south these remnants had to compete with the Indian culture and Buddhist religion introduced by Mauryan rulers. Most of Afghanistan was ruled during this period by feuding Greek satraps. From these satrapies arose the Greco-Bactrian kingdom (225–55 B.C.E.) whose greatest ruler, Demetrius, expanded its boundaries eastward into India about 187 B.C.E.

By the middle of the first century B.C.E. the Greek power had waned. Five nomadic tribes from Central Asia, called Yueh-chi by the Chinese, invaded Bactria. One of these tribes, the Kushans, gained supremacy and established a dynasty that dominated the Hindu Kush for nearly four centuries. Under their most famous king, Kanishka (c.110–162), the Kushans adopted the Mahayana form of Buddhism and took over what remained of the Graeco-Bactrian culture. The Kushan Empire was destroyed about 425 by the Ephthalites, or White Huns, a Mongol people. They, in turn, were dislodged by the Persian Sassanids in the seventh century.

In the seventh century, Islam reached Afghanistan, then known as Iranian Khorasan. After initial forays, the Arab general Yakub ibn Layth occupied Kabul, Herat, and Balkh. By the ninth century, Arabs had gained control of the region, ensuring the triumph of Islam.

In the mid-10th century, Alptagin, a former Turkish slave and commander in chief of the army of the Samanid dynasty (874–999) in eastern Persia gained control of the principality of Ghazni and founded the Ghaznivid dynasty (962–1140), the first great Islamic kingdom in Afghanistan. The most renowned of his successors was Mahmud of Ghazni (983–1030), nicknamed the "Destroyer of Idols," who led 17 predatory expeditions to India. A patron of arts and learning, he founded a university in Ghazni with the distinguished historian al-Biruni as its head. The empire lasted for some 125 years after Mahmud's death and it was supplanted by the rival principality of Ghorid, southeast of Herat, in the mountains of Ghor. The Ghorids ascended to prominence under Muizuddin, known also as Mohammad of Ghor, who established a permanent empire in India in 1192.

In the early 13th century, Mongols from the eastern plains of Central Asia swept through Afghanistan under Genghis Khan. Under the Il-Khans, as Genghis Khan's descendants were known, a local Tajik dynasty, called Karts, ruled over most of Afghanistan for two centuries until the rise of Timur (1336–1404), known to the West as Tamarlane. Timur's descendant, Babur, went on to establish the Mughal dynasty in India. Although Babur died in India, he was buried in his beloved city of Kabul.

For the next two centuries, Afghanistan was the bone of contention between the Sefavid rulers of Iran and the Mughal rulers of India. The conflict set a pattern of foreign rivalry and intervention that continued well into the 20th century. Northwest and southeast Afghanistan with Herat and Kandahar as centers lay in Iran's sphere of influence; the east with Kabul, Ghazni, and Jalalabad as centers lay within the Indian sphere. The Uzbeks held sway in the north outside these two spheres of influence. During this period, the Pushtun tribes, particularly the Abdali and Ghilzai, steadily increased in numbers and influence and spread from their original mountain habitat in the Sulaiman Range into the more fertile valleys of Kandahar, Zaminawar, and the Tarnak-Arghandab. Although fiercely independent, the Pushtun tribes retained a long tradition of internecine fighting, and both the Mughals and the Iranians played off one tribe against the other to advance their own interests. Thus the Abdali tribes near Kandahar were favored by the Iranian ruler Shah Abbas the Great who recognized Sado Khan, an Abdali, as chief. Sado's descendants, the Sadozai, rebelled against the Iranians after Shah Abbas II reconquered Kandahar in 1648. As the Sadozai lost Iranian support, the rival Ghilzai tribes became ascendant. Both the Ghilzai and the Abdalis were overpowered by Nadir Shah (1732–47), one of Iran's greatest monarchs, who captured Kabul and severed it from the Mughal Empire in 1738.

Ahmad Shah Sadozai, a chief of the Sadozai *kheyl* (lineage group) of the Abdali tribe, was one of Nadir Shah's commanders. When the shah was assassinated in 1747, Ahmad Khan marched to Kandahar with a contingent of troops and was elected by the chieftains as the ruler of all Afghans. In 1748 he made Kandahar his capital and took the title of Dur-i-Duran (Pearl of Pearls) and the throne name of Ahmed Shah Durani. Since then the Abdalis have been called the Durani and their leaders have held the title of *amir*, Arabic for chief. An able administrator, Ahmed Shah Durani forged a unified Afghan state based on the ascendancy of the Pushtuns. His son, Timur, moved his capital to Kabul, but after his death, the dynasty was weakened by the quarrels of his 23 sons over succession to the throne. The Sadozai power ended in 1818 with the revolt of the Mohammadazai *kheyl* of the Durani. The Mohammadazai leader Dost Mohammad Khan (1793–1863) declared himself amir in 1835.

It was during Dost Mohammad's reign that the country experienced its earliest contacts with European powers. The British, now well established in India, sought to contain Russian expansion into Afghanistan. For the next century, Anglo-Russian rivalry shaped Afghan history. The British invaded Afghanistan in 1838 in what became known as the First Afghan War (1838–42), the first of three wars. British troops took Kandahar and Kabul, drove Dost Mohammad north, and installed a Sadozai rival on the throne. The British occupation ended in 1842 in complete disaster as the Afghans massacred all but a few of the British troops. The British returned the same year to burn Kabul in retaliation and to restore Dost Mohammad to the throne. During the latter years of his rule, Dost Mohammad recovered Herat and Kandahar, and succeeded in unifying and pacifying the Afghans.

Sher Ali succeeded Dost Mohammad in 1863, but his relations with the British soon deteriorated. Sher Ali's refusal to allow entry to a British mission led to the Second Afghan War (1878–79) in which he was deposed in favor of his son, Yakub Khan (1879–80). Yakub Khan was later ousted and replaced by Abdur Rahman Khan, who was forced to accept the Treaty of Gandamak of 1879, which made the country a virtual British protectorate and mandated cession of the Khyber Pass to the British. The boundaries of Afghanistan were settled at this time. The Anglo-Russian Pact of 1895 established the border with Russia along the River Amu Darya. Two years earlier, Sir Mortimer Durand demarcated the Afghan border with British India along the so-called Durand Line, which cut Pushtun tribal areas in half.

Abdur Rahman Khan was the first modern ruler of Afghanistan who built the country's first standing army and police force and broke the independent power of the tribal chiefs. His policies were continued by his son Habibullah Khan, who introduced Western medicine and surgery, automobiles, telephones, and opened the first European school. The Anglo-Russian Convention of 1907 recognized Afghanistan as an independent buffer state. It remained neutral in World War I, although popular sympathies were with the Ottomans.

When Habibullah was assassinated in mysterious circumstances in 1919 the mantle of amir fell first on his brother, Nasrullah Khan, and later on his son, Amanullah Khan. Intensely anti-British, Amanullah Khan attacked the British forces, causing the Third Afghan War (May–August 1919). Although the British were victorious, they granted Afghanistan complete independence by the Treaty of Rawalpindi in 1919. Amanullah thereupon used his popularity as a hero who had wrested independence to launch a series of social and economic reforms, including the emancipation of women, prohibition of polygamy, compulsory education of both sexes, stipulation of Western dress as the national dress, and creation of the nation's first parliament. Outraged by the reforms, the mullahs (Muslim religious leaders) staged an open revolt and drove Amanullah out of the country. In 1929 the throne was seized by Sardar Mohammad Nadir Khan, who became amir under the name of Nadir Shah (1929–33). A pious Muslim, he abrogated the reforms of Amanullah and restored the power of the tribal chiefs.

Nadir Shah was assassinated in 1933 and was succeeded by his 19-year-old son Mohammad Zahir Shah. He inherited a state riven by factional and tribal conflicts, but he lasted for 40 years until 1973. Under the leadership of his cousin, Sardar Mohammad Daoud Kahn, who became prime minister in 1953, the nation began a series of economic plans for modernization with financial help from the Soviet Union. Daoud resigned in 1963 and was replaced by Mohammad Yusuf, who introduced a democratic constitution in 1964 that combined Western political ideas with traditional Islamic values. Parliamentary elections were held in 1965. Nevertheless, the king never permitted political parties to operate. In 1973, financial problems, recurrent famine, restiveness among the small middle class, and military impatience with civilian rule led to the overthrow of the monarchy. King Zahir was replaced by Daoud who took office as president, prime minister, and minister of foreign affairs and defense.

The national assembly, appointed from among notable elders by provincial governors, adopted a new constitution in 1977. It called for a presidential government and one-party rule. Daoud was elected to a six-year term as president, and military rule ended. Disaffection among the military culminated in a left-wing coup in April 1978, led by the deputy air force commander, Colonel Abdul Khadir. Daoud and members of his family were killed during the coup. A Revolutionary Council installed Nur Mohammad Taraki, imprisoned leader of the formerly banned People's Democratic Party of Afghanistan (PDPA), as president of the party and prime minister. The constitution was abolished, the nation was renamed the Democratic Republic of Afghanistan, and all parties except the communist PDPA were banned. Under Taraki, Afghanistan's already close ties with the Soviet Union were strengthened. Opposition to the new regime, led by Muslim tribesmen known collectively as the Mujahiddin, resulted in armed insurrection throughout the country. In March 1979, party hard-liner Hafizullah Amin took over the office of prime minister with Taraki remaining titular head of state. The Revolutionary Council designated Amin president in September. Amin's attempts to impose hard-line communist policies were widely unpopular and led to armed rebellion. In December 1979, he was killed in a coup supported by the introduction of 80,000 Soviet troops. Former deputy prime minister Babrak Karmal, who had been in exile in Eastern Europe, was flown into the country by the Soviets and installed as president. Karmal's regime won little acceptance from the Afghan people, and his government depended on the presence of Soviet troops—estimated at 110,000 in 1982—for survival. The Mujahiddin continued their rebellion from rural bases and supply camps in Pakistan.

In an attempt to broaden its support, the government convened the National Assembly in 1985. It immediately ratified a new constitution and endorsed the Soviet presence. Elections were held on the local level.

Unable to stop rebel fighting or generate domestic support, Karmal stepped down as general secretary of the PDPA in May 1986 and was replaced by Mohammad Najibullah. In November Karmal asked to be relieved of his other posts, including the presidency of the Revolutionary Council. He was succeeded by Haji Mohammad Chamkani. Najibullah was made president of the Republic of Afghanistan in 1987. That year political reforms were effected along with a cease-fire extension. In November a new constitution was ratified that permitted the formation of political parties. Najibullah also announced that he was prepared to share power with the opposition in a coalition government. In April 1988 a multiparty election was held with about one-fifth of the legislative seats left vacant in hope of Mujahideen occupation. In 1988 Afghanistan, the Soviet Union, Pakistan, and the United States came to agreement on the withdrawal of Soviet troops, which was completed in 1989. The rebel Mujaheddin continued hostilities, demanding the installation of an Islamic regime in Kabul and proclaiming a "free Muslim state." Factional infighting among the Mujahideen limited its military and political influence, although its military victories in 1990 and 1991 did compel Najibullah to propose a truce in May 1991, which the rebel leaders rejected.

With the fall of the Najibullah government in 1992 the seven-party alliance of Islamic groups based in Pakistan announced plans to set up an interim government, but soon the parties were embroiled in a virtual civil war. By 1992 more than 3,000 Afghans died in the fighting and over 700,000 fled Kabul. By 1994 Burhanuddin Rabbani and his defense minister, Ahmed Shah Masud, were in control of Kabul, although the rest of the country was in a state of anarchy. Disaffected theology students (Taliban) based in Pakistan banded together into a militant armed group and went on to capture Kandahar, the country's second largest city. Pakistan supported the Taliban with ammunition, fuel, and food. By 1996 the Taliban had captured Kabul after driving out Rabbani, and its members were in control of 21 out of 32 provinces. Taliban's opponents, mainly from the Tajik, Uzbek, Hazara, and Turkoman ethnic groups, retreated to the northeastern provinces. In 1997 the Taliban entered Mazar-i-Sharif, the largest town north of the Hindu Kush and stronghold of the Uzbek warlord Rashid Dostum. Dostum was ousted by his lieutenant, Malik Pahlawan, who managed to drive the Taliban out of Mazar. By 2000 the Taliban controlled about 75 percent of the country.

For a number of years the Taliban encouraged and offered asylum to a militant Islamic terrorist group called al-Qaeda (The Cell), led by a Saudi millionaire, Osama bin Laden. Al-Qaeda had cells and branches in more than 60 countries and was dedicated to waging a jihad against Christians and Jews, who were described as infidels and crusaders. The group was responsible for a number of terrorist attacks against the United States in the 1990s, including the World Trade Center bombing in 1993, the bombing of the U.S. embassies in Tanzania and Kenya, and a sneak attack against the U.S. destroyer *Cole* while docked in Aden harbor. Emboldened by apparent U.S. failure to respond adequately to these attacks, al-Qaeda struck again on September 11, 2001. Four groups of 19 suicide bombers hijacked four U.S. passenger planes; two of them were flown into the World Trade Center in New York City and one into the Pentagon in Washington, D.C., and the fourth crashed in Pennsylvania as a result of an apparent scuffle between the hijackers and the passengers. The twin towers of the World Trade Center, New York's tallest buildings, collapsed in the attack, resulting in the deaths of nearly 3,000 persons of all nationalities; the Pentagon was severely damaged, with more than 100 persons killed. It was the worst attack on the United States since Pearl Harbor, 1941.

The United States responded decisively and quickly. The Bush administration put together an antiterrorism coalition of nations, including Pakistan, Russia, India, Uzbekistan, Tajikistan, and other neighboring nations. It demanded that the Taliban government in Kabul hand over bin Laden and his top lieutenants and also destroy terrorist training camps in Afghanistan. When the Taliban government failed to comply, the coalition forces, led by the United States and Great Britain, launched in the first week of October a massive air assault on Afghan military installations and al-Qaeda training camps. The coalition also supported the Northern Alliance, still in power near the Uzbek and Tajik borders, to regroup and resume their campaign against the Taliban. The Northern Alliance managed to break Taliban resistance and recapture Mazar-i-Sharif, the northern city, and also Kabul, the capital, in November. Kandahar, the last remaining Taliban stronghold, fell in December. In the same month, a conference of all non-Taliban Afghan factions was convened in Bonn, Germany. The conference set up an interim government for the next six months, to be led by a respected Pushtun leader, Hamid Karzai. However, the warlords are still in power in the various provinces, and the important ministries of defense, foreign affairs, and internal affairs are assigned to non-Pushtun Northern Alliance leaders. Although the war against the Taliban was virtually won by the end of 2001, neither Mullah Muhammad Omar, the former Taliban head of state, nor Osama bin Laden had been captured, and pockets of resistance continued to hamper the pacification of the country.

CONSTITUTION

The last constitution of Afghanistan was promulgated in 1990 after the withdrawal of Soviet forces. The new multiparty Islamic-oriented constitution amended the constitution of 1987, which had reaffirmed Afghanistan's nonaligned status, strengthened the post of president, and permitted other parties to participate in government. When the Taliban took control in 1996, the constitution was suspended. The current government of Afghanistan is a transitional one, set up by a conference held in Bonn, Germany, in December 2001 by four non-Taliban factions. It includes 30 representatives of various ethnic factions and is to be replaced with a permanent government by June 2002.

LOCAL GOVERNMENT

Afghanistan is divided into 30 provinces, each under an appointed governor.

Local Government

Principal administrative divisions, area, population

AREA AND POPULATION

	area		population 1993
Regions	**sq mi**	**sq km**	**estimate**
Central	11,657	30,192	3,481,400
East	9,802	25,386	1,567,500
East-central	21,739	56,304	685,000

(*continued*)

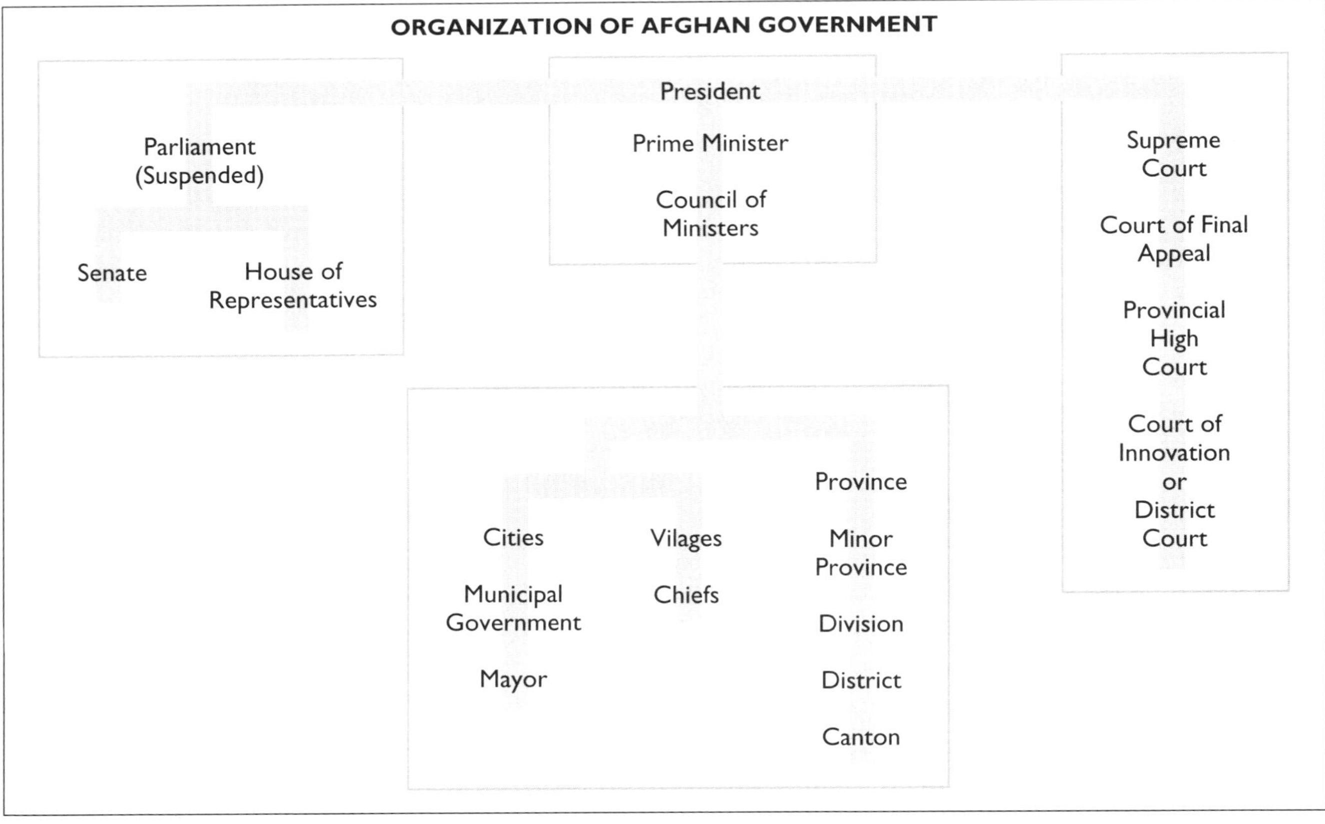

North	29,520	76,457	2,421,900
Northeast	30,233	78,304	2,518,300
South	19,525	50,569	1,659,600
Southwest	77,000	199,430	2,188,700
West	46,187	119,624	1,497,500
TOTAL	251,825	625,225	16,020,500

PARLIAMENT

Not applicable.

POLITICAL PARTIES

Not applicable.

Political Parties (Former)

United National Islamic Front for the Salvation of Afghanistan, 1997, consisting of the Tajik-controlled Islamic Afghan Society, National Front, and the Islamic Party.

Islamic Unity Party, 1987, representing the Hazara Shiites and consisting of the following Iran-based parties:
- Afghan Nasr Organization,
- Da'wa Party of Islamic Unity of Afghanistan,
- Guardians of the Islamic Jihad of Afghanistan,
- Islamic Force of Afghanistan,
- Islamic Movement of Afghanistan,
- Islamic Struggle for Afghanistan

United Islamic Front of Afghanistan
National Islamic Front
Islamic Party-Khalis
Islamic Unity
Islamic Revolutionary Movement
National Liberation Front
Homeland Party

LEGAL SYSTEM

Not applicable.

LAW ENFORCEMENT

Law Enforcement

Offenses reported to the police per 100,000:
- Murder: —
- Assault: —
- Burglary: —
- Automobile Theft: —
- Population per police officer: 540

Death Penalty: Yes.

HUMAN RIGHTS

In terms of civil and political rights, Afghanistan is classified as a country that is not free. It is a country torn by civil war, depleted of manpower by the flight of thousands of refugees, and isolated from its neighbors.

FOREIGN POLICY

Under the Taliban regime, Afghanistan turned inward, so it may be years before the country is able to reestablish itself as a member of the international community. The interim government of Hamid Karzai is apparently aligned with the United States if only because of the coalition military presence in the country and the dire need for Western financial aid. The Northen Alliance, which has a strong representation in the cabinet, has strong ties with Russia. Pakistan's influence over Afghanistan is likely to diminish under the arrangements set up by the Bonn Conference.

DEFENSE

Military organization disintegrated after 1992 with the fall of Najubullah's government. Much of the advanced equipment, including combat aircraft and helicopters, have fallen into a state of disrepair.

Military Indicators

Total Active Duty Personnel:
Military Manpower per 1,000:
Military Expenditures $: 408 million
- as % of GNP: 9.1
- per capita $: 24
- as % of central government expenditures: 64.4

Arms Imports $: 20 million
Arms Exports $: 0

ECONOMY

Afghanistan is an extremely poor, landlocked country, highly dependent on farming and livestock raising (sheep and goats). Economic considerations have played second fiddle to political and military upheavals during two decades of war, including the nearly 10-year Soviet military occupation (which ended February 15, 1989). During that conflict one-third of the population fled the country, with Pakistan and Iran sheltering a combined peak of more than 6 million refugees. In early 2000, 2 million Afghan refugees remained in Pakistan and about 1.4 million in Iran. Gross domestic product has fallen substantially over the past 20 years because of the loss of labor and capital and the disruption of trade and transport. The majority of the population continues to suffer from insufficient food, clothing, housing, and medical care. Inflation remains a serious problem throughout the country. International aid can deal with only a fraction of the humanitarian problem, let alone promote economic development. The economic situation did not improve in 1998–2000, as internal civil strife continued, hampering both domestic economic policies and international aid efforts. Numerical data are likely to be either unavailable or unreliable. Afghanistan was by far the largest producer of opium poppies in 2000, and narcotics trafficking is a major source of revenue.

Principal Economic Indicators

Gross National Product: $5.666 billion
GNP per capita: $250
GNP Average Annual Growth Rate (1990–97) %: —
GNP per capita Average Annual Growth Rate (1990–97) %: —
Origin of Gross Domestic Product %
- Agriculture: 48
- Mining: —
- Manufacturing: 26
- Construction: 10
- Public Utilities: —
- Transportation and Communications: 4
- Trade: 10
- Financial Services: 2
- Other Services: 2
- Government: 2

Gross Domestic Product by Type of Expenditure %
- Private Consumption: —
- Government Consumption: —
- Gross Domestic Investment: —
- Foreign Trade: Exports: —
- Imports: —

% of Income Received by Poorest 20%: —
% of Income Received by Richest 10%: —

Price and earnings indexes (1990 = 100)

	1988	1989	1990	1991	1992	1993	1994
Consumer price index	64.3	83.1	100.0	266.0	420.8	563.9	676.7

Finance

National Currency: Afghani (Af)
Exchange Rate: $1 = Af 17,000
Money Supply Stock in National Currency billion: —
M1 per capita: —
Central Bank Discount Rate %: —
Total External Debt $thousand: 2,300
Debt Service Ratio %: —

Balance of Payments $million: —
International Reserves SDRs million: —
Ratio of External Debt to Total Reserves: —

Average Annual Rate of Inflation/Consumer Price Index Growth Rate %: 240

Official Development Assistance

ODA: —
as % of GNP: —
per capita: $—
Foreign Direct Investment $million: —

Central Government Revenues and Expenditures

Fiscal Year: 21 March–20 March

Revenues $million: —
Expenditures $million: —
Budget Deficit/Surplus $: —
Tax Revenues as % of GDP: —
Highest Tax Bracket %
Individual: —
Corporate: —

Employment and Labor

Economically Active Population: 3,941,000
Female Participation Rate %: 7.9
Activity Rate %: 30.3
Labor by Sector: %
Agriculture, Forestry, Fishing: 60.1
Manufacturing, Mining: 12.5
Construction: 1.3
Transportation and Communications: 1.6
Trade, Hotels, and Restaurants: 3.5
Finance, Insurance, Real Estate: —
Public Administration, Defense: —
Services: 19.0

Unemployment %: 8

Agriculture

Agriculture's Share of GDP %: 48
Average Annual Rate of Growth (1965–98) %: —
Number of Farms 000: 126
Average Size of Farm ha: 3.5
Number of Tractors per 1,000 hectares: 0.1
Irrigation, % of Farms having: 35
Artificial Fertilizer kg/hectare: 7
Total Farm land as % of land area: 58.4
Livestock: Cattle 000: 1,500
Sheep 000: 14,300
Hogs 000: —
Chickens 000: 7,200
Forests: Production of Roundwood (000 cubic meters): 7,680
Fisheries: Total Catch tons: 1.3

Mining

% of GDP: —
Value of Mineral Production $million: 16.2

Manufacturing

Value Added $million: 435
Industrial Production Growth Rate %: —

Energy

Commercial Energy Production metric tons of oil equivalent 000: —
Commercial Energy Consumption metric tons of oil equivalent 000: —
Commercial Energy Consumption per capita kg: —
Average Annual Growth Rate 1980–97%: —
Net Energy Imports % of use: —
Electricity Installed Capacity kW 000: 494
Production kW-hr million: 625
Coal Reserves tons million: 66
Production tons 000: 5
Natural Gas Proven Reserves cubic meters billion: 99
Production cubic meters million: 294
Crude Petroleum Reserves barrels million: —
Production barrels million: —
Consumption barrels million: —
Refinery Capacity barrels per day 000: —
Pipelines Length km: —

Foreign Trade

Imports $million: 936.4
Exports $million: 235.1
Export Volume % Annual Growth Rate (1990–97): —
Import Volume % Annual Growth Rate (1990–97): —
Balance of Trade $

Balance of trade (current prices)

	1992	1993	1994	1995	1996	1997
U.S. $000,000	−217	+263	−263	−197	−495	−376
% of total	37.5%	23.6%	55.6%	37.2%	66.3%	55.3%

Major Trading Partners

	Imports	Exports
European Union %	4.8	7.3
United States %	0.2	0.5
Eastern Europe %	59.9	70.2
Japan %	7.9	0.3
Others %	27.2	21.8

Transportation

Roads Total Length mi: 13,000 km 21,000
Paved %: 13
Automobiles: 31,000
Trucks and Buses: 34,000
Persons per vehicle: 332
Railroad; Track Length mi: 16 km: 25

Passenger-mi million: 25
Freight-mi million: —
Merchant Marine: No of Vessels: —
Total Deadweight Tonnage 000: —
International Cargo Loaded tons 000: —
International Cargo Off-loaded tons 000: —
Airports with Scheduled Flights: 3
Traffic: Passenger-mi million: 122
Freight-mi million: 7.5
Length of Canals mi: 750 km 1,200

Tourism

Number of Tourists to 000: —
Number of Tourists from 000: —
Tourist Receipts $million: 1
Tourist Expenditures $million: 1

Communications

Telephones 000: —
Cost of Local Calls 3 mins $0: —
Cellular Telephones 000: —
Fax Machines 000: —
Personal Computers 000: —
Internet Hosts per million persons: 352
Mail: Post Offices: 352
Pieces of Mail Handled million: —
Pieces of Mail Handled per person: —

EDUCATION

Afghanistan has one of the lowest literacy rates in the world, with only 31.5 percent of its population literate (males 47.2 percent and females 15 percent).

Until civil war broke out in 1989, schooling was free and compulsory for eight years, from ages seven to 15. Elementary education consisted of eight years and secondary school of four years. From 1981 to 1986, the enrollment in primary and secondary school dropped from 29 percent of school-age population to less than half that number. Outside of Kabul, most education was limited to just the elementary years. In 1986 only 6 percent of children in the secondary school-age group were in attendance and that figure has dropped. In both primary and secondary schools, attendance by female students was significantly below that of males.

Twenty years of war have had a drastic impact on education. Most rural schools were destroyed by the resistance when the Soviet-backed regime attempted to turn them into political indoctrination centers. Many others were closed because of the danger of regime teachers. Formal education even in major cities, such as Kandahar, had been brought to a virtual standstill as a result of daily firefights. In 1995, there were five universities in operation. The oldest and largest is the University of Kabul (Pohantoon), founded in 1946. It has nine faculties. The University of Nangargarth at Jallalabad has only a faculty of medicine.

The Taliban further eroded educational standards by barring women, who form a majority of Afghan teachers, from work and education. With the fall of the Taliban and the installment of a transitional government in December 2001, schools reopened for girls, and female teachers returned to work.

Education

Literacy Rate %: 31.5
Male %: 47.2
Female %: 15.0
First Level: Primary schools: 1,753
Teachers: 20,055
Students: 1,312,197
Student-Teacher Ratio: —
Net Enrollment Ratio: 29
Second Level: Secondary Schools:
(included in First Level) 819
Teachers: 17,548
Students: 512,815
Student-Teacher Ratio: —
Net Enrollment Ratio: —

Vocational Level: Schools: 33
Students: —

Third Level: Institutions: 5
Teachers: 444
Students: 9,367
Student-Ratio Level: 21.1
Gross Enrollment Ratio: 1.8
Students per 100,000: 165
% of Population Age 25 and over with Postsecondary Education: —

Public Expenditure on Education as % of GDP: —

SCIENCE AND TECHNOLOGY

Science and Technology

Scientists and Engineers in R&D per 1 million persons: —
Expenditures in R&D as % of GDP: —
High-Tech Exports $: —
Patent Applications by Residents: —

MEDIA

The media in all its forms (radio, television, and newsprint) is controlled by the government.

Media

Daily Newspapers: 15
- Total Circulation 000: 216
- Circulation per 1,000: 4

Books Published: —
Magazines: —
Radio Receivers 000: —
- per 1,000: —

Television sets 000: 180
- per 1,000: 10

MOST IMPORTANT MEDIA:

Press. The following were government dailies published at Kabul prior to the formation of the Islamic Republic: *Haqiqat-i-Inqilab-i-Sawr* (Truth of the April Revolution, 50,000), in Pushtu and Dari; *Watan* organ founded 1980; *Anis* (Friendship, 25,000), in Pushtu and Dari; *Kabul New Times* (formerly *Kabul Times,* 5,000), in English.

News agencies. The official domestic facility is the Bakhtar News Agency.

Radio and television. Prior to 1996 Radio Afghanistan broadcast domestically in Pushtu, Dari, Uzbeki, Nuristani, Turkmani, and Baluchi. Following the Taliban takeover of Kabul, the facility was renamed the Voice of Shari'a. Television Afghanistan broadcasts over one station at Kabul.

CULTURE

Cultural Indicators

Public Libraries
- Number: 55
- Volumes: 350,000
- Registered borrowers: 11,331

Museums
- Number: 7
- Annual Attendance: 7,000

Cinema
- Production of Long Films: 3
- Number of Cinemas: —
- Seating Capacity: —
- Annual Attendance: —
- Annual Attendance per capita: —

STATUS OF WOMEN

The establishment of a strict fundamentalist Islamic regime has meant a loss of rights for women. Under prior governments, women were, in theory, equal to men in their right to vote and to receive an education. However, these advancements no longer exist. Decrees by the Taliban government in 1996 banned girls and women attending school, work, and other places outside the home without a male relative. In fact, reports indicate that women are regularly beaten if they attempt to work outside the home. The regime has become one of the most repressive in terms of the status of women. Violating Taliban decrees can result in beating, stoning, and death. In June 2001, a ban was put in place restricting foreign women from driving in Afghanistan.

The new transitional government, in place since December 2001, includes two women. Sima Samar was elected minister of women's affairs, and independent candidate Suhaila Seddiqi, minister of public health.

Women

Gender Empowerment Measure: —
Seats Held in Parliament by Women %: —
Female Administrators and Managers %: —
Female Professional and Technical Workers %: —
Women's Share of Earned Income %: —
Women in Government %: 0.1

HEALTH, FOOD, AND NUTRITION

Health

Number of Physicians: 2,233
Number of Dentists: 267
Number of Nurses: 1,451
Number of Pharmacists: 510
Population per Physician: 6,701
Number of Hospitals: —
Hospital Beds per 10,000: 3
Hospital Bed Occupancy Rate: —
Infant Mortality Rate per 1,000 live births: 248
Maternal Mortality Rate per 100,000 live births: —
Total Health Expenditures as % of GDP: —
Health Expenditures per capita $: —
HIV Infected % of adults: —
Cigarette Consumption per smoker per year: —
% of Smokers: Male: —
Female: —
Access to Safe Water %: 10

Food and Nutrition

Food Supply as % of FAO Requirements: —
% of Consumption Expenditures on Food: 33.9
Daily Available Calories per capita: —
% of Total Calories Derived From:
Cereals: —
Potatoes, cassava: —
Meat, poultry: —
Fish: —
Eggs, milk: —
Fruits, vegetables: —
Fats, oils: —

ENVIRONMENT

A long civil war and continuing political chaos in the country leave Afghanistan in a difficult situation environmentally. With less than 3 percent of their territory covered with trees in 1993, Afghanis have continued to cut forests for fuel and shelter at an alarming rate. Much of the land that was productive prior to the more than 20 years of fighting has been generally devastated by the war and its aftermath, including the continuing existence of many land mines.

Environment

Forest Area sq km: —
Average Annual Deforestation sq km: —
Nationally Protected Areas as % of Total Land Area: —
Freshwater Access cubic meters per capita: —
Emissions of Organic Water Pollutants kg per day: —
CO_2 Emissions per capita ton: —

CHRONOLOGY

1946 Shah Mahmud succeeds Mohammad Hashim Khan as prime minister.
Afghanistan is admitted to the United Nations.
1947 Afghanistan votes against the admission of Pakistan to the United Nations.
1948 Border pact is concluded with the Soviet Union.
1949 First free elections are held.
1950 Border clashes with Pakistan intensify conflict over Pushtunistan issue.
1951 United States halts economic aid to Afghanistan.
1953 Afghanistan establishes diplomatic relations with the People's Republic of China.
Daoud's policy leads to a crisis in diplomatic relations with Pakistan; the Soviet Union backs Afghanistan; anti-Pakistan riots occur in Kabul.
1956 Earthquake kills over 2,000.
Arms pacts with the USSR and Czechoslovakia are concluded.
1958 Transit treaty is concluded with Pakistan.
1959 Afghanistan signs aid pact with the USSR.
President Eisenhower visits Kabul.
1961 Afghanistan cuts diplomatic relations with Pakistan.
1962 Afghanistan reopens border with Pakistan to permit transshipment of U.S. aid materials.
1963 King dismisses Prime Minister Daoud; Mohammad Yusuf is appointed prime minister.
Diplomatic relations with Pakistan are resumed.
1964 New constitution is promulgated.
1965 Mohammad Hashim Maiwandwal succeeds Yusuf as prime minister.
All adults over age 21, including women, are enfranchised under new constitution.
1967 Supreme Court is established.
Nur Ahmad Etemadi replaces Maiwandwal as prime minister.
1969 Demonstrations by university and school students lead to suspension of the educational system.
1971 Etemadi resigns in face of growing criticism; Abdul Zahir takes over as prime minister.
1972 Widespread grain shortage and famine leads to deaths of tens of thousands.
Mohammad Musa Shafiq replaces Zahir as prime minister.
1973 An army coup d'état led by former prime minister Mohammad Daoud deposes Zahir Shah; loyal army general Abdul Ali Shah is executed; Daoud is elected president and prime minister of new Republic of Afghanistan by Central Committee; King Zahir abdicates.
1974 Conflict with Pakistan over Pushtunistan issue is renewed.
1975 Daoud announces general amnesty to plotters in 1973 conspiracy, including former prime minister Mohammad Musa Shafiq.
1977 Planning Minister Ahmad Khoram is assassinated in Kabul; one suspect is arrested.
1978 Daoud is overthrown in coup led by Khalq leader Nur Mohammad Taraki. The 1977 constitution is abolished; Afghanistan and the Soviet Union sign 20-year treaty of friendship and cooperation; heavy fighting is reported between Muslim rebels and government troops along the Pakistani border.
1979 U.S. ambassador Adolph Dubs is shot and killed in Kabul after being abducted by Muslim extremists.
President Taraki is ousted and killed in a coup.
Revolutionary Council names Hafizullah Amin as president; Amin is ousted in a second coup and executed for crimes against the state.
Deputy Prime Minister Babrak Karmal, a pro-Moscow hard-liner, is installed as president.
Citing an invitation by the Afghan government, the Soviet Union pours 30,000 troops across the border into Afghanistan.
Open fighting is reported between Soviet forces and Afghan rebels.
1980 An estimated 800,000 Afghans cross into Pakistan.
Heavy clashes between Soviets and rebels are reported.
Afghanistan is suspended from the Conference of Islamic States.
1982 The first congress of the ruling People's Democratic Party of Afghanistan calls for a purge of the Khalq dissidents and seizure of the estates of rich landowners.
1985 The Loya Jigah (National Assembly) ratifies a new constitution. Elections are held through March/

April 1986 for local organs with 60 percent of those elected not affiliated with the People's Democratic Party of Afghanistan (PDPA).

1986 Dr. Najibullah, former head of Khad, replaces Karmal as leader of the PDPA. The PDPA declares a unilateral cease-fire for six months, which is subsequently extended. However, the Mujaheddin alliances refused to honor the cease-fire or negotiate, demanding an unconditional Soviet withdrawal.

1987 The NFF is renamed the National Front (NF) and becomes a separate organization from the PDPA. Other political parties are allowed to form under the auspices of the NF. Najibullah proposes sharing power with representatives of the opposition groups if a coalition is formed. A draft of a new constitution is approved by the presidium of the Revolutionary Council. Further local elections are held throughout the country with many non-PDPA members being elected. Najibullah is unanimously reappointed president by the Loya Jirgah.

1988 The Soviets begin withdrawal of troops based on accords signed in Geneva in April. Direct talks begin for the first time between the Soviets and Mujaheddin in Pakistan. The Soviet insistence on a continued role for the PDPA caused a breakdown in negotiations.

1989 A state of emergency is declared by Najibullah based on accusations that Pakistan and the United States have violated the Geneva accords. The Mujahideen in Pakistan known as the IUAM forms a government-in-exile but receives no recognition from rebels in Afghanistan. Factional infighting amongst Mujaheddin groups has undermined their mutual goals.

1990 A coup attempt by Defense Minister Shahnawaz Tanai fails; leaders of moderate rebel groups form an alliance to counter Gulbuddin Hekmatyar's fundamentalist Muslim faction.

1991 Rebels seize the town of Khost; Najibullah proposes a truce that rebel leaders reject.

1992 The government falls to rebel troops who enter Kabul; a coalition names religious leader Sibghatullah Mujaddidi interim president. However, Hekmatyar's force continues to fight and in June Mujaddidi resigns. Burhanuddin Rabbani is elected president by the Leadership Council.
Kabul is subjected to continual fighting into 1993.

1993 Hekmatyar is named prime minister in the hopes of establishing peace.

1994 Fighting between rebel factions resumes.

1995 The United Nations brokers a deal to have the nine major factions share power in a council. The deal is of little use as a new force, the Taliban, a fundamentalist Islamic group, enters the fray. By the end of the year, the Taliban, which consists largely of students from Islamic schools, has overrun much of the country.

1997 Abdul Rashid Dostum, leader of opposition forces, continues to fight and inflicts severe damage on the Taliban, forcing a stalemate for power.

1998 Amid rumors of Russian support for the opposition, the Taliban is able to take control of 75 percent of the country and end the fighting.

2000 Taliban regime issues a religious edict that leads to the destruction of ancient Buddhist statues in central Afghanistan.

2001 Following attacks on the World Trade Center in New York City and the Pentagon in Washington, D.C., by suicide bombers linked to al-Qaeda, President Bush demands the Taliban administration in Kabul to surrender Osama bin Laden and his associates. On the Taliban's failure to comply, the United States and its coalition allies launch massive air bombardment of military and terrorist installations in the country. The Northern Alliance forces resume their campaign against the Taliban with U.S.- and Russian-supplied materiel. In November the Northern Alliance retakes Mazar-i-Sharif, Harat, and Kabul; in December, Kandahar, the last Taliban stronghold, falls. An international conference summoned by the coalition in Bonn, Germany, helps set up an interim post-Taliban government headed by Pushtun leader Hamid Karzai. The new interim government is sworn in on December 22, slotted to stay in power for six months.

BIBLIOGRAPHY

Gopalakrishnan, R. *The Geography and Politics of Afghanistan.* Atlantic Highlands, N.J., 1982.

Gupta, Bhabani S. *Afghanistan: Politics, Economics and Society.* Boulder, Colo., 1985.

Hyman, A. *Afghanistan Under Soviet Domination, 1964–1991.* 3rd edition. London, 1992.

Isby, David C. *War in a Distant Country: Afghanistan, Invasion and Resistance.* New York, 1989.

Maley, William. *Fundamentalism Reborn?: Afghanistan and the Taliban.* New York, 1998.

Mousavi, Sayed Askar. *The Hazaras of Afghanistan: An Historical, Cultural, Economic and Political Study.* New York, 1998.

Rashid, Ahmed. *Taliban.* New Haven, Conn., 2000.

Rubin, B. R. *The Fragmentation of Afghanistan: State Formation and Collapse in the International System.* New Haven, Conn., 1995.

OFFICIAL PUBLICATIONS

Afghanistan Rehabilitation Strategy: Action Plan (6 vols.; 1993); *Preliminary Results of the First Afghan Population Census* (1979).

CONTACT INFORMATION

Embassy of: —
Phone: —
Fax: —

INTERNET RESOURCES

- Afghanistan Today
  http://frankenstein.worldweb.net/afghan
- Afghanistan Directory
  http://www.afghana.com/Directories/Directory.htm
- Arthur Paul Afghanistan Collection
  http://www.unomaha.edu/-world/cas/collection.html

ALBANIA

BASIC FACT SHEET

OFFICIAL NAME:
Republic of Albania

ABBREVIATION:
AB

CAPITAL:
Tirana

HEAD OF STATE:
President Rexhep Meidani (from 1997)

HEAD OF GOVERNMENT:
Prime Minister Ilir Meta (from 1999)

NATURE OF GOVERNMENT:
Parliamentary democracy

POPULATION:
3,365,000 (1999)

AREA:
28,748 sq km (11,100 sq mi)

MAJOR ETHNIC GROUPS:
Albanian (97%) and Greek (2%)

LANGUAGE:
Albanian

RELIGIONS:
Muslim, Orthodox, Catholic

UNIT OF CURRENCY:
Lek

NATIONAL FLAG:
Red standard, at the center of which is a black double-headed eagle.

NATIONAL EMBLEM:
A black two-headed eagle supported on either side by golden sheaves of wheat

NATIONAL ANTHEM:
"Hymni I Flamurit" (Anthem of the flag)

NATIONAL HOLIDAYS:
November 28 (Proclamation of Independence)

DATE OF INDEPENDENCE:
November 28, 1912

DATE OF CONSTITUTION:
November 22, 1998

GEOGRAPHICAL FEATURES

Albania, on the western coast of the Balkan Peninsula, is separated from the heel of the Italian boot on the southwest and the west by the Strait of Otranto and the Adriatic Sea, respectively. Albania's total area is 28,748 sq km (11,100 sq mi). It shares a boundary with Yugoslavia and Greece.

Albania's boundaries were established in 1913 on the principle of nationality rather than geography: to separate Albanians from Serbians and Montenegrins, and to separate Albanians from Greeks.

Nearly 70 percent of Albania is mountainous and inaccessible. The North Albanian Alps form an extension of the Dinaric alpine chain and, specifically, the Montenegro limestone plateau. A low coastal belt extends from the northern boundary southward. The foothills of the central uplands contain fertile land. The mountains east of the serpentine zone are the highest in the country and among the most rugged in the Balkan Peninsula.

Albania

BOSNIA-HERZEGOVINA
CROATIA
YUGOSLAVIA
MONTENEGRO
SERBIA
0 25 Miles
0 25 Kms
N
Valbone
Han i Hotit
Bajram Curri
Koplik
Lake Scutari
Drin R.
Lake Fierzës
Shkoder
Puke
Kukes
Bushtrice
Lezhe
Rreshen
Drinit Bay
Peshkopi
Lac
Burrel
Mat R.
MACEDONIA
Kruje
Adriatic Sea
Shijak
Zerquan
Durres
Tirana
Kavaje
Librazhd
Shkumbin R.
Rrogozhine
Elbasan
Cerrik
Lake Ohrid
Lushnje
Gramsh
Pogradec
Seman R.
Kucove
Lake Prespa
Fier
Devoll R.
Patos
Berat
Maliq
Korce
Ballsh
Osum R.
Sazan
Selenice
Corovode
Strait of Otranto
Vlore
Mavrove
Kelcyre
Erseke
Tepelene
Permet
Vjosë R.
ITALY
Gjirokaster
GREECE
Delvine
Sarande
Corfu
(GREECE)
Ionian Sea

Geography

Area sq km: 28,748 sq mi: 11,100
World Rank: 142nd
Land Boundaries, km: Greece 282; Macedonia 151; Yugoslavia 287
Coastline, km: 362
Elevation Extremes meters
Lowest: Adriatic Sea 0
Highest: Maja e Korabit 2,753
Land Use % Arable land: 21
Permanent Crops: 5
Permanent Pastures: 15
Forest and Woodland: 38
Other: 21

Population of Principal Cities

Tirana	270,000

CLIMATE AND WEATHER

For a small country, Albania has an unusually large number of climatic regions. The coastal lowlands have a typically Mediterranean climate, whereas the highlands have a Mediterranean continental climate. In both climatic zones, weather changes markedly from north to south and from winter to summer. The lowlands have mild winters, averaging about 45°F; summer temperatures average 75°F. Humidity is high, and summers are oppressive.

Inland temperatures vary more widely with differences in elevation. Cold northerly and northeasterly winds cause frigid winters. Average precipitation is high. The central uplands receive the heaviest rainfall. There are also frequent thunderstorms accompanied by torrential downpours.

Climate and Weather

Temperature Range 45°F to 75°F
Average Rainfall
Lowlands 40 in to 60 in
Highlands 70 in to 100 in

POPULATION

Population Indicators

Total Population: 1999 3,365,000
World Rank: 128th
Density per sq mi: 303.2 per sq km: 117.1
% of annual growth (1994–99): 1.1
Male %: 41.5
Female %: 48.5
Urban %: 35.7
Age Distribution: % 0–14: 33.0
15–29: 28.9
30–44: 18.5
45–59: 11.7
60–74: 5.9
75 and over: 1.9
Population 2020: 4,155,000
Birth Rate per 1,000: 16.6
Death Rate per 1,000: 4.7
Population Doubling Time (years): 50

Infant Mortality Rate per 1,000 live births: 32.0
Rate of Natural Increase per 1,000: 11.9
Total Fertility Rate: 20.4
Expectation of Life (years): Males 68.0
Females 74.0
Marriage Rate per 1,000: 8.9
Divorce Rate per 1,000: 0.8
Total Number of Households: 2,110,000
Average Size of Households: 6.2
% of Illegitimate Children: —
Induced Abortions: —
Rate per 100 live births: —

ETHNIC COMPOSITION

The main cleavage in Albanian society is between two ethnic groups: Gegs and Tosks. Numerically, the Gegs are slightly in the majority.

Nearly 97 percent of the population is Albanian, with the remainder divided among Greeks, Vlachs, Bulgars, Serbs, and Gypsies.

Greeks, who constitute about 2 percent of the population, are most numerous closer to the Greek border. They have adopted Albanian customs and speak fluent Albanian. Vlachs, descendants of the Thracians of the pre-Christian era, are most numerous in the Pindus Mountains. Bulgars tend to live in the border area near Lake Prespa, and those of Serb origin live in the Shkoder area.

An estimated 2 million Albanians are believed to live outside the country. Until the Kosovo War, Yugoslavia alone had 1 million, of whom about 70 percent lived in the Kosovo area.

LANGUAGES

The national and official language is Albanian, a member of the Thraco-Illyrian group. Historically, it has been heavily influenced by Latin and Italian on the one hand and Turkish and Greek on the other. The first written document in Albanian did not appear until the 15th century, but the repressive policies of the rulers of the Turkish Ottoman Empire (1350–1918) restricted its growth until the 19th century. A standardized orthography was adopted in 1908 using a Latin-based alphabet of 36 letters approved by a linguistic congress at Monastir. The alphabet was made official by a government directive in 1924. The two principal dialects are Geg, spoken by about two-thirds of the population, and Tosk, spoken by most of the elite.

Principal Languages and Their Speakers

Albanian	3,296,000
Greek	62,000
Macedonian	5,000
Other	1,000

RELIGIONS

Until the 1940s, Albania was the only predominantly Islamic nation in Europe, with a legacy of five centuries of Ottoman rule. Christianity was introduced in Albania in the first century and the country remained Christian until the 14th century when Turkish invaders introduced Islam. During the next five centuries, Islam made steady inroads. By the 17th century Muslims outnumbered Christians in the population.

At the time of independence, in 1912, Albania became a secular state. The constitution guaranteed freedom of worship for all religions. The communist constitution of 1946 adopted the same liberal tenor. However, even before the adoption of the constitution, the first shots had been fired in the state's war against religion. The Agrarian Reform Law of 1945 confiscated all religious property. In 1967 mosques and churches were closed to worshipers. The ban was lifted in 1990.

Today, under the aegis of democracy all religions are again tolerated. Their followings are: Muslim 70 percent; Orthodox 20 percent; and Catholic 10 percent.

Religious Affiliations

Muslim	2,360,000
Albanian Orthodox	240,000
Roman Catholic	180,000
Other	590,000

HISTORICAL BACKGROUND

Until 168 B.C.E. Albania was composed of parts of the kingdom of Illyria, with its capital at Shkoder. During the succeeding nine centuries, invasions of Huns, Bulgarians, and Slavs drove the Illyrians to the mountain fastnesses on the Adriatic coast, where they are concentrated today. During the Crusades in the 12th and 13th centuries, Albania became a thoroughfare for the contending armies.

Albania's dark ages began with the defeat of the Serbs by the Ottoman Turks in 1389 at the Battle of Kosovo, after which the Turks asserted their suzerainty over the country and forced it to submit to Islam.

It was only when the Ottoman Empire was defeated in a Balkan war in 1912 that Albania became an independent nation. Virtually dismembered by the Treaty of San Stefano, Albania struggled to ward off the territorial demands of Serbia, Austria-Hungary, Italy, Russia, and Montenegro. In 1912, Albanians staged a series of revolts and proclaimed Albania's independence.

At the end of World War 1, Albania was occupied by the Allied armies. On April 7, 1939, Italy invaded Albania. King Zog fled the country, never to return.

In the chaotic conditions created by the Italian occupation and World War II, the Communists created the National Liberation Movement on September 16, 1942, to coordinate the activities of various guerrilla bands. Having accomplished this goal, the National Liberation Front seized control of the whole country.

On January 11, 1946, the People's Assembly proclaimed the People's Republic of Albania and approved the first Albanian constitution.

During the following 45 years, Albania became the most reclusive (and most repressive) of the European communist regimes. The first leader of this totalitarian state, Enver Hoxha, earned a reputation for marxist ideological authoritarianism more rigid than that of either the Soviet Union or China.

With the collapse of the last communist government in 1992, Albania entered a period of political instability. This was worsened by the sudden national obsession with financial schemes promising instant riches for unwary investors. The pyramid schemes failed, plunging the country into bankruptcy and severe disorder. This situation descended into chaos in 1997 when citizens distributed thousands of military weapons, and armed factions divided the country into local fiefdoms. More than 10,000 Albanians fled to Italy. In time, the army reasserted a measure of control and a central government was elected and installed.

In 1998, Serbian police and the Yugoslav army attacked Albanian separatists and civilians in Kosovo. When the Federal Republic of Yugoslavia (FRY) refused to sign a peace accord, NATO began air strikes against Yugoslav targets in 1999. By the time a peace agreement was signed in June 1999, an estimated 444,000 refugees had fled from Kosovo into neighboring Albania, placing an enormous burden on the country's economy.

CONSTITUTION

The Albanian constitution approved in a national referendum in 1998 abandoned virtually all the provisions of the communist constitution of 1976. The new basic law was a Western-style document modeled on German and Italian counterparts. It describes Albania as a democratic republic in which human rights, including religious freedom, are guaranteed. Private property rights are also protected and emphasis is given to a market-oriented economy.

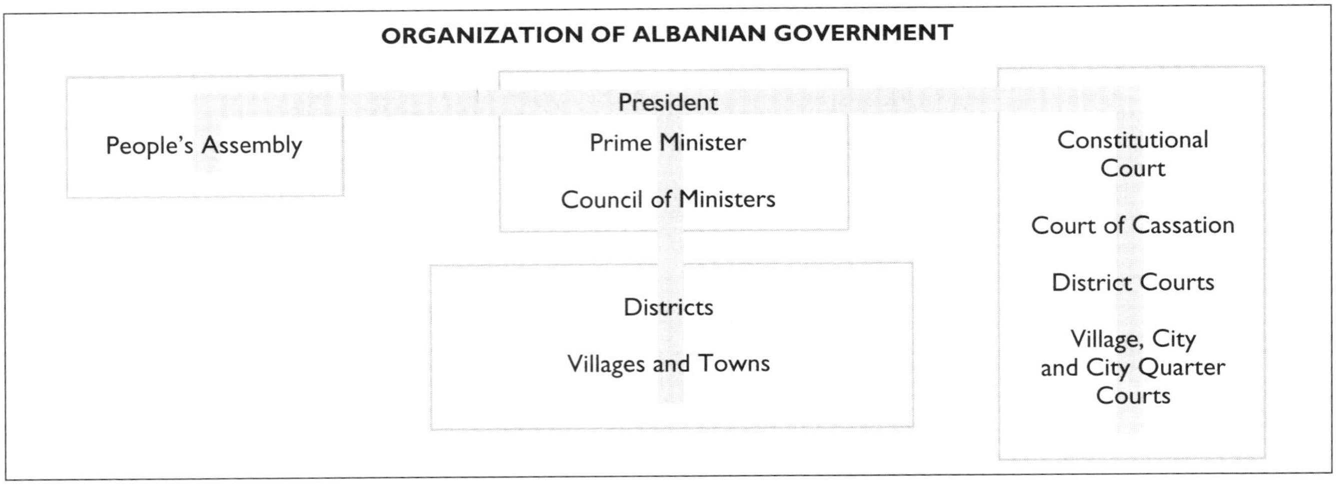

ORGANIZATION OF ALBANIAN GOVERNMENT

People's Assembly

President
Prime Minister
Council of Ministers

Districts
Villages and Towns

Constitutional Court
Court of Cassation
District Courts
Village, City and City Quarter Courts

LOCAL GOVERNMENT

For purposes of local administration, Albania is divided into 26 districts (*rrethet*), over 200 localities, and 2,500 villages. Local councils, elected by direct suffrage for three-year terms, are the governing bodies in each subdivision.

Local Government

Principal administrative divisions, capitals, area, population

AREA AND POPULATION

		area		population 1990
Provinces	**Capitals**	**sq mi**	**sq km**	**estimate**
Berat	Berat	396	1,027	180,489
Diber	Peshkopi	605	1,568	153,775
Durres	Durres	327	848	251,029
Elbasan	Elbasan	572	1,481	248,676
Fier	Fier	454	1,175	251,115
Gjirokaster	Gijrokaster	439	1,137	67,392
Gramsh	Gramsh	268	695	44,791
Kolonje	Erseke	311	805	25,291
Korce	Korce	842	2,181	218,219
Kruje	Kruje	234	607	109,876
Kukes	Kukes	514	1,330	104,731
Lezhe	Lezhe	185	479	63,505
Librazhd	Librazhd	391	1,013	73,871
Lushnje	Lushnje	275	712	137,830
Mat	Burrel	397	1,028	78,754
Mirdte	Rreshen	335	867	51,701
Pemet	Pemet	359	929	40,419
Pogradec	Pogradec	280	725	73,333
Puke	Puke	399	1,034	50,286
Sarande	Sarande	424	1,097	89,459
Shkoder	Shkoder	976	2,528	241,549
Skrapar	Corovoda	299	775	47,605
Tepelene	Tepelene	315	817	51,022
Tirane	Tirana (Tirane)	478	1,238	374,483
Tropoje	Bajram	403	1,043	45,965
Vlore	Vlore	621	1,609	180,725
TOTAL		11,100	28,748	3,255,891

PARLIAMENT

The 1998 constitution provides for a democratic form of government. The supreme organ of government is the unicameral People's Assembly. The president is elected by the assembly but is precluded from holding party office. The powers of the president, especially those regarding his authority to govern in times of emergency, were substantially diluted. The responsibility for the administration rests with the Council of Ministers, whose head serves as prime minister. The prime minister is appointed by the president, who, upon the proposal of the prime minister, also nominates the Council of Ministers for approval by the assembly. The assembly may pass a no-confidence motion against the Council of Ministers forcing it to resign.

POLITICAL PARTIES

The parliament that emerged from the 1997 elections was led by the Socialist Party, which took 101 of the 155 seats. The Democratic Party gained 27 seats, while the Social Democrats secured eight seats, and the Unity for Human Rights Party won four.

Political Parties

Socialist Party, 1941
Socialist Democratic Party, 1991
Democratic Alliance, 1992
Albanian Agrarian Party, 1991
Human Rights Union Party, 1992
Omonia, representing ethnic Greeks
Union for Democracy, 1997, a coalition of 5 opposition parties including
- Democratic Party, 1990
- Movement of Legality Party, 1991
- Party of National Unity, 1991
- Social Democratic Union, 1995
- Christian Democratic Party,

United Albanian Right, 1997
National Front Party, 1942
Albanian Republican Party, 1992
Republican Alternative Party, 1992
Right-wing Republican Party, 1992
Democratic Party of the Right, 1994
Movement for Democracy, 1997
Albanian Communist Party, 1991
Party of National Restoration, 1996
Albanian Green Party, 1991
Albanian Liberal Party, 1991
People's Party, 1991
Cameria Political and Patriotic Association, 1991
Right National Front Party, 1998

Political Parties: Strength in Parliament Most Recent Elections

The **People's Assembly** (Kuvend Popullore) is currently a unicameral body of 140 deputies, 100 of whom are chosen from single-member constituencies in two-stage balloting. The remaining 40 members are selected by proportional representation from party lists on the basis of first-round strength, assuming a minimum vote share of 3 percent. At the election of June 24, 2001, the Socialist Party of Albania won 73 seats; the Union for Victory, 46; Social Democratic Party of Albania, 4; Union for Human Rights, 3; Party of the Democratic Alliance of Albania, 3; Albanian Agrarian Party, 2; and independents, 2.

LEGAL SYSTEM

The court system consists of a Constitutional Court, the Court of Cassation, appeals courts, and district courts. The Constitutional Court is composed of nine judges appointed by the People's Assembly for maximum nine-year terms. The Constitutional Court determines the constitutionality of laws and resolves disagreements between local and federal authorities. The remaining courts are each divided into three jurisdictions: criminal, civil, and military. The Court of Cassation is the highest court of appeal and consists of 11 members appointed by the People's Assembly and serving seven-year terms. The president of the republic chairs the High Council of Justice, which is charged with appointing and dismissing judges.

A college of three judges renders Albanian court verdicts; there is no jury trial, though the college is sometimes referred to in the Albanian media as the "jury."

LAW ENFORCEMENT

Law Enforcement

Offenses reported to the police per 100,000: —
- Murder: —
- Assault: —
- Burglary: —
- Automobile Theft: —
- Population per Police officer: 550

Death Penalty: —

HUMAN RIGHTS

Under President Meidani, restrictions on Albanians' personal freedoms have been substantially relaxed. To a large extent, the war over Kosovo, with its huge migrations of refugees and the presence of large numbers of international aid workers and NATO military personnel, has had an influence on Albania's external and internal affairs.

Nevertheless, the improvement in the human rights situation is marginal overall and complaints continue to occur over violations. The principal area of concern centers on conditions in the prisons, which are known to be harsh. Long-term solitary confinement, for example, is common, and cells are cramped, with rudimentary sanitary facilities and often without heat in winter or fresh air in summer.

FOREIGN POLICY

The war over Kosovo probably did more to influence Albania's foreign relations than any other single event since the end of communist rule.

Albanian foreign policy has concentrated on maintaining good relations with its Balkan neighbors, gaining access to European-Atlantic security institutions, and securing close ties with the United States. The crisis of 1997 spurred an intensive period of international involvement in Albania—led by the Organization for Security and Cooperation in Europe (OSCE). Italy hosted a series of international conferences and led a multinational force of about 7,000 troops to help stabilize the country and facilitate OSCE election monitoring. The United States has worked closely with European partners and various multilateral forces to ensure that international efforts are coordinated.

During the forced mass exodus of Albanian refugees from Kosovo, Albania threw open its borders to accept as many as wanted to come. In addition, the government gave blanket permission to NATO to make whatever military use of Albania it saw fit. These and several other such gestures have resulted in Western governments adopting a much more positive attitude toward Albania.

In addition, bilateral relations with Greece have improved dramatically as have Tirana's relations with Macedonia.

DEFENSE

Albania's armed forces in 1991 comprised some 48,000 active-duty and 155,000 reserve personnel. The People's Army was thus made up of 35,000 active ground forces, 11,000 air and air defense personnel, and 2,000 naval personnel.

The defense budget accounts for about 4.1 percent of GNP. In addition to defense forces, the defense appropriation also accounts for 7,000 frontier guards and internal security personnel.

Military Indicators

Total Active Duty Personnel: 48,000
Military Manpower per 1,000: —
Military Expenditures: $157 million
as % of GNP: 4.1
per capita: $56
as % of central government expenditures: 11.3

Arms Imports: $20
Arms Exports: 0

ECONOMY

The collapse of communism in Albania produced an atmosphere more chaotic than that in other East European countries and was marked by a mass exodus of refugees in the early 1990s. At this point, with real Gross Domestic Product (GDP) having fallen by 50 percent, economic reforms began in earnest.

These included an ambitious program of market liberalization. Any progress that developed was halted for several years, however, because of the deleterious effects of financial pyramid schemes, all of which collapsed, leaving millions of people bankrupt.

International aid helped to defray the high cost of receiving and returning refugees from the Bosnia conflict. GDP grew by 8 percent in 1999 and 7.5 percent in 2000.

Principal Economic Indicators

Gross National Product: $2.540 billion
GNP per capita: $760
GNP Average Annual Growth Rate (1990–97): 2.2
GNP per capita Average Annual Growth Rate (1990–97): 2.0
Origin of Gross Domestic Product %
Agriculture: 55
Mining: —
Manufacturing: 13
Construction: 9
Public Utilities: —
Transportation and Communications: 3
Trade: 19
Financial Services: 19
Other Services: 19
Government: 19
Gross Domestic Product by Type of Expenditure %
Private Consumption: 170
Government Consumption: 170
Gross Domestic Investment: 10
Foreign Trade: Exports: 12
Imports: −92
% of Income Received by Poorest 20%: —
% of Income Received by Richest 10%: —

Price and earnings indexes (1995 = 100)

	1992	1993	1994	1995	1996	1997	1998
Consumer price index	40.9	75.7	92.8	100.0	112.7	150.1	181.1
Earnings index	—	—	—	—	—	—	—

Finance

National Currency: Lek (L)
Exchange Rate: $1 = L 152.28
Money Supply Stock in National Currency billion: 90.4
M1 per capita: 27,600
Central Bank Discount Rate %: 21.3
Total External Debt $million: 645
Debt Service Ratio %: 5.2

Balance of Payments $million: 272.2
International Reserves SDRs million: 202
Ratio of External Debt to Total Reserves: 2.3

Average Annual Rate of Inflation/Consumer Price Index
Growth Rate %: 40

Official Development Assistance

ODA: $242 million
as % of GNP: 7.8
per capita $: 7.8
Foreign Direct Investment $million: 45

Central Government Revenues and Expenditures

Fiscal Year: Calendar Year

Revenues $million: 624
Expenditures $million: 996
Budget Deficit: $372 million
Tax Revenues as % of GDP: 14.8
Highest Tax Bracket %
Individual: —
Corporate: —

Employment and Labor

Economically Active Population: 1,340,000
Female Participation Rate %: 47.0
Activity Rate %: 57.4
Labor by Sector: %
Agriculture, Forestry, Fishing: 60.1
Manufacturing, Mining: 12.5
Construction: 1.3
Transportation and Communications: 1.6
Trade, Hotels, and Restaurants: 3.5
Finance, Insurance, Real Estate: —
Public Administration, Defense: —
Services: 19

Unemployment %: 14

Agriculture

Agriculture's Share of GDP %: 55
Average Annual Rate of Growth (1965–98) %: 3.0
Number of Farms 000: 0.5
Average Size of Farm ha: 1,182
Number of Tractors per 1,000 ha: 15. 6
Irrigation, % of Farms having: 61
Artificial Fertilizer kg/ha: 158
Total Farmland as % of land area: 41.1
Livestock: Cattle 000: 780
Sheep 000: 1,890
Hogs 000: 98
Chickens 000: 4,600
Forests: Production of Roundwood
(000 cubic meters): 409
Fisheries: Total Catch tons 000: 3.2

Mining

% of GDP: —
Value of Mineral Production $million: 81.4

Manufacturing

Value Added $million: 224
Industrial Production Growth Rate %: 6

Energy

Commercial Energy Production metric tons of
oil equivalent 000: 912
Commercial Energy Consumption metric tons of
oil equivalent 000: 1,048
Commercial Energy Consumption per capita kg: 317
Average Annual Growth Rate 1980–97 %: −8
Net Energy Imports % of use: 13
Electricity Installed Capacity kW 000: 1,892
Production kW-hr million: 4,414
Coal Reserves tons million: 15
Production tons 000: 130
Natural Gas Proven Reserves cubic meters billion: 2
Production cubic meters million: 136
Crude Petroleum reserves barrels million: 165
Production barrels million: 3
Consumption barrels million: 3
Refinery Capacity barrels per day 000: 40
Pipelines Length km: —

Foreign Trade

Imports $million: 601
Exports $million: 141.3
Export Volume % Annual Growth Rate (1990–97): —
Import Volume % Annual Growth Rate (1990–97): —
Balance of Trade $

Balance of trade (current prices)

	1991	1992	1993	1994	1995	1996	1997
U.S.							
$000,000	−208	−470	−490	−460	−475	−678	−535
% of total	58.8%	77.1%	68.7%	62.0%	53.7%	58.2%	62.8%

Major Trading Partners

	Imports	Exports
European Union %	4.8	7.3
United States %	0.2	0.5
Eastern Europe %	59.9	70.2
Japan %	7.9	0.3
Others %	27.2	21.8

Transportation

Roads Total Length mi: 9,631 km: 15,500
Paved %: 30
Automobiles: 48,682
Trucks and Buses: 34,441
Persons per vehicle: 34
Railroad; Track Length mi: 419 km: 674
Passenger-mi million: 139
Freight-mi million: 0.3
Merchant Marine: No. of Vessels: 24
Total Deadweight Tonnage 000: 81.0
International Cargo Loaded tons 000: 1,065
International Cargo Off-loaded tons 000: 664
Airports with Scheduled Flights: 1
Traffic: Passenger-mi million: —
Freight-mi million: —
Length of Canals mi: 27 km: 43

Tourism

Number of Tourists to 000: 27
Number of Tourists from 000: 18
Tourist Receipts $million: 7
Tourist Expenditures $million: 5

Communications

Telephones 000: 42
Cost of Local Calls 3 mins $0.02
Cellular Telephones 000: —
Fax Machines 000: —
Personal Computers 000: 550
Internet Hosts per million persons:
Mail: Post Offices: 698
Pieces of Mail Handled million: 3.5
Pieces of Mail Handled per person: 1.0

EDUCATION

Upon taking power in late 1944, the communist regime gave high priority to reopening the schools and organizing the whole education system to reflect communist ideology.

The 1946 Education Reform Law provided specifically that Marxist-Leninist principles would permeate all school texts. This law also made the struggle against illiteracy a primary objective of the new school system.

Illiteracy had been virtually eliminated by the late 1980s. From a total enrollment of fewer than 60,000 students at all levels in 1939, the number of people in school had grown to more than 750,000 by 1987.

A reorganization plan was announced in 1990 to extend the compulsory education program from eight to 10 years. The following year, however, a major economic and political crisis in Albania, and the ensuing breakdown of public order, plunged the school system into chaos. Widespread vandalism and extreme shortages of textbooks and supplies had a devastating effect on school operations. Many teachers fled the country. The highly structured and controlled educational environment that the communist regime had painstakingly cultivated in the course of more than 46 years was abruptly shattered.

Since 1992, the government has focused on improving supplies and equipment and reconstructing buildings in urban centers, as well as training teachers and improving enrollment rates. New schools are being built in areas that currently have no facilities.

Education

Literacy Rate %: 91.8
- Male %: 95.5
- Female %: 88.0

First Level: Primary schools: 1,777
- Teachers: 32,098
- Students: 535,713
- Student-Teacher Ratio: 16.7
- Net Enrollment Ratio: 96

Second Level: Secondary Schools: 47
- Teachers: 4,149
- Students: 73,259
- Student-Teacher Ratio: 17.7
- Net Enrollment Ratio: —

Vocational Level: Schools: 466
- Students: 138,000

Third Level: Institutions: 8
- Teachers: 1,774
- Students: 30,185
- Student-Teacher Ratio Level: 17.0
- Gross Enrollment Ratio: 9.6
- Students per 100,000: 17.0
- % of Population Age 25 and over with Postsecondary Education: 9.6

Public Expenditure on Education as % of GDP: 3.4

SCIENCE AND TECHNOLOGY

Science and Technology

Scientists and Engineers in R&D per 1 million persons: —
Expenditures in R&D as % of GDP: —
High-Tech Exports $: 1 million
Patent Applications by Residents: —

MEDIA

In 1999 the People's Assembly voted to protect freedom of the press and abolished a 1993 law that restricted access to information and made editors liable to heavy fines for publishing antistate material. The principal source of domestic and foreign news is the Albanian Telegraph Agency. The government-owned Radio and Television of Albania controls all broadcasting. Radio Tirana transmits in a number of languages and television is broadcast in the four most populous districts.

Media

Daily Newspapers: 3
- Total Circulation 000: 185
- Circulation per 1,000: 54

Books Published: —
Magazines: 143
Radio Receivers 000: 550
- per 1,000: 157

Television sets 000: 300
- per 1,000: 89

MOST IMPORTANT MEDIA:

Press. The following are published at Tirana: *Zeri I Popullit* (Voice of the People, 105,000), PSS daily; *Rlindja Demokratike* (Democratic Revival, 50,000), PDS daily; *Koha Joné* (Our Time, 400,000), leading independent; *Rpublika* (Republic), PRS daily; *Progresi Agrar* (Agrarian Progress), twice-weekly PAS organ; *Laiko Vema* (People's Step), twice-weekly organ of the Greek minority; *Bashkimi* (Unity, 30,000); *Albanian Daily News*, daily in English; *Gazeta Shqiptare* (Albanian Gazette), daily; *Skekulli*, daily.

News agencies. The principal source for both domestic and foreign news is the official Albanian Telegraph Agency (Agiensi Telegrafike Shqiptar—ATS).

Radio and television. Radio and Television of Albania (Radiotelevisione Shqiptar), a government facility, controls all broadcasting and in March 1994 curtailed British Broadcasting Corporation (BBC) transmissions because of alleged left-wing bias. Radio Tirana transmits internationally in a number of languages, while television is broadcast in four districts. There were approximately 799,000 radio and 400,000 television receivers in 1998. In May 1997 the assembly passed a law providing for private ownership of radio and television stations but, since a government commission would control licensing, it was unclear if the state would still maintain control of all broadcast media. At least one private station, Radio Koha Jone owned by an independent candidate for the assembly, was established in time for the June/July 1997 elections, although subsequent developments in that arena have apparently been constrained by the nation's political turmoil.

CULTURE

Cultural Indicators

Public Libraries
- Number: 45
- Volumes: 5,712,000
- Registered borrowers: —

Museums
- Number: —
- Annual Attendance: —

Cinema
- Production of Long Films: 11
- Number of Cinemas: —
- Seating Capacity: —
- Annual Attendance: —
- Annual Attendance per capita: —

STATUS OF WOMEN

Violence against women and spousal abuse is common in Albania's male-dominated society. The rights of women are not protected by any government program. There is a facility for abused women in Tirana, but it can house only a few women at a time. There is also a hot line that women and girls can call for advice and help. The UNHCR reported cases of rape and sexual assault of Kosovar Albanian women in refugee camps. In the northeast the traditional code known as *kanum* prevails. Under this code women are considered as chattels and may be kidnaped to be sold as brides. Trafficking in women for purposes of prostitution is a major problem. More than 30,000 Albanian women are reported to be working abroad as prostitutes.

Women

Gender Empowerment Measure: —
Seats Held in Parliament by Women %: —
Female Administrators and Managers %: —
Female Professional and Technical Workers %: —
Women's Share of Earned Income %: —
Women in Government %: 12

HEALTH, FOOD, AND NUTRITION

Health

Number of Physicians: 4,467
Number of Dentists: 1,099
Number of Nurses: 6,801
Number of Pharmacists: 772
Population per Physician: 729
Number of Hospitals: 895
Hospital Beds per 10,000: 57
Hospital Bed Occupancy Rate: —
Infant Mortality Rate per 1,000 live births: 38
Maternal Mortality Rate per 100,000 live births: 65
Total Health Expenditures as % of GDP: 4.00
Health Expenditures per capita $: 26
HIV Infected % of adults: 0.01
Cigarette Consumption per smoker per year: —
% of Smokers: Male: 50
Female: 8
Access to Safe Water % —

Food and Nutrition

Food Supply as % of FAO Requirements: 96
% of Consumption Expenditures on Food: 680
Daily Available Calories per capita: 2,324
% of Total Calories derived from:
Cereals: 38.6
Potatoes, cassava: 1.8
Meat, poultry: 8.7
Fish: —
Eggs, milk: 22.9
Fruits, vegetables: 5.8
Fats, oils: 10.2

ENVIRONMENT

Although the continuing deleterious effects of decades of environmental neglect should not be discounted, Albania's most serious current environmental problems stem from the military conflict in Yugoslavia.

United Nations' studies have determined that the most serious threat is caused by leakages of highly toxic chemicals into the Drin from damaged industrial plants and by the sudden and uncontrolled influx of refugees.

In the case of river pollution, the leaking of high quantities and concentrations of ammonia, chlorides, and hydroxides are likely to cause sustained environmental damage for a long time to come. The unplanned construction of refugee camps has led to the destruction of protected natural habitat and the contamination of water supplies with untreated sewage. The generalized danger to precious water resources in Albania is now of heightened concern.

Environment

Forest Area sq km: 10,000
Average Annual Deforestation sq km: 0
Nationally Protected Areas as % of Total Land Area: 2.9
Freshwater Access cubic meters per capita: 12,758
Emissions of Organic Water Pollutants kg per day: 5,844
CO_2 Emissions per capita ton: 0.6

CHRONOLOGY

1943–44	Albania is under German rule following Italian surrender.
1946	Communists under Enver Hoxha proclaim a Communist republic.
1949	Albania joins COMECON.
1961	Albania breaks with Soviet Union in the wake of Nikita Khrushchev's denunciation of Stalin.
1978	Albania becomes a rogue state following suspension of diplomatic relations with China.
1982	Ramiz Alia, a protege of Hoxha, becomes head of state.
1985	Hoxha dies; Alia becomes head of Party of Labor.
1990	One-party system is abandoned as first opposition party is permitted to form.
1991	Communists win first multiparty elections; Alia is reelected.
1992	Presidential election is won by Sali Berisha of the Democratic Party; Alia and other Communist Party officials are charged with corruption and abuse of power; Totalitarian and Communist parties are banned.
1993	Conflict erupts between Albanians and ethnic Greeks following purge of Greeks from senior positions in civil service and army; Alia is sentenced to eight years' imprisonment.

1995 Alia is released from prison but is banned, along with fellow-Communists, from local and national elections until 2002.

1997 Antigovernment riots break out following collapse of bogus investment schemes, southern Albania falls under rebel control; national election is won by former Communist Party; Rexhep Meidani is elected president and Fatos Nano prime minister.

1998 Prime Minister Fatos Nano resigns and former student activist Pandeli Majko becomes new prime minister.

1999 NATO conducts air strikes against Yugoslav military targets. Hundreds of thousands flee from Kosovo into Albania. Prime Minister Majko resigns after losing a Socialist Party leadership vote; Iler Meta, 30, becomes Europe's youngest prime minister.

2001 Albania and Yugoslavia reestablish diplomatic ties broken off during the Kosovo crisis in 1999.

BIBLIOGRAPHY

Bland, William B. *Albania.* Santa Barbara, Calif., 1988.

Hall, Derek R. *Albania and the Albanians.* New York, 1994.

Logoreci, Anton. *The Albanians: Europe's Forgotten Survivors.* Boulder, Colo., 1978.

Marmallaku, Ramadan. *Albania and the Albanians.* Hamden, Conn., 1975.

Pano, Nicholas C. *Albania: Politics, Economics and Society.* Boulder, Colo., 1986.

Pollo, Stefanay, and Arben Puto. *The History of Albania.* London, 1981.

Sjoberg, Orjan. *Rural Change and Development in Albania.* Boulder, Colo., 1991.

OFFICIAL PUBLICATIONS

Albania. *Albanian Human Development Report 1996* (UNDP); *IMF Economic Reviews: Albania* (1994); *Population and Housing Census 1989; Statistical Yearbook of Albania.*

CONTACT INFORMATION

Embassy of Albania
2100 S Street NW
Washington, D.C. 20008
Phone: (202) 223-4942 Fax: (202) 628-7342

INTERNET RESOURCES

- Albanian Home Page http://albanian.com/main/
- Albanian Ministry of Foreign Affairs http://www.tirana.al/minjash/

ALGERIA

BASIC FACT SHEET

OFFICIAL NAME:
Democratic and Popular Republic of Algeria (Al-Jumhouriyya al-Jazariyya ad Dimocratiyya Ash-Sahbiyya; République Algérienne Démocratique et Populaire)

ABBREVIATION:
AE

CAPITAL:
Algiers

HEAD OF STATE:
President Abdelaziz Bouteflika (from 1999)

HEAD OF GOVERNMENT:
Prime Minister Ali Benflis (from 2000)

NATURE OF GOVERNMENT:
Democracy

POPULATION:
29,910,000 (1999)

AREA:
2,381,741 sq km (919,592 sq mi)

ETHNIC MAJORITY:
Arabs, Berbers

LANGUAGE:
Arabic (official)

RELIGION:
Sunni Islam

UNIT OF CURRENCY:
Algerian dinar

NATIONAL FLAG:
Red star and crescent superimposed on the center of two equal vertical fields, one white and the other green

NATIONAL EMBLEM:
The central motif is the "white hand of Fatima," an Arab sign of blessing and happiness. This insignia is flanked by two national flags with their gold staffs joined. On the outside are branches of palm and olive trees with a larger red crescent and star in the middle.

NATIONAL ANTHEM:
"We Pledge"

NATIONAL HOLIDAYS:
November 1 (National Day, Anniversary of the Revolution); January 1 (New Year's Day); May 1 (Labor Day); June 19 (Ben Bella's overthrow); July 5 (Independence Day); also variable Islamic festivals

DATE OF INDEPENDENCE:
July 3, 1962

DATE OF CONSTITUTION:
February 23, 1989; revised November 28, 1996

GEOGRAPHICAL FEATURES

Algeria is the second-largest country in Africa, with an area of 2,381,741 sq km (919,592 sq mi). It lies midway along the Mediterranean littoral in the Maghreb region of North Africa and extends south into the heart of the Sahara. It shares international borders with Libya, Mali, Mauritania, Morocco, Niger, and Tunisia.

The two parallel mountain ranges of the Tell (or Maritime) Atlas and the Saharan Atlas divide Algeria into three lateral zones: a narrow but fertile coastal plain, a high plateau, and the Sahara. The coastal plain is a narrow strip about 128 km (80 mi) wide to the east and 64 km (40 mi) to the west. The Tell Atlas consists of two distinct ranges: the Traras Mountains, the Sahel of Oran, and the Dahra Massif to the west; and the Djurdjura Massif, Greater and Lesser Kabylia, and the Biban and Hodna chains to the east. The eastern end of the Hodna Mountains leads into the Aures Massif, which includes the highest peaks in northern Algeria, several exceeding 2,133 m (7,500 ft). Behind the coastal hills lie a series of relatively low plains: Oran, Chelif Valley, Algier (Mitidja), Bejaia, Skikda, and

Algeria

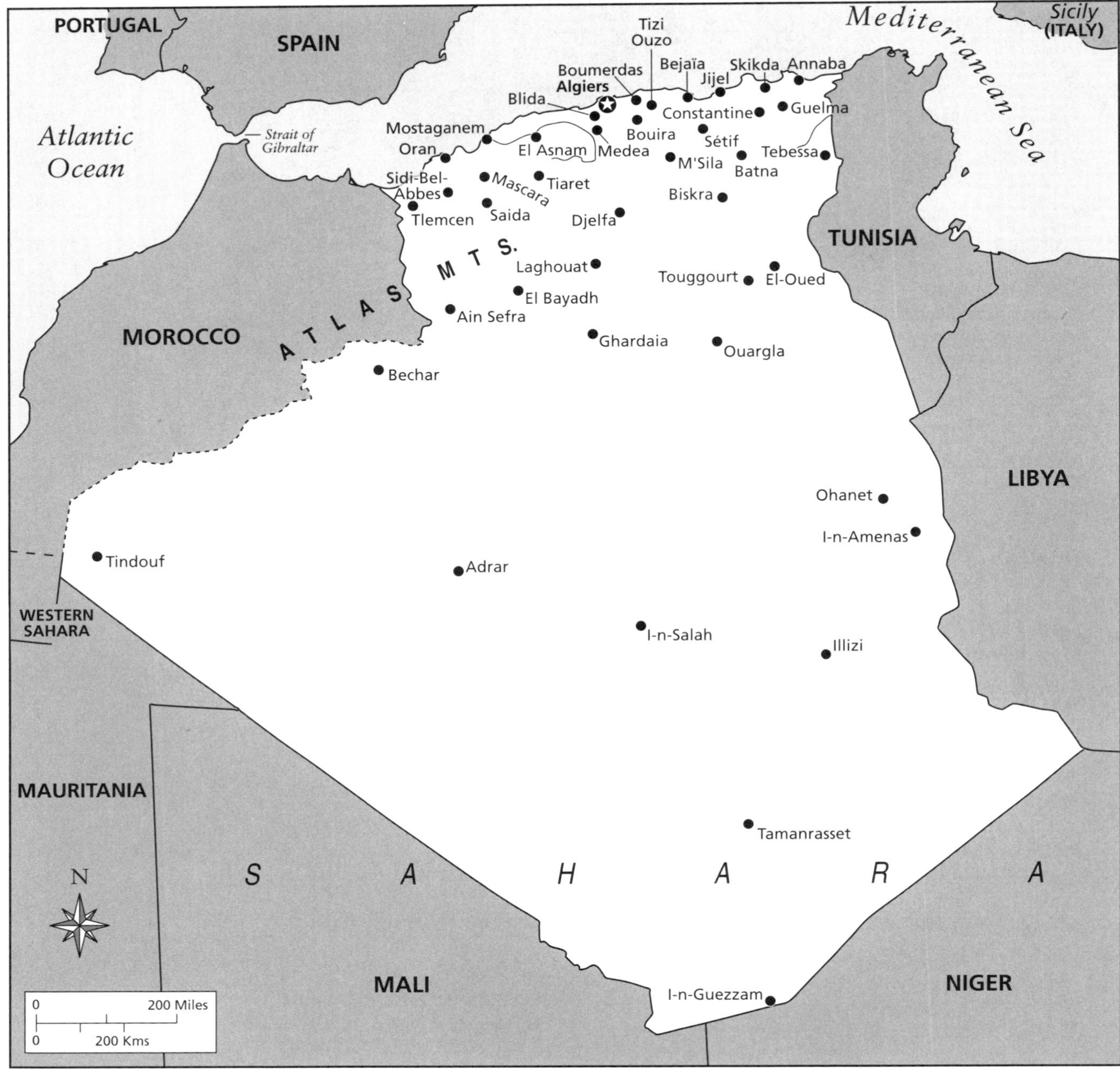

Annaba. South of the plains are the inland ranges of the Tell Atlas: Tlemcen, Djebel Ouarsenis, and Blida Atlas, whose altitude decline from west to east. They surround and isolate a series of inland basins and depressions such as Sidi Bel Abbes, Tiaret, Setif, Constantine, and Guelma Plains. The second zone is the high plateau, a vast, steppelike plain that forms a depression between the Tell Atlas and the Saharan Atlas. The plateau generally narrows and falls in height eastward and ends in the Hodna Basin. The plateau is covered by salt lakes and salt marshes, of which the largest is the Shott ech Chergui. To the south of the high plateau are the five massifs of the Saharan Atlas: Ksour, Amour, Ouled Nail, Ziban, and Aures, the last of which includes the highest peak in Algeria outside the Sahara, Chelia, 2,328 m (7,537 ft). The Algerian Saharan covers 2,071,990 sq km (800,000 sq mi), over 85 percent of Algeria's land area, and is one of the driest, hottest, and most arid regions on earth. Much of the Sahara is covered by rocky platforms known as *hammadas*, and two great sand deserts, the Great Western Erg and the Great Eastern Erg. To the southeast is the high Ahaggar Massif, surrounded by desolate sandstone plateaus.

With the exception of the Chelif River there are no permanent rivers but only wadis, rivers that have water only in the rainy season.

Geography

Area sq km: 2,381,741 sq mi 919,592
World Rank: 11th
Land Boundaries, km: Libya 982; Mali 1,376; Mauritania 463; Morocco 1,559; Niger 956; Tunisia 965; Western Sahara 42
Coastline, km: 998
Elevation Extremes
Lowest: Chott Melrhir -40
Highest: Tahat 3,003
Land Use % Arable land: 3
Permanent Crops: 0
Permanent Pastures: 13
Forest and Woodland: 2
Other: 82

Population of Principal Cities (1998)

Algiers	1,519,570
Annaba	348,554
Batna	242,514
Béchar	131,010
Bejaia	147,076
Biskra	170,956
Blida (el-Boulaida)	226,512
Constantine (Qacentina)	462,187
Mostaganem	124,399
Oran (Wahran)	692,516
Setif	211,859
Sidi bel Abbes	180,260
Skikda	152,335
Tébessa	153,246
Tlemcen (Tilimsen)	155,162

CLIMATE AND WEATHER

The climate of northern Algeria, including the coastal plains and the Tell Atlas, is Mediterranean, with hot, dry summers and mild, wet winters. Typical winter temperatures range from 10°C to 12°C (50°F to 54°F) and summer temperatures from 24°C to 26°C (75°F to 79°F), although summer temperatures of over 37.8°C (100°F) are not infrequent. Rainfall increases from west to east, with an average annual rainfall of 380 mm (15 in) in Oran, 660 mm (26 in) in Algiers, and 1,520 mm (60 in) in Kabylia. In the higher elevated areas of Kabylia snow is common in the winter. Winters are colder and summers are hotter in the Tell Atlas. Mean temperatures in the winter average 4°C to 6°C (39°F to 43°F) and rise to 26°C to 28°C (70°F to 82°F) in the summer. In the high plateau region the continental climate is dominant, with greater daily temperature ranges. The mean winter temperature is 4.4°C (40°F) and the mean summer temperature is 26.7°C (80°F). Rain is scanty, less than 400 mm (15 in), much of it falling within a brief period. The Sahara has a true desert climate, with temperatures going up to 50°C (122°F) on most days in summer. Rainfall is erratic and infrequent.

During the summer Algeria is subject to the scorching southern wind from the Sahara known as the *chehili*. It blows for 40 days a year over the high plateau and for 20 days a year near the coast. In the summer, a wind called the sirocco is accompanied by blinding swirls of dust.

Climate and Weather

Mean Temperature
Coastal Region Winter 50°F to 54°F
Summer 75°F to 79°F
Tell Atlas Winter 39°F to 43°F
Summer 79°F to 82°F
High Plateau Winter 40°F
Summer 80°F
Sahara Summer 122°F
Average Rainfall 15 in (Oran), 26 in (Algiers), 60 in (Kabylia)

POPULATION

Population Indicators

Total Population: 1999 29,910,000
World Rank: 35th
Density per sq mi: 32.5 Per sq km 12.6
% of annual growth (1994–99): 2.2
Male %: 49.9
Female %: 50.1
Urban %: 49.7
Age Distribution: % 0–14: 43.9
15–29: 28.0
30–44: 13.9
45–59: 8.4
60–74: 4.2
75 and over: 1.6
Population 2020: 43,045,000
Birth Rate per 1,000: 28.5
Death Rate per 1,000: 5.9
Population Doubling Time (years): 32
Infant Mortality Rate per 1,000 live births: 48.7
Rate of Natural Increase per 1,000: 22.6
Total Fertility Rate: 3.6
Expectation of Life (years):Males 62.5
Females 69.5
Marriage Rate per 1,000: 5.7
Divorce Rate per 1,000: —
Total Number of Households: 3,824,000
Average Size of Households: 6.9
% of Illegitimate Children: —
Induced Abortions: —
Rate per 100 live births: —

ETHNIC COMPOSITION

Arabs and Arabized Berbers constitute the largest ethnic community and about 80 percent of the population. Berbers constitute the remainder. Because both the

Arabized Berbers and the Berbers belong to the same racial stock, the dividing line between these two groups is neither rigid nor exclusive. However, the Berbers, with their weaker cultural identify, have tended to be easily assimilated into the stronger Arab group. Although Berbers do not constitute a homogeneous group in a cultural sense and do not exhibit a sense of peoplehood, they are proud of their separateness vis-à-vis the Arabs. Many Berber tribes are endogamous and have resisted the imposition of the Arabic language, preferring to learn French. Major Berber groups live in separate mountain regions: the Kabyles in Kabylia, the Chaouias in the Aures Mountains, the M'zabites in the northern Sahara, and the Tuareg in the central Sahara. Of these groups, the Kabyles, numbering over 2 million, are the most important. They also form the majority of the Algerian workers in France. The Chaouias number over 1 million, the M'zabites 80,000, and the Tuareg less than 10,000.

In 1982 the total non-Arab and non-Berber population was less than 100,000, a fraction of the 1 million Europeans and 150,000 Jews who lived in the country up to the time of independence. The once-flourishing Jewish community has been reduced to a few hundred. Most Europeans are of French (including Corsican) descent, with a sprinkling of Italians, Spaniards, and Maltese.

LANGUAGES

Arabic is the official language of Algeria and is spoken by 86 percent of the population.

During the long colonial rule French became entrenched as the language of the administrative and intellectual elite and also as the language of progress and civilization. The Algerian revolutionary movement and the governments since independence have been committed to a total replacement of French by Arabic in all areas of national life. However, as in France's other former colonies, French has proved difficult to dislodge for practical reasons, and it is likely to remain the semi-official language of Algeria for the foreseeable future.

Principal Languages and Their Speakers

Arabic	25,720,000
Berber	4,190,000
English	—
French	6,000,000

RELIGIONS

Islam in its Sunni form is the official religion of Algeria; 99 percent of Algerians are Muslim. A vigorous program of mosque construction was undertaken in the late 1960s. Within the Muslim community the Kharadjites comprise the major minority. The M'zabite tribe is almost entirely Kharadjite. Frequently referred to as the "Puritans of the Desert," they are governed by a stricter moral code than other Muslims. Friday sermons are not formally censored, but government monitoring constrains their freedom of expression. Religious travel, most notably the hajj (the Islamic pilgrimage to Mecca), is government-organized.

Except for a few converted berbers, mostly Kabyles, the Christian population is almost entirely foreign. There is one Roman Catholic archdiocese for all of Algeria. The ancient Jewish community comprises native converts to Judaism and descendants of refugees from Roman and, later, Spanish, persecution.

Religious Affiliations

Religion	Adherents
Sunni Muslim	29,770,000
Ibādiyah Muslim	110,000
Other	20,000

HISTORICAL BACKGROUND

At the beginning of recorded history Algeria was inhabited by Berber tribes. After the 8th century B.C.E. the region was controlled by Carthage and, after the fall of Carthage in 146 B.C.E. by Rome. Known as Numidia under Roman rule, the region was Christianized in the early years of the modern era. Roman influence declined, especially after the Vandal invasions of 430–31. The Arabs arrived on the scene in 637 and swept away all traces of the Roman past. The inhabitants were forcibly converted to Islam and Arabic was introduced as the national language. Another wave of Arabs in the 11th century brought widespread destruction until the Almoravids and Almohads from Morocco unified the country and consolidated it with Morocco and Spain. Spain conquered a part of the coast in the 16th century but the Spaniards were expelled by Barbarossa, a Turkish pirate, who made himself a sultan. His brother Khayr al-Din placed his territory under the suzerainty of the Ottoman sultan in Istanbul. From the mid-1500s Algeria was ruled by Turkish beylerbeys, pashas, aghas, and deys. By the 1800s Turkish power had waned and the French began to expand their control over the coastal areas.

Algeria was conquered by France in the 1830s and officially annexed to that country in 1842. In the following century white French settlers colonized the territory, became permanent residents, and assumed political and economic power, denying equal rights to the indigenous Muslim majority.

The nationalist movement under the auspices of the Front de Libération Nationale (FLN) instigated a war for independence on November 1, 1954. The eight-year conflict resulted in the deaths of 250,000 Algerians and injuries to an additional 500,000. Two million people were uprooted, and 1 million French settlers left the country. The French government declared a cease-fire in March 1962, and Algeria became independent on July 3, 1962. In August the political bureau of the FLN took control of the government. A single list of FLN candidates was proposed for election to the National Constituent Assembly in September, and the republic was established. Ahmed Ben Bella, founder of the FLN, was made prime minister of the new government.

In September 1963 a popular referendum was held in which a constitution providing for a presidential form of government and the FLN as the sole political party was approved. Ben Bella was elected president. During his presidency economic reconstruction was initiated, and Algeria emerged as a single-party socialist state.

Col. Houari Boumedienne, the minister of defense, led the army in a bloodless coup in June 1965, taking over the government as president of the Revolutionary Council of 26 members. During the next six years Boumedienne overrode the opposition of left-wing interests in the FLN and, by 1971, had nationalized French petroleum enterprises and undertaken agricultural reforms.

In 1976, in two separate referenda, a new National Charter and a new constitution were approved. These set forth the principles of government whereby a socialist system was to be established and Islam declared the state religion. Boumedienne, as the only candidate nominated, was elected president in December. In February 1977, in the first legislative election since 1964, the unicameral National People's Assembly was convened and, in February, Chadli Bendjedid was elected president. Bendjedid appointed Col. Muhammad Abd al-Ghani prime minister in anticipation of constitutional changes approved later, in June, requiring the appointment of a prime minister. A legislative election was held in March 1982 for the National People's Assembly, whose membership had increased to 281. Voters were offered a choice of three candidates for each seat. Government officials were elected to 142 seats and FLN party officials to 55, with expectations that executive control of the National People's Assembly would increase.

Bendjedid was elected to a second term as president on January 12, 1984, and he appointed Abd al-Hamid Brahimi prime minister. The National Charter was revised in 1985 to provide for encouragement of the private sector and a balance of socialism and Islam as state ideologies. It was adopted in a referendum in January 1986. The number of seats in the National People's Assembly was increased to 295, its present size, and a legislative election was held in February 1987.

Discontent among students, Islamic fundamentalists, and Berbers of the Kabyle region began to be expressed publicly in 1985 in the form of criticism of the government and violent protests. In separate trials, supporters of Ben Bella and Berber activists were found guilty of either threatening state security or of membership in illegal groups and given prison sentences. Riots in Constantine and Setif in November 1986 led to four deaths and 186 arrests. Economic problems, particularly the sharp drop in petroleum prices in 1986, caused the government to introduce austerity measures, leading to further discontent. Administrative reforms were announced in December 1987 to increase efficiency in the government structure, but the combination of rapid population growth, government austerity measures, food shortages, high prices, and high unemployment led to a series of strikes beginning in July 1988, and by October riots broke out in Algiers. Violent protests also were staged in Oran and Annaba. A state of emergency was declared by the government. The official death toll was announced as 176, but unofficial estimates ranged between 200 and 500. The state of emergency was ended after six days, with Benjedid promising political reforms. A referendum was held on November 3, and a number of constitutional amendments were approved, including provision for the prime minister to be responsible to the National People's Assembly instead of the FLN.

Kasdi Merbah was appointed prime minister in late 1988. The new government proposed an emergency plan for reforms intended to address the problems causing discontent among youths and the unemployed. Benjedid, as the sole candidate in the presidential election held in December, was elected to his third term in office.

In February 1989 Algerians approved a new constitution that dropped all references to socialism and cleared the way for a multiparty system. Islam remained the state religion. The new political reforms were seen in part as an effort to head off the growing influence of Muslim fundamentalist groups, especially among the young.

Benjedid dismissed Merbah in September, citing the prime minister's failure to implement the political and economic reforms promised after the 1988 riots and the plans intended to transform Algeria from a one-party socialist state into a multiparty democracy. He was replaced by Mouloud Hamrouche, one of Benjedid's top advisers.

The democratization process, begun by the nationwide riots in 1988, gathered speed in 1990. Municipal elections were held in June 1990, with the Islamic Salvation Front (FIS) winning 54 percent of the vote. Violent protests by Islamic fundamentalists in June 1991 caused Benjedid to declare a state of emergency and cancel the national parliamentary elections that had been scheduled for late June. In the same month, Benjedid dismissed Prime Minister Mouloud Hamrouche and replaced him with Sid Ahmed Ghozali.

In June 1992, Mohamed Boudiaf, the head of the government, was assassinated and was replaced by Ali Kafi, who in turn was replaced by a five-member presidential High Council. In 1994 the council named Algeria's defense minister, Liamine Zeroual, as interim president of Algeria for a three-year term, allowing him to negotiate with the FIS. In 1994 the government met with five opposition groups to negotiate a peace settlement. Negotiations continued in Italy and led to elections in 1995.

Open elections were held in November. However, the FIS boycotted them. Liamine Zeroual was elected president. In 1996, President Zeroual signed new constitutional reforms that, among other things, banned political parties based upon religion or language. Rather than curb violence, these reforms led to increased ethnic conflict. Elections were once again held in April 1999 with Abdelaziz Bouteflika, former foreign minister, winning the vote. President Bouteflika enjoys the widespread support of the military, but he was elected amid allegations of fraud. His election has not brought an end to the armed conflict between government forces and Islamic fundamentalists.

CONSTITUTION

The basis of the government of Algeria is the constitution of 1976, ratified in 1977, amended in 1979, and further amended in 1988 and 1989. The constitution originally established Algeria as a socialist, democratic, and popular republic and guaranteed the fundamental rights of its citizens. Voting is universal at the age of 18. The National Liberation Front (FLN) was recognized as the nation's sole political party and as "the leading force in society." Executive power is vested in the president of the republic as the chief executive, head of state, and president of the Political Bureau of the FLN. The constitution was suspended by the military government in January 1992, which ended the commitment to socialism embodied in the National Charter and earlier constitutions. Algeria has a political system based on strong presidential rule, which provides in theory for a multiparty system, the separation of church and state, and military subordination to civilian authority. The constitution was again revised in 1996, banning political parties based solely on ethnicity, religion, or another separatist feature and creating a new, bicameral legislature.

LOCAL GOVERNMENT

The major units of local governments are the *wilayat*, or provinces; the *da'iraat*, or districts; and communes. The largest unit is the *wilaya*, headed by a *wali*, or governor, appointed by the central government. The *wilayat* are divided into *da'iraat*, each of which is headed by a deputy governor. The commune is the basic unit of local government and is linked to the central and *wilaya* governments and also to the FLN through party units, thus functioning as a means of both administrative and political control.

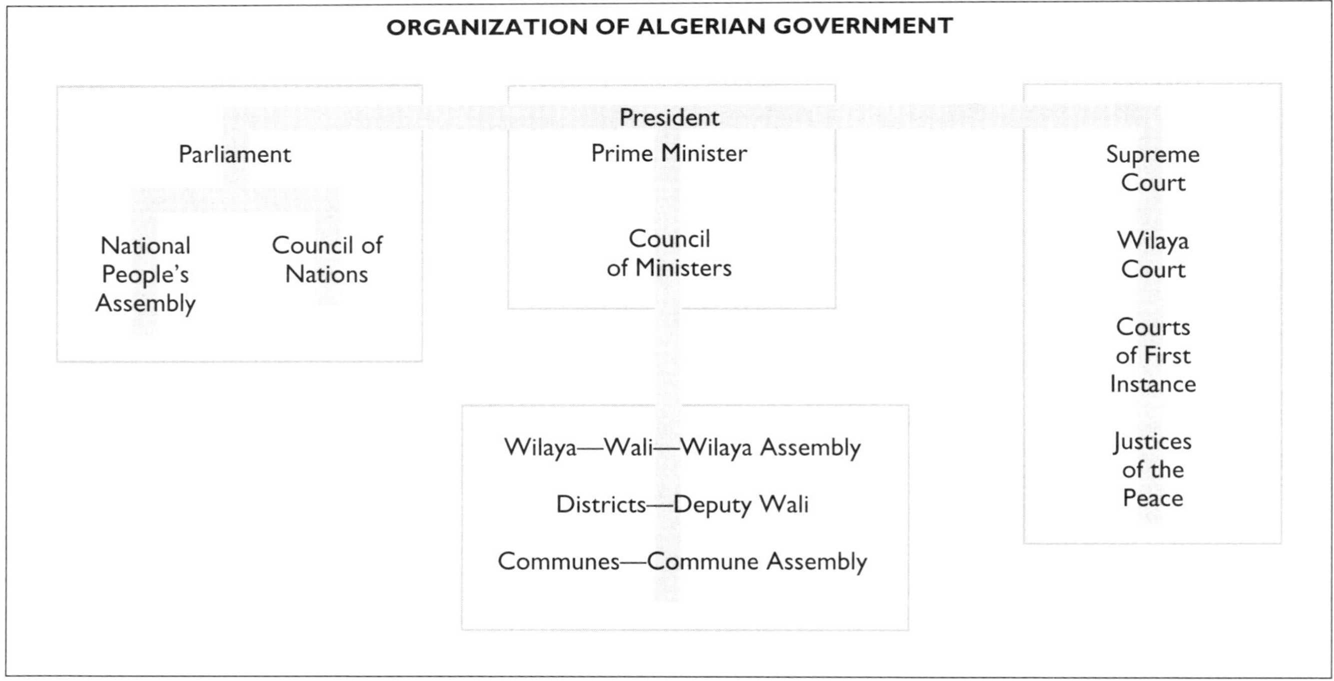

The organs of self-government at the local level include the commune assemblies in the communes and people's assemblies in the 48 *wilayat*. The commune's assemblies are elected for four years. Their administrative work is conducted through standing committees and an executive council.

Local Government

Principal administrative divisions, population

Population (1987 census)

Provinces	**population**
Adrar	217,678
Ain Delfia	537,256
Ain Temouchment	274,990
Algier	1,690,191
Annaba	455,888
Batina	752,617
El-Bayadh	153,254
Béchar	185,346
Bejaia	700,952
Biskra	430,202
Blida	702,188
Bordj Bou Arreridj	424,828
Bouira	526,900
Boumerdes	650,975
Ech-Chieff	684,192
Constantine	664,303
Djelfa	494,494
Ghardaia	216,140
Guelma	363,309
Illizi	18,930
Jijel	472,312
Khenchela	246,541
Laghouat	212,388
Mascara	566,901
Médéa	652,863
Mila	511,605
Mostaganem	505,932
M'Sila	604,693
Naāma	113,700
Oran	932,473
Ouargla	284,454
El-Oued	376,909
Oum el-Bouaghi	403,936
Relizane	544,877
Saida	235,494
Setif	1,000,694
Sidi bel-Abbes	446,277
Skikda	622,510
Souk Ahras	296,077
Tamanrasset	95,822
Et-Tarf	275,315
Tébessa	410,233
Tiaret	575,794
Tindouf	16,428
Tipaza	620,151
Tissemslit	228,120
Tizi Ouzou	936,948
Tiemcen	714,862
TOTAL	23,038,942

PARLIAMENT

The 1976 constitution described the National People's Assembly (APN) as a unicameral, elected, representative legislative body. Under the 1989 law, deputies are elected for five-year terms, and all Algerians "enjoying full civil and political rights" and over the age of 25 are eligible. Elections occur by secret, direct, and universal ballot. Until the country's first multiparty elections in December 1991, all candidates were drawn from a single party list, approved by the FLN, although multiple candidates could compete for a single constituency. Some legislative functions are exercised by the National Transitional Council, created in May 1994—a 200-member body which provides for political party, trade union, professional, and civil service representation. The bicameral parliament consists of the National People's Assembly, or Al-Majlis Ech-Chaabi Al-Watani (380 seats; members elected by popular vote to serve four-year terms), and the Council of Nations (144 seats; one-third of the members appointed by the president, two-thirds elected by indirect vote; members serve six-year terms; created as a result of the constitutional revision of November 1996). In 1997 multiparty elections to the parliament were held.

POLITICAL PARTIES

The number of legal parties in Algeria has dropped from 60 in 1991 to about 20 in 1999. The constitutional amendment of 1996 imposed a number of restrictions on the formation of political parties. There are three government parties: the National Democratic Rally, National Liberation Front (FLN), and the Movement for a Peaceful Society, formerly Movement for an Islamic Society. The principal opposition parties are Renaissance Movement (NAHDA), Movement for National Reform, Socialist Forces Front, Rally for Culture and Democracy, the latter two being primarily pro-Berber groups.

Political Parties

National Democratic Rally, 1997
National Liberation Front, 1954
Movement for a Peaceful Society, 1997
The main opposition parties are:

- Renaissance Movement, 1997
- Movement for National Reform, 1999
- Socialist Forces Front, 1998
- Rally for Culture and Democracy, 1989
- Workers' Party, 1995
- Progressive Republican Party
- Social Liberal Party
- Union for Democracy and Liberty
- Algerian Renewal Party, 1988
- Algerian Movement for Justice and Development, 1990
- Social Authenticity Movement

(continued)

Democratic and Social Movement, 1993
Social Democratic Party, 1989
Movement for Democracy in Algeria, 1984
Union of Democratic Forces, 1989
The Community, 1990
Party of Islamic and Democratic Arab Unity, 1990
Algerian People's Party, 1990
People's Association for Unity and Action
Republican National Alliance, 1995
National Party for Solidarity and Development
Socialist Workers Party, 1990
Algerian National Party, 1989
Illegal Groups include
Islamic Salvation Front, 1989
Islamic Salvation, 1992
Armed Islamic Group
Party of God

Political Parties: Strength in Parliament Most Recent Elections

Council of the Nation (Mailis al-Umma/Conseil de la Nation) Following the balloting of December 25, 1997, the distribution of the elected seats was as follows: National Democratic Rally, 80; National Liberation Front, 10; Socialist Forces Front, 4; Movement for a Peaceful Society, 2.

National People's Assembly (Majlis Ech Chaabi al-Watani, Assemblée Nationale Populaire) Following the election of June 5, 1997, the distribution of seats was as follows: National Democratic Rally, 156; Movement for a Peaceful Society, 69; National Liberation Front, 62; Renaissance Movement (*Nahda*), 34; Socialist Forces Front, 20; Rally for Culture and Democracy, 19; Workers' Party, 4; Progressive Republican Party, 3; Union for Democracy and Liberty and Social Liberal Party, 1 each; independents, 11.

LEGAL SYSTEM

The legal system is in transition. All legislation dating from the colonial era was reviewed and amended by a national commission, and a revised code was issued in 1975. Algerianization of the judiciary was completed in 1963. Despite these efforts the bulk of Algerian law remains French in origin and substance.

At the apex of the legal structure is the Supreme Court. It serves as the final court of appeal and also as the body that sets standards of procedure. However, it has no right to decide on the legality of government actions. Below the Supreme Court there is one court for each *wilaya*, (province; 48 in total); there are more than 180 courts of first instance at the district (*daira*) level and justices of the peace at the commune level. Three special courts have been set up in Oran, Constantine, and Algiers to deal with economic crimes against the state. There is no appeal from decisions of these courts. In 1975 the Cour de Sûreté de l'Etat, composed of magistrates and army officers was set up to try cases against state security. The Higher Court of the Magistrature, presided over by the president of the republic, is the constitutional body concerned with the integrity and discipline of the judiciary. Judges are appointed by the executive branch, and their appointment may be challenged only by the High Judicial Council.

LAW ENFORCEMENT

Law Enforcement

Offenses reported to the police per 100,000: 584
Murder: 1.0
Assault: 19.7
Burglary: 39.7
Automobile Theft: 8.5
Population per Police officer: 840
Death Penalty: Yes

HUMAN RIGHTS

Although democratic in principle, Algeria is a military state. The military establishment strongly influences domestic and foreign policy and security forces are actively involved in counterinsurgency and counterterrorism operations, in the course of which they have committed serious human rights abuses, including extrajudicial killings, torture of detainees, and arbitrary arrest and detention. Although the constitution provides for an independent judiciary, prolonged pretrial detention, lack of due process, and absence of privacy rights are serious problems.

There is no overt censorship, but the electronic media are entirely state-owned and the print media exercise self-censorship out of fear. Freedoms of press and speech are restricted in practice.

Islamic insurgents pose the greatest threat to human rights. During the past eight years, more than 100,000 people have been killed by armed groups who target both security personnel and civilians, especially women. In many cases, terrorists randomly targeted civilians in an apparent attempt to create social disorder. There are reports of disappearances involving both security forces and armed Islamic groups. Police beatings of detainees are a common practice. Muslim terrorists committed numerous abuses, such as beheading, mutilation, disemboweling, and dismembering their victims, including infants, children, and pregnant women. They also rape female victims whom they murder afterward.

Freedom of assembly and association are curtailed in practice. Islam is the official faith and the law limits sharply the practice of other faiths. Islam is taught compulsorily in schools and the government appoints preachers in mosques, gives general guidance on sermons, and provides financial support for the promotion of Islam.

Citizens do not have the ability to change the government peacefully. The executive branch is dominated by the military and the bureaucracy. Opposition parties are harassed, and the government sometimes disconnects their phone services. The opposition has only limited access to state-controlled radio and television. Under the present state of emergency, the police operate checkpoints throughout the country and routinely stop vehicles and detain people at will.

FOREIGN POLICY

Algeria's foreign policy has undergone a sea change since the military takeover in 1992. In the immediate post-independence period foreign policy was dominated by Ben Bella's anti-imperialist ideology. It changed into a low-profile moderate policy after the 1965 coup led by Boumedienne. But following the 1967 Arab-Israeli war Boumedienne became more pro-Arab, and Algeria joined the Steadfastness Front as a charter member in opposition to any rapprochement with Israel. During the 1970s and 1980s foreign policy was dominated by disputes with Morocco over Western Sahara and disputes with Libya. Relations with France were always uneasy until the military takeover. Algeria's efforts to contain the fundamentalist movement has received the support of not merely France and the United States but also Arab countries such as Morocco, Tunisia, and Egypt.

DEFENSE

The defense structure is headed by the president as supreme commander of the armed forces. He is assisted by the Higher Council of Defense and the General Staff. The Ministry of National Defense includes a Political Commissariat, an arm of the FLN charged with providing ideological indoctrination for the armed forces. Territorially, Algeria is divided into five military regions: Blida (I), Oran (II), Bechar (III), Ouargla (IV), and Constantine (V). Each is headed by a colonel who is directly subordinate to the minister of defense rather than to the General Staff.

Military manpower is provided by voluntary conscription for a period of six months at age 19.

The total strength of the armed forces is 124,000. In 1998, the annual military budget was $1.238 billion. This constituted 6.9 percent of the national budget. Total arms imports in 1998 cost the government $230 million.

The Algerian army is the most important and representative national institution, with both a political and a military mission. In its political role the army is designated the guardian of the revolution, and it determines the ideological direction of the nation.

Military Indicators

Total Active Duty Personnel: 124,000
Military Manpower per 1,000: 4.2
Military Expenditures $million: 1.238 billion
- as % of GNP: 3.2
- per capita $: 43
- as % of central government expenditures: 6.9

Arms Imports $million: 230
Arms Exports $million: 0

ECONOMY

The hydrocarbons sector is the backbone of the economy, accounting for roughly 52 percent of budget revenues, 25 percent of gross domestic product, and over 95 percent of export earnings. Algeria has the fifth-largest reserves of natural gas in the world and is the second-largest gas exporter; it ranks 14th for oil reserves. Algiers' efforts to reform one of the most centrally planned economies in the Arab world stalled in 1992 as the country became embroiled in political turmoil. Burdened with a heavy foreign debt, Algiers concluded a one-year standby arrangement with the IMF in April 1994 and, the following year, signed onto a three-year extended fund facility, which ended on April 30, 1998. Some progress on economic reform, Paris Club debt reschedulings in 1995 and 1996, and oil and gas sector expansion contributed to a recovery in growth since 1995. Still, the economy remains heavily dependent on volatile oil and gas revenues. In 2000 Algeria's finances benefited from the spike in oil prices and the government's tight fiscal policy, leading to a large increase in the trade surplus, the near tripling of foreign-exchange reserves, and reduction in foreign debt. The government has continued efforts to diversify the economy by attracting foreign and domestic investment outside the energy sector, but it has had little success in reducing high unemployment and improving living standards.

Principal Economic Indicators

Gross National Product: $43.927 billion
GNP per capita $: 1,500
GNP Average Annual Growth Rate (1990–97) %: −1.6
GNP per capita Average Annual Growth Rate (1990–97) %: −3.9
- Agriculture: 10
- Mining: 23
- Manufacturing: 9
- Construction: 12
- Public Utilities: —
- Transportation and Communications: 2
- Trade: 33
- Financial Services: 33
- Other Services: 13
- Government: 13

(continued)

Gross Domestic Product by Type of Expenditure %
Private Consumption: 56
Government Consumption: 17
Gross Domestic Investment: 32
Foreign Trade: Exports: 24
Imports: −28
% of Income Received by Poorest 20%: 6.9
% of Income Received by Richest 10%: 31.5

Price and earnings indexes (1995 = 100)

	1992	1993	1994	1995	1996	1997	1998
Consumer price index	48.6	58.6	75.7	100.0	121.6	126.3	129.0
Earnings index	75.9	88.8	90.9	100.0	110.0	—	—

Finance

National Currency: Algerian Dinar (DA)
Exchange Rate: $1 = DA 58.969
Money Supply Stock in National Currency billion: 520.3
M1 per capita: 18,300
Central Bank Discount Rate %: —
Total External Debt $million: 33,000
Debt Service Ratio %: 24.4
Balance of Payments $million: 3,500
International Reserves SDRs million: 4,835
Ratio of External Debt to Total Reserves: 13.3
Average Annual Rate of Inflation/Consumer Price Index
Growth Rate %: 7

Official Development Assistance

Donor ODA $million: 420
as % of GNP: 0.9
per capita $: 13
Foreign Direct Investment $million: 5

Central Government Revenues and Expenditures

Fiscal Year:
Revenues $million: 13,700
Expenditures $million: 13,100
Budget Surplus $million: 600
Tax Revenues as % of GDP: 30.7
Highest Tax Bracket %
Individual: —
Corporate: —

Employment and Labor

Economically Active Population: 5,341,000
Female Participation Rate %: 9.2
Activity Rate %: 23.6
Labor by Sector: %
Agriculture, Forestry, Fishing: 13.6
Manufacturing, Mining: 11.6
Construction: 12.9
Transportation and Communications: 4.1
Trade, Hotels, and Restaurants: 7.3
Finance, Insurance, Real Estate: 2.7
Public Administration, Defense: —
Services: 22.1
Unemployment %: 28

Agriculture

Agriculture's Share of GDP: 10
Average Annual Rate of Growth (1965–98) %: 4.8
Number of Farms 000: 899
Average Size of Farm ha: 6.2
Number of Tractors per 1,000 hectares: 13.2
Irrigation, % of Farms having: 7
Artificial Fertilizer kg/hectare: 13
Total Farm land as % of land area: 16.6
Livestock: Cattle 000: 1,250
Sheep 000: 16,750
Hogs 000: 6
Chickens 000: 132,000
Forests: Production of Roundwood
(000 cubic meters): 2,517
Fisheries: Total Catch tons: 135.4

Mining

% of GDP: 25.7
Value of Mineral Production $million: 10628.8

Manufacturing

Value Added $million: 4,084
Industrial Production Growth Rate %: —

Energy

Commercial Energy Production metric tons of
oil equivalent 000: 125,576
Commercial Energy Consumption metric tons of
oil equivalent 000: 26,497
Commercial Energy Consumption per capita kg: 904
Average Annual Growth Rate 1980–97 %: 0.9
Net Energy Imports % of use: −374
Electricity Installed Capacity kW 000: 6,007
Production kW-hr million: 19,714
Coal Reserves tons million: 43
Production tons 000: 22
Natural Gas Proven Reserves cubic meters billion: 3,690
Production cubic meters million: 51,817
Crude Petroleum Reserves barrels million: 9,200
Production barrels million: 298
Consumption barrels million: 164
Refinery Capacity barrels per day 000: 465
Pipelines Length km: 6,910

Foreign Trade

Imports $million: 9,830.6
Exports $million: 8,555.5
Export Volume % Annual Growth Rate (1990–97): 2.4
Import Volume % Annual Growth Rate (1990–97): 0.6
Balance of Trade $

Balance of trade (current prices)

	1992	1993	1994	1995	1996	1997
U.S. $000,000	+2,489	+1,337	−1,005	+299	+4,270	+5,034
% of total	12.6%	7.1%	5.5%	1.5%	20.1%	22.1%

Major Trading Partners

	Imports	Exports
European Union %	59.3	64.8
United States %	13.2	16.7
Eastern Europe %	2.5	2.7
Japan %	3.4	0.7
Others %	21.6	15.1

Transportation

Roads Total Length mi: 63,643 km 102,424
Paved %: 69
Automobiles: 871,000
Trucks and Buses: 566,000
Persons per vehicle: 20
Railroad; Track Length mi: 2,965 km 4,772
Passenger-mi million: 1,568
Freight-mi million: 1,644
Merchant Marine: No. of Vessels: 149
Total Deadweight Tonnage 000: 1,093.4
International Cargo Loaded tons 000: 57,607
International Cargo Off-loaded tons 000: 14,284
Airports with Scheduled Flights: 28
Traffic: Passenger-mi million: 1,643
Freight-mi million: 10.1
Length of Canals mi: — km

Tourism

Number of Tourists to 000: 678
Number of Tourists from 000: 1,377
Tourist Receipts $million: 27
Tourist Expenditures $million: 135

Communications

Telephones 000: 1,146
Cost of Local Calls 3 mins $0.02
Cellular Telephones 000: 4.7
Fax Machines 000: 5.2
Personal Computers 000: 85
Internet Hosts per million persons: 0.6
Mail: Post Offices: 3,145
Pieces of Mail Handled million: 564
Pieces of Mail Handled per person: 20

EDUCATION

Education is, in principle, free, compulsory, and universal for nine years, from ages six to 15. Primary education lasts for six years and secondary education for four years in the technical stream and seven years in the general stream, leading to the baccalaureat.

The academic year runs from September to July. The medium of instruction is Arabic in the first two grades of primary school, partly Arabic and partly French in the next four years in primary school, and almost entirely French from the secondary grades up. Promotion is automatic in all primary grades. In the intermediate and secondary schools promotion is determined by monthly, midyearly, and annual examinations. There are three leaving examinations: at the end of primary school, the end of elementary school, and the end of secondary school. At the primary level all the teachers are now Algerian, but about half of the secondary school teachers are recruited abroad.

Several types of vocational training are offered by different institutions. Six-year programs are available at technical schools, agricultural training programs at agricultural schools and nine regional agricultural colleges, and two- and three-year technical programs with 11 months of intensive practical training at technical institutes. Only 1.5 percent of secondary school students are enrolled in the technical and vocational stream.

Traditional religious schools known as *kuttabs* have been incorporated into the school system. Koranic study centers offer programs in Arabic, and Islamic secondary schools have developed a curriculum with a strong religious emphasis. A total of 2 percent of primary school students are enrolled in private schools.

The educational system is administered by three ministries: the Ministry of Primary and Secondary Education, the Ministry of Higher Education and Scientific Research, and the Ministry of Traditional Education and Habus (religious affairs). In addition, the Ministry of Agriculture and the Ministry of Labor and Social Affairs run vocational training and special education centers.

There are more than a dozen universities and campuses, including the University of Algiers, the University of Oran, the University of Annaba, and the University of Constantine.

Education

Literacy Rate %: 61.6
Male %: 73.9
Female %: 49.0
First Level: Primary schools: 11,186
Teachers: 169,010
Students: 4,617,000
Student-Teacher Ratio: 27.3
Net Enrollment Ratio: 95
Second Level: Secondary Schools: 3,954
Teachers: 150,397
Students: 2,544,864
Student-Teacher Ratio: 16.9
Net Enrollment Ratio: 56

Vocational Level: Schools: —
Students: —

Third Level: Institutions: —
Teachers: 14,475
Students: 233,019
Student-Ratio Level: 16.1
Gross Enrollment Ratio: 10.9
Students per 100,000: 1,126
% of Population Age 25 and over with Postsecondary Education: —

Public Expenditure on Education as % of GDP: 5.6

SCIENCE AND TECHNOLOGY

Science and Technology

Scientists and Engineers in R&D per 1 million persons: —
Expenditures in R&D as % of GDP: —
High-Tech Exports $million: 5
Patent Applications by Residents: 34

MEDIA

All news media are government-controlled. Among the major newspapers are *el-Moudjahid* (The Fighter), the organ of the FLN, published in Arabic and French; the Arabic dailies *Ach Cha'ab* (The People, also an FLN organ), *Al Badil* (The Alternate), *Al-Joumhouria* (The Republic), and *An Nasr* (The Victory); and the French dailies *Horizons* and *Le Soir d'Algérie* (Algerian Evening). The combined circulation of the newspapers is approximately 1 million.

Censorship of all news is implicit in state ownership. News coverage is limited largely to officially approved material. The official news agency is Algérie Presse Service (APS).

Broadcasting is a state monopoly operated by Radiodiffusion-Télévision Algérienne (RTA), which has three radio networks broadcasting in Arabic and French. International programs consist of daily Arabic broadcasts beamed to Morocco and the Middle East and broadcasts in French beamed to Algerian workers in Europe.

RTA's television service, introduced in 1956, is available to 80 percent of the population in the region north of the Sahara through a network of transmitters. The system is connected with Eurovision and with Maghrebovision. The national programs are in French, Arabic, and Kabyle.

Media

Daily Newspapers: 6
- Total Circulation 000: 1,250
- Circulation per 1,000: 46

Books Published: 323
Magazines: 48
Radio Receivers 000: 3,500
- per 1,000: 125

Television sets 000: 1,945
- per 1,000: 71

Most Important Media:

Press. The following are dailies published at El Djazair (Algiers) unless otherwise noted: *el-Moudjahid* (The Fighter, 400,000), former FLN organ in French; *an-Nasr* (The Victory, Qacentina, 340,000), in Arabic; *Algérie Actualité* (255,000), government weekly in French; *Horizons* (200,000), in French; *al-Massa* (100,000), in Arabic; *al-Jumhuriyah* (The Republic, Wahran, 70,000), former FLN organ in Arabic; *al-Chaab* (The People, 25,000), former FLN information journal in Arabic. Other independent dailies include: *Le Soir de l'Algérie* (150,000), in French; *El Watan* (The Nation, 130,000), in French; *Al Khabar* (The News, 120,000), in Arabic; *Al Djazair al-Joum* (54,000), in Arabic; *Le Matin*, in French; and *La Tribune*, in French.

News agencies. The domestic agency is the Algerian Press Service (Wikalat al-Anba' al-Jaza 'iriyah/Algérie Presse Service—APS). A number of foreign agencies maintain offices at Algiers.

Radio and television. The government-controlled Broadcasting Service of the Algerian Republic (Idha 'at al-Jumhuriyat al-Jaza 'iriyah) maintains a television network (Télévision Algérie) servicing about a dozen stations and four radio networks.

CULTURE

Cultural Indicators

Public Libraries Number: —
- Volumes: —
- Registered borrowers: —

Museums Number: 32
- Annual Attendance: 260,000

Cinema Production of Long Films: 3
- Number of Cinemas: —
- Seating Capacity: —
- Annual Attendance: —
- Annual Attendance per capita: —

STATUS OF WOMEN

After 1962 the status of women began improving, primarily because of the increased education of family members, broader economic and social development, and the willingness or necessity for ever-larger numbers of women to seek gainful employment. In the mid-1950s, about 7,000 women were registered as wage earners; by 1977 a total of 138,234 women, or 6 percent of the active work force, were engaged in full-time employment. Corresponding figures for the mid-1980s were about 250,000, or 7 percent of the labor force. Many women were employed in the state sector as teachers, nurses, physicians, and technicians. The number of women in the workforce, however, may be much higher than official statistics have suggested. Women in the rural workforce were not counted; only 140 were listed in official statistics.

Women

Gender Empowerment Measure: 93
Seats Held in Parliament by Women %: 3.2
Female Administrators and Managers %: 5.9
Female Professional and Technical Workers %: 27.6
Women's Share of Earned Income %: 19
Women in Government %: 2

HEALTH, FOOD, AND NUTRITION

Health

Number of Physicians: 25,796
Number of Dentists: 7,763

Number of Nurses: —
Number of Pharmacists: 3,425
Population per Physician: 1,066
Number of Hospitals: 181
Hospital Beds per 10,000: 19
Hospital Bed Occupancy Rate: 49.3
Infant Mortality Rate per 1,000 live births: 54
Maternal Mortality Rate per 100,000 live births: 160
Total Health Expenditures as % of GDP: 6.95
Health Expenditures per capita $: 149
HIV Infected % of adults: 0.07
Cigarette Consumption per smoker per year: —
% of Smokers: Male: —
Female: —
Access to Safe Water %: 78

Food and Nutrition

Food Supply as % of FAO Requirements: 127
% of Consumption Expenditures on Food: 52.3
Daily Available Calories per capita: 3,042
% of Total Calories derived from:
Cereals: 59.3
Potatoes, cassava: 1.5
Meat, poultry: 3.0
Fish: 0.3
Eggs, milk: 5.1
Fruits, vegetables: 3.8
Fats, oils: 16.9

ENVIRONMENT

Algeria suffers from growing desertification caused by widespread soil erosion because of overgrazing and other poor farming practices. The rivers and coastal waters of the country are being polluted by the dumping of raw sewage, petroleum refining wastes, and other industrial effluents. The Mediterranean Sea, in particular, is becoming polluted from oil wastes, soil erosion, and fertilizer runoff. Most Algerians do not have an adequate supply of potable water.

Environment

Forest Area sq km: 19,000
Average Annual Deforestation sq km: 234
Nationally Protected Areas as % of Total Land Area: 2.5
Freshwater Access cubic meters per capita: 478
Emissions of Organic Water Pollutants kg per day: 102,069
CO_2 Emissions per capita ton: 3.3

CHRONOLOGY

1962 The Evian Agreement establishes a provisional government for Algeria; in a referendum 91 percent of the electorate vote for full independence; France proclaims independence for Algeria.
Internal struggles among Algerian leaders intensify as Muhammad Ahmed Ben Bella and Houari Boumedienne of the National Liberation Front (FLN) assert opposition to the provisional government of Ben Yusuf Ben Khedda.
Ben Bella and Boumedienne march at the head of the FLN forces on Algiers and occupy the capital.
The Republic of Algeria is proclaimed, with Ferhat Abbas as president and Ben Bella as prime minister.
Hundreds of thousands of French Algerians flee the country.

1963 The Algerian dinar is introduced.
Vacant French estates are handed over to workers' committees.
A new constitution is promulgated, establishing a presidential form of government; Ben Bella is elected the first president.
In war with Morocco, Algerian forces are badly defeated.

1964 The Algiers Charter is adopted at the historic FLN Congress.
Two revolts against the regime are crushed.

1965 In a swift and bloodless coup, Boumedienne ousts Ben Bella and assumes power at head of Council of the Revolution.

1967 An armed uprising led by Colonel Tahar Zbiri, chief of army staff, is put down.
Algeria suspends diplomatic relations with the United States in the aftermath of the Arab-Israeli War.

1970 The Tlemcen Accord settles the border dispute with Morocco.

1971 Boumedienne signs into law the Charter of the Agrarian Revolution, initiating a comprehensive land reform program.

1974 Diplomatic ties with the United States are resumed.

1976 A new constitution is promulgated, restoring the National Assembly.
Boumedienne is elected president.
Mauritania and Morocco break ties with Algeria over Algeria's formal recognition of the Saharan Arab Democratic Republic (SADR) in Western Sahara and support of Polisario, Western Sahara's national independence movement.

1977 The first legislative election since 1964 is held to form the unicameral National People's Assembly.

1978 President Boumedienne dies of natural causes and Speaker of the National Assembly Rabah Bitat is named interim president.
Diplomatic relations between Algeria and Egypt are severed.

1979 Chadli Bendjedid is elected president; Colonel Muhammad Ben Ahmed Abdelghani is named prime minister; the constitution is amended, reducing the presidential term to five years.
Former president Ben Bella is released from prison.
Diplomatic ties with Mauritania are restored after Mauritania relinquishes claims to Western Sahara (formerly Spanish Sahara).

1980 In a cabinet reshuffle, influential foreign minister Abdelaziz Bouteflika is removed.
The government shifts economic priorities away from heavy industry and toward consumer goods.
The Berbers, charging discrimination and repression, break out into violence in the city of Tizi-Ouzou.
1983 President Chadli Bendjedid visits France. The Moroccan border is reopened.
1984 President Chadli Bendjedid is reelected to a second term in office.
1985 Algeria boycotts Arab summit meeting over the Polisario issue.
President Chadli Bendjedid visits the United States.
1986 In a national referendum, voters approve by a vote of 98.37 percent the Revised National Charter, which encourages the private sector and balances Islam against socialism as state ideologies. National People's Assembly seats are increased to 295.
1988 In a joint meeting, the heads of state of Algeria, Libya, Mauritania, Morocco, and Tunisia form the Great Arab Maghreb and plan to harmonize legislation within the region and share in joint economic projects. Algeria experiences its worst riots and internal unrest since independence in 1962, and at least 500 are killed in army attacks on rioters. Full diplomatic relations with Egypt are restored.
1989 A new constitution is approved by a national referendum.
1990 The Islamic Salvation Front (FIS) earns sweeping victories in municipal elections throughout the country; the government formally recognizes at least 25 political parties as they prepare for the 1991 multiparty National Assembly elections.
1991 Islamic fundamentalists riot in Algiers; Bendjedid declares a state of emergency and postpones national elections; Prime Minister Mouloud Hamrouche and his cabinet are dismissed and Sid Ahmed Ghozali is named prime minister.
1992 The head of the government, Mohamed Boudiaf, is assassinated.
1995 Gen. Liamine Zeroual wins the first contested presidential elections in more than 30 years.
1997 A multiparty parliament is elected, but the ruling military council maintains control.
1998 Islamic fundamentalists continue to slaughter their opponents.
1999 Abdelaziz Bouteflika is elected president amid allegations of fraud.
A law on civil concord, the result of negotiations with the armed wing of the FIS, is approved in a referendum.
2000 Attacks on civilians and security forces continue and are thought to be the work of small groups still opposed to the civil concord.
2001 Many demonstrators are killed in violent clashes between security forces and Berber protestors in the mainly Berber region of Kabylie following the death of a teenager in police custody. The Rally for Culture and Democracy, a pro-Berber group, withdraws from the government in protest against the authorities' handling of the riots.

BIBLIOGRAPHY

Ciment, James. *Algeria: The Fundamentalist Challenge*. New York, 1997.

Heggoy, A. A., and R. R. Crout. *Historical Dictionary of Algeria*. Metuchen, N.J., 1995.

Ruedy, John. *Modern Algeria: The Origins and Development of a Nation*. Bloomington, Ind., 1992.

Martinez, Luis. *The Algerian Civil War, 1990–1998*. New York, 2000.

Stone, M. *The Agony of Algeria*. New York, 1997.

Willis, Michael. *The Islamist Challenge in Algeria: A Political History*. New York, 1997.

OFFICIAL PUBLICATIONS

Algeria. *Annuaire statistique; Recensement general de la population et de l'habitat,* 1987.

CONTACT INFORMATION

Embassy of Algeria
2118 Kalorama Road NW
Washington, D.C. 20008
Phone: (202) 265-2800 Fax: (202) 667-2174

INTERNET RESOURCES

- Office National des Statistiques (French)
  http://www.ons.dz
- Permanent Mission of Algeria to the UN
  http://www.algeria-un.org/nspage.html

ANDORRA

BASIC FACT SHEET

OFFICIAL NAME:
Principality of Andorra, Principat d'Andorre (French); Principado de Andorra (Spanish)

ABBREVIATION:
AD

CAPITAL:
Andorra la Vella

HEAD OF STATE:
French co-prince President Jacques Chirac (from 1975); Spanish Episcopal Co-Prince Msgr. Joan Martí y Alanis (from 1971)

HEAD OF GOVERNMENT:
Marc Forné Molné (from 1994)

NATURE OF GOVERNMENT:
Parliamentary democracy

POPULATION:
66,100 (1999)

AREA:
487 sq km (188 sq mi)

MAJOR ETHNIC GROUPS:
Catalan, Spanish, French

LANGUAGES:
Spanish, French, Catalan

RELIGION:
Roman Catholicism

UNIT OF CURRENCY:
French franc and Spanish peseta

NATIONAL FLAG:
Tricolor of blue, yellow, and red vertical stripes; on the yellow stripe is the coat of arms.

NATIONAL ANTHEM:
"Himne Andorra" beginning "The great Charlemagne, my father, has delivered me from the Arabs."

NATIONAL HOLIDAYS:
National Festival, September 8

DATE OF INDEPENDENCE:
December 6, 1288

DATE OF CONSTITUTION:
May 4, 1993 (effective)

GEOGRAPHICAL FEATURES

Andorra is a landlocked country on the southern slopes of the Pyrenees Mountains between the French departments of Ariège and Pyrenées-Orientales to the north and the Spanish provinces of Gerona and Lerida to the south. Andorra has a total area of 487 sq km (188 sq mi), extending 30.1 km (18.7 sq mi) east to west and 25.4 km (15.8 mi) north to south. The total boundary length of 125 km (77.8 mi) is shared with France (60 km; 37.3 mi) and Spain (65 km; 40.4 mi).

The capital is Andorra la Vella, with a population of 21,984 in 1998.

Most of Andorra's rugged terrain consists of gorges, narrow valleys, and defiles surrounded by mountain peaks rising higher than 2,900 m (9,500 ft) above sea level. All the valleys are at least 914 m (3,000 ft) high, and the mean altitude is over 1,829 m (6,000 ft). Of the several lofty peaks, the highest is Coma Pedrosa (3,100 m; 10,170 ft).

The country is drained by a single basin whose main stream, Riu Valira, has two branches and six smaller open basins; hence the term "valleys" is used to describe the republic. The section of the river flowing through la Serrat by way of Ordino and La Massana is the Valira del Norts; that flowing through Canilo, Encamp, and Les Escaldes is the Valira del Orien.

Andorra

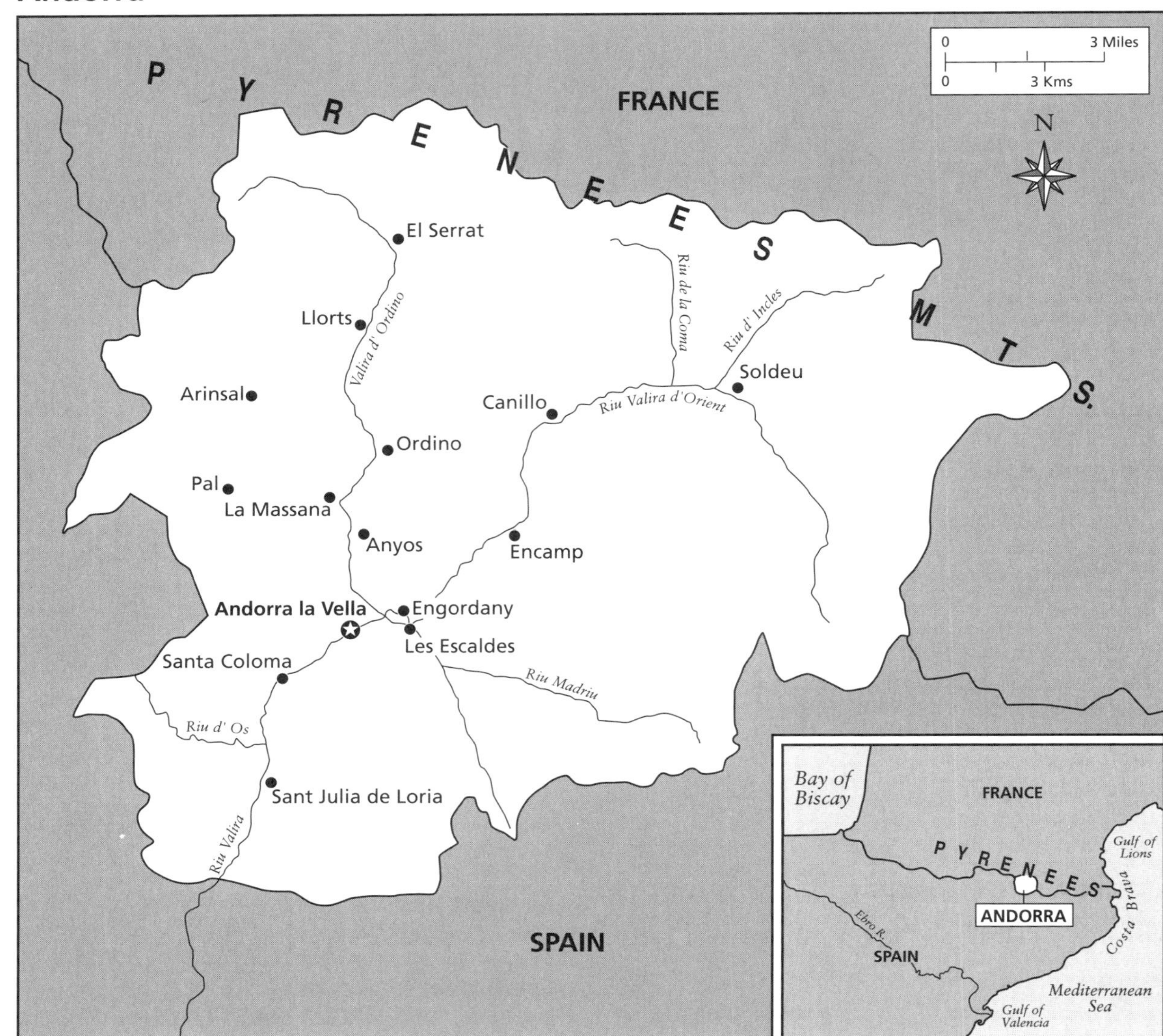

Geography

Area sq km: 487
World Rank: 193rd
Land Boundaries, km: France 60; Spain 65
Coastline, km: 0
Elevation Extremes meters
- Lowest: Riu Valira 840 m
- Highest: Coma Pedrosa 2,945 m

Land Use % Arable land: 2
- Permanent Crops: 0
- Permanent Pastures: 56
- Forest and Woodland: 22
- Other: 20

Population of Principal Cities

Andorra la Vella	21,984

CLIMATE AND WEATHER

Because of its high elevation, Andorra has an alpine climate with severe winters and mild or warm summers, depending on the altitude. The rainfall is heavy, most of it falling in April and October, and it accounts for the lush mountain pastures. The northern valleys are completely snowed in for at least six months a year, and there is a thriving ski resort industry.

Climate and Weather

Mean Temperature
Winter 30°F to 40°F
Summer 54°F to 79°F
Average Rainfall 35 in

POPULATION

Population Indicators	
Total Population: 1999	66,100
World Rank:	203rd
Density per sq mi:	365.2
% of annual growth (1994–99):	0.4
Male %:	53.1
Female %:	46.9
Urban %:	62.5
Age Distribution: % 0–14:	16.3
15–29:	27.7
30–44:	27.2
45–59:	15.1
60–74:	9.9
75 and over:	3.8
Population 2020:	78,000
Birth Rate per 1,000:	11
Death Rate per 1,000:	3.4
Population Doubling Time (years):	85
Infant Mortality Rate per 1,000 live births:	7.7
Rate of Natural Increase per 1,000:	7.6
Total Fertility Rate:	1.7
Expectation of Life (years): Males	75.6
Females	81.7
Marriage Rate per 1,000:	2.0
Divorce Rate per 1,000:	—
Total Number of Households:	7,000
Average Size of Households:	7.0
% of Illegitimate Children:	—
Induced Abortions:	—
Rate per 100 live births:	—

ETHNIC COMPOSITION

Native Andorrans, who make up about one-third of the population, are of Catalan stock. The majority are Spanish residents.

LANGUAGES

The official language is Catalan, a Romance language related to Provençal. Both Spanish and French are spoken widely.

Principal Languages and Their Speakers	
Catalan (Andorran)	21,000
French	4,000
Portuguese	7,000
Spanish	29,000
Other	4,000

RELIGIONS

The population is almost entirely Roman Catholic. The constitution guarantees religious liberty.

Religious Affiliations	
Roman Catholic	61,000
Other	6,000

HISTORICAL BACKGROUND

Andorra is historically associated with Charlemagne, who in the national anthem is referred to as "The great Charlemagne, my father, has delivered me from the Arabs." Charlemagne is believed to have christened the principality after the biblical town of Endor and to have granted the Andorrans a charter. Charles the Bald, grandson of Charlemagne, appointed the count of Urgel overlord of Andorra with the right to collect the imperial tribute. The same right was claimed by the bishop of Urgel. When, in 1226, the lords of the county of Foix, in present-day France, became heirs of the counts of Urgel, the contest between the two claimants became intense. In 1278 the dispute was resolved by the adoption of a pareage, a federal institution recognizing the equal rights of two lords to a seignorage. In 1505 Germaine of Foix married Ferdinand V of Spain, thus bringing the overlordship under Spain, but it went back to France when Henry II of Navarre, also a count of Foix, ascended the French throne in 1589 as Henry IV. In 1793 the French revolutionary government refused the traditional Andorran tribute as a legacy of feudalism and renounced French suzerainty, overriding the wishes of the Andorrans. French coprincipalityship was restored in 1806 by Napoleon on the express petition of the Andorrans. With the demise of the monarchy, the president of France functions as the coprince along with the Spanish bishop of Urgel.

In 1970 suffrage was extended to women and in 1977 to all first-generation Andorrans of foreign parentage who were aged 28 and over. In 1982 an executive council of six ministers was formed in the first institutional reform in modern Andorran history. In 1993 a new constitution was promulgated approved by 74.2 percent of Andorrans. In 1993 Andorra was admitted to the Council of Europe and the United Nations. In the same year both France and Spain explicitly acknowledged the sovereignty of Andorra and established embassies in Andorra la Vella.

CONSTITUTION

Andorra has one of the most unusual systems of government in the world. The two heads of state, or coprinces, who have equal authority in Andorran matters, are both non-Andorrans: One is the president of France and the other the bishop of Urgel. Andorra pays a biennial *questia* (tribute) of 960 French francs to the president of France and 460 Spanish pesetas to the bishop, who also receives from each of the six parishes two capons, two hens, and four cheeses, which he then returns.

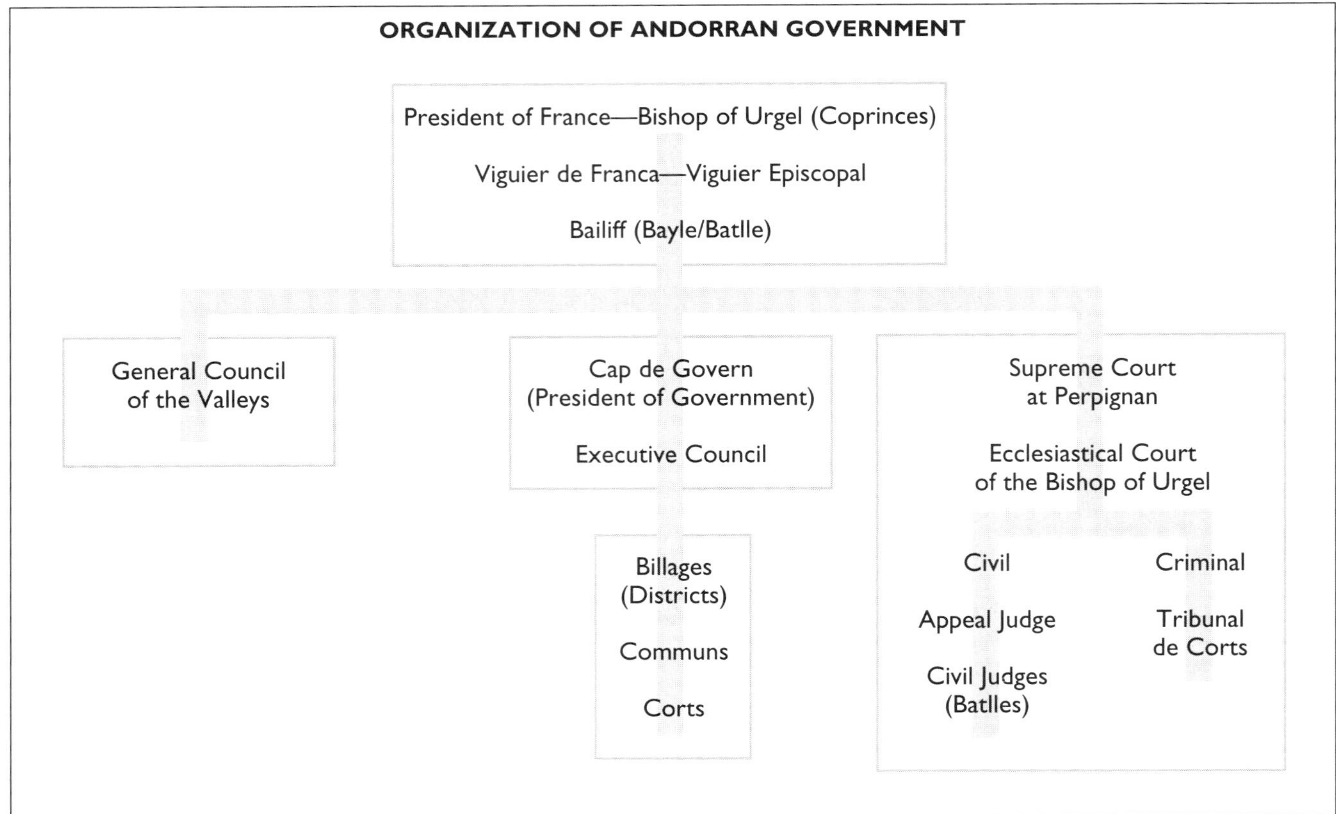

The constitution adopted in 1993 created a constitutional monarchy. A parliament is elected by universal suffrage. The General Council of the Andorran Valleys, as it is called, has 28 seats with two members elected from each of the seven parishes and 14 elected at large. The members serve for four years.

LOCAL GOVERNMENT

For the purpose of local administration, Andorra is divided into seven villages or districts, each of which has a parish council whose members are elected by universal suffrage. Below the districts are *communs* and *corts*. The former are 10-member bodies elected by universal suffrage and headed by an elected senior consul and junior consul. The latter are submunicipal advisory bodies that function primarily as administrators of communal property.

Local Government

Principal administrative divisions, capitals, area, population

Area and population

Parishes	Capitals	area sq/mi	area sq/km	population 1998 estimate
Andorra la Vella	Andorra la Vella	49	127	21,630
Canillo	Canillo	74	191	2,645
Encamp	Encamp	74	191	10,163
La Massana	La Massana	25	65	5,874
Les Escaldes-Engordany	—	3	3	15,259
Ordino	Ordino	33	85	2,098
Saint Julia de Loria	Saint Julia de Loria	181	468	65,306

PARLIAMENT

Andorra has a unicameral legislature of which only one-half are elected in national elections. The remaining members of the General Council are elected to represent one of the country's seven parishes.

POLITICAL PARTIES

Political parties were sanctioned under the 1993 constitution. The largest parties include The Liberal Union headed by Marc Forné Molné, the National Democratic Initiative, and the National Democratic Organization, which succeeded the Democratic Party of Andorra, founded in 1979.

Political Parties

Liberal Party of Andorra
Social-Democratic Party
Democratic Party
Lauredian Union

Political Parties: Strength in General Council Most Recent Elections (March 4, 2001)

Liberal Party, 16; Social-Democratic Party, 6; Social Democratic Party, 5; Union Lauredian, 2.

LEGAL SYSTEM

The legal system is based on customary Catalan law supplemented by Roman law. Traditional laws are codified in the Namual Digest of 1748 and the Politar of 1763, and legal standards are found in the Instructions to Bailiffs of 1740. Civil cases in the first instance are heard in the Court of the Bailiff (Tribunal del Batlle), presided over by two bayles, one appointed by the viguier de franca of France and the other by viguier episcopal of Spain. Appeals are heard in the Court of Appeal, headed by a single judge appointed alternately by each of the two coprinces. Final appeals in civil cases lie with the Supreme Court of Andorra (Tribunal Supremo) at Perpignan, France, or the ecclesiastical court of the bishop of Urgel. Criminal cases are heard in Andorra la Vella by the Tribunal des Corts, consisting of the two viguiers, the judge of appeal, the two bailiffs, and two members of the General Council. There is a parallel system of labor and administrative courts.

LAW ENFORCEMENT

Law Enforcement

Offenses reported to the police per 100,000: 2,795
- Murder: 1.6
- Assault: 36.5
- Burglary: 796.8
- Automobile Theft: 111.1
- Population per Police officer: 220

Death Penalty: Abolished 1990

HUMAN RIGHTS

Under the constitution, all human and civil rights are respected and protected. All citizens are equal before the law and enjoy full liberties. Discrimination on the grounds of race, sex, religion, and national origin is prohibited.

FOREIGN POLICY

Apart from France and Spain, Andorra has no diplomatic relations with the rest of the world.

DEFENSE

Andorra has no defense forces. All able-bodied men who own firearms must serve without remuneration and without uniforms in the small army that presents the Andorran flag at official ceremonies. The army, which has not seen battle in 700 years, is unique in that all its men are officers.

Military Indicators

Total Active Duty Personnel: —
Military Manpower per 1,000: —
Military Expenditures $: —
- as % of GNP: —
- per capita $: —
- as % of central government expenditures: —

Arms Imports $: —
Arms Exports $: —

ECONOMY

Andorra has a capitalist economy superimposed on a feudal political system. The economy is based primarily on trade and tourism. Owing to Andorra's duty-free status, its economy expanded rapidly after World War II. However, Spain's accession to the European Union (EU) in 1986 and the consequent removal of Spanish tariff barriers has threatened its lucrative trade. Failing to reach an agreement with the EU by 1988 on a special status within the Union, Andorra has requested that it be allowed to continue as a free trade area in exchange for modifications in the coprincipality's fiscal and social policies.

With minimal company laws or regulations and little or no enforcement of laws that do exist, Andorra also has been a tax haven for foreign financiers and investors. Land speculation has led to rapid growth of the construction industry. The country's prosperity is based as much on smuggling and laundering of money as on legitimate activities.

There are no accurate estimates of Andorra's gross national product, but the best available one is $1 billion, or $16,000 per capita.

Principal Economic Indicators

Gross National Product: $1.155 billion
GNP per capita: 18,000
GNP Average Annual Growth Rate (1990–97) %: —
GNP per capita Average Annual Growth Rate (1990–97) %: —
Origin of Gross Domestic Product %
- Agriculture: —
- Mining: —
- Manufacturing: —
- Construction: —
- Public Utilities: —
- Transportation and Communications: —
- Trade: —
- Financial Services: —
- Other Services: —
- Government: —

(continued)

Gross Domestic Product by Type of Expenditure %
Private Consumption: —
Government Consumption: —
Gross Domestic Investment: —
Foreign Trade: Exports: —
Imports: —
% of Income Received by Poorest 20%: —
% of Income Received by Richest 10%: —

Price and earnings indexes (1995 = 100)

	1993	1994	1995	1996	1997	1998	1999
Consumer price index	91.2	95.5	100.0	103.6	105.6	107.5	109.7
Earnings index	94.4	96.6	100.0	105.0	—	—	—

Finance

National Currency: Peseta (pta)
Exchange Rate: $1 = 6.0836 pta
Money Supply Stock in National Currency billion: —
M1 per capita: —
Central Bank Discount Rate %: —
Total External Debt $million: $125 million
Debt Service Ratio %: —

Balance of Payments $million: —
International Reserves SDRs million: —
Ratio of External Debt to Total Reserves: —

Average Annual Rate of Inflation/Consumer Price Index Growth Rate %: —

Official Development Assistance

ODA $: —
as % of GNP: —
per capita: $ —
Foreign Direct Investment $million: —

Central Government Revenues and Expenditures

Fiscal Year: Calendar Year

Revenues $million: 138
Expenditures $million: 177
Budget Deficit $: 39 million
Tax Revenues as % of GDP: —
Highest Tax Bracket % —
Individual:
Corporate:

Employment and Labor

Economically Active Population: 25,000
Female Participation Rate %: 45.6
Activity Rate %: 55.1
Labor by Sector: %
Agriculture, Forestry, Fishing: 1.2
Manufacturing, Mining: 11.0
Construction: 11.8
Transportation and Communications: —
Trade, Hotels, and Restaurants: 24.2
Finance, Insurance, Real Estate: 5.4
Public Administration, Defense: 10.3
Services: 16.7

Unemployment %: 0

Agriculture

Agriculture's Share of GDP %: —
Average Annual Rate of Growth (1965–98) %: —
Number of Farms 000: —
Average Size of Farm ha: —
Number of Tractors per 1,000 hectares: —
Irrigation, % of Farms having: —
Artificial Fertilizer kg/hectare: —
Total Farm land as % of land area: 2.2
Livestock: Cattle 000: —
Sheep 000: —
Hogs 000: —
Chickens 000: —
Forests: Production of Roundwood (000 cubic meters): —
Fisheries: Total Catch tons 000: —

Mining

% of GDP: —
Value of Mineral Production $million: —

Manufacturing

Value Added $million: 38
Industrial Production Growth Rate %:

Energy

Commercial Energy Production metric tons of oil equivalent 000:
Commercial Energy Consumption metric tons of oil equivalent 000:
Commercial Energy Consumption per capita kg:
Average Annual Growth Rate 1980–97 %:
Net Energy Imports % of use:
Electricity Installed Capacity kW 000:
Production kW-hr million:
Coal Reserves tons million:
Production tons 000:
Natural Gas Proven Reserves cubic meters billion:
Production cubic meters million:
Crude Petroleum Reserves barrels million:
Production barrels million:
Consumption barrels million:
Refinery Capacity barrels per day 000:
Pipelines Length km:

Foreign Trade

Imports $million: 48.9
Exports $million: 1.055
Export Volume % Annual Growth Rate (1990–97): —
Import Volume % Annual Growth Rate (1990–97): —
Balance of Trade $1.006 billion

Balance of trade (current prices)

	1992	1993	1994	1995	1996	1997
Ptas 000,000	−112,179	−113,282	−117,786	−125,507	−129,579	−150,016
% of total	93.02%	91.1%	89.7%	91.1%	91.7%	91.4%

Major Trading Partners

	Imports	Exports
European Union %	85.7	99.6
United States %	4.2	—
Eastern Europe %	0.1	0.1
Japan %	3.4	—
Others %	6.6	0.3

Transportation

Roads Total Length mi: 187
Paved %: 74
Automobiles: 35,941
Trucks and Buses: 4,186
Persons per vehicle: 1.6
Railroad; Track Length mi: —
Passenger-mi million: —
Freight-mi million: —
Merchant Marine: No. of Vessels: —
  Total Deadweight Tonnage 000: —
  International Cargo Loaded tons 000: —
  International Cargo Off-loaded tons 000: —
Airports with Scheduled Flights: —
Traffic: Passenger-mi million: —
  Freight-mi million: —
Length of Canals mi: —

Tourism

Number of Tourists to 000: —
Number of Tourists from 000: —
Tourist Receipts $million: —
Tourist Expenditures $million: —

Communications

Telephones 000: 30,000
Cost of Local Calls 3 mins $0. —
Cellular Telephones 000: 2,800
Fax Machines 000: 1,300
Personal Computers 000: —
Internet Hosts per million persons: 147
Mail: Post Offices:
  Pieces of Mail Handled million: —
  Pieces of Mail Handled per person: —

EDUCATION

Education is provided in both French- and Spanish-language schools. Instruction in Catalan has only recently become available. French-language schools are partially subsidized by the French government and Spanish-language schools by the Roman Catholic Church.

Education

Literacy Rate %: 100
  Male %: 100
  Female %: 100
First Level: Primary schools: 12
  Teachers: —
  Students: 5,424
  Student-Teacher Ratio:
  Net Enrollment Ratio: —
Second Level: Secondary Schools: 6
  Teachers: —
  Students: 2.655
  Student-Teacher Ratio: —
  Net Enrollment Ratio: —
Vocational Level: Schools:
  Students:
Third Level: Institutions:
  Teachers:
  Students:
  Student-Ratio Level:
  Gross Enrollment Ratio:
  Students per 100,000:
  % of Population Age 25 and over with Postsecondary Education:
Public Expenditure on Education as % of GDP:

SCIENCE AND TECHNOLOGY

Science and Technology

Scientists and Engineers in R&D per 1 million persons: —
Expenditures in R&D as % of GDP: —
High-Tech Exports $: —
Patent Applications by Residents: —

MEDIA

The oldest Andorran newspaper is the *Poble Andorra*, a weekly that was founded in 1974 on the demise of the daily newspaper of the same name. A private TV company, Antenna 7, transmits one hour of Andorran-interest programs from the Spanish side of the border. Andorra Television, founded in 1995, is an Andorran-owned commercial television service. Radio Andorra, a commercial public broadcasting service, replaced two stations that closed down in 1981 after the expiration of their contracts with French and Spanish companies.

Media

Daily Newspapers: 3
  Total Circulation 000: 4,000
  Circulation per 1,000: 63
Books Published: 57
Magazines: —
Radio Receivers 000: 10,000
  per 1,000: 5.7
Television sets 000: 22,000
  per 1,000: 360

MOST IMPORTANT MEDIA:

Press. The domestic press consists of two dailies, *Diari d'andorra* (Andorran Diary, 3,000) and *Correu Andorra* (Andorran Post, 2,000), plus the weekly *Poble Andorra* (Andorran People, 3000), all issued at Andorra la Vella.

Radio and television. In 1981 the question of control over Andorran airwaves resulted in the government ordering the principality's two radio

(continued)

stations, the French-owned Sud-Radio and the commercial, privately owned Spanish Radio Andorra, off the air. The dispute arose over the co-princes' refusal to permit effective nationalization of the broadcast facilities, which had extensive audiences in both France and Spain. Under a compromise approved by the General Council in September, the right of the Andorran people to operate (but not necessarily own) radio stations was acknowledged, and the General Council was granted full sovereignty over any stations broadcasting solely within Andorra. In 1984 Radio Andorra returned to the air, with an Antena 7 television facility initiating programs of Andorran interest from the Spanish side of the border in 1987. In January 1991 a domestic service, Televisiode Andorra, initiated four hours of daily programming.

CULTURE

Cultural Indicators

Public Libraries
- Number: —
- Volumes: —
- Registered borrowers: —

Museums
- Number: —
- Annual Attendance: —

Cinema
- Production of Long Films: —
- Number of Cinemas: —
- Seating Capacity: —
- Annual Attendance: —
- Annual Attendance per capita: —

STATUS OF WOMEN

There is no legal discrimination against women either privately or professionally. The recently established Association of Andorran Women actively promotes women's issues.

Women

Gender Empowerment Measure: —
Seats Held in Parliament by Women %: —
Female Administrators and Managers %: —
Female Professional and Technical Workers %: —
Women's Share of Earned Income %: —
Women in Government %: —

HEALTH, FOOD, AND NUTRITION

Health

Number of Physicians: 132
Number of Dentists: —
Number of Nurses: —
Number of Pharmacists: —
Population per Physician: 491
Number of Hospitals: 1
Hospital Beds per 10,000: 18
Hospital Bed Occupancy Rate: —
Infant Mortality Rate per 1,000 live births: —
Maternal Mortality Rate per 100,000 live births: —
Total Health Expenditures as % of GDP: —
Health Expenditures per capita $: —
HIV Infected % of adults: —
Cigarette Consumption per smoker per year: —
% of Smokers: Male: —
Female: —
Access to Safe Water %: —

Food and Nutrition

Food Supply as % of FAO Requirements: —
% of Consumption Expenditures on Food: —
Daily Available Calories per capita: —
% of Total Calories derived from:
Cereals: —
Potatoes, cassava: —
Meat, poultry: —
Fish: —
Eggs, milk: —
Fruits, vegetables: —
Fats, oils: —

ENVIRONMENT

Andorra is subject to snowslides and avalanches. The principle environmental concern is deforestation as a result of overgrazing of mountain meadows. Andorra has not signed any international environmental agreements.

Environment

Forest Area sq km: —
Average Annual Deforestation sq km: —
Nationally Protected Areas as % of Total Land Area: —
Freshwater Access cubic meters per capita: —
Emissions of Organic Water Pollutants kg per day: —
CO_2 Emissions per capita-ton: —

CHRONOLOGY

1970 Women gain the right to vote and the right to hold public office.

1973 The first personal meeting between the two co-princes since 1278 takes place at Cahors, France.

1978 Andorra celebrates the 700th anniversary of its founding.

1981 Women are granted the franchise in a sweeping electoral reform. An executive, separate from the legislature, is established with a head of government and an executive council.

1987 A meeting of Europe's six small nations is held in Andorra.

1993 A constitutional referendum is held and a written constitution is approved by 74 percent of the electorate.

1994 Don Marc Forné Molné is elected prime minister of a coalition government.

1997 The Liberal Union Party of Prime Minister Molné wins a majority of seats in the general election and ends the coalition government.
2001 Marc Forné Molné is reelected prime minister.

BIBLIOGRAPHY

Cameron, Peter. *Andorra.* New York, 1997.
Carrick, Noel. *Andorra.* New York, 1997.
Morgan, Bryan. *Andorra, The Country in Between.* Nottingham, England, 1964.
Taylor, Barry. *Andorra.* Santa Barbara, Calif., 1993.

OFFICIAL PUBLICATIONS

Andorra. *Estadistiques* (annual); *Recull Estadistic General de la Poblacio Andorra 90.*

CONTACT INFORMATION

Embassy of Andorra
Two United Nations Plaza, 25th Floor
New York, N.Y. 10017
Phone: (212) 750-8064 Fax: (212) 750-6630

INTERNET RESOURCES

- Andorra National Information Centre
  http://www.andorra.ad/cniauk.html
- Informes economics ("Economic Information")
  http://www.andorra.ad/ccis/fineco.htm

ANGOLA

BASIC FACT SHEET

OFFICIAL NAME:
Republic of Angola (República de Angola)

ABBREVIATION:
AO

CAPITAL:
Luanda (Huambo has been designated as the future capital)

HEAD OF STATE & GOVERNMENT:
President José Eduardo dos Santos (from 1979)

NATURE OF GOVERNMENT:
Parliamentary democracy (transitional government)

POPULATION:
11,178,000 (1999)

AREA:
1,246,700 sq km (481,351 sq mi)

ETHNIC MAJORITY:
Bantu

LANGUAGE:
Portuguese (official)

RELIGIONS:
Christianity and animism

UNIT OF CURRENCY:
Kwanza (K.)

NATIONAL FLAG:
Red over black horizontal stripes with an arc of cogwheel, crossed by a machete, and a star (all in yellow) in the center.

NATIONAL EMBLEM:
A machete and a spade crossed over a rising sun with a star at the top and an open book at the bottom, all enclosed by an arc of cogwheel and a stalk of grain. The legend "República Popular de Angola" appears at the bottom.

NATIONAL ANTHEM:
"O Fatherland, We Shall Never Forget the Heroes of the Fourth of February"

NATIONAL HOLIDAYS:
November 11 (Independence Day), January 1 (New Years Day), February 4 (anniversary of the outbreak of struggle against Portuguese colonialism), March 27 (Victory Day), May 1 (Workers' Day), September 17 (National Hero's Day), December 10 (Anniversary of the foundation of the MPLA), December 25 (Family Day)

DATE OF INDEPENDENCE:
November 11, 1975

DATE OF CONSTITUTION:
November 11, 1975; revised 1978, 1980, 1991, and 1992

GEOGRAPHICAL FEATURES

Angola is on the western coast of southern Africa, south of the equator, and occupies an area of 1,246,700 sq km (481,351 sq mi). Angola proper excluding the exclave of Cabinda, extends 1,758 km (1,092 mi) southeast to northwest and 1,491 km (927 mi) northeast to southwest. The total Atlantic coastline is 1,434 km (891 mi) long.

Angola proper shares its total international land boundary of 4,747 km (2,950 mi) with three countries: Democratic Republic of the Congo (Zaire) (2,511 km; 1559 mi); Zambia (1,086 km; 675 mi); and Namibia (formerly South-West Africa) (1,376 km; 855 mi). Cabinda shares its international land boundary of 426 km (265 mi) with two nations: Democratic Republic of the Congo (Zaire) (225 km; 140 mi) and Republic of Congo (201 km; 125 mi).

The sparsely watered coastal plain extends for 50 to 160 km (30 to 100 mi) inland. North of the mouth of the Kwanza the coast is hilly; to the south it is for the most part flat, with occasional cliffs. The coastal plain is separated from the inland plateau by a series of irregular terraces forming a subplateau. Two-thirds of Angola is composed of the central plateau, which has an average height of 1,050 to 1,350 m (3,445 to 4,430 ft). The highest point is Mount Moco (2,620 m; 8,596 ft). The Namib Desert occupies the coastal plain above Mocamedes. The Cassange Depression is a sedimentary hollow toward the Kwango Basin in Zaire. The northwestern section of the Angolan

Angola

Plateau and the Cabinda exclave are covered by equatorial jungles.

Geography

Area sq km: 1,246,700 sq mi 481, 351
World Rank: 24th
Land Boundaries, km: Democratic Republic of the Congo 2,511; Republic of the Congo 201; Namibia 1,376; Zambia 1,110
Coastline, km: 1,600
Elevation Extremes meters
- Lowest: Atlantic Ocean 0
- Highest: Morro de Moco 2,620

Land Use % Arable land: 2
- Permanent Crops: 0
- Permanent Pastures: 23
- Forest and Woodland: 43
- Other: 32

Population of Principal Cities (1993 est.)

City	Population
Huambo	400,000
Luanda	2,081,000
Lubango	105,000
Benguela	155,000
Lobito	155,000

CLIMATE AND WEATHER

Angola has a tropical climate with two seasons: a cool season from June to September and a rainy season from October to May. There are, however, considerable regional variations. The northern region from Cabinda to Ambriz has a damp, tropical climate; the region from Luanda to Mocamedes has a moderate tropical climate; the southern strip between the plateau and Namibia has a desert climate. The interior uplands in Bie, Huambo, and Huila have a pleasant climate similar to that of Portugal. The Benguela Current along the coast reduces rainfall in the coastal regions and makes them arid or semiarid. The mean annual temperature is 22.5°C (72.5°F) in the north, 23.5°C (74.3°F) in Luanda, and 19.5°C (67.2°F) in the south. The mean annual rainfall is 203 mm (8 in) in the southwest and 2,030 mm (80 in) in the northeast. The prevailing winds are west, southwest, and south-southwest.

Climate and Weather

Mean Temperature
North 72.5°F
Luanda 74.3°F
South 67.2°F
Average Rainfall: 8 in (the Southwest)
80 in (the Northeast)

POPULATION

Population Indicators

Total Population: 1999 11,178,000
World Rank: 64th
Density per sq mi: 23.2 per sq km 9.0
% of annual growth (1994–99): 3.3
Male %: 52.1
Female %: 47.9
Urban %: 14.2
Age Distribution: % 0–14: 41.7
15–29: 23.2
30–44: 17.0
45–59: 7.4
60–74: 3.8
75 and over: 1.0
Population 2020: 19,207,000
Birth Rate per 1,000: 47.7
Death Rate per 1,000: 18.7
Population Doubling Time (years): 26
Infant Mortality Rate per 1,000 live births: 124
Rate of Natural Increase per 1,000: 29.0
Total Fertility Rate: 6.7
Expectation of Life (years): Males 44.9
Females 48.1
Marriage Rate per 1,000: 4.5
Divorce Rate per 1,000: —
Total Number of Households: —
Average Size of Households: 4.8
% of Illegitimate Children: —
Induced Abortions: —
Rate per 100 live births: —

ETHNIC COMPOSITION

Angolans are almost entirely of Bantu stock and are composed of numerous tribal groupings. Three-fourths of the African population are accounted for by the four most important tribes.

The largest group is the Ovimbundu, in central and southern Angola, who make up almost 33 percent of the population. The Bakingo, in the northwest, making up 25 percent of the population, also spill over into the Democratic Republic of the Congo (Zaire) and Republic of Congo. The Kimbundu (Mbundu), who occupy the terrain inland from Luanda, are culturally but not ethnically related to the Bakongo. The Kimbundu are among the more detribalized groups in Angola and make up 25 percent of the population. The Chokwe, of eastern Angola, make up 8 percent of the population; sometimes they are grouped together with the Luanda. Other prominent groups are the Nganguela, Nyaneka, Humbe, Ovambo, Luvale, Ambo, Bunda, Luchazi, Kangala, Kwangare, Cuanhama, and Herero.

Under the Portuguese the population was officially divided until 1961 into indigenas, or native Africans, and assimilados, including mesticos. Under the colonial regime the European population was almost entirely Portuguese and constituted close to 6 percent of the total population. Nearly 90 percent of Portuguese settlers and mesticos were repatriated to Portugal just before independence. The foreign community after independence included 50,000 Cuban soldiers and advisers and an undetermined number of Soviets. These forces were withdrawn in 1991.

LANGUAGES

The official language is Portuguese. No African language extends beyond its tribal area, and few have written scripts of any kind. The principal Bantu languages and their dialects are Kikongo, Kimbundu, Umbundu, Kioko, and Nganguela.

Principal Languages and Their Speakers

Ambo (Ovambo)	270,000
Chokwe	470,000
Herero	80,000
Kongo	1,470,000
Luchazi	270,000
Luimbe-Nganguela	600,000
Lunda	130,000
Luvale (Luena)	400,000
Mbunda	130,000
Mbundu	2,410,000
Nyaneka-Nkhumbi	600,000
Ovimbundu (Umbundu)	4,160,000
Portuguese	3,900,000
Other	170,000

RELIGIONS

Although the constitution guarantees the inviolability of freedom of conscience and belief and provides for separation of church and state, the Movimento Popular de Libertacão de Angola (MPLA), the controlling political party, publicly emphasizes the importance of propagating "atheism" and has been critical of religious activities. A large portion (70 percent) of the Angolan population is Christian, however, and the MPLA has not moved to close down churches. Church services are regularly held, and there is widespread attendance. Foreign and Angolan missionaries are allowed to carry out activities. Reportedly, the União Nacional para a Independencia Total de Angola (UNITA) allows religious liberty in the areas it controls and in which it operates, but obviously the ability of religious personnel to carry out activities in Angola has been circumscribed by the intensification of the civil war.

Over 35 percent of the population still adhere to traditional African religions.

Religious Affiliations

Roman Catholic	5,670,000
Protestant	1,640,000
African Christian	480,000
Other (mostly traditional beliefs)	3,390,000

HISTORICAL BACKGROUND

Although the precolonial history of many parts of Africa has been carefully researched and preserved, there is relatively little information on the region that forms contemporary Angola as it was before the arrival of the Europeans in the late 1400s. The limited information that is available indicates that the original inhabitants of present-day Angola were hunters and gatherers. Their descendants, called Bushmen by the Europeans, still inhabit portions of southern Africa, and small numbers of them may still be found in southern Angola. These Khoisan speakers lost their predominance in southern Africa as a result of the southward expansion of Bantu-speaking peoples during the first century.

The Bantu settled in Angola between 1300 and 1600, and some may have arrived even earlier. The Bantu formed a number of historically important kingdoms. The earliest and perhaps most important of these was the Kongo Kingdom, which arose between the mid-1300s and the mid-1400s in an area overlapping the present-day border between Angola and the Democratic Republic of the Congo (Zaire). Other important kingdoms were Ndongo, located to the south of Kongo; Matamba, Kasanje, and Lunda, located east of Ndongo; Bié, Bailundu, and Ciyaka, located on the plateau east of Benguela; and Kwanhama (also spelled Kwanyama), located near what is now the border between Angola and Namibia. Although they did not develop a strong central government, the Chokwe (also spelled Cokwe) established a significant cultural center in the northeast of present-day Angola.

Parts of Angola were exposed to Portuguese influence as early as the late 15th century. Luanda was founded as a trading settlement in 1575, and the king of Kongo, Nzinga-a-Cuum, was converted to Christianity. Meanwhile, the Portuguese, having failed to find gold and other precious metals, became deeply involved in the slave trade. Portugal's attempts to consolidate its rule over the whole interior of Angola was strongly resisted by the Angolans; the first concerted resistance to Portuguese rule lasted from 1872 to 1902, when the Ovimbundu were beaten in the Bailundo War.

Portugal's colonial policy was to bind its colonies rigidly to the mother country. The doctrine of Luso-African unity argued that what was good for Portugal was good for the colonies. Portugal also emphasized its antiracism compared to the racial practices of Britain, France, and other colonial powers. In 1951 Angola was declared to be an integral part of Portugal, and in 1952 the first of a series of planned settlement projects known as colonatos was begun for Portuguese immigrants.

Armed resistance to Portuguese rule began on February 4, 1961, when partisans of the Movimento Popular de Libertacão de Angola (MPLA), headed by a physician, Dr. Antonio Agostinho Neto, attacked the São Paulo fortress and police headquarters in Luanda. Within six weeks the war had spread to the north. Another guerrilla organization, the Frente Nacional de Libertacão de Angola (FNLA), headed by Holden Roberto, set up a government-in-exile in the Democratic Republic of the Congo (Zaire) in 1962. Insurgency spread to the south through the partisans of a third organization, the União Nacional para a Independencia Total de Angola (UNITA). The drawn-out guerrilla warfare had forced Portugal to the limits of military and psychological exhaustion when the coup of April 25, 1974, brought a new and radical government into power in Lisbon, one committed to ending all Portugal's colonial wars. The transfer of sovereignty to African hands in 1975 was completed with few upsets and in a reasonable spirit of tolerance.

In the wake of the coup in Portugal, the leaders of Angola's three nationalist movements signed an agreement with Portugal calling for independence in late 1975. However, the alliance soon broke down, and the FNLA and UNITA formed an alliance in opposition to the MPLA. The conflict soon involved the cold war superpowers, as the Soviet Union and Cuba sent in troops and advisers whereas South Africa, with the support of Western nations, backed UNITA. On independence, Dr Agostinho Neto, whose MPLA controlled the capital, announced the formation of the People's Republic of Angola. The two other nationalist groups announced the formation of a Democratic People's Republic of Angola with the capital in Huambo. In early 1976, the MPLA launched a major offensive into UNITA territory that resulted in the withdrawal of South African troops and the capture of major UNITA centers. UNITA continued its resistance as a guerrilla movement.

Neto established a socialist regime and in 1977 reconstituted the MPLA as a Marxist-Leninist party with a state subordinate to the party. Neto died in 1979 and was succeeded by MPLA chairman Jose Eduardo dos Santos. Legislative elections were held in 1980 and again in 1986, but real power continued in the hands of the MPLA hierarchy.

During the 1980s, South Africa periodically invaded and occupied Angola, purportedly in pursuit of Namibian rebels. Its troops withdrew in 1988 as part of the peace process designed to bring independence to Namibia. Cuba also agreed to a gradual withdrawal of its troops. In 1988 UNITA rejected a one-year amnesty offered by dos Santos to UNITA supporters, and fighting continued despite attempts at a cease-fire. In late 1989, the UNITA leaders agreed to peace talks with the Angolan government.

During 1990, the Angolan government and UNITA met for five rounds of peace talks under the sponsorship of Portugal, the Soviet Union, and the United States. By the end of the year the parties had reached a tentative agreement on ending the civil war. Under the final accord, which was signed in May 1991, multiparty elections would take place by November 1992. In the meantime, the MPLA would continue to administer the government's daily affairs. In addition, both sides agreed to merge their ground forces into an army of no more than 50,000 members. The air force and navy would remain in MPLA hands until the elections, under close independent supervision of a commission made up of delegates from the MPLA and UNITA as well as the three mediating governments.

While negotiations were underway in 1990 the MPLA formally abandoned its Marxist-Leninist ideology and declared itself a social democratic force. It approved the establishment of a multiparty government, direct presidential elections, and a large degree of free enterprise. It also endorsed proposals for a year-long process of constitutional revision that would start after a cease-fire had been signed. UNITA was to participate in the revision process. In 1991 UNITA decided to transform its movement from a guerrilla force into a political party.

A peace settlement signed in Washington in 1991 provided for free multiparty elections in Angola in 1992 under the supervision of a joint commission with Portuguese, U.S., Russian, MPLA-PT, and UNITA representatives. In 1992 the MPLA-PT endorsed constitutional revisions formalizing the government's commitment to a democratic system. It also approved a united armed force, Angolan Armed Forces, drawn from both Popular Armed Forces for the Liberation of Angola and UNITA's Armed Forces for the Liberation of Angola. However, the 1992 election was marred by widespread violence and armed clashes in the capital. In the polling MPLA-PT gained a 2 to 1 majority and dos Santos won 49.57 percent of the vote compared to Savimbi's 40.07 percent. Savimbi, however, charged that the elections were rigged and stated that he would not accept defeat. By 1993 tens of thousands were reported killed, with Savimbi's forces on the defensive. In a pitched 55-day battle that left 12,000 dead, UNITA recaptured its headquarters in Huambo. The insurgents were now in control of over 70 percent of Angolan territory and the UNITA guerrilla forces had become as powerful as a conventional army. The next several years were marked by successive peace talks at Addis Ababa, Abidjan, and Lusaka, all ending in a stalemate. In response to UNITA's intransigence, the United States recognized the dos Santos government and ended its support for UNITA. Subsequently UNITA intensified its military operations, capturing oil-rich Soyo. In the Lusaka-2 agreement, the government made key concessions to UNITA, including the award of 11 government portfolios and three governorships. President dos Santos and Savimbi met in 1995 and further talks were held. Despite reported agreements, the two sides continued to drift apart on issues such as disarming of civilians and integration of UNITA forces into the army. Meanwhile both UNITA and MPLA-PT continued to launch new offensives. In 1997 the United Nations Angola Verification Mission (UNAVEM) charged with monitoring and organizing elections was replaced by UN Observer Mission at Angola (UNOMA). UNOMA's mandate expired in 1998 and UN's involvement in Angola completely ended. Savimbi refused to relinquish rebel-held territory or completely disarm his troops. However, in 1997, a final resolution appeared near as the National Assembly met for the first time with a full complement of UNITA legislators and with Savimbi as "the leader of the largest opposition party." At the same time, dos Santos named a Government of Unity and National Reconciliation with Fernando Van Dunem as prime minister and including 11 UNITA members. This government was suspended in 1998 because of reported UNITA noncompliance with the Lusaka accord. Some UNITA cabinet members are reported to have deserted Savimbi and stayed on in the government. By 2000 the government was reported to be planning a final offensive against UNITA.

CONSTITUTION

Angola is a sovereign, democratic, and independent republic according to the constitution, promulgated in 1975 and amended in 1978 and 1980. The supreme organ of state is the unicameral National People's Assembly, which is chosen by an electoral college whose members are directly elected. In 1992 the MPLA-PT approved a revised constitution that provided for a presidentially appointed

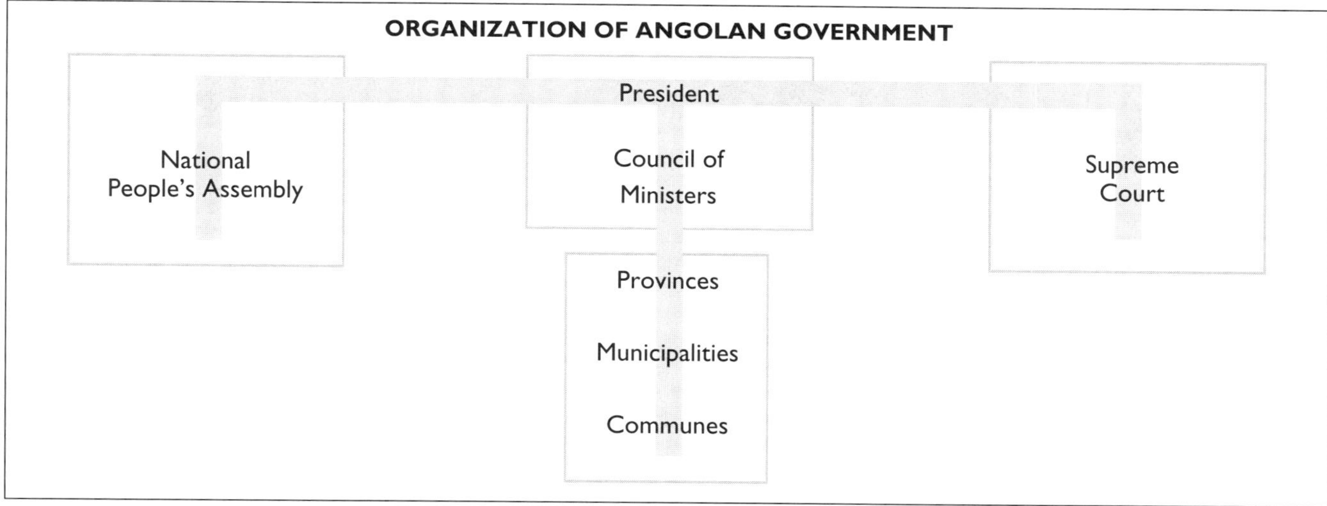

prime minister to head a transitional government, the abolition of the death penalty, the removal of *People's* from the republic's formal name, and the deletion of all constitutional references to *people* and *popular* as reflecting former marxist tendencies.

The president is head of state and government, commander-in-chief of the armed forces, and leader of Angola's sole political party, the MPLA. Real political power is exercised by the MPLA, which is responsible for the nation's political, economic, and social leadership. The chairman of the party is the head of state.

LOCAL GOVERNMENT

Under the MPLA regime, Angola is administratively divided into provinccias (provinces), concelhos (councils), comunas (communes), circulos (circles), bairros (neighborhoods), and povoacaos (villages). The government is represented in the provinces by the provincial commissioner, in the district by the local commissioner, and in the commune by the commune commissioner, all of whom are appointed on the recommendation of the MPLA. The administrative bodies of the district, commune, neighborhood, and villages are the local commission, the commune commission, the neighborhood commission, and the village commission, respectively.

Local Government

Principal administrative divisions, capitals, area, population

Area and population

Provinces	Capitals	area sq mi	area sq km	population 1997 census
Bengo	Caxito	12,112	31,371	—
Benguela	Benguela	12,273	31,788	—
Bié	Kuito	27,148	70,314	—
Cabinda	Cabinda	2,807	7,270	—
Cunene	N'Giva	34,495	89,342	—
Huambo	Huambo	13,233	34,274	—
Huila	Lubango	28,958	75,002	—
Kuando Kubango	Menongue	76,853	199,049	—
Kuanza Norte	N'Dalatando	9,340	24,190	—
Kuanza Sul	Sumbe	21,490	55,660	—
Luanda	Luanda	934	2,418	—
Luanda Norte	Lucapa	39,685	102,783	—
Luanda Sul	Saurimo	17,625	45,649	—
Malanje	Malanje	37,684	97,602	—
Moxico	Lwena	86,110	223,023	—
Namibe	Namibe	22,447	58,137	—
Uige	Uige	22,663	58,698	—
Zaire	M'Banza Kongo	15,494	40,130	—
TOTAL		481,345	1,246,700	10,624,000

PARLIAMENT

In accordance with the constitution of 1975, the National People's Assembly was established in 1980 as successor to the Council of the Revolution. The unicameral legislature is indirectly elected for a term of five years. Nearly all the 289 full and 29 alternate members are directly or indirectly affiliated with the MPLA.

POLITICAL PARTIES

While Angola has a number of political parties, the two most important are the ones that have shaped much of its history since independence. The ruling party is the leftist Popular Movement for the Liberation of Angola, or MPLA, which has ruled the country since 1975. The second largest party is the formerly U.S.-backed National Union for the Total Independence of Angola (UNITA), which spent years of armed resistance before joining the current unity government in April 1997.

Political Parties

Popular Movement for the Liberation of Angola-Labor Party
National Union for the Total Independence of Angola
National Front for the Liberation of Angola, 1962
Social Renewal Party
Democratic Renewal Party, 1977
Liberal Democratic Party
Angolan Democratic Forum, 1992
Angolan National Democratic Party, 1992
Democratic Alliance of Angola
Democratic Party for Progress-Angolan National Alliance
Party of the Alliance of the Youth, Workers, and Farmers of Angola
Social Democratic Party
Angolan Democratic Party
Angolan Labor Party, 1995
Social Democratic Center 1995
Union Front for the Salvation of Angola, 1996

Political Parties: Strength in Parliament Most Recent Elections

At balloting on September 29–30, 1992, for 220 seats (three seats reserved for overseas Angolans not being filled by mutual agreement of the parties) the distribution was as follows: Popular Liberation Movement of Angola-Labor Party, 129; National Union for the Total Independence of Angola, 70; Social Renewal Party, 6; National Front for the Liberation of Angola, 5; Liberal Democratic Party, 3; Angolan Democratic Forum, Angolan National Democratic Party, Democratic Alliance of Angola, Democratic Party for Progress-Angolan National Alliance, Democratic Renewal Party, Party of the Alliance of Youths, Workers, and Farmers of Angola, and the Social Democratic Party, 1 each.

LEGAL SYSTEM

The judiciary is headed by a Supreme Court and Court of Appeals in Luanda. There are also military, civil, and revolutionary people's courts. The rule of law is based upon Portuguese civil law system and customary law. In the last few years there have been attempts to accommodate political pluralism and increased use of free markets.

LAW ENFORCEMENT

Law Enforcement

Offenses reported to the police per 100,000: 31
- Murder: 3.4
- Assault: 6.1
- Burglary: —
- Automobile Theft: —
- Population per Police officer: 14

Death Penalty: Abolished 1992

HUMAN RIGHTS

In terms of civil and political rights, Angola is classified as a country that is not free.

There is very little reliable information on human rights practices in Angola. The United States does not maintain diplomatic relations with Angola, and of the major human rights organizations only Amnesty International has reported on this country.

The freedoms of expression, religion, assembly, and belief are qualified by the condition that they must conform to and promote "fundamental national interests and objectives." The domestic media are entirely in government hands. Entry of foreign correspondents is restricted, and those who are in the country are subject to immediate expulsion if they write articles critical of MPLA policies. The labor movement also is an MPLA organ; the right to strike is prohibited by law as a crime against the security of the state. The government has instituted a pass system for travel within Angola; foreigners are generally prohibited from traveling outside cities. The visa policy also is extremely restrictive and stringent. Applications for visas are subject to long delays, if they are not rejected outright or ignored. As in other authoritarian states, participation in the political process is limited to members of the MPLA-Labor Party.

FOREIGN POLICY

Although battered by a decade-old civil war, Angola has been an active player in regional affairs. Its support for Kabila was a factor in the overthrow of Mobutu in Congo (Zaire), and the later withdrawal of this support contributed to the disintegration of the Kabila administration. Relations with the United States, which had opposed the Marxist basis of the Neto government, became more positive after the exit of Cuban troops from Angola in 1991. One of the major goals of Angolan foreign policy has been to isolate UNITA, the principal opposition, and to deny it any aid from abroad. In 1998 Luanda alleged that Burkina Faso, Rwanda, Togo, Uganda, and Zambia were either supplying UNITA rebels or providing them safe haven. Relations with Zambia especially deteriorated in 1999 to the point of armed conflict. Although the issue was later defused, Angola's aggressive involvement in the Congolese civil wars is a matter of serious concern to its neighbors.

DEFENSE

The defense structure is headed by the president. The armed forces, known as FAPLA (Forcas Armadas Populares de Libertacão de Angola), are integrated within the MPLA. The government has announced a universal draft for two years for all Angolans between the ages of 18 and 35. The total strength of the armed forces was reported at 110,500 in 1999.

The country is divided into six military divisions: North, East, Central and West, Luanda, South, and Cabinda.

Military Indicators

Total Active Duty Personnel: 110,500
Military Manpower per 1,000: 10.4
Military Expenditures $: 225 million
as % of GNP: —
per capita $: 22
as % of central government expenditures: 3.0

Arms Imports $: 90 million
Arms Exports $: 0

ECONOMY

Angola is an economy in disarray because of a quarter century of nearly continuous warfare. Despite its abundant natural resources, output per capita is among the world's lowest. Subsistence agriculture provides the main livelihood for 85 percent of the population. Oil production and the supporting activities are vital to the economy, contributing about 45 percent to GDP and 90 percent of exports. Notwithstanding the signing of a peace accord in November 1994, violence continues, millions of landmines remain, and many farmers are reluctant to return to their fields. As a result, much of the country's food must still be imported. To take advantage of its rich resources—gold, diamonds, extensive forests, Atlantic fisheries, and large oil deposits—Angola will need to implement the peace agreement and reform government policies. Despite the increase in the pace of civil warfare in late 1998, the economy grew by an estimated 5 percent in 2000.

The government introduced new currency denominations in 1999, including a 1 and 5 kwanza note. Expanded oil production brightens prospects for 2000, but internal strife discourages investment outside of the petroleum sector.

Principal Economic Indicators

Gross National Product: $3.012 billion
GNP per capita: $260
GNP Average Annual Growth Rate (1990–97) %: −10.0
GNP per capita Average Annual Growth Rate (1990–97) %: −13.3
Origin of Gross Domestic Product %
Agriculture: 12
Mining: 51
Manufacturing: 3
Construction: 2
Public Utilities: —
Transportation and Communications: 2
Trade: 10
Financial Services: —
Other Services: 19
Government: 19
Gross Domestic Product by Type of Expenditure %
Private Consumption: 56
Government Consumption: 34
Gross Domestic Investment: 14
Foreign Trade: Exports: 60
Imports: −70
% of Income Received by Poorest 20%: —
% of Income Received by Richest 10%: —

Price and earnings indexes (1995 = 100)

	1991	1992	1993	1994
Consumer price index	100.0	595.0	11,534.0	123,639.0
Earnings index	100.0	150.0	1,000.0	8,800.0

Finance

National Currency: Kwanza (NKz)
Exchange Rate: $1 = Nkz 265,000
Money Supply Stock in National Currency billion: —
M1 per capita: —
Central Bank Discount Rate %: 58
Total External Debt $million: 12,500
Debt Service Ratio %: 15

Balance of Payments $million: −866
International Reserves SDRs million: —
Ratio of External Debt to Total Reserves: —

Average Annual Rate of Inflation/Consumer Price Index Growth Rate %: 92

Official Development Assistance

ODA: $451 million
as % of GNP: 8.2
per capita: $28
Foreign Direct Investment $million: 360

Central Government Revenues and Expenditures

Fiscal Year: Calendar Year

Revenues $million: 928
Expenditures $million: $2,500
Budget Deficit/Surplus $: 1,573 million
Tax Revenues as % of GDP: —
Highest Tax Bracket %
Individual: —
Corporate: —

Employment and Labor

Economically Active Population: 4,166,000
Female Participation Rate %: 38.4
Activity Rate %: 40.3
Labor by Sector: %
Agriculture, Forestry, Fishing: 69.4
Manufacturing, Mining: 10.5
Construction: —
Transportation and Communications: —
Trade, Hotels, and Restaurants: —
Finance, Insurance, Real Estate: —
Public Administration, Defense: —
Services: 20.1

Unemployment %: NA

Agriculture

Agriculture's Share of GDP %: 12
Average Annual Rate of Growth (1965–98) %: —
Number of Farms 000: 1,067
Average Size of Farm ha: 3.9
Number of Tractors per 1,000 hectares: 3.4
Irrigation, % of Farms having: 89
Artificial Fertilizer kg/hectare: 7
Total Cropland as % of Farmland: 2.8
Livestock: Cattle 000: 3,500
Sheep 000: 245
Hogs 000: 810
Chickens 000: 6,500
Forests: Production of Roundwood (000 cubic meters): 7,005
Fisheries: Total Catch tons 000: 77.9

Mining

% of GDP: 52.1
Value of Mineral Production $million: 2610.9

Manufacturing

Value Added $million: 319
Industrial Production Growth Rate %: NA

Energy

Commercial Energy Production metric tons of oil equivalent 000: 41,430
Commercial Energy Consumption metric tons of oil equivalent 000: 6,848
Commercial Energy Consumption per capita kg: 587
Average Annual Growth Rate 1980–97 %: −0.6
Net Energy Imports % of use: −505
Electricity Installed Capacity kW 000: 617
Production kW-hr million: 1,870
Coal Reserves tons million: —
Production tons 000: —
Natural Gas Proven Reserves cubic meters billion: 68
Production cubic meters million: 561
Crude Petroleum Reserves barrels million: 5,412
Production barrels million: 258
Consumption barrels million: 11
Refinery Capacity barrels per day 000: 32
Pipelines Length km: 179

Foreign Trade

Imports $million: 2,041.9
Exports $million: 3,178.9
Export Volume % Annual Growth Rate (1990–97): 5.0
Import Volume % Annual Growth Rate (1990–97): −0.7
Balance of Trade $

Balance of trade (current prices)

	1993	1994	1995	1996	1997
U.S. $000,000	+1,437	+1,553	+1,863	+2,879	+2,531
% of total	32.9%	35.0%	33.4%	39.5%	33.9%

Major Trading Partners

	Imports	Exports
European Union%	79.7	25.3
United States %	7.2	64.4
Eastern Europe %	0.9	0.5
Japan %	2.2	1.3
Others %	10.0	8.5

Transportation

Roads Total Length mi: 45,128 km: 72,626
Paved %: 25
Automobiles: 197,000
Trucks and Buses: 26,000
Persons per vehicle: 52
Railroad; Track Length mi: 1,739 km: 2,798
Passenger-mi million: 203
Freight-mi million: 1,178
Merchant Marine: No. of Vessels: 113
Total Deadweight Tonnage 000: 123.5
International Cargo Loaded tons 000: 23,288
International Cargo Off-loaded tons 000: 1,261
Airports with Scheduled Flights: 17
Traffic: Passenger-mi million: 589
Freight-mi million: 77
Length of Canals mi: 805 km: 1,295

Tourism

Number of Tourists to 000: 52
Number of Tourists from 000: 3
Tourist Receipts $million: 13
Tourist Expenditures $million: 66

Communications

Telephones 000: 60
Cost of Local Calls 3 mins $0.14
Cellular Telephones 000: 2.0
Fax Machines 000: —
Personal Computers 000: —
Internet Hosts per million persons: —
Mail: Post Offices: 62
Pieces of Mail Handled million: 2.6
Pieces of Mail Handled per person: 0.2

EDUCATION

Education is, in principle, universal, free, and compulsory for five years between ages six and 14.

Schooling lasts for 10 years, divided into four years of primary school, four years of middle school, and two years of secondary school. The MPLA regime has announced plans to reorganize the educational structure and nationalize all educational services. Revolutionary cadres of students are being formed, and the entire educational system is being politicized.

The academic year runs from September to July. The medium of instruction is Portuguese. The shortage of teachers created by the departure of Portuguese teachers has been met by Cuban teachers. Higher education is provided by the Universidade de Luanda, founded in 1963.

Education

Literacy Rate %: 41.7
 Male %: 55.6
 Female %: 28.5
First Level: Primary schools: —
 Teachers: 31,062
 Students: 900,155
 Student-Teacher Ratio: 31.9
 Net Enrollment Ratio: —
Second Level: Secondary Schools: —
 Teachers: 5,138
 Students: 166,812
 Student-Teacher Ratio: 30.2
 Net Enrollment Ratio: —

Vocational Level: Schools: —
 Students: 6,534

Third Level: Institutions: —
 Teachers: 439
 Students: 6,534
 Student-Ratio Level: 14.9
 Gross Enrollment Ratio: 0.7
 Students per 100,000: 71
 % of Population Age 25 and over with Postsecondary Education: —

Public Expenditure on Education as % of GDP: 4.9

SCIENCE AND TECHNOLOGY

Science and Technology

Scientists and Engineers in R&D per 1 million persons: —
Expenditures in R&D as % of GDP: —
High-Tech Exports $: —
Patent Applications by Residents: —

MEDIA

Two daily newspapers are published in Luanda: *Diario da República* and *O Jornal de Angola*. Under the MPLA regime, the press has been brought under Marxist ideological control and serves as an organ of government.

Radio Nacional de Angola broadcasts in Portuguese, English, French, Spanish, and native languages. Television service began in 1975 and is provided by the parastatal company, Televisão Popular de Angola.

The public libraries are the National Library of Angola with 25,000 volumes, and the Municipal Library in Luanda, with 18,000 volumes.

Media

Daily Newspapers: 4
 Total Circulation 000: 117
 Circulation per 1,000: 11
Books Published: —
Magazines: —
Radio Receivers 000: 450
 per 1,000: 39
Television sets 000: 550
 per 1,000: 51

Most Important Media:

Press. The following are Portuguese-language dailies published at Luanda: *O Jornal de Angola* (42,000), official newspaper; *Diario de República* (8,500), government news sheet.

News agencies. The domestic facility is the government-operated Angolan News Agency (Agência Noticiosa N'gola Press-Angop). A limited number of foreign agencies maintain offices at Luanda.

Radio and television. The principal broadcasting services are Radio Nacional de Angola and Télevisão Popular de Angola, both controlled by the government.

CULTURE

Cultural Indicators

Public Libraries
 Number: 2
 Volumes: 43,000
 Registered borrowers: —
Museums
 Number: —
 Annual Attendance: —
Cinema
 Production of Long Films: —
 Number of Cinemas: —
 Seating Capacity: —
 Annual Attendance: —
 Annual Attendance per capita: —

STATUS OF WOMEN

The general economic status of women is low. Women play a role in all aspects of the political process. They make up 6 percent of the People's Assembly and increasingly are voicing their concern for participation in higher governmental offices. It has been reported that they participated in the military vanguard during the war for independence. Women participate in the MPLA, not only in the Angolan Women's Organization but also at higher levels of the party. Social, cultural, and traditional factors tend to limit the participation of women at the highest level of the party, however. Three members of the Central Committee are women.

Women

Gender Empowerment Measure: —
Seats Held in Parliament by Women %: 15.5
Female Administrators and Managers %: —
Female Professional and Technical Workers %: —
Women's Share of Earned Income %: —
Women in Government %: 6

HEALTH, FOOD, AND NUTRITION

Health

Number of Physicians: 662
Number of Dentists: 10
Number of Nurses: 9,334
Number of Pharmacists: —
Population per Physician: 15,136
Number of Hospitals: 58
Hospital Beds per 10,000: 12
Hospital Bed Occupancy Rate: 44.5
Infant Mortality Rate per 1,000 live births: 179
Maternal Mortality Rate per 100,000 live births: 1,500
Total Health Expenditures as % of GDP: —
Health Expenditures per capita $: —
HIV Infected % of adults: 2.12
Cigarette Consumption per smoker per year: —
% of Smokers: Male: —
Female: —
Access to Safe Water %: 32

Food and Nutrition

Food Supply as % of FAO Requirements: 82
% of Consumption Expenditures on Food: 74.1
Daily Available Calories per capita: 1.927
% of Total Calories derived from:
Cereals: 28.1
Potatoes, cassava: 36.3
Meat, poultry: 3.6
Fish: 1.2
Eggs, milk: 1.7
Fruits, vegetables: 3.3
Fats, oils: 10.8

ENVIRONMENT

Angola suffers from a number of environmental problems that have resulted from nearly 40 years of warfare. Deforestation claims around 440 square km a year, and only small patches of natural forest remain. Poaching in woodlands and burning of trees are widespread. Water shortages are common, despite abundant rivers and wetlands. Also, many important endemic species are overhunted or receive no protection, and Angola's protected area system has almost completely disintegrated due to the civil war.

Environment

Forest Area sq km: 222,000
Average Annual Deforestation sq km: 2,370
Nationally Protected Areas as % of Total Land Area: 6.6
Freshwater Access cubic meters per capita: 15,783
Emissions of Organic Water Pollutants kg per day: 1,472
CO_2 Emissions per capita ton: 0.5

CHRONOLOGY

1956 Movimento Popular de Libertacão de Angola (MPLA) is founded.

1960 Dr. Agostinho Neto, chairman of the MPLA Steering Committee, is arrested.
Portuguese troops fire on Neto's supporters, killing 30 and wounding 300.
Neto is imprisoned in Cape Verde and later is transferred to Portugal.

1961 MPLA guerrillas attack São Paulo fortress and police station, killing seven Portuguese and 40 Angolans, and a plantation in Uige Province, killing 21 Portuguese.

1962 Neto escapes from Portuguese prison and returns to Angola via Rabat.
União das Populaçoes de Angola and Partido Democratico Angolano merge to form the Frente Nacional de Libertacão de Angola (FNLA), which sets up a government-in-exile, Governo Revolucionario de Angola no Exillo (GRAE), with Holden Roberto as prime minister.

1963 Zaire recognizes GRAE and is followed by the OAU.
MPLA is expelled from Zaire and moves its headquarters to Brazzaville, Republic of Congo.

1964 Dr. Jonas Savimbi, foreign minister of GRAE, resigns after accusing Roberto of corruption.

1966 Savimbi organizes the União Nacional para a Independencia Total de Angola (UNITA).

1972 MPLA and FNLA form Supreme Council for the Liberation of Angola under OAU auspices, with Roberto as president and Neto as vice president.

1975 Portugal grants complete independence to Angola.
A coalition government is formed headed by a three-member presidential council consisting of the three rival political parties: MPLA, FNLA, and UNITA.
The coalition breaks up and FNLA and UNITA proclaim the Popular Democratic Republic of Angola, with the capital at Huambo.
Agostinho Neto is inaugurated as president of the republic by MPLA.
The United States, Zaire, South Africa, and China support the UNITA-FNLA government, whereas the Soviet Union and Cuba airlift arms and equipment to MPLA forces.

1976 MPLA captures Huambo and other key cities as FNLA-UNITA forces disintegrate.
MPLA units clear the country of all opposition and foreign forces.
OAU recognizes MPLA.
President Neto takes over post of prime minister.

1977 A short-lived rebellion led by anti-Cuban and pro-Soviet dissidents is put down after severe fighting in Luanda and the provinces; three provincial administrations are suspended.
UNITA forces claim minor victories.
MPLA-backed forces cross into Zaire on what is described as an invasion.
Andrew Young, U.S. representative to the United Nations, claims that Cuban forces are a stabilizing element in Angola.
Kwanza is introduced as new national monetary unit.
Cuba's Fidel Castro, visiting Angola, promises unlimited aid.
MPLA, in national conference, restructures itself as a Leninist party under the name Movimento Popular de Libertacão de Angola-Partido de Trabalho (MPLA-PT).

1978 Prime Minister Lopo de Nascimento is dismissed as President Neto strengthens hold on MPLA.
United States bars recognition of regime, citing Cuban influence over MPLA.
Relations with Zaire are normalized and President Neto visits Kinshasa.
Three-year friendship and cooperation agreement is signed with Portugal.

1979 President Neto dies of cancer and is succeeded in office by José Eduardo dos Santos, minister of planning.

1982 President dos Santos assumes emergency powers in the face of increasing South African attacks.

1983 Beijing recognizes the MPLA-PT regime.

1985 U.S. Congress lifts ban on aid to UNITA rebels.

1986 The United States decides to give UNITA $15 million in military aid.

1988 Angola and South Africa declare a cease-fire. South African troops withdraw from Angola. An agreement is reached for the phased withdrawal of Cuban troops. African nations push peace initiatives.

1989 UNITA leaders agree to peace talks with the Angolan government.

1990 Following five separate rounds of talks, representatives of the Angolan government and UNITA reach a tentative agreement to end the civil war. The MPLA discards its Marxist-Leninist ideology and adopts democratic socialism as its new ideology.

1991 The Angolan government and UNITA sign an agreement ending the civil war; UNITA decides to transform its movement from a guerrilla force into a political party.

1992 In Angola's first multiparty elections, neither candidate gains a majority, but the required runoff between dos Santos of the MPLA and Jonas Savimbi of UNITA is never held; dos Santos retains the presidency and UNITA denounces the elections, resuming the civil war.

1993 The U. N. Security Council adopts an embargo on arms and fuel to UNITA.

1994 Successful government offenses early in the year aid in the signing of a UN-brokered peace treaty between UNITA and the government of Angola.

1995 The United Nations sends 7,000 peacekeeping troops to Angola.

1997 The 70 UNITA members elected to the National Assembly take their seats.

1998 UNITA leader Jonas Savimbi refuses to participate in peace talks.

1999 The United Nations terminates its peacekeeping mision in Angola, citing the tepid efforts of both Savimbi and dos Santos toward promoting peace.

BIBLIOGRAPHY

Anstee, M.J. *Orphan of the Cold War: The Inside Story of the Collapse of the Angolan Peace Process, 1992–93*. London, 1996.

Bloomfield, Richard J. *Regional Conflict and U.S. Policy: Angola and Mozambique*. Algonac, Mich., 1988.

Ebinger, Charles K. *Foreign Intervention in Civil War: The Politics and Diplomacy of the Angolan Conflict*. Boulder, Colo., 1986.

Heywood, Linda. *Contested Power in Angola, 1840s to the Present*. Rochester, N.Y., 2000.

Keller, Edmond J., ed. *Afro-marxist Regimes: Ideology and Public Policy*. Boulder, Colo., 1987.

Martin, Phyllis M. *Historical Dictionary of Angola*. Metuchen, N.J., 1980.

Munslow, Barry, and Jan Marsh. *Angola: Politics, Economics and Society*. Boulder, Colo., 1986.

Somerville, Keith. *Angola: Politics, Economics and Society*. Boulder, Colo., 1986.

Tvedten, Inge, Stephen Wright, and Larry W. Bowman. *Angola: Struggle for Peace and Reconstruction*. Boulder Colo., 1997

OFFICIAL PUBLICATIONS

Angola. *Angola—Recent Economic Developments* (IMF Staff Country Report [1995]); *Perfil estatistico de Angola* (annual).

CONTACT INFORMATION

Embassy of Angola
1615 M Street NW, Suite 900
Washington, D.C. 20036
Phone: (202) 785-1156 Fax: (202) 785-1258

INTERNET RESOURCES

- Official Home Page of the Republic of Angola http://www.angola.org/

ANTIGUA AND BARBUDA

BASIC FACT SHEET

OFFICIAL NAME:
Antigua and Barbuda

ABBREVIATION:
AB

CAPITAL:
St. John's

HEAD OF STATE:
Queen Elizabeth II, represented by Governor-General Sir James B. Carlisle (from 1993)

HEAD OF GOVERNMENT:
Prime Minister Lester Bryant Bird (from 1994)

NATURE OF GOVERNMENT:
Parliamentary democracy in the Commonwealth recognizing Elizabeth II as head of state

POPULATION:
69,100 (1999)

AREA:
442 sq km (171 sq mi)

ETHNIC MAJORITY:
African black

LANGUAGES:
English (official), English patois

RELIGION:
Christianity

UNIT OF CURRENCY:
East Caribbean dollar

NATIONAL FLAG:
An inverted triangle centered on a red ground and divided horizontally into three bands of black, blue, and white, the black stripe bearing a symbol of the rising sun in gold

NATIONAL EMBLEM:
The main elements are two antelopes flanking a shield. The shield bears a golden sun on a black-field motif with wavy bands of white and blue beneath it; there is a sugar mill in the foreground. The motto on the scroll at the bottom reads: "Each Endeavouring, All Achieving."

NATIONAL ANTHEM:
"Fair Antigua and Barbuda, We Thy Sons and Daughters Stand"

NATIONAL HOLIDAYS:
Easter; Labor Day; Whit Monday; Queen's Official Birthday; Carnival; Independence Day (November 1); Christmas

DATE OF INDEPENDENCE:
November 1, 1981

DATE OF CONSTITUTION:
November 1, 1981

GEOGRAPHICAL FEATURES

Antigua and Barbuda are part of the Leeward Islands chain in the eastern Caribbean and include the islands of Antigua and Barbuda as well as the uninhabited Redonda. The capital city is St. John's on the northwestern edge of the island of Antigua. Both islands are volcanic and coral. Antigua has deeply indented shores marked by reefs and shoals. Its highest point is Boggy Peak (1,329 ft). The central part of the island is a fertile plain and there are numerous islets dotting the eastern coastline. Barbuda is a coral island.

Antigua and Barbuda

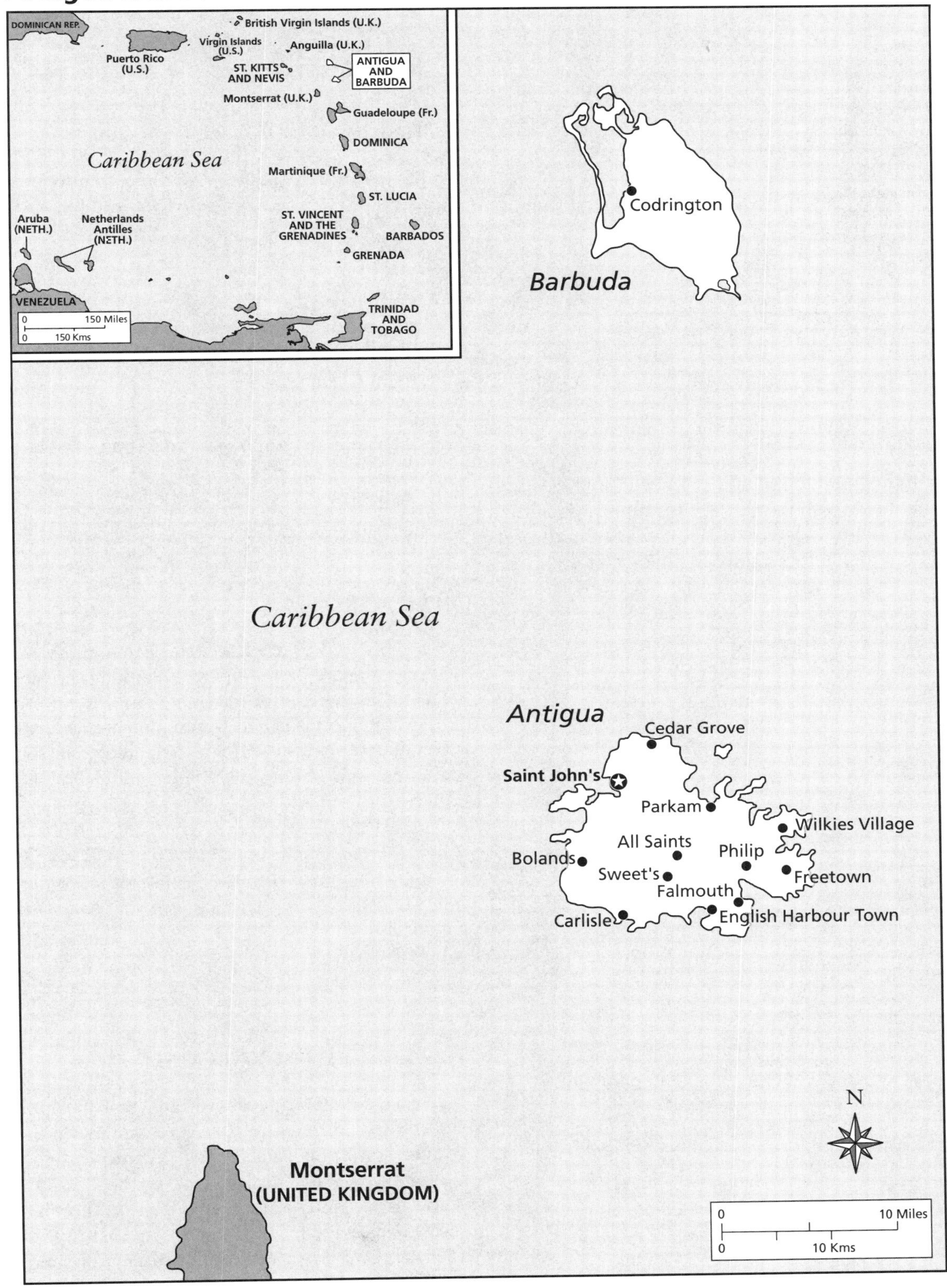
DOMINICAN REP.
British Virgin Islands (U.K.)
Puerto Rico (U.S.)
Virgin Islands (U.S.)
Anguilla (U.K.)
ST. KITTS AND NEVIS
ANTIGUA AND BARBUDA
Montserrat (U.K.)
Guadeloupe (Fr.)
DOMINICA
Caribbean Sea
Martinique (Fr.)
ST. LUCIA
Aruba (NETH.)
Netherlands Antilles (NETH.)
ST. VINCENT AND THE GRENADINES
BARBADOS
GRENADA
VENEZUELA
TRINIDAD AND TOBAGO
0 150 Miles
0 150 Kms
Codrington
Barbuda
Caribbean Sea
Antigua
Cedar Grove
Saint John's
Parkam
Wilkies Village
All Saints
Philip
Bolands
Sweet's
Freetown
Falmouth
Carlisle
English Harbour Town
N
Montserrat (UNITED KINGDOM)
0 10 Miles
0 10 Kms

Geography

Area sq km: 442 sq mi 171
World Rank: 195th
Land Boundaries, km: 0
Coastline, km 153
Elevation Extremes meters
Lowest: Caribbean Sea 0
Highest: Boggy Peak 402
Land Use % Arable land: 18
Permanent Crops: 0
Permanent Pastures: 9
Forest and Woodland: 11
Other: 62

Population of Principal Cities

St. John's	22,342

CLIMATE AND WEATHER

Cooling winds from the east and the northeast moderate the temperatures, which rise to 84°F in summer and 75°F in winter. The rainfall averages 40 inches, with most of it falling between September and November.

Climate and Weather

Mean Temperature 81°F to 93°F
Average Rainfall: 40 in

POPULATION

Population Indicators

Total Population: 1999 69,100
World Rank: 202nd
Density per sq mi: 405.3 per sq km 156.5
% of annual growth (1994–99): 1.5
Male %: 48.2
Female %: 51.8
Urban %: 36.2
Age Distribution: % 0–14: 30.4
15–29: 27.8
30–44: 20.5
45–59: 10.2
60–74: 7.7
75 and over: 3.4
Population 2020: 71,000
Birth Rate per 1,000: 20.9
Death Rate per 1,000: 6.7
Population Doubling Time (years): 47
Infant Mortality Rate per 1,000 live births: 17.2
Rate of Natural Increase per 1,000: 14.2
Total Fertility Rate: 1.7
Expectation of Life (years): Males 71.5
Females 75.8
Marriage Rate per 1,000: 4.9
Divorce Rate per 1,000: 0.2
Total Number of Households: 18,000
Average Size of Households: —
% of Illegitimate Children: 76.6
Induced Abortions: —
Rate per 100 live births: —

ETHNIC COMPOSITION

Antiguans and Barbudans are almost entirely of African descent. Minorities include East Indians, Arabs, and Britons.

LANGUAGES

English is the official language spoken by virtually all Antiguans.

Principal Languages and Their Speakers

English	69,000
English/English Creole	66,000
Other	3,000

RELIGIONS

The Anglican Church has historically enjoyed the status of the dominant denomination, claiming the membership of about 32 percent of the population. A variety of other Protestant groups make up another 42 percent. Roman Catholics are in a minority at 10 percent. St. John's is the episcopal seat of both the Anglican and Roman Catholic dioceses.

Religious Affiliations

Protestant	29,000
Anglican	22,000
Roman Catholic	7,000
Other	11,000

HISTORICAL BACKGROUND

The early inhabitants of Antigua and Barbuda in pre-Columbian times were the Arawak and Carib Indians, whom Columbus met on his second voyage in 1493. Columbus named the island after the Church of Santa Maria de la Antigua, in Seville, Spain. The first Western settlements were by the Spanish in 1520, the French in 1629, and the British in 1632. Antigua became a British colony in 1677 under the Treaty of Breda. In 1674 Sir Christopher Codrington established a large sugar estate on Antigua worked by slaves from Barbuda. In 1860 Barbuda was formally annexed to Antigua and 11 years later both were merged into the Federation of Leeward

Islands for the next 75 years until 1956. From 1958 the name of the federation was changed to the federation of the West Indies and a system of ministerial government was introduced. Vere Cornwall Bird, leader of the Antigua Labour Party, became chief minister. Antigua became an associated state with full internal self-government in 1967 despite opposition from Barbudans who sought constitutional guarantees for autonomy. In 1981 Antigua and Barbuda became an independent state within the British Commonwealth.

Since independence Antigua and Barbuda has been governed by the Bird family. The senior Vere Cornwall Bird's most remarkable achievement was in ruling the country for more than four decades and in surviving a series of corruption charges that would likely have brought down a government in any other country. He was succeeded in 1994 by his son Lester Bird, whose cabinet also includes other members of the Bird family. The Birds have also maintained their hold over the ruling Antigua Labour Party, which won its sixth consecutive electoral victory in 1999.

CONSTITUTION

Under the constitution of 1981, the government is headed by the British monarch as head of state, represented on the island by a governor-general. The executive is headed by a prime minister, who, in the British parliamentary tradition, is the leader of the largest party in the House of Representatives. He heads a cabinet whose members are appointed by the governor general on his recommendation.

LOCAL GOVERNMENT

Antigua is divided into six parishes and the two dependencies of Barbuda and Redonda. Local government is directed by 29 community councils, each with five elected members and four appointed members.

Local Government

Principal administrative divisions, area, population

AREA AND POPULATION

	area		population 1991
Parishes	**sq mi**	**sq km**	**census**
Saint George	9.3	24.1	4,473
Saint John's	28.5	73.8	35,636
Saint Mary	22.0	57.0	5,303
Saint Paul	18.5	47.9	6,117
Saint Peter	12.7	32.9	3,622
Saint Philip	17.0	44.0	2,964
Islands			
Barbuda	62.0	160.6	1,241
Redonda	0.5	1.3	3
TOTAL	170.5	441.6	59,355

PARLIAMENT

The bicameral legislature consists of a 17-member House of Representatives elected from single-member constituencies for five-year terms by universal adult suffrage, and a 17-member Senate, appointed by the governor general of whom 11 are named on the recommendation of the prime minister, four on the advice of the Leader of the Opposition, one on the governor general's discretion, and one by the Barbuda Council.

POLITICAL PARTIES

The Antigua Labour Party has been in power since independence. The principal opposition is the United Progressive Party, which won four seats (out of 17) in the House of Representatives in 1999.

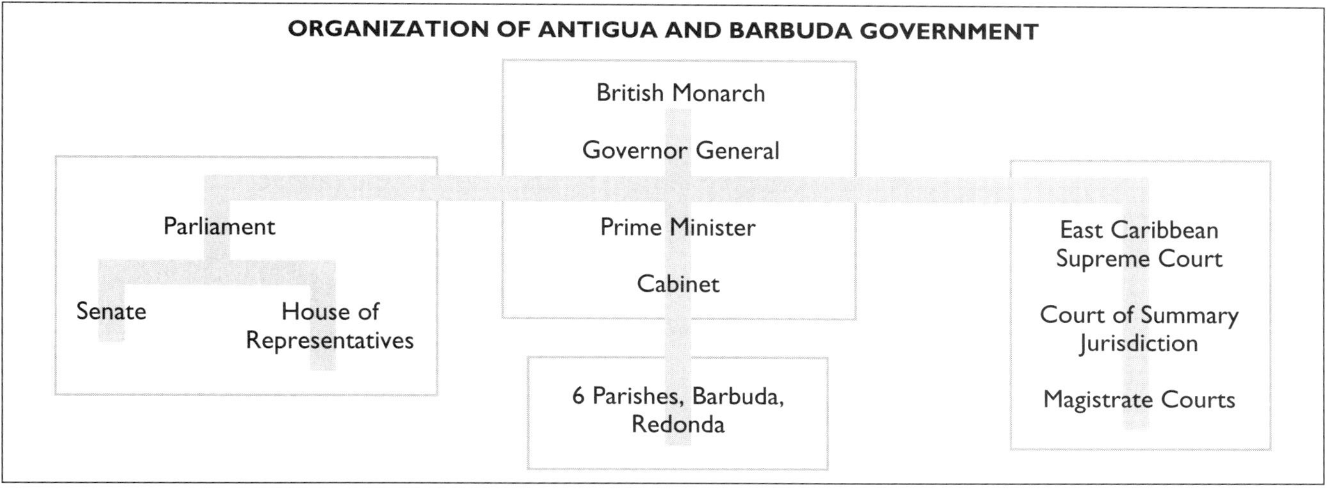

Political Parties

Antigua Labor Party, 1967
United Progressive Party, 1992
Other parties include
People's Democratic Movement, 1995
Barbuda People's Movement
Barbuda National Party
Barbuda Independence Movement, 1987

Political Parties: Strength in Parliament Most Recent Elections

House of Representatives. The lower house has 17 members chosen every five years (subject to dissolution) from single-member constituencies. At the most recent election of March 9, 1999, the Antigua Labour Party won 12 seats; the United Progressive Party, 4; and the Barbuda People's Movement 1.

LEGAL SYSTEM

The court system operates on three levels. At the bottom level are three magistrates' courts dealing with summary offenses and civil cases with a value of EC$500 or less. At the intermediate level is the court of summary jurisdiction, which sits without a jury and deals with civil cases. At the apex of the system is the Eastern Caribbean Supreme Court, based in St. Lucia, which serves as a high court and a court of appeal. Final appeals may be made to the Queen's Privy Council in the United Kingdom. The Industrial Court arbitrates and settles trade disputes. The Antigua and Barbuda legal system is based on English common law.

LAW ENFORCEMENT

Law Enforcement

Offenses reported to the police per 100,000: 4,977
- Murder: 4.7
- Assault: 475
- Burglary: 1984.4
- Automobile Theft: 35.9
- Population per Police officer: 120
- Death Penalty: Yes

HUMAN RIGHTS

The Bird family has controlled the government since 1976. They have been notoriously corrupt and have managed to amass an enormous fortune through drug dealing and arms trafficking. They have managed to hold on to power by inflating electoral rolls and through intimidation of political opponents. Several of the Birds have been the target of criminal investigations and Vere Bird was banned from public life for his association and support of Colombian drug bosses. The Bird family also controls the media and has successfully denied the opposition access to the media. The government also engages in arson against opposing political parties. Prison condition are inhumane and there are allegations of physical abuse of prisoners by the guards.

FOREIGN POLICY

Prime Minister V. C. Bird was a strong believer in regional cooperation and played a leading role in the Caribbean Free Trade Association, its successor, the Caribbean Community and Common Market, and the Organization of Eastern Caribbean States. There is a U.S.–backed regional military training center on the main island.

DEFENSE

Antigua and Barbuda is an active member of the Organization of Eastern Caribbean States. It maintains close ties to the United States, which maintains a military training base on the main island.

Military Indicators

Total Active Duty Personnel: 200
Military Manpower per 1,000: 2.3
Military Expenditures $million: —
- as % of GNP: —
- per capita $: —
- as % of central government expenditures: —

Arms Imports $million: —
Arms Exports $million: —

ECONOMY

Tourism is the mainstay of the economy, contributing about half of the gross domestic product. The number of annual tourist arrivals, mainly from the United States, determines the health of the economy. The older agricultural economy is directed to the domestic market but is hobbled by a lack of water and labor shortage. Manufacturing is primarily for export, of which the principal products are bedding, handicrafts, and electronic components.

Principal Economic Indicators

Gross National Product: $489 million
GNP per capita: $7,380
GNP Average Annual Growth Rate (1990–97) %: 1.8
GNP per capita Average Annual Growth Rate (1990–97) %: 1.3
Origin of Gross Domestic Product %
- Agriculture: 4
- Mining: 1
- Manufacturing: 2

Construction: 9
Public Utilities: 4
Transportation and Communications: 20
Trade: 25
Financial Services: 15
Other Services: 7
Government: 18

Gross Domestic Product by Type of Expenditure %
Private Consumption: 53
Government Consumption: 21
Gross Domestic Investment: 24
Foreign Trade: Exports: 106
Imports: −104

% of Income Received by Poorest 20%:
% of Income Received by Richest 10%:

Price and Earnings Indexes (1995 = 100)

	1991	1992	1993	1994	1995	1996
Consumer price index	105.7	108.9	112.2	116.2	119.5	124.3
Weekly earnings index	100.0	112.7	—	—	—	—

Finance

National Currency: EC Dollar (EC$)
Exchange Rate: $1 = EC$ 2.7
Money Supply Stock in National Currency billion: 0.255
M1 per capita: 3,960
Central Bank Discount Rate %: 7.0
Total External Debt $million: 225
Debt Service Ratio %: —

Balance of Payments $million: −24.7
International Reserves SDRs million: 32
Ratio of External Debt to Total Reserves: —
Average Annual Rate of Inflation/Consumer Price Index Growth Rate %: 2.5

Official Development Assistance

ODA $million: 12
as % of GNP: 2.6
per capita: $184
Foreign Direct Investment $million: —

Central Government Revenues and Expenditures

Fiscal Year: 1 April–31 March
Revenues $million: 107
Expenditures $million: 132
Budget Deficit $million: 15
Tax Revenues as % of GDP: —
Highest Tax Bracket %
Individual: —
Corporate: —

Employment and Labor

Economically Active Population: 26,800
Female Participation Rate %: 45.6
Activity Rate %: 45.1
Labor by Sector: %
Agriculture, Forestry, Fishing: 3.9
Manufacturing, Mining: 7.3
Construction: 11.6
Transportation and Communications: 9.0
Trade, Hotels, and Restaurants: 31.9
Finance, Insurance, Real Estate: 5.4
Public Administration, Defense: —
Services: 23.9

Unemployment %: 10

Agriculture

Agriculture's Share of GDP %: 4
Average Annual Rate of Growth (1965–98) %: —
Number of Farms 000: 2.3
Average Size of Farm ha: 2.1
Number of Tractors per 1,000 hectares: 30.0
Irrigation, % of Farms having: —
Artificial Fertilizer kg/hectare: —
Total Farmland as % of land area: 5.7
Livestock: Cattle 000: 16
Sheep 000: 12
Hogs 000: 2
Chickens 000: 90
Forests: Production of Roundwood (000 cubic meters): —
Fisheries: Total Catch tons 000: 0.6

Mining

% of GDP: 1.5
Value of Mineral Production $million: 7.6

Manufacturing

Value Added $million: 8.4
Industrial Production Growth Rate %: —

Energy

Commercial Energy Production metric tons of oil equivalent 000: —
Commercial Energy Consumption metric tons of oil equivalent 000: 131
Commercial Energy Consumption per capita kg: 2,017
Average Annual Growth Rate 1980–97 %: —
Net Energy Imports % of use: 100
Electricity Installed Capacity kW 000: 26
Production kW-hr million: 98
Coal Reserves tons million: —
Production tons 000: —
Natural Gas Proven Reserves cubic meters billion: —
Production cubic meters million: —
Crude Petroleum Reserves barrels million: —
Production barrels million: —
Consumption barrels million: —
Refinery Capacity barrels per day 000: —
Pipelines Length km: —

Foreign Trade

Imports $million: 245.9
Exports $million: 39.8
Export Volume % Annual Growth Rate (1990–97): —
Import Volume % Annual Growth Rate (1990–97): —

(continued)

Balance of Trade (current prices)

	1992	1993	1994	1995	1996	1997
U.S.$.000,000	−347	−375	−403	—	−279	−296
% of total	71.4%	78.6%	83.1%	—	82.8%	83.6%

Major Trading Partners

	Imports	Exports
European Union %	41.3	15.0
United States %	29.5	15.4
Eastern Europe %	—	—
Japan %	—	—
Others %	29.2	69.5

Transportation

Roads Total Length mi: 721 km 1,161
Paved %: 33
Automobiles: 13,588
Trucks and Buses: 1,342
Persons per vehicle: 4.3
Railroad; Track Length mi: —
Passenger-mi million: —
Freight-mi million: —
Merchant Marine: No. of Vessels: 292
Total Deadweight Tonnage 000: 997.4
International Cargo Loaded tons 000: 28
International Cargo Off-loaded tons 000: 113
Airports with Scheduled Flights: 2
Traffic: Passenger-mi million: 140
Freight-mi million: 14
Length of Canals mi: — km —

Tourism

Number of Tourists to 000: —
Number of Tourists from 000: —
Tourist Receipts $million: 329
Tourist Expenditures $million: 24

Communications

Telephones 000: 120
Cost of Local Calls 3 mins $0
Cellular Telephones 000: —
Fax Machines 000: —
Personal Computers 000: —
Internet Hosts per million persons: 2,424
Mail: Post Offices: —
Pieces of Mail Handled million: —
Pieces of Mail Handled per person: —

EDUCATION

Education is compulsory between the ages of five and 16. The majority of the schools are public. There are three institutions of higher learning: The University of Health Sciences, Antigua, the University of the West Indies School of Continuing Studies, and the Antigua State College.

Education

Literacy Rate%: 90
Male %: —
Female %: —
First Level: Primary schools: 43
Teachers: 439
Students: 11,506
Student-Teacher Ratio: 26.2
Net Enrollment Ratio: —
Second Level: Secondary Schools: 12
Teachers: 277
Students: 4,294
Student-Teacher Ratio: 15.5
Net Enrollment Ratio: —

Vocational Level: Schools: 1
Students: 46

Third Level: Institutions: —
Teachers: —
Students: —
Student-Ratio Level: —
Gross Enrollment Ratio: —
Students per 100,000: —
% of Population Age 25 and over with Postsecondary Education: —
Public Expenditure on Education as % of GDP: —

SCIENCE AND TECHNOLOGY

Science and Technology

Scientists and Engineers in R&D per 1 million persons: —
Expenditures in R&D as % of GDP: —
High-Tech Exports $million: —
Patent Applications by Residents: —

MEDIA

Freedom of the press is guaranteed by the constitution. Three of the newspapers are published by political parties: *The Outlet* by the Antigua Caribbean Liberation Movement, *The Workers' Voice* by the ruling Antigua Labor Party, and *Rappore by* the United National Democratic Party. There is no domestic news agency. Most media rely on the Caribbean News Agency. Radio ZDK is a private radio facility controlled by Prime Minister Bird's family. The government-run Antigua and Barbuda Broadcasting Service (ABBS) transmits over one radio station and television facility.

Media

Daily Newspapers: 1
Total Circulation 000: 6.0
Circulation per 1,000: 94
Books Published: —
Magazines: —
Radio Receivers 000: 50
per 1,000: 778
Television sets 000: 27
per 1,000: 419

MOST IMPORTANT MEDIA:

Press. The following are published at St. John's: *The Outlet* (5,500), ACLM weekly; *The Herald* (2,500), progovernment weekly; *The Worker's Voice* (2,200), twice-weekly organ of the ALP and AT&LU; *The Nation* (1,500), government weekly; *Rappore*, UPP weekly. A weekly, *Antigua Today*, was launched in December 1993.

News agency. There is no domestic facility. Most media rely on the regional Caribbean News Agency (CANA) for international coverage.

Radio and television. Radio ZDK is a private station broadcasting from St. John's. The government-operated Antigua and Barbuda Broadcasting Service (ABBS) transmits over one radio station and one TV facility, the latter providing the most sophisticated full-color service in the Commonwealth Caribbean. Other radio facilities include Voice of America, BBC Caribbean, and Deutsche Welle relays, plus a religious station, Caribbean Radio Lighthouse.

CULTURE

Cultural Indicators

Public Libraries Number:
Volumes:
Registered borrowers:
Museums Number:
Annual Attendance:
Cinema Production of Long Films:
Number of Cinemas:
Seating Capacity:
Annual Attendance:
Annual Attendance per capita:

STATUS OF WOMEN

Antigua has an official agency, the Directorate of Women's Affairs, to monitor the status of women in the islands. Violence against women is common. In 1999 parliament approved antidomestic violence legislation, but in many cases women are unwilling to testify against their husbands. Progress in implementing new programs to assist women in bettering their economic opportunities is slow.

Women

Gender Empowerment Measure: —
Seats Held in Parliament by Women %: —
Female Administrators and Managers %: —
Female Professional and Technical Workers %: —
Women's Share of Earned Income %: —
Women in Government %: 30

HEALTH, FOOD, AND NUTRITION

Health

Number of Physicians: 59
Number of Dentists: 13
Number of Nurses: 179
Number of Pharmacists: 13
Population per Physician: 1,083
Number of Hospitals: 2
Hospital Beds per 10,000: 58
Hospital Bed Occupancy Rate: 49.9
Infant Mortality Rate per 1,000 live births: 22
Maternal Mortality Rate per 100,000 live births: —
Total Health Expenditures as % of GDP: 4.55
Health Expenditures per capita $: 241
HIV Infected % of adults: —
Cigarette Consumption per smoker per year: —
% of Smokers: Male: —
Female: —
Access to Safe Water %: 95

Food and Nutrition

Food Supply as % of FAO Requirements: 102
% of Consumption Expenditures on Food: 4,050
Daily Available Calories per capita: 2,406
% of Total Calories derived from:
Cereals: 26.7
Potatoes, cassava: 1.0
Meat, poultry: 14.5
Fish: 4.4
Eggs, milk: 11.0
Fruits, vegetables: 7.2
Fats, oils: 16.0

ENVIRONMENT

The principal ecological problem in Antigua and Barbuda is shortage of water. The islands are subject to periodic drought and existing facilities and underground sources are contaminated by industrial polluters. Deforestation contributes not only to soil erosion as water quickly runs off but also compounds the water shortage. Waste disposal is antiquated, and untreated sewage runs in open trenches and empties into the sea. There is an official Environmental Commission which exists mainly on paper and does little to solve these problems.

Environment

Forest Area sq km: —
Average Annual Deforestation sq km: 0
Nationally Protected Areas as % of Total Land Area: —
Freshwater Access cubic meters per capita: —
Emissions of Organic Water Pollutants kg per day: —
CO_2 Emissions per capita ton: 4.9

CHRONOLOGY

1946 Antigua Labour Party (ALP) is formed by Vere Bird, Sr.
1958 The Leeward Islands Federation becomes the West Indies Federation.
1967 Antigua and Barbuda become an associated state within the Commonwealth.

1971 Progressive Labor Movement wins elections with George Walter as prime minister.
1976 ALP regains power and remains in power for the rest of the century.
1981 Antigua and Barbuda become sovereign states.
1993 Lester Bird succeeds his father as prime minister.
1995 Hurricane Luis damages or destroys at least 75 percent (worth approximately $300 million) of homes in Antigua and Barbuda.
1996 Antigua establishes an office of the control of illicit drugs to improve its tarnished antinarcotics image.
1997 Antigua and Barbuda takes steps to eliminate money laundering and organized crime within its borders, closing 11 offshore banks and initiating legislation to close loopholes used by international criminal organizations.
1999 Lester Bird is reelected, representing the sixth term for his party, the ALP.
2000 The UN criticizes the courts' decision to impose the death penalty in convicting two men of murdering four tourists.

BIBLIOGRAPHY

Coram, Robert. *Caribbean Time Bomb: The United States' Complicity in the Corruption of Antigua.* New York, 1993.

Henry, Paget. *Peripheral Capitalism and Underdevelopment in Antigua.* New Brunswick, N.J., 1985.

Lazarus-Black, Mindie. *Legitimate Acts and Illegal Encounters: Law and Society in Barbuda and Antigua.* Washington, D.C., 1994.

OFFICIAL PUBLICATIONS

Antigua. *Antigua and Barbuda—Statistical Annex* (IMF Staff Country Report [1996]); *Statistical Yearbook: 1991 Population and Housing Census.*

CONTACT INFORMATION

Embassy of Antigua and Barbuda
3216 New Mexico Avenue NW
Washington, D.C. 20016
Phone: (202) 362-5211 Fax: (202) 362-5225

INTERNET RESOURCES

- Antigua and Barbuda High Commission (London)
http://antigua-barbuda.com/
- The Commonwealth OnLine: Antigua and Barbuda
http://www.tcol.co.uk/antig/index.htm

ARGENTINA

BASIC FACT SHEET

OFFICIAL NAME:
Republic of Argentina (República Argentina)

ABBREVIATION:
AG

CAPITAL:
Buenos Aires

HEAD OF STATE & HEAD OF GOVERNMENT:
Interim President Eduardo Duhalde (2002)

NATURE OF GOVERNMENT:
Constitutional democracy

POPULATION:
36,578,000 (1999)

AREA:
2,791,810 sq km (1,077,921 sq mi)

ETHNIC MAJORITY:
Caucasian

LANGUAGE:
Spanish

RELIGION:
Roman Catholicism (official)

UNIT OF CURRENCY:
Argentine peso

NATIONAL FLAG:
Tricolor consisting of middle white horizontal stripe between two light blue horizontal stripes emblazoned with the "Sun of May"

NATIONAL EMBLEM:
An oval shield divided horizontally into two halves, light blue in the upper portion and white in the lower. In the center is a liberty pole held by clasped hands. On the top of the staff is a red liberty cap worn by 19th-century patriots in the wars of liberation. Surmounting the oval is a golden "Sun of May" and enclosing it is a laurel wreath of victory.

NATIONAL ANTHEM:
"Hear, O mortals, the sacred cry of liberty"

NATIONAL HOLIDAYS:
July 9 (Independence Day, National Day); January 1 (New Year's Day); May 1 (Labor Day); May 25 (Anniversary of the 1810 Revolution); June 20 (Flag Day); August 17 (Death of Gen. José de San Martín); Variable Christian festivals and Christmas.

DATE OF INDEPENDENCE:
July 9, 1816

DATE OF CONSTITUTION:
May 1, 1853; revised August 1994

GEOGRAPHICAL FEATURES

Argentina, located in the southern part of the South American continent, is the eighth largest country in the world and one-fourth the size of Europe with an area of 2,791,810 sq km (1,077,921 sq mi) extending 3,650 km (2,268 mi) north to south and 1,430 km (889 mi) east to west. Argentina also claims a section of Antarctica of about 1,235,430 sq km (477,000 sq mi). Argentina also claimed the Falkland Islands as part of its territory. The total length of the Atlantic coastline is 4,970 km (3,088 mi).

Argentina is bordered by: Chile (5,150 km; 3,198 mi), Bolivia (832 km; 517 mi), Paraguay (1,880 km; 1,167 mi), Brazil (1,224 km; 760 mi), and Uruguay (579 km; 353 mi). These international borders generally coincide with natural features, and all have been demarcated except along certain watercourses.

Argentina

BOLIVIA
PARAGUAY
CHILE
BRAZIL
URUGUAY
Pacific Ocean
Atlantic Ocean
ANDES
La Quiaca
Embarcacion
San Salvador de Jujuy
Salta
Rio Bemejo
Rio Salado del Norte
Clorinda
Formosa
Resistencia
San Miguel de Tucuman
Bernardo de Irigoyen
Corrientes
Posadas
Catamarca
Santiago del Estero
Chilecito
Rio Parana
Goya
Santo Tome
Reconquista
Curuzu Cuatia
Pasos de los Libres
San Jose de Jachal
Chamical
Concordia
San Juan
Cordoba
Villa Maria
Santa Fe
Parana
Mendoza
Rio Cuarto
Rosario
Colon
San Luis
San Rafael
Mercedes
Junin
Lujan
Buenos Aires
La Plata
Realico
Rio de la Plata
Telen
Las Flores
Santa Rosa
Olavarria
Tandil
Dolores
Rio Colorado
Bahia Blanca
Puerto Belgrano
Mar del Plata
Zapala
Neuquen
Rio Colorado
Puerto Rosales
Necochea
Rio Negro
San Antonio Oeste
Carmen de Patagones
San Carlos de Bariloche
Las Plumas
Rawson
Sarmiento
Comodoro Rivadavia
Colonia Las Heras
Gobernador Gregores
Puerto Deseado
Rio Chico
San Julian
Santa Cruz
FALKLAND IS. (UNITED KINGDOM)
Yacimientos de Rio Turbio
Rio Gallegos
N
Rio Grande
Ushuaia
Tierra del Fuego
Cape Horn
0
100 Miles
0
100 Kms

Argentina is generally divided into four topographical regions: the Pampas, Patagonia, the lowland region of the northeast, and the northwest Andes (including the piedmont).

The Pampas, extending 800 km (497 mi) north to south and east to west, is the heartland of Argentina, containing the richest agricultural land in South America. The region is an unbroken plain, which is exactly what Pampa means in the Quechua language. The plain is bounded by the Chaco Plain to the north, the Colorado River to the south, the Atlantic to the east, and the Sierra de Córdoba to the west. However, when Argentinians refer to *la pampa* they are more often than not referring to the gaucho and cattle country of the Dry Pampa rather than to the Humid Pampa around Buenos Aires. They also distinguish three subregions within the Pampas: the Littoral, immediately to the north of Buenos Aires along the west bank of the Paraná River; the Comahue, comprising the province of La Pampa and the Patagonian provinces of Neuquén and Río Negro; and the Campo, or rural region, of the Pampa.

The second region is Patagonia, a semiarid, windswept land, including the barren island of Tierra del Fuego. Patagonia fans out southward from the Colorado River to the Strait of Magellan and from the Atlantic to the Chilean border. Rising from a narrow coastal plain in tiers toward the west, Patagonia reaches elevations of over 1,500 m (5,000 ft). In the north the Granbajo de Gualicho depression between the Colorado and Río Negro rivers drops to 32 m (105 ft) below sea level. In the extreme south the land is dotted with glaciers and ice fields.

The third region is the northeastern lowlands lying north of the Pampa and east of the Andes Mountains between the Paraná and Uruguay Rivers. Because of its location between two rivers, the region is sometimes known as the Argentine Mesopotamia. It also includes the Argentine portion of the Gran Chaco Plain, which extends northward across Paraguay into Bolivia.

The fourth region is the northwest Andes and piedmont extending along the western half of the country from Bolivia in the north to Patagonia in the south, and from the Chilean border to Gran Chaco and Pampa. Along the Chilean border Jujuy, Catamarca, and Tucumán Provinces have elevations of 6,100 m (20,000 ft); the province of Mendoza contains Aconcagua (7,021 m; 20,035 ft), the highest peak in the Western Hemisphere. The mountainsides are cut by broad valleys known as *quebradas*, but otherwise the land is generally inhospitable.

Geography

Area sq km: 2,791,810 sq mi: 1,077,921
World Rank: 8th
Land Boundaries, km: Bolivia 832; Brazil 1,224; Chile 5,150;
Paraguay 1,880; Uruguay 579
Coastline, km: 4,989
Elevation Extremes meters
Lowest: Salinas Chicas −40
Highest: Cerra Aconcagua 6,962
Land Use % Arable land: 9
Permanent Crops: 1
Permanent Pastures: 52
Forest and Woodland: 19
Other: 19

Population of Principal Cities (1991)

City	Population
Avellaneda	346,620
Bahía Blanca	260,096
Buenos Aires	2,988,006
Catamarca	110,269
Rivadavia	124,104
Concordia	116,485
Córdoba	1,208,718
Corrientes	268,103
Formosa	148,074
General San Martín	407,506
La Matanza	1,111,811
La Plata	642,979
La Rioja	103,727
Lanus	466,755
Lomas de Zamora	572,769
Mar del Plata	512,880
Mendoza	773,113
Morón	641,541
Neuquén	243,803
Paraná	211,936
Posadas	210,755
Quilmes	509,445
Resistencia	292,350
Río Cuarto	138,853
Rosario	1,118,984
Salta	370,904
San Fernando	132,626
San Isidro	299,022
San Juan	352,691
San Luis	110,136
San Miguel de Tucumán	622,324
San Nicolas de los Arroyos	119,302
San Salvador de Jujuy	180,102
Santa Fe	406,388
Santiago del Estero La Banda	263,471
Vicente Lopez	289,142

CLIMATE AND WEATHER

The climate varies from subarctic in the south to subtropical in the north. January is the warmest month, and June and July are the coolest. Summer lasts from December through February and winter from June through August. Temperatures and rainfall become progressively lower from north to south. The highest temperature recorded in the country is 49°C (120°F). The average daily temperature is about 16.7°C (62°F). The Chaco area has a mean annual temperature of 23°C (73°F), while Puna de Atacama has a temperature average of 14°C (57°F). Rainfall diminishes from east to west; Buenos Aires receives 939.8 mm (37 in), Chaco 762 mm (30 in), and Puna de Atacama 50 mm (2 in). Snow falls rarely.

Most of the piedmont and Patagonia are dry and the Patagonian winters relatively mild.

Both the Pampas and the northeast are subject to violent windstorms known as the *pamperos*, which are usually accompanied by thunder and rain.

Climate and Weather

Mean Temperature
Buenos Aires 62°F
Chaco 73°F
Puna de Atacama 57.2°F
Average Rainfall: Buenos Aires 37 in
Chaco 30 in
Puna de Atacama 2 in

POPULATION

Population Indicators

Total Population: 1999 36,578,000
World Rank: 31st
Density per sq mi: 34.1 per sq km: 13.2
% of annual growth (1994–99): 1.3
Male %: 48.9
Female %: 51.1
Urban %: 88.4
Age Distribution: % 0–14: 30.6
15–29: 23.3
30–44: 19.3
45–59: 13.9
60–74: 9.6
75 and over: 3.3
Population 2020: 45,347,000
Birth Rate per 1,000: 19.9
Death Rate per 1,000: 7.9
Population Doubling Time (years): —
Infant Mortality Rate per 1,000 live births: 22.0
Rate of Natural Increase per 1,000: 12.0
Total Fertility Rate: 2.6
Expectation of Life (years): Males 69.6
Females 76.8
Marriage Rate per 1,000: 6.0
Divorce Rate per 1,000: —
Total Number of Households: 10,097,000
Average Size of Households: 3.2
% of Illegitimate Children: 32.5
Induced Abortions: —
Rate per 100 live births: —

ETHNIC COMPOSITION

The Argentines are overwhelmingly Caucasian by racial origin. Of the many European national groups, Italians and Spaniards predominate, but British, West and East Europeans, Jews, and Middle Easterners are also represented in the population. Together they make up 85 percent of the population. The remaining 15 percent consists of mestizos, Indians, and others. The pureblooded Indian population, estimated at 50,000, is concentrated in the provinces of the north, northwest, and south.

LANGUAGES

The official language is Spanish, but spoken Spanish has a distinctively Argentinian flavor and differs in pronunciation and grammar from Castilian Spanish. Among the many peculiarities of Argentinian Spanish is the trait known as *yeísmo*, in which the double *l* and *y* sounds are spoken like *z*, as in *azure*. The *porteños* ("people of the port," as inhabitants of Buenos Aires are called) also speak Spanish with a peculiar accent called Río Platense. Many variations are due to Italian and French influences. Italian, particularly, has contributed numerous words to the Argentine vocabulary, and an Italianized Spanish dialect known as *lunfardo* has evolved in urban slums. English is spoken by an increasing number of people, particularly within the business and professional communities. English, French, and German immigrants have managed to retain their own mother tongue and all of the larger communities run their own newspapers.

Three Indian languages still survive in the country: Tehuelche in southern Patagonia, Guaraní in Misiones Province, and Quechua, a modified form of the ancient Inca language, in Jujuy and Salta Provinces. These languages receive no official encouragement and may die out in course of time.

Principal Languages and Their Speakers

Amerindian languages	110,000
Italian	640,000
Spanish	35,420,000
Other	410,000

RELIGIONS

Roman Catholicism is the state religion, adhered to by 88 percent of the population. However, less than 20 percent of the population are believed to be actively practicing Christians. The government retains "National Patronage" over the church derived form the royal patronage of Spanish times. Bishops are appointed by the president of the republic from a panel of three submitted by the Senate, and papal bulls and decrees are proclaimed by the president, and, sometimes, incorporated in acts of the Congress. The hierarchy consists of two cardinal archbishops, 11 archbishops, and 46 bishops.

Non-Catholic religious groups are small, but all creeds enjoy freedom of worship. Supervision of religious bodies is the responsibility of the Ministry of Foreign Affairs and Worship. Two percent of the population, generally members of ethnic minorities, is listed as Protestant. Interchurch cooperation is very rare despite the existence of the Argentine Federation of Evangelical Churches. Nearly one-half of the Protestants belong to the Anglican, Congregationalist, Seventh-Day Adventist, Lutheran, and Methodist Churches.

Argentina's constitution states that all have the right to practice their religion, but it also states that the federal government supports Roman Catholicism. The constitution requires the president and vice president to be members of the Roman Catholic Church. Religions other than Catholicism must register with the government to obtain the legal recognition required to operate freely in Argentina. In July 1984 the government granted long-pending legal recognition to the Jehovah's Witnesses.

Argentina's 450,000 Jews constitute the second largest Jewish community in the Americas and the largest in Latin America. The bulk of the Jews are descendants of Ashkenazim who arrived form Russia in the 19th century. Anti-Semitism has been an ever-present factor in Argentine politics, but it has been more a nuisance than a threat.

In 1978 the government required all religions other than Roman Catholicism to register with the Ministry of Foreign Affairs. Religious sects "injurious to public order, national security, morality and customs" are banned.

Religious Affiliations

Roman Catholic	32,090,000
Protestant	2,740,000
Muslim	540,000
Jewish	260,000
Other	950,000

HISTORICAL BACKGROUND

Argentina's recorded history began with the visit of the first Spaniards in 1516. Permanent settlement began when colonists from Chile established the town of Santiago del Estero in 1553 and settlers from Peru established Tucumán (1565) and Córdoba (1573). Juan de Garay, governor of Asunción, founded Santa Fe in 1573 and Buenos Aires in 1580 on the site of an older Spanish settlement. These scattered settlements did not coalesce into a province until 1776 when a viceroy was sent to Buenos Aires to thwart Portuguese expansion to the south. In 1886 an English naval force under Gen. William Beresford captured Buenos Aires, but was later driven out.

The Spanish colonies in Latin America won independence in 1810–19, and Argentines date their independence from 1816 when they wrested independence from Spain. A long period of disorder during the early and mid-century was followed by strong centralized government at the end of the century. Argentina witnessed a large-scale Italian, German, and Spanish immigration after 1810. Modernization followed, and Argentina soon became the most prosperous, educated, and industrialized of the Latin American nations. Military coups prevailed during the 1930s and 1940s until the election of General Juan Perón as president. Perón with his wife, Eva Duarte (known as Evita), worked for social welfare and labor reforms but became increasingly authoritarian. As the economy worsened in the early 1950s he repressed strikes, drove down wages, and harassed opposition leaders. The military overthrew Perón in 1955. After an 18-year exile (1955–73) in Spain, Perón was once again elected the president of Argentina in 1973. He died after 10 months in office, and he was succeeded by his third wife, Isabel Perón, who thus became the world's first woman president.

A military junta ousted Isabel Perón on charges of corruption in 1976. The new military government battled guerrillas and leftists, engaged in the killing of some 5,000 people, and jailed thousands of political opponents. In December 1981, Lieutenant General Leopoldo Galtieri, the commander in chief of the army, became president. During his presidency Argentina witnessed a severe worsening of economic conditions throughout the country. Largely to distract public attention from the unstable domestic situation, President Galtieri ordered the invasion of the Falkland Islands in April 1982. The islands had been a source of contention between Great Britain and Argentina. The defeat in the Falklands War brought humiliation to the Argentine armed forces, and President Galtieri was forced to resign on June 17.

Democratic rule returned to Argentina in 1983 when Doctor Raúl Alfonsín took office as president in December of that year. The most pressing problems facing the new administration included a need to refinance the country's $40 billion debt, bring runaway inflation under control, and resolve thorny foreign conflicts involving the Falkland Islands and the Beagle Channel. Soon after his election, President Alfonsín announced a radical reform of the armed forces and prosecution of military officials engaged in human rights abuses during the "dirty war" between the former military regime and its opponents in the late 1970s and early 1980s. On December 9, 1985, five former junta members were found guilty of murder and human rights abuses. Alfonsín's attempts at prosecuting military personnel were limited by unrest in the army. Three army rebellions linked to discontent over prosecutions were crushed in 1988–89.

Alfonsín was unable to deal with Argentina's economic problems, which worsened during his administration. Inflation reached 100 percent in 1985 and foreign debt topped $60 billion by the end of 1988. The government issued a new monetary unit, the australe, to replace the peso in 1985 but the measure was unable to curb inflation permanently, and the peso was reinstated.

In the campaign for the May 1989 elections, the Peronist presidential candidate Carlos Saúl Menem attracted popular votes with his promise of "productive revolution." The Peronists returned to power on May 14, 1989, by securing 48.5 percent of the votes and 310 of the 600 seats in the electoral college. President Alfonsín resigned from office five months earlier than scheduled and Carlos Saúl Menem took office as president on July 8, 1989. By September, Menem's drastic economic policies brought the rate of inflation down to 37 percent compared with the July level of 197 percent. In 1990 Menem pardoned the junta members convicted of human rights abuses, saying it was time to close a black period in Argentine history. President Fernando de la Rúa of the UCR center-left Alliance, elected to a four-year term in 1999, has promised a crackdown on corruption and tough fiscal measures to balance Argentina's budget. His austerity measures were met with protest, and, in 2001 congressional elections, the opposition Peronists took control of both houses of parliament. In December, after having declared a state of emergency to stop protests against his government's economic policies, de la Rúa resigned. Adolfo Rodríguez Saa, who was named interim president, stepped down after only 10 days in office and was replaced for a day by caretaker president Eduardo Camaño and, later, by Eduardo Duhalde (January 1, 2002).

CONSTITUTION

With the return to civilian rule in 1983 the constitution of 1853, as amended, was reintroduced. In 1994, the constitution was amended. The amendments relate mostly to electoral details. The most important was the removal of the ban on consecutive presidential terms. Executive power is once again in the hands of an elected president, serving a four-year term and chosen by direct universal suffrage. The president is eligible to serve two terms. Legislative power is vested in Congress, comprising a Chamber of Deputies with 259 directly elected members and a Senate with 72 members with three members chosen by each provincial legislatures and three from the federal district. Each province has its own constitution.

Voting is compulsory for all citizens 18 years of age or older. Some 85 percent to 90 percent of those eligible vote in most elections. Elections are generally fair and honest and are administered by an electoral board headed by a federal judge called an electoral judge.

During the 20th century, Argentina has been plagued by violence, civil strife, unstable governments, and economic chaos. Since the 1930 revolution led by Gen. José Felix Uriburu, 10 of the 13 presidents have been military officers.

The country has witnessed systematic violence, kidnappings, and bombings by both left-wing and right-wing terrorists. Left-wing terrorism is exemplified by the activities of two organizations: the Montonero guerrillas and ERP (Ejército Revolucionario del Pueblo, People's Revolutionary Army). The government's operations against the guerrillas were marked by mass arrests and suppression of human rights.

During the 1980s terrorism no longer was the number one threat to the country. The principal subversive movements, ERP and the Montoneros, were forced to move their bases of operations abroad. The latter were unable to launch even one significant military action after 1978, except for an occasional grenade or bomb attack, whereas the former began to concentrate on propaganda efforts to isolate the military government, principally through the bulletin, *Che Guevara*, and the information center Centro Argentino de Información y Solidaridad (CAIS) set up in Paris.

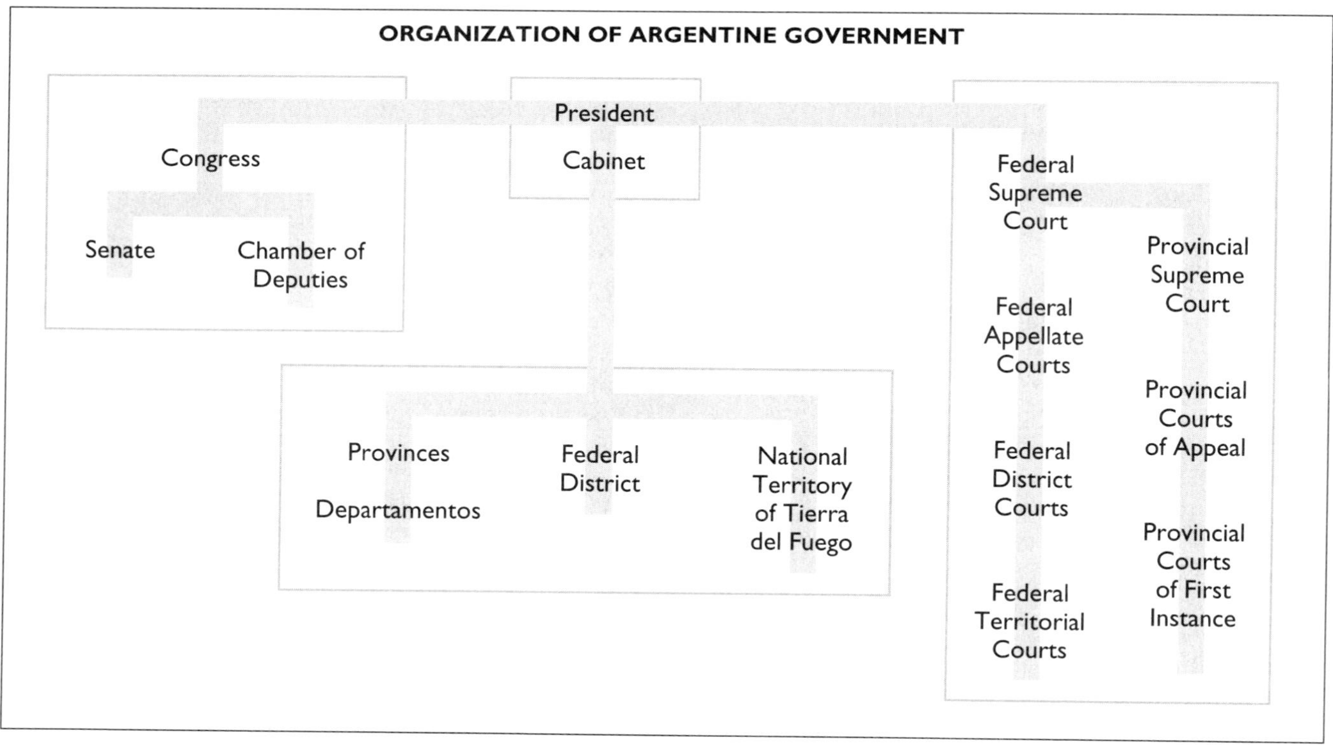

LOCAL GOVERNMENT

For purposes of regional administration Argentina is divided into 23 provinces and the federal capital, Buenos Aires. Under the constitution of 1853 the provinces have their own constitutions and retain all powers not explicitly delegated to the central government. The provincial governors are elected directly for four-year terms and enjoy extensive powers, including the right to issue executive decrees, prepare provincial budgets, and pardon offenders of provincial laws. The governor is also the commander-in-chief of the local militia. Each province has its own legislature, and those provinces with a population of more than half a million have bicameral legislatures. The powers of provincial legislatures include approval of provincial budgets and supervision of education and health-related activities. However, the federal government retains the right to intervene in provincial administrations "to guarantee the republican form of government."

Local Government

Principal administrative divisions, capitals, area, population

AREA AND POPULATION

Provinces	Capitals	area sq mi	area sq km	population 1999 estimate
Buenos Aires	La Plata	118,754	307,571	14,047,483
Catamarca	Catamarca	39,615	102,602	312,269
Chaco	Resistencia	38,469	99,633	940,901
Chubut	Rawson	86,752	224,686	438,236
Córdoba	Córdoba	63,831	165,321	3,059,115
Corrientes	Corrientes	34,054	88,199	909,207
Entre Ríos	Paraná	30,418	78,781	1,104,836
Formosa	Formosa	27,825	72,066	492,513
Jujuy	San Salvador de Jujuy	20,548	53,219	594,117
La Pampa	Santa Rosa	55,382	143,440	301,466
La Rioja	La Rioja	34,626	89,680	273,471
Mendoza	Mendoza	57,462	148,827	1,588,091
Misiones	Posadas	11,506	29,801	972,672
Neuquén	Neuquén	36,324	94,078	540,384
Río Negro	Viedma	78,384	203,013	606,575
Salta	Salta	60,034	155,488	1,044,973
San Juan	San Juan	34,614	89,651	574,053
San Luis	San Luis	29,633	76,748	354,959
Santa Cruz	Río Gallegos	94,187	243,943	201,642
Santa Fe	Santa Fe	51,354	133,007	3,068,765
Santiago del Estero	Santiago del Estero	52,645	136,351	720,982
Tierra del Fuego	Ushuaia	8,210	21,263	109,998
Tucumán	San Miguel de Tucumán	8,697	22,524	1,278,216
Other federal entity				
Distrito Federal	Buenos Aires	77	200	3,043,431
TOTAL		1,073,400	2,780,092	36,578,358

PARLIAMENT

The National Congress consists of a Senate and a Chamber of Deputies. The Senate has 72 members: three from the federal capital and three from each of the 23 provinces. The senators from the provinces are elected by the provincial legislatures and the senators form the Federal District by direct vote. Their term of office is nine years with one-third retiring every three years. The 259 representatives are elected directly (on the basis of one for every 85,000 inhabitants) for four years with one-half retiring every two years. The two chambers meet in ordinary sessions annually from April 1 through November 30.

POLITICAL PARTIES

Argentina's political parties are noted for their vigor and ideological variety. The oldest of these parties is the Unión Cívica Radical (UCR, Radical Civic Union), which has represented the moderate left in Argentine politics since the 19th century. For most of its existence the party has been in opposition. In the period following the deposition of Juan Perón, the party split into two factions: Unión Cívica Radical de Pueblo (UCRP, People's Radical Party) led by Arturo Illia and Unión Cívica Radical Intransigente (UCRI, Intransigent Radical Party) led by Arturo Frondizi. When partisan political activity was legalized in 1973, Frondizi led his followers into the Peronist coalition while UCR backed the candidacy of Richard Balbin.

The country's largest political movement is known by the broad name of Peronism, a label carried by a number of political parties: Partido Unión Popular, Partido Populista, Partido Laborista, Partido Justicialista, and Movimiento Nacional Justicialista. In 1983 these parties joined to form the Frente Justicialista de Liberación (FREJULI, Justicialist Liberation Front) to contest the elections.

Fragments of the traditional parties are scattered across the ideological spectrum. The conservatives are represented by the Union of Argentine People and the National Federation of Parties of the Center. The latter was known as the National Autonomist Party until 1914, the Conservative Party from 1914 until 1930, and the National Democratic Party from 1930 until 1955. The Catholic Church is represented by the Christian Democratic Party and the Federal Union Party, both nationalistic and traditionalistic in outlook. The Socialist Party, which dominated the labor movement from 1922 until the rise of Perón, has steadily lost ground to the Peronists. In 1959 the right wing of the party broke off to form the Democratic Socialist Party and the main party itself was split into two factions. The moderate and anticlerical Progressive Democratic Party derives its strength from the interior.

The government has formally outlawed all left-wing parties. These include the Marxist-Leninist Communist Party, the Revolutionary Communist Party, the Trotskyite Workers' Party, the Workers' Political Party, the Workers' Socialist Party, and the Authentic Peronista Party. The number of Communist Party members in the country is estimated at about 70,000, including a small nucleus of activists.

Political Parties

Justicialist Party, 1946, the former Peronista movement Alliance for Work, Justice and Education, 1997, an electoral alliance consisting of the
- Radical Civic Union, late 19th century
- Front for a Country in Solidarity, 1994
- Broad Front, 1993
- Christian Democratic Party
- Socialist Unity, 1994

Action for the Republic, 1997
New Direction, 1996
Open Politics for Social Integrity, 1994
Union of the Democratic Center, 1980
Republican Force, 1989
Progressive Democratic Party, 1983
Movement of Integration and Development
Intransigent Party
Movement for Dignity and Independence, 1990
Blue and White, 1994
Movement for National Identity and Ibero-American Integration, 1992
Communist Party of Argentina, 1918
Broad Current, 1994
Front for Patriotic Coincidence, 1995
Free Homeland Current

Political Parties: Strength in Parliament Most Recent Elections

Senate. The Senate consists of 72 seats. As of the October 14, 2001, election the Partido Justicialista held 40 seats; the Alianza (Unión Cívica Radical and Frente del País Solidario), 25; Alternativo por una República de Iguales, 1; Partido Neuvo, 1; Partido de Trabajadores por Socialismo, 1; Partido Renovador de Salta, 1; Movimiento Popular Neuquiño, 2; and Partido Liberal de Corrientes, 1.
President: Fernando de la Rúa (1999–2001)

Chamber of Deputies (Cámara de Diputados). The lower house currently consists of 257 deputies directly elected for four years, with one-half reelected every two years. As of the October 14, 2001, elections the Partido Justicialista held 116 seats; the Alianza (Unión Cívica Radical and Frente del País Solidario), 88; Alternativa por una República de Iguales, 17; Frente por el Cambio, 4; Izquierda Unida, 3; Acción por la República, 9; Autodeterminación y Libertad, 2; Fuerza Republicana, 2; and Others, 16.

LEGAL SYSTEM

The judicial system consists of federal and provincial courts. The federal court system is headed by the Supreme Court, whose members are appointed and dismissed by the president. The provincial court structure parallels the federal one with a supreme court, courts of appeal, and courts of first instance in each province. Although the federal and provincial judiciaries are independent of each other, a degree of centralized control is exercised by the secretary of state for justice in the National Ministry of Interior. Outside of both these systems are minor courts that handle petty offenses. These include juvenile courts and courts of justices of peace, or alcaldes.

Argentina is reported to run one of the outstanding prison systems in Latin America. The system consists of some 15 federal and 60 provincial institutions. Federal prisons are under the jurisdiction of the General Directorate of Penal Institutions. Although many of the prisons are overcrowded, the emphasis in the prison regimen is on rehabilitation. In addition, a number of prison farms, open-door institutions, and "homes" for women and minors are maintained.

LAW ENFORCEMENT

Law Enforcement

Offenses reported to the police per 100,000: 186.2
- Murder: 0.3
- Assault: 0.6
- Burglary: 1.5
- Automobile Theft: 19.9
- Population per Police officer: 1,270

Death Penalty: Yes.

HUMAN RIGHTS

Argentina continued to consolidate the dramatic improvements in its human rights record stemming from the successful 1983 transition from a military government to a freely elected civilian government. Argentina is once again a constitutional democracy with an executive branch, an independent bicameral legislature, and an autonomous judicial system. Political debate is free and open, and all parties have access to the media. There exists a high level of public participation in discussing the issues of the day.

Full respect for civil rights returned to Argentina in 1984. Press restrictions ended and controls on the largely government-owned electronic media were the least restrictive since the 1976 military coup. Freely elected national and provincial legislatures reopened. An independent judiciary functioned normally by the end of 1984. Trade union freedom was greater than at any time since 1976; strikes occurred, including one national strike on September 3, and most unions completed leadership elections by the end of the year.

There have also been improvements in respect for individual rights. Human rights groups continue to demand a complete accounting for past disappearances and punishment for those responsible.

Alfonsín also created a special, permanent office in the Ministry of the Interior to replace the commission and to continue its work. Other steps to institutionalize human rights have included instituting new laws strengthening the right of habeas corpus and making torture a crime, signing and ratifying the Inter-American Human Rights Convention, and supporting the United Nations

Convention on Torture. The provincial government in La Rioja began mandatory human rights courses at all schools and for all provincial policemen.

In 1984 Argentina signed and ratified the Inter-American Human Rights Convention. The Chamber of Deputies also approved the UN Convention on Civil and Political Rights and the UN Convention on Economic, Social and Cultural Rights.

FOREIGN POLICY

Argentina has traditionally followed an independent foreign policy and has been frequently out of step with the United States as well as its neighbors. Despite its defeat in the 1982 war with Britain, it continues to assert its longstanding claim to the Falkland Islands (Islas Malvinas). Nevertheless President Menem indicated that he was prepared to engage in a "civilized dialogue" with Britain if the latter abandoned its economic zone around the islands. In 1990 agreement was reached to restore full diplomatic relations. In 1998 Menem traveled to London for the first such visit by an Argentine executive in four decades. The dispute with Chile over three disputed islands in the Beagle Channel was resolved by an agreement in 1991 and an additional protocol in 1996. Argentina is linked to Paraguay, Uruguay, and Brazil in the Southern Cone Common Market, an ambitious economic integration effort. Brazil and Argentina also have an agreement to cooperate in the development of nuclear power although both nations have rejected the use of nuclear weaponry.

DEFENSE

The defense structure is headed by the president, assisted by the chiefs of all three services of the armed forces and a number of advisory bodies, including the National Security Council and the Board of Commanders in Chief of the Armed Forces. Day-to-day operations are the responsibility of the Joint General Staff (Estado Mayor Conjunto).

Argentina is divided into two army areas: the first headquartered at Santa Fe and responsible for the coastal regions, and the second headquartered at Mendoza and responsible for the mountains and the north. The two areas are further divided into six military regions: First (Federal Capital), Second (La Plata), Third (Paraná), Fourth (Córdoba), Fifth (Tucumán), and Sixth (Bahía Blanca). The regions are then divided into 68 military districts. The two mountain brigades are located at Mendoza and Neuquén in the foothills of the Andes. The army aviation battalion is based at Campo de Mayo.

Military manpower is provided by conscription. All Argentine males between the ages of 20 and 45 are required to serve in the military for one or two years' service. In actual practice, only those between 20 and 22 are inducted.

The total strength of the armed forces in 1998 was 73,000.

Military Indicators

Total Active Duty Personnel: 73,000
Military Manpower per 1,000: 2.1
Military Expenditures $million: 4,684
as % of GNP: 1.7
per capita: $137
as % of central government expenditures: 27.0

Arms Imports: $40
Arms Exports: $70

ECONOMY

Argentina benefits from rich natural resources, a highly literate population, an export-oriented agricultural sector, and a diversified industrial base. However, when President Carlos Menem took office in 1989, the country had piled up huge external debts, inflation had reached 200 percent per month, and output was plummeting. To combat the economic crisis, the government embarked on a path of trade liberalization, deregulation, and privatization. In 1991, it implemented radical monetary reforms, which pegged the peso to the U.S. dollar and limited the growth in the monetary base by law to the growth in reserves. Inflation fell sharply in subsequent years. In 1995, the Mexican peso crisis produced capital flight, the loss of banking system deposits, and a severe, but short-lived, recession; a series of reforms to bolster the domestic banking system followed. Real GDP growth recovered strongly, reaching 8 percent in 1997. In 1998, international financial turmoil caused by Russia's problems and increasing investor anxiety over Brazil produced the highest domestic interest rates in more than three years, halving the growth rate of the economy. Conditions worsened in 1999 with GDP falling by 3 percent. President Fernando de la Rua, who took office in December 1999, sponsored tax increases and spending cuts to reduce the deficit, which had ballooned to 2.5 percent of GDP in 1999. The new government also arranged a new $7.4 billion stand-by facility with the IMF for contingency purposes—almost three times the size of the previous arrangement. Growth in 2000 was a disappointing 0.8 percent, as both domestic and foreign investors remained skeptical of the government's ability to pay debts and maintain its fixed exchange rate with the U.S. dollar. At the end of 2001, Argentina was on the brink of default.

Principal Economic Indicators

Gross National Product: $319–293 billion
GNP per capita: $8,950
GNP Average Annual Growth Rate (1990–97) %: 4.2
GNP per capita Average Annual Growth Rate (1990–97): 2.9

(continued)

Origin of Gross Domestic Product %
- Agriculture: 6
- Mining: 2
- Manufacturing: 22
- Construction: 5
- Public Utilities: 2
- Transportation and Communications: 5
- Trade: 15
- Financial Services: 17
- Other Services: 26
- Government: 26

Gross Domestic Product by Type of Expenditure %
- Private Consumption: 82
- Government Consumption: 82
- Gross Domestic Investment: 20
- Foreign Trade: Exports: 7
  Imports: −9

% of Income Received by Poorest 20%: 4.4
% of Income Received by Richest 10%: 35.2

Price and earnings indexes (1995 = 100)

	1993	1994	1995	1996	1997	1998
Consumer price index	92.2	96.7	100.0	100.2	100.7	101.6
Monthly earnings index	95.2	101.7	100.0	100.7	—	—

Finance

National Currency: Nuevo Peso Argentino (NPA)
Exchange Rate: $1 = NPA 0.99950
Money Supply Stock in National Currency billion: 19.076
M1 per capita: 540
Central Bank Discount Rate %: 6.89
total External Debt $million: 115,000
Debt Service Ratio %: 40.1
Balance of Payments $million: −12,035
International Reserves SDRs million: 14,335
Ratio of External Debt to Total Reserves: 4.3
Average Annual Rate of Inflation/Consumer Price Index Growth Rate %: 0.3

Official Development Assistance

ODA $million: 77
- as % of GNP: 0.0
- per capita $: 2
- Foreign Direct Investment $million: 6,150

Central Government Revenues and Expenditures

Fiscal Year: Calendar Year
Revenues $million: 55,000
Expenditures $million: 59,000
Budget Deficit $million: 4,000
Tax Revenues as % of GDP: 12.4
Highest Tax Bracket %
- Individual: 35
- Corporate: 35

Employment and Labor

Economically Active Population: 14,345,000
Female Participation Rate %: 36.7
Activity Rate %: 41.5
Labor by Sector: %
- Agriculture, Forestry, Fishing: 12.0
- Manufacturing, Mining: 21.3
- Construction: 10
- Transportation and Communications: 4.6
- Trade, Hotels and Restaurants: 17.0
- Finance, Insurance, Real Estate: 3.9
- Public Administration, Defense: —
- Services: 23.9

Unemployment %: 13.7

Agriculture

Agriculture's Share of GDP %: 6
Average Annual Rate of Growth (1965–98) %: 1.6
Number of Farms 000: 421
Average Size of Farm ha: 469
Number of Tractors per 1,000 hectares: 11.2
Irrigation, % of Farms having: 7
Artificial Fertilizer kg/hectare: 4
Total Farmland as % of land area: 64.8
Livestock: Cattle 000: 54,600
- Sheep 000: 16,432
- Hogs 000: 3,200
- Chickens 000: 55,000

Forests: Production of Roundwood (000 cubic meters): 11,792
Fisheries: Total Catch tons 000: 949.3

Mining

% of GDP: 1.7
Value of Mineral Production $million: 4383.3

Manufacturing

Value Added $million: 29,622
Industrial Production Growth Rate %: 8.7

Energy

Commercial Energy Production metric tons of oil equivalent 000: 80,134
Commercial Energy Consumption metric tons of oil equivalent 000: 61,710
Commercial Energy Consumption per capita kg: 1,730
Average Annual Growth Rate 1980–97 %: 0.9
Net Energy Imports % of use: −30
Electricity Installed Capacity kW 000: 19,610
- Production kW-hr million: 67,169

Coal Reserves tons million: 130
- Production tons 000: 305

Natural Gas Proven Reserves cubic meters billion: 619
- Production cubic meters million: 17,336

Crude Petroleum reserves barrels million: 2,386
- Production barrels million: 275
- Consumption barrels million: 163

Refinery Capacity barrels per day 000: 665
Pipelines Length km: 6,990

Foreign Trade

Imports $million: 20121.7
Exports $million: 20962.6
Export Volume % Annual Growth Rate (1990–97): 9.6
Import Volume % Annual Growth Rate (1990–97): 25.1
Balance of Trade $

Balance of trade (current prices)

	1992	1993	1994	1995	1996	1997
U.S.$000,000	−1,388	−1,576	−4,002	+2,985	+1,621	−4,160
% of total	5.4%	5.7%	11.3%	7.7%	3.5%	7.4%

Major Trading Partners

	Imports	Exports
European Union %	29.9	21.4
United States %	20.9	8.6
Eastern Europe %	1.1	0.7
Japan %	3.5	2.2
Others %	44.6	67.2

Transportation

Roads Total Length mi: 134,278 km: 216,000
Paved %: 29
Automobiles: 4,665,229
Trucks and Buses: 1,181,569
Persons per vehicle: 5.9
Railroad; Track Length mi: 21,015 km: 33,821
Passenger-mi million: 4,014
Freight-mi million: 5,214
Merchant Marine: No. of Vessels: 423
Total Deadweight Tonnage 000: 1173.1
International Cargo Loaded tons 000: 55,572
International Cargo Off-loaded tons 000: 17,316
Airports with Scheduled Flights: 39
Traffic: Passenger-mi million: 7,323
Freight-mi million: 911
Length of Canals mi: 6,800 km 11,000

Tourism

Number of Tourists to 000: 4,860
Number of Tourists from 000: 5,522
Tourist Receipts $million: 4,306
Tourist Expenditures $million: 2,067

Communications

Telephones 000: 5,532
Cost of Local Calls 3 mins $0.10
Cellular Telephones 000: 341
Fax Machines 000: 50
Personal Computers 000: 850
Internet Hosts per million persons: 154
Mail: Post Offices: 5,676
Pieces of Mail Handled million: 420
Pieces of Mail Handled per person: 12

EDUCATION

Education is universal and compulsory for seven years from the ages of six to 14. From preschool to university level, education is available free of charge.

Schooling lasts for 12 years divided into seven years of primary school and five years of secondary school. More than 70 percent of grade 1 pupils completed primary school during 1975–82. The school curriculum is being periodically reformed, but, in general, the emphasis in the primary grades is on nonacademic subjects, such as etiquette, cooperation, civics, and thrift. Secondary schools are divided into general (or academic) and technical (including agriculture) schools. The large majority of the students are enrolled in courses leading to the baccalaureate (bachillerato) certificate, consisting of a three-year basic cycle of study and a two-year general (común) upper cycle of nonspecialized instruction. Other students are in specialized baccalaureate courses of from five to seven years.

Although Argentina has the highest literacy rate in Latin America, the government is actively engaged in systematic adult education. As a result of these efforts, almost all adults claim simple literacy: the ability to read and write simple sentences. Women and men have equal literacy rates. However, because of the high dropout rates in primary schools, functional illiteracy is widespread, and the principal thrust of the present adult education programs is to improve practical skills. These courses, known as parasistematica, are attended by over a half million adults, of whom women are in the majority.

Private schools run by ethnic groups and by the Roman Catholic Church are integrated within the school system. They adopt the curriculum prescribed by the government, are monitored by national inspectors, and, in most cases, receive public subsidies. The future of private schools is a sensitive political issue and is closely related to the fortunes of the anticlerical movement.

The national higher educational system consists of 29 state universities and 23 private universities. National universities are autonomous, but since 1966 students are excluded from their governing bodies. The rising tempo of student unrest in the late 1960s and early 1970s led to the dismissal of thousands of professors, the consequent crippling of faculties, and decline in the quality of instruction. Argentine students are acutely concerned over social and political issues and many of them are active in support of leftist and Marxist causes.

Education

Literacy Rate %: 96.2
Male %: 96.2
Female %: 96.2
First Level: Primary schools: 25,448
Teachers: 286,885
Students: 5,126,307
Student-Teacher Ratio: 17.9
Net Enrollment Ratio: —
Second Level: Secondary Schools: 7,239
Teachers: 233,564
Students: 2,238,091
Student-Teacher Ratio: 9.6
Net Enrollment Ratio: —

Vocational Level: Schools: —
Students: —

Third Level: Institutions: 1,705
Teachers: 118,695
Students: 926,793
Student-Ratio Level: 7.8
Gross Enrollment Ratio: 38.1
Students per 100,000: 3,116
% of Population Age 25 and over with Postsecondary Education: 12.0

Public Expenditure on Education as % of GDP: 4.5

SCIENCE AND TECHNOLOGY

Science and Technology

Scientists and Engineers in R&D per 1 million persons: 660
Expenditures in R&D as % of GDP: 0.38
High-Tech Exports $million: 491
Patent Applications by Residents: 824

MEDIA

The Argentine press is one of the largest in the Americas with more than 200 dailies with combined circulation of approximately 3.5 million. Greater Buenos Aires alone had some 60 daily newspapers with a combined circulation of 1.5 million. Four of these have national reputations: *La Razón*, *Clarín*, *La Prensa*, and *La Nación*. Dailies are published in all the 24 provincial capitals and 60 other towns. Buenos Aires also has a vigorous ethnic-oriented and foreign language press, including the *Buenos Aires Herald*.

Historically, the Argentine press had been noted for its independence and its boldness in discussing politically controversial issues. The first break from this tradition took place under Perón, who used a number of methods, such as withholding newsprint and state-inspired strikes and expropriation, to bring the press under government control as an instrument to rally the masses behind his policies. The fall of Perón brought a general relaxation, but censorship was revived under President Ongania and became even more oppressive. In 1968 TELAM, the national news agency, was nationalized and given control over state-enterprise advertising as a means of bringing indirect pressure on errant media.

There are three types of radio stations: state, private, and municipal and provincial. Of the two state-owned networks, Radio Nacional is the largest. The second state system is operated by the Dirección General de Emisoras Comerciales. External broadcasting is conducted by Radio Nacional. There are more than 52 private stations grouped under Asociación de Radiodifusoras Privadas Argentinas. In addition, there are a number of university stations.

Television, introduced in 1951, now reaches almost three-fourths of the population. There are no national networks, but there are nationwide hookups by affiliated stations. Foreign programs are limited by law to 50 percent.

Media

Daily Newspapers: 187
Total Circulation 000: 4,705
Circulation per 1,000: 138
Books Published: 9,065
Magazines: —
Radio Receivers 000: 21,500
per 1,000: 637
Television sets 000: 12,000
per 1,000: 34.7

Most Important Media:

Press. Unless otherwise noted, the following are Spanish-language dailies published at Buenos Aires: *Clarín* (490,000 daily, 750,000 Sunday), reportedly the world's largest-selling Spanish-language paper; *Página 12*(280,000), highly regarded investigative paper launched in 1987; *Crónica* (190,000 daily, 440,000 Sunday); *La Nación* (197,000), founded 1870; *Diario Popular* (145,000); *El Cronista Comercial* (100,000); *La Prensa* (80,000), founded 1869; *Buenos Aires Herald* (22,500), in English. In August 1988 the *Herald* launched a Spanish-language evening edition, *El Heraldo de Buenos Aires*, with an initial print run of 40–60,000 copies; however, it was forced to close down in June 1989 because of unanticipated costs attributed to the country's burgeoning inflation. In 1990 *La Razón*, which reportedly had a circulation of 1 million a decade earlier, was also forced to close.

News agencies. The domestic agencies include Diarios y Noticias (DyN), Noticias Argentinas (NA), and the official Agencia TELAM. There are also a number of foreign agencies with bureaus at Buenos Aires.

Radio and television. All broadcasting is supervised by the secretary of state for communications and the Comité Federal de Radiodifusión (Comfer). Approximately two-thirds of the more than 260 radio stations but only one-third of the 42 television stations are privately owned. Radio Nacional is an official government service providing local, national, and international programming. Government-owned commercial radio and television stations are grouped under the Dirección General de Radio y Televisión, while most privately owned stations belong to the Asociación de Radiodifusoras Privadas Argentinas and the Asociación de Teleradiodifusoras Argentinas

CULTURE

Cultural Indicators

Public Libraries Number: —
Volumes: —
Registered borrowers: —
Museums Number: —
Annual Attendance: —
Cinema Production of Long Films: 21
Number of Cinemas: 280
Seating Capacity: 69,000
Annual Attendance: 7.8
Annual Attendance per capita: 0.2

STATUS OF WOMEN

Women possess the same constitutional rights as do men. Their participation in politics, business, and education is quite extensive especially when compared to other countries in the region. Argentina has the distinction of having had the first elected woman president in the world.

Women

Gender Empowerment Measure: —
Seats Held in Parliament by Women %: 21.3
Female Administrators and Managers %: —
Female Professional and Technical Workers %: —
Women's Share of Earned Income %: —
Women in Government %: 3

HEALTH, FOOD, AND NUTRITION

Health

Number of Physicians: 88,800
Number of Dentists: 21,900
Number of Nurses: 18,000
Number of Pharmacists: —
Population per Physician: 376
Number of Hospitals: —
Hospital Beds per 10,000: 44
Hospital Bed Occupancy Rate: 51.9
Infant Mortality Rate per 1,000 live births: 25
Maternal Mortality Rate per 100,000 live births: 100
Total Health Expenditures as % of GDP: 4.21
Health Expenditures per capita $: 137
HIV Infected % of adults: 0.69
Cigarette Consumption per smoker per year: 2,771
% of Smokers: Male: 40
Female: 23
Access to Safe Water % 64

Food and Nutrition

Food Supply as % of FAO Requirements: 132
% of Consumption Expenditures on Food: 40.1
Daily Available Calories per capita: 3,110
% of Total Calories derived from:
Cereals: 30.6
Potatoes, cassava: 3.7
Meat, poultry: 16.3
Fish: 0.4
Eggs, milk: 10.2
Fruits, vegetables: 4.2
Fats, oils: 14.8

ENVIRONMENT

Argentina's current environmental issues include soil erosion resulting from inadequate flood controls and improper land use practices. The latter is also leading to growing desertification. In the large cities like Buenos Aires, air pollution from emissions and industrial activity is also a problem. The nation's rivers are becoming polluted due to increased pesticide and fertilizer use.

Environment

Forest Area sq km: 339,000
Average Annual Deforestation sq km: 1.7
Nationally Protected Areas as % of Total Land Area: 1.7
Freshwater Access cubic meters per capita: 186,844
Emissions of Organic Water Pollutants kg per day: 3.7
CO_2 Emissions per capita ton: 3.7

CHRONOLOGY

1945 The military arrest Vice President Juan Domingo Perón; the General Confederation of Labor calls for a general strike in support of Perón; the army is cowed, and Perón is restored to power.

1946 Perón is elected president, defeating a coalition of radical, socialist, and communist parties.

1947 Perón launches the First Five-Year Plan.

1952 Perón is reelected to the presidency, winning 65 percent of all votes cast.
Eva Perón dies.

1953 Perón antagonizes the Catholic Church by proposing to legalize divorce and prostitution and by opposing church influence in labor unions.
Perón is ousted in an army coup and replaced by General Eduardo Lonardi.
Lonardi is deposed in a bloodless second coup led by General Pedro Eugenio Aramburu.
The constitution of 1949 is abrogated and the constitution of 1853 is reinstated.

1958 Arturo Frondizi is elected president in the first post-Perón national elections.

1962 Reinstated Peronist party wins 34 percent of popular vote, 11 governorships, and 42 seats in Congress in elections; the army, alarmed at the revival of Peronism, deposes and arrests Frondizi; José Mario Guido is named president.
In internal struggle the Azul (blue, or Catholic) faction purges the armed forces of the Colorado (red, or anti-constitutionalist) faction.

1963 Arturo Umberto Illia is elected president under new electoral laws that bar Peronists from standing as candidates.

1965 Illia is forced out in a coup led by Azul leader Gen. Juan Carlos Ongania; Congress is dissolved; all political parties are banned; university autonomy is abolished; provincial governors and legislatures are dismissed.

1970 Ongania attempts to dismiss the army's commanding general, Gen. Alejandro Augustín Lanusse, but is himself dismissed by the army.
Brig. Gen. Roberto Marcelo Levingston succeeds to the presidency.

1971 Levingston is forced to step down, and Lanusse assumes the presidency; Lanusse announces plans for national elections and return to civilian rule.

1972 Perón returns to Argentina after an 18-year exile.

1973 Hector Campora, a candidate of the Peronist coalition, Frente Justicialista de Liberación (FREJULI), wins presidential election with almost 50 percent of the vote; FREJULI candidates win large majorities in legislative and gubernatorial elections.
Campora resigns to enable Perón to stand as candidate; Perón wins 62 percent of the vote and is inaugurated president.

1974 Perón dies and is succeeded in office by his wife Isabel (Maria Estela) Martínez de Perón.

1976 Mrs. Perón's turbulent presidency is terminated by an army coup.

Military junta suspends many of the provisions of the 1853 constitution.
Lt. Gen. Jorge Rafael Videla is named president.
1977 432 political prisoners are freed out of an estimated 18,000 held in jail without trial.
Guerrillas step up kidnappings, bombings, and other acts of terrorism.
Montoneros form a political party in exile.
1978 The territorial dispute between Chile and Argentina over three islands at the extreme south of the continent intensifies into crisis.
Videla quits army but receives an extension of term as president until 1981.
Mrs. Perón, accused of embezzlement, is placed under house arrest.
1979 Unions are banned from political activities.
Diplomatic relations are resumed with the United Kingdom.
Publisher Jacobo Timerman is freed from prison and expelled from the country.
1980 Argentina's two largest private banks are declared bankrupt.
Roberto Eduardo Viola, a former commander-in-chief of the army, is named to succeed President Videla in March 1981.
1981 Roberto Eduardo Viola assumes presidency but is ousted within a few months and is replaced by Gen. Leopoldo Galtieri.
1982 Argentina invades and occupies the Falkland Islands. In brief but bloody conflict, United Kingdom recovers the islands.
Galtieri resigns and is succeeded by Reynaldo Benito Antonio Bignone.
Bignone lifts ban on political parties and promises return to civilian rule.
Junta rule is reimposed.
Peso is devalued.
Government announces plan to return state companies to the private sector.
Labor protests austerity measures to curb inflation.
General strike paralyzes nation.
1983 Police strike in Tucumán province.
Raúl Alfonsín of the Radical Party is elected president, winning 51 percent of the national vote.
Radicals also win majority in Chamber of Deputies.
The junta is dissolved as Alfonsín takes office.
The Peso Argentina is introduced to replace the old peso.
1984 Argentina and Chile reach accord over the Beagle Channel.
The Peronist CGT and Alfonsín reach agreement over proposed labor reforms.
Alfonsín appoints a National Commission on the Disappearance of Persons.
The Ley de Pacificación National is repealed and members of the three juntas that ruled the country since 1976 are tried before military tribunal.
1985 Isabel Perón, former president, steps down as leader of the Peronists.
Argentina obtains bridge loan from IMF.
Radicals fare well in midterm elections.
1986 Three members of the military junta are found guilty and receive prison sentences.
1987 Divorce is legalized; gubernatorial and legislative elections are held as scheduled.
1988 A rebellion at the garrison town of Monte Caberos is crushed in April. The World Bank approves and unprecedented $1.25 billion loan package in September. Annual inflation rate reaches about 390 percent.
1989 In January an attack on the military base at La Tablada is crushed by the army. Inflation reaches crisis level of more than 5,000 percent, sparking a week of looting and rioting in several cities. President Menem takes office on July 8. IMF guarantees a stand-by loan of $1.5 billion. In October, Galtieri and two other senior military leaders are pardoned of war crimes.
1990 Menem authorizes the military to suppress civil unrest for the first time since 1983.
In December a bloody uprising by several hundred Argentine army troops is quashed by forces loyal to Menem.
Menem grants pardons to eight military men, including former junta members responsible for the "dirty war."
1991 Argentine workers stage wildcat strikes to protest economic austerity measures.
1993 The country's 11-year debt crisis comes to an end.
1994 Argentina adopts several changes to its constitution including the direct election of the president.
1995 Though inflation is down to 4 percent, the government braces for Mexican devaluation with a new austerity plan.
1997 Violent protests erupt in several major cities over growing unemployment (20 percent in some areas); the governing Peronist party suffers heavy losses in midterm legislative elections; the economy pulls out of recession, posting 8 percent GDP.
1998 Judge Roberto Marquevich orders the arrest of former army chief Jorge Videla over the theft of babies of disappeared persons, crimes not protected by the amnesty laws passed after the end of military rule.
1999 Fernando de la Rúa is elected president; President de la Rúa arranges a new $7.4 billion stand-by facility with the IMF for contingency purposes.
2001 President de la Rúa forms a government of national unity incorporating several parties from across Argentina's political spectrum. He appoints three finance ministers in as many weeks. Protests greet planned austerity measures. The opposition Peronists take control of both houses of parlia-

ment in congressional elections. In December, the IMF announces it won't disburse $1.3 billion in aid for the month, pushing Argentina closer to the brink of default. On December 20, President de la Rúa resigns after widespread street protests and rioting leave at least 25 people dead. Within two weeks, on January 2, 2002, Eduardo Duhalde becomes the fifth Argentine president.

BIBLIOGRAPHY

Crawley, Eduardo. *A House Divided: Argentina 1880–1980*. New York, 1984.

Decker, David R. *The Political, Economic and Labor Climate in Argentina*. Philadelphia, Pa., 1983.

Foster, David William, and Melissa Fitch Lockhart. *Culture and Customs of Argentina*. Westport, Conn., 1998.

Gillespie, Richard. *Soldiers of Perón: Argentina's Montoneros*. New York, 1982.

Lewis, Paul H. *The Crisis of Argentina Capitalism*. Chapel Hill, N.C., 1990.

Schoultz, Lars. *The Populist Challenge: Argentine Electoral Behavior in the Postwar Era*. Durham, N.C., 1983.

Simpson, John, and Jana Bennet. *The Disappeared and the Mothers of the Plaza: The Story of the 11,000 Argentinians Who Vanished*. New York, 1985.

Tulchin, Joseph S. *Argentina and the United States: A Conflicted Relationship*. Boston, Mass., 1990.

Vacs, Aldo C. *Discreet Partners: Argentina and the USSR since 1917*. Pittsburgh, Pa., 1984.

OFFICIAL PUBLICATIONS

Argentina. *Anuario estadístico de la República Argentina; Censo nacional de población y vivienda, 1991; Encuesta permanente de hogares* (irreg.)

CONTACT INFORMATION

Embassy of Argentina
1600 New Hampshire Avenue NW
Washington, D.C. 20009
Phone: (202) 238-6400 Fax: (202) 238-6471

INTERNET RESOURCES

- National Institute of Statistics and Censuses
  http://www.indec.mecon.ar/default.htm

ARMENIA

BASIC FACT SHEET

OFFICIAL NAME:
Republic of Armenia (Havastani Hanrapetoutioun)

ABBREVIATION:

CAPITAL:
Yerevan

HEAD OF STATE:
President Robert Kocharyan (from 1998)

HEAD OF GOVERNMENT:
Andranik Markaryan

NATURE OF GOVERNMENT:
Parliamentary Democracy

POPULATION:
3,804,000 (1999)

AREA:
29,743 sq km (11,484 sq mi)

MAJOR ETHNIC GROUPS:
Armenian

LANGUAGES:
Armenian

RELIGIONS:
Christianity

UNIT OF CURRENCY:
Dram

NATIONAL FLAG:
Three equal horizontal bands of red (top), blue, and gold.

NATIONAL ANTHEM: —

NATIONAL HOLIDAY:
Referendum Day September 21

DATE OF INDEPENDENCE:
September 23, 1991

DATE OF CONSTITUTION:
July 5, 1995

GEOGRAPHICAL FEATURES

Armenia is a landlocked nation in the Caucasus region in southeastern Europe. It shares borders with Georgia on the north, Azerbaijan on the east, Iran on the south, and Turkey on the west. Its capital city is Yerevan, located near its southeast border. The country is a high plateau region of rugged mountains and extinct volcanoes and has an average elevation of 5,900 ft. The perpetually snow-capped Mount Ararat is the highest point in Armenia. The chief rivers are the Aras and its tributary the Razdan. Lake Sevan, in the northeast, supports an important fishing industry.

Geography

Area sq km: 29,743 sq mi 11,484
World Rank: 141st
Land Boundaries, km: Azerbaijan 787; Georgia 164; Iran 35; Turkey 268
Coastline, km: 0
Elevation Extremes meters
- Lowest: Debed River 400
- Highest: Aragats Ler 4,095

Land Use % Arable land: 17
- Permanent Crops: 3
- Permanent Pastures: 24
- Forest and Woodland: 15
- Other: 41

Armenia

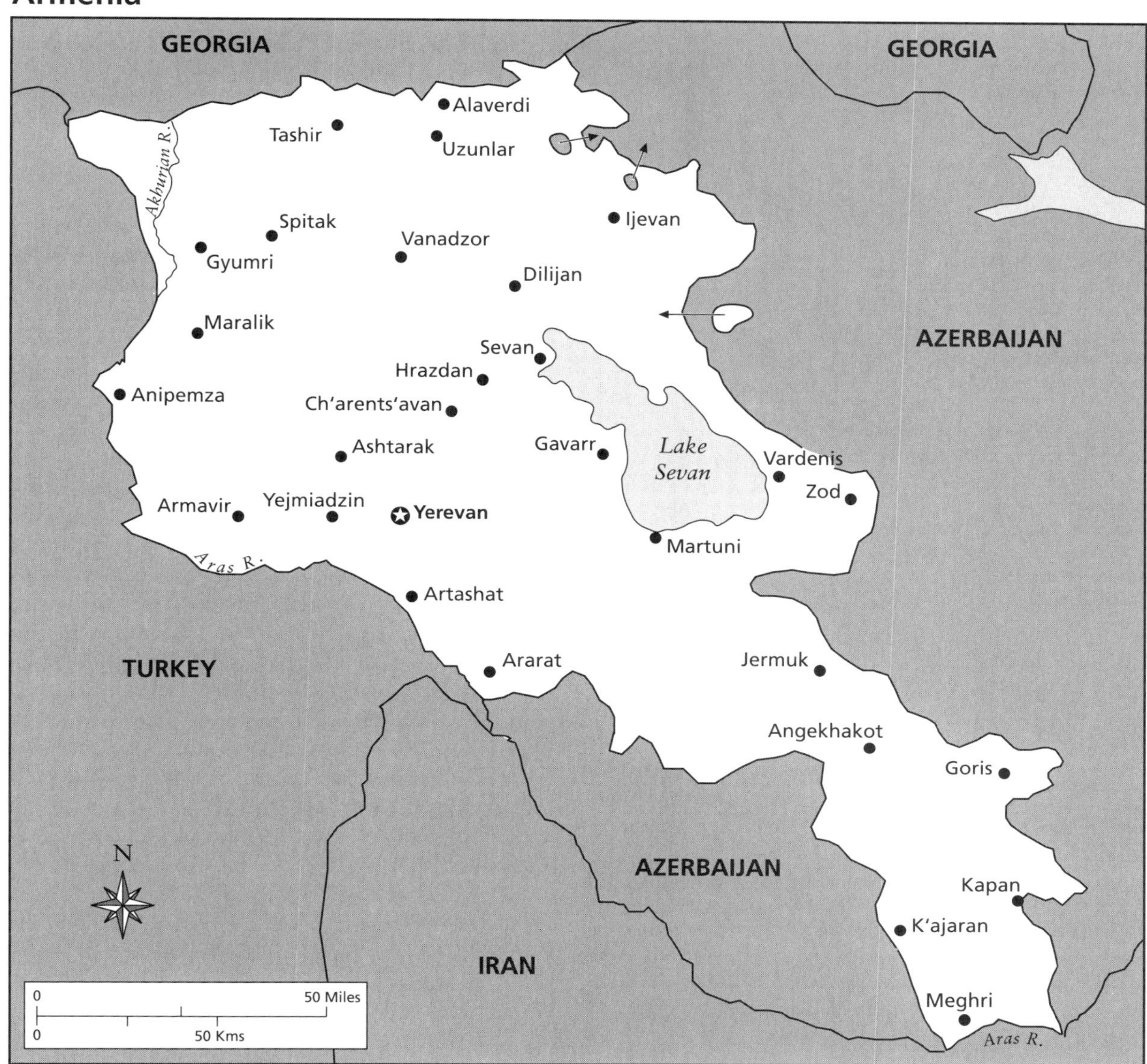

Population of Principal Cities (1995 est.)	
Gyumri (Kumayri; Leninakan)	120,000
Yerevan	1,248,700

Climate and Weather

Mean Temperature (August) 77°F
Mean Temperature (January) 27°F
Annual Rainfall 13 in

CLIMATE AND WEATHER

Armenia's climate ranges from subtropical to alpine. The mean temperature is 77°F in August and 27°F in January. Rainfall is infrequent. Yerevan receives 13 inches of rain annually, though the surrounding mountains receive more rainfall.

POPULATION

Population Indicators

Total Population: 1999 3,804,000
World Rank: 122nd
Density per sq mi: 331.2 per sq km 127.9

(continued)

% of annual growth (1994–99): 0.3
Male %: 49.3
Female %: 50.7
Urban %: 67.8
Age Distribution: % 0–14: 30.3
15–29: 25.7
30–44: 20.8
45–59: 13.6
60–74: 6.4
75 and over: 3.2
Population 2020: 3,838,000
Birth Rate per 1,000: 13.3
Death Rate per 1,000: 7.5
Population Doubling Time (years): —
Infant Mortality Rate per 1,000 live births: 25.0
Rate of Natural Increase per 1,000: 5.8
Total Fertility Rate: 1.7
Expectation of Life (years): Males 67.2
Females 74.0
Marriage Rate per 1,000: 4.2
Divorce Rate per 1,000: 0.8
Total Number of Households: 559,000
Average Size of Households: 4.7
% of Illegitimate Children: 12.3
Induced Abortions: 27,958
Rate per 100 live births: 39.6

ETHNIC COMPOSITION

Armenia is ethnically homogeneous, with Armenians making up 93 percent of the population. Major minorities are Azerbaijans, Kurds, and Russians. Minorities include Azeris (2.6 percent), Kurds (1.7 percent), and Russians (1.6 percent).

LANGUAGES

Armenian is an Indo-European language. It has two main dialects: East Armenian, the official language of Armenia, and West or Turkish Armenian. The alphabet is of Greek and Persian origin. It is highly inflective, with a complex system of declensions, agglutinative, and rich in consonants. Armenian has a rich literature dating from the fifth century.

Principal Languages and Their Speakers

Armenian	3,500,000
Azerbaijani (Azeri)	100,000
Other	150,000

RELIGIONS

Armenia is one of the oldest Christian countries in the world, and it was the first to declare Christianity as its national religion. The Armenian Orthodox Church belongs to the Lesser Eastern Churches and is headed by a Catholicos (the head or patriarch) resident in the ancient city of Etchmiadzin.

Religious Affiliations

Armenian Apostolic (Orthodox)	2,450,000
Other	1,350,000

HISTORICAL BACKGROUND

According to tradition the kingdom of Armenia was founded in the region of Lake Van by Haig or Haik, a descendant of Noah. By the sixth century B.C.E. it was a homogeneous nation. Until the fourth century B.C.E. it was a Persian satrapy. It was conquered in 330 B.C.E. by Alexander the Great and, after his death, became a part of the Syrian kingdom of Seleucus I. After the defeat of the Seleucids the Armenians declared their independence under a native dynasty, the Artashesids. The imperialistic ambitions of King Tigranes led to a war with Rome and his defeat by Pompey in 67 B.C.E. Tiridates, a Parthian prince, was confirmed as king of Armenia by Nero in A.D. 66. Christianity was introduced early in the first century. In the third century Ardashir I, founder of the Sassanid dynasty, overran Armenia and with that began the long history of persecutions that has lasted until the 20th century. Attempts at independence were short-lived and the country found itself the constant prey of the Persians, Byzantines, White Huns, Khazars, and Arabs. During the Mongol invasions, the invaders massacred a large part of the population. After the Mongols, the Ottoman Turks invaded Armenia and by the 16th century occupied all of it. The eastern portion of Armenia was chronically disputed between Turkey and Persia until 1828 when Persia ceded to Russia what is now the Republic of Armenia. Between 1894 and 1915 Armenians were subjected to their Holocaust when the Turks attempted to exterminate the entire Armenian population. More than 600,000 were killed and the rest were forcibly deported. With the collapse of the Russian and Ottoman Empires Armenia declared its independence in 1918 and its independence was recognized by the Treaty of Sèvres in 1920. In the same year, however, communists gained control of Armenia and proclaimed it a Soviet republic, thus ending the country's independence. With the collapse of the Soviet Union in 1990, Armenia declared its independence in 1991.

In the same year Levon Ter-Petrosian, the incumbent Supreme Soviet chairman, was elected president of the republic and Khosrov Haroutiunian as prime minister. In May 1992 Armenian forces captured Azerbaijan's last major urban stronghold in Nagorno-Karabakh and proceeded to open a corridor to Armenia proper. Concurrently an attack was launched on the Azeri enclave of Nakhichevan near Armenia's border with Turkey. In 1993 Hrand Bagratian replaced Haroutiunian as prime minister. The opposition parties mounted large antigovernment demonstrations in 1993 and 1994. In Armenia's first postindependence legislative elections in 1995 Ter-

Petrosian's Pan Armenian National Movement won a substantial legislative majority while a constitutional amendment gave the president more powers. In the 1996 presidential election, Ter-Petrosian was elected with 51.75 percent vote over Vasken Manukian of the National Democratic Union. Opposition leaders alleged widespread electoral fraud, which was confirmed by outside election observers. In 1996 Prime Minister Bagratian resigned and was replaced first by Armen Sarkisian and later by Robert Kocharian, president of the self-proclaimed Republic of Nagorno-Karabakh. President Ter-Petrosian himself resigned, leaving Kocharian as president. In the presidential balloting in 1998 Kocharian was elected with 60 percent of the vote. He later named Armen Darbinian as prime minister. The May 30, 1999, parliamentary elections resulted in a convincing victory for the Unity Coalition led by Vazgen Sarkisian, who thereupon became prime minister. However, Sarkisian, two cabinet ministers, and five other parliamentary deputies were shot dead on October 27, 1999. President Kocharian named the slain prime minister's brother, Aram Sarkisian, to replace him. There was further political violence when the deputy minister of the interior and national security, Artsun Markkaryan, was found shot dead. Armenia became a full member of the Council of Europe in 2001.

CONSTITUTION

Armenia adopted its first post-Soviet constitution on July 5, 1995. The constitution is based largely on the French model with a strong president and a legislature elected by popular suffrage. The president is directly elected for five-year terms. His veto can be overridden by a simple majority in the house. The prime minister is the head of government. He is nominated by the president, subject to parliamentary approval. The cabinet of ministers as well as the chairman of the state administration are appointed by the prime minister with presidential and parliamentary approval.

LOCAL GOVERNMENT

Armenia is divided into 11 provinces headed by governors and 67 rayons or districts, all centrally controlled. There are legislative bodies at the local level with some fiscal powers.

Local Government

Principal administrative divisions, area, population

Area and population

	area		population 1995
Regions	**sq mi**	**sq km**	**estimate**
Aragafsotn	1,064	2,755	161,700
Ararat	812	2,104	302,100
Armavir	479	1,241	314,000
Gegharkunik	1,573	4,073	255,800
Lori	1,464	3,791	391,700
Kotayk	811	2,100	327,100
Shirak	1,034	2,679	357,600
Syunik	1,739	4,505	161,400
Vayots-Dzor	891	2,308	69,700
Tavush	1,043	2,702	170,000
Cities			
Yerevan	81	210	1,248,700
Other	493	1,278	
TOTAL	11,484	29,743	3,759,800

PARLIAMENT

The unicameral National Assembly (Azgayin Zhaghov) is elected for a five-year term and has a membership of 131, of whom 56 are elected from national party lists on a proportional basis and 75 from constituencies on a majoritarian basis.

POLITICAL PARTIES

Political Parties

Unity a coalition of two parties
- People's Party, 1998
- Republican Party, 1998

Republic Bloc, 1995, a coalition of
- Pan-Armenian National Movement, 1989
- Armenian Christian Democratic Union, 1991
- Democratic Liberal Party, 1991

Shamiram Women's Movement
Armenian Communist Party, 1994
Democratic Party, 1991
Armenian Revolutionary Federation, 1891
National Democratic Union, 1991
National Self-Determination Union

Political Parties: Strength in Parliament Most Recent Election

The National Assembly has 131 members elected for four-year terms., 75 in single-seat constituencies and 56 by proportional representation. In the elections of May 30, 1999, the Unity Party won 55 seats; Communist Party of Armenia, 11; Law and Unity, 6; Armenian, Revolutionary Federation, 9; Rule of Law Country, 6; National Democratic Union of Armenia, 6; Armenian National Movement, 1; Democratic Party of Armenia, 1; Mission, 1; National Concord Party, 1; Nonpartisans, 32; and invalid, 2.

LEGAL SYSTEM

The court system consists of three levels: district courts of first instance, appellate courts, and a Supreme Court. The Supreme Court consists of three sections: criminal, civil, and appellate. The presidium of the court reviews cases first tried in the other sections of the court. The new constitution provides for review courts and a court of appeals to handle cases previously sent to the Supreme Court. Soviet-era judicial practices persist even as the new constitution has tried to fashion a new legal system. The courts are viewed largely as a rubber stamp for the prosecutors and not as a defender of citizens' rights. The courts are subject to pressure from the executive branch. A new criminal code went into effect in 2000. The civil code and the criminal procedure code went into effect in 1999. The latter permits the right to an attorney, right to a public trial, right to question witnesses, and right to appeal, but does not guarantee bail or trial by jury. A constitutional court has been established. It has the right to review the constitutionality of legislation and approve international treaties.

LAW ENFORCEMENT

Law Enforcement

Offenses reported to the police per 100,000: 160.4
- Murder: 5.4
- Assault: 3.4
- Burglary: —
- Automobile Theft: 2.1
- Population per Police officer: —

Death Penalty: Yes

HUMAN RIGHTS

The government's human rights record is poor in several important respects. In some cases, extrajudicial killings by security forces are reported, and some persons are arbitrarily arrested and detained without warrants. Prison conditions are harsh and lengthy pretrial detention is common. The judiciary is subject to political pressures and does not enforce constitutional protections consistently. There are some limits on press freedoms and many journalists practice self-censorship. Registration requirements hinder freedom of association. The law places some restrictions on religious freedom, including a prohibition against proselytizing by groups other than the Armenian Orthodox Church.

FOREIGN POLICY

Armenia is a founding member of the Commonwealth of Independent States. It is also a member of the Conference on Security and Cooperation in Europe and the United Nations. The major foreign policy issue in the 1990s was the dispute with Azerbaijan over the Nagorno-Karabakh enclave. The 1994 cease-fire has left the Armenians in control of much of the territory.

DEFENSE

Military Indicators

Total Active Duty Personnel: 58,600
Military Manpower per 1,000: 15.5
Military Expenditures $ million: 7.9
- as % of GNP: 0.9
- per capita $: 23
- as % of central government expenditures: —

Arms Imports $million: 30
Arms Exports $million: 0

ECONOMY

Under the old Soviet central planning system, Armenia had developed a modern industrial sector, supplying machine tools, textiles, and other manufactured goods. Since the collapse of the Soviet Union and the independence of Armenia that followed, the economy has switched to small-scale agriculture and away from heavy industry. The privatization of industry has proceeded at a slow pace, but ahead of most other former Soviet republics. Armenia is a food importer and its mineral deposits are small. The Nagorno-Karabakh dispute and the embargoes imposed by Turkey and Azerbaijan contributed to a severe economic decline in the early 1990s. By 1994, however, the Armenian government had launched an ambitious IMF-sponsored economic program that has since produced positive growth rates. Armenia also managed to slash inflation and to privatize small and medium enterprises. The chronic energy shortages Armenia suffered in recent years have been partially offset by one of its nuclear plants at Metsamor. Unemployment is high and women form a disproportionately large number of the unemployed.

Principal Economic Indicators

Gross National Product: $2.112 billion
GNP per capita: $560
GNP Average Annual Growth Rate (1990–97) %: 10.7
GNP per capita Average Annual Growth Rate (1990–97) %: 11.6
Origin of Gross Domestic Product %
- Agriculture: 43
- Mining: —
- Manufacturing: 29
- Construction: 7
- Public Utilities: —
- Transportation and Communications: 1
- Trade: 4
- Financial Services: 15
- Other Services: 15
- Government: 15

Gross Domestic Product by Type of Expenditure %
- Private Consumption: 87
- Government Consumption: 16
- Gross Domestic Investment: 9
- Foreign Trade: Exports: 44
  Imports: 57

% of Income Received by Poorest 20%: —
% of Income Received by Richest 10%: —

Price and Earnings Indexes (1995 = 100)

	1993	1994	1995	1996	1997	1998
Consumer price index	1	36	100	119	135	147
Earnings index	—	—	—	—	—	—

Finance

National Currency: Dram
Exchange Rate: $1 = Dram 499.89
Money Supply Stock in National Currency billion: —
M1 per capita: —
Central Bank Discount Rate %: 52
Total External Debt $million: 820
Debt Service Ratio %: 5

Balance of Payments $million: 306.5
International Reserves SDRs million: —
Ratio of External Debt to Total Reserves: —
Average Annual Rate of Inflation/Consumer Price Index Growth Rate %: 13.2

Official Development Assistance

ODA $million: 138
- as % of GNP: 7.3
- per capita: $36
- Foreign Direct Investment $million: 232

Central Government Revenues and Expenditures

Fiscal Year: Calendar Year

Revenues $million: 322
Expenditures $million: 424
Budget Deficit $million: 102
Tax Revenues as % of GDP: —
Highest Tax Bracket %: —
- Individual: —
- Corporate: —

Employment and Labor

Economically Active Population: 1,618,000
Female Participation Rate %: —
Activity Rate %: 43.1
Labor by Sector: %
- Agriculture, Forestry, Fishing: 33.3
- Manufacturing, Mining: 20.0
- Construction: 6.7
- Transportation and Communications: 30
- Trade, Hotels, and Restaurants: 4.0
- Finance, Insurance, Real Estate: 1.8
- Public Administration, Defense: 1.9
- Services: 21.6

Unemployment %: 10.6

Agriculture

Agriculture's Share of GDP %: 43
Average Annual Rate of Growth (1965–98) %: —
Number of Farms 000: 316
Average Size of Farm ha: 1
Number of Tractors per 1,000 hectares: 11.2
Irrigation, % of Farms having: 7
Artificial Fertilizer kg/hectare: 4
Total Farmland as % of land area: 64.8
Livestock: Cattle 000: 505
- Sheep 000: 550
- Hogs 000: 52
- Chickens 000: 2,800

Forests: Production of Roundwood (000 cubic meters): —
Fisheries: Total Catch tons 000: 4.1

Mining

% of GDP: —
Value of Mineral Production $million: —

Manufacturing

Value Added $million: 368
Industrial Production Growth Rate %: 0.7

Energy

Commercial Energy Production metric tons of oil equivalent 000: 537
Commercial Energy Consumption metric tons of oil equivalent 000: 1,804
Commercial Energy Consumption per capita kg: 476
Average Annual Growth Rate 1980–97 %: 6.0
Net Energy Imports % of use: 70
Electricity Installed Capacity kW 000: 3,583
  Production kW-hr million: 5,561
Coal Reserves tons 000: —
  Production tons 00: —
Natural Gas Proven Reserves cubic meters million: —
  Production cubic meters million: —
Crude Petroleum Reserves barrels million: —
  Production barrels million: —
  Consumption barrels million: 1
  Refinery Capacity barrels per day 000: —
Pipelines Length km: —

Foreign Trade

Imports $million: 673.9
Exports $million: 270.9
Export Volume % Annual Growth Rate (1990–97): —
Import Volume % Annual Growth Rate (1990–97): —

Balance of trade (current prices)

	1993	1994	1995	1996	1997
U.S. $000,000	−98.0	−178.3	−403.0	−565.5	−659.8
% of total	23.9%	29.3%	42.7%	49.3%	58.7%

Major Trading Partners

	Imports	Exports
European Union %	13.2	17.8
United States %	17.0	0.2
Eastern Europe %	22.6	33.3
Japan %	—	—
Others %	47.2	48.7

Transportation

Roads Total Length mi: 4,797 km 7,720
Paved %: 97
Automobiles: 1,590
Trucks and Buses: 5,950
Persons per vehicle: 499
Railroad Track Length mi: 515 km 829
Passenger-mi million: 196
Freight-mi million: 3,345
Merchant Marine: No of Vessels: —
  Total Deadweight Tonnage 000: —
  International Cargo Loaded tons 000: —
  International Cargo Off-loaded tons 000: —
Airports with Scheduled Flights: 1
Traffic: Passenger-mi million: 3,453
  Freight-mi million: 34
Length of Canals mi: — km —

Tourism

Number of Tourists to 000: 32
Number of Tourists from 000: —
Tourist Receipts $million: —
Tourist Expenditures $million: —

Communications

Telephones 000: 583
Cost of Local Calls 3 mins $0.12
Cellular Telephones 000: —
Fax Machines 000: 0.3
Personal Computers 000: —
Internet Hosts per million persons: 46
Mail: Post Offices: —
  Pieces of Mail Handled million: 1.8
  Pieces of Mail Handled per person: 0.5

EDUCATION

Education is compulsory between ages six and 17 and is free at both the primary and secondary levels. The education system is based on the old Soviet system, but since independence more emphasis has been placed on Armenian history and culture. There are two universities in Yerevan: the Yerevan State University, founded in 1919, and the State Engineering University of Armenia.

Education

Literacy Rate %: 98.8
  Male %: 99.4
  Female %: 98.1
First Level: Primary schools: 1,400
  Teachers: 54,000
  Students: 574,500
  Student-Teacher Ratio: 11.0
  Net Enrollment Ratio: —
Second Level: Secondary Schools: —
  Teachers: —
  Students: —
  Student-Teacher Ratio: —
  Net Enrollment Ratio: —

Vocational Level: Schools: 69
  Students: 25,200

Third Level: Institutions: 14
  Teachers: —
  Students: 36,500
  Student-Ratio Level: —
  Gross Enrollment Ratio: 41.8
  Students per 100,000: 3,225
  % of Population Age 25 and over with Postsecondary Education: —

Public Expenditure on Education as % of GDP: 7.2

SCIENCE AND TECHNOLOGY

Science and Technology

Scientists and Engineers in R&D per 1 million persons: 1,485
Expenditures in R&D as % of GDP: —
High-Tech Exports $million: 6
Patent Applications by Residents: 63

MEDIA

Before independence Armenia had over 90 newspapers, but many of them have folded since then and only 80 have survived. The leading paper is *Hayastani Hanrapetoutioun* (Republic of Armenia), founded in 1990. Other important newspapers include *Hayots Ashkar*, *Hasg* (Nation), and *Haystani Kommunist* (Armenian Communist). The domestic news agency is the Armenian Press Agency (Armenpress). The electronic media comprise Radio Yerevan and Armenian TV.

Media

Daily Newspapers: 7
    Total Circulation 000: 80
    Circulation per 1,000: 23
Books Published: 224
Magazines: 40
Radio Receivers 000: —
    per 1,000: —
Television sets 000: 900
    per 1,000: 241

MOST IMPORTANT MEDIA:

Press. Prior to independence there were more than 90 newspapers published in Armenia, most of which were controlled by the Communist Party and affiliated organizations. At present, the leading paper is *Hayastani Hanrapetoutioun* (Republic of Armenia), founded in 1990 by the Supreme Council. Others are *Hayk* (Armenia), PANM organ; *Hayots Ashkhar*, HHD/Dashnak organ; *Hazg* (Nation), PDF organ; *Hayastani Kommunist* (Armenian Communist), ACP organ.

News agencies. The domestic facility is the Armenian Press Agency (Armenpress), headquartered at Yerevan.

Radio and television. Radio Yerevan and Armenian TV broadcast from Yerevan in Armenian and a number of other languages. There were approximately 17,000 radio and 5,000 television receivers in 1995.

CULTURE

Cultural Indicators

Public Libraries Number: —
    Volumes: —
    Registered borrowers: —
Museums Number: —
    Annual Attendance: —
Cinema Production of Long Films: —
    Number of Cinemas: —
    Seating Capacity: —
    Annual Attendance million: —
    Annual Attendance per capita: —

STATUS OF WOMEN

There is no specific law banning violence against women, and only a few cases of rape, spousal abuse, or other types of violence are reported. Domestic violence cases usually are not reported to the police, and women have no specific legal recourse. At least one nongovernmental organization in the Gyumuri area provides shelter and assistance to battered women. The public prosecutor's office registers fewer than 20 cases of rape in a normal year. Prostitution is not illegal, and, according to anecdotal evidence, street walkers are simply sent to a hospital or a physician for a checkup. There are reports of trafficking in women by Middle Eastern Arabs. In the workplace, women receive equal pay for equal work but are generally not afforded the same professional opportunities given to men and are often relegated to menial or low-skill jobs. Women make up 65 percent of those officially registered as unemployed. Currently there are more women than men receiving university and postgraduate education but this may be due to the fact that more young men emigrate in search of jobs.

Women

Gender Empowerment Measure: —
Seats Held in Parliament by Women %: —
Female Administrators and Managers %: —
Female Professional and Technical Workers %: —
Women's Share of Earned Income %: —
Women in Government %: 2

HEALTH, FOOD, AND NUTRITION

Health

Number of Physicians: 19,000
Number of Dentists: —
Number of Nurses: 34,900
Number of Pharmacists: —
Population per Physician: 198
Number of Hospitals: 183
Hospital Beds per 10,000: 82
Hospital Bed Occupancy Rate: —
Infant Mortality Rate per 1,000 live births: 23
Maternal Mortality Rate per 100,000 live births: 50
Total Health Expenditures as % of GDP: 4.17
Health Expenditures per capita $: 152
HIV Infected % of adults: 0.01
Cigarette Consumption per smoker per year: —
% of Smokers: Male: —
    Female: —
Access to Safe Water %: —

Food and Nutrition

Food Supply as % of FAO Requirements: —
% of Consumption Expenditures on Food: 47.3
Daily Available Calories per capita: —
% of Total Calories derived from:
Cereals: —
Potatoes, cassava: —
Meat, poultry: —
Fish: —
Eggs, milk: —
Fruits, vegetables: —
Fats, oils: —

ENVIRONMENT

Armenia's chief environmental problems have resulted from natural disasters, pollution, and war. The disastrous 1988 earthquake, which left 55,000 dead, set environmental cleanup progress back by a decade. Pollution was caused principally by the Chernobyl nuclear reactor meltdown, and the Metsamor nuclear power plant continues to add to the problem. Chemical pollution affects the Hrazdan and Aras Rivers.

Environment

Forest Area sq km: 3
Average Annual Deforestation sq km: 84
Nationally Protected Areas as % of Total Land Area: 7.4
Freshwater Access cubic meters per capita: 2,767
Emissions of Organic Water Pollutants kg per day: 12,858
CO_2 Emissions per capita ton: 1.0

CHRONOLOGY

1920 The Allies recognize Armenia as a sovereign nation; the Turks, who refuse to recognize the independence of Armenia, seize the regions of Kars and Alexandropol and continue the forced repatriation of ethnic Armenians, a process begun in 1915 and in which 1.5 million perish; the government of Armenia, a coalition of communists and Dashnaks, pronounces Armenia a Soviet republic.

1921 Communists force out of government the Dashnaks, who stage a revolt but fail to regain power.

1922 Armenia, Georgia, and Azerbaijan form the Transcaucasian Soviet Federated Socialist Republic, then join the Soviet Union.

1923 The Soviet Union assigns control of Nagorno-Karabakh, a region disputed by Armenia and Azerbaijan, to Azerbaijan.

1926 Joseph Stalin comes to power in Moscow and initiates both the industrialization of Armenia and the systematic suppression and murder of the country's political and intellectual elite, a campaign known as the Great Terror.

1936 The Soviet Union makes Armenia, Georgia, and Azerbaijan distinct republics within the union.

1953 Stalin dies; Nikita Khrushchev becomes the leader of the Soviet Union.

1974 Moscow appointee Karen Demirchian assumes control of the Communist Party of Armenia (CSA), further entrenching its notorious corruption.

1985 Mikhail Gorbachev becomes leader of the Soviet Union.

1988 A massive earthquake kills 55,000 in Armenia.

1989 Soviet authorities arrest members of the Karabakh Committee, a political group dedicated to regaining the Nagorno-Karabakh region from Azerbaijan; the dispute with Azerbaijan over the Nagorno-Karabakh enclave escalates into war.

1991 Armenia declares its independence following the collapse of the Soviet Union; Levon Ter-Petrosian is elected president; Armenia joins 10 other former Soviet countries as a member of the Commonwealth of Independent States.

1992 The Armenian army carves a supply route, the "Lachin corridor," through Azerbaijan and occupies Nagorno-Karabakh.

1994 Russia brokers a cease-fire between Armenia and Azerbaijan in which Armenia retains control over most of the Nagorno-Karabakh enclave.

1998 President Ter-Petrosian resigns unexpectedly; the government legalizes the Dashnak party, which Ter-Petrosian had outlawed; Prime Minister Robert Kocharian is elected president.

1999 Five terrorists enter the National Assembly and open fire, killing the prime minister, speaker, and six other members of parliament.

2001 Armenia becomes a full member of the Council of Europe.

BIBLIOGRAPHY

Bernoutian, George A. *A History of the Armenian People*. Costa Mesa, Calif., 1993.

International Monetary Fund. *Armenia*. Washington, D.C., 1992.

Narsessian, Vrej. *Armenia*. Santa Barbara, Calif., 1993.

Suny, Ronald Grigor. *Armenia in the 20th Century*. Decatur, Ga., 1983.

Walker, Christopher J. *Armenia: The Survival of a Nation*. New York, 1990.

OFFICIAL PUBLICATIONS

Armenia. *Armenia Human Development Report* (UNDP; 1996); *Economic Reviews: Armenia* (IMF [irreg.]); *Statisticheskii Yezhegodnik Armenii* (Statistical Yearbook of Armenia).

CONTACT INFORMATION

Embassy of Armenia
2225 R Street NW
Washington, D.C. 20008
Phone: (202) 319-1976 Fax: (202) 319-2982

INTERNET RESOURCES

- The Embassy of the Republic of Armenia
  http://www.armeniaemb.org/

AUSTRALIA

BASIC FACT SHEET

OFFICIAL NAME:
Commonwealth of Australia

ABBREVIATION:
AT

CAPITAL:
Canberra (ACT Australian Capital Territory)

HEAD OF STATE:
Queen Elizabeth II, represented by Governor-General Peter Hollingworth

HEAD OF GOVERNMENT:
Prime Minister John Winston Howard (from 1996)

NATURE OF GOVERNMENT:
Parliamentary democracy

POPULATION:
18,943,000 (1999)

AREA:
7,686,850 sq km (2,967,124 sq mi)

MAJOR ETHNIC GROUPS:
Caucasian, Aboriginal, Asian

LANGUAGE:
English

RELIGION:
Christianity (mainly Protestant and Roman Catholic)

UNIT OF CURRENCY:
Australian dollar

NATIONAL FLAG:
The red, white, and blue Union Jack in the upper left canton; in the remaining blue field a white, five-star Southern Cross (four stars with seven points and one with five points) appears in the right fly, and the white, seven-pointed federal star appears immediately below the Union Jack.

NATIONAL EMBLEM:
Standing on green eucalyptus branches surrounded by the gold and blue wattle blossoms of the national flower are two native creatures: a kangaroo and an emu. Most prints show the two creatures in shades of brown, the pouched animal in lighter color than the swift, flightless bird. The base sometimes is depicted as a green, grassy mound. Between the two facing animals is an ermine-bordered shield surmounted by a seven-pointed gold Union star having one point for each Australian state and one for the Northern Territory. The star rests on a blue and white candy-striped wand, or heraldic wreath. Beneath the emblem the country's name appears in black letters on a white scroll. The coats of arms of the six states are displayed in equal segments on the central shield. In the top, from left to right, New South Wales is first, with a St. George's Cross on a white field with a gold lion in the center. Each arm of the cross contains a gold, five-pointed star. Victoria's gold and red royal crown is placed against a blue background, which also contains the white stars of the Southern Cross. Queensland's coat of arms is a Maltese Cross against a white background, "defaced," in heraldic usage, by a gold and red royal crown. The coat of arms of South Australia is a black-and-white crow shrike or magpie in flight against a yellow background. Also against a yellow background is the black swan of Western Australia. Tasmania is represented by a red lion on a white field.

NATIONAL ANTHEM:
"Advance Australia Fair"

NATIONAL HOLIDAYS:
Australia Day (January 26); the queen's birthday is celebrated in June except in Western Australia, where it is observed in November; all Christian festivals, and also December 26 as Boxing Day.

DATE OF INDEPENDENCE:
January 1, 1901

DATE OF CONSTITUTION:
July 9, 1900

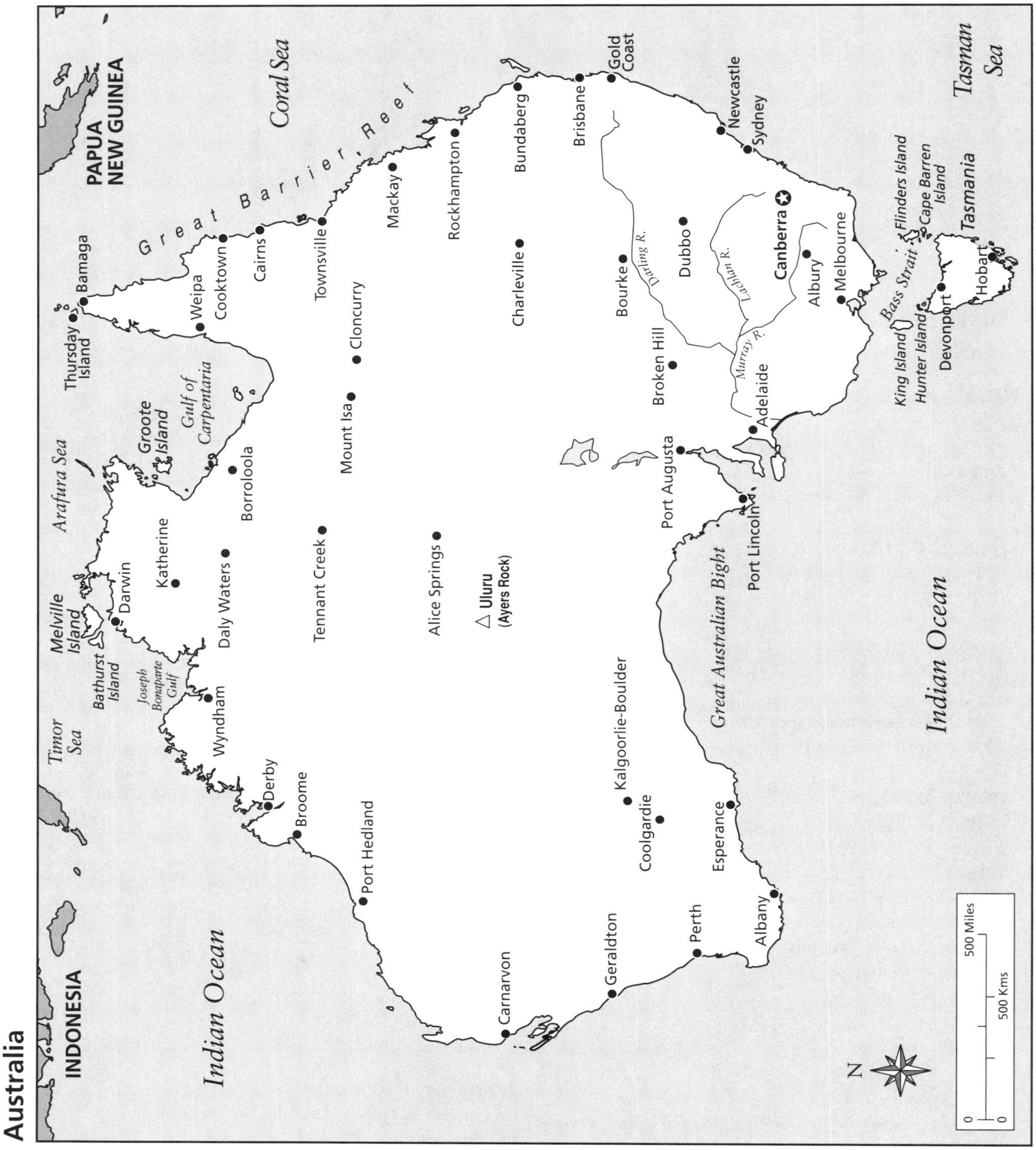

Australia

INDONESIA
Timor Sea
Melville Island
Arafura Sea
Thursday Island
Bamaga
PAPUA NEW GUINEA
Bathurst Island
Darwin
Groote Island
Joseph Bonaparte Gulf
Katherine
Gulf of Carpentaria
Weipa
Indian Ocean
Wyndham
Daly Waters
Cooktown
Borroloola
Great Barrier Reef
Derby
Cairns
Coral Sea
Broome
Tennant Creek
Townsville
Mount Isa
Cloncurry
Port Hedland
Mackay
Alice Springs
Rockhampton
Uluru (Ayers Rock)
Carnarvon
Charleville
Bundaberg
Brisbane
Geraldton
Kalgoorlie-Boulder
Bourke
Gold Coast
Coolgardie
Darling R.
Broken Hill
Port Augusta
Dubbo
Perth
Esperance
Great Australian Bight
Newcastle
Murray R.
Lachlan R.
Port Lincoln
Adelaide
Sydney
Albany
Canberra
Albury
Melbourne
N
Bass Strait
King Island
Flinders Island
Hunter Island
Cape Barren Island
Indian Ocean
Devonport
0 500 Miles
0 500 Kms
Tasmania
Tasman Sea
Hobart

GEOGRAPHICAL FEATURES

Australia is the world's smallest continent but its sixth-largest country, lying southeast of Asia between the Pacific and Indian Oceans. Its total area of 2,967,124 sq mi (7,686,850 sq km) is nearly as large as that of the continental United States and half the size of Europe. Including Tasmania, the country extends 2,486 mi (4,000 km) east to west and 2,385 mi (3,837 km) north to south. On the eastern coast the Great Barrier Reef extends for 1,243 mi (2,000 km) comprising an important ecosystem of islands and coral reefs containing many rare forms of life.

The country is customarily divided into three principal topographical regions: the large Western Plateau, underlain by ancient rock shield; the Central Lowlands, or Central Plains, underlain by horizontal sedimentary rocks, and the Eastern Highlands, of more complex geological origin. A smaller fourth region sometimes is known as the Southern Faultlands east of the Australian Bight. These regions are known popularly designated by different terms. The Outback applies generally to the interior, specifically to the arid center of the Western Plateau and its semiarid northern plains. The name Red Center is applied to an area with characteristic red, brown, and tan soils located in the heart of the continent.

Australia is one of the flattest continents, with just 6 percent of its area lying over 2,000 ft (610 m) above sea level. Only in the southern corner is there any considerable area over 5,000 ft (1,524 m), with Mount Kosciusko rising to 7,134 ft (2,229 m). This inaptly named Australian Alps area is far from alpine, and the summit of Mount Kosciusko is easy to reach by car. These mountains form part of an extensive area of high relief known as the Great Dividing Range, consisting of fretted margins of plateaus and cones and plugs of long-extinct volcanoes. The wetter seaward flanks of these highlands are much more desiccated than the western slopes, which fall away to the interior plains in long ridges. The coast, especially in New South Wales, often is backed by massive scarps cut by wild gorges.

The vast desert and semidesert region of the Western Plateau covers almost two-thirds of the continent. Averaging about 1,000 ft (305 m) above sea level, it is relieved by widely separated mountains. These mountains include the Hamersley Range to the west and, in the north-central rim, the irregular ranges of the Kimberley Plateau. Toward the east of the Western Plateau are three notable ranges—Macdonnell, Musgrave, and Petermann. From the western rocky ranges, the Western Plateau stretches eastward as a continuous flatland with occasional stark outcroppings of granite or sandstone. The most impressive outcropping is Ayers Rock, a massive, rounded monolith rising over 1,100 ft (335 m). There are four major deserts—Gibson, Great Sandy, Great Victoria, and Tanamy—on the Western Plateau. The plateau is also rimmed by escarpments, including the singular Nullarbor Plain and the Darling Scarp.

The Central Eastern Lowlands extend from the Gulf of Carpentaria in the north to Western Victoria in the south. This lowland belt averages only about 500 ft (152 m) above sea level. Beneath the Central Eastern Lowlands are several artesian basins, one of which, the Great Artesian Basin, underlies approximately one-fifth of the entire continent and is the largest in the world.

The Eastern Highlands are inaccurately designated as the Great Dividing Range, though they do not form a true range and have an average altitude of 3,000 ft (914 m). They consist of a complex of tablelands, ridges, and coastal ranges. Nevertheless, they are rugged and spectacular in parts. The Eastern Highlands are low and broad in the north and rise as they progress southward. The island of Tasmania, lying about 150 mi (241 km) southeast of the continent, is geologically part of the Eastern Highlands. The island has a rugged terrain, with a large central plateau, and with some mountains rising to over 5,000 ft (1,524 m)

Australia is one of the world's driest continents, with only a few permanent rivers and streams. More than 60 percent of the annual runoff is from the Tasmania, Gulf of Carpentaria, and Timor Sea drainage basins. In nearly three-fourths of the country, stream flow is intermittent or dependent on seasonal rains, and for months or even years streams and rivers dry up. The Murray-Darling river system is the most important drainage system in the country.

Geography

Area sq km: 7,686,850 sq mi 2,967,124
World Rank: 6th
Land Boundaries, km: —
Coastline, km 25,760
Elevation Extremes meters
- Lowest: Lake Eyre 15
- Highest: Mount Kosciusko 2,229

Land Use % Arable land: 6
- Permanent Crops: 0
- Permanent Pastures: 54
- Forest and Woodland: 19
- Other: 21

Population of Principal Cities (1995 est.)

City	Population
Adelaide	1,081,000
Bankstown	162,600
Blacktown	228,400
Brisbane	1,489,100
Cairns	100,900
Campbeltown	149,100
Canberra	303,700
Canterbury	134,500
Fairfield	186,100
Geelong	152,600
Gold Coast-Tweed	326,900

(continued)

Gosford	142,150
Hobart	194,700
Keilor	114,639
Knox	132,686
Lake Macquarie	175,510
Liverpool	106,750
Melbourne	3,218,100
Moorabbin	100,389
Newcastle	466,000
Parramatta	137,450
Penrith	163,500
Perth	1,262,600
Randwick	117,600
Stirling	178,734
Sydney	3,772,700
Townsville	124,900
Wanneroo	190,965
Wollongong	253,600

CLIMATE AND WEATHER

Australia has a warm climate with little rainfall, clear skies, and much sunshine. The temperature range is moderate, and intense winter cold is absent for the most part. Summer and winter rainfall systems tend to be weak. Toward the interior of the country rainfall not only decreases but also becomes increasingly variable. Months or years may pass without any rainfall. Droughts are common but generally affect limited areas.

Atmospheric systems influencing the climate include the prevailing southeasterly trade winds. These loose much of their moisture over the Eastern Highlands, which constitute an effective barrier over the inland spread of moisture. In the winter months, the north of the continent is affected by trade winds from the southeast, and the south by westerly winds that bring high rainfall over the southwestern area and the western mountain slopes of Tasmania. In the summer months easterly winds prevail over most of the continent, though the north has a wet summer through the influence of the northeastern monsoons. Australia experiences hurricanes and cyclones on both coasts, in the northeast and northwest. They occur mainly between November and March, the southern summer.

The vast interior and much of the west and south have high temperatures and very low rainfall. Summer temperatures are particularly high in the northern zone above the tropic of Capricorn, with daytime maximums of 90°F (32°C) and higher. Encircling this arid zone to the north, east, and southwest is a large, semiarid belt with slightly higher rainfall and somewhat greater seasonal variations. In the north the maximum rainfall occurs in the summer and is followed by a cooler, drier period extending through August, and warm weather with dusty windstorms in September and October. In the south the rainfall is somewhat more evenly distributed, with a drier summer in the west and southwest.

The monsoonal north comprising Arnhem Land, the Cape York Peninsula, and northern parts of the eastern coast has a hot, humid tropical climate with rainfall concentrated in the summer months. The entire region is subject to seasonal floods. In the longer, drier winter season, only slightly cooler in temperature, rain is infrequent. Along the northern parts of the eastern coast the winter season is pleasant and mild. The eastern and southeastern coast has relatively abundant rainfall well distributed throughout the year and usually reliable. Droughts there are infrequent and winters are mild.

The area to the west of the humid coastal zone has abundant rainfall and considerable temperature variations. Summers there are hot, with maximum temperatures of about 100°F (38°C) common, but winters are cool and frosts may occur between April and September. Drought is a continuing hazard since rainfall in many places is rendered ineffective by evaporation and seepage. The southwestern corner of the country and the Southern Faultlands experience a subtropical Mediterranean climate, with sunny summers and mild winters. Tasmania has a middle latitude climate, with cold winters and warm summers. Rainfall generally is abundant.

Climate and Weather

Mean Temperature
Melbourne July 49°F January 68°F
Darwin July 53°F January 84°F
Interior Summer High 100°F to 115°F
Average Rainfall
North and Northeast 60 in
West 30 in to 50 in
Southwest 20 in to 45 in
Tasmania 40 to 100 in

POPULATION

Population Indicators

Total Population: 1999 18,943,000
World Rank: 51st
Density per sq mi: 6.4 per sq km 2.5
% of annual growth (1994–99): 1.2
Male %: 49.5
Female %: 50.5
Urban %: 85.3
Age Distribution: % 0–14: 22.1
15–29: 24.2
30–44: 23.4
45–59: 15.0
60–74: 11.1
75 and over: 4.4
Population 2020: 22,672,000
Birth Rate per 1,000: 14.1
Death Rate per 1,000: 6.9
Population Doubling Time (years): 99
Infant Mortality Rate per 1,000 live births: 5.7
Rate of Natural Increase per 1,000: 7.2
Total Fertility Rate: 1.8
Expectation of Life (years): Males 75.4
Females 81.1

Marriage Rate per 1,000: 5.9
Divorce Rate per 1,000: 2.7
Total Number of Households: 6,636,000
Average Size of Households: 2.6
% of Illegitimate Children: —
Induced Abortions: —
Rate per 100 live births: —

ETHNIC COMPOSITION

Australia is perhaps the most homogeneous of former British dominions, next to New Zealand. The racial stock is overwhelmingly Causasian and of British descent, making up 92 percent of the population. Immigrants from Southeast Asia compose a sizable part of the population, numbering 7 percent.

Aboriginals, making up 1 percent of the population, are the only true ethnic minority. In 1788, when Europeans first established a permanent settlement in Australia, there were between 250,000 and 300,000 indigenous Aborigines or Aboriginals living there. These peoples are believed to have lived on the continent for over 30,000 years, coming originally from mainland Asia. They are thought to form a distinct race known as Australoid, and generally are of short stature, with black skin and fine, straight hair that often is blond among children but later becomes black.

In the late 1700s the Aboriginals were divided into over 500 tribes, each ranging from 100 to 1,500 members. Each tribe spoke a different but related language and occupied a defined territory. The Aboriginal material culture was limited to the bare essentials. The people were nomadic and depended entirely on hunting, fishing, and gathering for subsistence. The arid climate, lack of natural resources, and lack of plants or animals meant a constant struggle for existence in a harsh environment. There was no economic specialization, but sharing and generosity were highly prized virtues. Kinship was of paramount importance and determined all social relationships. Religion was totemistic and animistic, and totems and culture heroes governed the life cycles.

Within the first century of the arrival of the Europeans, the Aboriginals were decimated in numbers. By 1876, all the Tasmanian Aboriginals had died, and disease, loss of hunting grounds, and expulsion from hospitable coastal areas brought the mainland Aboriginals close to extinction. Most Aboriginals were segregated from the rest of Australia by the establishment of Aboriginal reserves in the 19th century. Until the end of World War II, they were treated as second-class citizens and openly discriminated against. However, in the 1950s and 1960s public concern over Aboriginal rights forced the government to reverse many of the former discrimination laws. In the 1970s, provisions were made to educate their children in white schools. Australia became committed to the full development of the Aboriginals' providing them medical care and legal aid. Government boards were established to further Aboriginals' economic and social development and to preserve their cultural heritage.

LANGUAGES

The official language is English. Although there are no dialects, Australian English has established itself during recent decades as a distinct branch of the Queen's English, with its own many picturesque idioms and expressions.

Many first-generation immigrants continue to use their own languages at home, and there are numerous non-English newspapers and periodicals published in the major urban centers. The Aboriginal languages and dialects are dying out despite official efforts to preserve them.

Principal Languages and Their Speakers

Aboriginal languages	50,000
Arabic	185,000
Cantonese	217,000
Dutch	46,000
English	15,381,000
English (lingua franca)	18,300,000
French	43,000
German	110,000
Greek	295,000
Hungarian	29,000
Indonesian Malay	30,000
Italian	419,000
Macedonian	78,000
Maltese	51,000
Mandarin	99,000
Pilipino (Filipino)	77,000
Polish	70,000
Portuguese	27,000
Russian	34,000
Serbo-Croatian	116,000
Spanish	99,000
Turkish	48,000
Vietnamese	153,000
Other/not stated	1,287,000

RELIGIONS

Nearly 87 percent of Australians are affiliated with some religious denomination. The major religious groups are Roman Catholics (27 percent), Anglican Church members (21.9 percent), and other Protestants (18.6 percent).

Roman Catholics are predominantly Irish and South and East European. This group has increased over the years as a percentage of the population from 21 percent in 1941 to 27 percent in 1998. This increase has been due to the large number of immigrants from predominantly Catholic countries such as Italy, Poland, and Malta. Among Aboriginals, about 26 percent are Catholics.

The oldest religious denomination is the Anglican Church. Anglican chaplains arrived with the first convict immigrants in 1781. Most Anglicans are of British origin. The highest proportion of Anglicans is in Tasmania, with 45 percent. As elsewhere, Anglicanism is the professed religion of many Australians who do not practice any religion.

Of the Protestant churches outside Anglicanism, the largest are the Methodists and Presbyterians. The early Methodists were Welsh settlers, and the first Presbyterian church was built by Scottish settlers in 1809. Other Christian denominations include Lutherans, Congregationalists, Eastern Orthodox, and Pentecostals.

Patterns of religious practice are similar to those in the United Kingdom. The percentage of regular churchgoers is about 30 percent, of whom Catholics form the predominant majority. Attendance is lowest among Anglicans, only 10 percent of whom are active churchgoers.

Australia is a secular state, and there is little friction between church and state. Church properties and funds are exempt from taxes, and the clergy and seminary students, prior to the establishment of an all-volunteer force, were exempted from military service. Churches receive no financial aid from the government, though they are given assistance for social services and missions to the Aboriginals. Since 1974 church schools have received government subsidies under certain conditions.

Religious Affiliations

Roman Catholic	5,120,000
Anglican	4,160,000
Uniting Church	1,420,000
Presbyterian	720,000
Other Protestant	1,380,000
Orthodox	530,000
Nonreligious	3,150,000
Other	2,460,000

HISTORICAL BACKGROUND

On January 26, 1988, Australia celebrated its bicentennial, commemorating the settlement of the first British penal colony of 700 convicts at Port Jackson (later Sydney). Captain Arthur Philip, the settlement's commander, was to be the first governor of the colony, later known as New South Wales. The eastern coast of Australia had been explored by Captain James Cook in 1770, only 18 years before this event, and most of the continent was still unexplored. Hobart, Tasmania, was founded in 1803, but it was not until 1813 that a way was found over the Blue Mountains for westward expansion into the continent itself. Then new settlements were established on the Brisbane River in Queensland in 1824 and on the Swan River in Western Australia in 1829. Melbourne was established on Port Phillip Bay in 1835 and Adelaide on Gulf St. Vincent in 1836. These settlements formed a series of starting points for further exploration of the north and west.

Meanwhile, more shiploads of convicts from England arrived—161,000 in all—until the penal system itself was abolished between 1840 and 1868. Sheep-raising and wheat-growing became the backbone of a flourishing economy that attracted free settlers from the British Isles. This flow of immigrants increased following the Ripon Land Regulations of 1831, which provided land grants to settlers. By 1850, Australia's population had grown to 500,000 inhabitants (not including Aboriginals). Within a few years the population quadrupled under the stimulus of the discovery of gold in Victoria in 1851.

Self-government became an early objective of the colonies as the population grew. The Australian Colonies Government Act, passed by the British Parliament in 1850, empowered the colonies to establish legislatures, determine voting rights, and frame their constitutions as desired. New South Wales was the first to draft a constitution, in 1855. All other colonies except Western Australia became self-governing by 1859; the latter's desire to remain a penal colony delayed its constitution until 1890.

The need for a continental federation was felt even by 1863, when the first intercolonial conference of the premiers of the six colonies began. A draft federal constitution was drawn up in 1891, and it was approved at a convention in 1897–98. On the basis of this constitution, the Commonwealth of Australia came into being on January 1, 1901. The federal parliament sat in Melbourne until 1927. In 1911 a federal capital territory was selected and established as Australian Capital Territory, and the foundation stone for the present federal capital of Canberra was laid in 1913.

Three political parties competed for power in the new commonwealth: the Conservative Free Traders, the Liberal Protectionist Party, and the Australian Labor Party (ALP). The ALP came to power in the first decade and dominated Australian politics for the next several decades, until the end of World War II. Through its extensive social legislation, it set the pattern for Australia's future development.

In the later decades of the 1900s, Australia's social welfare state gradually changed as reliance on government controls decreased and private sector economics became more dominant. The need for budgetary constraints and caps on spending forced the government to impose limits on social programs and subsidies. Changes in public opinion toward a centrist view of the proper role of government also influenced the nation's political outlook. After 13 years in power, the Australian Labor Party (ALP) was defeated by a coalition of the more conservative Liberal Party and Nationalist Party in 1996. This coalition won a large majority in the House of Representatives under the leadership of John Howard of the Liberal Party, who became prime minister.

The Liberal administration of John Howard faced opposition for its treatment of Aborigines, especially the practice of leasing tribal lands to outsiders. Faced with the probability that the Asian financial crisis would seriously damage his electoral prospects, Howard called an early election in 1998. The Liberal-National Coalition again prevailed at the polls but with a reduced majority. In 1999 55 percent of Australians voted against the country's becoming a republic although a constitutional convention had recommended that course in 1998.

CONSTITUTION

The legal foundation of the Australian government is the Commonwealth of Australia Act of 1900. The constitution is based essentially on the British model, but it borrows heavily from the U.S. Constitution, especially in provisions regarding federal versus state powers. From the British model, it adopted the parliamentary system of government, under which the cabinet is responsible to the legislature. From the U.S. model came the idea of a decentralized, federal system of government in which the powers of government are divided between the federation and the states, and the states retain their constitutional and political structures.

The powers of the federal government are divided among legislative, executive, and judicial branches, though there is not a strict separation of powers. In the British tradition, the distinction between the legislative and executive branches is nominal in as much as leadership of both branches belongs to the same political party or coalition of parties commanding a majority in the popularly elected lower house of parliament.

Relations between the federal and state authorities are specified in great detail. Federal powers are enumerated, and powers not constitutionally delegated to the federal government remain with the states. The constitution empowers the federal government to legislate and act on all matters relating to foreign affairs, defense, immigration, foreign trade and interstate commerce, taxation, currency, banking, weights and measures, marriage and divorce, and enforcement of the judgments of state courts.

State governments are given wide responsibilities over education, public health, housing, agriculture, transportation, law enforcement, child welfare, welfare of the Aboriginals, tourism, and exploitation of natural resources. However, since 1900 the trend has been toward a steady enlargement of federal powers at the expense of the states, stemming principally from the unlimited federal taxation power and the relative financial weakness of the states.

Questions relating to the interpretation and application of the constitution are resolved by the High Court of Australia, which has original jurisdiction in any constitutional case as well as appellate jurisdiction in cases brought from the state supreme courts.

The terms associated with cabinet government, including prime minister and cabinet, as well as the principle of collective cabinet responsibility to parliament, are not mentioned in the constitution, but they are the foundations of Australian government. By convention, the chief executive officer of the federal government is the prime minister, not the governor-general appointed by the British sovereign, as stated in the constitution. The prime minister works with a cabinet of a dozen or so senior ministers that initiates all major government bills in parliament. The ministers are party loyalists less concerned with day-to-day running of their departments than with legislative and political oversight.

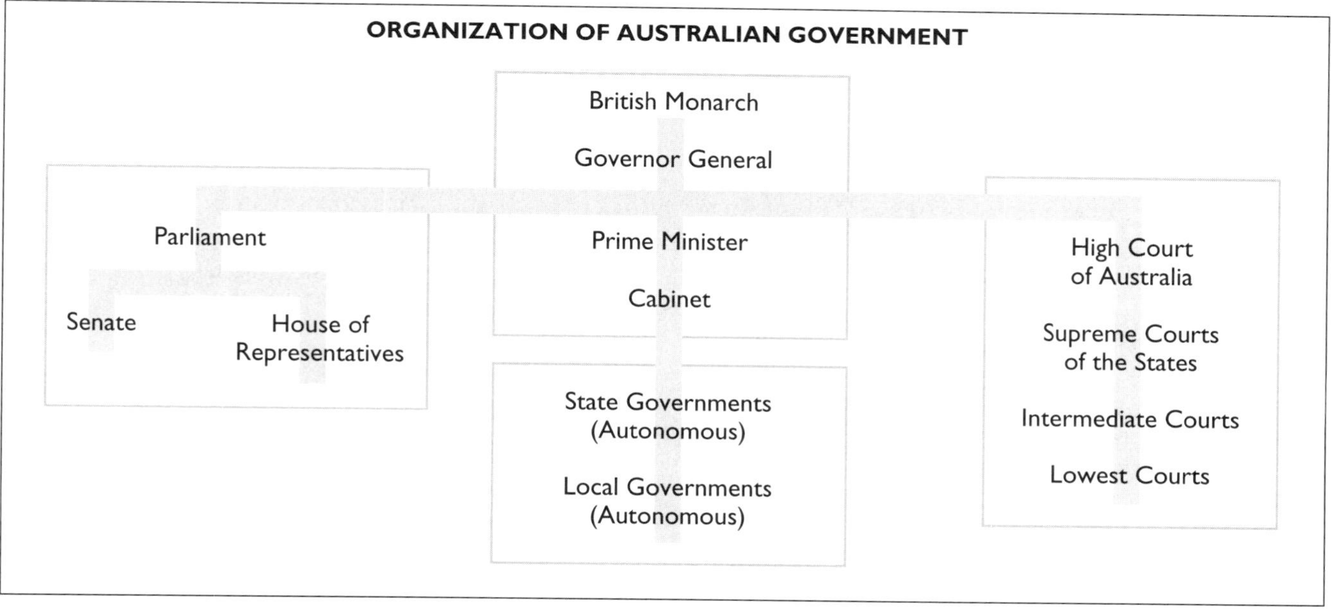

State governments are much older than the federal government and each has its own constitutional framework. The term "state" refers to Australia's six political divisions: New South Wales, Victoria, Queensland, South Australia, Western Australia, and Tasmania. In addition, there are two mainland territories fully dependent on the federal government: Australian Capital Territory and Jervis Bay Territory, and Northern Territory, which became self-governing in 1978.

LOCAL GOVERNMENT

Each state is subdivided into self-governing local units called cities, counties, municipalities, towns, shires, district councils, or road districts. These units are created by the state parliament and are subject to the supervision of the state department of local government. The governing councils of these local areas are popularly elected.

The principal functions of local councils include construction and maintenance of roads, bridges, water and sewage systems, and sanitation and garbage collection services. The more important functions, such as education, public housing, and law enforcement, are performed directly by the state government.

Local Government

Principal administrative divisions, capitals, area, population

AREA AND POPULATION

		area		population 1996
States	**Capitals**	**sq mi**	**sq km**	**census**
New South Wales	Sydney	309,500	801,600	6,038,696
Queensland	Brisbane	666,900	1,727,200	3,368,850
South Australia	Adelaide	379,900	984,000	1,427,936
Tasmania	Hobart	26,200	67,800	459,659
Victoria	Melbourne	87,900	227,600	4,373,520
Western Australia	Perth	975,100	2,525,500	1,726,095
Territories				
Australian Capital Territory	Canberra	900	2,400	299,243
Northern Territory	Darwin	519,800	1,346,200	195,101
TOTAL		2,966,200	7,682,300	17,892,423

PARLIAMENT

The legislative power of government is vested in the federal parliament, with a lower house, the House of Representatives, and an upper house, the Senate. The constitution limits the duration of the House of Representatives to three years, subject to earlier dissolution. It provides that the House, as the national chamber, should have twice the membership of the Senate, which represents states and territories. The House's 148 members are elected directly by the people in single-member constituencies. The leader of the party or party coalition commanding the majority in the House after an election is chosen as prime minister. The second largest party in the House is the official opposition, and its leader is known as the leader of the opposition. The government party in the House also is the government party in the Senate regardless of whether it has a majority in the upper house.

Both houses use a system of committees to oversee their work and to consider proposed legislation. The fundamental stages in legislation, or the enactment of a bill, are: presentation and first reading, second reading, committee proceedings, and third reading. The bill is then transmitted to the other house, where it goes through the same stages in committee.

On the British model, the most effective mechanism of legislative, parliamentary control over the executive is question time, during which ministers are questioned as a demonstration of the accountability of the executive.

All state parliaments are bicameral except Queensland, which has a unicameral body called the Legislative Assembly. The functions of state parliaments and their procedures are almost the same as those of the federal parliament.

POLITICAL PARTIES

Like most English-speaking countries, Australia has a two-party system in which a right-wing party, the Liberal Party, has alternated in government with a left-wing party, the Australian Labor Party. There is a third group, the National Party, which generally sides with the conservatives, and is part of any right-wing coalition. The Liberal Party was founded in 1944 as the successor to the United Australia Party and is actually an amalgam of traditional liberals (in the European sense) and conservatives (in the Anglo-Saxon sense) with strong ties to the business community. The Australian Labor Party is the oldest of Australian political parties, founded in the 1890s as the political arm of the trade union movement. Its traditional constituency comprises immigrants, feminists, and workers. The party has long been divided between a moderate, pragmatic wing and a dogmatic, socialist wing, but the moderates generally carry the day at election times. The National Party was founded in 1920 as the Country Party and assumed its present name in 1982 in an effort to widen its appeal. It is conservative in outlook and its constituency includes rural residents and farmers.

Political Parties

Liberal Party, 1944
National Party, 1920
Australian Labor Party, 1890s
Australian Democrats, 1977
Australian Greens
Australia First Party, 1996
Pauline Hanson's One Nation

Political Parties: Strength in Parliament Most Recent Elections

Senate. The Senate currently consists of 76 members (12 from each state plus 2 each from the Australian Capital Territory and the Northern Territory), who are elected from state or territorial lists by proportional representation. Balloting is normally conducted every three years, with members of the state delegations serving staggered six-year terms. Following the balloting of November 10, 2001, the LP/NP Alliance held 35 seats (Liberal Party, 31; National Party, 3; Northern Territory Country Liberal Party, 1), Australian Labor Party, 28; Australian Democrats, 8; Australian Greens, 2; Pauline Hanson's One Nation, 1; Country Labor Party, 1; and non-partisans, 1.

LEGAL SYSTEM

Australia's legal system is based on English common law. The two principal sources of its law are the statutes of the federal parliament and state parliaments and the decisions of the judicial committee of the Privy Council in London, the High Court of Australia, and the supreme courts of the states.

The constitution vests judicial power in the High Court of Australia and other courts created by the federal parliament. At the judicial apex, the High Court has both appellate and original jurisdiction. It handles all cases arising under a treaty, those in which the federal government is a party, those involving disputes between states or residents of different states, and those involving the interpretation of the constitution. The High Court's appellate jurisdiction covers appeals from other federal courts, from state courts within federal jurisdiction, and from state supreme courts. The High Court is presided over by the chief justice and six other justices.

The superior courts include the Family Court and the Federal Court. The Federal Court handles cases involving copyright law, trade practices, bankruptcy, industrial law, and administrative review. The Family Court deals with divorce, custody of children, family maintenance, and property disputes. There is no separate system of federal courts paralleling state courts. Instead, existing state courts are vested with jurisdiction over most federal matters.

All states and the Northern Territory have their own court systems headed by the state supreme court. Capital punishment was abolished by the federal government in 1973 but is retained by some states. All Australian prisons are maintained by the states, and there are no federal prisons.

LAW ENFORCEMENT

Law Enforcement

Offenses reported to the police per 100,000: 6,279
Murder: 1.8
Assault: 560.3
Burglary: 2,131.9
Automobile Theft: 703
Population per Police officer: 453
Death Penalty: Abolished 1985

HUMAN RIGHTS

As a multiparty parliamentary democracy, Australia is a country where all basic human rights are guaranteed by law. However, not until the mid-1970s did the federal and state governments enact equal opportunity and antidiscrimination legislation. The reason for this delay lies in the historic belief that Australia was a classless society free of violent racial tensions and serious breaches of human rights. This belief masked the fact that a silent minority, the native Australian peoples, suffered disguised discrimination without any legal remedies.

The indigenous people, the Aboriginals, have an average life expectancy 20 years less than nonindigenous Australians, higher rates of unemployment, and inferior access to medical and educational institutions. In recent years, a wide variety of government initiatives have sought to improve these conditions. In 1997, the government spent over $1.1 billion on health, welfare, education, and regional development to assist Aboriginal people. In 1998, Prime Minister Howard declared that reconciliation with Aboriginals was one of his government's highest priorities.

FOREIGN POLICY

Since World War II, Australia has played an active role in world affairs. As one of the founders of the UN, Australia has strongly supported that body and the work of its agencies. It has taken a key role in the UN's peace-keeping activities, drug control programs, and disarmament initiatives. Australia has devoted special attention to conflicts and disputes involving Asian nations. It contributed soldiers to the UN force during the Korean War, helped suppress a communist revolt in Malaya in the 1950s, sent combat troops to fight in the Vietnam War, and took the lead in helping restore peace in East Timor after Indonesian forces tried to overturn a vote for independence in 1999.

Australia's foreign policy reflects its national interests and defense needs as well. It has signed security agreements with Britain and New Zealand to protect Singapore and Malaysia. It has given large grants of aid to Papua New Guinea, a former Australian trust territory and another neighbor to the north.

Australia also has maintained close ties with the United States in the decades since World War II. This special relationship was reflected in Australia's strong support of the United States during the Gulf War in 1991 and the two countries' mutual belief that their national security depended on this power alliance. Foreign commerce also played a key role, with trade between the two countries totaling over $18 billion in 1996.

DEFENSE

Australia's Department of Defense supervises the three services—army, navy, and air force—each a separate branch of the military forces but with joint services for operations, equipment, communications intelligence, and systems analysis. The Defense Logistics Organization operates the government aircraft factories, which produce about one-third of the nation's aircraft, and is also the principal procurer of defense equipment.

The Royal Australian Army consists of the all-volunteer Australian regular army and the citizen military force, the reserve element. Military age is 17 years of age, and military service has been based on volunteers since 1972. The Royal Australian Navy is the senior service, dating from 1910, and is the smallest of the three services. There is no separate coast guard. The Royal Australian Air Force was created in 1921.

The nation's volunteer military service offers the choice of a military career. Initial enlistment is for six years, with reenlistment at the end of a further three or six years up to age 55. Men and women may enlist at any age between 17 and 43.

Australia's military expenditures are relatively high, reaching $8.2 billion in 1997–98, or 1.9 percent of the national GDP.

Military Indicators

Total Active Duty Personnel: 57,400
Military Manpower per 1,000: 3.1
Military Expenditures $: 8.401billion
as % of GNP: 2.5
per capita $: 465
as % of central government expenditures: 8.8

Arms Imports $: 930 million
Arms Exports $: 50 million

ECONOMY

Australia has a prosperous capitalist economy that ranks it with the highly industrialized countries of Western Europe. Australia's Gross Domestic Product (GDP) was growing at an annual rate of 2.4% in 1990–97, totaling $382.7 billion, with a per capita GDP of $20,650.

Australia has abundant mineral and energy resources and is the world's leading exporter of coal as well as a major exporter of aluminum bauxite, copper, industrial diamonds, iron ore, lead, nickel, gold, and silver. It is a major exporter of agricultural products such as wheat, barley, sugarcane, cattle, and sheep. Commodities account for 57 percent of the total value of Australian exports, making its economy subject to major movements in world commodity prices. To offset such downturns in commodity prices, government policies have helped increase the share of manufactured goods in Australian exports.

Australia suffered from low economic growth and high unemployment in the early 1990s, though prosperity returned by the late 1990s despite the economic slump in many Southeast Asian countries. Foreign investments have spurred the development of Australian transport, manufacturing, and ranching. The United States is the leading source of such business investments, accounting for more than $65 billion in 1996, or 40 percent of the total. In the 1990s the government privatized the national airline, telecommunication system, and national bank, which marked significant steps toward greater emphasis on the private sector in the nation's economy.

Principal Economic Indicators

Gross National Product: $382.705 billion
GNP per capita: $20,650
GNP Average Annual Growth Rate (1990–97) %: 2.4
GNP per capita Average Annual Growth Rate (1990–97) %: 1.2
Origin of Gross Domestic Product %
Agriculture: 3
Mining: 4
Manufacturing: 16
Construction: 7
Public Utilities: 3
Transportation and Communications: 9
Trade: 19
Financial Services: 22
Other Services: 14
Government: 4
Gross Domestic Product by Type of Expenditure %
Private Consumption: 62
Government Consumption: 18
Gross Domestic Investment: 22
Foreign Trade: Exports: 19
Imports: −20
% of Income Received by Poorest 20%: 3.8
% of Income Received by Richest 10%: 28.0

Price and earnings indexes (1995 = 100)

	1992	1993	1994	1995	1996	1997	1998
Consumer price index	92.1	93.8	95.6	100.0	102.6	102.9	103.7
Weekly earnings index	90.4	92.1	95.1	100.0	104.0	108.3	112.7

Finance

National Currency: Australian Dollar ($A)
Exchange Rate: $1 = A 1.4865
Money Supply Stock in National Currency billion: 95,650
M1 per capita: 5,200
Central Bank Discount Rate %: 4.69
Total External Debt $ million: 150,000
Debt Service Ratio %: —
Balance of Payments $million: −12.731 billion
International Reserves SDRs million: 10,511
Ratio of External Debt to Total Reserves: —
Average Annual Rate of Inflation/Consumer Price Index Growth Rate %: 1

Official Development Assistance

Donor ODA $: 1.43 billion
as % of GNP: —
per capita: $ —
Foreign Direct Investment $million: 6,165

Central Government Revenues and Expenditures

Fiscal Year: 1 July–30 June
Revenues $million: 89,350
Expenditures $million: 91,920
Budget Deficit/Surplus $: 2,570 million
Tax Revenues as % of GDP: 22.7
Highest Tax Bracket %
Individual: 47
Corporate: 36

Employment and Labor

Economically Active Population: 9,066,000
Female Participation Rate %: 42.9
Activity Rate %: 49.9
Labor by Sector: %
Agriculture, Forestry, Fishing: 4.7
Manufacturing, Mining: 14.1
Construction: 6.6
Transportation and Communications: 6.0
Trade, Hotels, and Restaurants: 23.2
Finance, Insurance, Real Estate: 12.3
Public Administration, Defense: 4.2
Services: 20.3

Unemployment %: 8.4

Agriculture

Agriculture's Share of GDP %: 3
Average Annual Rate of Growth (1965–98) %: 1.8
Number of Farms 000: 150
Average Size of Farm ha: 3,710
Number of Tractors per 1,000 hectares: 6.8
Irrigation, % of Farms having: 5.0
Artificial Fertilizer kg/hectare: 28
Total Farmland as % of land area: 60.3
Livestock: Cattle 000: 26,710
Sheep 000: 119,600
Hogs 000: 2,680
Chickens 000: 83,000
Forests: Production of Roundwood (000 cubic meters): 22,458
Fisheries: Total Catch tons 000: 210.5

Mining

% of GDP: 4.4
Value of Mineral Production $million: 14,150.8

Manufacturing

Value Added $million: 47,563
Industrial Production Growth Rate %: 1.2

Energy

Commercial Energy Production metric tons of oil equivalent 000: 199,167
Commercial Energy Consumption metric tons of oil equivalent 000: 101,626
Commercial Energy Consumption per capita kg: 5,484
Average Annual Growth Rate 1980–97 %: 0.9
Net Energy Imports % of use: −96
Electricity Installed Capacity kW 000: 39,693
Production kW-hr million: 173,404
Coal Reserves tons million: 90,940
Production tons 000: 241,806
Natural Gas Proven Reserves cubic meters billion: 550
Production cubic meters million: 29,554
Crude Petroleum Reserves barrels million: 1,800
Production barrels million: 195
Consumption barrels million: 205
Refinery Capacity barrels per day 000: 771
Pipelines Length km: 3,000

Foreign Trade

Imports $million: 65,427
Exports $million: 60,534
Export Volume % Annual Growth Rate (1990–97): 7.9
Import Volume % Annual Growth Rate (1990–97): 8.7
Balance of Trade $

Balance of Trade (current prices)

	1994	1995	1996	1997	1998	1999
$A 000,000	−3,183	−5,810	−1,424	−1,423	−7,808	3,294
% of total	2.4%	3.9%	0.9%	0.8%	4.2%	7.5%

Major Trading Partners

	Imports	Exports
European Union %	24.9	10.8
United States %	23.0	6.4
Eastern Europe %	0.2	0.4
Japan %	13.0	20.1
Others %	39.0	62.2

Transportation

Roads Total Length mi: 556,145 km 895,030
Paved %: 39
Automobiles: 8,370,000
Trucks and Buses: 2,640,300
Persons per vehicle: 1.6
Railroad; Track Length mi: 22,385 km 38,026
Passenger-mi million: 7,152
Freight-mi million: 67,593
Merchant Marine: No. of Vessels: 695
Total Deadweight Tonnage 000: 3857.3
International Cargo Loaded tons 000: 13,536
International Cargo Off-loaded tons 000: 22,740
Airports with Scheduled Flights: 400
Traffic: Passenger-mi million: 44,687
Freight-mi million: 1,257
Length of Canals mi: 5,200 km 8,368

Tourism

Number of Tourists to 000: 4,167
Number of Tourists from 000: 3,161
Tourist Receipts $million: 7,100
Tourist Expenditures $million: 4,604

Communications

Telephones 000: 9,200
Cost of Local Calls 3 mins $0.16
Cellular Telephones 000: 2,305
Fax Machines 000: 475
Personal Computers 000: 4,979
Internet Hosts per million persons: 17,146
Mail: Post Offices: 3,954
Pieces of Mail Handled million: 4,556
Pieces of Mail Handled per person: 252

EDUCATION

School attendance is compulsory from the ages of six to 15 in all states except Tasmania, where it is six to 16. Completion of the final two years of secondary school, while not compulsory, is achieved by at least one-third of students.

At the primary and secondary levels, about 22 percent of Australian children attend private schools, the majority run by the Catholic Church. Approved private schools receive substantial financial assistance from federal and state governments. Most government schools are coeducational; the proportion of single-sex schools is far greater among private schools.

Higher education comprises traditional universities as well as "tertiary" educational institutions, including teachers' colleges, agricultural colleges, fine arts institutions, and technical institutes. The three "old" universities are Sydney, Melbourne (both founded in the 1850s), and Adelaide (founded in 1874), and the three "middle" universities are Tasmania, Queensland, and Western Australia.

Until 1986 all tertiary institutions were state-run and secular. Bond University of Technology was the first private university, established in 1988. It was only in 1945 that the first doctoral program was instituted, at the University of Melbourne. Since then, all universities have offered courses of higher degree and research.

Education

Literacy Rate %: 99.5
Male %: —
Female %: —
First Level: Primary schools: 9,865
Teachers: 202,401
Students: 3,109,337
Student-Teacher Ratio: 15.4
Net Enrollment Ratio: 98
Second Level: Secondary Schools:
Teachers:
Students:
Student-Teacher Ratio:
Net Enrollment Ratio: 89

Vocational Level: Schools: —
Students: 917,801

Third Level: Institutions: 95
Teachers: 25,916
Students: 604,177
Student-Ratio Level: —
Gross Enrollment Ratio: 71.7
Students per 100,000: 5,401
% of Population Age 25 and over with Postsecondary Education: —

Public Expenditure on Education as % of GDP: 5.6

SCIENCE AND TECHNOLOGY

Science and Technology

Scientists and Engineers in R&D per 1 million persons: 3,357
Expenditures in R&D as % of GDP: 1.80
High-Tech Exports $: 1,564 million
Patent Applications by Residents: 8,937

MEDIA

The country's most influential newspapers are the *Sydney Morning Herald, The Age*, and *The Australian*. The national press agency is the Australian Associated Press (AAP), established in 1935.

The Australian Broadcasting Corporation (ABC) provides nationwide noncommercial radio and television service. The Australian Broadcasting Tribunal regulates commercial and public radio and the country's 139 television stations.

Australia has an extensive book-publishing industry, with over 150 publishers, many of them British publishing houses.

Media

Daily Newspapers: 69
Total Circulation 000: 4,600
Circulation per 1,000: 255
Books Published: 10,835
Magazines: —
Radio Receivers 000: 21,000
per 1,000: 1,152
Television sets 000: 11,565
per 1,000: 641

MOST IMPORTANT MEDIA:

Press. Newspapers are privately owned and almost all are published in the state capitals for intrastate readers; *The Australian* and the *Australian Financial Review* are the only genuinely national daily newspapers. The leading dailies are as follows: *Herald-Sun* (Melbourne, 560,000), sensationalist; *Daily Telegraph* (Sydney, 440,000); *The Age* (Melbourne, 240,000), independent; *Sunday Morning Herald* (Sydney, 230,000), oldest morning newspaper (founded 1831), conservative; *The West Australian* (Perth,

230,000), conservative; *Courier Mail* (Brisbane, 220,000), conservative; *Advertiser* (Adelaide, 200,000), conservative; *The Australian* (Sydney, Adelaide, Perth, Melbourne, Townsville, Brisbane, 150,000), first national daily, independent; *Australian Financial Review* (Sydney, 80,000); *Mercury* (Hobart, 50,000), conservative; *Canberra Times* (Canberra, 40,000 daily), conservative; *Northern Territory News* (Darwin, 20,000). The leading Sunday papers are *Sunday Telegraph* (Sydney, 675,000); *Sunday Mail* (Brisbane, 580,000); *Sunday Herald* (Sydney, 550,000); *Sunday Times* (Perth, 350,000); *Sunday Mail* (Adelaide, 340,000); *Sunday Tasmanian* (Hobart, 53,000); *Sunday Territorian* (Darwin, 24,000).

News agencies. The domestic agency is the Australian Associated Press (AAP), a Reuters-affiliated international news service owned by the country's principal metropolitan dailies; in addition, most leading foreign agencies maintain bureaus at Sydney or elsewhere.

Radio and television. The federal Australian Broadcasting Authority determines and guarantees technical and programming standards for radio and television stations. Broadcasting services are provided both by private stations and by those of the Australian Broadcasting Corporation, whose status is comparable to that of the British Broadcasting Corporation. The Federation of Australian Radio Broadcasters is an association of privately owned radio stations; its television counterpart is the Federation of Australian Commercial Television Stations.

CULTURE

Cultural Indicators

Public Libraries
- Number: —
- Volumes: —
- Registered borrowers: —

Museums
- Number: 15
- Annual Attendance: 5,279,000

Cinema
- Production of Long Films: 18
- Number of Cinemas: 1,137
- Seating Capacity: 332,000
- Annual Attendance: 69 million
- Annual Attendance per capita: 3.8

STATUS OF WOMEN

Women in Australia have equal status under the law, and Australia was a pioneer in women's political rights. South Australia was the first British colony to give women the vote and the right to sit in parliament. Yet in practice, historical patterns of bias against women have contributed to their underrepresentation in government and politics. In 1998, only 24 percent of federal parliamentarians were women.

Although women's rights organizations, both public and private, exist at the federal, state, and local levels, discrimination exists in the workplace. In 1994 it was estimated that women received approximately 90 percent of wages paid to men for similar work. Women generally work at lower-paying jobs in most professions and also hold jobs most at risk from technological change. Numerous government programs aid women who are homeless or are victims of abuse. Working mothers also have access to government-operated child-care facilities.

Women

Gender Empowerment Measure: 12
Seats Held in Parliament by Women %: 20.5
Female Administrators and Managers %: 43.3
Female Professional and Technical Workers %: 25.5
Women's Share of Earned Income %: 40
Women in Government %: 24

HEALTH, FOOD, AND NUTRITION

Health

Number of Physicians: 45,800
Number of Dentists: 9,100
Number of Nurses: 1,605,000
Numberr of Pharmacists: 12,900
Population per Physician: 400
Number of Hospitals: 1,071
Hospital Beds per 10,000: 89
Hospital Bed Occupancy Rate: —
Infant Mortality Rate per 1,000 live births: 8
Maternal Mortality Rate per 100,000 live births: 9
Total Health Expenditures as % of GDP: 7.67
Health Expenditures per capita $: 1,294
HIV Infected % of adults: 0.14
Cigarette Consumption per smoker per year: 4,951
% of Smokers: Male: 29
Female: 21
Access to Safe Water %: 95

Food and Nutrition

Food Supply as % of FAO Requirements: 115
% of Consumption Expenditures on Food: 18.7
Daily Available Calories per capita: 3,068
% of Total Calories derived from: —
Cereals: 24.6
Potatoes, cassava: 3.0
Meat, poultry: 15.3
Fish: 1.0
Eggs, milk: 14.2
Fruits, vegetables: 5.5
Fats, oils: 11.9

ENVIRONMENT

Australia's size and physical isolation have given it an assemblage of plants and animals found nowhere else in the world. However, many of its unique mammals, birds, fish, and plants are endangered, primarily from a loss of natural habitat. In South Australia alone nearly 80 percent of the natural vegetation has been lost in areas cleared for agricultural purposes. It is estimated that 68 percent of the 102 species of native mammals there have become extinct or are endangered.

Key environmental issues in Australia are soil erosion and soil salinity. Erosion of the continent's limited arable land continues, caused by industrial development, urbanization, poor farming practices, and overgrazing. Soil salinity often results from the use of poor quality water. Increasing desertification and the continent's limited fresh water sources pose other environmental concerns.

The Great Barrier Reef off the northeast coast, the largest coral reef in the world, is endangered by increased shipping and its growing popularity as a tourist attraction.

Australia has joined with other nations in agreements to limit ocean pollution and protect the ozone. However, as in most of these nations as well, Australia's economic development as an industrial, urban nation has taken priority over environmental issues.

Environment

Forest Area sq km: 409,000
Average Annual Deforestation sq km: −170
Nationally Protected Areas as % of Total Land Area: 7.3
Freshwater Access cubic meters per capita: 18,772
Emissions of Organic Water Pollutants kg per day: 173,269
CO_2 Emissions per capita ton: 16.7

CHRONOLOGY

1939 Australia begins participation in World War II operations against Germany and Japan; the United States provides military aid.

1944 Robert Menzies founds the Liberal Party.

1945 World War II ends; Prime Minister Curtin dies; Joseph B. Chifley and the Labor Party come to power and strengthen relations with the United States; Australia takes part in the founding of the United Nations.

1946 An influx of postwar immigration begins, bringing 800,000 non-British Europeans to Australia by 1968.

1949 Robert Menzies becomes prime minister, a post he will hold for the next 17 years.

1950 Australia contributes troops to the UN's Korean War effort.

1951 Australia joins the United States and New Zealand in a regional security arrangement known as ANZUS; the Colombo Plan, which provides aid for Australia's neighbor countries in Southeast Asia, goes into effect, spurring immigration of Asian students to Australia.

1953 The Korean War ends and Australian troops return home.

1954 Australians enthusiastically receive the visit of Queen Elizabeth II; Australia helps to found the Southeast Asia Treaty Organization (SEATO).

1956 Television is introduced in Australia, with the Melbourne-hosted Olympics as its first broadcast.

1965 Australia sends troops to fight communism in the Vietnam War.

1966 Prime Minister Menzies steps down; his protégé Harold Holt becomes prime minister.

1967 Prime Minister Holt drowns; John Gorton, also of the Liberal Party, becomes prime minister; a referendum gives Australian Aborigines full citizenship rights; Australia becomes a full member of the Association of South East Asian Nations (ASEAN); Japan replaces Britain as Australia's main trading partner.

1971 William McMahon of the Liberal Party becomes prime minister.

1972 Gough Whitlam of the Labor Party becomes prime minister; Australia formally recognizes the People's Republic of China; troops are withdrawn from Vietnam.

1974 The Immigration Restriction Bill of 1901, known as the "White Australia" policy, is repealed, ending the racially based process for allowing entrance to Australia.

1975 A constitutional crisis erupts when the Senate blocks the financial legislation necessary to implement the programs of Prime Minister Gough Whitlam; Governor General John Kerr dismisses Whitlam and appoints Malcolm Fraser, the leader of the opposition, as interim prime minister; elections confirm Fraser, with a Liberal-Country coalition, as prime minister; Papua New Guinea becomes independent.

1976 The Aboriginal Land Rights Act awards historic lands in Northern Territory to Aboriginal claimants.

1977 SEATO dissolves.

1978 Northern Territory achieves self-government.

1983 The Labor Party returns to power under Bob Hawke.

1984 Japan surpasses the United States as the largest provider of imports to Australia.

1986 The British Parliament passes the Australia Act, eliminating the last vestiges of British authority in Australia.

1988 Australia signs a free trade agreement with New Zealand.

1990 Carmen Lawrence and Joan Kirner become Australia's first female leaders of governments.

1992 Parliament passes the Citizenship Act, which removes the oath of allegiance to the British Crown from the requirements for Australian citizenship.

1993 The Labor Party wins record fifth election victory.

1996 A coalition of the Liberal and National (formerly Country) parties under John Howard ousts Labor.

1999 Australians vote against cutting the links with the British monarchy and the establishment of a republic.

2000 Australia hosts the Olympic Games in Sydney.
2001 National elections are held on 10 November.

BIBLIOGRAPHY

Alpin, Graeme. *Australians and Their Environment*. Oxford, 1998.

Bambrick, Susan, ed. *The Cambridge Encyclopedia of Australia*. Cambridge, 1994.

Castles, Francis G., ed. *Australia Compared: People, Politics, Policies*. London, 1992.

Dollery, Brian. *Australian Local Government: Reform and Renewal*. Sydney, 1999.

Forster, Clive. *Australian Cities: Continuity and Change*. Oxford, 1996.

Kriesler, Peter, ed. *The Australian Economy*. New York, 1996.

Meredith, David, and Barrie Dyster. *Australia in the Gobal Economy*. Cambridge, 1999.

Sturman, A. P., and N. J. Tapper. *The Weather and Climate of Australia and New Zealand*. Oxford, 1996.

Uhr, John, and Gregory Uhr. *Deliberative Democracy in Australia*. Cambridge, 1998.

OFFICIAL PUBLICATIONS

Australia. *Monthly Summary of Statistics, Australia; Social Indicators* (annual); *Year Book Australia; 1996 Census of Population and Housing.*

CONTACT INFORMATION

Embassy of Australia
1601 Massachusetts Avenue NW
Washington, D.C. 20036
Phone: (202) 797-3000 Fax: (202) 797-3168

INTERNET RESOURCES

- Australian Bureau of Statistics
  http://www.abs.gov.au

AUSTRIA

BASIC FACT SHEET

OFFICIAL NAME:
Republic of Austria (Republik Österreich)

ABBREVIATION:
AS

CAPITAL:
Vienna

HEAD OF STATE:
President Thomas Klestil (from 1992)

HEAD OF GOVERNMENT:
Wolfgang Schüsgel

NATURE OF GOVERNMENT:
Federal parliamentary democracy

POPULATION:
8,080,000 (1999)

AREA:
83,583 sq km (32,376 sq mi)

ETHNIC MAJORITY:
German

LANGUAGE:
German

RELIGION:
Christian; predominantly Roman Catholic

UNIT OF CURRENCY:
Euro

NATIONAL FLAG:
White horizontal stripe between two red stripes.

NATIONAL EMBLEM:
A black eagle with a golden beak and long red tongue, a three-merlon mural crown on its head; a hammer in its right hand and a sickle in its left hand; a severed silver chain hanging from each of its hands and a shield with the national colors of red and white on bars on its breast.

NATIONAL ANTHEM:
"Land der Burge, Land am Strome" (Land of the mountains, land on the river)

NATIONAL HOLIDAYS:
October 26, National Day; all major Christian holidays

DATE OF INDEPENDENCE:
October 30, 1918

DATE OF CONSTITUTION:
October 1, 1920

GEOGRAPHICAL FEATURES

Austria is a small, landlocked alpine country in south-central Europe with an area of 83,853 sq km (32,376 sq mi). Austria's geographical importance lies as the crossroads of Europe. Austrians place the country in the exact center rather than in the south-central part of Europe. The Hahneckkogel, a peak in the province of Salzburg, is not only claimed to be the highest wooded mountain in Europe but also is said to mark the geographic center of the continent. Austria shares international borders with the Czech Republic, Germany, Hungary, Italy, Liechtenstein, Slovakia, Slovenia, and Switzerland.

Austria generally is divided topographically into the eastern Alps, the northern alpine forelands, the Bohemian Plateau, the Vienna Basin, and the eastern and southeastern lowland. Although nearly three-quarters of the country is mountainous, 17 percent is arable; 23 percent is meadow and pasture; 39 percent is forest; a little more than 1.6 percent is vineyards, orchards, and small garden plots; and about 14.5 percent consists of built-up areas and wasteland.

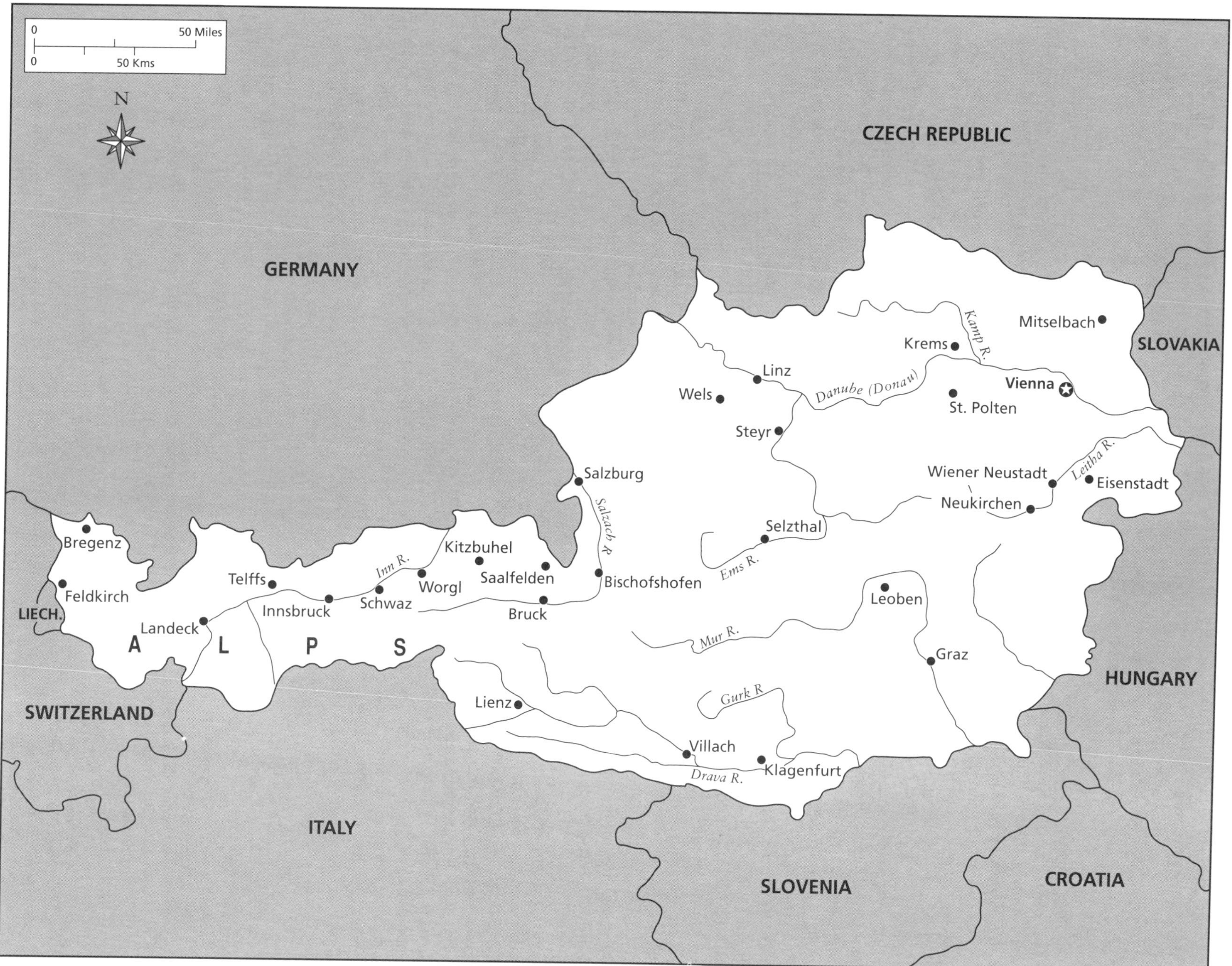
Austria
0 50 Miles
0 50 Kms
N
CZECH REPUBLIC
GERMANY
SLOVAKIA
HUNGARY
SWITZERLAND
LIECH.
ITALY
SLOVENIA
CROATIA
A L P S
Mitselbach
Krems
Kamp R.
Linz
Danube (Donau)
Vienna
Wels
St. Polten
Steyr
Salzburg
Wiener Neustadt
Leitha R.
Eisenstadt
Neukirchen
Selzthal
Salzach R
Bregenz
Kitzbuhel
Inn R.
Telffs
Saalfelden
Bischofshofen
Ems R.
Feldkirch
Worgl
Schwaz
Innsbruck
Bruck
Leoben
Landeck
Mur R.
Graz
Gurk R
Lienz
Villach
Klagenfurt
Drava R.

The eastern Alps consist of a group of mountains that begin at the Swiss border and become three ranges that fan out as they cross the country. The central range is the largest, containing the highest elevations in Austria, topped by the Grossglöckner, at 3,797 m (12,461 ft).

The northern and central ranges separate near Landeck, where the Inn River takes up its generally eastward course. Much of the northern range consists of either limestone or dolomite, like the southern range.

The northern alpine forelands are foothills of the Alps that extend between the mountains and the Danube River from the country's border north of the city of Salzburg to the Vienna Basin. Nearly all of the highlands northwest of Vienna and north of the Danube River form part of the Bohemian massif rather than the alpine system. They are referred to as the Bohemian Plateau, as they form a ring around the Bohemian portion of the Czech Republic. The northern alpine forelands ultimately terminate in the foothills bordering the Vienna Basin. The basin itself is not completely flat, but the terrain is gentle. The basin extends into the Leitha River valley in a southeasterly direction toward the Semmering Pass and is separated from the Neusiedler See by the Leitha Mountains.

Because Austria contains a greater part of the eastern Alps, precipitation drains in all directions with all except a minute fraction of it eventually reaching the Danube River.

The Danube is Austria's grand river. The major alpine tributaries of the Danube—including the Inn River, which joins the Danube near the German border—flow eastward, through central Austria. To the east of the Inn are the Salzach and the Enns. The Danube bisects Lower Austria and receives a large number of lesser streams. To the south, the Leitha flows northeast, draining the area from the Semmering Pass to the Hungarian border. From the other side of the Semmering Pass the Murz drains to the south, joining the Danube farther downstream.

Geography

Area sq km: 83,853 sq mi 32,376
World Rank: 115th
Land Boundaries, km: Czech Republic 362; Germany 784; Hungary 366; Italy 430; Liechtenstein 35; Slovakia 9; Slovenia 330; Switzerland 164
Coastline, km: 0
Elevation Extremes meters
Lowest: Neusiedler Sea 115
Highest: Grossglöckner 3,797
Land Use % Arable land: 17
Permanent Crops: 1
Permanent Pastures: 23
Forest and Woodland: 39
Other: 20

Population of Principal Cities (1991)

Graz	237,810
Innsbruck	118,112
Linz	203,044
Salzburg	143,978
Vienna	1,560,471

CLIMATE AND WEATHER

Austria's weather is determined by three systems—the North Atlantic maritime, the Mediterranean, and the continental—but each dominates in a particular section of the country. The weather of the Danube valley and the northern alpine forelands is mostly from the North Atlantic maritime system. The low-pressure air masses that move with relative rapidity eastward across northern Europe affect climatic activity in a broad way, but weather is determined largely by local factors in the valleys and basins. In deep valleys without air circulation, temperature inversions occur, while sunbathed mountaintops enjoy clean, crisp air and warmer temperatures. The phenomenon known as foehn (warm winds) is common, especially in the valleys on the northern slopes of the mountain ranges. On the southern slopes foehn occur more frequently in winter and spring, while on the northern slopes they occur more frequently in spring and autumn. These strong, hot, dry, and dusty winds cause much discomfort to people and also cause avalanches.

Vienna has an average annual temperature of just under 10°C (50°F). In January, the coldest month, the average is about −2°C (28°F), and in July, the warmest month, 20°C (68°F). Vienna's temperatures are slightly higher than the country's average, but mean annual temperatures vary surprisingly little in low-elevation areas all over the country—less than 4°F in a typical year. At about 2,743 m (9,000 ft), average annual temperatures drop to the freezing point, but clear air and bright sunshine make life tolerable at these elevations.

Precipitation varies considerably more than average temperatures—from about 457 mm (18 in) annually in easternmost Burgenland to 2,032 mm (80 in) or more in mountain spots. Vienna receives about 610 mm (24 in) annually, the southeastern alpine foothills about 1,016 mm (40 in), and Salzburg and the northern alpine forelands about 889 to 1,016 mm (35 to 40 in). Much winter precipitation occurs as snow. Annual snowfalls average from 508 to 1,016 mm (20 to 40 in) in the east, 2,032 mm (80 in) in the low Alps, and 10,160 mm (400 in) or more at high elevations.

Climate and Weather

Mean Temperature
Vienna 50°F (January 28°F, July 68°F)
Average Rainfall

Burgenland 80 in
Vienna 24 in
Southeastern Alpine Foothills 40 in
Salzburg and the Northern Alpine Footfills 35 to 40 in
Snowfall 20 to 40 in (East), 80 in (Low Alps) 400 in (Higher elevations)

POPULATION

Population Indicators

Total Population: 1999 8,080,000
World Rank: 87th
Density per sq mi: 249.6 per sq km 96.4
% of annual growth (1994–99): 0.1
Male %: 48.2
Female %: 51.8
Urban %: 64.5
Age Distribution: % 0–14: 17.4
15–29: 23.7
30–44: 21.6
45–59: 17.2
60–74: 13.4
75 and over: 6.7
Population 2020: 8,076,000
Birth Rate per 1,000: 10.8
Death Rate per 1,000: 9.9
Population Doubling Time (years): —
Infant Mortality Rate per 1,000 live births: 5.0
Rate of Natural Increase per 1,000: 0.9
Total Fertility Rate: 1.5
Expectation of Life (years): Males 73.5
Females 80.1
Marriage Rate per 1,000: 5.1
Divorce Rate per 1,000: 2.2
Total Number of Households: 3,131,000
Average Size of Households: 2.5
% of Illegitimate Children: 24.8
Induced Abortions: —
Rate per 100 live births: —

ETHNIC COMPOSITION

Virtually all Austrians consider themselves German. Minority groups excluding the over 200,000 guest workers, account for only 2 percent of the total population and are made up of Croatians, Slovenians, Hungarians, Czechs, and Slovaks. The rights of the Slovene and Croat minorities are guaranteed by the Austrian State Treaty of 1955. They are entitled to complete equality as Austrian citizens, education in their own language, their own cultural and social organizations, and bilingual signs.

LANGUAGES

Austrians are 92 percent German-speaking. All are literate and, by law, receive at least nine years of formal education.

Austria's apparent linguistic unity belies its actual diversity. The standard German, sometimes called "school German," is the same as that of Germany, although the Austrian speech is softer. The majority of Austrians use a Bavarian dialect at home. Alemannic German is spoken in Vorarlberg, Frankish German in Lower Austria, and polyglot German in Vienna. In Tirol German is mixed with Latin words and in eastern areas with Slavic words.

The different dialects also are associated with class distinctions. The Viennese speak a Slavicized dialect that was spoken in the days of the Habsburg empire. The varieties of Austrian German reflect the country's mixed ethnic heritage, drawn from diverse elements such as the Avars, Illyrians, Romans, Teutons, Huns, Bayuvarians, and Franks. Dialectal differences are the sole vestiges of the various groups that held sway at various times over what is present-day Austria.

Principal Languages and Their Speakers

Czech	19,000
German	7,434,000
Hungarian	34,000
Polish	19,000
Romanian	17,000
Serbo-Croatian	175,000
Slovene	30,000
Turkish	123,000
Other	229,000

RELIGIONS

Statistically, Austria is a Roman Catholic country, with an estimated 75 percent professing the Catholic faith. Throughout the country, Catholicism is evident in cathedrals and churches; crucifixes at crossroads; and in monasteries, convents, and wayside shrines. Throughout the year, the many religious holidays are marked by festivals, processions, pageants, and ceremonies.

The real influence of the Catholic Church on the lives of Austrians has been steadily decreasing in this century. More than 20,000 Austrians withdraw annually from church membership, and only one-third of baptized Catholics (15 percent in Vienna) participate in Sunday Mass. Only 10 percent belong to Catholic organizations, such as Katholische Aktion. The number of young people following a calling to the priesthood or a religious order also has been decreasing. The number of priests has declined from one for 1,347 Catholics in 1945 to one for 1,700 Catholics in 1985.

The Protestant percentage of the population has doubled since the end of World War II to more than 6 percent, primarily as a result of immigration. The principal Protestant body is the Evangelical Church, which is a loose union of the Helvetian Reformed and Augsburg Lutheran churches. Protestants are strongest in the alpine regions and in Burgenland. Only two other Protestant groups are officially recognized: the Moravians and the Methodists. The Old Catholic Church, founded in 1871 as a protest movement against the doctrine of papal infallibility, was given legal recognition in 1877. Eastern Orthodoxy is represented by Armenian, Bulgarian, Greek, Romanian, Russian, and Serbian Orthodox churches.

Of the non-Christian religions, Judaism is the oldest. On the other hand, Islam has increased in numbers, most of whose adherents are guest workers from Turkey and Yugoslavia.

Religious Affiliations

Roman Catholic	6,060,000
Protestant (mostly Lutheran)	430,000
Atheist and nonreligious	700,000
Other	890,000

HISTORICAL BACKGROUND

At the beginning of the Christian era, the Romans organized the region that is present-day Austria into a number of provinces, including Noricum, Pannonia, and Ilyria, and founded its major urban settlements: Vindobona (Vienna), Juvavum (Salzburg), Valdidena (Innsbruck), and Brigantim (Bregenz). After the fall of the Roman Empire Austria became in the ninth century a province of Charlemagne's empire and two centuries later, under the name Österreich, or Kingdom of the East, was joined to the Holy Roman Empire.

Austria's rise to greatness began in 1282 when Rudolf von Habsburg (Rudolf I, German emperor) gave Austria (Upper and Lower Austria, Styria, Carinthia, and Carniola) to his sons Albrecht and Rudolf, launching a dynastic rule that lasted until 1918. The zenith of Habsburg power came in the 1500s under Charles V (Charles I of Spain, the grandson of Emperor Maximilian I on the agnate side and King Ferdinand and Queen Isabella of Spain on the enate side), whose dominions included Austria, Spain, the Netherlands, and Spanish America. Charles gave Austria to his brother Ferdinand, who had already been elected king of Hungary and Bohemia in 1526. When the last Habsburg king of Spain died in 1700, France and Austria both claimed the throne. In the ensuing War of the Spanish Succession (1701–14), Austria lost Spain but retained control of the Spanish Netherlands, Naples, Milan, and Sardinia. In the War of the Polish Succession (1733–35) Austria lost Naples and Sicily. The death of Charles VI in 1740 led to the War of the Austrian Succession (1740–48), at the end of which Maria Theresa was recognized as ruler. Both she and her son Joseph II (1780–90) instituted a number of major reforms, including the abolition of serfdom and the extension of religious freedom, and their reigns spanned the golden age of the Austrian cultural renaissance.

The rise of Napoleon signaled the end of Austria's power and the slow dismemberment of its empire. In 1797 France took Belgium and Milan and in 1805 Austria lost Venice, the Tyrol, and land in Dalmatia to Napoleon. The Congress of Vienna (1814–15) awarded Lombardy, Venetia, Istria, and Dalmatia to Austria but denied the return of former Austrian possessions in Baden and the Netherlands.

From 1815 to 1848 Austria was dominated by Prince Klemens von Metternich, one of the most famous European statesmen of the age. His extremely repressive rule was ended by revolutions that broke out in 1848 in Hungary, Bohemia, and in Vienna itself. Metternich resigned and fled to London. Emperor Ferdinand I abdicated the Austrian crown in favor of Francis Joseph I, his 18-year old nephew, who held the throne for the next 68 years until his death in 1916. Although Francis Joseph I set up a strong central government, the Habsburg empire continued to shrink. In 1859 French and Sardinian troops defeated the Austrians in Italy, thus ending their rule in the peninsula. In 1866 Austria lost its influence in Germany after being defeated in the Seven Weeks' War. In 1867 the Magyars revolted and forced the Habsburgs to concede a separate Kingdom of Hungary under the Austrian crown. Enfeebled by these losses, the empire was ripe for the final coup de grace, which came on June 28, 1914, when Archduke Francis Ferdinand, heir to the Austrian throne, was assassinated in Sarajevo by Serbian nationalists. The event set off World War I, in which Austria was joined by Germany, an ally since 1879.

Austria emerged from World War I defeated and impoverished with neither the empire nor the Habsburg dynasty. In 1918 Austria was proclaimed a republic confined to its German-speaking provinces. Like Germany, Austria faced both political and economic chaos for the next 20 years. The two major parties, the Christian Socialist Party and the Social Democratic Party, were almost equal in strength, and both had private armies. A third group, the Austrian Nazi Party, advocated union with Germany; such a union was prohibited by the Treaty of Versailles and the Treaty of Saint-Germain. The democratic constitution of 1920 was suspended in 1933 when Chancellor Engelbert Dollfuss dissolved the Austrian parliament and began to rule by decree. In 1934, following civil strife, Dollfuss established Austria as a corporate state along fascist lines. A few months later, Dollfuss was assassinated by the Nazis in a coup, and Kurt von Schuschnigg succeeded to the leadership. Schuschnigg struggled for the next four years to keep Austria independent, but in 1938 German troops entered the country and annexed it to the Third Reich. Eighteen months later, Austria entered World War II as part of the Axis powers.

Allied troops entered Vienna in 1945 and the country was divided, like Germany, into U.S., British, French, and Soviet zones. Although the Austrians were permitted to set up a provisional central government, the exercise of

Austrian sovereignty was limited to the four occupying powers under a 1946 agreement.

The provisional government was established under the Social Democrat Karl Renner. Following a general election in November 1945, Leopold Figl became chancellor of a coalition government with the Austrian People's Party (ÖVP) and the Austrian Social Democratic Party (SPÖ) as partners. In 1955, the Austrian State Treaty formally ended the occupation and declared Austria's independence. During the same year Austria joined the United Nations.

The postwar coalition government endured until 1966 when the ÖVP won a legislative majority. Thereafter a succession of ÖVP and SPÖ governments held power. The 1970s were dominated by SPÖ chancellor Bruno Kreisky. The 1980s saw the rise of the far-right Freedom Party of Austria (FPÖ) under Jörg Haidar. To keep the FPÖ out of office ÖVP and SPÖ agreed to a coalition under Franz Vranitzky. Austria became an EU member in 1995. In the first direct election for the European parliament in 1995 the SPÖ finished second to the ÖVP while the FPÖ secured a high 27.6 percent. This led to Vranitzky's resignation in 1997 and the election of Viktor Klima as chancellor. In legislative elections in 1999 the FPÖ won 27 percent of the vote, securing an equal number of parliamentary seats as the ÖVP. This time, however, talks between the ÖVP and the SPÖ were unsuccessful prompting the ÖVP to form a coalition government with the FPÖ, with Wolfgang Schüssel as chancellor. Following international protest, Haidar resigned as leader of the FPÖ in 2000.

CONSTITUTION

Austrian constitutional development has undergone many changes. After the demise of the Habsburg monarchy in 1918, a new constitution was proclaimed in 1920, establishing a federal democratic republic. The so-called First Republic collapsed in the face of fascism in 1934. The Second Republic was recreated on an identical basis in 1945.

The constitution of 1920 provides for three separate branches of government: executive, legislative, and judicial. The federal president, as the head of state, is directly elected by the people. He in turn appoints the chancellor, who is the head of government. The president names the cabinet, which usually includes the vice chancellor, on the recommendation of the chancellor. These officials, plus state secretaries, constitute the executive branch.

The constitution of 1920 delegates powers not specifically assigned to the federal government to the nine provinces (Länder; sing. Land). Each of the provinces has a constitution and an elected provincial diet (Landtag). Below the provinces are local communities (Gemeinden).

The constitution of 1920 has been amended several times. In 1929 the federal president's powers were enhanced by granting him the formal power to appoint and dismiss the chancellor, and, on the chancellor's recommendation, the cabinet. It also provided for the popular election of the president.

According to the constitution, federal and provincial legislative and administrative authority is apportioned four ways. Such matters as foreign affairs, justice, finance, civil and criminal law, public peace and order, and security are federal concerns. Some laws are enacted at the federal level but are administered by provincial authorities, including those on elections, highway, police, and housing. Other laws are made and administered at the provincial level but under federal guidelines, such as social welfare and land reform. Matters not specifically assigned to federal control are reserved for the provinces, including municipal affairs, buildings, theaters, fire control, and tourism.

The constitution does not include a bill of rights as such, but it does guarantee equality before the law and prohibits discrimination of any kind.

Constitutional amendments may be made through laws designated constitutional laws or through constitutional provisions if the amendment is part of another law. They require a two-thirds majority vote in the Nationalrat, with at least half of the members present. Constitutional laws or provisions are accompanied by a national referendum only if requested by one-third of the deputies of either the Nationalrat or the Bundesrat.

In addition to the constitution, two laws—a constitutional law and a treaty—are particularly important in Austria's constitutional development. The first is the Federal Constitutional Law on the Neutrality of Austria of 1955; the second is the Austrian State Treaty, signed by the four occupying powers and Austria in 1955.

Since 1951 the president of Austria has been elected by popular vote for a six-year term, limited to two consecutive terms. Members of reigning or formerly reigning dynasties are barred from running for election. Presidential candidates are nominated by parties, and the winner must poll over 50 percent of the vote. If no candidate succeeds on the first ballot, a runoff election is held between the two candidates receiving the highest number of votes.

Presidential duties include convoking, proroguing, and dissolving the Nationalrat; appointing the chancellor and, on his recommendation, the cabinet; signing treaties; and granting reprieves and pardons. Although the president cannot veto legislation, he is empowered to reject a cabinet proposal or delay enactment of a bill. The official acts of the president generally require the countersignature of the chancellor or the concerned minister. During national emergencies when the Nationalrat is not in session, the president may issue ordinances countersigned by the cabinet. The president may be recalled or dismissed from office by popular referendum and by a two-thirds vote of the Bundesversammlung

(Federal Assembly). There is no office of vice president; hence new elections are held if the presidency is vacated for any reason.

The chancellor is appointed or dismissed by the federal president but is responsible to the Nationalrat and is the leader of the majority party. Cabinet ministers, also appointed by the president, are generally but not necessarily members of the Nationalrat. Ministers can participate in sessions of either house. Committee meetings also are open to ministers, with the exception of the Main Committee, where they must be specifically invited.

State secretaries are appointed and leave office in the same manner as ministers. They aid ministers in parliamentary business and are nonvoting participants in cabinet sessions.

The basic features of the Austrian constitution are those of Western democracies: separation of powers, federalism, local autonomy, and liberalism. All the institutions of representative parliamentary democracy are present and place basic human rights over those of the state. However, there are countervailing tendencies within the political process, especially from the entrenched bureaucracy, corporatist interest groups, powerful political parties, and the growing power of the interventionist welfare state.

In addition to the parliamentary opposition, there are a number of constitutional checks on federal authority. These include the Constitutional Court and the administrative courts (which are more fully described in the Legal System section); the Central Auditing Authority; and the people's lawyer, the Austrian equivalent of the ombudsman.

LOCAL GOVERNMENT

Each of the nine provinces has its own constitution and an elected Landtag (provincial legislature). The number of delegates in the Landtag varies according to the population. A Landtag may be dissolved by the president with the consent of the Bundesrat.

A Landtag elects an executive composed of a governor (Landeshauptmann) and councillors (Landesrate). If there is no federal agency in the province, the governor also acts as the federal representative. Article 15(1) of the constitution states that all matters not expressly designated as under federal authority lie within provincial jurisdiction. These include primary education, housing, health, and conservation. In cases where there is a dispute regarding jurisdiction, the Constitutional Court has ultimate authority. Interprovincial policies are coordinated by compacts and treaties.

Provinces are divided into districts (Bezirke) and local communities (Gemeinden). Each district is headed by a district commissioner (Bezirkshauptmann), usually a career civil servant who is appointed by the provincial governor. Local communities are self-governing, each with a popularly elected community council (Gemeinderat) chosen by proportional representation on the basis of political party strength. Members serve a five- or six-year term. Community council meetings are presided over by a mayor (Burgermeister) elected by the council. Local communities with a population of 20,000 or more have a charter. Each local community has a board whose members are elected on the basis of proportional representation by the community council. The actual authority of these bodies is quite limited because federal and provincial regulations are so pervasive and their supervision and controls so extensive.

Local Government

Principal administrative divisions, capitals, area, population

Area and population

States	Capitals	area sq mi	area sq km	population 1998 estimate
Burgenland	Eisenstadt	1,531	3,966	279,752
Carinthia	Klagenfurt	3,681	9,533	564,431
Niederösterreich	Sankt Pölten	7,403	19,174	1,534,001
Oberösterreich	Linz	4,626	11,980	1,373,470
Salzburg	Salzburg	2,762	7,154	513,853
Steiermark	Graz	6,327	16,388	1,204,904
Tirol	Innsbruck	4,883	12,647	661,901
Vorarlberg	Bregenz	1,004	2,601	345,272
Wien (Vienna)	—	160	415	1,609,631
TOTAL		32,378	83,858	8,087,215

PARLIAMENT

The Austrian Bundesversammlung (Federal Assembly; parliament) is comprised of two chambers: the upper house (Bundesrat) and the lower house (Nationalrat).

The Bundesrat consists of 63 delegates elected for terms varying from four to six years by the provincial legislatures. Representation reflects party strength in the provincial legislatures. At least one seat must be given to the second largest party in each legislature.

The Bundesrat, like the upper houses in many other countries, is the less powerful of the two chambers. Its authority is only that of a delaying veto, which can be overridden by the Nationalrat.

The Nationalrat consists of 183 members elected by universal suffrage from nine electoral districts for minimum terms of four years. Two sessions are convoked annually by the federal president, in spring and autumn. Special sessions may be called if requested by the cabinet, by one-third of the Nationalrat, or by one-third of the Bundesrat. Deputies elect a president and second and third presidents from among their members. The president and the third president usually belong to the majority party, while the second president usually belongs to the opposition party. The three presidents preside over plenary sessions in two-hour shifts and join with the chairmen of the parliamentary groups to form a conference that directs Nationalrat activities and decides the time and agenda of plenary sessions and committees.

Universal male suffrage has been in force in Austria since 1907, but women did not gain full voting rights until after 1917. Voting is compulsory for citizens 21 or over. All elections are supervised by electoral boards on which political parties are represented on the basis of their performance in the previous elections.

Party lists are submitted for the Nationalrat elections. Each voter can list as a preferred choice, thereby increasing his chances for election. Turnout usually is heavy; it has not fallen below 92 percent since 1945.

POLITICAL PARTIES

The Austrian political party system has been described as the "two-and-a-half system," with two major parties, the Austrian People's Party (ÖVP) and the Socialist Party of Austria (SPÖ), and a third party in the Freedom Party of Austria (FPÖ). The primary characteristics of the system are continuity and concentration: continuity reflecting the historical roots of the major groups in the 19th century, and concentration reflecting the limited ideological spectrum covered by these parties.

The Austrian People's Party (Österreichische Volkspartei, ÖVP) was founded in 1945 as the successor to the pre–World War II Christian Social Party. Its overall policies support a free-market economy with some government intervention, low taxes, a balanced budget, and low wage increases. Although it advocates free enterprise, it favors some nationalization programs and workers' profit-sharing.

The Socialist Party of Austria (Sozialistische Partei Österreichs, SPÖ) was founded in 1945 as the successor to the Social Democratic Party, established in 1888. The SPÖ retains very little of its predecessor's dogmatic Marxism; after the end of World War II it became pragmatic and reformist, as evidenced by its Grand Coalition government alliance with the ÖVP from 1945 to 1966.

Led by moderates such as Karl Renner and Adolf Scharf, each of whom eventually served as federal president, the SPÖ program stressed humane and liberal policies such as full employment, a reduced work week, electoral reform, lower food prices, and increased government spending on social welfare. The party also softened its former anticlerical position to become acceptable to Catholics and even supported state subsidies to Catholic schools. A new party program adopted in 1958 claimed the SPÖ was the party of "all those who work for a living" and stated the party's opposition to both communism and fascism.

The Freedom Party of Austria (Freiheitliche Partei Österreichs, FPÖ) was founded in 1955 by a former Nazi, Anton Reinthaller, and represents the nationalist-liberal camp in Austrian politics. It is an offshoot of the League of Independents, a postwar party that broke up in 1955 over internal disagreements.The party is composed of right-wing nationalists and moderate liberals, between whom there are frequent factional disputes. It contested the presidential election for the first time in 1980, when it won 17 percent of the vote. Although a weak opposition party, it was able to parlay its Nationalrat votes as a power broker and participate in the government in 1983.

The FPÖ is a defender of pan-German interests and opposes all forms of non-German, especially Slavic, influences. It is antagonistic to guest workers, who are seen as threats to Austria's Germanness. It is an advocate of free enterprise but has supported social reforms, including granting workers a voice in management. It has endorsed cooperation with Western European countries, particularly the European Union. It is strongly anticlerical, opposing Catholicism as a constraint on individual liberty.

The United Greens of Austria, an ecological party, was founded in 1982 by Professor Alexander Tollman and Alois Englander. Another ecological party is the Alternative List of Austria, also founded in 1982. These two parties won 19 percent and 1.2 percent, respectively, of the Nationalrat vote in 1983.

The National Democratic Party, founded in 1966, is a radical right-wing group that advocates reintroduction of the death penalty, abolition of abortion, and withdrawal of civil rights from conscientious objectors. It is violently anticommunist and anti-Slav and opposed to the presence of guest workers.

Political Parties

Austrian Social Democratic Party, 1889
Austrian People's Party, 1945, formerly the Christian Social Party
Freedom Party of Austria, 1956
Liberal Forum, 1993
Green Alternative, 1987
United Greens, 1982
Austrian Communist Party, 1918
Economy Party, 1992

Political Parties: Strength in Parliament Most Recent Elections

Federal Council (Bundesrat). The upper chamber currently consists of 64 members representing each of the provinces on the basis of population, but with each province having at least three representatives. Chosen by provincial assemblies in proportion to party representation, members serve for terms ranging from five to six years, depending on the life of the particular assembly.The presidency of the council rotates among the nine provinces for a six-month term. In the present council, the Austrian People's Party holds 26 seats; the Austrian Social Democratic Party, 24; and the Freedom Movement, 14.

National Council (Nationalrat). The lower chamber consists of 183 members elected by universal suffrage from 25 electoral districts for maximum terms of four years.At the most recent election of October 3, 1999, the Austrian Social Democratic Party won 65 seats; the Austrian People's Party, 52; Freedom Party of Austria, 52; and the Greens, 14.The next election was scheduled for all 2003.

LEGAL SYSTEM

Austrian law belongs to the system of European continental law, which has its basis in Roman law. In this system, legal codes play an important role. Austrian civil law is based largely on an 1812 civil code and its amendments, especially those introduced by the Socialist government from 1970 to 1980. The most important of these amendments relate to family law, consumer law, and legal procedure.

The court system is independent of the executive and the legislature. Judges, although administratively subject to the Ministry of Justice, are not bound by instructions from the executive, and they cannot be dismissed or transferred except in accordance with procedures established by law. Judges are chosen by the federal president or the cabinet from lists submitted by the judiciary.

The judicial hierarchy consists of the following courts:

Constitutional Court (Verfassungsgerichtshof)
Administrative Court (Verwaltungsgerichtshof)
Supreme Court (Obserster Gerichtshof)
Appeals courts (Oberlandesgerichte)
Provincial courts (Kreisgericht or Landesgericht)
District courts (Bezirksgericht)

Cases outside the jurisdiction of these courts are heard in special courts.

The Constitutional Court decides the constitutionality of laws and decrees passed at the federal, provincial, and local levels, and hears cases involving jurisdictional conflicts between the federal government and the provinces and between or among provinces. Individuals can present cases to the court if they believe that the decision of an administrative agency violated their constitutional rights. Monetary claims against the state as well as cases regarding disputed elections are also brought before this court. In addition, the court decides impeachment of the federal president and charges of illegality against members of the federal government and provincial governments.

The highest ordinary court (distinct from military or other special courts) is the Supreme Court, which is the court of last resort for all civil and criminal cases. Justices hear cases in five-person panels. Four appellate courts, in Vienna, Graz, Linz, and Innsbruck, are courts of second instance for civil and criminal cases and final appellate courts for district court cases. Usually a three-judge panel hears cases. On the lower level are 18 provincial and district courts. Provincial courts serve as courts of first instance for civil and criminal cases carrying penalties of up to 10 years' imprisonment and as appellate courts for some cases from district courts.

District courts hear minor cases, such as misdemeanors and guardianship, adoption, paternity, probate, registry of lands, and boundary disputes. Juries, usually consisting of eight persons, are employed in criminal cases. Certain criminal cases are subject to a hearing by two lay assessors and a judge.

LAW ENFORCEMENT

Law Enforcement

Offenses reported to the police per 100,000: 6,314
- Murder: 2.5
- Assault: 2.5
- Burglary: 1128.2
- Automobile Theft: 31.8
- Population per Police officer: 470

Death Penalty: Abolished 1968

HUMAN RIGHTS

Austria is a constitutional parliamentary democracy in which most basic human rights are guaranteed and respected in practice.

Although arbitrary detention is constitutionally prohibited, the law provides for investigative, pretrial, or preventive detention for up to 48 hours. The investigative judge may authorize continued detention before trial for up to two years.

The human rights of Austria's minorities are fully respected. However, the Slovenes are concerned about government efforts to end teaching of the Slovenian language in local elementary schools attended by them.

Austria plays a major role in monitoring human rights issues in Eastern Europe. Both Amnesty International and the Bruno Kreisky Foundation are active in this regard.

FOREIGN POLICY

The Austrian State Treaty of 1955 ended the four-power occupation of Austria, reestablished the country as a sovereign republic, and prohibited any union with Germany. During the same year the Federal Assembly approved a constitutional amendment declaring Austria's permanent neutrality, rejecting military alliances, and banning the establishment of foreign military bases on national soil. Austria formally submitted an application to join the European Community in 1989, and accession to the European Union was endorsed by the voters in a referendum by 66.4 percent. In 1995 Austria joined NATO's Partnership for Peace and signed the Schengen Accord providing for free movement between EU states.

DEFENSE

The Austrian military establishment is relatively small, and its forces are lightly armed and organized into small basic units. The Austrian State Treaty of 1955 placed limitations on armaments. For example, it prohibited weapons of mass destruction and guided missiles. Also in 1955, the Nationalrat enacted a constitutional law on Austrian neutrality that prohibits membership in military alliances but permits participation in peacekeeping efforts outside the country, such as in Cyprus. There are no foreign military bases in Austria.

Legislation in 1962 separated national defense into regular military, civil defense, economic, and psychological sectors. The president is the supreme commander of the Bundesheer (Defense Forces), but operational control is vested in the minister of defense. The four sectors are responsible to the National Defense Council, presided over by the minister of defense.

Conscription is compulsory under the Armed Forces Law of 1955. The period of service is six months under a revised law of 1971.

Austria has only a limited armaments industry, and most of the military hardware is imported. The country does not receive military aid.

Observers rate the conditions of military service and the morale reasonably good, even though military pay is low by West European standards, and a lack of mission and the poor quality of material reduce the sense of purpose among all ranks. The military budget is austere, allowing little room for sophisticated weaponry. Austrian troops have not engaged in military action since World War II.

Military Indicators

Total Active Duty Personnel: 45,500
Military Manpower per 1,000: 56
Military Expenditures $ million: 2,106
- as % of GNP: 0.9
- per capita $: 264
- as % of central government expenditures : 2.2

Arms Imports $million: 120
Arms Exports $million: 0

ECONOMY

Austria, with its well-developed market economy and high standard of living, is closely tied to other EU economies, especially Germany's. Membership in the EU has drawn an influx of foreign investors attracted by Austria's access to the single European market. Through privatization efforts, the 1996–98 budget consolidation programs, and austerity measures, Austria has brought its total public sector deficit down to 2.1 percent of gross domestic product (GDP) in 1999 and public debt—at 63.1 percent of GDP in 1998—more or less in line with the 60 percent of GDP required by the European Market Union's Maastricht criteria. Cuts mainly have affected the civil service and Austria's generous social benefit system, the two major causes of the government's deficit. To meet increased competition from both EU and central European countries, Austria will need to emphasize knowledge-based sectors of the economy and deregulate the service sector. Growth is remained at about 3 percent in 2001.

Principal Economic Indicators

Gross National Product $: 225.373 billion
GNP per capita $: 27,920
GNP Average Annual Growth Rate (1990–97) %: 1.1
GNP per capita Average Annual Growth Rate (1990–97) %: 0.5
Origin of Gross Domestic Product %
- Agriculture: 2
- Mining: —
- Manufacturing: 24
- Construction: 8
- Public Utilities: 3
- Transportation and Communications: 6
- Trade: 16
- Financial Services: 19
- Other Services: 5
- Government: 14

Gross Domestic Product by Type of Expenditure %
- Private Consumption: 55
- Government Consumption: 19
- Gross Domestic Investment: 27
- Foreign Trade: Exports: 37
  Imports: −37

% of Income Received by Poorest 20%: 4.0
% of Income Received by Richest 10%: 28.7

Price and earnings indexes (1995 = 100)

	1993	1994	1995	1996	1997	1998	1999
Consumer price index	95.0	97.8	100.0	101.8	103.2	104.1	104.6
Earnings index	93.4	96.7	100.0	102.4	104.2	—	—

Finance

National Currency: Austrian Schilling (AS)
Exchange Rate: $1 = AS 12.776
Money Supply Stock in National Currency billion: 401.9
M1 per capita: 49,800
Central Bank Discount Rate %: 2.50
Total External Debt $million: 29,400
Debt Service Ratio %: —

Balance of Payments $million: −4,996
International Reserves SDRs million: 15,221
Ratio of External Debt to Total Reserves: —
Average Annual Rate of Inflation/Consumer Price Index Growth Rate %: 1.3

Official Development Assistance

Donor ODA $million: 480
- as % of GNP: 0.2
- per capita $ 59.40
- Foreign Direct Investment $million: 6,034

Central Government Revenues and Expenditures

Fiscal Year: Calendar Year

Revenues $million: 53,600
Expenditures $million: 61,600
Budget Deficit $million: 8,000
Tax Revenues as % of GDP: 34.8
Highest Tax Bracket %
- Individual: 50
- Corporate: 34

Employment and Labor

Economically Active Population: 3,881,000
Female Participation Rate %: 42.8
Activity Rate %: 48.3
Labor by Sector: %
- Agriculture, Forestry, Fishing: 7
- Manufacturing, Mining: 23.1
- Construction: 9.6
- Transportation and Communications: 6.5
- Trade, Hotels, and Restaurants: 20.9
- Finance, Insurance, Real Estate: 9.1
- Public Administration, Defense: —
- Services: 23.5

Unemployment %: 7.1

Agriculture

Agriculture's Share of GDP %: 2
Average Annual Rate of Growth (1965–98) %: 0.8
Number of Farms 000: 267
Average Size of Farm ha: 26.4
Number of Tractors per 1,000 hectares: 242
Irrigation, % of Farms having: 0.3
Artificial Fertilizer kg/hectare: 201
Total Farmland as % of land area: 91.4
Livestock: Cattle 000: 2,198
- Sheep 000: 384
- Hogs 000: 3,680
- Chickens 000: 13,950

Forests: Production of Roundwood (000 cubic meters): 14,405
Fisheries: Total Catch tons 000: 4.6

Mining

% of GDP: 0.4
Value of Mineral Production $million: 515.1

Manufacturing

Value Added $million: 33,371
Industrial Production Growth Rate %: 1

Energy

Commercial Energy Production metric tons of oil equivalent 000: 8,007
Commercial Energy Consumption metric tons of oil equivalent 000: 27,761
Commercial Energy Consumption per capita kg: 3,439
Average Annual Growth Rate 1980–97 %: 0.9
Net Energy Imports % of use: 71
Electricity Installed Capacity kW 000: 17,440
  Production kW-hr million: 56,587
Coal Reserves tons million: 31
  Production tons 000: 1,297
Natural Gas Proven Reserves cubic meters billion: 22
  Production cubic meters million: 1,475
Crude Petroleum Reserves barrels million: 76
  Production barrels million: 8
  Consumption barrels million: 61
  Refinery Capacity barrels per day 000: 210
Pipelines Length km: 725

Foreign Trade

Imports $million: 65,662.5
Exports $million: 57,141.5
Export Volume % Annual Growth Rate (1990–97): —
Import Volume % Annual Growth Rate (1990–97): —

Balance of trade (current prices)

	1993	1994	1995	1996	1997	1998
$ 000,000,000	−97.7	−116.4	−88.0	−100.6	−75.3	−67.4
% of total	9.5%	10.2%	7.1%	7.6%	5.0%	4.2%

Major Trading Partners

	Imports	Exports
European Union %	75.5	58.6
United States %	3.1	2.8
Eastern Europe %	6.4	11.1
Japan %	1.7	1.2
Others %	13.3	26.2

Transportation

Roads Total Length mi: 80,792 km 130,023
Paved %: 100
Automobiles: 3,593,588
Trucks and Buses: 300,042
Persons per vehicle: 2.1
Railroad; Track Length mi: 3,524 km 5,672
Passenger-mi million: 6,509
Freight-mi million: 9,526
Merchant Marine: No. of Vessels: 26
  Total Deadweight Tonnage 000: 208.5
  International Cargo Loaded tons 000: 1,311
  International Cargo Off-loaded tons 000: 5,122
Airports with Scheduled Flights: 6
Traffic: Passenger-mi million: 4,701
  Freight-mi million: 120.3
Length of Canals mi: 277 km 446

Tourism

Number of Tourists to 000: 17,352
Number of Tourists from 000: 13,263
Tourist Receipts $million: 14,618
Tourist Expenditures $million: 11,687

Communications

Telephones 000: 3,749
Cost of Local Calls 3 mins $0.19
Cellular Telephones 000: 384
Fax Machines 000: 285
Personal Computers 000: 1,000
Internet Hosts per million persons: 6,623
Mail: Post Offices: 2,634
  Pieces of Mail Handled million: 3,627
  Pieces of Mail Handled per person: 425

EDUCATION

Since 1962, compulsory education has lasted for nine years (ages six to 15 and grades one through nine). The elementary school consists of a four-year lower school and a four-year Hauptschule (high school). The latter also functions as the lower level of the eight-year secondary school (grades five through 12), leading to the certificate of maturity (Matura or Reifezeugnis), which qualifies students for university admission. Children who complete the eight-year elementary school may complete their ninth year of compulsory education in a polytechnical (prevocational) course. There are three types of vocational education: apprenticeships; middle-level technical or vocational full-time schooling, one to four years in length; and upper-level vocational or technical schools, with a five-year program leading to the Matura. The educational system is rounded out by an extensive adult education program.

The School Organization Act of 1962 divided the secondary schools into special and regular categories. The upper five-year curricula vary widely. The regular category usually offers six different curricula, three of which are in the classical arts, two in science and mathematics, and one in home economics for female students.

The Private Schools Act of 1962 regulates the establishment and operation of private schools and private student boardinghouses. It also provides for accreditation, subsidies, and inspection. Private schools exist at every level of the educational system except universities. Private-school enrollment in compulsory general education is about 3 percent, but it increases to 12 percent in upper-level academic secondary schools, 20 percent in vocational schools, and 59 percent in middle-level vocational schools. In teacher training 36 percent of the students at the secondary level and about 29 percent of the students at the postsecondary level are in private schools.

The language of instruction is German in 99 percent of the schools, but the rights of the Croatians, Slovenes, Hungarians, Czechs, and Slovaks are respected, and elementary schools for minority groups are conducted in their native language. Croatian and Slovenian are offered as electives in academic secondary schools.

Higher education comprises universities (Universitäten) and colleges of fine arts (Hochschulenkünstlicher Richtung), which have equivalent status. The general German term for a higher-education institution is Hochschule, which includes universities and all other institutions of university rank. There are 12 universities and six colleges of fine arts.

The federal government has complete financial responsibility for academic secondary schools, medium- and upper-level vocational schools and higher education. In regard to the costs of other schools and levels, the federal government pays the majority of the personnel costs, while the province and district pay the rest. Districts are primarily responsible for preschool and compulsory general education and the provinces for compulsory vocational schools. On average, federal funds provide about two-thirds of total public expenditures on education at all levels. About 60 percent of the costs of private schools are reimbursed by the federal government.

Education

Literacy Rate %: 100
- Male %: 100
- Female %: 100

First Level: Primary schools: 4,557
- Teachers: 65,977
- Students: 649,994
- Student-Teacher Ratio: 9.9
- Net Enrollment Ratio: 100

Second Level: Secondary Schools: 693
- Teachers: 39,553
- Students: 295,473
- Student-Teacher Ratio: 7.5
- Net Enrollment Ratio: 90

Vocational Level: Schools: —
- Students: —

Third Level: Institutions: 44
- Teachers: 14,322
- Students: 222,095
- Student-Ratio Level: 15.9
- Gross Enrollment Ratio: 44.8
- Students per 100,000: 2,933
- % of Population Age 25 and over with Postsecondary Education: —

Public Expenditure on Education as % of GDP: 5.5

SCIENCE AND TECHNOLOGY

Science and Technology

Scientists and Engineers in R&D per 1 million persons: 1,627
Expenditures in R&D as % of GDP: 1.53
High-Tech Exports $million: 5,877
Patent Applications by Residents: 2,681

MEDIA

Austrian newspapers can be divided into three distinct groups: the big, popular, mass-appeal dailies, all in Vienna; the provincial press; and a small group of independent quality papers, of which Vienna's *Die Presse* and Salzburg's *Salzburger Nachrichten* are the best known. Strong political party leanings, if not actual affiliations, characterize most newspapers.

Newspaper readership is highest in Vienna, where it reaches 500 per 1,000 inhabitants, whereas it is only 116 per 1,000 in Tirol and Vorarlberg. In rural areas broadcasting is a more important medium.

The press exhibits three types of ownership: private, political party, and government. None is directly tied to any commercial enterprise, although there is some cross interest. Austria has not been spared the trend toward press concentration that most advanced countries have experienced since the 1950s, although it has tended to take the form of increased concentration in the hands of political parties rather than chains. The disappearance of a number of papers, such as *Express*, a mass-appeal daily, and the Austrian People's Party paper *Volksblatt* in the 1970s reflected the fragile economic base of the Austrian press. The Press Promotion Law of 1975 was designed to give the government power to help ailing newspapers.

Freedom of the press is guaranteed by the constitution, which states, "Every person has the right of free expression of opinion in speech, writing, print and visual media within the limits of legal regulations. The press must not be subjected to censorship nor restricted by rule of the licensing system." Because the space devoted to advertising is not high—about 25 percent—advertisers do not exert much influence on editorial policies.

The national news agency is the Österreichische Presse-Agentur (APA), a cooperative jointly owned by all newspapers (except *Neue Kronen Zeitung*) and the Austrian Broadcasting Corporation (Österreichischer Rundfunk, ORF), a public corporation whose shares are held by the provincial governments. It does not have foreign bureaus but has a number of part-time correspondents in major cities abroad. It also has contracts for the supply of news with Reuters, AFP, AP, and dpa.

Media

Daily Newspapers: 23
- Total Circulation 000: 3,736
- Circulation per 1,000: 465

Books Published: 7,987
Magazines: 2,481
Radio Receivers 000: 4,710
- per 1,000: 584

Television sets 000: 4,000
- per 1,000: 497

Most Important Media:

Press. The following are published daily at Vienna, unless otherwise noted: *Neue Kronen-Zeitung* (1,080,500 daily, 1,332,400 Sunday), independent; *Kurier* (385,000 daily, 607,000 Sunday), independent; *Kleine Zeitung* (Graz and Klagenfurt, 277,000), independent; *Salzburger Nachrichten* (Salzburg, 135,000), independent; *Oberösterreichische Nachrichten* (Linz, 120,000), independent; *Tiroler Tageszeitung* (Innsbruck, 100,000), independent; *Die Presse* (100,000), independent; *Der Standard* (100,000 daily, 152,000 Sunday); *Neue Zeit* (Graz, 71,000), Socialist; *Vorarlberger Nachrichten* (Bregenz, 65,000); *Wiener Zeitung* (40,000), government organ, world's oldest daily (f. 1703); *Kartner Tageszeitung* (Klagenfurt, 36,000), Socialist.

News agencies. The domestic agency is *Austria Presse-Agentur* (APA); numerous foreign agencies also maintain bureaus at Vienna.

Radio and television. The Austrian Broadcasting Company (Österreichischer Rundfunk-ORF), which controls both media, is state owned but protected in its operation from political interference under the broadcasting law. In October 1989 the government moved to end the ORF's monopoly by licensing private broadcasting.

CULTURE

Cultural Indicators

Public Libraries Number: 2,081
- Volumes: 7,442,000
- Registered borrowers: 802,337

Museums Number: 209
- Annual Attendance: 8,943,000

Cinema Production of Long Films: 22
- Number of Cinemas: 412
- Seating Capacity: 72,700
- Annual Attendance million: 11.9
- Annual Attendance per capita: 1.5

STATUS OF WOMEN

The position of Austrian women is not markedly different from that of women in other western European countries. Legal and other barriers to their full participation in public life are disappearing, although vestiges remain. Violence against women is a problem and it is reported that more than 300,000 women are abused annually and that one-fifth of the country's 1.5 million women have suffered from violence at some time. The 1997 Law on Protection against Violence in the Family provides special protection to women. Although prostitution is legal in Austria, the country is a transit point for women sold into sexual slavery from the former Soviet republics to western Europe and North America. There is a Women's Affairs Ministry that oversees the condition of women. In addition there is a Federal Equality Commission and a Federal Commissioner for Equal Treatment. Sixty percent of the women between 15 and 60 are in the labor force, but they typically earn less than 30 percent than do men. Since 1998 women are allowed to serve in the military. Sexual harassment is punishable by law and women may be awarded compensation of up to four months' salary if discriminated against because of their sex.

Women

Gender Empowerment Measure: 10
Seats Held in Parliament by Women %: 24.7
Female Administrators and Managers %: 23.9
Female Professional and Technical Workers %: 46.1
Women's Share of Earned Income %: 34
Women in Government %: 7

HEALTH, FOOD, AND NUTRITION

Health

Number of Physicians: 27,869
Number of Dentists: 3,687
Number of Nurses: 40,756
Number of Pharmacists: 2,068
Population per Physician: 289
Number of Hospitals: 330
Hospital Beds per 10,000: 93
Hospital Bed Occupancy Rate: 79.4
Infant Mortality Rate per 1,000 live births: 8
Maternal Mortality Rate per 100,000 live births: 10
Total Health Expenditures as % of GDP: 8.38
Health Expenditures per capita $: 1,711
HIV Infected % of adults: 0.18
Cigarette Consumption per smoker per year: 3,041
% of Smokers: Male: 42
Female: 27
Access to Safe Water %: 100

Food and Nutrition

Food Supply as % of FAO Requirements: 130
% of Consumption Expenditures on Food: 28.1
Daily Available Calories per capita: 3,417
% of Total Calories derived from:
Cereals: 22.2
Potatoes, cassava: 3.3
Meat, poultry: 13.4
Fish: 0.7
Eggs, milk: 12.0
Fruits, vegetables: 6.0
Fats, oils: 20.7

ENVIRONMENT

Austria is actively engaged in the protection of the national environment. Forests cover about 39 percent of the territory, and there are 129 protected areas or nature reserves covering 28.3 percent of the country; 302 plant species and 108 animal species are protected by law. Along with Hungary and the Czech Republic, Austria is planning a trinational park along the floodplain areas of the Danube, Thaya, and March rivers.

Forest damage is caused by a combination of air and soil pollution. It is estimated that some 25 percent of the country's forests have suffered some damage. Like many postindustrial nations, Austria is taking an active role in reducing pollutants including those that contribute to the greenhouse effect. Legislation has been passed to reduce emission by more than 20 percent over the next five years and greater care is being taken of the country's remaining undeveloped lands.

Environment

Forest Area sq km: 39,000
Average Annual Deforestation sq km: 0
Nationally Protected Areas as % of Total Land Area: 28.3
Freshwater Access cubic meters per capita: 10,399
Emissions of Organic Water Pollutants kg per day: 78,040
CO_2 Emissions per capita ton: 7.4

CHRONOLOGY

1945 A provisional government is established under Socialist leader Karl Renner; following general elections in November, Chancellor Leopold Figl forms a coalition government with the OVP and the SPO as partners.

1946 Government nationalizes major industrial firms to prevent Soviet confiscation; denazification laws are enacted; Salzburg festival is revived.

1947 Austria joins UNESCO, but its application to join the United Nations is vetoed; United States begins to pay its own occupation costs.

1948 Austria qualifies for aid under the Marshall Plan.

1949 Former Nazis are allowed to participate in national elections in parties free of Nazi ideology, including the Union of Independents (later renamed the Freedom Party); a new coalition cabinet is formed.

1950 President Renner dies and Theodor Körner of the Socialist Party is elected president; Reds lose Soviet Zone elections; the death penalty is abolished.

1951 Theodor Körner is elected president.

1953 Julius Raab is named chancellor, and he pursues a modified free-market economy for Austria; the Soviet Union begins to pay its own occupation costs, and France and Britain follow suit.

1955 Four-power occupation of Austria ends as the Austrian State Treaty proclaims an independent Austria; Nationalrat votes for permanent neutrality; Austria joins the United Nations; Austrian defense forces are established.

1956 Austria becomes a member of the Council of Europe.

1957 Adolf Schärf of the Socialist Party is elected president.

1958 Austria joins the European Free Trade Association (EFTA).

1961 Raab resigns and is succeeded as chancellor by Alfons Gorbach.

1962 Austria applies to join the European Economic Community (EEC).

1964 Josef Klaus is named chancellor.

1965 Franz Jonas of the Socialist Party is elected president.

1966 People's Party wins elections and forms a minority government under Josef Klaus.

1969 Austria and Italy agree on a policy guaranteeing the rights of the German-speaking population of South Tirol.

1970 Socialists win a plurality and form a the first all-Socialist government under Chancellor Bruno Kreisky; *Volksblatt* ceases publication.

1971 New civil code liberalizes divorce and marriage laws; Socialists win a clear majority in snap elections.

1972 Austria joins the EEC.

1974 President Jonas dies; Rudolf Kirchschläger is elected president on the Socialist ticket.

1975 Socialists sustain their Nationalrat majority in elections as the economy continues its upward trend.

1978 In a national referendum, voters reject a program for nuclear power.

1979 Socialists increase their Nationalrat majority in elections.

1983 Socialists lose parliamentary majority in national elections; Bruno Kreisky steps down as chancellor and is succeeded by Fred Sinowatz heading a Socialist Party–Freedom Party coalition government.

1986 Jörg Haidar becomes the leader of the Freedom Party; despite charges that he was an active Nazi military officer, Austrian People's Party candidate Kurt Waldheim is elected president; Sinowatz resigns as chancellor and Socialist leader Franz Vranitzky calls for new elections, in which the Green Party participates for the first time; following elections, the Socialist and People's parties form a grand coalition.

1990 The government revokes some of the neutrality provisions of the 1955 State Treaty.

1991 Austria supports UN forces in the Persian Gulf War by permitting air and land transportation through Austrian territory; President Waldheim announces that he will not run for reelection; the Socialist Party is renamed the Social Democratic Party.

1992 Thomas Klestil of the People's Party, a proponent of European Union (EU) membership for Austria, is elected president.

1994 In October legislative elections, the anti-immigrant, anti-EU Freedom Party wins 42 seats at the expense of the Social Democratic and People's parties.

1995 Austria enters the European Union.

1997 Chancellor Vranitsky resigns and is succeeded by Socialist finance minister Viktor Klima; Austria implements the Schengen accord, lifting all customs and immigration controls with the eight other accord member-countries.

1998 Klestil is elected to a second six-year term as president.

1999 The Freedom Party wins 27 percent of the vote in legislative elections for a total of 52 seats, equaling the People's Party's number of seats.

2000 After talks with the Social Democrats break down, the People's Party forms a coalition government with the Freedom Party, with Wolfgang Schüssel of the People's Party as chancellor; foreign and domestic groups protest the Freedom Party's participation in the government; the EU imposes diplomatic sanctions on Austria; Haidar resigns as leader of the Freedom Party and is replaced by Susanne Reiss-Passer; EU lifts sanctions.

BIBLIOGRAPHY

Bischof, Gunter, and Anton Pelinka. *Austria in the New Europe* New Brunswick, N.J., 1993.

Brook-Shepherd, Gordon. *The Austrians: A Thousand-Year Odyssey.* London, 1996.

Jardos, Havald. *Some Aspects of Cultural Policy in Austria.* Paris, 1981.

Steiner, Kurt. *Modern Austria.* Palo Alto, Calif., 1981.

Sully, Melanie. *Political Parties and Elections in Austria.* New York, 1981.

OFFICIAL PUBLICATIONS

Austria. *Grosszahlung* 1991 (General Census 1991). *Sozialstatistische Daten* (irreg.); *Statistisches Jahrbuch für die Republik Österreich.*

CONTACT INFORMATION

Embassy of Austria
3524 International Court NW
Washington, D.C. 20008
Phone: (202) 895-6700 Fax: (202) 895-6750

INTERNET RESOURCES

- Austrian Central Office of Statistics
  http://www.oestat.gv.at
- Austrian Press and Information Service (Washington, D.C.)
  http://www.austria.org/index.html

AZERBAIJAN

BASIC FACT SHEET

OFFICIAL NAME:
Azerbaijani Republic (Azarbaycan Respublikasi)

ABBREVIATION:
AJ

CAPITAL:
Baku

HEAD OF STATE:
President Heydar Aliyev (from 1993)

HEAD OF GOVERNMENT:
Prime Minister Artur Rasizade (from 1993)

NATURE OF GOVERNMENT:
Emerging Democracy

POPULATION:
7,993,000 (1999)

AREA:
86,600 sq km (33,400 sq mi)

MAJOR ETHNIC GROUPS:
Azeri

LANGUAGES:
Azeri

RELIGIONS:
Shiite Muslim

UNIT OF CURRENCY:
Manat

NATIONAL FLAG:
Three equal horizontal bands of blue (top) red, and green. A crescent and eight-pointed star in white are centered in red band

NATIONAL ANTHEM: —

NATIONAL HOLIDAY:
May 28 (Independence Day)

DATE OF INDEPENDENCE:
August 30, 1991

DATE OF CONSTITUTION:
November 12, 1995

GEOGRAPHICAL FEATURES

Azerbaijan is situated in southwestern Asia in Transcaucasia. It has a total area of 86,600 sq km (33,440 sq mi), including the exclave of the Naxcivan Autonomous Republic and the disputed Nagorno-Karabakh region. Naxcivan is separated from the rest of Azerbaijan by Armenia. Azerbaijan shares land borders with five countries: 787 km (489 mi) with Armenia, including 221 km (137 mi) of border between Armenia and the Naxcivan enclave; 323 km (200 mi) with Georgia; 284 km (176 mi) with Russia; 9 km (5.5 mi) with Turkey; and 611 km (379 mi) with Iran. The country also has an 800 km (500 mi) coastline on the Caspian Sea.

Nearly half of the country is covered by mountains and the three main relief features of the Transcaucasian region—the Greater Caucasus mountains in the northeast, the Lesser Caucasus in the southwest, and the Kura River depression in between—converge within the country. Of the more than 1,000 rivers in Azerbaijan, only 21 are longer than 97 km (60 mi). The capital, Baku, and its surrounding metropolitan region had an estimated population of 2,500,000 in 2000. Only two other cities have populations over 200,000, namely, Ganca (291,000) and Sumqayit (268,000).

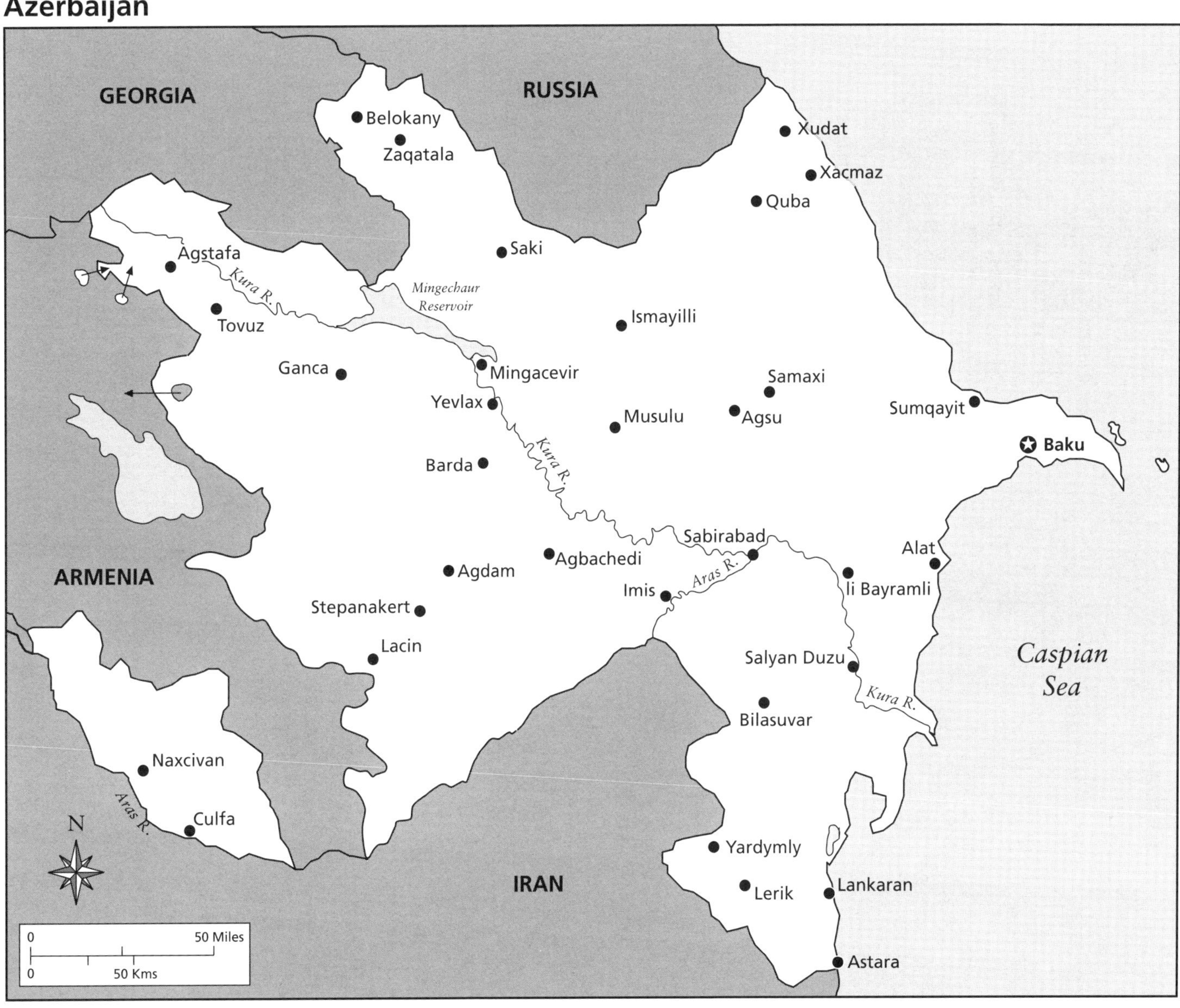

Azerbaijan
GEORGIA
RUSSIA
ARMENIA
IRAN
Caspian Sea
Belokany
Zaqatala
Xudat
Xacmaz
Quba
Saki
Agstafa
Kura R.
Tovuz
Mingechaur Reservoir
Ismayilli
Ganca
Mingacevir
Samaxi
Yevlax
Musulu
Agsu
Sumqayit
Baku
Barda
Kura R.
Sabirabad
Alat
Agdam
Agbachedi
Imis
Aras R.
Ii Bayramli
Stepanakert
Lacin
Salyan Duzu
Kura R.
Bilasuvar
Naxcivan
Aras R.
Culfa
N
Yardymly
Lerik
Lankaran
Astara
0 50 Miles
0 50 Kms

Geography

Area sq km: 86,600 sq mi 33,400
World Rank: 113th
Land Boundaries, km: Armenia 787; Georgia 322; Iran 611; Russia 284; Turkey 9
Coastline, km: 0
Elevation Extremes meters
- Lowest: Caspian Sea −28
- Highest: Bazarduzu Dagi 4,485

Land Use % Arable land: 18
- Permanent Crops: 5
- Permanent Pastures: 25
- Forest and Woodland: 11
- Other: 41

Population of Principal Cities (1995 est.)

Baku (Baky)	1,739,900
Ganca (Gyandzha)	292,500
Sumqayit (Sumgait)	270,000

CLIMATE AND WEATHER

Azerbaijan has a wide range of climates and weather zones considering its relatively small size. The climate zones range from the arid subtropical to the mountainous tundra. In the lowlands near the Caspian Sea coast, the mean annual temperature is 15°C (59°F) while in the mountains the mean is 0°C (32°F). During July, the hottest month, the mean lowland temperature is 26°C (79°F) and the mean mountain temperature 5°C (41°F). Rainfall distribution is also uneven with the lowlands receiving between 300 mm and 900 mm (8 to 12 in) on an annual basis and the southern slopes of the Greater Caucasus mountains getting 1,200 to 1,400 mm (47 to 55 in) of rain a year. Winter is the rainy season in the lowlands while in the highlands and mountains most of the precipitation falls in winter, much of it in the form of snow.

Climate and Weather

Mean Temperature
July 81°F
January 34°F
Average Rainfall 14.3 in

POPULATION

Population Indicators

Total Population 1999: 7,998,000
World Rank: 88th
Density per sq mi: 239.3 per sq km 92.3
% of annual growth (1994–99): 1.0
Male %: 48.7
Female %: 51.3
Urban %: 53.8
Age Distribution: %
- 0–14: 32.8
- 15–29: 29.7
- 30–44: 16.8
- 45–59: 12.8
- 60–74: 5.7
- 75 and over: 2.2

Population 2020: 9,169,000
Birth Rate per 1,000: 19.2
Death Rate per 1,000: 6.6
Population Doubling Time (years): 54
Infant Mortality Rate per 1,000 live births: 33.0
Rate of Natural Increase per 1,000: 12.6
Total Fertility Rate: 2.3
Expectation of Life (years): Males 66.5
Females 74.5
Marriage Rate per 1,000: 6.3
Divorce Rate per 1,000: 0.8
Total Number of Households: 1,381,000
Average Size of Households: 4.8
% of Illegitimate Children: 2.5
Induced Abortions: 42,134
- Rate per 100 live births: 23.2

ETHNIC COMPOSITION

Azerbaijan has a relatively homogeneous population with 90 percent of the population ethnic Azeris belonging to the Caspian type of the southern European race. The country's principal minority groups are the Dagestani (3.2 percent), Russian (2.5 percent), and Armenian (2 percent). Virtually all Armenians reside in the breakaway region of Nagorno-Karabakh.

LANGUAGES

The official language is Azerbaijani—one of the South Turkic group of languages that are a branch of the Altaic language family. It is the least Russified of all the Turkic languages spoken in the former USSR and there has been a steady campaign to purge all Russian words still in the vocabulary. There are eight distinct dialects of Azerbaijani spoken in the country and in northern Iran. As part of the de-Sovietization of the country, the Turkish version of the Latin script replaced the Cyrillic alphabet in 1992. Azerbaijani has nine vowels and 23 consonants. Russian and Armenian are also spoken by their respective ethnic minorities but are shunned by most Azerberjanis.

Principal Languages and Their Speakers

Armenian	160,000
Azerbaijani (Azeri)	7,110,000
Lezgi (Lezgian)	180,000
Russian	240,000
Other	300,000

RELIGION

The religious mix in Azerbaijan is based primarily on the ethnic origins of the population. Virtually all ethnic Azeris and Dagestanis are Muslim with 65 percent being Shiite and 28 percent Sunni. The Russian minority follows the Russian Orthodox religion and the Armenian community is mostly Armenian Orthodox. Despite the overwhelming number of Muslims, religion is less of a factor than might be expected because of the secular nature of society—another holdover from the years of Soviet domination.

Religious Affiliations

Shiite Muslim	5,230,000
Sunni Muslim	2,240,000
Other	520,000

HISTORICAL BACKGROUND

Azerbaijan has been, over the centuries, an area of confrontation and the object of disputes and wars between the region's three powers, Iran, Turkey, and Russia. The roots of present day Azerbaijan can be traced back to the fourth century B.C.E. with the emergence of two kingdoms: Caucasian Albania in the north and Antropan in the south. By the second century C.E. Caucasian Albania had developed into a regional power. Its borders were in essence the same borders as modern day Azerbaijan. During the seventh century, Caucasian Albania fell to the Arab Caliphate leading to the Islamization of the region. The succeeding centuries saw Azerbaijan ruled by a series of Turkic empires from Central Asia.

In the beginning of the 16th century Azerbaijan was under the rule of the Safavid dynasty which by now had also assumed leadership in neighboring Persia. Wars between the Turkish Ottoman Empire and the Safavid in Persia led to Ottoman occupation of Azerbaijan between 1578 and 1603. As Safavid authority began to wane in the region, the Russians and the Ottomans fought for control. With the breakup of the Safavid dynasty in the middle of the 18th century, the remains of the empire in the Caucasus, including Azerbaijan, fell to a number of independent khanates or fiefdoms.

Catherine the Great sought to extend the Russian empire into the region and as a result two Russo-Iranian wars were fought from 1804–13 and from 1826–28. The first war ended with the Treaty of Gulistan, which ceded the majority of the northern khanates to Russia. The Treaty of Turkmanchi in 1828, ending the second war, extended Russian influence into present-day Armenia and southwestern Azerbaijan. The net effect of the two treaties saw Azerbaijan divided in half with the north being under Russian colonial rule and the south governed by Iran.

In 1918, the end of World War I saw Azerbaijan change hands from Russian to Ottoman Turk and finally to British control. With British blessing Azerbaijan declared its independence from Russia. The first independent Republic of Azerbaijan existed for just 23 months, between May 28, 1918, and April 28, 1920. That first Azerbaijan Republic is considered by historians to be the first truly secular state in the Orient with the first European-like parliament and the first cabinet of ministers. In April 1920, units of the Russian Bolshevik 11th army invaded Azerbaijan and overthrew the government. Under Red Army occupation, Azerbaijan was incorporated into the Soviet Union with the signing of the Treaty of Formation of the USSR on December 30, 1922. For the next 70 years the country remained a republic within the Soviet empire.

In 1945 with both Armenia and Azerbaijan members of the Soviet Union, Moscow, by fiat, tried to settle control over Nagorno-Karabakh—a mostly ethnic Armenian enclave within Azerbaijan's borders. The Soviet Bureau of Caucasian Affairs awarded the territory to Armenia, but Soviet leader Josef Stalin reversed the decision declaring the region an autonomous oblast or county within Azerbaijan.

The Azerbaijani political reawakening began in 1988, sparked by an outbreak of ethnic violence between Azerbaijanis and Armenians over Armenian claims to the Nagorno-Karabakh region and the refusal of Moscow to heed Armenian demands to cede the territory to Soviet Armenia. Moscow sent 5,000 troops to the region to quell the violence that left hundreds dead.

In 1991, Azerbaijan again declared its independence from Russia under the presidency of former communist Ayaz Mutalibov, who won a hastily called election that many believed was rigged by the former Communist Party. The country immediately became embroiled in an armed conflict with now independent Armenian over Nagorno-Karabakh. The failure to hold back Armenian advances in the region led to the replacement of Mutalibov by Abulfaz Elchibey of the Popular Front of Azerbaijan through a multiparty general election in 1992. However, continued military defeats led to more internal dissent.

In June 1993, rebel army units seized Baku, the capital, in a bloodless revolt. A national referendum of no confidence was held in August on Elchibey's rule with 97.5 percent of the electorate voting against him. The National Assembly endorsed the result and called for another election in June. This time Heydar Aliyev, a former member of the Soviet KGB secret police, and leader of the New Azerbaijan Party, was declared the winner with 98.9 percent of the votes cast.

In December of 1993, Azerbaijani forces launched a counteroffensive into Nagorno-Karabakh and recaptured some of the territory that it had lost to the Armenians. In May 1994 the Bishkek Protocol was signed, which led to a cease-fire between Azerbaijan and Armenia. Russian troops arrived as peacekeepers in the disputed territory.

In 1997 and 1998, the Organization for Security and Cooperation in Europe brokered a settlement between Armenia and Azerbaijan but both sides have refused to sign, claiming reservations about territorial division and home rule issues. The May 1994 cease-fire has generally remained in effect with only minor violations into the new century.

CONSTITUTION

In a national referendum in 1995, 91.9 percent of voters gave approval to a new constitution, which mandated a strong presidency and an independent legislature based on a division of powers. However, in reality both parliament and the judiciary are subservient to the president's office. Under the 1995 constitution, which replaced the Soviet constitution of 1978, the president is head of state and commander-in-chief of the armed forces. The president, who is elected by popular vote for a five-year term, holds supreme executive authority in conjunction with a Council of Ministers appointed by the president. The council is headed by a prime minister. President Heydar Aliyev of the New Azerbaijan Party won the October 1998 presidential election, gaining 77.61 percent of the vote compared to Etibar Mamedov of the National Independence Party, who came second with 11.83 percent. In November 2000, Aliyev's son, Ilham, looked set to eventually succeed his father as president, leading the New Azerbaijan Party to victory in disputed parliamentary elections and claiming the speaker of parliament position. Both men and women over the age of 18 have the right to vote.

LOCAL GOVERNMENT

The country is divided into 59 rayons, which are Soviet-era administrative districts, 11 cities with locally elected officials, and one autonomous republic.

Local Government

Principal administrative divisions, capitals, area, population

Area and population

Administrative/ Geographic units	Capitals	area sq mi	area sq km	population 1991 estimate
Autonomous republic				
Naxcivan	Naxcivan	2,100	5,500	305,700
Geographic region				
Nagorno-Karabakh	Xankándi (Stepanakert)	1,700	4,400	193,300
Capital city				
Baku	—	—	—	1,713,300
Others	—	29,600	76,700	4,924,300
TOTAL		33,400	86,600	7,136,600

PARLIAMENT

The unicameral National Assembly, or Milli Mejlis, is comprised of 125 seats with 25 seats filled by proportional representation according to party lists and 100 seats elected in single-member constituencies. Members serve five-year terms.

POLITICAL PARTIES

Political parties include the following:

The New Azerbaijan Party the dominant force in the government and is headed by President Aliyev. Other key political parties:

Popular Front of Azerbaijan once controlled the government but unable to deliver victory over Armenia. Headed by Abulfaz Elchibey.

National Independence Party anticorruption party headed by Etibar Mamedov

Independent Azerbaijan Party headed by Nizami Suleymanov

Communist Party of Azerbaijan eager to return to the previous form of government and closer ties with Russia. Headed by Firudin llasanov

Association of Victims of Illegal Political Repressions critical of government's human rights policy. It is headed by Ashraf Mehdiyev.

Political Parties

New Azerbaijan Party, 1992
Azerbaijan Popular Front, 1989
New Muslim Democratic Party, 1992
Azerbaijan National Independence Party, 1992
Azerbaijan United Communist Party, 1993

Political Parties: Strength in Parliament Most Recent Elections

The unicameral National Assembly (Milli Mejlis) created under the 1995 constitution is elected for a five-year term and has 125 members, of whom 100 are elected from single-member constituencies and are elected by proportional representation. In the elections of November 5, 2000, and January 7, 2001, the New Azerbaijan Party won 75 seats; Popular Front of Azerbaijan, 6; Citizens Solidarity Party, 3; Azerbaijan Communist Party, 2; New Equality Party, 2; Alliance for the Sake of Azerbaijan, 1; Social Prosperity Party, 1; Motherland Party, 1; Ana Vatan, 1; Yurddash Partiyasi, 1; and nonpartisans, 29.

LEGAL SYSTEM

The legal system is based on a code of civil law. The president appoints Supreme and Constitutional Court judges subject to confirmation by the National Assembly. The president directly appoints lower level judges and there is no independent confirmation required—a fact that gives the judiciary little independence from the executive branch. Lower level courts are considered corrupt and open to outside influences. Cases at the district or rayon level are tried by a judge and two civilian assessors. The constitution provides for a presumption of innocence and a defendant's right to legal counsel. The death penalty is enforced.

LAW ENFORCEMENT

Law Enforcement

Offenses reported to the police per 100,000: 247
- Murder: 8.1
- Assault: 5.6
- Burglary: 8.4
- Automobile Theft: 4.1
- Population per Police officer: —

Death Penalty: Yes.

HUMAN RIGHTS

The government's human rights record improved considerably toward the end of the 1990s as a semblance of political stability returned to the country. In 1998, for example, there were no reports of political or extrajudicial killings by security forces or politically motivated disappearances. Torture is illegal but international human rights organizations have accused police of routinely using coercion to win confessions from suspects. Prison conditions are harsh. Security forces continue to arbitrarily arrest and detain suspects despite constitutional guarantees against such practices.

The constitution provides for freedom of speech and the press but in reality these freedoms have often been ignored by the government. Through intimidation and threats many journalists exercise self-censorship. The government, keen to control the flow of international opinion, has also limited internet access by licensing only two service providers.

The government requires political parties to register and has on occasion forbidden opposition political rallies. The government also requires religious organizations and congregations to register and there have been credible claims of harassment of non-Islamic religious groups. Generally, international human rights organizations are granted free access to monitor and investigate abuse claims.

FOREIGN POLICY

Since gaining independence in 1991, Azerbaijan has had a difficult relationship with Russia. Although a charter member of the Commonwealth of Independent States (CIS), the Azerbaijani parliament refused to ratify the treaty in 1992 and instead voted to leave the grouping of former Soviet republics. However, with the accession to power of Aliyev, that course was reversed and in 1993 Azerbaijan formally rejoined the group. Relations with Russia have been rather one-sided. In 1996, Russia sealed its border with Azerbaijan to prevent arms shipments reaching rebels in Chechnya. Russian companies remain closely involved in the country's oil and gas industry, especially in the transportation sector. Russia is eager to see Azeri oil flow through its territory in order to reach world markets. Russian troops continued to monitor the cease-fire in Nagorno-Karabakh at the end of the 1990s.

In the early 1990s, the primary criterion governing Azerbaijan's relations with foreign countries was their stance on Azerbaijani sovereignty in Nagorno-Karabakh. The strengthening of relations with Turkey since independence has been a cornerstone of this policy. Turkey helped to enforce Azerbaijan's economic blockade of Armenia during the war.

Iran has also played an increasing role in Azerbaijani foreign policy. With a large number of Azerbaijanis living and working in Iran that country is now one of Azerbaijan's leading trading partners. After the U.S. Congress placed restrictions on aid to Azerbaijan pending the lifting of its economic blockade against Armenia, relations between the two countries were strained. However, once the blockade was lifted, relations between Azerbaijan and the United States improved significantly. In 1997 Aliyev paid an official visit to Washington and signed a military cooperation agreement. The state oil company also signed agreements with major U.S. oil companies to help in the exploration of the Caspian oil fields.

Azerbaijan was admitted to the United Nations in 1992, and in 1996, along with Georgia and Armenia, the country signed an economic cooperation pact with the European Union.

DEFENSE

Prior to independence in 1991, Azerbaijan had no national defense force, relying instead on the Soviet army for border protection. Military service is compulsory for males over the age of 18 and individuals serve 17 months. The army makes up the largest sector of the national defense forces, followed by the navy. Naval units operate under Russian command as part of the Commonwealth of Independent States protocols. In 1994, Azerbaijan joined NATO's Partnership for Peace—a program of military aid and cooperation. Iranian, Turkish, and Russian officers have all assisted with the training of the national defense forces.

Military Indicators

Total Active Duty Personnel: 66,700
Military Manpower per 1,000: 8.8
Military Expenditures $million: 304
- as % of GNP: 2.8
- per capita $: 40
- as % of central government expenditures: 3.8

Arms Imports $: 0
Arms Exports $: 0

ECONOMY

The first years following independence in 1991 were an economic nightmare for Azerbaijan, which was far less developed industrially than the neighboring Caucasian states of Armenia and Georgia. The collapse of trade between the former Soviet republics and Azerbaijan's war with Armenia led to a drastic decline in economic activity for the newly independent nation. Gross domestic product (GDP) declined every year since 1988 and by 1994 and stood at just 37 percent of 1988 levels. Agricultural output was off by 43 percent and industrial output had fallen about 60 percent. The oil and gas sectors were particularly hard hit with production falling to 9.6 million metric tons from 13.8 million metric tons.

By the latter half of the 1990s, there were signs of improvement following a general political stabilization, a cease-fire in the war with Armenia, and the launching of government structural reforms, including a limited privatization program, sanctioned by the World Bank and the IMF. Inflation, which hit 1,664 percent in 1994, fell to less than 1 percent in 1997 and was negative in 1998 and again in 1999. GDP growth was 10 percent in 1998, reversing years of double digit decline. Despite low world oil prices at the end of the decade, there were signs of a revival in Azerbaijan's oil sector after the state-run oil company signed a 30-year production-sharing agreement with an international consortium of oil companies to develop the oil fields of Chirag, Azeri, and Gunashli in the Caspian Sea. The country has also switched its trading focus away from the former Soviet states toward Turkey, Iran, the European Union, and the Middle East.

Principal Economic Indicators

Gross National Product: $3.886 billion
GNP per capita: $510
GNP Average Annual Growth Rate (1990–97) %: −16.0
GNP per capita Average Annual Growth Rate (1990–97) %: −16.9
- Agriculture: 30
- Mining: —
- Manufacturing: 25
- Construction: 4
- Public Utilities: —
- Transportation and Communications: 7
- Trade: 34
- Financial Services: 34
- Other Services: 34
- Government: 34

Gross Domestic Product by Type of Expenditure %
- Private Consumption: 69
- Government Consumption: 24
- Gross Domestic Investment: 21
- Foreign Trade: Exports: 58
- Imports: −71

% of Income Received by Poorest 20%: —
% of Income Received by Richest 10%: —

Price and earnings indexes (1995 = 100)

	1995	1996	1997	1998
Consumer price index	100.0	119.9	99.5	98.7
Earnings index	—	—	—	—

Finance

National Currency: Manat
Exchange Rate: $1 = Manat 3,936
Money Supply Stock in National Currency billion: —
M1 per capita: —
Central Bank Discount Rate %: 14
Total External Debt $million: 100
Debt Service Ratio %: 6

Balance of Payments $million: 915.8
International Reserves SDRs million: —
Ratio of External Debt to Total Reserves: —
Average Annual Rate of Inflation/Consumer Price Index Growth Rate %: 3.7

Official Development Assistance

ODA $million: 89
as % of GNP: 2.3
per capita: $11
Foreign Direct Investment $million: 1,023

Central Government Revenues and Expenditures

Fiscal Year: Calendar Year

Revenues $million: 565
Expenditures $million: 682
Budget Deficit $million: 117
Tax Revenues as % of GDP: 18.2
Highest Tax Bracket %
Individual: 40
Corporate: 30

Employment and Labor

Economically Active Population: 2,698,000
Female Participation Rate %: —
Activity Rate %: 36.2
Labor by Sector: %
Agriculture, Forestry, Fishing: 6.7
Manufacturing, Mining: 17.3
Construction: 7.4
Transportation and Communications: 6.7
Trade, Hotels, and Restaurants: 6.3
Finance, Insurance, Real Estate: 0.4
Public Administration, Defense: —
Services: 21.8

Unemployment %: 20

Agriculture

Agriculture's Share of GDP %: 30
Average Annual Rate of Growth (1965–98) %: —
Number of Farms 000: 3.2
Average Size of Farm ha: 19
Number of Tractors per 1,000 hectares: 20.6
Irrigation, % of Farms having: 62
Artificial Fertilizer kg/hectare: —
Total Farmland as % of land area: 48.5
Livestock: Cattle 000: 1,843
Sheep 000: 5,867
Hogs 000: 21
Chickens 000: 13,000
Forests: Production of Roundwood (000 cubic meters): —
Fisheries: Total Catch tons 000: 35.0

Mining

% of GDP: —
Value of Mineral Production $million: —

Manufacturing

Value Added $million: 512
Industrial Production Growth Rate %: 0.3

Energy

Commercial Energy Production metric tons of oil equivalent 000: 4,027
Commercial Energy Consumption metric tons of oil equivalent 000: 11,987
Commercial Energy Consumption per capita kg: 1,529
Average Annual Growth Rate 1980–97 %: 6.3
Net Energy Imports % of use: 17
Electricity Installed Capacity kW 000: 5,239
Production kW-hr million: 17,000
Coal Reserves tons million: —
Production tons 000: —
Natural Gas Proven Reserves cubic meters billion: 100
Production cubic meters million: 3,896
Crude Petroleum Reserves barrels million: 3,300
Production barrels million: 190
Consumption barrels million: 74
Refinery Capacity barrels per day 000: 442
Pipelines Length km: 1,760

Foreign Trade

Imports $million: 667.6
Exports $million: 547.4
Export Volume % Annual Growth Rate (1990–97): —
Import Volume % Annual Growth Rate (1990–97): —
Balance of Trade $

Balance of trade (current prices)

	1992	1993	1994	1995	1996	1997
U.S.$000,000	+573.3	+357.6	−140.4	−122.0	−329.4	−13.0
% of total	22.3%	22.0%	9.9%	10.1%	20.7%	0.8%

Major Trading Partners

	Imports	Exports
European Union %	12.7	17.2
United States %	2.0	0.2
Eastern Europe %	24.4	26.9
Japan %	0.2	—
Others %	60.7	55.7

Transportation

Roads Total Length mi: 35,879 km 57,770
Paved %: 94
Automobiles: 289,000
Trucks and Buses: 88,800
Persons per vehicle: 20
Railroad; Track Length mi: 1,305 km 2,100
Passenger-mi million: 516
Freight-mi million: 1,055
Merchant Marine: No of Vessels: —
Total Deadweight Tonnage 000: —
International Cargo Loaded tons 000: —
International Cargo Off-loaded tons 000: —
Airports with Scheduled Flights: 1
Traffic: Passenger-mi million: 1,259
Freight-mi million: 34
Length of Canals mi: 3,600 km 5,300

Tourism

Number of Tourists to 000: 170
Number of Tourists from 000: 232
Tourist Receipts $million: 146
Tourist Expenditures $million: 70

Communications

Telephones 000: 640
Cost of Local Calls 3 mins: $0.13
Cellular Telephones 000: 6.0

(continued)

Fax Machines 000: 2.5
Personal Computers 000: —
Internet Hosts per million persons: 2.1
Mail: Post Offices: 1,857
Pieces of Mail Handled: 7.5
Pieces of Mail Handled per person: 1.0

EDUCATION

Education is free and compulsory for children from the age of six to the age of 17. Primary education covers a period of four years, while secondary education is in two phases of five and two years. The country has 17 institutes of higher learning. In 1994, two-thirds of all people between the ages of six and 23 were enrolled in school. The education level of the general population is relatively high for the region, with a mean education of nine years for males and females. A total of 97 percent of the adult population is considered to be literate.

Education

Literacy Rate %: 97.3
Male %: 98.9
Female %: 95.9
First Level: Primary schools: 4,502
Teachers: 156,000
Students: 1,486,000
Student-Teacher Ratio: 9.5
Net Enrollment Ratio: —
Second Level: Secondary Schools: —
Teachers: —
Students: —
Student-Teacher Ratio: —
Net Enrollment Ratio: —
Vocational Level: Schools: 78
Students: 73,000
Third Level: Institutions: 23
Teachers: —
Students: 89,100
Student-Ratio Level: —
Gross Enrollment Ratio: 19.8
Students per 100,000: 1,619
% of Population Age 25 and over with Postsecondary Education: —
Public Expenditure on Education as % of GDP: 3.0

SCIENCE AND TECHNOLOGY

Science and Technology

Scientists and Engineers in R&D per 1 million persons: 2,791
Expenditures in R&D as % of GDP: 0.21
High-Tech Exports $million: —
Patent Applications by Residents: —

MEDIA

Azerbaijan has a lively and healthy mix of government-run and independently owned media in print and broadcast, but the government continues to intimidate independent journalists through unofficial means. In 1998 the government officially ended censorship of the press, creating a boom in independent newspapers and magazines despite attempts at unofficial intimidation. By 1999 there were more than 370 registered newspapers in the country (but only about 100 actually publish). There are seven television stations, including the government-run Azerbaijan National Television and six independently owned ones, including BM-TI TV. However, the government refuses to grant licenses to about a dozen independent television stations wishing to broadcast. Radio Baku, the state-run radio network, broadcasts in Azerbaijani, Arabic, English, and Turkish.

Media

Daily Newspapers: 3
Total Circulation 000: 210
Circulation per 1,000: 28
Books Published: 375
Magazines: 49
Radio Receivers 000: —
per 1,000: —
Television sets 000: 1,600
per 1,000: 212

MOST IMPORTANT MEDIA:

Press. Prior to independence more than 150 newspapers were published in Azerbaijan, most of them in Azeri. The following are Azeri dailies issued at Baku, unless otherwise noted: *Khalq Gazeti* (former ACP organ); *Kommunist*, 254,000; *Azadlig* (Liberty, 142,000), APF weekly; *Bakinsy Rabochy* (Baku Worker, 68,000), former ACP organ; *Respublika* (Republic, 57,000), government weekly; *Hayat* (Life, 40,000), published by the Azerbaijan National Assembly.

News agencies. The domestic facility is the Azerbaijan Information Agency (Azerinform), headquartered at Baku.

Radio and television. Radio Baku and Baku Television broadcast from Baku in Azeri and a number of other languages. A nominally independent television station, BMTI, was closed down May 15, 1994.

CULTURE

Cultural Indicators

Public Libraries Number:
Volumes: —
Registered borrowers: —
Museums Number:
Annual Attendance: —
Cinema Production of Long Films:
Number of Cinemas: —
Seating Capacity: —
Annual Attendance: —
Annual Attendance per capita: —

STATUS OF WOMEN

Perhaps as a result of the country's Soviet legacy, women nominally enjoy the same legal protections as men and they do participate in all aspects of economic, social, and political life, though women are generally underrepresented in higher political offices as well as executive business positions. Despite traditional Muslim views of the place of women in society, females do have opportunities for work and education. There are several active women's political and social organizations in the country. In rural areas women who appear in public unaccompanied, smoke in public, or drive cars are still, however, subject to harassment.

Women

Gender Empowerment Measure: —
Seats Held in Parliament by Women %: 10.5
Female Administrators and Managers %: —
Female Professional and Technical Workers %: —
Women's Share of Earned Income %: —
Women in Government %: 5

HEALTH, FOOD, AND NUTRITION

Health

Number of Physicians: 29,300
Number of Dentists: —
Number of Nurses: 70,100
Number of Pharmacists: —
Population per Physician: 256
Number of Hospitals: 787
Hospital Beds per 10,000: 96
Hospital Bed Occupancy Rate: —
Infant Mortality Rate per 1,000 live births: 37
Maternal Mortality Rate per 100,000 live births: 22
Total Health Expenditures as % of GDP: 4.27
Health Expenditures per capita $: 99
HIV Infected % of adults: 0.01
Cigarette Consumption per smoker per year: —
% of Smokers: Male: —
Female: —
Access to Safe Water %: —

Food and Nutrition

Food Supply as % of FAO Requirements: —
% of Consumption Expenditures on Food: 42.2
Daily Available Calories per capita: —
% of Total Calories derived from:
Cereals: —
Potatoes, cassava: —
Meat, poultry: —
Fish: —
Eggs, milk: —
Fruits, vegetables: —
Fats, oils: —

ENVIRONMENT

The Apsheron Peninsula that includes the cities of Baku and Sumqayit is considered to be one of the world's gravest ecological disaster areas. Soviet-era water, air, and soil pollution, caused by unregulated industry and uncontrolled use of toxic fertilizers and DDT in the agricultural sector, especially in the cotton industry, has led to a shortage of potable water and unsafe toxin levels in the soil.

Environment

Forest Area sq km: 10,000
Average Annual Deforestation sq km: 0.0
Nationally Protected Areas as % of Total Land Area: 5.5
Freshwater Access cubic meters per capita: 3,831
Emissions of Organic Water Pollutants kg per day: 45,025
CO_2 Emissions per capita ton: 3.9

CHRONOLOGY

1945 With both Armenia and Azerbaijan members of the Soviet Union, Moscow's Bureau of Caucasian Affairs awards the territory of Nagorno-Karabakh to Armenia, but Soviet leader Josef Stalin reverses the decision, declaring Nagorno-Karabakh an autonomous region.

1988 The Azerbaijani political reawakening begins, sparked by an outbreak of ethnic violence between Azerbaijanis and Armenians over Armenian claims to the Nagorno-Karabakh region in which hundreds die; Moscow sends 5,000 troops to the region to quell the violence.

1991 Azerbaijan declares its independence from Russia; Ayaz Mutalibov wins a hastily called election that many believed was rigged by the former Communist Party; the conflict with Armenia over the disputed Nagorno-Karabakh region intensifies.

1992 Azerbaijan joins the United Nations and signs a friendship treaty with Russia; Mutalibov's failure to hold back Armenian advances in Nagorno-Karabakh leads to his replacement by Abulfaz Elchibey of the Popular Front of Azerbaijan in a multiparty general election; Armenian forces seize much of the Nagorno-Karabakh region, equivalent to 20 percent of Azerbaijan's total territory.

1993 Reydar Aliyev ousts Elchibey in a bloodless coup; Azerbaijan forces launch a counteroffensive in Nagorno-Karabakh.

1994 In May Azerbaijan signs the Bisbkek Protocol, a cease-fire agreement regarding Nagorno-Karabakh, which remains in force through the 1990s.

1995 Internal Affairs Ministry militia stage an unsuccessful coup attempt in Baku.

1996 Azerbaijan signs an economic cooperation pact with the European Union.

1997 Aliyev becomes the first Azerbaijani leader to make an official visit to Washington; Azerbaijan's state-owned oil company signs agreements on oil exploration with U.S. and international companies; the Organization for Security and

Cooperation in Europe brokers a draft peace proposal between Armenia and Azerbaijan.

1998 President Reydar Aliyev of the New Azerbaijan Party wins the presidential election with 77.61 percent of the vote.

1999 The government's privatization policy shows signs of success, with the IMF noting in June that consumer prices had fallen by 11 percent in the 12 months ending in April 1999.

2000 In November, Aliyev's son, Ilham, leads the New Azerbaijan Party to victory in disputed parliamentary elections to claim the speaker of parliament position.

2001 Azerbaijan becomes a full member of the Council of Europe.

BIBLIOGRAPHY

Croissant, Cynthia, *Azerbaijan, Oil and Geopolitics*. San Francisco, 1998.

Kelly, Robert C, Debra Ewing, and Stanton Doyle. *Azerbaijan Country Review 1999*. New York, 1999.

Martin, Robert J. *The Economy and International Relations of Azerbaijan: The International Influence*. Washington, D.C., 1999.

Swietochowski, Tadeusz. *Historical Dictionary of Azerbaijan*. New York, 1999.

Swietochowski, Tadeusz. *Russia and Azerbaijani*. New York, 1995.

OFFICIAL PUBLICATIONS

Azerbaijan. *Azerbaijan—Recent Economic Developments* (IMF Staff Country Report [1997]); *Azerbaijan Human Development Report* (UNDP; 1996); *Statistical Yearbook of Azerbaijan.*

CONTACT INFORMATION

Embassy of Azerbaijan
927 15th Street NW, Suite 700
Washington, D.C. 20005
Phone: (202) 842-0001 Fax: (202) 842-0004

INTERNET RESOURCES

- Statistical Committee of Azerbaijan Republic
http://statcom.baku-az.com/
- Azerbaijan Republic
http://www.president.az/azerbaijan/azerbaijan.htm

BAHAMAS

BASIC FACT SHEET

OFFICIAL NAME:
The Commonwealth of the Bahamas

ABBREVIATION:
BF

CAPITAL:
Nassau

HEAD OF STATE:
Queen Elizabeth II, represented by Governor-General Ivy Dumont (from 2001)

HEAD OF GOVERNMENT:
Prime Minister Hubert Alexander Ingraham (from 1992)

NATURE OF GOVERNMENT:
Parliamentary democracy within the British Commonwealth

POPULATION:
297,000 (1999)

AREA:
13,935 sq km (5,380 sq mi)

ETHNIC MAJORITY:
Blacks

LANGUAGE:
English

RELIGION:
Christianity

UNIT OF CURRENCY:
Bahamian dollar

NATIONAL FLAG:
Three horizontal stripes of blue, gold, and blue, with a black triangle at the hoist

NATIONAL EMBLEM:
A shield on which appears Christopher Columbus's flagship, the *Santa Maria*, with a shining sun at the top. The shield is supported by a flamingo and a leaping silver-blue marlin. At the crest appears a conch shell with a mantling of palm fronds. The shield rests on the ground on which a ribbon carries the national motto: "Forward, Upward, Onward, Together."

NATIONAL ANTHEM:
"March On, Bahamaland"

NATIONAL HOLIDAYS:
July 10 (National Day, Independence Day); January 1 (New Year's Day); June 7 (Labor Day); August 5 (Emancipation Day); October 12 (Discovery Day); Christian festivals include Christmas, Boxing Day, Good Friday, Easter Monday, and Whitmonday

DATE OF INDEPENDENCE:
July 10, 1973

DATE OF CONSTITUTION:
July 10, 1973

GEOGRAPHICAL FEATURES

The Bahamas make up an archipelago of 700 islands (of which 29 are inhabited) between southeastern Florida and northern Hispaniola. From the north of the chain, which lies 96 km (60 mi) off the Florida coast, the archipelago extends 950 km (590 mi) southeast to northwest and 298 km (185 mi) northeast to southwest, with a total land area of 13,935 sq km (5,380 sq mi). The most populous island is New Providence (150 sq km; 58 sq mi). Of the other islands or island groups, known as the Family of Islands, the 15 largest are Grand Bahama, the Biminis, the Berry Islands, the Abacos group, Andros, Eleuthera, the Exumas, Cat Island, Rum Cay, San Salvador (also known as Watlings Island), Long Island, Acklins Island, Mayguana, the Ragged Island Range, and the Inaguas. In

The Bahamas

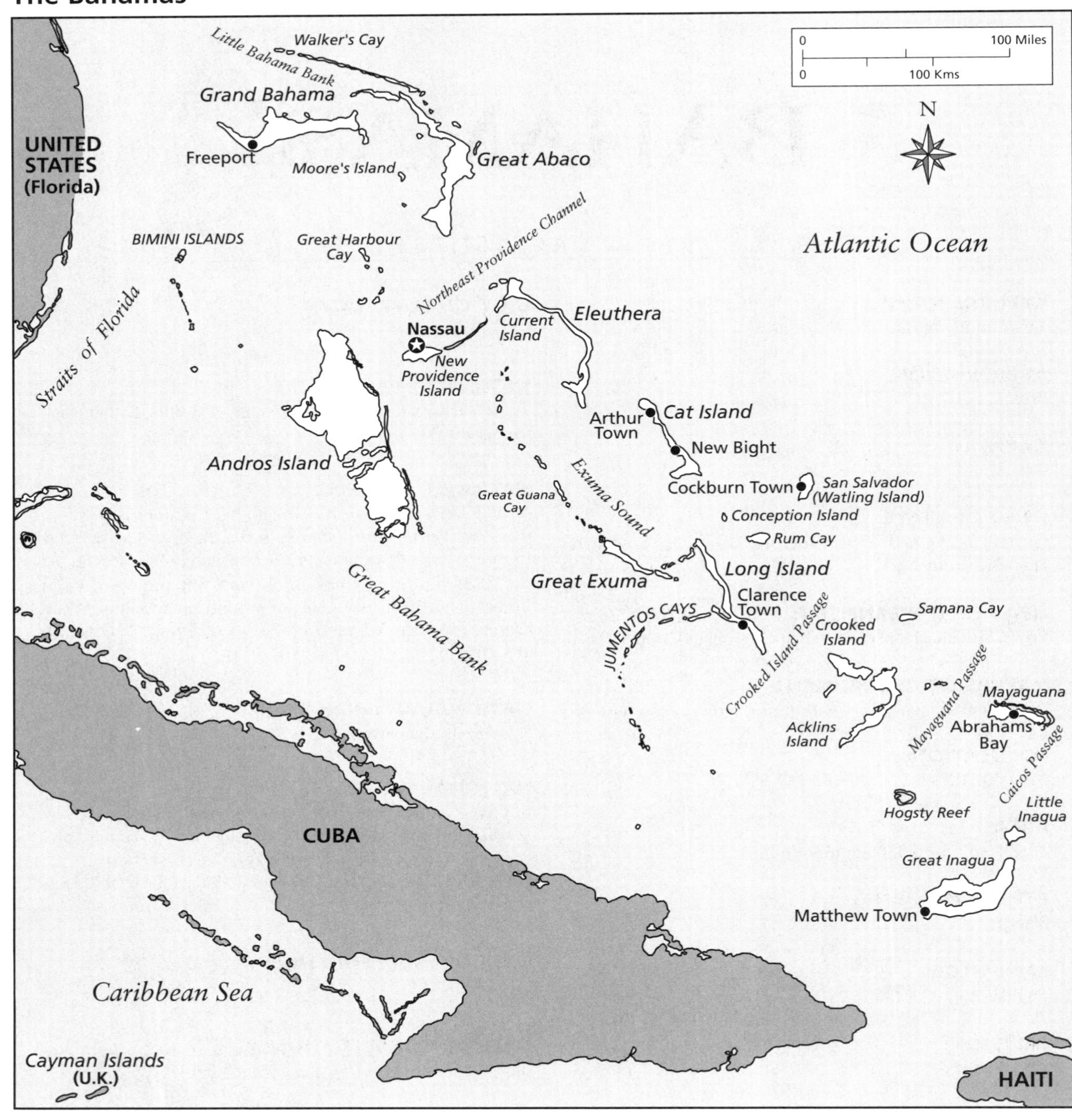

addition, more than 2,000 small cays and rocks protrude from the shallow seas (the name *Bahamas* is derived from the Spanish *bajamar*, "shallow sea"). The total length of the coastline is 2,543 km (1,580 mi).

The capital, Nassau, on New Providence Island, had an estimated population of 178,000 in 1996. The only other major urban center is Freeport (45,000), on the island of Grand Bahama. The islands are for the most part low and flat, with the terrain only occasionally broken by small lakes and mangrove swamps. The shoreline is marked by coral reefs. There are no navigable rivers, and the islands lack sufficient freshwater.

Geography

Area sq km: 13,935 sq mi 5,380
World Rank: 158th
Land Boundaries, km: 0
Coastline, km 3,542

Elevation Extremes meters
Lowest: Atlantic Ocean 0
Highest: Mount Alvernia on Cat Island 63
Land Use % Arable land: 1
Permanent Crops: 0
Permanent Pastures: 0
Forest and Woodland: 32
Other: 67

Population of Principal Cities

Nassau	172,196

CLIMATE AND WEATHER

The Bahamas enjoy a semitropical climate and have only two seasons: Winter extends from December through April, and summer extends from May through November. The warm waters of the Gulf Stream keep temperatures comfortably high during the winter months, and the sea breezes temper even the warmest summer day. Temperatures range from 21.1°C (70°F) to 34.4°C (94°F) in summer and from 15.6°C (60°F) to 23.9°C (75°F) in winter. Relative humidity in summer varies from 60 percent to 100 percent. Annual rainfall averages 1,320 mm (52 in.), concentrated from May to June and from September to October. Gales are uncommon except during the hurricane season, which lasts from June to November.

Climate and Weather

Mean Temperature
Summer 70°F to 94°F
Winter 60°F to 75°F
Average Rainfall: 52 in

POPULATION

Population Indicators

Total Population: 1999 297,000
World Rank: 174th
Density per sq mi: 55.2 per sq km 21.3
% of annual growth (1994–99): 1.7
Male %: 49.0
Female %: 51.0
Urban %: 64.3
Age Distribution: % 0–14: 32.2
15–29: 30.8
30–44: 19.7
45–59: 10.6
60–74: 5.0
75 and over: 1.8
Population 2020: 377,000
Birth Rate per 1,000: 22.5
Death Rate per 1,000: 5.9
Population Doubling Time (years): 46
Infant Mortality Rate per 1,000 live births: 19.0
Rate of Natural Increase per 1,000: 16.6
Total Fertility Rate: 2.0
Expectation of Life (years): Males 66.0
Females: 77.2
Marriage Rate per 1,000: 9.2
Divorce Rate per 1,000: 1.7
Total Number of Households: 68,000
Average Size of Households: 3.7
% of Illegitimate Children: 55.3
Induced Abortions: —
Rate per 100 live births: —

ETHNIC COMPOSITION

The population is predominantly black, constituting close to 85 percent of Bahamians. Many of their ancestors arrived in the islands when it was a major staging area for the slave trade or were brought over by British loyalists during the American Revolution. The remainder of the population is divided evenly between whites and persons of mixed descent.

LANGUAGES

The official language is English (still British English, despite the creeping American influences).

Principal Languages and Their Speakers

English/English Creole	260,000
French/Haitian Creole	30,000

RELIGIONS

The chief Christian denominations represented in the islands are Baptist (32 percent), Anglican (20 percent), and Roman Catholic (19 percent). The remainder is divided among other Protestant groups and Greek Orthodox and Jewish groups. Freedom of religion is guaranteed by the constitution.

Religious Affiliations

Protestant	167,000
Roman Catholic	50,000
Other	80,000

HISTORICAL BACKGROUND

The earliest inhabitants of the Bahamas were a group of Arawak Indians known as Lucayan. Christopher Columbus discovered the islands for the Europeans in 1492. The Spanish made no permanent settlement but conducted slave raids on the peaceful Arawak that depopulated the islands. By the time the British arrived in the 17th century, the Bahamas were uninhabited. In 1717 the Bahamas became a crown colony. Its parliamentary system dates from 1729. Internal self-government was implemented in 1964.

In 1973 the Bahamas became an independent nation within the Commonwealth. Lynden Pindling, leader of the Progressive Liberal Party (PLP), which had won preindependence elections, became prime minister. Pindling remained head of government throughout the 1980s.

During the 1980s, illegal drug trading and government corruption became the dominant issues in Bahamian politics. Responding to allegations of drug-related corruption among government officials, Pindling appointed a commission in 1983 to investigate the problem. Within two years 51 suspects, including the assistant police commissioner, had been indicted Following revelations that Pindling had accepted several million dollars' worth of gifts and loans from businessmen, Deputy Prime Minister Arthur Hanna called for Pindling's resignation. Hanna resigned his post when the prime minister refused to step down.

An early general election was held in June 1987. Despite the continuing prominence of the drug issue, the PLP won a fifth consecutive term. In 1988, in the wake of violent drug-related crimes, allegations of bribery again were leveled at Pindling. However, the Judicial Committee of the Privy Council rejected the claims.

In 1992 a quarter of a century of Progressive Liberal Party rule under Lynden Oscar Pindling came to end when Hubert Alexander Ingraham of the Free National Movement (FNM) was sworn in as prime minister. The FNM retained control by an even wider margin in the 1997 elections.

CONSTITUTION

The constitution of 1973, under which the Bahamas became independent, establishes a parliamentary form of government on the British model. The head of state is the British sovereign, represented in the islands by the governor-general. The governor-general appoints the prime minister (who also is the leader of the majority party in the House), the cabinet, and the leader of the opposition.

The bicameral parliament, composed of the nominated Senate and the elected House of Assembly, is the national legislative body.

The Bahamas' judicial system is made up of the following main courts: the Judicial Committee of the Privy Council (which sits in London), the Bahamas Court of Appeal, the Supreme Court, and magistrates' courts. All courts have jurisdiction over both civil and criminal cases.

Suffrage is universal over age 18. Elections are held at least every five years.

The Bahamas has enjoyed stable government since independence, and the country has been relatively free of violent racial strife that has afflicted many other West Indian states.

LOCAL GOVERNMENT

The Family Islands (islands other than New Providence) are administered by district commissioners, who also exercise limited legal jurisdiction. There are senior commissioners in Grand Bahama, Andros, Abaco, Exuma, and Ragged Island; commissioners in Harbour Island, Grand Bahama, Eleuthera, Berry Islands, Andros, Inagua, Abaco, the Biminis, Cat Island, and Long Island; and assistant commissioners in Abaco, Crooked Island, Exuma, Grand Bahama, Mayaguana, and San Salvadore.

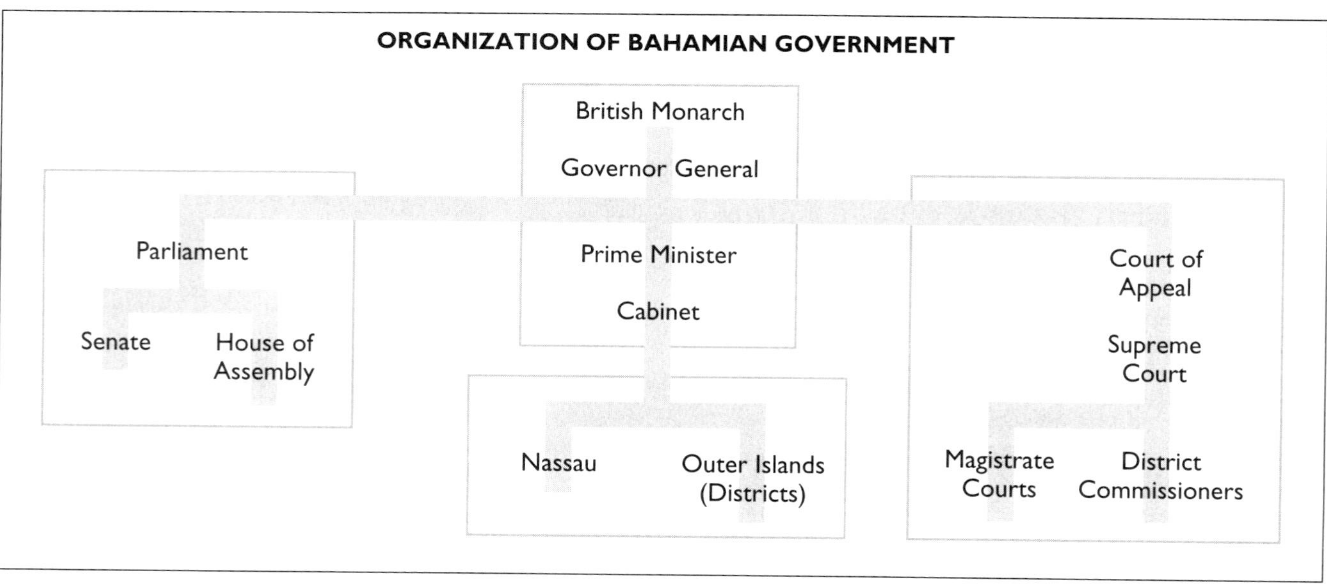

Local Government

Principal administrative divisions, area, population

AREA AND POPULATION

Islands/Island groups	area sq mi	area sq km	population 1990 estimate
Abaco, Great and Little	649	1,681	10,034
Acklins	192	497	405
Andros	2,300	5,957	8,187
Berry Islands	12	31	628
Bimini Islands	9	23	1,639
Cat Island	150	388	1,698
Crooked and Long Cay	93	241	412
Eleuthera	187	484	7,993
Exuma, Great, and Exuma Cays	112	290	3,556
Grand Bahama	530	1,373	40,898
Harbour Island	3	8	1,219
Inagua, Great and Little	599	1,551	985
Long Island	230	596	2,954
Mayaguana	110	285	312
New Providence	80	207	172, 196
Ragged Island	14	36	89
Rum Cay	30	78	53
San Salvador	63	163	465
Spanish Wells	10	26	1,372
Other uninhabited cays and rocks	9	23	—
TOTAL	5,382	13,939	255,095

PARLIAMENT

The bicameral parliament consists of the Senate and the House of Assembly. The Senate consists of 16 members appointed by the governor-general, of whom nine are appointed on the advice of the prime minister, four on the advice of the opposition leader, and three on the advice of the prime minister after consultation with the opposition leader. The House of Assembly consists of 40 members elected on the basis of universal suffrage over age 18. Following the 1997 elections the party position in the House of Assembly was: Free National Movement, 34 seats; Progressive Liberal Party, six seats.

The normal term of the House is five years, but elections may be called and the House dissolved at any time. The House performs all legislative duties, and the majority leader serves as the prime minister.

POLITICAL PARTIES

There are four major political organizations in the Bahamas. For the most part, the politics of the islands are centrist in nature. The Free National Movement is headed by the current prime minister Hubert Ingraham and was founded in 1970. The Progressive Liberal Party, the only other party with seats in parliament, is also a centrist party. The Vanguard Nationalist and Socialist Party was founded in 1971. The most recent political party formed is the Bahamian Freedom Alliance.

Political Parties

Free National Movement, 1972
Progressive Liberal Party, 1953
Vanguard Socialist Party, 1971
People's Democratic Force, 1989

Political Parties: Strength in Parliament Most Recent Elections

House of Assembly. At the most recent election of March 14, 1997, the Free National Movement won 34 seats and the Progressive Liberal Party, 6. At a by-election on September 5, the FNM won the parliamentary seat vacated by the PLP's Lynden Pindling.

LEGAL SYSTEM

Bahamian jurisprudence is based on British common law. The highest court is the Court of Appeal, composed of three nonresident judges. Appeals from this court go in certain instances to the Judicial Committee of the Privy Council in the United Kingdom. The Supreme Court is composed of a chief justice, one senior justice, and two other justices. Appointments to the Supreme Court and the Court of Appeal are made by the governor-general. Magistrates' courts in New Providence and Grand Bahama are presided over by professionally qualified magistrates. Magisterial powers on other islands are exercised by the district commissioners.

The main prison is at Fox Hill in New Providence, but there are smaller lockups in the larger settlements in each district.

LAW ENFORCEMENT

Law Enforcement

Offenses reported to the police per 100,000: 6,752
- Murder: 17.6
- Assault: 115.7
- Burglary: 1336.5
- Automobile Theft:—
- Population per Police officer: 125

Death Penalty: Yes.

HUMAN RIGHTS

In terms of civil and political rights the Bahamas is classified as a free country. A British-style democracy, the Bahamas is noted for unqualified observance of all human as well as political rights. Notwithstanding the transfer of power from the white elite to the black majority, whites continue to play an active role in the political process, both elective and appointive. Similarly, women hold key judicial, civil service, and elective positions. While being seriously tested by the continued influx of Haitians, the government has for the most part maintained a humane approach to the issue.

FOREIGN POLICY

Bahamian foreign relations are determined in part by the islands' proximity to Cuba, Haiti, and the United States. Haitian illegal immigration has been described as the greatest threat to the national security of the islands. Disputes over fishing rights with Cuba have been settled and there are no outstanding issues. Relations with the United States are generally cordial, although there are periodic strains over accusations that high-level Bahamian officials, including the prime minister, are involved in drug trafficking. In 1997 Bahamas opened its first embassy in Beijing and withdrew its ambassador in Taipei.

DEFENSE

The Bahamas has no standing army. The Commonwealth has the 850-man Royal Bahamian Defense Force, which is a paramilitary coast guard. In addition, there is the 2,000-man Royal Bahamas Police Force.

Military Indicators

Total Active Duty Personnel: 900
Military Manpower per 1,000: 3.0
Military Expenditures $: 9 million
- as % of GNP: 0.5
- per capita $: 40
- as % of central government expenditures: 2.5

Arms Imports $: 0
Arms Exports $: 0

ECONOMY

The Bahamas is a middle-income country with a free-market economy in which the dominant sector is private. Its 1999 per capita GNP of 11,830 was the highest among Caribbean nations. The two main economic sectors are tourism and offshore banking. Moderate growth in tourism receipts and a boom in construction of new hotels, resorts, and residences led to an increase in the country's GDP by an estimated 3 percent in 1998, 6 percent in 1999, and 4.5 percent in 2000.

Tourism accounts for 50 percent of the GDP and employs 58,000 people, 40 percent of the workforce.

As one of the first and largest offshore "tax havens," the Bahamas is an important financial center and currently has about 425 financial institutions and over 100 Eurocurrency branches of foreign banks. With no current corporate, capital gains, or personal income taxes it is an attractive location for offshore banking activities. Operating fees paid to banks are a significant revenue source.

Principal Economic Indicators

Gross National Product: $3.288 billion
GNP per capita: $11,830
GNP Average Annual Growth Rate (1990–97) %: —
GNP per capita Average Annual Growth Rate (1990–97) %: —
Origin of Gross Domestic Product %
- Agriculture: 1
- Mining: 15
- Manufacturing: 17
- Construction: 6
- Public Utilities: 2
- Transportation and Communications: 11
- Trade: 11
- Financial Services: 19
- Other Services: 5
- Government: 19

Gross Domestic Product by Type of Expenditure %
- Private Consumption: 76
- Government Consumption: 15
- Gross Domestic Investment: 21
- Foreign Trade: Exports: 44
- Imports: −56

% of Income Received by Poorest 20%: 3.6
% of Income Received by Richest 10%: 32.1

Price and earnings indexes (1995 = 100)

	1993	1994	1995	1996	1997	1998	1999
Consumer price index	96.6	98.0	100.0	101.4	101.9	103.3	104.1
Annual earnings index	—	—	—	—	—	—	—

Finance

National Currency: Bahamian Dollar (B $)
Exchange Rate: $1 = B $1
Money Supply Stock in National Currency billion: 0.445
M1 per capita: 1,560
Central Bank Discount Rate %: 5.75
Total External Debt $million: 381.7
Debt Service Ratio %: —

Balance of Payments $million: −472.1
International Reserves SDRs million: 220
Ratio of External Debt to Total Reserves: —

Average Annual Rate of Inflation/Consumer Price Index
Growth Rate %: 0.4

Official Development Assistance

ODA: $ —
- as % of GNP: —
- per capita: $ —
- Foreign Direct Investment $million: —

Central Government Revenues and Expenditures

Fiscal Year: 1 July–30 June

Revenues $million: 687.5
Expenditures $million: 827.0

Budget Deficit/Surplus $: 139.5
Tax Revenues as % of GDP: —
Highest Tax Bracket %
Individual: —
Corporate: —

Employment and Labor

Economically Active Population: 139,000
Female Participation Rate %: 47.5
Activity Rate %: 50.7
Labor by Sector: %
Agriculture, Forestry, Fishing: 5.0
Manufacturing, Mining: 5.3
Construction: 8.3
Transportation and Communications: 8.1
Trade, Hotels, and Restaurants: 31.8
Finance, Insurance, Real Estate: 9.3
Public Administration, Defense: 7.7
Services: 21.4
Unemployment %: 10

Agriculture

Agriculture's Share of GDP %: 1
Average Annual Rate of Growth (1965–98) %: —
Number of Farms 000: 1.8
Average Size of Farm ha: 8.5
Number of Tractors per 1,000 hectares: 13.3
Irrigation, % of Farms having: 10
Artificial Fertilizer kg/hectare: —
Total Farmland as % of land area: 2
Livestock: Cattle 000: .1
Sheep 000: .6
Hogs 000: 5
Chickens 000: 3,800
Forests: Production of Roundwood (000 cubic meters): 117
Fisheries: Total Catch tons 000: 10.0

Mining

% of GDP: —
Value of Mineral Production $million: —

Manufacturing

Value Added $million: 95
Industrial Production Growth Rate %: —

Energy

Commercial Energy Production metric tons of oil equivalent 000: –
Commercial Energy Consumption metric tons of oil equivalent 000: 1,867
Commercial Energy Consumption per capita kg: 5,864
Average Annual Growth Rate 1980–97 %:—
Net Energy Imports % of use: 100
Electricity Installed Capacity kW 000: 401
Production kW-hr million: 1,028
Coal Reserves tons million: —
Production tons 000: —
Natural Gas Proven Reserves cubic meters billion: —
Production cubic meters million: —
Crude Petroleum Reserves barrels million: —
Production barrels million:—
Consumption barrels million: —
Refinery Capacity barrels per day 000: —
Pipelines Length km: —

Foreign Trade

Imports $million: 2,919.9
Exports $million: 2,592.6
Export Volume % Annual Growth Rate (1990–97):
Import Volume % Annual Growth Rate (1990–97):
Balance of Trade $

Balance of trade (current prices)

	1993	1994	1995	1996	1997	1998
B$000,000	−792	−904	−1,067	−1,163	−1,441	−1,572
% of total	70.9%	73.0%	75.2%	76.4%	79.9%	72.4%

Major Trading Partners

	Imports	Exports
European Union %	5.9	2.6
United States %	36.2	93.8
Eastern Europe %	0.2	—
Japan %	0.5	0.6
Others %	57.3	3.0

Transportation

Roads Total Length mi: 1,522 km 2,450
Paved %: 57
Automobiles: 46,089
Trucks and Buses: 11,858
Persons per vehicle: 4.7
Railroad: Track Length mi:—km —
Passenger-mi million: —
Freight-mi million: —
Merchant Marine: No of Vessels: 1,061
Total Deadweight Tonnage 000: 3,3081.7
International Cargo Loaded tons 000: 5,920
International Cargo Off-loaded tons 000: 5,705
Airports with Scheduled Flights: 23
Traffic: Passenger-mi million: 119
Freight-mi million: 0.01
Length of Canals mi: km —

Tourism

Number of Tourists to 000: —
Number of Tourists from 000: —
Tourist Receipts $million: 1,346
Tourist Expenditures $million: 213

Communications

Telephones 000: 77
Cost of Local Calls 3 mins $0.
Cellular Telephones 000: 2.4

(continued)

Fax Machines 000: 0.5
Personal Computers 000: —
Internet Hosts per million persons: 989
Mail: Post Offices: 136
Pieces of Mail Handled million: 61
Pieces of Mail Handled per person: 216

EDUCATION

Education is compulsory, free, and universal for 10 years, from ages five to 14. Schooling lasts for 12 years, divided into six years of primary school, three years of lower secondary school, and three years of upper secondary school. The academic year runs from September to June. The medium of instruction is English.

There are two teacher training colleges. Technical education is provided by C. R. Walker Technical College. Higher education is provided by the University of the West Indies in Jamaica. The university opened a branch in the Bahamas in 1979.

Education

Literacy Rate %: 98.2
Male %: 98.5
Female %: 98.0
First Level: Primary schools: 115
Teachers: 1,581
Students: 33,343
Student-Teacher Ratio: 2.1
Net Enrollment Ratio: 95
Second Level: Secondary Schools: —
Teachers: 1,775
Students: 28,363
Student-Teacher Ratio: 16.0
Net Enrollment Ratio: 8.7

Vocational Level: Schools: —
Students: —

Third Level: Institutions: 1
Teachers: 300
Students: 3,201
Student-Ratio Level: 10.7
Gross Enrollment Ratio: —
Students per 100,000: —
% of Population Age 25 and over with Postsecondary Education: 13.5

Public Expenditure on Education as % of GDP: 4.0

SCIENCE AND TECHNOLOGY

Science and Technology

Scientists and Engineers in R&D per 1 million persons:—
Expenditures in R&D as % of GDP: —
High-Tech Exports $: —
Patent Applications by Residents: —

MEDIA

In 1995 two national newspapers and two nondailies were published in the Bahamas, with combined circulations of 35,000 and 50,000, respectively. Per capita circulations are 143 per 1,000 inhabitants for dailies and 270 per 1,000 inhabitants for nondailies. The principal dailies are the *Nassau Guardian* (11,800) and the *Freeport News* (5,000).

Annual consumption of newsprint totaled 400 metric tons in 1987, or 1,581 kg (3,485 lb.) per 1,000 persons. The press enjoys substantial freedom, including the right to oppose the government on national issues.

Media

Daily Newspapers: 3
Total Circulation 000: 35
Circulation per 1,000: 126
Books Published: —
Magazines: —
Radio Receivers 000: 80
per 1,000: 282
Television sets 000: 65
per 1,000: 233

MOST IMPORTANT MEDIA:

Press. The following are published daily at Nassau, unless otherwise noted: *Nassau Daily Tribune* (13,500); *Nassau Guardian* (12,300); *Freeport News* (Freeport, 3,000); *Bahama Journal; Official Gazette*, weekly government publication. In August 1998 the *Tribune* concluded a partnership agreement with the *Miami Herald* to produce a combined edition of the two papers.

Radio and television. The government-owned Broadcasting Corporation of the Bahamas, which operates two commercial radio stations at Nassau and one at Freeport, transmitted to approximately 261,000 receivers in 1998. Bahamas Television began broadcasting from Nassau in 1977, while the Canadian-owned Cable Bahamas commenced cable TV transmission in March 1995.

CULTURE

Cultural Indicators

Public Libraries
Number: —
Volumes: —
Registered borrowers: —
Museums
Number: 7
Annual Attendance: —
Cinema
Production of Long Films: —
Number of Cinemas: —
Seating Capacity: —
Annual Attendance: —
Annual Attendance per capita: —

STATUS OF WOMEN

Like most modern democracies, women legally share in all rights equally with their male counterparts. While most political rights and access to education are secure, real economic inequalities do exist.

Women

Gender Empowerment Measure: 15
Seats Held in Parliament by Women %: 19.6
Female Administrators and Managers %: 34.7
Female Professional and Technical Workers %: 51.4
Women's Share of Earned Income %: 40
Women in Government %: 34

HEALTH, FOOD, AND NUTRITION

Health

Number of Physicians: 373
Number of Dentists: 58
Number of Nurses: 1,067
Number of Pharmacists: 52
Population per Physician: 709
Number of Hospitals: 5
Hospital Beds per 10,000: 40
Hospital Bed Occupancy Rate: 83.7
Infant Mortality Rate per 1,000 live births: 24
Maternal Mortality Rate per 100,000 live births: —
Total Health Expenditures as % of GDP: —
Health Expenditures per capita $: —
HIV Infected % of adults: —
Cigarette Consumption per smoker per year: —
% of Smokers: Male: —
Female: —
Access to Safe Water %: 97

Food and Nutrition

Food Supply as % of FAO Requirements: 103
% of Consumption Expenditures on Food: 13.8
Daily Available Calories per capita: 2,498
% of Total Calories derived from:
Cereals: 29.0
Potatoes, cassava: 1.5
Meat, poultry: 17.5
Fish: 1.7
Eggs, milk: 7.3
Fruits, vegetables: 7.9
Fats, oils: 9.6

ENVIRONMENT

While the Bahamas has long recognized the need to protect its natural resources—it created a flamingo habitat and marine nursery park in 1959—growing population and increased tourism have caused concern over soil and coastal erosion. The government continues its long tradition of aggressively protecting the environment and finding creative ways to reward good usage of natural resources.

Environment

Forest Area sq km: —
Average Annual Deforestation sq km: —
Nationally Protected Areas as % of Total Land Area: —
Freshwater Access cubic meters per capita: —
Emissions of Organic Water Pollutants kg per day: —
CO_2 Emissions per capita ton: 6.0

CHRONOLOGY

1953 Bahamians of African descent form the Progressive Liberal Party (PLP).

1961 Men who do not own property and all women win the right to vote.

1964 The United Kingdom grants the Bahamas self-government.

1973 The Bahamas is granted full independence by the United Kingdom and is admitted as the 33rd member of the Commonwealth.

1976 Chester Whitfield is elected leader of the opposition Free National Movement.
Gerald C. Cash succeeds Milo B. Butler as governor-general.

1977 Lynden O. Pindling's Progressive Liberal Party wins 30 of 38 seats in the House of Assembly in national elections.

1978 An economic commission is created to promote investment and review economic policies of the government.

1979 Legislation restricting land sales to foreigners is approved.

1982 In national elections Pindling's Progressive Liberal Party wins 32 of 43 seats.

1984 Royal Commission of Inquiry is appointed to investigate charges of corruption in government and extensive influence-peddling by drug dealers. The commission finds no direct evidence of Pindling's association with drug traffic but releases damaging data of unaccounted wealth in the prime minister's account. Deputy Prime Minister Arthur D. Hanna resigns and two other cabinet ministers are dismissed following publication of the report.

1985 Howard Smith, assistant police commissioner, is indicted along with 50 others for involvement in illegal drug trade and is dismissed from the force.

1986 A joint U.S.-Bahamian task force on drug interdiction is created following a two-year inquiry into the cocaine-smuggling problem.

1987 Pindling's Progressive Liberal Party wins 31 of the 49 House Assembly seats despite the issue of drug related corruption. Statistics for the year reveal unprecedented levels of violence and drug-related crimes.

1988 The Judicial Committee of the Privy Council in the United Kingdom rejects opposition accusations that Pindling's financial affairs had not been adequately investigated.

1989 The Bahamas ratifies the 1988 Vienna Convention on Narcotics Trafficking; a Bahamian member of Parliament, his wife, an associate of Prime Minister Pindling, and five others are indicted in two separate U.S. drug-related cases.

1990 Sir Cecil Wallace-Whitfield, leader of the opposition Free National Movement, dies and is replaced by Hubert Ingraham; Minister of Agriculture, Trade and Industry Ervin Knowles resigns after accusations of nepotism and misuse of public funds.

1992 After 25 years in power, Pindling's Progressive Liberal Party is defeated by the Free National Movement and Hubert Ingraham becomes prime minister.

1995 Sir Orville Turnquist is appointed governor-general.

1997 The Free National Movement wins 34 of 40 House Assembly Seats.

2000 Pindling dies at age 70.

BIBLIOGRAPHY

Albury, P. *The Story of the Bahamas*. London, 1975.

Craton, Michael. *A History of the Bahamas*. Waterloo, Ont. 1986.

Craton, Michael, and G. Saunders. *Islanders in the Stream*. Athens, Ga., 1992.

Dupuch, S. P. *Bahamas Handbook and Businessman's Annual*. New York, 1979.

Evans, F. C., and N. Young. *The Bahamas*. New York, 1977.

Smith, Anastasia P. *Aspects of Bahamian Culture*. New York, 1978.

OFFICIAL PUBLICATIONS

Bahamas, The. *Census of Population and Housing 1990; Statistical Abstract* (annual).

CONTACT INFORMATION

Embassy of the Bahamas
2220 Massachusetts Avenue NW
Washington, D.C. 20008
Phone: (202) 319-2660 Fax: (202) 319-2668

INTERNET RESOURCES

- The Commonwealth Online: The Bahamas
  http://www.tcol.co.uk/baha/index.htm

BAHRAIN

BASIC FACT SHEET

OFFICIAL NAME:
State of Bahrain (Dawlat al-Bahrayn)

ABBREVIATION:
BA

CAPITAL:
Manama

HEAD OF STATE:
Emir Sheikh Hamad ibn Isa al-Khalifa (from 1999)

HEAD OF GOVERNMENT:
Prime Minister Sheikh Khalifa ibn Salman al-Khalifa (from 1970)

NATURE OF GOVERNMENT:
Constitutional monarchy

POPULATION:
646,000 (1999)

AREA:
622 sq km (240 sq mi)

ETHNIC MAJORITY:
Arab

LANGUAGES:
Arabic (official), English

RELIGION:
Islam

UNIT OF CURRENCY:
Bahraini dinar

NATIONAL FLAG:
Red field covering three-fourths of the flag separated by a vertical serrated line from a white vertical stripe on the hoist

NATIONAL EMBLEM:
A red shield with a serrated white upper border surrounded by a red and white mantling

NATIONAL ANTHEM:
"Our Bahrain, Country of Security, Nation of Hospitality, Protected by Our Courageous Emir . . ."

NATIONAL HOLIDAYS:
December 16 (National Day); January 1 (New Year's Day); also variable Islamic holidays

DATE OF INDEPENDENCE:
December 16, 1971

DATE OF CONSTITUTION:
June 1973

GEOGRAPHICAL FEATURES

The Bahrain archipelago covers a total area of 622 sq km (240 sq mi) and lies at the entrance of the Gulf of Salwa between Saudi Arabia's Hausa Province and the Qatar Peninsula. The group includes six principal islands—Bahrain, Muharraq, Sitrah, Umm al-Nassan (the personal property and private game preserve of the emir), Jidda, and Nabi Salih—as well as 27 minor islands, including the Muhammadiyah and the Hwar groups. The total length of the coastline is 126 km (78 mi).

In 1986 the King Fahd Causeway was opened, linking Bahrain and Saudi Arabia. Except for a narrow strip of land along the northern coast, Bahrain is a desert. Toward the interior, the land rises gradually toward a central range of hills, which reaches its highest elevation at Jebel Dukhan (130 m, 440 ft). Most of the smaller islands are flat and sandy.

Bahrain is blessed with a number of freshwater springs or artesian wells whose source still is a mystery. These springs are most numerous along the northern coast of Bahrain Island, and they make permanent cultivation possible on a narrow strip of land.

Bahrain

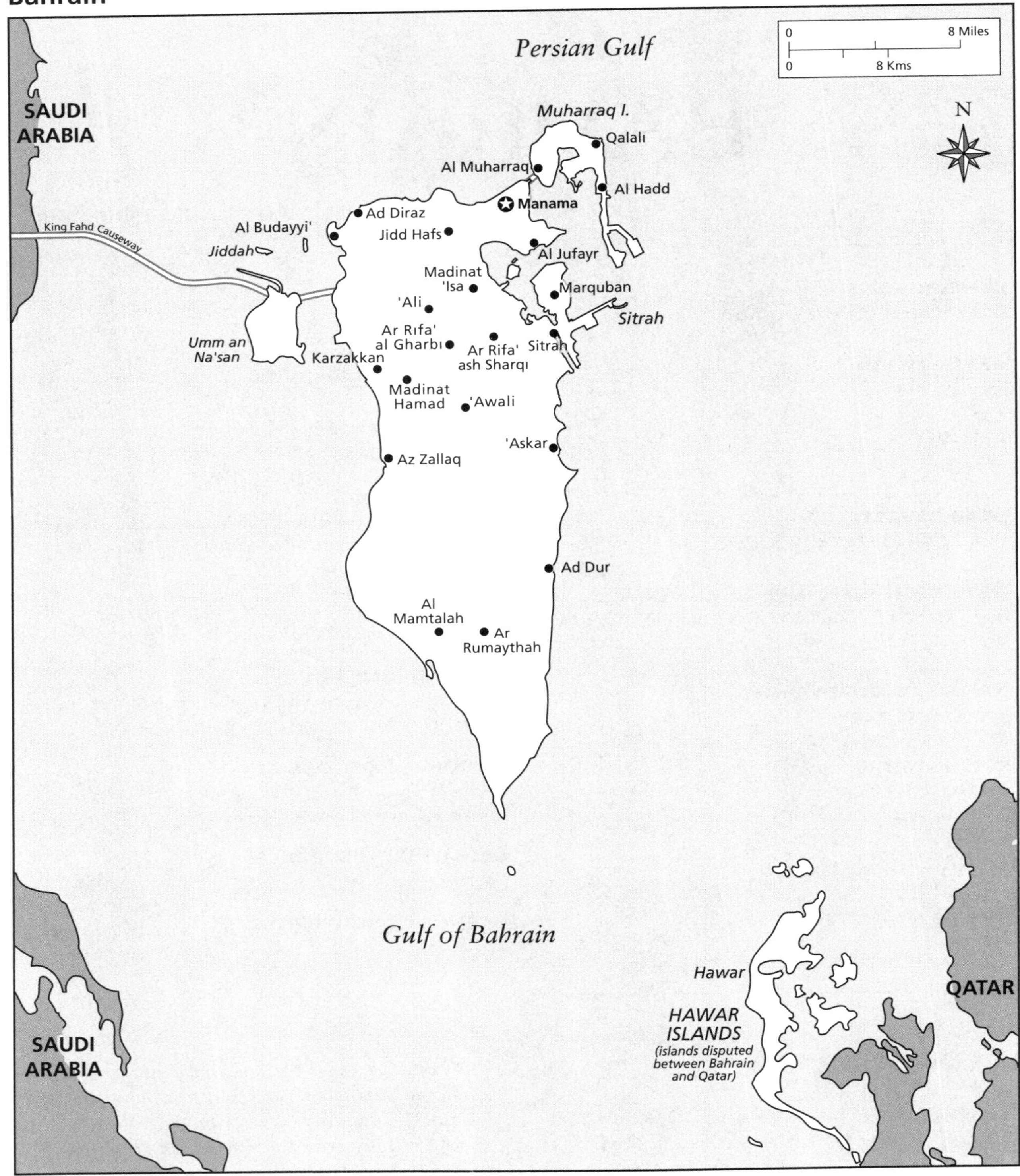
Persian Gulf
0
8 Miles
0
8 Kms
N
SAUDI ARABIA
Muharraq I.
Qalali
Al Muharraq
Al Hadd
Manama
Ad Diraz
Al Budayyi'
King Fahd Causeway
Jidd Hafs
Jiddah
Al Jufayr
Madinat 'Isa
Marquban
'Ali
Sitrah
Ar Rifa' al Gharbi
Ar Rifa' ash Sharqi
Sitrah
Umm an Na'san
Karzakkan
Madinat Hamad
'Awali
'Askar
Az Zallaq
Ad Dur
Al Mamtalah
Ar Rumaythah
Gulf of Bahrain
Hawar
HAWAR ISLANDS
(islands disputed between Bahrain and Qatar)
QATAR
SAUDI ARABIA

Geography

Area sq km: 622 sq mi 240
World Rank: 186th
Land Boundaries, km: 0
Coastline, km: 161
Elevation Extremes meters
 Lowest: Persian Gulf 0
 Highest: Jabal ad Dukhan 122
Land Use % Arable land: 1
 Permanent Crops: 1
 Permanent Pastures: 6
 Forest and Woodland: 0
 Other: 92

Population of Principal Cities

Manama	148,000

CLIMATE AND WEATHER

Bahrain has an arid, desert climate, with maximum summer temperatures in July reaching 44°C (111°F). Winters are relatively cooler, with temperatures in December between 10°C and 20°C (50°F and 68°F). Average annual rainfall is only 76 mm (3 in). A dry, southwestern wind known locally as the qaws periodically raises dust storms.

Climate and Weather

Mean Temperature
Summer High 111°F
Winter 50° to 68°F
Average Rainfall 3 in

POPULATION

Population Indicators

Total Population: 1999 646,000
World Rank: 161st
Density per sq mi: 2,410.4 per sq km 930.6
 % of annual growth (1994–99): 3.0
Male %: 57.9
Female %: 42.1
Urban %: 88.4
Age Distribution: % 0–14: 31.7
 15–29: 28.4
 30–44: 28.2
 45–59: 8.0
 60–74: 3.1
 75 and over: 0.6
Population 2020: 895,000
Birth Rate per 1,000: 21.0
Death Rate per 1,000: 3.6
Population Doubling Time (years): 37
Infant Mortality Rate per 1,000 live births: 18.0
Rate of Natural Increase per 1,000: 17.4
Total Fertility Rate: 3.0
Expectation of Life (years): Males 71.1
 Females 75.3
Marriage Rate per 1,000: 6.4
Divorce Rate per 1,000: 1.3
Total Number of Households: 67,000
Average Size of Households: 6.5
% of Illegitimate Children: —
Induced Abortions: —
 Rate per 100 live births: —

ETHNIC COMPOSITION

Indigenous Arabs constitute the majority of the population, though their percentage has decreased. Indigenous Bahrainis include blacks who have intermarried with local Arabs, and the Bahanrah, descendants of the original inhabitants of the islands who sought refuge there from Nebuchadnezzar's persecution.

Ethnic diversity among the minority groups is a pronounced feature of Bahrain's population. Among the groups represented are Saudi Arabians, Omanis, Iranians, Asians (including Baluchis, Pakistanis, Indians) and British or continental Europeans. The ethnic mix is continuing to change as a steady flow of immigration brings more aliens into the country.

LANGUAGES

The official language is Arabic, which is universally spoken in its Gulf dialect. English is widely understood and taught in secondary schools. English also dominates the media. Other languages are spoken by immigrants to Bahrain, principally from South and East Asia.

Principal Languages and Their Speakers

Arabic	440,000
English	—
Other	210,000

RELIGIONS

The national religion is Islam, and a majority of Bahrainis are Shiite Muslims. The Shiites constitute 75 percent of the Muslim population; the Sunnis, 25 percent. Further, a number of Iranian Shiites were naturalized in the early 1970s. Sunni-Shiite conflicts have been common.

The emirs of Bahrain have shown remarkable toleration for the Christian denominations. There are Catholic and Anglican churches at Manama as well as a Catholic school and a Dutch Reformed mission. There are also a few Hindu temples. The number of Christians in the emirate is estimated at 6,570; members of other faiths number about 100,000.

Religious Affiliations	
Shiite Muslim	400,000
Sunni Muslim	130,000
Other	110,000

HISTORICAL BACKGROUND

The earliest recorded reference to Bahrain dates back to the third millennium B.C., when it was known as Dilmun. The era has been chronicled in the Epic of Gilgamesh, who called Dilmun the land of immortality when he visited it in his quest for eternal life. With its lush vegetation and abundant fresh water springs, not to speak of its ideal location between Mesopotamia and the Indian subcontinent, Dilmun became a popular haven on the sea trade route. As trade between Mesopotamia and the Indus Valley civilizations in the subcontinent continued to flourish, Dilmun also grew in prosperity. A city, Qalat Al Bahrain, began to spring up at the site where the Bahrain Fort now exists.

The good times were not to last; between 1800 and 1600 B.C.E., Aryan forces invaded and destroyed the cities of the Indus Valley Civilization, bringing trade to a halt. For a long period thereafter Bahrain remained isolated, forced to depend on its own resources. It would not be until the early first millennium that Bahrain would flourish again, as part of the Assyrian empire. Bahrain became an important pearling and fishing port, but the high quality and abundance of pearls in its waters attracted some unwelcome attention.

By 600 B.C.E., Bahrain was drawn into the expanding Babylonian empire. The Greeks, who called the island Tylos, soon began settling in Bahrain. Trade began to play an important part after the fall of Babylonia to the Persians—who now controlled much of the region between India and the Mediterranean—and by 323 B.C.E., Bahrain regained its independence.

There followed a period of relative calm, up until the 15th century when the Europeans began exploring new sea trade routes. Bahrain was also known as Awal during that pre-Islamic era. The name is associated with a pagan idol worshipped by the Wael tribe.

The islands first became known as Bahrain in the early Islamic era, when the name was used for the entire region stretching from Basra (Iraq) in the north to Oman in the south. By the early 1500s, the Portuguese viewed Bahrain as a key point to protect their trade routes between India, Africa, and Europe. They invaded the island and set up a military base at the Bahrain Fort. The fort, which ironically had been used by the people of Bahrain to defend themselves against the Portuguese, was strengthened and new stone towers erected. The Bahrain Fort remains widely known as the Portuguese Fort.

The Portuguese were, however, unable to protect the islands, which fell to the Persians in 1603. Then came a long period of turmoil, with Bahrain changing hands between the warring Persians and Arabs until it was finally conquered in 1783 by Shaikh Ahmed bin Mohammed Al Khalifa, better known as Ahmed bin Mohamed Al Fateh, the conqueror.

The British gained a foothold in Bahrain by offering naval protection from the Ottoman empire in the 1830s. Conflict between Bahrain and Britain was rare. However, there was conflict between the two nations when the British sought to install their choice for emir in 1869. Oil was discovered in Bahrain in 1902, but large-scale drilling did not begin until the 1930s. The production of oil brought wealth to the country. Additionally, the British increased their presence. Growing anti-British sentiment in the 1950s led to the British announcing their plans to depart the Persian Gulf in 15 years. On August 14, 1971, Bahrain declared itself independent from Britain.

As the price of oil continued to grow in the 1970s and 1980s, the country's wealth and infrastructure also improved. The opening of the King Fahd Causeway between Bahrain and Saudi Arabia in 1986 both increased tourism and improved the economy. During the Gulf War, Saddam Hussein ordered Scud missile attacks on the country. However, the missiles largely missed targets and landed harmlessly in the sea. Bahrain also cooperated with the United Nation's attempt to monitor Iraq after the Gulf War. However, U.S. troop buildups in 1998 strained relations between the United States and Bahrain.

In 1999, Emir Isa bin Sulman al-Khalifa was succeeded by his son Hamad ibn Isa al-Khalifa, who commissioned the drafting of a new national charter and pardoned more than 800 political prisoners. In a national referendum in February 2001, voters overwhelmingly endorsed the political reforms stipulated in the national charter, which called for a European-style constitutional monarchy. Emir Hamad abolished the State Security Law and the State Security Court, which had been set up in 1995 after unrest by Shiite Muslims demanding reform. On February 15, he declared Bahrain a constitutional monarchy.

CONSTITUTION

Bahrain has been ruled since the 18th century by the Khalifa family. The only restraint on the absolute power of the emir, until the state became independent in 1971, was the British political agent. Political unrest inspired by the Arab Nationalist Movement and the pro-Iraqi Baath Party in the late 1960s led to the convening of a Constituent Assembly in 1972 and to the ratification of the constitution of 1973, which provides for a National Assembly composed of elected members and cabinet ministers. The constitution created the post of financial comptroller, responsible to the National Assembly and not to the emir, and guarantees freedom of the press, speech, conscience, and religious belief. In theory it also permits national labor unions to be organized "on peaceful lines." None of these provisions served, in practice, to reduce the power of the emir, who remains as absolute a ruler as

ever. The Assembly was dissolved in 1975, and the emir rules through the cabinet alone.

Bahrain's leadership has been torn between two aims: its desire to foster the open social and commercial environment needed to attract international business, and its urge to protect the ruling family's preeminence, prevent potential sectarian violence, and thwart efforts by Iran and other revolutionary states to destabilize Bahrain.

The government is administered by a cabinet appointed by the emir, the head of state, and presided over by the prime minister, head of government.

Bahrain has had one popular election in its history—in 1973—on the basis of the new constitution. Suffrage was restricted to men over 21. Upon the dissolution of the National Assembly in 1975, the emir promised a revised electoral law providing for a more representative body.

Beginning in the mid-1990s, pressure on the government to restore a liberal constitution increased. In 1999, Emir Isa bin Sulman al-Khalifa was succeeded by his son Hamad ibn Isa al-Khalifa, who began to release political prisoners and noticeably declined the use of the state security courts. In 2001, his National Action Charter for a European-style constitutional monarchy was put to a referendum and won overwhelming approval from the populatce. The charter calls for a partially elected legislature and an independent judiciary. Both men and women over the age of 20 vote. The charter is expected to go into effect no later than 2004. The principal threat to the state comes from the Iran-oriented Shiite community, which forms the numerical majority but has been excluded from power.

LOCAL GOVERNMENT

The country's six towns are administered by municipal councils. Half the councilmen are elected, and the other half are appointed by the emir. Council presidents are invariably members of the Khalifa family. Villages are administered by mukhtars (headmen), appointed by the emir.

On May 9, 2002, the first elections in 32 years for municipal council members took place. For the first time Bahrain women voted and ran for office.

Local Government

Principal administrative divisions, area, population

Area and population

	area		population
Regions	**sq mi**	**sq km**	**1991 census**
Al-Gharbiyah (Western)	60.3	156.1	22,034
Al-Hadd	2.3	6.0	8,610
Jidd (Judd) Hafs	8.3	21.6	44,769
Al-Manāmah (Manama)	10.0	25.8	136,999
Al-Muharraq	6.2	16.0	74,245
Ar-Rifa	112.6	291.6	49,752
Ash-Shamāliyah (Northern)	14.2	36.8	33,763
Ash-Sharqiyah (Eastern)	—	—	3,242
Sitrah	11.1	28.8	36,755
Al-Wusta (Central)	13.6	35.2	34,304
Towns with special status			
Hammād	5.1	13.1	29,055
Madfinat 'Isā	4.8	12.4	34,509
Islands			
Hawār and other	19.5	50.6	2
TOTAL	268.0	694.2	508,037

PARLIAMENT

The National Assembly consists of 30 members elected for four-year terms, cabinet ministers, and ministers of state. According to the constitution, the financial comptroller is responsible to the National Assembly. The first election to the National Assembly was held in 1973, when 30,000 electors chose 30 members from 114 candidates, all of whom ran as independents because political parties were not allowed. The membership of the 1973 National Assembly was almost equally divided between conservatives and radicals. Its powers were few and insubstantial, and even its rights of debate were subject to government control. Nevertheless, it was dissolved in 1975 "for being dominated by ideas alien to the society and values of Bahrain." For this act Bahrain was expelled from the International Parliamentary Union in 1976. In 1977 Bahrain was cited by Amnesty International as one of the countries in which legislators had been jailed without trial.

The National Action Charter, approved in a national referendum on February 12 and 15, 2001, stipulates the creation of a bicameral legislature and calls for suffrage for men and women over the age of 20. The first parliamentary elections are scheduled for October 2002.

POLITICAL PARTIES

There are five political parties in Bahrain: Islamic National Al Wefaq Society, National Democratic Action, Progressive Democratic Forum, Islamic National Forum, and Islamic Arab Democratic Wassat Society.

LEGAL SYSTEM

The legal system is based on the Shari'a, Islamic law, but has been influenced by British traditions and codes. The emir and the Ministry of Justice constitute the apex of the judicial system. Local Shari'a courts dispense justice at lower levels. Equality before the law is guaranteed by the constitution. A number of judges and lawyers are non-Bahraini Arabs. The main penal settlement is on the rocky islet of Jidda.

LAW ENFORCEMENT

Law Enforcement

Offenses reported to the police per 100,000: 1,714
- Murder: 1.8
- Assault: 547.1
- Burglary: 86.7
- Automobile Theft: 8.2
- Population per Police officer: 180

Death Penalty: Yes.

HUMAN RIGHTS

There continue to be serious problems in Bahrain's human rights record. However, the situation has improved measurably in the last few years. The government continues to deny citizens the right to change their government; however, the political situation improved and political and civil unrest decreased following an effort by the new emir to develop relations with the Shia community. In the 1990s, there were no extrajudicial killings by security forces; however, security forces continued to torture, beat, and otherwise abuse prisoners. Impunity of security forces personnel remains a problem; there are no known instances of any security forces personnel being punished for human rights abuses. The government continued to use arbitrary arrest and detention, incommunicado and prolonged detention, and involuntary exile. However, one of the new emir's first official acts was to pardon or release more than 800 prisoners, detainees, and exiles. In November and December of 1999 the emir pardoned a combined total of approximately 800 prisoners and detainees, some of whom had been detained for political reasons. The judiciary remains subject to government pressure, and there are limits on the right to a fair, public trial, especially in the security court. The government continues to infringe on citizens' privacy rights. The government has also imposed some restrictions on freedom of speech and of the press and restricted freedom of assembly and association. In addition, the government imposes some limits on freedom of religion and movement. Violence against women and discrimination based on sex, religion, and ethnicity remain problems. The government restricts worker rights, and there have been instances of forced labor.

FOREIGN POLICY

Since independence Bahrain has followed Saudi Arabia's lead in foreign policy, but the country has proven more moderate than most Arab states on the Palestinian question. It has a running dispute with Qatar over the small uninhabited island of Fasht al-Dibal that had been reclaimed from a coral reef. Bahrain and the United States have a defense cooperation agreement that provides for a U.S. airbase in Bahrain.

DEFENSE

The defense command is headed by the emir, and the line of command runs through the defense minister to the chief of staff. Both the defense minister and the chief of staff are members of the ruling Khalifa family. Military manpower is provided by voluntary enlistment. The total strength of the armed forces is 2,800, or 5 per 1,000 inhabitants.

The Bahrain military is designed for internal peacekeeping only. For defense against possible external attack, Bahrain depends on Saudi forces. Bahrain has permitted Saudi Arabia to establish a major air base south of the Awali-Zalaq road. It is Saudi Arabia's first military establishment outside its own borders.

Most of the equipment is of British origin. Britain also provides training for defense personnel. The U.S. Navy's base in Bahrain was closed in 1977. The United States is currently assisting in the construction of a major air base.

Military Indicators

Total Active Duty Personnel: 11,000
Military Manpower per 1,000: 17.7
Military Expenditures $million: 273
  as % of GNP: 5.4
  per capita $: 473
  as % of central government expenditures: 14.8

Arms Imports $million: 40
Arms Exports $million: 0

ECONOMY

Bahrain has a free-market economy in which the private sector is dominant. In Bahrain, petroleum production and processing account for about 60 percent of export receipts, 60 percent of government revenues, and 30 percent of gross domestic product. Economic conditions have fluctuated with the changing fortunes of oil since 1985, for example, during and following the Gulf crisis of 1990–91. With its highly developed communication and transport facilities, Bahrain is home to numerous multinational firms with business in the Persian Gulf region. A large share of exports consists of petroleum products made from imported crude. Construction proceeds on several major industrial projects. Unemployment, especially among the young, and the depletion of both oil and underground water resources are major long-term economic problems.

Principal Economic Indicators

Gross National Product $: 4.514 billion
GNP per capita $: 7,820
GNP Average Annual Growth Rate (1990–97) %: —
GNP per capita Average Annual Growth Rate (1990–97) %: —
Origin of Gross Domestic Product %
  Agriculture: 1
  Mining: 15
  Manufacturing: 15
  Construction: 6
  Public Utilities: 3
  Transportation and Communications: 11
  Trade: 8
  Financial Services: 22
  Other Services: 5
  Government: 20
Gross Domestic Product by Type of Expenditure %
  Private Consumption: 30
  Government Consumption: 25
  Gross Domestic Investment: 26
  Foreign Trade: Exports: 107
    Imports: −88
% of Income Received by Poorest 20%: —
% of Income Received by Richest 10%: —

Price and earnings indexes (1995 = 100)

	1990	1991	1992	1993	1994	1995	1996
Consumer price index	93.6	94.4	94.1	96.5	97.3	100.0	99.8
Monthly earnings index	—	—	—	—	—	—	—

Finance

National Currency: Bahraini Dinar (BD)
Exchange Rate: $1 = BD 0.3760
Money Supply Stock in National Currency billion: 0.291
M1 per capita: 480
Central Bank Discount Rate %: 5.6
Total External Debt $million: 3,200
Debt Service Ratio %: —
Balance of Payments $million: −303.7
International Reserves SDRs million: 1,045
Ratio of External Debt to Total Reserves: —
Average Annual Rate of Inflation/Consumer Price Index
  Growth Rate %: −0.2

Official Development Assistance

ODA $million: 5
  as % of GNP: 0.1
  per capita: $9
  Foreign Direct Investment $million: —

Central Government Revenues and Expenditures

Fiscal Year: Calendar Year
Revenues $million: 1,700
Expenditures $million: 1,900
Budget Surplus $million: 200
Tax Revenues as % of GDP: —
Highest Tax Bracket %
  Individual: —
  Corporate: —

Employment and Labor

Economically Active Population: 226,000
Female Participation Rate %: 17.5
Activity Rate %: 44.6
Labor by Sector: %
  Agriculture, Forestry, Fishing: 2.3
  Manufacturing, Mining: 14.6
  Construction: 11.8
  Transportation and Communications: 6.1
  Trade, Hotels, and Restaurants: 13.2
  Finance, Insurance, Real Estate: 7.6
  Public Administration, Defense: 18.1
  Services: 19.0
Unemployment %: 15

Agriculture

Agriculture's Share of GDP %: 1
Average Annual Rate of Growth (1965–98) %: —
Number of Farms 000: 0.8
Average Size of Farm ha: 4.4
Number of Tractors per 1,000 hectares: —
Irrigation, % of Farms having: 100
Artificial Fertilizer kg/hectare: 333
Total Farmland as % of land area: 5.2
Livestock: Cattle 000: 13
  Sheep 000: 17
  Hogs 000: —
  Chickens 000: 450
Forests: Production of Roundwood (000 cubic meters): —
Fisheries: Total Catch tons 000: 7.6

Mining

% of GDP: 15.1
Value of Mineral Production $million: 763.8

Manufacturing

Value Added $million: 1,730
Industrial Production Growth Rate %: 3.4

Energy

Commercial Energy Production metric tons of oil equivalent 000: —
Commercial Energy Consumption metric tons of oil equivalent 000: 140,840
Commercial Energy Consumption per capita kg: 1,561
Average Annual Growth Rate 1980–97 %: —
Net Energy Imports % of use: −48
Electricity Installed Capacity kW 000: 1,080
Production kW-hr million: 4,750
Coal Reserves tons million: —
Production tons 000: —
Natural Gas Proven Reserves cubic meters billion: 147
Production cubic meters million: 5,250
Crude Petroleum Reserves barrels million: 210
Production barrels million: 38
Consumption barrels million: 91
Refinery Capacity barrels per day 000: 249
Pipelines Length km: 72

Foreign Trade

Imports $million: 3,624.8
Exports $million: 4,092.1
Export Volume % Annual Growth Rate (1990–97): —
Import Volume % Annual Growth Rate (1990–97): —

Balance of trade (current prices)

	1992	1993	1994	1995	1996	1997
U.S.						
$000,000	−300.3	−50.6	−49.3	+149.3	+160.5	+134.6
% of total	10.3%	1.87%	1.8%	5.1%	4.8%	4.3%

Major Trading Partners

	Imports	Exports
European Union %	19.7	4.0
United States %	8.2	3.2
Eastern Europe %	0.2	—
Japan %	4.1	8.2
Others %	67.8	84.6

Transportation

Roads Total Length mi: 1,762 km 2,835
Paved %: 75
Automobiles: 141,901
Trucks and Buses: 29,584
Persons per vehicle: 3.4
Railroad; Track Length mi: — km
Passenger-mi million: —
Freight-mi million: —
Merchant Marine: No. of Vessels: 87
Total Deadweight Tonnage 000: 192.5
International Cargo Loaded tons 000: 13,285
International Cargo Off-loaded tons 000: 3,512
Airports with Scheduled Flights: 1
Traffic: Passenger-mi million: 1,714
Freight-mi million: 72.5
Length of Canals mi: —km

Tourism

Number of Tourists to 000: —
Number of Tourists from 000: —
Tourist Receipts $million: 268
Tourist Expenditures $million: 163

Communications

Telephones 000: 141
Cost of Local Calls 3 mins: $0
Cellular Telephones 000: 28
Fax Machines 000: 5.7
Personal Computers 000: 29
Internet Hosts per million persons: 244
Mail: Post Offices: 12
Pieces of Mail Handled million: 72
Pieces of Mail Handled per person: 122

EDUCATION

Education is free and universal, but not compulsory, for nine years, between ages six and 15. Schooling consists of six years of primary school, three years of intermediate school, and three years of secondary school, for a total of 12 years.

The academic year runs from October to June. The medium of instruction is Arabic, but English is taught as a second language from the intermediate grades on.

The state system is supplemented by an independent program sponsored by the Bahrain Petroleum Company, which runs vocational centers for workers, provides education for the children of working families, and finances overseas training for Bahraini students. Private schools account for 100 percent of preprimary enrollment and 7 percent of primary enrollment. In addition, boys can be enrolled at kuttabs, or Muslim schools attached to mosques. Educational administration is centralized in the Ministry of Education.

There are four higher-education institutions: the Arabian Gulf University, the University of Bahrain, the Men's Teacher Training College, and the Gulf Technical College.

Education

Literacy Rate %: 85.2
Male %: 89.1
Female %: 79.4
First Level: Primary schools: 124
Teachers: 3,536
Students: 72,329
Student-Teacher Ratio: —
Net Enrollment Ratio: 100

Second Level: Secondary Schools: —
Teachers: 2,305
Students: 48,944
Student-Teacher Ratio: —
Net Enrollment Ratio: 85

Vocational Level: Schools: —
Students: 7,113

Third Level: Institutions: —
Teachers: 655
Students: 7,676
Student-Ratio Level: 11.7
Gross Enrollment Ratio: 20.2
Students per 100,000: 1,445
% of Population Age 25 and over with Postsecondary Education: 10.3

Public Expenditure on Education as % of GDP: 4.8

SCIENCE AND TECHNOLOGY

Science and Technology

Scientists and Engineers in R&D per 1 million persons: —
Expenditures in R&D as % of GDP: —
High-Tech Exports $million: —
Patent Applications by Residents: —

MEDIA

The Bahraini press consists of two dailies, eight non-dailies, and 11 other periodicals. One of the weeklies is in English. An English daily, the *BAPCO Daily News*, is published by the Bahrain Petroleum Company. The media are subject to the supervision of the Ministry of Information, but there is no active censorship. Bahrain has no national news agency. Bahrain has a small book publishing industry, but it does not adhere to any copyright convention.

The state-owned Bahrain Broadcasting Station operates two medium-wave transmitters, which broadcast in Arabic. The Bahrain Petroleum Company also broadcasts daily programs in English.

Television broadcasting was begun in 1975 by a private station, which was taken over by the government in 1983. There are now two television stations in operation.

There are 11 public libraries in the urban centers of Manama and Muharraq.

Media

Daily Newspapers: 3
Total Circulation 000: 70
Circulation per 1,000: 128
Books Published:
Magazines: 26
Radio Receivers 000: 320
per 1,000: 542
Television sets 000: 255
per 1,000: 442

MOST IMPORTANT MEDIA:

Press. The following newspapers are published at Manama unless otherwise noted; *al-Ayam* (The Days, 21,400), daily; *Sada al-Usbu* (Weekly Echo, 20,000), Arabic weekly; *Akhbar al-Khalij* (Gulf News, 17,000), first Arabic daily, founded 1976; *al-Adhwaa* (Lights, 7,000), Arab weekly; *al-Bahrain al-Yawm* (Bahrain Today, 5,000), Arabic weekly, published by the Ministry of Information.

News agencies. There is no domestic facility; Agence France-Presse, the AP, the Gulf News Agency, and Reuters maintain offices at Manama.

Radio and television. The Bahrain Broadcasting Service (Idha 'at al-Bahrayn), a government facility that transmits in Arabic and English, and Radio Bahrain (Radiyu al-Bahrayn), an English-language commercial station, are the principal sources of radio programs and were received by approximately 351,000 sets in 1998. The government-operated Bahrain Television (Tilifiziyun al-Bahrayn), which has provided commercial programming in Arabic since 1973, added an English-language channel in 1981.

CULTURE

Cultural Indicators

Public Libraries Number:
Volumes: —
Registered borrowers: —
Museums Number:
Annual Attendance: —
Cinema Production of Long Films:
Number of Cinemas: —
Seating Capacity: —
Annual Attendance million: —
Annual Attendance per capita: —

STATUS OF WOMEN

Bahraini women have traditionally constituted a "separate society," in keeping with the nation's Islamic heritage. Integration of male and female societies began with the development of a modern economy, and women have increasingly taken on roles previously reserved for men. The government has encouraged the trend toward equality, has enacted special labor laws to encourage female entry into the workforce, and is itself a leading employer of women. Most of these position are clerical, but a small number of senior positions are held by women. Labor law grants women 60 days paid maternity leave and nursing periods during the working day. Women may not be discharged for marriage or pregnancy. However, women generally do not enjoy equal access to many government benefits. In 1984 complaints were aired in the press that women were discriminated against in the award of scholarships for study abroad. The responsible government official defended the discrimination and indicated it would continue. Many legal rights of concern to women are subject to *sharia* law: women have rights to their own property but daughters receive less inheritance than sons, and widows must share their husband's estate with their children. Although a wife may divorce, she must specify grounds for the plea, whereas a man may divorce without cause. In the case of a male child, custody remains with the mother until he reaches age 12; a girl stays with her mother until the daughter marries. Women are allowed to drive and appear in public without a male escort. However, permission from a male family member sometimes is required if a woman wishes to leave the country.

Bahrain had no birth control programs or policies prior to the mid-1970s; however, since then the government has supported the Family Planning Association, with commercial access to modern contraceptives and health and welfare services.

Women

Gender Empowerment Measure: —
Seats Held in Parliament by Women %: —
Female Administrators and Managers %: 6
Female Professional and Technical Workers %: 26
Women's Share of Earned Income %: —
Women in Government %: 0

HEALTH, FOOD, AND NUTRITION

Health

Number of Physicians: 482
Number of Dentists: 40
Number of Nurses: 1,608
Number of Pharmacists: 101
Population per Physician: 1,115
Number of Hospitals: 12
Hospital Beds per 10,000: 28
Hospital Bed Occupancy Rate: —
Infant Mortality Rate per 1,000 live births: 23
Maternal Mortality Rate per 100,000 live births:
Total Health Expenditures as % of GDP: 4.6
Health Expenditures per capita $: 324
HIV Infected % of adults:
Cigarette Consumption per smoker per year: —
% of Smokers: Male:
Female:
Access to Safe Water %: 100

Food and Nutrition

Food Supply as % of FAO Requirements: —
% of Consumption Expenditures on Food: 32.4
Daily Available Calories per capita: —
% of Total Calories derived from:
Cereals: —
Potatoes, cassava: —
Meat, poultry: —
Fish: —
Eggs, milk: —
Fruits, vegetables: —
Fats, oils: —

ENVIRONMENT

A desert country, Bahrain's limited arable lands have been subject to drought, dust storms, and other forms of degradation that have intensified desertification of the country. The oil industry has also caused some environmental concern, as oil spills and discharge from tankers, refineries, and distribution centers have caused coastal pollution.

Environment

Forest Area sq km: —
Average Annual Deforestation sq km: 0
Nationally Protected Areas as % of Total Land Area: —
Freshwater Access cubic meters per capita: —
Emissions of Organic Water Pollutants kg per day: —
CO_2 Emissions per capita ton: 26.6

CHRONOLOGY

1970 A 12-member Council of State is established as Bahrain's supreme executive authority; only four of the 12 directors are of royal descent, but all are Bahrainis.
Iran's claims over Bahrain are referred to the United Nations; UN representatives report popular opinion as overwhelmingly in favor of independence; Iran accepts UN report.
1971 The United Kingdom withdraws from the Persian Gulf region and ends its treaty obligations to the Trucial States; Bahrain declares its independence.
The sheikh of Bahrain assumes the title emir.
1972 In response to popular demand, the emir convenes a Constituent Assembly to draft a new constitution for Bahrain.
1973 New constitution is ratified; elections are held for the newly created National Assembly; the radical Popular Bloc of the Left gains 10 of the 30 elected seats.
The Bahrain Monetary Agency is established.
1975 The National Assembly is dissolved by the emir, who promises new elections and a new electoral apparatus.
Television is introduced.
1976 International Parliamentary Union expels Bahrain for its autocratic dissolution of the National Assembly.
1977 Bahrain terminates a six-year agreement permitting U.S. naval ships to be based in Bahrain.
1981 Bahrain joins the Gulf Cooperation Council.
1984 The emirate bans the Shiite Islamic Enlightenment Society, charging it with pro-Iranian subversive plots.
1988 Bahrain holds its first official talks with the USSR.

1989 Bahrain establishes diplomatic relations with the People's Republic of China.

1990 Iraq invades Kuwait; Bahrain supports UN economic sanctions against Iraq and permits the stationing of U.S. combat aircraft in Bahrain; Bahrain establishes diplomatic relations with the USSR.

1991 Bahrain sends troops and air support to Saudi Arabia; Bahrain fights alongside international troops against Iraq; Bahrain joins seven moderate Arab states in agreeing to a U.S.-backed postwar plan for collective security in the Persian Gulf region.

1992 The emir establishes an advisory council as a replacement for the National Assembly that was dissolved in 1975.

1995 Uneven economic and social conditions lead to rioting against the government of Bahrain; the State Security Law is established to suppress unrest.

1996 The government cracks down on antigovernment protests, arresting over 600 dissenters.

1999 Emir Isa bin Salman al-Khalifa dies and is succeeded by his son Hamad bin Isa al-Khalifa; Bahrain begins negotiations with Qatar over the disputed Hawar Islands.

2000 The emir promises to restore a democratically elected parliament.

2001 The emir pardons more than 800 political prisoners and exiles; in a national referendum, 98 percent of voters support a proposal for a new national charter providing for free elections and restoration of the National Assembly; the emir abolishes the State Security Law.

2002 First elections in 32 years are held on May 9 to decide municipal representatives. Women vote and run for office for the first time.

BIBLIOGRAPHY

Al-Khalifa, A., and M. Rice eds. *Bahrain through the Ages*. London, 1993.

Al-Khalifa, H. bin I. *First Light: Modern Bahrain and Its Heritage*. London, 1995.

Belgrave, James H. D. *Welcome to Bahrain*. London, 1970.

Lawson, Fred Haley. *Bahrain: The Modernization of Autocracy*. Boulder, Colo., 1989.

Nugent, Jeffrey B. *Bahrain and the Gulf: Past Perspectives and Alternative Futures*. New York, 1985.

OFFICIAL PUBLICATIONS

Statistical Abstract (annual); *The Population, Housing, Buildings and Establishments Census—1991*.

CONTACT INFORMATION

Embassy of Bahrain
3502 International Drive NW
Washington, D.C. 20008
Phone: (202) 342-0741 Fax: (202) 362-2192

INTERNET RESOURCES

- The World Factbook
  http://www.odci.gov/cia/publications/factbook/ba.html

BANGLADESH

BASIC FACT SHEET

OFFICIAL NAME:
People's Republic of Bangladesh (Gana Prajātantri Bangladesh)

ABBREVIATION:
BG

CAPITAL:
Dhaka

HEAD OF STATE:
President A.Q.M. Budruddoza Chowdhury (from 2001)

HEAD OF GOVERNMENT:
Prime Minister Khaleda Zia (from 2001)

NATURE OF GOVERNMENT:
Republic

POPULATION:
127,118,000

AREA:
142,776 sq km (55,126 sq mi)

ETHNIC MAJORITY:
Bengali

LANGUAGES:
Bangla (official)

RELIGION:
Islam

UNIT OF CURRENCY:
Taka (Tk.)

NATIONAL FLAG:
A bright red circle on a dark green field

NATIONAL EMBLEM:
A seven-petaled stylized water lily rising from a series of five wavy lines representing the Ganges and Brahmaputra rivers enclosed within wreaths of rice and jute. The design is created by a sprig of tea flanked by four stars.

NATIONAL ANTHEM:
"My Golden Bengal"

NATIONAL HOLIDAYS:
March 26 (Independence Day), January 1 (New Year's Day); December 16 (National Day); Christian festivals include Christmas, Boxing Day, Good Friday, and Easter Monday; also variable Hindu, Muslim, and Buddhist festivals

DATE OF INDEPENDENCE:
December 16, 1971

DATE OF CONSTITUTION:
November 4, 1972 (amended 1973, 1974, 1975, 1977, 1979, 1981, 1988, 1989)

GEOGRAPHICAL FEATURES

Bangladesh, at the eastern end of the Indo-Gangetic Plain in southern Asia, extends 767 km (477 mi) south-southeast to north-northwest and 429 km (267 mi) east-northeast to west-southwest. It has a total land area of 142,776 sq km (55,126 sq mi). The highly irregular deltaic coastline runs 574 km (357 mi).

Bangladesh's total international land boundary of 2,816 km (1,750 mi) is shared with two countries: India (4,053 km; 2,517 mi) and Myanmar (193 km; 120 mi).

Topographically Bangladesh may be divided into the vast alluvial plain comprising most of the country and the small Chittagong Hill Tracts in the extreme southeast. The Bengal Plain, also known as the Lower Indo-Gangetic Plain, is the largest delta in the world. The Chittagong Hill Tracts constitute roughly one-sixth of

Bangladesh

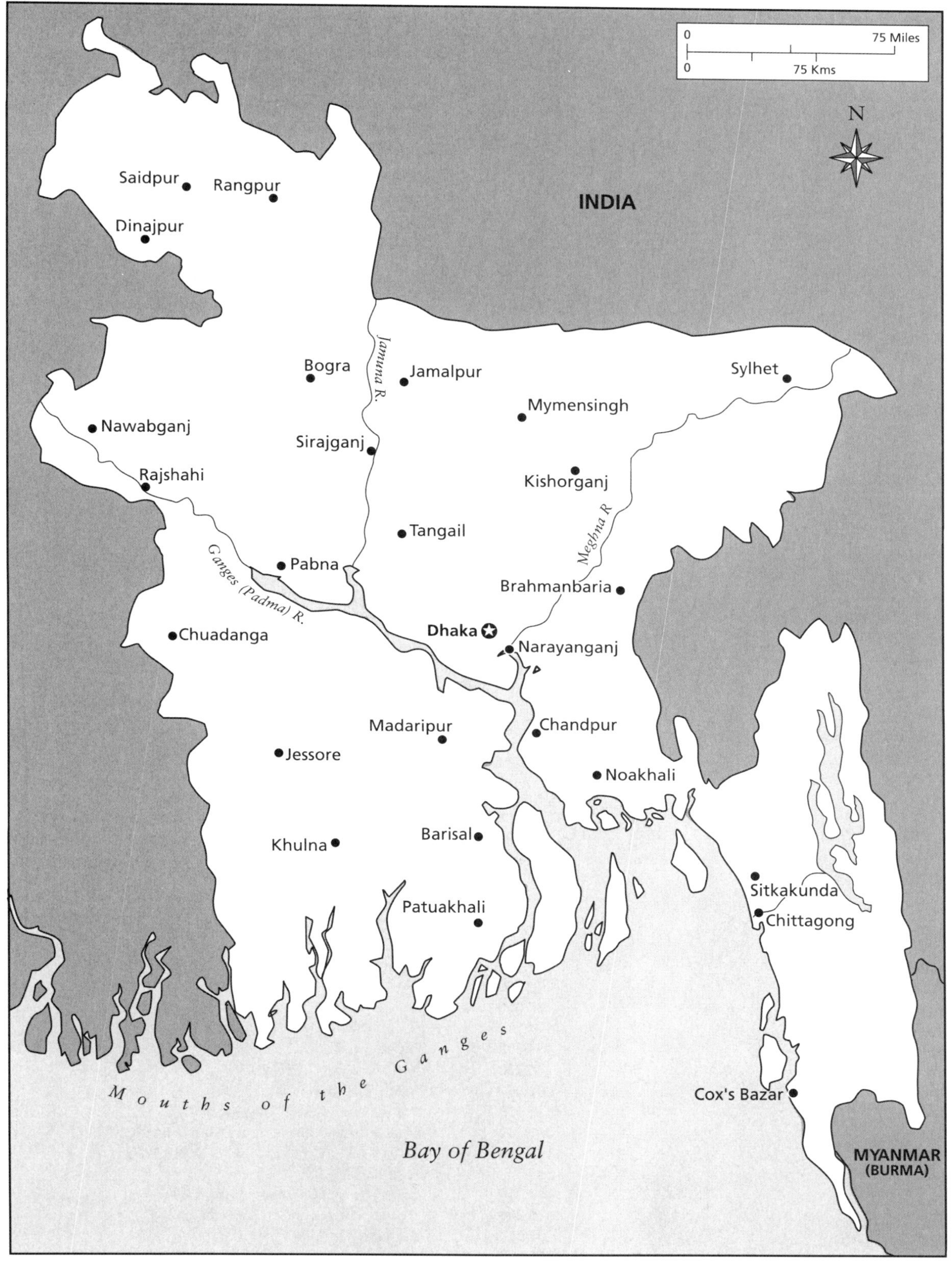
0
75 Miles
0
75 Kms
N
INDIA
Saidpur
Rangpur
Dinajpur
Bogra
Jamuna R.
Jamalpur
Sylhet
Mymensingh
Nawabganj
Sirajganj
Rajshahi
Kishorganj
Meghna R.
Tangail
Pabna
Ganges (Padma) R.
Brahmanbaria
Chuadanga
Dhaka
Narayanganj
Chandpur
Madaripur
Jessore
Noakhali
Barisal
Khulna
Sitkakunda
Patuakhali
Chittagong
Mouths of the Ganges
Cox's Bazar
Bay of Bengal
MYANMAR
(BURMA)

the country. They form a minor hill system, with its greatest elevation at Keodradong (1,229 m; 4,034 ft). Toward the east they form a series of parallel hill chains, while toward the west they slope gradually into a small coastal plain.

Bangladesh has one of the most complex river systems in the world, forming an interlacing grid. The three principal rivers of this network are: the Ganges (known as Padma in Bangladesh), the Brahmaputra (known as Jamuna in Bangladesh), and the Meghna.

From the junction of the three rivers below Dhaka to the Bay of Bengal is the stem of the river system. The triangular estuary contains a number of temporary islands known as chars, as well as permanent islands. The largest of the permanent islands are Shahbazpur, North Hatia, South Hatia, and Sandwip. The tides from the Bay of Bengal are felt as far inland as Kalipur, 270 km (168 mi) away. These tidal waves, called bores, often cause disastrous floods.

Geography

Area sq km: 142,776 sq mi 55,126
World Rank: 93rd
Land Boundaries, km: Myanmar 193; India 4,053
Coastline, km: 580
Elevation Extremes meters
 Lowest: Indian Ocean 0
 Highest: Reng Tlang 957
Land Use % Arable land: 75
 Permanent Crops: 2
 Permanent Pastures: 5
 Forest and Woodland: 15
 Other: 5

Population of Principal Cities (1991)

Barisal	188,000
Bogra	130,000
Brahmanbaria	125,000
Chittagong	1,599,000
Comilla	156,000
Dhākā (Dacca)	3,839,000
Dinājpur	138,000
Gāzpur	104,000
Jamālpur	111,000
Jessore	154,000
Khulna	731,000
Mymensingh	202,000
Naogaon	110,000
Nārāyanganj	296,000
Narsinghdi	106,000
Nawābganj (Nowābgoni)	141,000
Pābna	112,000
Rājshāhi	318,000
Rangpur	207,000
Saidpur	105,000
Savar	115,000
Sirājgangj	108,000
Sythet	109,000
Tangail	114,000
Tongi	181,000

CLIMATE AND WEATHER

Bangladesh has a tropical climate governed by the monsoons. Though it is comparatively temperate and equable, there are marked seasonal variations. The three main seasons are a hot summer season from March to June; a cooler but still warm and humid monsoon season from June through September; and a cool, dry winter season from October to February.

The average temperatures range from 7°C (45°F) in January to 31°C (90°F) in May. Temperatures up to 40.6°C (105°F) have been recorded occasionally. Daily temperature changes are moderate.

Nearly 80 percent of the annual rain falls from June through September, when the moisture-laden monsoon blows from the south and the southwest. The average annual rainfall varies between 1,270 and 1,520 mm (50 to 60 in) in the west to over 2,540 mm (100 in) elsewhere. The Sylhet district, in the northeast, is believed to receive the highest rainfall in the world.

Climate and Weather

Mean Temperature:
January 45°F
May 90°F
August 88°F
Average Rainfall 50 in to 60 in the west
 100 in the north and east.

POPULATION

Population Indicators

Total Population: 1999 127,118,000
World Rank: 8th
Density per sq mi: 2,231 per sq km 861.4
% of annual growth (1994–99): 1.6
Male %: 51.4
Female %: 48.6
Urban %: 20.2
Age Distribution: % 0–14: 41.5
 15–29: 25.2
 30–44: 16.2
 45–59: 8.1
 60–74: 4.3
 75 and over: 1.1
Population 2020: 170,879,000
Birth Rate per 1,000: 26.8
Death Rate per 1,000: 12.2
Population Doubling Time (years): 39
Infant Mortality Rate per 1,000 live births: 79.0
Rate of Natural Increase per 1,000: 14.6
Total Fertility Rate: 3.2
Expectation of Life (years): Males 58.0
 Females 58.0
Marriage Rate per 1,000: 10.1
Divorce Rate per 1,000: 3.6
Total Number of Households: 19,980,000
Average Size of Households: 5.6
% of Illegitimate Children: —
Induced Abortions: —
 Rate per 100 live births: —

ETHNIC COMPOSITION

Bangladesh is noted for the remarkable ethnic homogeneity of its population. Over 97 percent of its people are Bengali. The remaining almost 2 percent are Biharis and tribals. The term *Bihari* designates non-Bengali, Urdu-speaking Muslims who fled to Bangladesh from eastern India in 1947. The tribals, racially distinct from the Bengali, have facial features and language closer to those of the Burmese.

In the coastal areas there are scattered communities of Arab, Dutch, and Portuguese settlers. Apart from these groups there are no numerically significant foreign communities.

LANGUAGES

Bengali is the official language of Bangladesh. Bangalees identify themselves with their national language very closely. Bengali has a rich literature; at least two Bengali writers are well known in the West: Nobel laureate Rabindranath Tagore and Kazi Nazrul Islam. English remains the language of the modern sector, but its cultural use seems to be declining.

Principal Languages and Their Speakers

Bengali	124,230,000
Chakmā	470,000
English	3,300,000
Gāro	110,000
Khāsi	100,000
Marma (Magh)	240,000
Mro	40,000
Santhāli	90,000
Tripuri	90,000
Other	1,740,000

RELIGIONS

Bangladesh also is remarkably homogeneous in religious affiliations. Approximately 88 percent of the people are Muslim mainly of the Sunni sect, making Bangladesh the second largest Islamic country in the world, after Indonesia. Although loyalty to Islam is deep-rooted, the content and social structure of Islam have been influenced by Hinduism. Although Islam does not recognize caste, Bengali Muslim society is divided into three groups: *ashraf* (better class), *ajlaf* (lower class), and *arzal* (lowest class). Each group is subdivided into smaller groups.

The percentage of Hindus, the largest religious minority, has been steadily decreasing since 1947. Hindus are concentrated in areas bordering India, such as Khulna, Jessore, Sylhet, and Dinajpur, where they constitute nearly 25 percent of the population. The bulk of the Hindus belong to one of the lowest castes, the Namashudra, and they occupy low social and economic positions and generally follow the more inferior professions.

Smaller minorities include Zoroastrians (also known as Parsis) and tribal animists. There is a Roman Catholic archbishopric at Dhaka. The secular constitution guarantees the religious rights of all minorities.

Religious Affiliations

Muslim	112,250,000
Hindu	13,370,000
Other	1,500,000

HISTORICAL BACKGROUND

Prior to 1971, Bangladesh was the province of East Pakistan, one of five Pakistani provinces formed when the British Indian empire was partitioned in August 1947. However, East Pakistan was separated from the four western provinces of Pakistan by about 1,600 km (1,000 mi) of Indian territory. By 1952 tensions within the province flared not only because East Pakistan was more populous and the central government was situated in distant West Pakistan but also because Urdu was declared the official language of Pakistan, an affront to the Bengali-speaking East Pakistanis. Bengali was made a joint official language in 1954, and in 1955 the country was divided into two sections, east and west, each equally represented in the central legislative body.

The Awami League, under the leadership of Sheikh Mujibur Rahman, won an overwhelming victory in the general elections of December 1970, and thus gave the east a majority in the nation's legislative assembly. The election results meant that Sheikh Mujib should have become the prime minister, but the president, Gen. Yahya Khan, prevented that, and the newly elected assembly was not convened. Violent protests ensued in the east, and when the Awami League decided that the province should secede, Mujib declared the independence of the People's Republic of Bangladesh ("Bengal Nation") on March 26, 1971.

Civil war followed with President Yahya Khan blaming the Awami League and the Pakistani army taking over the eastern province. By December 16, Pakistan had surrendered, and Bangladesh was independent. In January 1972 Sheikh Mujib, who had been imprisoned in West Pakistan, was freed by Pakistan's president, Zulfiquar Ali Bhutto, and assumed the position of prime minister of Bangladesh. The new country was rapidly recognized by the international community, leading Pakistan to withdraw from the Commonwealth and Bangladesh to join the Commonwealth in April. The Bangladesh Constituent Assembly was made up of those members who had been elected in December 1970 to the Pakistan National Assembly, and a new constitution was approved by that body in November, taking effect in December. The first general election to the country's Jatiya Sangsad (Parliament) was held in March 1973. The Awami League won 292 of the 300 directly elected seats, and, in February 1974, Pakistan officially recognized Bangladesh. Terrorism by both right- and left-wing opposition groups led to the declaration of a state of emergency and a suspension of constitutional rights in December. President Mujib assumed complete power, and the country became a one-party state in February.

In August 1975 a right-wing coup led by a number of Islamic army officers assassinated Sheikh Mujib and his family. The former minister of commerce, Khandakar Mustaque Ahmed, assumed the presidency, declaring martial law and outlawing all political parties. On November 3, a second coup led to the appointment of Brigadier Khalid Musharaf as army chief of staff. Major General Ziaur Rahman (General Zia) was reinstated as chief of army staff and became the leader of the neutral nonparty government. In July 1976 political parties were legalized.

General Zia gradually assumed increased power, taking on the role of chief martial law administrator and taking over the presidency by April 1, 1977. He made Islam the first basic principle of the constitution and in June 1978 was overwhelmingly elected president in the nation's first direct presidential election. In parliamentary elections held in February 1979, Zia's Bangladesh Nationalist Party (BNP) won 207 of the directly elected seats in the Jatiya Sangsad. A new prime minister was named in April, and martial law was lifted. In November the state of emergency was ended.

The assassination of General Zia on May 30, 1981, during an attempted military coup resulted in the promotion of Justice Abdus Satta to acting president. He was later overwhelmingly elected to the position of president in November, but was unable to maintain civilian control, and, on March 24, 1982, Lt. Gen. Hussain Mohammad Ershad came to power in a bloodless coup. Martial law was declared once again, and Ershad became chief martial law administrator. In October Ershad took the position of prime minister and named Justice Abul Chowdhury to the presidency.

Two major opposition groups emerged in the aftermath, a 15-party coalition led by Sheikh Hasina Wajed (daughter of the late Sheikh Mujib) and a seven-party alliance under the leadership of Begum Khalida Zia (widow of General Zia). The two groups joined forces in September 1983 to form the Movement for the Restoration of Democracy (MRD). On December 11, President Chowdhury resigned his position in favor of Ershad, and a new party, Jana Dal, was established in support of the regime. Subsequent struggles between progovernment and opposition parties led to the cancellation of presidential and parliamentary elections scheduled for April 1, 1985, and martial law was once again imposed on March 1. Three weeks later, Ershad was again elected president in a referendum.

On March 2, 1986, President Ershad scheduled parliamentary elections for late April. Opposition parties refused to participate unless martial law was completely lifted. However, the Awami League coalition and the fundamentalist Jama'at-i-Islam later agreed to participate in an election scheduled for May 7, although the BNP alliance led by Begum Khalida Zia refused to take part. The Jatiya Dal won a narrow majority of the directly elected seats and also filled the 30 seats reserved for women. Extensive fraud, which characterized the parliamentary elections, was also operative in the presidential election of October in which Ershad won an overwhelming victory over his 11 opponents. In November Ershad lifted martial law and restored the 1972 constitution. In order to quiet growing unrest, Ershad reshuffled the Council of Ministers in December, adding four new ministers from the Awami League.

The Jatiya Sangsad was dissolved by Ershad on December 6, 1987, following the resignation of 12 opposition members and 73 Awami League members. Ershad scheduled a general election for February 28, but continued opposition threats to boycott the election forced a postponement to March 3. Widespread violence disrupted the general election, and participation by voters was estimated at less than 50 percent. The Jatiya Dal took a large majority of the seats.

A further reshuffling of the cabinet in March included the naming of a new prime minister, Moudid Ahmed. Ershad repealed the state of emergency in April because of a lessening of the opposition antigovernment demonstrations. In June a majority of the Jatiya Sangsad approved a constitutional amendment making Islam Bangladesh's state religion, even though the opposition strongly opposed the measure.

Disastrous monsoon floods in August once again overshadowed political troubles, and further severe flooding in December 1988 and January 1989 resulted in at least 2,100 casualties.

In July 1989 the Jatiya Sangsad acted to limit the term of the president to two electoral terms of five years each and also established the position of a directly elected vice president. Moudid Ahmed, who had been prime minister, was appointed vice president by Ershad in August, and Kazi Zafar Ahmed was named prime minister.

Following eight weeks of violent protests against his government, Ershad resigned in December 1990. Shortly thereafter, he and his wife were arrested on charges of theft of public funds, nepotism, and gold smuggling. An interim president, Shahabuddin Ahmed, headed a caretaker government until elections in 1991. The general elections were won by the conservative Bangladesh National Party (BNP), whose leader, Khaleda Zia, became prime minister.

While many hoped that the election of Zia would bring democratic stability to Bangladesh, it has not happened. After a few years, the people grew tired of the Zia

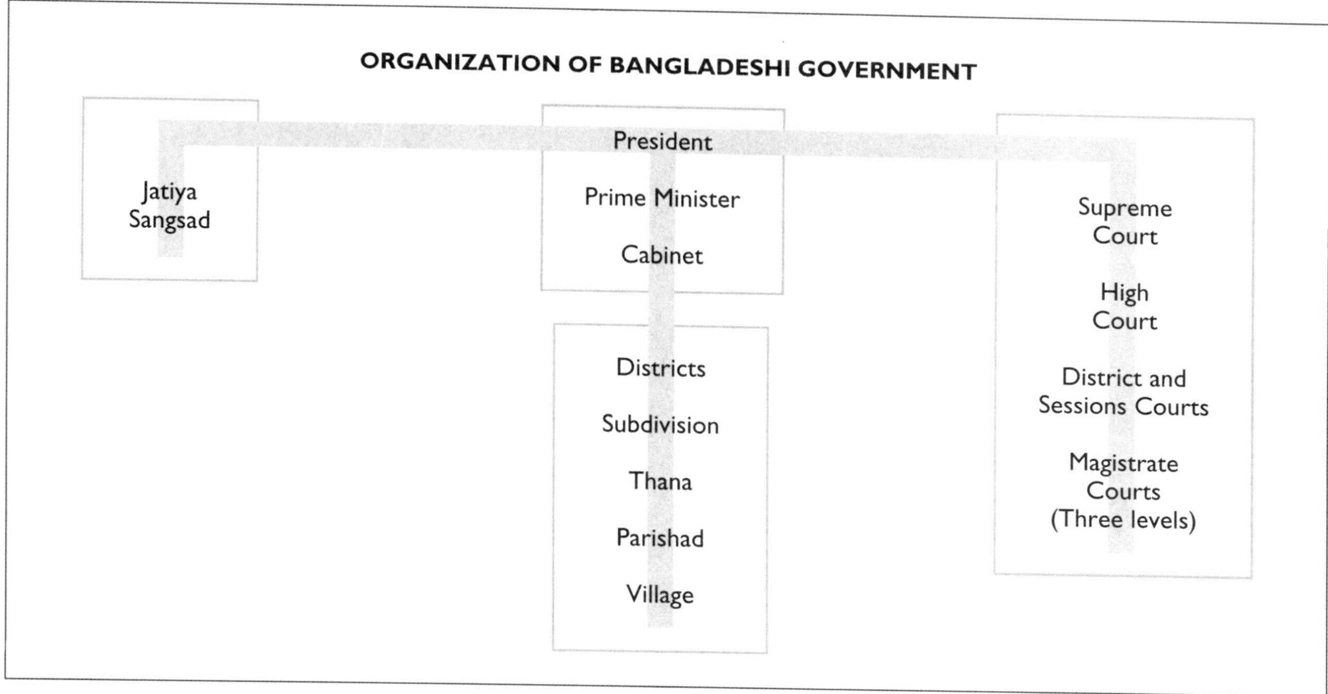

government. The government did not repeal the 1974 Special Powers Act that allows for the detention of individuals for 120 days without charges. Elections were finally held in February 1996, but they were boycotted by opposition parties and only five percent of the population turned out to vote. Zia was reelected but was forced to resign under protests in March. Elections were once again held in June and a coalition government headed by Sheikh Hasina Wazed of the Awami League was elected. Political stability has still not been achieved and the country has been racked by natural disasters, including widespread flooding in 1998. In 2001, the BNP won a majority of seats in parliamentary elections, and Zia became prime minister a second time.

CONSTITUTION

Bangladesh is governed by the constitution of 1972 (as amended in 1973, 1974, 1975, 1977, 1979, 1981, 1988, and 1989), which established a parliamentary democracy. The constitution was suspended after the military coup of March 24, 1982, and it was revived following the repeal of martial law on November 10, 1986. The constitution incorporates four basic principles of state policy: nationalism, Islam, socialism, and democracy.

The president and vice president are elected by universal adult suffrage for a five-year term and may be elected to a single additional five-year term. In addition to the president and vice president, the executive branch of the government includes a prime minister appointed by the president and council of ministers, all of whom are appointed by the president and may be dismissed by him.

The Jatiya Sangsad is a unicameral legislature. It is made up of 300 members who are directly elected by universal suffrage for a five-year term, unless the president chooses to dissolve parliament sooner. Additionally, 30 women members of the Jatiya Sangsad are elected by the other members of the Jatiya Sangsad in order to ensure some representation by women in the Jatiya Sangsad. The approval of the Jatiya Sangsad is required for any declaration of war.

LOCAL GOVERNMENT

The basic units of regional administration are, in descending order, division, district, and thana. The divisions number five, each headed by a commissioner. The districts number 64, each of which is headed by a deputy commissioner. The deputy commissioner is the linchpin of the regional administration and also the most important government representative at the local level.

The districts are divided into 64 zillas or subdistricts, each headed by a subdistrict officer. These subdistricts are further divided into 490 thanas, union parishads, and villages.

Local Government

Principal administrative divisions, capitals, area, population

AREA AND POPULATION

Divisions	Administrative centres	area sq mi	area sq km	population 1991 census
Barisal	Barisal	5,134	13,297	7,757,334
Chittagong	Chittagong	7,906	20,476	20,823,477
Dhākā	Dhākā	12,015	31,119	33,939,848
Khulna	Khulna	8,600	22,274	13,243,054
Rājshāhi	Rājshāhi	13,326	34,513	27,499,727
Sythet	Sythet	4,863	12,596	7,149,372
Tribal region				
Chittagong Hill Tracts	Rangamati	5,133	13,295	1,042,373
TOTAL		56,977	147,570	111,455,185

PARLIAMENT

The national legislature is the unicameral Jatiya Sangsad, with a membership of 300 elected members and—to ensure that their sex has some representation—30 women elected by the other members. Members of the Jatiya Sangsad are elected from single-member constituencies on the basis of universal adult suffrage over age 18. Their legislative term lasts five years unless the Jatiya Sangsad is dissolved sooner by the president. The Jatiya Sangsad was dissolved in 1982 following the seizure of power by the army and the imposition of martial law. Constitutional government was revived in November 1986 when martial law ended.

POLITICAL PARTIES

Bangladesh is a multiparty country in which two parties control most of the elected seats in the parliament. The Awami League is a nationalistic secular party that arose in opposition to the National Party that ruled Bangladesh for most of the 1970s and 1980s. The Bangladesh Nationalist Party has an Islamic orientation to its membership. In addition to these two major parties, there are more than a dozen smaller ones. The Bangladesh Islamic Assembly is the nation's ultra-religious right-wing Islamic party, which secured three seats of the 330 available in 1996. The Jatiya Party helped form the most recent government by building a coalition with the Awami League. The Jatiya are a centrist party that seeks national consensus for governing.

Political Parties

- Awami League, 1948
- National Socialist Party, 1972
- Bangladesh Nationalist Party, 1978
- Jatiya Dal, 1985
- Bangladesh Islamic Assembly, 1979
- Islamic Unity Front
- National Democratic Alliance, 1993, a conservative alliance of 10 Islamic groups
  - Democratic League, 1976
  - Freedom Party, 1987
  - Islamic Constitutional Movement
  - Progressive Democratic Force
  - National Democratic Party, 1986
  - Bangladesh Caliphate Movement 1981
- Democratic Unity Front, 1994, a coalition of nine diverse parties
  - National People's Party, 1978
  - National Awami Party-Bhashani
- People's Forum, 1993
- National Awami Party-Muzaffar
- Left Democratic Front, 1994, an alliance of six leftist parties
  - Communist Party, 1978
  - Equalitarian Party
  - Bangladesh Workers' Party
  - Bangladesh Socialist Party-Zaman
  - Bangladesh Socialist Party-Mahbub
  - Workers' and Peasants' Socialist Party, 1969

Political Parties: Strength in Parliament Most Recent Elections

The **National Parliament.** In the elections of October 1, 2001, the Bangladesh Nationalist Party won 191 seats; Islam Conference Bangladesh, 18; National Party (Naziur), 4; Islamic Unity Front, 2; Bangladesh People's League, 62; National Party (Ershad), 14; National Party (Manju), 1; Peasants' and Worker's People's League, 1; nonpartisan and others, 9.

LEGAL SYSTEM

The judicial system inherited from Pakistan and Britain has been retained almost unchanged by independent Bangladesh. The chief court of the land is the Supreme Court, which is composed of the Appellate Division and the High Court Division. The Supreme Court consists of the chief justice and 11 other judges, all appointed by the president. The subordinate courts consist of district and sessions courts in every district and three lower levels of magistrate courts.

LAW ENFORCEMENT

Law Enforcement

- Offenses reported to the police per 100,000: 64
  - Murder: 1.9
  - Assault: 3.6
  - Burglary: 4.6
  - Automobile Theft: 0.6
  - Population per Police officer: 2,560
- Death Penalty: Yes

HUMAN RIGHTS

Institutional weakness, political instability, and unchecked police brutality appeared to be the major factors in continued widespread human rights violations. Despite election promises made by the Zia government, the 1974 Special Powers Act, allowing detention without charge for 120 days, has never been repealed. There have been claims that the government has rigged by-elections, and military and police repression of dissenters appear to be on the rise. According to Amnesty International, hundreds of people were injured and dozens killed, some as a result of police action, in nationwide strikes (*hartals*) called by opposition parties during 1999. Political party activists and student groups with links to the ruling and opposition parties continue to perpetrate acts of violence, including beating political opponents to death.

FOREIGN POLICY

Bangladesh's foreign policy reflects the twin realities of geography and religion. Soon after independence, it signed a 25-year treaty of friendship, cooperation, and peace with India, but within a few years, the two nations were embroiled in disputes over water from the Ganges and Teesta rivers and rights of transit from Nepal. Relations with Pakistan, initially characterized by mutual hatred and suspicion born out of the war of independence, slowly improved. The question of the repatriation of pro-Pakistani Biharis from Bangladesh to Pakistan was settled in the early 1990s but has not been fully resolved. There are also repatriation issues with Myanmar over the Rohingya Muslims who were being persecuted and forced to flee from Myanmar.

DEFENSE

The defense structure is headed by the president, who is the minister of defense and chief of the army staff and who thus dominates the defense establishment. Military manpower is provided by voluntary enlistment. The total strength of the armed forces in 1998 was 121,000.

The combat-worthiness of the Bangladesh armed forces is limited by a number of factors, including severe budgetary restrictions and the small number of professionals with field experience. The operational effectiveness of both the army and the air force is inhibited by lack of spare parts. The armed forces also are plagued by factionalism and lack of discipline.

Military Indicators

Total Active Duty Personnel: 121,000
Military Manpower per 1,000: 1.0
Military Expenditures $million: 502
  as % of GNP: 1.7
  per capita $: 4.0
  as % of central government expenditures: 9.9
Arms Imports $million: 60
Arms Exports $million: 0

ECONOMY

Despite sustained domestic and international efforts to improve economic and demographic prospects, Bangladesh remains one of the world's poorest, most densely populated, and least developed nations. The economy is largely agricultural, with the cultivation of rice the single most important activity in the economy. Major impediments to growth include frequent cyclones and floods, the inefficiency of state-owned enterprises, a rapidly growing labor force that cannot be absorbed by agriculture, delays in exploiting energy resources (natural gas), inadequate power supplies, and slow implementation of economic reforms. Prime Minister Sheikh Hasina Wajed's Awami League government has made some headway improving the climate for foreign investors and liberalizing the capital markets; for example, it has negotiated with foreign firms for oil and gas exploration, better country-wide distribution of cooking gas, and the construction of natural gas pipelines and power plants. Progress on other economic reforms has been halting because of opposition from the bureaucracy, public sector unions, and other vested interest groups. The especially severe floods of 1998 increased the country's reliance on large-scale international aid.

Principal Economic Indicators

Gross National Product $: 44.090 billion
GNP per capita $: 360
GNP Average Annual Growth Rate (1990–97) %: 3.3
GNP per capita Average Annual Growth Rate (1990–97) %: 1.7
Origin of Gross Domestic Product %
  Agriculture: 30
  Mining:—
  Manufacturing: 10
  Construction: 6
  Public Utilities: 2
  Transportation and Communications: 12
  Trade: 8
  Financial Services: 2
  Other Services: 24
  Government: 5
Gross Domestic Product by Type of Expenditure %
  Private Consumption: 78
  Government Consumption: 14
  Gross Domestic Investment: 14
  Foreign Trade: Exports: 12
    Imports: −18
% of Income Received by Poorest 20%: 9.4
% of Income Received by Richest 10%: 23.7

(continued)

Price and earnings indexes (1995 = 100)

	1992	1993	1994	1995	1996	1997	1998
Consumer price index	91.3	91.2	94.5	100.0	102.7	108.5	—
Earnings index	84.3	88.5	93.9	100.0	—	—	

Finance

National Currency: Taka (TK)
Exchange Rate: $1 = T45.450
Money Supply Stock in National Currency billion: 141,676
M1 per capita: 1,140
Central Bank Discount Rate %: 8
Total External Debt $million: 17,100
Debt Service Ratio %: 8.7

Balance of Payments $million: −327.3
International Reserves SDRs million: 1,226
Ratio of External Debt to Total Reserves: 6.6
Average Annual Rate of Inflation/Consumer Price Index
Growth Rate %: 2.5

Official Development Assistance

ODA $million: 1.475 billion
as % of GNP: 2.8
per capita $ 10
Foreign Direct Investment $million: 308

Central Government Revenues and Expenditures

Fiscal Year: 1 July–30 June
Revenues $million: 3,600
Expenditures $million: 5,300
Budget Deficit $million: 1.7 billion
Tax Revenues as % of GDP: —
Highest Tax Bracket %
Individual: —
Corporate: —

Employment and Labor

Economically Active Population: 51,155,000
Female Participation Rate %: 39.3
Activity Rate %: 46.0
Labor by Sector: %
Agriculture, Forestry, Fishing: 65.1
Manufacturing, Mining: 11.7
Construction: 1.0
Transportation and Communications: 3.1
Trade, Hotels, and Restaurants: 8.4
Finance, Insurance, Real Estate: 0.6
Public Administration, Defense: —
Services: 3.7

Unemployment %: 35.2

Agriculture

Agriculture's Share of GDP %: 30
Average Annual Rate of Growth (1965–98) %: 2.1
Number of Farms 000: 10,045
Average Size of Farm ha: 0.9
Number of Tractors per 1,000 hectares: 0.6
Irrigation, % of Farms having: 35
Artificial Fertilizer kg/hectare: 98
Total Farmland as % of land area: 70.2
Livestock: Cattle 000: 23,400
Sheep 000: 1,158
Hogs 000: —
Chickens 000: 152,875
Forests: Production of Roundwood (000 cubic meters): 32,044
Fisheries: Total Catch tons 000: 1,090.6

Mining

% of GDP: —
Value of Mineral Production $million: 5.2

Manufacturing

Value Added $million: 1,899
Industrial Production Growth Rate %: 5.3

Energy

Commercial Energy Production metric tons of
oil equivalent 000: 21,894
Commercial Energy Consumption metric tons of
oil equivalent 000: 24,327
Commercial Energy Consumption per capita kg: 197
Average Annual Growth Rate 1980–97 %: 0.9
Net Energy Imports % of use: 10
Electricity Installed Capacity kW 000: 3,284
Production kW-hr million: 11,689
Coal Reserves tons million: 1,054
Production tons 000: —
Natural Gas Proven Reserves cubic meters billion: 288
Production cubic meters million: 7,365
Crude Petroleum Reserves barrels million: 5
Production barrels million: 0.5
Consumption barrels million: 10
Refinery Capacity barrels per day 000: 31
Pipelines Length km: —

Foreign Trade

Imports $million: 2,708
Exports $million: 2,137.6
Export Volume % Annual Growth Rate (1990–97): 12.9
Import Volume % Annual Growth Rate (1990–97): 9.1

Balance of trade (current prices)

	1993	1994	1995	1996	1997	1998
Lm						
$000,000	−51,872	−59,233	−107,720	−110,988	−99,478	−118,772
% of total	22.3%	21.7%	29.7%	28.7%	23.0%	24.8

Major Trading Partners

	Imports	Exports
European Union %	11.1	37.4
United States %	5.2	35.0
Eastern Europe %	1.3	1.6
Japan %	6.7	2.6
Others %	75.8	23.4

Transportation

Roads Total Length mi: 104,709 km 168,513
Paved %: 9
Automobiles: 82,198
Trucks and Buses: 104,860
Persons per vehicle: 634
Railroad; Track Length mi: 1,681 km 2,706
Passenger-mi million: 2,508
Freight-mi million: 521
Merchant Marine: No. of Vessels: 301
  Total Deadweight Tonnage 000: 566.8
  International Cargo Loaded tons 000: 1,848
  International Cargo Off-loaded tons 000: 10,608
Airports with Scheduled Flights: 8
Traffic: Passenger-mi million: 1,763
  Freight-mi million: 82
Length of Canals mi: 5,000 km 8,046

Tourism

Number of Tourists to 000: 172
Number of Tourists from 000: 992
Tourist Receipts $million: 23
Tourist Expenditures $million: 229

Communications

Telephones 000: 287
Cost of Local Calls 3 mins: $0.04
Cellular Telephones 000: 2.5
Fax Machines 000: 4.0
Personal Computers 000: —
Internet Hosts per million persons: —
Mail: Post Offices: —
  Pieces of Mail Handled million: 261
  Pieces of Mail Handled per person: 2.2

EDUCATION

Education is free, but not compulsory for the five years from five to 10. Schooling consists of five years of primary education, five years of lower secondary education, and two years of higher education, for a total of 12 years. There is a high dropout rate at all levels. Although primary education is free, fees are charged by secondary schools.

The academic year is the calendar year. The medium of instruction is Bangla in the primary grades and Bangla and English in the secondary grades.

Educational standards have been steadily declining since 1947, partly because of the lack of trained teachers. Only 30 percent of the teachers in primary schools are believed to possess minimum professional training.

Private secondary institutions and colleges vastly outnumber government institutions. In 1996 government high schools constituted only 29 percent of the total and government colleges numbered only 34 of a total of 636. In addition, Muslim religious schools are maintained by both private and public funds. Separate schools also are run by Hindus and Buddhists. Vocational education has received little emphasis.

Affiliated with Bangladesh's seven universities are 636 colleges, of which seven are medical colleges and nine are law colleges.

Education

Literacy Rate %: 38.1
  Male %: 49.4
  Female %: 26.1
First Level: Primary schools: 66,168
  Teachers: 242,252
  Students: 15,185,000
  Student-Teacher Ratio: 62.7
  Net Enrollment Ratio: 62
Second Level: Secondary Schools: 11,019
  Teachers: 135,217
  Students: 4,884,000
  Student-Teacher Ratio: 36.1
  Net Enrollment Ratio: 20.0

Vocational Level: Schools: 152
  Students: 29,923

Third Level: Institutions: 1,268
  Teachers: 36,000
  Students: 1,032,635
  Student-Ratio Level: 28.7
  Gross Enrollment Ratio: 4.4
  Students per 100,000: 399
  % of Population Age 25 and over with Postsecondary Education: —

Public Expenditure on Education as % of GDP: 2.3

SCIENCE AND TECHNOLOGY

Science and Technology

Scientists and Engineers in R&D per 1 million persons: 52
Expenditures in R&D as % of GDP: 0.03
High-Tech Exports $million: 3
Patent Applications by Residents: 70

MEDIA

Bangladesh has a flourishing newspaper industry with more than 179 dailies. Thirteen of the newspapers are published in English. Aggregate circulation is nearly 2 million.

The largest-selling dailies are the *Dainik Ittefaq* (195,000) in Bengali and the *Bangladesh Observer* (43,000) and *Bangladesh Daily Star* (20,000) in English.

The national news agency is Bangladesh Sangbad Sangstha (Bangladesh News Agency), with headquarters at Dhaka. The other agency is Eastern News Agency.

The official broadcasting organization is the National Broadcasting Authority, which was formed in 1984 through the merger of Radio Bangladesh and

Bangladesh Television. It operates seven medium-wave transmitters, four shortwave transmitters, and five FM transmitters. Bangladesh Television (BTV), founded in 1971, has a transmitter at Dhaka, and relay stations.

Media

Daily Newspapers: 51
Total Circulation 000: 710
Circulation per 1,000: 6.0
Books Published: —
Magazines: —
Radio Receivers 000: 8,000
per 1,000: 67
Television sets 000: 850
per 1,000: 7.0

Most Important Media:

Press. The following are among the dozens of Dhaka dailies, all published in Bangla unless otherwise noted: *Dainik Ittefaq* (200,000); *Dainik Inqilab* (180,000); *Dainik Janakantha* (Dhaka, 100,000), also published at four other cities; *Sangbad* (70,000); *Dainik Bangla* (60,000); *Dainik Bhorer Kagoj* (50,000); *Bangladesh Observer* (40,000), in English; *Daily Star* (30,000), in English.

News agencies. There are two domestic news agencies located at Dhaka: the government-owned Bangladesh News Agency (Bangladesh Sangbad Sangstha—BSS) and the independent United News of Bangladesh; in addition, many of the leading foreign agencies maintain offices at the capital.

Radio and television. The government-controlled Bangladesh Betar operates domestic radio stations at Dhaka, Chittagong, Khulna, and other leading cities while providing overseas service in six languages. Bangladesh Television, also operated by the government, broadcasts from Dhaka and Chittagong as well as from relay stations.

CULTURE

Cultural Indicators

Public Libraries Number: 63
Volumes: 384,000
Registered borrowers: —
Museums Number: —
Annual Attendance: —
Cinema Production of Long Films: 77
Number of Cinemas: —
Seating Capacity: —
Annual Attendance million: —
Annual Attendance per capita: —

STATUS OF WOMEN

By customs and Muslim-influenced tradition, women occupy a subordinate, dependent place and receive unequal treatment before the law on a widespread basis. The ability of a family to seclude its women is a key symbol of social status. The daily press testifies to a pattern of domestic violence (murder, rape, torture), breach of matrimonial contract, denial of inheritance rights, and desertion, which victimize women, particularly among the poor. The rate of suicide among women is reportedly almost three times higher than among men. In October 1983 the government promulgated a stringent ordinance aimed at deterring cruelty to women. To check murder, kidnapping, abduction, and trafficking (including international trafficking) in women, the ordinance brings together the various statutes applicable to women and stiffens the penalties for abuse. It provides the death penalty for those directly responsible for a "dowry killing" or for killing of a woman in the course of rape, although it does not address the abuse of a woman that stops short of murder or rape or that takes place within the family or home. "Dowry killings," as reported in the press, usually share a common theme: the bride's family has not made full payment of a supposedly promised dowry, so the husband or his family attacks and often murders the bride.

Women

Gender Empowerment Measure: 80
Seats Held in Parliament by Women %: 9.1
Female Administrators and Managers %: 4.9
Female Professional and Technical Workers %: 34.7
Women's Share of Earned Income %: 23
Women in Government %: 3

HEALTH, FOOD, AND NUTRITION

Health

Number of Physicians: 24,911
Number of Dentists: 812
Number of Nurses: 9,630
Number of Pharmacists: 7,485
Population per Physician: 4,759
Number of Hospitals: 919
Hospital Beds per 10,000: 3
Hospital Bed Occupancy Rate: —
Infant Mortality Rate per 1,000 live births: 144
Maternal Mortality Rate per 100,000 live births: 850
Total Health Expenditures as % of GDP: 3.19
Health Expenditures per capita $: 6
HIV Infected % of adults: 0.03
Cigarette Consumption per smoker per year: 351
% of Smokers: Male: 60
Female: 15
Access to Safe Water %: 83

Food and Nutrition

Food Supply as % of FAO Requirements: 87
% of Consumption Expenditures on Food: 63.3
Daily Available Calories per capita: 2,017
% of Total Calories derived from:
Cereals: 82.4
Potatoes, cassava: 1.4
Meat, poultry: 0.8

Fish: 0.8
Eggs, milk: 1.4
Fruits, vegetables: 1.1
Fats, oils: 5.8

ENVIRONMENT

High population density is a major factor contributing to extensive overuse of the country's forests, fisheries, and even soil and water resources. These problems are especially serious, given that most Bangladeshis are still directly dependent economically on natural resources. Already a majority of households are without sufficient land to produce their food needs, and fuelwood stocks have been depleted to the point where most domestic energy requirements must be met by crop residues and dung, with only a small fraction met by fuelwood. Floods and storms also inflict severe socioeconomic and environmental damage on the country.

Environment

Forest Area sq km: 10,000
Average Annual Deforestation sq km: 88
Nationally Protected Areas as % of Total Land Area: 0.8
Freshwater Access cubic meters per capita: 9,636
Emissions of Organic Water Pollutants kg per day: 186,852
CO_2 Emissions per capita ton: 0.2

CHRONOLOGY

1970 In legislative elections, Awami League candidates win 167 of East Pakistan's 169 seats in the 313-seat Pakistan National Assembly; President Yahya Khan postpones opening the assembly; the Awami League launches provincewide agitation.

1971 Sheikh Mujibur Rahman is imprisoned in West Pakistan on treason charges; the government outlaws the Awami League, declares martial law in East Pakistan, and begins a reign of terror, attempting to suppress the Bengali nationalist movement; millions of Bengalis seek refuge in India as war breaks out; the combined armies of India and East Pakistan compel West Pakistani forces to surrender; East Pakistan becomes the independent state of Bangladesh.

1972 Mujibur Rahman is released from prison in Pakistan and sworn in as interim prime minister of Bangladesh; a treaty of friendship and cooperation is signed with India; Bangladesh joins the British Commonwealth; Bangladesh nationalizes all banks and Pakistani-owned industries and introduces the taka as the national currency; the Jatiya Sangsad ratifies a new constitution.

1973 In the first nationwide elections, the Awami League wins 308 of 315 seats in the Jatiya Sangsad.

1974 As protests become violent, Mujibur Rahman declares a state of emergency; Pakistan recognizes Bangladesh; Bangladesh joins the United Nations.

1975 Mujibur Rahman has the constitution amended to make himself a virtual dictator; Mujibur Rahman is killed in a pro-Pakistani coup; Brig. Khalid Musharaf stages a pro-Indian coup and names Abu Sadat Mohammad Sayem as president; Col. Abu Taher leads a third coup in which Musharaf is killed.

1977 Sayem steps down as president and is replaced by army chief of staff General Zia Rahman; President Zia Rahman's martial law policies win approval in a nationwide referendum; 92 soldiers are executed for their role in an attempted coup against Zia Rahman; opposition parties are banned.

1978 Zia Rahman is elected president for a five-year term; a refugee pact is reached with Burma.

1979 The Bangladesh Nationalist Party, led by President Zia Rahman, wins in elections to the Jatiya Sangsad; martial law is lifted.

1981 President Zia Rahman is assassinated by dissident army officers at Chittagong; Vice President Adbus Sattar is installed as acting president.

1982 Lt. Gen. Hussain Mohammad Ershad ousts the Sattar government, installs Ahsanuddin Chowdhury as president and himself as martial law administrator, dissolves the Jatiya Sangsad, and suspends the constitution.

1983 Ershad dissolves the cabinet and names himself president.

1985 Ershad enforces the ban on political parties, jailing opposition leaders; a cyclone described as "the worst in the country's history" strikes Bangladesh, killing 10,000.

1986 Ershad lifts the ban on political activity; the five parties of the National Front unite to form the pro-government Jatiya Dal (National Party); in May legislative elections, the Jatiya Dal wins 153 of the 300 elected seats and all 30 of the seats reserved for women, and Mizanur Rahman Chowdhury becomes prime minister; Ershad wins the October presidential election by an overwhelming majority; President Ershad repeals martial law and restores the 1972 constitution.

1987 Violent opposition to a bill allowing army representation in the 64 district councils forces President Ershad to withdraw it; the worst floods in 40 years bring widespread devastation; in November Ershad declares a 120-day state of emergency, banning antigovernment protests; in December Ershad dissolves the Jatiya Sangsad.

1988 Monsoon rains leave 30 million homeless and cause nearly $2 billion in damage; the Jatiya Dal wins 250 of the 300 seats in the Jatiya Sangsad; President Ershad repeals the state of emergency; a constitutional amendment establishes Islam as the state religion of Bangladesh; Buddhist Chakma rebels seeking autonomy for the Chittagong Hill region kill 200 people.

1989 Jatiya Sangsad legislation limits the tenure of presidency to two five-year terms and makes the vice presidency a directly elected position; Moudud Ahmed assumes vice presidency and Kazi Zafar Ahmed becomes prime minister.

1990 After violent protests against his government, President Ershad declares a national state of emergency in November; in December Ershad dissolves the legislature and resigns; Chief Justice Shahabuddin Ahmed heads a caretaker government; Ershad and his wife are convicted of theft of public funds, nepotism, and gold smuggling.

1991 The conservative Bangladesh National Party wins the February general elections and BNP leader Khaleda Zia Rahman, widow of former president Zia Rahman, becomes prime minister; the constitution is changed to make the position of president merely ceremonial, with the prime minister holding primary executive power; a cyclone kills over 100,000 and causes billions of dollars in damage.

1994 Nearly 150 members of the opposition resign their seats in parliament hoping to force new elections.

1996 Under the leadership of Sheik Hasina Wazed, daughter of Sheikh Mujibur Rahman, the Awami League wins control of the government for the first time since 1975.

1997 The opposition BNP organizes a series of strikes to protest the government.

1998 Monsoons cause severe flooding, killing over 1,000 and leaving millions homeless; 15 military officers involved in the assassination of Sheikh Mujibur Rahman are sentenced to death.

2001 In parliamentary elections the BNP wins a majority of seats. Khaleda Zia becomes prime minister for a second time.

BIBLIOGRAPHY

Alam, S. M. Shamsul. *The State, Class Formation, and Development in Bangladesh.* Lanham, Md., 1995.

Baxter, Craig. *Bangladesh.* Boulder, Colo., 1984.

Brauns, Claus-Dieter. *Mru: Hill People On the Border of Bangladesh.* Boston, 1990.

Khan, Mohammad, and John P. Thorp. *Bangladesh: Society, Politics and Bureaucracy.* Riverdale, Md., 1985.

Khan, Zillur R. *Leadership in the Least Developed Nation: Bangladesh.* Syracuse, N.Y., 1983.

O'Donnell, Charles P. *Bangladesh: Biography of a Nation.* Boulder, Colo., 1984.

Sisson, Richard. *War and Secession: Pakistan, India, and the Creation of Bangladesh.* Berkeley, Calif., 1990.

Wallace, Ben J. *The Invisible Resource: Women and Work in Rural Bangladesh.* Boulder, Colo., 1987.

Zaheer, Hasan. *The Separation of East Pakistan: The Rise and Realization of Bengali Muslim Nationalism.* New York, 1994.

OFFICIAL PUBLICATIONS

Bangladesh. *Bangladesh Population Census, 1991; Statistical Yearbook of Bangladesh.*

CONTACT INFORMATION

Embassy of Bangladesh
2201 Wisconsin Avenue NW
Washington, D.C. 20007
Phone: (202) 342-8372

INTERNET RESOURCES

- Government of the People's Republic of Bangladesh
  http://bangladeshonline.com/gob

BARBADOS

BASIC FACT SHEET

OFFICIAL NAME:
Barbados

ABBREVIATION:
BB

CAPITAL:
Bridgetown

HEAD OF STATE:
Queen Elizabeth II, represented by Governor General Clifford Husbands (from 1995)

HEAD OF GOVERNMENT:
Prime Minister Owen Seymour Arthur (from 1994)

NATURE OF GOVERNMENT:
Parliamentary democracy within the Commonwealth recognizing Elizabeth II as head of state

POPULATION:
274,540 (July 2000 est.)

AREA:
430 sq km (166 sq mi)

ETHNIC MAJORITY:
Black

LANGUAGE:
English

RELIGIONS:
Christianity

UNIT OF CURRENCY:
Barbados dollar

NATIONAL FLAG:
Vertical tricolor of ultramarine blue stripes on the hoist and the fly sides and a gold stripe in the middle. A broken trident in black appears on the center stripe.

NATIONAL EMBLEM:
A shield in which red orchids flank the fig tree *Ficus barbata*, from which the name of the island is derived. Above the shield, from a silver helmet decorated with a red and ornamental wreath, rises a powerful black forearm grasping two crossed stalks of sugarcane. On either side of the shield are a red-finned dolphin and a pelican with one webbed foot supporting the shield. Beneath the device a golden scroll proclaims the motto "Peace and Industry."

NATIONAL ANTHEM:
"In Plenty and in Time of Need, When This Fair Land Was Young"

NATIONAL HOLIDAYS:
November 30 (National Day, Independence Day); January 1 (New Year's Day); May 1 (May Day); first Monday in July (Caribbean Day); first Monday in October (U.N. Day); Christian festivals, including Christmas, Good Friday, Easter Monday, Whitmonday, and Boxing Day.

DATE OF INDEPENDENCE:
November 30, 1966

DATE OF CONSTITUTION:
November 30, 1966

GEOGRAPHICAL FEATURES

Barbados is the most easterly of the Caribbean islands, lying in the Lesser Antilles east of the Windward Islands about 322 km (200 mi) north-northeast of Trinidad and 161 km (100 mi) east-southeast of St. Lucia. Barbados is the second smallest country in the Western Hemisphere, with an area of 430 sq km (166 sq mi), extending 34 km (21 mi) north to south and 23 km (14 mi) east to west. Its total coastline stretches 101 km (63 mi).

From the south and west the island presents a flat appearance, rising in a series of ridges up to about 100 m (325 ft) and then falling steeply toward the sea. The highest point is Mount Hillaby (336 m; 1,105 ft), near the center of the island. The coast is encircled with coral reefs.

Barbados

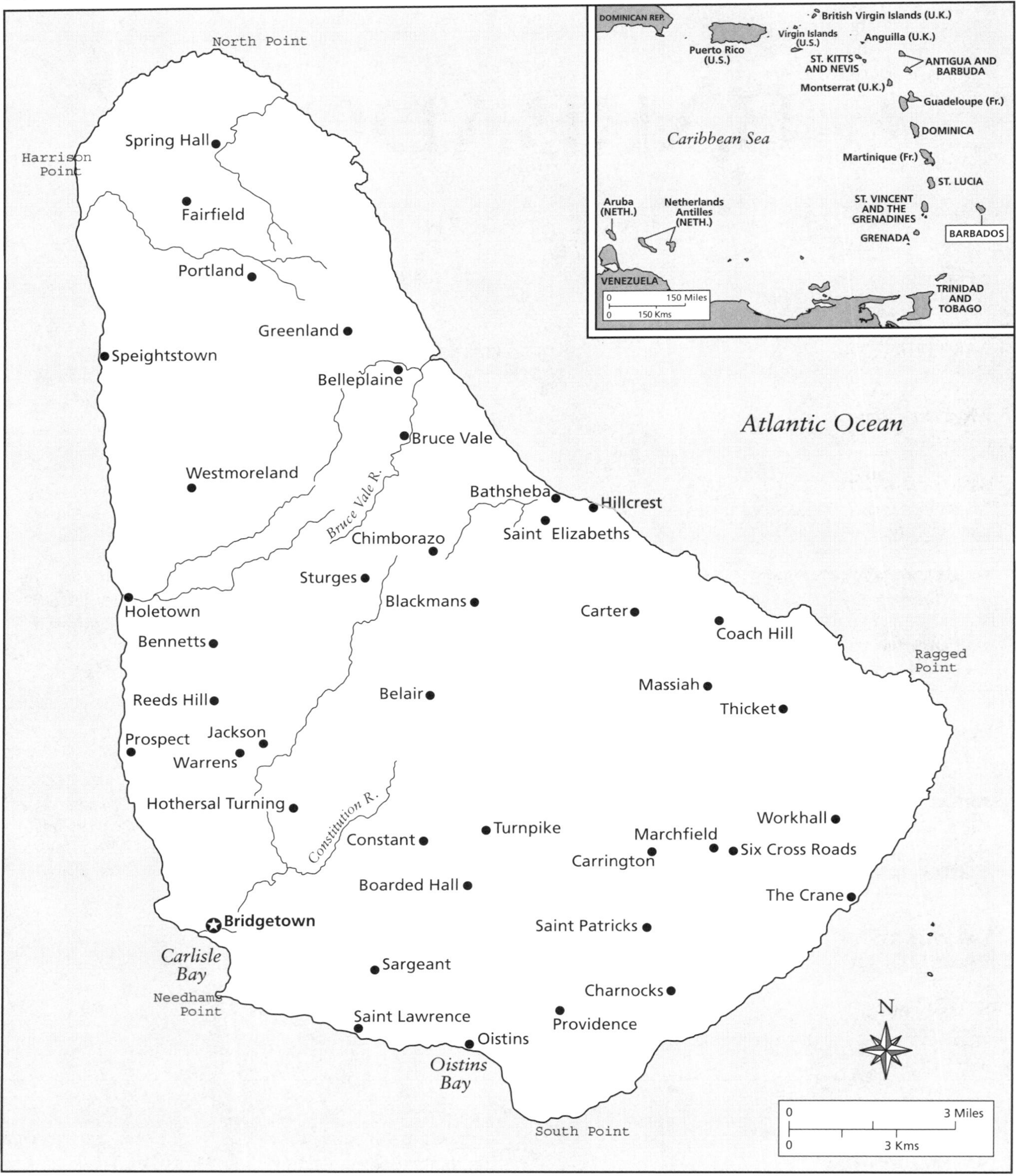
North Point
Harrison Point
Spring Hall
Fairfield
Portland
Greenland
Speightstown
Belleplaine
Bruce Vale
Westmoreland
Bruce Vale R.
Bathsheba
Hillcrest
Saint Elizabeths
Chimborazo
Sturges
Blackmans
Holetown
Carter
Coach Hill
Bennetts
Ragged Point
Massiah
Belair
Reeds Hill
Thicket
Jackson
Prospect
Warrens
Hothersal Turning
Constitution R.
Workhall
Turnpike
Marchfield
Constant
Six Cross Roads
Carrington
Boarded Hall
The Crane
Bridgetown
Saint Patricks
Carlisle Bay
Sargeant
Charnocks
Needhams Point
Saint Lawrence
Providence
Oistins
Oistins Bay
South Point
Atlantic Ocean
N
0 3 Miles
0 3 Kms
DOMINICAN REP.
Puerto Rico (U.S.)
British Virgin Islands (U.K.)
Virgin Islands (U.S.)
Anguilla (U.K.)
ST. KITTS AND NEVIS
ANTIGUA AND BARBUDA
Montserrat (U.K.)
Guadeloupe (Fr.)
DOMINICA
Caribbean Sea
Martinique (Fr.)
ST. LUCIA
Aruba (NETH.)
Netherlands Antilles (NETH.)
ST. VINCENT AND THE GRENADINES
GRENADA
BARBADOS
VENEZUELA
TRINIDAD AND TOBAGO
0 150 Miles
0 150 Kms

There are no rivers in the conventional sense but only gullies, watercourses, and underground channels. The best-known underground channel is Cole's Cave, in the middle of the island. Two rivulets known as Indian River and Joes River are no use for either fishing or navigation.

Geography

Area sq km: 430 sq mi 166
World Rank: 196th
Land Boundaries, km: 0
Coastline, km: 97
Elevation Extremes meters
  Lowest: Atlantic Ocean 0
  Highest: Mount Hillaby 336
Land Use % Arable land: 37
  Permanent Crops: 0
  Permanent Pastures: 5
Forest and Woodland: 12
Other: 46

Population of Principal Cities

Bridgetown	6,070

CLIMATE AND WEATHER

Barbados enjoys tropical temperatures tempered by the northeasterly trade winds. The average annual temperature is 25°C (77°F); daily temperatures rarely rise above 32.2°C (90°F). The dry season is relatively cool, while the wet season is a little warmer. The rains fall from July to November. Annual rainfall varies from 1,016 mm (40 in) in coastal areas to 2,286 mm (90 in) in the central ridge area.

Climate and Weather

Mean Temperature 77°F
Average Rainfall 40 in to 90 in

POPULATION

Population Indicators

Total Population: July 2000 (estimated) 274, 540
World Rank: 178th
Density per sq mi: 1602.4 per sq km 618.6
% of annual growth (1994–99): 0.1
Male %: 47.7
Female %: 52.3
Urban %: 37.9
Age Distribution: % (2000, estimated) 0–14: 22
  15–64: 25.6
  30–44: 22.1
  45–59: 11.4
  60–74: 9.9
  65 and over: 9
Birth Rate per 1,000: 14.45
Death Rate per 1,000: 8.68
Population Doubling Time (years): —
Infant Mortality Rate per 1,000 live births: 12.37
Rate of Natural Increase per 1,000: 4.2
Total Fertility Rate: 1.7
Expectation of Life (years): Males 70.43
  Females 75.6
Marriage Rate per 1,000 (1998): 8.5
Divorce Rate per 1,000: 16.7
Total Number of Households: 67,000
Average Size of Households: 3.5
% of Illegitimate Children: 73.1
Induced Abortions: 723
  Rate per 100 live births: 19.6

ETHNIC COMPOSITION

The ethnic configuration of Barbados consists of 80 percent blacks, 5 percent whites, and 15 percent mulattoes and East Indians.

LANGUAGES

The official language is English, spoken with a variety of accents and a vocabulary replete with Barbadianisms.

Principal Languages and Their Speakers

Bajan (English Creole)	253,000
English	—
Other	13,000

RELIGIONS

About 33 percent of the population is Anglican. The remainder belong to a number of denominations, of which the Moravian, Methodist, and Roman Catholic Churches claim the largest number of believers.

Religious Affiliations

Anglican	88,000
Protestant	79,000
Roman Catholic	12,000
Other	87,000

HISTORICAL BACKGROUND

The original inhabitants of Barbados were the Arawak Indians. They were subsequently replaced by invading Carib Indians in the 13th century. By the time Portuguese explorer Pedro a Campos stopped in Barbados in 1536 en route to Brazil, the Carib Indians were also gone. Some historians have suggested that even earlier contact with the Spanish led the Caribs to flee because some of them were taken as slaves by the Spanish.

Barbados was under the British Crown from 1624, although it was briefly the personal fief of the dukes of Marlborough and later Lords Carlisle and Pembroke. Its House of Assembly, which began meeting in 1639, is the third oldest legislative body in the New World by Bermuda's legislature and the Virginia House of Burgesses. By the time the British left after 342 years in 1966, the island had become completely English in culture.

When Barbados became independent, the government was dominated by the Democratic Labour Party (DLP), whose leader, Errol W. Barrow, was premier. Upon the country's independence he became prime minister. The DLP maintained power until 1976, when it was defeated in the general elections by the Barbados Labor Party (BLP), under the leadership of J. M. G. ("Tom") Adams, who became prime minister. Very few issues divided the rival parties; the campaign centered around alleged government corruption. It maintained its majority in close voting during the 1981 elections. Adams died in 1985 and was succeeded by H. Bernard St. John. St. John was unable to maintain party unity, and the BLP lost the elections in 1986. Barrow was returned to office. Following the sudden death of Barrow in 1987, Lloyd Erskine Sandiford succeeded as prime minister. He led the DLP to victory in 1991, although with a reduced margin. However, in the 1994 elections the DLP suffered an overwhelming defeat and Owen Seymour Arthur of the BLP was swept into power. Arthur won reelection in 1999.

CONSTITUTION

The constitution of 1966 provides for a governmental structure modeled on the British parliamentary system. The queen remains the titular head of state and is represented on the island by a governor-general, who appoints an advisory privy council. Executive authority is vested in the prime minister—the head of government—and his cabinet, who are collectively responsible to a bicameral legislature. The cabinet is required to consist of not fewer than five ministers in addition to the prime minister. The constitution also provides for a judiciary and legal service, and service commissions for judicial, public, and police services. These commissions are exempt from executive interference. The leader of the opposition is a salaried servant of the Crown. Legislative power is vested in the bicameral parliament, composed of the appointed Senate and the elected House of Assembly. Following adoption of a Canters Commission report in 1965, the island was divided into 24 single-member constituencies. House of Assembly elections are held every five years. The judicial system is headed by the Supreme Court of Judicature, which sits as both a high court and a court of appeal.

LOCAL GOVERNMENT

For the purpose of local government the island is divided into 11 parishes, which, until 1969, physically corresponded to ecclesiastical parishes and were administered by rectors and church wardens.

In 1969 all local government services were taken over by the central government, and statutory bodies were established to administer some of these services.

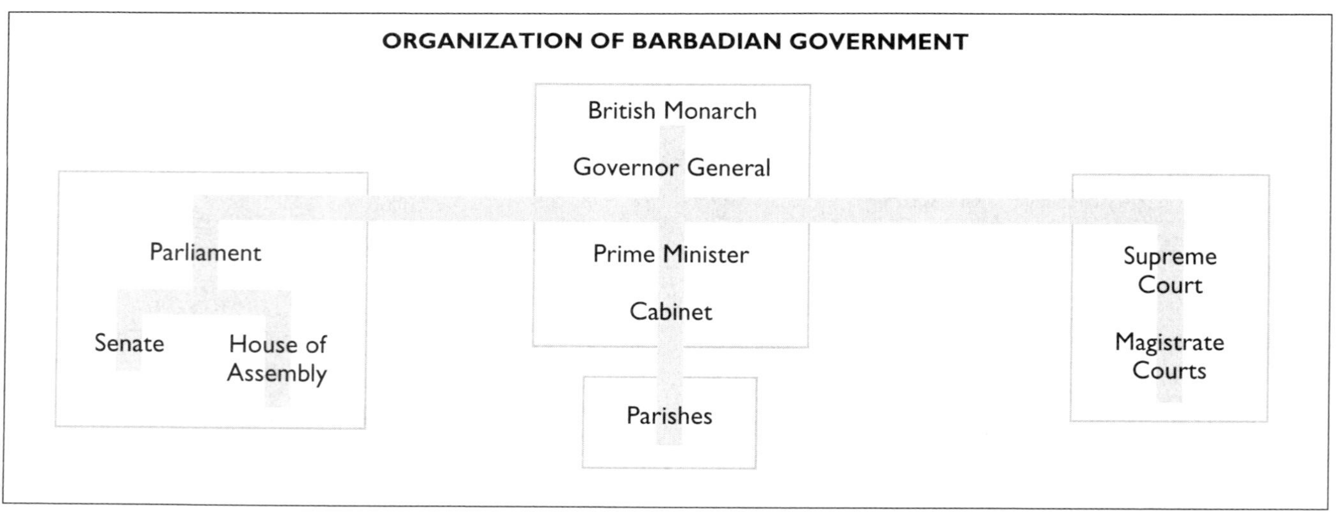

Local Government

Principal administrative divisions, area, population

AREA AND POPULATION

	area		population 1990
Parishes	**sq mi**	**sq km**	**estimate**
Christ Church	22	57	47,050
St. Andrew	14	36	6,346
St. George	17	44	17,905
St. James	12	31	21,001
St. John	13	34	10,206
St. Joseph	10	26	7,619
St. Lucy	14	36	9,455
St. Michael	15	39	97,516
St. Peter	13	34	11,263
St. Philip	23	60	20,540
St. Thomas	13	34	11,590
TOTAL	166	430	260,491

PARLIAMENT

The bicameral parliament consists of the appointed Senate and the elected House of Assembly. The Senate consists of 21 members, of whom 12 are drawn from the majority party; two are from the opposition; and seven are appointed to represent social, religious, and economic interests. The House of Assembly consists of 27 members elected by direct popular vote for five-year terms from the 11 parishes and the city of Bridgetown.

The electoral system is based on adult suffrage over age 18. In the 1986 elections the Democratic Labour Party won 24 seats and the Barbados Labor Party three seats.

POLITICAL PARTIES

There are five active political parties in Barbados. The largest and oldest is the Barbados Labour Party, founded in 1938 as a moderate social democratic party. The second oldest and largest is the Democratic Labour Party founded in 1955. A splinter group from the Democratic Labour Party formed the National Democratic Party in 1989. Two small left-wing organizations, the People's Pressure Movement and the Workers' Party of Barbados, were founded in 1979 and 1985, respectively.

Political Parties

Barbados Labor Party, 1938
Democratic Labor Party, 1955
National Democratic Party, 1989

Political Parties: Strength in Parliament Most Recent Elections

House of Assembly. The House currently consists of 28 members elected for five-year terms by direct popular vote. At the most recent election of January 20, 1999, the Barbados Labour Party won 26 seats and the Democratic Labour Party, 2.

LEGAL SYSTEM

Barbadian jurisprudence is based on English common law. However, the courts have no power of judicial review.

The highest court of the land is the Supreme Court of Judicature, with a chief justice and three puisne judges appointed by the governor-general on the recommendation of the prime minister and after consultation with the leader of the opposition. The Supreme Court sits as both a high court and a court of appeal. Appeals from the Supreme Court go to the Privy Council in the United Kingdom.

The country is divided into 11 magisterial districts, with 11 magistrate courts. Magistrates are appointed by the governor-general on the recommendation of the Judicial and Legal Service Commission, a constitutional body.

The Prisons Department is administered by a superintendent of prisons and consists of a penitentiary at Glendairy and two reformatories. The daily average prison population is 212.

LAW ENFORCEMENT

Law Enforcement

Offenses reported to the police per 100,000: 4,337
- Murder: 8.8
- Assault: 170.8
- Burglary: 1,267.2
- Automobile Theft: 34.2
- Population per Police officer: 280

Death Penalty: Yes.

HUMAN RIGHTS

In terms of civil and political rights Barbados is ranked as a free country. Barbados is a free and democratic state of the British model. The government respects all the freedoms and rights granted to Barbadians in the constitution. There have been no complaints of human rights violations in recent years.

FOREIGN POLICY

Barbados has pursued an active but nonaligned posture in the Caribbean. Nevertheless, it has maintained close relations with the United States and it was designated in early 1985 as the center of the Washington-funded Regional Security System (RSS). In 1998 the government announced that henceforth the primary focus of its relations would be with Asia and the Pacific.

DEFENSE

The island has no standing army. A citizens' militia, the Barbados Regiment, is composed of two companies with a combined strength of 206 volunteers. The Barbados Coast Guard began operations in 1974. It has two armed patrol boats. In the event of an emergency the United Kingdom is under contractual obligation to provide for the defense of the island, but such an emergency has not arisen.

Military Indicators

Total Active Duty Personnel: 600
Military Manpower per 1,000: 2.3
Military Expenditures $: 13 million
 as % of GNP: 0.8
 per capita $: 50
 as % of central government expenditures: 2.3

Arms Imports $: 0
Arms Exports $: 0

ECONOMY

Barbados has a free-market economy in which the dominant sector is private. It has achieved the highest standard of living of all the small island states of the eastern Caribbean. Historically, the Barbadian economy had been dependent on sugarcane cultivation and related activities, but production in recent years has diversified into manufacturing and tourism. The start of the Port Charles Marina project in Speightstown helped the tourism industry continue to expand in 1996–2000. Offshore finance and informatics are important foreign exchange earners, and there is also a light manufacturing sector. The government continues its efforts to reduce the unacceptably high unemployment rate, encourage direct foreign investment, and privatize remaining state-owned enterprises.

Principal Economic Indicators

Gross National Product: $1.741 billion
GNP per capita: $6,590
GNP Average Annual Growth Rate (1990–97) %: —
GNP per capita Average Annual Growth Rate (1990–97) %: —
Origin of Gross Domestic Product %
 Agriculture: 4
 Mining: 1
 Manufacturing: 6
 Construction: 4
 Public Utilities: 3
 Transportation and Communications: 8
 Trade: 27
 Financial Services: 14
 Other Services: 4
 Government: 15
Gross Domestic Product by Type of Expenditure %
 Private Consumption: 64
 Government Consumption: 20
 Gross Domestic Investment: 13
 Foreign Trade: Exports: 49
 Imports: −47
% of Income Received by Poorest 20%: 7.0
% of Income Received by Richest 10%: 44.0

Price and earnings indexes (1995 = 100)

	1992	1993	1994	1995	1996	1997	1998
Consumer price index	97.0	98.1	98.2	100.0	102.4	110.3	108.9
Hourly earnings index	—	—	—	—	—	—	—

Finance

National Currency: Barbadian Dollar (Bds $)
Exchange Rate: $1 = Bds $2
Money Supply Stock in National Currency billion: 0.627
M1 per capita: 2,370
Central Bank Discount Rate %: 10.0
Total External Debt $million: 359
Debt Service Ratio %: —

Balance of Payments $million: 7.1
International Reserves SDRs million: 249
Ratio of External Debt to Total Reserves: 1.7

Average Annual Rate of Inflation/Consumer Price Index
 Growth Rate %: 2.4

Official Development Assistance

ODA: $5 million
 as % of GNP: 0.3
 per capita: $ 19
 Foreign Direct Investment $million: —

Central Government Revenues and Expenditures

Fiscal Year: 1 April–30 March
Revenues $million: 600
Expenditures $million: 645
Budget Deficit $: 45 million
Tax Revenues as % of GDP:
Highest Tax Bracket %
 Individual: —
 Corporate: —

Employment and Labor

Economically Active Population: 137,000
Female Participation Rate %: 49.5
Activity Rate %: 51.8
Labor by Sector: %
 Agriculture, Forestry, Fishing: 4.6
 Manufacturing, Mining: 11.4
 Construction: 8.9
 Transportation and Communications: 4.3
 Trade, Hotels, and Restaurants: 25.8
 Finance, Insurance, Real Estate: 6.1

Public Administration, Defense: —
Services: 35.7

Unemployment %: 16.2

Agriculture

Agriculture's Share of GDP %: 4
Average Annual Rate of Growth (1965–98) %: —
Number of Farms 000: 17.2
Average Size of Farm ha: 95.8
Number of Tractors per 1,000 hectares: 38.0
Irrigation, % of Farms having: 6
Artificial Fertilizer kg/hectare: 91
Total Farmland as % of land area: 50.2
Livestock: Cattle 000: 22
Sheep 000: 41
Hogs 000: 30
Chickens 000: 3,400
Forests: Production of Roundwood (000 cubic meters): 5
Fisheries: Total Catch tons 000: 2.6

Mining

% of GDP: 0.6
Value of Mineral Production $million: 10.4

Manufacturing

Value Added $million: 95
Industrial Production Growth Rate %: 0.8

Energy

Commercial Energy Production metric tons of oil equivalent 000:
Commercial Energy Consumption metric tons of oil equivalent 000: 363
Commercial Energy Consumption per capita kg: 2,701
Average Annual Growth Rate 1980–97 %: —
Net Energy Imports % of use: 100
Electricity Installed Capacity kW 000: 140
Production kW-hr million: 613
Coal Reserves tons million:
Production tons 000:
Natural Gas Proven Reserves cubic meters billion: 0.1
Production cubic meters million: 17
Crude Petroleum Reserves barrels million: 2
Production barrels million: 0.4
Consumption barrels million: 2
Refinery Capacity barrels per day 000: 4
Pipelines Length km: —

Foreign Trade

Imports $million: 766
Exports $million: 235.7
Export Volume % Annual Growth Rate (1990–97): —
Import Volume % Annual Growth Rate (1990–97): —
Balance of Trade $

Balance of trade (current prices)

	1993	1994	1995	1996	1997	1998
BDS.$ 000,000	−777.1	−865.6	−1,063	−1,106	−1,425	−1,510
% of total	51.0%	54.4%	52.7%	49.6%	55.7%	59.7%

Major Trading Partners

	Imports	Exports
European Union %	17.1	20.5
United States %	40.7	16.0
Eastern Europe %	0.2	—
Japan %	6.7	0.6
Others %	35.2	62.8

Transportation

Roads Total Length mi: 1,000 km 1,610
Paved %: 95
Automobiles: 43,711
Trucks and Buses: 10,583
Persons per vehicle: 4.9
Railroad; Track Length mi: — km —
Passenger-mi million: —
Freight-mi million: —
Merchant Marine: No of Vessels: 37
Total Deadweight Tonnage 000: 84.0
International Cargo Loaded tons 000: 206
International Cargo Off-loaded tons 000: 538
Airports with Scheduled Flights: 1
Traffic: Passenger-mi million: 93
Freight-mi million: 0.8
Length of Canals mi: — km —

Tourism

Number of Tourists to 000: —
Number of Tourists from 000: —
Tourist Receipts $million: 680
Tourist Expenditures $million: 52

Communications

Telephones 000: 90
Cost of Local Calls 3 mins: $0.0
Cellular Telephones 000: 4.6
Fax Machines 000: 1.8
Personal Computers 000: 15
Internet Hosts per million persons: 7.7
Mail: Post Offices: 17
Pieces of Mail Handled million: 18
Pieces of Mail Handled per person: 68

EDUCATION

The national literacy rate is 97.4 percent. Education is free, universal, and compulsory for nine years, from ages five to 14. Schooling lasts 12 years, divided into six years of primary school, three years of lower secondary school, and three years of upper secondary school. The curriculum is based on the British model. No tuition fees are charged in secondary schools.

The academic year runs from September to July. The medium of instruction is English at all levels.

Vocational training is provided at the Barbados Technical Institute and the Samuel Jackson Prescod

Polytechnic. Private schools account for 14 percent of total primary and secondary enrollment. Higher education is provided at the University of the West Indies.

Education

Literacy Rate %: 97.4
- Male %: 98.0
- Female %: 96.8

First Level: Primary schools: 106
- Teachers: 1,553
- Students: 26,662
- Student-Teacher Ratio: 17.2
- Net Enrollment Ratio: 78

Second Level: Secondary Schools: 33
- Teachers: 1,406
- Students: 21,259
- Student-Teacher Ratio: 15.1
- Net Enrollment Ratio: 75

Vocational Level: Schools: —
- Students: —

Third Level: Institutions: 1
- Teachers: 153
- Students: 1,314
- Student-Ratio Level: 8.6
- Gross Enrollment Ratio: 28.1
- Students per 100,000: 2,501
- % of Population Age 25 and over with Postsecondary Education: —

Public Expenditure on Education as % of GDP: 7.2

SCIENCE AND TECHNOLOGY

Science and Technology

Scientists and Engineers in R&D per 1 million persons: —
Expenditures in R&D as % of GDP: —
High-Tech Exports $: —
Patent Applications by Residents: —

MEDIA

The island's two daily newspapers, the *Barbados Advocate* and *The Nation*, claim a circulation of 39,000, or 154 per 1,000 inhabitants. Five nondailies, with a circulation of 35,000 (or 136 per 1,000 inhabitants), and 50 periodicals also are published in the country.

The press is free and unfettered. A vigorous opposition press flourishes in the absence of government controls.

There is no national news service. Reuters's Caribbean desk is in Bridgetown.

Barbados has a small book publishing industry.

The Caribbean Broadcasting Corporation (CBC), a statutory body, operates two medium-wave transmitters and one FM transmitter. A privately owned commercial service, the Barbados Rediffusion Service, wires programs for 120 hours weekly to its nearly 26,000 subscribers. CBC's television service was introduced in 1964.

Media

Daily Newspapers: 2
- Total Circulation 000: 41
- Circulation per 1,000: 159

Books Published: —
Magazines: —
Radio Receivers 000: 300
- per 1,000: 1,132

Television sets 000: 75
- per 1,000: 284

MOST IMPORTANT MEDIA:

Press. The following are privately owned and published at Bridgetown: *Daily Nation* (23,000 daily, 43,000 Sunday, published as *Sunday Sun*); *The Beacon* (15,000), weekly BLP organ; *Barbados Advocate* (10,000 daily, 16,300 Sunday), independent. In addition, an *Official Gazette* is issued on Monday and Thursday.

News agencies. The regional Caribbean News Agency (Cana) is headquartered at St. Michael; Spain's *Agencia EFE* is also represented in Barbados.

Radio and television. Barbados Rediffusion Service, Ltd., has operated a wired radio system since the 1930s, and the government-owned Caribbean Broadcasting Corporation (CBC) has offered a wireless system since 1963. The Voice of Barbados, privately owned, began broadcasting in 1981, while Barbados Broadcasting Service (BBS), also private, began transmission in late 1982. In addition, a multidenominational religious system has sought licensing. The CBC operates the only television service, apart from two cable channels.

CULTURE

Cultural Indicators

Public Libraries
- Number: 10
- Volumes: 173,000
- Registered borrowers: 63,822

Museums
- Number: 1
- Annual Attendance: —

Cinema
- Production of Long Films: —
- Number of Cinemas: 4
- Seating Capacity: —
- Annual Attendance: —
- Annual Attendance per capita: —

STATUS OF WOMEN

The 1992 Domestic Violence Law affords protection to women suffering violence and abuse. It applies equally to married persons and those in common law relationships, the latter being in the vast majority. However, criminal law penalties for incest are less than those for rape or sexual assault on nonfamily members. Women's rights are monitored by the National Organization of Women (NOW) which is affiliated to the Caribbean Women's Association.

Women

Gender Empowerment Measure: 18
Seats Held in Parliament by Women %: 18.4
Female Administrators and Managers %: 38.7
Female Professional and Technical Workers %: 51.2
Women's Share of Earned Income %: 40
Women in Government %: 23

HEALTH, FOOD, AND NUTRITION

Health

Number of Physicians: 312
Number of Dentists: 38
Number of Nurses: 889
Number of Pharmacists: 138
Population per Physician: 842
Number of Hospitals: 10
Hospital Beds per 10,000: 75
Hospital Bed Occupancy Rate: 88.3
Infant Mortality Rate per 1,000 live births: 15
Maternal Mortality Rate per 100,000 live births: —
Total Health Expenditures as % of GDP: 5.04
Health Expenditures per capita $: 323
HIV Infected % of adults: —
Cigarette Consumption per smoker per year:
% of Smokers: Male: —
Female: —
Access to Safe Water %: 100

Food and Nutrition

Food Supply as % of FAO Requirements: 133
% of Consumption Expenditures on Food: 45.8
Daily Available Calories per capita: 3,207
% of Total Calories derived from:
Cereals: 28.1
Potatoes, cassava: 4.2
Meat, poultry: 13.7
Fish: 1.8
Eggs, milk: 6.3
Fruits, vegetables: 4.6
Fats, oils: 13.7

ENVIRONMENT

The single greatest environmental concern for Barbados is waste disposal. Its coastal waters are often at risk from the waste of ships and its aquifers are threatened by solid waste dumping. Barbados is one of the world's most densely populated countries, and coastal erosion is a growing concern at many of the built-up resort areas.

Environment

Forest Area sq km: —
Average Annual Deforestation sq km: —
Nationally Protected Areas as % of Total Land Area: —
Freshwater Access cubic meters per capita: —
Emissions of Organic Water Pollutants kg per day: —
CO_2 Emissions per capita ton: 3.2

CHRONOLOGY

1966 Barbados gains independence, with Errol W. Barrow as prime minister.

1969 National government takes over all local parish administration.

1971 Barrow's Democratic Labor Party (DLP) wins in national elections.

1973 The Barbados dollar is introduced, replacing the East Caribbean dollar.

1976 The Barbados Labor Party (BLP) wins an upset victory in national elections, gaining 17 seats in the House of Assembly; J. M. G. ("Tom") Adams is named prime minister; Frederick Smith is elected president of the DLP.

1978 Mercenary army led by Robert Denard is reported preparing for an invasion of the island.

1979 Britain announces formation of a special force to counter Cuban influence in the Barbados region.

1983 Barbados supports U.S. invasion of Grenada.

1984 Governor-General Sir Deighton Lisle dies and is succeeded in office by Sir Hugh Springer.

1985 Prime Minister Adams dies and is succeeded in office by H. Bernard St. John.

1986 The BLP loses the 1986 elections; Barrow returns as prime minister.

1987 Barrow dies and is succeeded as prime minister by Lloyd Erskine Sandiford.

1989 The National Democratic Party (NDP) is formed by members of the DLP.

1990 Dame Nita Barrow is named governor-general.

1991 General elections are held; Sandiford is elected to a five-year term as prime minister; the DLP wins 18 of 28 seats in the House of Assembly; the BLP wins the remaining 10.

1994 The BLP wins the general election and 19 of the 28 seats in the House of Assembly; Owen Arthur becomes prime minister.

1996 Sir Clifford Husbands is appointed governor-general.

1998 A constitutional commission undertaken by former foreign minister Sir Henry Fords recommends that Barbados should remain within the British Commonwealth, replace the British monarch with a Barbadian president as head of state, and establish a Caribbean or Barbadian court of appeals.

2000 The Organization for Economic Cooperation and Development (OECD) threatens trade sanctions on Barbados and 34 other territories for acting as tax havens.

2001 The 12 Caribbean Community (CariCom) countries, including Barbados, sever legal ties between the region and Britain and establish their own regional supreme court.

BIBLIOGRAPHY

Beckles, H. *A History of Barbados.* Cambridge, England, 1990.

Handler, Jerome S. *The Unappropriated People: Freedom in the Slave Society of Barbados.* Baltimore, 1971.

Harlow, V. T. *A History of Barbados, 1625–85.* London, 1972.

Hope, Kempe R. *Economic Development in the Caribbean.* New York, 1986.

Hoyos, Alexander, Sir. *Barbados Comes of Age: From Early Strivings to Happy Fulfillment.* London, 1987.

Kent, David L. *Barbados and America.* Arlington, Va., 1980.

Lynn, Bruce. *Barbados: A Smiling Island.* Farmington, N.Y., 1975.

Potter, Robert B. *Barbados.* Santa Barbara, Calif., 1987.

Tree, Ronald. *A History of Barbados.* London, 1972.

OFFICIAL PUBLICATIONS

Barbados. *Barbados Economic Report* (annual); *Monthly Digest of Statistics; 1993–2000 Development Plan.*

CONTACT INFORMATION

Embassy of Barbados
2144 Wyoming Avenue NW
Washington, D.C. 20008
Phone: (202) 939-9200

INTERNET RESOURCES

- Central Bank of Barbados
  http://www.centralbank.org.bb

BELARUS

BASIC FACT SHEET

OFFICIAL NAME:
Republic of Belarus (Respublika Byelarus)

ABBREVIATION:
BO

CAPITAL:
Minsk

HEAD OF STATE:
President Alyaksandr Lukashenko (from 1994)

HEAD OF GOVERNMENT:
Prime Minister Henadz Navitski (from 2001)

NATURE OF GOVERNMENT:
Authoritarian regime

POPULATION:
10,164,000 (1999)

AREA:
207,595 sq km (80,153 sq mi)

MAJOR ETHNIC GROUPS:
Byelorussian, Russian

LANGUAGES:
Belarusian

RELIGIONS:
Eastern Orthodoxy

UNIT OF CURRENCY:
Belarusian rubel

NATIONAL FLAG:
Red horizontal band (top) and green horizontal band one-half of the width of the red band; a vertical stripe of white on the hoist side bears in red the Belarusian national ornament

NATIONAL ANTHEM: —

NATIONAL HOLIDAY:
Independence Day July 3

DATE OF INDEPENDENCE:
August 25, 1991

DATE OF CONSTITUTION:
November 17, 1996

GEOGRAPHICAL FEATURES

Situated along the Western Dvina and the Driepr rivers, Belarus is the smallest of the three Slavic successor states of the former Soviet Union. Completely landlocked, the country shares borders with Latvia, 141 km (87 mi); Lithuania, 502 km (312 mi); Poland, 605 km (376 mi); Russia, 959 km (595 mi), and Ukraine, 891 km (553 mi). Its geography consists largely of flat lowlands with a ridge of higher ground running from the northeast to the southwest bisecting the country. This ridge contains the country's highest point, a hill named Dzerzhinskaya Gora (1,135 ft/346 m above sea level.) While the northern part of the country is covered in forests, the southern portion is a combination of marshes, swamps, and forests including a large forested swamp called the Pripyat Marshes. Along the country's southwestern border with Poland, the two countries jointly administer a nature preserve in the Belovezha Forest (Bialowieza in Polish).

Geography

Area sq km: 207,595 sq mi 80,153
World Rank: 85th
Land Boundaries, km: Latvia 114; Lithuania 502; Poland 605; Russia 959; Ukraine 891
Elevation Extremes meters
Lowest: Nyoman River 90
Highest: Dzerzhinskaya Gora 346

(continued)

Belarus

Land Use % Arable land: 29
Permanent Crops: 1
Permanent Pastures: 15
Forest and Woodland: 34
Other: 21

Population of Principal Cities (1996 est.)

Baranovichi (Baranavichy)	172,000
Bobruysk (Babrujsk)	227,100
Borisov (Baryasáu)	153,000
Brest (Bierascie)	293,000
Gomei (Homiel)	512,000
Grodno (Horadnia)	301,000
Lida	101,000
Minsk	1,700,000
Mogilyov (Mahilou)	367,000
Mozyr (Mazyr)	108,000
Orsha (Vorsha)	134,000
Pinsk	130,000
Soligorsk	101,000
Vitebsk (Viciebsk)	365,000

CLIMATE AND WEATHER

The relatively monolithic geography gives the entire country a similar climate. Belarus has cold winters and warm summers with temperatures ranging from about 22°F (−6°C) in January, the coldest month, to about 65°F (18°C) in July, the hottest. Annual precipitation ranges from 20 to 26 inches (50 to 66 centimeters).

Climate and Weather

Mean Temperature
July 65°F
January 22°F
Average Rainfall 20.5 in to 26.6 in

POPULATION

Population Indicators

Total Population: 1999 10,164,000
World Rank: 74th
Density per sq mi: 126.8 per sq km 49
% of annual growth (1994–99): −0.3
Male %: 46.9
Female %: 53.1
Urban %: 65.5
Age Distribution: % 0–14: 23.0
15–29: 22.4
30–44: 20.6
45–59: 18.0
60–74: 11.5
75 and over: 4.5
Population 2020: 10,132,000
Birth Rate per 1,000: 9.3
Death Rate per 1,000: 13.0
Population Doubling Time (years): —
Infant Mortality Rate per 1,000 live births: 12.6
Rate of Natural Increase per 1,000: −3.7
Total Fertility Rate: 1.7
Expectation of Life (years): Males 66
Females 75.7
Marriage Rate per 1,000: 7.3
Divorce Rate per 1,000: 4.3
Total Number of Households: 2,796,000
Average Size of Households: 3.2
% of Illegitimate Children: 9.0
Induced Abortions: 85,685
Rate per 100 live births: 73.0

ETHNIC COMPOSITION

The most dominant ethnic group in the country are Belarusians, a Slavic people who can trace their inhabitance of the area back nearly 1,500 years. Belarusians make up nearly 78 percent of the population. Slightly more than 13 percent of the population is Russian by nationality. The country also has small numbers of Poles (4 percent) and Ukrainians (3 percent).

LANGUAGES

The native and official language of the country is Belarusian, a Slavic language that closely resembles both Russian and Ukrainian. Like these two languages, Belarusian uses the Cyrillic alphabet. In addition to Belarusian, Russian is also an official language.

Principal Languages and Their Speakers

Belarusian	6,670,000
Polish	60,000
Russian	3,250,000
Ukrainian	130,000
Other	60,000

RELIGIONS

Most Belarusians are Eastern Orthodox Christians who belong to either the Russian Orthodox Church or the Belarusian Autocephalous Orthodox Church, a self-governing Orthodox church. Because the Belarusian Autocephalous Orthodox Church encouraged independence from the Soviet Union, it was banned from 1920 until 1990, except for a brief time in the 1940s. The second largest religious group is the Belarusian Catholic Church. These followers are also called Greek Catholics or Uniates because they follow the rituals of the Eastern Orthodox Church, but accept the authority of the Roman pontiff. These two groups account for more than 80 percent of the population. In addition to these two groups there are small numbers of Roman Catholics, Protestants, Jews, and Muslims.

Religious Affiliations

Belarusian	3,210,000
Orthodox	1,800,000
Roman Catholic	5,150,000
Other	5,150,000

HISTORICAL BACKGROUND

The history of the Belarus people begins when Slavic tribes moved into the area during the 500s. Belarusians, like the Ukrainians and Russians, constituted a portion of the Kievan Rus state that was formed during the 800s. For two centuries, Belarus formed the northwestern limits of the state that flourished as a major European political, economic, and military power. By the 13th century, the Kievan Rus state was falling apart due to invasions from the east by Mongol hordes and threats from the growing Germanic tribes from the west. Belarus sought protection by forming a military alliance with its western neighbor, Lithuania. Eventually, however, the alliance led to Belarus becoming part of Lithuania. In 1386 when the grand duke of Lithuania married the queen of Poland, the two countries began a process of merger into one country. In 1569, Lithuania and its protectorate Belarus were subsumed by Poland. For more than 200 years, Belarus remained part of the Polish empire until the empire was divided between Russia, Prussia, and Austria at the end of the 18th century. Russia received eastern Poland, which included Belarus. For nearly two centuries, the Russians practiced a policy of Russification that promoted Russian culture and language over those native cultures that made up its empire.

When the Bolsheviks overthrew the Russian czar in 1917, the Belarusians used the opportunity in 1918 to set up an independent state called the Belarusian National Republic. However, the communists invaded later that same year and established a state they named Bylelorussia (meaning White Russia). In January 1919, the communists officially declared the state the Belarusian Soviet Socialist Republic. The communists continued the policy of Russification begun under the czar. In 1939, the Soviets gained control of western Belarus, which had been under the control of the Polish state since 1919. During World War II, much of Belarus was occupied by Nazi Germany and formed part of the famed eastern front. The toll on the country was great with the city of Minsk nearly completely destroyed. With the defeat of Nazi Germany by Russia and Allied forces, Belarus returned to the control of the Soviet Union where it remained until 1990. Under Soviet rule, Belarus was converted from a largely agricultural republic to an industrial one. Stalin's collectivization activities were resisted by the Belarusians. In the end, Stalin won out. The Soviets also encouraged migration of Russians into Belarus. Belarusian was replaced by Russian as the official language of the republic. The relative prosperity of Belarus under the Soviet system made it a somewhat passive player in the disintegration of the USSR.

In 1990, the Belarusian parliament declared that the laws of the republic took precedence over those passed by the Soviet Union. In August 1991, still as part of the Soviet Union, the country failed to overthrow Mikhail Gorbachev. Belarus along with several other republics declared their independence from the Soviet Union. In September, it officially changed its name from Byelorussia to Belarus. In December it joined the Commonwealth of Independent States. Independence has not proven to be what many had hoped. The country's leaders were inexperienced in dealing with economic issues and their conversion to a market-driven economy was not nearly as fast as anticipated by both Belarusians and Westerners. As international aid began to dry up, Belarus sought to form closer ties with former Soviet republics, especially Russia. Aleksandr Lukashenko, who became president in 1994, worked for a new constitution that was adopted in 1996 and that increased his powers. In addition to adopting a new constitution, the people approved an extension of Lukashenko's term to 2001. In 1997, Lukashenko signed a charter with Russia's Boris Yeltsin calling for the merger of the two nations. In protest to the growing authoritarian power of Lukashenko, the United States cut off aid to Belarus. Lukashenko was reelected president in 2001. However, the elections were called undemocratic by opposition leaders and international observers.

CONSTITUTION

Under the constitution of Belarus, which became effective in 1996, a president is head of state and has broad powers over the government. The president appoints a prime minister, who heads the Council of Ministers. Since the election of Lukashenko, the country has largely been subservient to his will. He has sought closer ties

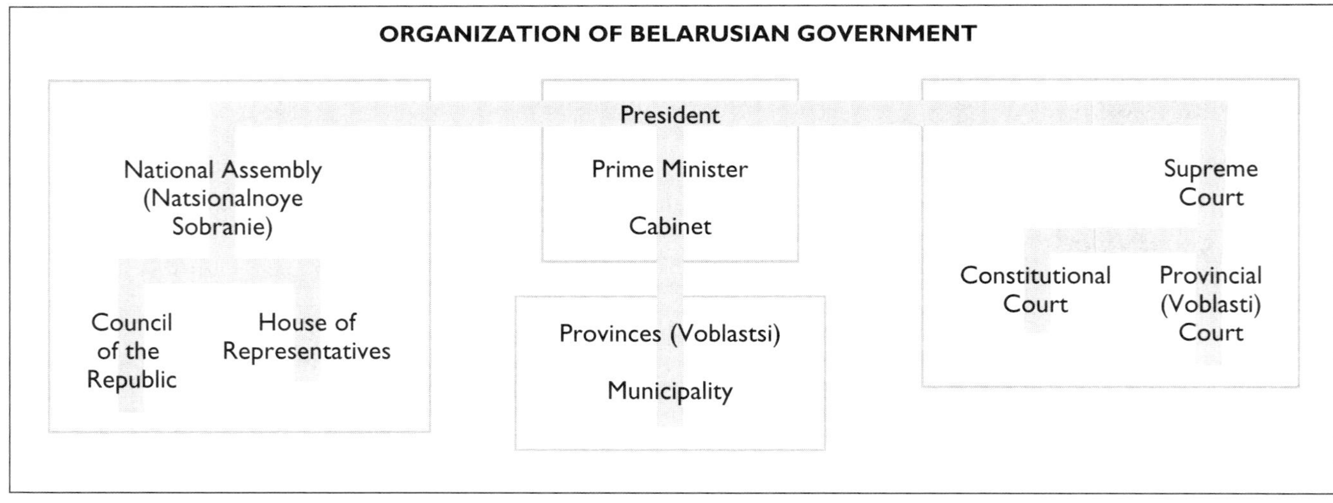

with the former Soviet Union and has gone so far as to agree in principle to a merger of the two countries. The country's legislature consists of two houses, an upper house called the Council of the Republic and a lower house called the House of Representatives. The council has 64 members. The House of Representatives has 110 members.

LOCAL GOVERNMENT

Belarus is divided into six provinces, each named for the capital of the province: (1) Brest, (2) Gomel, (3) Grodno, (4) Minsk, (5) Mogilev, and (6) Vitebsk. A council elected by the voters governs each province. The president, however, appoints regional executives, who supervise and appoint local executives. The appointed executives control the regional and local councils.

Local Government

Principal administrative divisions, capitals, area, population

AREA AND POPULATION

		area		population 1995
Provinces	**Capitals**	**sq mi**	**sq km**	**estimate**
Brest	Brest	12,700	32,800	1,508,000
Homei (Gomel)	Homel	15,600	40,400	1,594,000
Hrodno (Grodno)	Hrodno	9,700	25,000	1,209,000
Mahilyoū (Mogilyov)	Mahilyoū	11,200	29,100	1,259,000
Minsk (Mensk)	Minsk	15,500	40,200	3,288,000
Vitebsk	Vitebsk	15,500	40,100	1,439,000
TOTAL		80,200	207,600	10,297,000

PARLIAMENT

The Belarusian parliament—the National Assembly—comprises two houses: the House of Representatives, composed of 110 deputies, and the Supreme House, the Council of the Republic, composed of 64 representatives. The deputies are elected to the House of Representatives directly by the voters. Any citizen of the Republic of Belarus who has reached the age of 21 may become a deputy of the House of Representatives. The Council of the Republic is the house of territorial representation. Any citizen of the Republic of Belarus who has reached the age of 30, and who has been resident in the territory of a corresponding region (oblast) or the city of Minsk for no less than five years may become a member of the Council of the Republic. Eight members of the council are appointed by the president of the Republic of Belarus, while the rest are elected at the sittings of the deputies of the local Soviets of Deputies: eight from each of the six regions of the Republic and of the city of Minsk.

POLITICAL PARTIES

There are nearly a dozen political parties in Belarus. The main ones are as follows:

Abyadnanaya Grazhdanskaya Partiya Belarusi (United Civic Party of Belarus, liberal)
Agrarnaya Partiya Belarusi (Agrarian Party of Belarus, agrarian)
Belaruskaya Ekalagichnaya Partiya (Belarusian Ecological Party, ecologist)
Belaruskaya Narodnaya Partiya (Belarusian People's Party)
Belaruskaya Partiya Zyelenykh (Green Party of Belarus, ecologist)
Belaruskaya Satsiyalna-Sportjunaya Partiya (Belarusian Social Sport Party)
Belaruskaya Syalanskaya Partiya (Belarusian Peasants' Party, agrarian)
Belaruski Patryatychny Ruch (Belarusian Patriotic Movement, authoritarian)
Nadzeya (Hope–Belarusian Women's Political Party, feminist)
Kommunisticheskaya Partuya Belarusi (Communist Party of Belarus, communist)
Narodni Front Belarusi-Adradzhennie (Belarusian Popular Front–Revival, Christian-democratic)
Partiya Narodnaya Zgody (Party of People's Accord, liberal)
Respublikanskaya Partiya Pratsy y Spravyadivasti (Republican Party of Labour and Justice)
Satsiyal-Demokratychnaya Partiya Belarusi-Hramada (Belarusian Social Democratic Party-Assembly, social-democratic)
Usebelaruskaya Partiya Narodnaga Adzinstva i Zgody (All-Belarusian Party for Popular Unity and Accord, centrist)

Of the above parties the United Civic Party of Belarus was formed when the Democratic and Civil Parties merged. It has strong support among intellectuals and is committed to democracy while downplaying nationalism. The Belarusan Social-Democratic Union is modeled after the German Social Democratic Party. The Belarusian Peasant Party is an agrarian party that favors private farming. The Belarusian Popular Front is an umbrella group that contains members who generally support democracy and nationalism.

Political Parties

Belarusian Patriotic Movement, 1994
Belarusian Popular Patriotic Union, 1998, an alliance of three parties:
- Communist Party
- Liberal Democratic Party
- Slavic Assembly

(continued)

Agrarian Party, 1994
United Civic Party, 1995
Belarusian Christian Democratic Union, 1991
All-Belarusian Party of People's Unity and Accord, 1994
Belarusian Peasants' Party, 1990
Belarusian Social Democratic Party, 1991
Belarusian Ecological Party
Republican Party of Labor and Justice
Belarusian People's Party
Belarusian Social Sporting Party
Belarusian Green Party
Belarusian Popular Front-Revival, 1989
Socialist Party, 1994
Party of Popular Accord
Yabloko, 1997

Political Parties: Strength in Parliament Most Recent Elections

The National Assembly has two chambers. The **House of Representatives** has 110 members elected in single-seat constituencies for four-year terms. The **Council of the Republic** has 64 members, 56 indirectly elected and eight appointed by the president. In the House elections of October 15 and 29, 2000, the Communist Party of Belarus won 6 seats; Agrarian Party of Belarus, 5; Republican Party of Labor and Justice, 2; Liberal Democratic Party, 1; Social-Democratic Party of People's Accord, 1; Social and Sporting Party, 1; nonpartisans, 81; and vacant because of invalid elections, 13.

LEGAL SYSTEM

The system of government of Belarus establishes an independent judicial system that goes to great lengths to protect the appearance of propriety. The courts administer justice on the basis of the constitution, the laws, and other enforceable enactments such as presidential declarations. The trial of cases in all courts are stipulated to be open. The hearing of cases in closed court session are permitted only in the instances specified in law and in accordance with all the rules of legal procedure. Justice is administered on the basis of the adversarial proceedings and equality of the parties involved in the trial. The rulings of courts are mandatory for all citizens and officials. Parties have the right to appeal rulings, sentences, and other judicial decisions. The Constitutional Court of the Republic of Belarus consists of 12 judges from among highly qualified specialists in the field of law, who as a rule have a scientific degree.

LAW ENFORCEMENT

Law Enforcement

Offenses reported to the police per 100,000: 650
Murder: 2.9
Assault: 7.0
Burglary: —
Automobile Theft: —
Population per Police officer: —
Death Penalty: Yes.

HUMAN RIGHTS

Belarus has not had an easy transition to Western principles of freedom and human rights. Lukashenko's government continues to use Soviet-style repression in violations of a broad spectrum of basic civil and political rights. The government has censored the press and closed the only remaining independent press. There have been threats made against government critics. Restrictions on political freedoms have been codified. Demonstrators have been arrested. Academic freedom is nonexistent as discussion and research of controversial topics are forbidden. The government has hounded or disbanded opposition political parties and nongovernmental organizations, and it has stripped independent lawyers of their accreditation. State university authorities issue reprimands and warnings to politically active lecturers, independent historians, and other academics.

FOREIGN POLICY

Belarus is among the most pro-Russian of the former republics of the Soviet Union. In 1995 Belarus and Russia signed a friendship and cooperation treaty providing for bilateral reintegration. Among other things, the pact provided for the eventual creation of an economic and monetary union. The process was continued in 1996 by a far-reaching Treaty on the Formation of the Community of Sovereign Republics (CSR), which called for military and political cooperation as well as economic union and the establishment of a CSR Supreme Council and a CSR parliamentary assembly consisting of an equal number of Belarusian and Russian representatives. A Charter of the Union was ratified in 1997. Citizens of both nations were declared CSR citizens. However, there has been no recent progress in implementing the provisions of the charter.

DEFENSE

Belarusian military activities are coordinated with Russia under a 1993 treaty. The entire nuclear arsenal of the country was transferred to Russia in 1996. Belarusian males who have reached the age of 18 are subject to conscription, which lasts 18 months. The army has ground forces that number approximately 50,000 members and are organized under the ministry of defense. The air force has about 25,000 members and 200 combat aircraft of

Soviet design. Being a landlocked country, Belarus has no navy.

Military Indicators

Total Active Duty Personnel: 80,000
Military Manpower per 1,000: 7.7
Military Expenditures $million: —
as % of GNP: —
per capita $: —
as % of central government expenditures: —

Arms Imports $million: 0
Arms Exports $million: 170

ECONOMY

Belarus has seen little structural reform since 1995, when President Lukashenko launched the country on the path of "market socialism." In keeping with this policy, Lukashenko reimposed administrative controls over prices and currency exchange rates and expanded the state's right to intervene in the management of private enterprise. In addition to the burdens imposed by high inflation, businesses have been subject to pressure on the part of central and local governments, including, arbitrary changes in regulations, numerous rigorous inspections, and retroactive application of new business regulations prohibiting practices that had been legal. Additional economic problems include two consecutive bad harvests in 1998 and 1999 and persistent trade deficits. Close relations with Russia, possibly leading to reunion, color the pattern of economic developments. For the time being, Belarus remains self-isolated from the West and its open-market economies.

Principal Economic Indicators

Gross National Product: $22.082 billion
GNP per capita: $2,150
GNP Average Annual Growth Rate (1990–97) %: −5.6
GNP per capita Average Annual Growth Rate (1990–97) %: −5.6
Origin of Gross Domestic Product %
Agriculture: 16
Mining: —
Manufacturing: 45
Construction: 9
Public Utilities: —
Transportation and Communications: 5
Trade: 9
Financial Services: 8
Other Services: 7
Government: 2
Gross Domestic Product by Type of Expenditure %
Private Consumption: 63
Government Consumption: 21
Gross Domestic Investment: 29
Foreign Trade: Exports: 72
Imports: −85
% of Income Received by Poorest 20%: 11.1
% of Income Received by Richest 10%: 19.4

Price and earnings indexes (1995 = 100)

	1992	1993	1994	1995	1996
Consumer price index	100	1,290	29,946	242,349	370,043
Earnings index	100	1,207	1,936	14,888	23,899

Finance

National Currency: Belarusian rubel (BR)
Exchange Rate: $1 = BR 31,030
Money Supply Stock in National Currency billion: 15,708.4
M1 per capita: 1,519,000
Central Bank Discount Rate %: 5.8
Total External Debt $million: 970
Debt Service Ratio %: 1.4

Balance of Payments $million: −787.6
International Reserves SDRs: —
Ratio of External Debt to Total Reserves: —
Average Annual Rate of Inflation/Consumer Price Index Growth Rate %: 65

Official Development Assistance

ODA $million: 28
as % of GNP: 0.1
per capita: $3
Foreign Direct Investment $million: 149

Central Government Revenues and Expenditures

Fiscal Year: Calendar Year
Revenues $million: 4,000
Expenditures $million: 4,100
Budget Deficit $million: 100
Tax Revenues as % of GDP: 28.7
Highest Tax Bracket %
Individual: —
Corporate: —

Employment and Labor

Economically Active Population: 4,798,000
Female Participation Rate %: —
Activity Rate %: 46.5
Labor by Sector: %
Agriculture, Forestry, Fishing: 19.1
Manufacturing, Mining: 28.4
Construction: 7.7
Transportation and Communications: 6.6
Trade, Hotels, and Restaurants: 9.6
Finance, Insurance, Real Estate: 2.0
Public Administration, Defense: 1.9
Services: 19.8
Unemployment %: 3.3

Agriculture

Agriculture's Share of GDP %: 16
Average Annual Rate of Growth (1965–98) %: —
Number of Farms 000: 3.0
Average Size of Farm ha: 20
Number of Tractors per 1,000 hectares: 19.9

(continued)

Irrigation, % of Farms having: 2
Artificial Fertilizer kg/hectare: 119.0
Total Cropland as % of Farmland: 45.0
Livestock: Cattle 000: 4,801
Sheep 000: 127
Hogs 000: 3,682
Chickens 000: 40,000
Forests: Production of Roundwood (000 cubic meters): 10,015
Fisheries: Total Catch tons: 14.5

Mining

% of GDP: 0.1
Value of Mineral Production $million: 2.0

Manufacturing

Value Added $million: 3,006
Industrial Production Growth Rate %: 17

Energy

Commercial Energy Production metric tons of oil equivalent 000: 3,275
Commercial Energy Consumption metric tons of oil equivalent 000: 25,142
Commercial Energy Consumption per capita kg: 2,449
Average Annual Growth Rate 1980–97 %: 5.9
Net Energy Imports % of use: 87
Electricity Installed Capacity kW: 7,390
Production kW-hr million: 24,918
Coal Reserves tons million: —
Production tons 000: —
Natural Gas Proven Reserves cubic meters billion: —
Production cubic meters million: 262
Crude Petroleum Reserves barrels million: —
Production barrels million: 37
Consumption barrels million: 97
Refinery Capacity barrels per day 000: 473
Pipelines Length km: 2,570

Foreign Trade

Imports $million: 5,563.6
Exports $million: 4,706.8
Export Volume % Annual Growth Rate (1990–97): —
Import Volume % Annual Growth Rate (1990–97): —

Balance of trade (current prices)

	1992	1993	1994	1995	1996	1997	1998
CFAF 000,000	+64	−569	−556	−856	−1,287	−1,388	−1,493
% of total	0.9%	12.6%	10.0%	8.3%	10.2%	8.7%	9.6%

Major Trading Partners

	Imports	Exports
European Union %	16.7	12.2
United States %	1.7	1.2
Eastern Europe %	74.8	75.1
Japan %	0.4	—
Others %	6.4	11.5

Transportation

Roads Total Length mi: 32,030 km 51,547
Paved %: 99
Automobiles: 955,526
Trucks and Buses: 9,289
Persons per vehicle: 11
Railroad; Track Length mi: 3,480 km 5,600
Passenger-mi million: 7,770
Freight-mi million: 17,473
Merchant Marine: No. of Vessels: —
Total Deadweight Tonnage 000: 18,373
International Cargo Loaded tons 000: —
International Cargo Off-loaded tons 000: —
Airports with Scheduled Flights: 2
Traffic: Passenger-mi million: 864
Freight-mi million: 7
Length of Canals mi: —

Tourism

Number of Tourists to: 355
Number of Tourists from 000: 969
Tourist Receipts $million: —
Tourist Expenditures $million: —

Communications

Telephones 000: 1,968
Cost of Local Calls 3 mins: $0.
Cellular Telephones 000: 5.9
Fax Machines 000: 8.9
Personal Computers 000: —
Internet Hosts per million persons: 2.2
Mail: Post Offices: 3,894
Pieces of Mail Handled million: 6.7
Pieces of Mail Handled per person: 0.7

EDUCATION

The national educational system of Belarus consists of preschool upbringing and different levels of education (general, secondary, out-of-school, professional and technical, special secondary, higher education, training of scientists and lecturers, self-education for grown-ups). Primary and secondary education are compulsory in Belarus. Children from the ages of seven to 16 are provided with free public education. The state also maintains a number of universities and vocational centers. In the 1996–97 academic year there were 55,000 teachers employed in Belarus, 35 percent of them in higher education and 60 percent in special secondary education. In 4,500 preschool institutions there were 444,300 children. There were 4,900 general secondary schools of all types with 1.6 million pupils, including 26 lyceums (15,600 pupils), 68 gymnasiums (63,500 pupils), and two colleges (1,500 pupils). There are 123,900 students in 248 professional and technical colleges and 125,000 students in 150 special secondary educational institutions, including 2,000 students in four private institutions. There were 55 higher educational institutions in Belarus as of January 1, 1998, 13 private ones among them. The largest state higher educational institutions are the Belarusian University, the University of Informatics and Radio-electronics, and economic, technological, agricultural, technological, and pedagogical universities. All of them are located in Minsk.

Education

Literacy Rate %: 97.9
  Male %: 99.4
  Female %: 96.6
First Level: Primary schools: 4,900
  Teachers: 127,000
  Students: 1,561,000
  Student-Teacher Ratio: 12.3
  Net Enrollment Ratio: 9.5
Second Level: Secondary Schools: —
  Teachers: —
  Students: —
  Student-Teacher Ratio: 12.3
  Net Enrollment Ratio: 95

Vocational Level: Schools: 149
  Students: 122,400

Third Level: Institutions: 59
  Teachers: 16,900
  Students: 197,400
  Student-Ratio Level: 10.5
  Gross Enrollment Ratio: 42.6
  Students per 100,000: 3,031
  % of Population Age 25 and over with Post secondary Education: —

Public Expenditure on Education as % of GDP: 5.6

SCIENCE AND TECHNOLOGY

Science and Technology

Scientists and Engineers in R&D per 1 million persons: 2,248
Expenditures in R&D as % of GDP: 1.07
High-Tech Exports $million: 204
Patent Applications by Residents: 755

MEDIA

There is an active newspaper industry in Belarus with more than 220 papers in print in 1989. This number has declined as the government of Lukashenko has cracked down on the independent and opposition press. Despite this crackdown, there exists a circulation of more than 1.5 million papers daily in Belarusian and another 3 million in other languages (largely Russian).

Both radio and television are controlled by the government. Belarus Radio broadcasts two national programs. It also shares a relay with Radio Moscow. Belarus Television broadcasts a single color channel.

There are 5,200 public libraries with 79.5 billion books, 24 theaters, 4,600 clubs, and 149 museums, including the National Arts Museum, the Belarusan State Museum of the Great Patriotic War History, the Museum of the Brest Hero-Fortress, and museums of famous writers (Y. Kolas, Y. Kupala, M. Bogdanovich, and others).

Media

Daily Newspapers: 10
  Total Circulation 000: 1,899
  Circulation per 1,000: 187
Books Published: 3,346
Magazines: 155
Radio Receivers 000: 3,200
  per 1,000: 311
Television sets 000: 727
  per 1,000: 13.98

MOST IMPORTANT MEDIA:

Press. The following are published daily at Minsk in Belarusian, unless otherwise noted: *Narodnaya Hazeta* (People's Newspaper, 603,000), government organ in Belarusian and Russian; *Zvyazda* (Star, 173,000), government organ; *Vechernil Minsk* (Evening Minsk, 169,000); *Republika* (Republic, 143,000), government organ; *Dobry Vechar* (Good Evening, 40,000), independent. There are also a number of party organs, including *Naviny BNF* (Belarusian popular Front News).

News agencies. The domestic facility is the Belarus Telegraph Agency (BelTA), headquartered at Minsk.

Radio and television. Radio Minsk and Belarus Television broadcast from Minsk in Belarusian and Russian. There were approximately 3.2 million radio and 2.1 television receivers in 1998.

CULTURE

Cultural Indicators

Public Libraries Number: 52
  Volumes: —
  Registered borrowers: —
Museums Number: 149
  Annual Attendance: —
Cinema Production of Long Films: —
  Number of Cinemas: —
  Seating Capacity: —
  Annual Attendance: —
  Annual Attendance per capita: —

STATUS OF WOMEN

Belarus has made a considerable step in the last five years to improve the status of women. In that period, the government adopted the Women of the Republic of Belarus program and the National Plan of Action to Improve the

Status of Women for 1996–2000 and established the Gender Information and Policy Center. Parliament passed laws aimed at defending women's rights. Women are almost completely unrepresented in the government and parliament. In Lukashenko's government, there is only one female minister and 10 deputy ministers. Women account for only about 5 percent of members of the House of Representatives of the Belarusian National Assembly. Women make up 31 percent of members of the Council of the Republic, the upper house of the National Assembly.

Women

Gender Empowerment Measure: —
Seats Held in Parliament by Women %: 18.4
Female Administrators and Managers %: —
Female Professional and Technical Workers %: —
Women's Share of Earned Income %: —
Women in Government %: 4

HEALTH, FOOD, AND NUTRITION

Health

Number of Physicians: 45,000
Number of Dentists: —
Number of Nurses: 117,000
Number of Pharmacists: —
Population per Physician: 222
Number of Hospitals: 880
Hospital Beds per 10,000: 122
Hospital Bed Occupancy Rate: —
Infant Mortality Rate per 1,000 live births: 19
Maternal Mortality Rate per 100,000 live births: 37
Total Health Expenditures as % of GDP: 3.19
Health Expenditures per capita $: 157
HIV Infected % of adults: 0.17
Cigarette Consumption per smoker per year: —
% of Smokers: Male: —
Female: —
Access to Safe Water %: —

Food and Nutrition

Food Supply as % of FAO Requirements: —
% of Consumption Expenditures on Food: 29
Daily Available Calories per capita: —
% of Total Calories derived from:
Cereals: —
Potatoes, cassava: —
Meat, poultry: —
Fish: —
Eggs, milk: —
Fruits, vegetables: —
Fats, oils: —

ENVIRONMENT

The biggest ongoing environmental problem facing Belarus is the continuing contamination from the fallout from the 1986 nuclear reactor at Chernobyl in northern Ukraine. However, as an industrial state, Belarus also suffers from air and water quality issues since much of the economic industrialization in the country was done when environmental factors were not taken into consideration.

Environment

Forest Area sq km: 74
Average Annual Deforestation sq km: −688
Nationally Protected Areas as % of Total Land Area: 4.1
Freshwater Access cubic meters per capita: 5,665
Emissions of Organic Water Pollutants kg per day: —
CO_2 Emissions per capita ton: 6.0

CHRONOLOGY

1944	The Soviet Red Army drives Nazi forces out of Belarus.
1945	Belarus is reunited with the Soviet Union and admitted as a founding member of the United Nations.
1960s–70s	The Soviet government closes Belarusian language schools and emphasizes the Russian language.
1986	An explosion at the nuclear power station at Chernobyl, in the neighboring Soviet state of Ukraine, contaminates 20 percent of Belarus's territory and a large portion of its population with high-radiation fallout; Mikhail Gorbachev initiates his programs of glasnost and perestroika.
1988	The Belarusian Popular Front (BPS) is formed with the goals of restoring Belarusian culture and language and eliminating repressive Stalinist policies.
1990	The Byelorusian parliament declares that the laws of the republic take precedence over those passed by the Soviet Union.
1991	On August 19 the BSSR is renamed the Republic of Belarus . . . . seven days later, the Supreme Soviet of the BSSR suspends the Communist Party of Belarus.
1994	In March the Supreme Soviet adopts a constitution that declares Belarus a unitary, democratic, social-oriented, and legal state. In July Alyaksandr Lukashenko is elected as the first president of Belarus.
1996	The 1994 constitution is amended to extend Lukashenko's term until 2001.
1997	The Treaty on Union of Belarus and Russia, calling for the merger of Belarus with Russia, is signed . . . The United States cuts off aid to Belarus because of the new authoritarian government.
1998	The United States and all 15 European Union countries ban officials from Belarus.

2000 Parliamentary elections are criticized by election observers as undemocratic. Turnout in some constituencies is so low that new elections will be necessary.

2001 Lukashenko is reelected to a second term. Opposition leaders and international electoral observers allege irregularities.

BIBLIOGRAPHY

Marples, David R. *Belarus: From Soviet Rule to Nuclear Catastrophe.* New York, 1996.

Zaprudnik, J. *Belarus at the Crossroads in History.* Boulder, Colo., 1993.

OFFICIAL PUBLICATIONS

Belarus. *Economic Reviews: Belarus* (IMF [irreg.]); *Narodnoye Khozyaystvo Respubliki Belarus; Statisticheskiy Yezhegodnik* (National Economy of the Republic of Belarus: Statistical Yearbook).

CONTACT INFORMATION

Embassy of Belarus
1619 New Hampshire Avenue NW
Washington, D.C. 20009
Phone: (202) 986-1606 Fax: (202) 986-1805

INTERNET RESOURCES

- Ministry of Statistics and Analysis
  http://president.gov.by/minstat/en/main.html
- The Native Byelorussian WWW-server for Businessmen
  http://www.belarus.net/

BELGIUM

BASIC FACT SHEET

OFFICIAL NAME:
Kingdom of Belgium (Koninkrijk België; Royaume de Belgique; Königreich Belgien)

ABBREVIATION:
BE

CAPITAL:
Brussels

HEAD OF STATE:
King Albert II (from 1993)

HEAD OF GOVERNMENT:
Prime Minister Guy Verhofstadt (from 1999)

NATURE OF GOVERNMENT:
Constitutional monarchy

POPULATION:
10,224,000 (1999)

AREA:
30,540 sq km (11,781 sq mi)

MAJOR ETHNIC GROUPS:
Flemings and Walloons

LANGUAGES:
Dutch and French

RELIGION:
Roman Catholicism

UNIT OF CURRENCY:
Euro

NATIONAL FLAG:
Tricolor of black, yellow, and red vertical stripes

NATIONAL EMBLEM:
A lion rampant on a shield forms the central design of the coat of arms. The lion is in gold emblazoned on a black field. Encircling the shield is the ornate collar of the Order of Leopold. Behind it, golden scepters form a saltire or diagonal cross. A royal gold and red crown tops the design, and a gold and white ribbon decorates it. The national motto in gold letters on a red riband at the base appears in both French and Dutch. The English translation reads, "Union Provides Strength."

NATIONAL ANTHEM:
"La Brabançonne" (The Song of Brabant)

NATIONAL HOLIDAYS:
National Independence Day (July 21); National Dynasty Day (November 15); Labor Day; January 1; all major Catholic festivals

DATE OF INDEPENDENCE:
July 21, 1831

DATE OF CONSTITUTION:
February 7, 1831 (revised August 8–9, 1980)

GEOGRAPHICAL FEATURES

Belgium occupies an area of 30,540 sq km (11,781 sq mi). Its borders are formed by the North Sea and the neighboring states of France, Germany, the Netherlands, and Luxembourg. Almost one-fifth of the country was reclaimed from the North Sea between the eighth and 13th centuries. Salt marshes became rich plowland behind a legendary barrier of dikes. A coastal strip 48 km (30 mi) wide was thus added to the country; at the same time rivers like the Schelde, which had spread out in broad, shallow deltas, were made navigable.

Belgium

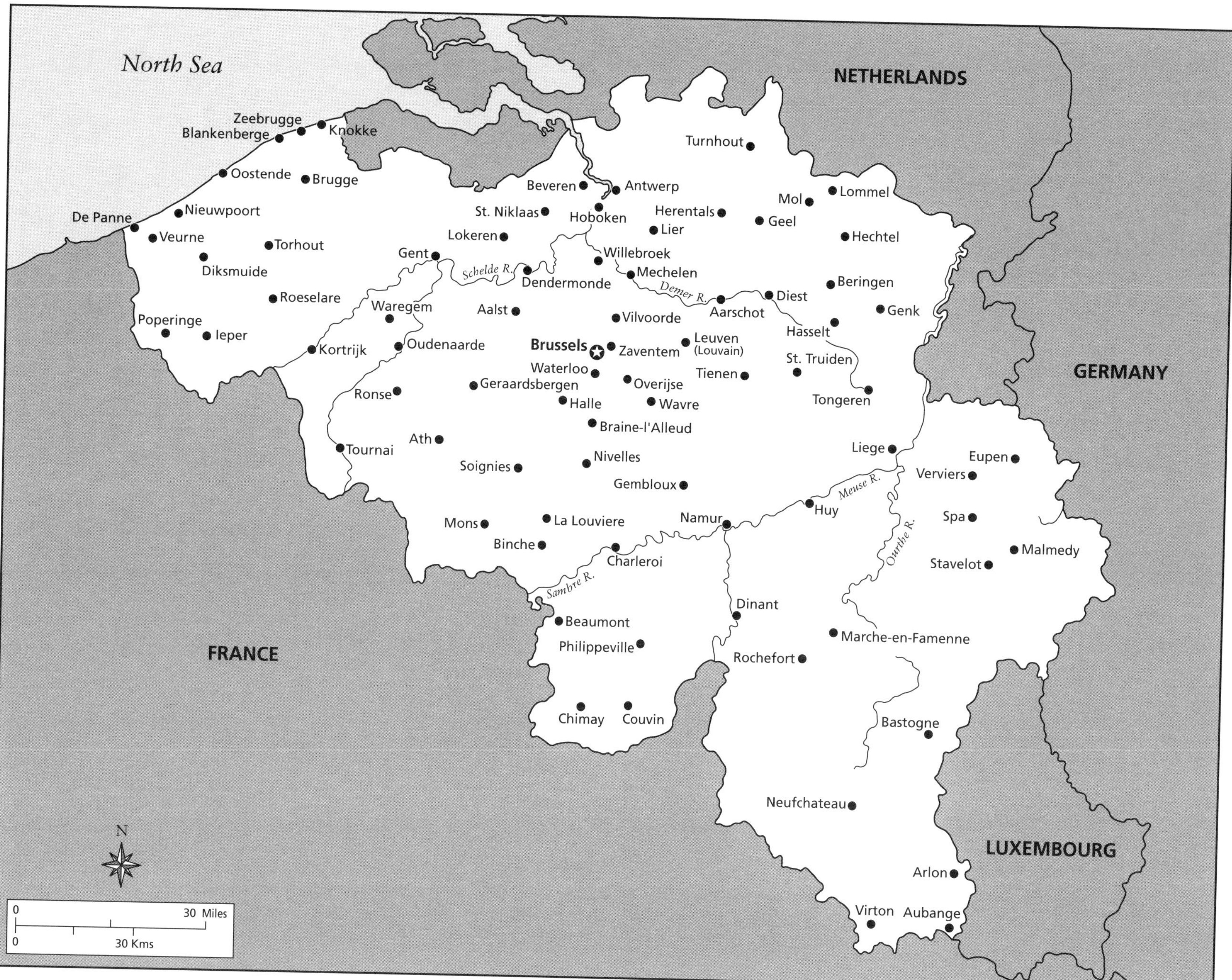
North Sea
NETHERLANDS
GERMANY
LUXEMBOURG
FRANCE
Zeebrugge
Blankenberge
Knokke
Oostende
Brugge
De Panne
Nieuwpoort
Veurne
Torhout
Diksmuide
Roeselare
Poperinge
Ieper
Kortrijk
Waregem
Oudenaarde
Ronse
Tournai
Ath
Gent
Schelde R.
Lokeren
St. Niklaas
Beveren
Antwerp
Hoboken
Turnhout
Herentals
Lier
Mol
Lommel
Geel
Hechtel
Willebroek
Mechelen
Dendermonde
Demer R.
Aalst
Vilvoorde
Aarschot
Diest
Beringen
Genk
Hasselt
Brussels
Zaventem
Leuven
(Louvain)
St. Truiden
Waterloo
Overijse
Tienen
Geraardsbergen
Halle
Wavre
Tongeren
Braine-l'Alleud
Soignies
Nivelles
Gembloux
Liege
Eupen
Verviers
Meuse R.
Huy
Spa
Ourthe R.
Mons
La Louviere
Namur
Binche
Charleroi
Malmedy
Stavelot
Sambre R.
Beaumont
Dinant
Philippeville
Marche-en-Famenne
Rochefort
Chimay
Couvin
Bastogne
Neufchateau
Arlon
Virton
Aubange
N
0
30 Miles
0
30 Kms

Geography

Area sq km: 30,540 sq mi 11,781
World Rank: 139th
Land Boundaries, km: France 620; Germany 167; Luxembourg 148; Netherlands 450
Coastline, km: 64
Elevation Extremes meters
Lowest: Northeast 0
Highest: Signal de Botrange 694
Land Use % Arable land: 24
Permanent Crops: 1
Permanent Pastures: 20
Forest and Woodland: 21
Other: 34

Population of Principal Cities (1996 est.)

Antwerp	455,852
Brugge (Bruges)	115,815
Brussels	136,424
Agglomeration	948,122
Charleroi	205,591
Ghent	226,464
Liege (Luik)	190,525
Namur	105,059

CLIMATE AND WEATHER

Lowland Belgium has a climate similar to that of Britain because of the passage of air depressions, which result from a combination of tropical and polar air masses. They cause characteristic weather features such as changing winds, summer thunderstorms, winter drizzle, and overcast skies. The Flemish oceanic region has a mild climate because of the warm waters of the North Atlantic Drift, which is responsible for fogs. The interior has more extreme summers and winters, while the uplands have more severe frost and more cold and rain.

Climate and Weather

Temperature Range
Brussels 30.6°F to 76.5°F
Brugge 30.0°F to 73.9°F
Kempenland 26.6°F to 75.9°F
Ardennes 24.4°F to 74.8°F
Average Rainfall
North of the Sambre and Meuse Rivers 20 in to 30 in
Southern Foothills 47 in

POPULATION

Population Indicators

Total Population: 1999 10,224,000
World Rank: 73rd
Density per sq mi: 867.4 per sq km 334.9
% of annual growth (1994–99): 0.2
Male %: 48.9
Female %: 51.1
Urban %: 96.6
Age Distribution: % 0–14: 18.2
15–29: 21.8
30–44: 22.5
45–59: 15.9
60–74: 14.1
75 and over: 6.6
Population 2020: 9,819,000
Birth Rate per 1,000: 11.4
Death Rate per 1,000: 10.4
Population Doubling Time (years): —
Infant Mortality Rate per 1,000 live births: 5.6
Rate of Natural Increase per 1,000: 1.0
Total Fertility Rate: 1.6
Expectation of Life (years): Males 73.0
Females 79.8
Marriage Rate per 1,000: 5.1
Divorce Rate per 1,000: 2.2
Total Number of Households: 3,613,000
Average Size of Households: 2.7
% of Illegitimate Children: 11.3
Induced Abortions: —
Rate per 100 live births: —

ETHNIC COMPOSITION

The original population of Belgium was of Celtic stock, who were almost entirely wiped out during the Norse invasions of the early Christian era. During the fourth century the area was settled by the Salian Franks, who also constitute the basic racial stock of France. It is generally agreed that there are no ethnic differences between the Dutch and French language groups.

Since the end of World War II, immigration into Belgium increased significantly, and these immigrants account for approximately 10 percent of the total population.

LANGUAGES

Belgium's three official languages are Dutch, French, and German. Linguistic and political boundaries do not coincide: German is spoken in the eastern part of the country bordering Germany; Dutch in the northern area bordering the Netherlands; and French in the southern and western areas bordering France. The provinces of West Flanders, East Flanders, Antwerp, Limburg, and northern Brabant constitute Dutch-speaking Flanders, while those of Liège, Luxembourg, Hainaut, Namur, and southern Brabant constitute French-speaking Wallonia. The German speakers, using Low German and Franco-Mosellan dialects, live in the eastern cantons of Eupen and Malmedy, and account for less than 1 percent of the population. Today, the number of Italian and Arabic speakers has surpassed the number of German speakers. In Brussels, linguistic minorities are given special status in a bilingual context.

Principal Languages and Their Speakers	
Arabic	160,000
Dutch (Flemish Netherlandic)	6,060,000
French (Walloon)	3,340,000
German	100,000
Italian	250,000
Spanish	50,000
Turkish	90,000
Other	180,000

RELIGIONS

Belgium has no state church, and the constitution grants state aid to officially recognized religions. These include Roman Catholicism (88 percent of the population), Anglicanism (1.4 percent), Protestantism (1.0 percent), Judaism (0.3 percent), Islam (2.5 percent), and Greek and Russian Orthodoxy. These religions receive state subsidies for the maintenance of the clergy and upkeep of buildings, as well as for the cost of providing teachers for religious instruction in schools. The second largest group for religious affiliation is actually "Other," at 6.9 percent, and includes those of other religions as well as those with no religious affiliation. The third largest religious group is Muslim, many of whom emigrated from Turkey and North Africa. In 1974, Islam was recognized as an official religion. However, it was not until 1998 that Muslims held nationwide elections to choose representatives for their dealings with the Belgian government.

In 1997, a parliamentary commission issued a report on dangers and problems with harmful religious sects or cults, defined as a religious group that would harm individuals or society, especially children. A clearinghouse is being established that will undertake to collect information on many religious groups, as well as provide information regarding a Belgian citizen's right to freely choose his or her religion and associate with other like-minded people.

Religious Affiliations	
Roman Catholic	8,990,000
Other	1,230,000

HISTORICAL BACKGROUND

The Belgae were a Celtic people whose land was conquered by Julius Caesar in 57 B.C. and constituted Gallia Belgica, a province of the Roman Empire. In the fifth century it was overrun by the Franks and in the eighth century it became a part of the Carolingian empire. When the empire fell apart on the death of Charlemagne, several independent principalities emerged, including Flanders, Hainaut and Namur, Brabant and Liège. During the following three centuries, the towns of Flanders became prosperous through trade. In the 15th century, all of the present Benelux countries came under the rule of the Dukes of Burgundy and, later, under the Habsburg crown. When Emperor Charles V divided his empire, the Benelux territories were united with Spain under Philip II, whose energies were devoted to the suppression of Protestantism. This led to a Protestant revolt ended only by the Treaty of Westphalia (1648), which granted independence to the northern Protestant provinces. The southern half remained Catholic and under Spanish rule.

For the next 150 years, the southern Low Countries became a pawn in Franco-Austrian rivalries. French armies invaded Belgium in 1792 for the third time in a century and annexed it, by the 1797 Treaty of Campo Formio. Belgium was reunited with The Netherlands by the Congress of Vienna, which led to widespread discontent and uprisings. The Dutch were compelled to retreat, and on October 4, 1830, Belgium was declared independent. However, William I, king of the United Netherlands, invaded Belgium and was repulsed by the French army. In 1839 he was forced to accept the Treaty of XXIV Articles, by which Belgian independence was guaranteed under a system of constitutional monarchy with Leopold of Saxe-Coburg-Gotha as king. His successor, Leopold II, financed the exploration and settlement of the Congo basin, thereby laying the foundations of Belgium's colonial empire, which eventually extended to Rwanda and Burundi.

Belgium was invaded by Germany during World Wars I and II, even though it had maintained its neutrality before both invasions. After the capitulation of Germany in 1945, a constitutional crisis rose over the return of King Leopold III amidst questions over his wartime conduct. A rash of strikes, riots, and demonstrations led to his abdication, and in 1951, his son, Baudouin I, was formally proclaimed king.

The country successfully balanced the recognition of its diverse linguistic and cultural communities through four constitutional reforms in the second half of the 20th century (in 1970, 1981, 1988–89, and 1993–94). The reforms have led to the creation of three linguistic communities (French, Flemish, and German) as well as three cultural regions (Flanders, Wallonia, and Brussels). Under the 1993–94 reforms, the central government retains responsibility for defense, taxation, foreign policy, and social welfare policies. The regional governments oversee transport, environmental, and economic development matters. The community governments are empowered to deal with cultural concerns, including education.

On July 31, 1993, a reign that had spanned four decades came to an end with the death of King Baudouin, who was childless. His brother, Albert, prince of Liège, ascended the throne as Albert II. In 1994 the government was rocked by the Agusta scandal, in which Socialist parties were alleged to have received huge kickbacks from government contractors. In the 1995 general elections, the coalition headed by Jean-Luc Dehaene retained power despite the scandals. However, in the 1999 general elections, the Dehaene coalition was ousted, ending decades of dominance by Christian Democrats. Dehaene was replaced by the first Liberal prime minister in half a century, the Flemish Liberal leader Guy Verhofstadt. He presided over a six-party rainbow coalition representing Socialists, Liberals, and Greens.

CONSTITUTION

Belgium is a constitutional monarchy. The original constitution was written in 1831 and has been amended, usually to address voting rights or cultural differences. The king is the head of state and commander in chief of the armed forces. Executive power lies in the crown, but is practiced by the cabinet. The king appoints and dismisses ministers, but the prime minister countersigns his successor's appointment. The king's role has grown somewhat since World War II, as coalition governments and cultural differences have called for an honest broker to conduct negotiations. The king does not have veto power and cannot act against the advice of the cabinet. The post of prime minister has a variable amount of power, depending on the actual coalition of the government, and the post was not mentioned in the constitution until 1970.

LOCAL GOVERNMENT

Local government consists of several layers, in order to deal with the cultural and linguistic variations in the country. There are three linguistic communities (French, Flemish, and German) and three cultural regions (Wallonia, Flanders, and Brussels). The communities have no geographic boundaries, but include all people who speak each language as their native tongue. Within the regions are nine provinces (four Flemish, four Walloon, one bilingual). These provinces are further divided into 43 arrondissements. Within the arrondissements are numerous communes, municipalities, and boroughs. Disputes between the communities and regions are handled by a court of arbitration, and they can also be handled by the Council of State and Court de Cassation.

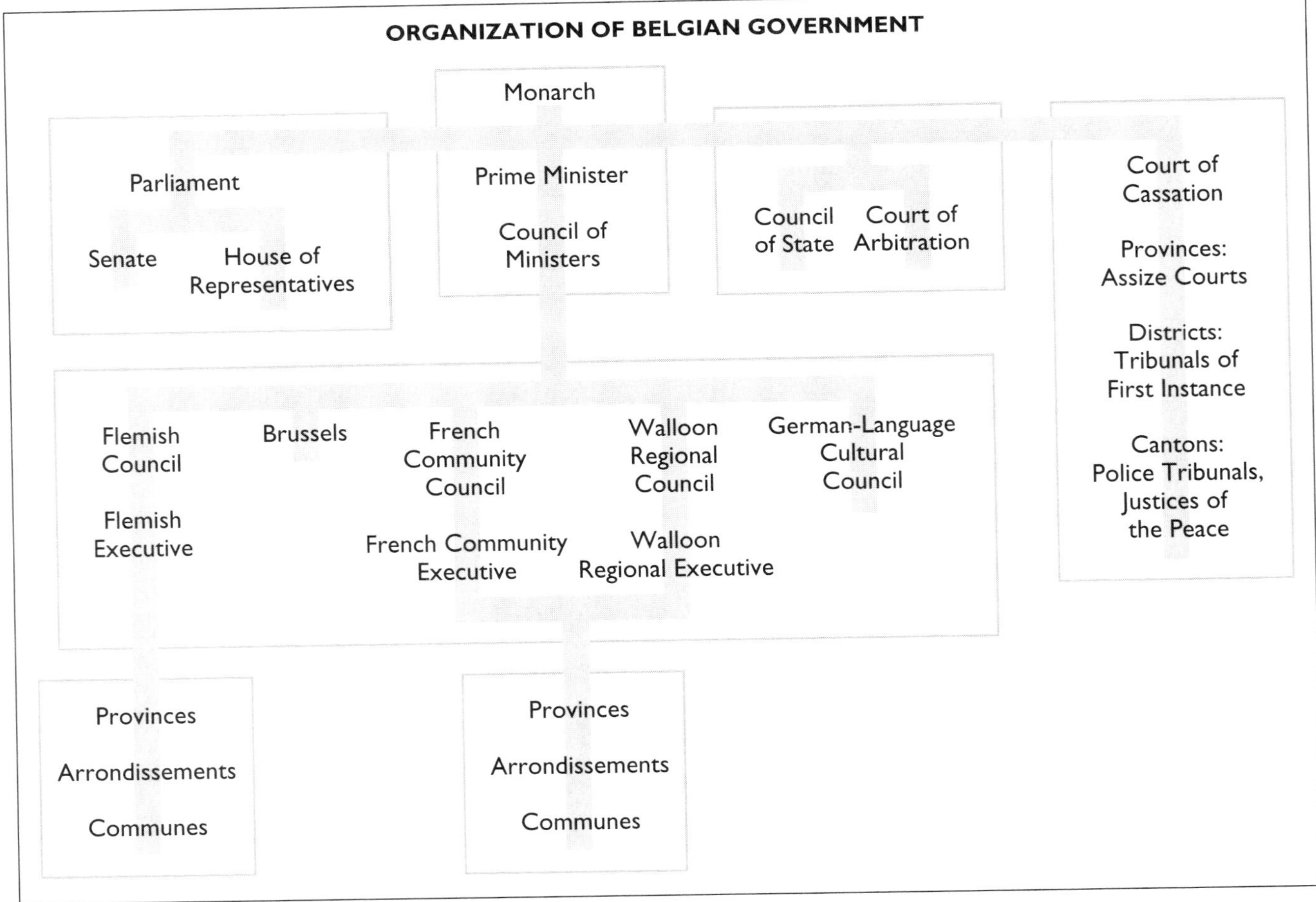

Local Government

Principal administrative divisions, capitals, area, population

AREA AND POPULATION

Regions / Provinces	Capitals	area sq mi	area sq km	population 1998 estimate
Brussels-Capital	—	62	161	953,175
Flanders	—	5,221	13,522	5,912,382
Antwerp	Antwerp	1,107	2,867	1,637,857
East Flanders	Ghent	1,151	2,982	1,357,576
Flemish Brabant	Leuven	813	2,106	1,007,982
Limburg	Hassett	935	2,422	783,927
West Flanders	Brugge	1,214	3,145	1,125,140
Wallonia	—	6,504	16,844	3,326,707
Hainaut	Mons	1,462	3,786	1,282,783
Liège	Liège	1,491	3,862	1,016,762
Luxembourg	Arlon	1,714	4,440	243,790
Namur	Namur	1,415	3,666	483,864
Walloon Brabant	Wavre	421	1,091	344,508
TOTAL		11,787	30,528	10,192,264

PARLIAMENT

The Belgian parliament is made up of two houses: a Senate (upper house) and a House of Representatives (lower house). Members of both houses are elected to their positions. However, the king's children in the line of succession are senators by right at age 18. They are not allowed to speak in chambers until they are 25.

Members of the upper house serve a four-year term. There are 71 members, of whom 40 are directly elected (25 from Flanders and 15 from Wallonia); 21 are indirectly elected (10 each by the Flemish Council and the French Council and 1 by the German Council); and 10 are appointed (six Flemish and four Walloon) by the elected senators. Members of the lower house serve a four-year term. There are 150 deputies, directly elected by proportional representation from multimember electoral districts whose complement of deputies is in proportion to the population size.

POLITICAL PARTIES

Belgian political parties are historically divided into Dutch- and French-speaking divisions that subscribe to common programs during general elections. Beginning in the 1960s, the cleavages became more pronounced leading to formal separation as the country moved toward creation of a federal structure. At the same time, the dominance of the three principal groupings (Christian Democratic, Liberal, and Socialist) has eroded somewhat as numerous smaller ethnic and special interest groups have made gains.

Political Parties

Christian People's Party
Christian Social Party
Parti Socialiste, 1885
Socialistische Partij, 1978
Flemish Liberals and Democrats, 1961
Liberal Reformation Party, 1979
Democratic Front of French Speakers, 1964
Ecologists, 1978
Live Differently
People's Union, 1954
Flemish Bloc, 1979
National Front, 1983

Political Parties: Strength in Parliament Most Recent Elections

Senate. There are 71 seats in the Senate. As of the elections of June 13, 1999, the Flemish Liberals and Democrats held 6 seats; Christian People's Party, 6; PRL-FDF-MCC (Liberal Reformist Party-Democratic Front of Francophones-Citizens' Movement for Change), 5; Socialist Party (French), 4; Socialist Party (Flemish), 4; Ecolo, 3; Agalev, 3; Christian Social Party, 3; People's Union-ID21, 2; senators indirectly elected, 31.

House of Representatives. There are 150 seats in the House. As of the June 13, 1999, elections, the Flemish Liberals and Democrats held 23 seats; Christian People's Party, 22; Socialist Party (French), 19; PRL-FDF-MCC, 18; Flemish Block, 15; Socialist Party (Flemish), 14; Ecolo, 11; Agalev, 9; Christian Social Party, 10; People's Union-ID21, 8; and National Front/Front for the Nation, 1.

LEGAL SYSTEM

Belgium's legal system is based on the Napoleonic Code and patterned on the French judicial model. The country is divided into nine judicial provinces (with assize courts), 26 districts (each with a tribunal of first instance), and 222 cantons (with justices of the peace and police tribunals). Judges are appointed for life and cannot be removed except through due process. The highest court is the Court of Cassation, which takes appeals from lower courts.

LAW ENFORCEMENT

Law Enforcement

Offenses reported to the police per 100,000: 5,769
- Murder: 3.1
- Assault: 33.0
- Burglary: 1,529.5
- Automobile Theft: 310.7
- Population per Police officer: 640

Death Penalty: Yes. Last execution in 1950.

HUMAN RIGHTS

Belgium's constitution guarantees respect for human rights. Belgium's key human rights challenges concern its prison system, police procedures, and handling of immigrants. There is no limit as to how long a defendant may be held prior to trial. Human rights groups claim this is abusive, as many defendants are held for extended periods of time. Some prisons remain in substandard condition. In the late 1990s, Belgian soldiers came to trial for torture and unlawful killing of Somali citizens while they were part of a UN peackeeping mission in 1993. A sergeant was charged with crimes associated with the incident. In 1998, a Nigerian woman was killed while being forcibly repatriated by Belgian authorities. This led to further investigations and reforms (some implemented, some proposed) regarding police conduct and restraint procedures.

The primary goal of human rights organizations has been to eliminate two previously standard procedures, hog-tying and covering of the mouth, which have led to death and injury in some cases. The new government, which took power in 1999, has adopted most of these recommendations. However, reports of inappropriate handling and police abuse continue. In addition, reports of racially based mistreatment by police have been reported throughout the late 1990s.

FOREIGN POLICY

The cornerstone of Belgian foreign policy is active participation in the European Union and support for NATO. Belgium was a prime mover of the Schengen Accord providing for the abolition of border controls, which has been in effect since 1995. Former Belgian colonies in Africa—the Congo, Rwanda, and Burundi—were the scenes of considerable violence in the 1960s and 1990s. Belgian troops were sent to the Congo and Rwanda in an effort to evacuate Belgian nationals.

DEFENSE

Eighteen and nineteen year olds are subject to the draft, and serve part of their time with NATO forces. Military officers and senior officials must be bilingual in French and Flemish. The Belgian navy is larger than would be expected, as a Belgium's shallow waters makes Belgian ports vulnerable to mine and submarine attacks. Historically, Belgium has been a major exporter of arms, and today those weapons find their way to the Middle East, Africa and other regions in conflict. Defense accounts for 1.7% of the Gross Domestic Product (GDP).

Military Indicators

Total Active Duty Personnel: 44,500
Military Manpower per 1,000: 4.4
Military Expenditures $ million: 4,449
as % of GNP: 1.7
per capita $: 439
as % of central government expenditures: 3.5

Arms Imports $million: 340
Arms Exports $million: 130

ECONOMY

Belgium's highly developed private enterprise economy has capitalized on its central geographical location, highly developed transport network, and diversified industrial and commercial base. Industry is concentrated mainly in the populous Flemish area in the north. With few natural resources, Belgium must import substantial quantities of raw materials and export a large volume of manufactures, making its economy unusually dependent on world markets. This accounts for Belgium's keen support of free trade and European integration. The major problems of the Belgian economy stem from its antiquated industrial structure and high labor costs. The constitutional process of regionalization also has placed additional strains on the economy. In one sense Belgium is trying to adjust to the dislocations caused by the demise of its industrial power based on coal mining and heavy industry along the Sambre-Meuse and Wallonia, one of the most prosperous regions on the continent in the late 19th century. However, a virtual revolution took place in industrial geography after World War II. With the replacement of coal by petroleum, the Walloon areas lost much of their prominence and the Brussels-Antwerp axis became the country's economic core. The rise of the modern service sector also favored the Flemish region. Flanders also benefited from state support and foreign investment. Thus the industrial sector now consists of a modern sector in Flanders and a traditional sector in Wallonia. Official economic policy is complicated by linguistic and regional rivalries. As industrial loci shifted to Flanders, coalition governments were forced to balance regional interests and to dole out public funds for nonviable projects in the Walloon region. Although the Belgian economy is a free enterprise one, the state is an active partner in economic development. State intervention, however, remains discreet and is felt primarily only in the weak sectors, with the exception of transportation and communications which are traditional state domains. Government role in the economy is overseen by the Economic Planning Bureau within the Ministry of Economic Affairs. The financial arm of the government's industrial policy is the National Investment Company, created in 1962 to provide venture capital. A key element in national economic policy is regionalization, which has led to the establishment of separate ministerial departments, regional economic councils, and regional development corporations.

Principal Economic Indicators

Gross National Product: $272.382 billion
GNP per capita: $26,730
GNP Average Annual Growth Rate (1990–97) %: 1.3
GNP per capita Average Annual Growth Rate (1990–97) %: 1.0
Origin of Gross Domestic Product %
- Agriculture: 2
- Mining: —
- Manufacturing: 22
- Construction: 5
- Public Utilities: 2
- Transportation and Communications: 8
- Trade: 13
- Financial Services: 18
- Other Services: 18
- Government: 7

Gross Domestic Product by Type of Expenditure %
- Private Consumption: 63
- Government Consumption: 15
- Gross Domestic Investment: 18
- Foreign Trade: Exports: 72
  Imports: −67

% of Income Received by Poorest 20%: 7.9
% of Income Received by Richest 10%: 21.5

Price and earnings indexes (1995 = 100)

	1992	1993	1994	1995	1996	1997	1998
Consumer price index	93.7	96.3	98.6	100.9	102.1	103.7	104.7
Earnings index	—	—	—	—	—	—	—

Finance

National Currency: Belgian Franc (BF)
Exchange Rate: $1 = BF 37.459
Money Supply Stock in National Currency billion: 1,439.2
M1 per capita: 141,000
Central Bank Discount Rate %: 2.75
Total External Debt $million: 31,300
Debt Service Ratio %: —
Balance of Payments $million: 13,939
International Reserves SDRs million: 12,610
Ratio of External Debt to Total Reserves: —
Average Annual Rate of Inflation/Consumer Price Index Growth Rate %: 1.7

Official Development Assistance

Donor ODA $million: 808
- as % of GNP: 0.29
- per capita: $80.8
- Foreign Direct Investment $million: —

Central Government Revenues and Expenditures

Fiscal Year: Calendar Year
Revenues $million: —
Expenditures $million: —
Budget Deficit/Surplus $: —
Tax Revenues as % of GDP: 43.3
Highest Tax Bracket %
- Individual: 55
- Corporate: 39

Employment and Labor

Economically Active Population: 4,237,000
Female Participation Rate %: 42.3
Activity Rate %: 42.2
Labor by Sector: %
- Agriculture, Forestry, Fishing: 2.2
- Manufacturing, Mining: 18.6
- Construction: 5.8
- Transportation and Communications: 6.1
- Trade, Hotels, and Restaurants: 15.0
- Finance, Insurance, Real Estate: 8.1
- Public Administration, Defense: 7
- Services: 32.9

Unemployment %: 12.75

Agriculture

Agriculture's Share of GDP %: 2
Average Annual Rate of Growth (1965–98) %: 1.9
Number of Farms 000: 73
Average Size of Farm ha: 16.5
Number of Tractors per 1,000 hectares: 144
Irrigation, % of Farms having: 0.1
Artificial Fertilizer kg/hectare: 496
Total Cropland as % of Farmland: 45.6
Livestock: Cattle 000: 3,184
- Sheep 000: 155
- Hogs 000: 7,436
- Chickens 000: 48,000

Forests: Production of Roundwood (000 cubic meters): 4,185
Fisheries: Total Catch tons: 34.6

Mining

% of GDP: 0.2
Value of Mineral Production $million: 541

Manufacturing

Value Added $million: 44,163
Industrial Production Growth Rate %: 9.7

Energy

Commercial Energy Production metric tons of oil equivalent 000: 13,153
Commercial Energy Consumption metric tons of oil equivalent 000: 57,125
Commercial Energy Consumption per capita kg: 5,611
Average Annual Growth Rate 1980–97 %: 1.5
Net Energy Imports % of use: 77
Electricity Installed Capacity kW 000: 14,916
- Production kW-hr million: 74,428

Coal Reserves tons million: 410
- Production tons 000: 637

Natural Gas Proven Reserves cubic meters billion: —
- Production cubic meters million: 1.4

(continued)

Crude Petroleum Reserves barrels million: —
Production barrels million: —
Consumption barrels million: 192
Refinery Capacity barrels per day 000: 630
Pipelines Length km: 1,328

Foreign Trade

Imports $million: 150,624.7
Exports $million: 165,173.1
Export Volume % Annual Growth Rate (1990–97): 6.2
Import Volume % Annual Growth Rate (1990–97): 5.4
Balance of Trade $

Balance of trade (current prices)

	1993	1994	1995	1996	1997	1998
U.S.						
$000,000	+370,500	+513,000	+427,700	+402,000	+404,000	+562,000
% of total	4.5%	5.9%	4.4%	4.5%	3.5%	4.6%

Major Trading Partners

	Imports	Exports
European Union %	74.5	71.2
United States %	5.6	3.7
Eastern Europe %	2.1	2.3
Japan %	2.6	1.3
Others %	15.1	21.4

Transportation

Roads Total Length mi: 88,579 km 142,555
Paved %: 97
Automobiles: 4,339,231
Trucks and Buses: 431,376
Persons per vehicle: 2.1
Railroad; Track Length mi: 2,093 km 3,368
Passenger-mi million: 4,199
Freight-mi million: 5,334
Merchant Marine: No. of Vessels: 232
Total Deadweight Tonnage 000: 218.5
International Cargo Loaded tons 000: 291,540
International Cargo Off-loaded tons 000: 5,077
Airports with Scheduled Flights: 2
Traffic: Passenger-mi million: 5,599
Freight-mi million: 221.9
Length of Canals mi: 1,269 km 2,043

Tourism

Number of Tourists to 000: 6,179
Number of Tourists from 000: 7,773
Tourist Receipts $million: 5,719
Tourist Expenditures $million: 9,215

Communications

Telephones 000: 4,632
Cost of Local Calls 3 mins: $0.17
Cellular Telephones 000: 235
Fax Machines 000: 165
Personal Computers 000: 1,400
Internet Hosts per million persons: 3,024
Mail: Post Offices: 1,635
Pieces of Mail Handled million: 3,557
Pieces of Mail Handled per person: 352

EDUCATION

Education is required for nine years, ages six through 15; another three years of part-time education are required from ages 15 through 18. The school year runs from September through June. There are six universities and numerous vocational and technical schools for postsecondary education.

Education

Literacy Rate %: 100
Male %: 100
Female %: 100
First Level: Primary schools: 4,453
Teachers: 72,589
Students: 731,527
Student-Teacher Ratio: —
Net Enrollment Ratio: 98
Second Level: Secondary Schools: 1,950
Teachers: 110,599
Students: 796,914
Student-Teacher Ratio: —
Net Enrollment Ratio: 98
Vocational Level: Schools: 304
Students: 155,192
Third Level: Institutions: 21
Teachers: —
Students: 123,320
Student-Ratio Level: —
Gross Enrollment Ratio: 49.1
Students per 100,000: 3,206
% of Population Age 25 and over with Post-secondary Education: —
Public Expenditure on Education as % of GDP: 5.7

SCIENCE AND TECHNOLOGY

Science and Technology

Scientists and Engineers in R&D per 1 million persons: 2,272
Expenditures in R&D as % of GDP: 1.60
High-Tech Exports $million: 11,115
Patent Applications by Residents: 1,687

MEDIA

The Belgian press dates back to 1649, when *Courrier véritable des Pays Bas* was published. It was the only Belgian newspaper until 1791. The country went through a "golden period" of newspapers in the 1800's and early

1900's. During the 1970's and 1980's many newspapers folded and ownership concentration grew. Today there are fewer than 20 regional and national newspapers, including those imported from The Netherlands and France.

In spite of the ongoing cultural and linguistic struggles, Belgium has continued to make an impressive contribution to the arts. From painters Peter Paul Rubens and René Magritte, to music by César Franck, literature by Georges Simenon, and present-day movie action hero Jean-Claude Van Damme, Belgium has produced a number of well-known artists.

Media

Daily Newspapers: 32
Total Circulation 000: 3,231
Circulation per 1,000: 321
Books Published: —
Magazines: 13,706
Radio Receivers 000: 5,000
per 1,000: 500
Television sets 000: 4,700
per 1,000: 464

Most Important Media:

Press. The following are published daily at Brussels, unless otherwise noted: *Krantengroep De Standard* (including *De Gentenaar, Het Nieuwsblad,* and *De Standard,* 377,400), in Dutch, independent; *Het Laatste Nieuws* (including *De Nieuwe Gazet,* 307,500), in Dutch, independent; *Le Soir* (183,100), in French, independent; *Gazet van Antwerpen* (Antwerp, 177,900), in Dutch, Christian Democratic; *Het Volk* (Ghent, including *De Nieuwe Gids,* 164,800), in Dutch, Christian Democratic; *La Meuse* (Liége, including *La Lanterne,* 124,600), in French, independent; *La Dernière Heure* (101,800), in French, Liberal; La Libre Belgique (90,500), in French, independent.

News agencies. The official agency is Agence Télégraphique Belge de Presse/Belgisch Pers-telegraaf-agentschap (Agence Belga/Agentschap Belga); private facilities include *Centre d'Information de Presse* (Catholic), Agence Europe, and Agence Day. Numerous foreign agencies also maintain bureaus in Belgium.

Radio and television. The French-language Radio-Télévision Belge de la Communauté Française (RTBF), the Dutch-language Belgische Radio en Televisie (BRT), and the German-language Belgisches Rundfunk und Fernsehzentrum (BRF) are government-owned systems operated by cultural councils, under grants made by the parliament.

CULTURE

Cultural Indicators

Public Libraries
Number: 2,351
Volumes: 24,140,000
Registered borrowers: 1,731,256
Museums Number: —
Annual Attendance: —
Cinema Production of Long Films: 81
Number of Cinemas: 423
Seating Capacity: 96,800
Annual Attendance: 19.2
Annual Attendance per capita: 1.9

STATUS OF WOMEN

Women received full voting rights in 1948, and beginning in 1999, Belgian law requires one-third of all political candidates to be women. Domestic violence against women is still underreported. In 1998, the Belgian government passed a law that both defines and provides stiff penalties for domestic violence. The law, which covers both married and unmarried partners, allows organizations to represent women. It also requires the government to keep statistics on domestic violence.

Women

Gender Empowerment Measure: 19
Seats Held in Parliament by Women %: 15.8
Female Administrators and Managers %: 18.8
Female Professional and Technical Workers %: 50.5
Women's Share of Earned Income %: 34
Women in Government %: 8

HEALTH, FOOD, AND NUTRITION

Health

Number of Physicians: 38,363
Number of Dentists: 6,983
Number of Nurses: —
Number of Pharmacists: 13,926
Population per Physician: 264
Number of Hospitals: 363
Hospital Beds per 10,000: 76
Hospital Bed Occupancy Rate: 84.4
Infant Mortality Rate per 1,000 live births: 7
Maternal Mortality Rate per 100,000 live births: 10
Total Health Expenditures as % of GDP: 7.50
Health Expenditures per capita $: 1,449
HIV Infected % of adults: 0.14
Cigarette Consumption per smoker per year: 5,300
% of Smokers: Male: 31
Female: 19
Access to Safe Water %: 100

Food and Nutrition

Food Supply as % of FAO Requirements: 134
% of Consumption Expenditures on Food: 18.3
Daily Available Calories per capita: 3,530
% of Total Calories derived from:
Cereals: 21.2
Potatoes, cassava: 5.4
Meat, poultry: 9.9
Fish: 1.2
Eggs, milk: 9.3
Fruits, vegetables: 6.3
Fats, oils: 26.2

ENVIRONMENT

Water protection laws in effect since 1971 have not stopped factories in steel-making areas from releasing wastes into the Meuse. The Meuse supplies drinking water to 6 million people, yet it is highly polluted. Pollution from agricultural sources—especially excess fertilizers and animal manures—has increased algal growth in surface waters. Belgium is the home of a number of smokestack industries that contribute to Europe's air pollution. However, there has been significant progress as a result of legislation. In Brussels, for example, average concentrations of sulfur dioxide have declined to about one-fifth the 1975 levels.

Environment

Forest Area sq km: —
Average Annual Deforestation sq km: —
Nationally Protected Areas as % of Total Land Area: —
Freshwater Access cubic meters per capita: 1,228
Emissions of Organic Water Pollutants kg per day: 113,460
CO_2 Emissions per capita ton: 10.4

CHRONOLOGY

1940	Germany invades Belgium and Holland. While the Belgian government escapes to London, Leopold III remains and surrenders to the Germans.
1944	Allied forces liberate Belgium.
1949	NATO is founded, with Belgium as a founding member. G. Eyskens is named prime minister.
1950	Second School Conflict begins. J. Duvieusart is elected prime minister, but resigns after two months in favor of J. Pholen.
1951	Leopold III abdicates in favor of his son, Baudouin.
1951	The Queen Elizabeth Contest is founded, named after Albert's widow, Elizabeth. It offers support to up-and-coming young musicians to this day.
1952	J. van Houtte is sworn in as prime minister.
1954	A. van Acker returns as prime minister.
1957	The Benelux Union is formed with Luxembourg and The Netherlands
1958	School Pact ends Second School Conflict. EEC is established. G. Eyskens returns as prime minister.
1960	Austerity budget is announced following general strike in Wallonia.
1961	T. Lefevre takes office as prime minister.
1962	Belgium's African colonies—Congo, Rwanda and Burundi—become independent. Linguistic boundaries are delimited.
1965	P. Harmel is sworn in as prime minister.
1966	P. van den Boeynants is named prime minister.
1968	G. Eyskens begins new term as prime minister. Violence erupts at the University of Louvain as Flemish students call for the removal of French as medium of instruction. Social Christians split into French and Flemish sections.
1971	Third reform of the constitution establishes four linguistic regions and three cultural communities.
1972	Liberals split into Flemish, Walloon, and Brussels wings.
1974	Leo Tindemans is elected prime minister.
1977	The Egmont Pact is signed by Social Christians, Socialists, and Liberals, but collapses following persisting party differences. The country is divided into three regions: Wallonia, Flanders, and Brussels.
1978	P. van den Boeynants returns as prime minister. Socialists split into Flemish and Walloon wings.
1979	Wilfried Martens forms his first cabinet as prime minister.
1980	Regionalization takes effect as major national powers are devolved to regional and communal councils. The Belgian constitution is changed accordingly.
1981	M. Eyskens is prime minister for nine months, but Wilfried Martens returns to office as head of a coalition government following general elections.
1982	Martens coalition government is granted special power to establish an austerity regime.
1985	In new elections, the Martens center-right coalition retains majority.
1986	Former prime minister Boeynants is convicted of tax evasion and fraud.
1988–89	Further linguistic and cultural reforms are enacted.
1993	King Baudouin dies. His brother, Albert, becomes king.
1993–94	Another round of linguistic and cultural reforms are passed.
1995	Belgium creates Flemish Brabant and Walloon Brabant from the former Brabant province.
1998	Belgium agrees to adopt the euro currency, effective January 1, 1999, for electronic transactions and January 1, 2002, for coin and paper money; the judiciary comes under heavy fire after a notorious pedophile escapes.
1999	A contamination scandal prompts Belgium's trading partners to ban Belgian food imports; Prime Minister Jean-Luc Dahaene's center-left coalition resigns; a new center-right coalition comes to power led by Guy Verhofstadt of the Liberal Party.

BIBLIOGRAPHY

Cowie, Donald *Belgium: The Land and the People.* Cranberry, N.J. 1977
Fitzmaurice, John *The Politics of Belgium.* New York, 1996
Huggett, Frank E. *Modern Belgium.* London 1969
Liphart, Arend *Conflict and Coexistence in Belgium: The Dynamics of a Culturally Divided Society.* Berkeley, Calif. 1981
Mallinson, V. *Belgium.* London, 1969
OECD Belgium-Luxembourg, Pairs, Annual
Riley, Raymond *Belgium.* Boulder, Colo., 1976

OFFICIAL PUBLICATIONS

Belgium. *Annuaire statistique de la Belgique; Recensement de la population et des logements au 1er mars 1991.*

CONTACT INFORMATION

Embassy of Belgium
3330 Garfield St. NW
Washington, D.C. 20008
Phone: (202) 333-6900 Fax: (202) 333-3079

INTERNET RESOURCES

- Belgian Federal Government On line
  http://belgium.fgov.be

BELIZE

BASIC FACT SHEET

OFFICIAL NAME:
Belize

ABBREVIATION:
BE

CAPITAL:
Belmopan

HEAD OF STATE:
Queen Elizabeth II, represented by Governor-General Colville Young (from 1993)

HEAD OF GOVERNMENT:
Prime Minister Said Musa (from 1998)

NATURE OF GOVERNMENT:
Parliamentary democracy

POPULATION:
250,000 (1999)

AREA:
22,963 sq km (8,864 sq mi)

ETHNIC COMPOSITION:
Black, mestizo, and Amerindian

LANGUAGE:
English (official), Spanish

RELIGION:
Christianity

UNIT OF CURRENCY:
Belize dollar

NATIONAL FLAG:
Dark blue with narrow horizontal red stripes at the upper and lower edges; at the center is a white disk containing the state coat of arms bordered by a wreath of leaves.

NATIONAL EMBLEM:
The shield of the coat of arms is divided into three sections by a vertical line and an inverted V. The base represents a ship in full sail. The two upper sections show the tools of the timber industry, a paddle and a squaring ax to the left and a saw and a beating ax to the right. Supporting the shield are two woodcutters; the one to the left holds a beating ax, and the one to the right holds a paddle. Above this shield rises a mahogany tree and beneath it on a scroll is the motto *Sub Umbra Floreo* (Under the Shade I Flourish).

NATIONAL ANTHEM:
"O the Land of the Free by the Carib Sea"

NATIONAL HOLIDAYS:
Baron Bliss Day; Easter; Labor Day; Commonwealth Day; St. George's Caye Day; Independence Day (September 21); Columbus Day; Carib Settlement Day; Christmas

DATE OF INDEPENDENCE:
September 21, 1981

DATE OF CONSTITUTION:
September 21, 1981

GEOGRAPHICAL FEATURES

Belize, on the eastern coast of Central America just below the Yucatán Peninsula, is bounded on the north and west by Mexico and on the south and west by Guatemala, with a total boundary length of 995 km (618 mi). Belize extends 288 km (179 mi) north-northeast to south-southwest and 109 km (68 mi) west-northwest to east-southeast. The waters immediately offshore are shallow; they are sheltered by the second longest barrier reef in the world, dotted with a large number of islands known as *cayes*. The total land area of the mainland and the cayes is 22,963 sq km (8,864 sq mi).

The most notable topographical feature is the Maya Mountains, rising to heights of 1,000 to 1,100 m (3,400 to 3,700 ft) and running northeast to southwest across the central and southern parts of the country. The highest point is Victoria Peak (1,104 m; 3,680 ft). The country

Belize

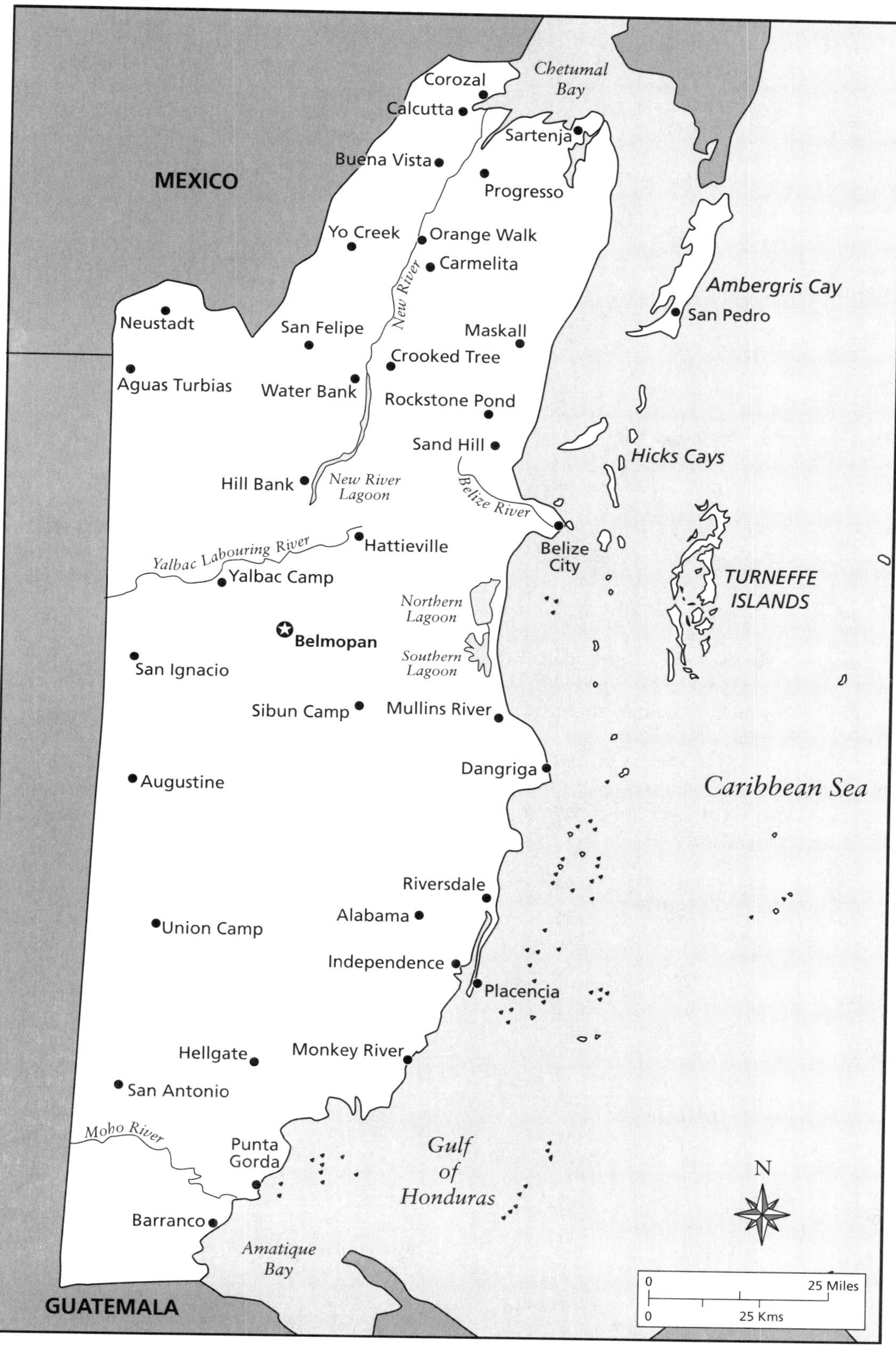

MEXICO
Chetumal Bay
Corozal
Calcutta
Sartenja
Buena Vista
Progresso
Yo Creek
Orange Walk
Carmelita
New River
Ambergris Cay
San Pedro
Neustadt
San Felipe
Maskall
Crooked Tree
Aguas Turbias
Water Bank
Rockstone Pond
Sand Hill
Hicks Cays
Hill Bank
New River Lagoon
Belize River
Yalbac Labouring River
Hattieville
Belize City
Yalbac Camp
TURNEFFE ISLANDS
Northern Lagoon
Belmopan
San Ignacio
Southern Lagoon
Sibun Camp
Mullins River
Dangriga
Augustine
Caribbean Sea
Riversdale
Alabama
Union Camp
Independence
Placencia
Hellgate
Monkey River
San Antonio
Mobo River
Punta Gorda
Gulf of Honduras
N
Barranco
Amatique Bay
0
25 Miles
0
25 Kms
GUATEMALA

north of Belize City is mostly level, interrupted only by the Manatee Hills. The coast is flat and swampy and indented by many lagoons. The land is drained by over 17 rivers.

Geography

Area sq km: 22,963 sq mi 8,864
World Rank: 150th
Land Boundaries, km: Guatemala 266; Mexico 250
Coastline, km 386
Elevation Extremes meters
Lowest: Caribbean Sea 0
Highest: Victoria Peak 1,160
Land Use % Arable land: 2
Permanent Crops: 1
Permanent Pastures: 2
Forest and Woodland: 92
Other: 3

Population of Principal Cities

Belmopan	6,490

CLIMATE AND WEATHER

Belize has a subtropical climate moderated by the Caribbean trade winds, which keep the temperatures between 15.6°C and 32°C (60°F and 90°F) in the coastal regions and slightly higher inland. The seasons are marked more by differences in humidity than by differences in temperature. The average humidity is 83 percent, and the average annual rainfall varies from 1,270 mm (50 in) in the north to 4,445 mm (175 in) in the south. There are two dry seasons, from February to May and from August to September. The hurricane season extends from July to October.

Climate and Weather

Mean Temperature 60°F to 90°F
Average Rainfall 50 in to 175 in

POPULATION

Population Indicators

Total Population: 1999 250,000
World Rank: 179th
Density per sq mi: 28.2 per sq km 10.9
% of annual growth (1994–99): 3.7
Male %: 50.9
Female %: 49.1
Urban %: 47.5
Age Distribution: % 0–14: 43.9
15–29: 27.9
30–44: 14.9
45–59: 7.2
60–74: 4.4
75 and over: 1.6
Population 2020: 383,000
Birth Rate per 1,000: 32.8
Death Rate per 1,000: 5.7
Population Doubling Time (years): 28
Infant Mortality Rate per 1,000 live births: 33.9
Rate of Natural Increase per 1,000: 27.1
Total Fertility Rate: 4.2
Expectation of Life (years): Males 66.6
Females 70.6
Marriage Rate per 1,000: 6.3
Divorce Rate per 1,000: 0.6
Total Number of Households: 38,000
Average Size of Households: 4.9
% of Illegitimate Children: 58.4
Induced Abortions: 990
Rate per 100 live births: 15.1

ETHNIC COMPOSITION

Most Belizeans are of multiracial descent. About two-fifths are of African or partly African ancestry. Somewhat more than one-third are of mixed local Indian and Caucasian descent. Less than one-fifth are composed of Carib, Mayan, or other Amerindian ethnic groups. The remainder, about 6 percent, includes East Indians, Syrians, Lebanese, Chinese, and Caucasians.

LANGUAGES

English is the official language and is spoken by the entire population. Spanish is the native tongue of about 40 percent of the people and is spoken as a second language by another 20 percent. The various Indian groups speak their indigenous languages, and a Creole dialect, similar to the Creole of the English-speaking Caribbean islands, is spoken by many. Some of the older Mennonites in the Mennonite colony speak German.

Principal Languages and Their Speakers

English	127,000
English Creole (lingua franca)	190,000
Garifuna (Black Carib)	17,000
German	4,000
Mayan languages	24,000
Spanish	79,000
Spanish (lingua franca)	140,000

RELIGIONS

Most of the population is Christian, divided between 60 percent Roman Catholic and 40 percent Protestant. Most of Belize's primary and secondary schools are operated by churches. Church leaders have close ties to the political establishment.

Religious Affiliations

Roman Catholic	144,000
Protestant	68,000
Anglican	17,000
Other	21,000

HISTORICAL BACKGROUND

Numerous ruins indicate that for hundreds of years Belize was heavily populated by the Maya Indians, whose relatively advanced civilization reached its height between A.D. 250 and 900. Eventually the civilization declined leaving behind small groups whose offspring still exist in Belize, contributing positively to the culturally diverse population.

The first recorded European settlements were made by shipwrecked English seamen in 1638. Over the next 150 years more English settlements were established. Although a series of agreements permitted British settlers to engage in the logwood industry, Spain claimed sovereignty and occasionally supported the claim with military action. The decisive victory of the settlers over the Spanish in the Battle of St. George's Caye in 1798 firmly established British control, although it was not until 1862 that the colony of British Honduras was formally declared. Initially, the colony came under the jurisdiction of the governor of Jamaica, but in 1884 a separate post of governor of British Honduras was created. A broad-based suffrage was introduced in 1935 and universal adult suffrage in 1954. From 1961 the system of government was a ministerial one, supported by an elected majority in the National Assembly. In June 1974 the country's name was changed from British Honduras to Belize. Belize became independent within the British Commonwealth on September 21, 1981. George Cadle Price, head of the People's United Party (PUP), which was first organized in 1951, became prime minister.

Territorial disputes with Guatemala, which had been particularly heated prior to independence, remained Belize's most important issue. The inability of the PUP to secure any treaty agreements with Guatemala along with internal disputes culminated in a change of government. In December 1984, the United Democratic Party (UDP) received 53 percent of the general election vote, and the UDP leader, Manuel Esquivel, became prime minister. By 1988, however, the government was weakened because of a controversy over the legislative creation of the Security and Intelligence Service (SIS). Though the SIS was mandated to fight large-scale drug activity and deal with illegal immigrants, the UDP was accused by its opponents of creating a "police state." The PUP won the general elections held in 1989 by a slight margin.

In the snap assembly elections in 1993 the opposition United Democratic Party was returned to power under Manuel Esquivel. In 1998, the PUP won a decisive victory by gaining 26 of the 29 assembly seats. Shortly thereafter, Said Musa was named to succeed Esquivel as prime minister.

CONSTITUTION

Under the constitution of 1981 Belize is a constitutional monarchy, with the British sovereign represented by the governor-general as the head of state. The sovereign appoints the governor-general, who must be a Belizean

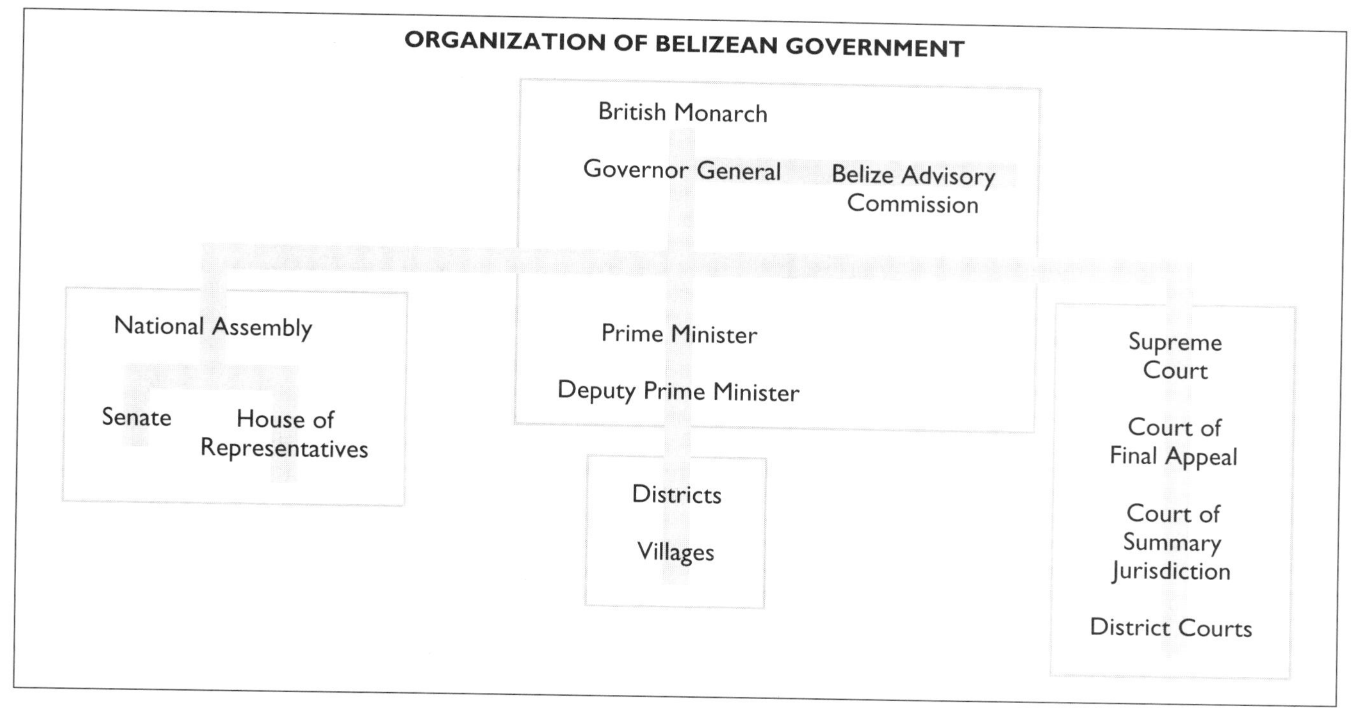

national, on the advice of the Belizean prime minister, the head of government. The governor-general appoints the prime minister and, on the latter's recommendation, other ministers; the governor-general also appoints the leader of the opposition. There are a number of parastatal bodies, such as the Belize Advisory Council, an advisory body of no less than six members who advise the governor-general; the Election and Boundaries Commission; and the Public Services Commission.

LOCAL GOVERNMENT

For purposes of local government Belize is divided into six districts and eight municipal councils. The six districts are: Belize, Cayo, Corozal, Orange Walk, Stann Creek, and Toledo.

Local government at the village level is conducted through village councils.

Local Government

Principal administrative divisions, capitals, area, population

Area and Population

		area		population 1994
Districts	**Capitals**	**sq mi**	**sq km**	**estimate**
Belize	Belize City	1,663	4,307	62,939
Cayo	San Ignacio	2,006	5,196	41,594
Corozai	Corozai	718	1,860	31,412
Orange Walk	Orange Walk	1,790	4,636	33,855
Stann Creek	Dangriga	986	2,554	19,957
Toledo	Punta Gorda	1,704	4,413	19,243
Total		8,867	22,965	209,000

PARLIAMENT

The National Assembly is a bicameral body consisting of an appointed Senate and a directly elected House of Representatives, both of which serve five-year terms. The Senate has eight members, five of whom are appointed on the advice of the prime minister, two on the advice of the leader of the opposition, and one on the advice of the Belize Advisory Council. The House of Representatives has 28 members.

POLITICAL PARTIES

There are three active political organizations in Belize. The People's United Party was formed in 1950 by organized labor and merged with the Christian Democratic Party in 1988. The conservative party, United Democratic Party, was formed by the merger of several smaller organizations, including the People's Development Movement, the Liberal Party, and the National Independence Party. The National Alliance for Belizean Rights is a small organization formed in 1992 that opposes any territorial compromise with Guatemala over land disputes.

Political Parties

United Democratic Party, 1974
National Alliance for Belizean Rights, 1992
People's United Party, 1950

Political Parties: Strength in Parliament Most Recent Elections

House of Representatives. The lower house currently has 29 members elected by universal adult suffrage. At the election of August 27, 1998, the People's United Party won 26 seats, while the United Democratic Party won 3.

LEGAL SYSTEM

The judicial system includes the Supreme Court, whose chief justice is appointed on the advice of the prime minister after consultation with the leader of the opposition and the Court of Appeal, from which final appeal may in certain cases be made to the Judicial Committee of the U.K. Privy Council. There also are courts of summary jurisdiction and civil courts in each of the six districts.

The constitution guarantees the right of habeas corpus and prohibits arbitrary imprisonment. Release on bail is allowed for all but the most serious criminal offenses. The constitution also guarantees due process and the rights of accused persons, such as the presumption of innocence, protection against self-incrimination, the right to counsel, and public trial. Trial by jury is mandatory in criminal cases. The judiciary is independent in theory and in fact. Its major shortcoming is an insufficient number of trained personnel at all levels.

No information is available on the penal system.

LAW ENFORCEMENT

Law Enforcement

Offenses reported to the police per 100,000: —
- Murder: 33.2
- Assault: 275.6
- Burglary: 833.6
- Automobile Theft: —
- Population per Police officer: 290

Death Penalty: Yes

HUMAN RIGHTS

Belize's overall record in human rights is good. Belize has a parliamentary form of government with a competitive political system and regular local and national elections.

Elections are open, peaceful, and honest. Constitutional protections for fundamental rights and freedoms of the individual are upheld by an independent judiciary and monitored by a free press. There have been no incidents of political violence since independence.

FOREIGN POLICY

Belize's long-standing dispute with Guatemala over territorial rights has never been settled and bilateral talks continue to be held. In 1991 Belize was admitted to the OAS over Guatemala's objections. In 1993 Guatemalan president José Serrano Elias committed himself to a resolution of the "sterile dispute" and extended diplomatic recognition to Belmopan. In 1993 the two countries reached agreement on a nonaggression pact and the United Kingdom withdrew its army garrison from Belize. A rapprochement of sorts appeared to have come after Belize agreed to limit its southern territorial limit to three miles in addition to granting its neighbor access to the sea from the northern department of Petén and the use of the port facilities at Stann Creek. But the accord remains unpopular in both countries, and in February 2000 Guatemala announced that it would pursue its claim to half of Belize through international courts.

DEFENSE

The Belize Defense Force was formed in 1978 with the merger of the Police Special Forces and the Belize Volunteer Guard. Military service is voluntary. As of mid-2000, members of the regular armed services numbered 1050 with an additional 700 reservists.

Military Indicators

Total Active Duty Personnel: 1,050
Military Manpower per 1,000: 4.6
Military Expenditures $: 9 million
- as % of GNP: 1.6
- per capita $: 41
- as % of central government expenditures: 5.0

Arms Imports $: 0
Arms Exports $: 0

ECONOMY

Belize has a mixed economy in which the government cooperates with the private sector. Because of its open nature and because of the fixed relationship between the Belize dollar and the U.S. dollar, movements in domestic prices reflect external rather than domestic trends.

The economy is an open one with agriculture accounting for almost one-quarter of Gross Domestic Product (GDP) and three-quarters of its exports.

There also is a comparatively high level of investment, with gross domestic investment accounting for an average of 20 percent of GDP in recent years. The sectoral contributions to the GDP also have remained fairly stable.

Principal Economic Indicators

Gross National Product 000: $614
GNP per capita: $2,670
GNP Average Annual Growth Rate (1990–97) %: 0.3
GNP per capita Average Annual Growth Rate (1990–97) %: −2.5
Origin of Gross Domestic Product %
- Agriculture: 19
- Mining: —
- Manufacturing: 14
- Construction: 7
- Public Utilities: 4
- Transportation and Communications: 11
- Trade: 17
- Financial Services: 11
- Other Services: 6
- Government: 13

Gross Domestic Product by Type of Expenditure %
- Private Consumption: 66
- Government Consumption: 17
- Gross Domestic Investment: 23
- Foreign Trade: Exports: 53
- Imports: −59

% of Income Received by Poorest 20%: —
% of Income Received by Richest 10%: —

Price and earnings indexes (1995 = 100)

	1993	1994	1995	1996	1997	1998	1999
Consumer price index	94.7	97.2	100.0	106.4	107.5	106.6	106.3
Earnings index	—	—	—	—	—	—	—

Finance

National Currency: Belizean Dollar (Bz $)
Exchange Rate: $1 = Bz $2.0
Money Supply Stock in National Currency billion: 0.164
M1 per capita: 730
Central Bank Discount Rate %: 12.0
Total External Debt $million: 217
Debt Service Ratio %: 7.7

Balance of Payments $million: −31.9
International Reserves SDRs million: 43
Ratio of External Debt to Total Reserves: 5.9

Average Annual Rate of Inflation/Consumer Price Index Growth Rate %: 1

Official Development Assistance

ODA $: 18 million
- as % of GNP: 3.2
- per capita: $ 83
- Foreign Direct Investment $million: —

Central Government Revenues and Expenditures

Fiscal Year: 1 April–31 March
Revenues $million: 140
Expenditures $million: 142
Budget Deficit/Surplus $: −2 million
Tax Revenues as % of GDP: 21
Highest Tax Bracket %
Individual: —
Corporate: —

Employment and Labor

Economically Active Population: 75,500
Female Participation Rate %: 30.8
Activity Rate %: 34.1
Labor by Sector: %
Agriculture, Forestry, Fishing: 31.4
Manufacturing, Mining: 12.0
Construction: 7.0
Transportation and Communications: 5.0
Trade, Hotels, and Restaurants: 17.2
Finance, Insurance, Real Estate: 3.1
Public Administration, Defense: 9.2
Services: 10.3
Unemployment %: 13

Agriculture

Agriculture's Share of GDP %: 19
Average Annual Rate of Growth (1965–98) %: —
Number of Farms 000: 11
Average Size of Farm ha: 26.7
Number of Tractors per 1,000 hectares: 144
Irrigation, % of Farms having: 0.1
Artificial Fertilizer kg/hectare: 496
Total Farmland as % of land area: 10
Livestock: Cattle 000: 60
Sheep 000: 3
Hogs 000: 23
Chickens 000: 1,500
Forests: Production of Roundwood (000 cubic meters): 188
Fisheries: Total Catch tons 000: 1.9

Mining

% of GDP: 0.6
Value of Mineral Production $million: 3.5

Manufacturing

Value Added $million: 59
Industrial Production Growth Rate %: 0.2

Energy

Commercial Energy Production metric tons of oil equivalent 000: —
Commercial Energy Consumption metric tons of oil equivalent 000: 88
Commercial Energy Consumption per capita kg: 417
Average Annual Growth Rate 1980–97 %: —
Net Energy Imports % of use: 100
Electricity Installed Capacity kW 000: 25
Production kW-hr million: 148
Coal Reserves tons million: —
Production tons 000: —
Natural Gas Proven Reserves cubic meters billion: —
Production cubic meters million: —
Crude Petroleum Reserves barrels million: —
Production barrels million: —
Consumption barrels million: —
Refinery Capacity barrels per day 000: —
Pipelines Length km: —

Foreign Trade

Imports $million: 258.3
Exports $million: 161.7
Export Volume % Annual Growth Rate (1990–97): —
Import Volume % Annual Growth Rate (1990–97): —
Balance of Trade $

Balance of trade (current prices)

	1993	1994	1995	1996	1997	1998
BZ$ 000,000	−288.9	−217.9	−193.6	−175.7	−220.3	−271.4
% of total	34.6%	26.5%	23.0%	20.8%	23.9%	26.4%

Major Trading Partners

	Imports	Exports
European Union %	15.5	51.4
United States %	54.1	36.6
Eastern Europe %	—	—
Japan %	1.3	0.1
Others %	29.0	12.0

Transportation

Roads Total Length mi: 1,721 km 2,770
Paved %: 19
Automobiles: 10,667
Trucks and Buses: 6,108
Persons per vehicle: 12
Railroad; Track Length mi: — km —
Passenger-mi million: —
Freight-mi million: —
Merchant Marine: No. of Vessels: 32
Total Deadweight Tonnage 000: 45.7
International Cargo Loaded tons 000: 178
International Cargo Off-loaded tons 000: 241
Airports with Scheduled Flights: 9
Traffic: Passenger-mi million: —
Freight-mi million: —
Length of Canals mi: 513 km 825

Tourism

Number of Tourists to 000: —
Number of Tourists from 000: —
Tourist Receipts $million: 78
Tourist Expenditures $million: 21

Communications

Telephones 000: 29
Cost of Local Calls 3 mins: $0.
Cellular Telephones 000: 1.2
Fax Machines 000: 0.5
Personal Computers 000: 6.0
Internet Hosts per million persons: 4.6
Mail: Post Offices: 113
  Pieces of Mail Handled million: 3.8
  Pieces of Mail Handled per person: 18

EDUCATION

Education is compulsory for children aged between six and 14. Primary and secondary education is free. In 1997 there were 53,110 pupils enrolled in 280 primary schools, 10,912 in 30 secondary school, and 2,500 in 11 post-secondary institutions. The government runs some of the schools but most schools are run by the churches. The government maintains one special school for mentally disabled children and another for children with physical disabilities.

A Centre for Employment Training (CET) has been established in Belize City to provide a mechanism to reach the student population that has not had the advantage of completing secondary school. The Belize Technical College offers craft and technical courses and the Belize Teachers College runs a two-year diploma course leading to trained teacher status.

The Belize Vocational Training Centre in Belize City provides courses for primary school-leavers, while the Belize Youth Development Centre and the Belize College of Agriculture offer training for those interested in entering the field of agro-industry. Advanced training is provided to Belizeans in the professional and technical fields at Belize's first university, the University College of Belize, which opened in 1986. The University of the West Indies maintains a School of Continuing Education (SCE) in Belize City.

Education

Literacy Rate %: 70.3
  Male %: —
  Female %: —
First Level: Primary schools: 245
  Teachers: 1,939
  Students: 52,994
  Student-Teacher Ratio: 25.9
  Net Enrollment Ratio: 99
Second Level: Secondary Schools: 30
  Teachers: 740
  Students: 10,648
  Student-Teacher-Ratio: 13.7
  Net Enrollment Ratio: 36
Vocational Level: Schools: —
  Students: —
Third Level: Institutions: 11
  Teachers: —
  Students: 2,469
  Student-Ratio Level: —
  Gross Enrollment Ratio: —
  Students per 100,000: —
  % of Population Age 25 and over with Postsecondary Education: 6.6
Public Expenditure on Education as % of GDP: 6.1

SCIENCE AND TECHNOLOGY

Science and Technology

Scientists and Engineers in R&D per 1 million persons: —
Expenditures in R&D as % of GDP: —
High-Tech Exports $: —
Patent Applications by Residents: —

MEDIA

No dailies are published in Belize, but four weekly newspapers are published, including the pro-PUP *Belize Sunday Times*, the pro-UDP *The People's Pulse*, *The Reporter*, and the independent *Amandala*. Aggregate circulation of the nondaily press is 35,000, or 301 per 1,000 inhabitants.

Freedom of speech and press are guaranteed by the constitution and assured in practice. The government controls the country's only radio station, but there are 14 privately owned and operated television stations. Following the enactment of a broadcasting law in 1983, the six-member Belize Broadcasting Authority was appointed to license existing stations.

Book publishing is undeveloped in the country, and title output is negligible.

There is no national news agency. Only EFE is represented in the capital.

Radio Belize is a government-operated service that provides daily programming on a semicommercial basis in English and Spanish. Television was introduced in 1985.

The National Library of Belize contains over 100,000 volumes.

Media

Daily Newspapers: 4
  Total Circulation 000: 23.5
  Circulation per 1,000: 0.5
Books Published: 70
Magazines: —
Radio Receivers 000: 30
  per 1,000: 140
Television sets 000: 36
  per 1,000: 167

(continued)

MOST IMPORTANT MEDIA:

Press. The following are weeklies published at Belize City; *Amandala* (8,500), independent; *The Reporter* (6,500), pro-UDP; *Belize Times* (6,000), PUP organ; *People's Pulse* (5,000), UDP organ; *Government Gazette*.

Radio and television. The Belize Broadcasting Network (BBN) provides daily programming on a semicommercial basis in English and Spanish; formerly government operated, the BBN was privatized in November 1998. In mid-1986 licenses were issued to eight operators for 14 privately owned television channels retransmitting U.S. satellite programs, all of which had theretofore been technically illegal; two additional licenses for the operation of nationwide television services were issued in late 1994.

CULTURE

Cultural Indicators

Public Libraries
- Number: 1
- Volumes: 120,000
- Registered borrowers: 25,000

Museums
- Number: 1
- Annual Attendance (000): 1

Cinema
- Production of Long Films: —
- Number of Cinemas: —
- Seating Capacity: —
- Annual Attendance: —
- Annual Attendance per capita: —

STATUS OF WOMEN

There are no legal barriers to equality in Belize. The government actively supports the educational and economic empowerment of women through special programs. Women already hold positions of leadership in the government and in industry in Belize.

Women

Gender Empowerment Measure: 40
Seats Held in Parliament by Women %: 10.8
Female Administrators and Managers %: 36.6
Female Professional and Technical Workers %: 38.8
Women's Share of Earned Income %: 18
Women in Government %: 10

HEALTH, FOOD, AND NUTRITION

Health

Number of Physicians: 139
Number of Dentists: 12
Number of Nurses: 300
Number of Pharmacists: 17
Population per Physician: 1,546
Number of Hospitals: 7
Hospital Beds per 10,000: 29
Hospital Bed Occupancy Rate: —
Infant Mortality Rate per 1,000 live births: —
Maternal Mortality Rate per 100,000 live births: 37
Total Health Expenditures as % of GDP: 5.88
Health Expenditures per capita $: 23
HIV Infected % of adults: —
Cigarette Consumption per smoker per year: —
% of Smokers: Male: —
Female: —
Access to Safe Water %: 82

Food and Nutrition

Food Supply as % of FAO Requirements: 123
% of Consumption Expenditures on Food: 34.0
Daily Available Calories per capita: 2,791
% of Total Calories Derived From:
Cereals: 31.2
Potatoes, cassava: 1.6
Meat, poultry: 8.2
Fish: 0.4
Eggs, milk: 8.8
Fruits, vegetables: 7.5
Fats, oils: 11.1

ENVIRONMENT

Compared to other Central American countries, Belize is in relatively good shape environmentally. However, the growing population and its environmentally based economy pose certain threats, including increased solid and liquid waste, the overfishing of its waters, and deforestation due to development. Of particular concern is the state of its water supply, which in its major city is often mixed with sewage. Also of concern is the number of endangered species in its rain forests, which currently numbers more than 50. The government of Belize has committed to consider environmental impact in its ongoing planning, including reviewing the status of land usage and the protection of certain habitats.

Environment

Forest Area sq km: —
Average Annual Deforestation sq km: —
Nationally Protected Areas as % of Total Land Area: —
Freshwater Access cubic meters per capita: 109
Emissions of Organic Water Pollutants kg per day: —
CO_2 Emissions per capita ton: 1.9

CHRONOLOGY

1950 In response to the devaluation of the Belize dollar, the People's United Party (PUP) is formed, led by Leigh Richardson, George Price, and Philip Goldson.

1952 The General Workers Union (GWU) and the PUP call the first national strike.

1954 Universal adult suffrage is established; PUP wins eight of the nine elected seats and 67 percent of the vote.

1964 Belize is granted internal self-government; Guatemala continues to assert its claim to the territory.

1971 Belmopan becomes the capital of Belize; the government initiates decade-redistribution of land from large landowners to tenants.

1973 The country's name is legally changed from British Honduras to Belize; the Alien Landholding Ordinance is passed, limiting foreign purchase and development of land.

1981 Belize becomes independent, with George Price, People's United Party (PUP) leader, as prime minister. Guatemala refuses to recognize Belize's independence as legal and presses territorial claims.

1984 The PUP is unseated in the National Assembly elections as the opposition United Democratic Party (UDP) wins a landslide victory.
UDP leader Manuel Esquivel is sworn in as prime minister.

1988 The UDP is weakened by PUP accusations about the government-created Security and Intelligence Service and about suppression of the PUP newspaper.
The Joint Commission is established to examine territorial dispute issues. This is an unofficial recognition by Guatemala of Belize sovereignty.

1989 In general elections, the PUP wins over the UDP and Price regains the prime ministry.

1990 Belize holds official talks with Guatemala in an effort to settle their long-standing border dispute.

1991 Belize becomes a member of the Organization of American States (OAS).

1992 Guatemala formally recognizes Belize.

1993 The UDP once again defeats the PUP in general elections and Manuel Esquivel becomes prime minister.
Sir Colville Norbert Young is appointed governor-general.

1994 The last remaining British forces are withdrawn from the country.
Guatemala reasserts its territorial claims.

1995 The Violent Crime/Counternarcotics Intelligence Unit (VIU) is formed to reduce drug trafficking through Belize's borders.

1998 The PUP wins a landslide victory in the general elections and Said Musa becomes prime minister.

2000 Guatemala announces that it will pursue its claim to half of Belize through international courts.

BIBLIOGRAPHY

Bolland, O. Nigel. *Belize: A New Nation in Central America.* Boulder, Colo., 1986.

Fernandez, Julio A. *Belize: Case Study for Democracy in Central America.* Brookfield, Vt., 1989.

Miller, E. Willard. *The Third World: Guatemala, Honduras, Belize, Costa Rica, Panama, a Bibliography.* Monticello, Ill., 1990.

Stetzekorn, William David. *Formerly British Honduras: A Profile of the New Nation of Belize.* Athens, Ohio, 1981.

Waddell, David A. *British Honduras:, A Historical and Contemporary Survey.* Westport, Conn., 1981.

Woodward, Ralph L. *Belize* (World Bibliographical Series). Santa Barbara, Calif., 1980.

OFFICIAL PUBLICATIONS

Belize. *Abstract of Statistics* (annual); *Belize Economic Survey* (annual); *Belize—Statistical Appendix* (IMF Staff Country Report [1997]); *Development Plan 1990–94; Labour Force Survey (1993);* 1991 *Population Census: Major Findings.*

CONTACT INFORMATION

Embassy of Belize
2535 Massachusetts Avenue NW
Washington, D.C. 20008
Phone: (202) 332-9636 Fax: (202) 232-6888

INTERNET RESOURCES

- Government of Belize http://www.belize.gov.bz
- http.//www.belizenet.com (unofficial)

BENIN

BASIC FACT SHEET

OFFICIAL NAME:
Republic of Benin (République du Bénin) (formerly Dahomey)

ABBREVIATION:
BN

CAPITAL:
Porto-Novo (official); Cotonou (de facto)

HEAD OF STATE & GOVERNMENT:
President Mathieu Kérékou (from 1996)

NATURE OF GOVERNMENT:
Parliamentary democracy

POPULATION:
6,306,000 (1999)

AREA:
112,622 sq km (43,483 sq mi)

ETHNIC MAJORITY:
Fon, Adja, Bariba, and Yoruba

LANGUAGE:
French (official)

RELIGIONS:
Animism, Christianity, and Islam

UNIT OF CURRENCY:
Communauté Financière Africaine franc (C.F.A.F.)

NATIONAL FLAG:
Green horizontal strip on left; two vertical stripes, yellow above red on right

NATIONAL EMBLEM:
The principal elements of the national coat of arms are a five-pointed star in a green circle enclosed within an ornamental wreath with the letters RPB, standing for République Populaire du Benin

NATIONAL ANTHEM:
"The New Dawn"

NATIONAL HOLIDAYS:
August 1 (Independence Day, National Day); May 1 (Labor Day); December 4 (Proclamation of the Republic Day); Christian holidays include Assumption, All Saints' Day, Christmas, Ascension, Easter Monday, and Pentecost Monday; also variable Islamic festivals

DATE OF INDEPENDENCE:
August 1, 1960

DATE OF CONSTITUTION:
December 1990

GEOGRAPHICAL FEATURES

Benin, in southern West Africa, has an area of 112,622 sq km (43,483 sq mi), extending 665 km (413 mi) north to south and 333 km (207 mi) east to west. Its coastline, on the Bight of Benin, runs for 125 km (78 mi). Benin shares an international boundary of 1,830 km (1,137 mi) with four countries: Togo (644 km; 400 mi); Burkina Faso (306 km; 190 mi); Niger (266 km; 165 mi); and Nigeria (773 km; 483 mi).

Benin has four natural topographical regions. The first is the coastal belt. Behind this belt is a lagoon region with four lagoons (Cotonou or Nadoue, Ouidah, Grand Popo, and Porto-Novo), all of which join the sea at Grand Popo. Farther north is the *terre de barre*, a fertile clay plateau divided by a wide, marshy depression known as the Lama. The third region, in the northwest, is composed of the Atakora Mountains, with an elevation of 654 m

Benin

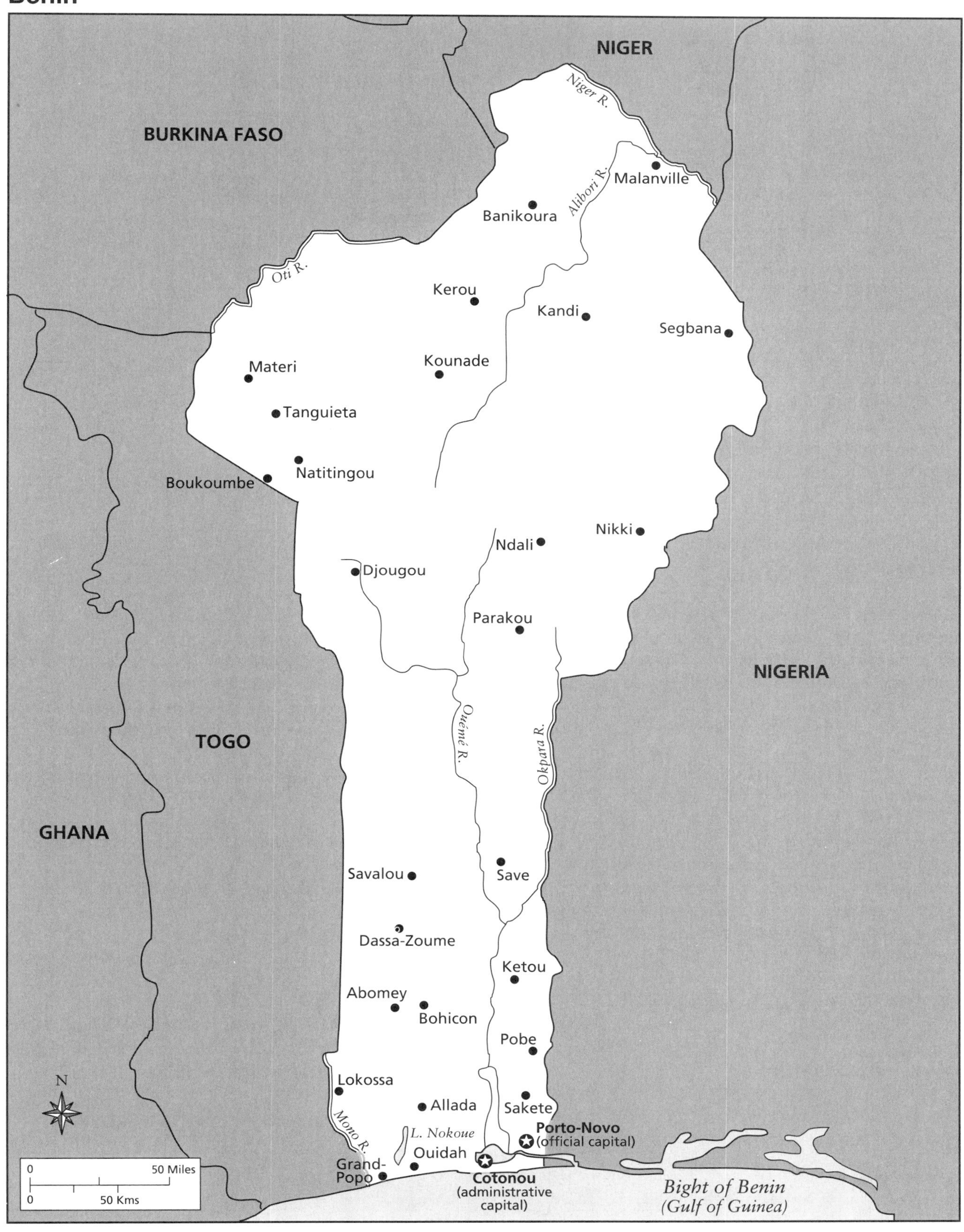
NIGER
Niger R.
BURKINA FASO
Alibori R.
Malanville
Banikoura
Oti R.
Kerou
Kandi
Segbana
Materi
Kounade
Tanguieta
Natitingou
Boukoumbe
Nikki
Ndali
Djougou
Parakou
NIGERIA
Ouémé R.
Okpara R.
TOGO
GHANA
Savalou
Save
Dassa-Zoume
Ketou
Abomey
Bohicon
Pobe
N
Lokossa
Allada
Sakete
Mono R.
L. Nokoue
Porto-Novo
(official capital)
Ouidah
Grand-Popo
Cotonou
(administrative capital)
0
50 Miles
0
50 Kms
Bight of Benin
(Gulf of Guinea)

(2,146 ft). Mt. Sokbaro (658 m) is the highest peak. Last, there are the eastern plains, the Borgu and the Plain of Kandi, sloping toward the Niger Basin.

Geography

Area sq km: 112,622 sq mi 43,483
World Rank: 101st
Land Boundaries, km: Burkina Faso 306; Niger 266; Nigeria 773; Togo 644
Coastline, km: 121
Elevation Extremes meters
Lowest: Atlantic Ocean 0
Highest: Mount Sokbaro 658
Land Use % Arable land: 13
Permanent Crops: 4
Permanent Pastures: 4
Forest and Woodland: 31
Other: 48

Population of Principal Cities (1994 est.)

Abomey-Calavi	125,565
Cotonou (official capital)	750,000
Djougou	132,000
Parakou	120,000
Porto-Novo (de facto capital)	200,000

CLIMATE AND WEATHER

The coastal region of Benin has an equatorial climate with four seasons: the long rainy season between March and July, the short dry season from August through mid-September, the short rainy season from October through mid-November, and the long dry season from November through March. Away from the coast, the length of the dry season increases. In the north there are two seasons, with the rains falling between May and September. The maximum midday temperature in January often reaches 43.3°C (110°F) in the north, but the coastal region has a steady temperature of 22°C to 34°C (72°F to 93°F) throughout the year. Rainfall varies between 965.2 mm (38 in) in the north and 1346.2 mm (93 in) in the south.

The prevailing wind is the *harmattan*, a hot and searing wind that drives down from the Sahara between December and March.

Climate and Weather

Mean Temperature
Coastal Ragion: 72°F to 93°F
Average Rainfall 38 in to 93 in

POPULATION

Population Indicators

Total Population: 1999 6,306,000
World Rank: 95th
Density per sq mi: 145.0 per sq km 56
% of annual growth (1994–99): 3.4
Male %: 48.7
Female %: 51.3
Urban %: 39.6
Age Distribution: % 0–14: 48.3
15–29: 26.9
30–44: 13.3
45–59: 7.4
60–74: 3.2
75 and over: 0.8
Population 2020: 11,920,000
Birth Rate per 1,000: 46
Death Rate per 1,000: 13
Population Doubling Time (years): 30
Infant Mortality Rate per 1,000 live births: 103
Rate of Natural Increase per 1,000: 33
Total Fertility Rate: 6.6
Expectation of Life (years): Males 50.7
Females 54.7
Marriage Rate per 1,000: 12.8
Divorce Rate per 1,000: 0.8
Total Number of Households: —
Average Size of Households: 5.9
% of Illegitimate Children: —
Induced Abortions: —
Rate per 100 live births: —

ETHNIC COMPOSITION

Benin is an ethnic mosaic of 42 groups, of whom the four largest—the Fon, the Adja, the Bariba, and the Yoruba—constitute 54 percent of the population. These groups may be broadly divided into five clusters: Voltaic, Sudanese, Fulani, Ewe, and Yoruba.

The foreign community in Benin is estimated at more than 5,500, of whom the French constitute the largest group.

Interethnic relations are characterized by a carryover of historic animosities. This has led to shifting and uneasy alliances between groups, often directed against other similar alliances of groups. The northern groups have invariably suffered as the southern tribes sought to advance their regional interests through national political institutions.

LANGUAGES

The official language of Benin is French. Fon and Yoruba are used as lingua francas in the south, and Bariba and Fulani are used as lingua francas in the North.

Principal Languages and Their Speakers

Adja	700,000
Aizo (Ouidah)	550,000
Bariba	550,000
Dendi	130,000
Djougou	190,000
Fon	2,510,000

French	600,000
Fula (Fulani)	350,000
Somba (Ditamari)	420,000
Yoruba (Nago)	770,000
Other	150,000

RELIGIONS

In statistical terms, over 62 percent of Beninese follow traditional African, or animist, religions, about 21 percent are Christian (mostly in the south), and 12 percent are Muslim. Catholic missionary activities began in the middle of the 19th century, when the apostolic vicariate of Benin and Dahomey was set up. Benin was the scene of intense missionary efforts from 1860, when the Pères des Missions Africaines de Lyon began their activities. Since 1975 spiritualist cults have been discouraged.

Muslim influence in the country is disproportionately higher than the number of its adherents. Most Muslims belong to the Fulani, Bariba, and Dendi tribes.

Religious Affiliation

Traditional beliefs	3,910,000
Roman Catholic	1,320,000
Muslim	760,000
Other	320,000

HISTORICAL BACKGROUND

The history of Benin begins in the 17th century when Onegbajda (c. 1645–85), chief of the Fon people, after fighting with his brother, moved to Abomey and then conquered the Kingdom of Dan, which became Dahomey. Successful rulers were pledged to continue to expand Benin territory, which led to constant war and conflict, especially with the powerful Yoruba of Nigeria. The Dahomey became an integral part of the slave trade by selling its prisoners of war to Europeans, largely the Portuguese, in exchange for weapons. Southern Benin became known as "the Slave Coast."

The first French trading post is what is now Benin was established in 1851, but a French protectorate was firmly imposed only after the defeat of King Behanzin of Abomey in 1892. Benin—or Dahomey, as it was then known—became a component colony of French West Africa in 1902. French rule ended in 1958, when the territory accepted the French-drafted constitution proposed by Charles de Gaulle and opted for the status of an autonomous republic within the French Community. It achieved independence in 1960 but did not remain part of the French Community.

Benin is one of the most politically unstable nations in western Africa. Since independence, it has had four successful coups (1963, 1967, 1969, and 1972) as well as two unsuccessful coup attempts (1974 and 1988) and 11 presidents (one was in power for only one month). The instability of the governments and their vulnerability have been due in part to the fragility of political institutions and the constant intervention of ethnic interests in politics. None of the Beninese leaders has attempted to build a broad popular base.

The leader of the Parti Dahoméen de l'Unité, Hubert Maga, was elected the country's first president late in 1960. President Maga's term was interrupted by a military coup in 1963 following worker and student riots. The vice president under Maga, Sourou-Migan Apithy, was elected president in January 1964. Unrest in the northern part of Benin over this southern-born president led military leader General Christophe Soglo to set up, in November 1965, an interim government, which he eventually headed. This was followed by another coup consisting of young officers led by Maj. (later Lt.-Col.) Maurice Kouandete, who took over as prime minister.

Attempts were made to reestablish civilian rule in 1968, but because former presidents and leading politicians were excluded from taking part in the presidential poll, a boycott of the election was called. With only a quarter of the population voting, the election was voided, and a military appointee, Dr. Emile Derlin Zinsou, formerly minister of foreign affairs, was sworn in as president in July 1968. In little over a year, Zinsou was deposed by Lt.-Col. Kouandete, and civilian rule was replaced by a military directorate.

Indecisive results in the presidential election of March 1970 led to a compromise. The Presidential Council was organized, and power was shared by the three main candidates. In 1972, however, civilian rule was once again overturned, this time by a military coup under the leadership of Maj. (later Brig.-Gen.) Mathieu Kérékou, who abolished the constitution and established a military regime in which all the country's regions would be equally represented in the newly formed National Council of the Revolution (CNR).

In November 1974, Kérékou moved the country toward Marxism-Leninism, with the state taking over all major economic sectors. An unsuccessful military coup in January 1975 led to the merging of the army and the gendarmerie to form the National Defense Force.

In that same month, the Parti de la Révolution Populaire de Benin (PRPB) was organized as the "highest expression of the political will of the people of Benin," followed by a change in the country's name to the People's Republic of Benin, after an ancient African kingdom.

In January 1977, an airborne attack led by French mercenary Col. Robert Denard was repelled. In May, a Loi Fondamentale was announced by the PRPB in preparation for the "people's democratic revolution." In August, the Loi Fondamentale was approved by the CNR, which was replaced by a National Revolutionary Assembly

(ANR). In February 1980 the ANR unanimously elected Kérékou as president. In that same year, Kérékou is said to have converted to Islam, taking the first name of Ahmed. Official documents, though, still refer to him as Mathieu.

In February 1984, the Loi Fondamentale was amended to extend the terms of the president and ANR members, along with a reduction of the number of members in the ANR. In July, Kérékou, as the sole candidate, was reelected president.

School riots in May led to the closing of all educational establishments. In November, 100 people, including teachers, engineers, and high-ranking officials, were arrested for belonging to the banned Parti Communiste Dahoméen (PCD).

In January 1987, Kérékou resigned from the army so that he could become the civilian head of state. Dissatisfaction within the military over government corruption led to a coup attempt in March 1988 and another one in June.

A lessening of popular support of the official list of candidates in the 1989 ANR elections was probably caused by the country's persistent economic problems. Nonetheless, Kérékou was reelected president by the ANR in August.

In 1989, though suggestions were made within Kérékou's ministry to create a multiparty system, Kérékou maintained that such a change would lead to a resurgence of tribalism and regionalism.

Economic problems and austerity programs led to strikes early in 1989 by public-sector workers, including teachers and civil servants. Classes were boycotted by students demanding disbursements of promised grants and scholarships. Pressure by the military gave way to a payment of back salaries. But despite agreements with the IMF and the World Bank, strikes by civil servants continued. Classes resumed in October but were disrupted again in December when the government did not fulfill its promises.

Faced with widespread public disillusionment with his government and mounting street protests, Kérékou, in December 1989, announced that Benin would abandon its Marxist-Leninist ideology and that a national conference would be held early in 1990 to draft a new constitution. The conference, convened in February, voted to abolish the Loi Fondamentale and appoint a High Council of the Republic to assume the functions of the National Revolutionary Assembly, which was abolished. Nicephore Soglo, a former official of the World Bank, was designated prime minister. The conference also voted to change the country's name to Republic of Benin. A political organization, the Union des Forces du Progrès (UFP) was established in May to replace the former PRPB. The nation, in December, approved a new constitution that provided for separation of powers of the executive, legislature, and judiciary in the context of a multiparty state.

In March 1990 Soglo defeated Kérékou in the final round of elections—the country's first free presidential elections in nearly 30 years and the first time an incumbent president was defeated in a reelection bid in Africa. He assumed office in April. However, Soglo's term was plagued by legislative infighting and his opponents captured the majority of the seats in parliamentary elections in 1995. In the 1996 presidential elections, Kérékou staged a comeback, winning 52.5 percent of the vote. In 1999, Soglo's Benin Renaissance Party and its allies captured a one-seat majority in the Assembly. Kérékou was reelected in 2001.

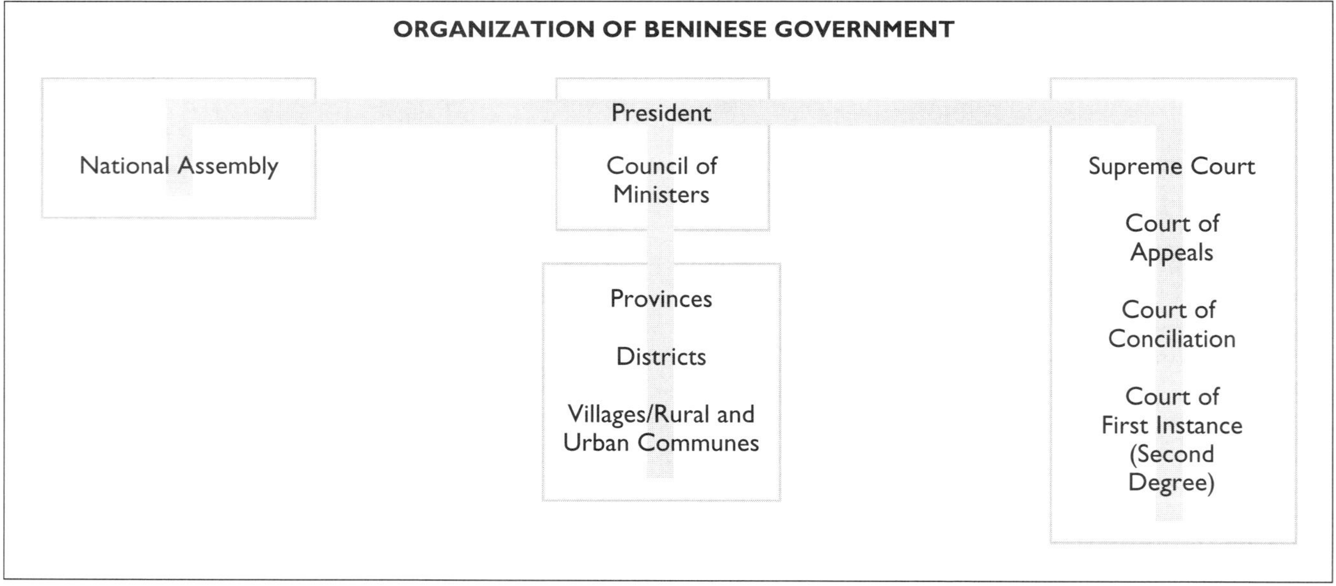

CONSTITUTION

Benin has had six constitutions since independence. In 1990 Benin adopted its newest constitution. It provides for an executive directly elected for a five-year term. The president is limited to two terms and must be between 40 and 70 years old. He is advised by a council composed of former heads of state. Legislative power is vested in a unicameral National Assembly, which is directly elected. The constitution established the principle of an independent judiciary.

LOCAL GOVERNMENT

For purpose of regional administration, Benin is divided into six provinces, within which there are 78 districts.

Each province is headed by a civilian prefect. In addition, the country has five urban constituencies: Abomey, Cotonou, Ouidah, Parakou, and Porto-Novo.

At the lower levels, rural and urban communes and villages are run by elected committees.

Local Government

Principal administrative divisions, capitals, area, population

Area and population

Provinces	Capitals	area sq mi	area sq km	population 1992 census
Altacora	Natitingou	12,050	31,200	648,330
Atlantique	Cotonou	1,250	3,200	1,060,310
Borgou	Parakou	19,700	51,000	816,278
Mono	Lokossa	1,500	3,880	646,954
Ouémé	Porto-Novo	1,800	4,700	869,492
Zou	Abomey	7,200	18,700	813,965
TOTAL		43,500	112,680	4,855,349

PARLIAMENT

The 1990 constitution provided for a unicameral National Assembly composed of 83 deputies chosen by direct election. Deputies serve four-year terms and may be reelected indefinitely. There are two ordinary sessions starting within the first fortnight of April and the second fortnight of October, respectively. Each session cannot exceed three months. The decisions are made by a simple majority.

POLITICAL PARTIES

Benin had throughout its history been a single-party state. However, that changed in 1990 when the parliament provided for a multiparty system. There are currently more than 100 active political parties in the country. The largest of them include Benin Renaissance Party (PRB), Democratic Renewal Party (PRD), Front for Renewal and Development (FARD-ALAFIA), and the Alliance of the Social Democratic Party (PSD).

Political Parties

Social Democratic Party
Rally of Liberal Democrats for National Reconstruction
Action Front for Renewal and Development, 1994
Cardunya, 1998
Our Common Cause, 1991
Party of Democratic Renewal
Benin Renaissance Party, 1992
African Assembly for Progress and Solidarity, 1993
Communist Party, 1977
Marxist-Leninist Communist Party, 1999
Combat for Development and Unity
Party of Beninese Workers, 1994
National Rally for Democracy, 1990
Union of the Forces of Progress, 1990
Republican Party
Rally for Democracy and Pan-Africanism, 1994

Political Parties: Strength in Parliament Most Recent Elections

At the most recent election of March 30, 1999, declared supporters of former president Soglo captured 42 seats (Benin Renaissance Party, 27; Party of Democratic Renewal, 11; and Star Alliance, 4) while so-called presidential (pro-Kérékou) tendency parties secured 41 (Action Front for Renewal and Development-Alafia, 10: Social Democratic Party, 9; African Movement for Development and Progress, 6; Impulse for Progress and Democracy, 4; Car-DUNYA, 3; Movement for Citizens' Commitment and Awakening, 2; Together Party and others, 7).

LEGAL SYSTEM

The legal system is based on French civil law and customary law. The constitution of 1990 established an independent judiciary. It provides for a Supreme Court, which is the highest court in the nation, and a High Court of Justice with the power to impeach government officials. The High Court is composed of six members of the legislature and the president of the Supreme Court.

LAW ENFORCEMENT

Law Enforcement

Offenses reported to the police per 100,000: 125
- Murder: 0.9
- Assault: 37.9
- Burglary: 3.4
- Automobile Theft: 1.3
- Population per Police officer: 3,250

Death Penalty: Yes.

HUMAN RIGHTS

For a country that had a poor record on human rights for most of the 1960s through the 1980s, Benin has made remarkable progress. The country has successfully made the transition from a single-party, authoritarian, Marxist-Leninist state. The constitution provides for a number of protections of citizens from abuse and these have largely been respected.

FOREIGN POLICY

Throughout the cold war era Benin followed nonaligned policies, although military and economic ties with France continued to be strong. Relations with neighboring Nigeria are occasionally strained by frequent expulsions of Beninese workers. Benin is a strong supporter of the Economic Community of West African States (ECOWAS) and has initiated bilateral ventures with Ghana, Mauritania, and Togo.

DEFENSE

The defense structure is headed by the president, who also is the defense minister and commander in chief. Military manpower is provided by voluntary enlistment for a period of 18 months. The army headquarters is at Parakou.

Benin's armed forces have no offensive capability, and their combat-worthiness is largely untried in the field. The major role of the military in the history of modern Benin has been as a political arbiter and as a power base for ambitious colonels.

The bulk of military aid has been received from France. Token assistance has been received from the United States and Israel. Benin has no domestic defense production.

Military Indicators

Total Active Duty Personnel: 4,800
Military Manpower per 1,000: 0.8
Military Expenditures $: 24 million
- as % GNP: 1.2
- per capita $: 4
- as % of central government expenditures: 8.6

Arms Imports $: 0
Arms Exports $: 0

ECONOMY

The economy of Benin remains underdeveloped and dependent on subsistence agriculture, cotton production, and regional trade. Growth in real output has averaged a sound 4 percent in 1990–95 and 5 percent in 1996–99. Rapid population growth has offset much of this increase in output. Inflation has subsided over the past several years. Commercial and transport activities, which make up a large part of gross domestic product, are vulnerable to developments in Nigeria, particularly fuel shortages. The Paris Club and bilateral creditors have eased the external debt situation in recent years. While high fuel prices constrained growth in 2000, increased cotton production—enabled by a major restructuring program—and an expansion of the Cotonou port, may lead to increased growth in 2001.

Principal Economic Indicators

Gross National Product: $2.227 billion
GNP per capita: $380
GNP Average Annual Growth Rate (1990–97) %: 1.7
GNP per capita Average Annual Growth Rate (1990–97) %: −1.2
Origin of Gross Domestic Product %
- Agriculture: 33
- Mining: —
- Manufacturing: 8
- Construction: 4
- Public Utilities: 1
- Transportation and Communications: 8
- Trade: 20
- Financial Services: 11
- Other Services: 11
- Government: 9

Gross Domestic Product by Type of Expenditure %
- Private Consumption: 78
- Government Consumption: 12
- Gross Domestic Investment: 20
- Foreign Trade: Exports: 31
- Imports: −41

% of Income Received by Poorest 20%: 8
% of Income Received by Richest 10%: 39.0

Price and earnings indexes (1995 = 100)

	1992	1993	1994	1995	1996	1997	1998
Consumer price index	62.8	63.1	87.4	100.0	104.9	108.6	114.8
Earnings index	—	—	—	—	—	—	—

Finance

National Currency: CFA Franc (CFAF)
Exchange Rate: $1 = CFAF 608.36
Money Supply Stock in National Currency billion: 161.7
M1 per capita: 28,800
Central Bank Discount Rate %: 5.75
Total External Debt $: 1,700 million
Debt Service Ratio %: 7.5

Balance of Payments $: −96.6
International Reserves SDRs: 184 million
Ratio of External Debt to Total Reserves: 7.6

Average Annual Rate of Inflation/Consumer Price Index Growth Rate %: 3.5

Official Development Assistance

ODA: $210 million
- as % of GNP: 9.2
- per capita: $35
- Foreign Direct Investment $million: 34

Central Government Revenues and Expenditures

Fiscal Year: Calendar Year
Revenues $: 299 million
Expenditures $: 445 million
Budget Deficit/Surplus $: 246 million
Tax Revenues as % of GDP: 13.7
Highest Tax Bracket %
Individual: —
Corporate: —

Employment and Labor

Economically Active Population: 2,085,000
Female Participation Rate %: 42.6
Activity Rate %: 43.0
Labor by Sector: %
Agriculture, Forestry, Fishing: 55.0
Manufacturing, Mining: 7.8
Construction: 2.5
Transportation and Communications: 2.5
Trade, Hotels, and Restaurants: 20.7
Finance, Insurance, Real Estate: 0.1
Public Administration, Defense: —
Services: 35.9

Unemployment %: —

Agriculture

Agriculture's Share of GDP %: 33
Average Annual Rate of Growth (1965–98) %: 4.0
Number of Farms 000: 408
Average Size of Farm ha: —
Number of Tractors per 1,000 hectares: 0.1
Irrigation, % of Farms having: 0.7
Artificial Fertilizer kg/hectare: 2.0
Total Cropland as % of Farmland: 29.3
Livestock: Cattle 000: 1,400
Sheep 000: 605
Hogs 000: 580
Chickens 000: 27,000
Forests: Production of Roundwood (000 cubic meters): 5,899
Fisheries: Total Catch tons: 37

Mining

% of GDP: 0.7
Value of Mineral Production $: 14.7 million

Manufacturing

Value Added $: 59 million
Industrial Production Growth Rate %: —

Energy

Commercial Energy Production metric tons of oil equivalent: 1,897
Commercial Energy Consumption metric tons of oil equivalent: 2,182
Commercial Energy Consumption per capita kg: 377
Average Annual Growth Rate 1980–97 %: −0.6
Net Energy Imports % of use: 13
Electricity Installed Capacity kW: 15,000
Production kW-hr: 6 million
Coal Reserves tons million: —
Production tons 000: —
Natural Gas Proven Reserves cubic meters billion: 1.2
Production cubic meters million: —
Crude Petroleum Reserves barrels million: 29
Production barrels million: 0.7
Consumption barrels million: —
Refinery Capacity barrels per day 000: —
Pipelines Length km: —

Foreign Trade

Imports $: 408 million
Exports $: 43 million
Export Volume % Annual Growth Rate (1990–97): 31.6
Import Volume % Annual Growth Rate (1990–97): 9.7
Balance of Trade $

Balance of trade (current prices)

	1992	1993	1994	1995	1996	1997
CFAF 000,000,000	−64.20	−53.2	−22.2	−138.8	−123.3	−136.5
% of total	26.6%	19.7%	4.9%	25.2%	22.1%	22.3%

Major Trading Partners

	Imports	Exports
European Union %	30.6	18.6
United States %	4.5	18.7
Eastern Europe %	0.7	—
Japan %	2.4	0.4
Others %	61.8	62.3

Transportation

Roads Total Length mi: 5,257 km: 8,460
Paved %: 31
Automobiles: 22,200
Trucks and Buses: 12,400
Persons per vehicle: 160
Railroad; Track Length mi: 359 km: 578
Passenger-mi: 66 million
Freight-mi: 173 million
Merchant Marine: No. of Vessels: 12
Total Deadweight Tonnage: 0.2
International Cargo Loaded tons: 339
International Cargo Off-loaded tons 000: 1,738
Airports with Scheduled Flights: 1
Traffic: Passenger-mi: 139.6 million
Freight-mi: 11.2 million
Length of Canals mi: — km: —

Tourism

Number of Tourists to 000: 152
Number of Tourists from 000: 420
Tourist Receipts $: 27 million
Tourist Expenditures $: 6 million

Communications

Telephones 000: 28
Cost of Local Calls 3 mins: $0.12
Cellular Telephones 000: 1.1
Fax Machines 000: 0.8
Personal Computers 000: —
Internet Hosts per million persons: —
Mail: Post Offices: 159
Pieces of Mail Handled: 8.4 million
Pieces of Mail Handled per person: 1.5

EDUCATION

Education is free, universal, and compulsory, in principle, from ages five to 11. Schooling consists of 13 years, divided into six years of primary school, four years of lower secondary school, and three years of upper secondary school. The curricula are modeled on those of France, but changes gradually are being introduced to adapt to local needs and traditions.

The academic year runs from November to July. The medium of instruction is French, but the government has proposed a gradual shift to regional vernaculars as part of its de-Westernization policy.

One of the more significant changes made by the Kérékou government was the introduction of technical education at the secondary level. Benin's sole institution of higher learning, the University of Benin, is 70 percent supported by France. The national literacy rate is estimated to be 37 percent.

Education

Literacy Rate %: 37.0
- Male %: 48.7
- Female %: 25.8

First Level: Primary schools: 2,889
- Teachers: 12,343
- Students: 602,069
- Student-Teacher Ratio: 48.8
- Net Enrollment Ratio: 59

Second Level: Secondary Schools: 145
- Teachers: 2,384
- Students: 97,480
- Student-Teacher Ratio: 40.9
- Net Enrollment Ratio: —

Vocational Level: Schools: 14
- Students: 4,873

Third Level: Institutions: 16
- Teachers: 602
- Students: 9,964
- Student-Ratio Level: 16.5
- Gross Enrollment Ratio: 2.6
- Students per 100,000: 208
- % of Population Age 25 and over with Postsecondary Education: 1.3

Public Expenditure on Education as % of GDP: 3.1

SCIENCE AND TECHNOLOGY

Science and Technology

Scientists and Engineers in R&D per 1 million persons: 176
Expenditures in R&D as % of GDP: 0.00
High-Tech Exports $: —
Patent Applications by Residents: —

MEDIA

Benin has two daily newspapers. *Ehuzu* is the official government organ with a circulation of about 10,000. All are located in Cotonou. There are four nondailies, with a total circulation exceeding 5,000. All are published in French and, except for the Official Journal, all are published at Cotonou. Fifteen periodicals also are published, with a total circulation of 4,000.

The national news agency is Agence Béninoise de Presse, which is located in a section of the Ministry of Information. AFP and Tass have regional bureaus in Cotonou. Reuters, UPI, DPA, and AP have correspondents.

The official broadcasting organization is the Office de Radiodiffusion et Télévision du Bénin (RTB).

Media

Daily Newspapers: 1
- Total Circulation 000: 12
- Circulation per 1,000: 2

Books Published: 84
Magazines: 37
Radio Receivers 000: 400
- per 1,000: 73

Television sets 000: 400
- per 1,000: 73

MOST IMPORTANT MEDIA:

Press. Current publications include *La Gazette du Golfe* (18,000), independent fortnightly; *Tam-Tam Express* (15,000), independent fortnightly; *Bénin*, Catholic fortnightly; and *Les Echos du Jour*, independent. More than a dozen new press organs commenced publication in 1990, following abandonment of the prior censorship that had been imposed by the Kérékou regime. More recently, *Le Matin*, an independent daily, was launched in May 1994 and in August 1997 *Le Point au Quotidien*, another independent daily, was founded.

News agencies. The Agence Bénin-Presse operates as a section of the Ministry of Information.

Radio and television. The government's Office de Radiodiffusion et de Télévision du Bénin broadcasts in French, English, and a number of indigenous languages throughout the country.

CULTURE

Cultural Indicators

Public Libraries
- Number: 31
- Volumes: 148,000
- Registered borrowers: 2,730

Museums
- Number: 28
- Annual Attendance: —

Cinema
- Production of Long Films: 5
- Number of Cinemas: 23
- Seating Capacity: 9,400
- Annual Attendance: —
- Annual Attendance per capita: —

STATUS OF WOMEN

Although the constitution provides for equality for women in the political, economic, and social spheres, women experience extensive societal discrimination, especially in rural areas where they occupy a subordinate role and are responsible for much of the hard labor on subsistence farms. In urban areas, women dominate the trading sector in the open-air markets. By law women have equal inheritance and property rights, but local custom in some areas prevents them from inheriting real property. Women do not enjoy the same educational opportunities as men, and female literacy is about 26 percent (compared with 49 percent for males). However, elementary school pass rates in recent years highlighted significant progress by girls in literacy and scholastic achievement. Violence and abuse of women are considered a family matter. Female genital mutilation is practiced in the northern provinces of the country.

Women

Gender Empowerment Measure: —
Seats Held in Parliament by Women %: 6
Female Administrators and Managers %: —
Female Professional and Technical Workers %: —
Women's Share of Earned Income %: —
Women in Government %: 10

HEALTH, FOOD, AND NUTRITION

Health

Number of Physicians: 363
Number of Dentists: 16
Number of Nurses: 1,236
Number of Pharmacists: 86
Population per Physician: 14,216
Number of Hospitals: —
Hospital Beds per 10,000: 2
Hospital Bed Occupancy Rate: —
Infant Mortality Rate per 1,000 live births: 158
Maternal Mortality Rate per 100,000 live births: 990
Total Health Expenditures as % of GDP: 4.32
Health Expenditures per capita $: 19
HIV Infected % of adults: 2.06
Cigarette Consumption per smoker per year: —
% of Smokers: Male: —
Female: —
Access to Safe Water %: 70

Food and Nutrition

Food Supply as % of FAO Requirements: 105
% of Consumption Expenditures on Food: 37
Daily Available Calories per capita: 2,405
% of Total Calories derived from:
Cereals: 35.1
Potatoes, cassava: 37.2
Meat, poultry: 2.3
Fish: 0.8
Eggs, milk: 0.9
Fruits, vegetables: 2.8
Fats, oils: 5.4

ENVIRONMENT

Benin's environmental problems are ones common to Africa. The country suffers from growing deforestation and desertification. Severe droughts in the north have further marginalized archaic agricultural activities. Finally, the country lacks adequate supplies of potable water.

Environment

Forest Area sq km: 46,000
Average Annual Deforestation sq km: 596
Nationally Protected Areas as % of Total Land Area: 7.1
Freshwater Access cubic meters per capita: 42,459
Emissions of Organic Water Pollutants kg per day: 1,646
CO_2 Emissions per capita ton: 0.1

CHRONOLOGY

1960 Republic of Dahomey is proclaimed, with Hubert C. Maga as president.
1963 Col. Christophe Soglo leads the first of the country's six coups; Maga is placed under house arrest.
1964 The constitution of the Second Republic is approved by referendum.
Following presidential and legislative elections, a two-headed executive emerges with Sourou-Migan Apithy as president and Justin Tometin Ahomadegbé as virtual copresident.
1965 The completed port of Cotonou is inaugurated. Soglo leads his second coup; Apithy and Ahomadegbé are dismissed, and the government is entrusted to Tairou Congacou, president of the National Assembly. Within a month Soglo leads his third coup, assumes full powers, and sets up his own administration.
1967 Soglo is toppled in a coup led by Maurice Kouandete, and an interim military administration is formed under the dual leadership of Kouandete and Colonel Alphonse Amadou Alley, who is the official president.
1968 A new constitution—the country's fourth—is approved by referendum; after 74 percent of eligible voters abstain, the election of President-elect Moumouni Adjou is annulled; the military appoints Emile Derlin Zinsou as president, and his appointment is confirmed in a plebiscite.
1969 Kouandete unseats Zinsou in a coup but is himself ousted in an interfactional struggle in the army; an

interim three-man military directorate is formed under the chairmanship of Paul Emile de Souza. A new provisional constitution is adopted.

A new presidential election is held but is later suspended; a presidential triumvirate is set up with Maga, Apithy, and Ahomadegbé as members, with rotating terms of office.

1970 Maga is inaugurated as first president of the presidential council. A new constitution is promulgated.

1972 Maga transfers power to Ahomadegbé. Within five months Major Mathieu Kérékou seizes power in the nation's sixth coup.

1973 A new decree decentralizes local administrative structures.

1974 Kérékou proclaims a Marxist-Leninist state and nationalizes banks and major industries.

1975 Dahomey is renamed the People's Republic of Benin and the Parti de la Révolution Populaire de Bénin (PRPB) is founded as the country's sole political party and as the supreme organ of state. Key junta officer, Major Michel Aikpe, is killed. The government is rocked by two serious coup attempts.

1977 Government troops reportedly foil a coup attempt by "mercenaries in the pay of international imperialism"; a curfew is imposed throughout the country, and borders and airports are closed.

The National Council of Revolution approves the Loi Fondamentale, which replaces the council with a National Revolutionary Assembly (ANR).

1978 Gabon expels Beninese workers.

1979 Single-party balloting is held for electing members of the National Revolutionary Assembly.

1982 Pope John Paul II visits Benin.

1983 Nigeria expels illegal Beninese immigrants.

1984 Kérékou is reelected to a new term in office.

1985 Nigeria expels further Beninese immigrants, souring relations between the two countries.

In April and May students boycott classes, followed by riots at the University of Benin. The government closes schools. A ministerial reshuffling follows. In November, 100 people are arrested, suspected of belonging to the banned Parti Communiste Dahoméen.

1986 Benin reschedules external debt in meetings with the IMF and World Bank.

1987 Kérékou resigns from the army to become a civilian leader of government.

1988 After an abortive military coup, nearly 150 officers are arrested.

1989 The ANR reelects Kérékou president. Public-sector workers strike to protest economic problems and austerity programs. Kérékou announces that Benin is abandoning its Marxist-Leninist ideology.

1990 The Loi Fondamentale is abolished, and a High Council of the Republic replaces the National Revolutionary Assembly. The PRPB is abolished and replaced with a new political organization, the Union des Forces de Progrès. The nation approves a new constitution.

1991 Nicephore Soglo defeats Kérékou in the first free presidential elections in nearly 30 years.

1996 Kérékou is elected president in the country's second free election.

1998 Civil servants seeking back pay and wage increases stage a four-day strike.

1999 The IMF extends an additional $14 million to Benin.

2001 Kérékou is reelected president.

BIBLIOGRAPHY

Allen, Chris. *Benin and the Congo*. New York, 1989.

Decalo, Samuel. *Historical Dictionary of Dahomey*. Metuchen, N.J., 1995.

OFFICIAL PUBLICATIONS

Benin. *Annuaire statistique; Recensement général de la population et de l'habitation* (1992).

CONTACT INFORMATION

Embassy of Benin
2737 Cathedral Avenue NW
Washington, D.C. 20008
Phone: (202) 232-6656 Fax: (202) 265-1996

INTERNET RESOURCES

- Découvrez la République du Bénin
  http://planben.intnet.bj/

BHUTAN

BASIC FACT SHEET

OFFICIAL NAME:
Kingdom of Bhutan (Druk-Yul)

ABBREVIATION:
BT

CAPITAL:
Thimphu (Tashi Chho Dzong)

HEAD OF STATE & HEAD OF GOVERNMENT:
King Jigme Singhye Wangchuk (from 1972) and Foreign Minister Jigme Yoeser Thinley (since June 1998)

NATURE OF GOVERNMENT:
Absolute monarchy

POPULATION:
658,000 (1999)

AREA:
46,620 sq km (18,000 sq mi)

ETHNIC MAJORITY:
Bhotias

LANGUAGE:
Dzongkha (official)

RELIGION:
Druk Kargue sect of Buddhism

UNIT OF CURRENCY:
Ngultrum; the Indian rupee is used in external transaction

NATIONAL FLAG:
Two triangles, one orange-yellow and the other maroon, divided diagonally with a white dragon superimposed in the center

NATIONAL EMBLEM:
The *khorlo,* or Buddhist Wheel of Law also symbolic of the monarchy, is flanked in a circular pattern by two dragons, at the sides, representing spiritual and secular authority; by the Jewel Umbrella at the top; and by a lotus flower at the bottom. Latticelike designs are at each corner of the square outer portion of the emblem.

NATIONAL ANTHEM:
"In the Thunder Dragon Kingdom"

NATIONAL HOLIDAYS:
December 17 (National Day); November 11 (the *druk gyalpo's* birthday); also variable Buddhist festivals

DATE OF INDEPENDENCE:
Never under direct foreign rule in modern times

DATE OF CONSTITUTION:
None

GEOGRAPHICAL FEATURES

Bhutan, a landlocked country in the Himalayas, has a total land area of 46,620 sq km (18,000 sq mi) extending 306 km (190 mi) east to west and 145 km (90 mi) north to south.

Bhutan's total international boundary of 1,019 km (633 mi) is shared with two countries: India (607 km; 377 mi) and China 412 km; 256 mi). The border with India was established by the British in the 18th and 19th centuries. The border with China, running along the crest of the main Himalayan range, has never been surveyed and has been the subject of repeated disputes since 1947.

Bhutan is entirely mountainous except for the southern Duars Plain, which extends into the Himalayan foothills in India. The country is almost equally divided in two by the Black Mountain Range, a spur of the Himalayas jutting southward. In the north is a series of north-to-south ranges, with four peaks over 6,100 m (20,000 ft). The loftiest of these peaks are Gangri (7,540 m; 24,740 ft) and Chomo Lhari (7,314 m; 23,997 ft).

Bhutan is drained by a series of parallel rivers flowing south through narrow valleys and gorges into the Brahmaputra River. From west to east these are the Amo, Raidak (with its tributaries the Paro, Wong, and Ha),

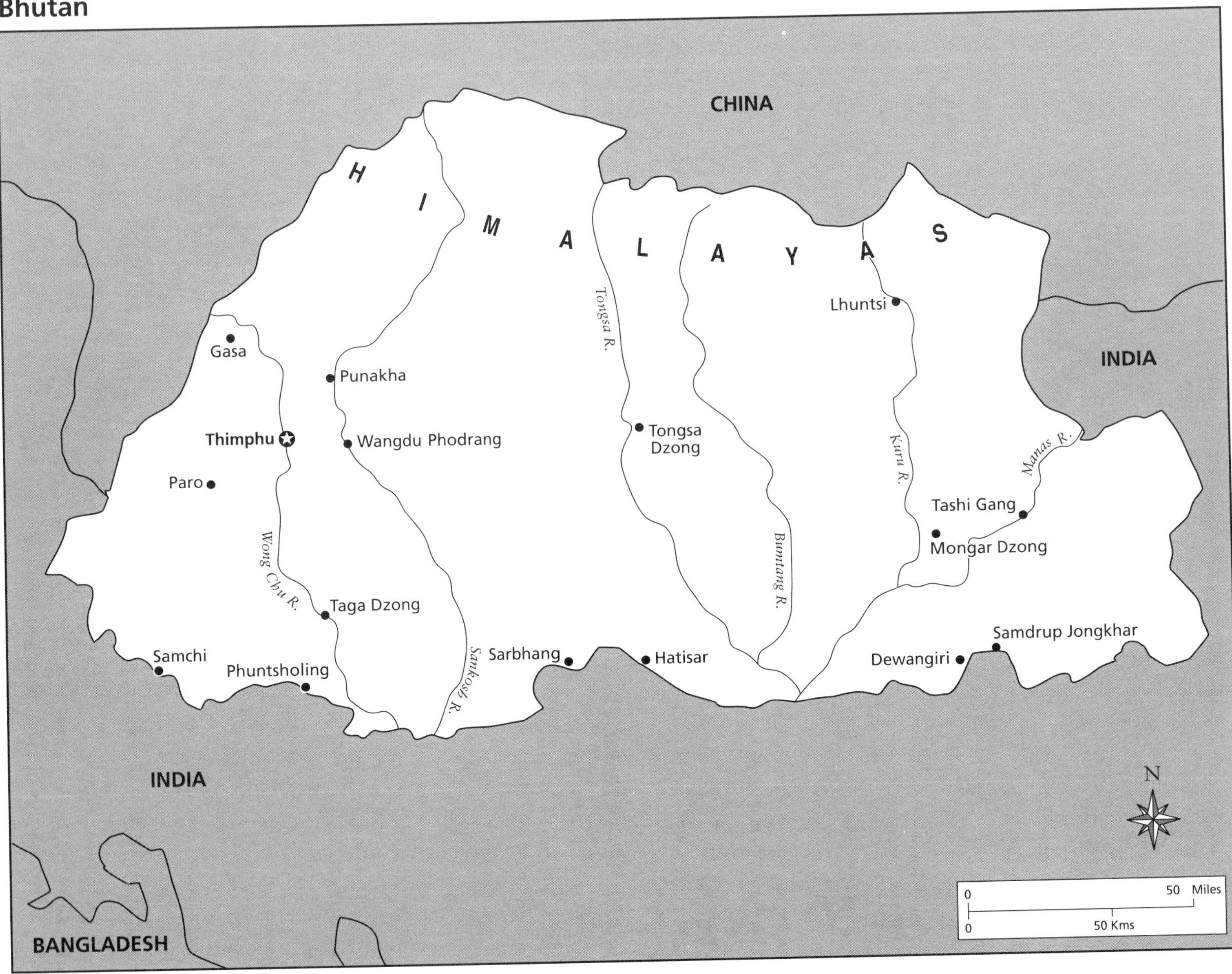
Bhutan
CHINA
H I M A L A Y A S
INDIA
Gasa
Punakha
Thimphu
Wangdu Phodrang
Paro
Tongsa R.
Tongsa Dzong
Lhuntsi
Kuru R.
Manas R.
Tashi Gang
Mongar Dzong
Bumtang R.
Wong Chu R.
Taga Dzong
Sankosh R.
Samchi
Phuntsholing
Sarbhang
Hatisar
Dewangiri
Samdrup Jongkhar
INDIA
BANGLADESH
N
0 50 Miles
0 50 Kms

Sankosh, Ai, Tongsa, Bumtang, Kuru, and Dangma. None of these rivers is navigable.

Geography

Area sq km: 46,620 sq mi 18,000
World Rank: 131st
Land Boundaries, km: China 470; India 605
Coastline, km 0
Elevation Extremes meters
Lowest: Dangme Chu 97
Highest: Khula Kangri 7,553
Land Use % Arable land: 2
Permanent Crops: 0
Permanent Pastures: 6
Forest and Woodland: 66
Other: 26

Population of Principal Cities (2000 est.)

Paro	4,300
Thimphu	53,600

CLIMATE AND WEATHER

Bhutan has three climatic zones. The Duars Plain in the outer foothills has a subtropical climate with high humidity and heavy rainfall, averaging 5,080 to 6,290 mm (200 to 250 in.) a year. The central belt of flat valleys has cool winters and hot summers with moderate rainfall. The uplands and high valleys over 3,650 m (12,000 ft) have cold winters and cool summers with an annual average rainfall of 1,020 to 1,520 mm (40 to 60 in). Over 5,000 m (15,000 ft), the land is permanently covered with snow and glaciers. A major feature of the climate is the frequency of violent thunderstorms, from which Bhutan gets its name. (In the Dzongkha language Bhutan means "Land of the Thunder Dragon.") Temperatures vary widely because of the enormous range of elevation; no specific temperature information is available.

Climate and Weather

Mean Temperature 40°F to 50°F
Average Rainfall Duars Plain 200 in to 250 in
High Valleys 40 to 60 in

POPULATION

Population Indicators

Total Population: 1999 658,000
World Rank: 100th
Density per sq mi: 36.3 per sq km 14.0
% of annual growth (1994–99): 3.0
Male %: 50.6
Female %: 49.0
Urban %: 5.3
Age Distribution: % 0–14: 40.6
15–29: 26.5
30–44: 17.1
45–59: 10.4
60–74: 4.6
75 and over: 0.8
Population 2020: 1,031,000
Birth Rate per 1,000: 41.3
Death Rate per 1,000: 13.9
Population Doubling Time (years): 31
Infant Mortality Rate per 1,000 live births: 105.0
Rate of Natural Increase per 1,000: 27.4
Total Fertility Rate: 5.9
Expectation of Life (years): Males 51.0
Females 53.0
Marriage Rate per 1,000: —
Divorce Rate per 1,000: —
Total Number of Households: —
Average Size of Households: 5.4
% of Illegitimate Children: —
Induced Abortions: —
Rate per 100 live births: —

ETHNIC COMPOSITION

The largest homogeneous ethnic group in Bhutan are the Bhotias (known in the Dzongkha language as Sharchops), who constitute 54 percent of the population and who are concentrated in the eastern regions. Direct descendants of Tibetan immigrants live west of the Sankosh River and make up about 32 percent of the population. The largest ethnic minority is the Nepali community, made up largely of the Rai, Gurung, and Limbu castes. They have resisted assimilation and have maintained their own settlements. They are prohibited from moving into the northern regions, where the Bhotias predominate. Smaller ethnic groups include Lepcha immigrants from Sikkim and Santals and Paharias from India.

LANGUAGES

The official language is Dzongkha (also spelled Denjongke), whose written form is identical to Tibetan. Three other languages are spoken in the country: Bumthangka in the central region, Sarachapkha in the eastern region, and Nepalese in the southern region.

Indian influence is reflected in the use of Hindi and Bengali near the southern border. English is taught in schools, and many educated Bhutanese are fluent in Hindi and English as well as in their native dialect.

Principal Languages and Their Speakers

Assamese	100,000
Dzongkha (Bhua)	330,000
Nepaii (Hindi)	230,000

RELIGIONS

The official religion is a Tibetan form of Buddhism of the Mahayana branch, known as Lamaism, which is followed by the dominant Bhotias. The monks and clerics belong to the Druk Kargue branch of the Kagyutpa, one of the "red hat" orders of Tibetan Buddhism. Monasteries are numerous, and the number of monks is estimated at 4,000 to 5,000. By custom each family devotes at least one offspring to a monastery.

Though the monarch—the druk gyalpo (dragon king)—is the secular as well as spiritual head of Bhutan, the head of the monastic order—the jey khampo—is a dominant force in national life and is a member of the Royal Advisory Council. Monks in the lower echelons also serve as the social, cultural, and religious leaders in their respective dzongs as well as functioning as physicians and astrologers.

The Nepali minority follows a form of Hinduism with Buddhist overtones.

Religious Affiliations

Lamaistic Buddhist	490,000
Hindu	160,000

HISTORICAL BACKGROUND

Little is known of the history of Bhutan before the modern era. The Bhotes probably came from Tibet in the 9th century when the Tibetans overran the area that was inhabited by the native Tephu tribe. Bhutan first appears in history when the British repelled a Bhutanese invasion of the Indian princely state of Cooch Behar and later concluded a peace treaty with Bhutan. But the Bhutanese continued their inroads into the Duars, the low-lying areas of north Assam and Bengal. In 1866 the British finally defeated the Bhutanese and forced them to withdraw in return for an annual payment. In 1907 the Bhutanese leader Ugyen Dorji was installed as king, with British blessings. Under the Punakha Treaty of 1910 the United Kingdom agreed not to interfere in Bhutanese affairs but took over the management of Bhutan's external relations. When India became independent in 1949 the treaty was replaced by the Indo-Bhutan Treaty of Friendship. King Jigme Dorji Wangchuk, installed in 1952, established the National Assembly in 1953 and a Royal Advisory Council in 1965. He died in 1972 and was succeeded by the Western-educated 16-year-old crown prince Jigme Singye Wangchuk. During the last 40 years, Bhutan has had to deal with illegal emigration from Tibet on the one hand and from Bhutan on the other. A Citizenship Act was passed in 1985 that set stringent conditions for citizenship, including linguistic and other tests of commitment to the Bhutanese community. Illegal Nepali immigrants have tried to organize themselves into a political party to wrest civil rights and legal citizenship. Violence continued in southern Bhutan during the 1990s leading to strained relations with Nepal. Bhutan's plans for modernization of its institutions are supported and financially underwritten by India.

CONSTITUTION

Though Bhutan has no constitution and is an absolute monarchy—the king is both head of state and head of government—the nation has taken some hesitant steps toward constitutionalism by introducing certain features of representative government. These include the Tsongdu, or National Assembly, created in 1953; the Royal Advisory Council, created in 1965; and the Council of Ministers, or cabinet, formed in 1968. At the same time the monarch voluntarily surrendered some of his traditional powers to strengthen the Tsongdu. Specifically, the right to veto by the king was removed, full freedom of parliamentary speech was guaranteed, and the king was required to seek a vote of confidence of the Tsongdu every three years. In the event of a vote of no confidence by a two-thirds majority, the king is to abdicate, but the crown is to remain in the Wangchuk dynasty in order of succession. The Tsongdu subsequently abrogated the right to remove the monarch and then reinstated the right in 1998. The impact of these measures, however, has been minimal.

The most powerful organ of government after the druk gyalpo is the Royal Advisory Council, whose eight members are appointed by the king. Five of its members represent the people, two the Buddhist hierarchy, and one is the personal representative of the king. The council only submits recommendations to the king, who either accepts or rejects them as he sees fit. Next in authority is the five-member Council of Ministers selected, in principle, from the Tsongdu.

Popular elections are held at the village level every three years. Each family is granted one vote.

The Wangchuk dynasty seems to be confronted with no serious or visible opposition. Almost all the changes initiated during the past 30 years have come from the monarch himself. The intention behind these reforms has been to create a semblance of popular participation in the political process without actually diluting royal power. Feudal and theocratic forces remain in control of the country, and a possible internal threat to the monarchy would likely arise only from conservative forces who may feel that the pace of modernization is too fast. The nearest Bhutan came to a political crisis in recent times was in 1964, when Prime Minister Jigme Polden Dorji was assassinated and his successor and younger brother Prime Minister Lhendup Dorji was involved in a power struggle with the king and was forced to flee to Nepal. Although there has been occasional Chinese-inspired guerrilla activity, it is not a serious problem.

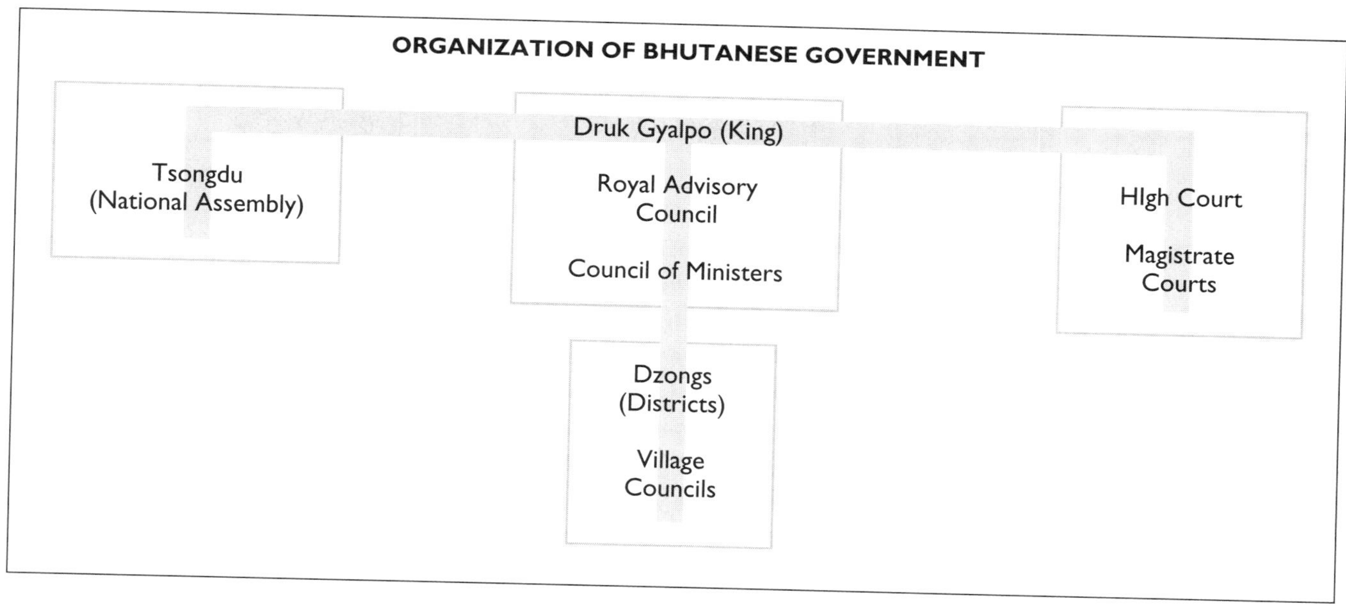

LOCAL GOVERNMENT

For purposes of local administration Bhutan is divided into 20 districts known as *dzongs*, each headed by a *dzongda* (in charge of administration and law and order) and a commissioner known as a *trimpong* (in charge of judicial matters). The trimpongs are assisted by tax collectors known as *nyer-chens*.

Each village has a council consisting of one member from each family. The council elects a village headman, who also dispenses justice. Elections are held at the village level at three-year intervals.

Local Government

Principal administrative divisions, capitals, area, population

Area and population

Districts	Capitals	area sq mi	area sq km	population 1998 estimate
Bumthang	Jakar	1,150	2,990	—
Chhukha	Chhukha	—	—	—
Chirang	Damphu	310	800	—
Dagana	Dagana	540	1,400	—
Gaylegphug	Gaylegphug	1,020	2,640	—
Ha	Ha	830	2,140	—
Lhuntshi	Lhuntshi	1,120	2,910	—
Mongar	Mongar	710	1,830	—
Paro	Paro	580	1,500	—
Pema Gatsei	Pema Getsei	150	380	—
Punakha	Punakha	2,330	6,040	—
Samchi	Samchi	830	2,140	—
Samdrup Jongkhar	Samdrup Jongkhar	900	2,340	—
Shemgang	Shemgang	980	2,540	—
Tashigang	Tashigang	1,640	4,260	—
Thimphu	Thimphu	630	1,620	—
Tongsa	Tongsa	570	1,470	—
Wangdi Phodrang	Wangdi Phodrang	18,140	47,000	633,000

PARLIAMENT

The national assembly, known as the Tsongdu, established in 1953, seats members on the basis of a three-year term and meets twice yearly, in spring and autumn, for sessions that last no more than two weeks each. The strength of the Tsongdu is 150 members, of whom 105 are indirectly elected by village headmen; 10 represent the Buddhist clergy and monks; and the remaining seats are occupied by officials, ministers, deputy ministers, and judicial officers. The Tsongdu enjoys broad powers, comparable in theory to those of the best representative institutions abroad. It debates freely all important issues and advises the king on political and constitutional matters. Both the Royal Advisory Council and the Council of Ministers are responsible to it. Bills passed by the Tsongdu may not be vetoed by the king. The Tsongdu also has the right to force the abdication of the king through a no-confidence motion. But because most of its members are illiterate, the Tsongdu remains an otiose and ineffective organ.

POLITICAL PARTIES

Political parties are banned in Bhutan. However, there are a number of antigovernment organizations that are based in Nepal.

LEGAL SYSTEM

Bhutan's court systems dates from 1968, when the king established the first High Court (Thimkhang Gongma). At the same time judges were appointed for each of the country's administrative districts. The High Court was empowered to review the decisions of the king.

Below the High Court local headmen and magistrates hear cases in the first instance. At this level, justice is dispensed according to customary and religious laws.

No information is available on correctional facilities.

LAW ENFORCEMENT

Law Enforcement

Offenses reported to the police per 100,000: —
- Murder: —
- Assault: —
- Burglary: —
- Automobile Theft: —
- Population per Police officer: —

Death Penalty: Yes; Last execution in 1964

HUMAN RIGHTS

Although information is not readily available on political conditions in the nation, Bhutanese society has a reputation for nonviolence and tolerance. However, civil and political liberties have no constitutional basis, and the role of the state is that of a benign patriarch. The basic freedoms have not been guaranteed on paper but are enjoyed in practice.

FOREIGN POLICY

Although bound by treaty with India, Bhutan has established direct relations with China, India's archenemy. It has negotiated with the People's Republic of China over the Bhutan-China border. The ninth round of these border talks were held in 1993. Demarcation of the southern border has been agreed with India. Bhutan became a member of the United Nations in 1971 and has diplomatic relations with 19 nations and with the European Union. It is a founder-member of the South Asian Regional Cooperation (SARC) organization.

DEFENSE

The defense structure is headed by the druk gyalpo, who also is the commander in chief. Military manpower is provided by conscription.

The strength of the armed forces is estimated at 4,000, or 0.003 percent of the population. No information is available on annual military expenditures.

The capability of the army is limited to internal security missions, manning of border posts, and suppression of any opposition movements or guerrilla activities inspired by Chinese Communists. Bhutanese soldiers are noted for their stamina and fighting qualities, which partially offset their weakness in equipment and supplies.

Though the defense of Bhutan is the responsibility of the Indian army, there is no agreement to station Indian troops in Bhutanese territory. India provides military training to Bhutanese officers and men.

Military Indicators

Total Active Duty Personnel: 4,000
Military Manpower per 1,000: 3.1
Military Expenditures $: —
- as % of GNP: —
- per capita $: —
- as % of central government expenditures: —

Arms Imports $:
Arms Exports $:

ECONOMY

Bhutan is one of the low-income countries of the world and also is one of the least-developed countries of the world. Because the economy is incompletely monetized, few statistical indicators can be constructed from existing data.

Bhutan has a free-market economy in which the dominant sector is private. The economy is based on agriculture and forestry, which employ 90 percent of the population and account for about 51 percent of the gross domestic product.

Balance of payments statistics are limited to imports and exports. Trade deficits are made up through credits from the Indian government.

Principal Economic Indicators

Gross National Product: $315 million
GNP per capita: $430
GNP Average Annual Growth Rate (1990–97) %: 2.0
GNP per capita Average Annual Growth Rate (1990–97) %: −0.9
Origin of Gross Domestic Product %
- Agriculture: 38
- Mining: 1
- Manufacturing: 10
- Construction: 12
- Public Utilities: 7
- Transportation and Communications: 7
- Trade: 8
- Financial Services: 6
- Other Services: 9
- Government: 9

Gross Domestic Product by Type of Expenditure %
- Private Consumption: 53
- Government Consumption: 18
- Gross Domestic Investment: 45
- Foreign Trade: Exports: 31
  - Imports: −47

% of Income Received by Poorest 20%: —
% of Income Received by Richest 10%: —

Price and earnings indexes (1995 = 100)

	1990	1991	1992	1993	1994	1995	1996
Consumer price index	59.0	66.1	76.8	85.40	91.3	100.0	108.8
Earnings index	—	—	—	—	—	—	—

Finance

National Currency: Ngultran (Nu)
Exchange Rate: $1 = Nu 39.358
Money Supply Stock in National Currency billion: 2,074
M1 per capita: 2,440
Central Bank Discount Rate %: 8
Total External Debt $million: 129
Debt Service Ratio %: 5.0
Balance of Payments $million: −46.5
International Reserves SDRs million: 119
Ratio of External Debt to Total Reserves: 0.7
Average Annual Rate of Inflation/Consumer Price Index Growth Rate %: 7

Official Development Assistance

ODA $62 million
- as % of GNP: 23.5
- per capita: $ 89
- Foreign Direct Investment $million: —

Central Government Revenues and Expenditures

Fiscal Year: 1 July–30 June

Revenues $million: 146
Expenditures $million: 94
Budget Surplus $: 52 million
Tax Revenues as % of GDP: 6
Highest Tax Bracket %
- Individual: —
- Corporate: —

Employment and Labor

Economically Active Population: —
Female Participation Rate %: —
Activity Rate %: —
Labor by Sector: %
- Agriculture, Forestry, Fishing: 93%
- Manufacturing, Mining: —
- Construction: —
- Transportation and Communications: —
- Trade, Hotels, and Restaurants: —
- Finance, Insurance, Real Estate: —
- Public Administration, Defense: —
- Services: 5%

Unemployment %: NA

Agriculture

Agriculture's Share of GDP %: 38
Average Annual Rate of Growth (1965–98) %: —
Number of Farms 000: 160
Average Size of Farm ha: 0.8
Number of Tractors per 1,000 hectares: 2.5
Irrigation, % of Farms having: 5
Artificial Fertilizer kg/hectare: 3
Total Farm land as % of land area: 20.6
Livestock: Cattle 000: 435
- Sheep 000: 59
- Hogs 000: 75
- Chickens 000: 310

Forests: Production of Roundwood (000 cubic meters): 1,399
Fisheries: Total Catch tons 000: 0.3

Mining

% of GDP: 1.9
Value of Mineral Production $million: 60

Manufacturing

Value Added $million: 21
Industrial Production Growth Rate %: 7.6

Energy

Commercial Energy Production metric tons of oil equivalent 000: —
Commercial Energy Consumption metric tons of oil equivalent 000: 22
Commercial Energy Consumption per capita kg: 33
Average Annual Growth Rate 1980–97 %: —
Net Energy Imports % of use: 95
Electricity Installed Capacity kW 000: 366
- Production kW-hr million: 1,717

Coal Reserves tons million: —
- Production tons 000: 2

Natural Gas Proven Reserves cubic meters billion: —
- Production cubic meters million: —

Crude Petroleum Reserves barrels million: —
- Production barrels million: —
- Consumption barrels million: —
- Refinery Capacity barrels per day 000: —

Pipelines Length km: —

Foreign Trade

Imports $million: 128.0
Exports $million: 67.1
Export Volume % Annual Growth Rate (1990–97): —
Import Volume % Annual Growth Rate (1990–97): —
Balance of Trade $

Balance of trade (current prices)

	1989–90	1990–91	1991–92	1992–93	1993–94	1994–95
Nu 000,000	−48.6	−583.5	−687.9	−1,633.6	−966.2	−1,337.4
% of Total	17.5%	18.3%	17.4%	30.8%	18.7%	23.1%

Major Trading Partners

	Imports	Exports
European Union %	25.5	0.1
United States %	0.8	—
Eastern Europe %	—	—
Japan %	10.8	—
Others %	62.9	99.9

Transportation

Roads Total Length mi: 1,998 km 3,216
Paved %: 79
Automobiles: 2,590
Trucks and Buses: 1,367
Persons per vehicle: 348
Railroad; Track Length mi: —
Passenger-mi million: —
Freight-mi million: —
Merchant Marine: No. of Vessels: —
  Total Deadweight Tonnage 000: —
  International Cargo Loaded tons 000: —
  International Cargo Off-loaded tons 000: —
Airports with Scheduled Flights: 1
Traffic: Passenger-mi million: 29
  Freight-mi million: —
Length of Canals mi: —

Tourism

Number of Tourists to 000: —
Number of Tourists from 000: —
Tourist Receipts $million: 5
Tourist Expenditures $million: —

Communications

Telephones 000: 5.2
Cost of Local Calls 3 mins: $0
Cellular Telephones 000: —
Fax Machines 000: 0.3
Personal Computers 000: —
Internet Hosts per million persons: —
Mail: Post Offices: 103
  Pieces of Mail Handled million: 1.9
  Pieces of Mail Handled per person: 1.2

EDUCATION

Though education is neither universal nor compulsory, it is free for the first 10 years. Of the 10 years of schooling, primary school lasts for five years, lower secondary school for three years, and upper secondary school for two years. There are no mission or private schools, and all schools are subsidized by the government. A few schools are co-educational and are run on the lines of American private schools but using a British syllabus. The kingdom's only postsecondary institution is named the Junior College, as there is no university in Bhutan. Two vocational institutes exist as teacher training schools. These are the Kharbandi Technical School and the Royal Bhutan Polytechnic.

The academic year is the calendar year. The medium of instruction is Dzongkha, but English is taught in selected schools.

Education

Literacy Rate %: 42.2
  Male %: 56.2
  Female %: 28.1
First Level: Primary schools: 235
  Teachers: 1,859
  Students: 56,773
  Student-Teacher Ratio: 30.5
  Net Enrollment Ratio: —
Second Level: Secondary Schools: 31
  Teachers: 662
  Students: 15,984
  Student-Teacher Ratio: 24.1
  Net Enrollment Ratio: —

Vocational Level: Schools: 8
  Students: 1,822

Third Level: Institutions: 2
  Teachers: 57
  Students: 519
  Student-Ratio Level: 9.1
  Gross Enrollment Ratio: —
  Students per 100,000: —
  % of Population Age 25 and over with Postsecondary Education: —

Public Expenditure on Education as % of GDP: 2.7

SCIENCE AND TECHNOLOGY

Science and Technology

Scientists and Engineers in R&D per 1 million persons: —
Expenditures in R&D as % of GDP: —
High-Tech Exports $: —
Patent Applications by Residents: —

MEDIA

The only newspaper in the country is the weekly *Kuensel*, published by the government in English, Dzongkha, and Nepalese and with a total circulation at about 12,500 copies.

Bhutan has no national news agency. There are no foreign news bureaus in the capital.

Bhutan has 52 radio stations. The Bhutan Broadcasting Service airs programs in English, Sharchopkha, Dzongkha, and Nepali on a daily basis. There is no local television.

Bhutan has no public library, but most monasteries have collections of Buddhist manuscripts.

Media

Daily Newspapers: 1
Total Circulation 12,500
Circulation per 1,000:
Books Published: —
Magazines: —
Radio Receivers 000: 34
per 1,000: 34
Television sets 000: —
per 1,000: —

MOST IMPORTANT MEDIA:

Press. The country's only newspaper, *Kuensel* (Thimphu, 10,000), was founded in 1967 as a bimonthly government bulletin but is now an independent weekly published in English, Dzongkha, and Nepali.

Radio and television. The Bhutan Broadcasting Service (BBS), now operated by an autonomous corporation, transmits in Dzongkha, Sarachapkha, Nepali, and English to approximately 34,000 receivers; there is no domestic television service.

CULTURE

Cultural Indicators

Public Libraries
Number: —
Volumes: —
Registered borrowers: —
Museums
Number: —
Annual Attendance: —
Cinema
Production of Long Films: —
Number of Cinemas: —
Seating Capacity: —
Annual Attendance: —
Annual Attendance per capita: —

STATUS OF WOMEN

Although officially the government has encouraged greater participation of women in political and administrative life, male members of the traditional aristocracy dominate the social system. By 1989 nearly 5 percent of government employees were women. Reflecting the dominance of males in society, girls were outnumbered three to two in primary and secondary-level schools. The government founded the National Women's Association of Bhutan in 1981 primarily to improve the socioeconomic status of women, particularly those in rural areas. Starting in 1985, the association became a line item in the government budget.

Women

Gender Empowerment Measure: —
Seats Held in Parliament by Women %: —
Female Administrators and Managers %: —
Female Professional and Technical Workers %: —
Women's Share of Earned Income %: —
Women in Government %: 5

HEALTH, FOOD, AND NUTRITION

Health

Number of Physicians: 100
Number of Dentists: 9
Number of Nurses: 233
Number of Pharmacists: 5
Population per Physician: 8,000
Number of Hospitals: 27
Hospital Beds per 10,000: 12
Hospital Bed Occupancy Rate: —
Infant Mortality Rate per 1,000 live births: 145
Maternal Mortality Rate per 100,000 live births: 1,600
Total Health Expenditures as % of GDP: 5.05
Health Expenditures per capita $: 10
HIV Infected % of adults:
Cigarette Consumption per smoker per year:
% of Smokers: Male: —
Female: —
Access to Safe Water %: 21

Food and Nutrition

Food Supply as % of FAO Requirements: —
% of Consumption Expenditures on Food: 72.3
Daily Available Calories per capita: —
% of Total Calories Derived From:
Cereals: —
Potatoes, cassava: —
Meat, poultry: —
Fish: —
Eggs, milk: —
Fruits, vegetables: —
Fats, oils: —

ENVIRONMENT

Like those of most other developing nations, Bhutan's fertile valleys suffer from continuing soil erosion as antiquated agricultural techniques are employed. Another environmental concern is the country's limited amount of potable water.

Environment

Forest Area sq km: —
Average Annual Deforestation sq km: —
Nationally Protected Areas as % of Total Land Area: —
Freshwater Access cubic meters per capita: 13
Emissions of Organic Water Pollutants kg per day: —
CO_2 Emissions per capita ton: 0.1

CHRONOLOGY

1949 India and Bhutan sign Treaty of Perpetual Peace and Friendship.
1952 Maharaja Jigme Dorji Wangchuk ascends to the throne.
1958 The maharaja abolishes slavery.
1961 Bhutan's first five-year plan is launched.

1962 Bhutan joins the Colombo Plan.
1963 The ruler of Bhutan adopts the title of *druk gyalpo*.
1964 Prime Minister Jigme Polden Dorji is assassinated; Brigadier Bahadur Namgyal, deputy commander in chief, is implicated and arrested along with 40 other members of the military. Namgyal is executed.
Lhendup Dorji is named prime minister but becomes involved in a power struggle with the *druk gyalpo* and flees to Nepal with the army commander, Brigadier Ugyen Tyangbi.
The *druk gyalpo* names himself prime minister.
1965 The Royal Advisory Council is established along with the Council of Ministers in an effort to broaden the political decision-making process.
1968 Bhutan's first High Court is established.
In a major governmental reform, the druk gyalpo renounces his royal prerogative to veto bills passed by the Tsongdu and also declares that he would step down if two-thirds of its members demanded his abdication through a vote of no confidence.
The Bank of Bhutan is established.
1969 Bhutan holds its first census.
1971 Bhutan is admitted to the United Nations.
1972 Druk Gyalpo Jigme Dorji Wangchuk dies; his son, 17-year-old Jigme Singhye Wangchuk, ascends the throne.
1974 The ngultrum is introduced as the national currency.
Jigme Singhye Wangchuk is crowned king.
1979 Following the breakdown of talks with the dalai lama, the Tsongdu passes a directive requiring Tibetan settlers to become citizens or face repatriation to Tibet.
1983 Bhutan becomes a founding member of the South Asian Regional Cooperation (SARC) along with Bangladesh, India, Maldives, Nepal, Pakistan, and Sri Lanka.
1985 Bhutan hosts the first meeting of ministers of foreign affairs from SARC member countries; SARC is renamed the South Asian Association for Regional Cooperation (SAARC).
1989 King Wangchuk issues the "Driglam Manzha," an edict that lays down strict rules pertaining to dress and social codes.
1990 Alarmed by restoration of democracy in Nepal, King Wangchuk bans viewing of foreign television and orders strict enforcement of the Driglam Manzha, subjecting violators to fines and imprisonment; demonstrations are held.
1991–93 Thousand of illegal immigrants, mostly Nepali-speaking Hindus, are expelled.
1997 Nearly 80,000 Bhutanese refugees in United Nations camps in Nepal claim they were forced out of their homeland.
1998 King Wangchuk agrees to some constitutional governmental reforms including the election of a cabinet.
1999 Bhutan releases 200 prisoners that human rights groups had identified as political detainees.

BIBLIOGRAPHY

Aris, Michael. *Bhutan: The Early History of a Himalayan Kingdom*. Portland, Ore., 1980.

Das, B. N. *Mission to Bhutan: A Nation in Transition*. New Delhi, 1995.

Deb, Arabinda. *India and Bhutan: Study in Frontier Political Relations*. Columbia, Mo., 1976.

Edmunds, Tom Owen. *Bhutan: Land of the Thunder Dragon*. London, 1988.

Gibbons, Robert and Bob Ashford. *Himalayan Kingdoms: Nepal, Sikkim and Bhutan*. New York, 1983.

Sauada, A. M., ed. *Nepal and Bhutan: Country Studies*. Washington, D.C., 1993.

White, J. *Sikkim and Bhutan*. Highland Park, N.J., 1984.

OFFICIAL PUBLICATIONS

Bhutan. *Bhutan—Selected Issues* (IMF Staff Country Report [1997]); *Statistical Yearbook of Bhutan.*

CONTACT INFORMATION

Consulate General of Bhutan
2 United Nations Plaza, 27th Floor New York, NY 10017
Phone: (212) 826-1919 Fax: (212) 826-2998

INTERNET RESOURCES

- The Library of Congress Country Studies: Bhutan http://lcweb2.loc.gov/frd/cs/bttoc.html
- National Institute of Statistics http://www.ine.es/

BOLIVIA

BASIC FACT SHEET

OFFICIAL NAME:
Republic of Bolivia (República Boliviana)

ABBREVIATION:
BO

CAPITAL:
Sucre (de jure); La Paz (administrative and de facto)

HEAD OF STATE AND GOVERNMENT:
President Jorge Quiroga Ramírez (from 2001)

NATURE OF GOVERNMENT:
Parliamentary democracy

POPULATION:
8,137,000 (1999)

AREA:
1,098,579 sq km (424,162 sq mi)

ETHNIC MAJORITY:
Indian

LANGUAGES:
Spanish, Aymara, Quechua

RELIGION:
Roman Catholicism

UNIT OF CURRENCY:
Boliviano (B.)

NATIONAL FLAG:
Tricolor of horizontal red, gold and green stripes with the national emblem at the center.

NATIONAL EMBLEM:
A condor of the Andes, with wings outstretched, perches on a blue and gold oval shield flanked by branches of olive and laurel. In the upper rim of the shield is the word Bolivia and in the lower rim nine stars appear. The upper half of the inner shield shows Mount Potosí illuminated by a rising sun. In the foreground are a breadfruit tree, a sheaf of corn, a farm house, and an alpaca. In the background of the emblem are an array of crossed cannon, bayonet-armed rifles, an Inca war axe, red cap and pike, and six national flags, three on either side.

NATIONAL ANTHEM:
"O Bolivia, Now a Kindly Fate Has Crowned Our Long-felt Hopes"

NATIONAL HOLIDAYS:
August 6 (Independence Day, National Day); August 5 to 7 (National Festival); January 1 (New Year's Day); May 1 (Labor Day); July 21 (Martyrs' Day); October 12 (Discovery of Americas Day); Christian festivals include All Saints' Day, All Souls' Day, Christmas, Good Friday, Holy Saturday, and Corpus Christi.

DATE OF INDEPENDENCE:
August 5, 1865

DATE OF CONSTITUTION:
February 2, 1967

GEOGRAPHICAL FEATURES

Bolivia is located in the heart of South America. It is the fifth-largest country in the continent with an area of 1,098,579 sq km (424,162 sq mi) extending 1,529 km (950 mi) north to south and 1,448 km (900 mi) east to west. Because of its landlocked position, it is sometimes described as the "Tibet of South America."

Bolivia shares its total international land border of 6,532 km (4,059 mi) with five countries: Brazil (2,400 km; 1,490 mi); Paraguay (756 km; 470 mi); Argentina (832 km; 517 mi); Chile (861 km; 535 mi); and Peru (900 km; 559 mi). Bolivia has served throughout its history as a buffer state amid these five neighbors but in the process has lost more than half of the national territory it originally claimed to all neighbors except Argentina.

Bolivia is divided into three topographical regions by most geographers and into four regions by others. The three commonly cited regions are the high plateau region known as the altiplano; an intermediary region comprising semitropical rain forests on the eastern slopes, or yungas, of the Andean mountain system; and the drier valleys

Bolivia

While the constitution has established Sucre as the legal capital and the seat of the judiciary, La Paz is the de facto capital.

and the llanos, or the Amazon-Chaco lowlands. The intermediate region south of Cochabamba is sometimes identified as a separate region under the name of Valles.

The altiplano, which crosses the country in a northwest to southeast direction, parallels and splits the Andes into two mountain chains, or cordilleras, straddling the country on its eastern and western sides. The western mountain chain, the Cordillera Occidental, forms the border with Chile and has crests and peaks that often rise to 4,900 m (16,000 ft), the highest peak being Sajama (6,519 m; 21,388 ft). On the other flank of the altiplano is the even higher Cordillera Real, or Cordillera Oriental, an impressive array of peaks with an average elevation of over 5,500 m (18,000 ft). The most majestic of these mountains are those around Lake Titicaca, especially Illimani and Illampu, both of which rise to over 6,400 m (21,000 ft) overlooking the city of La Paz. The altiplano itself is 800 km (500 mi) long and 130 km (80 mi) wide, with an average altitude of 3,650 m (11,975 ft) above sea level. This region cradles the famed Lake Titicaca, 222 km (138 mi) long and 113 km (70 mi) wide with a surface elevation of 3,657 m (12,000 ft), making it the highest navigable lake in the world. It is also South America's largest lake.

The second region, the yungas (meaning "warm lands" in Aymara), is made up of sharply tilted mountain valleys with an altitude of between 490 m (1,608 ft) and 2,750 m (9,022 ft). The yungas consists of three zones, of which the highest, called ceja (eyebrow) is similar to the altiplano, whereas the intermediate zone consists of fertile river valleys. The valleys and basins of the Valles region, which is often treated as part of the yungas, are broader and more densely populated.

The lowland plain, or llano, region consists of tropical rain forests and the Plains of Moxos with alternating savannas and cultivated areas. Because the drainage is poor, much of this region is converted periodically to swamp. Farther south, the llano merges with the La Plata River basin, constituting a northward extension of the Pampas of Argentina.

The altiplano is an inland drainage basin drained by the Desaguadero River, which flows into Lake Poopó. The yungas and the Valles regions are drained by the Pilcomayo River, which flows south to join the Paraguay, and the Chaparé, Ichilo, and Río Grande, which join to form the Mamoré, a tributary of the Amazon. The Guaporé, Beni, and Madre de Dios rivers also converge in the northeast to form the Madeira in Brazil.

CLIMATE AND WEATHER

Bolivia is entirely within the tropics, but extreme differences in elevation produce a variety of climatic conditions. In general, temperatures and rainfall increase from west to east. During most of the year, the altiplano is parched and inhospitable. The valleys of the Cordillera Oriental have a warmer, semiarid Mediterranean climate. The yungas have a semitropical and moist climate, and the lowlands become drier to the south near the Argentina border. The mean annual temperature at La Paz is about 8°C (47°F); at Trinidad in the eastern lowlands, it is 26°C (79°F). In the altiplano, the nights are cold even in summer, and freezing temperatures are recorded during most winter nights. The thinness of the air in the altiplano and the intense sunlight combine to produce a kind of luminosity in the atmosphere that has a stimulating visual quality.

The rainy season lasts from December to February, but the amount of rainfall varies seasonally as well as annually. Rainfall is heaviest in the Cordillera Oriental and lightest in the altiplano; it also tends to decrease from north to south. Lake Titicaca receives around 1,010 mm (40 in), the yungas 1,520 mm (60 in), the Valles 760 mm (30 in), the Santa Cruz Plains 1,020 mm to 1,520 mm (40 in to 60 in), and the Chaco 890 mm to 1,020 mm (35 in to 40 in). Because of seasonal variations, both floods and droughts are common. The Chaco particularly becomes a swamp during the rainy season and a parched desert during the summer.

The rain-bearing winds are easterlies from the Amazon basin. Dust-laden winds called the surazos blow from Paraguay across the Santa Cruz plains.

Geography

Area sq km: 1,098,579 sq mi 424,162
World Rank: 28th
Land Boundaries, km: Argentina 832; Brazil 2,400; Chile 861; Paraguay 750; Peru 900
Coastline, km: 0
Elevation Extremes meters
- Lowest: Río Paraguay 90
- Highest: Cerro Illimani 6,882

Land Use % Arable land: 2
- Permanent Crops: 0
- Permanent Pastures: 24
- Forest and Woodland: 53
- Other: 21

Population of Principal Cities (2001 est.)

City	Population
Cochabamba	1,475,400
El Alto	695,200
La Paz (administrative capital)	792,600
Oruro	392,400
Potosí	708,800
Santa Cruz	2,033,700
Sucre (judicial capital)	194,900

Climate and Weather

Mean Temperature
La Paz 47°F
Trinidad 79°F
Average Rainfall:
Lake Titicaca 40 in
Yungas 60 in
Valles 30 in
Santa Cruz Plains 40 in to 60 in
Chaco 35 in to 40 in

POPULATION

Population Indicators

Total Population: 1999 8,137,000
World Rank: 85th
Density per sq mi: 19.2 per sq km 7.4
% of annual growth (1994–99): 2.4
Male %: 49.4
Female %: 50.6
Urban %: 57.5

(continued)

Age Distribution: % 0–14: 41.2
15–29: 26.2
30–44: 16.8
45–59: 8.9
60–74: 6.5
75 and over: 6.5
Population 2020: 12,193,000
Birth Rate per 1,000: 33.2
Death Rate per 1,000: 9.1
Population Doubling Time (years): 33
Infant Mortality Rate per 1,000 live births: 66.0
Rate of Natural Increase per 1,000: 20.4
Total Fertility Rate: 4.4
Expectation of Life (years): Males 59.8
Females 63.2
Marriage Rate per 1,000: 4.8
Divorce Rate per 1,000: —
Total Number of Households: 1,655,000
Average Size of Households: 3.8
% of Illegitimate Children: 19.1
Induced Abortions: —
Rate per 100 live births: —

ETHNIC COMPOSITION

Indians constitute the ethnic majority in Bolivia, with an estimated 52 percent to 70 percent of the population. Cholos, or mestizos, make up 32 percent, whites from 5 percent to 15 percent, blacks 2 percent, and others 1 percent. These disparate ethnic groups have never quite melded together into one people, and cultural, racial, and linguistic differences persist in most areas of national life.

The Indians of Bolivia are broadly divided into Highland and Lowland Indians. The two largest highland groups are the Aymara and the Quechua, the former the oldest and the latter the largest among all Indian tribes in the country. The Quechua are predominantly rural and are noted for their industriousness and friendliness.

The lowland tribes are characterized by extreme diversity, and many tribes remain unknown to ethnographers. They are generally classified into four linguistic groups: Panoan, Tacanan, Mojoan (or Arawakan), and Guaranian. These, in turn, are divided into 30 extant tribes of from 10 to 20,000 members. The largest of these groups is the Guaranian with six subgroups.

Mestizos constitute a transitional group between whites and Indians. Although they make up almost one-third of the population and are widely distributed, they occupy an equivocal position in Bolivian society. The terms mestizo and cholo were applied formerly only to persons of mixed Indian and Spanish descent, but over the years the terms have been applied indiscriminately to any upwardly mobile Indian who has attained a certain economic and cultural status. Both terms are now defined by criteria such as the ability to speak Spanish, urban orientation, occupation, manners, and dress. Nevertheless, most cholos continue to maintain certain Indian traditions and to practice certain rituals associated with Indian folk religion, magic, and festivals.

Although they represent less than 15 percent of the population, whites (also known as *gente decente*, or *gente buena*, "decent" or "good people"), dominate the political and economic life of the country. The white elite remains socially and culturally homogeneous and jealously protective of their Spanish heritage. The 1952 revolution, which altered the political equation in favor of the Indians, also mitigated some of the rigidity of the Bolivian social system.

Ethnic aliens include Brazilians, Germans (some of whom are members of a 500-family Mennonite agricultural colony), Jews who fled Nazi Germany in the 1930s, Lebanese, Canadians, Italians, and Poles. Relatively prominent among foreign communities are 700 Japanese and Okinawan families, who immigrated to Bolivia after World War II and settled in the Santa Cruz area. Almost all aliens live in urban centers.

LANGUAGES

The official languages are Spanish, Aymara, and Quechua. Spanish is spoken as a first language by only a little more than a third of the population. Bolivian Spanish conforms to standard Castilian and is purer than that spoken in most parts of South America. An estimated 40 percent of Indians cannot speak or read Spanish.

Quechua was the royal language of the Incas and is still the most widespread of the Indian languages. Guaraní is also a principal Indian language. Many isolated Indian groups speak languages so distinctive that they do not fit into conventional classifications and are therefore described by linguists as unrelated.

Principal Languages and Their Speakers

Aymara	260,000
Guaraní	10,000
Quechua	660,000
Spanish	3,400,000
Spanish-Amerindian (multilingual), of which	3,740,000
Spanish-Aymara	1,610,000
Spanish-Guaraní	30,000
Spanish-Quechua	2,110,000
Other	70,000

RELIGIONS

Over 88 percent of the population is estimated to be nominally Roman Catholic, but the church's influence on national life is marginal. The 1961 constitution formally separated church and state. The government relinquished the right to mediate in church affairs, to approve the appointment of major church officials, and to control the issuance of conciliar decrees. However, the church continues to receive financial support through the national budget.

Roman Catholicism, although claiming 2.1 million members in 1998, admits that only about 15 percent of the population actually practices the faith.

Protestants constitute 9.0 percent of the population but the Protestant growth rate has tended in recent years to exceed the population growth. During the last 30 or 40 years, Protestant churches have seen increased social acceptance. The Aymaras, for example, have shown great receptivity to the Protestant missions, and nearly 3 percent of them are professing Protestants.

Some Indians practice a mixture of Catholic and traditional beliefs based upon the pantheism of pre-Columbian religion.

Religious Affiliations

Roman Catholic	7,200,000
Protestant	740,000
Other	200,000

HISTORICAL BACKGROUND

Bolivia's earliest inhabitants were Aymara-speaking Colla Indians who settled around the southern end of Lake Titicaca around 600. They developed the Tiahuanaco civilization, which flourished until 900. Around 1300 the Quechua-speaking Incas conquered the region. In 1527 Inca emperor Huayna Capac divided his empire between his two sons and the southern part with its capital of Cuzco became a distinct region. The civil war between the two sons gave an opportunity for the Spaniards under Pizarro to overrun the land. In 1539 Pedro de Anzures established La Plata, now Sucre. The discovery of a rich silver mine called Cerro Rico de Potosí in 1545 brought the Spaniards to Upper Peru (as Bolivia was known during the colonial period). In 1548 La Paz was founded on the main silver transport route between Potosí and the coast. In 1559 Upper Peru became the audiencia of Charcas under the Viceroyalty of Lima, but in 1776 it was transferred to the Viceroyalty of Rio de la Plata.

The major event in the colonial period was the insurrection of Tupac Amaru, heir to the Inca throne, which was put down brutally. Bolivia was one of the first Spanish-American countries to revolt against Spain in 1809. Fifteen years later, Antonio José de Sucre, Simón Bolívar's young general, defeated the royalists in Upper Peru and convened a congress, which, in 1825, formally proclaimed the Republic of Bolívar, later changed to Bolivia. In 1826, Bolívar gave the new nation its first constitution. Sucre was chosen as the first president and Chuquisaca was renamed Sucre in his honor. Sucre was ousted in 1828 by Gen. Andrés de Santa Cruz, who formed the short-lived Peruvian-Bolivian Confederation, dissolved in 1839. For most of the 19th century, Bolivia was racked by civil and foreign wars as a result of which it lost much of its original land to Brazil and Chile. Between 1899 and 1920, Bolivia's rich tin deposits were extensively mined, leading to the construction of its fabled mountain railroads. During this period, the Liberals were in power and they changed the capital from Sucre to La Paz, a Liberal stronghold. In a war with Paraguay between 1932 and 1935 over the Chaco Boreal region Bolivia lost its outlet on the Paraguay River. The unrest following the war led to the rise of the left-wing governments of David Toro and German Busch, who nationalized the large oil industry and three large tin-mining interests. One of Busch's major accomplishments was the liberal constitution of 1938.

In 1952 the National Revolutionary Movement (MNR) seized power and, in a coalition with the Labor Party, began a program of extensive social reform. Under the leadership of presidents Victor Paz Estenssoro and Hernán Siles Zuazo, the government nationalized the tin mines, introduced land reform, and established universal suffrage. As a result of opposition from powerful trade unions and growing social disorder, Estenssoro was overthrown by Vice President René Barrientos Ortuño with the support of the army. Barrientos shared the presidency with Gen. Alfredo Ovando Candia until January 1966 when he resigned to run for president. He won election in July 1966. Barrientos was killed in a helicopter crash in April 1969. Later, Victor Paz Estenssoro, a runner-up in the race, dropped out of the contest, thus virtually ensuring Siles the necessary majority in congress. At this point the military again seized control of the government, ordered the disbanding of the congress and declared the country a military zone. The coup was led by Gen. Luis García Meza, the commander of the army, who then proceeded to establish a military government. The junta immediately moved to consolidate power and to eliminate opposition within the army as well as among the labor force. The new regime was promptly recognized by the other military dictatorships in the so-called Southern Cone of South America—Argentina, Chile, Paraguay, and Uruguay. Argentina was reported to have been actively involved in the coup, masterminding the takeover strategy as well as supplying the coup leaders with 200 military and intelligence personnel.

In May 1981, President García Meza resigned, naming Gen. Humberto Cayoja Riart as his successor. A month later, General Cayoja was arrested for his involvement in the plot to remove García Meza from the presidency, and Brig. Gen. Celso Torrelio Villa was named president. Torrelio himself resigned on August 4 in favor of Gen. Waldo Bernal Pereira but was restored to office on September 4. On July 19, 1982, General Torrelio was ousted and replaced by Gen. Guido Vildoso Calderón, who announced on September 17 the restoration of civilian rule. The congress elected in 1980 was reconvened and it elected Hernán Siles Zuazo as president. During the two ensuring years, numerous government changes only helped to worsen economic conditions, and in December 1984 Siles Zuazo announced his early retirement from the presidency following general elections on June 16, 1985. These elections brought Siles's old rival, Victor Paz Estenssoro, back to the presidential office.

On taking office Paz Estenssoro attacked the staggering inflation rate estimated at 11,750 percent. His program was rejected by the trade unions, which called for a countrywide strike that was banned by the government and followed by the arrest and banishment of union leaders. Thousands of strikers were arrested. The strike was called off in October and was to be followed by talks. In the same month, the right-wing Acción Democrática Nacionalista (ADN) aligned with the governing party, the Movimiento Nacionalista Revolucionario (MNR).

A joint campaign by Bolivia and the U.S. military to eradicate illegal coca growing was actively protested by trade unions and opposition groups. Despite $100 million in U.S. aid, coca operations continued unchecked.

In 1986 the government's economic austerity programs led to further strikes and the imposition of a 90-day state of siege. Unrest continued in 1987 with several ministers being replaced. Strikes were banned in November 1989.

Displeasure with the MNR programs was reflected in ADN and Leftist Revolutionary Movement (MIR) victories in the December 1987 municipal elections. Nevertheless, the pact between the ruling MNR and ADN kept the ADN in power. Further economic troubles, fired by rising oil prices early in 1988, led to a national hunger strike in April instigated by the COB trade union. Following this, the cabinet resigned, though all but four members were reappointed.

The presidential elections in May 1989 resulted in defeat for the three candidates—General Banzer (ADN), Gonzalo Sánchez de Lozada (MNR), and Jaime Paz Zamora (MIR). All candidates agreed on MNR policy—its economic austerity programs, campaign against coca production, and finding of alternative employment and crops for coca growers. Despite the fact that Paz Zamora received the least votes of the three presidential candidates, support from Banzer (who initially was aligned with Sanchez) assured a majority vote for Paz Zamora in the newly elected congress. A coalition government was set up in which ADN members occupied strategic ministries. General Banzer held on to a certain amount of power through his leadership of a newly established joint political council.

Harsher measures were taken in 1988 to fight Bolivia's drug trafficking. In April an antinarcotic agency and drug-control troops (UMOPAR) were established and empowered by a coca limitation law restricting the allowable acreage for traditional legal coca growing. At the same time, Roberto Suárez, Bolivia's foremost drug trafficker, was arrested. This was followed by the exposure of leading ADN members' involvement in drug trading.

In 1989 an inability to make inroads against the powerful coca growers culminated in a cutoff of U.S. aid and a meeting in October of the presidents of the three major coca-growing countries—Bolivia, Colombia, and Peru—to discuss a common strategy. In 1993 Gonzalo Sánchez de Lozada won the presidential election. During his tenure, he implemented a number of reforms in favor of Bolivia's indigenous majority. His government's plan to privatize the oil industry led to heavy protests in 1995 and 1996. In response, the government declared a state of siege and suspended civil rights. Presidential elections in 1997 brought former dictator Hugo Banzer Suárez to office as a candidate of the ADN. In a program largely funded by the United States, the government announced plans to eradicate the coca plant by 2002, leading to angry protests by coca producers. Suffering from cancer, Banzer stepped down as president in 2001 and was replaced by Jorge Quiroga Ramírez.

CONSTITUTION

Bolivia is governed by the constitution of 1967 (the nation's 16th constitution since independence), which provides for a democratic centralist republic. Although the constitution calls for elected governments, frequently elected governments have not been allowed by the military to take office. Furthermore, the separation of governmental powers and the equal status of the three branches of government have become legal fictions as presidents have gained power through coups and maintained it by decree. Suffrage is at 18 years of age for married individuals and 21 for single ones.

The constitution of 1967 provides for a president elected for a four-year term (amended in 1995 to a five-year term) by direct suffrage and by simple majority. A vice president is elected with the president on the same party ticket. Neither the president nor the vice president can be reelected for a succeeding term. The constitution was amended in 1995 to provide for a five-year term of office. Although an effort is made in the constitution to blend the presidential and cabinet forms of government, presidential powers are virtually unrestricted. The president commands the armed forces, controls the local governments, appoints all major public servants, administers the national taxes, disburses state revenues, and negotiates treaties. He may also, under certain conditions and for a limited period of time, declare a state of siege and suspend the constitution. As head of the cabinet he appoints and dismisses cabinet members whose number is fixed by law at 12.

The political system is dominated by persons of largely European origin. Those following a traditional Indian lifestyle and speaking Aymara or Quechua as a primary language, who make up an estimated 60 percent of the population, have little opportunity to advance to top positions because of economic disadvantages and cultural isolation. However, Indians have served in cabinet-level positions, and there are several Indian congressmen.

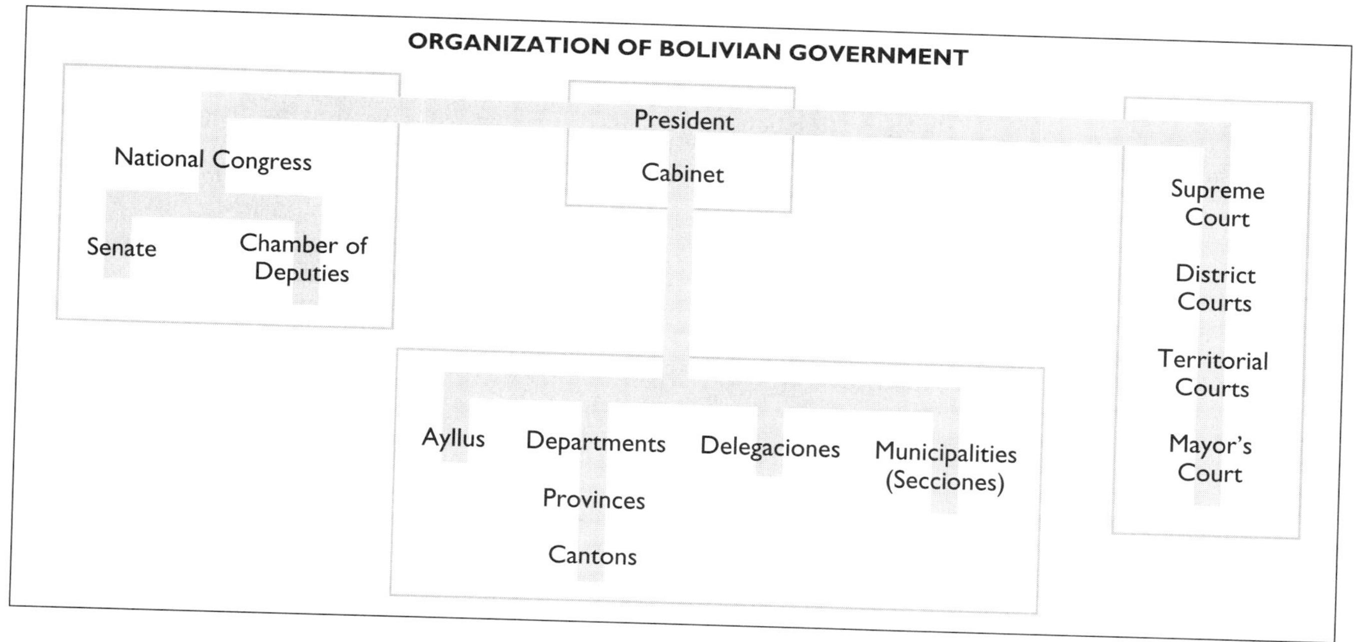

LOCAL GOVERNMENT

Bolivia is divided into nine departments, each headed by a prefect who is appointed by the president for a term of four-years. The departments are subdivided into provinces headed by appointed officials called subprefects. The 94 provinces are further divided into about 1,000 cantons, led by officials known as corregidors. Three underpopulated and remote areas are designated as delegacions and administered by officials whose duties include promoting the welfare of Indian tribes in the area and the fostering of colonization.

Local Government

Principal administrative divisions, capitals, area, population

AREA AND POPULATION

Departments	Capitals	area sq mi	area sq km	population 1997 estimate
Beni	Trinidad	82,458	213,564	336,633
Chuquisaca	Sucre	19,893	51,524	549,835
Cochabamba	Cochabamba	21,479	55,631	1,408,071
La Paz	La Paz	51,732	133,985	2,268,824
Oruro	Oruro	20,690	53,588	383,498
Pando	Cobija	24,644	63,827	53,124
Potosí	Potosí	45,644	118,218	746,618
Santa Cruz	Santa Cruz	143,098	370,621	1,651,950
Tarija	Tarija	14,526	37,623	368,506
TOTAL		424,164	1,098,581	7,767,059

PARLIAMENT

The National Congress is a bicameral body consisting of a Senate and a Chamber of Deputies. The Senate consists of 27 members and the Chamber of Deputies of 130 members. According to the constitution, each of the country's nine departments (states) is represented by three senators. Members of both houses are elected for four-year terms. The regular session of congress lasts for 90 days, beginning on August 6 every year. The constitution also provides for a legislative committee composed of nine deputies and five senators to function when the congress is not in session.

Minority representation in the congress is ensured by a proportional system under which the party winning the most seats in each department is awarded two seats, and the party with the second-highest vote is awarded the third seat. Candidates who fail to win the elections to the Chamber of Deputies serve as alternates and fill in vacancies as they occur.

Suffrage is universal with no property or literacy qualifications for married persons over 18 and single persons over 21. All electoral procedures, including the registration of candidates and political parties, are supervised by the National Electoral Court. Below the National Electoral Court are departmental electoral courts, electoral judges, electoral notaries, and juries. Electoral juries consist of five persons chosen by lot from among the literate voters registered in each polling place. Each ballot has a distinctive color and symbol to make voting easier for illiterates. Voters cast their ballots for parties instead of candidates.

POLITICAL PARTIES

Bolivia's five major political parties are the Acción Democrática Nacionalista (ADN); the Movimiento Nacionalista Revolucionario (Histórico)(MNR); the Movimiento de la Izquerda Revolucionaria (MIR); the Conciencia de Patria (Condepa); and Izquierda Unida (IU). The ADN is a right-wing party founded in 1979 by Hugo Banzer Suárez under the slogan, "peace, order and work." The MNR is a center-right party founded in 1942 and led by Victor Paz Estenssoro. The MIR is a noncommunist, marxist party founded in 1971. It is led by former vice president Jaime Paz Zamora. Condepa, founded in 1988, is a populist party formed by a popular La Paz broadcast personality. The IU is an eight-party coalition formed for the 1989 campaign. Among the parties included were the left-wing Alianza Patriótica, the left-wing Movimiento Bolivia Libre, the communist Partido Communista de Bolivia, and the left-wing Partido Socialista-Uno.

Political Parties

- Civic Solidarity Union, 1988
- Nationalist Democratic Action, 1979
- Nationalist Revolutionary Movement, 1941
- Christian Democratic Party
- New Republican Force
- Leftist Nationalist Revolutionary Movement
- Movement of the Revolutionary Left
- Conscience of the Fatherland, 1988
- Patriotic Condepa Movement, 1993
- United Left, an alliance of leftist groups
    - Patriotic Alliance
    - Socialist Party–One, 1971
    - Bolivian Communist Party, 1952
- Free Bolivia Movement, 1985
- Socialist Vanguard
- Tupaj Katari Revolutionary Movement
- Tupaj Katari Revolutionary Movement - Liberation
- National Leftist Revolutionary Party, 1964
- Left Revolutionary Front
- People's Revolutionary Party
- Revolutionary Workers' Party
- Workers' Vanguard Party
- Workers' Socialist Movement
- Revolutionary Vanguard of 9 April
- Pachakutic Axis

Political Parties: Strength in Parliament Most Recent Elections

Senate. At the 1997 election the Nationalist Democratic Action won 13 seats; the Movement of the Revolutionary Left, 6; the Nationalist Revolutionary Movement, 3; the Conscience of the Fatherland, 3; and the Civic Solidarity Union, 2.

Chamber of Deputies. At the 1997 election the Nationalist Democratic Action won 33 seats; the Nationalist Revolutionary Movement, 26; the Movement of the Revolutionary Left, 25; the Civic Solidarity Union, 21; the Conscience of the Fatherland, 17; and the Free Bolivian Movement and United Left, 4 each.

LEGAL SYSTEM

The legal system is based on Spanish law and the Napoleonic Code. The judiciary comprises the Supreme Court, superior district courts, and local courts.

The Supreme Court, which sits at Sucre, is divided into four sections of three justices each. Its 12 judges, called ministros, and the chief justice are chosen for 10-year terms by a two-thirds vote of the Chamber of Deputies from a list of three names submitted for each vacancy by the Senate. They may be reelected indefinitely. District court judges are elected by the Senate for six-year terms from a list of three names submitted for each vacancy by the Supreme Court. The jurisdiction of the nine district courts is chiefly appellate. All major towns and cities have territorial courts whose judges are chosen by the Supreme Court from lists submitted by the district courts. At the bottom of the judicial system are small claims courts and mayor's courts in every parish.

LAW ENFORCEMENT

Law Enforcement

Offenses reported to the police per 100,000: —
- Murder: —
- Assault: —
- Burglary: —
- Automobile Theft: —
- Population per Police officer: —

Death Penalty: Yes; last execution 1974.

HUMAN RIGHTS

In terms of political and civil rights, Bolivia is classified as a free country. Bolivia's most notable progress since the end of military government in 1982 has been in the area of human rights. Political parties are now free to organize and criticize the government. Both congress and the court system function independently and fulfill an active monitoring function. After several delays, municipal elections were held in June 1985. The excesses of the former security police apparatus are a thing of the past. No political prisoners are being held.

The press continues to operate without government restriction. The government has dealt with general strikes, road blockades, and labor protests with restraint. It has been less effective in protecting property rights and providing guarantees for private-sector activities. There have also been charges of corruption and intimidation in the judicial system.

FOREIGN POLICY

The central issue in Bolivian foreign policy for the last 100 years has been the question of a corridor to the Pacific, which had been lost to Chile in the War of the Pacific (1879–84). In 1975 relations with Chile were resumed after a 12-year lapse and Santiago announced an agreement in principle to grant Bolivia an outlet to the sea in exchange for territory elsewhere. However, the agreement had not taken effect by 2001 and a territorial corridor to the sea has eluded Bolivia. Bolivia is a member of both the Andean Pact and the Southern Cone Common Market. Relations with the United States are complicated by Bolivia's involvement in the cocaine trade. Bolivia is a major producer of cocaine, and has resisted U.S. attempts to eliminate its trade.

DEFENSE

The defense structure is headed by the president. He also presides over the Supreme Council of National Defense, the highest policy-making body in military affairs. The line of command runs through the minister of national defense to the commanders of the three services. The Ministry of Defense does not exercise any operational command. The country is divided into nine military regions corresponding to the administrative departments. The army is divided into 10 divisions with one based in each of these regions with an additional division at Viacha. The main bases are at Miraflores barracks in La Paz and at Cochabamba.

Military manpower is provided by selective conscription at age 18. However, in practice, few of the registered youths are called for service. The conscript service period is 12 months. The total strength of the armed forces is 33,500, as of 1998.

Military Indicators

Total Active Duty Personnel: 33,500
Military Manpower per 1,000: 4.3
Military Expenditures $million: 132
- as % of GNP: 2.3
- per capita $: 19
- as % of central government expenditures: 9.5

Arms Imports $million: 10
Arms Exports $million: 0

ECONOMY

Bolivia, long one of the poorest and least developed Latin American countries, has made considerable progress toward the development of a market-oriented economy. Successes under President Sánchez de Lozada (1993–97) included the signing of a free trade agreement with Mexico and the Southern Cone Common Market (Mercosur) as well as the privatization of the state airline, telephone company, railroad, electric power company, and oil company. His successor, Hugo Banzer Suárez has tried to further improve the country's investment climate with an anticorruption campaign. Growth slowed in 1999, in part due to tight government budget policies, which limited needed appropriations for antipoverty programs, and the fallout from the Asian financial crisis. In 2000, violent protests in April, September, and October held down overall growth to 2.5 percent.

Principal Economic Indicators

Gross National Product $: 7.564 billion
GNP per capita $: 970
GNP Average Annual Growth Rate (1990–97) %: 2.0
GNP per capita Average Annual Growth Rate (1990–97) %: −0.4
Origin of Gross Domestic Product %
- Agriculture: 10
- Mining: 10
- Manufacturing: 14
- Construction: 4
- Public Utilities: 2
- Transportation and Communications: 11
- Trade: 11
- Financial Services: 11
- Other Services: 7
- Government: 9

Gross Domestic Product by Type of Expenditure %
- Private Consumption: 75
- Government Consumption: 14
- Gross Domestic Investment: 16
- Foreign Trade: Exports: 23
- Imports: −28

% of Income Received by Poorest 20%: 5.6
% of Income Received by Richest 10%: 31.7

Price and earnings indexes (1995 = 100)

	1992	1993	1994	1995	1996	1997
Consumer price index	77.5	84.1	90.8	100.0	112.4	117.7
Annual earnings index	66.1	76.7	89.2	100.0	—	—

Finance

National Currency: Boliviano ($B)
Exchange Rate: $1 = $B 5.3724
Money Supply Stock in National Currency billion: 4.759
M1 per capita: 620
Central Bank Discount Rate %: 14.30
Total External Debt $million: 4,200
Debt Service Ratio %: 21.7

Balance of Payments $million: −550.8
International Reserves SDRs million: 781
Ratio of External Debt to Total Reserves: 6.3
Average Annual Rate of Inflation/Consumer Price Index Growth Rate %: 7

Official Development Assistance

Donor ODA $million: 588
- as % of GNP: 7.5
- per capita $ 79
- Foreign Direct Investment $million: 872

Central Government Revenues and Expenditures

Fiscal Year: Calendar Year
Revenues $million: 3,750
Expenditures $million: 3,750
Budget Deficit $million: 0
Tax Revenues as % of GDP: 15.1
Highest Tax Bracket %
- Individual: 13
- Corporate: 25

Employment and Labor

Economically Active Population: 2,530,000
Female Participation Rate %: 36.2
Activity Rate %: 39.4
Labor by Sector: %
- Agriculture, Forestry, Fishing: 38.9
- Manufacturing, Mining: 11.1
- Construction: 5.1
- Transportation and Communications: 4.6
- Trade, Hotels, and Restaurants: 9.2
- Finance, Insurance, Real Estate: 2.1
- Public Administration, Defense: 2.3
- Services: 13.8

Unemployment %: 10

Agriculture

Agriculture's Share of GDP %: 16
Average Annual Rate of Growth (1965–98) %: —
Number of Farms 000: 519
Average Size of Farm ha: 72.1
Number of Tractors per 1,000 hectares: 2.5
Irrigation, % of Farms having: 5.0
Artificial Fertilizer kg/hectare: 30
Total Farmland as % of land area: 20.6
Livestock: Cattle 000: 6,387
- Sheep 000: 8,409
- Hogs 000: 2,637
- Chickens 000: 58,796

Forests: Production of Roundwood (000 cubic meters): 2,567
Fisheries: Total Catch tons 000: 6.0

Mining

% of GDP: 5.3
Value of Mineral Production $million: 369.6

Manufacturing

Value Added $million: 880
Industrial Production Growth Rate %: 4

Energy

Commercial Energy Production metric tons of oil equivalent 000: 5,953
Commercial Energy Consumption metric tons of oil equivalent 000: 4,254
Commercial Energy Consumption per capita kg: 548
Average Annual Growth Rate 1980–97 %: 0.4
Net Energy Imports % of use: −40
Electricity Installed Capacity kW 000: 805
- Production kW-hr million: 3,020

Coal Reserves tons million: 1
- Production tons 000: —

Natural Gas Proven Reserves cubic meters billion: 128
- Production cubic meters million: 3,279

Crude Petroleum Reserves barrels million: 132
- Production barrels million: 11
- Consumption barrels million: 10
- Refinery Capacity barrels per day 000: 48

Pipelines Length km: 2,380

Foreign Trade

Imports $million: 1,396.3
Exports $million: 1,181.4
Export Volume % Annual Growth Rate (1990–97): 2.8
Import Volume % Annual Growth Rate (1990–97): 10.2

Balance of trade (current prices)

	1993	1994	1995	1996	1997	1998
U.S. 000,000	−384.1	−89.3	−162.5	−313.4	−531.6	−721.1
% of total	20.9%	4.1%	6.9%	12.1%	18.6%	24.6%

Major Trading Partners

	Imports	Exports
European Union %	19.6	25.9
United States %	22.3	27.8
Eastern Europe %	0.5	0.1
Japan %	12.3	0.3
Others %	45.3	45.9

Transportation

Roads Total Length mi: 34,478 km 55,487
Paved %: 5
Automobiles: 213,666
Trucks and Buses: 133,984
Persons per vehicle: 21
Railroad; Track Length mi: 2,295 km 3,694
Passenger-mi million: 216.8
Freight-mi million: 521.9
Merchant Marine: No. of Vessels: 1
- Total Deadweight Tonnage 000: 15.8
- International Cargo Loaded tons 000: —
- International Cargo Off-loaded tons 000: —

Airports with Scheduled Flights: 14
Traffic: Passenger-mi million: 912
- Freight-mi million: 31.7

Length of Canals mi: 6.214 km 10,000

Tourism

Number of Tourists to 000: 434
Number of Tourists from 000: 298
Tourist Receipts $million: 146
Tourist Expenditures $million: 148

Communications

Telephones 000: 348
Cost of Local Calls 3 mins: $0
Cellular Telephones 000: 7.2
Fax Machines 000: —
Personal Computers 000: —
Internet Hosts per million persons: 8.9
Mail: Post Offices: 159
- Pieces of Mail Handled million: 21
- Pieces of Mail Handled per person: 2.8

EDUCATION

Education in theory is universal, free, and compulsory for eight years from the ages of six to 14. The entire educational system is under the control of the Ministry of Education and Culture.

Schooling lasts for 12 years, divided into eight years of primary school and four years of secondary school. The rural primary schools are nuclear schools, each consisting of a core, full-program central school surrounded by 15 to 30 outlying units in which all the classes are taught by a single teacher. The primary curriculum is designed to make the student a more useful member of the rural community rather than to train him or her for further studies. Attrition rates are high and in urban classrooms grade repeaters exceed the number of regular students. Secondary schools for boys are known as colegios and those for girls are known as liceos. Almost all secondary school curriculum is adapted to prepare the students for university studies.

Literacy and adult education programs are directed by the National Office for Literacy and Adult Education, established in 1956. A number of educational broadcasts are being transmitted for new literates, the most successful of which is one conducted by the Maryknolls (a Catholic order), which combines broadcasts with short training programs in which both Indian languages and Spanish are used. At the secondary level, centers of intermediate adult education offer courses of study leading to a "bachelor by maturity" certificate in three years.

Vocational training is provided in commercial schools, industrial schools, agricultural schools, and labor secondary schools.

Private education plays a significant role in the school system. About 17 percent of primary school and 25 percent of secondary school students are in private institutions, most of which are run by Roman Catholic orders as well as large business enterprises, which are required by law to maintain their own schools. The quality of education in private secondary schools is reportedly higher than that in public schools. In order to qualify for state subsidies, private schools are required to provide scholarships to at least 10 percent of their enrollments.

The entire school system is under the centralized control of the Ministry of Education and Culture. Rural schools are administered by a school assistance board headed by a school mayor. All public educational expenditures are met by the central government. Higher education is provided in nine states universities and five private universities.

Education

Literacy Rate %: 83.1
- Male %: 90.5
- Female %: 76.0

First Level: Primary schools: —
- Teachers: 51,763
- Students: 1,278,775
- Student-Teacher Ratio: 24.7
- Net Enrollment Ratio: 91.0

Second Level: Secondary Schools: —
- Teachers: 12,434
- Students: 219,232
- Student-Teacher Ratio: 17.6
- Net Enrollment Ratio: 29.0

Vocational Level: Schools: —
- Students: —

Third Level: Institutions: —
- Teachers: 4,261
- Students: 109,503
- Student-Ratio Level: 25.7
- Gross Enrollment Ratio: 22.2
- Students per 100,000: 2,154
- % of Population Age 25 and over with Postsecondary Education: 9.9

Public Expenditure on Education as % of GDP: 6.6

SCIENCE AND TECHNOLOGY

Science and Technology

Scientists and Engineers in R&D per 1 million persons: 172
Expenditures in R&D as % of GDP: 0.50
High-Tech Exports $million: 15
Patent Applications by Residents: 17

MEDIA

La Paz has three morning and three evening dailies, which together represent almost 80 percent of the national newspaper circulation. Other towns with daily newspapers are Cochabamba, Santa Cruz, Potosí, and Oruro. The principal dailies are *Presencia* (91,000), *El Diario* (55,000), *Los Tiempos* (18,000), *Hoy* (40,000), and *Ultima Hora* (36,000). *Presencia* is Catholic and all the others are independent.

In television, the network of state and university channels has been controlled by the government. Unauthorized private TV stations have been functioning in Santa Cruz, Sucre, and Cochabamba, and the government has been unwilling to legalize them.

Radio broadcasting is controlled by the state. In 1996 there were 235 radio stations, the majority of which were commercial. Most broadcast in Spanish, but a few offer programs in Quechua, Aymara, German, and English. Of the many networks and stations belonging to religious organizations, the largest is La Cruz del Sur, owned and operated by the Canadian Baptist Foreign Mission Board, which is on the air for 120 hours a week. Many universities conduct their own radio schools. Television, introduced in 1969, is supplied by Empresa Nacional de Televisión with stations in La Paz, Oruro, Cochabamba, Potosí, Sucre, Pando, Beni, Tarija, and Santa Cruz. Educational programs are broadcast by Televisión Universitaria, founded in 1980.

The government does not exercise formal censorship, and freedom of the press is formally guaranteed by the constitution. There are no government restrictions on free speech or the press. The views of opposition parties, leaders, and organizations—often harshly critical of the government—are given free play in the press, and on radio, and most television stations. Some extremist political and labor groups, taking exception to these liberties, have called for the closing or takeover of certain newspapers and radio stations.

Media

Daily Newspapers: 11
Total Circulation 000: 500
Circulation per 1,000: 69
Books Published: —
Magazines: —
Radio Receivers 000: 4,250
per 1,000: 553
Television sets 000: 1,500
per 1,000: 202

Most Important Media:

Press. The following papers are published daily at La Paz, unless otherwise notied: *Presencia* (91,000), Catholic; *El Diario* (55,000); *Hoy* (40,000), independent; *Ultima Hora* (36,000), independent; *El Mundo* (Santa Cruz, 20,000), business oriented; *Los Tiempos* (Cochabamba, 18,000), independent; *Jornada* (12,000), independent.

News agencies. The domestic facility is the Agencia de Noticias Fides (ANF); a number of foreign agencies, including AFP, ANSA, AP, and UPI, maintain bureaus at La Paz.

Radio and television. In 1996 Bolivia had 235 radio and 66 television outlets.

CULTURE

Cultural Indicators

Public Libraries Number: 99
Volumes: 125,000
Registered borrowers: 119,618
Museums Number: —
Annual Attendance: —
Cinema Production of Long Films: 4
Number of Cinemas: 130
Seating Capacity: —
Annual Attendance million: 2.2
Annual Attendance per capita: 0.3

STATUS OF WOMEN

Women do not enjoy a status in society equal to that of men. The main obstacles to advancement are cultural traditions, social conditions, and a lack of political power. In rural families women contribute significantly to economic activities but are considered subordinate and rarely participate in cooperatives, community meetings, or training programs. In Hispanic urban families, women are more likely to stay at home and are not economically active. However, women are slowly achieving a greater role in Bolivian business life.

Although Bolivian laws generally do not discriminate against women, under the agrarian reform law, title to land cannot pass to a woman even if she is widowed or divorced. Also, agricultural credit to women is restricted by most banks and lending institutions. Although by law women workers have the right to three months maternity leave, in practice most are unaware of this right or are concerned that they will lose their salaries or jobs if they take such a leave.

Even though there is no overt political discrimination against women, they are rarely named to high-ranking positions in the government. The most notable exception was Lidia Gueiler, who served as interim president from November 1979 to July 1980.

Women

Gender Empowerment Measure: 65
Seats Held in Parliament by Women %: 6.4
Female Administrators and Managers %: 28.3
Female Professional and Technical Workers %: 42.2
Women's Share of Earned Income %: 27
Women in Government %: 9

HEALTH, FOOD, AND NUTRITION

Health

Number of Physicians: 3,392
Number of Dentists: 1,643
Number of Nurses: 1,869
Number of Pharmacists: —
Population per Physician: 2,083
Number of Hospitals: 336
Hospital Beds per 10,000: 10
Hospital Bed Occupancy Rate: 45.9
Infant Mortality Rate per 1,000 live births: 88
Maternal Mortality Rate per 100,000 live births: 650
Total Health Expenditures as % of GDP: 4.01
Health Expenditures per capita $: 25
HIV Infected % of adults: 0.07
Cigarette Consumption per smoker per year: —
% of Smokers: Male: 50
Female: 21
Access to Safe Water %: 60

Food and Nutrition

Food Supply as % of FAO Requirements: 92
% of Consumption Expenditures on Food: 46.6
Daily Available Calories per capita: 2,192
% of Total Calories derived from:
Cereals: 44.4
Potatoes, cassava: 7.0
Meat, poultry: 10.4
Fish: 0.1
Eggs, milk: 3.1
Fruits, vegetables: 7.5
Fats, oils: 9.9

ENVIRONMENT

Bolivia suffers from a number of environmental problems. Perhaps the most important is the clearing of land for agricultural purposes and the international demand for tropical timber, which contributes to deforestation. The use of slash-and-burn agriculture combined with overgrazing is causing soil erosion and desertification. The cutting of lumber and the clearing of land is also impacting the biodiversity of the country. Industrial pollution has contaminated water supplies used for drinking and irrigation.

Environment

Forest Area sq km: 483,000
Average Annual Deforestation sq km: 5,814
Nationally Protected Areas as % of Total Land Area: 14.4
Freshwater Access cubic meters per capita: 38,625
Emissions of Organic Water Pollutants kg per day: 10,251
CO_2 Emissions per capita ton: 1.3

CHRONOLOGY

1946 President Gualberto Villarroel is murdered by a rioting mob; a civilian junta headed by Nestor Guillén names Tomás Manje Gutiérrez provisional president.

1947 A constitutionally elected government under President Enrique Hertzog takes office.

1949 The arrest and exile of leftist leader Juan Lechín Oquendo provoke a nationwide strike; in widespread civil war the Movimiento Nacionalista Revolucionario (MNR) gains control of Oruro, Potosí, Cochabamba, Sucre, and Santa Cruz until the army intervenes.

1950 Hertzog resigns in the wake of a general strike and Vice President Mamerto Urriolagoitia assumes power; MNR candidate Victor Paz Estenssoro wins a 43 percent plurality in the presidential election; to forestall a Paz presidency, a military junta led by Hugo Bollivian assumes power.

1952 Tin miners and Paz supporters overthrow the government after several days of bloody fighting in which nearly 3,000 are killed; Paz is inaugurated president; in a series of reforms tin mines are nationalized, universal adult suffrage is proclaimed, and a program of land reform is begun.

1956 Hernán Siles Zuazo, the MNR candidate, is elected to the presidency, succeeding Paz.

1960 Paz is reelected president.

1962 Bolivia breaks diplomatic relations with Chile over the Lauca River hydroelectric project.

1963 Using the army, Paz breaks a violent strike by the tin miners; the peso replaces the boliviano as the national currency.

1964 Paz is reelected to a second consecutive term with the help of the army and police; workers and students rise against Paz, joined by Vice President René Barrientos Ortuño; the army intervenes in favor of the dissidents and Paz flees to Lima; Barrientos is sworn in as president with General Alfredo Ovando Candia as copresident.

1965 Lechín is exiled.

1966 Barrientos resigns his copresidency and is elected president.

1967 Bolivia adopts a new constitution; Che Guevara dies after a battle between his guerrillas and government units.

1969 Barrientos dies in a helicopter crash; Vice President Siles Salinas is named president; four months later Siles is dismissed by Ovando.

1970 Ovando is overthrown in a rightist army coup led by Gen. Rogelio Miranda who is, in turn, replaced by leftist-backed Gen. Juan José Torres Gonzalez; Torres weathers attempts by rightist Gen. Hugo Banzer Suárez to unseat him; Banzer is exiled.

1971 Banzer returns to La Paz and leads successful coup in which over 200 persons are killed; Banzer forms the Nationalist Popular Front, which incorporates Paz's MNR.

1972 Andres Selich, head of the Rangers, unleashes a reign of terror; Selich is dismissed and transferred to Paraguay as ambassador.

1973 Selich is murdered as he returns to La Paz.

1974 Paz leaves the coalition and is exiled.

1977 Banzer announces that elections will take place in 1978.

1978 Banzer declares a state of siege after discovering "subversive plots," but declares a general amnesty and lifts the ban on trade unions; in general elections Gen. Pereda Asbun wins a clear lead but elections are invalidated due to claims of fraud; General Pereda ousts General Banzer in a coup, and is installed as president; in a second coup General Pereda is overthrown and Gen. Padilla Arancibia is named president; diplomatic relations with Chile are broken over the issue of a Bolivian corridor to the sea.

1979 After no candidate wins a clear victory, congress installs the president of the Senate, Walter Guevara Arze, as president of Bolivia for one year; army forces led by Col. Alberto Natusch Busch depose Guevara, occupy the capital, and dissolve congress; more than 200 people are killed in street fighting in the capital; Natusch steps down in the face of opposition from the military; civilian government is restored with Bolivia's first woman president, Lidia Gueiler; army commander Luis García Meza defies a presidential order to resign.

1980 In national elections, the leftist Siles wins a plurality, but the military intervenes again and takes over the government; Gen. Luis García Meza establishes a junta and receives prompt support from other military regimes in the Southern Cone region of South America; the United States withdraws all but humanitarian aid.

1981 President García Meza resigns under duress and Gen. Humberto Cayoja Riart assumes the presidency; within a month Cayoja is arrested and charged with involvement in the plot that ousted García Meza; Brig. Gen. Celso Torrelio Villa is designated president.

1982 Gen. Torrelio is forced to step down in favor of Gen. Guido Vildoso Calderón, who reconvenes the congress elected in 1980 to name a civilian government; congress elects Hernán Siles Zuazo.

1983 Near bankruptcy, intracabinet power struggles, military mutinies, and labor strikes plague Siles's administration; Siles is kidnapped by an army faction but later released unharmed; the peso is devalued and external debt rescheduled.

1984 The government sets austerity measures; Bolivia defaults on external debt repayments but obtains a moratorium; fuel and food subsidies are removed; the peso is devalued by 75 percent; congress approves a wage increase of 130 percent while food prices rise 450 percent.

1985 Siles retires and Victor Paz Estenssoro is elected president; President Paz Estenssoro allows the peso to float; following a general strike by the trade union organization COB, the government calls a state of siege for 90 days and arrests thousands; the strike is called off; the world tin market collapses.

1986 Protests throughout the country over the government's austerity plans continue through 1987; opposition groups and trade unions protest a joint military campaign with the United States, ultimately unsuccessful, to fight illegal coca production.

1988 COB calls a nationwide hunger strike over plans to decentralize social services; Bolivia establishes an antinarcotics department; Roberto Suárez, Bolivia's foremost drug trafficker, is captured.

1989 No clear winner emerges from the presidential elections; congress awards the presidency to Paz Zamora, the third-place candidate.

1990 The presidents of Bolivia, Peru, Colombia, and the United States pledge to cooperate in the fight against illegal narcotics trafficking; the Chamber of Deputies impeaches eight of the nation's 12 Supreme Court justices for declaring a law unconstitutional for purely political reasons.

1991 Officials from across Latin America combine efforts to fight the region's cholera epidemic.

1993 MNR candidate Gonzalo Sánchez de Lozada wins the presidential election and successfully fights the country's hyperinflation.

1995 The country's continuing movement toward a free market sparks a general strike by leftists; the government declares a state of siege and suspends civil rights; in December, Bolivia joins the free trade region of South America's Southern Common Market (MERCOSUR).

1997 Presidential elections bring to office former leader Hugo Banzer Suárez, who promises to continue free-market reforms while protecting Bolivia's poor.

1998 Torrential rains induce disastrous mudslides near the Peru border in February; in May, a series of earthquakes strikes central Bolivia; supported by the United States, the government destroys a record 11,000 hectares of coca leaf; coca-leaf producers march on La Paz in protest.

1999 Bolivia and Brazil inaugurate a natural gas pipeline stretching 3,000 miles from Santa Cruz, Bolivia, to Porto Alegre, Brazil.

2000 After violent protests break out over the price of water, the government imposes a state of emergency for two weeks; President Banzer meets with President Ricardo Lagos Escobar of Chile to discuss the two countries' century-old territorial dispute; storms result in severe flooding and declaration of half the country as a disaster area.

2001 President Banzer, who is suffering from cancer, resigns and is replaced by Vice President Jorge Quiroga Ramírez.

BIBLIOGRAPHY

Alexander, Robert J. *Bolivia: Past, Present and Future of Its Politics*. New York, 1982.

Blair, David Nelson. *The Land and People of Bolivia*, Philadelphia, 1990.

Clayton, Lawrence A. *The Bolivarian Nations*. Arlington Heights, Ill., 1984.

Dunkerley, James. *Rebellion in the Veins: Political Struggle in Bolivia, 1952–1982*. New York, 1984.

Gill, Lesley. *Peasants, Entrepreneurs and Social Change: Frontier Development in Lowland Bolivia*. Boulder, Colo., 1987.

Jemino, Luis Carlos. *Debt, Crisis and Reform in Bolivia*. Hampshire, U.K., 2001.

Klein, Herbert S. *Haciendas and Ayllus: Rural Society in the Bolivian Andes in the Eighteenth and Nineteenth Centuries*. Stanford, Calif., 1993.

Ladman, Jerry R. *Modern Day Bolivia: The Legacy of the Past and Prospects for the Future*. Tempe, Ariz., 1982.

Morales, Waltraud Q. *Bolivia: Land of Struggle*. Boulder, Colo., 1992.

Morner, Magnus. *The Andean Past: Land, Societies & Conflict*. New York, 1984.

Musgrave, Richard A. *Fiscal Reform in Bolivia*. Cambridge, Mass., 1980.

Preston, David A. *Farmers & Towns; Rural-Urban Relations in Highland Bolivia*. New York, 1980.

Stearman, Allyn MacLean. *Yuqui: Forest Nomads in a Changing World*. Fort Worth, Tex., 1989.

OFFICIAL PUBLICATIONS

Bolivia. *Anuario estadístico; Censo nacional de población y vivienda 1992; Compendio estadístico* (annual); *Estadísticas socioeconómicas* (annual); *Resumen estadístico* (annual).

CONTACT INFORMATION

Embassy of Bolivia
3014 Massachusetts Avenue NW
Washington, D.C. 20008
Phone: (202) 483-4410 Fax: (202) 328-3712

INTERNET RESOURCES

- Instituto Nacional de Estadística http://www.ine.gov.bo/
- UNDP Bolivia http://guf.pnud.bo/bolbrief.htm http://www.rbz.co.zw

BOSNIA AND HERZEGOVINA

BASIC FACT SHEET

OFFICIAL NAME:
Republic of Bosnia and Herzegovina
(Republika Bosna i Hercegovina)

ABBREVIATION:
BK

CAPITAL:
Sarajevo

HEAD OF STATE:
President: Zivko Radistic, Serb member of the presidency (from 1998)
Bosnian member of the presidency: Alija Izetbegovic (1998)
Croatian member of the presidency: Ante Jelavic (1998)

HEAD OF GOVERNMENT:
Chairman of the Council of Ministers: Zlatko Lagumdzija (from 2001)

1. Federation of Bosnia and Herzegovina
   President: Ejup Ganic (from 1999)
   Prime Minister: Edhem Bicakcic (from 1996)
2. Serb Republic of Bosnia and Herzegovina
   President: Nikola Poplasen (from 1998)
   Prime Minister: Milorad Dodik (from 1998)

NATURE OF GOVERNMENT:
Emerging Democracy

POPULATION:
3,838,000 (1999)

AREA:
51,129 sq km (19,741 sq mi)

MAJOR ETHNIC GROUPS:
Serb (40%); Muslim (38%); Croat (22%)

LANGUAGES:
Bosnian (Serbo-Croatian)

RELIGIONS:
Muslim (40%); Orthodox (31%); Catholic (15%); Protestant (4%)

UNIT OF CURRENCY:
Marka

NATIONAL FLAG:
A wide medium blue vertical band on the fly side with a yellow isosceles triangle abutting the band and the top of the flag; the remainder of the flag is medium blue with seven full five-pointed white stars and two half stars top and bottom along the hypotenuse of the triangle

NATIONAL ANTHEM: —

NATIONAL HOLIDAYS:
Serb Republic, January, 9; Federation Day, November 25

DATE OF INDEPENDENCE:
April 1992

DATE OF CONSTITUTION:
December 14, 1995

GEOGRAPHICAL FEATURES

The modern country of Bosnia and Herzegovina consists of a landmass of approximately 19,741 sq mi (51,129 sq km). The nearly completely landlocked country is carved out of the former Yugoslavia. It is bordered on the east by the modern state of Yugoslavia, which consists of Serbia and Montenegro. It is surrounded on its other three sides by Croatia. A narrow corridor gives Herzegovina outlet to the sea at Neum, on the Neretva Channel of the Adriatic Sea; the corridor splits Croatia along the Dalmatian coast about 25 mi (40 km) northwest of Dubrovnik. The country consists of two distinct land areas. The northern portion, Bosnia, is mountainous and covered with thick forests. The southern part, Herzegovina, is largely rocky hills and farmland.

Bosnia-Herzegovina

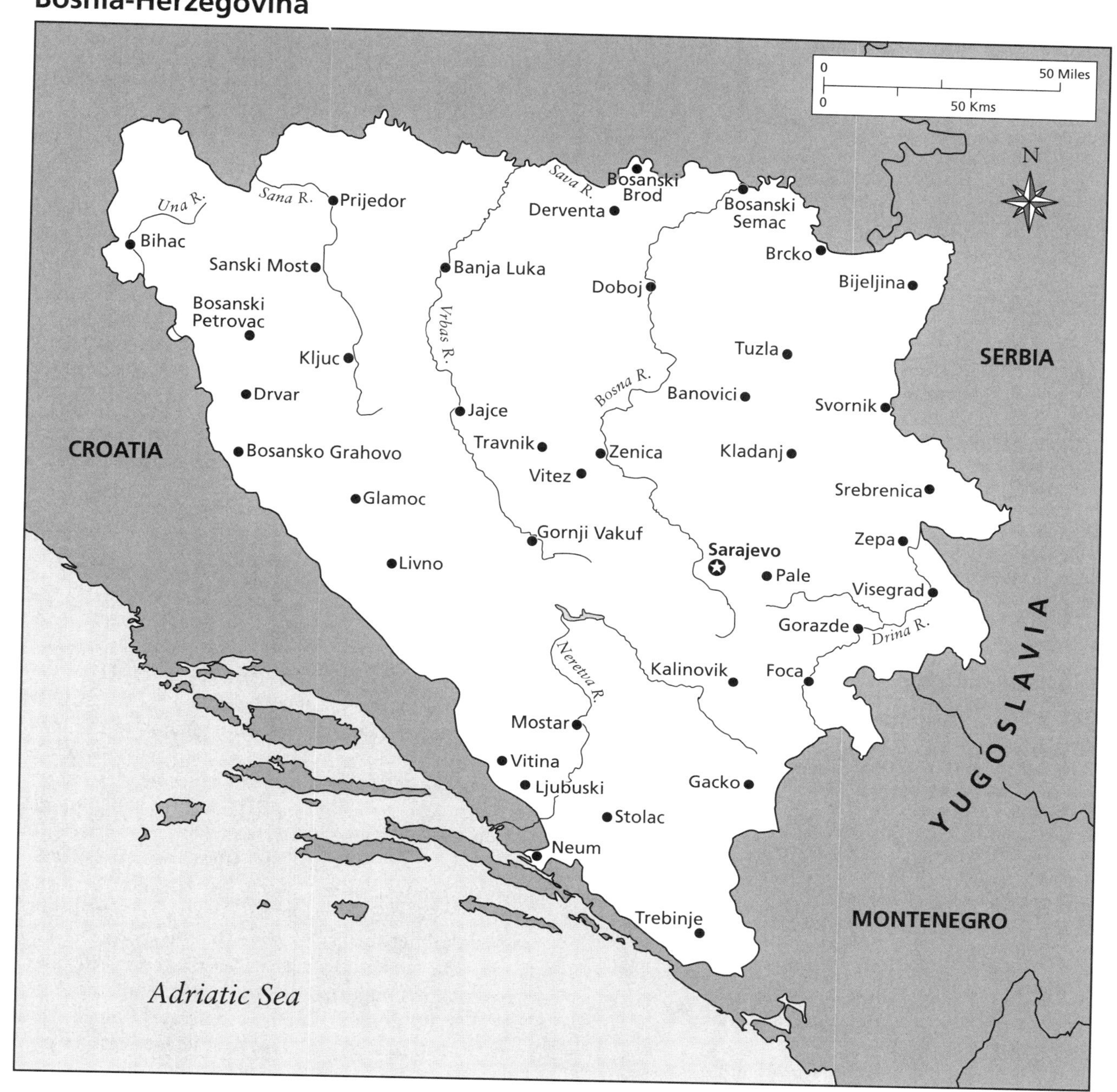

Geography

Area sq km: 51,129 sq mi 19,741
World Rank: 127th
Land Boundaries, km: Croatia 932
Serbia 527
Coastline, km: 20
Elevation Extremes meters
Lowest: Adriatic Sea 0
Highest: Maglic 2,386
Land Use % Arable land: 14
Permanent Crops: 5
Permanent Pastures: 20
Forest and Woodland: 39
Other: 22

Population of Principal Cities (2002 est)

Banja Luka	179,200
Sarajevo	434,000

CLIMATE AND WEATHER

Bosnia-Herzegovina's climate is marked by its exceptionally cold and snowy winters. The summers are warm in the mountain valleys, but cooler at higher elevations. There is a period of heavy rainfall in early summer. The far northern part of Bosnia has cold winters and dry, hot summers. The average January temperature in

Sarajevo is 30°F (−1°C). The average July temperature is 68°F (20°C).

Climate and Weather

Mean Temperature
July 72.5 in
January 32°F
Average Rainfall 24.6 in

POPULATION

Population Indicators

Total Population: 1999 3,838,000
World Rank: 121st
Density per sq mi: 194.9 per sq km 75.1
% of annual growth (1994–99): 0.8
Male %: 49.9
Female %: 50.1
Urban %: 39.6
Age Distribution: % 0–14: 23.5
15–29: 26.3
30–44: 22.6
45–59: 16.2
60–74: 8.9
75 and over: 2.7
Population 2020: 3,918,000
Birth Rate per 1,000: 6.5
Death Rate per 1,000: 15.5
Population Doubling Time (years): —
Infant Mortality Rate per 1,000 live births: 43.2
Rate of Natural Increase per 1,000: −9.0
Total Fertility Rate: 1.0
Expectation of Life (years): Males 72.1
Females 77.7
Marriage Rate per 1,000: 6.0
Divorce Rate per 1,000: 0.3
Total Number of Households: 1,203,000
Average Size of Households: 3.6
% of Illegitimate Children: —
Induced Abortions: —
Rate per 100 live births: —

ETHNIC COMPOSITION

While Bosnia and Herzegovina is home to many people of differing ethnic backgrounds, there are three major groups that make up more than 90 percent of the population. The largest single group are Bosniacs (formerly called Muslims) who constitute nearly 40 percent of the population. The Bosniacs are descended from Slavic people who converted to Islam at some point during the lengthy period of Ottoman rule. The second largest group are the Serbs who form nearly 33 percent of the population. Many of these people relocated to Bosnia and Herzegovina during the period of Tito's rule. The Serbs are largely Orthodox Christians. The third largest ethnic group, constituting 20 percent of the population, are Croats, who are generally Roman Catholic. These three groups have often intermingled with one another and it is often difficult to distinguish membership in a group except on the basis of religious affiliation. In addition to these three major groups, there are small numbers of Albanians, Gypsies, and Ukrainians who live in Bosnia.

LANGUAGES

The principal language of the country is Serbo-Croatian (though it is now known as Serbian, Croatian, or Bosnian, depending on the speaker's ethnic and political affiliation). The most distinctive aspect of language is that the Serbs use the Cyrillic alphabet and the Bosniacs and Croats use the Roman alphabet when writing Serbo-Croatian.

Principal Languages and Their Speakers

Serbo-Croatian (Bosnian)	3,810,000
Other	30,000

RELIGIONS

Sitting at the crossroads of east and west, the religious traditions of Bosnia and Herzegovina are reflective of their geopolitical location. A major segment of the population of the country represent the three major religious forces in the region. Most Croats are Roman Catholic while the Serbians are Orthodox Christian. The largest ethnic group, the Bosniacs, also represent the largest religious group, Muslims. Many Bosniacs were converted to Islam during the occupation of Bosnia by the Ottoman Empire. All three religions have a deep heritage in the country. Catholic Croats, for example, observe religious holidays and make pilgrimages to sites like the village of Medjugorje, near Mostar in southern Bosnia, where, in 1981, six Croat children reported that the Virgin Mary had appeared to them. While the country is religiously diverse, its diversity has often led to violent conflict between the groups.

Religious Affiliations

Sunni Muslim	1,360,000
Serbian Orthodox	1,090,000
Roman Catholic	520,000
Other	870,000

HISTORICAL BACKGROUND

The area of modern-day Bosnia and Herzegovina came under Roman rule in the second century B.C.E., ending the rival territorial ambitions of the Thracians, Illyrians, Celts, and Greeks. The division of the Roman Empire in 395 C.E. brought the region under the control of the Byzantine emperor in Constantinople. In the fifth century,

Slavic tribes from the Carpathian Mountains began regularly settling in the Balkan Peninsula, establishing a firm Slavic presence in the area.

As Catholicism dominated the western area of Croatia in the ninth century, the eastern region of Serbia adopted Eastern Orthodox Christianity, leaving the Bosnian area as a buffer between the two religious groups. In the 11th century, the Bosnian principality of Rama struggled to create its own regional identity. Despite the efforts of Byzantium to control the Bosnian region, Bosnian rulers of the 14th century temporarily established a powerful Bosnian state. In 1389 the Ottoman Empire thwarted the efforts of Stjepan Tvrtko, self-proclaimed czar of the Bosnians and Serbs, to unify Bosnian and Serb lands. Bosnia finally succumbed to Ottoman rule in 1463. Twenty years later, the Ottoman Turks gained control of Herzegovina (an Austrian border duchy since 1448) and confirmed their domination over the region. From the 15th to the 19th centuries, the Ottoman Empire ruled Bosnia and Herzegovina through a system that allocated responsibility for religious groups to the leader of each group. Many Bosnians converted to Islam to maintain control over their property and acquire membership in the Muslim ruling class. Persecution of Christians through heavy taxation, a Koran-based legal system, forced conversion to Islam, and, for girls, servitude in harems, contributed to hostile uprisings and violent repression.

Also during the 15th through the 19th centuries, the Habsburg Empire encouraged Serb settlement of the bordering Krajina region to prevent the expansion of the Turks. As the Ottoman Empire began to crumble, the 1878 Congress of Berlin gave the Habsburg Empire administrative rights in the six regions of Bosnia and Herzegovina (Sarajevo, Travnik, Bihac, Dinja Tuzia, Banja Luka, and Mostar).

In 1908 Austria-Hungary officially annexed Bosnia and Herzegovina as a province to counter the threat of Serbian expansion. The empire reversed the Ottoman policy of Muslim privilege. Political organizations were banned and the nationalistic tendencies of Serbs and Croats were suppressed. The Austro-Hungarian Empire attempted to insulate Bosnia and Herzegovina from the influence of its increasingly disgruntled neighbor—Serbia—while trying to prevent the creation of a Muslim state. Tensions in the area erupted when a student member of the Serb nationalist Black Hand organization, Gavrilo Princip, assassinated Archduke Francis Ferdinand, heir to the Habsburg monarchy, and his wife Sophie during a visit to Sarajevo. Austria-Hungary, supported by Germany, subsequently declared war on Serbia, igniting World War 1.

Despite having sided with the losing Austrians during World War I, Bosnia and Herzegovina joined the newly formed Kingdom of Serbs, Croats, and Slovenes in 1918. The kingdom lasted until 1929, when King Alexander established a royal monarchy. The area of Bosnia and Herzegovina, no longer recognized as a political region, was divided into four administrative units. Agrarian reforms freed peasants from the Muslim-led feudal hierarchy, but the centralized, Serb-dominated government dissatisfied many Muslims, Croats, and Slovenes.

A coalition government of Serbs, Muslims, and Slovenes took control in 1939 after the assassination of King Alexander in France. Tensions between the Serbs and the Croats steadily increased until the outbreak of World War II. Croats collaborated with German and Italian fascists and formed the independent state of Croatia, forcing the Serbs to vacate the region in order to create a "Greater Croatia." The Serbs countered with aggression by both the nationalist Cetnik organization, led by Draza Mihajlovic, and the communist Partisan movement, led by Josip Broz Tito. At the end of the war, Tito's partisans brought about the formation of the Federal Republic of Yugoslavia, comprising Serbia, Croatia, Slovenia, Macedonia, Montenegro, and the reunited region of Bosnia and Herzegovina.

Throughout the period of communist rule, Tito and his League of Communists of Yugoslavia suppressed nationalist sentiments and forcibly promoted an ideology of "unity and brotherhood." The 1974 constitution increased the autonomy of each member republic. The death of Tito in 1980 brought a powerful resurgence of long-suppressed nationalistic sentiments. Unlike the five other, ethnically more homogeneous, constituent republics, Bosnia and Herzegovina comprised significant numbers of Muslims, Serbs, Croats, and people of mixed ethnicity. In an attempt to increase their ranks, both the Serbs and the Croats claimed the Bosnian Muslims to be either converted Serbs or converted Croats. The Muslims resisted being identified with either group and claimed the right to a Muslim state within Bosnia and Herzegovina.

Because of its relative strength within the federal republic, Serbia sought to reassert the dominance of the federal government over the individual republics through legal, economic, communication, and voting reforms. Serbia also campaigned to reunify the decentralized League of Communists. By 1990 ethnic Serbs in Croatia and Bosnia had begun planning for a "Greater Serbia." Relations between the member republics rapidly disintegrated, culminating in the secession of Slovenia and Croatia in 1991.

In Bosnia and Herzegovina, dissatisfied Serb delegates in the regional Assembly deserted the coalition government and walked out during initial discussions of the region's independence. Following the example set by Slovenia and Croatia, the Muslim-dominated assembly of Bosnia and Herzegovina declared independence in December 1991. A referendum held two months later, boycotted by Serbs, confirmed the country's independence. In April and May, the United States, the European Union, and the United Nations joined in recognizing the independence of the Republic of Bosnia and Herzegovina.

Following the declaration of sovereignty by the Republic of Bosnia and Herzegovina, the Bosnian Serbs declared the formation of the Serbian Republic of Bosnia and Herzegovina, entitled the Republic of Srpska. Initially, Bosnian Croats remained united with the Bosnian Muslims in the Republic of Bosnia and Herzegovina against the rebel Serbs, despite proposals to Croatia from Serbian leader Radovan Karadzic to partition Bosnia. Bosnian government forces joined with Bosnian Croats to recapture the southern city of Mostar from the Bosnian Serbs. President Franjo Tudjman of Croatia, acting in support of Bosnian Croats, signed a cooperation treaty with the president of Bosnia and Herzegovina, Alija Izetbegovic, and formed a joint defense committee against the Bosnian Serbs. However, the cooperation did not last long, and the Bosnian Croats declared independence for the Croatian Union of Herzeg-Bosna (a year later renamed the Croatian Republic of Herzeg-Bosna) in the area west of Mostar.

Relations between Bosnian government and Bosnian Croat forces broke down in October 1992, as Bosnian Croats, backed up by Croatian army troops, took over Mostar and other towns in Croatian-held areas of Bosnia. The Bosnian government battled both the rebel Serbs and rebel Croats for almost a year before the Bosnian Muslim government and the Bosnian Croats renewed their cooperation against the Bosnian Serbs. In March 1994, under international pressure, Prime Minister Haris Silajdzic of Bosnia and Kresimir Zubak, leader of the Bosnian Croats, met in Washington to sign an agreement creating the Federation of Bosnia and Herzegovina ("Federation"). Bosnian president Izetbegovic and Croatian president Tudjman then signed a second agreement that established a loose confederation. The new federation, approved by the Bosnian Assembly on March 31, 1994, was designed to replace the governance structure of the Republic of Bosnia and Herzegovina. The Bosnian Federation held together, albeit precariously, despite political and military tensions between Bosnian Muslims (Bosniacs) and Bosnian Croats.

In December 1995 the Dayton peace agreement was signed by the governments of Serbia, Croatia, and Bosnia-Herzegovina, bringing a formal end to the war in Bosnia. The agreement called for the continuance of a single Bosnia-Herzegovina state based on a new constitution.

Approximately 34,000 NATO troops remain stationed in Bosnia-Herzegovina, and a large international civilian presence is working to rebuild the country. More than 80 political parties registered for the September 1997 municipal elections. More than 25 suspected war criminals have been arrested and are to stand trial before the International Court of Justice at the Hague. For the foreseeable future, international troops will remain in the region in order to ensure stability and prevent the return of open conflict between the major ethnic groups.

CONSTITUTION

Bosnia and Herzegovina comprises two autonomous entities: the Federation of Bosnia and Herzegovina and the Republic of Srpska. There are three constitutions in force in Bosnia and Herzegovina. The constitution of the Federation of Bosnia and Herzegovina (1994, hereafter referred to as the "Federation constitution") established the Federation government and eight cantonal governments. The constitution of the Republic of Srpska (1992) set forth the legal principles, rights, and duties upon which

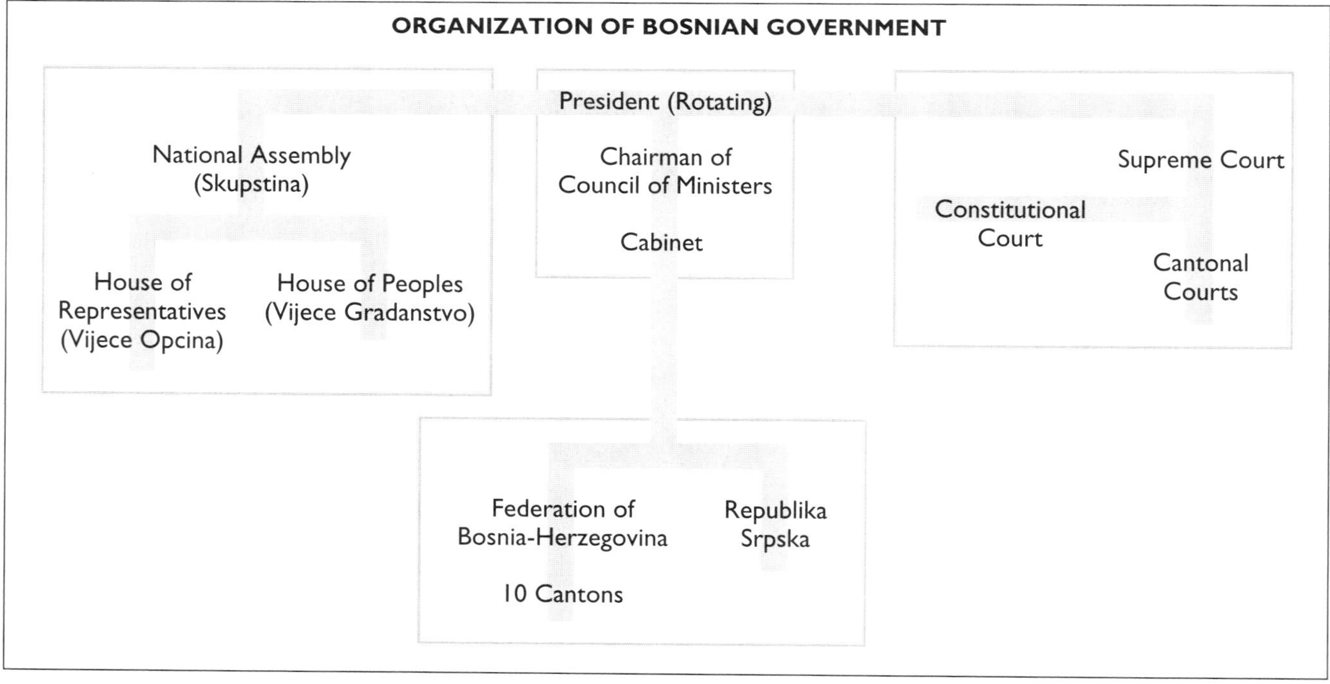

that republic is based and the powers of the respective bodies within the Republic of Srpska. The 1995 Constitution of Bosnia and Herzegovina governs the two entities within the state.

The 1995 constitution of Bosnia and Herzegovina was part of the Dayton Peace Agreement. It replaced the previous constitution of the Republic of Bosnia and Herzegovina and governs the relations between the two entities (the Federation of Bosnia and Herzegovina and the Republic of Srpska). The constitutions of the Federation and the Republic of Srpska, adopted in 1994 and 1992, respectively, were subsequently amended to bring them into compliance with the 1995 constitution.

The government of Bosnia and Herzegovina is headed by a three-person presidency, which comprises a representative of the Bosnians, a representative of the Croats, and a representative of the Republic of Srpska. Bosnia and Herzegovina has a parliamentary assembly comprising two chambers: a House of Representatives and a House of Peoples.

LOCAL GOVERNMENT

The Federation of Bosnia-Herzegovina is divided into 10 cantons, or autonomous regions. Republika Sprska has only one canton. The basic unit of local government is the commune (opstina), each governed by a commune assembly. The commune assembly elects an executive body with administrative responsibilities.

Local Government

Principal administrative divisions, capitals, area, population

AREA AND POPULATION

Autonomous regions / Cantons	Principal city	area sq mi	area sq km	population 1991 estimate
Federation of Bosnia and Herzegovina	Sarajevo	10,080	26,100	2,742,000
Central Bosnia	Travnik	1,240	3,200	305,000
Gorazde	Gorazde	170	440	253,000
Neretva	Mostra	1,680	4,360	253,000
Posavina	Orasje	90	240	61,000
Sarajevo	Sarajevo	460	1,190	526,000
Tuzia-Podrinje	Tuziallero	1,120	2,890	555,000
Una-Sava	Bihac	1,690	4,390	358,000
Western Bosnia	Livno	1,910	4,930	117,000
Western Herzegovina	Libuski	450	1,160	60,000
Zenica-Dobjoj	Zenica	1,270	3,300	429,000
Republika Srpska	Banja Luka	9,650	25,000	1,628,000
TOTAL		19,730	51,100	4,370,000

PARLIAMENT

The House of Peoples is made up of 15 delegates. One-third of the delegates (five) are selected from the Republic of Srpska, and two-thirds (five Croats and five Bosniacs) are selected from the Federation. The delegates from the Federation are selected, respectively, by the Croat and Bosniac delegates to the House of Peoples of the Federation. Delegates from the Republic of Srpska are selected by the National Assembly of the Republic of Srpska.

There are 42 members in the House of Representatives. As with the House of Peoples, one-third of the House of Representatives delegates come from the Republic of Srpska, and two-thirds are elected from the Federation. Each chamber of the parliamentary assembly of Bosnia and Herzegovina must convene in Sarajevo no more than 30 days after the selection or election of members. Although the first election to the House was held in September 1996, parliament's first session was not held until January 1997.

The parliamentary assembly has the responsibility to enact legislation necessary to implement decisions of the presidency; establish and approve a budget for the operations of the institutions of Bosnia and Herzegovina; and consent to the ratification of all international treaties. Other duties may be assigned to the Parliamentary Assembly by mutual agreement of the Federation of Bosnia and Herzegovina and the Republic of Srpska.

Each chamber adopts its internal rules by a majority vote of its members. In 1997 each chamber adopted provisional rules of procedure. There are also provisions in the constitution that regulate some important aspects of the legislative process. Each chamber selects from among its members one Serb, one Bosniac, and one Croat to serve as its chair and deputy chairs. The position of chair automatically rotates among the three selected persons every eight months. At no time can the chair of both chambers represent the same constituent people. In each chamber, the chair and deputy chairs comprise the Collegium of Chair and Deputy Chairs. The collegia have the responsibility to prepare the proposed legislative agenda, provide the delegates at least seven-days' notice of each session sitting, and ensure that draft legislative proposals are presented to the appropriate committees of the respective chambers. In case of undue delays in the legislative process, either chamber may call for a joint meeting. Both collegia are expected to make their best effort to overcome deadlocks.

All legislation requires the approval of both chambers. Unless otherwise proposed by the initiator of the draft legislation, a bill is first introduced in the House of Representatives. However, laws may be initiated in either chamber. Laws may be proposed by any member of parliament, by one or more committees, by any member of the presidency, or by the Council of Ministers. Upon approval by one chamber, the draft law is transferred within seven days to the other chamber, which may approve the legislation or return it to the originating chamber with suggested amendments.

POLITICAL PARTIES

In 1990 the Communist Party in Yugoslavia had given way to the smaller nationalist parties of the republics, including the Croatian Democratic Union of Bosnia and Herzegovina (HDZBiH), named after Franjo Tudjman's party in Croatia; the Muslim Party of Democratic Action (SDA), led by Alija Izetbegovic; and Radovan Karadzic's Serbian Democratic Party of Bosnia and Herzegovina (SDS-BiH), modeled after the SDS in the Croatian region of Krajina. Although there are more than 55 political parties in Bosnia and Herzegovina, the HDZBiH, SDA, and SDS-BiH continue to play the most important roles. They dominated the September 1996 elections.

The SDA, led by Izetbegovic, was founded on two main principles. The party chose religion as the vehicle to implement its first goal of strengthening Muslim nationalism. By appealing to the feature certain to distinguish the SDA from other parties, the SDA was able to rally the majority of Muslims behind the banner of Islam. The second goal was promoting the preservation of a multinational and multireligious state.

The HDZBiH was initially founded on the principle of keeping the borders of Bosnia and Herzegovina inviolate. However, as Bosnian Croats cooperated with Bosnian Serbs, inviolate borders appeared to be merely a step in creating a "Greater Croatia." The HDZBiH has not given up on the idea of an independent Herzeg-Bosna. The president of Croatia, Franjo Tudjman, initially controlled the party. The SDS-BiH was initially created in Croatia by Croatian Serbs to combat rising Croat nationalism.

Political Parties

Coalition for a Unified and Democratic Bosnia and Herzegovina, 1997
Party of Democratic Action, 1990
Party for Bosnia and Herzegovina, 1996
Croatian Democratic Union, 1990
Unity, 1998, a coalition consisting of
 Serbian People's Alliance, 1997
 Socialist Party of the Serb Republic,
 Party of Independent Social Democrats
Serbian Democratic Party, 1990
Serb Radical Party
Social Democratic Party, 1999
Radical Party of the Serb Republic
New Croatian Initiative, 1998
Democratic People's Union, 1996
Bosnian-Herzegovinian Patriotic Party
Democratic Party of Pensioners
Croatian Party of Rights
Bosnian Party
Center Coalition
Bosnian Rights Party
Croatian Peasants' Party, 1991
Serb Coalition
Coalition for King and Fatherland
Muslim Bosniac Organization, 1990
Democratic League of Greens
Party of Independent Social Democrats, 1999
Liberal Social Party, 1998
Croatian Pure Party of Rights

Political Parties: Strength in Parliament Most Recent Elections

REPUBLIC OF BOSNIA AND HERZEGOVINA

House of Peoples. The upper chamber has 15 members elected by the legislatures of the republic's two constituent entities (10 from the Federation and 5 from the Serb Republic).

House of Representatives. The lower chamber consists of 42 members directly elected by proportional representation (28 from the Federation and 14 from the Serb Republic). The balloting on November 11, 2000, yielded the following seat distribution: Party of Democratic Action, 8; Social Democratic Party BiH, 9; Serb Democratic Party, 6; Croatian Democratic Community, 5; Party for BiH, 4; Party for Democratic Progress RS, 2; SNSD-DSP (Party of Independent Social Democrats-Democratic Socialist Party), 1; Socialist Party RS, 1; Serbian People's Union RS-Biljana Plavsic, 1; New Croatian Initiative, 1; Democratic People's Community, 1; Bosnian-Herzegovinian Patriotic Party, 1; Democratic Party of Pensioners BiH, 1.

FEDERATION OF BOSNIA AND HERZEGOVINA

House of Peoples of the Federation. The chamber has 74 members who are directly elected, of whom at least 30 must be Bosniacs and at least 30 must be Croats.

House of Representatives of the Federation. The chamber consists 140 members who are directly elected by proportional representation. The elections of November 11, 2000, yielded the following distribution of seats: Party of Democratic Action, 38; Social Democratic Party BiH, 37; Croatian Democratic Community, 25; Party for BiH, 21; Democratic People's Community, 3; Bosnian-Herzegovinian Patriotic Party, 2; New Croatian Initiative, 2; Pensioners' Party of the BiH Federation, 2; Bosnian Party, 2; Croatian Party of Rights, 1; Democratic Party of Pensioners BiH, 1; Liberal Democratic Party, 1; Republican Party, 1; Croatian Peasants Party, 1; Croatian Christian Democratic Union, 1; Civic Democratic Party, 1; Party of Independent Social Democrats, 1.

SERB REPUBLIC OF BOSNIA AND HERZEGOVINA

National Assembly. The unicameral legislature consists of 83 members who are directly elected by proportional representation. The voting of November 11, 2000, yielded the following distribution of seats: Serbian Democratic Party, 31; Party of Independent Social Democrats, 11; Party for Democratic Progress RS, 11; Party of Democratic Action, 6; Party for BiH, 4; Social Democratic Party BiH, 4; Socialist Party RS, 4; Democratic Socialist Party, 4; Democratic People's League, 3; Serbian People's Union RS-Biljana Plavsic, 2; Pensioners's Party RS, 1; New Croatian Initiative, 1; Democratic Party RS, 1.

LEGAL SYSTEM

The Bosnian legal system is based on the civil law system. The highest court in the country is the Constitutional Court, which consists of nine members: four members are selected by the Bosniac/Croat Federation's House of Representatives, two members by the Republika Srpska's National Assembly, and three non-Bosnian members by the president of the European Court of Human Rights.

LAW ENFORCEMENT

Law Enforcement

Offenses reported to the police per 100,000: 402
- Murder: 2.5
- Assault: 2.6
- Burglary: —
- Automobile Theft: —
- Population per Police officer: —

Death Penalty: Yes.

HUMAN RIGHTS

There were significant improvements in several areas of concern with regard to human rights in Bosnia and Herzegovina during 1999, the fourth year of implementation of the Dayton Peace Agreement. The arrest and prosecution of war criminals increased as six persons indicted for war crimes were arrested, and one extradited to the Hague, including several high-ranking officials. The return of those who were displaced during the fighting that rocked the area began to accelerate with the support of international efforts. The Federation enacted legislation that abolished the death penalty and called for its abolishment in the Republic Srpska. Despite these improvements, there are still lingering hostilities between the ethnic-religious groups. Much of the resentment is not acted upon because of the deployment of international forces and continuing international pressure to keep the peace.

FOREIGN POLICY

Bosnia's independence is secured by the 1995 Dayton Accords. The Office of the High Representative oversees the implementation of the Dayton Accords. Hostility to Serbia is the cornerstone of Bosnian foreign policy although the two countries have diplomatic relations. Bosnia has extensive trade and other agreements with Croatia.

DEFENSE

The current strength of the Bosnian army is approximately 40,000 soldiers who are organized into five corps headquarters. This number does not include the Croatian Defense Council, which has approximately 16,000 personnel. The equipment of the army is largely Soviet-made and includes tanks, aircraft, and missiles.

Military Indicators

Total Active Duty Personnel: 40,000
Military Manpower per 1,000: 12.8
Military Expenditures $million: —
- as % of GNP: —
- per capita $: —
- as % of central government expenditures: —

Arms Imports $million: 270
Arms Exports $million: 0

ECONOMY

Bosnia and Herzegovina ranked next to the former Yugoslav Republic of Macedonia as the poorest republic in the old Yugoslav federation. Although agriculture has been almost all in private hands, farms have been small and inefficient, and the republic traditionally has been a net importer of food. Industry has been greatly overstaffed, one reflection of the socialist economic structure of Yugoslavia. Tito had pushed the development of military industries in the republic with the result that Bosnia hosted a large share of Yugoslavia's defense plants. The bitter interethnic warfare in Bosnia caused production to plummet by 80 percent from 1990 to 1995, unemployment to soar, and human misery to multiply. With an uneasy peace in place, output recovered in 1996–98 at high percentage rates on a low base; but output growth slowed appreciably in 1999 and 2000, and gross domestic product remains far below the 1990 level. Economic data are of limited use because, although both the Federation and the Republic of Srpska issue figures, national-level statistics are not available. Moreover, official data do not capture the large share of activity that occurs on the black market. In 1999, the convertible mark—the national currency introduced in 1998—gained wider acceptance, and the Central Bank of Bosnia and Herzegovina dramatically increased its reserve holdings. Implementation of privatization, however, has been slower than anticipated. Banking reform accererated in early 2001 as all the communist-era payments bureaus were shut down. The country receives substantial amounts of reconstruction assistance and humanitarian aid from the international community but will have to prepare for an era of declining assistance.

Principal Economic Indicators

Gross National Product: $4.455 billion
GNP per capita $: 1090
GNP Average Annual Growth Rate (1990–97) %: —
GNP per capita Average Annual Growth Rate (1990-97) %: —
- Agriculture: —
- Mining: —
- Manufacturing: —
- Construction: —
- Public Utilities: —
- Transportation and Communications: —
- Trade: —
- Financial Services: —
- Other Services: —
- Government: —

(continued)

Gross Domestic Product by Type of Expenditure %
Private Consumption: —
Government Consumption: —
Gross Domestic Investment: —
Foreign Trade: Exports: —
Imports: —
% of Income Received by Poorest 20%: —
% of Income Received by Richest 10%: —

Price and earnings indexes (1995 = 100)

	1994	1995	1996	1997
Consumer price index	—	—	—	—
Monthly earnings index	142.3	100.0	170.1	307.7

Finance

National Currency: Marka
Exchange Rate: $1 = —
Money Supply Stock in National Currency billion: —
M1 per capita: —
Central Bank Discount Rate %: —
Total External Debt $million: 3,500
Debt Service Ratio %: —
Balance of Payments $million: —
International Reserves SDRs million: —
Ratio of External Debt to Total Reserves: —
Average Annual Rate of Inflation/Consumer Price Index Growth Rate %: —

Official Development Assistance

ODA $million: 876
as % of GNP: —
per capita $: 232
Foreign Direct Investment $million: —

Central Government Revenues and Expenditures

Fiscal Year: Calendar Year
Revenues $million: —
Expenditures $million: —
Budget Deficit/Surplus $million: —
Tax Revenues as % of GDP: —
Highest Tax Bracket %
Individual: —
Corporate: —

Employment and Labor

Economically Active Population: 1,026,000
Female Participation Rate %: 36.9
Activity Rate %: 22.7
Labor by Sector: %
Agriculture, Forestry, Fishing: 3.8
Manufacturing, Mining: 50.5
Construction: 7.3
Transportation and Communications: 6.7
Trade, Hotels, and Restaurants: 12.8
Finance, Insurance, Real Estate: 3.8
Public Administration, Defense: —
Services: 15.1
Unemployment %: 50

Agriculture

Agriculture's Share of GDP: —
Average Annual Rate of Growth (1965–98) %: —
Number of Farms 000: 540
Average Size of Farm ha: —
Number of Tractors per 1,000 hectares: 48.3
Irrigation, % of Farms having: 0.3
Artificial Fertilizer kg/hectare: —
Total Farmland as % of land area: 49.4
Livestock: Cattle 000: 260
Sheep 000: 276
Hogs 000: 70
Chickens 000: 3,870
Forests: Production of Roundwood (000 cubic meters): 5,379
Fisheries: Total Catch tons: 2.4

Mining

% of GDP: —
Value of Mineral Production $million: —

Manufacturing

Value Added $million: 4,021
Industrial Production Growth Rate %: —

Energy

Commercial Energy Production metric tons of oil equivalent 000: 626
Commercial Energy Consumption metric tons of oil equivalent 000: 1,750
Commercial Energy Consumption per capita kg: —
Average Annual Growth Rate 1980–97 %: —
Net Energy Imports % of use: 64
Electricity Installed Capacity kW 000: 2,407
Production kW-hr million: 2,203
Coal Reserves tons million: —
Production tons 000: 1,640
Natural Gas Proven Reserves cubic meters billion: —
Production cubic meters million: —
Crude Petroleum Reserves barrels million: —
Production barrels million: —
Consumption barrels million: 15
Refinery Capacity barrels per day 000: —
Pipelines Length km: 174

Foreign Trade

Imports $million: 1,879.0
Exports $million: 1,71.0
Export Volume % Annual Growth Rate (1990–97): —
Import Volume % Annual Growth Rate (1990–97): —
Balance of Trade $

Balance of trade (current prices)

	1992	1993	1994	1995	1996	1997
U.S. $000,000	—	−339	−739	−898	−1,742	−2,004
% of total	—	66.6%	91.1%	89.6%	82.9%	69.9%

Major Trading Partners

	Imports	Exports
European Union %	35.8	45.6
United States %	3.4	5.3
Eastern Europe %	8.6	2.3
Japan %	0.1	1.2
Others %	52.2	45.6

Transportation

Roads Total Length mi: 13,153 km 21,168
Paved %: 54
Automobiles: 438,080
Trucks and Buses: 50,578
Persons per vehicle: 8.9
Railroad; Track Length mi: 634 km 1,021
Passenger-mi million: 344
Freight-mi million: 1,333
Merchant Marine: No. of Vessels: —
  Total Deadweight Tonnage 000: —
  International Cargo Loaded tons 000: —
  International Cargo Off-loaded tons 000: —
Airports with Scheduled Flights: 1
Traffic: Passenger-mi million: —
  Freight-mi million: —
Length of Canals mi: —

Tourism

Number of Tourists to 000: 100
Number of Tourists from 000: —
Tourist Receipts $million: —
Tourist Expenditures $million: —

Communications

Telephones 000: 238
Cost of Local Calls 3 mins: $0.03
Cellular Telephones 000: —
Fax Machines 000: —
Personal Computers 000: —
Internet Hosts per million persons: —
Mail: Post Offices: 159
  Pieces of Mail Handled million: 0.5
  Pieces of Mail Handled per person: 0.1

EDUCATION

Prior to the outbreak of civil war in Bosnia, education was universal and free from the age of seven until 18. The system had more than 700,000 students enrolled. Most of these were in the elementary school. There are four universities in the country. Since the Dayton Accords, schools have been reestablished where possible, however, the formal state structure that predated the war is largely gone. There are nearly 600,000 school-age children in the country.

Education

Literacy Rate %: 86.5
  Male %: 96.5
  Female %: 76.6
First Level: Primary schools: 2,205
  Teachers: 23,369
  Students: 539,875
  Student-Teacher Ratio: 23.1
  Net Enrollment Ratio: 98
Second Level: Secondary Schools: 238
  Teachers: 9,030
  Students: 172,063
  Student-Teacher Ratio: 19.1
  Net Enrollment Ratio: —

Vocational Level: Schools: —
  Students: —

Third Level: Institutions: 44
  Teachers: 2,802
  Students: 37,541
  Student-Ratio Level: 13.4
  Gross Enrollment Ratio: —
  Students per 100,000: —
  % of Population Age 25 and over with Postsecondary Education: —

Public Expenditure on Education as % of GDP: —

SCIENCE AND TECHNOLOGY

Science and Technology

Scientists and Engineers in R&D per 1 million persons: —
Expenditures in R&D as % of GDP: —
High-Tech Exports $million: —
Patent Applications by Residents: —

MEDIA

The Federation constitution guarantees the freedom of the media and press, and, with the exception of the government press center, media agencies operate freely and independently. The award-winning Sarajevo daily paper *Obslobodjenje* has continued its operations despite production difficulties imposed by the war. The Federation constitution also lists freedom of the press as a fundamental national freedom.

The Bosnia and Herzegovina constitution also provides for freedom of expression. The constitution of the Republic of Srpska also sets forth this freedom. Although the latter constitution guarantees freedom of communication, this may be limited by a court order if it is deemed crucial for criminal proceedings or for the Republic of Srpska's security.

The Office of the High Representative in Bosnia (OHR), a body created by the Dayton Accord and approved by the UN Security Council and other international bodies, has been active in promoting an independent media. For example, the OHR, Organization for Security and Cooperation in Europe, and the European Monitoring Commission have been working toward the establishment of an independent and self-sufficient publishing house in the Republic of Srpska.

Bosnia's first independent television station, the Open Broadcast Network, began broadcasting on September 7, 1996. TV-IN, a joint venture company that represents independent journalists in Bosnia and Herzegovina and five commercial television stations, was also launched in late 1996. By 1998, there were eight AM radio stations and 16 FM stations in operation in Bosnia.

Media

Daily Newspapers: 2
  Total Circulation 000: 518
  Circulation per 1,000: 131
Books Published: —
Magazines:
Radio Receivers 000: 840
  per 1,000: 263
Television sets 000: 385
  per 1,000: 111

MOST IMPORTANT MEDIA:

Press. As of early 1993 the circulation of Sarajevo's one remaining daily, *Oslobodjenje* (Liberation), had declined from 50,000 to 4,000, with supplies of newsprint nearing exhaustion. In May 1994 an English-language edition commenced publication at Bel Air, Maryland, the proceeds of which were to help the Sarajevo edition meet its operating costs. Circulation has subsequently rebounded to 56,000. Other dailies include *Dnevni Avaz* (Daily Voice), Bosnian; *Slobodna Dalmacija* (Free Dalmatia), Croatian; *Vjesnik* (The News), Serbian; *Vecernje Novine* (Nightly Report, 15,000), Serbian; *Glas Srpski* (Serbian Voice), Serbian; *Horizont* (Horizon), Croatian; *Nasa Borba* (Our Battle), Serbian. Weekly publications include *Ljiljan* (Lily), Bosnian; *Hratska Rijec* (Croatian Word), Croatian; and *Nevavisne Novine* (Independent News), Serbian.

News agencies. The Herceg-Bosna News Agency at Mostar and the Western Bosnian Information Agency (Zapadno Bosanska Informativna Agencija-ZBIA) at Velika Kladusa were both launched in 1993. The state news agency is BH Press.

Radio and television. Radio-Television of Bosnia and Herzegovina (Radio-Televizija Bosne I Hercegovine) broadcasts over four radio and two television channels in Serbo-Croat.

CULTURE

Cultural Indicators

Public Libraries
  Number:
  Volumes:
  Registered borrowers:
Museums
  Number:
  Annual Attendance:
Cinema
  Production of Long Films:
  Number of Cinemas:
  Seating Capacity:
  Annual Attendance:
  Annual Attendance per capita:

STATUS OF WOMEN

Legally women have the same rights as do men. The imposition of peace by international forces has brought to an end one of the tragedies of the war, mass rape. The country is still dealing with the emotional and cultural scars of the war.

Women

Gender Empowerment Measure: —
Seats Held in Parliament by Women %: 7.1
Female Administrators and Managers %: —
Female Professional and Technical Workers %: —
Women's Share of Earned Income %: —
Women in Government %: 2.8

HEALTH, FOOD, AND NUTRITION

Health

Number of Physicians: 4,500
Number of Dentists: 550
Number of Nurses: 11,900
Number of Pharmacists: —
Population per Physician: 703
Number of Hospitals: —
Hospital Beds per 10,000: 46
Hospital Bed Occupancy Rate: 82.4
Infant Mortality Rate per 1,000 live births: 20
Maternal Mortality Rate per 100,000 live births: —
Total Health Expenditures as % of GDP: —
Health Expenditures per capita $: —
HIV Infected % of adults: 0.04
Cigarette Consumption per smoker per year: —
% of Smokers: Male: —
  Female: —
Access to Safe Water %: —

Food and Nutrition

Food Supply as % of FAO Requirements: —
% of Consumption Expenditures on Food: 44.7
Daily Available Calories per capita: —
% of Total Calories derived from:
Cereals: —
Potatoes, cassava: —
Meat, poultry: —
Fish: —
Eggs, milk: —
Fruits, vegetables: —
Fats, oils: —

ENVIRONMENT

The environment of Bosnia and Herzegovina has suffered greatly because of the civil strife. The infrastructure for the removal of waste in urban areas and the provision of clean drinking water has been destroyed. Pollution is growing due to discharges from metallurgical plants.

Environment

Forest Area sq km: 27,000
Average Annual Deforestation sq km: 0
Nationally Protected Areas as % of Total Land Area: 0.4
Freshwater Access cubic meters per capita: 9,952
Emissions of Organic Water Pollutants kg per day: 8,903
CO_2 Emissions per capita ton: 0.9

CHRONOLOGY

1941 Axis powers incorporate Bosnia into the independent state of Croatia, a puppet state run by the Ustase, a Croat fascist group; the Ustase attempts to exterminate the region's two million Serbs; civil war breaks out, with the multiethnic communist Partisans led by Josip Broz Tito fighting both the Ustase and the Serb royalist Cetniks.

1943 The Partisans proclaim a federation of South Slav peoples, known as Yugoslavia, with Tito as marshal and prime minister.

1945 World War II ends; Tito organizes the Yugoslavia Socialist Federation as six republics: Bosnia-Herzegovina, Croatia, Serbia, Slovenia, Montenegro, and Macedonia; political representation within Bosnia-Herzegovina is strictly apportioned among the state's three constituent peoples, Croats, Serbs, and Muslims.

1948 Tito breaks relations with the Soviet Union's Joseph Stalin and begins a gradual process of decentralization of Yugoslavia.

1968 Muslims are officially recognized as one of Yugoslavia's six national groups.

1980 Tito dies; Yugoslavia's economy takes a turn for the worse.

1985 Yugoslavia's economic crisis hits its nadir, with production and living standards at 1965 levels.

1988 Slobodan Milosevic, the president of Serbia, embarks on a campaign to recentralize Yugoslavia.

1989 Croatia and Slovenia resist centralization and call for multiparty elections.

1990 In the first multiparty national elections since World War II, communist candidates are easily defeated by new parties representing the three national communities of Bosnia-Herzegovina, which gain seats roughly in proportion to their populations; Alija Izetbegovic, a Bosniac (Muslim), leads the resulting tripartite government and joint presidency.

1991 The Serbian Democratic Party of Bosnia-Herzegovina, led by Radovan Karadzic, boycotts joint presidential meetings and declares a Serb National Assembly in Banja Luka; Slovenia and Croatia declare their independence and are recognized by the European Union (EU).

1992 In a referendum boycotted by Serbs, 97 percent of voters endorse independence for Bosnia-Herzegovina; in April the United States and the EU recognize Bosnia-Herzegovina; within a week the combined Serb forces of the Yugoslavian army, Serb paramilitary groups, and Bosnian Serbs begin bombarding Sarajevo; Serbia and Montenegro declare themselves the Federal Republic of Yugoslavia (FRY); Serb forces begin a process of "ethnic cleansing" to clear non-Serbs from Serb-claimed areas; by mid-May Serb forces control two-thirds of Bosnia-Herzegovina.

1993 The UN imposes economic sanctions on the FRY; war breaks out between Croats and Bosniacs, formerly allied against the Serbs, over control of central Bosnia-Herzegovina; Serb ethnic cleansing is nearly complete by mid-year.

1994 Bosniacs and Croats agree to form a Bosniac-Croat federation in Bosnia-Herzegovina; a cease-fire with Serb forces is negotiated in December.

1995 Serbian forces massacre some 6,000 Muslim men in the UN-declared "safe haven" at Srebrenica; NATO carries out major air strikes on Serb positions; the United States brokers a peace agreement, the Dayton Accords, retaining Bosnia-Herzegovina's prewar boundaries but distinguishing two separate entities within it: one Serb, the other Croat-Bosniac.

1996 Voters choose candidates on essentially ethnic lines in national elections observed by the Organization for Security and Cooperation in Europe.

1998 NATO extends indefinitely its peacekeeping operations in Bosnia-Herzegovina, which were scheduled to expire in June.

1997 Candidates are selected on essentially ethnic lines in municipal elections.

2000 Non-nationalist parties gain a slim majority in national elections.

BIBLIOGRAPHY

Bert, Wayne. *The Reluctant Superpower*. New York, 1997.

Burg, Steven L. *The War in Bosnia-Herzegovina: Ethnic Conflict and International Intervention*. Armonk, N.Y., 1999.

Malcolm, N. *Bosnia: A Short History*. London, 1996.
O'Balance, E. *Civil War in Bosnia*. London 1995.

OFFICIAL PUBLICATIONS

No official publications are available.

CONTACT INFORMATION

Embassy of Bosnia and Herzegovina
2109 E Street NW
Washington, D.C. 20037
Phone: (202) 337-1500 Fax: (202) 337-1502

INTERNET RESOURCES

- Central Bank of Bosnia and Herzegovina
  http://www.cbbh.gov.ba
- Embassy of Bosnia and Herzegovina (Washington, D.C.)
  http://www.bosnianembassy.org/
- Office of the High Representative in Bosnia and Herzegovina
  http://www.ohr.int/

BOTSWANA

BASIC FACT SHEET

OFFICIAL NAME:
Republic of Botswana (formerly Bechuanaland)

ABBREVIATION:
BS

CAPITAL:
Gaborone

HEAD OF STATE AND HEAD OF GOVERNMENT:
President Festus Mogae (from 1998)

NATURE OF GOVERNMENT:
Parliamentary democracy

POPULATION:
1,464,000 (1999)

AREA:
600,372 sq km (231,804 sq mi)

ETHNIC MAJORITY:
Bamangwato, Batawana, Bakwena, Bangwaketsi, Bakgatla, Barolong, Bamalete, and Batalokwa

LANGUAGES:
English (official); Setswana (national)

RELIGIONS:
Christianity and animism

UNIT OF CURRENCY:
Pula (P.)

NATIONAL FLAG:
Five horizontal stripes of varying widths. Light blue top and bottom stripes are separated from a smaller black middle stripe by thin white stripes.

NATIONAL EMBLEM:
The main elements of the national coat of arms are a white oval shield flanked by a zebra and an elephant tusk on the left and zebra and a stem of millet with red crown and green stalk on the right; on the shield are three wavy black stripes, three cogwheels, and a reddish-brown oxhead with long silver horns; beneath is the legend *Pula,* meaning rain.

NATIONAL ANTHEM:
"Blessed Country"

NATIONAL HOLIDAYS:
September 30 (Botswana Day, National Day); May 24 (President's Day); first Monday in August (Commonwealth Day); Christian festivals include Good Friday, Holy Saturday, Holy Monday, Ascension Day, Whitmonday, Christmas, and Boxing Day

DATE OF INDEPENDENCE:
September 30, 1966

DATE OF CONSTITUTION:
Effective 1966

GEOGRAPHICAL FEATURES

Botswana, a landlocked country in southern Africa, occupies an area of 600,372 sq km (231,894 sq mi), extending 1,115 km (693 mi) north-northeast to south-south west and 951 km (591 mi) east-southeast to west-northwest.

Botswana shares its total international boundary of 4,052 km (2,518 mi) with South Africa (1,840 km; 1,142 mi), Namibia (formerly South-West Africa) (1,360 km; 844 mi), and Zimbabwe (813 km; 505 mi). Botswana touches Zambia at the confluence of the Zambezi and Chobe Rivers in the extreme north. This part of the border is a source of controversy with South Africa.

The capital is Gaborone, with an estimated 1999 population of 182,000. Gaborone is a comparatively new city and until 1975 had a much smaller population than Serowe (28,267) or Francistown (49,396). Other population centers are Lobatse (25,689), Selibe-Pikwe (49,490), Kanye (26,300, including seasonal migrants), Maun (18,470), Molepolole (29,212), Ramotswa (17,961), and Mochudi (26,320).

Botswana

Botswana is a vast tableland at a mean altitude of 1,000 m (3,300 ft). A gently undalating plateau running from the South African border near Lobatse to a point west of Kanye and from there northward to Bulawayo on the Zimbabwean border forms the watershed between the two main natural divisions of Botswana. The fertile land to the south of this plateau is hilly bush country and grassland, or veld. To the west of the country plateau, stretching over the border into Namibia, is the Kalahari (also known as Kgaladi) Desert. The Kalahari Desert is more accurately a semidesert, or sandy tract, covered with thorn bush and grass. In the extreme northwest lies the area known as Ngamiland, dominated by the Okavango Swamps, a great inland delta of some 16,835 sq km (6,500 sq mi) and the Makgadikgadi Salt Pans. Around the swamps and along the northeastern border from Kasane to Francistown there is forest and dense bush.

Most of Botswana is without surface drainage, and apart from the Limpopo and Chobe rivers the country's rivers never reach the sea. The major interior river system is the Okavango, which flows into Botswana from Angolan Highlands in the northwest to form the Okavango Swamps, a delta covering about 3 percent of the total land area of the country. About half of this area is perennially flooded; the rest is seasonally flooded. From this marsh there is a seasonal flow of water into the ephemeral Lake Ngami and, along the Botletle River, to Lake Dow and the Makgadikgadi Salt Pans. Much of the water is, however, lost through evaporation. The Chobe River, in the north, flows into the Zambezi after marking the border of the Caprivi Strip for part of its course.

Geography

Area sq km: 600,327 sq mi: 231,804
World Rank: 47th
Land Boundaries, km: Namibia 1,360; South Africa 1,840; Zimbabwe 813
Coastline, km: 0
Elevation Extremes meters
Lowest: Limpopoana shashe rivers 513
Highest: Tsodilo Hill 1,489
Land Use % Arable land: 1
Permanent Crops: 0
Permanent Pastures: 46
Forest and Woodland: 47
Other: 6

Population of Principal Cities

Gaborone	182,000

CLIMATE AND WEATHER

The climate is generally subtropical, although the northern part of the country lies within the tropics. The dry season lasts from September to April, the hottest month being in January, with mean maximum temperatures from 30° (86°F) to 34.4°C (94°F). Winters are cool, with frost common in the desert. In July, the coldest month, mean minimum temperatures range from 0.5°C (33°F) in the Kalahari to 8.3°C (47°F) in the far north. The rains usually begin in late October and continue until the end of April. Average rainfall is about 460 mm (18 in) but most of the Kalahari receives only 230 mm (9 in). The country often suffers long periods of drought, sometimes lasting up to five years.

In the winter the prevailing wind system is a dry wind from the Atlantic, sweeping across the Kalahari and bringing sandstorms.

Climate and Weather

Mean Temperature
Summer 86°F to 94°F
Winter 33°F to 47°F
Average Rainfall 18 in
Kalahari Desert 9 in

POPULATION

Population Indicators

Total Population: 1999 1,464,000
World Rank: 146th
Density per sq mi: 6.5 per sq km: 2.5
% of annual growth (1994–99): 1.2
Male %: 47.8
Female %: 52.2
Urban %: 23.9
Age Distribution: % 0–14: 42.8
15–29: 27.3
30–44: 14.3
45–59: 7.3
60–74: 4.1
75 and over: 2.2
Population 2020: 1,601,000
Birth Rate per 1,000: 37.1
Death Rate per 1,000: 6.6
Population Doubling Time (years): 27
Infant Mortality Rate per 1,000 live births: 39.0
Rate of Natural Increase per 1,000: 30.5
Total Fertility Rate: 4.5
Expectation of Life (years): Males 59.5
Females 65.6
Marriage Rate per 1,000: 1.6
Divorce Rate per 1,000: —
Total Number of Households: 256,842
Average Size of Households: 5.7
% of Illegitimate Children: 71.2
Induced Abortions: 17
Rate per 100 live births: 0.1

ETHNIC COMPOSITION

Botswana is one of the most ethnically homogeneous states in Africa. About 90 percent of the population are Tswana, of Tswana-speaking descent; most of the rest are Kalanga-speaking in origin, which links them with their counterparts in neighboring Zimbabwe. The remainder are Basarwa (San People), the Herero, who are linked to the larger Herero community in Namibia, whites, consisting mainly of Afrikaner farmers in the northeast of the country, and Asians.

LANGUAGES

Setswana is the national language but English is used in business and higher education and is widely spoken. In South Africa's North-West Province there are about 3 million Setswana-speaking people, representing some 66 percent of the province's population (which includes the former Tswana homeland of Bophuthatswana) and 7 percent of South Africa's population.

Principal Languages and Their Speakers

English (lingua franca)	590,000
Khoekhoe (Hottentot)	36,000
Ndebele	19,000
San (Bushman)	51,000
Shona	180,000
Tswana (lingua franca)	1,170,000
Other	71,000

RELIGIONS

The majority of the Tswana are nominally Christian, although less than 20 to 30 percent are practicing. The rest combine some form of traditional beliefs with Christian elements. Most Christians are affiliated with the United Congregational Church. There is a Roman Catholic diocese at Gaborone with 18,000 members.

Religious Affiliations

African Christian	400,000
Protestant	180,000
Roman Catholic	60,000
Other (mostly traditional beliefs)	820,000

HISTORICAL BACKGROUND

The earliest inhabitants of what is now Botswana were almost certainly the nomadic Basarwa (commonly known as the Bushmen or the San people). During the 17th and 18th centuries the area was settled by Tswana-speaking peoples whose communities overlapped into what are now South Africa's North-west and Northern provinces as well as Zimbabwe. Europeans began to venture into the region in the early 19th century. In 1872 King Khama III emerged as the most prominent indigenous leader and built up a powerful army. As expansionary pressures from Afrikaners in South Africa increased, intensified by the discovery of gold near Francistown, Khama III sought protection from the British. In 1885 Britain declared a protectorate, British Bechuanaland, over Khama's people, while annexing Tswana-inhabited territory in the northern Cape region to its own Cape Colony. After the Cape Colony became part of the South African Union in 1910, white South African leaders pushed for the incorporation of Bechuanaland into the union.

Khama III retained control of local administration, law, and justice, He also resisted pressure to grant mining concessions to the British South Africa Company and successfully prevented unification with South Africa. Economically, however, the protectorate remained neglected, and became little more than a labor reservoir for South African mines and farms. Cattle ownership remained at the core of Botswana society.

A grandson of Khama III, Seretse Khama, founded the Botswana Democratic Party (BDP), which won most of the elected seats in the preindependence poll of 1965. At independence in September 1966 Khama became the country's first president. He was a conservative and favored the creation of a multiracial democratic society, in which traditional laws would retain their due place. His policies included the transfer of tribal land rights to elected district committees for white leasehold farmers, encouragement of foreign investment, and a neutral stance toward racist regimes in South Africa and Rhodesia (now Zimbabwe), reflecting Botswana's strategic vulnerability. He did, however, refuse to open diplomatic relations with apartheid South Africa, despite strong commercial links. His leadership and statesmanship in the British Commonwealth earned him a knighthood from the British government, after which he was referred to as "Sir" Seretse Khama. He held office until his death in 1980. His deputy, Vice President Quette Ketumile Masire, a co-founder of the BDP, succeeded him. In March 1998, Sir Ketumile Masire retired and his vice president, Festus Mogae, took over as president. Mogae chose Ian Khama, Seretse's son and previous head of the army, as his vice president. BDP policy has remained fairly constant throughout these leadership transitions.

CONSTITUTION

Botswana is a presidential democracy. The constitution that was adopted at independence in 1966 vests legislative power in a parliament comprising the National Assembly, with 40 elected members, the president, the speaker, the attorney-general, and four members nominated by the president. The assembly is elected every five years on the basis of universal adult suffrage, with full freedom to organize political parties. A 15-member House of Chiefs has advisory power only. Executive power lies with the president, who is elected by parliament. The constitution may be amended in minor ways on a simple parliamentary majority vote. More substantive amendments require a two-thirds majority, while major alterations have to be put to a national referendum. Under a local government system introduced at independence, there are nine district councils (Gaborone and Francistown) and four town councils. Local elections coincide with national elections and are also conducted on a party basis.

Full protection of the fundamental rights and freedoms of the individual is provided under the constitution, although criticisms about the treatment of minority Basarwa have emerged. An independent judiciary interprets and administers the constitution and other laws. Roman-Dutch law is the common law, while criminal law is largely based on English law. Customary law cases in rural areas are heard by tribal courts associated with the village kgotla (an assembly of elders), the traditional chiefs acting as court presidents.

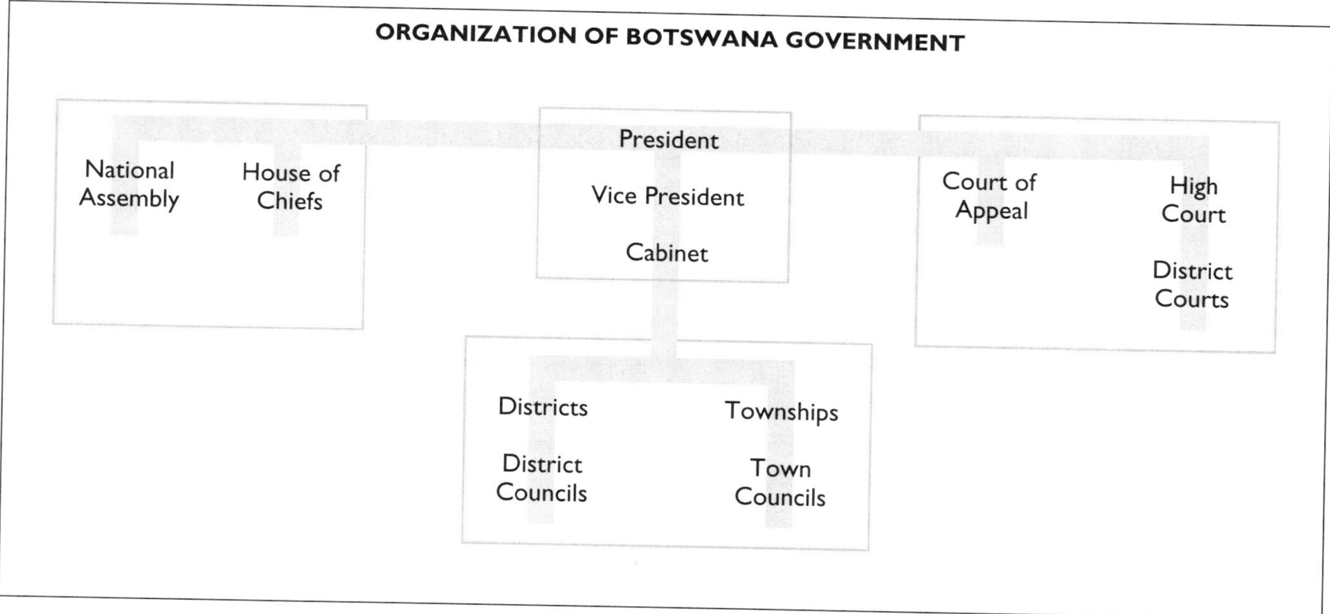

The Botswana Democratic Party's (BDP) hold on power is secure. In the 1999 general election it won 33 of the 40 elected seats. Although this was an improvement on the 27 it had won in 1994, it was largely a reflection of opposition weakness rather than strong BDP support. The BDP's urban support is quite weak, as rising unemployment and poverty are major issues, and it is the BDP's rural base that ensures its continued success. Internally, traditional BDP factions appear to have lost ground in recent years, although the party's conservative policies and constituency remain unchanged. Sir Quett Masire selected Festus Mogae, a former bureaucrat, as his successor in a bid to neutralize the internal factions. Mogae's subsequent choice of former army commander Ian Khama as his vice president was made for similar reasons. BDP faction leaders have thus taken more of a back seat, but they remain powerful. The main opposition Botswana National Front is led by aging Kenneth Koma, who has promised to stand down soon. The future of the party without its long-standing leader, especially as there is no obvious successor, remains in doubt. Other political parties, including those that fought the 1999 elections grouped in a coalition, are in a very weak position, and their prospects for gaining political power will rest heavily on their ability to forge successful alliances, probably with the BNF.

LOCAL GOVERNMENT

For purposes of regional administration, Botswana is divided into nine districts, whose boundaries follow the tribal divisions very closely. Five of the district councils are headed by chiefs and four by elected leaders. The district councils vary in size from 12 to 38 members; each council has an elected majority. Chiefs and tribal authorities are ex officio members of the council. The chief official on the district level is the district commissioner, a civil servant appointed by the central government. Each district also has a district development committee.

There are also three townships—Francistown, Gaborone, and Lobatse—with town councils. Each town council consists of eight elected members and varying numbers of nominated members.

Local Government

Principal administrative divisions, capitals, area, population

AREA AND POPULATION

		area		population
Districts	**Capitals**	**sq mi**	**sq km**	**1991 estimate**
Barolong	—	773	2,003	18,400
Central	Serowe	57,039	147,730	412,970
Ghanzi	Ghanzi	45,525	117,910	24,719
Kgalagadi	Tsabong	41,290	106,940	31,134
Kgatleng	Mochudi	3,073	7,960	57,770
Kweneng	Molepolole	13,857	35,890	170,437
Ngwaketse	Kanye	10,219	26,467	128,989
North East	Masunga	1,977	5,120	43,354
North West				
Chobe	Kasane	8,031	20,800	14,126
Ngamiland	Maun	33,359	86,400	57,811
Okavango	Orapu	8,776	22,730	36,723
South East	Ramotswa	687	1,780	43,584
Towns				
Francistown	—	31	79	65,244
Gaborone	—	65	169	133,468
Jwaneng	—	39	100	11,188
Lobatse	—	16	42	26,052
Orapa	—	7	17	8,827
Selebi-Pikwe	—	19	50	39,772
Sowa	—	61	159	2,228
TOTAL		224,607	581,730	1,326,796

PARLIAMENT

The national legislature is a bicameral parliament, consisting of an elective National Assembly and a consultative House of Chiefs.

The National Assembly consists of the president of the republic and the attorney general serving ex officio, and 38 elected members, of whom 34 are elected directly and four are elected indirectly. The term of the National Assembly is five years. The president may withhold his assent to a bill passed by the National Assembly, but if it is again presented to him after six months he is required to assent to it unless he dissolves parliament within 21 days.

The House of Chiefs is a largely advisory body consisting of the chiefs of the eight principal tribes serving ex officio, four members elected by the subchiefs from among their own number, and three members elected by the other 12 members of the House. Bills affecting tribal interests and chieftaincy matters must be referred to the House. Under the constitution, suffrage is universal over age 18.

POLITICAL PARTIES

The ruling party is the Botswana Democratic Party (BDP), founded in 1962 by Sir Seretse Khama and currently led by Quett K. J. Masire. The BDP favors parliamentary democracy, multiracialism, racial moderation, and close relations with Great Britain. It had supported a dialogue with white-dominated South Africa prior to the end of apartheid. There are five other parties: the Botswana National Front, the Botswana People's Party, the Botswana Independence Party, the Botswana Progressive Union, and the Botswana Liberal Party.

The Botswana National Front is a leftist party formed in 1965 by Kenneth Koma. It has been categorized as pro-communist, but Koma has termed its members social democrats who are not Marxist. Its supporters are primarily the urban working class. The Botswana People's Party (BPP), led by Knight Naripe, was once the dominant opposition party but it retained only one seat in the 1984 election. Its main planks are Africanization of the administration, an end to rule by the chiefs, and nationalization of foreign companies. Its primary strength is among minorities in northeast Botswana. The Botswana Independence Party was formed in 1964 by dissidents from the BPP. The party's main platforms are similar to those of the BPP. The Botswana Progressive Union was formed in 1982. The Botswana Liberal Party, which does not align itself with other opposition parties, was founded in 1984 to combat what the founders declared was economic stagnation since independence.

Political Parties

Botswana Democratic Party, 1962
Botswana National Front, 1965
Botswana Congress Party, 1998
Botswana People's Party, 1998
Botswana People's Party, 1960
Botswana Progressive Union, 1982
Independent Freedom Party, 1964
Botswana Liberal Party, 1983
Botswana Labor Party, 1989
United Action Party, 1997

Political Parties: Strength in Parliament Most Recent Elections

National Assembly. The National Assembly has 47 members, 40 elected for five-year terms in single-seat constituencies, 4 co-opted by the elected members, and 2 ex-officio and the Speaker (if elected from outside parliament). At the elections of October 16, 1999, the Botswana Democratic Party won 33 seats; Botswana National Front, 6; Botswana Congress Party, 1; and co-opted members, ex-officio members, and the Speaker, 7.

LEGAL SYSTEM

The legal system is headed by the High Court of Botswana, whose chief justice is also the chairman of the Judicial Service Commission, which advises the president on matters relating to the appointment, discipline, and removal of judges. The Botswana Court of Appeal has jurisdiction over civil and criminal appeals emanating from the High Court. In certain circumstances further appeals lie with the Judicial Committee of the Privy Council in London. There are subordinate first-, second-, and third-class courts with limited jurisdiction in each district. Under the African Courts Proclamation Act of 1961, tribal law and custom are dispensed in native and customary courts, but their jurisdiction is limited to Africans.

The judiciary is independent, and its separation from the executive has been upheld even in controversial and sensitive cases. There are no special courts to deal with security or political offenses. No information is available on the correctional facilities in the penal system in Botswana.

LAW ENFORCEMENT

Law Enforcement

Offenses reported to the police per 100,000: 8,281
- Murder: 12.7
- Assault: 431.9
- Burglary: 1.9
- Automobile Theft: 73.1
- Population per Police officer: 750

Death Penalty: Yes

HUMAN RIGHTS

In terms of civil and political rights, the country is ranked as a free nation. Botswana has conformed to the fundamental principles of rule of law, political democracy, and respect for human rights since independence. The constitution provides for a bill of rights, and the courts have consistently upheld these rights in practice. There are no political prisoners, and preventive detention is illegal. The right to a fair trial is honored in practice. Defendants are entitled to counsel, and consultation may be held in private. All trials are public.

While all of Botswana's information media are owned by the government, editorial staffs enjoy considerable independence. Articles strongly critical of the government are frequently published, and activities and statements of the political opposition are adequately covered. There is no censorship. Labor unions have the right to strike, organize, bargain collectively, and lobby. No religious or other groups experience discrimination.

FOREIGN POLICY

In the past Botswana maintained a delicate balancing posture between its natural affinity to black liberation movements in southern Africa and the economic realities of its geographical location as a landlocked nation bordering and economically heavily dependent on white-dominated South Africa. While rejecting apartheid, Botswana made a special effort to maintain good relations with South Africa, both as a trading partner and as a source of employment for Tswana. Botswana cooperates with South Africa in the South African Customs Union but has pulled out of the rand currency area and established its own monetary unit, the pula. Botswana now has established diplomatic relations with South Africa following the new regime in place in that country after 1994. Sir Seretse Khama also spoke out vigorously against the Ian Smith regime in Rhodesia (now Zimbabwe), apartheid in Rhodesia, and sale of arms to South Africa. Botswana continues to give conditional asylum to political refugees from Namibia guerrillas, illustrating its commitment to a peaceful resolution of racial problems.

Relations between South Africa and Botswana were extremely strained through the 1980s because of Botswana's asylum policy. The South African government alleged that Botswana had aided South African guerrilla insurgents, a charge Botswana denied. Border fire was exchanged between the two countries, and during 1985, 1986, and 1987, South Africa sent troops to attack alleged ANC bases in Botswana. In 1987 Botswana established diplomatic relations with Zimbabwe.

Botswana's main contacts farther afield are Tanzania and Zambia. Botswana and Zambia established a permanent consultative committee in 1973. A joint commission also was established with Lesotho and Swaziland in 1974. While retaining very close links with the United Kingdom and other Western powers, Botswana, following independence, demonstrated its nonalignment by establishing full diplomatic relations with the Soviet Union, China, North Korea, Romania, Yugoslavia, and Czechoslovakia.

Botswana joined the United Nations in 1966. It is a member of nine UN organizations, and also the Commonwealth and the OAU.

Botswana and the United States are parties to three agreements and treaties covering economic and technical operation, investment guarantees, and the Peace Corps.

Beginning in 1992, Botswana was involved in a border dispute with Namibia, which was referred to the International Court of Justice in 1995 and decided in Botswana's favor in 1999.

DEFENSE

Botswana established its first permanent defense force in 1977, and by 1998 it consisted of 7500 men.

Military Indicators

Total Active Duty Personnel: 7,500
Military Manpower per 1,000: 5.0
Military Expenditures $million: 225
as % of GNP: 5.3
per capita: $155
as % of central government expenditures: 12.7

Arms Imports: $0
Arms Exports: $0

ECONOMY

Botswana is one of the low-income countries of the world; it also is one of the countries considered by the United Nations as the least developed in the world. Since independence, however, Botswana has combined an impressive record of economic growth and political stability. Its 15 percent annual growth during the 1973–78 development plan period surpassed the growth rate of many other countries more generously.endowed with natural resources.

Botswana has a free-market economy in which the dominant sector is private. Traditionally Botswana's economy has been based on cattle raising and crops. Agriculture employs over four-fifths of the population but contributes less than 5 percent to the gross domestic product (GDP) and satisfies only about half of domestic food requirements. This sector is limited by overgrazing, poor soils, and limited water resources as well as periodic droughts and plagues of locusts. Botswana achieved dramatic economic growth during the 1970s and 1980s, primarily as a result of the growth in mining (principally diamonds). Mining's contribution to the GDP has grown from 25 percent in 1980 to over

35 percent in 1997. Despite rapid growth, unemployment remains high—about 40 percent—and a very limited resource base hampers diversification into labor-intensive industries.

The Botswana fiscal year runs from April 1 through March 31. Almost half of the government's revenues are from mineral royalties and dividends. Customs and excise taxes account for another 15 percent. Almost 16 percent of expenditures go to recurrent expenditures. Development expenditures account for over 40 percent, of which almost one-quarter go to economic services.

The first National Development Plan (1968–73) called for increased state intervention in economic development, creation of new job opportunities in the private sector, budgetary self-sufficiency, and equitable distribution of income. The plan exceeded its 15 percent per annum rate of growth in real terms, achieved budgetary self-sufficiency in 1972–73, and reached the 1975 employment target in 1972. Encouraged by the results, the government launched still more ambitious development plans designed to develop the infrastructure and expand social services. The 1997–2003 development plan aims at diversifying the economy in order to create jobs, especially for unskilled workers. It also focuse on further developing infrastructure and improving the quality of education.

The most important sources of foreign aid have been the United Kingdom, Sweden, Denmark, the Netherlands, the IBRD, the IDA, and the United States. Until 1972, budgetary deficits were met by the United Kingdom. From 1990 to 1998 the United States and other Western nations contributed $106 million in aid.

Principal Economic Indicators

Gross National Product: $5.070 billion
GNP per capita: $3,310
GNP Average Annual Growth Rate (1990–97) %: 1.3
GNP per capita Average Annual Growth Rate (1990–97): −1.3
Origin of Gross Domestic Product %
- Agriculture: 5
- Mining: 35
- Manufacturing: 4
- Construction: 5
- Public Utilities: 3
- Transportation and Communications: 3
- Trade: 16
- Financial Services: 5
- Other Services: 3
- Government: 22

Gross Domestic Product by Type of Expenditure %
- Private Consumption: 43
- Government Consumption: 31
- Gross Domestic Investment: 26
- Foreign Trade: Exports: 51
- Imports: −51

% of Income Received by Poorest 20%: 3.7
% of Income Received by Richest 10%: 42.9

Price and earnings indexes (1995 = 100)

	1992	1993	1994	1995	1996	1997	1998
Consumer price index	71.6	81.9	90.5	100.0	110.1	119.6	127.6
Monthly earnings index	73.5	89.2	93.5	100.0	—	—	—

Finance

National Currency: Pula (P)
Exchange Rate: $1 = P 3.8547
Money Supply Stock in National Currency billion: 0.951
M1 per capita: 640
Central Bank Discount Rate %: 13.25
Total External Debt $million: 619
Debt Service Ratio %: —
Balance of Payments $million: 721.5
International Reserves SDRs million: 3,961
Ratio of External Debt to Total Reserves: 0.1
Average Annual Rate of Inflation/Consumer Price Index Growth Rate %: 10

Official Development Assistance

ODA $million: 106
- as % of GNP: 2.3
- per capita $: 68
- Foreign Direct Investment $million: 95

Central Government Revenues and Expenditures

Fiscal Year: 1 April–31 March

Revenues $million: 1,600
Expenditures $million: 1,800
Budget Deficit $million: 200
Tax Revenues as % of GDP: 14.7
Highest Tax Bracket %
- Individual: 30
- Corporate: 15

Employment and Labor

Economically Active Population: 441,000
Female Participation Rate %: 38.5
Activity Rate %: 33.3
Labor by Sector: %
- Agriculture, Forestry, Fishing: 22.1
- Manufacturing, Mining: 10.7
- Construction: 13.2
- Transportation and Communications: 2.6
- Trade, Hotels, and Restaurants: 8.0
- Finance, Insurance, Real Estate: 30
- Public Administration, Defense: —
- Services: 24.2

Unemployment %: 40

Agriculture

Agriculture's Share of GDP %: 5
Average Annual Rate of Growth (1965–98) %: 3.3
Number of Farms 000: 90.3
Average Size of Farm ha: 5
Number of Tractors per 1,000 hectares: 14.3

Irrigation, % of Farms having: 0.2
Artificial Fertilizer kg/hectare: 1
Total Farmland as % of land area: 5.94
Livestock: Cattle 000: 2,330
Sheep 000: 210
Hogs 000: 4
Chickens 000: 1,800
Forests: Production of Roundwood (000 cubic meters): 1,584
Fisheries: Total Catch tons 000: 2.0

Mining

% of GDP: 35.5
Value of Mineral Production $million: 1,478.7

Manufacturing

Value Added $million: 186
Industrial Production Growth Rate %: 4.6

Energy

Commercial Energy Production metric tons of oil equivalent 000: —
Commercial Energy Consumption metric tons of oil equivalent 000: —
Commercial Energy Consumption per capita kg: —
Average Annual Growth Rate 1980–97 %: —
Net Energy Imports % of use: —
Electricity Installed Capacity kW 000: —
Production kW-hr million: 522
Coal Reserves tons million: 3,500
Production tons 000: —
Natural Gas Proven Reserves cubic meters billion: —
Production cubic meters million: —
Crude Petroleum reserves barrels million: —
Production barrels million: —
Consumption barrels million: —
Refinery Capacity barrels per day 000: —
Pipelines Length km: —

Foreign Trade

Imports $million: 1,636.6
Exports $million: 1,848.8
Export Volume % Annual Growth Rate (1990–97): 7.2
Import Volume % Annual Growth Rate (1990–97): −1.9
Balance of Trade $

Balance of trade (current prices)

	1993	1994	1995	1996	1997	1998
P 000,000	668.4	1,216.3	1,623.6	2,398.9	2,140.7	217.7
% of total	8.4%	14.0%	15.6%	17.3%	11.5%	1.1%

Major Trading Partners

	Imports	Exports
European Union %	7.5	28.8
United States %	1.9	0.7
Eastern Europe %	0.1	—
Japan %	2.1	—
Others %	88.5	70.5

Transportation

Roads Total Length mi: 11,388 km: 18,327
Paved %: 25
Automobiles: 27,058
Trucks and Buses: 42,696
Persons per vehicle: 20
Railroad; Track Length mi: 603 km: 971
Passenger-mi million: 53
Freight-mi million: 1,171
Merchant Marine: No. of Vessels: —
Total Deadweight Tonnage 000: —
International Cargo Loaded tons 000: —
International Cargo Off-loaded tons 000: —
Airports with Scheduled Flights: 4
Traffic: Passenger-mi million: 36.3
Freight-mi million: 0.3
Length of Canals mi: —

Tourism

Number of Tourists to 000: 100
Number of Tourists from 000: —
Tourist Receipts $million: 162
Tourist Expenditures $million: 145

Communications

Telephones 000: 60
Cost of Local Calls 3 mins: $0.03
Cellular Telephones 000: —
Fax Machines 000: 3.1
Personal Computers 000: —
Internet Hosts per million persons: —
Mail: Post Offices: 193
Pieces of Mail Handled million: 36
Pieces of Mail Handled per person: 25

EDUCATION

Compulsory, universal, and free education is the eventual goal of government, but its introduction has been delayed for economic reasons. Schooling consists of seven years of primary grades, three years of middle grades, and two years of secondary grades for a total of 12 years. Radical changes have taken place in both primary and secondary school curricula to make them more relevent to Botswana. Greater emphasis is being placed on agricultural subjects.

The academic year runs from January to December. The medium of instruction is English. The school system continues to depend heavily on expatriate teachers in secondary schools.

Vocational training is provided by the Botswana Training Centre. A unique feature of vocational education is brigade training, a system of job training where the expenses are met by sale of products.

Mission schools maintained by the Dutch Reformed and Catholic Churches are integrated with the school system.

All schools are controlled by the Department of Education. Botswana is divided into 10 educational circuits. Statutory responsibility for the maintenance and construction of primary schools lies with elected local authorities.

Higher education is provided by the University of Botswana and Swaaziland, formerly the University of Botswana, Lesotho, and Swaziland, from which Lesotho withdrew in 1975.

Education

Literacy Rate %: 69.8
- Male %: 80.5
- Female %: 59.9

First Level: Primary schools: 669
- Teachers: 11,726
- Students: 310,050
- Student-Teacher Ratio: 26.4
- Net Enrollment Ratio: 96

Second Level: Secondary Schools: 188
- Teachers: 4,712
- Students: 86,684
- Student-Teacher Ratio: 18.4
- Net Enrollment Ratio: 45

Vocational Level: Schools: 45
- Students: 6,373

Third Level: Institutions: 1
- Teachers: 507
- Students: 5,062
- Student-Ratio Level: 10.0
- Gross Enrollment Ratio: 4.1
- Students per 100,000: 403
- % of Population Age 25 and over with Postsecondary Education: 1.4

Public Expenditure on Education as % of GDP: 9.6

SCIENCE AND TECHNOLOGY

Science and Technology

Scientists and Engineers in R&D per 1 million persons: —
Expenditures in R&D as % of GDP: —
High-Tech Exports $million: —
Patent Applications by Residents: 1

MEDIA

Botswana's only daily newspaper, the *Botswana Daily News*, is published by the government in English and Setswana. It has a circulation of 30,000. Five weeklies and two monthlies are also published.

There is no official censorship and there is a vigorous opposition press. The Botswana Press Agency, the nation's first news agency, and Italy's Interpress Service have bureaus in the capital.

Botswana has a small book publishing industry. Botswana does not adhere to any copyright convention.

The official broadcasting organization, Radio Botswana, which has three transmitters, is on the air for 102 hours a week, with programs in English and Setswana. All programs are of national origin. Botswana has no television service, but television programs are received from South Africa.

The Botswana National Library Services acts as the national library and provides a nationwide library service. The Gaborone Library is the central library for southern Botswana, and the Francistown Library is the central library for northern Botswana.

Media

Daily Newspapers: 1
- Total Circulation 000: 40
- Circulation per 1,000: 29

Books Published: —
Magazines: 14
Radio Receivers 000: 300
- per 1,000: 206

Television sets 000: 35
- per 1,000: 24

MOST IMPORTANT MEDIA:

Press. All papers are published at Gaborone, except as noted: *Botswana Daily News/Dikgang Tsa Gompieno* (40,000), published by the Department of Information and Broadcasting in English and Setswana; *Kutlwano* (23,000), published monthly by the Department of Information and Broadcasting in English and Setswana; *Botswana Guardian* (17,000), weekly; *The Gazette* (16,000) weekly; *Midweek Sun* (13,800), weekly; *Northern Advertiser* (Francistown, 5,500), weekly; *Botswana Advertiser*, weekly; *The Reporter/Mmegi*.

News agencies. The Botswana Press Agency (Bopa) was established at Gaborone in 1981.

Radio and television. The government-owned Radio Botswana operates six stations broadcasting in English and Setswana to approximately 219,000 radio receivers. The TV Association of Botswana operates two low-power transmitters near Gaborone that relay programs from South Africa, to about 32,000 TV sets. Plans are under way to establish a commercial radio network and local television broadcasting.

CULTURE

Cultural Indicators

Public Libraries
- Number: 17
- Volumes: 108,000
- Registered borrowers: 30,000

Museums
- Number: 2
- Annual Attendance: 52,000

Cinema
- Production of Long Films: —
- Number of Cinemas: —
- Seating Capacity: —
- Annual Attendance: —
- Annual Attendance per capita: —

STATUS OF WOMEN

Women hold more than one-third of paid employment positions. An estimated 41 percent of central government employees are women, many of them in high-level positions. While there is little overt discrimination, statistics suggest that social customs elevate the rights and privileges of men above those of women. Some 40 percent of rural households are headed by women, but generally their economic situation—access to capital, seeds, labor, and draft animals—is significantly worse than that of households headed by men. Women about to marry may choose civil marriage, in which all property is held in common, or customary marriage, which recognizes individual property brought to a marriage. Most women are not aware, however, of the implications of these alternatives. Often a married woman is unable to obtain a bank loan without the signature of her husband or father. The government has participated in the preparation of a handbook outlining women's rights in Botswana and established preference points for women who seek government-sponsored development loans. The political rights of women and minority groups generally are observed.

Women

Gender Empowerment Measure: 48
Seats Held in Parliament by Women %: 8.5
Female Administrators and Managers %: 36.1
Female Professional and Technical Workers %: 61.4
Women's Share of Earned Income %: 39
Women in Government %: 11

HEALTH, FOOD, AND NUTRITION

Health

Number of Physicians: 339
Number of Dentists: —
Number of Nurses: 3,329
Number of Pharmacists: —
Population per Physician: 4,395
Number of Hospitals: 30
Hospital Beds per 10,000: 23
Hospital Bed Occupancy Rate: 93.1
Infant Mortality Rate per 1,000 live births: 57
Maternal Mortality Rate per 100,000 live births: 200
Total Health Expenditures as % of GDP: 6.19
Health Expenditures per capita $: 139
HIV Infected % of adults: 25.10
Cigarette Consumption per smoker per year: —
% of Smokers: Male: —
Female: —
Access to Safe Water %: 70

Food and Nutrition

Food Supply as % of FAO Requirements: 93
% of Consumption Expenditures on Food: 39.5
Daily Available Calories per capita: 2,153
% of Total Calories derived from:
Cereals: 52.9
Potatoes, cassava: 1.6
Meat, poultry: 5.9
Fish: 0.6
Eggs, milk: 8.1
Fruits, vegetables: 2.6
Fats, oils: 7.5

ENVIRONMENT

Landsat imagery reveals devegetated areas throughout the country as a result of overgrazing. Based on recent trends, more than half of Botswana's land area could be degraded and its productivity permanently impaired within 25 years. Rapid expansion of livestock farming has meant opening up new areas in the west and north, reducing the habitats available for wildlife. Especially damaging is the expanding network of cordon fences established by ranchers that block wildlife migration paths. Up to 50,000 wildebeest died along cordon fences in one year alone. The country also faces serious water shortages.

Environment

Forest Area sq km: 139,000
Average Annual Deforestation sq km: 708
Nationally Protected Areas as % of Total Land Area: 18.5
Freshwater Access cubic meters per capita: 9,413
Emissions of Organic Water Pollutants kg per day: 4,386
CO_2 Emissions per capita ton: 1.4

CHRONOLOGY

1966 Republic of Botswana is proclaimed, with Sir Seretse Khama as first president.

1969 New customs agreement is signed with South Africa granting Botswana, Lesotho, and Swaziland more favorable terms as members of the Southern African Customs Union.
Sir Seretse's Botswana Democratic Party (BDP) is returned to power in election.
Botswana declines to subscribe to international sanctions against Rhodesia.

1971 Botswana holds first national population census.

1974 Sir Seretse and BDP win another term in office at the polls.

1976 The pula is introduced as the new national currency, replacing the South African rand at par.

1977 Relations with Rhodesia worsen as the two countries accuse each other of armed attacks across the borders.

1979 President Khama is reelected in national elections, with increased majority for his Botswana Democratic Party.

1980 President Khama dies of cancer and is succeeded in office by Vice President Quett K. J. Masire.

1983 Martin Chakaliso launches a new political party, the Botswana Liberal Party.

1984 In national elections, the ruling Botswana Democratic Party retains commanding legislative majority, but the incumbent foreign affairs and home ministries are defeated.

1989 The ruling Botswana Democratic Party wins national elections by a landslide.

1990 Following the release of ANC leader Nelson Mandela from prison in South Africa, the government frees 16 members of South African liberation movements who had been held in detention.

1991 Leaders of Botswana join hundreds of American and African leaders at the first-ever summit of Africans and African Americans in Abidjan, Côte d'Ivoire.

1995 The informal Botswana Stockmarket is converted into a formal stock exchange

1997 The Eighth National Development Plan (NDP8) is presented to the National Assembly. The first referendum on constitutional reform lowers the voting age to 18, limits presidential terms to two, and provides for the automatic succession of the vice-president.

1998 President Quett Masire retires and is replaced by Festus Mogae, the vice-president. Mr. Mogae selects Ian Khama as vice president. The main opposition, BNF, officially splits following factional in-fighting. The majority of its MPs join the the Botswana Congress Party (BCP), which becomes the official opposition.

1999 The BDP easily wins legislative election and Festus is confirmed as president. The BCP loses most of its seats and the BNF regains its position as the official parliamentary opposition. In a cabinet reshuffle Mr. Mogae moves a key BDP faction leader, Pontashego Kedikilwe, from the finance ministry to education. Baledzi Gaolathe, who, like Mr. Mogae, is a former bureaucrat from outside the BDP inner circle, replaces Mr. Kedikilwe. Southern Africa's first female central bank governor, Linah Mohohlo, takes over from Mr. Geolathe. The International Court of Justice finds in Botswana's favor in a long-standing border disagreement with Namibia.

2000 The vice president, Ian Khama, takes a year's sabbatical leave leading to rumors, vigorously denied, of a rift with the president. Botswana's flagship manufacturing enterprise, the Hyundai car assembly plant, closes down owing to liquidation of its South African parent. The project to double diamond production at Orapa, Botswana's single largest private investment, is completed.

BIBLIOGRAPHY

Chirenje, J. Mutero. *A History of Northern Botswana, 1850–1910*. Teaneck, N.J., 1976.

Colclough, Christopher, and Stephen McCarthy. *The Political Economy of Botswana*. New York, 1980.

Dale, Richard. *Botswana's Search for Autonomy in Southern Africa*. Westport, Conn. 1995.

Holm, John D. A. *Comparative Study of Political Involvement in Three African States: Botswana, Ghana and Kenya*. Syracuse, N.Y., 1979.

Morton, Fred, Andrew Murray, and Jell Ramsay. *Historical Dictionary of Botswana*. New edition. Metuchen, N.J., 1989.

Morton, Fred, and Jell Ramsay (eds.). *The Birth of Botswana. A History of the Bechuanaland Protectorate from 1910 to 1966*. Gaborone, 1987.

Picard, Lois A. *The Politics of Development in Botswana: A Model for Success?* Boulder, Colo., 1987.

Sillery, Anthony, *Botswana: A Short Political History*. London, 1974.

OFFICIAL PUBLICATIONS

Finance and Development Planning Ministry. *Estimates of Expenditure from the consolidated and developments funds revenues.*

———. *Financial statements, Tables and Estimates of the Consolidated and Development Fund Revenues.*

———. *National Development Plan 7, 1991–1997; 1991 Population and Housing Census.*

Local Government and Lands Ministry. *Town and District Council Estimates of Revenue and Expenditure*

CONTACT INFORMATION

Embassy of Botswana
1531–1533 New Hampshire Avenue NW
Washington, D.C. 20036
Phone: (202) 244-4990 Fax: (202) 244-4164

INTERNET RESOURCES

- Republic of Botswana: The Government of Botswana Web Site
  http://www.gov.bw/home.html

BRAZIL

BASIC FACT SHEET

OFFICIAL NAME:
Federative Republic of Brazil (República Federativa do Brasil)

ABBREVIATION:
BL

CAPITAL:
Brasilia

HEAD OF STATE AND HEAD OF GOVERNMENT:
President Fernando Henrique Cardoso (from 1995)

NATURE OF GOVERNMENT:
Constitutional democracy

POPULATION:
163,947,000 (1999)

AREA:
8,511,965 sq km (3,286,470 sq mi)

ETHNIC MAJORITY:
Luso-Brazilians

LANGUAGES:
Portuguese (official); also Indian languages

RELIGION:
Christianity

UNIT OF CURRENCY:
Real

NATIONAL FLAG:
A large yellow diamond, twice as wide as high, in the center of a green field. In the center of the diamond is a blue globe showing the constellations of the southern sky with 23 stars representing the 22 states and the capital. Encircling the globe is a white banner bearing the national motto: *Ordem e Progresso* (Order and Progress).

NATIONAL EMBLEM:
A gold five-pointed star in the center of which is a blue orb representing the five white stars of the Southern Cross. The encircling blue rim of the orb carries 22 stars, one for each state. Concealed partly by the gold star is a silver sword and blue cross-hilt bearing in a red panel another white star. Sheaves of coffee and tobacco leaves wreathe design with the sun shining behind the emblem. A blue ribbon bears the name of the country and the date, 15 de Novembro de 1889, when the republic of Brazil was proclaimed.

NATIONAL ANTHEM:
"Listen to the Cry of Iparanga"

NATIONAL HOLIDAYS:
September 7 (Independence Day); January 1 (New Year's Day); May 1 (Labor Day); April 21 (Tiradentes or Toothpuller Day in honor of Joaquin José da Silva Xavier, an army officer and dentist whose conspiracy of the 1780s advanced the cause of Brazilian independence); November 15 (Proclamation of the Republic); also variable Catholic festivals and Christmas.

DATE OF INDEPENDENCE:
September 7, 1822

DATE OF CONSTITUTION:
October 5, 1988

GEOGRAPHICAL FEATURES

Brazil is in eastern central South America, occupying nearly half of the South American continent. It is the largest country in Latin America and ranks as the fifth largest in the world in continuous area after Russia, Canada, China, and the United States. The total land area is 8,511,965 sq km (3,286,470 sq mi) extending 4,328 km (2,689 mi) north to south and 4,320 km (2,684 mi) east to west. The total length of the Atlantic coastline is 7,491 km (4,652 mi). It shares international borders with the following countries: Argentina, Bolivia, Colombia, French Guiana, Guyana, Paraguay, Peru, Suriname, Uruguay, and Venezuela.

Brazil

The only offshore territory is the island of Fernando de Noronha in the Atlantic.

Although 59 percent of the land area is classified as highlands over 200 m (656 ft), only 0.5 percent is above 1,200 m (3,937 ft). The Central Highlands is a vast territory covering all of Brazil south of the Amazon basin, with the exception of a narrow coastal belt and the swamps of Mato Grosso State. The northern and western halves of this zone comprise broad rolling terrain relieved by only low, rounded hills. Southward the terrain becomes more mountainous, and three mountain ranges stand out: the Serra do Mar, with a mean crest of 1,525 m (5,003 ft); the Serra da Mantiqueira; and the Serra do Espinhaco. From the city of Salvador south to Porto Alegre, the highlands meet the Atlantic in a steep, wall-like slope called the Great Escarpment. The only elevated territory in the north is the Guiana Highlands, which extend into Venezuela and Guyana. It contains Brazil's highest mountain, the Pico da Neblina (3,014 m; 9,888 ft).

Northern Brazil is dominated by the Amazon River basin, which occupies two-fifths of the national territory. Although stretches of swampy land along the course of the river are subject to flooding, swampland is limited and most of the region is known as terra firma (high ground). The lowlands constitute the world's largest rain forest, supplying 15 percent of the planet's oxygen. There are three smaller lowland areas: between the Xingu and Tapajos Rivers, the Pantanal in western Mato Grosso, and the narrow strip of coastal plain extending along the Atlantic seaboard from Guyana to Uruguay. At some places the plain disappears entirely, and there are few large level areas except at the mouths of the Amazon, Doce, and Paraiba Rivers.

Brazil's river system is dominated by the Amazon, the world's second largest river in terms of length (6,275 km/3,900 mi) and the world's largest in terms of water flow. Together with its tributaries, it drains a vast basin equal to three-fifths of the national territory. The Amazon is also one of the least polluted rivers in the world, and its water has a chemical purity superior to tap water in many countries. It is navigable by oceangoing vessels as far as Iquitos in Peru, and smaller craft can reach Porto Velho near the Bolivian frontier. It has 18 major tributaries, including 10 larger than the Mississippi River. Altogether the 200 rivers of the Amazon system cover a basin of 6,993,000 sq km (2,700,000 sq mi).

The second largest river and the largest entirely within Brazil is the São Francisco, which is navigable for about 1,600 km (1,000 mi) of its total length of 1,900 km (1,180 mi). The Central Highlands are drained by two smaller rivers, the Paraiba and the Doce. The Paraná and the Uruguay Rivers rise in Brazil and flow south to form part of the Rio de la Plata basin.

Geography

Area sq km: 8,511,965 sq mi 3,286,470
World Rank: 5th
Land Boundaries, km: Argentina 1,224; Bolivia 3,400; Columbia 1,643; French Guiana 673; Guyana 1,119; Paraguay 1,290; Peru 1,560; Suriname 597; Uruguay 985; Venezuela 2,200
Coastline, km: 7,491
Elevation Extremes meters
- Lowest: Atlantic Ocean 0
- Highest: Pico da Neblina 3,014

Land Use % Arable land: 5
- Permanent Crops: 1
- Permanent Pastures: 22
- Forest and Woodland: 58
- Other: 14

Population of Principal Cities (1991)

City	Population
Alvorada	132,582
Americana	153,592
Anapolis	222,400
Aracaju	401,676
Aracatuba	145,751
Arapiraca	124,790
Araraquara	101,302
Barra Mansa	145,112
Bauru	254,211
Belém	765,476
Belo Horizonte	1,529,566
Belim	152,846
Blumenau	185,200
Boa Vista	118,928
Brasilia	1,492,542
Cachoeiro de Itapemirim	112,099
Campina Grande	298,331
Campinas	748,076
Campo Grando	516,403
Campos	275,508
Canoas	269,234
Carapiculba	207,264
Caruaru	180,654
Cascavel	175,294
Caxias do Sul	262,983
Colombo	105,464
Contagem	195,705
Cuiabá	252,784
Curitiba	841,862
Diadema	305,068
Divinopolis	141,984
Dourados	116,754
Duque de Caxias	325,903
Embu	155,851
Feira de Santana	340,034
Florianopolis	191,664
Fortateza	743,335
Foz do Iguacu	186,362
Franca	227,613
Goiania	912,136
Governador Valadares	210,396
Gravatal	166,954
Guarapuava	107,046
Guaruhos	544,698
Iihéus	135,117
Imperatriz	209,970
Ipatinga	120,025
Itabuna	170,434
Itajai	114,558
Itapevi	107,983
Itaquaquecetuba	164,665
Jaboatao	217,905
Jacarei	143,468
Jequié	114,542
Joao Pessoa	497,306
Joinville	326,208
Juazeiro do Norte	163,527
Juiz de Fora	377,538
Jundial	253,177
Lages	137,169
Limeira	177,016
Londrina	355,062
Luziania	194,128
Macapá	146,523
Macelo	554,727
Manaus	1,005,634
Marabá	102,364
Maracanau	133,206
Marlia	144,906
Maringá	225,516
Mauá	294,631
Mogi das Cruzes	125,992
Montes Claros	223,046
Mossoro	117,020
Natal	459,827
Nilopolis	104,671

(continued)

Niteroi	400,586
Nova Friburgo	111,020
Nova Iguacu	562,062
Novo Hamburgo	199,479
Olinda	341,059
Osasco	566,949
Parnalba	105,131
Passo Fundo	135,158
Pelotas	260,510
Petrolina	123,857
Petropolis	164,849
Piracicaba	223,170
Pocos de Caidas	204,800
Ponta Grossa	219,648
Porto Alegre	1,237,223
Porto Velho	226,198
Presidente Prudente	157,618
Recite	1,296,995
Ribeirao Preto	416,186
Rio Branco	167,457
Rio Claro	130,364
Rio de Janeiro	5,473,909
Rio Grande	157,608
Salvador	2,070,296
Santa Bárbara d'Oeste	140,208
Santa Maria	193,294
Santarém	168,153
Santo André	518,272
Santos	415,554
São Bernardo do Campo	550,030
São Caetano do Sul	149,203
São Carlos	100,502
São Goncalo	296,021
São João de Meriti	220,742
São José do Rio Préto	263,454
São José dos Campos	385,879
São Leopoldo	160,228
São Luis	164,334
São Paulo	9,393,753
São Vincente	268,467
Sapucaia do Sul	104,414
Sele Lagoas	137,537
Sorocaba	348,952
Susano (Suzano)	110,414
Taboão de Serra	159,894
Taubaté	185,790
Teresina	556,073
Uberaba	198,565
Uberiandia	354,710
Uruguaiana	103,160
Vila Velha	263,897
Vitoria	258,243
Vitoria da Conquista	179,868
Volta Redonda	219,968

CLIMATE AND WEATHER

Brazil has a tropical and equatorial climate characterized by high temperatures and moderate to high rainfall. There are three major climatic zones: the tropical north, the subtropical southeast, and the temperate southeast uplands.

The coolest period is from May to September, and the hottest period is from December to March. The rainy season lasts from October to May. Frost and snowfalls occur in the south.

Except in the south, the country is subject to little temperature variations. The highest temperatures are recorded on the northern coast. The mountainous areas of the Central Highlands, the Amazon basin, and the coastal belt have relatively cool nights. The average maximum temperature in Rio de Janeiro in February is 29.4°C (85°F), and the average low in July is 17°C (63°F).

Rainfall is fairly evenly distributed throughout the year and the average annual precipitation nationwide is between 1016 mm (40 in) and 2032 mm (80 in). The upper limit is common in the Amazon basin and the lower in the central-west highlands. The northeast region experiences periodic droughts caused by erratic rainfall. More than 30 serious droughts have been recorded in this region, known as the *sertao,* including one that caused the death of 500,000 people in 1877–79.

The coastal areas receive the trade winds.

Climate and Weather

Mean Temperature
Suimmer 85°F
Winter 63°F
Average Rainfall 40 in to 80 in

POPULATION

Population Indicators

Total Population: 1999 163,947,000
World Rank: 5th
Density per sq mi 49.7 per sq km 19.2
% of annual growth (1994–99): 1.4
Male %: 49.4
Female %: 50.6
Urban %: 75.6
Age Distribution: % 0–14: 34.7
15–29: 28.1
30–44: 19.3
45–59: 10.6
60–74: 5.7
75 and over: 1.6
Population 2020: 194,793,000
Birth Rate per 1,000: 20.8
Death Rate per 1,000: 9.2
Population Doubling Time (years): 60
Infant Mortality Rate per 1,000 live births: 55.3
Rate of Natural Increase per 1,000: 11.6
Total Fertility Rate: 2.3
Expectation of Life (years): Males 56.7
Females 66.8
Marriage Rate per 1,000: 4.7
Divorce Rate per 1,000: 0.6
Total Number of Households: 39,768,000
Average Size of Households: 3.7
% of Illegitimate Children: —
Induced Abortions: —
Rate per 100 live births: —

ETHNIC COMPOSITION

Brazilians have a complex racial background, yet are considered as a distinct and integrated people with few unassimilated minority groups. The racial elements present in the population are diverse and heterogeneous in origin. The main ingredient in the melting pot is what is generally described as Luso-Brazilian, representing descendants of original Portuguese settlers. Others of Caucasian stock include Italians, Spaniards, Germans, Russians, and Lebanese. Together the Caucasians make up about 60 percent of the population. Arabs, mostly of Lebanese descent, are estimated to constitute about 2 percent of the Caucasian population.

Portuguese settlers have been, historically, free of racial prejudice and have intermingled freely with the indigenous Indians and with the imported black slaves. Centuries of large-scale intermarriage have created a large mulatto population, and about one-third of the population is believed to have some Indian ancestry. Brazil's genetic mix is reflected in the rich ethnic terminology used to describe the various racial blends. Censuses until 1950 (when ethnic origin was deleted from the questionnaire) divided the population into *branco* (white), *pardo* (brown), *preto* (black), *indio* (Indian) and *amarelo* (yellow). Those of partial Indian ancestry are further subdivided into *mamelucos* (white father and Indian mother), *caboclos* (acculturated Indians), and *cafusos* or *curibacos* (Indian and African descent).

The proportion of blacks is estimated at about 7 percent concentrated in the state of Bahia. Blacks are also found in great numbers in Rio de Janeiro, São Paulo, Minas Gerais, and Espirito Santo. They are the descendants of between four to 18 million slaves imported into the colony from the 17th through the 19th centuries.

Brazilian society has minimal race prejudice, and racial violence is unknown. Blacks occupy many positions of importance. Nevertheless, discrimination does exist, especially in the business and social worlds.

The Japanese form the largest unassimilated minority group. Three-fourths of the Japanese live in the state of São Paulo, where they constitute an impressive economic and political force. Although they number only about 700,000, they have two members in the national cabinet, and they make up 10 percent of university enrollment in São Paulo. The younger generation of Japanese, the Nissei, are succumbing to the pressures of assimilation, and their sense of separate identity has been declining. All of them speak Portuguese, and most have been baptized as Roman Catholics and bear Brazilian names.

Indians form the second largest unassimilated group, and their number is estimated at about 200,000. There are approximately 150 tribes speaking over 90 languages and 300 dialects. Most of them live in isolated traditional communities in the interior, national reservations, or in religious missions. Indians who remain in their traditional villages are under the protection of the National Indian Foundation (Fundacão Nacional dos Indio, FUNAI), successor to the Indian Protection Service. Many Indian tribes are faced with extinction as the interior is being gradually opened to road builders, ranchers, and miners.

LANGUAGES

The official and national language is Portuguese, which is spoken by virtually all Brazilians except Indians. The principal Indian languages are Tupi, Ge, Garib, Arawak, and Nambicuara.

Although literary Portuguese differs slightly from the language as used in Portugal, spoken Portuguese differs markedly in vocabulary and pronunciation. There are also regional variations, and the speech of cariocas (natives of Rio de Janeiro) exhibits the most differences from traditional Portuguese.

Tupi, the main Indian language, belongs to the Tupi-Guarani family. It was the lingua franca of Brazil until the end of the 17th century.

English competes with French as the second language of educated Brazilians.

Principal Languages and Their Speakers

Amerindian languages	280,000
German	900,000
Italian	690,000
Japanese	620,000
Portuguese	159,930,000
Other	1,520,000

RELIGIONS

Brazil is the largest Roman Catholic nation in the world. At the time of the 1970 census, 85.4 million professed themselves as Roman Catholic. However, in 1989 reports indicated that the percentage of Catholics had dropped from 93 percent to 72 percent of the population. The hierarchy consists of six cardinals heading metropolitan sees, 26 archbishops, 126 dioceses, and 4,700 parishes. In 1970 there were over 13,000 priests, 40 percent of whom were foreigners.

The constitution provides for complete religious freedom, However, the church, although not established as official, exerts a strong influence on national affairs. Since the military takeover in 1964, there has been increasing friction between church and state. A growing number of priests, headed by Dom Helder Camara, archbishop of Recife and Olinda, have become outspoken critics of the government's social and political policies and have denounced the continuing violations of human rights in the country. The liberal clergy have defined the church's involvement in social problems as a "leavening role for the construction of a better world." The church has actively aligned itself with the poor and the disadvantaged and has tried to act as a vanguard of reform in the creation of labor unions, elimination of illiteracy, improved treatment of Indians and prisoners, and the reduction of economic disparities. The National Conference of Bishops of Brazil has become increasingly concerned with agrarian reform, mass education, and freedom of expression. Priests have been arrested for alleged subversive activities and subjected to torture, and confrontations between the military and the clergy are common. The government's displeasure is particularly directed toward Popular Action, the most radical Catholic group, which has advocated a revolution led by peasants and workers.

Protestants constitute the second largest religious group, numbering over 4.8 million in 1970, concentrated in the south and east. Protestant denominations, particularly the Pentecostal churches, have achieved a rapid rate of growth, estimated at 5.6 percent annually. In 1970 there were 16,800 ordained Protestant ministers and over 25,000 local churches. There are more practicing Evangelicals in Brazil than practicing Catholics and more Evangelical pastors than Catholic priests. Of the over 100 Protestant denominations represented in Brazil, the largest are the Assemblies of God and the Pentecostal Congregação Crista. They also report greater church attendance (73 percent as against 3 percent among Catholics) and a greater ratio of priests to believers (1:177).

Fringe religious groups include nearly one million Spiritualists, who follow the philosophy of spiritualism developed by the Frenchman Allen Kardec, Afro-Brazilian cults, such as Canpomble-Umbanda and Gege-Nago, and Buddhists. The number of Jews is estimated at close to 150,000, concentrated in urban areas. Anti-semitism is not a significant factor in national life.

Religious Affiliations

Roman Catholic (including syncretic Afro-Catholic cults having Spiritist beliefs and rituals)	118,600,000
Evangelical Protestant	38,000,000
Other	7,300,000

HISTORICAL BACKGROUND

About 2 million Indians inhabited the area that is now Brazil when the Portuguese first discovered the region in 1500. Chief among them were the Tupi, inhabitants of the tropical forest region along the coast. The Portuguese claim to Brazil was established by a papal bull of Alexander VI in 1493 and by the Treaty of Tordesillas (1494), which divided the New World between Spain and Portugal and awarded the latter all territory 370 leagues west of Cape Verde. On Easter Sunday 1500 the Portuguese admiral Pedro Alvares Cabral formally claimed the land for the Portuguese Crown. In 1532 the first Portuguese settlers arrived along with slaves from Africa. In 1549 the city of San Salvador was founded and the Jesuits began their work among the Indians. In 1640 Portugal appointed its first viceroy with his seat first in Bahia and after 1763 in Rio de Janeiro. The first effort to secure independence was the failed conspiracy of Joaquim José de Silva Xavier, better known as Tiradentes or Toothpuller, in Ouro Preto in 1789. In 1807 the invading armies of Napoleon forced the royal family to flee to Brazil. After the fall of Napoleon, the king returned to Portugal in 1821 leaving his son Pedro to rule Brazil. In 1822 Pedro proclaimed Brazil's independence, established the Braganza dynasty, and assumed the title of Pedro I, constitutional emperor of Brazil. The constitution of 1824, Brazil's first, was drawn up early in his reign. In 1831 a military revolt forced him to abdicate and the throne passed to his five-year-old son who in 1840 was crowned Emperor Pedro II. Under Pedro II, Brazil enjoyed half a century of peace, prosperity, and progress. New frontiers were opened, new cities such as Belem and Manaus were founded, new immigrants arrived from Europe, slavery was abolished in 1888, and railways were built. However, an economic crisis in 1889 led to a bloodless military coup, organized by the republican opposition and former slave owners angered by abolition, in which Pedro II was deposed and the Republic of the United States of Brazil was established. In 1891, a new constitution, based on the U.S. federal model, was promulgated.

The first republic (1889–1930) was organized in a weak federal system dominated by southern coffee interests. It drafted a federal structure of 20 self-governing states, which had complete jurisdiction in internal affairs; the central government was primarily responsible for trade and national security.

Severe economic problems followed World War I and the growth of a broad movement opposed to the oligarchies that controlled government led to a coup that brought Getulio Vargas to power in 1930. Initially Vargas encouraged democratic participation. However, unable to balance irreconcilable interest groups, he became increasingly authoritarian and, in 1935, in response to an abortive leftist uprising, he established a fascist-modeled new state. Vargas's dictatorship lasted until 1945, when he was forced to resign by the armed forces. During his dictatorship, he continued a policy of modernization and industrialization, with strong emphasis on development through foreign aid.

In 1946 General Eurico Dutra was elected president, and a new constitution was adopted. Vargas was reelected in 1950. He committed suicide in 1954 and was succeeded by Juscelino Kubitschek and then Janio Quadros. Kubitschek continued his policy of modernization through massive foreign—particularly U.S.—loans, which ultimately crippled the country. Quadros attempted to lessen dependence on support by the U.S. government.

The military, first under Gen. Castello Branco (1964–67), then Marshal Arthuro da Costa e Silva (1967–69), Gen. Emilio Garrastazú-Médici, and Gen. Ernesto Geisel (1974–78) banned unapproved political parties and all union activities. Political activities were limited to two authorized parties, the progovernment Alianca Renovadora Nacional (ARENA) and the opposition Movimento Democrático Brasileiro (MDB). During the 1960s, increasing political dissent was countered by increasing authoritarianism, and in 1969 the president assumed virtually unlimited powers.

The country's economic growth failed during the 1970s as its burden of foreign debt grew. Discontent, fueled by a deep recession, prompted President João Baptista de Figueiredo (1979–85) to dissolve the ARENA and the MDB in 1979 and permit a broad-based political participation and party formation. The January 1985 presidential election was won by a civilian, Tancredo Neves, for the first time in 21 years. The new president died soon after his inauguration, and his vice president, José Sarney, took office in April. The following month, a constitutional amendment restored direct elections by universal suffrage. (Previously, the president had been elected by an electoral college.) A new constitution, which prepared the way for a return to full democracy in 1990, was promulgated in 1988.

Sarney inherited an economy crippled by ruinous inflation and staggering foreign debt. His attempts to curb inflation through devaluation, wage and price freezes, dismissal of up to 60,000 civil servants, and privatization of state-run industry met with failure. He was also unable to deal with gross inequities in interior land ownership and environmental concerns over the development of the rain forest.

The nation's first direct vote presidential elections were held in December 1989. The winner was Francisco Collor de Mello, head of the conservative National Reconstruction Party (PRN), who promised to renegotiate the massive foreign debt and privatize state industries. During 1990–91 he instituted a series of economic austerity programs designed to reduce the annual inflation rate of almost 2,000 percent and curb the debt. His plans were unsuccessful, and the economy continued to decline. He was forced to resign in December 1992 as the economy continued to slide into recession.

Vice President Itamar Franco became president in December 1992 on Collor's resignation. He served only until November 1994 when Fernando Cardoso was elected president. Cardoso has reduced the inflation rate significantly. However, there has been the loss of nearly two million jobs between 1989–96 and ongoing problems with agrarian reform. Cardoso easily won a second four-year term in 1998. In June 1999 the military was placed under direct civilian control for the first time.

CONSTITUTION

In October 1988 a new constitution, Brazil's eighth, was promulgated with several major changes from the previous constitution of 1969. Significant among its 245 articles, the new constitution assures the National Congress certain presidential powers; abolished censorship; freed political dissidents with the ending of the National Security Law; included universal suffrage by a direct, secret ballot; lowered the minimum voting age to 16 years; and incorporated the principle of habeas corpus. The presidential term was limited to five years, and the incumbent cannot run for a second term.

Legislative powers are contained in the National Congress made up of the Chamber of Deputies and the federal Senate. Membership in the first branch is determined by a system of proportional representation, and the second branch consists of three representatives of each state and the Federal District.

The president presides over the cabinet as well as the National Defense Council whose other members are the vice president, the presidents of the Chamber of Deputies and federal Senate, the ministers of justice, foreign affairs, and planning, as well as the military ministers. This council advises the president on national sovereignty and defense.

LOCAL GOVERNMENT

Local government in Brazil is divided into 26 states, three territories, and a federal district. The federal district and the three territories have governors directly appointed by the president.

The framework of the state and local governments closely parallels that of the federal government. Governors, directly elected for four-year terms, have broad powers analogous to those of the president. All powers not explicitly or implicitly forbidden them by the constitution are reserved to the states, and each state has its own constitution and court system. The states may also contract foreign loans within a federal Senate centralized system in which only the wealthiest states have a measure of real autonomy. Intervention in the affairs of the states by the central government has been permitted on certain grounds, such as suppression of civil war, reorganization of state finances, execution of judicial orders, maintenance of national integrity, and corruption of public state power, and then only after referring to the National Congress. The growing financial weakness of states and municipalities has resulted in the strengthening of the federal government.

The unicameral state assemblies have powers comparable to those of the national congress. Their members are elected for four-year terms on the basis of proportional representation. State legislation may supplement federal legislation but not conflict with it.

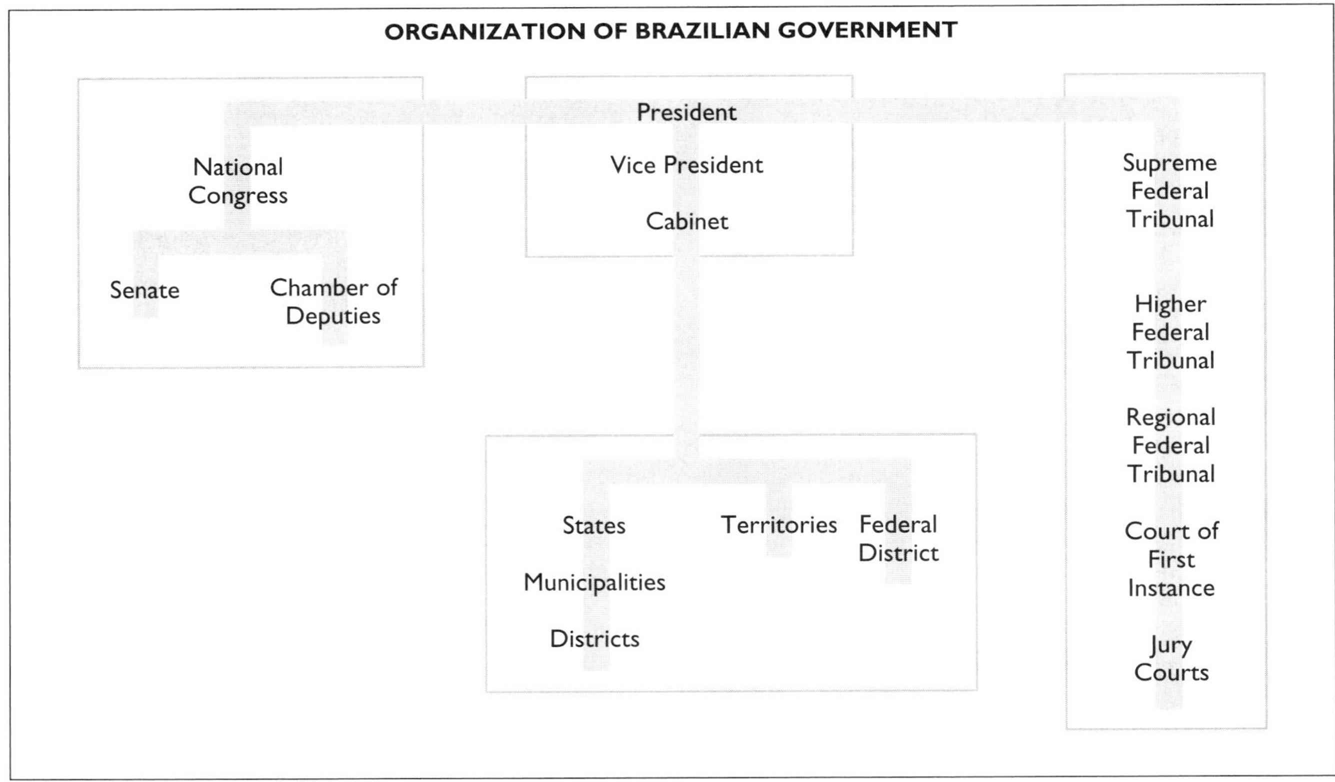

The chief administrative subdivision of a state is the municipio, corresponding to a U.S. county. Each of the 5,507 municipios is headed by a mayor (prefeito). The mayors of small municipios are elected by popular vote for four-year terms, and the executives of larger municipalities (camara de vereadores) consist of five to 50 members elected directly for four-year terms. Municipal authorities are responsible for the construction of roads, creation and upkeep of public parks and museums, and provision of primary education. Municipal revenues are derived from local taxes, fines, and federal grants-in-aid and subsidies. The Federal District is under an appointed governor, but there is a legislative council of 20 councilmen elected for four-year terms that is in session for four months every year.

Local Government

Principal administrative divisions, capitals, area, population

Area and population

		area		population 1996
States	**Capitals**	**sq mi**	**sq km**	**estimate**
Acre	Rio Branco	59,132	153,150	483,593
Alagoas	Maceio	10,785	27,933	2,633,251
Amapá	Macapá	55,388	143,454	379,459
Amazonas	Manaus	609,200	1,577,820	2,389,279
Bahia	Salvador	219,034	567,295	12,541,675
Ceará	Fortateza	56,505	146,348	6,809,290
Espirito Santo	Vitoria	17,836	46,194	2,802,707
Goiás	Goiánia	131,772	341,289	4,514,967
Maranhão	São Luis	128,713	333,366	5,222,183
Mato Grosso	Culabā	350,120	906,807	2,235,832
Mato Grosso do Sul	Campo Grande	138,286	358,159	1,927,834
Minas Gerais	Belo Horizonte	227,176	588,384	16,672,613
Pará	Belém	483,850	1,253,165	5,510,849
Paraiba	João Pessoa	21,848	56,585	3,305,616
Paraná	Curitiba	77,108	199,709	9,003,804
Permambuco	Recife	38,200	98,938	7,399,071
Piaui	Teresina	97,444	252,379	2,673,085
Rio de Janeiro	Rio de Janeiro	16,954	43,910	13,406,308
Rio Grande do Norte	Natal	20,582	53,307	2,558,660
Rio Grande do Sul	Porto Alegre	108,905	282,062	9,634,688
Rondonia	Porto Velho	92,090	238,513	1,229,306
Santa Catarina	Florianopolis	36,851	95,443	4,875,244
São Paulo	São Paulo	96,066	248,809	34,119,110
Sergipe	Aracaju	8,514	22,050	1,624,020
Tocantins	Palmas	107,499	278,421	1,048,642
Federal district				
Distrito Federal	Brasilia	2,248	5,822	1,821,946
Disputed areas		1,149	2,977	—
TOTAL		3,000,171	8,547,404	157,070,163

PARLIAMENT

The National Congress consists of the Senate (Senado) and the Chamber of Deputies (Camara dos Deputados). Members of the National Congress are elected by universal suffrage. The former literacy qualification for voters was removed in 1977. Elections for the National Congress occur every four years.

The Senate has 81 members, three from each state, and the Federal District, elected for eight-year terms, with one-third retiring after four years and the remaining two-thirds retiring after another four years. Two alternates, or suplente, are elected with each senator as replacements in the event of resignation or death. Each party runs three candidates for each seat and the party with the largest total wins the seat.

The Chamber of Deputies consists of 513 members elected on the basis of one for each 300,000 inhabitants with a minimum of seven and a maximum of 50 for each state and one for each territory. The term of office is four years. Alternates are elected with each member.

The legislature meets in ordinary session from March 15 to December 15. The National Congress is responsible for fiscal and budgetary concerns and all levels of planning. It also is responsible for resolutions authorizing the president to declare war.

Suffrage is universal and by direct secret ballot. Those between 18 and 69 are required to vote, and those who are illiterate and/or over 70 years of age or 16 or 17 are given an option to vote. Prior to the new constitution of 1988, there were about 30 million voters.

POLITICAL PARTIES

In November 1979 Congress passed a bill disbanding both ARENA and the opposition MDB as a prelude to the formation of popular democratic parties. To gain legal recognition, the new parties were required to swear allegiance to the democratic system, give six months prior notice of a national congress, win 5 percent of the vote in at least nine states and/or have the support of 10 members of each house of congress. On these bases, none of the existing parties have achieved legal recognition. In May 1985 the National Congress passed a constitutional amendment that allowed for an open participation of political parties. Major parties include the following:

- Partido do Movimento Democrático Brasileiro (PMDB) was formed by moderate elements in the Movimento Democrático Brasileiro (MBD). The MBD was a token opposition, and its members were nationalistic, statist, or socialistic, depending on the issues. In 1982 it merged with Partido Popular. It is a left of center party.
- Partido da Frente Liberal (PFL) was founded in 1984 by moderate members of the PDS and PMDB. It is slightly right of center in its philosophy.
- Partido Democrático Social (PDS) was formed in 1980 as a progovernment party succeeding Alianca Renovadora Nacional (ARENA). ARENA was designed as a government party, deeply conservative, and pro–United States in outlook.
- Partido Democrático Trabalhista (PDT) was founded in 1980 under the title Partido Trabalhista Brasileiro (PTB). It was a successor to the pre-1965 Brazilian Labor Party.
- Partido Trabalhista Brasileiro (PTB) was awarded its name by judicial proceedings.
- Partido dos Trabalhadores (PT) was founded in 1980 and was the first independent labor party. It has 350,000 members.

In addition there are at least four known terrorist groups of mainly Castroite orientation: the Revolutionary Popular Vanguard, the National Liberation Action, the Revolutionary Brazilian Communist Party, and the Tiradents Revolutionary Movement. These groups have claimed responsibility for a number of terrorist acts, including arson, bank robberies, and kidnappings.

Political Parties

Party of the Brazilian Democratic Movement, 1979
Brazilian Social Democratic Party, 1988
Brazilian Progressive Party, 1995
Liberal Front Party, 1984
Popular Socialist Party, 1992
Brazilian Socialist Party
National Reconstruction Party, 1989
Liberal Party
Democratic Labor Party, 1979
Brazilian Labor Party, 1980
Workers' Party
Communist Party, 1991
Communist Party of Brazil, 1961
Green Party, 1988

Political Parties: Strength in Parliament Most Recent Elections

Federal Senate. Following the replenishment of October 4,1998, the Party of the Brazilian Democratic Movement held 27 seats; the Liberal Front Party, 20; the Brazilian Social Democratic Party, 16; the Workers' Party, 7, the Brazilian Progressive Party, 4; the Brazilian Socialist Party, 3; the Democratic Labor Party, 2; the Brazilian Labor Party, 1.

Chamber of Deputies. At the conclusion of the most recent balloting on October 4, 1998, the Liberal Front Party held 105 seats; the Brazilian Social Democratic Party (PSDB), 99; the Party of the Brazilian Democratic Movement, 82; the Brazilian Progressive Party, 60; the Workers' Party, 58; the Brazilian Labor Party, 31; the Democratic Labor Party, 26; the Brazilian Socialist Party, 19; the Popular Socialist Party, 3; others, 30.

LEGAL SYSTEM

The legal system is based on Latin codes. The judicial branch is composed of federal, state, and municipal courts. By 1995 small claims courts augmented some municipal courts. Only appointments to the superior courts are political and therefore subject to approval by the legislature. The minimum and maximum ages for appointment to the superior courts are 35 and 65; mandatory retirement is at age 70. These federal courts have no chief justice or judge. The two-year presidency of each court is by rotation and is based on respecting seniority.

The 1988 constitution produced five significant modifications in Brazil's judicial system. First, it converted the old Federal Court of Appeals (Tribunal Federal de Recursos—TFR) into the Superior Court of Justice (Superior Tribunal de Justiça—STJ). Second, it created an intermediate-level Regional Federal Court (Tribunal Regional Federal—TRF) system. Third, the federal general prosecutor was given a two-year renewable term, subject to confirmation by the Senate, without the possibility of removal by the president. Fourth, the STF (Federal Supreme Court) can issue a warrant of injunction (*mandado de injunção*) to ensure rights guaranteed by the constitution but not regulated by ordinary legislation. And fifth, the STF can decide on matters of constitutionality without waiting for appeals to come through the federal courts.

LAW ENFORCEMENT

Law Enforcement

Offenses reported to the police per 100,000: 116
- Murder: —
- Assault: —
- Burglary: —
- Automobile Theft: —
- Population per Police officer: —

Death Penalty: For exceptional crimes. Last execution in 1855

HUMAN RIGHTS

Improvements in the human rights situation are most visible in the fields of speech, press, and assembly. There is a broad acceptance on the part of the administration of public protest and dissent. Opposition viewpoints are freely ventilated. The constitution of 1988 abolished the National Security Law used to detain political dissidents. In the so-called alternative, or leftist, press, criticism is often scathing and highly personal. Although no censorship exists, the print media are legally accountable for what they publish. The administration took action several times during the early 1980s against what it considered unacceptably blatant attacks, confiscating one edition of a leftist weekly and bringing lawsuits in half a dozen other instances. Labor unions have the right to organize, negotiate, and strike. However, strikes are not permitted in essential industries (broadly defined), and union rights are generally circumscribed by a ban on partisan political activity.

Perhaps the greatest human rights threat comes from violence and abuse by police. For the past several years, cases of police abuse have been well documented in the media. Massive public outcry has led to the approval of a national public security package loaded with crime-fighting measures but lacking in reforms to control police abuse or professionalize the security forces.

FOREIGN POLICY

Brazil is generally regarded as the bellwether of Latin America but its leadership is more symbolic than real. Its general external policies are aligned with those of the United States, except when they conflict with the interests of Brazil or Latin America. Brazil's arms industry is one of the largest sectors of its economy, and it is sensitive to U.S. restrictions on the sale of Brazilian arms. Brazil is linked to its neighbors through the Amazon Pact. Relations with Argentina, its main rival on the continent, have improved after the establishment of a Southern Cone Common Market, which also includes Paraguay and Uruguay. In 1994 Brazil signed a nuclear accord with Argentina proscribing the use of nuclear weapons in Latin America and the Caribbean. Diplomatic relations were restored with Cuba after a 22-year lapse.

DEFENSE

The defense structure is headed by the president. In June 1999, the military was placed under direct civilian control. The separate army, navy, and air force ministries, which had been led by military men, were combined into one Defense Ministry headed by a civilian cabinet minister appointed by the president.

The army minister heads the high command of the army, which includes the chief of staff, department heads, and the commanding generals of the other fields of the army. The navy, the senior service, is commanded by the navy minister assisted by the chief of navy staff, the commander of naval operations, the commandant of the marine corps and the commanders of the seven naval districts. The air force minister is assisted by an air cabinet as well as the air chief of staff and the air general staff.

The territorial organization of the armed forces is based on the strategic needs of the country. The army is divided into four numbered armies, the first with headquarters at Rio de Janeiro, the second at São Paulo, the third at Porto Alegre, and the fourth at Recife. These armies are further divided into military regions of which there are 11. The underpopulated north and northwest are controlled by the Amazon Military Command, and the capital falls under the Brasilia Military Command. The navy is divided into three operations districts with Brasilia as a separate naval command. The fleet air arm has its headquarters at São Pedro de Aldeia Naval Air Station. The air force consists of six regional air commands and the three specialized commands: Air Defense Command, Tactical Air Command, and Coastal Command.

Military manpower is provided by compulsory military service between the ages of 18 and 45. The period of service is one year.

The Brazilian armed forces are the largest and the best equipped in Latin America. The military have not been involved in combat operations in the 20th century other than in World War I and II. But they are maintained in a high state of combat readiness. About 85 percent of the army, including the powerful Third Army, is located on the southern border with Argentina and Uruguay. Operational capability around the River Plate basin is one of the two strategic priorities of the Brazilian high command, the other being a defensive shield around the Rio–São Paulo–Brasilia complex.

Defense production capability has expanded since the 1960s and now includes small arms and armaments, ammunition, naval craft and aerospace main systems, and components and engines. At least 40 percent of Brazilian arms and equipment are now manufactured internally. Brazil is the largest and technically the most advanced arms producer to the Third World. The country is now capable of producing such advanced and sophisticated military hardware as antitank missiles, armored personnel carriers, combat aircraft, rockets, and jet engines. A substantial portion of the arms industry is controlled by the military, but the two giants are the private firms Embraer and Engesa.

Military Indicators

Total Active Duty Personnel: 314,700
Military Manpower per 1,000: 2.0
Military Expenditures $million: 10,900
- as % of GNP: 1.7
- per capita $: 68
- as % of central government expenditures: 3.9

Arms Imports $million: 170
Arms Exports $million: 10

ECONOMY

Possessing large and well-developed agricultural, mining, manufacturing, and service sectors, Brazil's economy outweighs that of all other South American countries and is expanding its presence in world markets. In the late 1980s and early 1990s, high inflation hindered economic activity and investment. The Real Plan, instituted in the spring of 1994, sought to break inflationary expectations by pegging the real to the U.S. dollar. Inflation was brought down to single digit annual figures, but not fast enough to avoid substantial real exchange rate appreciation during the transition phase of the Real Plan. This appreciation meant that Brazilian goods were now more expensive relative to goods from other countries, which contributed to large current account deficits. However, no shortage of foreign currency ensued because of the financial community's renewed interest in Brazilian markets as inflation rates stabilized and the debt crisis of the 1980s faded from memory. The maintenance of large current account deficits via capital account surpluses became problematic as investors became more risk averse to emerging market exposure as a consequence of the Asian financial crisis in 1997 and the Russian bond default in August 1998. After crafting a fiscal adjustment program and pledging progress on structural reform, Brazil received a $41.5 billion IMF–led international support program in November 1998. In January 1999, the Brazilian Central Bank announced that the real would no longer be pegged to the U.S. dollar. This devaluation helped moderate the downturn in economic growth in 1999 that investors had expressed concerns about over the summer of 1998. Brazil's debt to gross domestic product ratio of 48 percent for 1999 beat the IMF target and helped reassure investors that Brazil will maintain tight fiscal and monetary policy even with a floating currency. The economy continued to recover in 2000, with inflation remaining in the single digits and an expected growth for 2001 of 4.5 percent. Foreign direct investment set a record of more than $30 billion in 2000.

Principal Economic Indicators

Gross National Product $: 784.044 billion
GNP per capita $: 4,790
GNP Average Annual Growth Rate (1990–97) %: 1.9
GNP per capita Average Annual Growth Rate (1990–97) %: 0.5
Origin of Gross Domestic Product %
- Agriculture: 14
- Mining: 1
- Manufacturing: 23
- Construction: 8
- Public Utilities: 6
- Transportation and Communications: 6
- Trade: 7
- Financial Services: 9
- Other Services: 25
- Government: 10

Gross Domestic Product by Type of Expenditure %
- Private Consumption: 63
- Government Consumption: 15
- Gross Domestic Investment: 21
- Foreign Trade: Exports: 9
  - Imports: −7

% of Income Received by Poorest 20 %: 2.1
% of Income Received by Richest 10 %: 51.3

Price and earnings indexes (1995 = 100)

	1994	1995	1996	1997	1998	1999
Consumer price index	60.2	100.0	115.8	123.8	127.7	132.2
Monthly earnings index	73.9	100.0	120.0	130.0	141.7	—

Finance

National Currency: Real (R$)
Exchange Rate: $1 = R$ 1.120
Money Supply Stock in National Currency billion: 39.591
M1 per capita: 250
Central Bank Discount Rate %: 23.15
Total External Debt $million: 192,900
Debt Service Ratio %: 25.2

Balance of Payments $million: −33,840
International Reserves SDRs million: 41,445
Ratio of External Debt to Total Reserves: 1.9
Average Annual Rate of Inflation/Consumer Price Index
Growth Rate %: 4.8

Official Development Assistance

ODA $million: 329
as % of GNP: 0.0
per capita $ 2
Foreign Direct Investment $million: 31,913

Central Government Revenues and Expenditures

Fiscal Year: Calendar Year
Revenues $million: 87,500
Expenditures $million: 96,000
Budget Surplus $million: 8,500
Tax Revenues as % of GDP: —
Highest Tax Bracket %
Individual: 28
Corporate: 15

Employment and Labor

Economically Active Population: 70,965,000
Female Participation Rate %: 39.6
Activity Rate %: 47.9
Labor by Sector: %
Agriculture, Forestry, Fishing: 25.7
Manufacturing, Mining: 13.4
Construction: 6.0
Transportation and Communications: 3.2
Trade, Hotels, and Restaurants: 11.9
Finance, Insurance, Real Estate: 2.0
Public Administration, Defense: —
Services: 31.6
Unemployment %: 7

Agriculture

Agriculture's Share of GDP %: 14
Average Annual Rate of Growth (1965–98) %: 3.4
Number of Farms 000: 5,835
Average Size of Farm ha: 64.5
Number of Tractors per 1,000 hectares: 17.0
Irrigation, % of Farms having: 7
Artificial Fertilizer kg/hectare: 43
Total Farmland as % of land area: 44.5
Livestock: Cattle 000: 161,000
Sheep 000: 18,300
Hogs 000: 31,427
Chickens 000: 900,000
Forests: Production of Roundwood (000 cubic meters): 285,295
Fisheries: Total Catch tons 000: 820

Mining

% of GDP: 1.0
Value of Mineral Production $million: 7,171.9

Manufacturing

Value Added $million: 154,425
Industrial Production Growth Rate %: 4.5

Energy

Commercial Energy Production metric tons of
oil equivalent 000: 120,236
Commercial Energy Consumption metric tons of
oil equivalent 000: 172,030
Commercial Energy Consumption per capita kg: 1,051
Average Annual Growth Rate 1980–97 %: 1.1
Net Energy Imports % of use: 30
Electricity Installed Capacity kW 000: 59,036
Production kW-hr million: 275,399
Coal Reserves tons million: 2,845
Production tons 000: 5,173
Natural Gas Proven Reserves cubic meters billion: 154
Production cubic meters million: 2,880
Crude Petroleum Reserves barrels million: 4,800
Production barrels million: 285
Consumption barrels million: 452
Refinery Capacity barrels per day 000: 1,256
Pipelines Length km: 5,804

Foreign Trade

Imports $million: 53,736.7
Exports $million: 46,505.4
Export Volume % Annual Growth Rate (1990–97): 4.5
Import Volume % Annual Growth Rate (1990–97): 24.9

Balance of trade (current prices)

	1993	1994	1995	1996	1997	1998
U.S.						
$000,000	+13,299	+10,466	−3,466	−5,554	−8,372	−6,430
% of total	20.8 %	13.7 %	3.6 %	5.5 %	7.3 %	5.9 %

Major Trading Partners

	Imports	Exports
European Union %	27.9	27.8
United States %	23.7	18.9
Eastern Europe %	1.0	2.1
Japan %	5.1	6.7
Others %	42.3	41.5

Transportation

Roads Total Length mi: 1,205,000 km 1,939,000
Paved %: 9
Automobiles: 12,000,000
Trucks and Buses: 3,160,689
Persons per vehicle: 10
Railroad; Track Length mi: 18,578 km 29,899
Passenger-mi million: 9,009
Freight-mi million: 93,455
Merchant Marine: No. of Vessels: 634

Total Deadweight Tonnage 000: 9,348.3
International Cargo Loaded tons 000: 168,026
International Cargo Off-loaded tons 000: 52,570
Airports with Scheduled Flights: 139
Traffic: Passenger-mi million: 22,471
Freight-mi million: 1,118
Length of Canals mi: 31,069 km 50,000

Tourism

Number of Tourists to 000: 4,818
Number of Tourists from 000: 4,598
Tourist Receipts $million: 2,171
Tourist Expenditures $million: 4,245

Communications

Telephones 000: 12,083
Cost of Local Calls 3 mins: $0.09
Cellular Telephones 000: 1,286
Fax Machines 000: 200
Personal Computers 000: 2,000
Internet Hosts per million persons: 12.4
Mail: Post Offices: 10,905
Pieces of Mail Handled million: 5,564
Pieces of Mail Handled per person: 36

EDUCATION

Education is free, universal, and compulsory for eight years from the ages of seven to 14. Schooling lasts for 11 years divided into eight years of primary school (technically known as first grade) and three to four years of second grade, or middle school. The term secondary school is applied to university-level institutions. The course of study is divided into hours rather than years, permitting students to proceed at a pace suited to their capabilities after completing the mandatory first grade. There are three types of primary schools: *escolas isoladas*, or one-room rural schools, *escolas reunida*, or collective schools in small towns, and *grupos escolares* in larger towns and cities. Attrition rates are high in the primary school, especially in the first grade where nearly one-third drop out, one-third are repeaters, and only one-third are promoted. Of the population over 25, more than 40 percent have no schooling. More than 25 percent have attended school but have not completed the first level, with only a very small percent completing postsecondary education.

The academic year runs from March to the middle of December. The medium of instruction is Portuguese throughout.

Private schools are operated by Roman Catholic orders, Protestant denominations, and commercial organizations. Enrollment in private institutions has been falling and now stands at 8 percent in the first level and 40 percent in the second level. Private primary schools offer a higher quality of schooling than public ones, but their record at the middle level is mixed.

Under the educational reforms introduced in 1971, the second grade is vocation-oriented, and general studies are supplemented by vocational courses designed to meet the requirements of the labor market in the region. Students are required to enroll in specialized technical programs and to undergo supervised apprenticeship in a specific vocation. Upper grades of primary schools have been converted into work-oriented institutions with shop courses in industrial arts, commercial arts, agriculture, and home economics. The result is that 59 percent of secondary school enrollment is in the vocational stream. The bulk of the full-time vocational enrollments are in private schools.

Responsibility for public education is divided between federal, state, and municipal governments. Primary and middle schools (now called first and second grades) are controlled by the states and municipal governments, whereas higher education is the responsibility of the federal government. The formulation and implementation of educational policies rest with the Federal Council of Education, whose members are appointed by the president. There are also state councils of education with comparable functions. Under the 1961 Directives and Standards for National Education, 12 percent of the national budget and 20 percent of state and municipal budgets must be devoted to education.

Higher education is offered in 68 universities and over 555 independent postsecondary institutions known as *establecimentos isolados*. The university system includes 35 federally approved and partly federally supported universities and 11 Catholic universities.

Education

Literacy Rate %: 83.3
Male %: 83.3
Female %: 83.2
First Level: Primary schools: 195,545
Teachers: 1,335,270
Students: 31,101,662
Student-Teacher Ratio: 23.3
Net Enrollment Ratio: 90
Second Level: Secondary Schools: 13,449
Teachers: 295,542
Students: 4,510,199
Student-Teacher Ratio: 15.3
Net Enrollment Ratio: 19

Vocational Level: Schools: —
Students: —

Third Level: Institutions: 851
Teachers: 155,776
Students: 1,661,034
Student-Ratio Level: 10.7
Gross Enrollment Ratio: 11.3
Students per 100,000: 1,094
% of Population Age 25 and over with Postsecondary Education: —

Public Expenditure on Education as % of GDP: 4.6

SCIENCE AND TECHNOLOGY

Science and Technology

Scientists and Engineers in R&D per 1 million persons: 168
Expenditures in R&D as % of GDP: 0.81
High-Tech Exports $million: 2,554
Patent Applications by Residents: 36

MEDIA

Most of the newspapers have small circulations because of distribution problems, and there are five national newspapers—*O Estado de São Paulo*, *Folha de São Paulo*, *Gazeta Mercantil*, *O Globo*, and *Jornal do Brasil*. All dailies, except two, are published in Portuguese. About 95 towns and cities have their own newspapers, and the larger ones have several morning and evening papers One of the most striking features of the Brazilian press is the dominance of chains and media dynasties, such as Chateaubriand's Associated Daily Newspapers, the Mesquita Brothers, and the Octavio Frias de Oliveira group.

There are a number of domestic news agencies: Agencia Nacional (AN), Agencia Meridional (AM), Agencia J. B. Servicos de Imprensa, Transpress, Argus Press, Asapress, Brastele, and Agencia Noticiosa. AN is the official news agency.

Broadcasting is conducted by three types of organizations: government stations, commercial stations, and religious foundations. All broadcasting stations are required to be licensed by the state and come under the control of Departmento Nacional de Telecommunicaçoes (Dentel). The government station, Radio Nacional, broadcasts an international short-wave program in six languages on the Voice of America model.

Television was first introduced in 1950. In 1998 there were 237 stations of which 118 were in state capitals and six in Brasilia. There are six main television networks and a number of chains. There are educational stations in Recife, Caceio, and São Paulo.

Media

Daily Newspapers: 317
 Total Circulation 000: 7,200
 Circulation per 1,000: 45
Books Published: 21,574
Magazines: —
Radio Receivers 000: 55,000
 per 1,000: 340
Television sets 000: 45,000
 per 1,000: 278

MOST IMPORTANT MEDIA:

Press. No Brazilian paper enjoys truly national distribution. The following are Portuguese-language dailies, unless otherwise noted: *Folhade São Paulo* (São Paulo, 557,000, daily, 1,401,000 Sunday); *O Globo* (Rio de Janeiro, 350,000, daily, 520,000 Sunday), conservative; *O Dia* (Rio de Janeiro, 250,000 daily, 500,000 Sunday), popular labor; *O Estado de São Paulo* (São Paulo 250,000, 470,000 Sunday), independent; *Jornal do Brasil* (Rio de Janeiro, 205,000, daily, 330,000 Sunday), Catholic conservative; *Noticias Populares* (São Paulo, 150,000); *Ultima Hora* (Rio de Janeiro, 57,000); *Diario de Pernambuco* (Recife, 31,000), oldest paper in Latin America (founded 1825), independent.

News agencies. There are a number of domestic agencies, including Agencia Globo and Agencia Jornal do Brasil, both headquartered at Rio de Janeiro; Agencia ANDA, headquartered at Brasilia; and Agencia o Estado do São Paulo and Agencia Folha de São Paulo. Numerous foreign agencies also maintain bureaus at Brasilia, Rio de Janeiro, and São Paulo.

Radio and television. The government's National Telecommunications Department (Departamento Nacional de Telecommunicaçoes-Dentel) oversees television and radio broadcasting. Most of the country's nearly 2,000 radio stations are commercial, but several are owned by the government or the Catholic Church. Commercial broadcasting, encompassing most of Brazil's 237 television stations, is organized into a national association, Associaçao Brasileira de Emissoras de Radio e Televisão (ABERT), and a number of regional groups. Although there are a number of television networks, TV Globo dominates with an audience share of about 70 percent.

CULTURE

Cultural Indicators

Public Libraries Number: 3,600
 Volumes: 18,106,000
 Registered borrowers: 2,919,155
Museums Number: 778
 Annual Attendance: 26,652
Cinema Production of Long Films: 86
 Number of Cinemas: —
 Seating Capacity: —
 Annual Attendance million: —
 Annual Attendance per capita: —

STATUS OF WOMEN

Under the constitution of 1988, women became entirely equal to men for all legal purposes. Despite persistent gender inequality, the status of women in Brazil is improving. Generally, females are staying in school longer than their male counterparts and thus achieving educational opportunities in law and medicine. The attitudes and practices of young people are generally not as sexist as those of their parents, at least among youths of families with higher income and education. Nevertheless, there are still relatively few women in positions of power. They have a significant, albeit limited, presence in high levels of federal government, although they have better representation at the state and municipal levels. Since the government of João Baptista do Oliveira Figueiredo (president, 1979–85), several female ministers have been in the cabinet, and in 1994 two women were candidates for vice president. However, by 1994 women made up only 7 percent of the Congress.

Women

Gender Empowerment Measure: 68
Seats Held in Parliament by Women %: 6.7
Female Administrators and Managers %: 17.3
Female Professional and Technical Workers %: 62.6
Women's Share of Earned Income %: 29.0
Women in Government %: 13

HEALTH, FOOD, AND NUTRITION

Health

Number of Physicians: 222,658
Number of Dentists: 160,000
Number of Nurses: —
Number of Pharmacists: 57,047
Population per Physician: 681
Number of Hospitals: 6,372
Hospital Beds per 10,000: 34
Hospital Bed Occupancy Rate: —
Infant Mortality Rate per 1,000 live births: 69
Maternal Mortality Rate per 100,000 live births: 220
Total Health Expenditures as % of GDP: 4.20
Health Expenditures per capita $: 146
HIV Infected % of adults: 0.63
Cigarette Consumption per smoker per year: —
% of Smokers: Male: 40
Female: 25
Access of Safe Water %: 92

Food and Nutrition

Food Supply as % of FAO Requirements: 119
% of Consumption Expenditures on Food: 25.3
Daily Available Calories per capita: 2,834
% of Total Calories derived from:
Cereals: 31.4
Potatoes, cassava: 5.5
Meat, poultry: 9.4
Fish: 0.3
Eggs, milk: 7.5
Fruits, vegetables: 5.2
Fats, oils: 13.1

ENVIRONMENT

Continuing deforestation in the Amazon Basin destroys the habitat and endangers the existence of a multitude of plant and animal species indigenous to the area. The air and water pollution in Rio de Janeiro, São Paulo, and several other large cities is a serious problem posing public health issues. Sanitation is also an issue in large urban areas where the poor generally do not have access to modern sewage systems. The exploitation of natural resources through activities like mining are also having adverse effects on land and water quality.

Environment

Forest Area sq km: 5,511,000
Average Annual Deforestation sq km: 25,544
Nationally Protected Areas as % of Total Land Area: 4.2
Freshwater Access cubic meters per capita: 42,459
Emissions of Organic Water Pollutants kg per day: 690,876
CO_2 Emissions per capita ton: 1.7

CHRONOLOGY

1945 The armed forces force President Getulio Vargas, the virtual dictator of Brazil since 1930, to step down; Chief Justice José Linhares becomes caretaker.

1946 General Eurico Dutra is elected president; a new constitution is promulgated.

1948 Brazilian Communist Party is proscribed.

1951 Vargas is reelected president as the candidate of the Labor Party.

1954 The armed forces and the cabinet demand Vargas's resignation; Vargas commits suicide and is succeeded in office by Vice President João Cafe Filho.

1955 In national elections Juscelino de Oliveira Kubitschek is elected president on the plank, "Power, Transportation, Food."

1960 Brasilia, the new capital of Brazil, is inaugurated.

1961 Janio Quadros is elected president with the largest plurality in the country's history.
Quadros resigns seven months later citing unnamed threats; João Goulart succeeds to the office of the president with reduced powers and in the face of wide opposition to his leftist policies.

1963 Full presidential powers are restored to Goulart through a national plebiscite.

1964 The armed forces depose Goulart, who flees to Uruguay; army chief of staff marshal Humberto de Alencor Castelo Branco is elected by a purged Chamber of Deputies to serve until 1966, a term subsequently extended to 1967.
Through a series of institutional acts, Castelo Branco gains virtually absolute powers.

1965 All existing political parties are banned.

1967 The military regime promulgates a new constitution.
President Castelo Branco steps down and is succeeded in office by Arturo da Costa e Silva.
U.S. Ambassador C. Burke Elbrick is kidnapped by extremists and is released only after the government meets their demands, which include release of certain political prisoners.

1969 President Costa e Silva suffers a stroke and dies; High Command of the Armed Forces selects General Emilio Garrastazú Médici as president.

Alianca Renovadoral National (ARENA) and Movimento Democrático Brasileiro (MDB) parties are permitted to function as the country's political parties.

1970 Work begins on the controversial Trans-Amazon Highway.

1974 General Ernesto Geisel is elected president by the electoral college.

1977 Brazil rejects U.S. military aid, reacting to U.S. criticisms of the regime's violations of human rights and nuclear development policies. . . .Geisel suspends Congress and decrees judicial and constitutional reforms.
Divorce is legalized. Amnesty International cites Brazil for torture and illegal detention of political prisoners.

1978 U.S. President Jimmy Carter visits Brazil.
General João Baptista de Figueiredo, the official nominee, is elected president to succeed Geisel in 1979. Institutional Act 5 is suspended as the regime initiates a process of moderate constitutional reform; press censorship is ended but broadcast curbs remain.
ARENA, the official party, retains control of Congress in parliamentary elections.
The Amazon Pact is concluded with Bolivia, Colombia, Ecuador, Guyana, Peru, Suriname, and Venezuela.

1979 The political parties, ARENA and MDB, are dissolved to make way for new political parties.
General Figueiredo is inaugurated as president.
As inflation tops annual rate of 70 percent the finance minister, Delfim Netto, outlines new anti-inflation plan including a maxidevaluation of the cruzeiro by 30 percent.
Tripartite accord is reached with Argentina and Paraguay over the Paraná River dispute.

1980 The pope visits Brazil and calls for social justice but warns against the social gospel.

1982 In national elections the opposition wins 10 states.

1983 Social Democrats regain control of the House of Representatives.

1984 The Itaipa Dam is inaugurated.

1985 Brazil's electoral college elects Tancredo de Almeida Neves as president.
Neves dies before taking office.
Vice President Jose Sarney is installed as the first civilian president in 20 years.
Angra I nuclear plant goes on stream. Approval is passed by Congress for a constitutional amendment that restores direct elections by universal suffrage.

1986 The Cruzado Plan is announced to fight inflation.

1987 A Constitutional Assembly is installed and is dominated by debate over the presidential mandate. A moratorium is announced on debts to commercial banks.

1988 Various strikes, some violent, occur throughout the country over recent economic policies. A new constitution is approved by the National Congress. Censorship is abolished, and the voting age is lowered to 16. Francisco (Chico) Mendes, the leader of the rubber-tappers' union, is killed.

1989 The Brazilian stock exchange experiences a serious setback as it suspends business for four months. In the latter part of the year Brazil is unable to make payments on its foreign debt. A meeting of the Amazon Pact nations denounces outside interference in the Amazon region. The Declaration of Manaus is signed by the Amazon Pact stating their rights over the Amazon environmental issues. The "Our Nation" environmental program is announced. The Summer Plan is abandoned.
The nation's inflation rate climbs to, 1,765 percent.

1990 Fernando Collor de Mello is sworn in as president, marking the beginning of the first democratically elected regime in Brazil in three decades. Amnesty International reports widespread human rights abuses by Brazilian law enforcement authorities between 1985 and 1990. Collor introduces an economic austerity program aimed at cutting government spending and reducing inflation. The inflation rate rises to 1,795 percent. The Group of Seven pledges to help Brazil preserve its rain forests. The Collor government says it will consider agreeing to preserve parts of its rain forest in return for forgiveness of some of its foreign debt.

1991 The government announces a new anti-inflation program as the economic situation worsens. Union leaders in the Amazon area are targeted in death plots.

1992 President Collor is impeached and Vice President Itamar Franco serves the remainder of the term as president.

1993 Former finance minister Fernando Henrique Cardoso wins the presidency on an anti-inflation platform.

1997 Congress passes a constitutional amendment allowing Cardoso to run for a second consecutive term; prisoners mutiny at the São Paulo jail, taking 600 hostages.

1998 A severe drought causes food shortages in northeast Brazil; the Brazilian economy collapses in the wake of the Asian fiscal crisis of 1997; Brazil receives an IMF–led international support program of $41.5 billion.

1999 Brazilian Central Bank announces that the real, which had tracked the value of the U.S. dollar, will be allowed to float; the government places the military under direct civilian control.

2000 Brazil celebrates its 500th anniversary amid protests by the indigenous population, who say that racial genocide, forced labor, and disease have dramatically cut their population from an estimated 5 million before the Europeans arrived in 1500 to the current 350,000.

BIBLIOGRAPHY

Baaklini, A. I. *The Brazilian Legislature and Political System*. London, 1992.

Baer, W. *The Brazilian Economy*. New York, 1995.

Dickenson, John. *Brazil*. Santa Barbara, Calif., 1997.

Eakin, Marshall. *Brazil: The Once and Future Country*. New York, 1997.

Stephan, A. *Democratizing Brazil*. Oxford, 1993.

OFFICIAL PUBLICATIONS

Brazil. *Anuario Estatistico do Brasil*; *Contagem da População 1996*.

CONTACT INFORMATION

Embassy of Brazil
3006 Massachusetts Avenue NW
Washington, D.C. 20008
Phone: (202) 238-2700 Fax: (202) 238-2827

INTERNET RESOURCES

- IBGE: Instituto Brasileiro de Geografia e Estatistica
  http://www.ibge.gov.br/
- Central Bank of Brazil: Economic Data
  http://www.bcb.gov.br/ingles/economic.shtm

BRUNEI

BASIC FACT SHEET

OFFICIAL NAME:
State of Brunei Darussalam (Negara Brunei Darussalam)

ABBREVIATION:
BD

CAPITAL:
Bandar Seri Begawan

HEAD OF STATE AND GOVERNMENT:
Sultan Muda Hassanal Bolkiah Mu'izzaddin Waddaulah (sultan from 1967; prime minister from 1984)

NATURE OF GOVERNMENT:
Absolute monarchy

POPULATION:
323,000 (1999)

AREA:
5,765 sq km (2,226 sq mi)

ETHNIC MAJORITY:
Malay

LANGUAGES:
Malay (official), English (lingua franca)

RELIGION:
Islam (official)

UNIT OF CURRENCY:
Brunei dollar

NATIONAL FLAG:
Yellow with two diagonal stripes of white and black running from the upper hoist to the lower fly; the national emblem, in red with yellow Arabic inscription, is superimposed in the center.

NATIONAL EMBLEM:
The crest consists of four elements: the *payong ubor-ubor* (royal umbrella); the *sayap* (wing); the *tangan* or *kimhap* (hand); and the *bulan* (crescent). On the crescent is inscribed in Arabic the national motto: "Always in Service with God's Guidance." The scroll beneath the crest reads, "Brunei Darussalam, Brunei, the Abode of Peace."

NATIONAL ANTHEM:
"Allah Peliharakan Sultan" (O God, long live our majesty, the sultan)

NATIONAL HOLIDAYS:
May 31 (Anniversary of the Royal Brunei Malay Regiment); Sultan's Birthday; Christmas; New Year's Day; Chinese New Year's Day; National Day (February 23); all major Islamic holy days

DATE OF INDEPENDENCE:
January 1, 1984

DATE OF CONSTITUTION:
None at present

GEOGRAPHICAL FEATURES

Brunei, on the northwestern coast of the island of Borneo (Kalimantan), has a total land area of 5,765 sq km (2,226 sq mi). It is composed of two enclaves separated by the Limbang River valley, a salient of the Malaysian state of Sarawak. Brunei's total boundary length is 579 km (360 mi).

Apart from the heavily populated narrow coastal strip to the west, the land is primarily tropical rain forest.

Geography

Area sq km: 5,765 sq mi 2,226
World Rank: 167th
Land Boundaries, km: Malaysia 381
Coastline, km 161
Elevation Extremes meters
- Lowest: South China Sea 0
- Highest: Bukit Pagon 1,850

Land Use % Arable land: 1
- Permanent Crops: 1
- Permanent Pastures: 1
- Forest and Woodland: 85
- Other: 12

Brunei

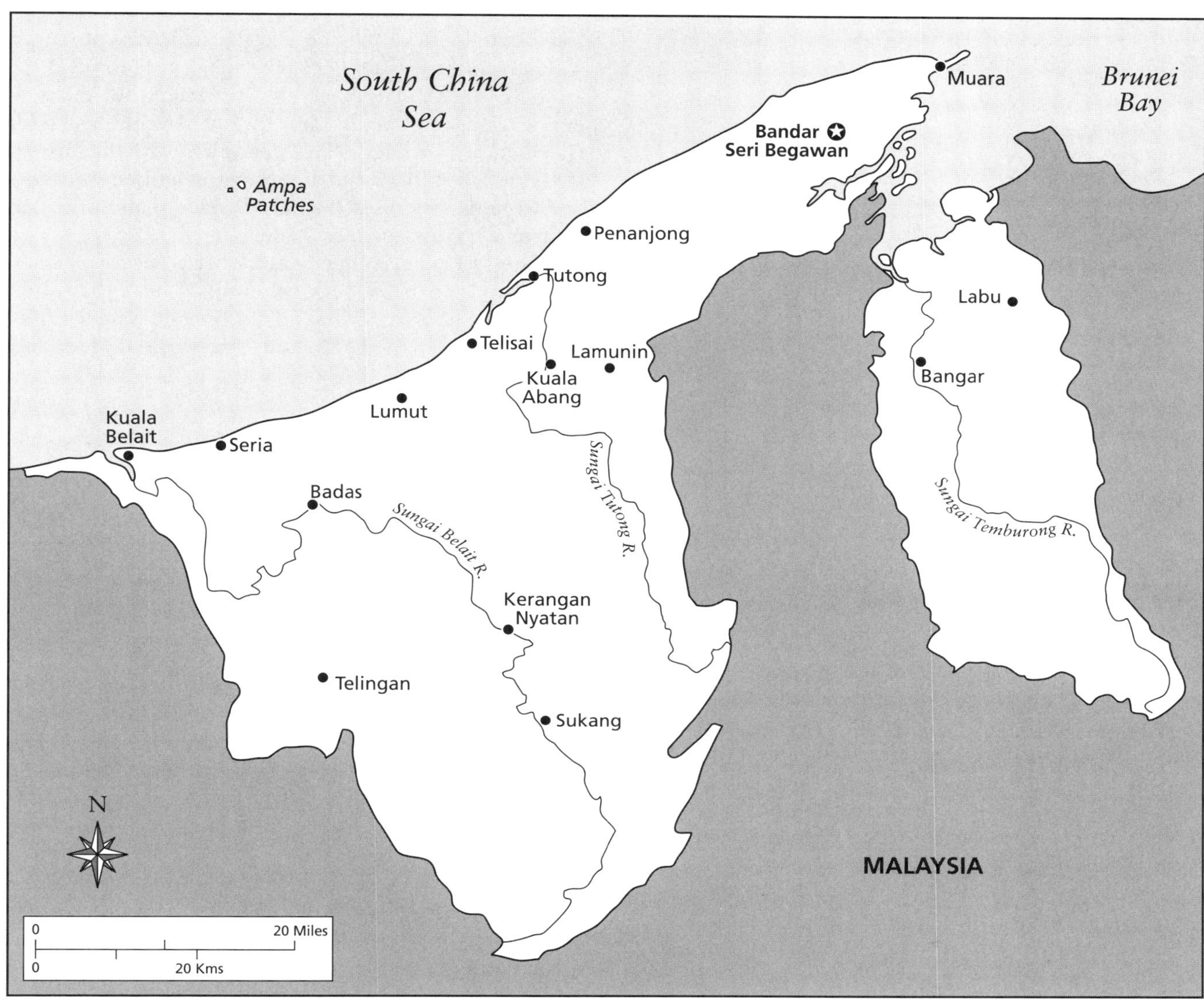

Population of Principal Cities (2002 est.)	
Bandar Seri Begawan	74,700

Climate and Weather

Mean Temperature 81°F to 90°F
Average Rainfall 95 in (lowlands) 158 (Interior)

CLIMATE AND WEATHER

Brunei has a tropical climate, with uniform temperatures ranging from 27°C to 32°C (81°F to 90°F). Humidity is constantly high, about 80 percent year-round. Rainfall is heaviest during the northeasterly monsoon season (*landas*), especially in November and December. Average annual rainfall ranges from 2,400 mm (95 in) in lowland areas to 4,000 mm (158 in) in the interior.

POPULATION

Population Indicators

Total Population: 1999 323,000
World Rank: 173rd
Density per sq mi: 145.1 per sq km 5.6
% of annual growth (1994–99): 2.6
Male %: 52.8
Female %: 47.2
Urban %: 66.6

(*continued*)

Age Distribution: % 0–14: 34.5
15–29: 29.3
30–44: 24.2
45–59: 7.9
60–74: 4.1
75 and over: 4.1
Population 2020: 490,000
Birth Rate per 1,000: 23.3
Death Rate per 1,000: 3.0
Population Doubling Time (years): 35
Infant Mortality Rate per 1,000 live births: 9.0
Rate of Natural Increase per 1,000: 20.3
Total Fertility Rate: 2.9
Expectation of Life (years): Males 73.0
Females 78.0
Marriage Rate per 1,000: 7.1
Divorce Rate per 1,000: 1.1
Total Number of Households: 45,000
Average Size of Households: 5.8
% of Illegitimate Children: 0.4
Induced Abortions: —
Rate per 100 live births: —

ETHNIC COMPOSITION

Brunei is officially described as a Malay nation, but Malays form only about 67 percent of the population. The minority of the populations are Chinese, who are officially "stateless noncitizens," although they have been in Brunei for many decades. Formerly they were "British-protected persons," but they lost that status on independence. Nevertheless, the Chinese community has prospered, and most commercial activity is in their hands. The Chinese form about 15% of the population.

Other minorities include about 6 percent Ibans, Dayak, and Kelabit, and about 12 percent other indigenous groups. There is a substantial Caucasian community, including temporary workers of English, U.S., Dutch, and Australian nationality.

LANGUAGES

Malay is the official language, but English is the effective lingua franca and the language of commerce. The principal Chinese dialect is Hokkien.

Principal Languages and Their Speakers

Chinese	30,000
English	10,000
Malay	147,000
Malay-Chinese	3,000
Malay-English	93,00
English-Chinese	7,000
Malay-Chinese-English	13,000
Other	17,000

RELIGIONS

Islam is the official religion and is extensively promoted with government funds. The percentage of Muslims is the same as that of Malays, about 67 percent, but the government acts as if the nation were 100 percent Muslim for all practical purposes. The Department of Religious Affairs is heavily funded and is in charge of building mosques and Koranic schools. There are monetary and other incentives for conversion to Islam.

The 31 percent religious minority comprises mostly Buddhists and tribal folk religionists; less than one-tenth are Christian. The constitution guarantees freedom of worship to non-Muslims, and this right is widely exercised.

Religious Affiliations

Muslim	217,000
Other	106,000

HISTORICAL BACKGROUND

From the 14th to the 16th centuries Brunei was the seat of a powerful sultanate extending over Sabah, Sarawak, and the lower Philippines. Thus the current sultan represents one of the oldest continuously ruling dynasties in the world. By the 19th century the Brunei empire had been whittled away by wars, piracy, and the colonial expansion of European powers.

In 1847 the sultan concluded a treaty with Great Britain, and in 1881 Brunei officially became a British protectorate. A new agreement, in 1959, recognized Brunei as fully self-governing, subject to Great Britain only for the conduct of its foreign affairs and defense. Great Britain exercised this right when an Indonesian-backed nationalist coup against the sultan was put down in 1962. The constitution of 1959 was effectively suspended and the sultan has ruled by decree since that time. In 1967 Sultan Omar abdicated in favor of his son Muda Hassan al-Bolkiah. On January 1, 1984, Brunei attained full independence and the sultan took office as prime minister, presiding over a cabinet of six (three of whom were close relatives).

Although the sultan's state of emergency remained in effect during 1985 and 1986, Brunei has moved toward a more progressive government. In October 1986 the cabinet was expanded to 11 members and included commoners for the first time. In 1988, however, the Brunei National Democratic Party (BNDP), which had been formed three years earlier, was dissolved by the state when it called for the sultan to drop his post as prime minister, end the 26 years of state emergency, and

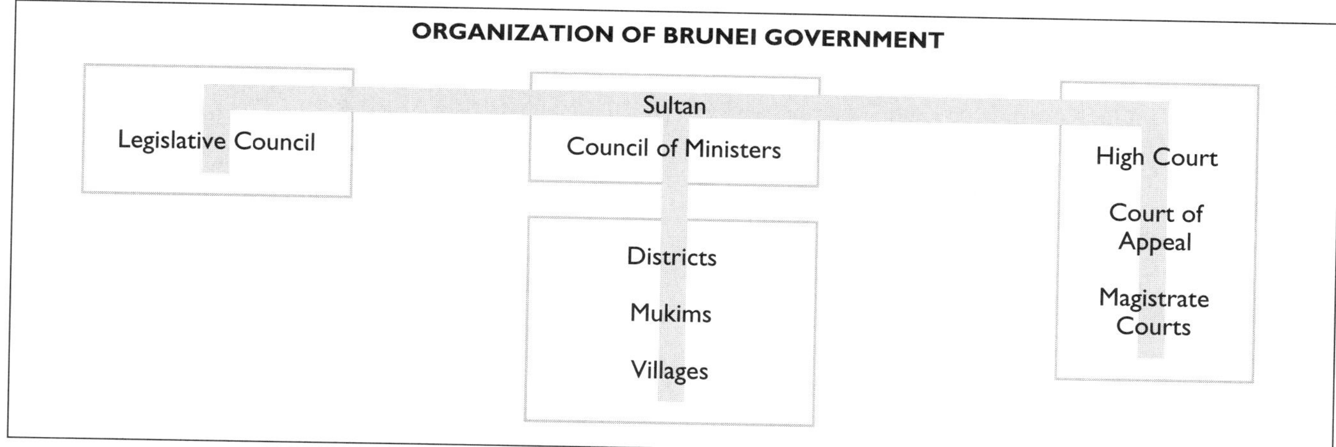

hold democratic elections. Since 1988 Brunei has adopted the name and style of an Islamic state and the sultan has emerged as a defender of Islam. In 1991 he undertook the great haj, or pilgrimage, to Mecca. The importation of alcohol and the public celebration of Christmas were banned, the female members of the royal family adopted Islamic headdress, and the name Islamic was added to the names of major public institutions.

CONSTITUTION

The constitution of 1959 was effectively suspended in 1962, and since then the sultan has ruled by invoking two-year states of emergency. The constitution provides for a number of constitutional bodies, including a Privy Council, Council of Ministers, Legislative Council, Religious Council, and Council of Succession. The present sultan, the head of state, also is the prime minister, the head of government. The sultanate is one of the most autocratic regimes outside the Middle East.

LOCAL GOVERNMENT

For purposes of local government Brunei is divided into four districts. Each district is headed by a district officer reporting directly to the sultan. District councils, in which a small number of the council is elected by the people, advise the district officials, as do the village headmen. A district consists of several mukims, each headed by a penghulu (subdistrict officer). A mukim is made up of several kampongs (villages), and each of these in turn is headed by a ketua (village officer), elected by the people of the village.

Local Government

Principal administrative divisions, capitals, area, population

AREA AND POPULATION

		area		population
Districts	**Capitals**	**sq mi**	**sq km**	**1995 estimate**
Belait	Kuala Belait	1,052	2,724	60,000
Brunei and Muara	Bandar Seri Begawan	220	571	195,000
Temburong	Bangar	504	1,304	8,500
Tulong	Tulong	450	1,166	32,500
Total		2,226	5,765	296,000

PARLIAMENT

The Legislative Council is a unicameral body of 22 members, all of whom are appointed by the sultan. This council is merely a ceremonial body, however, with no powers in theory or in practice. No elections have been held in the sultanate since the 1965 general elections.

POLITICAL PARTIES

Political parties have not fared well in Brunei. The government has often dissolved parties when they appear to be causing too much trouble. Currently there is only one active party, the Brunei National Unity Party, which was founded in 1986. It was forced out of existence in 1988. It reemerged in 1995.

LEGAL SYSTEM

The Bruneian legal system represents an amalgam of Anglo-Saxon and Islamic traditions and institutions.

Islamic courts deal with religious matters, and appeal goes to the Religious Council. The secular system is headed by the High Court and the Court of Appeals, both headed by British jurists. Minor civil and criminal cases are tried in magistrates' courts.

LAW ENFORCEMENT

Law Enforcement

Offenses reported to the police per 100,000: 1,148
- Murder: 1.5
- Assault: 27
- Burglary: 133.1
- Automobile Theft: 42.7
- Population per Police officer: 100

Death Penalty: Yes; last execution in 1957

HUMAN RIGHTS

Freedom House rates Brunei as partly free. Since 1962 there have been no political disturbances in the sultanate. Economic well-being has made the relative absence of political freedom tolerable for Bruneians. In its 1985 report, Amnesty International expressed concern about the continued detention without trial of eight persons allegedly involved in the armed uprising of 1962, and of 20 others arrested for political reasons between 1975 and 1978.

FOREIGN POLICY

Upon independence, Brunei became a member of the Commonwealth and in 1984 joined ASEAN. Soon after, it was admitted to the Organization of Islamic States. Since then, Brunei has moved closer to Muslim nations. Relations with the United Kingdom are cordial, and there is a 1983 agreement providing for a British army battalion to be stationed in the country. Relations with Malaysia and Indonesia were long marred by territorial claims, but talks in 1995 yielded an agreement for a bilateral approach to the resolution of territorial issues. In 1995 Brunei hosted the meeting of ASEAN that was attended by all countries in the region.

DEFENSE

With independence, Brunei established its own defense force for the first time since 1881, when Brunei become a British protectorate. The defense portfolio is in royal hands, with the sultan as minister of defense. There is no conscription, and enlistment is voluntary.

The Royal Brunei Malay Regiment consisted of 4,750 men and 250 women in 1998. Britain provides some officer corps, and a Gurkha battalion, which numbers 750 men, is stationed in Brunei. Agreements have been made with the British government for the purchase of military equipment totaling 250 million pounds sterling. In mid-1987 Brunei expressed some interest in joining the Five-Power Defense Agreement linking the United Kingdom, Malaysia, Singapore, Australia, and New Zealand.

The national defense budget in 1998 was $269 million, representing 6.0% of the GNP, 20% of the national budget, and $919 per capita.

Military Indicators

Total Active Duty Personnel: 5,000
Military Manpower per 1,000: 16.2
Military Expenditures $: 269 million
- as % of GNP: 6.0
- per capita $: 919
- as % of central government expenditures: 20.1

Arms Imports $: 5 million
Arms Exports $: 0

ECONOMY

This small, wealthy economy is a mixture of foreign and domestic entrepreneurship, government regulation and welfare measures, and village tradition. It is almost totally supported by exports of crude oil and natural gas, with revenues from the petroleum sector accounting for over half of gross domestic product (GDP). Per capita GDP is far above most other third world countries, and substantial income from overseas investment supplements income from domestic production. The government provides for all medical services and subsidizes food and housing. The government has shown progress in its basic policy of diversifying the economy away from oil and gas. Brunei's leaders are concerned that steadily increased integration in the world economy will undermine internal social cohesion although it has taken steps to become a more prominent player by serving as chair for the 2000 APEC (Asian Pacific Economic Cooperation) forum.

Principal Economic Indicators

Gross National Product: $7.151 billion
GNP per capita: $25,090
GNP Average Annual Growth Rate (1990–97) %: —
GNP per capita Average Annual Growth Rate (1990–97) %: —
Origin of Gross Domestic Product %
- Agriculture: 3
- Mining: —
- Manufacturing: 41
- Construction: 5
- Public Utilities: 1
- Transportation and Communications: 4
- Trade: 8
- Financial Services: 8
- Other Services: 32
- Government: 32

Gross Domestic Product by Type of Expenditure %
Private Consumption: —
Government Consumption: —
Gross Domestic Investment: —
Foreign Trade: Exports: —
Imports: —
% of Income Received by Poorest 20%: —
% of Income Received by Richest 10%: —

Price and earnings indexes (1995 = 100)

	1989	1990	1991	1992	1993	1994	1995
Consumer price index	84.1	85.8	87.2	88.3	92.1	94.3	100.0
Earnings index	—	—	—	—	—	—	—

Finance

National Currency: Bruneian Dollar (B$)
Exchange Rate: $1 = B$ 1.7533
Money Supply Stock in National Currency billion: —
M1 per capita: —
Central Bank Discount Rate %: —
Total External Debt $million: 0
Debt Service Ratio %: 16

Balance of Payments $million: 2,874
International Reserves SDRs million: —
Ratio of External Debt to Total Reserves: —
Average Annual Rate of Inflation/Consumer Price Index Growth Rate %: 2

Official Development Assistance

ODA $: 0
as % of GNP: —
per capita: $—
Foreign Direct Investment $million: —

Central Government Revenues and Expenditures

Fiscal Year: Calendar Year
Revenues $million: 2,500
Expenditures $million: 2,500
Budget Deficit $: —
Tax Revenues as % of GDP: —
Highest Tax Bracket %
Individual: —
Corporate: —

Employment and Labor

Economically Active Population: 112,000
Female Participation Rate %: 32.9
Activity Rate %: 43
Labor by Sector: %
Agriculture, Forestry, Fishing: 1.9
Manufacturing, Mining: 10.4
Construction: 12.6
Transportation and Communications: 4.8
Trade, Hotels, and Restaurants: 13.8
Finance, Insurance, Real Estate: 5.2
Public Administration, Defense: —
Services: 46.6
Unemployment %: 4.8

Agriculture

Agriculture's Share of GDP %: 3
Average Annual Rate of Growth (1965–98) %: —
Number of Farms 000: 6.3
Average Size of Farm ha: 2.6
Number of Tractors per 1,000 hectares: 24
Irrigation, % of Farms having: 33
Artificial Fertilizer kg/hectare: 57
Total Farmland as % of land area: 2.8
Livestock: Cattle 000: 2
Sheep 000: —
Hogs 000: 5
Chickens 000: 3,000
Forests: Production of Roundwood (000 cubic meters): 295
Fisheries: Total Catch tons 000: 4.5

Mining

% of GDP: 57.9
Value of Mineral Production $million: 1,437.7

Manufacturing

Value Added $million: 305
Industrial Production Growth Rate %: 4

Energy

Commercial Energy Production metric tons of oil equivalent 000: —
Commercial Energy Consumption metric tons of oil equivalent 000: 3,045
Commercial Energy Consumption per capita kg: 10,839
Average Annual Growth Rate 1980–97 %: —
Net Energy Imports % of use: −515
Electricity Installed Capacity kW 000: 473
Production kW-hr million: 1,560
Coal Reserves tons million: —
Production tons 000: —
Natural Gas Proven Reserves cubic meters billion: 399
Production cubic meters million: 9,922
Crude Petroleum Reserves barrels million: 1,350
Production barrels million: 55
Consumption barrels million: 2
Refinery Capacity barrels per day 000: 9
Pipelines Length km: 553

Foreign Trade

Imports $million: 1,820.5
Exports $million: 2,039.9
Export Volume % Annual Growth Rate (1990–97): —
Import Volume % Annual Growth Rate (1990–97): —
Balance of Trade $

Balance of Trade (current prices)

	1989	1990	1991	1992	1993	1994
B$ 000,000	+1,988	+2,197	+2,417	+1,946	+1,672	+886
% of total	37.4%	37.7%	39.2%	33.7%	29.3%	14.7%

Major Trading Partners

	Imports	Exports
European Union %	25.7	—
United States %	25.1	0.4
Eastern Europe %	17.1	—
Japan %	9.4	74.8
Others %	22.7	24.8

Transportation

Roads Total Length mi: 1,527 km 2,457
Paved %: 59
Automobiles: 141,371
Trucks and Buses: 16,557
Persons per vehicle: 1.9
Railroad; Track Length mi: —
Passenger-mi million: —
Freight-mi million: —
Merchant Marine: No. of Vessels: 51
Total Deadweight Tonnage 000: 349.7
International Cargo Loaded tons 000: 13,554
International Cargo Off-loaded tons 000: 1,325
Airports with Scheduled Flights: 1
Traffic: Passenger-mi million: 1,685
Freight-mi million: 74
Length of Canals mi: 130 km 209

Tourism

Number of Tourists to 000: —
Number of Tourists from 000: —
Tourist Receipts $million: —
Tourist Expenditures $million: —

Communications

Telephones 000: 68
Cost of Local Calls 3 mins: $0
Cellular Telephones 000: 36
Fax Machines 000: 2.0
Personal Computers 000: 8.0
Internet Hosts per million persons: 549
Mail: Post Offices: 6
Pieces of Mail Handled million: 13
Pieces of Mail Handled per person: 45

EDUCATION

Schooling is free, universal, and compulsory for 11 years, from ages five to 16 and covers six years of primary school and five years of lower secondary school. All children enter the government school system at age five at the kindergarten or preschool level. Government primary schools use Malay up to the fourth year and become bilingual (English and Malay) thereafter for three years. There is a national promotion examination at the end of the last year of primary school. Those who fail this examination are automatically promoted after a repeat year. At the end of the third secondary year, students take a junior certificate of education examination that qualifies them to pursue a further two-year course leading to the Brunei Cambridge General Certificate of Education (GCE "O" level). Those who pass this examination proceed to the sixth form center to follow another two-year course leading to the Brunei Cambridge Advanced General Certificate of Education (GCE "A" level), which qualifies them for university entrance.

Schools operate a five-day week with Fridays and Sundays off. The school year is divided into three terms, with a total of 202 school days. The longest break is during the month of Ramadan.

Islamic religious education is part of the curriculum in all educational institutions, including private schools, and religious knowledge is a subject in public examinations up to the GCE "A" level. In 1966 the first Arabic secondary school was established; it was followed by the Religious Teachers' Training College.

In May 1985 the University of Brunei Darussalam was founded, with two faculties, arts and education, and an enrollment of 200. Most of the staff are expatriates.

Education

Literacy Rate %: 87.8
Male %: 92.5
Female %: 82.5
First Level: Primary schools: 170
Teachers: 3,380
Students: 55,241
Student-Teacher Ratio: 16.3
Net Enrollment Ratio: 91
Second Level: Secondary Schools: 37
Teachers: 2,157
Students: 27,801
Student-Teacher Ratio: 12.9
Net Enrollment Ratio: 68

Vocational Level: Schools: 6
Students: 1,966

Third Level: Institutions: 4
Teachers: 325
Students: 1,606
Student-Ratio Level: 4.9
Gross Enrollment Ratio: 6.6
Students per 100,000: 518
% of Population age 25 and over with Postsecondary Education: —

Public Expenditure on Education as % of GDP: 3.1

SCIENCE AND TECHNOLOGY

Science and Technology

Scientists and Engineers in R&D per 1 million persons: —
Expenditures in R&D as % of GDP: —
High-Tech Exports $: —
Patent Applications by Residents: —

MEDIA

The only commercial weekly newspaper is *Borneo Bulletin*, with a circulation of 76,000. The government publishes the weekly *Pelita Brunei*, which is distributed free to 45,000 readers. Brunei Shell puts out the biweekly *Salam* in one combined English, Chinese, and Malay edition. Occasionally the government suspends the issue of offending foreign newspapers or periodicals and expels nonresident correspondents.

Radio Television Brunei broadcasts radio programs in English, Malay, Gurkha, and Chinese, and television programs in Malay and English. Educational television was introduced in 1978 and color television in 1975.

Media

Weekly Newspapers: 1
 Total Circulation 000: 20
 Circulation per 1,000: 71
Books Published: 45
Magazines: 15
Radio Receivers 000: 125
 per 1,000: 417
Television sets 000: 173
 per 1,000: 609

MOST IMPORTANT MEDIA:

Press. The following newspapers are published in Brunei: *Pelita Brunei* (Bandar Seri Begawan, 45,000), weekly in Romanized Malay; *Borneo Bulletin* (Kuala Belait, 30,000), progovernment weekly, in English; *Salam* (Seria, 9,000), monthly, in English and Romanized Malay, published by Brunei Shell Petroleum.

Radio and television. The government-controlled Radio Television Brunei, broadcasts in Malay, English, Chinese, and local dialects.

CULTURE

Cultural Indicators

Public Libraries
 Number: 1
 Volumes: 97,000
 Registered borrowers: 6,422
Museums
 Number: 3
 Annual Attendance: 112,000
Cinema
 Production of Long Films: —
 Number of Cinemas: —
 Seating Capacity: —
 Annual Attendance: —
 Annual Attendance per capita: —

STATUS OF WOMEN

In accordance with Koranic precepts, women are denied equal status with men in a number of important areas, such as divorce, inheritance, and custody of children. Under the Brunei Nationality Act, citizenship is transmitted through males only. Female citizens who are married to foreigners or bear children by foreign fathers cannot transmit citizenship to their children, even when such children are born in Brunei. However, some of this is changing. In 1999, the government passed the Emergency (Married Women) Order, which elevates women's rights, putting them on a more equal footing with men. According to the legislation, the husband and the wife shall have the right separately to engage in any trade or profession or in social activities, and the wife shall also have the right to use her own surname.

Women

Gender Empowerment Measure: —
Seats Held in Parliament by Women %: —
Female Administrators and Managers %: —
Female Professional and Technical Workers %: —
Women's Share of Earned Income %: —
Women in Government %: 2

HEALTH, FOOD, AND NUTRITION

Health

Number of Physicians: 251
Number of Dentists: 38
Number of Nurses: 1,288
Number of Pharmacists: 15
Population per Physician: 1,164
Number of Hospitals: 10
Hospital Beds per 10,000: 33
Hospital Bed Occupancy Rate: —
Infant Mortality Rate per 1,000 live births: 13
Maternal Mortality Rate per 100,000 live births: —
Total Health Expenditures as % of GDP: —
Health Expenditures per capita $: —
HIV Infected % of adults: —
Cigarette Consumption per smoker per year: —
% of Smokers: Male: —
 Female: —
Access to Safe Water %: 90

Food and Nutrition

Food Supply as % of FAO Requirements: 127
% of Consumption Expenditures on Food: 45.1
Daily Available Calories per capita: 2,849
% of Total Calories derived from:
Cereals: 43.6
Potatoes, cassava: 1.2
Meat, poultry: 14.2
Fish: 1.0
Eggs, milk: 6.1
Fruits, vegetables: 4.6
Fats, oils: 7.4

ENVIRONMENT

Brunei's main environmental problem is external to the country. It suffers from seasonal air pollution caused by forest fires in Indonesia.

Environment

Forest Area sq km: —
Average Annual Deforestation sq km: —
Nationally Protected Areas as % of Total Land Area: 3
Freshwater Access cubic meters per capita: —
Emissions of Organic Water Pollutants kg per day: —
CO_2 Emissions per capita ton: 28.1

CHRONOLOGY

1984 Brunei becomes an independent nation in accordance with its 1979 treaty with the United Kingdom.

1985 The Brunei National Democratic Party (BNDP) is formed.

1986 The Brunei National Unity Party (BNUP) is formed after splitting with the BNDP.

1988 The BNDP is dissolved after asking for political reforms.

1990 The outlawed Brunei People's Party writes to Sultan Hassanal Bolkiah from Malaysia demanding democracy for the kingdom; the sultan promptly issues warnings against criticism of the government, religion, or himself.

1991 As a result of pressure from the British government, the sultan releases six political prisoners who had been detained since the failed coup attempt in 1962.

1996 Brunei has successfully limited its economic dependence on oil revenue with nearly two-thirds of GNP coming from other diversified sources.

1998 Sultan Bolkhia's eldest son, Prince Al-Muhtadee Billah, becomes heir apparent.

BIBLIOGRAPHY

Cleary, M., and S. Y. Wong. *Oil, Economic Development and Diversification in Brunei*. London, 1994.

Krausse, Sylvia C. *Brunei*. Oxford, England, 1988.

Leake, David. *Brunei: The Modern Southeast-Asian Islamic Sultanate*. Jefferson, N.C., 1989.

Saunders, G. *History of Brunei*. Oxford, U.K., 1996.

Singh, D. Ranjit. *Brunei, 1839–1983: The Problems of Political Survival*. New York, 1984.

OFFICIAL PUBLICATIONS

Brunei. *Brunei Statistical Yearbook; Summary Tables of the Population Census 1991.*

CONTACT INFORMATION

Embassy of Brunei
2600 Virginia Avenue NW, Suite 300
Washington, D.C. 20037
Phone: (202) 342-0159 Fax: (202) 342-0158

INTERNET RESOURCES

- Brunei Darussalam http://www.brunet.bn/

BULGARIA

BASIC FACT SHEET

OFFICIAL NAME:
Republic of Bulgaria (Republika Bulgariya)

ABBREVIATION:
BU

CAPITAL:
Sofia

HEAD OF STATE:
President Petar Stoyanov (from 1997)

HEAD OF GOVERNMENT:
Chairman of the Council of Ministers Simeon Borisov Sakskobarggotski (from 2001)

NATURE OF GOVERNMENT:
Democracy

POPULATION:
8,206,000 (1999)

AREA:
110,911 sq km (42,823 sq mi)

MAJOR ETHNIC GROUP:
Bulgars

LANGUAGE:
Bulgarian

RELIGION:
Bulgarian Orthodox

UNIT OF CURRENCY:
Lev

NATIONAL FLAG:
Tricolor of white, green, and red horizontal stripes

NATIONAL EMBLEM:
Two sheaves of grain topped by a five-pointed star enclosing a rampant lion. A banner in the bottom contains two important dates: 681, the date of the nation's founding, and 1944, when Bulgaria was liberated from the Nazis.

NATIONAL ANTHEM:
"Proudly Rise the Balkan Peaks"

NATIONAL HOLIDAYS:
New Year's Day (January 1); Liberation Day (March 3); Labor Days (May 1–2); Education and Culture Day (May 24); Christmas (December 24–25)

DATE OF INDEPENDENCE:
October 5, 1908

DATE OF CONSTITUTION:
July 12, 1991

GEOGRAPHICAL FEATURES

Located in the Balkan Peninsula, Bulgaria occupies an area of 110,911 sq km (42,823 sq mi). Lying on the Black Sea, the country shares borders with Romania, Turkey, Greece, and Yugoslavia.

First called Serdica by the Thracians when it was founded 2,000 years ago, Sofia, the capital, stands on the direct trading route from Belgrade to Istanbul. Other important cities include Plovdiv, Varna, and Burgas, which are Bulgaria's principal Black Sea links with international maritime commerce.

Bulgaria contains four principal land regions: the Rodopi (the Rhodope Mountains); the Balkan Mountains; the Danubian Plateau; and the Central Thracian Plain.

The Rodopi, in southernmost Bulgaria, contain the country's tallest peak, Mount Musala, 2,925 m (9,596 ft) and topographically dominate the entire Balkan Peninsula.

Extending 595 km (370 mi) west to east, the Stara Planina (Balkan Mountains) encloses the Sredna Gora—

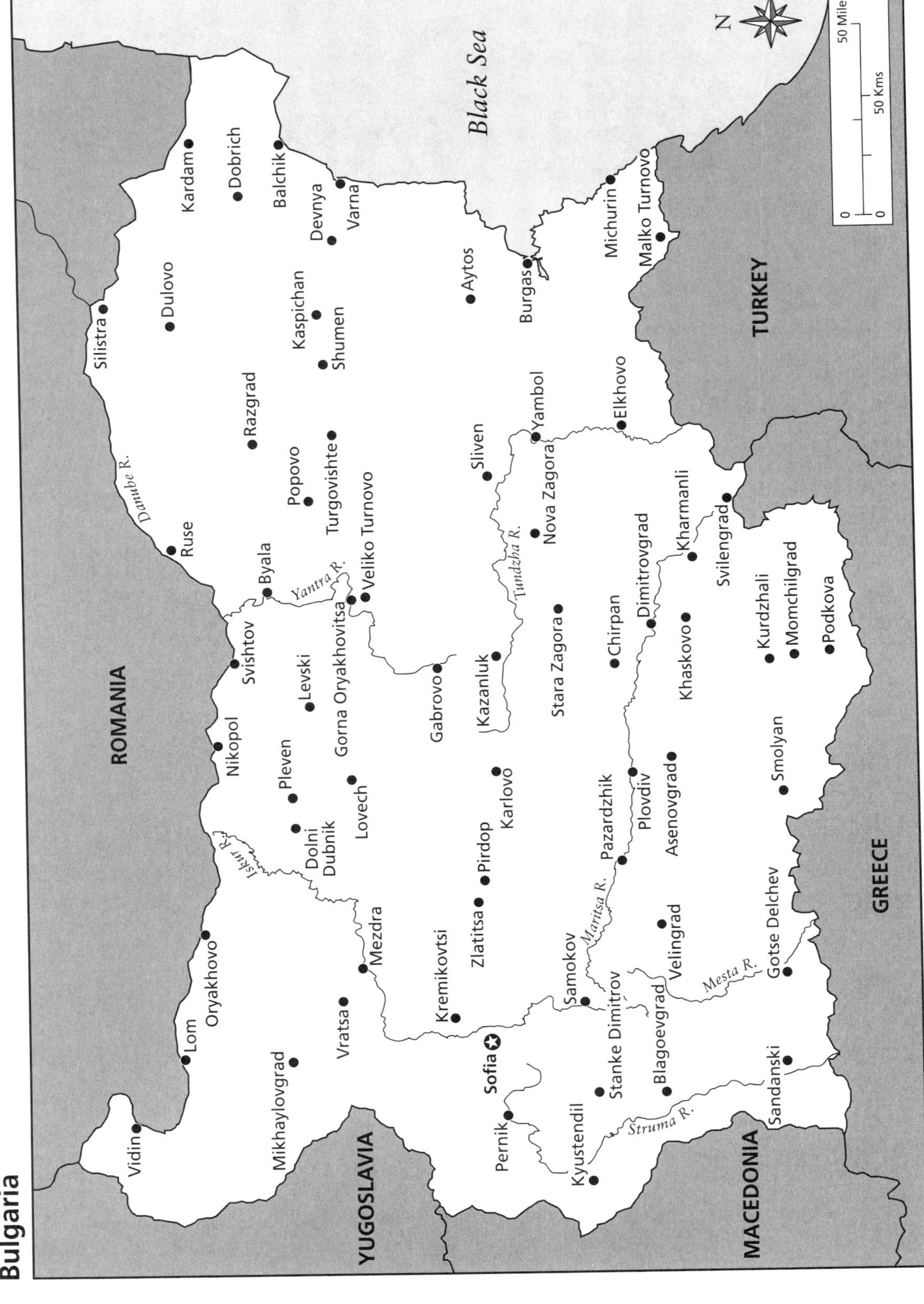

Bulgaria
ROMANIA
YUGOSLAVIA
MACEDONIA
GREECE
TURKEY
Black Sea
N
0
50 Miles
0
50 Kms
Danube R.
Yantra R.
Iskur R.
Tundzha R.
Maritsa R.
Mesta R.
Struma R.
Vidin
Lom
Oryakhovo
Nikopol
Svishtov
Ruse
Silistra
Kardam
Dobrich
Balchik
Dulovo
Razgrad
Devnya
Varna
Kaspichan
Shumen
Popovo
Turgovishte
Byala
Veliko Turnovo
Levski
Gorna Oryakhovitsa
Pleven
Dolni Dubnik
Lovech
Mikhaylovgrad
Vratsa
Mezdra
Kremikovtsi
Sofia
Pernik
Zlatitsa
Pirdop
Karlovo
Gabrovo
Kazanluk
Sliven
Aytos
Burgas
Yambol
Nova Zagora
Stara Zagora
Elkhovo
Michurin
Malko Turnovo
Chirpan
Dimitrovgrad
Kharmanli
Svilengrad
Khaskovo
Plovdiv
Pazardzhik
Asenovgrad
Kurdzhali
Momchilgrad
Podkova
Smolyan
Samokov
Velingrad
Stanke Dimitrov
Blagoevgrad
Kyustendil
Gotse Delchev
Sandanski

including the Shipka Pass (famous as the site of the battle between Russians and Turks that led to Bulgarian emancipation). The Stara Planina is also the location of the Valley of the Roses, which produce the attar used in perfumes.

The Danubian Plateau contains Bulgaria's most fertile farmland and extends from the Yugoslav border to the Black Sea.

The southern slopes of the Stara Planina and the Sredna Gora give way to the Thracian Plain. Roughly triangular in shape, the plain originates at a point east of the mountains ringing the Sofia basin and broadens as it fans eastward to the Black Sea.

Geography

Area sq km: 110,911 sq mi 42,823
World Rank: 103rd
Land Boundaries, km: Greece 494; Macedonia 148; Romania 608; Yugoslavia 318; Turkey 240
Coastline, km: 354
Elevation Extremes meters
Lowest: Black Sea 0
Highest: Musala 2,925
Land Use % Arable land: 37
Permanent Crops: 2
Permanent Pastures: 16
Forest and Woodland: 35
Other: 10

Population of Principal Cities (1996 est.)

Burgas	199,470
Dobrich	103,532
Pleven	125,029
Plovdiv	344,326
Ruse	168,051
Silven	107,011
Sofia	1,116,823
Stara Zagora	149,666
Varna	301,421

CLIMATE AND WEATHER

For a small country, Bulgaria has an unusually varied and complex climate, with six or more climatic zones. The north is characterized by hot summers and cold winters and with rainfall well distributed throughout the year. The Stara Planina represents the southern limits of this zone. The Rodopi mark the northern limits of Bulgaria's Mediterranean climate with mild, damp winters and hot, dry summers.

The area lying between these zones, including the Thracian Plain, has a climate characterized by long summers and high humidity. Average temperatures and precipitation are erratic. For Bulgaria as a whole, rainfall averages about 635 mm (25 in), with higher elevations receiving 1,016 mm (40 in) or more.

Throughout the uplands the many valley basins frequently experience temperature inversions, resulting in stagnant air. During winter there are many windy days and violent local storms, particularly along the Danube. The hard-blowing, hot, and dry Black Wind wreaks havoc on crops. It gets its name from the quantities of dust it carries, which often darken the skies.

Climate and Weather

Mean Temperature
January 32°F to 36°F
July 72°F to 75°F
Average Rainfall 25 in

POPULATION

Population Indicators

Total Population: 1999 8,206,000
World Rank: 83rd
Density per sq mi: 191.5 per sq km 73.9
% of annual growth (1994–99): −0.6
Male %: 49.1
Female %: 50.9
Urban %: 67.2
Age Distribution: % 0–14: 20.5
15–29: 19.2
30–44: 39.8
45–59: 39.8
60–74: 20.5
75 and over: 20.5
Population 2020: 7,517,000
Birth Rate per 1,000: 8.6
Death Rate per 1,000: 14.0
Population Doubling Time (years): —
Infant Mortality Rate per 1,000 live births: 15.6
Rate of Natural Increase per 1,000: −5.4
Total Fertility Rate: 1.2
Expectation of Life (years): Males 67.1
Females 74.9
Marriage Rate per 1,000: 4.3
Divorce Rate per 1,000: 1.3
Total Number of Households: 2,795,000
Average Size of Households: 3.0
% of Illegitimate Children: 25.7
Induced Abortions: 107,416
Rate per 100 live births: 217.3

ETHNIC COMPOSITION

Bulgaria is characterized by a remarkable ethnic, linguistic, and religious homogeneity. Some 85 percent of the population is Bulgarian. The most significant ethnic minorities are Turks, composing 8.5 percent, Roma (Gypsies), 2.5 percent, and Macedonians, 2.5 percent. The remainder is made up of Greeks, Romanians, Armenians, and others.

The Turks and the Pomaks (as the Islamized Bulgarians are known) represent the surviving elements of four centuries of Turkish rule, and their numbers have been steadily reduced by emigration to Turkey. In 1950–51 alone 150,000 were expelled from Bulgaria. An effort by the Zhivkov regime in the late 1980s to Bulgarianize the Turks resulted in protests by Turkey and mass emigration of Turks to Turkey. But many of the migrants later returned, as they found living conditions in Turkey more intolerable than at home. However, the Turks pose no serious problem to the Bulgarian government, and the Turks' cultural and other rights are guaranteed by the constitution.

Macedonians also are not recognized as a separate entity. They are considered to be ethnic Bulgarians and their language a dialect of Bulgarian. They live predominantly in the southwest. Romanians fall into two groups: the Romanian-speaking Vlachs of the northwest, and the Greek-speaking Karakatchans—nomadic mountain shepherds of Romanian descent. Another hybrid community is the Gagauzi of the northeast who are of Turkish origin but who follow the Orthodox faith.

LANGUAGE

Bulgarian, the national language, is classified as a Slavonic language of the southern group, which also includes Macedonian, Serbo-Croatian, and Slovenian. Old Bulgarian, also known as Old Church Slavonic, was the first Slavic language to acquire an alphabet, in the ninth century. The alphabet, created by Sts. Cyril and Methodius, two Greek missionaries, was based partly on Greek and was accordingly named Cyrillic. Both the grammar and the vocabulary of modern Bulgarian show the influence of non-Slavonic languages.

Principal Languages and Their Speakers

Bulgarian	6,820,000
Macedonian	210,000
Romany	300,000
Turkish	770,000
Other	100,000

RELIGIONS

By the second century, Christianity had become established in the area that is now Bulgaria. The Bulgars, who conquered the land in about 670, were converted when Boris, their king, was baptized by the Greek clergy. The introduction of the Cyrillic alphabet was a landmark in ecclesiastical history, enabling language, culture, and religion to converge. In 889, Boris abdicated to enter a monastery, while his son Simeon left a monastery to ascend the throne. Slavonic was substituted for Greek in the Bulgar liturgy. The Bulgar church was declared autocephalous, with its own patriarch. In 1018, the Bulgarian kingdom fell to Byzantine rulers, who suppressed the Bulgarian patriarchate. Bulgaria regained its independence in 1186, and the patriarchate was reestablished in 1235. In 1396 Bulgaria fell before a third wave of Muslim invaders, the Ottoman Turks. For the next 500 years the Bulgarian church was effectively silenced.

Prior to World War II and the Communist takeover, the Bulgarian Orthodox Church claimed a membership of 85 percent of the national population, but in the years since then, this percentage has dropped to below 20 percent.

The Armenian Apostolic Church has 12 congregations in the country. Protestantism was introduced by American Congregationalist missionaries in 1856, American Methodists in 1857, and Russian Baptists in 1865. From the ninth to the 14th centuries the Roman Catholic Church made repeated efforts to bring Bulgaria into its fold, but except for a brief 30-year union, these efforts were not fruitful. The majority of Bulgarian Catholics are descendants of the Bogomils, converted to Catholicism by the Franciscans in the 17th century. In 1926 an exarchate of Sofia was created for Catholics of the Byzantine rite, who number a few thousand and who are found in Sofia, Plovdiv, and along the Greek border. Immediately following World War II the church lost all its property as it became the target of the new Communist regime's hostility. All foreign religious personnel and priests were expelled, and many were arrested, sentenced to life imprisonment, or killed.

Religious Affiliations

Bulgarian Orthodox	3,000,000
Muslim (mostly Sunni)	1,070,000
Other	4,140,000

HISTORICAL BACKGROUND

Bulgarian history begins when the Bulgars, a central Asian Turkish tribe, overran what is present-day Bulgaria in the seventh century. They mixed with the Slavs, who had settled in the region earlier, and created a common polity. From this amalgam came the First Bulgarian Kingdom. In the ninth century Bulgaria was powerful enough to challenge Constantinople. Twice in this period Bulgars controlled areas of Greece, Turkey, Yugoslavia, Romania, and even Russia. In 924, after Serbia fell under Bulgarian rule, Simeon (893–927) claimed the title of czar. With territorial expansion came a resurgence of arts and letters, making Simeon's reign the Golden Age of Bulgaria. Toward the end of the 10th century the First Bulgarian Kingdom had vanished. From 1018 to 1185 all of Bulgaria was under Byzantine rule.

By the 13th century Bulgaria had become the largest state in the Balkans. Again, as in the time of Simeon, arts and culture flourished and reached a state of excellence.

Meanwhile, the nemesis of Christian Europe, the Turks, had begun to cross the Bosporus and advance on Thrace, Macedonia, and parts of Bulgaria. In 1371 they captured Sofia and in 1388 beat the Serbs. By 1396 all of Bulgaria was under Turkish rule.

The 482 years of Turkish rule were the darkest in Bulgarian history. Turkish rule was characterized by an enormous capacity for brutality and sustained by a religious and political system that institutionalized such aggression.

It was not until the 19th century that organized resistance to Turkish oppression began to show results. By then Ottoman power was in full retreat and large parts of eastern Europe had already been liberated. In 1872 the Bulgarian Revolutionary Central Committee was formed in Bucharest. As the revolutionary fervor grew, the Bulgarians turned to Russia for help.

The precursor to Bulgaria's liberation in 1878 was an unsuccessful rising in 1876. Thousands of Bulgarians were killed in April of that year. The savagery of these reprisals induced the Russians to invade Bulgaria soon after the Russo-Turkish War of 1877 and liquidate the Turkish army. In these battles for Bulgaria's liberation, the Russians lost over 200,000 soldiers.

Following the Russian intervention, Bulgaria was granted the status of an autonomous principality; complete independence was not established until 1908. However, the Congress of Berlin in 1878 took away from Bulgaria parts of Macedonia and Thrace that the Treaty of San Stefano had granted it. This set the tone for an irredentist foreign policy that led to Bulgaria's disastrous alliances with Germany in both world wars.

The post-independence government established a democratic government and a constitutional monarchy. Within four years, in 1912, Bulgaria was once again embroiled in war, this time essentially over Macedonia.

Macedonia remained a sore issue for Bulgaria, which was determined to regain the land that had escaped its grasp so often. Of all the Balkan states, Bulgaria was the only one to join the Central Powers in World War I, ironically siding with its former oppressor Turkey against her friend and benefactor Russia. It emerged from the war defeated and in a worse position.

The interwar period was one of political unrest and Macedonian terrorism.

Bulgaria entered World War II on the Axis side and again suffered defeat. The war ended for Bulgaria when, on September 4, 1944, Soviet troops entered Sofia. On October 28, 1944, an armistice was signed between Bulgaria and the Soviet Union by which the former surrendered all territories gained since 1941.

In 1944 the monarchy was rejected by the majority of Bulgarians and a People's Republic was formally established in 1947 under the premiership of Georgi Dimitrov, the "Father of Bulgarian Communism." Dimitrov died in 1949 and communist rule was consolidated under the successive regimes of Vulko Chervenko and Anton Yugov until 1954 and thereafter until 1989 by Todor Zhivkov. The collapse of East European communism did not impact Bulgaria until November 3, 1989, when demonstrators marched in Sofia in the country's first prodemocracy rally. One week later, Zhivkov was replaced as party general secretary by Petur Mladenov who later succeeded as head of state. In the first multiparty elections held in 1990 Bulgaria bucked the trend by reelecting the Communist Party to power. Nevertheless, Mladenov resigned and was succeeded in office by Zhelyu Zhelev. In 1991 a new democratic constitution was adopted. In 1996 Petar Stoyanov, the candidate of the opposition, won the presidency. In 1997, a deepening economic crisis led to mass protests and the demand for early elections. In general elections held on April 19, the United Democratic Forces (ODC) won 137 out of 240 seats, and its leader, Ivan Kostov, became prime minister. He promised to fight organized crime and corruption and implement rigorous economic reforms. His pro-Western government supported NATO action against Serbia, marking a departure from earlier pro-Serb policies. In 2001, the National Movement for Simeon II, the party of Bulgaria's former king, Simeon II, won a majority of seats in general elections. Simeon II became prime minister in a coalition government with the Movement for Rights and Freedoms. Georgi Parvanov won presidential elections in November.

CONSTITUTION

The theoretical foundation of the state is the 1991 constitution. The constitution established the basic institutions of government: the National Assembly and the Council of Ministers at the national level and the municipal councils at the local level.

The 1991 constitution is a far cry from Bulgaria's first constitution, the Turnovo Constitution of 1879, which was considered by its contemporaries one of the most liberal in the world. The parliament was supreme, and the king was bound by its laws. Even after the communist takeover, the Turnovo Constitution continued to be the charter of government until a new constitution was adopted in 1947.

Known as the Dimitrov Constitution after Georgi Dimitrov, who helped to draft it, the constitution of 1947 remained in force for 24 years. It established the National Assembly as the supreme organ of state power and the Council of Ministers as the supreme executive power. However, in actual practice the Presidium of the National Assembly was empowered with legislative, executive, and judicial authority. Following the Soviet model, the first secretary of the Bulgarska Komunisticheska Partiya (BKP) (Bulgarian Communist Party), also was chairman of the Council of Ministers and, as such, the country's prime minister.

With the 1971 constitution, the State Council became a more powerful body than the Presidium of the National Assembly that it replaced and overshadowed the Council of Ministers as well.

ORGANIZATION OF BULGARIAN GOVERNMENT

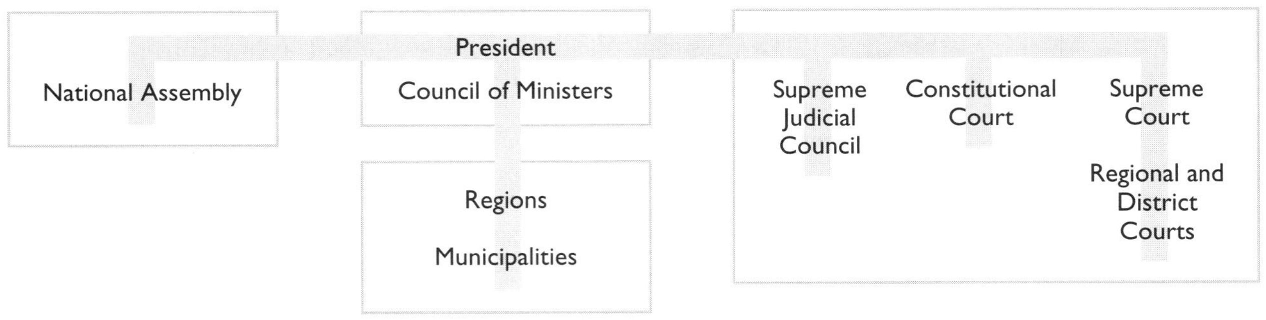

Following the collapse of communism in Eastern Europe in 1989–90, Bulgaria began to dismantle the constitutional structures of the authoritarian state. First, the Communist Party was stripped of its monopoly of power, called "the dominant role" in the constitution. The Communist Party lost its control over the police and the military. The State Council was dissolved. Finally, multiple parties were permitted to stand for free national and local elections.

The 1991 constitution defines Bulgaria as a parliamentary republic. The supreme legislative body is the National Assembly (the parliament). The president is the head of state, elected through direct and secret ballot for a five-year term of office.

The Council of Ministers is the supreme executive body for home and foreign affairs.

LOCAL GOVERNMENT

Bulgaria is divided into nine administrative regions and smaller municipalities. The municipality is the primary territorial administrative unit, being a legal entity where local self-government is exercised through a municipal council elected for a four-year term.

Local Government

Principal administrative divisions, capitals, area, population

AREA AND POPULATION

		area		population
Regions	**Capitals**	**sq mi**	**sq km**	**1996 estimate**
Burgas	Burgas	5,685	14,724	846,524
Khaskovo	Khaskovo	5,338	13,824	897,863
Lovech	Lovech	5,849	15,150	990,307
Montana	Mikhaylovgrad	4,095	10,607	615,629
Plovdiv	Plovdiv	5,245	13,585	1,213,966
Ruse	Ruse	4,187	10,843	760,029
Sofiya	Sofia (Sofiya)	7,344	19,021	966,502
Varna	Varna	4,606	11,929	901,160
City commune				
Sofiya	Sofia (Sofiya)	506	1,311	1,192,735
TOTAL		42,855	110,994	8,384,715

PARLIAMENT

The National Assembly (Narodno Sobraniye) is a 240-member unicameral legislature elected for a term of four years. Convened at least three times a year, its sessions are brief. The National Assembly has permanent commissions, the functions of some of which overlap those of the ministries.

The basic election law was adopted in 1953. It has been amended many times since then. Article 6 of the constitution extends the right to vote to every Bulgarian citizen who has reached 18. Members of both national and local representative bodies are elected by direct and secret ballot on the basis of universal, equal, and direct suffrage.

POLITICAL PARTIES

Until 1989 the only authorized political parties were the Bulgarian Communist Party and the Bulgarian Agrarian National Union, which formed the core of the Fatherland Front. The political landscape changed in the 1990s with the formation of numerous political parties on the left and right. The government coalition consists of a loose coalition of democratic parties, known as United Democratic Forces, which consists of three parties: Union of Democratic Forces, People's Union (itself an alliance of Bulgarian Agrarian National Union and Democratic Party), and the Bulgarian Social Democratic Party. The main opposition bloc is the Democratic Left, a coalition of the Bulgarian Socialist Party (formerly the Bulgarian Communist Party), Ecoglasnost Political Club, the Bulgarian Agrarian National Union, Alliance for National Salvation, an alliance of several smaller groups including the Movement for Rights and Freedoms representing the Turkish minority, New Choice Liberal Union, and the Green Party. There are hundreds of smaller title, most of them having the name Democratic in their title, such as the Liberal Democratic Union, Democratic Alternative for the Republic, Christian Democratic Union, and Turkish Democratic Party.

Political Parties

United Democratic Forces, 1994
Union of Democratic Forces, 1989
People's Union, 1994, an ailliance of
 Bulgarian Agrarian National Union Democratic Party, 1896
Bulgarian Social Democratic Party, 1891
Democratic Left, 1996
Bulgarian Socialist Party, 1990
Ecoglasnost Political Club
Bulgarian Agrarian National Union-Aleksandur Stamboliyski, 1899
Alliance for National Salvation
Movement for Rights and Freedoms-Turkish
New Choice Liberal Union, 1993
Green Party
Bulgarian Agrarian National Union-Nikola Petkov, 1989
Bulgarian Business Bloc, 1990
Euro-Left Coalition, 1997
United Labor Bloc, 1997
Liberal Democratic Union, 1996
Liberal Democratic Alternative, 1996
Democratic Alternative for the Republic, 1994
Christian Democratic Union
Fatherland Party of Labor
Turkish Democratic Party, 1993
New Democratic Party, 1995
Bulgarian Communist Party

Political Parties: Strength in Parliament Most Recent Elections

National Assembly. The National Assembly is a unicameral body of 240 members elected for four-year terms. At the most recent balloting of June 8, 2001, the National Movement for Simeon II won 120 seats; United Democratic Forces, 51; Coalition for Bulgarian 48; and Movement for Rights and Freedom, 21.

LEGAL SYSTEM

Bulgarian civil and criminal law is based on Roman law. The highest judicial organ is the Supreme Court. It is a court of original as well as appellate jurisdiction and is organized into civil, criminal, and military divisions. The chairman is appointed for a seven-year term by the president.

Below the Supreme Court are 28 regional and district courts. Lower court judges are elected by their respective municipal councils for five-year terms and are subject to recall by the voters.

The prosecutor general and senior judges are elected by the Supreme Judicial Council, established in 1992.

The maximum term of imprisonment is 20 years, but the death penalty may be allowed for exceptionally dangerous crimes. In 1996, 13,097 crimes were reported, of which 227 were murders.

There is also a Constitutional Court to review the constitutionality of laws, with 12 justices appointed or elected for a nine-year term.

LAW ENFORCEMENT

Law Enforcement

Offenses reported to the police per 100,000: 2,522
 Murder: 5.9
 Assault: 38.6
 Burglary: 1,174.9
 Automobile Theft: 208
 Population per Police officer: —
Death Penalty: Yes

HUMAN RIGHTS

Although Bulgaria is now a parliamentary democracy, some vestiges of former human rights abuses have survived. These include excessive use of force by the police. The judiciary continues to struggle with problems of antiquated procedures, corruption, and a heavy backlog of cases. Organized crime has some influence on the prosecutors' offices. Print journalism is generally free but the government exerts unduly heavy influence on the electronic media. Eastern Orthodox Christianity is designated as the "traditional religion" and other religions, like Islam, and sects like Jehovah's Witnesses, face some intolerance. Although the constitution guarantees protection against all forms of discrimination, Roma (Gypsies) are often discriminated against.

FOREIGN POLICY

Between 1945 and 1990, Bulgaria's foreign policy was completely subordinated to that of the Soviet Union. Todor Zhivkov once acknowledged that Bulgaria was bound "to the Soviet Union in life and death."

Since the end of the cold war, Bulgaria has sought to maintain a markedly Western foreign policy, joining the European Union as an associate member, making its presence better known at the United Nations, as well as seeking membership in NATO.

DEFENSE

The military forces of Bulgaria are composed of the following services: army, navy, air and air defense forces, border troops, and internal security troops

Manpower availability (conscription was reduced in 1992 from 18 to 12 months): males (aged 15–49): 2,155,332. Of this total, males fit for military service: 1,797,318. Males reach military age at 19.

Military equipment, such as vessels, aircraft, artillery, and missiles are generally ex-Soviet or Soviet-built, though much is relatively up-to-date.

Military Indicators

Total Active Duty Personnel: 75,800
Military Manpower per 1,000: 9.1
Military Expenditures $million: 1,073
as % of GNP: 2.8
per capita $: 125
as % of central government expenditures: 6.3

Arms Imports $million: 0
Arms Exports $million: 150

ECONOMY

In January 1992, almost the entire economy was still firmly under state control, despite the fact that the government stated that its goal was privatization. By the end of that year, 5 percent of state firms had been transferred to the private sector, along with another 500 by the end of 1993.

Privatization remains the stated objective of the present government and, but for the Kosovo War, the privatization process would have been dramatically accelerated in 1999.

In 1996, the gross domestic product (GDP) declined by 4 percent and in 1998 stood at $11.7 billion, or about $1,200 per capita. After several years of tumult, Bulgaria's economy has stabilized. Its better-than-expected economic performance in 1999—despite the impact of the Kosovo conflict, the 1998 Russian financial crisis, and structural reforms—and strong growth in 2000 portend solid growth over the next few years.

Principal Economic Indicators

Gross National Product $: 9.750 billion
GNP per capita $: 1,170
GNP Average Annual Growth Rate (1990–97) %: −2.0
GNP per capita Average Annual Growth Rate (1990–97) %: −1.3
Origin of Gross Domestic Product %
Agriculture: 12
Mining: —
Manufacturing: 29
Construction: 5
Public Utilities: —
Transportation and Communications: 7
Trade: 11
Financial Services: 15
Other Services: 20
Government: 20
Gross Domestic Product by Type of Expenditure %
Private Consumption: 71
Government Consumption: 16
Gross Domestic Investment: 13
Foreign Trade: Exports: 43
Imports: −44
% of Income Received by Poorest 20%: 8.3
% of Income Received by Richest 10%: 24.7

Price and earnings indexes (1995 = 100)

	1992	1993	1994	1995	1996	1997	1998
Consumer price index	18.2	31.5	61.7	100.0	223.0	2,636.6	3,224.3
Earnings index	28.6	44.5	68.4	100.0	—	—	—

Finance

National Currency: Lev (Lv)
Exchange Rate: $1 = Lv 1,740
Money Supply Stock in National Currency billion: —
M1 per capita: —
Central Bank Discount Rate %: 2.83
Total External Debt $million: 10,000
Debt Service Ratio %: 11.6

Balance of Payments $million: 427
International Reserves SDRs million: —
Ratio of External Debt to Total Reserves: —
Average Annual Rate of Inflation/Consumer Price Index
Growth Rate %: 579

Official Development Assistance

ODA $million: 232
as % of GNP: 1.9
per capita $28
Foreign Direct Investment $million: 401

Central Government Revenues and Expenditures

Fiscal Year: Calendar Year
Revenues $million: 2,700
Expenditures $million: 3,200
Budget Deficit $million: 500
Tax Revenues as % of GDP: 27
Highest Tax Bracket %
Individual: 40
Corporate: 27

Employment and Labor

Economically Active Population: 3,738,000
Female Participation Rate %: 48.4
Activity Rate %: 46.3
Labor by Sector: %
Agriculture, Forestry, Fishing: 20.9
Manufacturing, Mining: 26.8
Construction: 5.0
Transportation and Communications: 6.7
Trade, Hotels, and Restaurants: 9.5
Finance, Insurance, Real Estate: 1.4
Public Administration, Defense: 2.0
Services: 14.2

Unemployment %: 14

Agriculture

Agriculture's Share of GDP %: 12
Average Annual Rate of Growth (1965–98) %: −2.5
Number of Farms 000: 2.2
Average Size of Farm ha: 2,467

Number of Tractors per 1,000 hectares: 9.2
Irrigation, % of Farms having: 20
Artificial Fertilizer kg/hectare: 195
Total Farmland as % of land area: 55.8
Livestock: Cattle 000: 612
Sheep 000: 2,848
Hogs 000: 1,500
Chickens 000: 13,766
Forests: Production of Roundwood (000 cubic meters): 2,856
Fisheries: Total Catch tons 000: 22.0

Mining

% of GDP: —
Value of Mineral Production $million: 532.1

Manufacturing

Value Added $million: 5,889
Industrial Production Growth Rate %: −7.4

Energy

Commercial Energy Production metric tons of oil equivalent 000: 9,981
Commercial Energy Consumption metric tons of oil equivalent 000: 20,616
Commercial Energy Consumption per capita kg: 2,480
Average Annual Growth Rate 1980–97 %: −2.1
Net Energy Imports % of use: 52
Electricity Installed Capacity kW 000: 12,087
Production kW-hr million: 41,789
Coal Reserves tons million: 2,710
Production tons 000: 30,830
Natural Gas Proven Reserves cubic meters billion: 4
Production cubic meters million: 11
Crude Petroleum Reserves barrels million: 15
Production barrels million: 0.4
Consumption barrels million: 59
Refinery Capacity barrels per day 000: 300
Pipelines Length km: 718

Foreign Trade

Imports $million: 5,125.0
Exports $million: 5,184.4
Export Volume % Annual Growth Rate (1990–97): —
Import Volume % Annual Growth Rate (1990–97): —

Balance of trade (current prices)

	1992	1993	1994	1995	1996	1997
000,000,000	−12.8	−28.6	−10.8	−20.3	−32.3	+12.9
% of total	6.5%	12.2%	2.4%	2.8%	1.8%	0.0%

Major Trading Partners

	Imports	Exports
European Union %	37.2	37.7
United States %	2.1	3.0
Eastern Europe %	36.2	19.5
Japan %	0.8	0.3
Others %	23.7	39.5

Transportation

Roads Total Length mi: 23,190 km 37,320
Paved %: 32
Automobiles: 1,647,571
Trucks and Buses: 204,950
Persons per vehicle: 4.5
Railroad; Track Length mi: 4,043 km 6,507
Passenger-mi million: 3,147
Freight-mi million: 5,171
Merchant Marine: No. of Vessels: 222
Total Deadweight Tonnage 000: 1,938.2
International Cargo Loaded tons 000: 5,290
International Cargo Off-loaded tons 000: 20,080
Airports with Scheduled Flights: 3
Traffic: Passenger-mi million: 1,765
Freight-mi million: 24.1
Length of Canals mi: 292 km 470

Tourism

Number of Tourists to 000: 3,000
Number of Tourists from 000: 3,059
Tourist Receipts $million: 473
Tourist Expenditures $million: 195

Communications

Telephones 000: 2,563
Cost of Local Calls 3 mins: $0.00
Cellular Telephones 000: 21
Fax Machines 000: 15
Personal Computers 000: 180
Internet Hosts per million persons: 126
Mail: Post Offices: 3,579
Pieces of Mail Handled million: 156
Pieces of Mail Handled per person: 19

EDUCATION

Education (including university) is free and compulsory up to the age of 16. Bulgaria claims a literacy rate of 98 percent. There are four state universities, an American university, and various technical universities.

Education

Literacy Rate %: 97.9
Male %: 98.7
Female %: 97.1
First Level: Primary schools: 3,325
Teachers: 70,763
Students: 963,582
Student-Teacher Ratio: 13.6
Net Enrollment Ratio: 97
Second Level: Secondary Schools: —
Teachers: —
Students: —
Student-Teacher-Ratio: —
Net Enrollment Ratio: 75

(continued)

Vocational Level: Schools: 535
Students: 213,337

Third Level: Institutions: 88
Teachers: 25,339
Students: 248,571
Student-Ratio Level: 9.8
Gross Enrollment Ratio: 39.4
Students per 100,000: 2,942
% of Population Age 25 and over with Postsecondary Education: 15

Public Expenditure on Education as % of GDP: 4.2

SCIENCE AND TECHNOLOGY

Science and Technology

Scientists and Engineers in R&D per 1 million persons: 1,747
Expenditures in R&D as % of GDP: 0.57
High-Tech Exports $million: 111
Patent Applications by Residents: 400

MEDIA

From folk dancing to new developments in film, Bulgaria has shaken off its Soviet-era inferiority complex and begun to explore new cultural paths. In literature, music, and political expression, Bulgarians are seeking to identify both historic and untried avenues for national media and cultural expression.

In 1996, there were 1,053 newspapers with an annual circulation of 454 million. Some 5,000 book titles were published in 23 million copies during 1996. In addition, 219 cinemas were registered.

Broadcasting is under the aegis of the privatized National Radio and Television. There are two television programs and six national radio programs.

Media

Daily Newspapers: 17
Total Circulation 000: 1,179
Circulation per 1,000: 141
Books Published: 5,925
Magazines: 745
Radio Receivers 000: 3,920
per 1,000: 437
Television sets 000: 3,011
per 1,000: 359

MOST IMPORTANT MEDIA:

Press. The following are dailies published at Sofia unless otherwise indicated: *Glas* (Voice, Plovdiv, 900,000), city council organ; *24 Chasa* (24 Hours, 280,000), independent; *Duma* (Word, 210,000), formerly *Rabotnichesko Delo* (Workers' Cause), BSP organ; *Demokratsiya* (Democracy, 197,000), SDS organ; *Zemedelsko Zname* (Agrarian Banner, 178,000), BZNS organ; *Trud* (Labor, 100,000), trade union organ; *Narodno Delo* (People's Cause, Varna, 100,000), independent; *Zemya* (Earth, 60,000), former Ministry of Agriculture organ, now independent; *Chernomorsky Far* (Black Sea Lighthouse, Bourgas, 37,000); *Vecherni Novini* (Evening News, 35,000), former BKP organ.

News agencies. The official facility is the Bulgarian Telegraph Agency (Bulgarska Telegrafina Agentsiya—BTA). A number of foreign agencies, including Agence France-Presse and Reuters, maintain offices at Sofia.

Radio and television. Domestic broadcasting is regulated by the governmental Committee for Television and Radio. In the dominant public service sector, Bulgarsko Radio (BR) operates over four national networks, while Bulgarska Televiziya (BTV) transmits over two channels. There is also a regional commercial television channel (Rodopi), and a national commercial station was licensed in 1994.

CULTURE

Cultural Indicators

Public Libraries Number: 5,591
Volumes: 56,042,000
Registered borrowers: 2,216,839
Museums Number: 206
Annual Attendance: 15,535,000
Cinema Production of Long Films: 11
Number of Cinemas: 232
Seating Capacity: 108,000
Annual Attendance million: 4.7
Annual Attendance per capita: 0.6

STATUS OF WOMEN

Bulgarian attitudes toward women's aspirations remain complex, though improvements have been noted. The legal position is irreproachable, since such rights are enshrined in the constitution. The problem is that legal fact is not completely translated into reality.

Thus, within the bureaucracy women have made progress in securing jobs, so much so that in certain ministries they now outnumber men. Nevertheless, widespread gender discrimination is pernicious, especially when, in the context of deteriorating economic conditions, preference for scarce jobs is given to men or young women rather than to women supporting families. A corollary of this is systemic rural poverty, the effects of which are felt particularly strongly among women.

Domestic violence is still not recognized as a human rights issue, though parliament is attempting to draft laws criminalizing domestic abuse. There is also concern that induced abortion is being used as a method of family planning. Another concern is the unceasing traffic in females, and kidnapping for forced prostitution in Western countries and Israel.

Women

Gender Empowerment Measure: 43
Seats Held in Parliament by Women %: 10.8
Female Administrators and Managers %: 28.9
Female Professional and Technical Workers %: 57.0
Women's Share of Earned Income %: 41.0
Women in Government %: 9

HEALTH, FOOD, AND NUTRITION

Health

Number of Physicians: 29,529
Number of Dentists: 5,467
Number of Nurses: 51,269
Number of Pharmacists: 1,736
Population per Physician: 283
Number of Hospitals: 289
Hospital Beds per 10,000: 103
Hospital Bed Occupancy Rate: —
Infant Mortality Rate per 1,000 live births: 18
Maternal Mortality Rate per 100,000 live births: 27
Total Health Expenditures as % of GDP: 5.36
Health Expenditures per capita $: 121
HIV Infected % of adults: 0.01
Cigarette Consumption per smoker per year: 3,058
% of Smokers: Male: 49
Female: 17
Access to Safe Water %: 99

Food and Nutrition

Food Supply as % of FAO Requirements: 116
% of Consumption Expenditures on Food: 47
Daily Available Calories per capita: 2,907
% of Total Calories derived from:
Cereals: 40.3
Potatos, cassava: 1.9
Meat, poultry: 9.0
Fish: 0.1
Eggs, milk: 9.6
Fruits, vegetables: 6.3
Fats, oils: 15.6

ENVIRONMENT

As a signatory to several international environmental initiatives, Bulgaria has shown a serious intent to participate in such efforts and improve its own environment.

In reports to the United Nations (1995), Bulgaria has drawn attention to its worsening air and water quality and to a measurable decrease in its arable land. There are also concerns about disposal of solid industrial and household waste. In addition, there remain health consequences of the Chernobyl nuclear disaster in April 1986.

The World Bank is currently financing a long-term project to enable Bulgaria to phase out ozone-depleting substances (thereby helping to improve air quality), and serious planning is under way to upgrade the safety of the country's Soviet-era nuclear reactors.

Environment

Forest Area sq km: 32,000
Average Annual Deforestation sq km: −6
Nationally Protected Areas as % of Total Land Area: 4.4
Freshwater Access cubic meters per capita: 24,663
Emissions of Organic Water Pollutants kg per day: 88,729
CO_2 Emissions per capita ton: 6.6

CHRONOLOGY

1946 The monarchy is abolished and Bulgaria is declared to be a people's republic; Georgi Dimitrov is named head of government; agriculture is collectivized.

1947 New constitution is promulgated.

1948 Banks, industries, and mines are nationalized.

1949 Dimitrov dies; Vasil Kolarov takes over as prime minister.

1950 Dimitrov's brother-in-law Vulko Chervenkov is named prime minister.

1954 Chervenkov yields post of first secretary of the Bulgarion Communist Party (BKP) to Todor Zhivkov, a Khrushchev protege.

1956 Chervenkov loses post of prime minister to Anton Yugov.

1962 Yugov and Chervenkov fall from favor and Zhivkov takes over as prime minister.

1965 On Khrushchev's ouster in the Soviet Union, coup against Zhivkov is mounted by dissidents; coup is put down and is followed by a purge.

1971 Zhivkov is elevated to president and Stanko Todorov becomes prime minister. New constitution is promulgated.

1981 Grisha Filipov replaces Todorov as prime minister.

1985 Official Bulgarianization drive is launched and is directed against ethnic Turks.

1986 Georgi Ivanov Atanasov replaces Filipov as prime minister.

1987 BKP Congress approves extensive administrative reforms, including redrawing of local government jurisdictions.

1989 Zhivkov is ousted as regime yields to Soviet and popular pressures for reform; Petar Mladenov is named president.

1990 Grand National Assembly revokes the Communist Party's monopoly of power; the State Council is abolished; an executive presidency is created; the secret police is disbanded; the Bulgarian Communist Party (BKP) renames itself the Bulgarian Socialist Party; in free elections to the National Assembly the Bulgarian Socialist Party gains absolute majority by winning 211 out of 400 seats; President Mladenov steps down in the face of allegations that he ordered the shooting of protesters during anti-communist demonstrations in 1989; Zhelyu Zhelev, leader of the opposition Union of Democratic Forces, is elected president; Andrei Lukanov replaces Atanasov as prime minister.

1991 New constitution adopted and the Grand National Assembly is renamed National Assembly.
The prime minister is made the most important government official.

1992 Zhelu Zhelev becomes president and Zhan Videnov prime minister.

Some of the Bulgarian Orthodox bishops set up a rival synod.
Former Communist Party leader Todor Zhivkov is convicted of corruption and abuse of power, and imprisoned.

1996 An economic austerity program is launched in order to attract Western (primarily IMF) investment funds.
Former prime minister and Communist leader Andrei Lukanov is assassinated.
Petar Stoyanov is elected president.

1997 Despite attempts to stabilize the economy, deteriorating conditions lead to nationwide strikes and demonstrations.
The Union of Democratic Forces (UDF) wins parliamentary elections and Ivan Kostov becomes prime minister.
Bulgaria shows eagerness to join NATO and, meanwhile, signs an association agreement with the European Union.

1998 Todor Zhivkov dies in August.
The Turkish minority is allowed to broadcast in Turkish for the first time in 50 years.

1999 During the war for Kosovo, Bulgaria allows overflights of NATO jet fighters on their way to bomb Serbia.
The pro-Western government seeks international aid to offset economic disruption caused by the war.
The IMF and other Western donors promise $750 million to support Bulgaria's economy.

2001 Former king Simeon II's political party, National for Movement for Simeon II, wins a majority of seats in parliamentary elections, and Simeon becomes prime minister

BIBLIOGRAPHY

Bokov, Georgi *Modern Bulgaria*. Sofia, 1981.

Bristow, J. A. *Bulgarian Economy in Transition*. Brookfield, Vt., 1996.

Bulgaria: *A Country Study*. Washington, D.C., 1993.

Crampton, R. A. *A Short History of Modern Bulgaria*. Cambridge, Eng., 1987.

Jelavich, Barbara. *History of the Balkans*. Cambridge, Eng., 1983.

Lampe, John R. *The Bulgarian Economy in the 20th Century*. New York, 1996.

McIntyre, Robert J. *Bulgaria, Politics, Economics and Society*. London and New York, 1998.

Welsh, William A. *Bulgaria*. Boulder, Colo., 1986.

OFFICIAL PUBLICATIONS

Bulgaria. *Prebroyavaneto na naselenieto kum 4.12.1985 godina* (Census of Population of Dec. 4, 1985); *Naselenie* (Population; annual); *Statisticheskii godishnik na Republika Bulgariya* (Statistical Yearbook of the Republic of Bulgaria).

CONTACT INFORMATION

Embassy of Bulgaria
1621 22nd Street NW
Washington, D.C. 20008
Phone: (202) 387-7969 Fax: (202) 234-7973

INTERNET RESOURCES

- National Statistics Institute of the Republic of Bulgaria
http://www.acad.bg/BulRTD/nsi/index.htm

BURKINA FASO

BASIC FACT SHEET

OFFICIAL NAME:
Burkina Faso (formerly Upper Volta)

ABBREVIATION:
BF

CAPITAL:
Ouagadougou

HEAD OF STATE AND GOVERNMENT:
President Blaise Compaoré (from 1987)

HEAD OF GOVERNMENT:
Prime Minister Paramanga Ernest Vonli

NATURE OF GOVERNMENT:
Partial democracy

POPULATION:
11,576,000 (1999)

AREA:
274,200 sq km (105,870 sq mi)

ETHNIC MAJORITY:
Mossi

LANGUAGE:
French (official)

RELIGIONS:
Animism, Islam, and Christianity

UNIT OF CURRENCY:
Communauté Financière Africaine franc (C.F.A.F.)

NATIONAL FLAG:
Two equal horizontal stripes, of red and green, with a five-pointed gold star in the center.

NATIONAL EMBLEM:
A shield with black, white, and red horizontal bars representing the three main branches of the Volta River: the Black Volta, White Volta, and Red Volta. Behind the shield, silver-tipped spears are crossed in saltire. On the ground is a stalk of green sorghum flanked by the two native hoes. Black-hooved white stallions rear up to paw the shield. The design is crested by a banner proclaiming the national motto: *Unité, Travail, Justice* (Unity, Work, Justice).

NATIONAL ANTHEM:
"Proud Volta of My Ancestors"

NATIONAL HOLIDAYS:
December 11 (Proclamation of the Republic National Day); January 1 (New Year's Day); January 3 (1966 Revolution Day); May 1 (Labor Day); August 8 (Independence Day); Christian festivals include Assumption, All Saints' Day, Easter Monday, Pentecost Monday, Ascension and Christmas; also variable Islamic festivals

DATE OF INDEPENDENCE:
August 8, 1960

DATE OF CONSTITUTION:
June 11, 1991

GEOGRAPHICAL FEATURES

Burkina Faso, a landlocked nation located in West Africa, has an area of 274,200 sq km (105,870 sq mi), extending 873 km (542 mi) east-northeast to west-southwest and 474 km (295 mi) south-southeast to north-northwest.

Burkina Faso shares its international border of 3,301 km (2,051 mi) with six neighbors: Niger (628 km; 390 mi); Benin (306 km; 190 mi); Togo (126 km; 78 mi); Ghana (544 km; 338 mi); Côte d'Ivoire (584 km; 362 mi); and Mali (1,000 km; 621 mi).

The country is one vast plateau tilted toward the south. The average altitude is 400 m (1,312 ft), reaching the highest point at Tena Kourou (749 m; 2,457 ft).

The plateau is carved by the valleys of the three Voltas—the Black Volta, the White Volta, and the Red

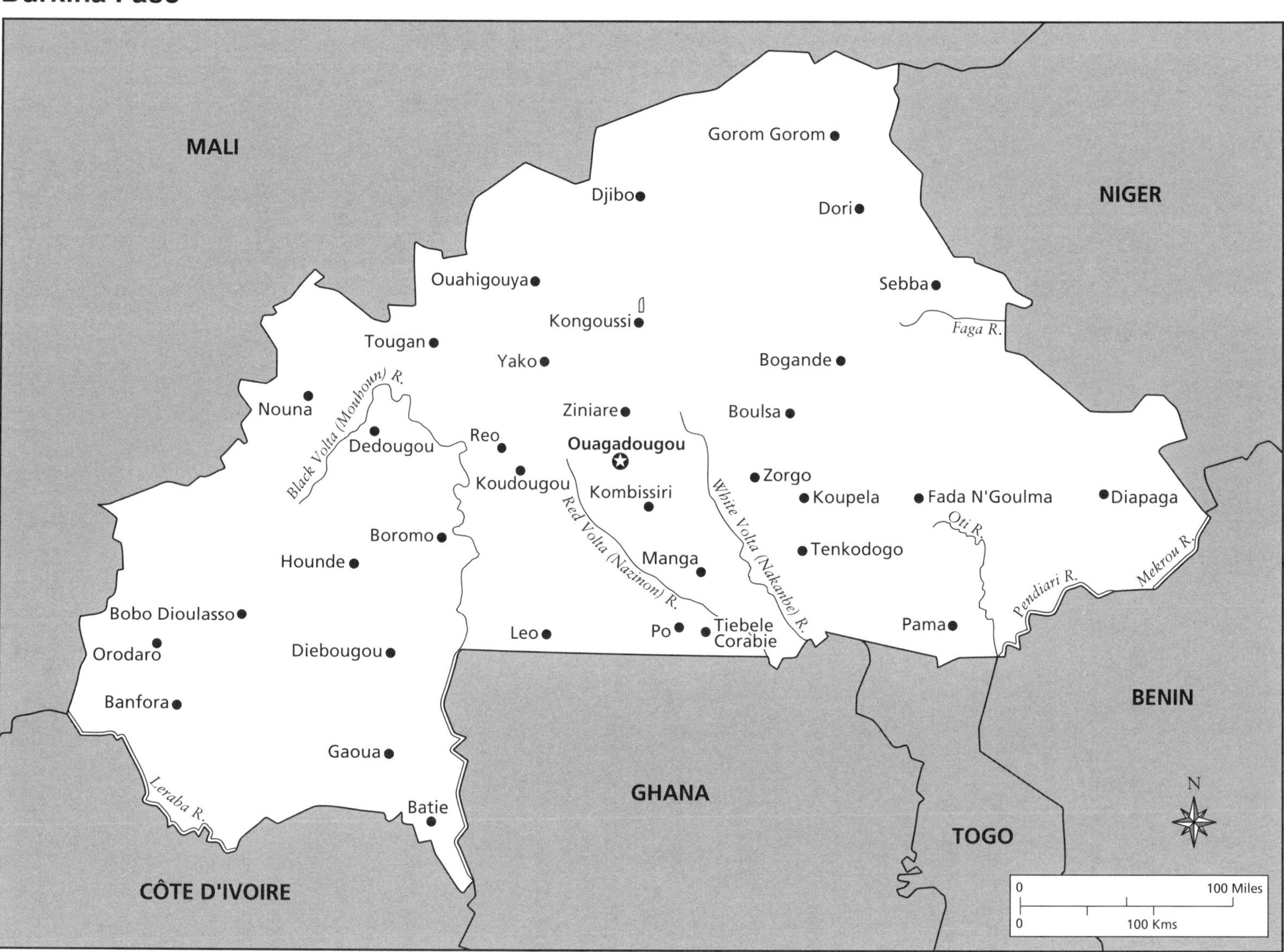
Burkina Faso
MALI
NIGER
BENIN
TOGO
GHANA
CÔTE D'IVOIRE
Gorom Gorom
Djibo
Dori
Ouahigouya
Sebba
Kongoussi
Tougan
Yako
Bogande
Nouna
Ziniare
Boulsa
Dedougou
Reo
Ouagadougou
Koudougou
Kombissiri
Zorgo
Koupela
Fada N'Goulma
Diapaga
Boromo
Hounde
Manga
Tenkodogo
Bobo Dioulasso
Orodaro
Leo
Po
Tiebele
Corabie
Pama
Diebougou
Banfora
Gaoua
Batie
Faga R.
Black Volta (Mouhoun) R.
Red Volta (Nazinon) R.
White Volta (Nakanbe) R.
Oti R.
Pendiari R.
Mekrou R.
Leraba R.
N
0 100 Miles
0 100 Kms

Volta—and their main tributaries, the Sourou and the Pendjari. The Volta, so named by the Portuguese because of its winding course, is a slow, meandering river, so unhealthy that people who live near its banks are highly susceptible to a variety of diseases. The most important river of the Volta system is the Black Volta, which rises not far from Bobo-Dioulasso as two streams called the Plandi and the Dienkoa. Before it reaches the border with Ghana at Ouessa it receives a number of tributaries, such as the Kou, the Sourou, the Tui, and the Bougouriba. The Pendjari, rising in Benin, forms the border between Benin and Burkina Faso for 170 km (110 mi). Burkina Faso has one of the few permanent lakes in West Africa, the Bama, on the White Volta.

Geography

Area sq km: 274,200 (105,870 sq mi)
World Rank: 73rd
Land Boundaries, km: Benin 306; Ghana 548; Côte d'Ivoire 584; Mali 1,000; Niger 628; Togo 126
Coastline, km: 0
Elevation Extremes meters
  Lowest: Mouhoun River 200
  Highest: Tena Kourou 749
Land Use % Arable land: 13
  Permanent Crops: 0
  Permanent Pastures: 22
  Forest and Woodland: 50
  Other: 15

Population of Principal Cities (1996 est.)

Bobo Dioulasso	309,800
Koudougou	72,500
Ouagadougou	709,700

CLIMATE AND WEATHER

Burkina Faso is within the tropical savanna zone, with two alternating seasons: a rainy season from June to October and a dry season from November to May. Temperatures are high in the north, especially at the end of the dry season. In March the mean temperature in Ouagadougou is 41°C (106°F); the heat is stoked by the dry east wind from the Sahara, called the *harmattan*, which blows from March to May. The climate is hot and wet from May to October and pleasant and dry from November to March. The lowest average temperature is recorded between December and January, when the mercury falls to 25°C (77°F).

The rainy season lasts a maximum of five months, from May to October. Rainfall progressively decreases from the high of 130 cm (51 in) per year in the southwest to 50 cm (20 in) per year in the northeast.

Climate and Weather

Mean Temperature
Summer 106°F
Winter 77°F
Average Rainfall 51 in (southwest); 20 in (northeast)

POPULATION

Population Indicators

Total Population: 1999 11,576,000
World Rank: 63rd
Density per sq mi: 109.3 (42.2 per sq km)
% of annual growth (1994–99): 2.8
Male %: 48.1
Female %: 51.9
Urban %: 11.7
Age Distribution: % 0–14: 48.3
  15–29: 23.4
  30–44: 13.4
  45–59: 8.7
  60–74: 4.7
  75 and over: 1.4
Population 2020: 19,239,000
Birth Rate per 1,000: 47.0
Death Rate per 1,000: 20.0
Population Doubling Time (years): —
Infant Mortality Rate per 1,000 live births: 117.8
Rate of Natural Increase per 1,000: 27.0
Total Fertility Rate: 6.8
Expectation of Life (years): Males 43.5
  Females 42.9
Marriage Rate per 1,000: —
Divorce Rate per 1,000: —
Total Number of Households: —
Average Size of Households: 6.2
% of Illegitimate Children: —
Induced Abortions: —
  Rate per 100 live births: —

ETHNIC COMPOSITION

The principal ethnic group is the Mossi, who make up about two-thirds of the total population. Other dominant tribes are the Bobo in the southwest and the Gourma in the east. The Mossi (singular: Moaga) are classified by anthropologists as a Voltaic people belonging to the Mole cluster. The Bobo, who called themselves Bwaba, are closely related to the Mande. The Gourounsi (singular: Gourounga) is a general name for those people who live between the Black Volta on the west and the Red Volta on the east, and Koudougou to the north and Ghana to the south.

Some 2,500 Europeans, mostly French, are reported resident in the country.

LANGUAGES

The official language is French, but its use is restricted to the elite. The dominant Mossi speak Moore, a language of the Voltaic or Gur subfamily of the Niger-Congo family of languages. These and other native African languages belonging to the Sudanic family are spoken by 90 percent of the population.

Principal Languages and Their Speakers

Dogon	40,000
French	30,000
French (lingua franca)	4,800,000
Fula (Fulani)	1,120,000
Gur (Voltaic) languages	
Bwamu	250,000
Gouin (Cerma)	70,000
Grusi (Gurunsi) group	
Ko	20,000
Lyele	280,000
Nuni	140,000
Sissala	10,000
Lobi	220,000
Mossi (Moore) group	
Dagara	360,000
Gurma	660,000
Kusaai	20,000
Mossi (Moore)	5,810,000
Senufo group	
Minianka	—
Senufo	160,000
Kru languages	
Seme (Siamou)	20,000
Mande languages	
Bobo	260,000
Busansi (Bisa)	410,000
Dyula (Jula)	300,000
Marka	200,000
Tamashek (Tuareg)	110,000
Other	820,000

RELIGIONS

Burkina Faso is one of the few countries in the world in which animism is widely prevalent, claiming nearly 40 percent of the population. Historically, the Burkinabe have successfully resisted the influence of Islam, which nevertheless claims some 50 percent of the population as believers. The remaining 10 percent are Christian.

Roman Catholicism was introduced into Burkina Faso in 1896 by the White Fathers, who founded their first mission in 1890. Abbé Yougbare became the first West African Catholic bishop in 1956 and in 1960 Abbé Paul Zoungrana was made an archbishop and later a cardinal, the first West African to be so appointed. There are 90 parishes, with 137 African priests and 256 non-African priests. American fundamentalist missionary groups have worked in the country since 1926, and Protestant denominations claim over 25,000 members. The Sudan Interior Mission and the Christian Missionary Alliance also are active.

Religious Affiliations

Muslim	5,790,000
Traditional beliefs	4,630,000
Christian	1,160,000

HISTORICAL BACKGROUND

Burkina Faso was founded by the descendants of the Mossi Empire who ruled the area in the 15th century. The empire was successful in resisting the Muslims who took control of much of West Africa. The country was relatively stable and developed a mature administrative apparatus to manage the empire.

The French expansion into Burkina Faso began around 1890 and was completed by Paul Gustave Lucien Voulet, who took Ouagadougou in 1896 and subjugated the entire territory. The Mossi accepted French domination as the best form of protection against their hostile neighbors. The French divided the country into administrative circles but maintained the chiefs in their traditional roles. At first attached to the French Sudan (or Upper Senegal-Niger, as it was called from 1904 to 1920), the country was organized as a separate colony in 1919. It was partitioned again among French Sudan, Côte d'Ivoire, and Niger between 1932 and 1947, but it was reestablished as an overseas territory in 1947, with a territorial assembly of its own. It became an autonomous republic within the French Community in 1958 and achieved full independence within two years.

In its years of independence, Burkina Faso has completed two full circles from authoritarian rule to democracy to authoritarian rule to democracy and back to authoritarian rule. However, under the new constitution of 1991, the country seems to be moving toward democracy once again. The nation's first government, formed by Maurice Yaméogo, a political disciple of Félix Houphouët-Boigny of Côte d'Ivoire, was incapable of handling economic problems and dealing with powerful trade unions. All parties in opposition to Yaméogo's Voltaic Democratic Union (VDU) were banned shortly after independence. Yaméogo was reelected in a one-party election in 1965, but in the wake of growing student and labor dissatisfaction, he was compelled to resign in 1966. The military, under Sangoulé Lamizana, took over, suspending the constitution and dissolving the National Assembly. In 1969, in preparation for a return to civilian rule, Lamizana removed all political restrictions. The nation adopted a new constitution the following year. Under the constitution, Lamizana was to retain his position as head of state with an elected assembly and a civilian prime minister governing the country. In the first elections following adoption, the VDU won a legislative majority and Gerard Ouédraogo became prime minister.

Ouédraogo's tenure was marked by corruption and conflict between government and opposition parties.

Government came to a standstill and was unable to respond to a severe drought in the Sahel region. In 1974 Lamizana and the army again seized control of the government. He suspended the constitution and dissolved the assembly. All political parties were banned, but trade unions were permitted to operate. Lamizana allowed political parties to resume activities in 1977, during which period a new constitution was prepared. He was reelected in elections held in 1978. The following year Lamizana banned all political parties except the Democratic Voltaic Union, the National Union for the Defense of Democracy, and the Voltaic Progressive Union.

In November 1980, the Military Committee for Reform and National Progress (CMRPN) under Col. Saye Zerbo seized power in a bloodless coup. The coup leaders abolished the constitution of 1977, banned all political parties, and dissolved the National Assembly.

In November 1982, Colonel Zerbo was ousted in another military coup, led by noncommissioned army officers, in which five people were killed. Maj. Jean-Baptiste Ouédraogo, who had not previously been involved in politics, emerged as leader of the new military regime, setting up the Conseil de Salut du Peuple (CSP). The CMRPN was dissolved, and a predominantly civilian government was formed. In February 1983, several soldiers and opposition figures were arrested following the discovery of an alleged plot to reinstate the Zerbo regime. A power struggle within the CSP became apparent with the arrest in May 1983 of radical left-wing elements within the government, including the prime minister, Capt. Thomas Sankara. Major Ouédraogo announced the withdrawal of the armed forces from political life and disbanded the CSP.

In August 1983, Sankara seized power in a coup in which an estimated 15 people were killed. Opposition politicians were placed under house arrest, a strict curfew was imposed, and the Conseil Nationale Revolutionnaire (CNR) was set up. Citizens were called to join local committees, Comités pour la Défense de la Révolution (CDRs), in attempt to mobilize popular support for the regime.

Sankara's regime consolidated its power through the local CDRs and brought extensive reforms to the administrative, judicial, education, and military systems. He celebrated the first anniversary of his regime by changing the country's name to Burkina Faso ("the land of free men"). Sankara was killed in a bloody coup in 1987. The coup was led by Capt. Blaise Compaoré, Sankara's closest friend, who established control through a Popular Front. In 1989 elements of the army staged an unsuccessful coup against Compaoré.

Under political pressure, Compaoré announced in 1990 plans for a new constitution as well as multiparty elections to be held at the end of 1991. The new constitution, which called for democratization, was approved by a national referendum and put into effect in June 1991. Compaoré was reelected without opposition in December 1991 for a seven-year term, and his party, the Organization of People's Democracy–Labor Movement, won a legislative majority in multiparty elections in May 1992. However, the transition to a fuller democratic system has been slowed, and the Compaoré administration has become a virtual one-party state. In 1997 the assembly approved constitutional amendments abolishing constitutional provisions limiting the number of presidential terms to two. In 1998 Compaoré, facing opposition candidates for the first time, easily won the presidential election with 87.5 percent of the vote.

CONSTITUTION

The new constitution, which was put into effect on June 11, 1991, provides for separate executive, legislative, and judicial branches of government that aimed to reduce the president's powers. It also calls for presidential elections to be held every seven years. In a separate decree on June

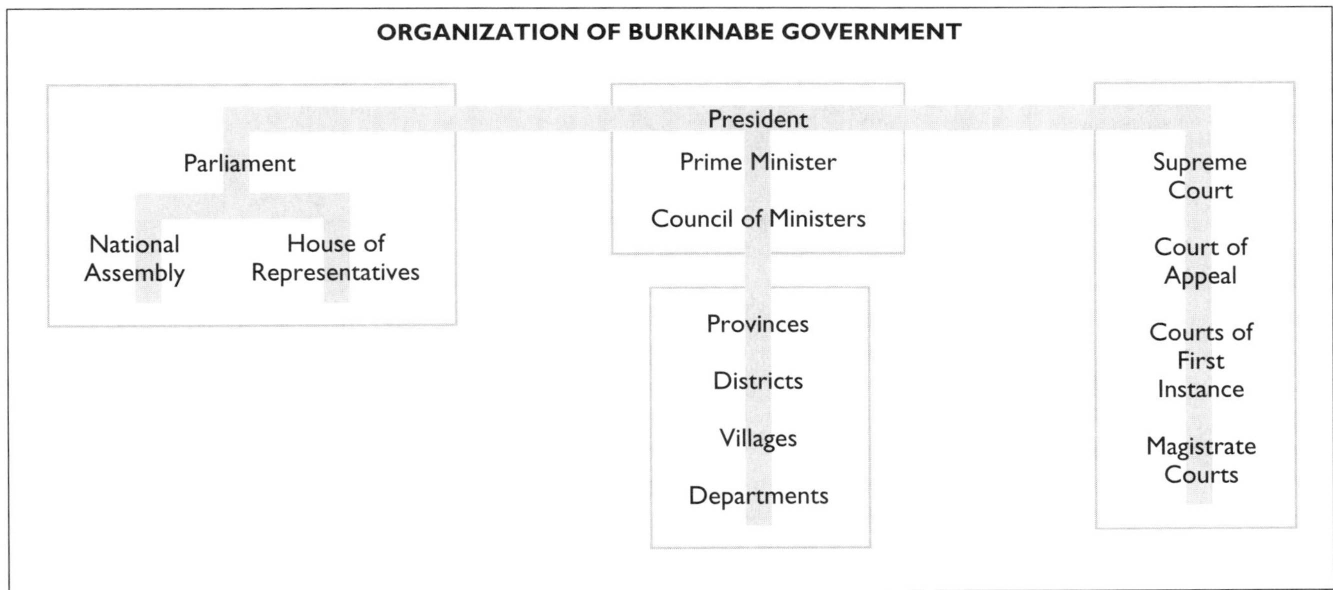

11, Capt. Blaise Compaoré dissolved the country's government, leaving the administration of ministerial affairs in the hands of permanent secretaries until new appointments could be made.

LOCAL GOVERNMENT

Burkina Faso is divided into 30 provinces, which are divided into 250 districts, villages, and departments. Revolutionary Committees (CRs) carry out local government.

Local Government

Principal administrative divisions, capitals, area, population

AREA AND POPULATION

Territorial provinces	Capitals	area sq mi	area sq km	population 1991 census
Bam	Kongoussi	1,551	4,017	173,516
Bazéga	Kombissiri	2,051	5,313	352,104
Bougouriba	Diébougou	2,736	7,087	242,986
Boulgou	Tenkodogo	3,488	9,033	465,845
Boulkiemde	Koudougou	1,598	4,138	393,900
Comoé	Banfora	7,102	18,393	296,083
Ganzourgou	Zorgho	1,578	4,087	223,555
Gnagna	Bogandé	3,320	8,600	272,203
Gourma	Fada N'Gourma	10,275	26,613	350,336
Houé	Bobo-Dioulasso	6,438	16,672	724,803
Kadiogo	Ouagadougou	451	1,169	652,377
Kénédougou	Orodara	3,207	8,600	272,203
Kossi	Nouna	5,088	13,177	389,360
Kouritenga	Koupéla	628	1,627	227,060
Mouhoun	Dédougou	4,032	10,442	329,115
Nahouri	Po	1,484	3,843	119,144
Namentenga	Boulsa	2,994	7,755	214,564
Oubritenga	Ziniaré	1,812	4,693	328,682
Oudalan	Gorom Gorom	3,879	10,046	123,495
Passoré	Yako	1,575	4,078	232,278
Poni	Gaoua	4,000	10,361	258,647
Sanguie	Réo	1,994	5,165	234,079
Sanmatenga	Kaya	3,557	9,213	404,563
Séno	Dori	5,202	13,473	269,892
Sissili	Léo	5,303	13,736	297,598
Soum	Djibo	5,154	13,350	217,972
Sourou	Tougan	3,663	9,487	313,355
Tapoa	Diapaga	5,707	14,780	187,785
Yalenga	Ouahigouya	4,746	12,292	558,318
Zoundwéogo	Manga	1,333	3,453	175,166
TOTAL		105,946	274,400	9,190,791

PARLIAMENT

Burkina Faso has a bicameral legislature. The lower house, the National Assembly, consists of 107 members who are elected by popular vote in 30 multimember districts. Members serve five years. The upper house, the House of Representatives, was created by the constitutional reforms of 1991, but was not formed until 1995. The House of Representatives consists of 178 members who are elected or appointed to represent particular constituencies within society.

POLITICAL PARTIES

While the country has numerous political parties, the Organization for People's Democracy–Labor Movement—an amalgam of former communist parties—controls the majority of seats in the National Assembly. In the most recent elections, the Organization for People's Democracy ran as the Popular Front. The second largest party is the National Convention of Progressive Patriots–Social Democrats.

Political Parties

- Congress of Democracy and Progress, 1996, and its allies
  - Organization for People's Democracy-Labor Movement, 1989
  - National Convention of Progressive Patriots-Social Democratic Party, 1991
  - Rally of Independent Social Democrats, 1990
  - Group of Revolutionary Democrats
  - Movement for Social Democracy
  - Movement of Progressive Democrats, 1990
- Party for Democracy and Progress, 1993
- Alliance for Democracy and Federation, 1990
- African Party for Independence
- Burkinabe Socialist Bloc
- Union of Greens for the Development of Burkina, 1991
- African Democratic Rally, 1946
- Refuser's Front of the African Democratic Rally
- United Social Democracy Party, 1994, an alliance of
  - Democratic Action Group
  - Ecological Party for Progress
  - Social Progress Party, 1987
- Social Forces Front, 1996
- Burkina Labor Party, 1990
- Alliance for Democracy and Social Development, 1991
- Patriotic League for Development, 1973
- Movement for Progress and Tolerance, 1990
- Union for Democracy and Social Progress, 1991

Political Parties: Strength in Parliament Most Recent Elections

The distribution of seats following the May 11, 1997, balloting was as follows: Congress of Democracy and Progress (CDP), 97; Party for Democracy and Progress, 6; African Democratic Rally, 2; Alliance for Democracy and Federation, 2. On June 19, 1997, fresh balloting was held in four constituencies where the Supreme Court had dismissed earlier results because of "electoral irregularities". The CDP secured all four seats, raising its total to 101.

LEGAL SYSTEM

The Burkinabe legal system is an amalgam of French civil law and African customary law.

Before 1984 the apex of the judiciary was the Supreme Court at Ouagadougou, with four chambers: constitutional, judicial, administrative, and fiscal. It was abolished in 1984 and replaced by two high appeals courts for public and private criminal and civil cases, in accordance with French judicial practice. There are four courts of first instance, at Ouagadougou, Bobo-Dioulasso, Ouahigouya, and Fada N'Gourma, with competence in criminal, commercial, and civil law. For cases involving common law there are several magistrate courts in the departments and a court at Ouagadougou.

The government's oft-stated aim is to ensure that European-imposed judicial procedures do not deny fair access to justice for an overwhelmingly illiterate, impoverished population. Meanwhile, the traditionally independent judiciary has continued to function for criminal and civil cases.

LAW ENFORCEMENT

Law Enforcement

Offenses reported to the police per 100,000: 41.0
- Murder: 0.2
- Assault: 4.1
- Burglary: —
- Automobile Theft: —
- Population per Police officer: —

Death Penalty: Yes. Last execution in 1982

HUMAN RIGHTS

In terms of political and civil rights Burkina Faso is classified as a country that is not free. Under the Third Republic, Burkina Faso had made considerable progress toward securing basic human rights for the people. Until the 1980 coup, there were no political prisoners, the right to a fair trial was guaranteed, the judiciary was independent of the executive, there were no political or security courts, arbitrary arrests and imprisonment were relatively uncommon, and searches of private homes could not take place at night and were permitted only with search warrants during the day. The media, although government owned, could comment freely and critically on government policies and actions, and labor unions often exercised their right to strike without fear of reprisal. Any group or organization could hold public meetings. Participation in the political process was open to all citizens. The 1980 and subsequent coups curtailed most, though not all, of these significant gains. Compaoré was widely criticized for the summary executions of those implicated in the 1989 coup.

FOREIGN POLICY

Burkina Faso's foreign relations have undergone two transformations in the last 17 years. After the 1983 coup, Sankara changed a moderately pro-French and pro-Western foreign policy into a radical, Libyan-influenced one. Sankara tried to rid the country of all vestiges of its colonial past (including the change of the country's name from Upper Volta to Burkina Faso), and he carried out widespread arrests of pro-French officials. Relations with neighbors also were strained, especially with Mali over Agacher Strip and with Togo over Burkinabe complicity in a coup attempt against President Eyadema.

The assassination of Sankara in 1987 led to an about-face in the nation's foreign relations. The new president, Compaoré, was a francophile who was a friend of Côte d'Ivoire's Coast's President Houphouët-Boigny. Relations with Ghana and Mali also improved, although the presence of Malian refugees in Burkina proved a continued irritant. Regional cooperation efforts have been the focus of Compaoré's foreign initiatives. He hosted the first summit of the West African Economic and Monetary Union in 1996.

DEFENSE

The defense structure is headed by the president as commander in chief. The chain of command runs through the minister of defense. Military service is compulsory for able-bodied men over the age of 18 and lasts for 18 months. The total strength of the armed forces is 7,200. There is no navy.

Burkinabe armed forces have no offensive capability. The bulk of the military aid is received from France.

Military Indicators

Total Active Duty Personnel: 10,000
Military Manpower per 1,000: 0.9
Military Expenditures $: 68 million
- as % of GNP: 2.9
- per capita $: 7
- as % of central government expenditures: 12.0

Arms Imports $: 0
Arms Exports $: 0

ECONOMY

One of the poorest countries in the world, landlocked Burkina Faso has a high population density, few natural resources, and a fragile soil. About 90 percent of the population is engaged in (mainly subsistence) agriculture, which is highly vulnerable to variations in rainfall. Industry remains dominated by unprofitable government-controlled corporations. Following the African franc currency devaluation in January 1994 the government updated its development program in conjunction with international agencies, and exports and economic growth have increased. Maintenance of its macroeconomic progress in 2001–2002 depends on continued low inflation, reduction in the trade deficit, and reforms designed to encourage private investment.

Principal Economic Indicators

Gross National Product: $2.579 billion
GNP per capita: $250
GNP Average Annual Growth Rate (1990–97) %: 0.8
GNP per capita Average Annual Growth Rate (1990–97) %: −1.6

(continued)

Origin of Gross Domestic Product %
- Agriculture: 30
- Mining: —
- Manufacturing: 18
- Construction: 5
- Public Utilities: 1
- Transportation and Communications: 4
- Trade: 18
- Financial Services: 20
- Other Services: 20
- Government: 20

Gross Domestic Product by Type of Expenditure %
- Private Consumption: 78
- Government Consumption: 16
- Gross Domestic Investment: 22
- Foreign Trade: Exports: 14
- Imports: −30

% of Income Received by Poorest 20%: —
% of Income Received by Richest 10%: —

Price and earnings indexes (1995 = 100)

	1992	1993	1994	1995	1996	1997	1998
Consumer price index	74.0	74.4	93.1	100.0	106.2	108.6	114.2
Earnings index	—	—	—	—	—	—	—

Finance

National Currency: CFA Franc (CFAF)
Exchange Rate: $ 1 = CFAF 608.36
Money Supply Stock in National Currency billion: 213.7
M1 per capita: 20,400
Central Bank Discount Rate %: 5.75
Total External Debt $: 715 million
Debt Service Ratio %: 21.0
Balance of Payments $: −122.2 million
International Reserves SDRs: 238 million
Ratio of External Debt to Total Reserves: 3.3
Average Annual Rate of Inflation/Consumer Price Index Growth Rate %: 3

Official Development Assistance

ODA: $397 million
- as % of GNP: 15.5
- per capita: $37
- Foreign Direct Investment $: 0

Central Government Revenues and Expenditures

Fiscal Year: Calendar Year
Revenues $: 277 million
Expenditures $: 492 million
Budget Deficit $: 215 million
Tax Revenues as % of GDP: —
Highest Tax Bracket %
- Individual: —
- Corporate: —

Employment and Labor

Economically Active Population: 4,679, 000
Female Participation Rate %: 49.4
Activity Rate %: 50.9
Labor by Sector: %
- Agriculture, Forestry, Fishing: 91.8
- Manufacturing, Mining: 1.2
- Construction: 0.2
- Transportation and Communications: 0.3
- Trade, Hotels, and Restaurants: 2.6
- Finance, Insurance, Real Estate: —
- Public Administration, Defense: —
- Services: 2.4

Unemployment %: NA

Agriculture

Agriculture's Share of GDP %: 30
Average Annual Rate of Growth (1965–98) %: 2.6
Number of Farms 000: 1,860
Average Size of Farm ha: 4.8
Number of Tractors per 1,000 hectares: 0.04
Irrigation, % of Farms having: 0.7
Artificial Fertilizer kg/hectare: 6
Total Cropland as % of Farmland: —
Livestock: Cattle 000: 4,522
- Sheep 000: 6,207
- Hogs 000: 587
- Chickens 000: 20,517

Forests: Production of Roundwood (000 cubic meters): 10,033
Fisheries: Total Catch tons: 8,000

Mining

% of GDP: 0.9
Value of Mineral Production $: 28.4 million

Manufacturing

Value Added $: 131 million
Industrial Production Growth Rate %: 4.2

Energy

Commercial Energy Production metric tons of oil equivalent: —
Commercial Energy Consumption metric tons of oil equivalent: —
Commercial Energy Consumption per capita kg: —
Average Annual Growth Rate 1980–97 %: —
Net Energy Imports % of use: —
Electricity Installed Capacity kW: 78,000
- Production kW-hr: 220 million

Coal Reserves tons: —
- Production tons: —

Natural Gas Proven Reserves cubic meters: —
- Production cubic meters: —

Crude Petroleum Reserves barrels: —
- Production barrels: —
- Consumption barrels: —
- Refinery Capacity barrels per day: —

Pipelines Length km: —

Foreign Trade

Imports $: 536 million
Exports $: 105.4 million

Export Volume % Annual Growth Rate (1990–97): 6.1
Import Volume % Annual Growth Rate (1990–97): 0.0
Balance of Trade $

Balance of trade (current prices)

	1991	1992	1993	1994	1995	1996
CFAF 000,000,000	+99.80	+93.10	+69.30	−22.90	+1.96	−122.85
% of total	22.8%	24.4%	18.1%	5.6%	0.3%	28.3%

Major Trading Partners

	Imports	Exports
European Union %	40.4	36.2
United States %	4.9	0.3
Eastern Europe %	0.3	—
Japan %	4.2	1.8
Others %	50.1	61.6

Transportation

Roads Total Length mi: 7,771 (12,506 km)
Paved %: 16
Automobiles: 16,800
Trucks and Buses: 17,222
Persons per vehicle: 304
Railroad; Track Length mi: 386 (622 km)
Passenger-mi: 126 million
Freight-mi: 31 million
Merchant Marine: No. of Vessels: —
Total Deadweight Tonnage: —
International Cargo Loaded tons: —
International Cargo Off-loaded tons: —
Airports with Scheduled Flights: 2
Traffic: Passenger-mi: 134.9 million
Freight-mi: 23.4 million
Length of Canals mi: —

Tourism

Number of Tourists to: 140,000
Number of Tourists from: —
Tourist Receipts $: 22 million
Tourist Expenditures $: 23 million

Communications

Telephones 000: 30
Cost of Local Calls 3 mins: $0.10
Cellular Telephones 000: —
Fax Machines 000: —
Personal Computers 000: —
Internet Hosts per million persons: —
Mail: Post Offices: 66
Pieces of Mail Handled: 14 million
Pieces of Mail Handled per person: 1.5

EDUCATION

Education is free, compulsory, and universal between the ages of seven and 13.

Schooling lasts for 13 years, divided into six years of primary school, four years of lower secondary school, and three years of upper secondary school, culminating in the baccalaureate. Nearly 7 percent of primary-school students and 43 percent of secondary-school students are enrolled in private schools. The literacy rate for males is estimated at 29 percent and for females 9 percent.

The school year runs from October to July. The language of instruction is French throughout. Higher education is provided by the University of Ouagadougou, with an enrollment of about 3,086 students.

Education

Literacy Rate %: 19.2
Male %: 29.5
Female %: 9.2
First Level: Primary schools: 2,971
Teachers: 10,300
Students: 600,032
Student-Teacher Ratio: 58.2
Net Enrollment Ratio: 31
Second Level: Secondary Schools: 173
Teachers: 3,346
Students: 116,033
Student-Teacher Ratio: 34.7
Net Enrollment Ratio: 7

Vocational Level: Schools: 22
Students: 8,808

Third Level: Institutions: 9
Teachers: 571
Students: 8,815
Student-Ratio Level: 15.4
Gross Enrollment Ratio: 1.1
Students per 100,000: 93
% of Population Age 25 and over with Postsecondary Education: —

Public Expenditure on Education as % of GDP: 3.6

SCIENCE AND TECHNOLOGY

Science and Technology

Scientists and Engineers in R&D per 1 million persons: 17
Expenditures in R&D as % of GDP: 0.19
High-Tech Exports $: —
Patent Applications by Residents: —

MEDIA

Three daily newspapers are published in the country, including the government funded daily *Sidwaya*. Aggregate daily circulation is 15,000. The press is characterized by active government participation and ownership but no overt censorship.

The national news agency is Agence Burkinabe de Presse (ABP). AFB, Reuters, UPI, and Tass maintain bureaus in the capital.

The state-owned Radiodiffusion-Télévision Burkina, founded in 1963, operates a television and radio service. Additionally Radio Bobo is a regional service and there is one commercial radio station.

Media

Daily Newspapers: 1
- Total Circulation 000: 17
- Circulation per 1,000: 1.6

Books Published: —
Magazines: 37
Radio Receivers 000: 513
- per 1,000: 48

Television sets 000: 46
- per 1,000: 4.4

MOST IMPORTANT MEDIA:

Press. Under the present regime, there is a Written Press Board (Direction de la Presse Ecrite) charged with overseeing the media. The following are published at Ouagadougou: *Observateur Paalga* (New Observer 8,000), independent daily; *Le Journal du Jeudi* (Thursday Journal, 8,000), independent weekly; *Sidwaya* (Truth, 5,000), government daily; *Le Pays* (The Country, 4,000), independent daily; *Bulletin de l'Agence d'Information du Burkina* (200), twice-weekly government organ; *L'Indépendent* (The Independent), independent weekly.

News agencies. Agence Burkinabê de Presse (AVP) is the domestic facility; Agence France-Presse and TASS maintain offices at Ouagadougou.

Radio and television. Radiodiffusion-Télévision du Burkina operates a number of radio and television stations, the latter concentrating on educational programming during the school year.

CULTURE

Cultural Indicators

Public Libraries —
- Number: —
- Volumes: —
- Registered borrowers: —

Museums
- Number: —
- Annual Attendance: —

Cinema
- Production of Long Films: 5
- Number of Cinemas: —
- Seating Capacity: —
- Annual Attendance: —
- Annual Attendance per capita: —

STATUS OF WOMEN

The role of women in Burkina Faso is still limited by the cultural orientation of a rural society. The current government has emphasized its strong commitment to expanding opportunities for women, including educational opportunities. The Ministry of Family Progress, for example, works to promote greater participation by women in the nation's economic, social, and political life.

Women

Gender Empowerment Measure: 77
Seats Held in Parliament by Women %: 10.8
Female Administrators and Managers %: 13.5
Female Professional and Technical Workers %: 25.8
Women's Share of Earned Income %: 40
Women in Government %: 10

HEALTH, FOOD, AND NUTRITION

Health

Number of Physicians: 341
Number of Dentists: 19
Number of Nurses: 2,627
Number of Pharmacists: 113
Population per Physician: 27,158
Number of Hospitals: 78
Hospital Beds per 10,000: 5
Hospital Beds Occupancy Rate: —
Infant Mortality Rate per 1,000 live births: 186
Maternal Mortality Rate per 100,000 live births: 930
Total Health Expenditures as % of GDP: 8.46
Health Expenditures per capita $: 7
HIV Infected % of adults: 7.17
Cigarette Consumption per smoker per year: —
% of Smokers: Male: —
Female: —
Access to Safe Water %: 78

Food and Nutrition

Food Supply as % of FAO Requirements: 95
% of Consumption Expenditures on Food: 36.7
Daily Available Calories per capita: 2,250
% of Total Calories derived from:
Cereals: 75.6
Potatoes, cassava: 0.7
Meat, poultry: 2.4
Fish: 0.1
Eggs, milk: 1.4
Fruits, vegetables: 1.0
Fats, oils: 4.1

ENVIRONMENT

The environment of Burkina Faso has suffered in recent years because of drought that has rapidly increased the rate of desertification and soil erosion. The country's growing population and uneven population distribution have also put a strain on natural resources.

Environment

Forest Area sq km: 43,000
Average Annual Deforestation sq km: 320
Nationally Protected Areas as % of Total Land Area: 10.5
Freshwater Access cubic meters per capita: 1,671
Emissions of Organic Water Pollutants kg per day: 2,385
CO_2 Emissions per capita ton: 0.1

CHRONOLOGY

1960 Burkina Faso (under the name Upper Volta) achieves independence, with Maurice Yaméogo as president. A new constitution is approved.

1965 Yaméogo is reelected president, with 99.98 percent of the votes cast.

1966 Following a general strike, mobs attack the National Assembly and other public buildings in the capital; army chief of staff Sangoulé Lamizana assumes supreme power and compels Yaméogo to resign; the constitution is dissolved; a consultative committee of 41 members replaces the National Assembly.

1969 Former president Yaméogo is sentenced to five years at hard labor.

1970 Lamizana announces a new constitution and renewal of political activities.

In the first elections since 1965, the Union Démocratique Voltaique (UDV) wins 37 of 57 seats.

1971 Gerard Kango Ouédraogo, head of the UDV, is elected premier by the National Assembly. Drought of unprecedented severity hits the Sahel.

1974 Military dismisses Premier Ouédraogo, suspends the constitution, and dissolves the National Assembly; Lamizana assumes the post of premier; all political parties are abolished; National Consultative Committee for Renewal is set up with 65 appointed members.

Border dispute between Mali and Burkina Faso erupts into border clashes; four West African heads of state, meeting in Lomé, order a truce in the border war; under the auspices of a mediation commission, Mali and Burkina Faso reach agreement.

1977 New constitution and a return to civilian rule are approved in popular referendum.

1978 In national elections, the UDV gains a clear majority in the restored National Assembly; Joseph Conombo is elected premier by the National Assembly; Lamizana is elected president for five-year term.

1980 President Lamizana is overthrown in an army coup led by Saye Zerbo; Zerbo abolishes the constitution of 1977, dissolves the National Assembly, and bans all political parties.

1982 Zerbo is ousted in an army coup led by Jean-Baptiste Ouédraogo, who sets up the Conseil de Salut du Peuple (CSP).

1983 Premier Thomas Sankara is arrested but later released.

The armed forces withdraw from politics and the CSP is disbanded.

Sankara ousts Ouédraogo and sets up a left-leaning regime called the Conseil National Revolutionnaire (CNR).

1984 Upper Volta is renamed Burkina Faso meaning "the land of free men."

1987 Sankara is overthrown in a bloody coup led by Blaise Compaoré.

1989 Seven men, including the minister of defense, are executed for attempting to overthrow Compaoré.

1990 Under pressure, Compaoré announces plans for a new constitution calling for democratization as well as plans for multiparty elections to be held at the end of 1991.

1991 A national referendum approves the new constitution, which immediately goes into effect.

1994 The World Bank reports that the country has made significant strides in economic progress.

1997 A constitutional amendment permits an unlimited number of presidential terms.

1998 Compaoré, facing opposition candidates for the first time, easily wins the presidential elections.

2000 Ernest Yonli is appointed prime minister.

BIBLIOGRAPHY

Englebert, Pierre. *Burkina Faso: Unsteady Statehood in West Africa*. Boulder, Colo., 1996.

McFarland, Daniel Miles. *Historical Dictionary of Upper Volta*. Metuchen, N.J., 1978.

Sankara, Thomas. *Thomas Sankara Speaks: The Burkina Faso Revolution 1983–1987*. New York, 1988.

OFFICIAL PUBLICATIONS

Burkina Faso. *Annuaire Statisque*; *Burkina Faso—Statistical Tables* (IMF Staff Country Report [1997]); *Recensement général de la population du 10 au 20 décembre 1985*.

CONTACT INFORMATION

Embassy of Burkina Faso
2340 Massachusetts Avenue NW
Washington, D.C. 20008
Phone: (202) 332-5577 Fax: (202) 667-1882

INTERNET RESOURCES

- Embassy of Burkina Faso
  http://burkinaembassy-usa.org

BURUNDI

BASIC FACT SHEET

OFFICIAL NAME:
Republic of Burundi (République de Burundi, Republika Y'Uburundi)

ABBREVIATION:
BD

CAPITAL:
Bujumbura

HEAD OF STATE & GOVERNMENT:
President Pierre Buyoya (from 1987)

NATURE OF GOVERNMENT:
Republic

POPULATION:
5,736,000 (1999)

AREA:
27,834 sq km (10,747 sq mi)

ETHNIC MAJORITY:
Hutu and Tutsi

LANGUAGES:
Kirundi and French

RELIGIONS:
Christianity and animism

UNIT OF CURRENCY:
Burundi franc (B.F.)

NATIONAL FLAG:
A white saltire extending from a central circle containing three green-bordered red stars. The upper and lower fields divided by the saltire are red, while the left and right fields are green.

NATIONAL EMBLEM:
A white-bordered red shield displaying the gold head of an African lion against a backdrop of native spears in the form of a tripod. Beneath is a white scroll with the national motto in black: "Unity, Work, Progress."

NATIONAL ANTHEM:
"Our Burundi, O Blessed Land"

NATIONAL HOLIDAYS:
July 1 (Independence Day, National Day); January 1 (New Year's Day); May 1 (Labor Day); September 18 (UPRONA Day); October 13 (Hero of the Nation, Prince Louis Rwagasore Day); November 28 (Republic Day); Christian festivals include All Saints' Day, Ascension, Pentecost, Assumption, and Christmas

DATE OF INDEPENDENCE:
July 1, 1962

DATE OF CONSTITUTION:
1962, 1974 (suspended in 1976); 1981, 1992; 1998

GEOGRAPHICAL FEATURES

Burundi, a landlocked country in the heart of Africa, has an area of 27,834 sq km (10,747 sq mi), extending 263 km (163 mi) north-northeast to south-southwest and 194 km (121 mi) east-southeast to west-northwest.

Burundi's total international border of 974 km (605 mi) is shared with three countries: Rwanda (290 km; 180 mi); Tanzania (451 km; 280 mi); and the Democratic Republic of the Congo (233 km; 145 mi).

Burundi is part of the Great East African Plateau, forming the divide between two watersheds: the Nile and the Zaire River basins. The western slopes of the Zaire-Nile ridgeline abruptly merge into the Great East African Rift Valley toward the Rusizi Plain and Lake Tanganyika, while the eastern slopes shelve toward the central uplands. There are three natural regions within this configuration: the Rift Valley, known as the Imbo, along the western border; the eastern zone, known as Kumoso; and the central mountain region.

Burundi

Burundi's rivers are connected to two major river basins: those of the Zaire and the Nile rivers. The most important river flowing into the Democratic Republic of the Congo system is the Rusizi, which has its source in Lake Kivu and forms the border between that country and Burundi.

Geography

Area sq km: 27,834 (10,747 mi)
World Rank: 45th

Land Boundaries, km: Democratic Republic of the Congo 233; Rwanda 290; Tanzania 451
Coastline, km: 0
Elevation Extremes meters
- Lowest: Lake Tanganyika 772
- Highest: Mount Heha 2,760

Land Use % Arable land: 9
- Permanent Crops: 36
- Permanent Pastures: 36
- Forest and Woodland: 3
- Other: 8

Population of Principal Cities

Bujumbura	300,000
Gilega	101,827

CLIMATE AND WEATHER

Despite its location within 5° of the equator, no region of Burundi is uncomfortably hot. The central plateau enjoys pleasant weather, with an average temperature of 20°C (68°F). The Imbo is warmer, averaging 23°C (73°F). The capital, Bujumbura, has an average annual temperature of 25°C (77°F). The upper elevations of the eastern plateau generally are cool, with temperatures below 19°C (66°F), but the easternmost savannas are hotter, with temperatures up to 23°C (73°F).

Although some rain falls every month, two wet seasons alternate with two dry seasons. June, July, August, January, and February are considered dry months, while the first wet season lasts from March to May and the second wet season from September to December. Rainfall is irregular, falling most heavily in the northwest. In the plateaus the average rainfall is 119.4 cm (47 in), but in the lower regions it declines to 76.2 cm (30 in) per year. Violent rainstorms are common at the higher elevations.

Climate and Weather

Mean Temperature
Central Plateau 68°F
Imbo and Savannah 73°F
Bujumbura 77°F
Eastern Plateau 66°F
Average Rainfall 30 in to 47 in

POPULATION

Population Indicators

Total Population: 1999 5,736,000
World Rank: 100th
Density per sq mi: 534.1 (206.2 per sq km)
% of annual growth (1994–99): 0.1
Male %: 48.6
Female %: 51.4
Urban %: 6.3
Age Distribution: % 0–14: 46.4
15–29: 25.3
30–44: 15.4
45–59: 7.0
60–74: 4.0
75 and over: 1.7
Population 2020: 9,432,000
Birth Rate per 1,000: 42.7
Death Rate per 1,000: 17.8
Population Doubling Time (years): 28
Infant Mortality Rate per 1,000 live births: 104.8
Rate of Natural Increase per 1,000: 24.9
Total Fertility Rate: 6.5
Expectation of Life (years): Males 44.3
Females 47.3
Marriage Rate per 1,000: —
Divorce Rate per 1,000: —
Total Number of Households: —
Average Size of Households: 4.6
% of Illegitimate Children: —
Induced Abortions: —
Rate per 100 live births: —

ETHNIC COMPOSITION

The ethnic composition of Burundi is relatively simple, especially in comparison with neighboring countries. The population is made up mainly of Hutu (properly Bahutu) and Tutsi (also known as Watutsi, Watusi, or Batutsi) peoples, who constitute 83 percent and 15 percent of the inhabitants, respectively. The Twa, a pygmoid group, and small numbers of Europeans and Asians account for the remaining 2 percent.

Burundi had, until quite recently, a feudal social system in which the Hutu, though numerically dominant, functioned as serfs and the Tutsi as masters. As a consequence, the Hutu have adopted a number of Tutsi cultural traits and social values. The two tribes differ markedly in physical appearance. The average Hutu is short and stocky, while the Tutsi are tall, slender, angular, and relatively light-skinned.

LANGUAGES

The two official languages of Burundi are Kirundi and French. Swahili is spoken as a lingua franca throughout the country.

Kirundi is closely related to Kinyarwanda, an official language of Rwanda. All Burundians speak Kirundi, but there are dialectical variations.

Principal Languages and Their Speakers

French	530,000
Kirundi	5,620,000
Hutu	4,730,000
Tutsi	830,000
Twa	60,000
Other	110,000

RELIGIONS

Burundi has no official religion. In terms of numbers, Christianity claims over 67 percent of the population, indigenous religions 23 percent, and Islam 10 percent. Of the Christians, nearly 89 percent are Roman Catholics and 11 percent are adherents of various Protestant denominations. Though Christian missions have been successful in proselytizing and in educational, medical, and social work, adherence to Christian beliefs among converts does not preclude retention of elements of traditional religions. The first Roman Catholic East African diocese was established at Kivu in 1912. The Anglicans form the largest Protestant denomination.

Burundi is a secular state, and religious freedoms are restricted by the government. All religious associations must receive approval from the government, and government authorities must be informed in advance of religious gatherings. Such gatherings are strictly limited to recognized places of worship (churches, mosques, or temples), and religious services are authorized only after midday on Saturday and Sunday. (In spite of this order, the government does not interfere with Muslim worship on Friday.)

The Jehovah's Witnesses sect is banned because its doctrines challenge certain precepts of civil authority. Seventh-Day Adventists' activities in Burundi were banned in 1986. Other churches have suffered various harassments. The government has made it clear that churches are to confine their activities to religion and social work and to stay out of political matters, which include Hutu/Tutsi relations.

Religious Affiliations

Roman Catholic	3,730,000
Nonreligious	1,070,000
Other (mostly Protestant)	940,000

HISTORICAL BACKGROUND

Burundi was settled by three waves of peoples: first the Twa, a pygmy tribe of hunters; then the Hutus, a Bantu group, who probably arrived around the 14th century; and lastly the Tutsis, a group of tall pastoral nomads who arrived between the 15th and 16th centuries. The Tutsis introduced a caste system to keep the original Hutus and Twa in subjection. The land was ruled by the Tutsi king, known as the *mwami,* who was always chosen from the elite Tutsi tribe, Ganwa. Prior to its colonial rulers, little is known of the history of Burundi. However, according to legend, Ntare Rushatsi, the founder of the original dynasty, came from Rwanda or Buha in the 17th century.

Burundi was under colonial rule for 77 years—from 1885 when the country, then known as Urundi, was designated a German sphere of interest at the Berlin Conference to 1962, when Belgium formally granted independence. However, it was not until the mid-1890s that German rule was officially extended over the whole country. In 1914 Germans in Burundi numbered only 190, of whom 130 were missionaries, 40 were soldiers, six were officials, and the rest were traders. Burundi was occupied by Belgium during World War I and in 1923 became a mandated territory of the League of Nations under Belgian supervision. Although under the terms of the mandate Burundi and Rwanda were to be maintained as a separate territory, Belgium was permitted to administer it as part of the Belgian Congo under a vice governor-general. The chief administrative officer in Rwanda and Burundi was the resident general. Belgium retained the traditional political organization under which the territory was divided into 36 chiefdoms under a mwami (king).

Belgian rule in Burundi was successful and intensive on all levels. The social structure was unalterably changed by the work of Christian missions, while the legal and administrative structures were rebuilt entirely on Belgian lines. The other major Belgian legacy was the French language, which supplanted existing Bantu languages in administration and education. The departure of the Belgians was peaceful, and there are no widespread anti-European feelings apparent in the country.

At independence, Burundi retained its monarchical form of government under the traditional Tutsi rulers. Elections held in 1961 prior to independence were won by the Union for National Progress party (UPRONA), which had been formed in 1958 by the king's son, Ganwa (Prince Rwagasore). Prince Rwagasore became prime minister but was assassinated after two weeks in office. He was succeeded by his brother-in-law, André Muhirwa.

Burundi politics are shaped by rivalry between the Hutus and the Tutsi. During the early years of independence, political stability was maintained by the monarchy, but in 1966 Mwami (King) Mwamba IV was deposed by his son Charles who reigned as Ntare V. Charles, in turn, was deposed a few months later by the prime minister, Michel Micombero, who declared a republic and took over the presidency of UPRONA, which was given monopoly status. Two alleged plots against the government in 1969 and 1972 culminated in an unsuccessful coup in 1972 in which Ntare V was killed. Micombero's Tutsi supporters held the Hutu responsible for the former king's death and initiated reprisals during which tens of thousands of Hutu, including all of the group's literate members, were killed.

Micombero was overthrown in 1976 in a bloodless coup that brought Jean-Baptiste Bagaza, another southern Tutsi, to power. He suspended the constitution, declared the second republic, and became president of the military Supreme Revolutionary Council. The council was abolished effective January 1980, and its functions given to the Central Committee of UPRONA, which adopted legislation that established a national assembly to be elected by universal adult suffrage. Elections held in 1982 and 1984 were mere formalities. Bagaza and UPRONA candidates ran unopposed. The president, in an effort to maintain stability, appointed several Hutu to important positions, but tension between the Hutu and Tutsi persisted.

Bagaza's second term was marked by increasingly strained relations with the Roman Catholic Church, which the president saw as a rival power aligned with the Hutu.

Priests were detained without trial, missionaries expelled, and parish councils abolished. The government also nationalized some of the seminaries, closed catechism classes, and banned the use of religious texts in education.

In 1987 Bagaza was overthrown in a coup lead by Major Pierre Buyoya. He suspended the constitution, dissolved the National Assembly, and set up a Military Committee for National Salvation to exercise power. The following year, a tribal dispute between the Hutu and the Tutsi resulted in the slaughter of tens of thousands of Hutu, including children. In response, Buyoya named a 23-member cabinet that, for the first time, had a Hutu majority. A Hutu was also appointed to the newly restored post of prime minister.

In 1992, Buyoya's government adopted a new constitution, which among its other provisions, banned political organizations based upon ethnicity. In June of that same year, free elections were held. Melchior Ndadaye, a Hutu, was elected president.

Ndadaye was assassinated in a military coup in October 1993. This coup marked the beginning of another period of ethnic fighting, with as many as 150,000 Tutsis being killed. Cyprien Ntaryamirs, a Hutu, was eventually chosen president and he took office in February of the following year. However, he was killed in a plane crash two months later. Fighting intensified until September when a new government was formed by Sylvestre Ntibantunganya, a Hutu.

In July 1996, the Tutsi-controlled army staged a coup and reinstalled Pierre Buyoya as president. The president was successful in having the economic sanctions eased in 1997 and lifted in 1999. However, the civil war continued into 2001.

CONSTITUTION

Burundi was a monarchy until 1966, when it was proclaimed a republic. The first republican constitution was promulgated in 1974, but it was suspended within two years following the military coup led by Lieutenant Colonel Jean-Baptiste Bagaza in 1976. A new constitution was approved by the National Assembly.

Following the 1987 coup, executive and legislative powers were assumed by the Military Committee for National Salvation, which elected its chairman president of the republic.

In 1991, the government proposed a new constitution, which was adopted in 1992. The new constitution called for a national assembly with 81 members elected from 16 constituencies by proportional representation. The government is overseen by a 10-member national security council. The president is elected by universal suffrage. In 1998, the size of the legislature was enlarged to 121 seats.

LOCAL GOVERNMENT

For purposes of regional administration Burundi is divided into 15 provinces. Each province is headed by an appointed governor. The provinces are subdivided into 114 communes headed by elected councils.

Local Government

Principal administrative divisions, capitals, area, population

AREA AND POPULATION

		area		population 1990
Provinces	**Capitals**	**sq mi**	**sq km**	**census**
Bubanza	Bubanza	420	1,089	222,953
Bujumbura	Bujumbura	509	1,319	608,931
Bururi	Bururi	952	2,465	385,490
Cankuzo	Cankuzo	759	1,965	142,707
Cibitoke	Cibitoke	631	1,636	279,843
Gitega	Gitega	764	1,979	565,174
Karuzi	Karuzi	563	1,457	287,905
Kayanza	Kayanza	476	1,233	443,116
Kirundo	Kirundo	658	1,703	401,103

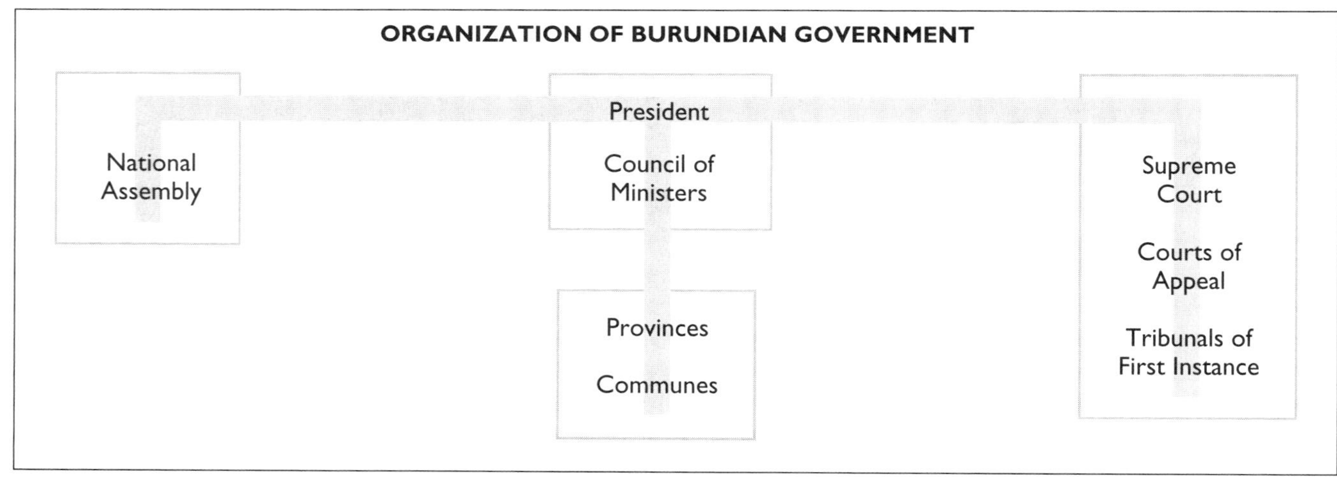

Makamba	Makamba	757	1,960	223,799
Muramvya	Muramvya	593	1,535	441,653
Muyinga	Muyinga	709	1,836	373,382
Ngozi	Ngozi	569	1,474	482,246
Rutana	Rutana	756	1,959	195,834
Ruyigi	Ruyigi	903	2,339	238,567
TOTAL LAND AREA		10,019	25,949	
INLAND WATER		721	1,867	
TOTAL		10,740	27,816	5,292,793

PARLIAMENT

The National Assembly is a unicameral legislature that is elected by universal suffrage and whose members serve five-year terms. The assembly has not been a very strong body. While it does have the right to propose legislation, it ceded its power to hold a vote of confidence in the government in 1994. The body was suspended by presidential decree in 1996. A new Transitional National Assembly was inaugurated in 1998. It has 121 members.

POLITICAL PARTIES

Burundi legalized multiple parties in 1992. Among the most important are: Union for National Progress or UPRONA, the largest party; the Burundi Democratic Front or FRODEBU; the Socialist Party of Burundi or PSB; and the People's Reconciliation Party or PRP. Opposition parties include: Burundi African Alliance for the Salvation or ABASA, Rally for Democracy and Economic and Social Development or RADDES, and the Party for National Redress or PARENA.

Political Parties

Union for National Progress, 1958
Front for Democracy in Burundi, 1992
Burundi People's Rally, 1992
Independent Workers' Party
People's Party
Rally for Democracy and Economic and Social Development
Guarantor of Speech and Freedom in Burundi, 1993
People's Reconciliation Party, 1991
Social Democratic Party
National Alliance for Rights and Development
Party for National Recovery, 1994
African Burundi Salvation Alliance, 1997
There are three exile groups:
- National Council for the Defense of Democracy
- Hutu People's Liberation Party
- Solidarity

Political Parties: Strength in Parliament Most Recent Elections

The National Assembly (Assemblée Nationale), then a one-party, 65-member body, was suspended following the September 1987 coup. Although President Buyoya promised to revive the body within "one to two years," the suspension remained in effect until the multiparty election of June 29, 1993, at which the Front for Democracy in Burundi (FRODEBU) won 65 seats in an enlarged body of 81 and the Unity for National Progress (UPRONA) won 16, no other formation meeting a threshold of 5 percent of the vote.

The assembly was once again suspended following the military coup of July 25, 1996. Although that decree was formally lifted in September, the assembly subsequently remained in disarray, many of its members having died in the recent violence or fled the country.

A **Transitional National Assembly** was inaugurated on July 18, 1998, under provisions of the June 6 transitional constitution. The assembly was expanded to 121 members; FRODEBU and UPRONA kept their 1993 allocations (65 and 16, respectively), although more than 20 vacant FRODEBU seats had to be filled with new members. Of the 40 new seats, 27 were filled by government-appointed representatives of social and political parties. The following parties were subsequently reported to have appointed legislators; the Alliance of the Brave, the Burundi People's Rally, the Guarantor of Freedom of Speech in Burundi, the Independent Workers' Party, the People's Party, the People's Reconciliation Party, the Rally for Democracy and Economic and Social Development, and the Social Democratic Party. Several other parties were apparently invited to participate but were unable to appoint legislators due to internal wrangling. Consequently, four seats were not filled upon the inauguration of the new assembly.

LEGAL SYSTEM

The judicial structure and the legal codes are based on the Belgian model. The judiciary is not entirely independent. In addition to appointing judges, the president can dismiss them. The judiciary is expected to adhere to the guidance and recommendations of the government. Nevertheless, there is a high degree of autonomy in the day-to-day administration of justice through the courts, and due process is largely observed. Court decisions cannot be overturned by the executive branch. The president can reduce sentences and can issue pardons.

LAW ENFORCEMENT

Law Enforcement

Offenses reported to the police per 100,000: 87
- Murder: 3.3
- Assault: 7.4
- Burglary: —
- Automobile Theft: —
- Population per Police officer: —

Death Penalty: Yes. Last execution in 1982

HUMAN RIGHTS

Burundi is faced with classic problems of an emerging nation: an ethnic imbalance where Tutsis, with 15 percent of the population, monopolize power; a history of genocide; limited natural resources; lack of access to the sea; and weak democratic traditions.

Torture and physical abuse occur occasionally during interrogation of violent prisoners or those who resist arrest. Preventive detention exists but is not commonly used. Legally, a person may be held for only five days before being charged. The separation of the judiciary and the executive is only a fiction, but trials are reasonably fair.

The government controls all domestic media. There is no television station, and in November 1980 the government seized all television sets used for watching telecasts from the Democratic Republic of the Congo. Freedom of religion is observed in principle. However, the involvement of many foreign missionaries in social work with the poor Hutu has aroused government suspicions and led to the missionaries being asked to leave the country.

FOREIGN POLICY

Burundi is the epicenter of one of the most violent ethnic conflicts in Central Africa, and this has influenced Burundi's foreign policy both toward its immediate neighbor, Rwanda, and also with other African nations. The 1993 presidential assassination set off a chain of events that led to the massacre of millions of Hutus and Tutsis, and it also had reverberations in Congo (then Zaire) where the two communities carried their struggle. International efforts to contain ethnic violence were frustrated by the intransigence of the combatants as well as the Tutsi military leadership's opposition to a foreign military presence. However, when Tutsi power was restored in Rwanda, cooperative security arrangements were restored between Burundi and Rwanda. Burundi is a member, along with Rwanda, Tanzania, and Uganda, of the Organization for the Management and Development of the Kagera River Basin and also the Economic Community of the Central African States.

DEFENSE

The defense structure is headed by the president, who is a professional military officer and commander in chief of the armed forces. Operational command is exercised through the commander of the armed forces. Military manpower is provided by voluntary enlistment. The officer corps is almost entirely Tutsi.

The total strength of the armed forces is 18,500. There are also 1,500 men in paramilitary units.

The army is organized in two infantry battalions, one parachute company, one commando company, and one armored car company. The navy has three patrol boats and the air force has three combat aircraft.

The army is trained by Belgian advisors, and most of the equipment is of Belgian origin. The army has no offensive capability and is weakened by traditional rivalry between Hutu enlisted men and Tutsi officers.

Military Indicators

Total Active Duty Personnel: 18,500
Military Manpower per 1,000: 3.1
Military Expenditures $: 46 million
- as % of GNP: 4.4
- per capita $: 8
- as % of central government expenditures: 24.8

Arms Imports $: 0
Arms Exports $: 0

ECONOMY

Burundi is a landlocked, resource-poor country with an underdeveloped manufacturing sector. The economy is predominantely agricultural with roughly 90 percent of the population dependent on subsistence agriculture. Its economic health depends on the coffee crop, which accounts for 80 percent of foreign exchange earnings. The ability to pay for imports therefore rests largely on the vagaries of the climate and the international coffee market. Since October 1993 the nation has suffered from massive ethnic-based violence, which has resulted in the death of perhaps 250,000 persons and the displacement of about 800,000 others. Foods, medicines, and electricity remain in short supply.

Principal Economic Indicators

Gross National Product: $924 million
GNP per capita: $140
GNP Average Annual Growth Rate (1990–97) %: −5.9
GNP per capita Average Annual Growth Rate (1990–97) %: −8.3
Origin of Gross Domestic Product %
- Agriculture: 47
- Mining: 1
- Manufacturing: 11
- Construction: 4
- Public Utilities: —
- Transportation and Communications: 4
- Trade: 4
- Financial Services: 2
- Other Services: 2
- Government: 15

Gross Domestic Product by Type of Expenditure %
- Private Consumption: 84
- Government Consumption: 16
- Gross Domestic Investment: 13
- Foreign Trade: Exports: 12
- Imports: −25

% of Income Received by Poorest 20%: —
% of Income Received by Richest 10%: —

Price and earnings indexes (1995 = 100)

	1992	1993	1994	1995	1996	1997	1998
Consumer price index	66.6	73.0	83.8	100.0	126.4	165.8	186.5
Earnings index	—	—	—	—	—	—	—

Finance

National Currency: Burundi Franc (FBu)
Exchange Rate: $1 = FBu 412.59
Money Supply Stock in National Currency billion: 43,644
M1 per capita: 7,280
Central Bank Discount Rate %: —
Total External Debt $: 1.1 billion
Debt Service Ratio %: 21.0
Balance of Payments $: 4.0 million
International Reserves SDRs: 103 million
Ratio of External Debt to Total Reserves: 5.2

Average Annual Rate of Inflation/Consumer Price Index
Growth Rate %: 26

Official Development Assistance

ODA: $77 million
as % of GNP: 8.8
per capita: $12
Foreign Direct Investment $: 1 million

Central Government Revenues and Expenditures

Fiscal Year: Calendar Year

Revenues $: 222 million
Expenditures $: 258 million
Budget Deficit $: 13.7
Tax Revenues as % of GDP: 13.7
Highest Tax Bracket %
Individual: —
Corporate: —

Employment and Labor

Economically Active Population: 2,780,000
Female Participation Rate %: 52.6
Activity Rate %: 52.5
Labor by Sector: %
Agriculture, Forestry, Fishing: 92.6
Manufacturing, Mining: 1.3
Construction: 0.7
Transportation and Communications: 0.3
Trade, Hotels, and Restaurants: 0.9
Finance, Insurance, Real Estate: 0.1
Public Administration, Defense: —
Services: 3.1
Unemployment %: NA

Agriculture

Agriculture's Share of GDP %: 47
Average Annual Rate of Growth (1965–98) %: 2.6
Number of Farms 000: —
Average Size of Farm ha: —
Number of Tractors per 1,000 hectares: 0.2
Irrigation, % of Farms having: 1.4
Artificial Fertilizer kg/hectare: 4.
Total Cropland as % of Farmland: 56.7

Livestock: Cattle 000: 346
Sheep 000: 320
Hogs 000: 73
Chickens 000: 4,600
Forests: Production of Roundwood (000 cubic meters): 4,969
Fisheries: Total Catch tons: 23,100

Mining

% of GDP: 0.6
Value of Mineral Production $: 5.4 million

Manufacturing

Value Added $: 94 million
Industrial Production Growth Rate %: NA

Energy

Commercial Energy Production metric tons of oil equivalent: —
Commercial Energy Consumption metric tons of oil equivalent: —
Commercial Energy Consumption per capita kg: —
Average Annual Growth Rate 1980–97 %: —
Net Energy Imports % of use: —
Electricity Installed Capacity kW: 43,000
Production kW-hr: 120 million
Coal Reserves tons: —
Production tons: —
Natural Gas Proven Reserves cubic meters: —
Production cubic meters: —
Crude Petroleum Reserves barrels: —
Production barrels: —
Consumption barrels: —
Refinery Capacity barrels per day: —
Pipelines Length km: —

Foreign Trade

Imports $: 204.5 million
Exports $: 68.7 million
Export Volume % Annual Growth Rate (1990–97): −2.5
Import Volume % Annual Growth Rate (1990–97): −3.6
Balance of Trade $

Balance of trade (current prices)

	1993	1994	1995	1996	1997	1998
CFAF 000,000,000	−34.683	−26.434	−24.018	−26.039	−12.482	−41.910
% of total	53.6%	30.6%	31.1%	53.6%	16.9%	42.4%

Major Trading Partners

	Imports	Exports
European Union %	45.4	63.8
United States %	1.8	2.0
Eastern Europe %	0.4	0.7
Japan %	9.2	0.7
Others %	43.3	33.6

Transportation

Roads Total Length mi: 8,997 (14,480 km)
Paved %: 7
Automobiles: 16,800
Trucks and Buses: 15,000
Persons per vehicle: 186
Railroad; Track Length mi: —
Passenger-mi: —
Freight-mi: —
Merchant Marine: No. of Vessels: 1
  Total Deadweight Tonnage: 400
  International Cargo Loaded tons: 35,000
  International Cargo Off-loaded tons: 188,000
Airports with Scheduled Flights: 1
Traffic: Passenger-mi: 1.2 million
  Freight-mi: —
Length of Canals mi: —

Tourism

Number of Tourists to: 14,000
Number of Tourists from: 16,000
Tourist Receipts $: 1 million
Tourist Expenditures $: 25 million

Communications

Telephones 000: 17
Cost of Local Calls 3 mins: $0.03
Cellular Telephones 000: 0.3
Fax Machines 000: 0.1
Personal Computers 000: —
Internet Hosts per million persons: —
Mail: Post Offices: 27
  Pieces of Mail Handled: 7.6 million
  Pieces of Mail Handled per person: 1.3

EDUCATION

Education is free and compulsory for six years, between ages seven and 13. The academic year runs from September through July. Schooling consists of 13 years, with six years of primary education, after which students enter a seventh year called the preparatory year and then six years of secondary education in two three-year cycles. Kirundi is the language of instruction in primary schools, although French is used in secondary schools.

Public schools directly administered by the government account for only 7 percent of the primary-school enrollment. The other 93 percent is provided by approved schools run by Roman Catholic and Protestant organizations. Approved schools must conform to government regulations regarding curriculum and qualifications of the teaching staff.

Vocational and technical training is provided at the Technical School at Kamenge and at craft schools.

The current literacy rate is 35 percent of the population.

Education

Literacy Rate %: 35.3
  Male %: 49.3
  Female %: 22.5
First Level: Primary schools: 1,418
  Teachers: 10,400
  Students: 651,086
  Student-Teacher Ratio: 62.6
  Net Enrollment Ratio: 52
Second Level: Secondary Schools: 113
  Teachers: 2,562
  Students: 55,713
  Student-Teacher Ratio: 21.7
  Net Enrollment Ratio: 5
Vocational Level: Schools: —
  Students: —
Third Level: Institutions: 8
  Teachers: 556
  Students: 4,256
  Student-Ratio Level: 7.6
  Gross Enrollment Ratio: 0.9
  Students per 100,000: 74
  % of Population Age 25 and over with Postsecondary Education: 0.6
Public Expenditure on Education as % of GDP: 2.8

SCIENCE AND TECHNOLOGY

Science and Technology

Scientists and Engineers in R&D per 1 million persons: 33
Expenditures in R&D as % of GDP: 0.31
High-Tech Exports $: —
Patent Applications by Residents: 1

MEDIA

The only daily publication in Burundi is the government bulletin *Le Renouveau de Burundi*, issued in French. It has a circulation of 20,000. The national news agency is Agence Burundaise de Presse (ABP).

The government controls all domestic media. There is no television station, and in November 1980 the government seized all television sets used for watching telecasts from the Democratic Republic of the Congo. The official broadcasting organization, Voix de la Révolution, broadcasts two programs in Kirundi, French, and Swahili, with a shortwave transmitter at Bujumbura.

Media

Daily Newspapers: 1
  Total Circulation 000: 20
  Circulation per 1,000: 3.0
Books Published: —
Magazines: —
Radio Receivers 000: 300
  per 1,000: 47
Television sets 000: 40
  per 1,000: 7.0

MOST IMPORTANT MEDIA:

Press. The following are published at Bujumbura: *Le Renouveau du Burundi* (20,000), government daily, in French; *Umbumwé* (20,000), weekly, in Kirundi; *Burundi Chrétien,* weekly publication of the Gitega Archbishopric, in French; *Ndongozi Yaburundi*, Catholic fortnightly, in Kirundi.

News agencies. Daily bulletins are issued by the official *Agence Burundaise de Presse.*

Radio and television. The government radio facility, La Voix de la Révolution, broadcasts in French, Kirundi, and Swahili to some 476,000 receivers; Télévision Nationale du Burundi offers programming from a station at Bujumbura.

CULTURE

Cultural Indicators

- Public Libraries
  - Number: 2
  - Volumes: 11,000
  - Registered borrowers: —
- Museums
  - Number: 4
  - Annual Attendance: —
- Cinema
  - Production of Long Films: —
  - Number of Cinemas: —
  - Seating Capacity: —
  - Annual Attendance: —
  - Annual Attendance per capita: —

STATUS OF WOMEN

Women in society hold a secondary position, although their status is undergoing considerable change from traditional patterns. The constitution provides for legal equality, and significant improvement in the legal status of women came in 1980 with the issuance of a new legal code on families. This code prohibits polygamy and the use of a dowry and allows women control of family matters in the absence of the husband. However, women still cannot inherit land and cannot work if forbidden to do so by their husbands. Although fewer women than men attain an education, once it is attained, women generally can find suitable employment. The government does not discriminate against women in hiring or with respect to the jobs open to them. Women are represented at all levels in the political life of the country. However, their main vehicle of political expression is the women's movement affiliated with the ruling UPRONA, which remains dominated by males.

Women

Gender Empowerment Measure: —
Seats Held in Parliament by Women %: 14.4
Female Administrators and Managers %: —
Female Professional and Technical Workers %: —
Women's Share of Earned Income %: —
Women in Government %: 4

HEALTH, FOOD, AND NUTRITION

Health

Number of Physicians: 354
Number of Dentists: 9
Number of Nurses: 1,270
Number of Pharmacists: 55
Population per Physician: 17,153
Number of Hospitals: —
Hospital Beds per 10,000: 7
Hospital Bed Occupancy Rate: —
Infant Mortality Rate per 1,000 live births: 143
Maternal Mortality Rate per 100,000 live births: 1,300
Total Health Expenditures as % of GDP: 3.28
Health Expenditures per capita $: 30
HIV Infected % of adults: 8.30
Cigarette Consumption per smoker per year: —
% of Smokers: Male: —
Female: —
Access to Safe Water %: 58

Food and Nutrition

Food Supply as % of FAO Requirements: 75
% of Consumption Expenditures on Food: 59.6
Daily Available Calories per capita: 1,749
% of Total Calories derived from:
Cereals: 17.0
Potatoes, cassava: 27.4
Meat, poultry: 1.3
Fish: 0.4
Eggs, milk: 0.7
Fruits, vegetables: 9.9
Fats, oils: 1.3

ENVIRONMENT

Burundi's environmental problems include soil erosion as a result of overgrazing and the expansion of agriculture into marginal lands. The country also suffers from deforestation; little forested land remains because of uncontrolled cutting of trees for fuel. Finally, the loss of forests has also meant a loss of habitat that threatens wildlife populations.

Environment

Forest Area sq km: 3,000
Average Annual Deforestation sq km: 14
Nationally Protected Areas as % of Total Land Area: 5.5
Freshwater Access cubic meters per capita: 561
Emissions of Organic Water Pollutants kg per day: 1,644
CO_2 Emissions per capita ton: 0.0

CHRONOLOGY

1961 UPRONA wins 58 of 62 seats in UN-sponsored legislative elections; Prince Rwagasore forms a new government; Rwagasore is assassinated.
1962 Burundi achieves independence, and the Belgian resident general leaves; Rwanda and Burundi agree on economic union; André Muhirwa is named the first prime minister of independent Burundi.
1963 Pierre Ngendendumwe replaces Muhirwa as prime minister.
1964 Rwanda withdraws from the Rwanda-Burundi currency union; fighting breaks out in the interior between Hutu and Tutsi, with the government supporting the Tutsi.
1965 In legislative elections Hutu win a majority in both houses but the king refuses to appoint a Hutu prime minister, dissolving the National Assembly and declaring an absolute monarchy; both Tutsi and Hutu groups attempt coups.
1966 Prince Charles deposes his father and is enthroned as Ntare V but is deposed after 89 days; Prime Minister Micombero becomes president of the newly proclaimed Republic of Burundi, with UPRONA as the sole official party.
1970 A new UPRONA charter assigns Burundi's presidency to the party secretary-general.
1971 A Supreme Military Council of 27 military officers is established.
1972 Former mwami Ntare V is arrested; Hutu-Tutsi hostilities are revived over the government's alleged discovery of monarchist plots; Ntare V is executed; fighting escalates into civil war between the poorly armed Hutu and government forces; an estimated 100,000 to 250,000 Hutu are killed, and approximately 400,000 refugees flee; Albin Nyamoya, a Tutsi, is named prime minister;.
1973 Hutu-Tutsi strife breaks out in neighboring Rwanda; Hutu begin guerrilla warfare against the Burundian army; Burundi receives aid from Libya; relations with Tanzania are strained as Burundian troops cross the border to attack Hutu camps there.
1974 Burundi compensates Tanzania for the 1973 attacks; a new constitution is adopted; President Micombero is granted a second seven-year term.
1976 Micombero is overthrown in a coup led by Lt. Col. Jean-Baptiste Bagaza, who suspends the constitution of 1974, dissolves the National Assembly, and vests executive and legislative powers in a Supreme Revolutionary Council.
1978 The post of prime minister is abolished; a national recovery program is launched.
1979 UPRONA holds the first National Congress under Bagaza and replaces the Supreme Revolutionary Council with a Central Committee; Protestant and Catholic missionaries are expelled from the country.
1981 A new constitution is approved in a popular referendum.
1982 A new National Assembly is elected in which all members belong to UPRONA.
1987 President Bagaza is overthrown in a coup led by Pierre Buyoya.
1988 Renewed tribal disputes lead to the death of over 1,000 Tutsi and 100,000 Hutu.
1990 The government issues a Charter of National Unity according equal rights to the country's three ethnic groups, the Hutu, Tutsi, and Twa.
1992 A new constitution is adopted.
1993 Melchior Ndadaye is elected the country's first Hutu president; a failed coup kills several ministers, and violence erupts between Tutsi and Hutu factions.
1996 The army seizes power in an attempt to restore peace; Major Pierre Buyoya is installed as president; the civil war between the Tutsi and Hutu continues.
2000 The government of Burundi and three Tutsi groups agree to a cease-fire, but the two major Hutu groups refuse to cooperate.
2001 Talks brokered by Nelson Mandela lead to the installation of a transitional, power-sharing government backed by a South African peacekeeping force carrying a UN mandate.

BIBLIOGRAPHY

Lemarchand, René. *Rwanda and Burundi*. New York, 1969.
Lemarchand, René. *Burundi: Ethnocide As Discourse and Practice*. New York, 1998.
Lemarchand, René. *Selective Genocide in Burundi*. London, 1974.
Melady, T. P. *Burundi: The Tragic Years*. Maryknoll, N.Y., 1974.
Weinstein, Warren. *Historical Dictionary of Burundi*. Metuchen, N.J., 1976.

OFFICIAL PUBLICATIONS

Burundi. *Annuaire statistique; Recensement général de la population, 1990.*

CONTACT INFORMATION

Embassy of Burundi
2233 Wisconsin Avenue NW, Suite 212
Washington, D.C. 20007
Phone: (202) 342-2574 Fax: (202) 342-2578

INTERNET RESOURCES

- Burundi: http://www.burundi.gov.bi

CAMBODIA

BASIC FACT SHEET

OFFICIAL NAME:
Kingdom of Cambodia

ABBREVIATION:
CB

CAPITAL:
Phnom Penh

HEAD OF STATE:
King Noradom Sihanouk (from 1973/1993)

HEAD OF GOVERNMENT:
Chairman of the Council of Ministers Hun Sen (from 1998)

NATURE OF GOVERNMENT:
Multiparty democracy under a constitutional monarch

POPULATION:
10,981,000 (1999)

AREA:
181,035 sq km (69,898 sq mi)

ETHNIC MAJORITY:
Khmer

LANGUAGE:
Khmer

RELIGION:
Theravada Buddhism

UNIT OF CURRENCY:
Riel (C.R.)

NATIONAL FLAG:
Two horizontal stripes, red above blue, with a yellow silhouette of the temple of Angkor Wat in the center

NATIONAL EMBLEM:
The main elements of the coat of arms are two golden cups stacked on top of each other with a sacred sword placed horizontally above. Above the sword is shown the symbol representing "om," the sound of creation. The cups are framed by two laurel branches united at the bottom by the star of the Royal Order of Cambodia.

NATIONAL ANTHEM:
"Heaven Protects Our King"

NATIONAL HOLIDAYS:
January 7 (National Day); April 17 (Victory over American Imperialism Day); May 1 (Labor Day); May 20 (Day of Hatred); September 22 (Feast of the Ancestors)

DATE OF INDEPENDENCE:
November 9, 1953

DATE OF CONSTITUTION:
September 21, 1993

GEOGRAPHICAL FEATURES

Cambodia, in the southwestern Indochinese peninsula, is an irregularly shaped country, with an area of 181,035 sq km (69,898 sq mi). It is bounded on the northeast by Laos, on the east and southeast by Vietnam, on the southwest by the Gulf of Thailand, and on the west and northwest by Thailand.

The capital city, also the largest, is Phnom Penh (1994 pop., est., 920,000). Other major cities are Battambang (1989 pop., est., 45,000) and Kompong Cham (1989 pop., est., 33,000). The major port is Kompong Saom, on the Gulf of Thailand.

The central three-fourths of the country is a level basin. The Mekong River, at 4,344 km (2,700 m) one of the longest in the world, flows north to south through the plain. In the center of the plain is the Tonle Sap, an inland lake that acts as a reservoir for the Mekong River. The lake floods during the rainy season; as it recedes, it leaves behind a rich sediment of alluvial soil. The area

Cambodia

southwest of the basin is mountainous; peaks in the Cardamom Range exceed 1,500 m (5,741 ft) and in the Elephant Range, 900 m (3,000 ft).

Geography

Area sq km: 181,035 sq mi 69,898
World Rank: 89th
Land Boundaries, km: Laos 541; Thailand 803; Vietnam 1,228
Coastline, km 443
Elevation Extremes meters
 Lowest: Gulf of Thailand 0
 Highest: Phnum Aoral 1,810
Land Use % Arable land: 13
 Permanent Crops: 0
 Permanent Pastures: 11
 Forest and Woodland: 66
 Other: 10

Population of Principal Cities (1998)	
Phnom Penh	999,800

CLIMATE AND WEATHER

Cambodia has a tropical climate with two distinct seasons. The rainy southwesterly monsoon season lasts from May through October; the dry northeasterly monsoon season lasts from November through April. Average temperatures range from 20°C to 35°C (68°F to 97°F), but in general the climate is more moderate than in other countries located at the same latitude. Average annual temperature is 26.7°C (80°F). Rainfall from April to September averages 1,270 mm (50 in) to 1,990 mm

(75 in) annually and is heaviest over the mountainous areas of the southwest.

Climate and Weather

Mean Temperature
Summer 97°F
Winter 68°F
Average Rainfall 60 in to 75 in
Southwest Mountains 200 in

POPULATION

Population Indicators

Total Population: 1999 10,981,000
World Rank: 68th
Density per sq mi: 156.3 per sq km 60.4
% of annual growth (1994–99): 2.4
Male %: 48.3
Female %: 51.7
Urban %: 21.0
Age Distribution: % 0–14: 42.8
15–29: 26
30–44: 17.2
45–59: 8.7
60–74: 4.2
75 and over: 1.1
Population 2020: 15,880,000
Birth Rate per 1,000: 43.0
Death Rate per 1,000: 15.0
Population Doubling Time (years): 28
Infant Mortality Rate per 1,000 live births: 106.0
Rate of Natural Increase per 1,000: 28.0
Total Fertility Rate: 5.8
Expectation of Life (years): Males 52
Females 55
Marriage Rate per 1,000: —
Divorce Rate per 1,000: —
Total Number of Households: —
Average Size of Households: 5.6
% of Illegitimate Children: —
Induced Abortions: —
Rate per 100 live births: —

ETHNIC COMPOSITION

Most of the population of Cambodia (approximately 90 percent) is Khmer. Most of the rest of the people are Vietnamese and Chinese, with a smattering of Laotians, Thai, and the Cham-Malays, who live in the rural mountainous regions.

LANGUAGES

Khmer, or Cambodian, is the official language. French was the official language until 1975, but its use has been discouraged by the government. Among the Chinese minority, a number of Chinese dialects are spoken.

Principal Languages and Their Speakers

Cham	260,000
Chinese	340,000
Khmer	9,730,000
Vietnamese	600,000

RELIGIONS

Approximately 90 percent of Cambodians practice Theravada Buddhism. Other religions followed in the country are Roman Catholicism, Islam, and Nahayana Buddhism; some Cambodians living in the mountainous regions practice animism.

Religious Affiliations

Buddhist	10,430,000
Muslim	240,000
Other	310,000

HISTORICAL BACKGROUND

There is archaeological evidence that Cambodia was inhabited as far back as the second millennium B.C. and that stable societies flourished there 2,000 years ago. Funan was the first Hindu-Buddhist kingdom to dominate in what is now Cambodia and is considered the first Khmer kingdom. The kingdom of Chenla conquered Funan in the sixth and seventh centuries but was itself later split in two, with its southern half, in the area of what is now Cambodia, under Javanese rule.

It was the reign of Jayavarman II (r. c. 802–50) that began the glorious Angkor era in Khmer history, and it was his successors who built the great temples at Angkor Wat. The kings of Angkor ruled over Cambodia and much of the rest of Southeast Asia until 1432, in what is known as the classical era in Khmer history. That civilization reached its peak in the 12th and early 13th centuries but then began to weaken, threatened by overextension of its irrigaton system, epidemics, and popular resentment against the well-entrenched bureaucracy, as well as the spread of Buddhism.

Over the next 400 years Siam (now Thailand) and Vietnam vied for control over Cambodia by the use of military occupations and puppet regimes. In 1863, France intervened, and Cambodia became a French colony under the Franco-Cambodian Treaty, which gave France exclusive control of foreign affairs and defense. A French *résident supérieur* was installed in Phnom Penh, and control of the country was exercised through a hierarchy of *résidents*, with the king as a powerless figurehead. The protectorate was not unopposed. Minor revolts in the 1860s and 1870s were put down with ease. After 1887 Cambodia became part of the Indochina Union, which included Annam, Tonkin, Cochin China, Laos, and Chanchiang.

France's primary interest in Cambodia was strategic—protection of French interests in Southeast Asia. Traditional political and social structures were left largely intact, although the French attempted a few economic reforms and introduced some cultural changes, especially social customs and education and architectural patterns. Debt slavery was abolished in 1884. From the 1920s secular education was entirely French in character and structure. At the same time, the French exhibited little interest in providing Cambodians with education beyond the primary level and did little to train Cambodians for administrative positions of responsibility. Although modern judicial and police systems were introduced, the French relied on the Vietnamese to staff them. Only after 1936 were Cambodians admitted to senior administrative positions.

France granted total independence to Cambodia in 1953. At that time the nation was led by King Norodom Sihanouk, who had been the reigning monarch since April 1941, when at the age of 18 he succeeded his grandfather. Eight years later, he personally negotiated independence. In order to increase his political role, Sihanouk abdicated in 1955 in favor of his father, Norodom Suramarit, and resumed his title of prince. Sihanouk established a mass political movement, Sangkum Reastr Niyum (People's Socialist Community), which won all National Assembly seats in elections held in 1955, 1958, 1962, and 1966. Sihanouk's government established close ties with North Vietnam and the People's Republic of China and opposed U.S. intervention in Asia. In June 1960 parliament elected Sihanouk head of state following the death of King Suramarit.

Beginning in 1964, the Khmer Rouge, a pro-communist insurgency movement, threatened the stability of Sihanouk's government. However, it was a conservative group led by prime minister Lon Nol that deposed Sihanouk in March 1970 and abolished the monarchy. In exile Sihanouk established the Royal Government of National Union of Cambodia (GRUNC), which was supported by the Khmer Rouge. Together the two groups, with the aid of North Vietnamese troops and South Vietnam's National Liberation Front, posed a serious threat to Lon Nol's government. Nevertheless, Lon Nol proclaimed the Khmer Republic in 1970. He was elected the first president of the republic in 1972 with U.S. and South Vietnamese support.

The GRUNC government of Sihanouk was recognized as the official government of Cambodia by several foreign nations in 1973, and its forces, along with those of the Khmer Rouge, prevented Lon Nol's government from controlling more than a few urban areas. By April 1975 the Khmer Rouge had taken control of Phnom Penh, and a regime headed by Pol Pot took power. The country was renamed Democratic Kampuchea in January 1976. The Khmer Rouge administered a radical and brutal program of social change, evacuating many of the towns and forcibly relocating residents to rural areas. Millions of Cambodians were tortured and murdered by the Khmer regime, and millions of others died from mistreatment, hunger, and disease as the Khmer Rouge tried to eradicate all Western influence from the country and to create a totally rural society.

In December 1978 Vietnam invaded Kampuchea with the assistance of the pro-communist Kampuchean National United Front for National Salvation (KNUFNS), using the murderous nature of the Khmer regime as its excuse. Within weeks Vietnamese troops had taken control of Phnom Penh, and in January 1979 the People's Republic of Kampuchea (PRK) was proclaimed under a puppet regime headed by Heng Samrin. However, pockets of Khmer resistance remained until the organization finally surrendered in 1998.

The Vietnamese occupied Cambodia for most of the 1980s, pulling out only in 1989. They restored much of Cambodian life, including Buddhism, but the country remained desperately poor and underdeveloped.

In 1991 all the parties involved signed a treaty calling for the United Nations and a Supreme National Council to govern the country temporarily, and Sihanouk temporarily assumed the office of president. In May 1993 the first democratic elections in Cambodia since 1972 were held, and Sihanouk's royalist party formed a coalition government with Hun Sen's Khmer People's National Liberation Front. A new constitution was approved in September 1993; the country was renamed the Kingdom of Cambodia, and Sihanouk once again took the throne. The new government was opposed by the Khmer Rouge, which continued to use armed violence in its struggle to regain power. A splinter faction within the Khmer Rouge announced its support for the monarch in 1996, however, and the Khmer Rouge rapidly lost public support after that, although it continued its armed opposition to the government until the last known unit surrendered to the government in December 1998.

In 1997 Hun Sen, co–prime minister in the Sihanouk government, staged a violent coup, ousting his rival, Prince Norodom Ranariddh, the king's son. Hun Sen party won the parliamentary elections held in July 1998, and he was sworn in as prime minister in November 1998. Pol Pot was arrested and convicted in a show trial in 1997; he died while under house arrest in 1998. Sihanouk, except for a brief abdication in 1997, remained king, although he had little power.

CONSTITUTION

Under the constitution approved in 1993, Cambodia is a multiparty liberal democracy under a constitutional monarchy. The monarch is advised by a Council of

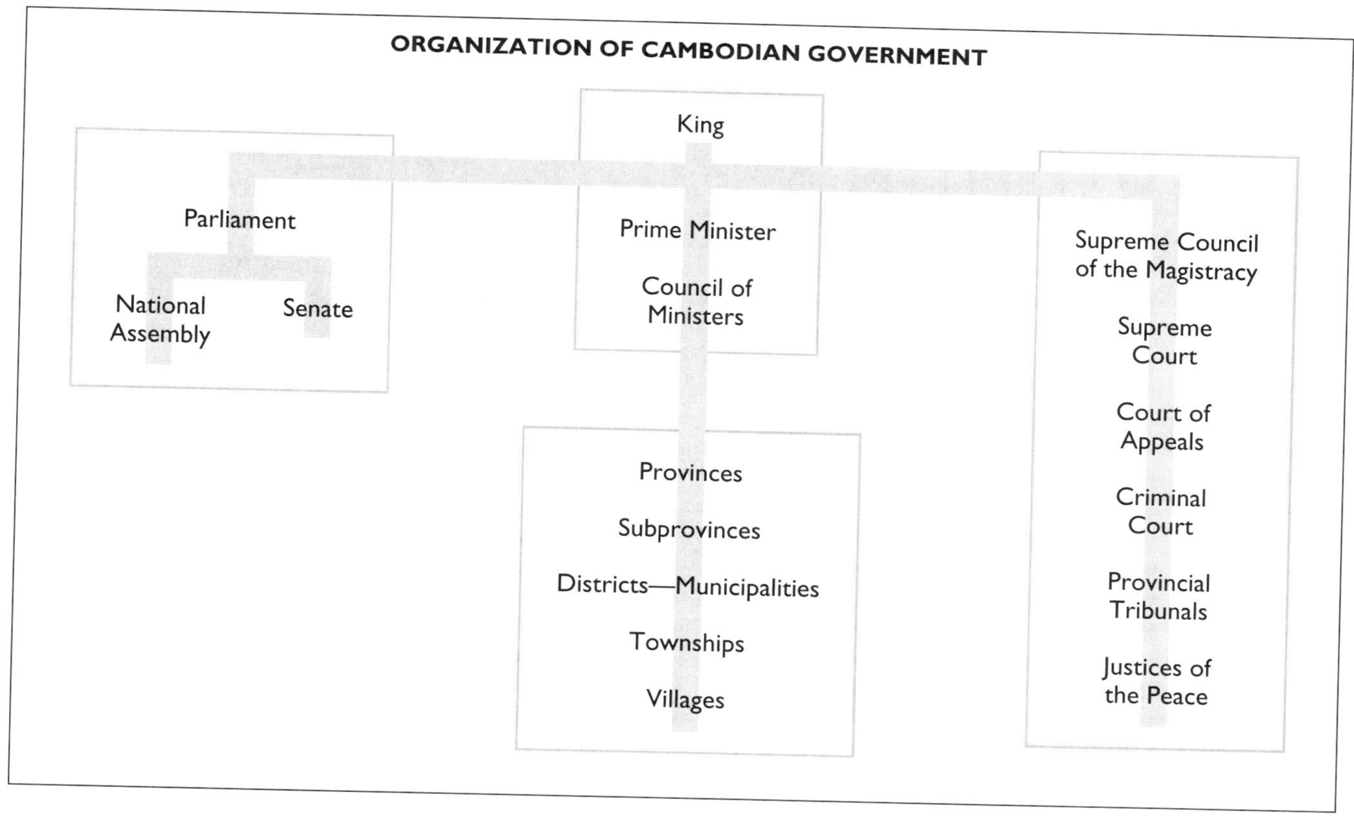

Ministers, which he appoints, but in practice, he has little power, and the first and second prime ministers are the true heads of state. There is universal suffrage for those age 18 and up.

LOCAL GOVERNMENT

Cambodia is divided for administrative purposes into five levels of government: 21 provinces (*khet*), each headed by a *chauvaykhet*; seven subprovinces (*anoukhet*); 147 districts (*srok*), each headed by a *chavausrok,* 1,200 townships (*sangkat* or *khum*), each headed by a *mekhum*, and villages (*phoumi*). Phnom Penh is an autonomous municipality with the status of a province, as are also Kirirom and Kompong Som.

Local Government

Principal administrative divisions, capitals, area, population

AREA AND POPULATION

Provinces	Capitals	area sq mi	sq km	population 1997 estimate
Baneay Mean Chealy	—	3	3	3
Baittambang	Baittambang	7,353	19,044	837,000
Kompong Cham	Kompong Cham	4,053	10,498	1,244,000
Kampong Chinang	Kampong Chinang	2,131	5,520	257,000
Kampong Spoe	Kampong Spoe	2,709	7,016	396,000
Kampong Thum	Kampong Thum	4,730	12,251	441,000
Kampot	Kampot	3,808	9,862	412,000
Kandal	—	1,472	3,813	838,000
Kaoh Kong	Krong Kaoh Kong	4,301	11,140	30,000
Kracheh	Kracheh	4,283	11,094	182,000
Mondoi Kiri	Senmonorom	5,517	14,288	18,000
Ordar Mean Cheay	—	—	—	—
Pouthsatndi	Pouthsat	4,900	12,692	204,000
Preah Vihear	Phnum Tbeng Mean Cheay	5,541	14,350	80,000
Prey Veng	Prey Veng	1,885	4,883	782,000
Rotanah Kiri	Lumphat	4,163	10,782	52,000
Siemreab	Siemreab	4,207	10,897	555,000
Sioeng Treng	Sioeng Treng	4,328	11,209	46,000
Svay Rieng	Svay Rieng	1,145	2,966	340,000
Takev	Takev	1,474	3,818	618,000
Municipalities				
TOTAL LAND AREA		68,045	176,238	
Phonm Penh		18	46	564,000
Preah Seihanu		27	69	61,000
Keb		—	—	—
INLAND WATER		2,192	5,678	
TOTAL		70,238	181,916	7,957,000

PARLIAMENT

Legislative power is vested in the bicameral parliament (Sepiacheat), consisting of a Senate (Pritsepia) made up of 61 members serving five-year terms and a National Assembly (Radsphea Ney Preah Recheanachakr) of 120 members elected for five-year terms. It meets in ordinary session at least twice a year, each session lasting at least two months. Extraordinary sessions may be convoked by the king at the request of the prime minister or by a majority in the National Assembly. Laws passed by parliament are subject to review by the Constitutional Council, which also has the right to interpret the constitution and settle electoral disputes. The National Assembly may not be dissolved unless the royal government has been dismissed twice within 12 months. The National Assembly may dismiss cabinet ministers or remove the royal government from office through a censure motion passed by two-thirds majority vote.

POLITICAL PARTIES

The dominant political parties are the National United Front for an Independent, Neutral, Peaceful, and Cooperative Cambodia (FUNCINPEC), the royalist party; the Cambodian People's Party (CPP); and the Sam Rainsi Party, previously the Khmer Nation Party, now named for a former finance minister who is the party head and leader of the opposition.

Political Parties

Cambodian People's Party, 1991
FUNCINPEC (United National Front for an Independent, Neutral, Peaceful and Cooperative Cambodia), 1989
Sam Rainsy Party, 1998
Buddhist Liberal Democratic Party, 1992
Cambodian National Unity Party, 1992
Khmer Nation Party, 1995, the former Communist Khmer
Rouge Party
Khmer Nation Party
National Liberation Movement of Kampuchea
Neutral Khmer Party
New Society Party, 1998
Populism Party, 1998
Son Sann Party

Political Parties: Strength in Parliament Most Recent Elections

National Assembly (Radhsphea Ney Reah Rcheanachakr). The current 122-member National Assembly was elected on July 26, 1998. Using a complicated seat allocation system, the National Election Commission officially awarded seats on August 5 as follows: Cambodian People's Party, 64; FUNCINPEC Party, 43; Sam Rainsy Party, 15. Thus no party achieved the two-thirds majority needed to form a government independently. In late December 30 cabinet ministers and other officials of the CPP-FP coalition government resigned their Assembly seats, arguing that they could not perform their executive and legislative duties simultaneously. The vacancies were immediately filed by other members of their parties.

LEGAL SYSTEM

A Supreme Court of the Magistracy, Cambodia's highest court, was created in 1997. A Supreme Court and lower courts handle cases at lower levels.

LAW ENFORCEMENT

Law Enforcement

Offenses reported to the police per 100,000: —
Murder: —
Assault: —
Burglary: —
Automobile Theft: —
Population per Police officer: 1,980
Death Penalty: Abolished 1989

HUMAN RIGHTS

During the years of the Khmer Rouge domination, Cambodians suffered under one of the most brutal, murderous, and totalitarian of governments. When the Vietnamese ousted Pol Pot, despite some liberalization, violations of human rights remained commonplace, with the provisions of the 1981 constitution ignored and police-state policies the rule.

The administration of justice in Cambodia is still problematic. Two human rights activists who were monitoring demonstrations in 1998 that developed in the wake of a revelation about dumping of toxic waste at a site in Sihanoukville were arrested and accused of inciting to riot. After international protests, the charges were dropped in July 1999. Other concerns about Cambodia's commitment to the balanced administration of justice have been raised in connection with efforts to bring to justice former members of the Khmer Rouge and those responsible for the murders of many associates of Prince Norodom Ranariddh in the months after the 1997 coup by Son Sann.

FOREIGN POLICY

Cambodia is a member of the United Nations. Its seat at the UN was left vacant by the General Assembly after the 1997 coup but is now taken by a representative of the new coalition government that took office in November 1998.

Cambodia is embroiled in border disputes with Vietnam and with Thailand. It is also under international pressure for money laundering and because it is a major producer of marijuana for the international market.

Land mine clearing operations have been under way in Cambodia since 1993, but land mines continue to be a major problem; an estimated 3,600 sq km (1,440 sq mi) of the country are believed to be mined, and several hundred people are maimed by mines each month. The United Nations estimates that there are still 6 million land mines buried in Cambodia.

DEFENSE

Military Indicators

Total Active Duty Personnel: 140,500
Military Manpower per 1,000: 13.5
Military Expenditures $: 90 million
- as % of GNP: 3.1
- per capita $: 9
- as % of central government expenditures: 16.7

Arms Imports $million: 20
Arms Exports $million: 0

ECONOMY

Cambodia's economy is based on agriculture, with rice the major crop. The national budget for 1995 was estimated to be $496 million. Although both the agricultural and the small manufacturing sectors have begun to recover from the disastrous years of warfare and social dislocation, the country remains among the world's poorest; gross domestic product in 1996 was estimated at $7.7 billion, and per capital gross domestic product was estimated to be approximately $710. Approximately 80 percent of the labor force is employed in agriculture.

Exports in 1996 were valued at $466 million; imports were $1.4 billion. Most foreign trade is with Singapore, Thailand, and Vietnam. The unit of currency is the new riel.

In 1999, the first full year of peace in 30 years, progress was made on economic reforms, and growth resumed at 4 percent. GDP growth for 2000 had been projected to reach 5.5 percent, but the worst flooding in 70 years severely damaged agricultural crops, and high oil prices hurt industrial production. Growth for the year is estimated at only 4 percent. Tourism is Cambodia's fastest-growing industry, with arrivals up 34 percent in 2000. The long-term development of the economy after decades of war remains a daunting challenge. The population lacks education and productive skills, particularly in the poverty-ridden countryside, which suffers from an almost total lack of basic infrastructure. Fear of renewed political instability and corruption within the government discourage foreign investment and delay foreign aid. On the brighter side, the government is addressing these issues with assistance from bilateral and multilateral donors.

Principal Economic Indicators

Gross National Product: $3.162 billion
GNP per capita: $300
GNP Average Annual Growth Rate (1990–97) %: 2.7
GNP per capita Average Annual Growth Rate (1990–97) %: 0.0
Origin of Gross Domestic Product %
- Agriculture: 51.0
- Mining: —
- Manufacturing: 5
- Construction: 8
- Public Utilities: 1
- Transportation and Communications: 30
- Trade: 15
- Financial Services: 13
- Other Services: 13
- Government: 4

Gross Domestic Product by Type of Expenditure %
- Private Consumption: 83
- Government Consumption: 11
- Gross Domestic Investment: 19
- Foreign Trade: Exports: 11
- Imports: −25

% of Income Received by Poorest 20%: —
% of Income Received by Richest 10%: —

Price and earnings indexes (1995 = 100)

	1992	1993	1994	1995	1996	1997	1998
Consumer price index	61.2	113.7	99.0	100.0	110.1	113.6	130.3
Earnings index	—	—	—	—	—	—	—

Finance

National Currency: New Riel (CR)
Exchange Rate: $1 = CR 3,537
Money Supply Stock in National Currency billion: 328,926
M1 per capita: 32,100
Central Bank Discount Rate %: 6.8
Total External Debt $million: 2,200
Debt Service Ratio %: 1.0

Balance of Payments $million: −209.9
International Reserves SDRs million: —
Ratio of External Debt to Total Reserves: —

Average Annual Rate of Inflation/Consumer Price Index Growth Rate %: 9.5

Official Development Assistance

ODA $: 337 million
- as % of GNP: 11.9
- per capita: $ 29
- Foreign Direct Investment $million: 121

Central Government Revenues and Expenditures

Fiscal Year: Calendar Year

Revenues $million: 261
Expenditures $million: 496
Budget Deficit/Surplus $: 235 million
Tax Revenues as % of GDP: —
Highest Tax Bracket %
Individual: 20
Corporate: 20

Employment and Labor

Economically Active Population: 4,010,000
Female Participation Rate %: 55.8
Activity Rate %: 43.1
Labor by Sector: %
Agriculture, Forestry, Fishing: 74.4
Manufacturing, Mining: 6.7
Construction: —
Transportation and Communications: —
Trade, Hotels, and Restaurants: —
Finance, Insurance, Real Estate: —
Public Administration, Defense: —
Services: 18.9

Unemployment %: NA

Agriculture

Agriculture's Share of GDP %: 51.0
Average Annual Rate of Growth (1965–98) %: —
Number of Farms 000: 840
Average Size of Farm ha: 3.6
Number of Tractors per 1,000 hectares: 0.4
Irrigation, % of Farms having: 4
Artificial Fertilizer kg/hectare: 1
Total Farmland as % of land area: 16.5
Livestock: Cattle 000: 2,900
Sheep 000: —
Hogs 000: 2,200
Chickens 000: 12,000
Forests: Production of Roundwood (000 cubic meters): 7,765
Fisheries: Total Catch tons 000: 103.2

Mining

% of GDP: 0.2
Value of Mineral Production $million: 4.4

Manufacturing

Value Added $million: 128
Industrial Production Growth Rate %: 7.0

Energy

Commercial Energy Production metric tons of oil equivalent 000: —
Commercial Energy Consumption metric tons of oil equivalent 000: —
Commercial Energy Consumption per capita kg: —
Average Annual Growth Rate 1980–97 %: —
Net Energy Imports % of use: —
Electricity Installed Capacity kW 000: 35
Production kW-hr million: 194
Coal Reserves tons million: —
Production tons 000: —
Natural Gas Proven Reserves cubic meters billion: —
Production cubic meters million: —
Crude Petroleum Reserves barrels million: —
Production barrels million: —
Consumption barrels million: —
Refinery Capacity barrels per day 000: —
Pipelines Length km: —

Foreign Trade

Imports $million: 403.9
Exports $million: 219.1
Export Volume % Annual Growth Rate (1990–97): —
Import Volume % Annual Growth Rate (1990–97): —
Balance of Trade $

Balance of trade (current prices)

	1991	1992	1993	1994	1995	1996
U.S.						
$000,000	−33.0	−86.0	−203.0	−275.0	−832.0	−395.0
% of total	7.1%	14.0%	31.7%	22.9%	19.1%	24.3%

Major Trading Partners

	Imports	Exports
European Union %	9.2	15.5
United States %	4.5	0.5
Eastern Europe %	2.5	0.5
Japan %	12.2	37.6
Others %	71.6	45.9

Transportation

Roads Total Length mi: 7,642 km 12,300
Paved %: 34
Automobiles: 42,210
Trucks and Buses: 9,005
Persons per vehicle: 197
Railroad; Track Length mi: 380 km 612
Passenger-mi million: 33.6
Freight-mi million: 6.9
Merchant Marine: No. of Vessels: 3
Total Deadweight Tonnage 000: 3.8
International Cargo Loaded tons 000: 11
International Cargo Off-loaded tons 000: 95
Airports with Scheduled Flights: 8
Traffic: Passenger-mi million: —
Freight-mi million: —
Length of Canals mi: 2,300 km 3,700

Tourism

Number of Tourists to 000: 576
Number of Tourists from 000: 41
Tourist Receipts $million: 100
Tourist Expenditures $million: 8

Communications

Telephones 000: 5.4
Cost of Local Calls 3 mins: $0.09
Cellular Telephones 000: 15
Fax Machines 000: 0.6
Personal Computers 000: —
Internet Hosts per million persons:
Mail: Post Offices: 30
  Pieces of Mail Handled million: 11
  Pieces of Mail Handled per person: 1.1

EDUCATION

Education is free and compulsory for children ages six to 12. The literacy rate was estimated in 1993 to be 65 percent. Approximately 1.5 million students were enrolled in the country's 4,500 elementary schools in the early 1990s. There are nine institutions of higher learning, with about 22,000 students enrolled in total.

Education

Literacy Rate %: 65.3
  Male %: 79.7
  Female %: 53.4
First Level: Primary schools: 4,539
  Teachers: 37,827
  Students: 1,703,316
  Student-Teacher Ratio: 45.0
  Net Enrollment Ratio: —
Second Level: Secondary Schools: 440
  Teachers: 16,349
  Students: 297,555
  Student-Teacher-Ratio: 18.2
  Net Enrollment Ratio: —

Vocational Level: Schools: 65
  Students: 16,356

Third Level: Institutions: 9
  Teachers: 784
  Students: 11,642
  Student-Ratio Level: 14.9
  Gross Enrollment Ratio: 1.6
  Students per 100,000: 119
  % of Population Age 25 and over with
  Postsecondary Education: —

Public Expenditure on Education as % of GDP: —

SCIENCE AND TECHNOLOGY

Science and Technology

Scientists and Engineers in R&D per 1
  million persons: —
Expenditures in R&D as % of GDP: —
High-Tech Exports $: —
Patent Applications by Residents: —

MEDIA AND CULTURE

The Cambodian print media consists of the following newspapers: *Cambodia Daily* in Khmer, Japanese, and English; *Cambodia Times*, weekly in English; *Phnom Penh Post*, daily in English; *Kampuchea*, weekly; *Pracheachon*, semiweekly; and *Rasmei Kampuchea*, daily. The Cambodian News Agency started functioning in 1978. The government-controlled National Radio of Cambodia, formerly the Voice of the Cambodian People, transmits over 11 stations.

Media

Daily Newspapers: —
  Total Circulation 000: —
  Circulation per 1,000: —
Books Published: —
Magazines: —
Radio Receivers 000: 1,500
  per 1,000: 150
Television sets 000: 80
  per 1,000: 8.0

MOST IMPORTANT MEDIA:

Press. The following newspapers circulate primarily at Phnom Penh: *Cambodia Daily*, in Khmer, Japanese, and English; *Cambodia Times*, weekly in English; *Kampuchea*, former KUFNCD weekly; *Phnom Penh Post*, daily in English; *Pracheachon* (The People), semiweekly CPP organ; *Rasmei Kampuchea*, pro-CPP daily.

News agencies. A Cambodian News Agency (Sapordamean Kampuchea) was established in late 1978.

Radio and television. The government-controlled National Radio of Cambodia (Vithyu Cheat Kampuchea), formerly known as the Voice of the Cambodian People, transmits over eleven stations. Clandestine broacasts by the Khmers Rouges ended in May 1998 when government forces captured their transitting antenna. Limited television service is offered via half a dozen government-dominated stations.

CULTURE

Cultural Indicators

Public Libraries
  Number: —
  Volumes: —
Registered borrowers: —
Museums
  Number: —
  Annual Attendance: —
Cinema
  Production of Long Films: —
  Number of Cinemas: —
  Seating Capacity: —
  Annual Attendance: —
  Annual Attendance per capita: —

STATUS OF WOMEN

In Khmer society, men have traditionally held positions of higher status than women. But women are gradually moving into mainstream Cambodian economic life, although traditional Cambodian culture calls for women to assume the vast bulk of child-rearing and other domestic responsibilities. The Cambodian Women Development Agency, a nongovernment-affiliated agency, is among those working to educate women about health, economic, and social issues and to help them improve their standing in society. Methods of birth control are generally well known, and are available to many women in the population. Divorce is legal and fairly easy to obtain, but not common.

Women

Gender Empowerment Measure: —
Seats Held in Parliament by Women %: 9.3
Female Administrators and Managers %: —
Female Professional and Technical Workers %: —
Women's Share of Earned Income %: —
Women in Government %: 5

HEALTH, FOOD, AND NUTRITION

Health

Number of Physicians: 5,642
Number of Dentists: 36
Number of Nurses: 9,950
Number of Pharmacists: 262
Population per Physician: 1,650
Number of Hospitals: 188
Hospital Beds per 10,000: 16
Hospital Bed Occupancy Rate: —
Infant Mortality Rate per 1,000 live births: 137
Maternal Mortality Rate per 100,000 live births: 900
Total Health Expenditures as % of GDP: —
Health Expenditures per capita $: —
HIV Infected % of adults: 2.40
Cigarette Consumption per smoker per year: 912
% of Smokers: Male: 70
Female: 10
Access to Safe Water %: 13

Food and Nutrition

Food Supply as % of FAO Requirements: 91
% of Consumption Expenditures on Food: —
Daily Available Calories per capita: 2,012
% of Total Calories derived from:
Cereals: 81.2
Potatoes, cassava: 1.7
Meat, poultry: 4.2
Fish: 0.8
Eggs, milk: 0.6
Fruits, vegetables: 2.9
Fats, oils: 3.9

ENVIRONMENT

The deforestation of Cambodia through illegal logging became an issue in the 1990s as the remnants of the Khmer Rouge sought profits from lumbering to support their operations. By the end of the decade, however, the Khmer Rouge no longer existed. Other environmental issues include the practice of strip mining for gems in the western region along the Thai border and soil erosion. An additional issue is the lack of safe drinking water in rural areas.

Environment

Forest Area sq km: 98,000
Average Annual Deforestation sq km: 1,638
Nationally Protected Areas as % of Total Land Area: 16.2
Freshwater Access cubic meters per capita: 41,407
Emissions of Organic Water Pollutants kg per day: 12,078
CO_2 Emissions per capita ton: 0.0

CHRONOLOGY

1953 Cambodia gains independence from the French.
1955 King Norodom Sihanouk becomes prime minister.
1970 Defense minister and premier Lon Nol leads a coup to oust Sihanouk; the U.S. military, at war with neighboring Vietnam, enters Cambodia in pursuit of Vietnamese communist guerrillas.
1975 The Khmer Rouge take over Cambodia, name Pol Pot the country's leader, and begin a forced evacuation of cities as part of a state experiment in agrarian communism.
1979 Vietnamese troops invade Cambodia, under the guise of opposing the Khmer Rouge regime.
1989 Vietnamese troops pull out of Cambodia.
1993 Elections are held for a new government; Prince Sihanouk resumes the throne at the head of a coalition government.
1997 Co–prime minister Hun Sen ousts his rival, Prince Norodom Ranariddh, in a coup.
1998 The last of the Khmer Rouge holdouts surrender to the government; Pol Pot dies while under house arrest, Hun Sen wins parliamentary elections and is sworn in as prime minister.
2001 The Senate passes a law requiring the creation of a tribunal to bring genocide charges against Khmer Rouge leaders.

BIBLIOGRAPHY

Chandler, David P. *The Land and People of Cambodia.* New York, 1991.

———. *The Tragedy of Cambodian History: Politics, War and Revolution since 1945*. New Haven, Conn., 1991.

———. *The History of Cambodia*. Boulder, Colo., 1992.

Ercheson, Craig. *The Rise and Demise of Democratic Kampuchea*. Boulder, Colo., 1984.

Peou, Serpong. *Conflict Neutralization in the Cambodian War: From Battle Field to Ballot Box*. Kuala Lumpur, 1997.

Pradhan, Bhagwan. *Super Powers and Non Alignment in Third World Conflicts: A Study of Kampuchea*. New Delhi, 1990.

Heder, Steven, and Judy Ledgerwood, eds. *Propaganda, Politics and Violence in Cambodia: Democratic Transition under United Nations Peacekeeping*. Armonk, N.Y., 1996.

Ross, Russell R. *Cambodia: A Country Study*. Washington, D.C., 1990.

Welaratna, Usha. *Beyond the Killing Fields: Voice of Nine Cambodia Survivors in America*. Stanford, Calif., 1993.

OFFICIAL PUBLICATIONS

Cambodia. *Cambodia: A Country Study* (1990); *Intersectoral Basic Needs Assessment Mission to Cambodia* (UNESCO; 1991); *Report of the Kampuchea Needs Assessment Study* (UNDP; 1989).

CONTACT INFORMATION

Embassy of Cambodia
4500 16th Street NW
Washington, D.C. 20011
Phone: (202) 726-7742 Fax: (202) 726-8381

INTERNET RESOURCES

- Cambodian Information Center
  http://www.cambodia.org
- Cambodian Women Development Agency Website
  www.bigpond.com/kh/users/cwda

CAMEROON

BASIC FACT SHEET

OFFICIAL NAME:
Republic of Cameroon (also Cameroun or Kamerun)

ABBREVIATION:
CM

CAPITAL:
Yaoundé

HEAD OF STATE:
President Paul Biya (from 1982)

HEAD OF GOVERNMENT:
Prime Minister Peter Mafany Musonge Mafani (from 1996)

NATURE OF GOVERNMENT:
Partial democracy

POPULATION:
15,456,000

AREA:
474,000 sq km (183,000 sq mi)

ETHNIC MAJORITY:
Approximately 200 ethnic groups

LANGUAGES:
French and English (official)

RELIGIONS:
Christianity, Islam, and animism

UNIT OF CURRENCY:
franc (C.F.A.F.)

NATIONAL FLAG:
Three vertical stripes, from left to right green, red, and yellow, with one yellow star in the middle of the red stripe.

NATIONAL EMBLEM:
A shield on which the principal element is a red triangle representing Mount Cameroon flanked by two inverted green triangles, each displaying a gold star. Within the red triangle is a golden map of Cameroon with a black upright sword balancing a pair of scales superimposed on it. Behind the shield are crossed golden fasces. On a scroll beneath appears the national motto *Paix, Travail, Patrie* (Peace, Work, Fatherland)

NATIONAL ANTHEM:
"O Cameroon, Thou Cradle of Our Fathers"

NATIONAL HOLIDAYS:
May 20 (National Day, Anniversary of the United Republic of Cameroon): January 1 (Independence Day); February 1 (Youth Day); May 1 (Labor Day); October 1 (Reunification Day); December 10 (Rights of Man Day); Christmas, Boxing Day, Good Friday, Easter Monday, Whit-Monday; also variable Islamic festivals

DATE OF INDEPENDENCE:
January 1, 1960

DATE OF CONSTITUTION:
May 20, 1972; revised January 1996

GEOGRAPHICAL FEATURES

Cameroon, known as the hinge of Africa, is in western-central Africa and extends like an irregular wedge northeastward from the Gulf of Guinea to Lake Chad. The total land area is 474,000 sq km (183,000 sq mi). The total length of international land borders is 4,450 km (2,765 mi), of which the longest is that with Nigeria (1,690 km; 1,050 mi). The other borders are with Chad (1,094 km; 679 mi), Central African Republic (797 km; 495 mi), Congo (523 km; 324 mi), Gabon (298 km; 185 mi), and Equatorial Guinea (189 km; 117 mi).

Cameroon is divided into four distinct topographical regions. In the south is a low coastal plain with equatorial rain forests and flat swamplands along its seaward edges. In the center of the country is an extensive savanna-covered plateau, known as the Adamaoua Plateau, extending from the eastern to the western border, with an average elevation of 1,370 m (4,500 ft). The western region is an area of mountainous forests and the site of

Cameroon

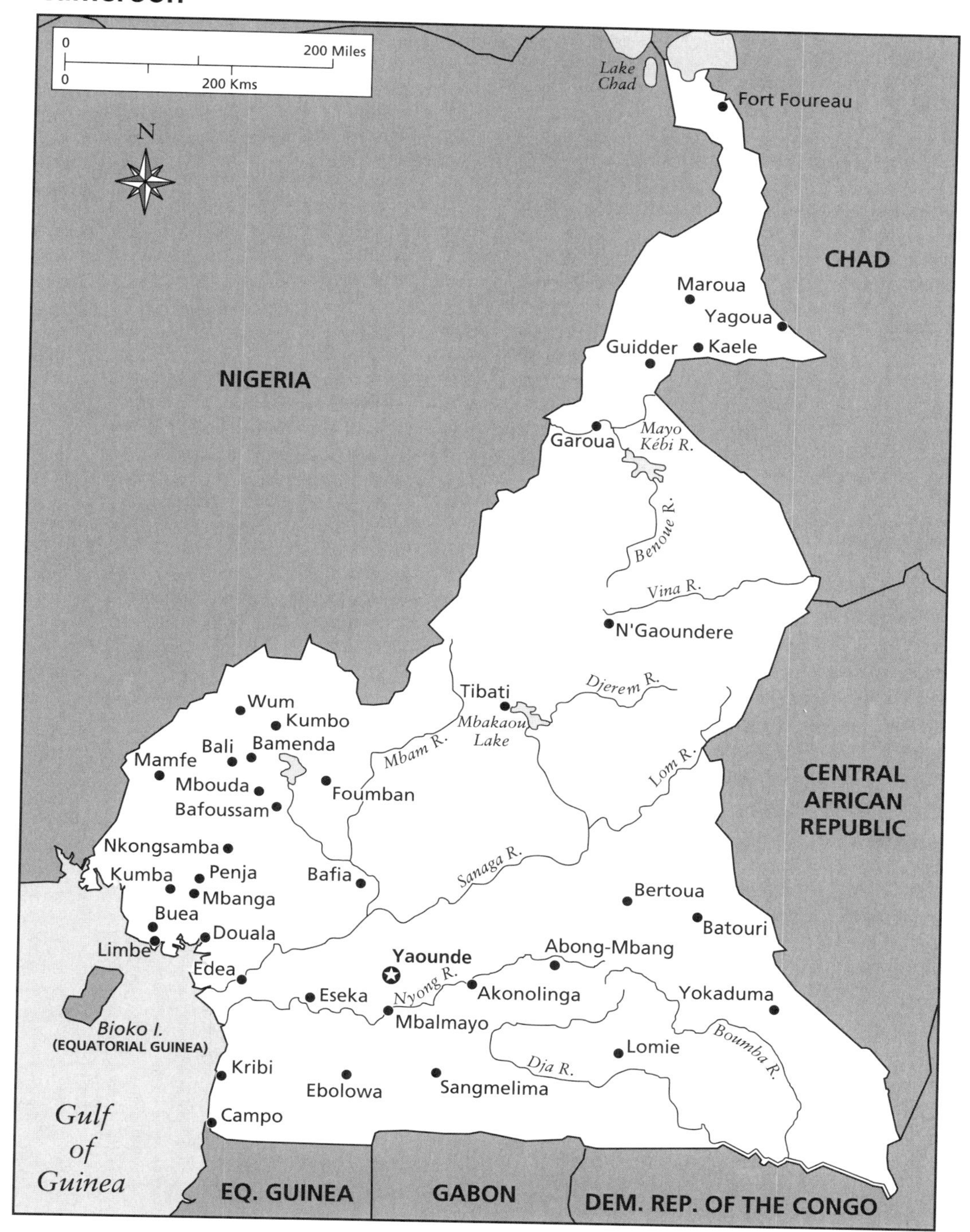

Mount Cameroon, a volcano that has been active on four occasions in this century and whose height of 4,069 m (13,350 ft) marks it as the highest peak in West Africa. Elsewhere in this region the elevations range from 1,524 m (5,000 ft) to 2,440 m (8,000 ft). The northern part of the country consists of a rolling subarid savanna sloping into a shallow inland basin.

Geography

Area sq km: 474,000 (183,000 sq mi)
World Rank: 53rd
Land Boundaries, km: Central African Republic 797; Chad 1094; Republic of the Congo 523; Equatorial Guinea 189; Gabon 298; Nigeria 1,690

(continued)

Coastline, km: 402
Elevation Extremes meters
Lowest: Atlantic Ocean 0
Highest: Fako 4,095
Land Use % Arable land: 13
Permanent Crops: 2
Permanent Pastures: 4
Forest and Woodland: 78
Other: 3

Population of Principal Cities (1992 est.)

Bafoussam	120,000
Bamenda	110,690
Douala	1,200,000
Garoua	160,000
Maroua	140,000
Yaoundé	800,000

CLIMATE AND WEATHER

The country exhibits a complete sequence of tropical climates, from equatorial in the south to Sahelian in the north. In the southern coastal region a wet equatorial climate prevails. There is no dry season and little daily variation in temperature or humidity. Temperatures range from an average daily low of 22°C (72°F) to 29°C (84°F), and the average humidity is 85 percent to 90 percent. Average annual rainfall ranges from 2,540 mm (100 in) to 4,010 mm (158 in). The western slopes of Mount Cameroon are among the wettest places in the world, receiving 6,096 mm (240 in) to 9,144 mm (360 in) of rainfall annually.

East and south of Yaoundé annual rainfall ranges from 1,524 mm (60 in) to 2,540 mm (100 in). Fluctuations in temperature and humidity are within narrower ranges, the average daily maximum temperature being 27.8°C (82°F) and the average daily minimum being 22.2°C (72°F).

In the transition zone of the high central plateau, elevation tends to moderate temperatures. At Ngaoundere daily maximums range from 27.8°C (82°F) in June during the rainy season to 35°C (95°F) in March at the end of the dry season, while the daily average is about 15.6°C (60°F) in the rainy season. Annual rainfall is about 1,524 mm (60 in), and the rainy season extends from April to October.

The northern plains are tropical, hot, and dry, with the rainfall dropping to 600 mm (24 in) annually toward Lake Chad. The dry season becomes longer and increasingly severe, with the temperature rising to 47°C (116°F) at Marona in the extreme north. The daily variations in temperature may be as much as 10°C (50°F). Most of the rain falls during the five months from May to September; for the rest of the year the region is under the influence of the dry winds of the Sahara.

Climate and Weather

Mean Temperature
Southern Coastal Region: 72°F to 84°F
East and South of Yaoundé 72°F to 82°F
High Central Plateau 82°F to 95°F
Northern Plains: Up to 116°F
Average Rainfall:
Southern Coastal Region: 100 in to 158 in
Western Slope of Mount Cameroon 240 in to 360 in
East and South of Yaoundé: 60 in to 100 in
High Central Plateau: 60 in
Northern Plains: 24 in

POPULATION

Population Indicators

Total Population: 1999 15,456,000
World Rank: 58th
Density per sq mi: 84.2 (32.5 per sq km)
% of annual growth (1994–99): 2.9
Male %: 49.0
Female %: 51.0
Urban %: 38.3
Age Distribution: % 0–14: 46.4
15–29: 24.5
30–44: 14.6
45–59: 8.7
60–74: 4.1
75 and over: 1.6
Population 2020: 26,059,000
Birth Rate per 1,000: 39.3
Death Rate per 1,000: 11.9
Population Doubling Time (years): 25
Infant Mortality Rate per 1,000 live births: 58
Rate of Natural Increase per 1,000: 27.4
Total Fertility Rate: 5.3
Expectation of Life (years): Males 54.5
Females 57.2
Marriage Rate per 1,000: —
Divorce Rate per 1,000: —
Total Number of Households: —
Average Size of Households: 5.2
% of Illegitimate Children: —
Induced Abortions: —
Rate per 100 live births: —

ETHNIC COMPOSITION

The ethnic composition of Cameroon is bewilderingly diverse. The country straddles the so-called Bantu Line, the northern limit of the Bantu peoples. In the south the Bantu stock dominates, with semi-Bantus prevailing to the north of them. Hamitic, Fulani, Arab Choas, and Sudanese Negroes predominate in the northern regions. Classification of the country's approximately 200 ethnic groups is extremely difficult, and in many cases ethnic affiliations and names have not been established.

Although numerically in the minority, the Fulani, descendants of Muslim conquerors of the 19th century, are the dominant group in the north and have retained their own political structure, composed of 21 lamidats (chiefdoms). The non-Muslim kirdi (pagan) peoples of the north have generally sided with the Fulani on political issues because of their long tradition of subservience to the latter. The Bamileke, also known as Grasslanders, dominate the cultural and economic life of the country. They hold 70 percent of the professional jobs and constitute 60 percent of the merchant class. The Doualas, after whom the country's principal port is named, are the most educated people in Cameroon and form the traditional elite in the coastal regions. The two other major ethnic groups are the Bassa and the Pahouin. Relations among all these groups are characterized by rivalry, suspicion, and hostility accentuated by regional, religious, and linguistic differences and memories of historic conflicts.

Ethnic aliens include more than 50,000 Africans, including Hausa and Ibo from Nigeria; Ewe from Ghana; and citizens of Benin, Central African Republic, Gabon, and Mauritania. There also are about 20,000 Europeans and North Americans in the country, including U.S., British, and French citizens, besides Canadians, Germans, Greeks, Cypriots, Syrians, and Lebanese. The Levantines control trade in the bush, and Europeans and North Americans control the major industries. Anti-Western feelings are not strong in the country.

LANGUAGES

The official languages of Cameroon are French and English. French is the dominant language, reflecting the French background of the ruling elite, drawn from the former East Cameroon. English is more widely spoken in the former West Cameroon

A number of local languages, such as Ful, or Fulfulde, in the north and Pahouin languages in the south, serve as lingua francas. Intergroup and interregional communication is through Wes Cos, a pidgin English that was developed during the slave trade and was popularized by missionaries.

Most of the peoples of the northern savanna speak Chadic languages, while the Moundang, Baya, and Douri speak Adamawa. Peoples of the south speak Bantu languages, of which Bamileke is the most important.

Principal Languages and Their Speakers

Chadic languages	
Buwai	300,000
Hausa	190,000
Kotoko	170,000
Mandara (Wandala)	880,000
Masana (Masa)	610,000
English	7,700,000
French	4,600,000
Niger-Congo languages	
Adamawa-Ubangi languages	
Baya (Gbaya)	190,000
Chamba	370,000
Mbum	200,000
Atlantic languages	
Fula (Fulani)	1,480,000
Benue-Congo languages	
Bamileke (Medumba)-Widikum (Moghamo)-Bamum (Mum)	2,870,000
Basa (Bassa)	170,000
Duala	1,690,000
Fang (Pangwe)-Beti-Bulu	3,040,000
Ibibio (Efik)	20,000
Igbo	90,000
Jukun	100,000
Lundu	420,000
Maka	760,000
Tikar	1,150,000
Tiv	400,000
Wute	50,000
Saharan languages	
Kanuri	50,000
Semitic languages	
Arabic	150,000
Other	120,000

RELIGIONS

Cameroon has no official religion. Animists constitute 26 percent of the population, Christians 52 percent, and Muslims 22 percent. In general, Christianity dominates in the south and Islam in the north. The main Christian tribes are the Pahouin, Douala, and Bamileke, while the main Muslim tribes are the Fulani, Koloko, Mousgoum, Mandara, and Bamoun. The Roman Catholic Church has an archbishopric at Yaoundé.

Religious Affiliations

Roman Catholic	5,370,000
Traditional beliefs	4,020,000
Muslim	3,370,000
Protestant	2,700,000

HISTORICAL BACKGROUND

Little is known of Cameroon prior to the arrival of the Portuguese in 1472. Bantu-speaking people arrived in the south in the first millennium B.C.E. Fulani pastoralists migrated to the north in the 16th century. Like most of the Atlantic seaboard of Africa, Cameroon served as an important stop on the slave trade. Today it is estimated that 200 distinct ethnic groups live in Cameroon, although most did not settle in the region until the late 18th and early 19th centuries. When the Germans arrived in the late 19th century, the northern portion of the country was under the control of the Islamic Fulani Empire.

Cameroon was under three Western colonial powers after 1884. All of Cameroon, or Kamerun, as it was then known, was a German protectorate until 1916. In 1919 the country was divided between the French and the English, with the larger eastern sector going to France. French Cameroon achieved independence in 1960 as the Republic of Cameroon. The British held a plebiscite in West Cameroon in 1961 under U.S. auspices, as a result of which the northern half opted to join Nigeria and the southern half voted to unite with the Republic of Cameroon as the Federal Republic of Cameroon.

Cameroon established a federal form of government with Ahmadou Ahidjo as president; he had served as prime minister before independence. Under his direction, regional political parties were merged into the Cameroon National Union (UNC), formed in 1966. The federal structure, originally developed to meet the problems created by the nation's tribal, religious, and ethnic diversity, was also phased out and abandoned in 1972 when a new constitution created a unitary state. Ahidjo was reelected in 1965, 1970, 1975, and 1980. He stepped down unexpectedly in 1982 and was succeeded by Prime Minister Paul Biya. Biya was reelected without opposition in 1984 and 1988.

In an effort to promote national unity, the UNC was restructured in 1985. At that time it also was renamed the Cameroon People's Democratic Movement (RDPC). Independents were permitted to run in that year's elections, but a return to multiple parties was not envisioned. Biya survived two coup attempts by the military in 1983 and 1984. By 1990, the people of Cameroon seemed to have had enough of Biya. More than 30 new political parties formed and strikes were called when Biya refused to call elections in 1991.

Giving into political pressure, Biya called for elections and several opposition parties were able to garner enough of the vote to form the government with Simon Achidi Achu as prime minister. However, later in 1992, Biya won reelection as the country's president. In 1997, Biya won reelection again under the newly expanded seven-year presidential term. The election was boycotted by main opposition parties.

CONSTITUTION

The constitution of 1972, as amended in 1975 and 1996, is the country's third basic document since 1960. It established a democratic and secular republic and radically altered the structure of power and government. It provided for a new unitary state headed by a strong executive. The National Assembly replaced the former Federal Assembly and the regional assemblies. It reaffirmed Cameroon's adherence to the Universal Declaration of Human Rights and specifically guaranteed freedom of religion, speech, press, movement, assembly, and association, as well as freedom from arbitrary arrest and discrimination and the right to hold private property. Finally, it barred any amendment to the constitution that would impair its democratic character or the unity and territorial integrity of the state.

National executive authority is vested in the president. He is elected by direct popular vote and may seek reelection for any number of terms. He serves as head of the

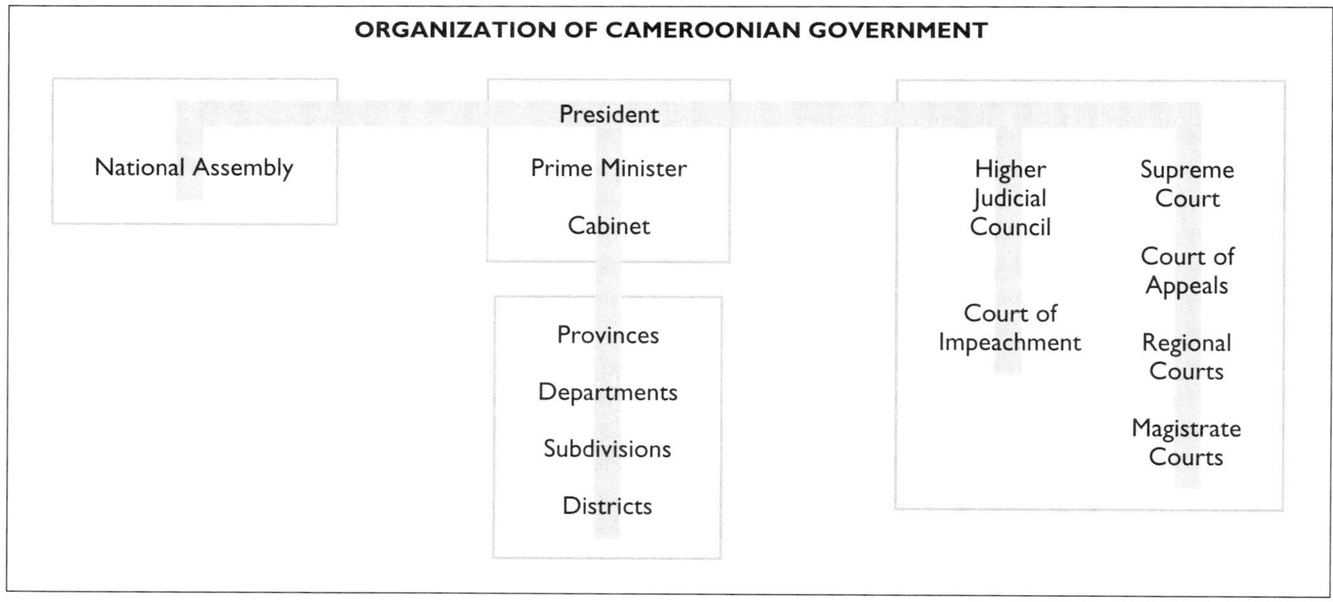

armed forces and can negotiate and ratify treaties without the concurrence of the National Assembly. He also can declare states of emergency and states of siege, when he may temporarily suspend civil rights and assume absolute powers. The members of the cabinet are appointed, and they are assigned duties by the president and are responsible only to him.

Although the office was not specifically provided for in the constitution, a prime minister was appointed in 1975 as head of a reorganized cabinet. In 1979 a constitutional amendment was passed incorporating the office of the prime minister and defining his status. The office of the prime minister was abolished in 1983 and reinstated in 1996. Cabinet members are not members of the legislature but of the civil service.

Since the creation of a single party in 1966, elections have been held on the basis of a single slate personally selected by the president. They serve only as occasions to demonstrate popular support for the government without offering real political choices to the electorate. Suffrage is universal over age 21.

LOCAL GOVERNMENT

For purposes of local government, Cameroon is divided into provinces, departments, departmental subdivisions, and districts. The provinces are supervised by a governor, the departments by a commissioner, subdivisions by a subcommissioner, and districts by a chief of district. All administrative officials are national civil servants responsible to the Ministry of the Interior.

At each level a chief administrative officer also is responsible for coordinating the work of the technical ministries within his territory. Development programs are coordinated by the Service for Rural Activation through provincial, departmental, and district development councils. The entire structure of regional government is supervised by the General Inspectorate of Administration.

Popular participation in regional government is channeled through elected communal councils, officially referred to as municipal councils, each representing a town, a rural area, or a mixed urban-rural area. A total of 126 municipal councils constitute the broadest local self-government structure in Francophone Africa. The councils levy taxes on produce and personal income and also receive back a portion of the national income taxes collected within their territories by the central government. The central government exercises close supervision over the councils through the mayors and the treasurers, both of whom are appointees of the Ministry of the Interior.

The primary areas of concern of the councils are education, health, and roads.

Local Government

Principal administrative divisions, capitals, area, population

AREA AND POPULATION

		area		population 1987
Regions	**Capitals**	**sq mi**	**sq km**	**census**
Adamoua	Ngaoundéré	24,591	63,691	495,200
Centre	Yaoundé	26,613	68,926	1,651,600
Est	Bertoua	42,089	109,011	517,200
Extrème-Nord	Maroua	13,223	34,246	1,855,700
Littoral	Douala	7,814	20,239	1,354,800
Nord	Garoua	25,319	65,576	832,200
Nord-Ouest	Bamenda	6,877	17,810	1,237,400
Ouest	Bafoussam	5,356	13,872	1,339,800
Sud	Ebolowa	18,189	47,110	373,800
Sud-Ouest	Buea	9,448	24,471	838,000
Land Area		179,519	464,952	
Inland Water		4,051	10,492	
TOTAL		183,569	475,442	10,495,700

PARLIAMENT

The National Assembly is a unicameral body consisting of 180 members elected by universal suffrage of those over age 21, for five-year terms. All members of the National Assembly belong to the Cameroon People's Democratic Movement (RDPC). Under the constitution specific areas of legislation are reserved to the National Assembly. These include civil rights; labor laws; civil, commercial, and property laws; civil and criminal codes; judicial organization; local government; national defense; currency; taxation and budgeting; education; and elections. Bills may be introduced either by the president of the republic or by any member of the National Assembly, which may override a veto of the president. The National Assembly may appoint commissions of inquiry on specific issues. The president of the republic may, after consultation with the National Assembly, submit certain propositions to national referenda. The National Assembly may empower the president of the republic to legislate by ordinance for a limited period.

The National Assembly meets twice a year; the duration of each session is limited to 30 days. However, the National Assembly may be recalled for an extraordinary session limited to 15 days.

The 1996 constitution calls for an upper chamber for the legislature, to be called a Senate, but it has yet to be established.

POLITICAL PARTIES

In the last elections held in 1997, 45 parties were represented by 3,000 candidates. Despite the large number of parties, the dominant Cameroon People's Democratic Movement, which from 1966 until 1990 was the only legal political party, under the leadership of Biya won an outright majority of the seats. The leading opposition party, the Social Democratic Front, won only 43 seats of 180 seats. Several other parties, including the Union Nationale pour la Démocratie et le Progrès (UNDP), won 13 seats and the Union Démocratique du Cameroun (UDC) won five seats.

Political Parties

Democratic Rally of the Cameroon People, 1966
National Union for Democracy and Progress, 1991
Cameroon People's Union, 1948
Social Democratic Front, 1990
Cameroonian Democratic Union, 1991
Movement for the Defense of the Republic, 1992
Cameroon National Party
Social Movement for the New Democracy, 1991
Allies' Front for Change, 1994
Liberal Democratic Party, 1991
Union of Democratic Forces of Cameroon
Movement for Democracy and Progress
Liberal Democratic Alliance, 1993
Cameroonian Party of Democrats
United Workers' Party
Movement for the Liberation of Cameroonian Youth
Action for Meritocracy and Equal Opportunity Party
Integral Democracy of Cameroon

Political Parties: Strength in Parliament Most Recent Elections

Following the May 17, 1997, balloting, the seats were distributed as follows (1992 figures are in parentheses): the Democratic Rally of the Cameroon People, 109 (88); the Social Democratic Front, 43 (0); the National Union for Democracy and Progress, 13 (68); the Cameroonian Democratic Union, 5 (0); the Movement for Democracy and the Republic, 1 (6); the Movement for the Liberation of Cameroonian Youth, 1 (0). Results for seven seats were nullified by the Supreme Court, and at new polling in early August the Democratic Rally secured all of the contested seats raising its total to 116.

LEGAL SYSTEM

The law of Cameroon is based primarily on the French Civil Code, with elements derived from British and local customary law. The court system consists of the Supreme Court, appeals courts, regional courts, and magistrates' courts. The duties of the Supreme Court are divided into two major parts, and its composition varies accordingly. The regular Supreme Court gives final judgment on appeals from decisions of appeals courts, while the expanded Supreme Court decides on the constitutionality of laws at the request of the president of the republic. The constitution also provides for a court of impeachment to try state officials for conspiracy against national security. The independence of the judiciary and its integrity are monitored by the Higher Judicial Council, whose concurrence is mandatory for appointments to the bench, which are made by the president.

LAW ENFORCEMENT

Law Enforcement

Offenses reported to the police per 100,000: 11
- Murder: 0.1
- Assault: 0.1
- Burglary: 1.2
- Automobile Theft: 0.2
- Population per Police officer: 1,170

Death Penalty: Yes.

HUMAN RIGHTS

In terms of civil and political rights Cameroon is ranked as a nation that is not free. Cameroon is an authoritarian state where political liberties are circumscribed. At the same time, Cameroon has managed to enjoy political stability and economic and social progress despite the ever-present threat of ethnic factionalism. As the only African state to fuse British and French traditions, Cameroon promotes national unity as its primary objective. To this end it has subordinated regional interests to the development of national institutions. As the threat of internal divisions has receded, some measure of civil liberties has been introduced into the political system.

Amnesty International has reported allegations of harsh prison conditions, ill treatment of detainees, unnecessary use of force, and even torture by the police, especially during interrogation and apprehension of suspects. Although habeas corpus is in effect, persons may be held in "administrative detention" under legislation relating to subversion. Cameroonian law guarantees criminal defendants a fair public trial, including legal representation at state expense. Courts are independent of executive and military control.

Except for independent weeklies in Douala, Limbe, and Bamenda, the Cameroonian radio and press is government owned and government controlled. Criticism of the government is discouraged, and the media are used as mouthpieces of the government. News reporters are often harassed and intimidated by the constant threat of censorship.

Freedoms of assembly and association are restricted by law and in practice.

Freedom of movement within the country is hampered by frequent police checkpoints, where travelers must produce identity cards and tax receipts.

FOREIGN POLICY

Cameroon, like Senegal, is one of the more Francophile states in Africa and ties with France are especially strong. On the other hand, Cameroon has disputes with almost all its neighbors. The civil war in Chad resulted in the influx of some 100,000 refugees into Cameroon's northern provinces. Cameroon was forced to evacuate 10,000 of its nationals from Gabon following a sports-related riot. Border conflicts with Nigeria have been more serious. In 1981 it led to a seven-month suspension of diplomatic relations. In 1993 it came to armed conflict. The matter was adjudicated by the International Court of Justice and the Organization of African Unity. In 1995 Cameroon was granted membership in the Commonwealth, which reflected the status of the western region as a former British colony.

DEFENSE

The defense structure is headed by the president; the line of command runs through the minister of defense to the commanders of the four military zones—central, north, west, and coastal—with regional headquarters at Yaoundé, Kutuba, Douala, and Battoussam, respectively.

Manpower is provided by volunteers, but all men are required to be registered for military service at age 18. Enlistment is for seven years, after which veterans are placed in on-call reserve status for 20 years. The armed forces have a high rate of literacy—60 percent—and are indoctrinated in the new national ideology. In addition to the regular army, there are 4,000 paramilitary troops.

Cameroon faces no external threat from its neighbors; therefore, its armed forces are designed for internal peacekeeping only. The armed forces have no offensive capability and have limited equipment and firepower. The air force is dependent on French personnel and supplies. The army has not yet seen field combat, but it was employed until 1970 in quelling internal dissident movements.

Military Indicators

Total Active Duty Personnel: 13,100
Military Manpower per 1,000: 0.9
Military Expenditures $: 102 million
- as % of GNP: 1.9
- per capita $: 8
- as % of central government expenditures: 10.2

Arms Imports $million: 10
Arms Exports $milliion: 0

ECONOMY

Because of its oil resources and favorable agricultural conditions, Cameroon has one of the best-endowed primary commodity economies in sub-Saharan Africa. Still, it faces many of the serious problems facing other underdeveloped countries, such as a top-heavy civil service and a generally unfavorable climate for business enterprise. Since 1990, the government has embarked on various IMF and World Bank programs designed to spur business investment, increase efficiency in agriculture, improve trade, and recapitalize the nation's banks. In June 2000, the government completed an IMF-sponsored, three-year structural adjustment program; however, the IMF is pressing for more reforms, including increased budget transparency and privatization. Higher oil prices in 2000 helped offset the country's lower cocoa export revenues. A rebound in the cocoa market should increase growth to more than 5 percent in 2001.

Principal Economic Indicators

Gross National Product: $8.610 billion
GNP per capita: $620
GNP Average Annual Growth Rate (1990–97) %: −3.3
GNP per capita Average Annual Growth Rate (1990–97) %: −6.1
Origin of Gross Domestic Product %
- Agriculture: 39
- Mining: 9
- Manufacturing: 10
- Construction: 2
- Public Utilities: 2
- Transportation and Communications: 24
- Trade: 24
- Financial Services: 24
- Other Services: 24
- Government: 13

Gross Domestic Product by Type of Expenditure %
- Private Consumption: 72
- Government Consumption: 8
- Gross Domestic Investment: 16
- Foreign Trade: Exports: 28
- Imports: −23

% of Income Received by Poorest 20%: —
% of Income Received by Richest 10%: —

Price and earnings indexes (1995 = 100)

	1992	1993	1994	1995	1996	1997
Consumer price index	67.1	65.0	87.8	100.0	104.7	106.3
Earnings index	—	—	—	—	—	—

Finance

National Currency: CFA Franc (CFAF)
Exchange Rate: $1 = CFAF 608.36
Money Supply Stock in National Currency billion: 319.2
M1 per capita: 22,700
Central Bank Discount Rate %: 7.60
Total External Debt $: 10 billion
Debt Service Ratio %: 16.8

Balance of Payments $: −101.1 million
International Reserves SDRs: 2 million
Ratio of External Debt to Total Reserves: 1,355.7

Average Annual Rate of Inflation/Consumer Price Index Growth Rate %: 3

Official Development Assistance

ODA: $424 million
as % of GNP: 5.1
per capita: $30
Foreign Direct Investment $: 50 million

Central Government Revenues and Expenditures

Fiscal Year: 1 July–30 June

Revenues $: 2.23 billion
Expenditures $: 2.23 billion
Budget Deficit $: 0.0
Tax Revenues as % of GDP: 13
Highest Tax Bracket %
Individual: 60
Corporate: 39

Employment and Labor

Economically Active Population: 4,740,000
Female Participation Rate %: 33.2
Activity Rate %: 40
Labor by Sector: %
Agriculture, Forestry, Fishing: 60.3
Manufacturing, Mining: 13.2
Construction: —
Transportation and Communications: —
Trade, Hotels, and Restaurants: —
Finance, Insurance, Real Estate: —
Public Administration, Defense: —
Services: 26.5
Unemployment %: NA

Agriculture

Agriculture's Share of GDP %: 39
Average Annual Rate of Growth (1965–98) %: 3.3
Number of Farms 000: 926
Average Size of Farm ha: 1.6
Number of Tractors per 1,000 hectares: 0.1
Irrigation, % of Farms having: 0.3
Artificial Fertilizer kg/hectare: 6.0
Total Cropland as % of Farmland: 100
Livestock: Cattle 000: 5,900
Sheep 000: 3,800
Hogs 000: 1,410
Chickens 000: 20,000
Forests: Production of Roundwood (000 cubic meters): 15,710
Fisheries: Total Catch tons: 66,000

Mining

% of GDP: 7.3
Value of Mineral Production $: 681.6 million

Manufacturing

Value Added $: 470 million
Industrial Production Growth Rate %: NA

Energy

Commercial Energy Production metric tons of oil equivalent: 11,250,000
Commercial Energy Consumption metric tons of oil equivalent: 5,756,000
Commercial Energy Consumption per capita kg: 413
Average Annual Growth Rate 1980–97 %: −0.5
Net Energy Imports % of use: −95
Electricity Installed Capacity kW: 627,000
Production kW-hr: 2,746 million
Coal Reserves tons: —
Production tons: 1,000
Natural Gas Proven Reserves cubic meters: 110 billion
Production cubic meters: —
Crude Petroleum Reserves barrels: 400 million
Production barrels: 33 million
Consumption barrels: 9 million
Refinery Capacity barrels per day: 42,000
Pipelines Length km: —

Foreign Trade

Imports $: 1.204 billion
Exports $: 1.757 billion
Export Volume % Annual Growth Rate (1990–97): 1.6
Import Volume % Annual Growth Rate (1990–97): 2.5
Balance of Trade $

Balance of trade (current prices)

	1992	1993	1994	1995	1996	1997
CFAF 000,000,000	+179.3	+221.3	+223.7	+398.8	+277.5	+290.6
% of total	22.6%	26.2%	15.7%	24.4%	18.1%	15.6%

Major Trading Partners

	Imports	Exports
European Union %	53.4	77.4
United States %	8.5	2.3
Eastern Europe %	1.8	0.2
Japan %	5.0	0.8
Others %	31.3	19.3

Transportation

Roads Total Length mi: 21,300 (34,300 km)
Paved %: 13
Automobiles: 92,200
Trucks and Buses: 60,000
Persons per vehicle: 91
Railroad; Track Length mi: 686 (1,104 km)
Passenger-mi: 247 million
Freight-mi: 405 million
Merchant Marine: No. of Vessels: 47
Total Deadweight Tonnage: 39,800
International Cargo Loaded tons: 126,000
International Cargo Off-loaded tons: 2,328,000
Airports with Scheduled Flights: 5
Traffic: Passenger-mi: 196 million
Freight-mi: 27 million
Length of Canals mi: 1,299 (2090 km)

Tourism

Number of Tourists to: 135,000
Number of Tourists from: —
Tourist Receipts $: 47 million
Tourist Expenditures $: 225 million

Communications

Telephones 000: 608
Cost of Local Calls 3 mins: $0.06
Cellular Telephones 000: 2.8
Fax Machines 000: —
Personal Computers 000: —
Internet Hosts per million persons: —
Mail: Post Offices: 261
Pieces of Mail Handled: 5.3 million
Pieces of Mail Handled per person: 0.4

EDUCATION

Education is, in theory, universal, free, and compulsory from ages six to 11.

The academic year runs from September to June in the east and from October to June in the west. The medium of instruction is French in the east and English in the west. Pupils in the north and east spend one year longer at school than those in the Center, Coastal, and Western provinces.

Schooling consists of a 13-year cycle, including six years of primary school divided into preparatory (two years), elementary (two years), and intermediate (two years), and seven years of secondary education in a lycée that offers a baccalaureate on the French model. The curriculum at all levels has been reoriented to reflect an African, and particularly Cameroonian, point of view.

The Cameroonian school system has a high dropout rate, partly attributable to a shortage of qualified teachers. Of every 1,000 pupils entering the first grade of the primary cycle, only 560 completed the sixth grade; of every 1,000 students entering the secondary cycle, only 312 earned the baccalaureate.

Nearly 27 percent of the school enrollment is in the vocational stream. Vocational and technical education is provided in two types of institutions: lower technical secondary schools and technical lycées. The former offer a four-year course, and the latter provide a three-year upper secondary course. The Ecole des Cadres at Douala provides training in development work to civil servants, and two colleges organized by the Pan-African Institute of Development (PAID) train middle-level executives in rural development.

Private schools of missionary origin continue to play a dominant role in secondary and primary education. Private-school enrollments constitute 40 percent of the total in East Cameroon, while the vast majority of primary and secondary schools and primary-school teacher training institutions are in private hands in West Cameroon. Approved private schools receive grants-in-aid and conform to official curricula and regulations. In Northern Province Koranic schools provide traditional instruction to Muslims.

Educational administration is centralized in the Ministry of Education.

The country's only university is the University of Yaoundé, founded in 1962 and financed until 1973 by the French government. The national literacy rate is 63 percent.

Education

Literacy Rate %: 63.4
Male %: 75.0
Female %: 52.1
First Level: Primary schools: 6,801
Teachers: 40,970
Students: 1,896,722
Student-Teacher Ratio: 46.3
Net Enrollment Ratio: —
Second Level: Secondary Schools: —
Teachers: 14,917
Students: 459,068
Student-Teacher Ratio: 30.8
Net Enrollment Ratio: —
Vocational Level: Schools:
Students: 91,779
Third Level: Institutions: —
Teachers: 1,086
Students: 33,177
Student-Ratio Level: 30.5
Gross Enrollment Ratio: 3.3
Students per 100,000: 289
% of Population Age 25 and over with Postsecondary Education: —
Public Expenditure on Education as % of GDP: 2.9

SCIENCE AND TECHNOLOGY

Science and Technology

Scientists and Engineers in R&D per 1 million persons: —
Expenditures in R&D as % of GDP: —
High-Tech Exports $: 2 million
Patent Applications by Residents: —

MEDIA

The Cameroonian press consists of one daily, the *Cameroon Tribune*, published by the government in French daily and in English weekly from Yaoundé, with a circulation of 66,000, and 25 nondailies with a total circulation of 315,000. Per capita circulation of the daily is four per 1,000. Some 54 periodicals also are published, almost all in French.

The national news agency is Société de Presse et d'Edition de Cameroun (SOPECAM), with four permanent bureaus. Foreign news agencies in Yaoundé include Tass, Agence France-Presse, Reuters, and China Nouvelle.

There are nine publishers, all but one in Yaoundé. Cameroon adheres to the Berne, UCC, and Florence copyright conventions.

The state-owned Radiodiffusion-Télévision Camerounaise operates four radio stations, at Yaoundé, Douala, Garoua, and Buea. The main services are in French and English, with some broadcasts in regional languages and Arabic. Television was introduced in 1985.

Media

Daily Newspapers: 1
  Total Circulation 000: 50
  Circulation per 1,000: 4.0
Books Published: —
Magazines: —
Radio Receivers 000: 1,500
  per 1,000: 115
Television sets 000: 960
  per 1,000: 75

MOST IMPORTANT MEDIA:

Press. The principal newspapers are *The Gazette* (Limbe, 70,000), weekly in English; *Le Tribune du Cameroun/Cameroon Tribune* (Yaoundé, 25,000), government daily in French and English; *Cameroon Post* (50,000), weekly in English; *La Gazette* (Douala, 35,000), French edition of *The Gazette*, twice weekly; *Le Combattant* (21,000), independent weekly in French; *Cameroon Outlook* (Victoria, 20,000), thrice weekly in English; *Le Messager* (19,000), independent fortnightly in French. In September 1992 *Le Messager* was one of several publications suspended by the government.

News agencies. The former Agence Camerounaise de Presse (ACAP) was replaced in 1978 by the Société de Presse et d'Edition du Cameroun (SOPECAM), which, under the Ministry of Information, is responsible for the dissemination of foreign news within Cameroon and also for publication of the Le Tribune du Cameroun. The principal foreign agency is Agence France-Presse.

Radio and television. The Office de Radiodiffusion-Télévision Camerounaise (CRTV) is a government facility operating under the control of the Ministry of Information and Culture. Programming is in French, English, and more than two dozen local languages. There were approximately 2.2 million radio and 354,000 television receivers in 1998.

CULTURE

Cultural Indicators

Public Libraries
Number: —
Volumes: —
Registered borrowers: —
Museums
  Number: 42
  Annual Attendance:
Cinema
  Production of Long Films: 2
  Number of Cinemas: 232
  Seating Capacity: 39,900
  Annual Attendance: —
  Annual Attendance per capita: —

STATUS OF WOMEN

Women enjoy equal rights with men under the constitution and are politically active in political parties and labor unions. The women's wing of the Cameroon People's Democratic Movement has created social and educational programs aimed at encouraging the economic and social productivity of Cameroonian women. Women are represented in the modern sector, although nor proportionately in the upper levels of administration and in the professions.

Women

Gender Empowerment Measure: 86
Seats Held in Parliament by Women %: 5.6
Female Administrators and Managers %: 10.1
Female Professional and Technical Workers %: 24.4
Women's Share of Earned Income %: 30
Women in Government %: 5

HEALTH, FOOD, AND NUTRITION

Health

Number of Physicians: 945
Number of Dentists: 55
Number of Nurses: 6,053
Number of Pharmacists: 206
Population per Physician: 11,848
Number of Hospitals: 629
Hospital Beds per 10,000: 27
Hospital Bed Occupancy Rate: —
Infant Mortality Rate per 1,000 live births: 109
Maternal Mortality Rate per 100,000 live births: 550
Total Health Expenditures as % of GDP: 2.62
Health Expenditures per capita $: 27
HIV Infected % of adults: 4.89
Cigarette Consumption per smoker per year: —
% of Smokers: Male: —
  Female: —
Access to Safe Water %: 41

Food and Nutrition

Food Supply as % of FAO Requirements: 95
% of Consumption Expenditures on Food: 49.1
Daily Available Calories per capita: 2,214
% of Total Calories derived from:
Cereals: 42.4
Potatoes, cassava: 16.0
Meat, poultry: 3.3
Fish: 0.7
Eggs, milk: 1.4
Fruits, vegetables: 13.7
Fats, oils: 7.9

ENVIRONMENT

Cameroon's major environmental problems are divided regionally. In the north and extreme north of the country, extensive desertification threatens the livelihood of nearly 25 percent of the country's population. On the coast and in the central areas, deforestation is a growing problem. In urban and industrial areas, there is growing concern over water purity and firewood supplies. In the mountainous zones of the west and northwest, over-farming of the soil in conjunction with soil erosion threatens food supplies. The country is largely unequipped to deal with these matters administratively.

Environment

Forest Area sq km: 196,000
Average Annual Deforestation sq km: 1,292
Nationally Protected Areas as % of Total Land Area: 4.5
Freshwater Access cubic meters per capita: 18,737
Emissions of Organic Water Pollutants kg per day: 12,796
CO_2 Emissions per capita ton: 0.3

CHRONOLOGY

1960 Cameroon becomes an independent nation, with Ahmad Ahidjo as first president.
Ahidjo's AN group wins an absolute majority in National Assembly elections. . . .New constitution is approved in national referendum.

1961 In UN–supervised plebiscite, Southern Cameroons region of the British Trust Territories votes to join the Republic of Cameroon, while Northern Cameroons votes to join Nigeria. The Federal Republic of Cameroon is formed with two states: West Cameroon and East Cameroon.
Ahidjo continues as president of the Federal Republic.

1964 First elections to the federal National Assembly are held.

1965 First federal presidential election is held, and Ahidjo is reelected.

1966 Cameroon joins the five-nation UDEAC (Union Douanière et Economique d'Afrique Centrale).
Union Nationale Camerounaise (UNC) is formed as the country's sole political party.

1968 Tandeng Muna is named premier.

1970 Ernest Ouandie, the last of the leaders of the UPC (Union des Populations de Cameroun) rebellion, is arrested along with Albert Ndongmo, Roman Catholic bishop of Nkongsamba; Ouandie and Ndongmo are sentenced to death, but Ndongmo's sentence is commuted to life imprisonment following an appeal by Pope Paul VI and by Secretary General U Thant of the United Nations.

1972 Federal Republic is replaced by the United Republic of Cameroon, with new unitary constitution providing for a strong presidential form of government; new constitution is approved overwhelmingly by the electorate.

1973 National Assembly elections are held.
Cameroon suspends ties with Israel.
Second stage of the Trans-Cameroon Railway, from Belabo to Ngaoundéré, is opened.

1975 Ahidjo is elected president for his fourth term.
Border treaty is signed with Nigeria.
Paul Biya is named prime minister.

1976 Border treaty is concluded with Gabon.

1978 In national elections UNC wins all seats.

1979 Constitutional amendment officially creates the post of prime minister.

1982 Ahidjo steps down as president and nominates Prime Minister Biya as his successor, but remains UNC leader.

1983 Biya rids the cabinet of Ahidjo supporters.
In bitter power struggle, Ahidjo is forced to leave the country.
Ahidjo and lieutenants are charged with plotting to overthrow Biya.
Ahidjo is tried in absentia along with military officers Ibrahim Oumarou and Adamou Salatou by a military tribunal.
More than 45 persons are executed in connection with the coup.
Members of the presidential security force loyal to Ahidjo stage a coup that is foiled by loyal army and paratroop regiments. As many as 1,000 civilians and soldiers are killed before the government regains control. The government deletes the word "United" from the name of the republic.
Three more provinces are added to the territorial administration.
The office of prime minister is abolished.

1984 Paul Biya is elected president in nationwide balloting, indicating strong popular support for his liberalization programs.

1985 Nigeria expels illegal Cameroonian residents. The Cameroon National Union is renamed the Cameroon People's Democratic Movement (RDPC).

1986 At least 1,700 people die as they sleep in a natural disaster when toxic gas from volcanic Lake Nyos engulfs lakeside villages.

1987 Electoral reforms allow legally constituted parties to contest elections, although the RDPC remains the only authorized party. Biya announces an austerity budget to deal with the country's growing economic crisis.

1988 Multiple candidates run for seats in the assembly. Biya is reelected unopposed.

1992 Biya is elected president in the first multiparty elections.

1994 Nigerian troops claim the petroleum-rich Bakasi Peninsula of Cameroon.

1996 Border skirmishes break out with Nigeria over the Bakasi Peninsula territorial dispute; Nigeria and Cameroon agree to adjudication by the International Court of Justice.

1997 In elections boycotted by most of the opposition, Biya's party, the Cameroon People's Democratic Movement (formerly the National Cameroonian Union), wins 60 percent of seats and Biya is reelected.

1998 Transparency International ranks Cameroon the world's most corrupt country.

2000 World Bank approves funding for an oil and pipeline project despite environmental and human rights criticism.

2001 Global Forest Watch reports that 80 percent of the country's indigenous forests have been allocated for logging. IMF offers debt relief worth $2 billion on the condition that corruption is checked and social services are improved

BIBLIOGRAPHY

Delancey, Mark. *Cameroon: Dependence and Independence*. Boulder, Colo., 1989.

Delancey, Mark D. *Historical Dictionary of the Republic of Cameroon*. Metuchen, N.J., 2000.

Manga, Ekema J. *The African Economic Dilemma: The Case of Cameroon*. Lanham, Md, 1998.

Staudinger, Paul. *In the Heart of the Hausa States*. Athens, Ohio, 1990.

OFFICIAL PUBLICATIONS

Cameroon. *Cameroon—Selected Issues and Statistical Appendix* (IMF Staff Country Report [1996]); *Recensement général de la population et de l'habitat 1987.*

CONTACT INFORMATION

Embassy of Cameroon
2349 Massachusetts Avenue NW
Washington, D.C. 20008
Phone: (202) 265-8790 Fax: (202) 387-3826

INTERNET RESOURCES

- Presidency of the Republic of Cameroon
  http://www.camnet.cm/celcom/anglais/homepr.htm

CANADA

BASIC FACT SHEET

OFFICIAL NAME:
Canada

ABBREVIATION:
CA

CAPITAL:
Ottawa

HEAD OF STATE:
Queen Elizabeth II, represented in Canada by Governor-General Adrienne Bing Chee Clarkson (from 1999)

HEAD OF GOVERNMENT:
Prime Minister Jean Chrétien (from 1993)

NATURE OF GOVERNMENT:
Parliamentary democracy

POPULATION:
30,626,000 (1999)

AREA:
9,976,610 sq km (3,848,654 sq mi)

MAJOR ETHNIC GROUPS:
British; French; Indian; Inuit

LANGUAGES:
English and French

RELIGIONS:
Roman Catholicism and Protestantism

UNIT OF CURRENCY:
Canadian dollar

NATIONAL FLAG:
A middle white field flanked by a red vertical field on each end, with a red maple leaf on the white field.

NATIONAL EMBLEM:
A heraldic shield divided into five parts: Three crouching lions on a red field in top left representing Britain; the erect red Scottish royal lion on gold surrounded by a decorated frame called a "double tressure" on the top right; a gold harp on blue for Ireland in the left center; three fleurs-de-lis for France in the right center; and at the bottom, with twice the width as the others, a cluster of three red maple leaves on white, representing Canada. A gold lion holding the red, white, and blue Union Jack and a silver unicorn with the flag of old France bearing three silver fleurs-de-lis support the shield. A gold helmet mantled in red and white rests on the upper part of the shield with a crowned lion on its top holding a red maple leaf in its forepaw. Above all is displayed St. Edward's jeweled gold crown. Underneath the emblem a blue scroll rests upon a design of Irish shamrocks and French lilies. In gold letters it carries the national motto: *A Mari Usque Ad Mare* ("From Sea to Sea").

NATIONAL ANTHEMS:
Canada has no official national anthem. Both "God Save the Queen" and "O Canada" have semiofficial status, with the latter more commonly used.

NATIONAL HOLIDAYS:
Dominion (or Confederation) Day (July 1); Victoria Day and the Sovereign's Birthday (Monday preceding May 25); Thanksgiving Day (first Monday in September); Remembrance Day (November 11); Labor Day (July 1); Christmas, Boxing Day, Good Friday, Easter, New Year's Day.

DATE OF INDEPENDENCE:
July 1, 1867

DATE OF CONSTITUTION:
April 17, 1982

GEOGRAPHICAL FEATURES

Canada occupies all of the North American continent north of the United States except Alaska and the small French islands of St. Pierre and Miquelon. The most striking geographical characteristic of Canada is its immense size. With a recorded area of 9,970,610 sq km (3,849,652 sq mi) for land and freshwater, it is the largest country in the Western Hemisphere and the second largest in the world, next to Russia. Canada's size is about the same as that of

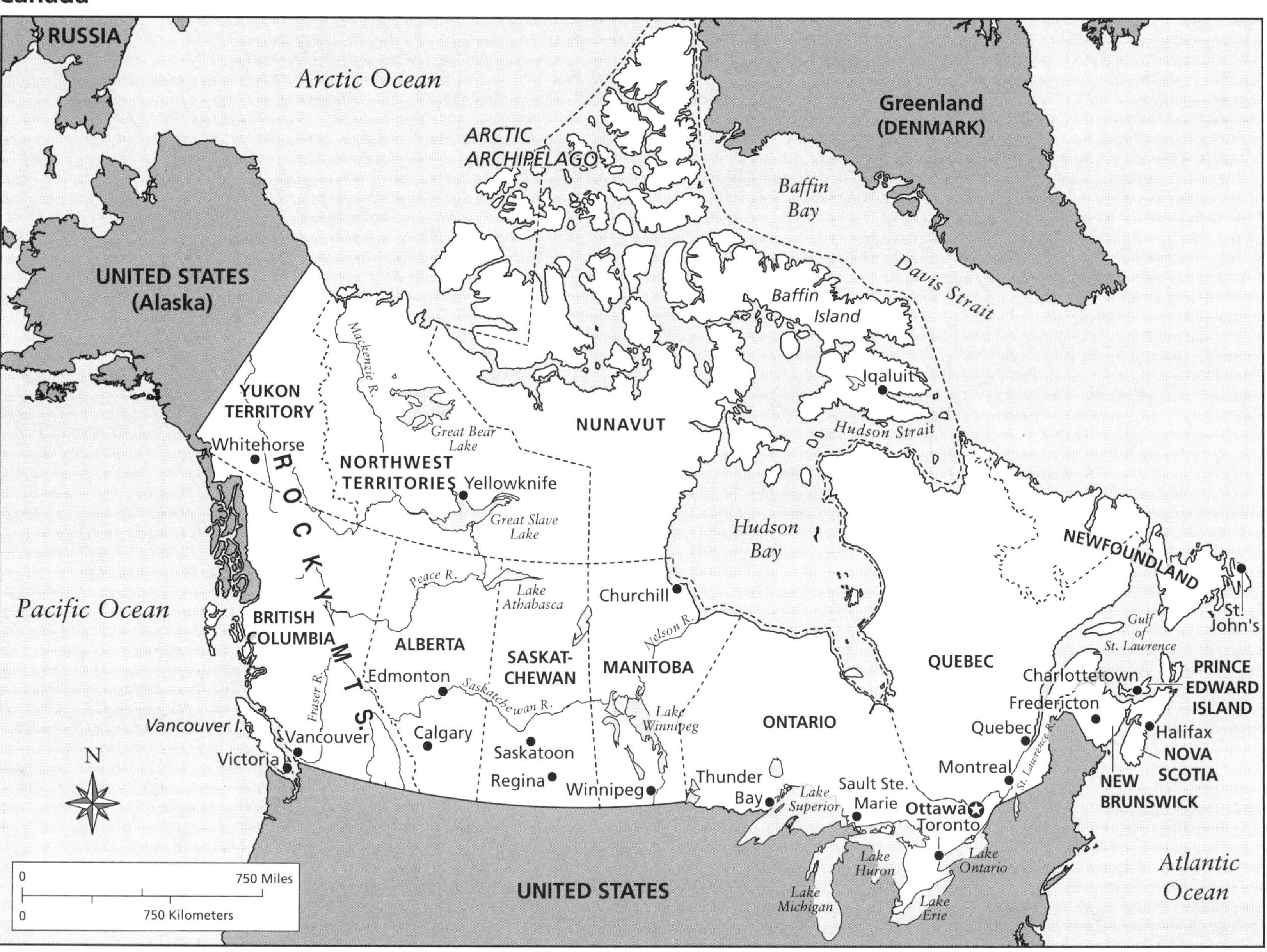
Canada
RUSSIA
Arctic Ocean
ARCTIC ARCHIPELAGO
Greenland (DENMARK)
Baffin Bay
Davis Strait
UNITED STATES (Alaska)
Baffin Island
Iqaluit
Mackenzie R.
YUKON TERRITORY
Whitehorse
Great Bear Lake
NUNAVUT
Hudson Strait
NORTHWEST TERRITORIES
Yellowknife
Great Slave Lake
ROCKY MTS.
Hudson Bay
NEWFOUNDLAND
Peace R.
Lake Athabasca
Churchill
Pacific Ocean
BRITISH COLUMBIA
St. John's
Nelson R.
Gulf of St. Lawrence
ALBERTA
SASKAT-CHEWAN
MANITOBA
QUEBEC
PRINCE EDWARD ISLAND
Charlottetown
Edmonton
Saskatchewan R.
Fredericton
ONTARIO
Lake Winnipeg
Fraser R.
Vancouver I.
Vancouver
Calgary
Quebec
Halifax
Saskatoon
NOVA SCOTIA
Victoria
St. Lawrence R.
Montreal
Regina
Thunder Bay
NEW BRUNSWICK
Winnipeg
Sault Ste. Marie
Lake Superior
Ottawa
Toronto
N
Lake Huron
Lake Ontario
Atlantic Ocean
0 750 Miles
0 750 Kilometers
UNITED STATES
Lake Michigan
Lake Erie

the continent of Europe. The border with the United States, the longest undefended border in the world, is 8,893 km (5,526 mi). The total coastline is divided into four segments: Arctic Ocean (9,286 km; 5,770 mi); Atlantic Ocean, including Baffin Bay and Davis Strait (9,833 km; 6,110 mi); Pacific coastline (2,543 km; 1,580 mi); and Hudson Bay and Hudson Strait (7,081 km; 4,400 mi).

Topographically, Canada is divided into the Atlantic provinces, the Great Lakes–St. Lawrence Lowlands, the Canadian Shield, the Interior Plains, the Western Cordillera, the Northwest Territories, and the Arctic Archipelago.

The foundation of Canadian geology is the Canadian Shield (sometimes called the Precambrian Shield or the Laurentian Plateau), which takes up almost half of Canada's total area. It extends beyond the Canadian boundary into the United States in two limited areas: at the head of Lake Superior and in the Adirondack Mountains. Structurally, the shield may be thought of as a huge saucer, the center of which is occupied by Hudson and James Bays. Most of the shield is relatively level and less than 610 km (2,000 ft) above sea level. Only along the dissected rim of the saucer rim are there major hills and mountains: the Torngat Mountains in northeastern Labrador, the Laurentian Highlands, and along the northern shores of Lake Superior. Except for the plains, the rest of the shield is composed of undulating terrain with rocky, knoblike hills and lakes interconnected by rapid streams.

The Canadian Shield is surrounded by a series of lowlands, the Atlantic region and the Great Lakes–St. Lawrence Lowlands to the east, the Interior Plains to the west, and the Arctic Lowlands to the north.

In the Far West is the Western Cordillera, composed of relatively young folded and faulted mountains and plateaus. It is only some 805 km (500 mi) wide in Canada, much narrower than in the United States, with less extensive interior plateaus. Generally, the mountains are much higher in Canada and contain some of the most beautiful alpine scenery in the world. The only other parts of Canada with comparable spectacular mountains are Baffin and Ellesmere Islands in the northeastern Arctic.

Between the Western Cordillera and the Canadian Shield is the region broadly known as the West, including the Manitoba and Mackenzie Lowlands. The Manitoba Lowland (leading to the Saskatchewan and Alberta Plains) is the only part of Canada that is as flat as a tabletop. The boundary between the Manitoba Lowland and the Saskatchewan Plain is marked by the Manitoba Escarpment. The Saskatchewan and Alberta Plains are divided in the south by the Missouri Couteau. The landscape of the two plains is similar to that of the U.S. Great Plains, with rolling plains; deeply incised rivers; water-filled depressions called sloughs; dry streambeds called coulees; and in the drier areas, mesas, buttes, and badlands.

The Northwest Territories is a political rather than a geographical term. It covers the region east of the Western Cordillera and north of the Interior Plains and the Canadian Shield. Within this large area there are two distinct subregions: the subarctic Mackenzie River valley to the west, and the arctic area of the islands and north-central mainland.

The Arctic Archipelago lies on a submerged plateau whose floor varies from flat to gently undulating. From the Alaskan border eastward to the mouth of the Mackenzie River the shelf is shallow and continuous. The deeply submerged continental shelf runs along the entire western coast of the Arctic Archipelago from Banks Island to Greenland.

The largest islands are those in the Arctic Archipelago, extending from St. James Bay to Ellesmere. The largest on the western coast are Vancouver Island and the Queen Charlotte Islands. The largest on the eastern coast are Newfoundland, Prince Edward Island, Cape Breton Island, the Grand Manan and Campbello Islands of New Brunswick, and Anticosti Island and the Îles de la Madeleine of Quebec.

Geography

Area sq km: 9,970,610 sq mi 3,849,652
World Rank: 2nd
Land Boundaries, km: United States 8,893
Coastline, km: 243,791
Elevation Extremes meters
- Lowest: Atlantic Ocean 0
- Highest: Mount Logan 5,950

Land Use % Arable land: 5
- Permanent Crops: 0
- Permanent Pastures: 3
- Forest and Woodland: 54
- Other: 38

Population of Principal Cities (1991)

Brampton	234,445
Brantford	81,997
Burlington	129,575
Burnaby	158,858
Calgary	710,677
Cambridge	92,772
Coquitlam	84,021
Delta	88,978
East York	102,696
Edmonton	616,741
Etobiocoke	309,993
Gatineau	92,284
Gloucester	101,677
Guelph	87,976
Halifax	114,455
Hamilton	318,499
Kelowna	75,950
Kitchener	168,282
Laval	314,398
London	303,165
Longueuil	129,874
Markham	153,811
Mississauga	463,388
Montreal	1,017,666

(continued)

Montreal-Nord	85,516
Nepean	107,627
Niagara Falls	75,399
North York	562,564
Oakville	114,670
Oshawa	129,344
Ottawa	313,987
Quebec	167,517
Regina	179,178
Richmond	126,624
Richmond Hill	80,142
Saanich	95,577
Saint Catharines	129,300
Saint John's	95,770
Saskatoon	186,058
Sault Sainte Marie	81,476
Scarborough	524,598
Sherbrooke	76,429
Sudbury	92,884
Surrey	245,173
Thunder Bay	113,746
Toronto	635,395
Vancouver	471,844
Vaughan	111,359
Windsor	191,435
Winnipeg	616,790
York	140,525

CLIMATE AND WEATHER

Canada has a great variety of climates. For example, British Columbia has moderate winter and summer temperatures, similar to those of England. The central and southern parts of the Western Plains, on the other hand, have great winter and summer temperature extremes and about as much precipitation as the Gobi Desert in Mongolia. In the north, winter temperatures plunge as low as −51°C (−60°F), but the summers are as hot as in the tropics in southern Ontario.

The conflict of the air masses that pour in from three directions east of the Rockies leads to continual cyclonic storms, producing much rain and snow. The Northwest Territories and the Prairies, having fewer and weaker storms, are the driest areas. The windward mountain slopes are exceptionally wet, and the protected slopes are very dry. Thus the western coast gets 1,524 to 3,048 mm (60 to 120 in) annually; the central Prairies area, less than 506 mm (20 in); the flat area east of Winnipeg, 508 to 1,016 mm (20 to 40 in); and the Maritime Provinces 1,143 to 1,524 mm (45 to 60 in). The average annual number of rainy days ranges from 252 along coastal British Columbia to 70 in the interior of the province. About 30 percent of the annual mean precipitation is snow.

In the province of Newfoundland, on the Atlantic coast, Labrador has a rigorous climate and is snow-covered for more than half the year. On the island of Newfoundland, however, summers are cool and winters are relatively mild.

On Prince Edward Island the climate is quite moderate except for occasional extreme lows in the winter.

In Nova Scotia summer and winter temperatures are more moderate than in the interior. Winters are stormy on the coast and fog is prevalent throughout the year.

In New Brunswick the seasons are somewhat delayed, and temperatures in the interior are more extreme than on the coast.

In Quebec the frost-free season extends from early May to late September. Northward and eastward, winter temperatures become more extreme and summers cool.

Ontario bears the brunt of severe winter cold waves moving east from the Prairies or south from the Arctic across Hudson Bay. Summers, though warm, are short. Peninsular Ontario has a much milder climate than the northern districts. Since Ontario lies in a major storm track, wide variations occur in weather, especially in winter, but extreme conditions are not prolonged

Mantioba and Saskatchewan have typically Prairie continental climates, with long, cold winters and warm summers. The frost-free period in the fertile lowland areas ranges from 80 to 100 days.

The south of Alberta is subject in the winter to cold, dry air masses of continental polar air, occasionally moderated by chinook winds. Summers are warm with abundant sunshine, but rainfall is meager and highly variable, particularly in the southwest.

British Columbia has the most moderate climate in Canada, with mild, wet winters, warm summers, and the maximum number of frost-free days. Semi-arid conditions sometimes occur in the interior.

Yukon is subject to wide temperature variations, but winters are remarkably mild for the latitude, and periods of intense cold are of short duration.

In the southern areas of the Northwest Territories summers last for about three months, with temperatures above 10°C (50°F). North of the tree line, freezing temperatures may occur during any month, and winters are long and bitterly cold. The climate is moderated by the sea in the Arctic Archipelago, so that extremes are not as severe as in a continental region of the same latitude. Temperatures in the Arctic Archipelago are generally below −18°C (0°F) for six months or more. Occasional mild periods occur, particularly in the western Arctic. Summers are short and cool. Winter nights and summer days are long, reaching a maximum of 24 hours. Precipitation is extremely light and falls mostly in late summer.

Climate and Weather

Mean Temperature Range
Newfoundland Jan 6°F to 22°F
July 49°F to 61°F
Maritime Provinces Jan 9°F to 27°F
July 47°F to 70°F
Ontario Jan 11°F to 25°F
July 61°F to 72°F
Prairie Provinces Jan 8°F to 11°F
July 63°F to 67°F

British Colombia Jan 12°F to 40°F
July 54°F to 63°F
Yukon Jan −22°F to −5°F
Jul 58°F to 60°F
Northwest Territories Jan −26°F to −14°F
July 38°F to 61°F

Average Rainfall
Western Coast 60 in to 120 in
Prairies 20 in
Winnipeg 20 to 40 in
Maritime Provinces 45 to 60 in

POPULATION

Population Indicators

Total Population: 1999 30,626,000
World Rank: 34th
Density per sq mi: 8.0 per sq km 3.1
% of annual growth (1994–99): 1.1
Male %: 49.3
Female %: 50.7
Urban %: 77.9
Age Distribution: % 0–14: 20.9
15–29: 22.7
30–44: 25.1
45–59: 15.3
60–74: 11.3
75 and over: 4.7
Population 2020: 36,454,000
Birth Rate per 1,000: 12.5
Death Rate per 1,000: 7.2
Population Doubling Time (years): —
Infant Mortality Rate per 1,000 live births: 6.1
Rate of Natural Increase per 1,000: 5.3
Total Fertility Rate: 1.7
Expectation of Life (years): Males 74.7
Females 81.7
Marriage Rate per 1,000: 5.4
Divorce Rate per 1,000: 2.7
Total Number of Households: 10,018,000
Average Size of Households: 2.7
% of Illegitimate Children: 16.2
Induced Abortions: 99,971
Rate per 100 live births: 25.7

ETHNIC COMPOSITION

Canada is a country with two founding peoples with distinct cultural and linguistic traditions: Anglo-Canadian and French-Canadian. The existence of two societies belies the belief of the fathers of the Confederation that they were creating a British (including Anglo-Celtic or Irish) nation in North America. In the 1870s more than 60 percent of the population was of British origin, almost double the size of the French. Further, the Anglo-Canadians were the ruling class economically and politically. The French constituted an enclave that simply would not disappear as well as a vulnerable but tenacious minority, who resisted all efforts at integration. The Anglo-Canadian dominance has suffered erosion during the past century. When the immigration of peoples from the British Isles did not reach the hoped-for proportions, immigration from eastern Europe, including the Ukraine, was encouraged. As a result, the prime farmlands of western Canada were settled by east Europeans. Having very little contact with Canadian government representatives or settled communities, they were forced to develop their own resources. They did not assimilate into a Canadian way of life because there were no social or institutional pressures to do so.

Amerindians bear a striking resemblance to East Asians. Their physical similarities and differences suggest that while related to Asians, Amerindians separated from Asians before many of the later Asian traits developed. Further, no clear relationship exists between Amerindian tongues and Asian languages except for the Inuit or Eskimo language, which bears a striking resemblance to some northeastern Asian tongues such as Kamchadal and Chukchi.

Anthropologists distinguish seven distinct cultural groups among the Canadian Indians: the Algonkin tribes of the northern woodlands, the agricultural tribes of the eastern woodlands, the Plains tribes, the tribes of the Pacific coast, the tribes of the Western Cordillera, the tribes of the basins of the Mackenzie and Yukon Rivers, and the Inuit along the Arctic coast.

The Indians of the eastern woodlands include the Beothuk, Micmac, Nasakapi, Cree, Montagnais, Algonkin, and Ojibwa The Iroquois are related groups and include the Huron, Neutral, and Tobacco. The Indians of the Plains are the Assiniboine, Plains Cree, Blackfoot, Sarcee, Gros-Ventre, and Sioux, all of whom are migratory hunters. The Indians of the northwestern coast include the Tsimshian, Haida, Kwakiutl (or Kwakwaka'waku), Bella Coola, and Nuu Chah-nulth ("people along the islands," Nootka). The Athabaskans of the Mackenzie and Yukon basins include the Chipewyan, Beaver, Slave, Yellowknife, Hare, Sekani, Dogrib, Nahani, and Kutchin. The Inuit live entirely north of the timberline. The most important Inuit groups are the Mackenzie, Copper, Central, and Labrador.

The one-third of the Canadian population who are neither French nor English are scattered into a number of groups, principally Italians, central and eastern Europeans, Chinese, Japanese, East Indians, blacks, and religious groups such as Hutterites, Mennonites, Doukhobors, and Jews. The immigration of these groups has had a profound impact on the nature of Canadian society. Cities such as Toronto became less British with a variety of languages and cultures enlivening its streets. At the same time, there remain pockets of racism and discrimination against non-British groups. Pressures to conform are more subtle than formerly but just as real. The degree of prejudice is in direct proportion to the cultural distance from the Anglo-Saxon center and is more persistent in the case of Asians and blacks and less in the case of more easily assimilable whites, such as Italians.

LANGUAGES

Canada has two official languages with coequal status: French and English, representing the dual origins of the nation. In the 1996 midterm census 63 percent of the population reported English as their only mother tongue and 11 percent a language other than English and French as their only mother tongue. Nearly 1 million persons, or 4 percent of the population, reported having more than one other tongue.

Language is a sensitive issue in Canada, and bilingualism is protected by legislation, particularly the Official Languages Act of 1969. The basic principles of the Official Languages Act are further buttressed in the Charter of Rights and Freedoms in the 1982 Constitution Act. It affirms that all public communications must be in both English and French and encourages bilingualism in nonofficial communications as well. The purpose of the official language policy is not to make all Canadians bilingual but to ensure that wherever there is a Francophone concentration, French speakers, who constitute 45 percent of all officially bilingual Canadians, may deal with the federal government in their own language. There is a commissioner of official languages to ensure the implementation of bilingualism in official practice. The result of this policy has been a modest increase in the overall number of persons who can speak both English and French with reasonable fluency.

Principal Languages and Their Speakers

English	18,113,000
French	7,125,000
English-French	116,000
English-other	268,000
French-other	38,000
English-French-other	10,000
Arabic	160,000
Chinese	768,000
Cree	83,000
Dutch	144,000
Eskimo (Inuktitut) languages	29,000
German	483,000
Greek	130,000
Italian	520,000
Pilipino (Filipino)	143,000
Polish	229,000
Portuguese	227,000
Punjābi	217,000
Spanish	229,000
Ukrainian	175,000
Vietnamese	114,000
Other	1,287,000

RELIGIONS

From the time of the British victory on the Plains of Abraham until the beginning of the 1960s, the Catholic Church was the pillar of French-Canadian society and made a profound contribution to the development of its identity. Beginning in about 1960, a rapid deconfessionalization of Catholic institutions has gained force and contributed to a disintegration of Catholic influence.

The largest Protestant denomination is the United Church of Canada (UCC), formed in 1925 through the merger of Methodist, Congregational, and nearly half the Presbyterian Churches. The second largest Protestant body is the Presbyterian Church, consisting of those Presbyterian congregations that refused union with the UCC in 1925. Lutherans and Baptists have widespread membership. Most of the 15 distinct Pentecostal churches are small offshoots of similar bodies in the United States. Mennonites are dispersed across Canada, with 15 distinct bodies. The Anglican Church is organized into 28 dioceses in four provinces. Immigration has helped to create a wide variety of Orthodox churches, of which the largest is the Greek.

In 1991 Catholics formed 48.2 percent of the population and Protestants 40.1 percent. Two provinces were predominately Catholic: Quebec, with 88.2 percent, and New Brunswick, with 53.9 percent. Of the 296,400 Jews, one-half lived in Ontario and one-third in Quebec. Of Christian denominations, the fastest growing were the Pentecostal, who grew by 54 percent between 1971 and 1981 compared to 13 percent for Catholics and 3 percent for Anglicans. The nearly 1.8 million people with no religious preferences were nearly double the number in this category in 1971. They were found mostly in the West, particularly in British Columbia, where they made up 20.5 percent of the population; Yukon (20.3 percent); and Alberta (11.7 percent).

Religious Affiliations

Roman Catholic	13,840,000
Protestant	8,520,000
Anglican	2,450,000
Eastern Orthodox	430,000
Jewish	360,000
Muslim	280,000
Buddhist	180,000
Hindu	180,000
Sikh	170,000
Nonreligious	3,840,000
Other	780,000

HISTORICAL BACKGROUND

The first inhabitants of North America came from Asia during the last Ice Age, around 20,000 to 35,000 years ago. Archaeological evidence and oral traditions indicate that some of the peoples who settled the west coast and the eastern woodlands, such as the Huron and Iroquois, created sophisticated political organizations as well as extensive trade systems.

At the end of the 10th century, Norse peoples from Europe, known as Vikings, created permanent settlements on the northern tip of Newfoundland and, after initial conflict, began trade relations with the local peoples. The settlements were abandoned around the mid-14th century.

The first European to set foot in Newfoundland, Canada, was the Venetian John Cabot (Giovanni Caboto), commissioned by England's Henry VIII to look for a short route to Asia. But his voyage was actually financed by Bristol merchants who were more interested in fisheries than in overseas colonies. Cabot reached the shores of Newfoundland in 1497 and his reports of codfish off the coast of Newfoundland brought fishing fleets from England, France, Spain, and Portugal.

In 1534 the French made their first stake in the New World when Jacques Cartier planted a cross on the tip of the Gaspé Peninsula and, the following year, discovered and ascended the St. Lawrence River.

Another 70 years passed before Sieur de Monts and Samuel de Champlain founded the first permanent French settlement, at Port Royal in Nova Scotia. In 1608 Champlain established the town of Quebec. By 1756 the French flag flew over a territory larger than France, and French settlers numbered more than 10,000. However, they suffered great depredations when their allies the Huron Indians were destroyed by the Iroquois.

In the 17th century the English began to press their claims to the French-held lands, and they conquered Quebec in 1629. Restored to France in 1632, Quebec, together with the rest of New France, as the territory was by now known, was placed under the control of a chartered company, the Company of One Hundred Associates, whose mandate was to exploit the fur trade and establish settlements. In 1663 the French Crown took over the territory and established a feudal system of government under which large grants of land were made to seigneurs who, in turn, made grants to settlers in return for specified dues. Meanwhile, explorers and missionaries such as Jacques Marquette, Louis Jolliet, and René-Robert Cavelier, sieur de La Salle expanded the royal domain, so that by the end of the 17th century it stretched north to the shores of the Hudson Bay, west to the Great Lakes, and south to the Gulf of Mexico. French dominance was complete except for the British Hudson's Bay Company, founded in 1670 to compete for the fur trade.

In the middle of the 18th century, French-British rivalry culminated in the historic defeat of the French general Montcalm on the Plains of Abraham by British forces led by James Wolfe in 1759. The French army surrendered in Montreal in 1760, and the 1763 Treaty of Paris ceded New France to Britain. The Quebec Act of 1774 established British rule and a system of government very favorable to the ruling seigneurs and the Roman Catholic Church. Concessions to the Quebecois paid off in the loyalty of the French aristocracy and the church during the American Revolution. However, the influx of 40,000 Loyalists from the American colonies changed the political character of the country permanently, as they took over the direction of the new government set up under the Constitutional Act of 1791. The act divided the British territories into Upper Canada (now southern Ontario) and Lower Canada (southern Quebec), each of which gained elected assemblies with limited powers.

The last decades of the 18th century witnessed another period of geographical expansion, which extended the borders to the Pacific coast. Between 1789 and 1793 Alexander Mackenzie undertook his journey to the northern reaches of the continent and the Pacific Ocean. British mariners, notably George Vancouver, secured for Britain a firm hold on what is now British Columbia. After amalgamating with the rival North West Company in 1821, the Hudson's Bay Company held undisputed sway over most of the North and West. Eastern border problems with the United States were settled by the Webster-Ashburton Treaty of 1842, and in the West the border was settled at 49°N in the face of considerable American public opposition.

The road to self-government began with two rebellions, one led by Louis J. Papineau in Lower Canada and the other by William Lyon Mackenzie in Upper Canada in 1838. The earl of Durham was sent to Canada in 1838 to recommend political reform. The Durham Report recommended the grant of some form of self-government and also the immediate union of the two Canadas for the purpose of Anglicizing the French-Canadians. Union of the two provinces was approved in 1840, and responsible government became effective in 1849.

Movement for a Canadian confederation gained strength in the 1860s. George A. MacDonald and George Brown, rival party leaders, agreed to merge Upper Canada and Lower Canada under a common dominion government. Later the Atlantic provinces were brought in and a confederation was established in 1867 through the British North America Act. The name *Canada* was chosen for the entire country, and Lower Canada and Upper Canada became the provinces of Quebec and Ontario, respectively. Prince Edward Island joined in 1873. In 1869 the Hudson's Bay Company relinquished its territorial rights to Rupert's Land and the Northwest Territories. In 1870 the province of Manitoba was established and admitted to the confederation, and the Northwest Territories were transferred to the central government. In 1871 British Columbia joined the confederation, thus spanning the continent. The formation of the federation was followed by an equally permanent link, the Canadian Pacific Railway (CPR), which helped to open up the West to new settlers. The two rebellions led by Louis Riel, in 1879–80 and 1885, provided a footnote to the creation of the second-largest nation in the world in the space of just under 25 years.

The long administration of Liberal prime minister Sir Wilfrid Laurier (1896–1911) witnessed the settlement of the Prairies and large-scale economic growth. Alberta and

Saskatchewan were made provinces in 1905. In 1911 Manitoba, Ontario, and Quebec were greatly enlarged through the allotment of all territory west of Hudson Bay and south of 60°N and all territory east of the bay, formerly known as Ungava. In 1931 Norway formally recognized Canadian title to the Sverdrup group of Arctic islands, giving Canada full sovereignty over the entire Arctic region north of the mainland. Newfoundland was the last province to join the confederation, in 1949.

The interwar years were marked by growth in self-government and the rise of radical political parties, such as the Social Credit Party. A major constitutional crisis arose in 1926 with the so-called King-Byng Affair. The governor-general, Lord Byng, tried to interfere in the government operations of Mackenzie King, the prime minister. Mackenzie King called for a new election; Lord Byng refused. The voters later voted for Mackenzie King, and the power of the governor-general to interfere in Canadian politics was reduced. The Statute of Westminster of 1931 gave all dominions equal status, with virtually complete legislative and executive independence.

Canada played an important part in World War II. It declared war three days after Great Britain. For a country of such a small population, Canada played a critical role in supplying Great Britain and in the liberation of Holland. After the war, the movement toward more independence from Great Britain continued as the Supreme Court of Canada replaced the House of Lords as Canada's highest court. Also in 1949 Newfoundlanders decided to join Canada as the 10th province.

Liberal governments successively headed by W. L. Mackenzie King and Louis St. Laurent were in office from 1935 to 1957 when the Conservatives returned to power under John Diefenbaker, prime minister until 1963. Liberals swept back under Lester Pearson (1963–68) and Pierre Trudeau. The Trudeau era lasted for 16 years until 1984 (except for a year's break in 1979), when the Conservatives won an overwhelming majority in the House of Commons and a new cabinet took office under Brian Mulroney.

In 1989, the United States and Canada signed a free-trade agreement that ultimately led to the formation of the North American Free Trade Agreement (which included Mexico) to create the world's single largest market. Canada has benefited greatly from this agreement. Its high-tech service economy has been a strong international player. Despite widespread opposition to its fiscal and defense policies and the embarrassment of a series of scandals, the Conservative government survived for nine years until 1993, when the pendulum swung again and the Liberals returned to power under Jean Chrétien. The principal event in the Mulroney administration was the Meech Lake Accord, which granted Quebec special privileges within the Canadian Federation and which was opposed by most of the Anglophone provinces. In 1994 Quebec voters turned down a referendum on separation from Canada by a narrow margin, 50.6 to 49.4 percent. In 1998 the Supreme Court of Canada held that Quebec could secede but only with the agreement of the federal government and the other provinces on such questions as the settlement of the national debt and the use of a common currency. In April 1999 the Northwest Territories were officially divided to create a new territory in the east to be governed by the Inuits, who constitute 85 percent of the area's population of 25,000. The new territory, Nunavut, has its capital at Iqaluit. In the 2000 elections, Jean Chrétien won a substantial victory with the help of large Liberal electorates in the eastern provinces.

CONSTITUTION

The foundation of the Canadian government is the British North America Act of 1867, renamed the constitution of 1867, which established the federal form of government as it exists today. It established the powers of the three branches of government and delimited the division of power between the federal government and the provinces.

The key phrase in the constitution is that Canada was to have a form of government "similar in principle to that of the United Kingdom." Yet, because Canada is a federal government, unlike the United Kingdom, the Canadian system of government has developed differently from that intended by the authors of the constitution. For instance, the existence of two Canadas, one French and the other British, required an elaborate system of protective clauses that have no parallel in Britain.

Federal constitutions lead to weak central governments, but Canada has been spared this development because the Constitution Act of 1867 clearly gives more powers to the federal Parliament than to the provincial legislatures. The efficient parts of the constitution are those that deal with the doctrine of "supremacy of Parliament," the principal British constitutional legacy to Canada. The principle is that Parliament can make or repeal any law it wishes on matters of federal jurisdiction. The courts have no right to declare illegal any statute passed by the federal Parliament. The main restraints on this supremacy are cultural and customary. One is that neither the federal nor any provincial government has the right to delegate its legislative authority to the other. The second is that parliamentary acts must be in harmony with the Canadian Bill of Rights. Third, the courts have built up rules of statutory interpretation that provide guidelines for legislators. However, the effect of judicial interpretation is quite limited because it is only in the event of lack of clarity in the wording of an act that the courts have the right to interpret the intention.

In addition to the Constitution Act of 1867, documents that contribute to the Canadian constitution include some statutes of the British Parliament (including the Statute of Westminster, which radically altered the relationship of the dominions to the mother country); some statutes of the Canadian Parliament, such as the Supreme Court Act and the Official Languages Act; the constitu-

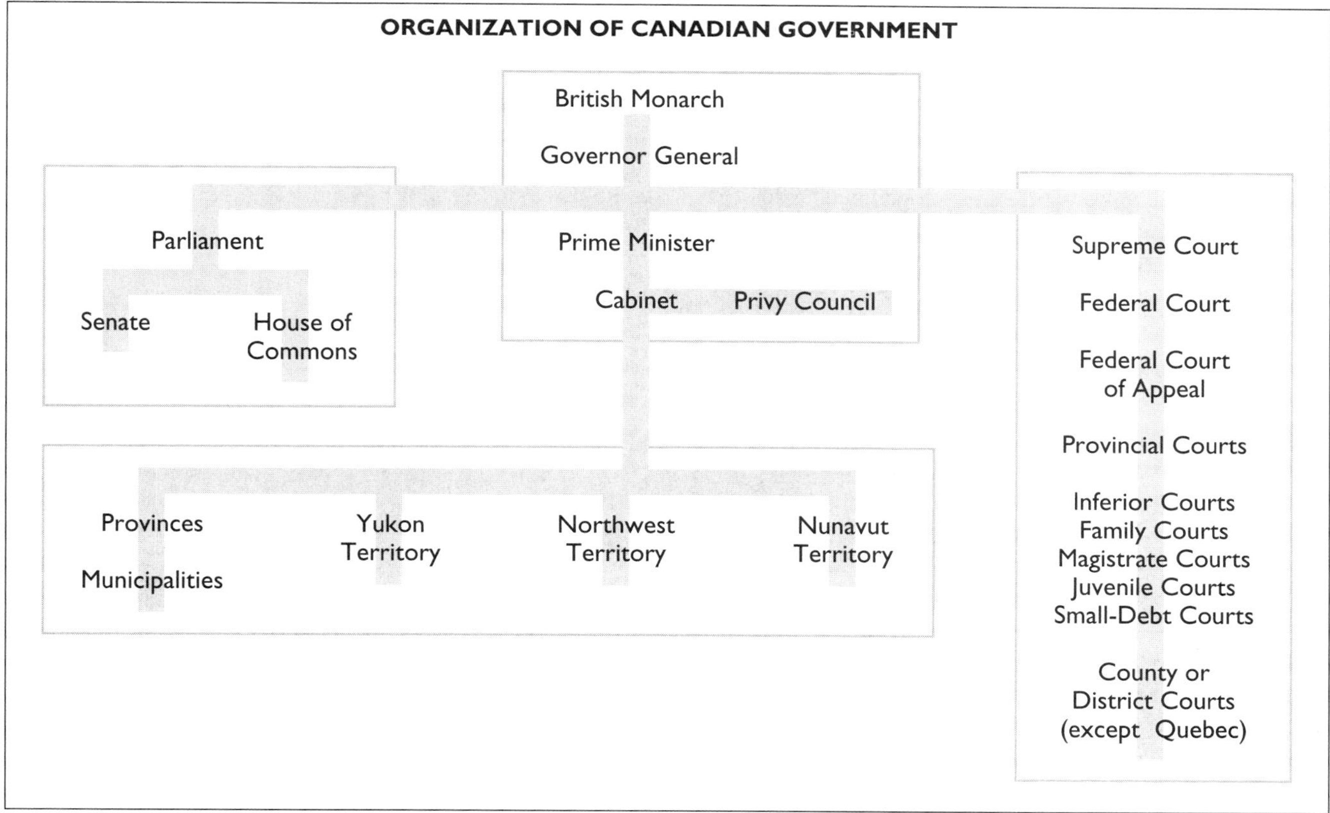

tions of the provinces; and some provincial statutes that establish provincial government institutions.

The Constitution Act of 1867 could be amended only by the British Parliament. Efforts to "patriate" the 1867 Constitution—i.e., to make it an authentically Canadian document—bore fruit in 1982, when the British Parliament approved a bill ending Canada's constitutional dependence on the United Kingdom for amendments. On the basis of this provision, the constitution of 1982 came into being. It included a charter of rights and freedoms and a provision for mechanisms to amend the constitution in the future. The first 15 clauses deal with fundamental freedoms, democratic rights, mobility rights, legal rights, and equality rights; clauses 15 through 24 deal with the status of English and French as co-official languages, and clauses 25 through 34 with general principles governing application of the charter and the removal of regional disparities. Clauses 38 through 51 deal with procedures for amending the 1982 and 1867 constitutions. Amendments require resolutions of the Senate and House of Commons and at least two-thirds of the provincial legislatures that have, in aggregate, at least 50 percent of the population of all the provinces.

As in the United Kingdom, there is a fusion of executive and legislative powers. Formal executive power is vested in the sovereign of Britain, who is head of state. The Crown is represented in Canada by a governor-general.

Even more so than in normal constitutional monarchies, the monarch is an entity with only a titular role in government. Such powers as the monarch has in theory—summoning, proroguing, and dissolving Parliament; inviting the leader of the majority in Parliament to form the government; and signing orders-in-council and other state documents—are done in her name by the governor-general, who is bound by constitutional convention to carry out these tasks in accordance with the advice of responsible ministers.

The 1867 constitution created an advisory body called the Queen's Privy Council for Canada, which includes, but is much larger than, the cabinet. Membership in the council is for life and includes cabinet ministers, former cabinet ministers, the chief justice, former chief justices, former speakers of the Senate and the House of Commons, and occasionally other distinguished persons, including members of the royal family, past and present Commonwealth prime ministers, and premiers of provinces. The Queen's Privy Council has met in plenary session only a few times, because its constitutional responsibilities to advise the Crown are discharged exclusively by the cabinet.

The linchpin of the governmental system is the prime minister, the head of government. By convention, the position is one of exceptional authority and influence. The prime minister also presides over cabinet meetings, sets its agenda, and recommends to the governor-general the dissolution of Parliament. The prime minister recommends the appointment of a new governor-general, the privy councillors, cabinet ministers, lieutenant governors, provincial administrators, speakers of the Senate, chief justices of all courts, senators, and certain senior executives in public service.

The most important federal institution is the cabinet, all of whose members are chosen by the prime minister from among the members of the House of Commons, although a few are chosen from the Senate. One of the most important considerations in putting together a viable cabinet is balance; although there is no requirement to give proportional representation to every group, every cabinet is expected to include Catholics as well as Protestants; Anglophones as well as Francophones; and, as far as possible, at least one representative from each of the provinces.

A typical cabinet consists of about 30 ministers whose work is carried out through a committee system. The prime minister determines the number, tasks, membership, and terms of reference of these committees. Legislative proposals first surface in the relevant committee, then move to the Justice Department, from where they go to the cabinet committee on legislation before reaching the cabinet, with the approval of which they are introduced as bills on the floor of the House or the Senate. The most important committees are Treasury Board, Priorities and Planning; Federal-Provincial Relations; Legislation and House Planning; External Policy and Defense; Economic Policy; Social Policy; Government Operations; and Science, Culture and Information.

The cabinet secretariat is the Queen's Privy Council Office, considered a government department under the prime minister. The Parliamentary Secretaries Act of 1959, as amended by the Government Organization Act of 1970, provides for one parliamentary secretary for each departmental minister. Parliamentary secretaries are appointed by the prime minister.

In each of the provinces, the Crown is represented by a lieutenant-governor appointed by the governor-general in council. The executive council is the provincial counterpart of the federal cabinet. The Legislative Assembly is known by that name in all provinces except Quebec, where it is known as the National Assembly, and Newfoundland and Nova Scotia, where it is the House of Assembly. In Yukon and the Northwest Territories, the central government is represented by the commissioner, who shares legislative power with the Legislative Assembly and has to approve all bills. In both territories there are executive councils or cabinets with limited powers, consisting of four members in Yukon and eight members in the Northwest Territories and headed by the leaders of the majority parties in the respective assemblies.

LOCAL GOVERNMENT

Under the Constitution Act of 1867, local government is the responsibility of the provincial legislatures, a responsibility later extended to territories. The unit of local government, apart from the school boards, is the municipality whose boundaries, powers, and responsibilities are assigned to them by provincial statutes. An increasing number of special agencies, joint boards, or commissions provide certain common services for groups of smaller municipalities. Certain other functions traditionally assigned to municipalities have reverted in whole or in part to the provinces. Some provinces, such as Ontario and British Columbia, also have established new intermediate or second-tier levels of regional government. In Prince Edward Island, Nova Scotia, New Brunswick, Ontario, and Quebec, the first order of municipalities consists of counties, which are further subdivided into cities, towns, villages, and townships. In Newfoundland and the four western provinces there are no counties; municipalities are either rural or urban, the latter being made up of cities, towns, and villages. Municipalities are usually administered by an elected council headed by a mayor, overseer, reeve, or warden.

Canada is made up of 10 provinces and three territories, each with its own premier and unicameral legislature. In each province, the sovereign is represented by a lieutenant governor appointed by the governor-general. The territories have become more autonomous since the 1980s

Local Government

Principal administrative divisions, capitals, area, population

AREA AND POPULATION

		area		population 1999
Provinces	**Capitals**	**sq mi**	**sq km**	**estimate**
Alberta	Edmonton	255,287	661,190	2,968,992
British Columbia	Victoria	365,948	947,800	4,029,253
Manitoba	Winnipeg	250,947	649,950	1,143,391
New Brunswick	Fredericton	28,355	73,440	754,741
Newfoundland	St. John's	156,649	405,720	541,164
Nova Scotia	Halifax	21,425	55,490	940,825
Ontario	Toronto	412,581	1,608,580	11,560,899
Prince Edward Island	Charlottetown	2,185	5,660	137,796
Quebec	Quebec	594,860	1,540,680	7,363,262
Saskatchewan	Regina	251,866	652,330	1,028,137
Territories				
Northwest Territories	Yellowknife	1,322,910	3,426,320	41,668
Nunavut	Iqaluit	1	1	27,146
Yukon Territory	Whitehorse	186,661	483,450	30,688
TOTAL		3,849,674	9,970,610	30,567,962

PARLIAMENT

The Canadian Parliament is a bicameral legislature consisting of a lower chamber, the elected House of Commons, and an appointed upper chamber, the Senate. The House of Commons consists of 282 members and the Senate of 104. Prior to 1965 the senators were appointed for life, but since then they have been required to retire at 75. The importance of the Commons relative to the

Senate is enhanced not only by its elected character but also by its role in the formation of the government and the latter's dependence on the House's confidence for its survival.

Representation in the Commons is roughly proportionate to population, but special provisions in the distribution of seats among the provinces as well as allowed variations in constituency size may create disparities. For example, no province may have fewer seats in the Commons than the fixed number of Senate seats to which it is entitled. Moreover, when the redistribution of seats occurs, normally after each decennial census, no province may be assigned 15 percent fewer seats than it had previously. All constituencies elect a single member to the Commons.

Except in cases of war or other national emergency, the life of a Parliament term may not extend beyond five years. However, Parliament terms frequently have been shorter because prime ministers generally seek a dissolution of the government, which follows when the cabinet loses the confidence of the House. Parliament must meet at least once each year, but there is no requirement as to the length of each session. As the business of government has increased in recent years it has become normal for sessions of Parliament to run for a whole year, with breaks in late summer and at Christmas and Easter.

Like its Westminster model and progenitor, the Canadian House of Commons is legally sovereign. However, this sovereignty is tempered by a number of factors, such as party discipline, the right of the prime minister to seek a dissolution, and control by the executive of the legislative agenda.

All bills go through five stages in the Commons and the same five stages in the Senate before they are passed on to the governor-general for royal assent. The first stage is a motion for leave to introduce the bill together with first reading. Debate at second reading concerns only the principle of legislation, and no amendments are permitted. When the bill has passed second reading, it is referred to one of the standing committees of the House for clause-by-clause examination. At this third stage the members are free to suggest amendments for the government to accept or reject, but since all committees have a government majority, few bills suffer anything more than minor changes. The bill then is reported back to the House for the fourth stage of clause-by-clause scrutiny and debate, when further amendments may be proposed. The fifth and final stage is the third readings, and debate is generally very brief at this stage. If the government does not feel confident that it can secure the passage of a bill at any stage it probably will withdraw the legislation rather than face defeat.

Of all the second chambers in Western democracies, the Canadian Senate is universally regarded as the most anachronistic and obsolete. Initially the Senate was a forum for the propertied classes, and senators were required to own real estate in the province they represented. In practice, however, Senate seats are not allocated by the prime minister as political plums for those who have done special service to the party or, less frequently, the nation. Mostly they are given to people who are near the end of their careers. When one party has been in power for a long period, as the Liberal Party has for most of this century, the Senate becomes lopsidedly in favor of that party. Further, few third-party members ever are nominated to the Senate, even though vacancies go begging many times.

Theoretically, Senate representation is based on the principle of equal regional representation. Accordingly, its 104 seats are distributed on a regional basis as follows: Ontario, 24; Quebec, 24; Atlantic provinces, 24 (Nova Scotia and New Brunswick, 10 each, and Prince Edward Island, four); Newfoundland, six; western provinces, 24 (six each from Manitoba, Saskatchewan, Alberta, and British Columbia); and one each from Yukon and the Northwest Territories.

The Senate performs three basic functions. In its legislative role, its major work is the revision of major government bills, either those passed by the House of Commons or those introduced in the Senate. In its deliberative role the Senate provides a national forum for the discussion of public issues. On two days' notice, a senator can start any debate, with no time limits, on any subject. In its investigative role, the Senate standing and special committees conduct thorough inquiries into social and economic issues, and their reports are considered authoritative.

The Senate's legislative powers are identical to those of the House, with two exceptions: Money bills must originate in the House and constitutional amendments may be passed by the House without the concurrence of the Senate after 180 days.

The Senate has no right, unlike the House of Lords, to delay legislation, but it has an absolute veto on nonmoney bills—i.e., it may reject or refuse to act on a bill passed by the House. Actually, the Senate does most of its useful work in tidying up legislation, and it seldom defeats a bill or amends it on matters of substance. It is a long-standing practice in the Senate when major government bills are introduced in the House to refer the "subject matter" of such bills to Senate committees in advance of their formal introduction later on. Although Liberals have dominated the chamber for most of this century, it operates with less partisanship and is less in a hurry than the lower chamber. Its lower political temperature no doubt helps it to do its tasks of legislative draftsmanship and investigation quite well.

Elections are governed by the Canada Elections Act of 1920, which also created the office of chief electoral officer. Elections to the House of Commons and provincial legislatures are direct. The age of suffrage is 18. Voter turnout ranges from 60 percent to 85 percent. All constituencies are single-member districts, and one is elected by a simply plurality. The system distorts actual voting support for the dominant party by giving it more seats than warranted by the votes and depresses the number of seats obtained by minority parties.

POLITICAL PARTIES

Canada has an effective two-party system at the federal level but multiple local parties at the provincial levels, reflecting the mosaic nature of Canadian political culture. Local parties are essentially parochial groups with little ideological content. As a result, the network of affiliated and subsidiary organizations that characterizes parties in other countries is absent in Canada. The organizational strength of federal parties rests on the local or constituent level, where the constituency associations are electoral clubs of volunteers who are active at election times At the top, each party is dominated by a handful of politicians with high visibility. Generally, constituency groups are responsible for nominating candidates, raising funds, and canvassing the electors. However, these groups exercise little influence at the national level, where the parliamentary party dominates, or at the provincial level, where the provincial legislative party dominates. One of the consequences of personal leadership in Canadian politics is that the more popular leaders are rarely displaced.

The Liberal Party (LP) emerged as the Canadian counterpart of the British Liberal Party soon after Canada gained dominion status in 1867. Its ideological bases were anticlericalism (in Quebec), free trade, and strong self-government.

The Progressive Conservative Party (PC) governed Canada for the first three decades of dominion status (1867–97) as the Conservative Party. Its constituency comprised the staunchly pro-British and anti-American British-Canadians on the one hand and the devoutly religious French-Canadians on the other. The Conservatives were pro-tariff, favoring trade restrictions as a means of building up national industrial power. Its rebirth began in 1942 when, following its merger with the Progressive Party of Manitoba, it became the Progressive Conservative Party and was able to build up a strong following in the Prairie provinces.

The New Democratic Party (NDP), known until 1961 as the Cooperative Commonwealth Federation, developed in 1933 out of the merger of the United Farmers Party, the Socialist Party, and a number of smaller political groups of European immigrants. It is a committed socialist party and a member of the Socialist International. Its twin political bases are in disparate areas: the Prairie farmers and the Ontario and British Columbia working classes. It has held political power in Saskatchewan and British Columbia under radical premiers.

The Reform Party is a right-wing populist group based in Alberta attracting broad western support. Its leader is Preston Manning, who deplores the commitment to bilingualism and opposes the dominance of Ontario and Quebec in Canadian politics.

Of the provincial parties, the most important is the Parti Québecois (PQ), which achieved power in Quebec in 1976, eight years after its founding. The party's success is closely tied to its dynamic leader, René Levesque, who helped to create the PQ from three organizations that had nothing in common except a commitment to Quebec's independence: Mouvement Souverainété, Ralliement National, and Rassemblement pour l'Indépendence Nationale.

Other minor parties include the Parti Nationaliste de Québec, the Western Canada Concept Party, the Social Credit Party (which has been in power in Alberta and British Columbia), the Union Nationale, the Confederation of Regions Western Party, the Libertarian Party, and the Communist Party.

Political Parties

Liberal Party
Quebec Bloc
Reform Party, 1988
New Democratic Party, 1961
Progressive Conservative Party, 1854
Social Credit Party, 1955
Green Party
Communist Party

Political Parties: Strength in Parliament Most Recent Elections

Senate. As of mid-1997 the distribution was as follows; Liberal Party, 52; Progressive Conservative Party, 44; independents, 3; vacant, 5. The powers of the Senate are coextensive with those of the Commons, save that all money bills must originate in the lower house.

House of Commons. Following the elections of November 27, 2000, the Liberal Party of Canada held 172 seats; Canadian Reform Conservative Alliance, 66; Progressive Conservative Party, 12; Quebec Bloc, 38, and New Democratic Party, 13.

LEGAL SYSTEM

Canada has two legal systems representing two great legal traditions: the common law derived from Anglo-Saxon traditions, and the *droit civil* (civil law), which has its roots in the legal code of the Roman emperor Justinian and later that of Napoleon Bonaparte. Criminal law is uniform throughout the country, and most of it is contained in the Criminal Code, which is derived almost exclusively from English sources.

Responsibility for the administration of the courts is divided between the federal and the provincial governments. The Constitution Act of 1867 gives each province exclusive powers over the administration of justice. Under this authority provincial legislatures have established courts of appeal, supreme courts, county courts, and provincial courts. The governments of Quebec and Nova Scotia have delegated some of this authority to the municipalities, and thus these provinces have, in addition, municipal courts.

The Supreme Court of Canada was created in 1875 by an act of Parliament and the Supreme Court Act of

1949 firmly established it as the ultimate court of appeal. The act also increased the number of judges from seven to nine, of whom three are to be Quebecois. The Supreme Court is a general court of appeal for both criminal and civil cases, with jurisdiction over both the *droit civil* of Quebec and the common law of the rest of Canada. The court sits in Ottawa. The quorum is five, but a full court of nine sits for most cases.

The Federal Court of Canada was established in 1971 as a court of law, equity, and admiralty and as a superior court of record, having both civil and criminal jurisdiction. It replaced the Exchequer Court of Canada, which had been in operation since 1875. The Federal Court of Canada has two divisions: an appeal division and a trial division. The former consists of the chief justice and nine other judges, and the latter of the associate chief justice and 13 other judges. Every judge is an ex officio member of the division of which he is not a regular member. The court may sit anywhere in Canada.

LAW ENFORCEMENT

Law Enforcement

Offenses reported to the police per 100,000: 10,351
- Murder: 5.2
- Assault: 769.1
- Burglary: 1,362.2
- Automobile Theft: 545.9
- Population per Police officer: 8,640

Death Penalty: Yes, but last execution in 1962.

HUMAN RIGHTS

The bulwark of civil rights in Canada is the 1982 constitution, which incorporates a charter of rights and freedoms. A major problem area in human rights is the influx of illegal immigrants from Asia without proper documentation. The government has found it necessary to move against these immigrant with measures considered harsh by civil rights activists. The government possesses exceptional powers to override constitutional guarantees in the event of war or national emergencies. These include the War Measures Act of 1914, augmented by a 1981 federal cabinet order permitting the federal government to declare a state of national emergency with suspension of certain basic civil liberties, as well as the Official Secrets Act of 1939. In 1987 civil rights groups and opposition parties complained that the Canadian Security and Intelligence Service (CSIS) maintained files on and performed unwarranted investigations into the activities of an unacceptably large group of Canadians who were members of peace organizations and also used false and misleading information to obtain authorization to perform a wiretap on suspected Sikh terrorists.

Freedom of speech and of press are generally respected except for provincial film censorship and legislation that specifically protects ethnic minorities against hate literature and guarantees them cultural and language rights. Although freedom of assembly and of association are freely acknowledged, the CSIS is charged with having paid informers within labor unions.

FOREIGN POLICY

Although a member of the Commonwealth, Canada's external relations are dominated by its geographical proximity to the United States. Both geography and economics as well as historical European legacies shape the common interests of the two countries. However, Canada has made strong efforts to carve a separate niche in foreign affairs and to give the impression that it is not tied to U.S. apron strings. Thus on a number of issues, it has taken a contrary position. In addition, anti–U.S. sentiments are openly expressed by Canadian policymakers in connection with the extensive U.S. ownership and control of Canadian economic enterprises and pervasive U.S. cultural and intellectual influences. There are also disputes with the United States centered on fishing rights, delimitation of the maritime boundaries in the Gulf of Maine, and the effects of acid rain from U.S. industries on Canadian forests. The two powers (as well as Mexico) are linked by the North American Free Trade Agreement (NAFTA), which entered into force in 1994. Canada has been one of the most active of the middle powers in the post–World War II period, and it enjoys an international influence far beyond what its population or economic wealth would suggest. It took the initiative in the successful completion of the international landmine treaty signed in 1997. Canadian peacekeepers serve in most UN peacekeeping forces around the world.

DEFENSE

Canada is one of the major members of the NATO alliance, and its defense forces are fully integrated into the Western system. Defense services are governed by the 1950 National Defense Act and the 1968 Canadian Forces Reorganization Act. The line of command runs from the Crown through the governor-general to the Department of National Defense and the Defense Staff. Within the unified structure there are no chiefs of individual services.

There are five functional commands, of which the first three are called environmental commands and correspond roughly to the traditional branches of navy, army, and air force: (1) Maritime Command, (2) Mobile Command, (3) Air Command, (4) Canadian Forces Europe, and (5) Communications Command. The Mobile Command consists of two brigade groups, each composed of one light artillery regiment, one light armored regiment, one combat engineer regiment, two or three infantry battalions, and supporting units. The command is headquartered at St. Hubert in Quebec, but units are stationed nationwide at Calgary, Alberta; Gagetown, New Brunswick; London, Ontario; Montreal, Quebec; Petawawa, Quebec; Shilo, Manitoba; Suffied, Alberta; and Valcartier, Quebec.

The Maritime Command is headquartered in Halifax, Nova Scotia. The commander of the maritime forces, Pacific, with headquarters at Esquimalt, British Columbia, exercises operational control over maritime forces in the Pacific.

The Air Command, with headquarters at Winnipeg, Manitoba, consists of several functional groups, such as the Fighter Group, the Air Transport Group, the Maritime Air Group, the Tactical Air Group, the Training Group, and the Air Reserve Group.

There is no conscription, and services, both regular and reserve, are voluntary.

There are two training facilities: one for English-speaking trainees and the other for French-speaking trainees. Officer recruits enter the forces through several programs, the most important of which is the Regular Officer Training Plan. The principal training institutions are the Forces Staff School for junior officers, the Land Forces Command and Staff College, the Forces Staff College, and the National Defense College.

Military Indicators

Total Active Duty Personnel: 61,600
Military Manpower per 1,000: 2.0
Military Expenditures $million: 9,077
as % of GNP: 1.7
per capita $: 319
as % of central government expenditures: 7.1

Arms Imports $million: 210
Arms Exports $million: 280

ECONOMY

As an affluent, high-tech industrial society, Canada today closely resembles the United States in its market-oriented economic system, pattern of production, and high living standards. Since World War II, the impressive growth of the manufacturing, mining, and service sectors has transformed the nation from a largely rural economy into one primarily industrial and urban. Real rates of growth have averaged nearly 3.0 percent since 1993. Unemployment is falling and government budget surpluses are being partially devoted to reducing the large public sector debt. The 1989 U.S.–Canada Free Trade Agreement (FTA) and 1994 North American Free Trade Agreement (NAFTA) (which included Mexico) have touched off a dramatic increase in trade and economic integration with the United States. With its great natural resources, skilled labor force, and modern capital plant Canada enjoys solid economic prospects. Two shadows loom, the first being the continuing constitutional impasse between English- and French-speaking areas, which has been raising the possibility of a split in the federation. Another long-term concern is the flow south to the United States of professional persons lured by higher pay, lower taxes, and the immense high-tech infrastructure.

Principal Economic Indicators

Gross National Product $: 594.976 billion
GNP per capita $: 19,640
GNP Average Annual Growth Rate (1990–97)%: 0.8
GNP per capita Average Annual Growth Rate (1990–97)%: −0.4
Origin of Gross Domestic Product %
Agriculture: 3
Mining: 4
Manufacturing: 19
Construction: 5
Public Utilities: 3
Transportation and Communications: 9
Trade: 12
Financial Services: 16
Other Services: 22
Government: 6
Gross Domestic Product by Type of Expenditure %
Private Consumption: 60
Government Consumption: 20
Gross Domestic Investment: 19
Foreign Trade: Exports: 33
Imports: −33
% of Income Received by Poorest 20%: 5.7
% of Income Received by Richest 10%: 24.1

Balance of trade (current prices)

	1992	1993	1994	1995	1996	1997	1998
Consumer price index	95.9	97.7	97.9	100.0	101.6	103.2	104.2
Monthly earnings index	95.6	97.7	98.6	100.0	103.2	104.1	106.3

Finance

National Currency: Canadian Dollar (Can $)
Exchange Rate: $1 = Can$ 1.4408
Money Supply Stock in National Currency billion: 155.8
M1 per capita: 5,170
Central Bank Discount Rate %: 4.75
Total External Debt $million: 253,000
Debt Service Ratio %: —
Balance of Payments $million: −10,304
International Reserves SDRs million: 15,315
Ratio of External Debt to Total Reserves: —
Average Annual Rate of Inflation/Consumer Price Index Growth Rate %: 1.8

Official Development Assistance

Donor ODA $million: 1,600
as % of GNP: 2.6
per capita $ 52.2
Foreign Direct Investment $million: 16,514

Central Government Revenues and Expenditures

Fiscal Year: 1 April–31 March

Revenues $million: 106,500
Expenditures $million: 117,200
Budget Deficit $million: 10,700
Tax Revenues as % of GDP: —
Highest Tax Bracket %
Individual: 29
Corporate: 38

Employment and Labor

Economically Active Population: 14,928,000
Female Participation Rate %: 45.1
Activity Rate %: 50.4
Labor by Sector: %
Agriculture, Forestry, Fishing: 3.7
Manufacturing, Mining: 15.9
Construction: 4.9
Transportation and Communications: 6.0
Trade, Hotels, and Restaurants: 21.2
Finance, Insurance, Real Estate: 11.2
Public Administration, Defense: 5.4
Services: 22.2
Unemployment %: 8.6

Agriculture

Agriculture's Share of GDP %: 3
Average Annual Rate of Growth (1965–98) %: —
Number of Farms 000: 277
Average Size of Farm ha: 246
Number of Tractors per 1,000 hectares: 16.3
Irrigation, % of Farms having: 1.6
Artificial Fertilizer kg/hectare: 47
Total Farmland as % of land area: 7.4
Livestock: Cattle 000: 13,357
Sheep 000: 634
Hogs 000: 11,843
Chickens 000: 139,000
Forests: Production of Roundwood (000 cubic meters): 186,195
Fisheries: Total Catch tons 000: 1,010.6

Mining

% of GDP: 4.4
Value of Mineral Production $million: 25,411.4

Manufacturing

Value Added $million: 103,690
Industrial Production Growth Rate %: 1.7

Energy

Commercial Energy Production metric tons of oil equivalent 000: 362,701
Commercial Energy Consumption metric tons of oil equivalent 000: 237,983
Commercial Energy Consumption per capita kg: 7,930
Average Annual Growth Rate 1980–97 %: 0.4
Net Energy Imports % of use: −52
Electricity Installed Capacity kW 000: 113,340
Production kW-hr million: 537,114
Coal Reserves tons million: 8,623
Production tons 000: 74,942
Natural Gas Proven Reserves cubic meters billion: 1,929
Production cubic meters million: 175,897
Crude Petroleum Reserves barrels million: 4,894
Production barrels million: 664
Consumption barrels million: 492
Refinery Capacity barrels per day 000: 1,852
Pipelines Length km: 23,564

Foreign Trade

Imports $million: 171,007.2
Exports $million: 201,573.7
Export Volume % Annual Growth Rate (1990–97): 9.1
Import Volume % Annual Growth Rate (1990–97): 8.6

Price and earnings indexes

	1992	1993	1994	1995	1996	1997	1998
Consumer price index	8.2	12.1	19.3	38.7	36.4	25.5	19.8
% of total	3.2%	3.4%	4.5%	7.9%	7.1%	4.5%	3.2%

Major Trading Partners

	Imports	Exports
European Union %	9.8	5.7
United States %	67.6	81.6
Eastern Europe %	0.4	0.3
Japan %	4.5	3.8
Others %	17.8	8.6

Transportation

Roads Total Length mi: 634,400 km 1,021,000
Paved %: 35
Automobiles: 14,280,000
Trucks and Buses: 3,895,600
Persons per vehicle: 1.6
Railroad; Track Length mi: 44,182 km 71,104
Passenger-mi million: 889
Freight-mi million: 185,641
Merchant Marine: No. of Vessels: 1,185
Total Deadweight Tonnage 000: 2,896.8
International Cargo Loaded tons 000: 176,667
International Cargo Off-loaded tons 000: 83,287
Airports with Scheduled Flights: 301
Traffic: Passenger-mi million: 35,364
Freight-mi million: 4,824
Length of Canals mi: 1,860 km 3,000

Tourism

Number of Tourists to 000: 18,837
Number of Tourists from 000: 17,648
Tourist Receipts $million: 8,012
Tourist Expenditures $million: 10,220

Communications

Telephones 000: 17,457
Cost of Local Calls 3 mins: $0
Cellular Telephones 000: 2,590
Fax Machines 000: 525
Personal Computers 000: 5,700
Internet Hosts per million persons: 12,595
Mail: Post Offices: 18,607
Pieces of Mail Handled million: 10,715
Pieces of Mail Handled per person: 370

EDUCATION

Schools were introduced into Canada by missionaries, both Catholic and Protestant (Anglican), in the French and British possessions, respectively. Even the Hudson's Bay Company encouraged missionary activity in its territory and subsidized denominational schools. It was only in the 19th century that the nondenominational public school system began to make headway, and soon it became well established in all provinces except Quebec and Newfoundland. The principle of public support for denominational schools was, nevertheless, accorded some recognition.

The constitutional basis of the educational system is found in the Constitution Act of 1867, which states that "in and for each province the legislature may exclusively make laws in relation to education." At the same time the act guaranteed denominational rights to education. The Charter of Rights and Freedoms of 1982 acknowledges language rights of both French and English speakers.

The evolution of the educational system has contributed to the gradual blurring of boundaries between elementary and secondary education in Canada. Among the developments that have brought about this integration are: the unification of the once-separate elementary and secondary school boards; the consolidation of all teacher training in the universities; the membership of both elementary and secondary teachers in the same professional associations; the shift in emphasis from subject-centered to child-centered curricula; and the insertion of an intermediate stage between the elementary and the secondary levels. The intermediate level retains some of the characteristics of elementary schooling, such as the home room, where the whole class studies together as a social unit for much of the day, and some features of the secondary school, such as a rotating schedule of instruction by a succession of subject specialists. Similarly, the traditional gap between secondary and vocational education has been bridged.

The point of transition to secondary school now varies among provinces and even among school boards. In some places there are six grades of elementary school followed by three middle grades known as junior high and three upper grades known as senior high. In other places, the pattern is 6-3-4. Although elementary education is compulsory throughout Canada, the starting age is six in Alberta, Nova Scotia, Ontario, and Quebec and seven elsewhere.

Secondary grades cover grades nine to 11 or nine to 12, while others begin at grade seven or eight. At least part of secondary education is compulsory everywhere except in the Northwest Territories, where children may leave school at age 12. Pupils must stay in school up to age 15 in British Columbia, Newfoundland, New Brunswick, Prince Edward Island, Quebec, and Yukon and up to age 16 in Alberta, Manitoba, Nova Scotia, Ontario, and Saskatchewan. In Quebec five years of secondary education (grades 7 to 11) are followed by two or three years at a collège d'enseignement général et professionnel (CEGEP).

The higher education sector comprises universities and community colleges. In 1998 there were 69 public universities, of which the five largest were the universities of Toronto, British Columbia, Alberta, Montreal, and McGill. Most are Anglophone. In addition, there are bilingual universities such as the University of Ottawa and Laurentian University, Sudbury. Private or religious universities affiliate with a public university while retaining their religious identity.

Three or four years of full-time study are required for a bachelor's degree in arts or science at general or honors levels. Community colleges offer the first two years of university study, after which students may transfer to a university. Community colleges have flexible admission policies, and their scale of tuition fees is much below that of universities.

Education

Literacy Rate %: 96.6
Male %: —
Female %: —
First Level: Primary schools: 12,700
Teachers: 148,724
Students: 2,413,126
Student-Teacher Ratio: 16.2
Net Enrollment Ratio: 95
Second Level: Secondary Schools: 3,324
Teachers: 133,358
Students: 2,469,552
Student-Teacher Ratio: 18.5
Net Enrollment Ratio: 92

Vocational Level: Schools: —
Students: —

Third Level: Institutions: 265
Teachers: 64,100
Students: 1,209,386
Student-Ratio Level: 14.4
Gross Enrollment Ratio: 102.9
Students per 100,000: 6,984
% of Population Age 25 and over with Postsecondary Education: 21.4

Public Expenditure on Education as % of GDP: 7.3

SCIENCE AND TECHNOLOGY

Science and Technology

Scientists and Engineers in R&D per 1 million persons: 2,719
Expenditures in R&D as % of GDP: 1.66
High-Tech Exports $million: 21,736
Patent Applications by Residents: 4,192

MEDIA

The first Canadian newspaper, published in Halifax in 1752, predated confederation by over a century. The press played an important role in the evolution of Canada's peculiar geographical and historical characteristics. The large physical size and small population dictated that the Canadian press would remain scattered and few in number and that the circulations of individual newspapers would be much smaller than those in Europe or the United States. Of the 99 communities with dailies, only 14 have more than one, and half the dailies have circulations under 25,000. Nonetheless, in terms of quality, Canada has at least half a dozen newspapers of world class, including the *Toronto Star*; *Le Devoir*, *Le Journal de Montreal*, the *Globe and Mail*, Toronto; and the *Winnipeg Free Press*, the last of which is included in *The World's Great Dailies*.

Three factors peculiar to Canada have influenced the evolution of the Canadian press. The first is the bilingual imperative, which means that although French speakers constitute less than 30 percent of the population, both French and English receive equal treatment in all public communications, backed up by constitutional provisions. French- and English-language media in Canada view the world in quite different ways. Francophone dailies and broadcast media have a much more insular outlook because of a preoccupation with Quebec's regional and provincial affairs. Even when the same stories are covered by the two language media, the French journalist is more likely to adopt a guiding rather than an informing function, following the continental European tradition of giving more analysis and comment than factual reportage.

The second major influence is that of the United States, a consequence of physical proximity. Two-thirds of Canadians live within 161 km (100 mi) of the U.S. border and are constantly exposed to U.S. electronic media. Hollywood films virtually dominate Canadian cinemas. American magazines outsell Canadian in Canada, and U.S. book imports make up two-thirds of total book sales. Even in dailies, some one-fifth of all news is about the United States, representing up to half of all foreign news printed, and most of the other foreign news originates with the U.S. wire services.

The third factor is regionalism in the context of Canada's strict federalism. The lack of a strong national identity or self-image has helped regionalist tendencies to flourish. The media are among the strongholds of regionalism, and complaints of inequalities and disparities are articulated and magnified by newspeople. Some regional newspapers resent the domination of the Toronto and Montreal elite press in the same way as third world media resent the hegemony of the Western media.

The Canadian press is as free as that of the United States even though no First Amendment infuses the Canadian media with the positive spirit of liberty that manifests itself in the no-malice libel defense or shield laws or the Freedom of Information Act. The Canadian Bill of Rights, however, does include a reference to freedom of the press as "a fundamental freedom." But it is rather in the due process of law that Canadian freedom of the press finds its strongest safeguard. This protection is invoked in regard to laws that apply to the press, such as contempt of court, civil defamation, criminal libel, obscenity, copyright, privacy, and government secrecy. Canada has no shield laws to protect journalists from having to disclose sources of information to courts or parliamentary bodies.

Canada's leading news agency, Canadian Press, has traditionally enjoyed a near monopoly and has been challenged only feebly by competitors, such as United Press Canada. Only a handful of foreign newspapers and magazines are represented in Ottawa.

The broadcast media are regulated by the Canadian Radio-Television and Telecommunications Commission, set up by the federal Broadcasting Act of 1968. The act established the Canadian Broadcasting Corporation (CBC) as the national, publicly owned broadcasting service, financed mainly by public funds supplemented by advertising revenues. Services are operated in both English and French.

CBC operates 10 AM and two FM networks, one each in English and in French. CBC's Northern Service provides both national network programming in English and French and special local and shortwave programs, some of which are broadcast in the language of the Indian and Inuit peoples. CBC radio is virtually free of commercials. Radio Canasa International is CBC's overseas shortwave service.

CBC operates two television networks, one in English and one in French. The Northern Service, created in 1958, reaches northern Quebec, the Northwest Territories, and Yukon, 60 percent of whose inhabitants are native Canadians, and programming is provided in Inuktitut languages as well as in English and French. Broadcast time is also made available to native groups who produce their own programs. Many privately owned stations have affiliation agreements with CBC. The major private television networks are CTV, TVA (which serves Quebec), and Global (which serves Ontario). Canadian Satellite Communications (CANCOM) was licensed in 1981 to carry on a multichannel radio and television operation via Anik satellite. There are five educational services: TV–Ontario, Radio Quebec, Access (in Alberta),

Knowledge Network (in British Columbia), and Sask-media (in Saskatchewan).

Media

Daily Newspapers: 107
Total Circulation 000: 5,500
Circulation per 1,000: 189
Books Published: 22,208
Magazines: 1,400
Radio Receivers 000: 22,600
per 1,000: 803
Television sets 000: 18,917
per 1,000: 647

MOST IMPORTANT MEDIA:

Press. Until the start of *The National Post* in October 1998, there were no national press organs; of the more than 1,200 newspapers in 1993, 108 were dailies, approximately one-third of the latter being owned by Thomson Newspapers, Ltd., the largest of Canada's major chains. The following (circulation figures for September 1993) are English-language dailies, unless otherwise noted: *Toronto Star* (Toronto, 510,336 daily, 510,100 Sunday); *Globe and Mail* (Toronto, 311,800 morning); *Le Journal de Montreal* (Montreal, 283,100 morning, 300,700 Sunday), in French; *Toronto Sun* (Toronto, 254,100 morning, 443,600 Sunday); *Vancouver Sun* (Vancouver, 200,500 evening); *La Presse* (Montreal, 187,800 morning, 186,600 Sunday), in French; *Ottawa Citizen* (Ottawa, 173,000 daily, 158,200 Sunday); *The Province* (Vancouver, 169,000 morning, 206,700 Sunday); *Edmonton Journal* (Edmonton, 156,300 morning, 148,300 Sunday); *The Gazette* (Montreal, 154,100 morning, 144,300 Sunday), oldest Canadian newspaper, founded 1788; *Free Press* (Winnipeg, 142,800 morning, 144,900 Sunday); *Free Press* (London, 110,200 morning); *The Spectator* (Hamilton, 108,900 evening); *Le Soleil* (Quebec, 95,800 morning, 82,500 Sunday), in French; *Windsor Star* (Windsor, 85,900 evening).

News agencies. In January 1985 the Canadian Press, a cooperative of over 100 daily newspapers, became Canada's only wire service after buying out its only competitor, United Press Canada. Numerous foreign agencies maintain offices in the leading cities.

Radio and television. Radio and television broadcasting is supervised by the Canadian Radio-Television and Telecommunications Commission (CRTC), which was formed by the 1968 Broadcasting Act. The publicly owned Canadian Broadcasting Corporation/Société Radio Canada (CBC/SRC) provides domestic radio and television service in both English and French. Most major television stations not associated with the CBC are affiliated with the CTV Television Network, Ltd., although there are several other smaller services, some emphasizing French-language and/or educational programming.

CULTURE

Cultural Indicators

Public Libraries Number: 997
Volumes: 56,860,000
Registered borrowers: —
Museums Number: 661
Annual Attendance: 16,165,000
Cinema Production of Long Films: 22
Number of Cinemas: 742
Seating Capacity: 722,000
Annual Attendance million: 79
Annual Attendance per capita: 2.8

STATUS OF WOMEN

Over the past decade, the government has demonstrated that improving the social and economic status of women is a top priority. The Ministry of Women's Equality was established in 1991 with a mandate to work in partnership with all government ministries, Crown corporations and agencies, community groups, and the private sector to build a society where women experience equality in all aspects of their lives. It is the only freestanding ministry for women in Canada, acting as an advocate for numerous economic, health, and safety matters, and social justice issues of importance to women.

Women

Gender Empowerment Measure: 7
Seats Held in Parliament by Women %: 21.2
Female Administrators and Managers %: 42.2
Female Professional and Technical Workers %: 56.1
Women's Share of Earned Income %: 38
Women in Government %: 19

HEALTH, FOOD, AND NUTRITION

Health

Number of Physicians: 63,700
Number of Dentists: 14,621
Number of Nurses: 262,288
Number of Pharmacists: 22,121
Population per Physician: 465
Number of Hospitals: 1,079
Hospital Beds per 10,000: 54
Hospital Bed Occupancy Rate: —
Infant Mortality Rate per 1,000 live births: 8
Maternal Mortality Rate per 100,000 live births: 6
Total Health Expenditures as % of GDP: 9.05
Health Expenditures per capita $: 1,945
HIV Infected % of adults: 0.33
Cigarette Consumption per smoker per year: 3,081
% of Smokers: Male: 31
Female: 29
Access to Safe Water %: 100

Food and Nutrition

Food Supply as % of FAO Requirements: 116
% of Consumption Expenditures on Food: 13.4
Daily Available Calories per capita: 3,093
% of Total Calories derived from:
Cereals: 22.1
Potatoes, cassava: 3.5
Meat, poultry: 11.5
Fish: 1.1
Eggs, milk: 9.7
Fruits, vegetables: 6.7
Fats, oils: 19.8

ENVIRONMENT

The country's greatest environmental concern is growing air pollution and the resulting acid rain severely affecting lakes and damaging forests. The origins of the pollutants that cause the acid rain have been a point of contention between Canadian officials and their U.S. counterparts. In addition to acid rain, metal smelting, coal-burning utilities, and vehicle emissions affect agricultural and forest productivity. Ocean waters are becoming contaminated due to agricultural, industrial, mining, and forestry activities.

Environment

Forest Area sq km: 2,446,000
Average Annual Deforestation sq km: −1,764
Nationally Protected Areas as % of Total Land Area: 10
Freshwater Access cubic meters per capita: 92,142
Emissions of Organic Water Pollutants kg per day: 295,525
CO_2 Emissions per capita ton: 13.8

CHRONOLOGY

1957 Long Liberal rule ends with Progressive Conservatives gaining power under John Diefenbaker as prime minister.
1963 Lester B. Pearson leads Liberals back into office.
1968 Pearson steps down and is succeeded by Pierre Trudeau as prime minister.
1970 The War Measures Act is promulgated to deal with Francophone terrorist activity in Quebec.
1974 Quebec declares French to be its official language.
1976 The Parti Qúebecois, a separatist party, gains power in Quebec under René Levesque as premier.
1979 A Progressive Conservative minority government under Joseph Clark displaces the Trudeau government.
1980 Progressive Conservatives lose elections, and Liberals return to power.
1982 The Constitution Act of 1867 is "patriated," and the Constitution Act of 1982 is passed along with the Charter of Rights and Freedoms:
1984 Trudeau yields office to John Turner, who is elected Liberal leader. Turner calls a snap election in which the Liberals suffer a decisive defeat; the Progressive Conservatives are elected to office with the largest majority in parliamentary history, under Brian Mulroney as prime minister.
1986 Canada proclaims sovereignty over the Arctic region, including interisland channels, despite opposition from the United States.
1987 A proposed division of the Northwest Territories into two regions, Nunavut and Denendah, is passed by the territorial assembly.
1989 The Canada-United States free-trade agreement comes into force.
1993 Liberal party candidate Jean Chrétien wins the prime ministry.
1994 Canada, the United States, and Mexico sign the North America Free Trade Agreement (NAFTA) creating the world's largest single market.
1999 Adrienne Clarkson is appointed governor-general .... A large region of the Northwest Territories officially becomes the separate territory of Nunavut, the only Canadian territory or province with a majority indigenous population. Paul Okalik becomes Nunavut's first territorial premier.
2000 Chrétien's Liberal Party wins the parliamentary election.

BIBLIOGRAPHY

d'Haenens, Leen. *Images of Canadianness: Visions on Canada's Politics, Culture, Economics,* Ottawa, 1998.
Mahand, Edelgard E., and Graeme S. Mount. *An Introduction to Canadian-American Relations.* New York, 1984.
Nossal, Kim R. *The Politics of Canadian Foreign Policy.* Englewood Cliffs, N.J., 1985.
Pryke, Kenneth G. *Profiles of Canada.* Toronto, 1992.
Riendeau, Roger E. *A Brief History of Canada.* New York, 2000.
Romney, Paul. *Getting It Wrong: How Canadians Forgot Their Past and Imperiled Confederation.* Toronto, 1999.
Savoie, Donald J. *Governing from the Centre: The Concentration of Power in Canadian Politics.* Toronto, 1999.
Smith, David E. *The Republican Option in Canada, Past and Present.* Toronto, 1999.

OFFICIAL PUBLICATIONS

Canada. *Canada Year Book* (biennial); *Census Canada 1996; Population.*

CONTACT INFORMATION

Embassy of Canada
501 Pennsylvania Avenue NW
Washington, D.C. 20001
Phone: (202) 682-1740 Fax: (202) 682-7726

INTERNET RESOURCES

- Statistics Canada http://www.statcan.ca

CAPE VERDE

BASIC FACT SHEET

OFFICIAL NAME:
Republic of Cape Verde (República de Cabo Verde)

ABBREVIATION:
CV

CAPITAL:
Praia

HEAD OF STATE:
President Pedro Verona Rodrigues Pires (from 2001)

HEAD OF GOVERNMENT:
Prime Minister José Maria Neves (from 2001)

NATURE OF GOVERNMENT:
One-party modified democracy

POPULATION:
406,000 (1999)

AREA:
4,033 sq km (1,557 sq mi)

ETHNIC MAJORITY:
Mesticos of mixed Portuguese and African descent

LANGUAGES:
Portuguese (official): Crioulo (national)

RELIGION:
Roman Catholicism

UNIT OF CURRENCY:
Cape Verde escudo (C.V. Esc.)

NATIONAL FLAG:
Three horizontal bands of (from top) blue (double width), white (with a horizontal red stripe in its middle), and blue; a circle of 10 yellow five-pointed stars is centered on the hoist end of the middle band, extending into the upper and lower blue bands.

NATIONAL EMBLEM:
The main elements of the coat of arms are a blue equilateral triangle with a white torch in its center; the words *Republic of Cape Verde* are inscribed from the bottom left angle up to the vertex and down to the bottom right angle of the triangle; three blue-colored line segments are parallel to the base of the triangle; a blue circle encloses these elements, with a yellow plummet, aligned with the vertex of the equilateral triangle; outside the circle are three yellow links placed on the composition base, followed by two green palms and 10 yellow five-pointed stars placed symmetrically in two groups of five.

NATIONAL ANTHEM:
"This Is Our Beloved Country"

NATIONAL HOLIDAYS:
July 5 (National Day, Independence Day); May 1 (Labor Day); September 12 (Day of the Nation); January 20 (National Heroes' Day); January 1 (New Year's Day); March 8 (Women's Day); June 1 (Children's Day); also variable Christian festivals

DATE OF INDEPENDENCE:
July 5, 1975

DATE OF CONSTITUTION:
September 25, 1992

GEOGRAPHICAL FEATURES

Cape Verde consists of an archipelago of 10 islands and five islets in the Atlantic Ocean about 595 km (370 mi) west of Dakar, Senegal, and with a total land area of 4,033 sq km (1,557 sq mi). The greatest distance across the archipelago southeast to northwest is 332 km (206 mi) and northeast to southwest is 299 km (186 mi). The total length of the coastline is 965 km (600 mi).

The archipelago is divided into two districts: Barlavento, or Windward Islands, and Sotavento, or Leeward Islands, named according to the direction of the prevailing northeasterly wind. Except for the low-lying islands of Sal, Boa Vista, and Maio, Cape Verde is mountainous, with rugged cliffs and deep ravines. The highest peaks are Pico da Cano, an active volcano reaching 2,829 m (9,278 ft), and two peaks reaching 1,935 m (6,348 ft) and 1,320 m (4,298 ft) on Santo Antao and São Tiago, respectively.

Cape Verde

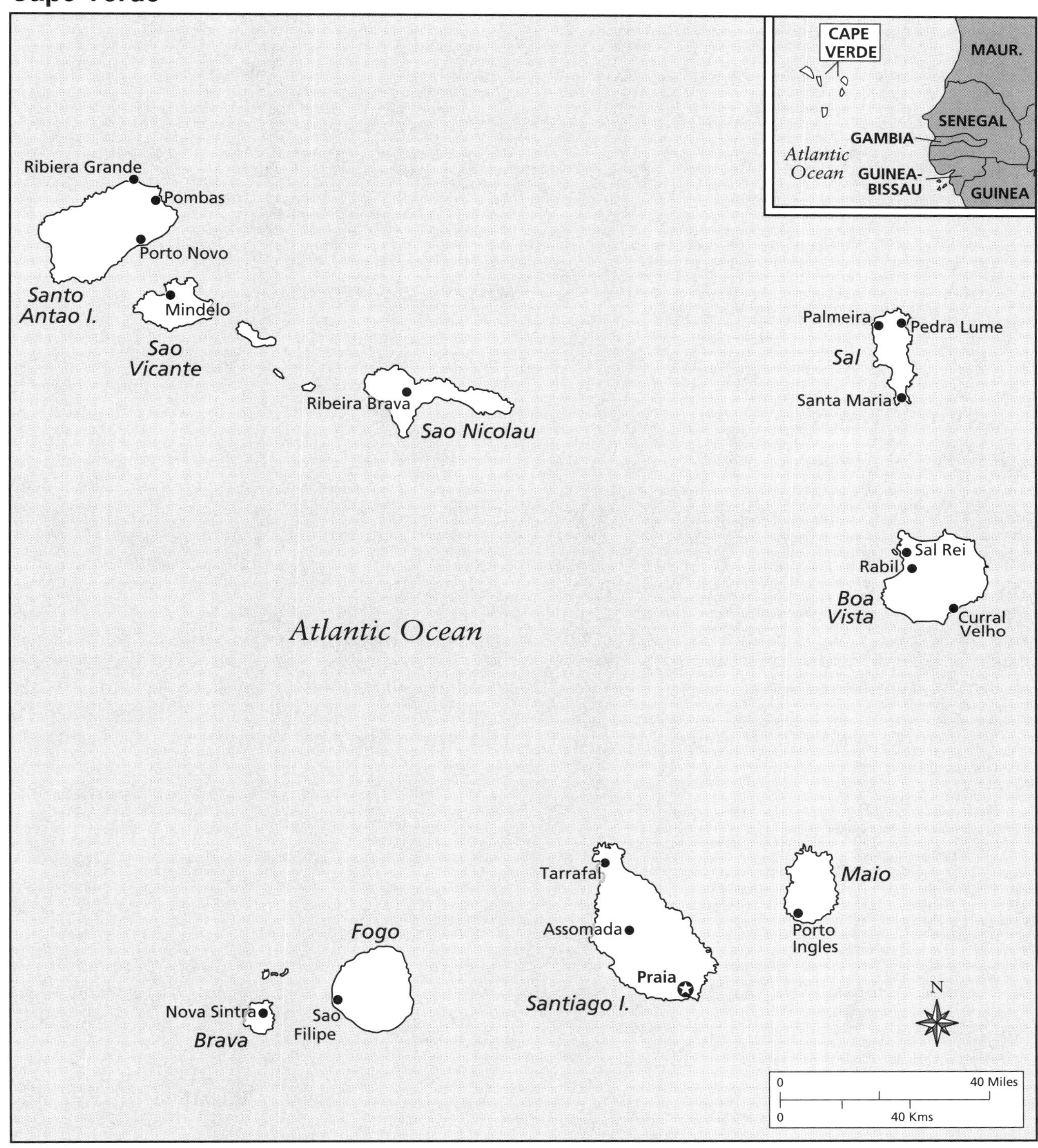
CAPE VERDE
MAUR.
SENEGAL
GAMBIA
Atlantic Ocean
GUINEA-BISSAU
GUINEA
Ribiera Grande
Pombas
Porto Novo
Santo Antao I.
Mindelo
Sao Vicante
Palmeira
Pedra Lume
Sal
Santa Maria
Ribeira Brava
Sao Nicolau
Sal Rei
Rabil
Boa Vista
Curral Velho
Atlantic Ocean
Tarrafal
Maio
Assomada
Porto Ingles
Fogo
Praia
Santiago I.
Nova Sintra
Sao Filipe
Brava
N
0
40 Miles
0
40 Kms

Geography

Area sq km: 4,033 sq mi 1,557
World Rank: 169th
Land Boundaries, km: 9
Coastline, km: 965
Elevation Extremes meters
Lowest: Atlantic Ocean
Highest: Pico 2,829
Land Use % Arable land: 11
Permanent Crops: 0
Permanent Pastures: 6
Forest and Woodland: 0
Other: 83

Population of Principal Cities

Praia	68,000

CLIMATE AND WEATHER

Cape Verde has an arid climate, with two seasons: a cool, dry season from December to June, with temperatures averaging 21°C (70°F); and a warm season from July to November, with temperatures averaging 26.6°C (80°F). Rainfall is sparse and rarely exceeds 127 mm (5 in) in the northern islands and 305 mm (12 in) in the southern islands. The islands suffer from chronic and severe shortages of water and rainfall, which cause catastrophic droughts periodically. São Vicente depends on a desalination plant for its drinking water.

Climate and Weather

Mean Temperature
Summer 80°F
Winter 70°F
Average Rainfall Northern Islands 5 in
Southern Islands 12 in

POPULATION

Population Indicators

Total Population: 1999 406,000
World Rank: 170th
Density per sq mi: 260.8 per sq km 100.7
% of annual growth (1994–99): 1.6
Male %: 47.3
Female %: 52.7
Urban %: 44.1
Age Distribution: % 0–14: 45.0
15–29: 27.3
30–44: 11.4
45–59: 8.0
60–74: 5.5
75 and over: 2.9
Population 2020: 512,000
Birth Rate per 1,000: 31.9
Death Rate per 1,000: 7.1
Population Doubling Time (years): 25
Infant Mortality Rate Per 1,000 live births: 41.0
Rate of Natural Increase per 1,000: 24.8
Total Fertility Rate: 3.6
Expectation of Life (years): Males 65.5
Females 67.5
Marriage Rate per 1,000: 4.5
Divorce Rate per 1,000: —
Total Number of Households: 59,000
Average Size of Households: 5.1
% of Illegitimate Children: 44.8
Induced Abortions: —
Rate per 100 live births: —

ETHNIC COMPOSITION

About 60 percent of the population are of mixed descent, except on São Tiago, where the population is of African Wolof stock. *Mesticos*, or Creoles, as persons of mixed descent are called, are a majority on all other islands. They are descendants of Portuguese settlers and of African slaves who were brought to work on the plantations. Whites represented 2 percent of the population until independence, but most of them have been repatriated. There are no Americans permanently resident in the country.

LANGUAGES

The official language is Portuguese. The national language is a creole Portuguese known as Crioulo, in which the vocabulary, syntax, and pronunciation have been Africanized. Crioulo spoken by 70 percent of the population. Portuguese is the language of the officials and educated elite.

Principal Languages and Their Speakers

Crioulo (Portuguese Creole)	406,000
Portuguese	—

RELIGIONS

Almost all the *mesticos* and the majority of the Africans adhere to the Roman Catholic faith. The Roman Catholic suffragan see of São Tiago de Cabo Verde is attached to the metropolitan see of Lisbon.

Religious Affiliations

Roman Catholic	390,000
Protestant	16,000

HISTORICAL BACKGROUND

Prior to the arrival of Europeans, there were no inhabitants of Cape Verde. Cape Verde was one of the earliest European colonies in Africa and one of the last to achieve independence. The archipelago was declared part of the

Portuguese royal dominions in 1495. From 1591 until independence in 1975 the islands formed a single overseas province of Portugal and were administered by a governor. However, the country had lost much of its importance as a strategic gateway to the Atlantic with the abolition of the slave trade in 1876.

Cape Verde achieved independence after a long and costly struggle, in the course of which Amilcar Cabral, the independence forces leader, was assassinated. There was little actual fighting in the islands; most of it occurred in Guinea-Bissau. Cape Verde's right to self-determination and independence was acknowledged by the new regime that was set up by the Armed Forces' Movement in Portugal in 1974. When independence finally was granted in 1975, relations between Portugal and its former colony became more cordial than ever before. At independence, the government was controlled by the Cape Verdean wing of the African Party for the Independence of Guinea and Cape Verde (PAIGC). Its leader, Aristides Pereira, became the first president. The PAIGC became the sole legal party and was given supremacy over government structures. This was confirmed by the constitution of 1980. Since its founding, the PAIGC had been a binational party that had the unification of Guinea-Bissau and Cape Verde as one of its principal objectives. However, in 1980 a coup in Guinea-Bissau, against a president who was Cape Verdean, shattered party unity. The following year the Cape Verdean wing of the party changed its name to the African Party for Independence of Cape Verde (PAICV) and abandoned the goal of unification. Relations between the two countries returned to normal in 1982.

In 1986 Aristides Pereira, who had been president since independence, was reelected to another five-year term by the National People's Assembly. Demonstrations for greater political freedom were held in 1988 and the following year a commission was established to consider proposals for constitutional change. As pressure from church and academic circles increased, the PAICV announced the convening of a special congress to abolish the constitutional provisions that gave it a monopoly of power. In September 1990 Cape Verde officially became a multiparty state, and the Movimento para Democracia (MPD), which had advocated a return to a multiparty system, received official recognition as a political party.

The MDP won 56 out of 79 seats in the 1991 legislative elections, the first since independence. The MPD candidate, Antonio Mascarenhas Monteiro, won the country's first free presidential elections in a contest that pitted him against Pereira. A new constitution endorsing the new multiparty system was adopted in 1992. The early 1990s were difficult for the country economically in large part due to devastating droughts. However, the MPD was successful in its 1995 reelections. In 1997, the country again suffered a drought that wiped out over 80 percent of the country's grain. In 2001 elections, the PAICV retook the majority of seats in the National Assembly, and PAICV candidate Pedro Pires was elected president. Pires appointed José Maria Neves prime minister.

CONSTITUTION

Cape Verde's newest constitution was adopted on September 25, 1992 and underwent revisions in 1995. December 28, 1994. The head of the state is the president, who is elected by the National People's Assembly for a five-year term, as is the prime minister, who is the head of government. Deputies of the National People's Assembly are elected by universal suffrage from a multiparty ballot.

Legislative power is vested in the 83-member National People's Assembly, which is elected by universal suffrage for five-year terms. The president, who is head of state, is

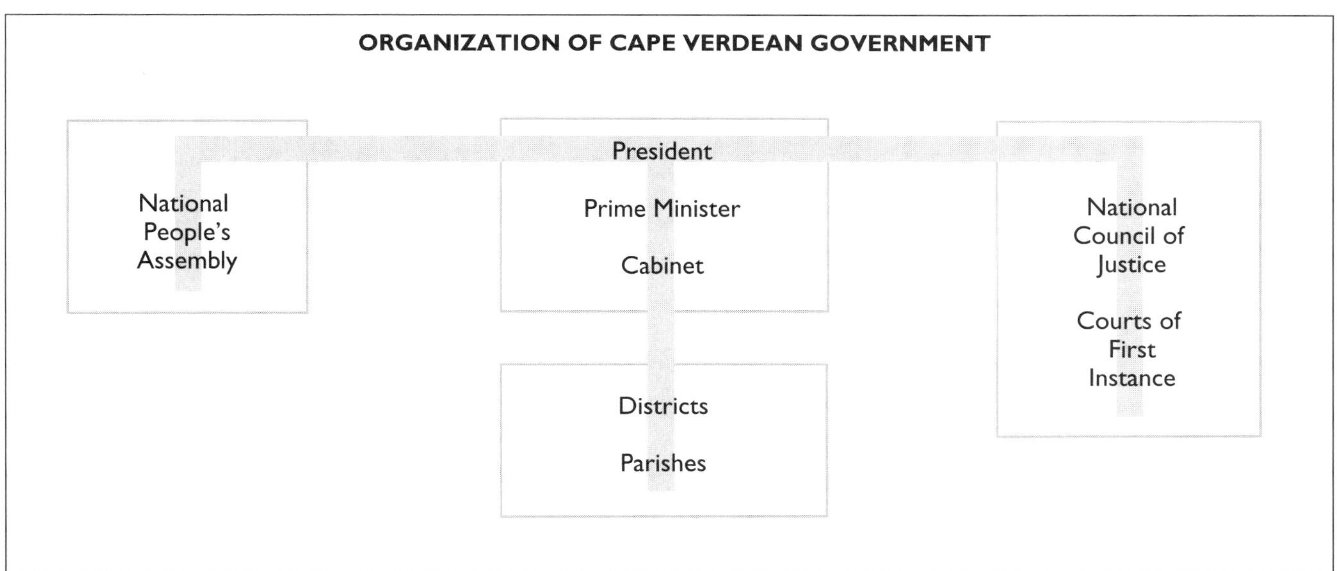

elected by universal suffrage and he must win two-thirds of the vote to secure election. If he does not, a runoff is scheduled within 21 days between the two candidates with the highest number of votes. The prime minister, who is head of government, is appointed by the president and elected by the National People's Assembly.

Suffrage is universal over age 18.

LOCAL GOVERNMENT

For purposes of local administration, Cape Verde is divided into 16 concelhos (districts) and 31 freguesias (parishes). Representative institutions are being gradually introduced at the regional level.

Local Government

Principal administrative divisions, capitals, area, population

AREA AND POPULATION

Island groups / Island/Counties / Counties	Capitals	area sq mi	area sq km	population 1990 estimate
Leeward Islands		696	1,803	221,537
Brava	Nova Sintra	26	67	6,975
Fogo				
Mosteiros	—	184	476	33,902
São Filipe	São Felipe	184	476	33,902
Maio	Porto Ingles	104	269	4,969
Santiago		383	991	175,691
Praia	Praia	153	396	82,802
Santa Catarna	Assomada	94	243	41,584
Santa Cruz	Pedra Badejo	58	149	25,892
São Domingos		—	—	—
Tarrafal	Tarrafal	78	183	25,413
Windward Islands		861	2,230	119,954
Boa Vista	Sal Rei	239	620	3,452
Sal	Santa Maria	83	216	7,715
Santo Antão		300	779	43,845
Paul	Pombas	21	54	8,121
Porto Novo	Porto Novo	215	558	14,873
Ribeira Grande	Ponta do Sol	64	167	20,851
São Nicolau	Ribeira Brava	150	388	13,665
São Vicente	Mindelo	88	227	51,277
TOTAL		1,557	4,033	341,491

PARLIAMENT

The national legislature is the Assembleia Nacional Popular (National People's Assembly), a unicameral body last elected in 1995. In that election, the Movimento para a Democracia (MPD) won 50 seats; the Partido Africano da Independência de Cabo Verde (PAICV), which had been the sole legitimate party until 1990, won 21 seats; and the Partido da Convergencia Democratica one a single seat.

Deputies of the National People's Assembly are elected by universal suffrage of those over age 18.

POLITICAL PARTIES

The three major political parties are: the Movimento para a Democracia founded in 1991, which advocates administrative decentralization; the Partido Africano da Independência de Capo Verde, which was the only authorized party from 1975–90; and the Partido da Convergencia Democrática founded in 1994 from splinter members of the Movimento para a Democracia. In addition to these three major parties, there are a number of smaller ones that in the last general election attracted less than 2.5 percent of the total vote as a group.

Political Parties

Movement for Democracy
Cape Verdean Independent and Democratic Union
African Party for the Independence of Cape Verde, 1956
People's Union for the Independence of Cape Verde, 1990
Democratic Socialist Party, 1995
Democratic Alliance for Change
Labor and Solidarity Party, 1998

Political Parties: Strength in Parliament Most Recent Elections

Elections to the 72-member **National People's Assembly** on January 14, 2001, gave the African Party of Independence of Cape Verde 40 seats; Movement for Democracy, 30; and Democratic Alliance for Change, 2.

LEGAL SYSTEM

The highest judicial body in the land is the National Council of Justice, composed of three judges appointed by the government and six assessors designated by the legislature. The council has original jurisdiction and also hears appeals from elected courts of first instance in each of the country's 224 administrative districts.

Trials are conducted by one judge; a public prosecutor presents the case against an accused, who is defended by counsel. There is no jury system. Appeal is possible, and trials appear to be handled expeditiously. There also is a system of popular tribunals to adjudicate minor disputes on a neighborhood or local level in rural areas. The "judges" usually are prominent local citizens without legal training who are appointees of the Ministry of Justice. Their decisions can be appealed within the regular court system.

The judiciary does not have the authority to determine the constitutionality of legislation. Although, according to the constitution, judges are independent, one former judge now living outside the country has claimed that one-party rule in practice has hampered the functioning of a truly independent judiciary. Most evidence suggests, however, that the courts protect individual rights in criminal cases.

Law Enforcement

Offenses reported to the police per 100,000: —
- Murder: —
- Assault: —
- Burglary: —
- Automobile Theft: —
- Population per Police officer: 110

Death Penalty: Abolished 1981

HUMAN RIGHTS

Despite the potential for human rights abuses, Cape Verde has a good track record in both civil and political rights. There are no political prisoners, no torture or physical abuse of prisoners has been reported, and no political opponents have "disappeared." Trials, both civil and criminal, are open to the public and defendants are afforded legal counsel, at state expense if need be. There have never been any allegations of forced entry into private homes by police officials. The news media are government monopolies and are used to reinforce support for the government programs.

FOREIGN POLICY

As a former Portuguese colony, Cape Verde's closest relations have been with other Lusophone countries, especially Guinea-Bissau, Angola, Mozambique, and São Tome and Príncipe. Relations with Guinea-Bissau, once close, have been frayed over the years. The 1980 constitution provides for the eventual merger of the two countries, but all island influences have been purged from the mainland party. However, diplomatic relations were resumed in 1982.

DEFENSE

The defense structure is headed by the president, who is the commander in chief of the Citizens' Army, a token force that replaced Portuguese troops on independence. The strength of the armed forces is 1,100.

Military Indicators

Total Active Duty Personnel: 1,100
Military Manpower per 1,000: 2.8
Military Expenditures $million: 4
- as % of GNP: 1.0
- per capita $: 9
- as % of central government expenditures: 1.3

Arms Imports $: 0
Arms Exports $: 0

ECONOMY

Cape Verde's low per capita gross domestic product (GDP) reflects a poor natural resource base, including serious water shortages exacerbated by cycles of long-term drought. The economy is service oriented, with commerce, transport, and public services accounting for almost 70 percent of GDP. Although nearly 70 percent of the population lives in rural areas, the share of agriculture in GDP in 1998 was only 18 percent, of which fishing accounts for 1.5 percent. About 90 percent of food must be imported. The fishing potential, mostly lobster and tuna, is not fully exploited. Cape Verde annually runs a high trade deficit, financed by foreign aid and remittances from emigrants; remittances constitute a supplement to GDP of more than 20 percent. Economic reforms, launched by the new democratic government in 1991, are aimed at developing the private sector and attracting foreign investment to diversify the economy. Prospects for 2001 depend heavily on the maintenance of aid flows, remittances, and the momentum of the government's development program.

Principal Economic Indicators

Gross National Product $: 436 million
GNP per capita: $1,090
GNP Average Annual Growth Rate (1990–97) %: 1.0
GNP per capita Average Annual Growth Rate (1990–97) %: −1.3
Origin of Gross Domestic Product %
- Agriculture: 18
- Mining: —
- Manufacturing: 6
- Construction: 18
- Public Utilities: 3
- Transportation and Communications: 11
- Trade: 21
- Financial Services: 3
- Other Services: 1
- Government: 7

Gross Domestic Product by Type of Expenditure %
- Private Consumption: 82
- Government Consumption: 24
- Gross Domestic Investment: 42
- Foreign Trade: Exports: 48
- Imports: 48

% of Income Received by Poorest 20%: —
% of Income Received by Richest 10%: —

Price and earnings indexes (1995 = 100)

	1993	1994	1995	1996	1997	1998
Consumer price index	89.0	92.0	100.0	106.0	115.0	120.0
Annual earnings index	85.8	87.9	100.0	—	—	—

Finance

National Currency: Cape Verdean Escudo (CVESc)
Exchange Rate: $1 = CVESc 95.4
Money Supply Stock in National Currency billion: 13.001
M1 per capita: 33,300
Central Bank Discount Rate %: 5.3

(continued)

Total External Debt $million: 202
Debt Service Ratio %: 22.3

Balance of Payments $million: −29.7
International Reserves SDRs million: —
Ratio of External Debt to Total Reserves: —
Average Annual Rate of Inflation/Consumer Price Index
Growth Rate %: 6.2

Official Development Assistance

ODA $million: 120
as % of GNP: 29.0
per capita: $316
Foreign Direct Investment $million: —

Central Government Revenues and Expenditures

Fiscal Year: Calendar Year
Revenues $million: 188
Expenditures $million: 228
Budget Deficit $million: 40
Tax Revenues as % of GDP: —
Highest Tax Bracket %
Individual: —
Corporate: —

Employment and Labor

Economically Active Population: 121,000
Female Participation Rate %: 37.1
Activity Rate %: 35.3
Labor by Sector: %
Agriculture, Forestry, Fishing: 24.8
Manufacturing, Mining: 5.7
Construction: 18.8
Transportation and Communications: 5.1
Trade, Hotels, and Restaurants: 10.6
Finance, Insurance, Real Estate: 0.7
Public Administration, Defense: —
Services: 14.4
Unemployment %: —

Agriculture

Agriculture's Share of GDP %: 18
Average Annual Rate of Growth (1965–98) %: —
Number of Farms 000: 32.2
Average Size of Farm ha: 1.3
Number of Tractors per 1,000 hectares: 0.4
Irrigation, % of Farms having: 7
Artificial Fertilizer kg/hectare: —
Total Farmland as % of land area: 10.2
Livestock: Cattle 000: 22
Sheep 000: 9
Hogs 000: 636
Chickens 000: 430
Forests: Production of Roundwood (000 cubic meters): —
Fisheries: Total Catch tons 000: 5.9

Mining

% of GDP: 0.3
Value of Mineral Production $million: 0.8

Manufacturing

Value Added $million: 14
Industrial Production Growth Rate %: —

Energy

Commercial Energy Production metric tons of
oil equivalent 000: —
Commercial Energy Consumption metric tons of
oil equivalent 000: 114
Commercial Energy Consumption per capita kg: 307
Average Annual Growth Rate 1980–97 %: —
Net Energy Imports % of use: 100
Electricity Installed Capacity kW 000: 7
Production kW-hr million: 39
Coal Reserves tons million: —
Production tons 000: —
Natural Gas Proven Reserves cubic meters billion: —
Production cubic meters million: —
Crude Petroleum Reserves barrels million: —
Production barrels million: —
Consumption barrels million: —
Refinery Capacity barrels per day 000: —
Pipelines Length km: —

Foreign Trade

Imports $million: 210.1
Exports $million: 5.0
Export Volume % Annual Growth Rate (1990–97): —
Import Volume % Annual Growth Rate (1990–97): —

Balance of trade (current prices)

	1990	1991	1992	1993	1994	1995
C.V. Esc.						
000,000	−9,097	−10,031	−11,907	−12,075	−13,678	−18,708
% of total	92.0%	92.9%	94.8%	95.1%	95.1%	93.2%

Major Trading Partners

	Imports	Exports
European Union %	40.0	98.3
United States %	—	0.1
Eastern Europe %	1.9	—
Japan %	5.7	—
Others %	52.4	1.6

Transportation

Roads Total Length mi: 680 km 1,095
Paved %: 78
Automobiles: 6,479

Trucks and Buses: 2,099
Persons per vehicle: 43
Railroad; Track Length mi: — km
Passenger-mi million: —
Freight-mi million: —
Merchant Marine: No. of Vessels: 42
Total Deadweight Tonnage 000: 30.9
International Cargo Loaded tons 000: 144
International Cargo Off-loaded tons 000: 299
Airports with Scheduled Flights: 9
Traffic: Passenger-mi million: 106
Freight-mi million: 13.2
Length of Canals mi: —

Tourism

Number of Tourists to 000: —
Number of Tourists from 000: —
Tourist Receipts $million: 10
Tourist Expenditures $million: 12

Communications

Telephones 000: 22
Cost of Local Calls 3 mins: $0
Cellular Telephones 000: —
Fax Machines 000: 0.5
Personal Computers 000: —
Internet Hosts per million persons: —
Mail: Post Offices: 55
Pieces of Mail Handled million: 1.7
Pieces of Mail Handled per person: 4.5

EDUCATION

In principle, education is free, universal, and compulsory for six years, from ages seven to 13. However, compulsory education is not enforced.

Schooling consists of six years of primary school (instrução primaria), three years of middle school (escola preparatoria), and either a three-year general course or a two-year preuniversity course, for a total of 11 or 12 years. The curriculum follows the Portuguese model. The academic year runs from October to July. The medium of instruction is Portuguese.

The building of new schools and improvement in teacher training are the two official priorities in educational planning.

In the absence of a local university, Cape Verdean students who wish to pursue higher studies go to Portugal.

Education

Literacy Rate %: 71.6
Male %: 81.4
Female %: 63.8
First Level: Primary schools: 370
Teachers: 2,657
Students: 78,173
Student-Teacher Ratio: 29.4
Net Enrollment Ratio: 100
Second Level: Secondary Schools: —
Teachers: 438
Students: 11,808
Student-Teacher Ratio: 27.0
Net Enrollment Ratio: 22

Vocational Level: Schools: —
Students: 2,289

Third Level: Institutions: —
Teachers: —
Students: —
Student-Ratio Level: —
Gross Enrollment Ratio: —
Students per 100,000: —
% of Population Age 25 and over with Postsecondary Education: —

Public Expenditure on Education as % of GDP: 4.4

SCIENCE AND TECHNOLOGY

Science and Technology

Scientists and Engineers in R&D per 1 million persons: —
Expenditures in R&D as % of GDP: —
High-Tech Exports $million: —
Patent Applications by Residents: —

MEDIA

Four weeklies are published: *Boletim Informativo*, *Boletim Oficial*, *Novo Journal Cabo-Verde*, *A Semana*, all in Portuguese. Cape Verde has no official news agency.

There are two radio stations, at Praia and Mindelo. Both are government owned.

Media

Daily Newspapers: —
Total Circulation 000: —
Circulation per 1,000: —
Books Published: —
Magazines: —
Radio Receivers 000: 57
per 1,000: 135
Television sets 000: 1.0
per 1,000: 3.0

MOST IMPORTANT MEDIA:

Press. The Cape Verdean press includes the following, all published at Praia, unless otherwise noted: *Novo Jornal Cabo Verde* (5,000), government-supported biweekly; *A Semana* (5,000), PAICV weekly; *Boletim Informativo* (1,500), published weekly by the Ministry of Foreign Affairs; *Boletim Oficial*, government weekly; *Terra Nova*, published monthly by the Catholic Church; *Unidade e Luta*, PAICV organ. An Independent bimonthly, *Noticias* ceased

(continued)

publication in March 1995 because of financial problems after the government had banned state enterprises from advertising in independent media.

News agencies. The domestic facility is Cabopress, headquartered at Praia; several foreign bureaus also maintain offices at the capital.

Radio and television. The government-controlled Radio Nacional de Cabo Verde broadcasts over two stations located at Praia and Mindelo, São Vicente to approximately 76,000 receivers; limited television service, launched in 1985 by Televisão Nacional de Cabo Verde, transmits from Praia.

CULTURE

Cultural Indicators

Public Libraries Number:
- Volumes: —
- Registered borrowers: —

Museums Number:
- Annual Attendance: —

Cinema Production of Long Films:
- Number of Cinemas: —
- Seating Capacity: —
- Annual Attendance: —
- Annual Attendance per capita: —

STATUS OF WOMEN

Sex discrimination exists sociologically, although banned by the constitution. Many of the traditional male-oriented values of the Portuguese and African ancestors of today's Cape Verdeans still are part of the country's culture. Women have been customarily excluded from certain types of work and often are paid less than men for comparable work. The government has included women in labor-intensive economic development projects financed by foreign grants. Both the government and the ruling party, African Party for the Independence of Cape Verde (PAICV), are making efforts to bring women into various economic and social activities where they have been traditionally absent. The Organization of Cape Verdean Women was founded in 1980, with PAICV encouragement, to sensitize the government and Cape Verdeans on issues affecting women. The Code of the Family, enacted in October 1981, prescribes full legal equality of men and women, including equal pay for equal work.

Women

Gender Empowerment Measure: 57
Seats Held in Parliament by Women %: 11.1
Female Administrators and Managers %: 23.3
Female Professional and Technical Workers %: 48.4
Women's Share of Earned Income %: 32
Women in Government %: 12

HEALTH, FOOD, AND NUTRITION

Health

Number of Physicians: 112
Number of Dentists: —
Number of Nurses: 205
Number of Pharmacists: 9
Population per Physician: 2,931
Number of Hospitals: 75
Hospital Beds per 10,000: 15
Hospital Bed Occupancy Rate: —
Infant Mortality Rate per 1,000 live births: 60
Maternal Mortality Rate per 10,000 live births: —
Total Health Expenditures as % of GDP: 6.32
Health Expenditures per capita $: 64
HIV Infected % of adults: —
Cigarette Consumption per smoker per year: —
% of Smokers: Male: —
Female: —
Access to Safe Water %: 51

Food and Nutrition

Food Supply as % of FAO Requirements: 129
% of Consumption Expenditures on Food: 60
Daily Available Calories per capita: 3,031
% of Total Calories derived from:
Cereals: 48.6
Potatoes, cassava: 1.9
Meat, poultry: 7.5
Fish: 0.8
Eggs, milk: 4.5
Fruits, vegetables: 2.6
Fats, oils: 17.1

ENVIRONMENT

Like many other developing nations, Cape Verde suffers from poor agricultural techniques, which have led to overgrazing and soil erosion. Additionally, the country suffers from growing deforestation as a result of a need for wood as a fuel and building material.

Environment

Forest Area sq km: —
Average Annual Deforestation sq km: —
Nationally Protected Areas as % of Total Land Area: —
Freshwater Access cubic meters per capita: —
Emissions of Organic Water Pollutants kg per day: —
CO_2 Emissions per capita ton: 0.3

CHRONOLOGY

1975 Cape Verde is granted independence by Portugal and is proclaimed a republic, with Aristides Pereira as president.

In national election 92 percent of the voters favor ultimate union with Guinea-Bissau.

1976 Cape Verde signs a judiciary protocol with Guinea-Bissau, merging the judicial systems of the two countries.

1980 Cape Verde's first constitution is approved in nationwide balloting.
New National People's Assembly is elected.

1981 Constitution is amended to revoke provisions designed to facilitate union with Guinea-Bissau.

1982 Cape Verde joins other Lusophone African nations in a summit at Praia and in setting up a joint committee to promote cooperation.

1984 The first distribution of land to landless peasants under the Land Reform Law of 1982 takes place, on São Tiago.

1985 National People's Assembly elections are held. Over 94 percent of the vote goes to candidates approved by the PAICV.

1986 President Pereira is reelected for another five-year term.

1988 Pereira is reelected secretary-general of the PAICV.

1989 A commission is established to consider constitutional changes.

1990 Pereira announces that the next presidential election will be based on universal suffrage. The nation officially becomes multiparty. The Movimento para Democracia (MPD) is given official recognition.

1991 MPD candidate Antonio Mascarenhas Monteiro defeats Pereira in the presidential election.

1994 The new constitution is adopted by 82 percent of the votes cast.

1995 MPD candidates capture 50 of the 72 seats in the parliament.

2001 In January legislative elections, PIACV candidates win 37 of the 72 seats; in February, Pedro Pires of the PIACV wins the presidency by a margin of 17 votes.

BIBLIOGRAPHY

Carreira, Antonio. *The People of the Cape Verde Island: Exploitation and Emigration*. Hamden, Conn., 1983.

Davidson, Basil. *No Fist Is Big Enough to Hide the Sky: The Liberation of Guinea-Bissau and Cape Verde*. London, 1984.

Lobban, Richard. *Historical Dictionary of the Republic of Cape Verde*. Metuchen, N.J., 1995.

Lobban, Richard. *Cape Verde: Crioulo Colony to Independent Nation*. Boulder, Colo., 1998.

Shaw Caroline S. *Cape Verde* (World Bibliographical Series). Santa Monica, Calif., 1991.

OFFICIAL PUBLICATIONS

Cape Verde. *Boletim Anual de Estantistica; Cape Verde—Recent Economic Developments* (IMF Staff Country Report [1996]); *I. Recenseamento Geral da População e Habitação—1990.*

CONTACT INFORMATION

Embassy of Cape Verde
3415 Massachusetts Avenue NW
Washington, D.C. 20007
Phone: (202) 965-6820 Fax: (202) 965-1207

INTERNET RESOURCES

- Cape Verde Home Page (unofficial)
http://www.umassd.edu/SpecialPrograms/capverdean.html
- Embassy of Cape Verde
http://www.capeverdeusaembassy.org

CENTRAL AFRICAN REPUBLIC

BASIC FACT SHEET

OFFICIAL NAME:
Central African Republic (formerly Central African Empire and Ubangi-Shari)

ABBREVIATION:
CX

CAPITAL:
Bangui

HEAD OF STATE & GOVERNMENT:
President Ange-Felix Patassé (from 1993)

HEAD OF GOVERNMENT:
Prime Minister Martin Ziguélé (from 2001)

NATURE OF GOVERNMENT:
Multiparty democracy

POPULATION:
3,445,000 (1999)

AREA:
622,984 sq km (240,534 sq mi)

ETHNIC MAJORITY:
Banda and Baya-Mandjia

LANGUAGES:
French (official); Snagho (national)

RELIGIONS:
Christianity and animism

UNIT OF CURRENCY:
Communauté Financière Africaine franc (C.F.A.F.)

NATIONAL FLAG:
Four horizontal blue, white, green, and yellow stripes divided at the center by a vertical red stripe. In the upper left corner is a yellow five-pointed star.

NATIONAL EMBLEM:
A central shield having four equal quarters with a white disk within a square red border at its center. Inside the white disk is a five-pointed gold star on a black map of Africa. The four quarters of the shield contain a white-tusked elephant dead on green; a green tree on a white background; a raised black hand, the symbol of Bokassa's Movement for the Social Evolution of Black Africa; and three diamonds against a gold field. The shield is flanked by two national flags, and the crest is illuminated by a blazing yellow sun marked with the date December 1, 1958 (the date on which Ubangi-Chari was granted self-governing status). Above the sun appears the legend *Zo Kwe Kox* (All Men Are Equal) in Sangho. Under the shield is a Maltese cross and a scroll containing the national motto, *Unité, Dignité, Travail* (Unity, Dignity, Labor).

NATIONAL ANTHEM:
"O Central Africa, O Cradle of the Bantus"

NATIONAL HOLIDAYS:
December 1 (Republic Day, National Day); March 29 (anniversary of Barthélémy Boganda's death); May 14 (anniversary of the First Republic); August 13 (Independence Day). Also, variable Christian festivals and Christmas.

DATE OF INDEPENDENCE:
August 13, 1960

DATE OF CONSTITUTION:
November 21, 1986

GEOGRAPHICAL FEATURES

The Central African Republic, a landlocked country in the heart of Africa, has an area of 622,984 sq km (240,535 sq mi) extending 1,437 km (893 mi) north to south and 772 km (480 mi) east to west. Its total international boundary of 5,232 km (3,251 mi) is shared with five countries, as follows: Cameroon (797 km; 511 mi); Republic of the Congo (467 km; 290 mi); Democratic Republic of the Congo (1,577 km; 495 mi); Sudan (1,167 km; 725 mi); and Chad (1,197 km; 741 mi).

Central African Republic

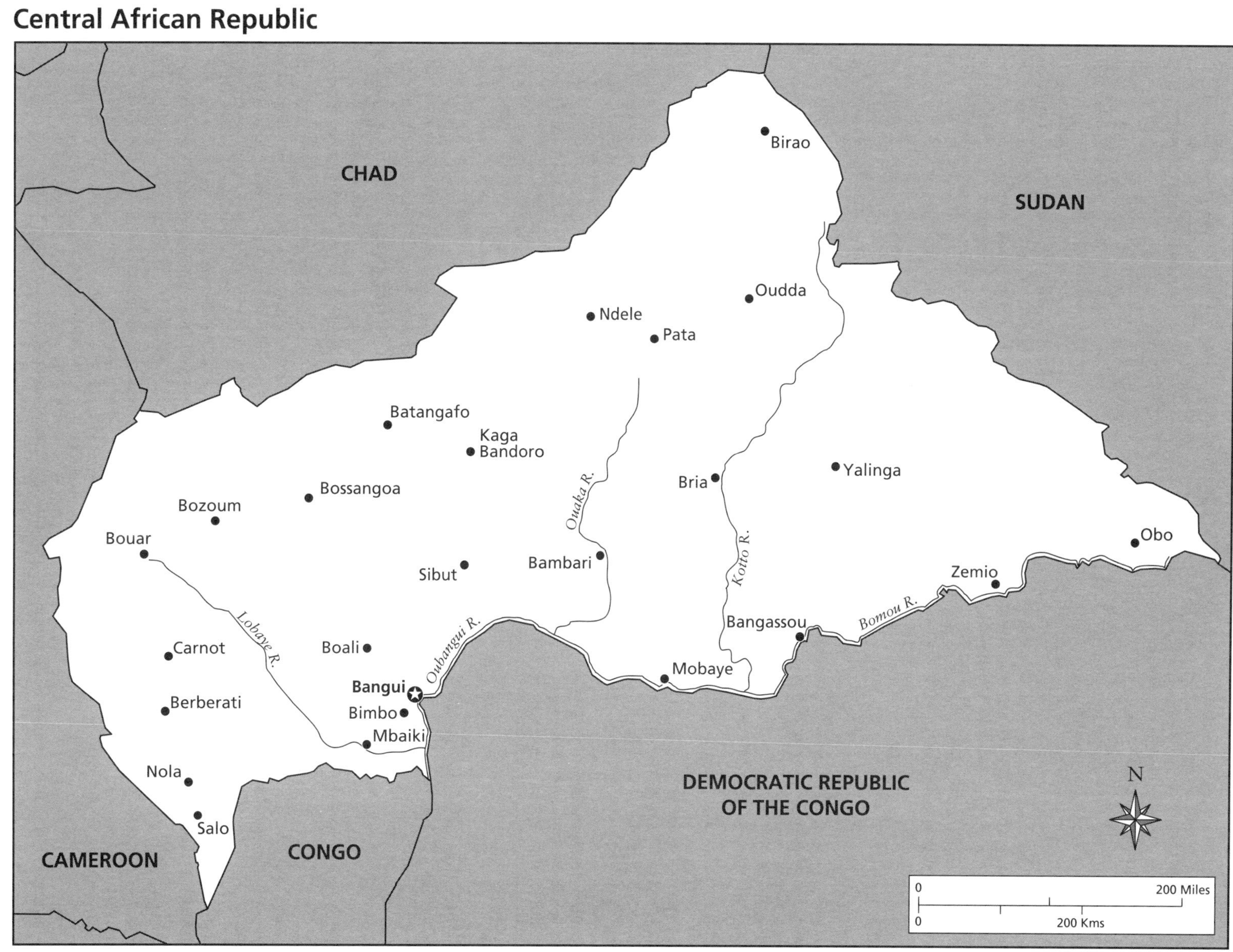

The country consists of a plateau with an average altitude of 600 to 700 m (1,969 to 2,297 ft). The most prominent topographical features are the Bongo Massif (1,370 m; 4,495 ft) in the northeast, the Yade Massif (1,400 m; 4,593 ft) in the northwest, and the Fertit Hills (1,280 m; 4,200 ft).

The Central African Republic is drained by two river systems, one flowing south, the other flowing north. Of those flowing south, the Chinko, Mbari, Kotto, Ouaka, and Lobaye are tributaries of the Ubangi River, and the Mambere and Kadei are tributaries of the Zaire. Two northern rivers, the Ouham and the Bamingui, are tributaries of the Chari River, which drains into Lake Chad.

Geography

Area sq km: 622,984 (240,534 sq mi)
World Rank: 43rd
Land Boundaries, km: Cameroon 797; Chad 1197; Democratic Republic of Congo 1577; Republic of Congo 467; Sudan 1165
Coastline, km: —
Elevation Extremes meters
- Lowest: Oubangui River 335
- Highest: Mount Gaou 1,420

Land Use % Arable land: 3
- Permanent Crops: 0
- Permanent Pastures: 5
- Forest and Woodland: 75
- Other: 17

Population of Principal Cities (2001 est.)

Bangui	636,300

CLIMATE AND WEATHER

Most of the country has a tropical climate, with alternate rainy seasons from May to June and from October to November, and with dry seasons from November to May and from June to October. The climate becomes Sahelian in the north, with a long, dry season lasting eight to nine months and slight and irregular rainfall. In the western highlands the climate is occasionally cool. Average temperatures at Bangui range from 21°C (70°F) to 32°C (90°F). Annual rainfall in the south is about 1,780 mm (70 in). In summer the heat is most oppressive when the country is subject to the *harmattan*, a hot, dry wind blowing from the Sahara.

Climate and Weather

Mean Temperature 70°F to 90°F
Average Annual Rainfall: 70 in

POPULATION

Population Indicators

Total Population: 1999, 3,445,000
World Rank: 127th
Density per sq mi: 14.3 (5.5 per sq km)
% of annual growth (1994–99): 2.0
Male %: 49.1
Female %: 50.9
Urban %: 36.5
Age Distribution: %
- 0–14: 43.2
- 15–29: 27.5
- 30–44: 15.0
- 45–59: 9.2
- 60–74: 4.1
- 75 and over: 0.8

Population 2020: 5,133,000
Birth Rate per 1,000: 39.2
Death Rate per 1,000: 17.0
Population Doubling Time (years): 32
Infant Mortality Rate per 1,000 live births: 108
Rate of Natural Increase per 1,000: 22.2
Total Fertility Rate: 5.2
Expectation of Life (years): Males 44.7
Females 48.3
Marriage Rate per 1,000: —
Divorce Rate per 1,000: —
Total Number of Households: —
Average Size of Households: 4.7
% of Illegitimate Children: —
Induced Abortions: —
- Rate per 100 live births: —

ETHNIC COMPOSITION

Central Africans belong to more than 80 ethnic groups, but three major groups account for 68 percent of the population. The largest group is Banda (32 percent), followed by Baya-Mandjia (29 percent), and Mbaka (7 percent). There are three ethnic zones in the country, each with its own dominant groups. The Bantu groups Mbaka, Lissongo, and Mbimu and the Babinga live in the forest region; the Sango, Yakoma, Baniri, and Buraka along the rivers; and the Banda, Zande, Sara, Ndle, and Bizao live in the savanna region.

The Western community in the country is estimated at 6,500, of whom 6,000 are French; the majority of the remainder are Portuguese.

LANGUAGES

French is the official language of the country, and Sango is the national language. Sango is the language of an ethnic group of the same name living in the south, and it is also used as a trade language and lingua franca for intertribal communication. French is spoken by 26 percent of the population.

Principal Languages and Their Speakers	
Banda	810,000
Baya (Gbaya)	820,000
French	900,000
Mandjia	510,000
Mbum	220,000
Ngbaka	260,000
Sango (lingua franca)	3,100,000
Sara	220,000
Zande (Azande)	70,000
Other	490,000

RELIGIONS

Religious statistics are generally unreliable, but it is estimated that 24 percent of the population follow traditional animist beliefs, 42 percent are Christian, and 15 percent are Muslim.

The Roman Catholic Church, which claims 16 percent to 17 percent of the population as adherents, is organized under the Archbishopric of Bangui, with four suffragan dioceses (Bambari, Bangassour, Berberati, and Bossangoa); 92 parishes; 1,452 mission stations; and 2,478 clergy. There are more than 1,000 Protestant mission centers, with nearly 2,000 missionaries and pastors.

Religious Affiliations	
Protestant	880,000
Traditional beliefs	830,000
Roman Catholic	580,000
Muslim	520,000
Other	630,000

HISTORICAL BACKGROUND

There is archaeological evidence that suggests the Central African Republic (CAR) was inhabited by a complex civilization before the rise of Egypt. However, little is known about the region and the first inhabitants, the Babinga. In the ninth and 10th centuries, there was widespread immigration from Sudan and Chad. However, by the 17th century the slave trade was depopulating entire towns in the north. Slave markets in Cairo were filled with slaves from the region now known as the CAR until the late 19th century. The result of the voracious slave trade is that the area making up the CAR is one of the most lightly populated regions in Africa.

The Central African Republic was under French rule as a province of French Equatorial Africa (Afrique Equatoriale Française, AEF) from 1908 and previously as a province of the French Congo from 1901. Economic development of the country, then known as Ubangi-Shari, was modeled on the policy adopted by the Belgians in the Congo. The country was parceled out among 40 concessionaires, who were granted rights of tenure and exploitation in return for a fixed annual payment and 15 percent of the profits. This system was abandoned in the 1920s following scandals exposed by René Maran in Batouala and André Gide in *Voyage au Congo*. Though AEF made considerable progress in health and education during the interwar years, much of the benefits were limited to Gabon and Middle Congo. Ubangi-Shari became independent about the same time as the other constituent units of AEF in 1960.

Prior to independence, the country experienced two years of self-government under Barthélémy Boganda, founder of the Social Evolution Movement of Black Africa (MESAN), and his nephew David Dacko, who became the nation's first president in 1960. Dacko established a one-party state in 1962. He was overthrown in 1966 by his cousin, Jean-Bédel Bokassa, commander in chief of the armed forces. Bokassa abrogated the constitution and assumed all executive power. In 1976 he announced that the republic was becoming an empire, and the following year he crowned himself emperor in a ceremony that consumed one-fourth of his poor country's income. The Bokassa regime was supported by substantial financial and military aid, particularly from France. His brutal regime was widely condemned, particularly after the role that he played in the massacre of almost 100 schoolchildren.

With the aid of the French, Dacko deposed Bokassa in 1979. Dacko was unable to deal with the nation's economic problems or the political discontent they generated. He was ousted by the military under the leadership of Gen. André Kolingba in 1981. Kolingba suspended the constitution and proscribed all political parties, although political leaders retained their freedom. He ruled through a Military Committee for National Recovery (CMRN). Kolingba promised to restore civilian rule as soon as conditions were favorable. When no action was forthcoming, opposition to his regime grew. In 1984 his opponents formed a government-in-exile and in 1986 promised a return to democracy. Kolingba responded to these actions by forming a new government in 1985 in which civilians held the majority of cabinet posts.

Kolingba dissolved the CMRN in 1985 and assumed the offices of president and prime minister. He was granted a six-year term under the constitution of 1986. The new constitution established a single-party state in which the Central African Democratic Assembly was the sole legitimate party. Legislative elections were held in 1987, but turnout was low because the opposition boycotted the polls.

In October 1993, Kolingba finally held elections and was defeated by Ange-Felix Patasse. Patasse, a civilian, did not bring calm to the country. Instead he built a government stacked with his own henchmen. Violence broke out in 1996 when some elements of the armed forces

ORGANIZATION OF CENTRAL AFRICAN REPUBLIC GOVERNMENT

National Assembly	President Prime Minister Council of Ministers	Supreme Court Criminal Court Civil Courts Justices of the Peace
	Prefectures Subprefectures Rural Communes	

challenged the government on at least four occasions. The ongoing conflicts have left the country broke and bereft of international aid.

In July 1997, the mutineers agreed to a truce, receiving amnesty and reintegration into the army in return. Soon thereafter France began withdrawing its military forces from the country, completing the process in 1998. Patasse was reelected president in the 1999 election, which the opposition claimed was rigged.

CONSTITUTION

The constitution adopted in November 1986 is a revised version of the constitution that was suspended in 1981. A new constitution was promulgated on December 29, 1994, and adopted on January 7, 1995. Under the constitution, executive power is vested in a president elected for a six-year term. The prime minister is appointed by the president. Legislative power is in the hands of a unicameral national assembly, whose 109 members are elected by popular vote to serve five-year terms. Although the constitution provides for separation of powers, the legislature is vulnerable to manipulation by the president, who dominates the government. The president can veto legislation, although two-thirds of the unicameral legislature can override his veto, and can rule by decree under special conditions. The constitution provides for an independent judiciary.

LOCAL GOVERNMENT

For purposes of local administration the republic is divided into 16 prefectures, 69 subprefectures, and 167 rural communes.

There are popular representative institutions at each level: prefectural councils, subprefectural councils, and municipal councils. Eight urban communes have full powers, and there are elected municipal councils at Bangui, Berberati, Bossangoa, Bambari, Bangassou, Bouar, and M'Baiki. Bangui, however, has a nominated mayor.

Local Government

Principal administrative divisions, capitals, area, population

Area and population

		area		population 1988
Prefectures	**Capitals**	**sq mi**	**sq km**	**census**
Bamingui-Bangoran	Ndélé	22,471	58,200	28,643
Basse-Kotto	Mobaye	6,797	17,604	194,750
Haut-Mbomou	Obo	21,440	55,530	27,113
Haute-Kotto	Bria	33,456	86,650	58,838
Kemo	Sibut	6,642	17,204	82,884
Lobaye	Mbaiki	7,427	19,235	169,554
Mambéré-Kadei	Berbérati	11,661	30,203	230,364
Mbomou	Bangassou	23,610	61,150	119,252
Nana-Gribizi	Kaga-Bandoro	7,721	19,996	95,497
Nana-Mabéré	Bouar	10,270	26,600	191,970
Ombella-M'poko	Boali	12,292	31,835	180,857
Ouaka	Bambari	19,266	49,900	208,332
Ouham	Bossangoa	19,402	50,250	262,950
Ouham-Pendé	Bozoum	12,394	32,100	287,653
Sangha-Mbaéré	Nola	7,495	19,412	65,961
Vakaga	Birao	17,954	46,500	32,118
Autonomous commune				
Bangui	Bangui	26	67	451,690
TOTAL		240,324	622,436	2,688,426

PARLIAMENT

Legislative power is vested in a unicameral parliament. The 109-member National Assembly is elected by direct universal suffrage for a five-year term. The National Assembly meets twice a year at the summons of the president. The National Assembly is advised by the Economic and Regional Council, an appointed body serving a five-year term. One-half of its members are elected by the National Assembly, and the other half are appointed by the president. When the two bodies sit together they are called the Congress.

POLITICAL PARTIES

More than 13 different political parties hold seats in the current National Assembly. The range of political ideology runs the gamut from left to right. Parties also have a tendency to take on a political cult of personality. The strongest parties include the Movement for the Liberation of the Central African People or MLPC (the party of the president), the Central African Democratic Assembly or RDC, and the Movement for Democracy and Development, or MDD.

Political Parties

Central African People's Liberation Movement, 1979
Liberal Democratic Party, 1993
National Convention, 1991
Central African Democratic Rally, 1986
Patriotic Front for Progress
Alliance for Democracy and Progress
Movement for Democracy and Development, 1994
Social Democratic Party
Civic Forum
Democratic Forum for Modernity, 1997
National Unity Party
People's Union for the Republic
Democratic Movement for the Renaissance and Evolution of Central Africa
Social Evolution Movement of Black Africa, 1949
Union of Democrats for Central African Renewal
Central African Republican Party
Central African Movement for National Liberation
Popular Rally for the Reconstruction of Central Africa

Political Parties: Strength in Parliament Most Recent Elections

At Assembly elections on November 22 and December 13, 1998, the Central African People's Liberation Movement (MLPC) captured 47 seats in the enlarged 109-seat body. The remainder of the seats were distributed as follows: the Central African Democratic Rally, 20; the Movement for Democracy and Development, 8; the Patriotic Front for Progress, 7; the Social Democratic Party (PSD), 6; the Alliance for Democracy and Progress, 5; the National Unity Party, 3; the Liberal Democratic Party, 2; the Democratic Forum for Modérnity, 2; the Civic Forum, 1; the People's Union for the Republic, 1; and independents, 7. In December an assemblyman affiliated with the PSD switched his allegiance to the MPLC, and in March 1999 it was reported that two other PSD legislators had renounced their PSD affiliation with the aim of joining the MLPC.

LEGAL SYSTEM

The highest judicial organ in the land is the Supreme Court, with three chambers: judicial, administrative, and accounts. It acts as a court of cassation in civil and penal cases and as a court of appeal in administrative cases. Subordinate courts include a criminal court in Bangui, seven civil courts (one in Bangui and six in other population centers), and justices of the peace in smaller population centers. The judiciary, like other branches of the government, is subject to the whims and dictates of the president.

Under local law political detainees can be held without charge for as long as two months, but at that point they must either be formally charged or released. If a suspect is charged, local judicial procedures (which are modeled on French procedures) allow for open-ended preventive detention while the public prosecutor prepares the state's case against the accused.

In most common criminal cases, the government permits the French-modeled legal procedures to be applied fairly and openly and the laws to be executed properly. Within this framework, Kolingba granted amnesty to about 100 petty criminals in September 1984. The courts are clearly dependent on the president.

A second tribunal comprising civilian magistrates and military advisers adjudicates political crimes. The special tribunal differs from ordinary courts in that there is no appeal except for the possibility of presidential clemency, and it can try a case only after being authorized by the president.

LAW ENFORCEMENT

Law Enforcement

Offenses reported to the police per 100,000: 135
- Murder: 1.6
- Assault: 22.8
- Burglary: 2.7
- Automobile Theft: —
- Population per Police officer: 2,740

Death Penalty: Yes. Last execution in 1981

HUMAN RIGHTS

In terms of civil and political rights, the Central African Republic is classified as a country that is not free. The Central African Republic still is recovering from the 13 years of Bokassa's dictatorship. General Kolingba's efforts to reconstitute the country's political and judicial institutions have generally been cautious and tentative. Several individuals closely connected with the Bokassa regime were imprisoned for over a year after the coup that overthrew him, but later they were tried and either sentenced or freed. Some of the verdicts were overturned by the Supreme Court because of judicial irregularities or errors in the initial proceedings. Mass media are extremely limited, and broadcast media are controlled by the government. There is no evidence of censorship.

FOREIGN POLICY

As a member of the French Community, CAR has retained close ties with France. A defense pact between the two states permits French intervention in times of crisis, and this clause was invoked against Bokassa and again in 1996 in defense of the government of Patasse. The civil war in neighboring Chad was the principal concern in foreign relations for two decades, and it prompted a rupture of diplomatic relations with Libya, which lasted until 1995. Similarly, the civil war in the Democratic Republic of the Congo spilled over into CAR and fighting was reported along the border. In 1998 the two countries signed a defense pact and CAR was reported to be supporting the Kabila regime.

DEFENSE

The defense structure is headed by the president, who also is the supreme commander of the armed forces. The line of command runs through the minister of defense to the unit commanders.

Military manpower is provided by voluntary enlistment. The total strength of the armed forces is estimated at 6,500, of which the army accounts for 3,500, the navy 85, and the air force 300. The remaining personnel are in paramilitary units.

The Central African Republic has no military capability other than for internal peacekeeping. Defense of the realm is guaranteed by a 1960 agreement with France, which also provides for military assistance in quelling internal revolts, base rights, and transit and overflight privileges. French officers are temporarily assigned as instructors and advisers, and French garrisons, numbering 1,100 troops, are stationed in Bangui and Bouar.

Military Indicators

Total Active Duty Personnel: 5,000
Military Manpower per 1,000: 1.5
Military Expenditures $: 30 million
- as % of GNP: 3.2
- per capita $: 10
- as % of central government expenditures: 6.6

Arms Imports $: 0
Arms Exports $: 0

ECONOMY

Subsistence agriculture, together with forestry, remains the backbone of the economy of the Central African Republic (CAR), with more than 70 percent of the population living in outlying areas. The agricultural sector generates half of gross domestic product (GDP). Timber has accounted for about 16 percent of export earnings and the diamond industry for nearly 54 percent. Important constraints to economic development include the CAR's landlocked position, a poor transportation system, a largely unskilled workforce, and a legacy of misdirected macroeconomic policies. The 50 percent devaluation of the currencies of 14 Francophone African nations on 12 January 1994 had mixed effects on the CAR's economy. Diamond, timber, coffee, and cotton exports increased, leading to an estimated rise of GDP of 7 percent in 1994 and nearly 5 percent in 1995. Military rebellions and social unrest in 1996 were accompanied by widespread destruction of property and a drop in GDP of 2 percent. Ongoing violence between the government and rebel military groups over pay issues, living conditions, and political representation has destroyed many businesses in the capital and reduced tax revenues for the government. The IMF approved an Extended Structure Adjustment Facility in 1998 and the World Bank extended further credits in 1999 and approved a $10 million loan in early 2001. The government has set targets of 3.5 percent GDP growth in 2001 and 2002. As of January 2001, many civil servants were owed as much as 30-months' pay, leading them to go on strike, which further damaged the economy.

Principal Economic Indicators

Gross National Product: $1.104 billion
GNP per capita: $320
GNP Average Annual Growth Rate (1990–97) %: −1.0
GNP per capita Average Annual Growth Rate (1990–97) %: −3.1
Origin of Gross Domestic Product %
- Agriculture: 53
- Mining: 6
- Manufacturing: 7
- Construction: 4
- Public Utilities: —
- Transportation and Communications: 3
- Trade: 12
- Financial Services: 5
- Other Services: 5
- Government: 5

Gross Domestic Product by Type of Expenditure %
- Private Consumption: 76
- Government Consumption: 15
- Gross Domestic Investment: 13
- Foreign Trade: Exports: 22
- Imports: 27

% of Income Received by Poorest 20%: —
% of Income Received by Richest 10%: —

Price and earnings indexes (1995 = 100)

	1991	1992	1993	1994	1995	1996	1997
Consumer price index	70.3	69.4	67.4	83.9	100.0	103.7	104.9
Earnings index	—	—	—	—	100.0	—	—

Finance

National Currency: CFA Franc (CFAF)
Exchange Rate: $1 = CFAF 608.36
Money Supply Stock in National Currency billion: 111.2
M1 per capita: 34,300
Central Bank Discount Rate %: 7.60
Total External Debt $: 890 million
Debt Service Ratio %: 1.9

Balance of Payments $: −43.5 million
International Reserves SDRs: 165 million
Ratio of External Debt to Total Reserves: 3.6

Average Annual Rate of Inflation/Consumer Price Index Growth Rate %: 4

Official Development Assistance

ODA: $120 million
as % of GNP: 11.6
per capita: $34
Foreign Direct Investment $: 5 million

Central Government Revenues and Expenditures

Fiscal Year: Calendar Year

Revenues $: 638 million
Expenditures $: 1.9 billion
Budget Deficit $: 1.262 billion
Tax Revenues as % of GDP: —
Highest Tax Bracket % —
Individual: —
Corporate: —

Employment and Labor

Economically Active Population: 1,187,000
Female Participation Rate %: 46.8
Activity Rate %: 48.2
Labor by Sector: %
Agriculture, Forestry, Fishing: 74.2
Manufacturing, Mining: 2.6
Construction: 0.5
Transportation and Communications: 0.6
Trade, Hotels, and Restaurants: 7.8
Finance, Insurance, Real Estate: 0.1
Public Administration, Defense: —
Services: 5.9

Unemployment %: 6

Agriculture

Agriculture's Share of GDP %: 53
Average Annual Rate of Growth (1965–98) %: 1.6
Number of Farms 000: 283
Average Size of Farm ha: 1.7
Number of Tractors per 1,000 hectares: 0.1
Irrigation, % of Farms having: —
Artificial Fertilizer kg/hectare: 2
Total Cropland as % of Farmland: 100
Livestock: Cattle 000: 2,992
Sheep 000: 201
Hogs 000: 622
Chickens 000: 3,875
Forests: Production of Roundwood (000 cubic meters): 3,864
Fisheries: Total Catch tons: 13,000

Mining

% of GDP: 5.8
Value of Mineral Production $: 65.5 million

Manufacturing

Value Added $: 27 million
Industrial Production Growth Rate %: NA

Energy

Commercial Energy Production metric tons of oil equivalent: —
Commercial Energy Consumption metric tons of oil equivalent: —
Commercial Energy Consumption per capita kg: —
Average Annual Growth Rate 1980–97 %: —
Net Energy Imports % of use: —
Electricity Installed Capacity kW: 43,000
Production kW-hr: 102 million
Coal Reserves tons: 4 million
Production tons: —
Natural Gas Proven Reserves cubic meters: —
Production cubic meters: —
Crude Petroleum Reserves barrels: —
Production barrels: —
Consumption barrels: —
Refinery Capacity barrels per day: —
Pipelines Length km: —

Foreign Trade

Imports $: 265.5 million
Exports $: 119.5 million
Export Volume % Annual Growth Rate (1990–97): 20.5
Import Volume % Annual Growth Rate (1990–97): 15.1
Balance of Trade $

Balance of trade (current prices)

	1990	1991	1992	1993	1994	1995
CFAF 000,000,000	−9.3	−13.0	−10.1	−4.5	+6.6	−1.6
% of total	12.4%	32.9%	15.2%	6.7%	4.1%	0.9%

Major Trading Partners

	Imports	Exports
European Union %	43.5	90.7
United States %	1.8	0.2
Eastern Europe %	—	—
Japan %	19.7	0.8
Others %	34.9	8.3

Transportation

Roads Total Length mi: 14,795 (23,810 km)
Paved %: 2
Automobiles: 2,500
Trucks and Buses: 7,000
Persons per vehicle: 195
Railroad; Track Length mi: —
Passenger-mi: —
Freight-mi: —
Merchant Marine: No. of Vessels: —
    Total Deadweight Tonnage: —
    International Cargo Loaded tons: 53,000
    International Cargo Off-loaded tons: 126,000
Airports with Scheduled Flights: 1
Traffic: Passenger-mi: 139.6 million
    Freight-mi: 11.2 million
Length of Canals mi: 500 (800 km)

Tourism

Number of Tourists to: 20,000
Number of Tourists from: —
Tourist Receipts $: 6 million
Tourist Expenditures $: 43 million

Communications

Telephones 000: 7.8
Cost of Local Calls 3 mins: $0.20
Cellular Telephones 000: 0.2
Fax Machines 000: —
Personal Computers 000: —
Internet Hosts per million persons: —
Mail: Post Offices: 31
    Pieces of Mail Handled: —
    Pieces of Mail Handled per person: —

EDUCATION

Education is free, universal, and compulsory, in principle, for eight years, from ages six to 14.

Schooling consists of six years of primary school, four years of middle school, and three years of secondary school for a total of 13 years. On completion of the secondary-school program, students are awarded a baccalaureate. The curricula are based on those of France, and Africanization has received a low priority. A few mission schools run by religious groups continue to operate within the school system.

The academic year runs from October to June. The medium of instruction is French, but the national language, Sango, is taught at all levels. The literacy rate is 60 percent for adults.

Adult education is provided by mobile teams.

The country's sole university is the National University. Specialized institutions include a national administration college, technical and agricultural colleges, and schools of nursing and forestry.

Education

Literacy Rate %: 60.0
    Male %: 58.5
    Female %: 52.4
First Level: Primary schools: 930
    Teachers: 4,004
    Students: 308,409
    Student-Teacher Ratio: 77.0
    Net Enrollment Ratio: 54.0
Second Level: Secondary Schools: 46
    Teachers: 845
    Students: 46,989
    Student-Teacher Ratio: 55.6
    Net Enrollment Ratio: —

Vocational Level: Schools:
    Students:

Third Level: Institutions: 1
    Teachers: 139
    Students: 2,923
    Student-Ratio Level: 21.0
    Gross Enrollment Ratio: 1.4
    Students per 100,000: 131
    % of Population Age 25 and over with Postsecondary Education: 2.0

Public Expenditure on Education as % of GDP: 2.5

SCIENCE AND TECHNOLOGY

Science and Technology

Scientists and Engineers in R&D per 1 million persons: 56
Expenditures in R&D as % of GDP: —
High-Tech Exports $: —
Patent Applications by Residents: —

MEDIA

Only one daily newspaper is published in the country: *E Le Songo*, with a circulation of 2,000. None of the six periodicals published in the country enjoys a circulation of more than a few hundred. The media are under the control and supervision of the state.

The national news agency is Agence Centrafricaine de Presse (ACAP), founded in 1974 through the nationalization of the French news agency AFP. Only Tass maintains a bureau in Bangui.

The official broadcasting organization, Radiodiffusion-Télévision Centrafricaine (RTC), formerly Radiodiffusion Nationale Centrafricaine, broadcasts a home service in both French and Sango. RTC is on the air for 130 hours a week.

Television broadcasts began in 1974.

Media

Daily Newspapers: 1
  Total Circulation 000: 2
  Circulation per 1,000: 1.0
Books Published: —
Magazines: —
Radio Receivers 000: 180
  per 1,000: 55
Television sets 000: 17.0
  per 1,000: 5.0

Most Important Media:

Press. The following are published at Bangui: *E Le Songo* (2,000), daily tabloid in Sango, launched in June 1986; *Renouveau Centrafricaine* (1,000), weekly in French; *Journal Officiel de la République Centrafricaine*, fortnightly in French; *Terre Africaine*, weekly in French; *Le Rassemblement*, RDC organ.

News agencies. The official facility is Agence Centrafricaine de Presse (ACAP).

Radio and television. The government-controlled Radiodiffusion-Télévision Centrafrique broadcasts in French and Sango to some 266,000 radio and 18,000 television receivers.

CULTURE

Cultural Indicators

Public Libraries
  Number: 6
  Volumes: 51,000
  Registered borrowers: 1,500
Museums
  Number: 7
  Annual Attendance:
Cinema
  Production of Long Films:
  Number of Cinemas:
  Seating Capacity:
  Annual Attendance:
  Annual Attendance per capita:

STATUS OF WOMEN

Women are generally accorded a lower status than men in the Central African Republic. Women's work at home and in the fields prevents many of them from receiving an education. Polygamy is common, but the legal system and traditional practice support the rights of wives and all children of such marriages. A national women's organization is supported by the government. There are no women cabinet members or high commissioners in the Kolingba government.

Women

Gender Empowerment Measure: 98
Seats Held in Parliament by Women %: 3.5
Female Administrators and Managers %: 9.0
Female Professional and Technical Workers %: 18.9
Women's Share of Earned Income %: 39
Women in Government %: 5

HEALTH, FOOD, AND NUTRITION

Health

Number of Physicians: 157
Number of Dentists: 8
Number of Nurses: 1,353
Number of Pharmacists: 22
Population per Physician: 18,660
Number of Hospitals: 133
Hospital Beds per 10,000: 15
Hospital Bed Occupancy Rate: —
Infant Mortality Rate per 1,000 live births: 149
Maternal Mortality Rate per 100,000 live births: 700
Total Health Expenditures as % of GDP: 4.9
Health Expenditures per capita $: 18
HIV Infected % of adults: 10.77
Cigarette Consumption per smoker per year: —
% of Smokers: Male: —
  Female: —
Access to Safe Water %: 18

Food and Nutrition

Food Supply as % of FAO Requirements: 83
% of Consumption Expenditures on Food: 70.5
Daily Available Calories per capita: 1,885
% of Total Calories derived from:
Cereals: 21.3
Potatoes, cassava: 31.5
Meat, poultry: 6.3
Fish: 0.4
Eggs, milk: 1.5
Fruits, vegetables: 6.5
Fats, oils: 16.1

ENVIRONMENT

The environmental status of the Central African Republic is a case study in problems and potentials. The problems are exacerbated by gaps in legislation, poaching (illegal wildlife traders and armed gangs from the Sudan), agricultural practices that impoverish the soil and cause erosion, a forestry code that does not provide for rational forest management, and the lack of environmental legislation. On the other hand, the country has considerable agricultural potential and mineral resources (diamonds and gold), along with an extensive protected areas system and strong potential for sustainable forest production.

Environment

Forest Area sq km: 299,000
Average Annual Deforestation sq km: 1,282
Nationally Protected Areas as % of Total Land Area: 8.2
Freshwater Access cubic meters per capita: 41,250
Emissions of Organic Water Pollutants kg per day:
CO_2 Emissions per capita ton: 0.1

CHRONOLOGY

1958 Ubangi-Shari votes to become an autonomous republic within the French community under the name Central African Republic.
Barthélémy Boganda is selected as the first prime minister.

1959 Boganda dies in an air crash and is succeeded in office by his nephew David Dacko.

1960 Central African Republic achieves full independence with Dacko as president.
Republic's first constitution is promulgated.

1962 The constitution is amended to establish Social Evolution Movement of Black Africa as the sole legal political party in the country.

1966 In a swift and bloodless coup Dacko is ousted by the army's commander in chief, Jean-Bédel Bokassa.
National Assembly and constitution are suspended.
Relations with People's Republic of China are broken.

1968 The Central African Republic leaves Union Douanière et Economique de l'Afrique Centrale (UDEAC) and joins with Chad and Zaïre in a new grouping called Union des Etats de l'Afrique Centrale but later returns to the UDEAC fold.

1969 Col. Alexandre Banza, a presidential associate, is implicated in an anti-Bokassa plot and is arrested and executed.

1972 Bokassa names himself president for life and marshal of the republic.

1973 The Central African Republic begins dialogue with South Africa.

1974 Bokassa begins a campaign against French influence; sale of French newspapers is forbidden; French consulate-general is closed down; French businesses are nationalized.

1975 Following the visit of French president Valéry Giscard d'Estaing for a Franco-African summit, good relations are restored with France.
Elisabeth Domitien is named as the Bokassa regime's first prime minister.

1976 Domitien is replaced by Ange Patasse as prime minister.
Bokassa survives attempt on his life at Bangui airport.
Bokassa renames the country the Central African Empire and proclaims himself emperor.

1977 Jonathan Randal and Michael Goldsmith, correspondents for the *Washington Post* and the Associated Press, respectively, are arrested and detained on charges of espionage and defamation of the emperor; Goldsmith is beaten unconscious by the emperor and his courtiers and is imprisoned for a month.
Bokassa holds coronation with pomp and circumstance, demonstrating his absolute hold over the country.

1978 Henri Maldou is named prime minister in place of Ange Patasse.

1979 Students riot in Bangui; Central African Empire ambassador to France resigns in the wake of mounting allegations of cruelty and brutality against the Bokassa regime; Bokassa is charged with the massacre of students; Bokassa is overthrown in a swift coup in which French troops play a prominent role; David Dacko is installed as president as the republic is reestablished; Bokassa, denied asylum in France, is granted one in Côte d'Ivoire.

1980 Central African Republic breaks diplomatic relations with the Soviet Union and Libya.
A new constitution for a multiparty system is approved by referendum.
Dacko wins presidential election and is sworn in for a six-year term.
Following accusations of electoral malpractice, rioting breaks out in Bangui and three people are killed in a bomb attack on a Bangui cinema.... State of siege is declared.
In a bloodless coup, President Dacko is ousted by an army group under General André Dieudonné Kolingba, who sets up Military Committee for National Recovery (CMRN) as the supreme organ of government.

1982 Ange Patasse, leader of the banned Movement for the Liberation of the Central African People (Mouvement pour la Libération du Peuple Centrafricain), is implicated in an unsuccessful coup attempt.
Patasse seeks asylum in the French embassy in Bangui, from where he is exiled.

1983 The three main opposition parties form a united opposition movement.

1984 President Kolingba announces amnesty for the leaders of banned political parties who had been under house arrest. Opposition leaders form a government-in-exile.

1985 President Kolingba gives civilians a majority of the portfolios in a new government formed in September.

1986 A new constitution provides for the establishment of the Rassemblement démocratique centrafricain as the sole political party and confers strong executive powers on the president. Bokassa returns from exile and is immediately arrested.

1987 The nation holds its first legislative elections in 20 years. Bokassa is convicted on charges of murder, illegal detention of prisoners, and embezzlement and is sentenced to death.

1988 Diplomatic relations with the USSR, suspended since 1980, are resumed. President Kolingba commutes Bokassa's sentence to one of life imprisonment at hard labor.

1989 The Central African Republic recognizes the Palestine Liberation Organization's declaration of an independent state of Palestine and reestablishes diplomatic relations with Israel.

1991 Political parties are legalized.

1993 Ange Félix Patasse is elected president and begins reforms to lessen the army's control of the country.

1996 Mutiny in the army leads to a French-brokered settlement between mutineers and President Patasse. The French twice send troops in an attempt to keep peace.

1997 United Nations sends peacekeeping troops to the country to stem further violence by army mutineers.

1999 Patasse is reelected.

2000 Civil servants strike over back pay; the coordinated protest of 15 opposition groups deteriorates into riots.

BIBLIOGRAPHY

Decalo, Samuel. *Psychosis of Power: African Personal Dictatorships*. Boulder, Colo., 1989.

Kalck, Pierre. *Historical Dictionary of the Central African Republic*. Metuchen, N.J., 1992.

O'Toole, Thomas. *The Central African Republic: The Continent's Hidden Heart*. Boulder, Colo., 1986.

OFFICIAL PUBLICATIONS

Central African Republic. *Annuaire statistique; Central African Republic—Recent Economic Developments* (IMF Staff Country Report [1997]); *Recensement général de la population 1988.*

CONTACT INFORMATION

Embassy of Central African Republic
1618 22nd Street NW
Washington, D.C. 20008
Phone: (202) 483-7800 Fax: (202) 332-9893

INTERNET RESOURCES

- Central African Republic
  http://www.africa.co.uk/country/cenafrep.htm

CHAD

BASIC FACT SHEET

OFFICIAL NAME:
Republic of Chad (République du Tchad)

ABBREVIATION:
CD

CAPITAL:
N'Djamena

HEAD OF STATE:
President Idriss Déby (from 1990)

HEAD OF GOVERNMENT:
Prime Minister Nagoum Yamassoum (from 1999)

NATURE OF GOVERNMENT:
Military dictatorship

POPULATION:
7,557,000 (1999)

AREA:
1,284,000 sq km (495,752 sq mi)

ETHNIC MAJORITY:
Arabs in the North; Sara in the South

LANGUAGES:
Arabic and French (official)

RELIGIONS:
Islam in the north; animism and Christianity in the south

UNIT OF CURRENCY:
Communauté Financière Africaine franc (C.F.A.F.)

NATIONAL FLAG:
A tricolor of blue, yellow, and red bands (from left to right)

NATIONAL EMBLEM:
The main elements of the national emblem are two heraldic animals holding a shield with serrated bands with the national motto underneath in French: *Unité, Travail, Progrès* (Unity, Work, Progress)

NATIONAL ANTHEM:
"Chadians, Up and to Work"

NATIONAL HOLIDAYS:
August 11 (Independence Day); January 1 (New Year's Day); May 1 (Labor Day); May 25 (Liberation of Africa Day); November 28 (Proclamation of the Republic); Christmas; also the movable Christian festivals of Ascension, Whitmonday, Easter Monday, Assumption and All Saints' Day, as well as variable Islamic festivals

DATE OF INDEPENDENCE:
August 11, 1960

DATE OF CONSTITUTION:
March 31, 1995 (adopted 1996)

GEOGRAPHICAL FEATURES

Chad, a landlocked country in north-central Africa, extends 1,765 km (1,097 mi) north to south and 1,030 km (640 mi) east to west. It covers an area of 1,284,000 sq km (495,752 sq mi).

Chad's total international border of 5,923 km (3,681 mi) is shared with six countries, as follows: Libya (1,055 km; 655 mi); Sudan (1,360 km; 845 mi); Central African Republic (1,197 km; 745 mi); Cameroon (1,094 km; 679 mi); Nigeria (87 km; 55 mi); and Niger (1,175 km; 730 mi).

The main feature of Chad is the broad, shallow central bowl of Lake Chad in the southern and southwestern half of the country. From the lake area and the central plains the land gradually rises to plateaus to the south, of which the Guera Massif (1,500 m; 4,900 ft) represents the highest point. To the north the basin rises to the clay plateau of the Ennedi and the volcanic Tibesti Range, whose highest point, Emi Koussi, rises to 3,415 m

Chad

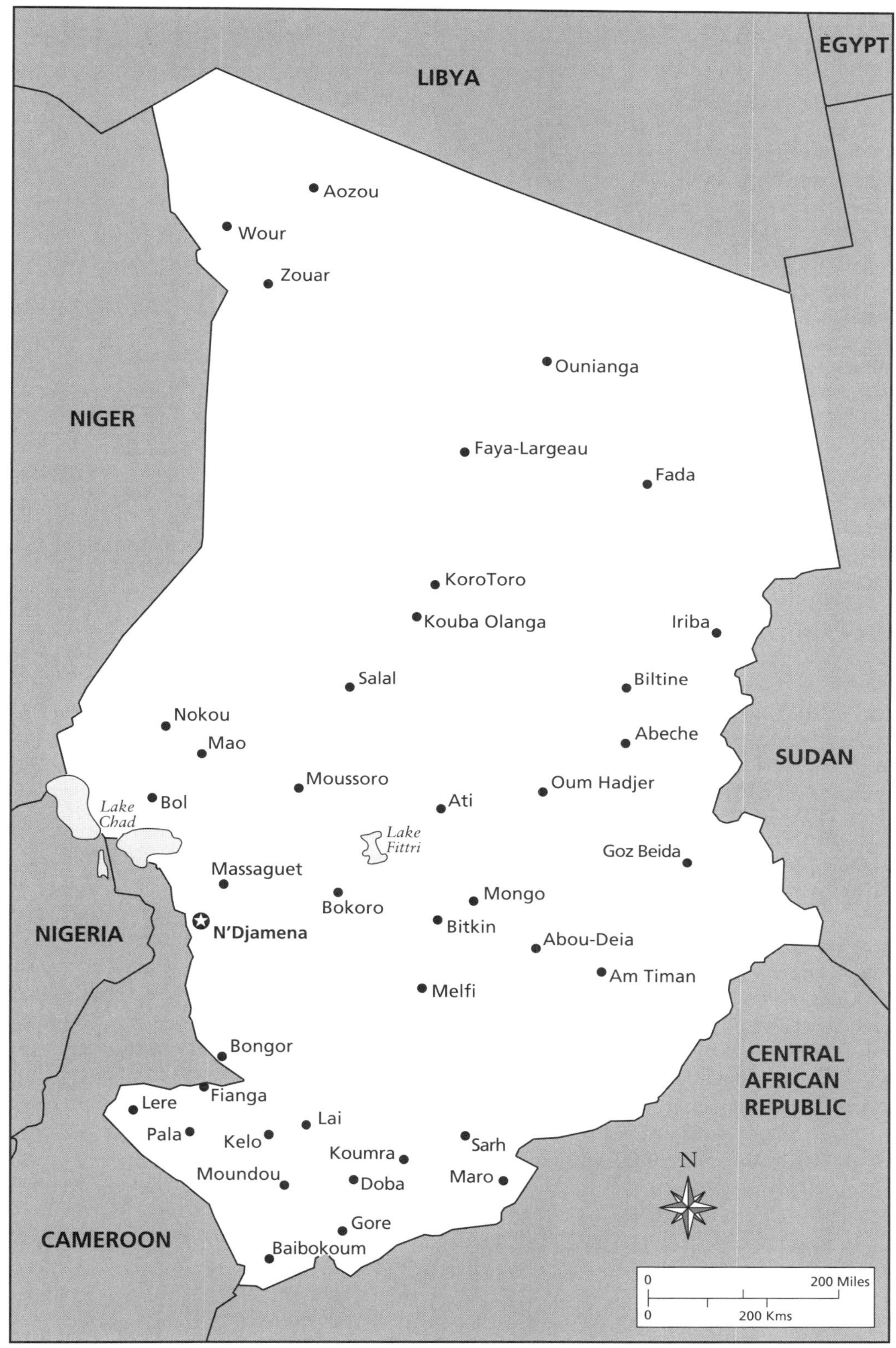
LIBYA
EGYPT
NIGER
SUDAN
NIGERIA
CAMEROON
CENTRAL
AFRICAN
REPUBLIC
Aozou
Wour
Zouar
Ounianga
Faya-Largeau
Fada
KoroToro
Kouba Olanga
Iriba
Salal
Biltine
Nokou
Mao
Abeche
Moussoro
Oum Hadjer
Bol
Ati
Lake
Chad
Lake
Fittri
Goz Beida
Massaguet
Mongo
Bokoro
N'Djamena
Bitkin
Abou-Deia
Am Timan
Melfi
Bongor
Fianga
Lere
Lai
Pala
Kelo
Sarh
Koumra
Moundou
Doba
Maro
Gore
Baibokoum
N
0
200 Miles
0
200 Kms

(11,204 ft). To the east the Ouaddai Range divides Chad from the Nile River drainage system. In the basin itself there are a few low mountains, such as Madjer El Hamis and Fianga-Moita.

Geography

Area sq km: 1,284,000 (495,752 sq km)
World Rank: 21st
Land Boundaries, km: Cameroon 1094; Central African Republic 1197; Libya 1055; Niger 1175; Nigeria 87; Sudan 1360
Coastline, km: 0
Elevation Extremes meters
  Lowest: Djourab Depression 175
  Highest: Emil Koussi 3,415
Land Use % Arable land: 3
  Permanent Crops: 0
  Permanent Pastures: 36
  Forest and Woodland: 26
  Other: 35

Population of Principal Cities (1993; MU)

Abéché	187,936
Bongor	196,713
Doba	185,461
Moundou	282,103
N'Djamena	530,965
Sarh	193,753

CLIMATE AND WEATHER

Chad has three climatic zones: the Guinean or subtropical zone within the equatorial rain belt, the Sahelian central zone, and the northern Saharan zone. The subtropical zone has a long rainy season from May to November, with rainfall between 900 and 1,200 mm (35 and 47 in) and a dry season lasting five to six months. The Sahelian zone has a longer dry season, of seven to eight months, and rainfall of 500 to 900 mm (20 to 35 in). The Saharan zone has a dry season of at least nine months and erratic rainfall between 200 and 500 mm (8 and 20 in). The northernmost areas have a true desert climate, with rainfall below 200 mm (8 in) and temperatures of up to 40°C (104°F). The minimum temperature drops to 0°C (32°F) in December.

Climate and Weather

Mean Temperature
Summer 104°F
Winter 32°F
Average Rainfall
Subtropical Zone: 35 in to 47 in
Sahelian Zone: 20 in to 35 in
Saharan Zone 8 in to 20 in

POPULATION

Population Indicators

Total Population: 1999 7,557,000
World Rank: 89th
Density per sq mi: 15.2 (5.9 per sq km)
% of annual growth (1994–99): 2.8
Male %: 47.9
Female %: 52.1
Urban %: 21.4
Age Distribution: % 0–14: 48.1
  15–29: 24.6
  30–44: 14.7
  45–59: 7.2
  60–74: 4.2
  75 and over: 1.3
Population 2020: 12,831,000
Birth Rate per 1,000: 41.6
Death Rate per 1,000: 17.3
Population Doubling Time (years): 26
Infant Mortality Rate per 1,000 live births: 115.0
Rate of Natural Increase per 1,000: 24.3
Total Fertility Rate: 5.5
Expectation of Life (years): Males 46.3
  Females 49.3
Marriage Rate per 1,000: —
Divorce Rate per 1,000: —
Total Number of Households: —
Average Size of Households: 3.9
% of Illegitimate Children: —
Induced Abortions: —
  Rate per 100 live births: —

ETHNIC COMPOSITION

The people of Chad are broadly divided into the Arab and Arabized northern groups and the pagan, or *kirdi*, groups of the south. The Arabs and the Arabized people form a relatively homogeneous cultural, religious, linguistic, and geographic group. The indigenous inhabitants of the south form a mosaic of infinite variety and number, consisting of some 200 distinct ethnic groups. No single group forms a majority in any region, and the largest group, the Sara, constitutes only 24 percent of the population. The ethnic composition has been altered over the years through invasions, migrations, warfare, intermarriage, slave raids, and epidemics.

An estimated 1,000 French live in Chad, constituting the major foreign community. There is no overt hostility toward foreigners in the south, but few Westerners venture into the north.

LANGUAGES

Arabic and French are Chad's official languages, though French is understood and spoken by only 30 percent of literate Chadians. No one language is spoken or understood by all Chadians. The language of northern and central Chad is Turku, a form of pidgin Arabic sometimes called Chadian Arabic. Sara is widely spoken in the south. The smaller dialects and languages are becoming extinct as the need for intertribal communication increases.

Principal Languages and Their Speakers

Arabic	930,000
Bagirmi	110,000
Fitri-Batha	350,000
French	2,270,000
Fula (Fulani)	190,000
Gorane	470,000
Hadjarai	510,000
Kanem-Bornu	680,000
Lac-Iro	40,000
Mayo-Kebbi	870,000
Ouaddai	660,000
Sara	2,090,000
Tandjile	490,000
Other	170,000

RELIGIONS

About 54 percent of the people are Muslims, mostly the northern and central tribes. Another 27 percent adhere to traditional African religions. Christianity, followed by about 35 percent of Chadians, is strongest among the Sara. There is a Roman Catholic archdiocese at N'Djamena, with three suffragan dioceses. Christian churches came into conflict with former president N'garta Tombalbaye's authenticity campaign in the early 1970s.

Islam, Christianity, and animism are freely practiced. The country has remained multireligious despite domestic and foreign pressures in favor of Islam. More than 50 percent of Chad's population profess faith in Islam, and the percentage is growing.

Religious Affiliations

Muslim	4,070,000
Roman Catholic	1,540,000
Protestant	1,090,000
Traditional beliefs	560,000
Other	300,000

HISTORICAL BACKGROUND

More than 2,500 years ago, the region had abundant water from Lake Chad. That resource has dwindled over the years. However, in the eighth and ninth centuries, people were migrating from the Nile River valley and the state of Kanem was founded. The kingdom lasted more than 1,000 years and was marked by its extensive trade in salt, copper, gold, and slaves. By the 13th century the region had adopted Islam. In 1812, the kingdom collapsed when the capital was attacked by the Fulani people.

Chad came under French rule in 1900 as part of French Equatorial Africa. The pacification of various Chadian areas, however, was not completed until 1915, and it was not until 1920 that an effective administrative system was established. The degree of French control was greatest in the south and nominal in the north. The extension of the French legal and administrative system was slow and halting because of the lack of French administrators willing to serve in Chad. The main legacy of French rule was the transfer of effective political power from the Muslim north to the animist and Christian south. The southerners, who were deeply influenced by French institutions and who readily availed themselves of the new opportunities for advancement that French culture offered, have retained the French political and economic system almost intact since independence on August 11, 1960.

Chad's political history has been marked by divisions based on ethnic, religious, and geographic lines, with the Muslims in the north traditionally in conflict with the black animists and Christians of the south. The governing elite traditionally have been drawn from the south, with the northern groups excluded. Unable to gain a role in national political life, in 1958 northerners launched a struggle that resulted in an ongoing civil war. Although nominally a republic, Chad has operated throughout most of its independent nationhood as a dictatorship.

Chad was made an autonomous state within the French community in November 1958. The following year François (later N'garta) Tombalbaye, a Christian from the south and the leader of the majority Parti Progressiste Tchadien (PPT), assumed the position of prime minister. With the exception of the northern province of Bourkou-Ennedi-Tibesti (BET), which remained under French control, the nation became independent in 1960 with Tombalbaye as president. Chad became a one-party state prior to the adoption of the constitution in 1962.

Tombalbaye's government faced civil disturbances in 1963 and outright rebellion in 1965 when the French ended their administration of BET. The Front de Libération Nationale de Tchad (FROLINAT), with covert support from Libya, which had historic ties to the northern region, led the rebellion. French military intervention in 1968 put a temporary end to the revolt, but despite Tombalbaye's attempts at reconciliation, disturbances continued. Resistance culminated in an attempted coup by FROLINAT in 1971, reportedly with Libya's backing. In another effort to consolidate his political power, Tombalbaye, in 1973, formed a new political party, the Mouvement National pour la Révolution Culturelle et Sociale (MNRCS), which replaced the PPT.

Tombalbaye was killed during an army coup in 1975 that brought the former army chief of staff, Félix Malloum, to power. Malloum dissolved the MNRCS and ruled through a newly instituted Supreme Military Council. FROLINAT, with support from Libya, occupied the Aozou Strip in the north, and continued, to oppose the government.

Temporary infighting in FROLINAT between the People's Armed Forces (FAP) led by Goukouni Oueddei and the Armed Forces of the North (FAN), loyal to Hissène Habré, temporarily weakened the party. However, by 1977, forces under Oueddei had captured much of the BET. In an effort to curb the rebellion by including factions from FROLINAT in government, Malloum appointed Habré, a Muslim from the BET, as prime minister. Nevertheless, Oueddei continued his advance on the capital, and French intervention was necessary to prevent a takeover.

In 1978 a serious rift between Habré and Malloum led to a breakdown in central authority. A three-way civil war erupted between Habré, Malloum, and Oueddei supporters, and rebellion also broke out in the south. French troops intervened in 1978 and 1979. External attempts by the French, Libyans, Nigerians, and Algerians to find a solution failed. A series of shaky coalition governments were formed, but the government was dominated by rivalry between Oueddei and Habré. Initially Oueddei, with Libyan support, controlled the capital, but by 1982, N'Djamena was under Habré's control. Oueddei reestablished his forces in the north and the following year led a major offensive against Habré. In 1983 France intervened in the armed conflict and declared the 15th parallel a line of interdiction between the warring factions. Further fighting forced the French to move the line to the 16th parallel.

The military situation eased in 1984, although there were reports of continued fighting in the south. In an effort to win over the region, Habré formed the Union Nationale pour l'Indépendance et la Révolution (UNIR) and carried out a major government reorganization in which a number of leading southerners were included. At the same time he carried out a major offensive that pushed many of the rebels into the Central African Republic.

In September 1987 a cease-fire was established, bringing the war to an end. The following year Chad and Libya agreed to reestablish diplomatic relations broken off in 1982 and to settle the Aozou question peacefully. Habré was overthrown in a military coup on December 1, 1990. Rebel leader Idriss Déby, a renegade general and former aide of Habré, declared himself president on December 4 and promised a multiparty democracy. He is now in exile in Senegal, but in early 1992 made a foray back into Chad, capturing two towns near Lake Chad before government troops and French paratroopers drove him back. The years 1992–93 saw five attempted coups and numerous government crackdowns. President Déby has brought some order to the country but at a high cost in terms of civil rights and government-sanctioned killing.

The Higher Transitional Council approved a new electoral code and draft constitution in 1995. A constitutional referendum was conducted in March 1996. A new constitution was approved by 63.5 percent of voters. Not surprisingly the no vote was heaviest in the south, which had preferred a federal status that gave the region substantial autonomy. As provided in the new constitution, presidential and legislative elections were held the following year. Fifteen candidates contested the first round of presidential voting with President Idriss Déby obtaining 43.9 percent of the vote. In the runoff Déby was reelected to another term by 69.1 percent of the vote. Nassour Ouaidou Guelenouksia was named prime minister, succeeding veteran politician Djimasta Koibla. Déby was reelected in May 2001.

CONSTITUTION

The Constitution of 1962 was suspended in 1975. In March 1991, Idriss Déby declared himself president and ruled the country almost single-handedly. A new constitution was adopted in 1996 that declared Chad a unitary state to be headed by a president. It also provided for a National Assembly consisting of 125 members elected for four-year terms.

LOCAL GOVERNMENT

Chad's territorial organization, devised by the French, combines traditional and modern units. The largest regional division is the prefecture, headed by a prefect appointed by the president. There are 14 prefectures.

The prefectures are divided into 54 subprefectures, each under a subprefect. N'Djamena is a separate prefecture known as a *délégation-générale*. Regions where traditional administrations were taken over as a unit are called administrative posts, of which there are 27. Their heads can be either a civil servant or a traditional chief or sultan.

Local Government

Principal administrative divisions, capitals, area, population

AREA AND POPULATION

Regions	Capitals	area sq mi	area sq km	population 1993 estimate
Batha	Ati	34,285	88,800	288,458
Blitine	Blitine	18,090	46,850	184,807
Borkou-Ennedi-Tibesti	Faya Largeau	231,795	600,350	73,185
Chari-Baguimi	N'Djamena	32,010	82,910	1,251,906
Guéra	Mongo	22,760	58,950	306,253
Kanem	Mao	44,215	114,520	279,927
Lac	Bol	8,620	22,320	252,932
Logone Occidental	Moundou	3,357	8,695	455,489
Logone Oriental	Doba	10,825	28,035	441,064
Mayo-Kebbi	Bongor	11,625	30,105	825,158
Moyen-Chari	Sarh	17,445	45,180	738,595

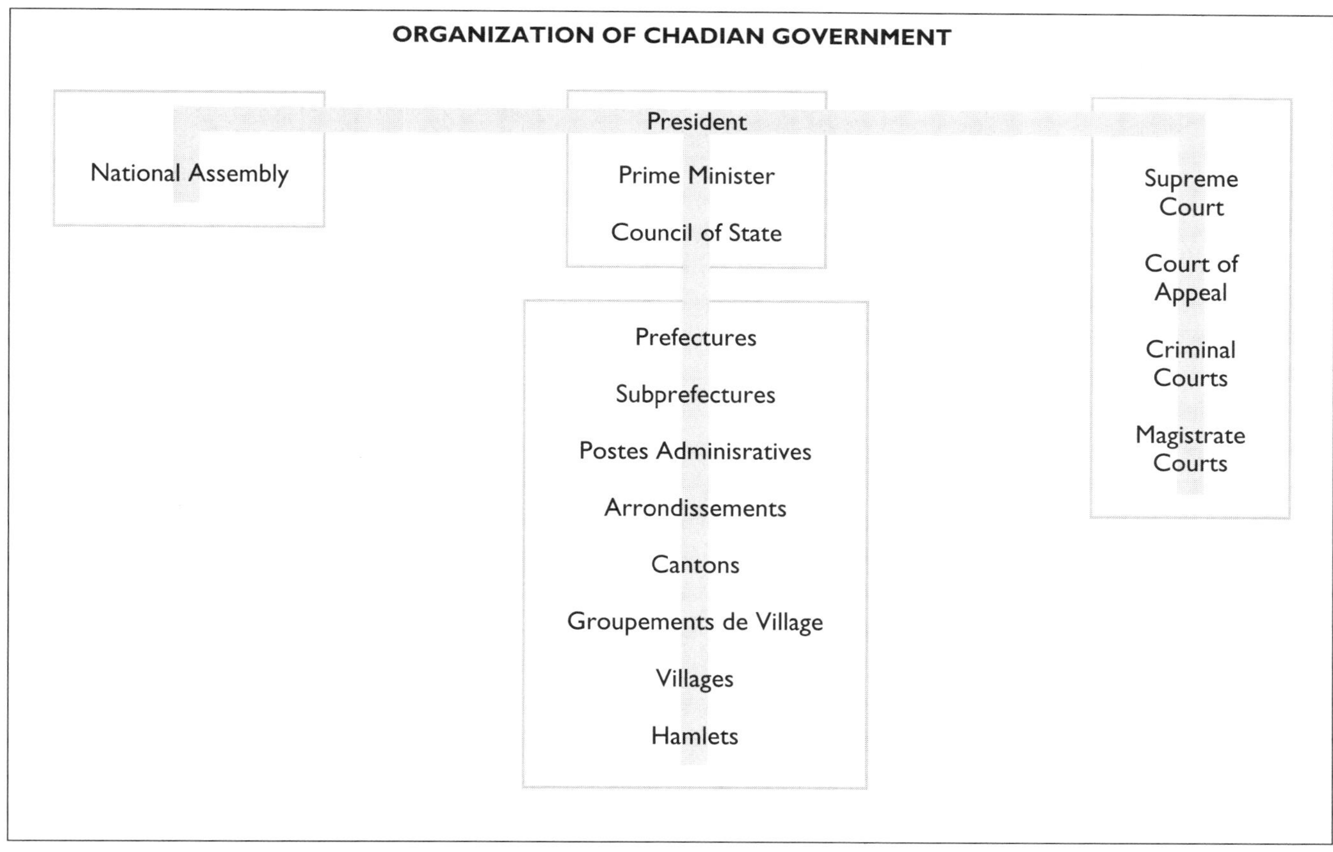

Ouaddai	Abéché	29,436	75,240	543,900
Salamat	Am Timan	24,325	63,000	184,403
Tandjilé	Lai	6,995	18,045	453,854
TOTAL		495,755	1,284,000	6,279,931

PARLIAMENT

The National Assembly was dissolved in 1975 following the coup. Traditionally, it enjoyed little power. A 30-member Conseil National Consultatif was formed in 1982. It was made up of two representatives from each of Chad's prefectures plus two representatives from the capital, N'Djamena. The president appointed all members of the council. The National Assembly was reinstated in 1997 after a new constitution was formed.

POLITICAL PARTIES

By mid-1996 Chad had about 60 political parties. The following are the most prominent in the new National Assembly: The Patriotic Salvation Movement or MPS, which was originally in opposition but now is the party in power and the party of the president; the National Union for Development and Renewal or UNDR; Rally for Democracy and Progress or RDP; and Union for Renewal and Democracy or URD.

Political Parties

Patriotic Salvation Movement, 1990
Union for Renewal and Democracy, 1992
National Union for Development and Renewal,
    National Alliance for Development
Rally for Democratic Action and Progress, an alliance of
    Action for Unity and Socialism
    Revolutionary Movement of the Chadian People
Union for Democracy and the Republic, 1992
Rally for Democracy and Progress, 1991
Party for Freedom and Development, 1993
National Convention for Social Democracy
Front of Action Forces for the Republic
Movement for Democracy and Socialism in Chad, 1988
Chadian Democratic Union
National Salvation Council for Peace and Democracy, 1992
Union of Democratic Forces
National Alliance for Democracy and Renewal, 1993
Rally of the Chadian People, 1992
National Assembly for Democracy and Progress, 1992
Convention of Chadian Social Democrats in Chad, 1992
National Union, 1992
Alliance for Chadian Democracy, 1992
Alliance of Political Parties for Democracy, 1994
Illegal groups engaged in insurrection against the government include
    Movement for Democracy and Justice in Chad, 1998
    Armed Forces for a Federal Republic
    Chadian National Front
    National Council for Chadian Recovery

Political Parties: Strength in Parliament Most Recent Elections

Elections (for a four-year term) to the new 125-member **National Assembly** were held on January 5 and February 23, 1997. According to the final official results, seats were distributed as follows: Patriotic Salvation Movement, 63; Union for Renewal and Democracy, 29; National Union for Development and Renewal, 15; Union for Democracy and the Republic, 4; Rally for Democracy and Progress, 3; Party for Freedom and Development, 3; National Alliance for Development, 2; Action for Unity and Socialism, 2; National Convention for Social Democracy, 1; Front of Action Forces for the Republic, 1; vacant, 2.

LEGAL SYSTEM

The Chadian legal system is marked by the continued coexistence of customary law, largely uncodified, and French law. In cases of conflict between the two, the French law prevails.

The court structure was extensively reorganized in 1967. The customary courts were replaced by justices of the peace, who were advised by two assessors on customary law. The Supreme Court, which functioned as the top judicial authority since 1963, was abolished in 1975 after the coup. In 1976 the permanent Court of State Security was established, comprising eight civilian and military members.

The judicial structure is controlled by the High Council of the Judiciary, which advises the president on judicial appointments and ensures the independence and integrity of the judges. Almost all the judges on the superior courts are French; there is a continuing shortage of qualified Chadian judges and magistrates.

LAW ENFORCEMENT

Law Enforcement

Offenses reported to the police per 100,000: —
- Murder: —
- Assault: —
- Burglary: —
- Automobile Theft: —
- Population per Police officer: 990

Death Penalty: Yes

HUMAN RIGHTS

In terms of civil and political rights Chad is classified as a country that is not free. Because of unsettled political conditions, it is difficult to speak of civil rights. The judicial system no longer functions, and there are no trials in the normal sense of the term. There are reports that all jails have been closed and civilian prisoners released. There is widespread looting of homes by armed combatants of all factions.

FOREIGN POLICY

Libya was one of the major players in the Chadian civil war, which was provoked by Libya's annexation of the Aozou Strip in northern Chad in 1978. Despite a 1989 agreement calling for mutual withdrawal from the disputed territory, Libya provided haven and support for Chadian rebels operating out of Sudan and Libya. Relations between the two countries improved after the 1990 victory of the Libyan-supported rebels in the civil war. Shortly thereafter the two countries signed a treaty of friendship and cooperation. Relations with France have been complicated by France's involvement in the civil war. French forces aided government troops until 1990 when the pro-Libyan MPS (Movement Patriotique du Salut) won. In 1991 the Chadian president invited French troops to remain in the country. In 1998 Chad sent more than 2,000 troops to support Kabila in the Democratic Republic of the Congo, but the force was withdrawn in 1999.

DEFENSE

The defense structure is headed by the president and chairman of the Supreme Military Council. The line of command runs through the chief of staff and the National Defense Commission to the head of the Tactical Bureau and the army and gendarmerie commanders. Military manpower is provided by voluntary enlistment. The total strength of the armed forces is 25,400.

Chad's army, deprived of French crutches, is small and neither staffed nor equipped to repel a concerted offensive by a foreign power.

Military Indicators

Total Active Duty Personnel: 25,400
Military Manpower per 1,000: 3.5
Military Expenditures $: 34 million
- as % of GNP: 3.1
- per capita $: 5
- as % of central government expenditures: 9.7

Arms Imports $: 10
Arms Exports $: 0

ECONOMY

Landlocked Chad's economic development suffers from it's geographic remoteness, drought, lack of infrastructure, and political turmoil. About 85 percent of the population depends on agriculture, including the herding of livestock. Of Africa's Francophone countries, Chad benefited least from the 50 percent devaluation of their currencies in January 1994. Financial aid from the World Bank, the African Development Fund, and other sources is directed largely at the improvement of agriculture, especially livestock production. Due to lack of financing, the development of the Doba Basin oil fields, originally due to finish in 2000, has been substantially delayed.

Principal Economic Indicators

Gross National Product: $1.629 billion
GNP per capita: $230
GNP Average Annual Growth Rate (1990–97) %: 1.0
GNP per capita Average Annual Growth Rate (1990–97) %: −2.1
Origin of Gross Domestic Product %
- Agriculture: 21
- Mining: —
- Manufacturing: 6
- Construction: 1
- Public Utilities: —
- Transportation and Communications: 12
- Trade: 12
- Financial Services: 12
- Other Services: 5
- Government: 5

Gross Domestic Product by Type of Expenditure %
- Private Consumption: 87
- Government Consumption: 14
- Gross Domestic Investment: 16

Foreign Trade: Exports: 22
Imports: −39
% of Income Received by Poorest 20%: 8
% of Income Received by Richest 10%: 30

Price and earnings indexes (1995 = 100)

	1991	1992	1993	1994	1995	1996	1997
Consumer price index	72.6	70.3	65.3	91.7	100.0	112.4	118.7
Earnings index	—	—	—	—	—	—	—

Finance

National Currency: CFA France (CFAF)
Exchange Rate: $1 = CFAF 608.36
Money Supply Stock in National Currency billion: 85.3
M1 per capita: 12,400
Central Bank Discount Rate %: 7.60
Total External Debt $: 875 million
Debt Service Ratio %: 7.8
Balance of Payments $: −228.2 million
International Reserves SDRs: 123 million
Ratio of External Debt to Total Reserves: 5.9
Average Annual Rate of Inflation/Consumer Price Index Growth Rate %: 15

Official Development Assistance

ODA: $155 million
- as % of GNP: 10
- per capita: $23
- Foreign Direct Investment $: 16 million

Central Government Revenues and Expenditures

Fiscal Year: Calendar Year

Revenues $: 198 million
Expenditures $: 218 million
Budget Deficit $: 20 million
Tax Revenues as % of GDP: —
Highest Tax Bracket % —
- Individual: —
- Corporate: —

Employment and Labor

Economically Active Population: 2,016,000
Female Participation Rate %: 18.2
Activity Rate %: 35.3
Labor by Sector: %
- Agriculture, Forestry, Fishing: 73.9
- Manufacturing, Mining: 7.4
- Construction: —
- Transportation and Communications: —
- Trade, Hotels, and Restaurants: —
- Finance, Insurance, Real Estate: —
- Public Administration, Defense: —
- Services: 18.7

Unemployment %: NA

Agriculture

Agriculture's Share of GDP %: 21
Average Annual Rate of Growth (1965–98) %: 1.7
Number of Farms 000: 366
Average Size of Farm ha: 2.6
Number of Tractors per 1,000 hectares: 0.05
Irrigation, % of Farms having: 0.4
Artificial Fertilizer kg/hectare: 2
Total Cropland as % of Farmland: 23.7
Livestock: Cattle 000: 5,582
Sheep 000: 2,432
Hogs 000: 23
Chickens 000: 4,700
Forests: Production of Roundwood (000 cubic meters): 4,531
Fisheries: Total Catch tons: 80,000

Mining

% of GDP: 0.5
Value of Mineral Production $: 5 million

Manufacturing

Value Added $: 98 million
Industrial Production Growth Rate %: 5.0

Energy

Commercial Energy Production metric tons of oil equivalent: —
Commercial Energy Consumption metric tons of oil equivalent: —
Commercial Energy Consumption per capita kg: —
Average Annual Growth Rate 1980–97 %: —
Net Energy Imports % of use: —
Electricity Installed Capacity kW: 29,000
- Production kW-hr: 89 million

Coal Reserves tons: —
- Production tons: —

(continued)

Natural Gas Proven Reserves cubic meters: —
Production cubic meters: —
Crude Petroleum Reserves barrels: —
Production barrels: —
Consumption barrels: —
Refinery Capacity barrels per day: —
Pipelines Length km: —

Foreign Trade

Imports $: 243 million
Exports $: 261 million
Export Volume % Annual Growth Rate (1990–97): −6.6
Import Volume % Annual Growth Rate (1990–97): −11.2
Balance of Trade $

Balance of trade (current prices)

	1993	1994	1995	1996	1997
CFAF 000,000,000	−19.6	+42.0	+13.1	+0.5	+2.8
% of total	20.8%	21.7%	5.0%	0.2%	0.9%

Major Trading Partners

	Imports	Exports
European Union %	46.5	42.9
United States %	2.5	0.8
Eastern Europe %	0.4	0.8
Japan %	1.6	7.3
Others %	49.0	48.2

Transportation

Roads Total Length mi: 20,319 (32,700 km)
Paved %: 1
Automobiles: 9,630
Trucks and Buses: 14,360
Persons per vehicle: 265
Railroad; Track Length mi: —
Passenger-mi: —
Freight-mi: —
Merchant Marine: No. of Vessels: —
Total Deadweight Tonnage: —
International Cargo Loaded tons: —
International Cargo Off-loaded tons: —
Airports with Scheduled Flights: 4
Traffic: Passenger-mi: 138 million
Freight-mi: 10.5 million
Length of Canals mi: 1,240 (2,000 km)

Tourism

Number of Tourists to: 11,000
Number of Tourists from: 10,000
Tourist Receipts $: 36 million
Tourist Expenditures $: 26 million

Communications

Telephones 000: 5.3
Cost of Local Calls 3 mins: $0
Cellular Telephones 000: 0.2
Fax Machines 000: —
Personal Computers 000: —
Internet Hosts per million persons: —
Mail: Post Offices: 34
Pieces of Mail Handled: 7.9 million
Pieces of Mail Handled per person: 1.3

EDUCATION

Education is free, universal, and compulsory, in principle, for six years, from ages eight to 14. However, actual school enrollment rates are abysmally low.

Schooling consists of six years of primary school, four years of middle school at a collège d'enseignement or lycée and three years of secondary school at a lycée for a total of 13 years. The curriculum in both primary and secondary schools is based on the French model and is standardized for both private and public schools.

The academic year runs from October to mid-June. The medium of instruction is French throughout, although Arabic is encouraged in areas with a Muslim majority.

About 88 percent of primary-level students attend public schools; the rest are in Roman Catholic mission schools. At the secondary level, 94 percent attend state schools and 4 percent Roman Catholic mission schools. Koranic schools offer limited primary education for northern Muslims. There also are a few Islamic secondary-education centers.

Chad's first university, the University of Chad, opened in N'Djamena in 1971 and graduated its first class in 1974.

Education

Literacy Rate %: 48.1
Male %: 62.1
Female %: 34.7
First Level: Primary schools: 2,447
Teachers: 9,404
Students: 591,784
Student-Teacher Ratio: 62.9
Net Enrollment Ratio: —
Second Level: Secondary Schools: 66
Teachers: 2,046
Students: 82,559
Student-Teacher Ratio: 40.4
Net Enrollment Ratio: —

Vocational Level: Schools: —
Students: 3,277

Third Level: Institutions: 4
Teachers: 311
Students: 3,049
Student-Ratio Level: 9.8
Gross Enrollment Ratio: 0.8
Students per 100,000: 70
% of Population Age 25 and over with Postsecondary Education: —

Public Expenditure on Education as % of GDP: 2.2

SCIENCE AND TECHNOLOGY

Science and Technology

Scientists and Engineers in R&D per 1 million persons: —
Expenditures in R&D as % of GDP: —
High-Tech Exports $: —
Patent Applications by Residents: —

MEDIA

A few news bulletins are issued by various government agencies, particularly *InfoTchad*, a mimeographed daily with a circulation of 1,600 copies. All printing facilities are owned by the government. The national news agency is Agence Tchadienne de Presse (ATP). Both AFB and Reuters have offices in N'Djamena.

Radiodiffusion National Tchadienne, until 1973 Radio Chad, operates transmitters at N'Djamena, Sarh, and Abeche. Chad's television service broadcasts over 800 hours annually, the majority of which is devoted to entertainment.

Media

Daily Newspapers: 1
Total Circulation 000: 2.0
Circulation per 1,000: 0.4
Books Published: —
Magazines: —
Radio Receivers 000: 1,310
per 1,000: 240
Television sets 000: 11
per 1,000: 2.0

Most Important Media:

Press. The following are published at N'Djamena: *Info-Tchad*, daily bulletin of the official news agency, ATP; *Al-Watan*, government weekly; *Contact*, independent weekly.

News agencies. The domestic agency is Agence Tchadienne de Presse (ATP). Agence France-Presse and Reuters also maintain offices at N'Djamena.

Radio and television. Radiodiffusion Nationale Tchadienne (RNT) broadcasts in French, Arabic, and local languages to some 1.7 million receivers; Télé-Chad transmits from N'Djamena.

CULTURE

Cultural Indicators

Public Libraries 4
Number: —
Volumes: 11,000
Registered borrowers: 300
Museums
Number: 5
Annual Attendance: —
Cinema
Production of Long Films: —
Number of Cinemas: —
Seating Capacity: —
Annual Attendance: —
Annual Attendance per capita: —

STATUS OF WOMEN

Women generally are subordinate to men in Chadian society. Females do attend school at all levels of the educational system. Some women participate in the political life of the country as, for example, the minister of social and women's affairs, who also is a member of the ruling UNIR's Executive Committee. Some women serve voluntarily in the armed forces, and some figure prominently in the labor movement. Although figures are not known, many women and their children have been left homeless and without adequate means of support, with their husbands missing or dead in civil strife. Widows and orphans are, however, often taken care of by extended family members.

Women

Gender Empowerment Measure: —
Seats Held in Parliament by Women %: 2.4
Female Administrators and Managers %: —
Female Professional and Technical Workers %: —
Women's Share of Earned Income %: —
Women in Government %: 3

HEALTH, FOOD, AND NUTRITION

Health

Number of Physicians: 217
Number of Dentists: 5
Number of Nurses: 878
Number of Pharmacists: 10
Population per Physician: 27,765
Number of Hospitals: —
Hospital Beds per 10,000: 7
Hospital Bed Occupancy Rate: —
Infant Mortality Rate per 1,000 live births: 172
Maternal Mortality Rate per 100,000 live births: 1,500
Total Health Expenditures as % of GDP: 6.22
Health Expenditures per capita $: 12
HIV Infected % of adults: 2.72
Cigarette Consumption per smoker per year: —
% of Smokers: Male: —
Female: —
Access to Safe Water %: 29

Food and Nutrition

Food Supply as % of FAO Requirements: 80
% of Consumption Expenditures on Food: 45.3
Daily Available Calories per capita: 1,913
% of Total Calories derived from:
Cereals: 54.0

(*continued*)

Potatoes, cassava: 12.1
Meat, poultry: 2.7
Fish: 0.6
Eggs, milk: 2.5
Fruits, vegetables: 1.9
Fats, oils: 6.2

ENVIRONMENT

The environment of Chad has suffered from both environmental and political factors. For more than 30 years, fighting has prevented any meaningful management of the environment to ensure the long-term sustainability of the agricultural lands. Severe droughts have also taken their toll on the land, particularly the ones between 1972 and 1983. The country suffers from growing desertification and poor agricultural practices.

Environment

Forest Area sq km: 110,000
Average Annual Deforestation sq km: 942
Nationally Protected Areas as % of Total Land Area: 9.1
Freshwater Access cubic meters per capita: 5,904
Emissions of Organic Water Pollutants kg per day:
CO_2 Emissions per capita ton: 0.0 ton

CHRONOLOGY

1960 Chad becomes an independent member of the French Community with François Tombalbaye as president.

1961 Tombalbaye's Parti Progressiste Tchadien (PPT) merges with the main opposition party, Parti Nationale Africaine (PNA).

1962 New constitution is promulgated.
All political parties except the PPT are banned.
Northern insurgent organization Front de Libération Nationale de Chad (FROLINAT) is founded.

1963 Five prominent northern politicians are arrested.
National emergency is declared in the wake of bloody riots in which 500 are killed.

1964 National Assembly passes resolution empowering the Political Bureau of the PPT to direct and control the actions of government and to choose all candidates for political office.

1965 Open revolt breaks out in the northern prefectures as secessionist movement gathers strength among Muslims.

1968 Tombalbaye invokes Franco-Chadian agreement of 1960 for military assistance against the rebels; French troops join in campaign against the insurgents.
Zaire, Chad, and Central African Republic join in a new union known as Union des Etats d'Afrique Centrale (UEAC).

1969 Tombalbaye is reelected president.

1972 Tombalbaye unleashes a new authenticity campaign calling for a return to "Tchaditude," or authentic Chadian traditions and values; he changes his name to N'garta Tombalbaye, the name of the capital to N'Djamena, and the name of the PPT to Mouvement Nationale pour la Révolution Culturelle et Sociale (MNRCS); Chad declares a drought emergency and appeals for international aid; nearly 20 percent of the national cattle herd is wiped out as a result of the drought that affected all of the Sahel since 1968.

1974 Françoise and Pierre Claustre, French archaeologists, are kidnapped by rebels led by Hissène Habré.

1975 Tombalbaye is overthrown in a swift coup; Félix Malloum is named the new president and chairman of the Supreme Military Council; the National Assembly is dissolved.

1976 New defense treaty is concluded with France.

1977 Attempted coup against the government is reported crushed.
Chad charges Libya with border violations; Françoise Claustre, the kidnapped French archaeologist, is released.

1978 Chad breaks diplomatic relations with Libya after accusing its northern neighbor of occupying a 78,000 sq km (30,000 sq mi) territory in the Tibesti region believed to hold uranium deposits.
FROLINAT launches major attack against government forces at Faya-Largeau; government concludes cease-fire with the Armed Forces of the North (FAN) led by Hissène Habré and later appoints Habré prime minister; the Malloum regime and Habré engage in a bloody but inconclusive confrontation.

1979 French forces are flown into N'Djamena as Malloum flees the country; a cease-fire is agreed on under Sudanese mediation; an agreement among the four main factions (FROLINAT, Malloum, Third Army, and Armed Forces of the North) breaks down when Libya attacks the Aozou Strip; an agreement among the 11 principal factions leads to formation of an interim government of national unity with Goukouni Oueddei, leader of the official FROLINAT, as president and Wadal Abdel Kader Kamougue, a former Malloum supporter, as vice president; N'Djamena is demilitarized and a neutral peacekeeping force from Benin, Congo, and Gabon is created to replace the departing French forces.

1980 Fighting resumes and over 700 die as violence escalates; Congo withdraws its troops; factional fighting breaks out between FAN and other FROLINAT rebel groups.
Libya moves into northern Chad and concludes defense treaty with President Oueddei.
Libyan offensive forces FAN to withdraw to Cameroon and Sudan border areas.

1981 Libya invades Chad, and Libyan troops occupy the capital; Libya and Chad announce a decision to "achieve full unity"; after OAU condemns the merger plan and sends a peacekeeping force, President Oueddei repudiates the merger plan; FAN takes N'Djamena and eventually controls most of the country; Oueddei flees the capital and sets up a rival government in the town of Bardai, near the Libyan border.

1982 Habré is sworn in as president; Oueddei forces regroup and advance to the south, taking strategic cities; France intervenes and stations its troops along the "Red Line" of the 16th parallel, which marks the division between the Habré-controlled south and the Oueddei-controlled north.

1984 Libya and France reach a mutual accord for withdrawal of troops from Chad; French troops evacuate the country, but Libya maintains a clandestine presence.

1985 Seven major antigovernment factions loyal to Goukouni unite to form the Conseil Suprème de la Révolution (CSR).

1986 Habré announces release of 122 political prisoners; Libyan-backed GUNT forces resume hostilities by attacking government positions; at Habré's request France again intervenes.

1987 OAU mediation culminates in cease-fire between Chad and Libya on September 11; fighting breaks out again in November, and the UN General Assembly declares OAU responsible for resolving the dispute.

1988 Diplomatic relations between Chad and Libya, severed in 1982, are restored in October; in December, military clashes resume near the Sudanese border.

1989 Libya and Chad sign an accord on August 31 agreeing to submit their border dispute over the Aozou Strip to the International Court of Justice.

1990 Habré is overthrown in a military coup on December 1; rebel leader Idriss Deby, a former Habré aide, declares himself president and promises a multiparty democracy.

1992 The govèrnment suppresses two attempted coups; opposition parties are legalized.

1996 Déby wins the nation's first multiparty presidential election.

1997 Déby's party, the Patriotic Salvation Movement, wins 63 of the 125 seats in legislative elections.

1998 The Movement for Democracy and Justice in Chad (MDJC) begins an armed rebellion against the government led by Déby's former defense minister, Youssouf Togoimi.

2000 In July, MDJC rebels capture the strategic town of Bardai in the north.

BIBLIOGRAPHY

Azevedo, Mario J., and Emmanuel U. Nnadozie. *Chad: A Nation in Search of Its Future.* Boulder, Colo., 1998.

Collins, Robert O., Millard J. Burr, and J. Burr. *Africa's Thirty Years War: Libya, Chad, and the Sudan 1963–1993.* Boulder, Colo., 1999.

Decalo, Samuel. *Historical Dictionary of Chad.* Metuchen, N.J., 1997.

Neuberger, Benyamin. *Involvement, Invasion and Withdrawal: Qaddhafi's Libya and Chad, 1969–81.* Syracuse, N.Y., 1982.

Thompson, Virginia, and Richard Adloff. *Conflict in Chad.* Berkeley, Calif., 1981.

Wright, John L. *Libya, Chad and the Central Sahara.* London, 1989.

OFFICIAL PUBLICATIONS

Chad. *Annuaire statistique; Chad: A Country Study (1990); Chad-Background Issues and Statistical Update* (IMF Staff Country Report [1995]).

CONTACT INFORMATION

Embassy of Chad
2002 R Street NW
Washington, D.C. 20009
Phone: (202) 462-4009 Fax: (202) 265-1937

INTERNET RESOURCES

- CIA World Factbook—Chad
  http://www.odci.gov/cia/publications/factbook/cd.html
- Chad—A Country Study
  http://lcweb2.loc.gov/frd/cs/tdtoc.html

CHILE

BASIC FACT SHEET

OFFICIAL NAME:
Republic of Chile (República de Chile)

ABBREVIATION:
CL

CAPITAL:
Santiago

HEAD OF STATE AND GOVERNMENT:
President Ricardo Lagos Escobar (from 2000)

NATURE OF GOVERNMENT:
Constitutional republic

POPULATION:
15,018,000 (1999)

AREA:
756,626 sq km (292,135 sq mi)

ETHNIC MAJORITY:
Mestizo

LANGUAGE:
Spanish

RELIGION:
Roman Catholicism

UNIT OF CURRENCY:
Peso

NATIONAL FLAG:
Divided horizontally; the upper left blue with a white star and the remaining upper half white; the lower half red

NATIONAL EMBLEM:
A gold-edged shield with its upper half red and the lower blue displaying a large white five-pointed star in the center. Three plumes in red, white, and blue form the crest of the design. On either side of the shield is a typical Chilean animal: the huemal, an Andean deer, to the right of the shield and the condor of the Andes to its left. Beneath the device is a white scroll with the legend in black letters: "Por La Razón O La Fuerza" ("By Right and by Might").

NATIONAL ANTHEM:
"Pure Chile, Thy Skies Spread Above Thee"

NATIONAL HOLIDAYS:
September 18 and 19 (National Days, Independence Days); January 1 (New Year's Day); May 1 (Labor Day); May 21 (Navy Day, Battle of Iquique Day); September 19 (Army Day); October 12 (Columbus Day); Christian festivals include Day of Saints Peter and Paul, Assumption, All Saints' Day, Immaculate Conception, Good Friday, Holy Saturday, Ascension, Corpus Christi, and Christmas.

DATE OF INDEPENDENCE:
September 18, 1810

DATE OF CONSTITUTION:
September 11, 1980, amended 1989, 1993, and 1997

GEOGRAPHICAL FEATURES

Chile is situated on the extreme southwestern coast of South America, and the name itself is believed to be a corruption of an Aymará Indian word meaning "where the land ends." It extends like a long ribbon between the Pacific and the towering Andes for 4,270 km (2,653 mi), but its median width is only 175 km (109 mi). The total land area of 756,945 sq km (292,258 sq mi) includes six dependencies: Easter Island (Isla de Pascua), a volcanic island famed for its massive monolithic stone heads of unknown origin; the Diego Ramírez Islands; the Juan Fernández Islands, famed as the scene of the shipwreck of Alexander Selkirk, the model for Daniel Defoe's Robinson Crusoe; Sale y Gomez Island; San Ambrosio Island; and San Félix Island. Chile also claims the section of Antarctica lying between 53°W and 90°W, the Palmer or O'Higgins Peninsula, parts of which are also claimed by Argentina and the United Kingdom. The Pacific coastline extends 5,338 km (3,317 mi).

Chile

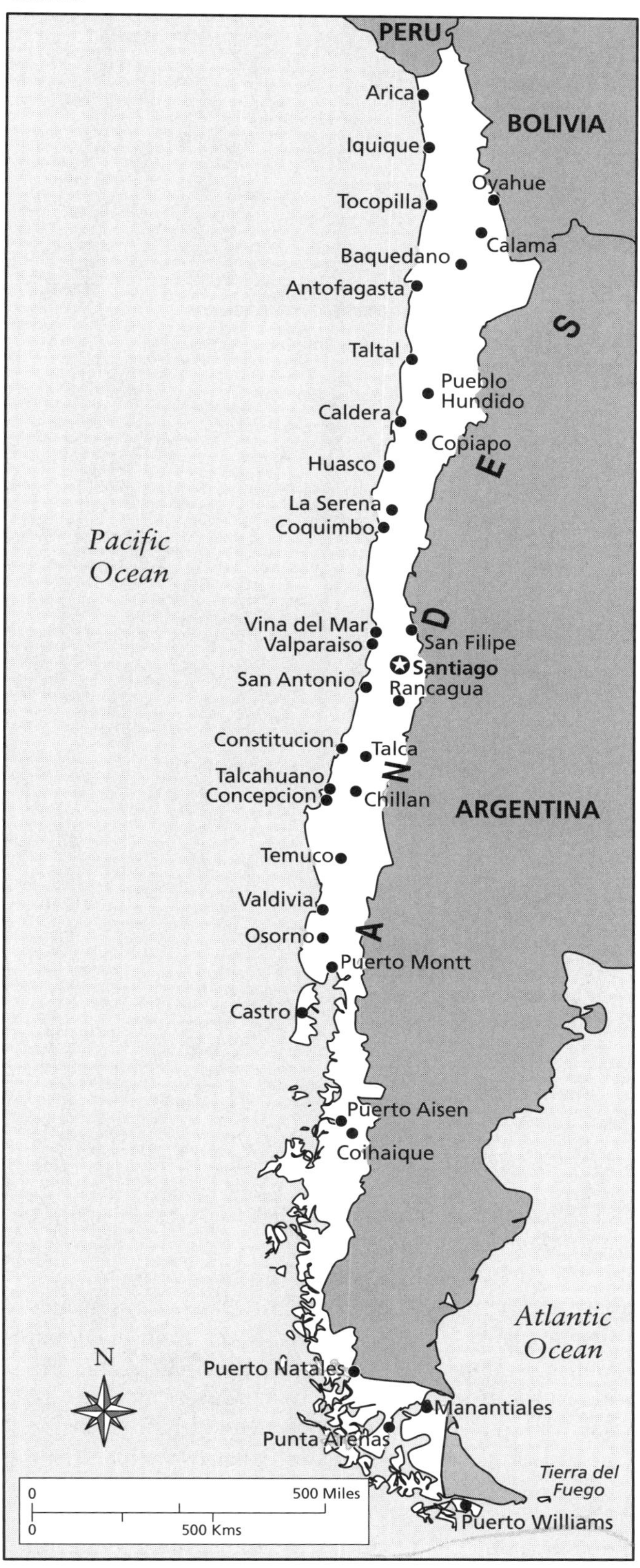

Chile shares its international border of 6,338 km (3,936 mi) with three neighbors: Bolivia (861 km, 535 mi), Argentina (5,308 km, 3,298 mi), and Peru (169 km, 105 mi).

The capital is Santiago, with a 1997 population of 4,640,635. Other large urban centers include Viña del Mar, population 303,589; Valparaíso, population 274,228; and Concepción, population 326,784.

Chile may be divided longitudinally into three regions and latitudinally into six regions. The three longitudinal regions are the Andean cordillera on the east, the low coastal mountains of the west, and the central valley in between. The Andes, occupying from one-third to the entire width of the country, rise to 7,034 m (23,077 ft) at Mt. Aconcagua (in Argentina), the highest peak in the Western Hemisphere. The coastal range, 300 m to 2,100 m (1,000 ft to 7,000 ft) in height, joins the Andean spurs to form a series of plateaus separated by deep valleys. In the south these valleys and ranges plunge into the sea to form a series of archipelagos. The central valley begins below the Atacama Desert in the north and ends at Puerto Montt in the south. The six latitudinal divisions are: the Great North, north of the Copiapó River; the Little North, also known as the Andean Fringe, a transitional zone made up of short transverse valleys; Central Chile, also known as the Vale of Chile, north of the Bío-Bío River; South-Central Chile between the Bío-Bío River and the Gulf of Reloncaví; the Far South, also known as Archipelagic Chile, dominated by fjords; and Patagonian or Atlantic Chile, an undulating plain at the tip of the continent.

Chile lies in an area of geologic instability and frequently suffers from earthquakes, tidal waves, volcanic eruptions, floods, avalanches, landslides, and violent storms. More than 100 major earthquakes have occurred since 1575. Valparaíso and Concepción have been leveled or shaken by earthquakes several times this century.

Some 30 rivers flow from the Andes, including the Loa in the Great North; the Huasco, Coquimba, and Limari in the Little North; the Mapoche, Maule, and Maipo in Central Chile; and the Bío-Bío in South-Central Chile. Few, if any of these rivers can be used for commercial navigation. Of the 12 lakes in the Lake District in South-Central Chile, Lake Llanquihue is the largest and Lake Todos los Santos the most beautiful.

Geography

Area sq km: 756,626 sq mi 292,135
World Rank: 38th
Land Boundaries, km: Argentina 5,150; Bolivia 861; Peru 160
Coastline, km: 6,435
Elevation Extremes meters
- Lowest: Pacific Ocean 0
- Highest: Cerro Aconcagua 6,962

Land Use % Arable land: 5
- Permanent Crops: 0
- Permanent Pastures: 18
- Forest and Woodland: 22
- Other: 55

Population of Principal Cities (1995 est.; MU)	
Antofagasta	236,730
Arica	173,336
Calama	120,602
Chillán	157,083
Concepción	350,268
Copiapó	100,946
Coquimbo	122,872
Curico	103,919
Iquique	152,592
La Serena	117,983
Los Angeles	142,136
Osorno	123,055
Puente Alto	318,898
Puerto Montt	122,399
Punta Arenas	117,206
Quilpue	110,340
Rancagua	193,755
San Bernardo	206,315
Santiago (administrative)	5,076,808
Talca	169,448
Talcahuano	260,915
Temuco	239,340
Valdivia	119,431
Valparaíso (legislative)	282,168
Viña del Mar	322,220

CLIMATE AND WEATHER

Because of its great length, Chile has a variety of climatic zones, ranging from subtropical to temperate and near polar. The variety is increased by the proximity of the Andean cordillera and the Humboldt, or Peru, Current, which flows along the coast northward. Generally, Chile is divided into three climatic zones: the north, including the Atacama Desert, one of the driest regions of the world; the middle, with a Mediterranean climate characterized by mild, wet winters and long, dry summers; and the south, with heavy winds and cyclones.

Rainfall, on the other hand, increases from virtually nothing in the Atacama Desert to 5,080 mm (200 in) in the south. Even Santiago in the middle has an annual precipitation of only 350 mm (14 in). Southward, the average rainfall rises to 1,270 mm (50 in) at Concepción and 2,540 mm (100 in) at Valdivia, but falls to 510 mm (20 in) in Chilean Patagonia. South of the Bío-Bío River, rain occurs almost all year round. Chiloé Island is perpetually shrouded in mists, giving rise to the legend that it is inhabited by disembodied spirits. Winds of gale force intensity are common in the south.

Climate and Weather

Mean Temperature
Arica on the Peruvian Border: 66°F
La Serena in the Little North and Santiago 57°F
Valdivia 53°F
Patagonia 43°F
Tierra del Fuego 20°F
Average Rainfall
Atacama Desert 0 in
South 200 in
Concepción 50 in
Valdivia 100 in
Patagonia 20 in

POPULATION

Population Indicators

Total Population: 1999 15,018,000
World Rank: 60th
Density per sq mi: 51.4 per sq km 19.8
% of annual growth (1994–99): 1.4
Male %: 49.1
Female %: 50.9
Urban %: 83.5
Age Distribution: % 0–14: 29.4
15–29: 27.3
30–44: 21.2
45–59: 12.2
60–74: 7.2
75 and over: 2.5
Population 2020: 18,774,000
Birth Rate per 1,000: 19.7
Death Rate per 1,000: 5.5
Population Doubling Time (years): 57
Infant Mortality Rate per 1,000 live births: 11.1
Rate of Natural Increase per 1,000: 14.2
Total Fertility Rate: 2.3
Expectation of Life (years): Males 71.8
Females 77.8
Marriage Rate per 1,000: 7.8
Divorce Rate per 1,000: —
Total Number of Households: 3,537,000
Average Size of Households: 3.8
% of Illegitimate Children: 38.1
Induced Abortions: 67
Rate per 100 live births: —

ETHNIC COMPOSITION

Chile has an uncomplicated ethnic mix, with white or white Amerindians (mestizos) constituting 95 percent of the population, Amerindians 3 percent, and other, mainly unmixed European, 2 percent. Early settlers intermarried with the Native Americans, notably the Araucanian, and European immigration was of less importance then elsewhere in Latin America. Of those Europeans who did come, the earliest non-Spanish settlers were from Britain, followed after 1845 by Germans, Italians, French, Austrians, Swiss, and Yugoslavs. Non-European settlers included the Lebanese and Jews. National enclaves exist in several cities, including the English in Valparaíso and Iquique; the Germans in Puerto Montt, Valdivia, Osorno, and Puerto Varas; and the Lebanese in Recoleta, a section of Santiago.

The largest Native American group in the country is known to ethnographers as Araucanian, but members of this group refer to themselves as *Mapuche* (around 1 million strong), a term that means "people of the land" in their language. After the Indian wars of the 19th century, the Mapuche were settled in more than 2,000 reservations in Cautin, Maleco, Valdivia, Arauco, Bío-Bío, and Llanquihue, which has isolated them from Western influences. Their customs and cultural heritage are protected by the Indigenous Peoples Law, which has also permitted their lands to be demarcated and preserved. However, the spread of education and transportation has meant that many Mapuche are succumbing to the pressures of assimilation. Other indigenous groups include the Aymara (35,000), Rapa Nui (3,000), Atacameños (about 4,000), Quechua, Colla, Alacalufe, and Yagán. Because of Chile's ethnic homogeneity, race by itself is not a divisive factor in politics or society, and there is little evidence of a race or color bar in the country. Class divisions do exist though, and are sharp, with only gradual eroding of dividing lines.

LANGUAGES

The official language is Spanish, which is spoken by almost everyone except a few Native Americans in the reservations. Chilean Spanish is corrupted by accretions of Native American and foreign words and is also characterized by wide variations in pronunciation and usage. The Mapuche speak the Araucan language, itself a family of languages with seven surviving dialects.

Principal Languages and Their Speakers

Araucanian (Mapuche)	1,440,000
Aymara	80,000
Rapa Nui	35,000
Spanish	13,470,000

RELIGIONS

Chile is predominantly Roman Catholic, with more than 77 percent of the population, although the church was disestablished in 1925. Protestants make up a further 12 percent of the population, with the remainder coming from Jewish, traditional Native American, or nonreligious backgrounds.

While the religious influence of the church varies among the various social classes and between the urban and rural population, the church has played an important role as a catalyst of social progress and as a defender of human rights when all other forms of opposition are silenced.

Protestantism has experienced rapid growth since the 1940s, and Chile is considered one of the most successful examples of Protestant missionary activity in Latin America. Religious minorities include a small Jewish community.

Religious Affiliations

Religion	Adherents
Roman Catholic	11,520,000
Evangelical Protestant	1,860,000
Other	1,640,000

HISTORICAL BACKGROUND

Chile's earliest inhabitants were the Araucanians in the south of the region, and subjects of the Inca Empire in the north. In 1536, the first Spanish expedition, led by Diego de Almagro, traveled across the Andes and into the central lowlands, but failed to establish a settlement. A subsequent attempt, led by Pedro de Valdivia, overcame Araucanian resistance and founded the cities of Santiago in 1541 and La Serena, Concepción, and Valdivia. A lack of precious metals meant Chile remained peripheral to Spanish interests, and development was focused on ranching and farming. Until 1778, Chile was a captaincy general ruled by the Viceroyalty of Peru, at which time it became a separate division virtually independent of Peru. Territorially, Chile's boundaries were ill-defined, and were the cause of many border disputes with Argentina, Peru, and Bolivia following independence. Chile declared its independence from Spain in 1810 but it was not until 1818 that it achieved independence. The country's geographic isolation has helped it to preserve its Spanish heritage virtually intact. This isolation has also helped it to maintain its independence.

Since independence, Chile has experienced alternating periods of authoritarian and parliamentary rule. From 1891 to 1924 the country was a parliamentary republic. But political corruption, the fragmentation of political parties, and increasing political chaos led to a military takeover in September 1924. Military strongman General Carlos Ibáñez del Campo ruled from 1927 to 1931, when a general strike precipitated by the effects of the Great Depression forced him to flee. From 1931 to 1973 the country was governed by a multiparty democratic system. In 1964 Eduardo Frei became president and implemented a series of social and economic changes that included partial nationalization of some industries and land reform. Frei was unable to control the inflation that was endemic to the nation and his reforms alienated the right. Salvador Allende Gossens, a Marxist, won the three-way 1970 presidential election with the largest share of the vote, 30 percent. The Allende government imposed an extensive nationalization program, froze prices, and raised wages.

Initially the program succeeded in improving economic conditions, but by 1972, the economy had again begun to lag. Middle- and upper-class resentment against government seizure of property grew, and, amid strikes and civil discontent (covertly promoted by the CIA acting to support U.S. interests), Allende's government was overthrown by the military in 1973. Depending on sources, Allende either committed suicide or was murdered in an attack by the military on the presidential palace.

Between 1973 and 1990, a military junta headed by General Augusto Pinochet Ugarte ruled Chile, suspending the constitution, dissolving congress, and banning political parties. Left-wing activists were arrested, tortured, and exiled in the thousands, in a campaign of terror that reached outside the country: the secret police, or DINA, was linked to the 1976 murder in Washington, D.C., of Orlando Letelier, a former Chilean ambassador to the United States.

Under Pinochet the government initiated a program of privatization that drastically reduced government; although his measures did not immediately improve the situation, by the end of the 1980s, the economy had begun to improve.

The Pinochet regime never faced a sustained revolutionary challenge. The great majority of its opponents were abroad in exile or sent underground. In September 1988 the government announced that all Chileans in political exile, about 430, were permitted to return to Chile. At this time Hortensia Bussi de Allende (President Allende's widow) and her daughter María Isabel Allende also returned to Chile from exile.

Pinochet faced constant criticism of his regime from political parties, trade unions, and the Catholic Church. In 1980 the electorate endorsed a new constitution designed to prepare the nation for a return to democracy in 1989. Pinochet expected this to reconfirm his hold over power, but opposition groups successfully united and campaigned against him. At a plebiscite in 1988 Chileans voted against a new eight-year term for Pinochet. Elections were held in 1989 that resulted in the victory of Patricio Aylwin Azócar, leader of the Christian Democratic Party and candidate of a 17-party Coalition for Democracy. He was inaugurated in March 1990. Pinochet was forced to accept the decision after the military had committed itself to recognizing the legitimacy of the ballot, and attempts to disrupt the election failed. Pinochet did maintain command of the armed forces until 1997 when he became a senator for life.

Fresh elections in 1993 brought Christian Democrat Eduardo Frei Ruiz-Tagle to the presidency, and continued the country's move toward civilian-controlled democracy. Investigations into the 1976 assassination of opposition leader Orlando Letelier in Washington, D.C., resulted in the convictions of the former head of the secret police and his deputy in November 1993. After a standoff between Pinochet and the government, the men were arrested in June 1995. The same year, investigations into disappearances during the Pinochet regime were begun.

In October 1998, General Pinochet was arrested in London on a warrant from Spain requesting his extradition on murder charges. For the next 18 months, the case moved from appeal to appeal, with British home secretary Jack Straw permitting extradition proceedings to begin following a Law Lords' decision in November. The British courts determined that Pinochet's immunity did not cover the charges against him. In January 2000, Pinochet was declared medically unfit to stand trial, and despite considerable pressure from domestic and international sources, Jack Straw released the general on March 1, when he returned to Chile. In June, the Chilean Appeals Court stripped Pinochet of his immunity, opening the way for criminal proceedings within Chile. He was subsequently indicted on charges of kidnapping and murder and placed under house arrest. In 2001 the Santiago Court of Appeals reduced the charges against Pinochet to accessory in the crimes by having covered them up. Pinochet was released from house arrest on bail while awaiting a possible trial.

In January 2000 Ricardo Lagos Escobar narrowly defeated his opponent in presidential elections, becoming the first socialist to be elected president since Salvador Allende.

CONSTITUTION

Chile has had only two constitutions since 1833, and although the continuity of democratic rule was interrupted once before, from 1924 to 1931, until the military junta, Chile had a notable record of adherence to parliamentary democracy, free elections, and separation of powers. While the balance of power favored the executive, the multiparty system made it virtually impossible for the executive to dominate the legislature.

After seizing power in 1973, the military junta suspended the 1925 constitution and ruled by three constitutional acts enacted in 1976. A new constitution was adopted in 1980 that gave executive and legislative power to the president and the junta. It also provided for what was described as a transition to democracy after a minimum period of eight years. It provided for presidential elections in 1989 and the reestablishment of a bicameral legislature. The constitution, which took effect in 1981, was approved and amended in 1989, when 54 reforms were passed. Among the provisions was a reduction in the term of office for the president from eight to four years. The president's right to dismiss congress and sentence to internal exile was also eliminated. In 1993, the legislature increased the president's term of office from four to six years.

Voting is universal over 18 and compulsory. Political parties, banned in 1977, were legalized again in 1987.

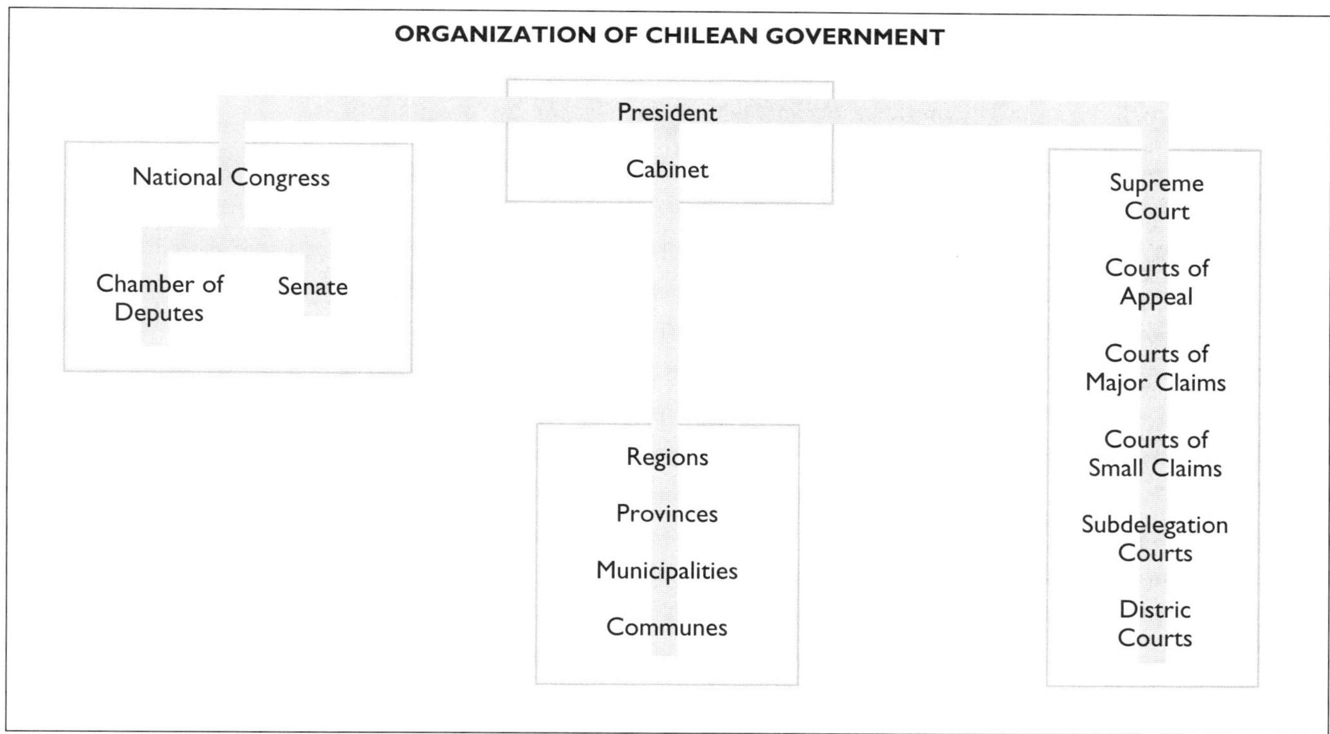

LOCAL GOVERNMENT

Chile is divided for purposes of local government into 12 numbered regions and the Santiago Metropolitan Region. Each numbered region is headed by an *intendente*, while Santiago is headed by a mayor. The regions are subdivided into 51 provinces, each headed by a governor, and further divided into 300 municipalities, headed by a mayor. The lowest subdivision is the *comuna*, or commune.

Local Government

Principal administrative divisions, capitals, area, population

Area and population

Regions	Capitals	area sq mi	area sq km	population 1995 census
Alsen del General Carlos Ibáñez del Campo	Colhaique	42,095	109,025	88,782
Antofagasta	Antofagasta	48,820	126,444	415,487
Araucania	Temuco	12,300	31,858	853,187
Atacama	Copiapó	29,179	75,573	202,810
Bío-Bío	Concepción	14,258	36,929	1,753,662
Coquimbo	La Serena	15,697	40,656	525,432
Libertador General Bernardo O'Higgins	Rancagua	6,319	16,365	684,179
Los Lagos	Puerto Montt	25,868	66,997	957,212
Magallanes y la Antártica Chilena	Punta Arenas	50,979	132,034	181,551
Maule	Talca	11,700	30,302	902,646
Santiago, Región Metropolitana de	Santiago	5,926	15,349	5,783,703
Tarapaca	Iquique	22,663	58,698	410,343
Valparaíso	Valparaíso	6,331	16,396	1,478,281
TOTAL		292,135	756,626	14,237,275

PARLIAMENT

The 1980 constitution had provided for a 120-member Chamber of Deputies and a 46-member Senate, 26 elected and eight appointed. Reforms in 1989 increased the number of elected senators to 38. Senators serve eight-year terms, while deputies serve four. The Chamber of Deputies carries out its duties by means of 13 permanent commissions, each one of which is composed of 13 deputies. The Senate has 18 commissions, each with five members.

Congress approves and rejects international treaties, states of siege or emergency imposed by the president, and selects a president if the office becomes vacant with less than two years until a scheduled election. The Chamber of Deputies can also initiate constitutional accusations by majority vote. The Senate, in turn, acts as a jury and finds the accused either innocent or guilty as charged. Further, the Senate can declare the physical or mental incapacity of the president or president-elect, once the Constitutional Tribunal has pronounced itself on the matter.

Congressional power was limited under the 1980 constitution, but many restrictions were removed in the

1989 amendments. Its role is limited in other areas, however, such as financial and budgetary administration, introduction of spending, public administration, and collective bargaining legislation. The president needs the approval of the majority of Congress to establish states of siege, but the president may declare a state of assembly, emergency, or catastrophe solely with the approval of Cosena.

POLITICAL PARTIES

The Communist Party of Chile (Partido Comunista de Chile–PCC), founded in 1922, is the oldest and largest communist party in Latin America and one of the most important in the West. Initially close to the Soviet Union and outlawed for a decade after 1948, the party helped elect Salvador Allende in 1970 and acted as a moderating influence in the move toward a communist society. By the 1990s, however, it enjoyed less than 5 percent support.

The Socialist Party (Partido Socialista, PS), founded in 1933, has drawn its support from blue-collar workers as well as intellectuals and members of the middle class. It also helped elect Salvador Allende and suffered under the military repression in the 1970s. Following numerous splits and schisms, the party formed a coalition with the Christian Democrats to oppose Pinochet in the 1988 referendum. As part of the ruling coalition since 1989, the party has moved more toward democratic socialism.

The Party for Democracy (Partido por la Democracia, PPD) was formed in 1988 to unite opposition to Pinochet. Subsequently becoming a party in its own right, it has sought a distinct position as a center-left secular force in Chilean society.

The Christian Democratic Party (Partido Demócrata Cristiano, PDC), founded in 1957, was heavily influenced by the progressive social doctrines of the Roman Catholic Church and the works of French Catholic philosopher Jacques Maritain. The PDC proclaimed a "third way" between Marxism and capitalism, a form of communitarian socialism of cooperatives and self-managed worker enterprises. After the military regime, the PDC emerged as Chile's largest party, retaining a commitment to social justice issues while embracing the free-market policies instituted by the military government.

The National Party (Partido Nacional, PN) was formed in 1965 from the merging of the Liberal and Conservative Parties. In 1987 it became the Renewal Party, a combination of three rightist organizations—the National Unity Movement, National Labor Front, and Independent Democratic Union

Other parties include the Radical Party (Partido Radical) and the Union of the Centrist Center (Unión de Centro Centro, UCC).

Political Parties

- Coalition of Parties for Democracy, 1983, an alliance of
  - Christian Democratic Party, 1957
  - Socialist Party, 1933
  - Party for Democracy, 1987
  - Social Democratic Radical Party, 1863
  - Social Democratic Party, 1973
  - Center Alliance Party, 1991
- Union for Chile, 1997, an alliance of right-wing parties
  - National Renovation, 1987
  - Independent Democratic Union
  - Progressive Center-Center Union
- Movement of the Allendist Democratic Left, 1991, an alliance of left-wing parties
  - Communist Party, 1922
  - Left Broad Force Party
- National Advance Guard
- National Party of Centrist Democracy, 1990
- Popular Christian Party, 1997
- Humanist-Green Alliance, 1993

Political Parties: Strength in Parliament Most Recent Elections

Senate (Senado de la República).The Senate consists of 48 members, 38 directly elected and up to 10 appointed. In the elections of December 16, 2001, the Consortium of Parties for the Democracy (Christian Democratic Party, Party for Democracy, Socialist Party of Chile, Social-Democratic Radical Party) won 20 seats; and Alliance for Chile (Independent Democratic Union, National Renewal), 18.

Chamber of Deputies (Cámara de Diputados).The lower house is currently contains 117 members. At the December 16, 2001, elections, the Consortium of Parties for Democracy (Christian Democratic Party, Party for Democracy, Socialist Party of Chile, Social-Democratic Radical Party) won 62 seats; and Alliance for Chile (Independent Democratic Union, National Renewal), 57.

LEGAL SYSTEM

The Chilean legal system is based on the Code of 1857 derived from Spanish jurisprudence. Subsequent codes have been influenced by French and Austrian laws.

The highest court of the land is the Supreme Court, which consists of 17 members, who select a president from their number for a three-year term. Members and prosecutors are appointed by the president from a list of five persons proposed by the court itself.

Chile has 16 appellate courts, each with jurisdiction over one or more provinces. The president is chosen from a slate of three candidates submitted by the Supreme Court, which also appoints the justices and prosecutors of each appellate court. Below this are major claims courts, and various local courts (juzgados de letras). There is also a series of special courts, such as the juvenile courts, labor courts, and military courts in time of peace. The local courts consist of one or more tribunals specifically assigned to each of the country's communes, Chile's smallest administrative units. In larger jurisdictions, the local courts may specialize in criminal cases or civil cases, as defined by law.

The courts faced few difficulties in dealing with the military regime, which left the court system virtually intact. Once the legitimacy of the military junta had been accepted, the courts adjudicated matters in conformity with the new decree laws, even when they violated the constitution. Since the return to democracy, attempts have been made to restore the courts' reputation and to address the deficiencies of the Pinochet years.

The correctional system is composed of around 140 prisons. The system is administered by the judicial police of Chile, or gendarmerie, reporting to the Ministry of Justice.

LAW ENFORCEMENT

Law Enforcement

Offenses reported to the police per 100,000: 1,066
- Murder: 11.0
- Assault: 96.3
- Burglary: —
- Automobile Theft: 13.1
- Population per Police officer: 470

Death Penalty: Yes

HUMAN RIGHTS

Many human rights groups consider Pinochet's regime as one of the most brutal in South American history. Immediately following the 1973 coup, the military government embarked on a campaign of extensive repression, including mass arrests, torture, exile, disappearances, and summary executions of prisoners. During this period, the number of people who were detained so exceeded the capacities of the existing penal institutions that for a time, stadiums, military grounds, and naval vessels were used as short-term prisons.

For the first four and a half years of military rule, Chile was officially in a state of siege and functioned under martial law. At the end of this period, the state of siege was replaced by a state of emergency, which restored a larger degree of authority to the civilian courts, although military tribunals continued to deal with cases involving public security. A state of siege was once again imposed after an attempt on Pinochet's life in 1984, and the level of repression increased once more.

Following the return to civilian government, judicial competence was returned to civilian courts. This opened the way for these courts to reexamine cases of human rights violations. The Aylwin government also established the National Commission on Truth and Reconciliation, or Rettig Commission, to inquire into human rights abuses during the 1973–90 period of military rule. The commission produced a report holding the security forces responsible for 2,115 deaths.

An amnesty law has protected military officers involved in human rights abuses committed between 1973 and 1978. However, by 1993 as many as 600 officers, mainly from the army, had been cited in 230 cases involving rights abuses.

In 1998 General Pinochet was arrested in England on a Spanish warrant, issued by a judge investigating the disappearance of Spanish citizens in Chile in the 1970s and 1980s. While Pinochet is unlikely to be tried in Chile, due to health as well as legal obstacles, the case has challenged existing views on international human rights prosecutions. Despite fears of a right-wing backlash, democracy in Chile has remained stable throughout the Pinochet case, a fact that bodes well for the future protection of human rights in the country.

FOREIGN POLICY

Since successfully reintegrating itself into the world political community after 1990, Chile's foreign policy has focused on deepening its international economic involvement and capitalizing on its trade and political ties with Latin and North America, Europe, and the Asia-Pacific region. In December 1994, Chile was invited by Canada, Mexico, and the United States to join the North American Free Trade Agreement, although entrance has subsequently been delayed. In June 1996, Chile became an associate of the Southern Common Market (Mercosur) and signed a framework agreement on cooperation with the European Union.

Chile is a founding member of the United Nations, belongs to the Organization of American States, and has provided forces for UN peacekeeping efforts in Cambodia, El Salvador, Israel, and along the Iraq-Kuwait border, among other missions. Chile is also a member of the WTO, and the Asia-Pacific Economic Cooperation (APEC) Forum.

The guiding principle of Chilean foreign economic policy is open regionalism. No other Latin American nation is so tightly integrated into the region's system of trade.

DEFENSE

Despite 17 years of military rule, Chile's armed forces are still exceptionally professional and generally free of factionalism or partisan politics. Their reputation, however, has suffered from the widespread human rights abuses that took place under the military junta, and credibility was badly damaged by allegations of financial wrongdoing by Pinochet's son, the discovery of mass graves containing corpses of individuals who died while in military hands, and the illegal export of arms to Croatia.

Chile was the first country in Latin America to organize a regular army, and the Chilean military takes great pride in its heritage. Within the Chilean state, the armed forces constitute an essentially autonomous power, with status comparable to that of Congress and the courts. Military service of one year in the army or two years in the navy or air force is compulsory in Chile for all able-bodied 18- or 19-year-old men

Military Indicators

Total Active Duty Personnel: 94,300
Military Manpower per 1,000: 6.5
Military Expenditures $million: 2,243
as % of GNP: 3.8
per capita $: 158
as % of central government expenditures: 17.5

Arms Imports $million: 380
Arms Exports $million: 0

ECONOMY

Chile's economy has been dominated by the production of copper since the early 20th century, which accounted for up to 50 percent of export revenues. Industry expanded since the 1940s in an attempt to diversify the economy, and Chile is one of the leading industrial nations in Latin America. Agriculture has played only a limited role, although efforts to increase production had some success in the 1970s. After the Marxist experiments of Allende's government were ended by the military coup of 1973, the government has played a less dominant role in the economy, with privatization a key policy. The financial market has become particularly strong, due largely to an effective reform of the pension system.

Under the Pinochet regime, influenced by U.S. economists, government expenditure was cut, regulatory functions and price controls ended, free trade promoted, and many state-owned companies privatized. The subsequent democratic governments of Aylwin and Frei have strayed little from this free-market economic policy, but have increased social spending on education, health, housing, and social security. The governments have pursued bilateral and multilateral free trade agreements throughout the world and have continued to privatize state enterprises and promote foreign investment.

In the 1990s, Chile was one of the strongest economies in South America, and enters the 21st century strengthened by its return to democracy.

Principal Economic Indicators

Gross National Product $: 70.510 billion
GNP per capita $: 4,820
GNP Average Annual Growth Rate (1990–97) %: 6.4
GNP per capita Average Annual Growth Rate (1990–97) %: 4.8
Origin of Gross Domestic Product %
Agriculture: 8
Mining: 8
Manufacturing: 17
Construction: 6
Public Utilities: 3
Transportation and Communications: 8
Trade: 17
Financial Services: 17
Other Services: 8
Government: 3
Gross Domestic Product by Type of Expenditure %
Private Consumption: 62
Government Consumption: 9
Gross Domestic Investment: 27
Foreign Trade: Exports: 28
Imports: −27
% of Income Received by Poorest 20%: 3.5
% of Income Received by Richest 10%: 46.1

Price and earnings indexes (1995 = 100)

	1992	1993	1994	1995	1996	1997	1998
Consumer price index	74.0	83.0	92.0	100.0	107.0	114.0	120.0
Earnings index	—	84.4	88.7	100.0	114.4	124.7	—

Finance

National Currency: Chilean Peso (CH$)
Exchange Rate: $1 = CH$ 452.60
Money Supply Stock in National Currency billion: 2,686.7
M1 per capita: 185,000
Central Bank Discount Rate %: 6.17
Total External Debt $million: 26,700
Debt Service Ratio %: 5.9
Balance of Payments $million: −4,057
International Reserves SDRs million: 11,928
Ratio of External Debt to Total Reserves: 0.5
Average Annual Rate of Inflation/Consumer Price Index Growth Rate %: 6

Official Development Assistance

Donor ODA $million: 105
as % of GNP: 0.1
per capita $ 7
Foreign Direct Investment $million: 4,638

Central Government Revenues and Expenditures

Fiscal Year: Calendar Year
Revenues $million: 17,000
Expenditures $million: 17,000
Budget Deficit $million: 0
Tax Revenues as % of GDP: 18.4
Highest Tax Bracket %
Individual: 45
Corporate: 15

Employment and Labor

Economically Active Population: 5,274,000
Female Participation Rate %: 32.4
Activity Rate %: 37.8

Labor by Sector: %
- Agriculture, Forestry, Fishing: 15.4
- Manufacturing, Mining: 18.6
- Construction: 7.8
- Transportation and Communications: 7.6
- Trade, Hotels, and Restaurants: 18.5
- Finance, Insurance, Real Estate: 6.4
- Public Administration, Defense: —
- Services: 25.1

Unemployment %: 6.1

Agriculture

Agriculture's Share of GDP %: 8
Average Annual Rate of Growth (1965–98) %: 3.5
Number of Farms 000: 306
Average Size of Farm ha: 94.1
Number of Tractors per 1,000 hectares: 10.4
Irrigation, % of Farms having: 32
Artificial Fertilizer kg/hectare: 69
Total Farmland as % of land area: 11.7
Livestock: Cattle 000: 3,755
Sheep 000: 3,754
Hogs 000: 1,771
Chickens 000: 70,000
Forests: Production of Roundwood (000 cubic meters): 31,365
Fisheries: Total Catch tons 000: 7,841.0

Mining

% of GDP: 8.0
Value of Mineral Production $million: 2,440

Manufacturing

Value Added $million: 11,841
Industrial Production Growth Rate %: 4.2

Energy

Commercial Energy Production metric tons of oil equivalent 000: 8,168
Commercial Energy Consumption metric tons of oil equivalent 000: 23,012
Commercial Energy Consumption per capita kg: 1,574
Average Annual Growth Rate 1980–97 %: 4.0
Net Energy Imports % of use: 65.0
Electricity Installed Capacity kW 000: 5,954
Production kW-hr million: 29,906
Coal Reserves tons million: 1,181
Production tons 000: 1,078
Natural Gas Proven Reserves cubic meters billion: 102
Production cubic meters million: 1,164
Crude Petroleum Reserves barrels million: 300
Production barrels million: 3
Consumption barrels million: 58
Refinery Capacity barrels per day 000: 192
Pipelines Length km: 1,540

Foreign Trade

Imports $million: 14,903.1
Exports $million: 15,901.1
Export Volume % Annual Growth Rate (1990–97): 10.1
Import Volume % Annual Growth Rate (1990–97): 15.0

Balance of trade (current prices)

	1993	1994	1995	1996	1997	1998
U.S. $000,000	−979	+660	+1,384	−1,147	−1,343	−2,483
% of total	5.1%	2.9%	4.5%	3.6%	3.8%	7.7%

Major Trading Partners

	Imports	Exports
European Union %	15.9	22.0
United States %	25.5	13.4
Eastern Europe %	0.2	0.5
Japan %	6.8	17.9
Others %	51.6	46.3

Transportation

Roads Total Length mi: 49,550 km 79,750
Paved %: 14
Automobiles: 888,645
Trucks and Buses: 459,142
Persons per vehicle: 10
Railroad; Track Length mi: 4,084 km 6,572
Passenger-mi million: 428
Freight-mi million: 1,595
Merchant Marine: No. of Vessels: 392
Total Deadweight Tonnage 000: 854.9
International Cargo Loaded tons 000: 21,768
International Cargo Off-loaded tons 000: 13,464
Airports with Scheduled Flights: 23
Traffic: Passenger-mi million: 3,935
Freight-mi million: 923
Length of Canals mi: 450 km 725

Tourism

Number of Tourists to 000: 1,757
Number of Tourists from 000: 1,351
Tourist Receipts $million: 990
Tourist Expenditures $million: 774

Communications

Telephones 000: 1,885
Cost of Local Calls 3 mins: $0.12
Cellular Telephones 000: 197
Fax Machines 000: 15
Personal Computers 000: 540
Internet Hosts per million persons: 632
Mail: Post Offices: 587
Pieces of Mail Handled million: 294
Pieces of Mail Handled per person: 21

EDUCATION

Education is free, universal, and compulsory for children between the ages of six and 14. Primary education lasts for eight years, secondary for four. Attendance is more than 95 percent at primary level, more than 75 percent at secondary.

Before the education reforms of 1980, Chile had eight universities. In 1980, the military regime split up the two state universities and fostered the development of new private universities, a policy that by 1989 had increased the number of universities to 41, along with 56 professional training institutes and 150 technical training centers. Few, if any, of these received state support. These changes led to greater competition, but also to greater disparities in standards, and a decline in overall quality. The top specialists in many fields moved to research institutes, depriving the university sector of innovative thinkers and writers. By the 1990s, the top schools included the University of Chile (1738), the University of Concepción (1919), the Catholic University of Chile (1888), and the Catholic University of Valparaíso (1928). Chilean universities are now widely recognized as being among the best in Latin America.

Preschool programs were introduced into Chile at the beginning of the 20th century by German advisers, and were increased greatly during the Pinochet years. The school system is administered by the national government under the Ministry of Education.

Education

Literacy Rate %: 95.2
  Male %: 95.4
  Female %: 95.0
First Level: Primary schools: 8,323
  Teachers: 78,813
  Students: 2,119,737
  Student-Teacher Ratio: 26.9
  Net Enrollment Ratio: 86
Second Level: Secondary Schools: —
  Teachers: 50,187
  Students: 664,498
  Student-Teacher Ratio: 13.2
  Net Enrollment Ratio: 55
Vocational Level: Schools: —
  Students: —
Third Level: Institutions: —
  Teachers: 18,084
  Students: 315,653
  Student-Ratio Level: —
  Gross Enrollment Ratio: 30.3
  Students per 100,000: 2,412
  % of Population Age 25 and over with Postsecondary Education: 12.3
Public Expenditure on Education as % of GDP: 2.9

SCIENCE AND TECHNOLOGY

Science and Technology

Scientists and Engineers in R&D per 1 million persons: 445
Expenditures in R&D as % of GDP: 0.68
High-Tech Exports $million: 92
Patent Applications by Residents: 189

MEDIA

Before 1973, most major political groups published their own daily or weekly journals, but when political parties were banned during the Pinochet years the journals were also restricted, except for those that did not criticize the government. Although freedom of expression and of the press were guaranteed under the 1980 constitution, and the courts constantly challenged government edicts concerning censorship, in practice the regime exercised considerable control over the media and simply blocked the legal dissent. During the 1980s, control was relaxed slightly and opposition groups were permitted a voice once more.

Since the return to democracy, modern press and communications have spread. By 1996 there were 52 daily newspapers, up from 33 in 1967, and *El Mercurio*, *La Nación*, and *La Tercera de la Hora*, all published in Santiago, have considerable influence. Television was introduced in 1958 and is operated by a national government network (started in 1967) and several independent stations. Many of the television and radio stations are operated by universities on a commercial basis. The country has more than 375 radio stations and 63 television broadcast stations.

In 1997, the number of people connected to the Internet in Chile was estimated to be 200,000, around 1.30 percent of the population. Usage, however, was growing rapidly, aided by good telecommunications infrastructure and the desire of Chileans to keep up with this latest technological development

Media

Daily Newspapers: 52
  Total Circulation 000: 1,411
  Circulation per 1,000: 99
Books Published: 1,820
Magazines: 417
Radio Receivers 000: 4,400
  per 1,000: 317
Television sets 000: 4,000
  per 1,000: 280

MOST IMPORTANT MEDIA:

Press. Unless otherwise noted, the following are published daily at Santiago: *La Tercera de la Hora* (190,000); *Las Ultimas Noticias* (145,000); *El Mercurio* (110,000), world's oldest Spanish-language paper (founded 1827), conservative; *La Nación* (45,000), financial; *La Segunda* (40,000); *¿Qué Pasa?* (30,000), weekly; *Diario Oficial* (10,000). *El Siglo*, a Communist Party fortnightly, claimed a clandestine circulation of 25,000 until September 4, 1989, when it resumed legal publication.

News agency. The domestic facility is Orbe Servicios Informativos; a number of foreign bureaus, including ANSA, AP, Reuters, TASS, and UPI, maintain offices at Santiago.

Radio and television. Radio Nacional de Chile is a government-operated network; the owners of more than 300 private stations are members of the Asociación de Radiodifusores de Chile (ARCHI). In 1988 it was reported that Televisión Nacionale de Chile would eventually be privatized. Four of the country's universities offer noncommercial TV programming.

CULTURE

Cultural Indicators

Public Libraries Number: 269
 Volumes: 940,000
 Registered borrowers: 23,153
Museums Number: —
 Annual Attendance: —
Cinema Production of Long Films: 1
 Number of Cinemas: 133
 Seating Capacity: 75,900
 Annual Attendance million: 8
 Annual Attendance per capita: 0.6

STATUS OF WOMEN

Traditional definitions of gender roles have been considerably challenged as women have won access to more education and have entered the labor force in larger numbers. By 1990 about half the students in the nation's primary and secondary schools were female; in higher education the proportion was lower at about 44 percent. A 1988 survey of workers found 70 percent of men and 92 percent of women accepted the notion that "men should participate more actively in housework so that women are able to work." Women can frequently be found in the professions even outside such traditionally female-dominated areas as primary and secondary education, nursing, and social work. For example, as physicians (around 27 percent), judges (around 48 percent), and journalism (over 50 percent).

Despite this, considerable pressures on women to have children remain. The proportion of the population favoring legal abortions remains small in Chile, except in cases of rape, danger to the mother, or malformations. Although illegal, abortions are commonly performed in Chile. Contraception is broadly accepted, even among practicing Catholics, and the distribution and use of birth control is facilitated by national health programs.

Women

Gender Empowerment Measure: 61
Seats Held in Parliament by Women %: 7.2
Female Administrators and Managers %: 20.1
Female Professional and Technical Workers %: 53.9
Women's Share of Earned Income %: 22
Women in Government %: 12

HEALTH, FOOD, AND NUTRITION

Health

Number of Physicians: 16,000
Number of Dentists: 5,200
Number of Nurses: 5,653
Number of Pharmacists: 230
Population per Physician: 875
Number of Hospitals: 198
Hospital Beds per 10,000: 31
Hospital Bed Occupancy Rate: 69.9
Infant Mortality Rate per 1,000 live births: 17
Maternal Mortality Rate per 100,000 live births: 65
Total Health Expenditures as % of GDP: 4.73
Health Expenditures per capita $: 100
HIV Infected % of adults: 0.20
Cigarette Consumption per smoker per year: 1,718
% of Smokers: Male: 38
 Female: 25
Access to Safe Water %: 96

Food and Nutrition

Food Supply as % of FAO Requirements: 113
% of Consumption Expenditures on Food: 27.9
Daily Available Calories per capita: 2,769
% of Total Calories derived from:
Cereals: 39.4
Potatoes, cassava: 3.6
Meat, poultry: 11.8
Fish: 2.0
Eggs, milk: 7.0
Fruits, vegetables: 6.0
Fats, oils: 10.8

ENVIRONMENT

Chile faces several environmental problems, not all of which are man-made. The country is affected by the socioeconomic consequences of climate variability, on a seasonal and annual scale, and particularly by the El Niño southern oscillation (ENOA). Agricultural production is based on extensive natural ecosystems in the region, and climate variability, both natural and influenced by development, impacts on natural resources. The country's most dynamic export sectors are natural resource–based, and expanded and intensified use of these resources—in forestry and agriculture particularly—has been accompanied by costly environmental degradation (e.g., soil loss and loss of native forests) and environmental contamination (e.g., the use of chemicals in agriculture and chemical wastes in mining).

Water pollution is also a problem, particularly in the river basins of the Elqui, Aconcagua, Maipo, Mapocho, Rapel, Maule, Bío-Bío, and Valdivia, where the largest demographic changes have occurred. Industrial waste discharges to lakes and rivers import excessive nutrients and heavy metals, although the majority of lakes in the south of Chile are transparent and clean.

A National Environmental Commission (Conema) coordinates the government's environmental management efforts. From 1990 through March 1996, a total of 147 investment projects worth almost US$16.6 billion (almost one-third of GDP) submitted to an environmental assessment system.

Environment

Forest Area sq km: 79,000
Average Annual Deforestation sq km: 292
Nationally Protected Areas as % of Total Land Area: 18.9
Freshwater Access cubic meters per capita: 32,007
Emissions of Organic Water Pollutants kg per day: 77,111
CO_2 Emissions per capita ton: 3.4

CHRONOLOGY

1946 Gabriel Gonzalez Videla of the Radical Party becomes president.
1948 Communist Party is outlawed.
1964 Eduardo Frei Montalva, Christian Democratic Party candidate, elected to presidency.
1970 Salvador Allende Gossens, of the left-wing Popular Unity Party, wins presidential election.
1971 Copper industry nationalized.
1973 Civil disorder, strikes, and civil war sweep the country. Army overthrows Allende, who dies in the process. Military junta under General Augusto Pinochet Ugarte assumes power. Congress is dissolved and political parties banned.
1974 Mass arrests, torture, and suppression of civil rights mark the junta's attempts to consolidate control.
1976 Former defense minister Orlando Letelier is killed in bomb explosion in Washington, D.C.
1978 Plebiscite supports Pinochet's policies; state of siege is lifted.
1980 New constitution introduced.
1984 Increased opposition to Pinochet results in state of emergency being declared.
1986 Pinochet survives assassination attempt.
1988 Presidential and congressional plebiscites are held.
1989 National referendum held in July. Presidential and congressional elections held in December.
1990 New president Patricio Aylwin Azócar takes office. Pinochet remains as head of army and life senator.
1991 President Aylwin accuses Pinochet regime of murdering 1,068 people during its rule.
1993 Christian Democrat Eduardo Frei Ruiz-Tagle, son of Eduardo Frei Montalva, is elected president. In November, the former head of the secret police and his deputy are sentenced to seven- and six-year sentences for the Letelier assassination in 1976.
1994 Canada, Mexico, and the United States invite Chile to join NAFTA.
1995 The convictions in the Letelier case are upheld by the Supreme Court, and Pinochet denounces the decision, challenging the court's authority. After a tense standoff, the two men are arrested in June 1995. In August legislation is introduced to reopen investigations into 542 cases of disappearance under the Pinochet regime.
1996 Chile becomes an associate member of Mercosur, the Southern Cone free-trade market, and concludes a free-trade agreement with Canada.
1998 October: Pinochet is arrested in London on a Spanish murder warrant. In December, Chile cuts contact with the United Kingdom following a legal decision to allow extradition proceedings to begin.
1999 January: the Law Lords in the United Kingdom rule that Pinochet's immunity does not extend to the charges against him. October: a U.K. court rules that Pinochet can be extradited to Spain to stand trial for torture and human rights charges. In presidential elections in December, neither of the two main candidates, Ricardo Lagos and Joaquín Lavín, secure an overall majority and face a run-off in January 2000.
2000 On January 16 Ricardo Lagos narrowly wins the second round of the presidential elections. January: Pinochet undergoes medical tests. March: Pinochet is declared unfit to stand trial and returns to Chile. June: The Chilean appeals court strips Pinochet of his immunity from prosecution. The Chilean army announces it will help to locate the bodies of some 1,200 people missing since the 1970s.
2001 Pinochet is indicted in January on charges of kidnapping and murder and placed under house arrest. In March, the Santiago Court of Appeals reduces the charges against Pinochet to acting as an accessory in the crimes. Pinochet is released from house arrest on bail while awaiting a possible trial.

BIBLIOGRAPHY

Collier, Simon, and William F. Sater. *A History of Chile, 1808–1994.* Cambridge, Mass., 1996.
Ensalaco, Mark. *Chile Under Pinochet: Recovering the Truth.* Philadelphia, Pa., 1999.
Hudson, Rex A. *Chile, A Country Study.* Area Handbook Series. Washington, D.C., 1995.
Martinez, Javier. *Chile: The Great Transformation.* Washington, D.C., 1996.
Oppenheim, Lois Hecht. *Politics in Chile: Democracy, Authoritarianism, and the Search for Development.* Boulder, Colo., 1993.
Spooner, Mary Helen. *Soldiers in a Narrow Land: The Pinochet Regime in Chile.* Los Angeles, 1999.
Wright, Thomas C., and Rody O'Nate, eds. *Flight from Chile: Voices of Exile.* Alberquerque, N.M. 1998.

OFFICIAL PUBLICATIONS

Chile. *Chile XVI censo nacional de población y de vivienda, 22 de abril 1992; Compendio estadístico* (annual).

CONTACT INFORMATION

Embassy of Chile
1732 Massachusetts Avenue NW
Washington, D.C. 20036
Phone: (202) 785-1746 Fax: (202) 887-5579

INTERNET RESOURCES

- Ministry General Secretariat of the Government; Communication and Culture Secretariat
  http://www.segegob.cl/seg-ingl/index2i.html

CHINA

BASIC FACT SHEET

OFFICIAL NAME:
People's Republic of China (Zhongguo Renmin Gonghehua)

ABBREVIATION:
CH

CAPITAL:
Beijing

HEAD OF STATE:
President Jiang Zemin (from 1993)

HEAD OF GOVERNMENT:
Premier of the State Council Zhu Rongji (from 1998)

NATURE OF GOVERNMENT:
Communist dictatorship

POPULATION:
1,251,238,000 (1999)

AREA:
562,904 sq km (3,692,244 sq mi)

MAJOR ETHNIC GROUPS:
Han Chinese (93.3%); Zhuang, Uygur, Hui, Yi, Tibetan, Miao, Manchu, Mongol, Puyi, and Korean

LANGUAGE:
Putonghua (Mandarin)

RELIGION:
Officially atheist; Confucianism, Buddhism, Taoism, Islam, and Christianity

UNIT OF CURRENCY:
Yuan

NATIONAL FLAG:
Red flag with five yellow stars in the upper left quadrant—one large star near the hoist and four smaller ones arranged in an arc to the right.

NATIONAL EMBLEM:
A large golden star partially encircled by four smaller stars, also in gold, against a circular red background, above a golden replica of Tiananmen Square. A gold decorative frame of ears of wheat and rice surrounds the emblem. At the base of the emblem is a gold cogwheel partially covered by red drapery.

NATIONAL ANTHEM:
"Yi Yong Ju Jin Xing Qu" (March of the volunteers)

NATIONAL HOLIDAYS:
National Day (October 1); May Day; Chinese New Year

DATE OF INDEPENDENCE:
1523 B.C.

DATE OF CONSTITUTION:
December 4, 1982

GEOGRAPHICAL FEATURES

The third-largest country in the world and the largest Asian country, the national territory includes approximately 5,000 islands, of which the largest is Hainan, off the southwestern coast; others are grouped among the Dongsha (Tungsha; Pratas) and the Sisha, Xisha (Paracels), Nansha (Spratly), (Chungsha) and Zhongsha archipelagoes. Mainland China's coastline extends from the mouth of the Yalu River in the northeast to the Gulf of Tonkin in the south in a sweeping arc, broken in the south by the Leizhou (Leichow) Peninsula, projecting into the South China Sea, and in the north by the Liadong (Liaotung) Peninsula and the Shandong (Shantung) Peninsula, projecting into the Yellow Sea.

The capital is Beijing, formerly known in English as Peking, or as Peiping or Shuntien-fu, founded by Khitan Tartars in the 10th century and the capital of China from the 15th century. There were 56 other cities with a population of 1 million or more, of which Shanghai is the

China

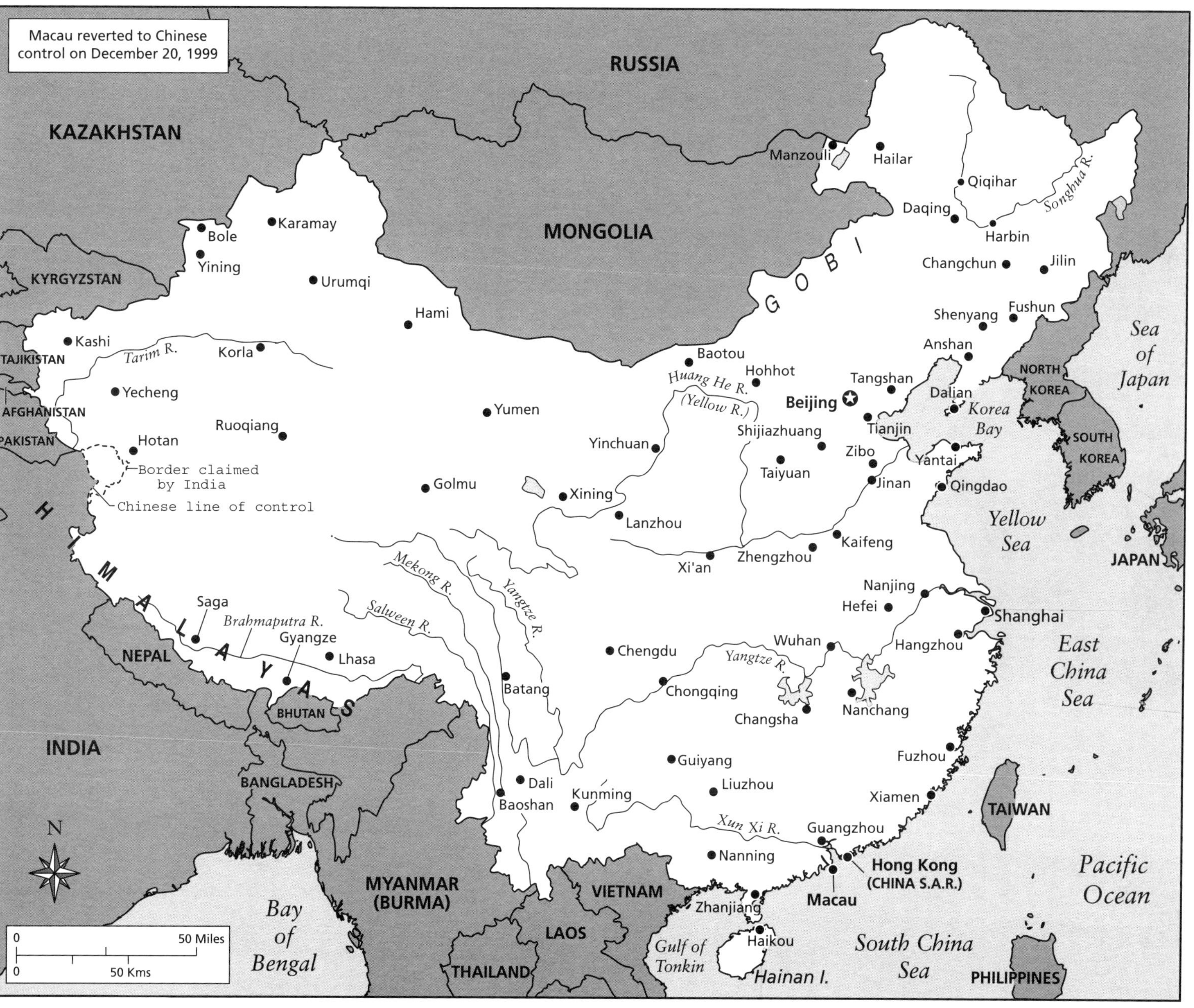
Macau reverted to Chinese control on December 20, 1999
RUSSIA
KAZAKHSTAN
MONGOLIA
KYRGYZSTAN
TAJIKISTAN
AFGHANISTAN
PAKISTAN
INDIA
NEPAL
BHUTAN
BANGLADESH
MYANMAR (BURMA)
THAILAND
LAOS
VIETNAM
PHILIPPINES
TAIWAN
NORTH KOREA
SOUTH KOREA
JAPAN
Sea of Japan
Yellow Sea
Korea Bay
East China Sea
Pacific Ocean
South China Sea
Gulf of Tonkin
Bay of Bengal
Hainan I.
GOBI
HIMALAYAS
Songhua R.
Huang He R. (Yellow R.)
Yangtze R.
Xun Xi R.
Mekong R.
Salween R.
Brahmaputra R.
Tarim R.
Beijing
Hong Kong (CHINA S.A.R.)
Macau
Manzouli
Hailar
Qiqihar
Harbin
Daqing
Jilin
Changchun
Fushun
Shenyang
Anshan
Dalian
Yantai
Qingdao
Tangshan
Tianjin
Zibo
Jinan
Kaifeng
Zhengzhou
Nanjing
Hefei
Shanghai
Hangzhou
Nanchang
Wuhan
Changsha
Fuzhou
Xiamen
Guangzhou
Zhanjiang
Haikou
Nanning
Liuzhou
Guiyang
Chongqing
Chengdu
Kunming
Dali
Baoshan
Batang
Lhasa
Gyangze
Saga
Xi'an
Taiyuan
Shijiazhuang
Hohhot
Baotou
Yinchuan
Lanzhou
Xining
Yumen
Golmu
Hami
Urumqi
Karamay
Bole
Yining
Korla
Ruoqiang
Kashi
Yecheng
Hotan
Border claimed by India
Chinese line of control
N
0 50 Miles
0 50 Kms

largest, with a population of more than 7 million in 2000. It is by far the largest port serving the vast hinterland of the Yangzi (Yangtze) River valley.

China is geographically one of the most diverse regions of the world, including vast areas of rugged, inhospitable terrain, broad plains, deserts, lofty mountain ranges, and steppe. Geographers have identified a number of topographical regions based on terrain and relief, divided broadly into plateaus and basins, the Great Plains, and the Southeast.

The four great plains of China are the Huanghe (Hwang Ho), the Yangtze (Yangzi), the Xijiang (Si Kiang), and the Northeast, or Manchurian. Mountains makeup more than two-thirds of the land area of China. They fall into three groups according to the direction in which they run: east-west, northeast-southwest, and north-south.

Since the general lie of the land is toward the east, all the great national rivers flow toward the Pacific. In the northeast, the Amur (Heilongjiang) drains a great part of the Manchurian basin as it winds along its 4,023-km (2,500-mi) course. The main river in northern China and the second largest in the country is the Yellow River (Huanghe; Hwang Ho), which acquired its name from the yellowish-color of its muddy waters—the result of its passage through the yellow loess plateau of Gansu (Kansu). From Gansu it winds 4,795 km (2,980 mi) through the northern provinces eastward to Shandong where it empties into the Gulf of Chihli (Boa Hai). Central China is drained by China's longest river, the Yangzi (Chiangjiang, Ch'ang Chiang). From its source about 80 km (50 mi) from that of the Yellow River, it wends 5,208 km (3,237 mi) to the East China Sea. Important rivers that drain the southwestern coastal regions are the Minjiang (Min Chiang) and the Zhujiang (Chu Chiang; Pearl River). The Pearl, the fourth largest river in China, is a general name for a network of three waterways that meet south of Guangzhou to form a big estuary consisting of many channels separated by islets. The main eastern channel, Hu Men (Boca Tigris), enters the sea near Hong Kong, while the main western channel flows close to Macao. Farther south are two independent rivers, the Mekong (Lancang; Lan-ts'ang) and the Red (Yuan) River, of which only the upper courses are in China.

Geography

Area sq km: 562,904 sq mi 3,692,244
World Rank: 3rd
Land Boundaries, km: Afghanistan 76 km, Bhutan 470 km, Burma 2,185 km, Hong Kong 30 km, India 3,380 km, Kazakhstan 1,533 km, North Korea 1,416 km, Kyrgyzstan 858 km, Laos 423 km, Macau 0.34 km, Mongolia 4,673 km, Nepal 1,236 km, Pakistan 523 km, Russia (northeast) 3,605 km, Russia (northwest) 40 km, Tajikistan 414 km, Vietnam 1,281 km
Coastline, km: 14,500
Elevation Extremes meters
Lowest: Turpan Pendi –154
Highest: Mount Everest 8,848
Land Use % Arable land: 10
Permanent Crops: 0
Permanent Pastures: 43
Forest and Woodland: 14
Other: 33

Population of Principal Cities (1998)

City	Population
Shanghai	7,830,000
Beijing (Peking)	7,000,000
Tianjin (Tientsin)	5,770,000
Shenyang	4,540,000
Wuhan	3,750,000
Guangzhou (Canton)	3,580,000
Chongqing (Chungking)	2,980,000
Harbin	2,830,000
Chengdu (Ch'eng-tu)	2,810,000
Xi'an (Sian)	2,760,000
Nanjing (Nanking)	2,500,000
Dalian (Ta-lien)	2,400,000
Zibo (Tzu-po)	2,460,000
Jinan (Chi-nan)	2,320,000
Changch'un	2,110,000
Jiutai (Ch'ing-tai)	2,060,000
Taiyuan	1,960,000
Zhengzhou (Cheng-chou)	1,710,000
Tangshan	1,500,000
Guiyang (Kuei-yang)	1,530,000
Kunming	1,520,000
Lanzhou (Lan-chou)	1,510,000
Anshan	1,500,000
Qiqihar (Tsitsihar)	1,380,000
Fushun	1,350,000
Nanchang	1,350,000
Hangzhou (Hang-chou)	1,340,000
Changsha	1,330,000
Shijiazhuang (Shih-chia-chuang)	1,320,000
Fuzhou (Fu-chou)	1,290,000
Jilin (Chi-lin)	1,270,000
Huainan	1,200,000
Baotou (Pao-t'ou)	1,200,000
Luoyang	1,190,000
Urmqi (Wu-lu-mu-chi)	1,160,000
Handan (Han-tan)	1,110,000
Dandong (Ta-tung)	1,110,000
Ningbo (Ning-po)	1,090,000
Nanning (Nan-ning)	1,070,000
Hefei (Ho-fei)	1,000,000

CLIMATE AND WEATHER

The diversity of China's terrain is matched only by the diversity of its climate. In a vast subcontinent such as China, with tremendous differences in latitude and longitude as well as altitude (from peaks 8 km [5 mi] in height to basins below sea level), there are sharp variations in climatic features. Leizhou Peninsula, Hainan Island, the South China Sea islands of Guangdong Province, and the southern part of Yunnan Province have a tropical climate, where summer reigns all year long. Heilongjiang Province, in the northeast, has a short and cool summer and a severe winter. The area around the Yangtze and Huai River valleys in the east is warm and humid, with four distinct seasons. The Inner Mongolia-Xinjiang area, in the northwest, experiences extremes of weather in a single day, giving rise to the saying "Fur coats in the morning and gossamer at noon." Some areas of the Yunnan-Guizhou Plateau, in the southwest, have a mild winter and cool summer, as does Kunming, which is justly named "City of Spring." The Tibet Plateau has a cold, dry climate and a strong sun; in some of its areas pronounced differences in climate are found between high and low altitudes.

In spite of these differences, the one constant that characterizes Chinese climate is the monsoon rhythm arising from the continentality of the Asian landmass. The monsoon denotes a wind system that, in China, changes from southeast in summer to north and northeast in winter. The cold air mass established in the autumn in Siberia and Mongolia forms an anticyclone or center of high pressure and spreads southward until it meets the warm air mass of the North Pacific trades along a front to the south of the China coast known as the West Pacific Polar Front. From this great anticyclone there is an outflow of dry northerly and northeasterly winds over China, bringing prolonged and bitter winters to the northern part of the country and cold weather as far south as the central and lower Yangzi River basins. In spring the movements are reversed. The cold air mass over the heart of the continent warms up, giving place to a continental low, while a high-pressure center is established over the eastern Pacific. Northerly and northwesterly winds give way to those from the south and southeast, and a great current of warm, humid air moves in from the south. Between May and July the summer monsoon extends over the Yangzi and the North China Plain. The characteristic weather of the summer monsoon over much of China is hot, calm days of high relative humidity, which are very oppressive. Inland the winds are light, but coastal regions in the south and southeast experience disastrous typhoons. The duration of the summer monsoon season varies between the north and the south, being shorter in the north because of the lateness of the onset.

Temperature patterns are determined by altitude, latitude, and landmass. There is a difference of 9,144 m (30,000 ft) between Mount Everest and the Turfan Basin and a difference of nearly 40° in latitude between Hainan and Moho on the Amur. In winter there is a large and steady fall in temperature from the south to the north. There is a remarkable unity of temperature in summer, the maximum differences being only 15°F compared to 60°F in winter. Every place is hot and humid. In the desert and semidesert regions of Xinjiang (Sinkiang), Mongolia, and Dzungaria, annual temperature ranges are very great, up to 76°F, compared to 22°F in Hong Kong.

Except for the small southwestern corner of Xizang (Sikang; Tibet) which shares the phenomenal rainfall of Assam across the border, rainfall in China shows a general decrease from southeast to northwest, ranging from 2,159 mm (85 in) in Hong Kong to 102 mm (4 in) in Kashgar.

Climate and Weather

Mean Temperature
Hainan, South Guanxi, South Giangdong 55°F
South and Central China 80°F
Northern Manchuria January −17°F to July 70°F
Hong Kong Summer 60°F
Average Rainfall Annual National 60 in
North China and Manchuria 25 in
Pearl River 80 in
Hong Kong 85 in

POPULATION

Population Indicators

Total Population: 1999 1,251,238,000
World Rank: 1st
Density per sq mi: 338.5 per sq km 130.7
% of annual growth (1994–99): 1.0
Male %: 51.6
Female %: 48.4
Urban %: 26.4

Age Distribution: %	
0–14:	27.7
15–29:	31.0
30–44:	20.7
45–59:	12.1
60–74:	6.9
75 and over:	1.7

Population 2020: 1,403,169,000
Birth Rate per 1,000: 16.2
Death Rate per 1,000: 7.1
Population Doubling Time (years): 77
Infant Mortality Rate per 1,000 live births: 38.0
Rate of Natural Increase per 1,000: 9.1
Total Fertility Rate: 1.8
Expectation of Life (years): Males 68.2
Females 71.7
Marriage Rate per 1,000: 7.6
Divorce Rate per 1,000: 0.9
Total Number of Households: 278,600,000
Average Size of Households: 4.1
% of Illegitimate Children: —
Induced Abortions: 10,500,000
Rate per 100 live births: 47.7

ETHNIC COMPOSITION

According to official data, 93.3 percent of the population is Han Chinese; the term *Han* referes to the ancient dynasty that ruled China from 206 B.C.E. to 220 C.E. Although there are sharp regional and cultural differences among the Han, who are a mingling of many races, they share a common language, social organization, and cultural characteristics universally recognized as the core of Chinese civilization.

Han is only one of 56 nationalities that officially make up the Chinese population; the other 55 are called minority nationalities. However, even while accounting for only 6.7 percent of the population, these minority nationalities are distributed over 50 percent of the national territory, mostly along the inland borders. The distinction between Han and some of the minorities is not clear because many have been totally or partially assimilated over the centuries. Some are found only in a single region, while others are spread over many regions. In general, Xinjiang, Inner Mongolia, and Tibet contain heavy concentrations of minorities, whereas minority groups in Yunnan and Guizhou provinces and the Guangxi-Zhuang Autonomous Region are more fragmented and inhabit smaller areas. There are special minority autonomous administrative regions on the Soviet model. They include five provincial-level units: Xizang (Tibet), Xinjiang, Guangxi, Nei Monggol, and Ningxia (named, respectively, for Tibetan, Uighur, Zhuang, Mongol, and Hui nationalities). In addition, there are over 29 autonomous prefectures and 73 autonomous counties.

With the exception of the Koreans, few ethnic nationalities have been able to preserve their identity in the face of the preponderance of the Han Chinese culture. Conflicts have been frequent between the majority and minority cultures, and the degree of Sinification reflects the outcome of these conflicts. The most Sinified groups are in the southeastern area and among the Tumet of former Suiyuan Province. There are no foreign communities as such in China.

LANGUAGES

The Chinese language is spoken by more people in the world than any other language, including English. Chinese is also a much older language and one that has undergone fewer changes in the course of its history, and one of the most important changes—the introduction of a *pinyin* script—is of recent date. Also, as every student of Chinese knows, it is one of the most difficult languages in the world to learn. As a result, illiteracy always has been high in the country, and literacy was among the privileges of the elite.

During the course of its evolution, the spoken language has undergone more modifications than the written one, particularly in pronunciation and modes of expression. A number of dialects have developed out of these changes. The spoken language also is more receptive to foreign influences. As a result, speech communities intermingle and overlap. Of the numerous dialects, the most important in terms of the number of speakers is Mandarin, followed by Wu, Hsiang, Hui, Kan, Hakka, Min, and Yueh. Although derived from a common core language, different pronunciation and linguistic structure make most of them mutually unintelligible. Even within Mandarin, there are three groups of subdialects: Northern Mandarin, spoken in Beijing and the entire Yellow River basin; Southwestern Mandarin, spoken in the southwestern hinterland, including the Sichuan (Szechwan) Red River basin, the Yunnan-Kweichow Plateau, and the central Yangzi River plains; and Southern Mandarin, spoken in the lower Yangzi River valley eastward to Nanjing (Nanking).

The cultural bond of language has led it to become one of the rallying standards of Chinese nationalism, embodied in the cry "One State, One People, One Language." Seeking to foster unity through language, each regime since 1911 has sought to (1) adopt Mandarin as a national language, (2) popularize Chinese among the non-Han minorities, (3) simplify the written words, (4) compile a list of basic Chinese characters and words, and (5) alphabetize the Chinese language.

An even more serious need was the introduction of a phonetic alphabet to replace the system of Chinese characters. In the absence of an alphabet, scholarly tools such as dictionaries, indexes, bibliographies, and catalogs have traditionally been arranged on the basis of a complex system of fundamental characters (radicals) or the number of strokes in each character. Chinese characters also create special problems in other areas. Telegraphic messages have to be sent in numerical codes. Typesetting machines and typewriters are vastly more complicated than those using an alphabet. In the 20th century, many alphabetic systems have been devised to overcome these deficiencies, ranging from romanizations to kanalike symbols used by the Japanese, shorthand systems, and picture scripts. In 1956 a committee of linguistic experts appointed by the Maoist regime recommended adoption of a 26-letter Latin alphabet for the Chinese written language. The new system, known as *pinyin*, was formally approved by the National People's Congress in 1958. It took another 21 years before the government decided to adopt it officially. In 1979 and following years the government issued a number of word lists and lists of places and persons with standard spellings. The switchover to *pinyin* posed problems not only for Chinese—particularly nationalists for whom language is a highly emotional issue—but also for Western readers accustomed to the Wade-Giles romanization system. Because it is based on the Beijing dialect, much education had to follow its introduction in all parts of China. As part of latinization, Chinese writing switched to left to right—i.e, horizontally—rather than in vertical lines from right to left, as in traditional Chinese. Pens and pencils also have replaced the time-honored writing brushes. Another part of the reform concerned punctuation. There were no punctuations in Chinese writing until a set of marks was introduced in the late 1910s. The new system was copied from the West, with the exception that the period is not a point but a small circle.

The introduction of a latinized script has not been an unmixed blessing. It has made classical Chinese virtually a foreign language for most Chinese and therefore constitutes a serious diminution of China's literary heritage. As it will be impossible to translate all the classic texts into the romanized form, most of them will be available only to scholars.

Principal Languages and Their Speakers

Language	Speakers
Achang	30,000
Bulang (Blang)	90,000
Ch'iang (Qiang)	220,000
Chinese (Han)	1,150,580,000
Cantonese (Yueh [Yue])	49,000,000
Hakka	27,000,000
Hsiang (Xiang)	38,000,000
Kan (Gan)	22,000,000
Mandarin	892,000,000
Min	38,000,000
Wu	82,000,000
Ching-p'o (Jingpo)	130,000
Chuang (Zhuang)	17,100,000
Daghur (Daur)	130,000
Evenk (Ewenki)	30,000
Gelo	480,000
Hani (Woni)	1,380,000
Hui	9,500,000
Kazak	1,230,000
Korean	2,120,000
Kyrgyz	160,000
Lahu	450,000
Li	1,230,000
Lisu	630,000
Manchu	10,840,000
Maonan	80,000
Miao	8,170,000
Mongol	5,310,000
Mulam	180,000
Na-hsi (Naxi)	310,000
Nu	30,000
Pai (Bai)	1,760,000
Pumi	30,000
Puyi (Chung-chia)	2,810,000
Salar	100,000
She	700,000
Shui	380,000
Sibo (Xibe)	190,000
Tai (Dai)	1,130,000
Tajik	40,000
Tibetan	5,070,000
Tu (Monguor)	210,000
Tu-chia (Tujia)	6,300,000
Tung (Dong)	2,780,000
Tung-hsiang (Dongxiang)	410,000
Uighur	7,960,000
Wa (Va)	390,000
Yao	2,350,000
Yi	7,250,000
Other	980,000

RELIGIONS

In China, organized religion is subordinated to a complex of folk beliefs and practices that provide the ritual setting to daily lives. They include ancestor worship, reverence for family altars and institutions, and more distinctly occult elements such as magic, sorcery, and divination. Over this substratum of core beliefs and practices lies a thin veneer of ethical rules of conduct by some of the greatest of classical masters, Confucius in particular. Some elements of theology and cosmogony were added from Buddhism, which was the first of the organized religions to reach China and which ranks with Confucianism and Taoism as one of the three main indigenous religious traditions. At the fringe of this religious landscape are the two major religions of the non-Chinese world—Islam and Christianity—neither of which was grafted onto the national consciousness and thus never properly took roots in the country. To complicate the picture even further is the hovering and brooding presence of Marxism, which negates religious belief and has waged a relentless campaign to uproot all established religions.

The most pervasive and the oldest of all Chinese religious practices—the distinction between religious practice and religion is quite important in the Chinese setting—is ancestor worship. Although ancestor worship is found in a variety of other cultures, nowhere else has it been so interwoven into the social fabric as to constitute an inseparable part of daily life. The personal and familial nature of ancestor worship precluded the suprafamilial aspect of most religions from taking roots in China. Formal religions such as Christianity were rejected because it could not be reconciled with ancestor worship and because its theological aspect overshadowed its social aspects. But while strong enough to resist the inroads of other religions, it was not vigorous enough to survive the decline of the patriarchal family in 20th-century Chinese society.

Folk religious systems antedate formal religious systems and coexist with them everywhere, even in the 20th century. But in China they flourish aboveground and have fewer linkages with organized religion. The world of folk religion is a kaleidoscope of dragons, demons, ghosts, gods, animals, and spirits jumbled together. In addition to folk deities, every family had its own tutelary deity, the kitchen god who kept an account of the good and bad deeds of the family and reported annually to the Tien. The kitchen god's periodical ascent to heaven was made easier by the burning of incense.

Folk religions did not concern themselves with theology, philosophy, or ethics other than in a rudimentary way. The philosophical and ethical bases were provided by Confucianism, Taoism, Buddhism, and other systems, none of which was organized in terms of doctrine, clergy, or believers. Although Confucianism is primarily a politico-intellectual tradition of statecraft (*ju-chia*), it was transformed by its followers into a religion with all the trappings of a cult: temples, sacrifices, and priests. But its inherent religious neutrality made Confucianism too impersonal to fill the emotional needs of the common people. In the 20th century Confucianism, closely identified with the imperial power, collapsed along with the monarchy.

Sacrifices in Confucian temples were discontinued in 1928. Reduced to a philosophical system, it was supplanted by Western philosophical and ethical traditions and even more so by dialectical materialism.

Taoism also is both a philosophy and a religion. Its conversion to a religion took place in the early centuries of the Christian era. Originally based on Persian Mazdaism in its early phase, it included confession of sins, healing, prayers to the spirits, and an elaborate angelology. Later, as a rival to Buddhism, it adopted an order of clergy and monks. Its philosophical character was gradually diluted as it became identified with folk religion. The organization and rituals of Taoism are blatant imitations of Buddhism. Strong Buddhist influences also permeated the architecture of Taoist temples, called *kuan* and *kung*, as well as liturgy and music. The Taoist pantheon was peopled by folk deities such as the Jade Emperor and lower gods and guardian spirits. The cult also embraced the rich reservoir of native superstitions such as geomancy, divination, witchcraft, astrology, communication with the dead, and, most important, alchemy, particularly the transmutation of base metals into gold and the manufacture of elixirs of immortality. From Indian cultures Taoism borrowed Yogic practices such as breathing controls, and special diets designed to prolong life. Taoism also quickly disintegrated in the early part of the 20th century. The official end came when the last hereditary *tien-shih*, presiding over Taoist headquarters in the Dragon and Tiger Mountain in Jiangxi, was expelled by the Nationalist government in 1927.

Although Buddhism originated in India and only spread into China after many centuries, it is considered a native religion for all practical purposes. Chinese Buddhism is of the Mahayana (Great Vehicle) school, which is more properly a religion than the Hinayana (Lesser Vehicle) school. In the Mahayana version, Buddha is a god whose image is worshiped and to whom sacrifices are offered. Buddhist temples and ceremonies are replicas of imperial palaces and court ceremonies. Nirvana is replaced by the Western Heaven ruled over by Amida Buddha (Amitabha). Hells and purgatories have been added as countervailing concepts. The Indian bodhisattva Avalokiteshvara, originally a male deity, became the goddess of mercy, Guanyin (Kuan-yin). Although persecuted at times by Taoist and Confucianist emperors, Buddhism was a useful political tool for China's rulers in their efforts to control the Mongol and Tibetan peoples who adhered to Lamaism, a form of Mahayana Buddhism corrupted by native shamanism. Suffering serious setbacks in the early 20th century, Buddhism enjoyed a brief revival in the 1930s and 1940s through the efforts of many abbots, such as Yin-guang and Tai-hsu.

Islam is considered a foreign religion known as Hui Hui jiao, which means "religion of the Uighur," the Turkic tribe of Xinjiang. About half of Chinese Muslims speak a Turkic language. Though distributed in most inland provinces, their most important traditional centers are in Yunnan, Gansu, Xinjiang, Ningxia, and Inner Mongolia. The Muslim community has avoided identifying itself with Chinese culture except for the sake of political expediency. Islam flourished under the Nationalist government when Muslims reestablished contacts with Arab countries, resulting in strong movements toward orthodoxy. The same period opened the way to political and military power for many Muslims. Even after the advent of communism, Islam has fared better than other religions. The Chinese Islamic Association operates under government aegis and disseminates communist propaganda in the Middle East. Muslim schools have been established as instruments of communist indoctrination. Islam also is taught in the Central Academy of Nationalities and the Chinese Muslim College in Beijing.

There is no accepted term for Christianity in Chinese. Catholicism and Protestantism, which were introduced separately, are called respectively *tien-chu jiao* (doctrine of the Heavenly Lord) and *chitu-jiao* (doctrine of Christ). Both groups evolved in isolation and operate as two different religions.

Religious Affiliations

Nonreligious	649,000,000
Chinese folk-religionist	251,000,000
Atheist	150,000,000
Buddhist	106,000,000
Christian	75,000,000
Muslim	18,000,000
Traditional beliefs	2,000,000

HISTORICAL BACKGROUND

Although earlier civilizations, now extinct, have flourished elsewhere, China is the world's oldest nation, with a continuance history that goes back to the second millennium B.C. The Chinese therefore have a strong sense of history and have kept voluminous records since very early times. An inward-looking people, the Chinese have constructed a China-centered view of the world reflected in the Chinese name for their own country—Zhonghua, literally the Middle Kingdom or the Central Nation.

The Chinese count time not in centuries, as in the West, but in dynasties. From the very first dynasty to 1911, when the first republic was established, there were 17 dynasties, many of them with subdivisions and periods.

The origins of Chinese civilization are shrouded in the mists of time. The first prehistoric dynasty is said to be the Xia, which ruled for about 500 years (2200–1700 B.C.E.). The first historical dynasty about which archaeological evidence exists is the Shang (or Yin), which ruled from 1700 to 1027 B.C.E. Two important Shang developments were the invention of writing and the use of bronze.

The last Shang ruler was overthrown by a chieftain of a frontier tribe called Zhou (Chou), settled along the banks of the Wei River valley in modern Shanxi Province. The Zhou dynasty had its capital at Hao, near the modern city of Xian (Sian). The Zhou dynasty ruled China for a longer period than any other. However, in 771 B.C.E. the Zhou court was sacked and its king killed, forcing the transfer of its capital eastward to Luoyang, in the modern province of Henan. Because of this shift the Zhou period is divided into Western and Eastern eras. The latter is further subdivided into the Spring and Autumn period (722–481 B.C.) and the Warring States period (403–221 B.C.E.). The Eastern Zhou period was a time of the flowering of Chinese culture, represented by such philosophers as Kongfuzi (K'ung-fu-tzu) or Master Kung (551–470 B.C.E.), known to the West as Confucius; Mencius, or Mengzi (Meng-tzu, 372–289 B.C.E.); Xunzi (Hsun-tzu, c. 300–237 B.C.E.), the Legalist whose ideas were developed by Hanfeizi (Hanfei-tzu, d. 233 B.C.E.) and Li Si (Li Ssu, d.208 B.C.E.); and Laozi (Lao-tsu or "Old Master"), the founder of Taoism, and his disciple Chuan Chu (369–286 B.C.E.).

The history of China as a united nation begins properly in 221 B.C.E. In that year the western frontier state of Qin (Ch'in, from which the name *China* is derived) subjugated the other warring states, and the king of Qin took on the grandiloquent title of "First Emperor of the Chin"—Qin Shi Huangdi. He set in motion a process of centralization and imperial expansion. To fend off barbarian invasions from the north, the various fortification walls built previously by the warring states were connected to make a 3,300-km (2,051-mi) Great Wall. The Qin dynasty did not outlast the death of its founder and lasted only 15 years—the shortest dynastic period in Chinese history.

The dynasty that replaced it was the Han—after whom the major nationality of China is named—with its capital at Chang'an, later known as Xian. The Han period is noted for the invention of paper and porcelain, the establishment of the Silk Route to the Roman imperial possessions in Asia Minor, and the introduction of Buddhism.

The collapse of the Han dynasty was followed by nearly four centuries of rule by warlords. This period began with the Three Kingdoms (220–80 C.E.), followed by the Jin dynasty, which through its western and eastern branches ruled until 420. From that time until the sixth century, power was shared by four southern and five northern dynasties. This period was noted for the spread of Buddhism, the invention of gunpowder and the wheelbarrow, and numerous advances in medicine, astronomy, and cartography.

China was reunified by the short-lived Sui dynasty, which ruled from 581 to 618. Their principal legacy was the Grand Canal, a monumental engineering feat. The Sui was supplanted by the Tang dynasty in 618. Most historians regard the Tang period as the high point in Chinese civilization, distinguished not only by the military exploits of its early rulers but also by the flowering of creativity in many fields. Block printing was invented, making the written word accessible to a larger audience. The Tang period also was the golden age of literature and art. The Tang rulers were the first to establish a cadre of civil servants selected through competitive examinations.

Tang power ebbed by the mid-eighth century, and the dynasty ended in 907. The next half century is known as the Five Dynasties and 10 Kingdoms period. This age of fragmentation gave way to a new power, the Song (Sung) (960–1279), notable for the development of cities and the mercantile class. At the same time there was a progressive revival of interest in the Confucian ideals, coinciding with the decline of Buddhism. The Confucian revival was spearheaded by Zhu Xi (Chu Hsi, 1130–1200), whose teachings became the official imperial ideology until the end of the Manchu dynasty. A rigid and unyielding creed, it stressed the one-sided obligations of obedience and compliance by subject to ruler, child to parents, and wife to husband. Before or during the Song period three other dynasties held power in various other parts of China: the Liao (Kitan) dynasty (907–1125), the Western Xia (Hsia) dynasty (1032–1227), and the Jin (Nurchen) dynasty (1032–1227).

At the beginning of the 13th century the Mongols were already ascendant in northern China. Chingiz Khan and his successors had established an empire that stretched from the Sea of Japan to the Black Sea and beyond. Kublai Khan, grandson of Chingiz Khan, began a drive against the Song, and even before the latter's extinction, established the first alien dynasty to rule all China, the Yuan (1279–1368). As in other parts of their empire, Mongol rule was brief and culturally barren. The period was notable only for the visit of the Venetian Marco Polo, whose account of his trip to Kublai Khan's court was the first Western glimpse into the fabulous land of Cathay. The Mongol rule was resented by the Han Chinese, who were discriminated against socially and politically.

Rivalry among the heirs to the Mongol khaganate, natural disasters, and numerous peasant uprisings led to the collapse of the Yuan dynasty. It was supplanted in 1368 by the Ming dynasty, founded by a Han Chinese peasant and former Buddhist priest. With its capital first at Nanjing and later at Beijing, its power reached its zenith during the first quarter of the 15th century. Chinese armies reconquered Annam in Southeast Asia, and the Chinese fleet ranged the China seas and the Indian Ocean as far as the eastern coast of Africa. Many Chinese historians consider the Ming period as the most stable and prosperous of Chinese eras. However, by the first half of the 17th century Ming power had weakened enough to allow invaders from the north to grasp the throne once again. In 1644 the Manchus took Beijing and became masters of northern China, thus establishing China's second and last alien dynasty. Known as the Qing (Ch'ing), it survived until 1911.

Although non-Han, the Manchus were Sinicized to a great degree, and they adopted Chinese customs and retained most of the Ming institutions. They continued the Confucian cult rituals over which they traditionally presided. In a series of bloody and costly campaigns, the Manchus gained control over most border and other outlying areas, including Xinjiang, Yunnan, Tibet, and Taiwan. A combination of military prowess and bureaucratic skills contributed to the early successes of the Manchus.

The Qing were suspicious of the Han, and Qing policy was directed toward preserving Manchu superiority. Han Chinese were prohibited from migrating to Manchuria. The Manchus were forbidden to engage in manual labor and trade, and no agriculture was permitted in northern Manchuria. Intermarriage between the two groups was forbidden. In many government positions a system of dual appointments was used, with Chinese officials being supervised by Manchus.

Even as the Manchu empire grew to include a larger area than ever before or since, it was sapped by new threats from within and without. The process of disintegration occurred throughout the entire 19th century through a series of incidents that cumulatively drained its resources and eventually toppled it. Beginning in the early 19th century, localized revolts erupted in various parts of the empire. Secret societies, such as the White Lotus sect in the north and the Hung Society in the south, gained ground, combining anti-Manchu subversion with banditry. Peace and stability had caused an explosion of population, but with no industry or trade of sufficient scope to absorb the surplus, there was widespread rural discontent and urban pauperism, aided by weakening of the Manchu bureaucratic and military systems through corruption. These problems were compounded by natural calamities of unprecedented proportions, including droughts, famines, and floods. These disasters were caused in part by misgovernment and neglect of public works. This was especially the case in southern China, the last area to yield to the Qing conquerors and the first place to be exposed to Western influence. It was the site of the most famous rebellion in Chinese history—the Taiping Rebellion, led by a misguided former Protestant convert, Hong Xiuquan, who proclaimed himself the Heavenly King of the Heavenly Kingdom of Great Peace in 1851. Over 25 million people were killed before the rebellion was finally crushed in 1864.

As the empire reeled under this revolt, the Western powers trying to get a foothold grew bolder. First the Portuguese gained Macao, where they monopolized the foreign trade at Guangzhou (Canton). Soon the "Celestial Empire" was humiliated by Great Britain in the Opium War (1839–42), provoked by illegal British trade in opium, which was prohibited by imperial decree. When the Chinese government confiscated and burned 20,000 chests of opium, the British retaliated with a punitive expedition in which the imperial army was disastrously defeated. The resulting Treaty of Nanjing (Nanking; 1842) was the first of a series of agreements with Western trading nations that the Chinese call "unequal treaties." Under its terms, the Chinese ceded Hong Kong, abolished the licensed monopoly system of trade, opened five ports to foreign trade, limited the tariff on trade to 5 percent ad valorem, granted British nationals extraterritoriality, and paid a large indemnity.

The treaty triggered a scramble among Western powers to carve up the vast empire. In the 1850s the Russians invaded the Amur watershed of Manchuria in violation of the Treaty of Nerchinsk (1689) and in 1860 forced the emperor to grant them all of Manchuria north of the Amur River and east of the Ussuri River. Foreign encroachments intensified after 1860 through a series of treaties imposed on China under one pretext or another. The catalog of concessions lengthened, and the foreign stranglehold on the economy deepened. The treaty ports became virtually foreign enclaves.

The official response of the tottering Manchu court to these humiliations was a series of half-hearted reforms designed to avert further decline. The first phase of the reforms was championed in the 1860s by such generals as Zeng Huofan (Tseng Kuo-fan), Zuo Zongtang (Chuo Chung-t'ang), and Li Hong Zhang (Li Hung-Chang). It attempted to reform the bureaucracy, modernize the army, expand public education, build railroads, telegraph lines, and new harbors, and create an industrial base. These efforts petered out, sabotaged by the Confucian bureaucrats, who saw in them only a threat to their own entrenched powers.

As the reforms failed to take hold, the foreign powers continued to dismember the empire. France, victorious in a war with China in 1883, took Annam; the British took Burma; Russia took Turkestan; and Japan, emerging from its centuries-long seclusion, took Taiwan, Korea, and the Liuqiu (Liu-Ch'iu; Ryukyu) Islands. In 1898 the British acquired a 99-year lease over the New Territories of Kowloon.

In 1898 the second phase of the reform movement was even briefer than the first; it lasted for just 102 days, from June 11 to September 21. Like the first, it was a self-strengthening movement, aimed at sweeping social and institutional changes. Opposition to the reform was intense among the Manchu ruling elite. Supported by the ultraconservatives, Empress Dowager Cixi (Tz'u-hsi) engineered a coup forcing young, reform-minded Emperor Guangxu (Khuang-hsu) into seclusion and took over the government as regent. The reform ended with the execution of six of its principal advocates and the flight of two to Japan.

The ultraconservatives then retaliated by backing an antiforeign and anti-Christian organization known to the West as the Boxers. In 1900 this group rampaged northern China in what became known as the Boxer Rebellion.

The uprising was crushed by the expeditionary forces of the foreign powers, and under the Boxer Protocol of 1901 the court was forced to pay the Western powers a large indemnity and consent to the stationing of foreign troops on Chinese soil.

The failure of the reform and the fiasco of the Boxer Rebellion set the stage for the Republican Revolution of 1911. The leader of the revolutionaries was Sun Zhongshan (Sun Yat-sen, 1866–1925), who as an exile in Japan had founded in 1905 the Tong Meng Hui (the United League or Brotherhood Society), a forerunner of the Guomindang (Kuomintang or KMT, the Nationalist Party). His followers included overseas Chinese and also military officers, among them a young cadet named Chiang Kai-shek. Sun's political philosophy centered on Three Principles of the People: nationalism, democracy, and socialism.

The Manchu dynasty fell on October 10, 1911, after having been in power for 267 years. Its anticlimactic exit was the result not of a massive popular uprising but of a minor mutiny by the imperial garrison at Wuchang, where 3,000 soldiers rose in revolt. The city fell without resistance, and the relatively bloodless revolution spread quickly. Sun was inaugurated on January 1, 1912, in Nanjing as the provisional president of the new Chinese Republic. But power in Beijing had already passed to Yuan Shikai (Yuan Shih-k'ai), the strongest warlord and commander in chief of the imperial army. To prevent possible bloodshed, Sun agreed to a united national government in Beijing under Yuan Shikai. On February 12, 1912, the last Manchu emperor, Puyi, abdicated, and on March 12 Yuan Shikai was inaugurated as provisional president of the republic.

Within two years Yuan Shikai became a virtual dictator by arranging the assassination of his political opponents and forcing Sun to flee to Japan. Yuan Shikai suspended parliament (in which the Guomindang had a majority of seats) and proceeded to establish a monarchy, and when that attempt failed, proclaimed himself president for life in 1915. He died a year later.

Yuan Shikai's death was followed by a scramble among the regional warlords for control of the Beijing government. In addition to internal chaos, the nation was threatened from without by Japan, who claimed Shandong and also sought to establish its protectorate over all of China through the so-called Twenty-one Demands. In 1917, the Beijing government conceded in a secret deal the Japanese claim to Shandong. When this sellout became public, there were massive student protest demonstrations, culminating in a national movement known as the May Fourth Movement or, in intellectual circles, as the New Culture Movement, which helped rekindle the fading cause of the republican revolution. In October 1919 Sun Zhongshan, who in 1917 had set up a rival government in Guangzhou in collaboration with southern warlords, reestablished the Guomindang. In 1922, a new alliance was forged under Soviet auspices between the Guomindang and the Chinese Communist Party (CCP), founded in 1921. Chiang Kai-shek (Jiang Jieshi), who became Sun's successor as Guomindang leader on his death in 1925, staged a coup in 1926, ousting the left-wing CCP elements in the party, but the Soviets nevertheless continued to support him. By 1928, Chiang was in control of most of China, receiving prompt international recognition as head of the sole legitimate government of China. The decade of 1928 to 1937 was an era of consolidation and accomplishment by the Nationalists.

But even as the nation was beginning to experience a strong, stable central government for the first time in a century, two forces were at work that would eventually undermine Chiang's regime: the rise of the CCP and Japanese aggression.

By mid-1927 CCP fortunes were at their lowest ebb in a decade. The CCP gave up its former policy of passivity and cooperation with Chiang in favor of armed insurrection in both urban and rural areas. Without waiting for the sanction of the CCP Center, then in Shanghai, a former librarian of Beijing University, Mao Zedong (Mao Tse-tung) began to establish peasant-based soviets along the border between Hunan and Jiangxi (Kiangsi) Province. By the winter of 1927–28, Mao's People's Liberation Army (PLA) had some 10,000 men. By 1932 Mao's control of the CCP was complete. Surviving a series of encirclement and extermination attacks mounted by the Guomindang forces, Mao, along with 100,000 to 190,000 supporters, began his epic retreat, celebrated in communist legend as the Long March, for some 10,000 km (6,215 mi) through southwestern China to the northern province of Shanxi (Shensi), where some 20,000 survivors arrived in 1935. The Communists then set up their headquarters in Yan'an, in southern Shanxi. The Yan'an era (1936–45) was one of rapid growth for the CCP, owing to a combination of internal and external circumstances, of which World War II was the most significant.

The Japanese had initiated a policy of conquering China piecemeal as early as 1917, and had pursued that policy relentlessly by seizing Manchuria in 1931 and then pushing down over the Great Wall into northern China and along the coastal provinces. In the first half of the 1930s the Guomindang was more preoccupied with campaigns to exterminate the Communists than resisting the Japanese invaders. Open hostilities between the two governments began only on July 7, 1937, when a clash, carefully engineered by the Japanese, occurred between Chinese troops and the invaders at the Marco Polo Bridge near Beijing. The Guomindang and the CCP patched up their differences to face the common enemy, but the uneasy alliance crumbled after 1938. By 1940 the Japanese controlled most of coastal and northern China and the rich Yangzi River valley. The Guomindang government moved its capital to Chongqing (Ch'ung-ch'ing). However, the Guomindang reverses greatly benefited Mao. The

Communists increased their party membership from 100,000 in 1937 to 1.2 million by 1945. The PLA troops became skilled guerrilla fighters able to wear down the enemy by alternating offensive and defensive actions.

China emerged from the war greatly enfeebled, economically prostrate, and politically divided. Despite massive economic aid from the United States, the economy was shattered by inflation and sabotaged by the Communists. Famines and floods left millions homeless and destitute. The civil war between the Communists and the Guomindang began in earnest within a year of the end of war. In 1947 the U.S. mission, headed by George C. Marshall, was withdrawn from Beijing as the United States decided not to intervene militarily in the conflict. Thereafter the Guomindang collapse was swift. In 1949 the PLA entered Beijing without a fight, and within months all the major cities passed into Communist hands. In December 1949 Chiang, with a few hundred thousand of his troops, fled from the mainland to Taiwan, proclaiming T'aipei as the capital of his republic.

The People's Republic of China was proclaimed on October 1, 1949, with its capital at Beijing. A year later, China entered the Korean War and pushed back the UN and U.S. troops to the South Korean border. It was the first successful military operation of the new republic. In 1950 China invaded Tibet, which had asserted its independence after the overthrow of the Manchus. Along the coast of Fujian (Fukien) province hostilities continued between the PRC and the Nationalists. In the early 1960s the Chinese fought intermittently with India over territorial claims along the Himalayas region. Growing discord between China and the Soviet Union continued throughout the 1960s and early 1970s and the two powers competed for support among the world's communist parties. Hostilities flared briefly along the Ussuri River.

In domestic affairs, a rapid program of industrialization and socialization was followed in 1958–59 by the Great Leap Forward, a crash program of collectivization. The program ended in three bitter years of economic crisis in 1960–62. Mao tried again to steer the country into a revolutionary path with the Cultural Revolution, 1966–69, the most convulsive period in modern Chinese history. In 1967 the Red Army intervened on the side of Mao and CCP and government organs were replaced by revolutionary committees and the Red Guard. Liu Shaoqi (Liu Shao-ch'i) in the Chinese hierarchy was dismissed from his position as chairman of the People's Republic and it was claimed that he died in suspicious circumstances in a plane crash while trying to flee to the Soviet Union.

The first half of the 1970s witnessed dramatic shifts in the course of Chinese diplomacy, particularly after it ousted Nationalist China at the United Nations in 1971. Henry Kissinger and then U.S. president Richard Nixon journeyed to Beijing as the first step toward normalization of relations between the two countries after a hiatus of 23 years.

The death of Mao and Prime Minister Zhou Enlai (Chou En-lai) in 1976 was followed by a power struggle in which the Maoists were dislodged by the moderates led by Deng Xiaoping (Teng Hsiao-Ping). During the next decade Deng consolidated his hold over the party and government by naming his allies to key posts in the CCP. Along with personnel changes, there was a sweeping reform in agricultural and economic policies, euphemistically termed rectification and consolidation. The Maoist commune system was nullified and family farms were restored. Leftist factionalism among party cadres was eliminated and an unprecedented program to reform the economic structure called for the adoption of many features of a "capitalistic" market system. These liberalization moves were set back in 1989 by a massive student demonstration in Tiananmen Square in Beijing in which several protesters died. This incident was followed by a hardening of the ideological positions within the CCP. At the 14th Party Congress in 1992 Jiang Zemin (Chiang Tse-min) was named as PRC president and as the successor to the ailing Deng. Deng himself died in 1997, but no major policy changes ensued, partly because the succession issue had long been settled. In the same year, Hong Kong was returned to China by the British government. In 1999, Macau was returned to China by Portugal. China agreed to trade reforms designed to open its economy to international competition and investment. In recognition of these reforms, China was admitted to the World Trade Organization on December 11, 2001.

CONSTITUTION

The People's Republic of China was established on October 1, 1949. For the first five years of its existence it had no constitution since, according to the regime, the revolution had not been consummated and the economy had not been completely socialized. In the place of a constitution, the state was governed by the Organic Law of the People's Political Consultative Conference. Both documents reflected Mao's ideas on "new democracy," which was a people's democratic dictatorship, a contradiction in terms that was justified as appropriate for a transition from a semifeudal and semi colonial stage to socialism. The first constitution was promulgated in 1954, and it was followed by three others, in 1975, 1978, and 1982.

The constitution of 1982, still in effect in 2001, is essentially a Deng constitution. It often is compared rather than contrasted with the constitution of 1954. The longest of the four constitutions, with 138 articles, it is more structural than programmatic, marking a radical departure from the heavily political preoccupations of its predecessors. The presidency was restored. China is defined as a "socialist state under people's democratic dictatorship." No reference is made to the preeminent role of the Communist Party, although it states that the state is "led by the

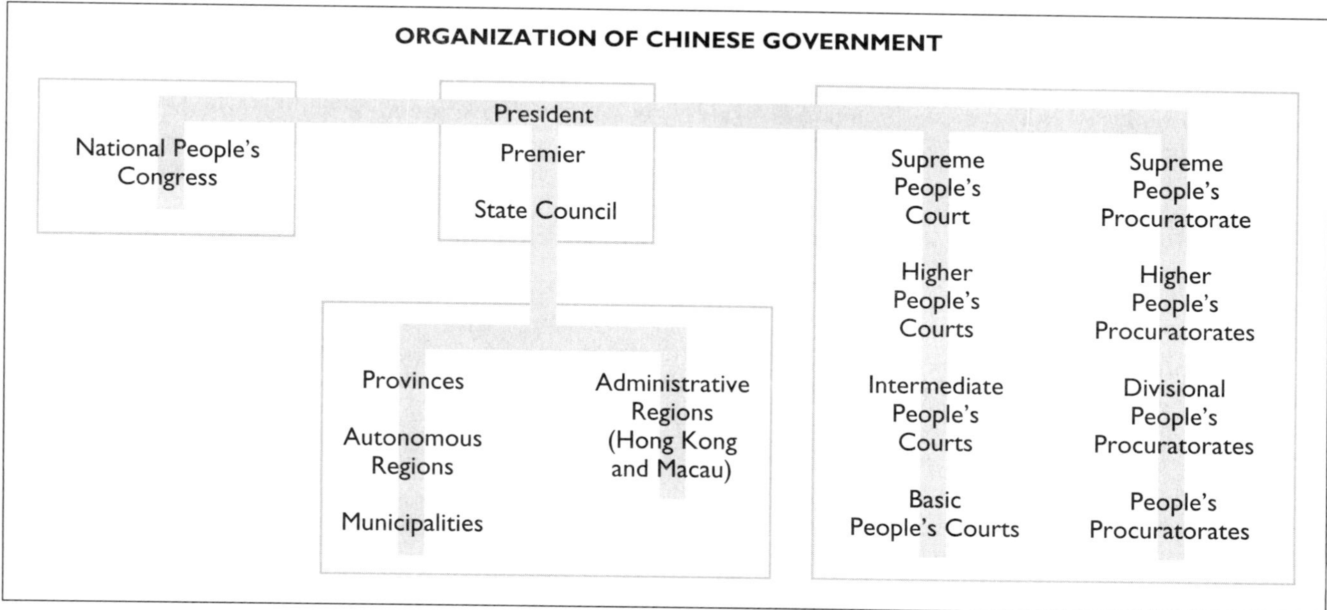

working class." Moreover, Article 5 states, "All state organs, the armed forces, all political parties and public organizations . . . must abide by the Constitution and the law." All civil liberties were restored, with the significant exception of the right to strike. The new constitution also reflects the post-Mao state by diminishing the political and governmental role of the people's communes by transferring their power to the townships.

Of the state organs specified in the constitution, the weakest is the presidency, which is largely ceremonial. The president is the head of state. The really efficient part of national government is the State Council (Guo Wu Yuan), which, according to the constitution, is the executive body of the National People's Congress and the "highest organ of state administration." It is chaired by the premier, nominated by the Central Committee, and approved by the National People's Congress, and it includes a number of vice premiers, ministers in charge of ministries, and ministers heading commissions. The premier of the State Council is the head of government. The functions of the State Council are defined as exercising "unified leadership" over the entire administration, including local governments. Most if not all of the ministries, commissions, bureaus, and agencies attached to the State Council are represented in some or all provincial-level administrative units and in some cases county- and commune-level units.

Although the functions and powers of the State Council are exceptionally broad, policy is largely determined by the Central Committee and Political Bureau, to both of which it is closely linked by concurrent memberships. This linkage facilitates the party's control over the state but at the same time obliterates the distinction between party and government.

The membership of the State Council has varied over the years, but the general trend has been toward a high degree of compartmentalization of jurisdictions, a top-heavy hierarchical structure, and a multiplication of units. The council is divided into ministries, commissions, bureaus, agencies, and departments. With the growing number of units it has become necessary to create intermediate offices between the state council and these units. Known as staff offices, they have supervisory responsibility over a group of related units. According to a high-ranking party leader, from 1950 to 1981 the number of ministries and commissions grew from 34 to 100, the number of ministries and deputy ministries to 1,000, and departments to 5,000. Under Deng this number was cut back but still remains unwieldy.

The State Council rarely meets as a whole. The long-standing practice is for major decisions to be made by an inner cabinet known as the Standing Conference of the State Council (Kuo-wu-yuan ch'ang'wu hui-yi), which generally consists of 15 members, including the premier and four vice premiers.

Directly attached to the State Council is the General Office, which appears to be a housekeeping organ corresponding to the Secretariat of the Central Committee. In addition, a number of specialized offices, subordinate directly to the State Council, deal with diverse matters such as science, environmental protection, and family planning.

LOCAL GOVERNMENT

On the whole, the communist regime has adopted without substantial change the previous local government divisions. Except for territorial adjustments, most of the provinces, municipalities, and counties remain as they were before 1949. There are, however, two important innovations: the organization of the people's communes on or below the county level; and the establishment of minority nationality areas, consisting of autonomous regions, districts, and counties.

The present system of local government is described in the constitution of 1982 and in local government laws. Article 30 of the constitution provides for the administrative division of the country into provinces, autonomous regions, and municipalities directly under the central government; provinces and autonomous regions into prefectures, counties, and cities; and counties into townships, nationality townships, and towns.

The 29 administrative units on the provincial level include 21 provinces (*sheng*); the three municipalities (centrally administered cities) (*chih-hsia-shih*) of Shanghai, Beijing, and Tianjin; and the five autonomous regions (*tzu-chih-ch'u*) of Xinjiang Uygur, Xizang, Ning-xia Hui, Guangxi Zhuang, and Nei Menggu, the home of the Uighurs, Tibetans, Hui, Zhuang, and Mongols, respectively.

Between the provincial and the *hsien* (county) levels, administrative entities without congresses have been established. There are 208 of these units: one administrative area (*hsing-cheng-ch'u*) on Hainan Island, eight leagues (*meng*) in Inner Mongolia, 29 autonomous areas (*tzu-chih-chou*), and 170 areas (*ti-chu'u*).

On the local administrative level there are 2,772 units, including three autonomous banners (*tzu-chih-ch'i*), 53 banners (*ch'i*), 71 autonomous *hsien* (*tzu-chih-hsien*), 431 city districts (*ch'u*), 214 provincially or area-administered cities (*shih*), and 2,000 regular *hsien*. On this level as well as on the *hsiang* (township) level, the party wields tight control.

The structure of local government is based on that of the national government. As presently constituted, the local people's congresses suffer from the same problems as the National People's Congress. The number of deputies is too large, ranging up to 1,000 and the standing committees also are large, with an average membership of 50 to 60, most of them far advanced in age. Local government organs are fifth wheels without any real power and hence burdened with a sense of superfluity. "The party has already made its decisions. Why should we go through the motions of debating them?" is a common complaint at local assemblies.

A noteworthy development, which took place in 1980–81, is the direct election by rural residents of deputies to county people's congresses. Before that only deputies to township (or commune) people's congresses were directly elected, and township deputies, in turn, elected deputies to county people's congresses from their own members. Although hailed as a measure to enhance democratic processes at the county level, these elections, like the others, are orchestrated by local Communist Party branches, with predictable results.

Official efforts to improve governmental performance at the local level have included strengthening standing committees of local people's congresses at and above the county level; institution of multiple candidacies in elections to local people's congresses; and reactivation of "basic-level mass autonomous organizations" such as urban neighborhood committees, people's mediation committees, and public security committees.

Local Government

Principal administrative divisions, capitals, area, population

Area and population

Provinces	Capitals	area sq mi	area sq km	population 1997 estimate
Anhwel (Anhui)	Ho-fei (Hefei)	54,000	139,900	61,270,000
Cheklang (Zhejiang)	Hang-chou (Hangzhou)	39,300	101,800	44,350,000
Fukien (Fujian)	Fu-chou (Fuzhou)	47,500	123,100	32,820,000
Hainan (Hainan)	Hai-k'ou (Haikou)	13,200	34,300	7,430,000
Heilungklang (Heilongjiang)	Harbin	179,000	463,600	37,510,000
Honan (Henan)	Cheng-chou (Zhengzhou)	64,500	167,000	92,430,000
Hopeh (Hebei)	Shih-chia-chuang (Shijiazhuang)	78,200	202,700	65,250,000
Hunan (Hunan)	Ch'ang-sha (Changsha)	81,300	210,500	64,650,000
Hupeh (Hubei)	Wu-han (Wuhan)	72,400	187,500	58,730,000
Kansu (Gansu)	Lan-chou (Lanzhou)	141,500	366,500	24,940,000
Kiangsi (Jiangxi)	Nan-ch'ang (Nanchang)	63,600	164,800	41,500,000
Kiangsu (Jiangsu)	Nanking (Nanjing)	39,600	102,600	71,480,00084
Kirin (Jilin)	Ch'ang-ch'un (Changchun)	72,200	187,000	26,280,000
Kwangtung (Guangdong)	Canton (Guangzhou)	76,100	197,100	70,510,000
Kweichow (Guizhou)	Kuei-yang (Guiyang)	67,200	174,000	36,060,000
Liaoning	Shen-yang (Shenyang)	58,300	151,000	41,380,000
Shansi (Shanxi)	Tai-yuan (Taiyuan)	60,700	157,100,	31,410,000
Shantung (Shandong)	Chi-nan (Jinan)	59,200	153,300	87,850,000
Shensi (Shaanxi)	Sian (Xi'an)	75,600	195,800	35,700,000
Szechwan (Sichuan)	Ch'eng-tu (Chengdu)	210,800	546,000	84,300,000
Tsinghai (Qinghai)	Hsi-ning (Xining)	278,400	721,000	4,960,000
Yunnan	K'un-ming (Kunming)	168,400	436,200	40,940,000
Autonomous regions				
Inner Mongolia (Nei Monggol)	Hu-ho-hao-t'e (Hohhot)	454,600	1,177,500	23,260,000
Kwangsi Chuang (Guangxi Zhuang)	Nan-ning (Nanning)	85,100	220,400	46,330,000
Ningsia Hui (Ningxia Hui)	Yin-ch'uan (Yinchuan)	25,600	66,400	5,300,000

Sinkiang Ulghur (Xinjiang Uygur)	Wu-lu-mu-chi (Urumqi)	635,900	1,646,900	17,180,000
Tibet (Xizang)	Lhasa	471,700	1,221,600	2,480,000
Municipalities				
Chungking (Chongqing)	—	8,900	23,000	30,420,000
Peking (Beijing)	—	6,500	16,800	12,400,000
Shanghai	—	2,400	6,200	14,570,000
Tientsin (Tianjin)	—	4,400	11,300	9,530,000
TOTAL		3,696,100	9,572,900	1,236,260,000

PARLIAMENT

The National People's Congress (NPC) is defined in the constitution of 1982 as "the highest organ of state power," without being identified, as in the constitution of 1975, as "under the leadership of the Communist Party of China." Among its 15 powers enumerated in Article 62 are amending the constitution; supervising enforcement of the constitution and the law; deciding on the choice of premier (on the recommendation of the CCP Central Committee); electing or removing the president of the Supreme People's Court and the chief procurator of the Supreme People's Procuratorate; examining and approving the national economic plan, the state budget, and the final state accounts; deciding on questions of war and peace; and approving administrative boundaries.

The NPC holds one session a year. Its deputies are elected by secret ballot for a term of five years by the people's congresses at the provincial-level administrative divisions. The provincial-level delegates themselves are indirectly elected. In 1997 the NPC had 2,977 members. Members of the National Committee of the Chinese People's Political Consultative Conference (CPPCC), a revolutionary united front organization led by the Communist Party, may be invited to attend the NPC as observers.

POLITICAL PARTIES

With a membership of 45 million—exceeding the population of all but 22 countries in the world—the Chinese Communist Party (CCP) is the largest political party in the world. It is the pivot of the Chinese political system, eclipsing even the government, and despite the debacle of the Cultural Revolution appears to be more firmly entrenched than at any time since 1949.

Despite apparent structural similarities with communist parties in other countries, the CCP is unique in several respects. First, the distinction between party and state is considerably blurred to the point where the two systems are identical. The post-Mao leadership has attempted with some success to re-create the distinction between party and state, but so pervasive is the party's power that the latter appears only as a shadow of the former. Another important distinction is the role of the military in the political system, a role that had been reduced in the Soviet Union to a purely professional one. At the top in China, many leaders hold concurrent civilian and military posts; the military also plays a large part in CCP activities at all subnational levels.

Political Parties

China Association for Promoting Democracy, 1945
China Democratic League, 1941
China Democratic National Construction Association, 1945
China Party for Public Interests
Chinese Peasants' and Workers' Democratic Party, 1947
Revolutionary Committee of the Kuomintang, 1948
September 3, 1945 Society
Taiwan Democratic Self-Government League, 1947

Political Parties: Strength in Parliament Most Recent Elections

The first session of the Eighth Congress (to which 2,977 deputies had been elected in early 1993) was held at Beijing on March 15–31, 1993. The first session of the Ninth Congress was held on March 5–19, 1998.

LEGAL SYSTEM

The State Constitution of 1982 and the Organic Law of the People's Courts provide for a four-tier court system. At the apex is the Supreme People's Court, which is not only the highest appellate forum of the land but also the supervisor of the administration of justice by subordinate courts. Local people's courts—the courts of first instance—handle civil and criminal cases. They consist of (1) higher people's courts at the level of provinces, autonomous regions, and municipalities directly under the central government; (2) intermediate people's courts at the level of prefectures; autonomous prefectures; and municipalities under the central government, provinces, or autonomous regions; and (3) basic people's courts at the level of autonomous counties, towns, and municipal districts. Special courts adjudicate military, railway transportation, water transportation, forest, and economic cases. The president and judges of the Supreme People's Court are elected by the National People's Congress and serve no more than two consecutive five-year terms. Local people's courts are similarly elected by the local state organs at their level.

China is perhaps the only major society without a written criminal or civil code. Although there are selected statutes, there is no comprehensive code. Law plays the dual role of resolving disputes between people and suppressing "enemies of the people." The definition of "enemies" varies with the times but has always included rightists, counterrevolutionaries, "bad elements," and revisionists. Although the constitution guarantees the independence of the judiciary, such independence is only a political fiction, and interference by party organs in judicial organs is common. The conception of equality before the law is seen as violating the Marxist theory of class struggle.

The court system is complemented by a structure of people's procuratorates, from the Supreme People's Procuratorate at the top to lower procuratorates established at the corresponding levels of the courts. The procuratorates represent the state in criminal proceedings and ensure that the judicial process of the courts and the execution of judgments and orders in criminal matters conform to the law.

Prisons were separated from the Ministry of Public Security and placed under the Ministry of Justice in 1983. The majority of the prisoners are sentenced to hard labor, of which there are two kinds: criminal and administrative. The former is for a fixed number of years, whereas the latter is for an indeterminate period, but usually three or four years. Both categories may be found at state farms, mines, and factory prisons. Prisoners are required to work eight hours a day, six days a week. They are forbidden to read anything not provided by the prison; to speak dialects not understood by the guards; or to keep cash, gold, or jewelry. Mail is censored, and generally only one visitor is allowed per month. Sentences may be reduced for up to half the original sentence, but at least 10 years of a life sentence have to be served. Both probation and parole are granted when certain conditions are met.

No detailed information is available on the criminal justice system.

LAW ENFORCEMENT

Law Enforcement

Offenses reported to the police per 100,000: 128
- Murder: 0.2
- Assault: 5.2
- Burglary: 45.2
- Automobile Theft: 6.9
- Population per Police officer: 1,360

Death Penalty: Yes

HUMAN RIGHTS

The major event affecting human rights in China since 1949 was the bloodbath in Tiananmen Square in Beijing in early 1989, which set the country back some 20 years in its evolution toward a less totalitarian government. The power struggle that preceded and followed this event has witnessed a leftward and more doctrinaire shift at the very apex of the power structure. The gradual relaxation of the political atmosphere that began with the ascent of Deng in the early 1980s has consequently slowed, and some of the gains made in this period have been lost.

This setback illustrates the fundamental weakness in China's so-called political modernization program. There is an entrenched intolerance of any criticism of the CCP and its aging leadership. Change can only be initiated at the top and then trickle down to the bottom rather than vice versa. The rigidity of institutional structures is as old as Chinese society, and it has been reinforced by the harshness of Marxist dogma.

The Code of Criminal Procedure specifically prohibits the use of torture. In 1986 China signed the UN Convention Against Torture and Other Cruel, Inhuman or Degrading Treatment, and the National People's Congress ratified the convention in 1988. But news reports of the use of torture by officials persist.

The law notwithstanding, persons accused of political crimes are often held for periods much longer than those sanctioned by the code. The provision requiring immediate notification of families or work units also is frequently ignored, and suspects are held incommunicado for long periods.

Under "labor education" provisions, those who commit minor theft or fraud or who have been expelled from their work units may be deprived of their civil liberties and subjected to one to four years of reform without trial. "Reform through labor" is a more severe sentence, similar to Soviet "internal exile" and imposed on those accused of more serious crimes.

The regime denies that there are any political prisoners, but this is only a semantic subterfuge, since "counterrevolutionaries" are classified as common criminals. Counterrevolutionary activity is defined as "inciting the overthrow of the socialist system." The total prison population is estimated at 2 million to 5 million, and of this total 1 percent to 3 percent are political prisoners according to Western standards.

Contacts between Chinese and foreigners had become free of official interference until the Tiananmen Square demonstrations brought a deterioration in the political climate. "English corners" where Chinese and foreigners can meet to talk in English attract large numbers of people.

The Code of Criminal Procedure allows officials wide latitude in emergency situations to enter and search living premises without warrants or notifications, use electronic eavesdropping, and seize mail or telegrams, although these powers are used sparingly.

After the excesses of the Cultural Revolution, freedom of religion was one of the major freedoms to be resuscitated. Although atheism is part of the official ideology, its enforcement and propagation have met with much resistance in a culture historically permeated with religious mores. The only major requirement is that religious bodies must not be subject to foreign domination, a proviso often used against Buddhism in Tibet and against the Catholic Church. Religious freedom, however, still is not a right, but a gift of the state, and it may be withdrawn at any time. The regime does not tolerate unsanctioned religious activity, defined as "counterrevolutionary sabotage perpetrated in the name of religion." In 1983 the death penalty was authorized for secret sects that spread "feudal and superstitious ideas," a broad rubric aimed at curbing any kind of religious zeal. Since the late 1990s, persecution of Fulan Gong, an indigenous religious sect, has intensified, leading to the incarceration of thousands of its followers.

Travel within China is restricted through various formal and informal regulations. Chinese citizens may not freely change their locality of residence or workplace. They are registered as residents of a particular jurisdiction, and permission to move to another locality is granted only for a change in employment. Because of the unwillingness of work units to lose employees, such permission is rarely granted.

Controls on foreign travel and emigration have been relaxed since the 1970s and further liberalized under the Citizens' Exit and Entry Control Law of 1985, which went into effect in 1986. The law authorizes exit for personal reasons but denies exit to those in criminal or civil cases or those whose exit may harm China's national security interests. Permission to travel may also be denied to the more vocal critics of the regime and to known dissidents. Restrictions on internal travel by foreigners also have been relaxed.

FOREIGN POLICY

Chinese foreign policy history exhibits a number of dichotomies and contradictions. China is a superpower without formal superpower status, it is a socialist country that does not belong to the socialist camp, and it is a developing country that does not belong to the third world proper. Reflecting the factional struggles within the party inner leadership, the policy also suffers from sudden shifts and breaks, as a result of which it lacks the consistency, coherence, and predictability of the foreign policies of other major powers. Such fluctuations reflect the fact that China has no urgent goals to achieve in foreign affairs, and foreign policy is merely an extension of internal political developments.

Chinese foreign policy thus is a product of three decades of trial and error, more failure than success perhaps, but nevertheless remarkable for snatching stability from the jaws of chaos. By 1990 Chinese foreign policy had reached a new threshold of maturity, flexibility, balance, and moderation. For the first time China was able to deal on a normal basis with both superpowers and had learned the art and wisdom of isolating troublesome issues and irritations so they did not impede the major thrust of policy. Given the historical ambivalence of China about the external world, this is a major achievement.

Relations between China and the United States deteriorated sharply in the late 1990s. The major irritants were the alleged Chinese efforts to influence U.S. presidential elections and attempts to obtain U.S. nuclear secrets. The incoming Bush administration was faced with a crisis when a U.S. spy plane was forced to land on Hainan Island after a midair collision with a Chinese fighter plane. The crew of the spy plane was detained for 11 days before release, and the two nations were embroiled in mutual recriminations following the reluctance of Chinese authorities to permit the return of the plane.

DEFENSE

The Chinese Communist Party came to power not through an election or revolution but through the successful military mission of the People's Liberation Army (PLA). The PLA is the world's largest standing army and has the world's third-largest air and naval forces. It provides China with a credible conventional defense-in-depth on land, at sea, and in the air but lacks offensive capability more than a short distance beyond its borders and is vulnerable to nuclear, biological, and chemical attack, as was the case particularly during the cold war period from its superior neighbor the Soviet Union. The small but effective nuclear deterrent is based on the policy of "no first use."

Deterrence is enhanced by a huge and well-organized population that can be mobilized at short notice. Coastal defense consists of successive rings of submarines, missile destroyers, and frigates supported by smaller missiles and torpedo boats. There are no military bases in foreign countries. The air force is strong in numbers but weak in equipment.

The PLA is organized as the armed forces of the party and remains under CCP control. The Common Program, the precursor of the constitution, placed control of the armed forces in the hands of the 22-member People's Revolutionary Military Council. Later constitutions confirmed this precedent, and the State Constitution of 1978 designated the party chairman as commander in chief of the armed forces. Until his resignation in 1989 Deng, although the virtual leader of the party, had no other official position than as chairman of the Military Affairs Committee. The chairmanship is currently vacant.

Military Indicators

Total Active Duty Personnel: 2,840,000
Military Manpower per 1,000: 2.3
Military Expenditures $million: 63,510
  as % of GNP: 2.3
  per capita $: 53
  as % of central government expenditures: 18.5

Arms Imports $million: 725
Arms Exports $million: 625

ECONOMY

Beginning in late 1978, the Chinese leadership has been trying to move from a sluggish Soviet-style centrally planned economy to a more market-oriented economy, but still within a rigid political framework of Communist Party control. To this end the authorities switched to a system of household responsibility in agriculture in place of the old collectivization, increased the authority of local officials and plant managers in industry, permitted a wide variety of small-scale enterprise in services and light manufacturing, and opened the economy to increased foreign trade and investment. The result has been a quadrupling of gross domestic product (GDP) since 1978. On the darker side, the leadership has often experienced in its hybrid system the worst results of socialism (bureaucracy, lassitude, corruption) and of capitalism (windfall gains and stepped-up inflation). Beijing thus has periodically backtracked, retightening central controls at intervals.

Popular resistance, changes in central policy, and loss of authority by rural cadres have weakened China's population control program, which is essential to maintaining growth in living standards. Another long-term threat to continued rapid economic growth is the deterioration in the environment, notably air pollution, soil erosion, and the steady fall of the water table especially in the north. China continues to lose arable land because of erosion and economic development; furthermore, the regime gives insufficient priority to agricultural research. The next few years may witness increasing tensions between a highly centralized political system and an increasingly decentralized economic system. Rapid economic growth likely will continue but at a declining rate. Hong Kong's reversion on July 1, 1997, to Chinese administration strengthened the already close ties between the two economies. China became the 143rd member of the World Trade Organization on December 11, 2001.

Principal Economic Indicators

Gross National Product $: 1,055.372 billion
GNP per capita $: 860
GNP Average Annual Growth Rate (1990–97) %: 10.0
GNP per capita Average Annual Growth Rate (1990–97) %: 8.9
Origin of Gross Domestic Product %
- Agriculture: 21
- Mining: —
- Manufacturing: 41
- Construction: 6
- Public Utilities: —
- Transportation and Communications: 6
- Trade: 9
- Financial Services: 17
- Other Services: 17
- Government: 17

Gross Domestic Product by Type of Expenditure %
- Private Consumption: 51
- Government Consumption: 9
- Gross Domestic Investment: 41

Foreign Trade: Exports: 24
Imports: −25
% of Income Received by Poorest 20%: 5.5
% of Income Received by Richest 10%: 30.9

Price and earnings indexes (1995 = 100)

	1992	1993	1994	1995	1996	1997	1998
Consumer price index	58.8	68.8	85.6	100.0	108.3	111.3	110.5
Monthly earnings index	126.7	157.5	212.1	257.0	290.2	—	—

Finance

National Currency: Yuan (¥)
Exchange Rate: $1 = ¥ 8.2796
Money Supply Stock in National Currency billion: 3,066.3
M1 per capita: 2,510
Central Bank Discount Rate %: 3.24
Total External Debt $million: 112,821
Debt Service Ratio %: 7.8
Balance of Payments $million: 29,718
International Reserves SDRs million: 88,926
Ratio of External Debt to Total Reserves: 1.2
Average Annual Rate of Inflation/Consumer Price Index Growth Rate %: 2.8

Official Development Assistance

ODA $million: 2,359
- as % of GNP: 0.3
- per capita $ 2.0
- Foreign Direct Investment $million: 43,751

Central Government Revenues and Expenditures

Fiscal Year: Calendar Year
Revenues $million: —
Expenditures $million: —
Budget Deficit $million: —
Tax Revenues as % of GDP: 5.7
Highest Tax Bracket %
- Individual: 45
- Corporate: 30

Employment and Labor

Economically Active Population: 657,290,000
Female Participation Rate %: 44.9
Activity Rate %: 57.9
Labor by Sector: %
- Agriculture, Forestry, Fishing: 71.2
- Manufacturing, Mining: 13.3
- Construction: 1.8
- Transportation and Communications: 1.8
- Trade, Hotels, and Restaurants: 3.9
- Finance, Insurance, Real Estate: 1.3
- Public Administration, Defense: —
- Services: 5.2

Unemployment %: 10

Agriculture

Agriculture's Share of GDP %: 21
Average Annual Rate of Growth (1965–98) %: 4.1
Number of Farms 000: 1,650
Average Size of Farm ha: —

Number of Tractors per 1,000 hectares: 7.7
Irrigation, % of Farms having: 53
Artificial Fertilizer kg/hectare: 261
Total Farmland as % of land area: 17.4
Livestock: Cattle 000: 96,193
Sheep 000: 118,152
Hogs 000: 485,898
Chickens 000: 3,010,535
Forests: Production of Roundwood (000 cubic meters): 300,360
Fisheries: Total Catch tons 000: 20,718.9

Mining

% of GDP: 2.7
Value of Mineral Production $million: 9,885.2

Manufacturing

Value Added $million: 146,612
Industrial Production Growth Rate %: 13.0

Energy

Commercial Energy Production metric tons of oil equivalent 000: 1,097,210
Commercial Energy Consumption metric tons of oil equivalent 000: 1,113,050
Commercial Energy Consumption per capita kg: 907
Average Annual Growth Rate 1980–97 %: 2.6
Net Energy Imports % of use: 1
Electricity Installed Capacity kW 000: 204,100
Production kW-hr million: 1,007,726
Coal Reserves tons million: 114,500
Production tons 000: 1,360,730
Natural Gas Proven Reserves cubic meters billion: 1,171
Production cubic meters million: 17,300
Crude Petroleum Reserves barrels million: 24,000
Production barrels million: 1,141
Consumption barrels million: 1,068
Refinery Capacity barrels per day 000: 2,867
Pipelines Length km: 10,800

Foreign Trade

Imports $million: 132,083.5
Exports $million: 148,779.6
Export Volume % Annual Growth Rate (1990–97): 12.1
Import Volume % Annual Growth Rate (1990–97): 11.3

Balance of trade (current prices)

	1993	1994	1995	1996	1997	1998
U.S.						
$000,000	−10,654	+7,290	+18,050	+19,535	+46,222	+46,613
% of total	6.6%	3.7%	7.6%	6.9%	14.5%	14.5%

Major Trading Partners

	Imports	Exports
European Union %	16.1	12.9
United States %	12.2	16.6
Eastern Europe %	3.7	2.0
Japan %	22.0	19.1
Others %	46.1	49.4

Transportation

Roads Total Length mi: 718,931 km 1,157,009
Paved %: 90
Automobiles: 4,179,000
Trucks and Buses: 5,213,270
Persons per vehicle: 128
Railroad; Track Length mi: 45,319 km 72,934
Passenger-mi million: 220,319
Freight-mi million: 881,539
Merchant Marine: No. of Vessels: 2,390
Total Deadweight Tonnage 000: 20,658.0
International Cargo Loaded tons 000: 105,852
International Cargo Off-loaded tons 000: 101,688
Airports with Scheduled Flights: 113
Traffic: Passenger-mi million: 42,334
Freight-mi million: 1,527
Length of Canals mi: 68,700 km 110,562

Tourism

Number of Tourists to 000: 25,073
Number of Tourists from 000: 8,426
Tourist Receipts $million: 8,733
Tourist Expenditures $million: 3,688

Communications

Telephones 000: 40,706
Cost of Local Calls 3 mins: $0.01
Cellular Telephones 000: 3,629
Fax Machines 000: 270
Personal Computers 000: 2,600
Internet Hosts per million persons: 1.8
Mail: Post Offices: 69,003
Pieces of Mail Handled million: 7,955
Pieces of Mail Handled per person: 6.5

EDUCATION

Three articles in the constitution of 1982 relate to education. Article 19 places on the state the responsibility of "developing socialist educational undertakings in order to raise the scientific cultural level of the whole nation." Article 46 states that citizens "have the duty as well as the right to receive education." Article 4 makes Putonghua (known as Mandarin in the West) the national language but guarantees minorities the right to employ their own languages under certain conditions.

Compulsory education covers in principle all of primary school, but in rural areas the goal of universal primary education has yet to be attained. Each academic year is divided into two parts: spring and fall semesters. Classes are held six days a week, with half a day on Saturday, nine months per year.

Since the end of the Cultural Revolution, private schools have reappeared, but they still maintain a low profile. Most of them teach foreign languages, but a few prepare students for examinations at various levels. They are funded mostly by private individuals, particularly overseas Chinese.

Kindergartens are available for children aged three to six. They function under the auspices of government authorities, army units, factories or agricultural production units, neighborhood communities, communes, or production brigades. Kindergartens are available from four to eight or 10 hours a day.

Primary education expanded rapidly after 1949. The net enrollment rate of 118 percent is close to those of advanced countries and 30 percent above the average rate for the rest of the developing world. Generally, primary schools are easily accessible, even in rural areas. The average commune has 15 primary schools, usually within walking distance. Access is difficult only in the remote areas of the north and west, partially inhabited by nomads. A common primary-school curriculum has been developed but local authorities may adjust the basic curriculum somewhat to meet their specific needs.

Students are expected to meet a portion of the costs for their schooling. Tuition fees are modest, but supplementary fees for books, transportation, food, and heating are collected. In fact, it is suggested that modest fees encourage parents to treat schooling seriously and to be certain that their children attend.

Secondary education has developed even more rapidly than primary education. The secondary enrollment rate has risen from 2 percent in 1949 to 37 percent. The rate compares favorably with the 26 percent enrollment ratio for 92 other developing countries but is lower than the 60 percent in China's East Asian neighbors or the 80 percent in OECD countries. Secondary education is biased toward general training. Less than 5 percent of the schools are vocational or technical, and they enroll 12 percent of the secondary-school population. The neglect of technical and vocational education is a fallout of the Cultural Revolution, during which 62,000 vocational and technical schools were dismantled.

China has 633 universities and other institutions of higher learning; the Ministry of Education directly manages 35, municipalities and provinces run 392, and 12 ministries run 206. Responsibility for research is shared between the Ministry of Education and the Chinese Academy of Sciences. Only 24 percent of college enrollees are women, a lower proportion than in the rest of the developing world (33 percent). In technical fields, the more prestigious institutions play a critical role. They enroll 45 percent and 60 percent of students in science and engineering, respectively, and graduate 56 percent and 70 percent, respectively, of all scientists and engineers.

Graduate education began only in the 1950s and was one of the casualties of the Cultural Revolution. Graduate institutions reopened in 1978, but the curriculum pattern was not fully defined for many years. Enrollment in graduate courses is low not only in agriculture but also in finance, law, business, trade, economics, and administration. Overall enrollment in higher education is very low by international standards.

The key universities recruit their students nationwide. Many other universities also recruit from outside their province. Until recently universities provided boarding for all their students. Some day students have been accepted in the past decade, but the percentage is low and restricted by lack of transportation in many university towns.

Education

Literacy Rate %: 81.5
  Male %: 89.9
  Female %: 72.7
First Level: Primary schools: 849,123
  Teachers: 6,539,000
  Students: 159,064,000
  Student-Teacher Ratio: 24.3
  Net Enrollment Ratio: 99
Second Level: Secondary Schools: 81,020
  Teachers: 3,334,000
  Students: 53,710,000
  Student-Teacher Ratio: 16.1
  Net Enrollment Ratio: —

Vocational Level: Schools: 14,196
  Students: 8,205,000

Third Level: Institutions: 1,054
  Teachers: 401,000
  Students: 2,906,000
  Student-Ratio Level: 7.2
  Gross Enrollment Ratio: 5.7
  Students per 100,000: 461
  % of Population Age 25 and over with Postsecondary Education: 2.0

Public Expenditure on Education as % of GDP: 2.3

SCIENCE AND TECHNOLOGY

Science and Technology

Scientists and Engineers in R&D per 1 million persons: 454
Expenditures in R&D as % of GDP: 0.66
High-Tech Exports $million: 23,308
Patent Applications by Residents: 12,786

MEDIA

The gap between law and practice is nowhere wider than in relation to freedom of speech and press. Prohibition in the constitutional preamble of criticism of the CCP or socialism takes precedence over the clause in the same constitution providing for both freedoms. As a result of this contradiction, official policy is punctuated by periodical campaigns against so-called press excesses. In such a climate, press freedom has not been able to take root. The bolder editors and authors who cross the bounds of officially permitted criticism are labeled as bourgeois and expelled from the party or jailed. Foreign periodicals are not available in newsstands but are available to subscribers in educational institutions. Coverage of foreign news in the open media is quite extensive and professional. Chinese citizens may freely listen to foreign broadcasts and receive Internet communication and millions do turn to the Voice of America and even Christian shortwave stations to learn or brush up on their English. Here again official policy appears erratic; foreign correspondents are invited at one time and ordered out at other times.

Media

Daily Newspapers: 38
- Total Circulation 000: 27,790
- Circulation per 1,000: 23

Books Published: 100,951
Magazines: 6,486
Radio Receivers 000: 215,950
- per 1,000: 178

Television sets 000: 300,000
- per 1,000: 247

MOST IMPORTANT MEDIA:

Press. The following are published daily at Beijing, unless otherwise noted: *Guangming Ribao* (Brightness Daily, 6,000,000), organ of minority parties; *Renmin Ribao* (People's Daily, 3,000,000), official CCP Central Committee organ; *Qingdao Ribao* (Qingdao Daily, Shandong Province, 2,600,000); *Gongren Ribao* (Workers' Daily, 2,400,000); *Nanfang Ribao* (South China Daily, Guangdong Province, 1,000,000); *Jiefang Ribao* (Liberation Daily, 1,000,000), organ of Shanghai CCP Municipal Committee; *Jiefang Junbao* (Liberation Army Daily, 800,000), PLA organ; *Beijing Ribao* (Beijing Daily, 700,000), organ of Peking CCP Municipal Committee; *Beijing Wanbao* (Beijing Evening News, 500,000); *Guangzhou Ribao* (Canton Daily, 500,000); *Liaowang/Outlook* (450,000), influential bilingual weekly; *China Daily* (150,000) began publication in July 1981 as an English-language daily; a New York edition was launched in June 1983 and a London edition in September 1986. The *Hong Kong Standard*, an independent English-language daily, was forced to suspend mainland publication in January 1995.

The only major newspaper to support the student protest movement, Shanghai's bilingual *Shijie Jingji Daobao/World Economic Herald*, was suspended in April 1989 and officially closed down one year later.

News agencies. The leading official facility is Xinhua She (New China News Agency—NCNA), which is attached to the State Council and has offices around the world; a number of other agencies service PRC-sponsored papers abroad. Some two dozen foreign agencies maintain offices at Beijing.

Radio and television. The Central People's Broadcasting Station (Zhongyang Renmin Guangbo Diantai) provides service in *putung hua* and various local dialects; the Central People's Television Broadcasting (Zhongyang Renmin Dianshi Tai) offers programming via some 400 television stations.

CULTURE

Cultural Indicators

Public Libraries Number: 2,406
- Volumes: 269,330,000
- Registered borrowers: —

Museums Number: —
- Annual Attendance: —

Cinema Production of Long Films: 469
- Number of Cinemas: 139,823
- Seating Capacity: —
- Annual Attendance million: 14,428.4
- Annual Attendance per capita: 12.3

STATUS OF WOMEN

Violence against women is a problem in China because there is no national spousal abuse law. Anecdotal evidence suggests that domestic abuse is on the rise, particularly in urban areas. Informal surveys indicate that 20 percent of wives may have been beaten by their husbands. Actual figures may be higher because many cases go unreported.

Trafficking in women and kidnaping of women for sale into prostitution is another major problem. According to reliable reports there are up to 10 million commercial sex workers in the country. There are 70,000 prostitutes in Beijing alone working in saunas, clubs, and hostess bars, and over 80 percent of them have hepatitis and AIDS. Xinhua News Agency reports that one in five massage parlors is involved in prostitution. In 1998 the Convention on the Elimination of Discrimination against Women highlighted the dangers women faced through forced prostitution. Actions to crack down on this lucrative business, involving organized crime, local officials, police, and the military, have been largely ineffective.

A third problem is a high female suicide rate. Some 56 percent of the world's female suicides occur in China at the rate of 500 per day. This rate is five times the global average.

The Chinese government has made gender equality a policy objective since 1949. The constitution states that "women enjoy equal rights with men in all walks of life." The 1992 Law on the Protection of Women's Rights and Interests provides for equality in ownership of property, inheritance rights, and access to education. However, since 1990 the pursuit of gender equality has become a low priority with the government as it concentrates on political stability and economic reform. The law notwithstanding, discrimination, sexual harassment, and wage discrepancies are significant problems. Although women are aware of their rights, they are encountering serious obstacles in getting the rights enforced. There are no statutes that outlaw sexual harassment in the workplace and the problem remains unaddressed in the legal system.

Women have borne the brunt of the workforce reduction in state enterprises. About 70 to 80 percent of the workers displaced as a result of downsizing are women although they make up only 36.4 percent of the workforce. Women between the ages of 35 and 50 are the most affected and the least likely to be rehired. Gender-discriminatory hiring practices are on the rise as unemployment rises. Many employers prefer to hire men to avoid the expense of maternity leave and childcare. On the average, Chinese women earn between 80 and 90 percent of the salaries of their male counterparts, but they generally work in lower-skilled and lower-paid jobs. The gap between the educational level of men and women is narrowing. At the end of 1997 women made up 36 percent of all university students and 30 percent of all graduate students. In some departments women are beginning to outnumber men. Women make up 70 percent of the 145 million illiterate Chinese. About 25 percent of all Chinese women are illiterate or semiliterate compared to 10 percent of men.

Women

Gender Empowerment Measure: 33
Seats Held in Parliament by Women %: 21.0
Female Administrators and Managers %: 11.6
Female Professional and Technical workers %: 45.1
Women's Share of Earned Income %: 38.0
Women in Government %: 4

HEALTH, FOOD, AND NUTRITION

Health

Number of Physicians: 1,918,000
Number of Dentists: —
Number of Nurses: 1,125,000
Number of Pharmacists: 418,000
Population per Physician: 633
Number of Hospitals: 67,807
Hospital Beds per 10,000: 24
Hospital Bed Occupancy Rate: 66.9
Infant Mortality Rate per 1,000 live births: 43
Maternal Mortality Rate per 100,000 live births: 95
Total Health Expenditures as % of GDP: 3.51
Health Expenditures per capita $: 11
HIV Infected % of adults: 0.06
Cigarette Consumption per smoker per year: —
% of Smokers: Male: —
Female: —
Access to Safe Water %: 46

Food and Nutrition

Food Supply as % of FAO Requirements: 116
% of Consumption Expenditures on Food: 49.9
Daily Available Calories per capita: 2,741
% of Total Calories derived from:
Cereals: 57.6
Potatoes, cassava: 5.5
Meat, poultry: 13.6
Fish: 0.8
Eggs, milk: 2.4
Fruits, vegetables: 4.9
Fats, oils: 6.3

ENVIRONMENT

Between 1957 and 1973 China lost one-fifth of its agricultural land from soil erosion as well as urban development. Since 1973 and the end of the Cultural Revolution, there have been efforts to reverse the environmental damage. Reforestation has included the construction of shelter belts and the restoration of erosion-prone loesslands in the middle reaches of the Yellow River. In 1979 the National People's Congress adopted an environmental protection law and a forestry law and 10 years later launched a reforestation program called the Great Green Wall. Water pollution is also serious. Nearly 436 of the 532 rivers are polluted and safe drinking water is unavailable to one-third of the population. The use of high-sulfur coal as the main energy source causes air pollution and contributes to acid rain. China has the world's second highest level of industrial carbon dioxide emissions at a per capita level of 2.27 metric tons. However, China has begun to impose more stringent environmental controls. Investment in pollution-reducing technology is required of all industrial enterprises, penalties are imposed for noncompliance, and incentives and tax reductions are offered for those enterprises that meet environmental standards. To protect the nation's flora and fauna, 300 new reserves have been established with a total area of 23.7 million acres.

Environment

Forest Area sq km: 1,333,000
Average Annual Deforestation sq km: 866
Nationally Protected Areas as % of Total Land Area: 6.4
Freshwater Access cubic meters per capita: 2,285
Emissions of Organic Water Pollutants kg per day: 7,396,000
CO_2 Emissions per capita ton: 2.8

CHRONOLOGY

1945 Japan surrenders, bringing World War II to a close.
1946 CCP-KMT representatives meet with Marshall mission; CCP-KMT civil war resumes.
1947 Marshall mission ends.
1948 CCP forces defeat KMT is many areas.
1949 CCP forces seize most major cities; People's Republic of China is established in Beijing; Chiang Kai-shek flees to Taiwan along with remaining KMT forces and sets up Republic of China, with seat at Taipei.
1950 North Korea invades South Korea; Chinese "people's volunteers" enter the fighting and push UN troops back into South Korea.
China invades Xizang (Tibet).
1951 China announces completion of the occupation of Xizang.
1952 Land reforms conclude.

The Three Anti and the Five Anti campaigns begin.
1953 Korean armistice is signed.
1954 Soviet-style collective farms are established.
1957 The Hundred Flowers campaign is launched.
1958 Mao launches Great Leap Forward campaign.
Communes are established. PRC forces shell Quemoy and Matsu.
Tibetan revolt against PRC rule is crushed, and Dalai Lama flees to India.
1960 PRC breaks with the Soviet Union; Soviet and Chinese troops clash on the Xinjiang border.
1962 Sino-Indian War erupts over Chinese occupation of areas in northern Kashmir.
1964 China conducts its first atomic test.
1965 Cultural Revolution begins; Many Chinese leaders, including Liu Shaoqi, Zhu De, and Deng Xiaoping, are disgraced.
1967 China explodes its first hydrogen bomb.
1969 Chinese and Soviet troops clash on the Wusuli Jiang border.
1971 PRC is seated in the Chinese seat at the United Nations, and the Republic of China is expelled . . . .
Vice Chairman Lin Biao dies under mysterious circumstances in a plane crash, following an abortive coup attempt.
1972 President Richard Nixon visits Beijing.
1975 Chiang Kai-shek dies.
1976 Zhou Enlai dies; Mao Zedong dies.
The Gang of Four is arrested.
Tangshan is devastated by an earthquake.
Hua Guofeng is sworn in as premier.
1978 China ends aid to Vietnam.
1979 United States recognizes PRC and breaks relations with Republic of China (Taiwan); China invades Vietnam in a brief war.
1981 The Gang of Four is convicted.
1982 Deng Xiaoping emerges as paramount ruler.
1983 China adopts new economic policy and strengthens relations with the West.
1984 U.S. president Reagan visits China.
Sino-British agreement is signed on reversion of Hong Kong to China in 1997.
1986 China launches “anticorruption” campaign.
1987 Hu Yaobang resigns as CCP general secretary and is replaced by Zhao Ziyang.
At the 13th National Congress, reformists led by Zhao gain the upper hand as only 90 of the 209 members of the outgoing Central Committee are reelected; Deng retires from the Central Committee but retains influential post of chairman of the Military Affairs Committee; Li Peng is named acting premier in place of Zhao Ziyang.
1988 Violent anti-Chinese demonstrations in Xizang are suppressed by force.
1989 Violent anti-Chinese demonstrations in Xizang are suppressed by force.
1989 Soviet president Gorbachev visits Beijing.
Prodemocracy demonstrators, numbering several thousands, gather in Tiananmen Square in Beijing and press for reforms; after initial vacillation, regime sends in the army and crushes the protest; China faces mounting international criticism for using force to quell the prodemocracy movement; antireform faction within the Politburo and the Central Committee gains strength; Zhao Ziyang is ousted and replaced by Jiang Zemin as party general secretary.
Deng resigns as chairman of the Military Affairs Committee.
1990 Martial law is lifted.
Dissident scientist Fang Lizhui is allowed into exile in the United Kingdom.
1991 China and Russia reach agreement over border dispute.
1996 Reunification of Taiwan is declared a priority.
1997 Deng Xiaoping dies at age 92.
Collective leadership assumes power headed by Jiang Zemin as president.
Hong Kong is returned to Chinese sovereignty.
President Clinton visits China and ZiangZemin visits the United States.
1998 Macau is returned to China.
1999 Chinese attack U.S. embassy in Beijing in retaliation for bombing of Chinese embassy in Belgrade.
2001 U.S. Navy reconnaissance plane collides with Chinese fighter jet sent to intercept it, forcing emergency landing on Hainan Island.
China becomes a member of the World Trade Organization.

BIBLIOGRAPHY

Bailey, Paul. *China in the Twentieth Century*. New York, 1988.

Bannister, Judith. *China's Changing Population*. Stanford, Calif., 1987.

Cotterell, Arthur. *China: A Cultural History*. New York, 1988.

Ebrey, Patricia B. *The Cambridge Illustrated History of China*. New York, 1996.

Evans, Richard. *Deng Xiaoping and the Making of Modern China*. New York, 1994.

Fairbank, John King. *The Great Chinese Revolution, 1800–1985*. New York, 1986.

———. *China: A New History*. Cambridge, Mass., 1992.

Grey, Jack. *Rebellion and Revolutions: China from the 1880s to the 1980s*. New York, 1990.

Howland, Douglas. *Borders of Chinese Civilization: Geography and History at Empire's End*. Durham, N.C. 1996.

Hsu, Immanuel Chung-yueh. *The Rise of Modern China*. New York, 1995.

Kaplan, Fredric M., and Julian M. Sobin. *Encyclopedia of China Today*. New York, 1981.

Leung, Edwin Pak-wah. *Historical Dictionary of Revolutionary China, 1839–1976*. Westport, Conn., 1992.

Lin Bih-jaw. *The Aftermath of the 1989 Tiananmen Crisis in Mainland China*. Boulder, Colo., 1992.

Mackerras, Colin. *China since 1978: Reform, Modernization and Socialism with Chinese*. New York, 1994.

———. *China's Minorities: Integration and Modernization in the Twentieth Century*. Boulder, Colo., 1994.

Michael, Franz. *China through the Ages: History of a Civilization*. Boulder, Colo., 1986.

Nathan, Andrew J. *Chinese Democracy*. Berkeley, Calif., 1985.

Rawski, Thomas G., and Lillian M. Li. *Chinese History in Economic Perspective*. Berkeley, Calif., 1992.

Reynolds, Bruce L. *Reform in China: Challenges and Choices*. Armonk, N.Y., 1987.

Schrecker, John E. *The Chinese Revolution in Historical Perspective*. Westport, Conn., 1991.

Worden, Robert L., Andreas Matles Savada, and Ronald E. Dolan. *China: A Country Study*. Washington, D.C., 1988.

OFFICIAL PUBLICATIONS

China, People's Republic of. *People's Republic of China Year-Book; Statistical Yearbook of China; 10 Percent Sampling Tabulation on the 1990 Population Census of the People's Republic of China.*

CONTACT INFORMATION

Embassy of China
2300 Connecticut Avenue NW
Washington, D.C. 20008
Phone: (202) 328-2500

INTERNET RESOURCES

- Embassy of The People's Republic of China http://www.china-embassy.org
- China Statistical Information Net http://www.stats.gov.cn/english/index.html

COLOMBIA

BASIC FACT SHEET

OFFICIAL NAME:
Republic of Colombia (República de Colombia)

ABBREVIATION:
CK

CAPITAL:
Bogotá

HEAD OF STATE AND HEAD OF GOVERNMENT:
President Álvaro Uribe Vélez (from 2002)

NATURE OF GOVERNMENT:
Parliamentary democracy

POPULATION:
38,297,000 (1999)

AREA:
1,141,748 sq km (440,829 sq mi)

ETHNIC MAJORITY:
Mestizos

LANGUAGES:
Spanish

RELIGION:
Roman Catholicism

UNIT OF CURRENCY:
Peso

NATIONAL FLAG:
Three horizontal stripes, the upper yellow stripe being twice as wide as the lower blue and red stripes

NATIONAL EMBLEM:
A silver-gray condor of the Andes holds in its golden beak a green laurel wreath from which a gold-rimmed shield is surrounded. The shield contains three panels, the first showing an open yellow-pomegranate, with two golden cornucopias on either side, the second the red Phrygian cap of liberty, and the third two white-sailed schooners separated by a narrow green strip of land. Beneath the talons of the eagle is a gold ribbon bearing the national motto: "Libertad y Orden" ("Liberty and Order"). The shield is flanked by two flags on either side.

NATIONAL ANTHEM:
"O Unwithering Glory, Immortal Joy"

NATIONAL HOLIDAYS:
January 1 (New Year's Day); May 1 (Labor Day); July 20 (Independence Day); August 7 (Battle of Boyaca); October 12 (Colombus Day); November 11 (Independence of Cartagena Day); Christian festivals include Epiphany, St. Joseph's Day, Day of Sts. Peter and Paul, Ascension, All Saints' Day, Immaculate Conception, Christmas, Holy Thursday, Good Friday, Easter, Assumption, Sacred Heart, and Corpus Christi

DATE OF INDEPENDENCE:
July 20, 1810

DATE OF CONSTITUTION:
July 5, 1991

GEOGRAPHICAL FEATURES

Located on the northwest corner of the South American continent, Colombia has a total area of 1,141,568 sq km (440,762 sq mi), extending 1,700 km (1,056 mi) north-northwest to south-southeast and 1,210 km (752 mi) north-northeast to south-southwest. The land area includes the islands of San Andrés and Providencia in the Caribbean and the islands of Malpelo, Gorgona, and Gorgonilla in the Pacific Ocean. The country fronts both the Caribbean Sea and the Pacific Ocean, with a 1,600-km (994-mi) Caribbean coastline and a 1,300-km (808-mi) Pacific coastline.

Colombia shares, its total international boundary of 7,408 km (4,593 mi) with five countries: Venezuela (2,050 km; 1,271 mi), Brazil (1,643 km; 1,019 mi), Peru

Colombia

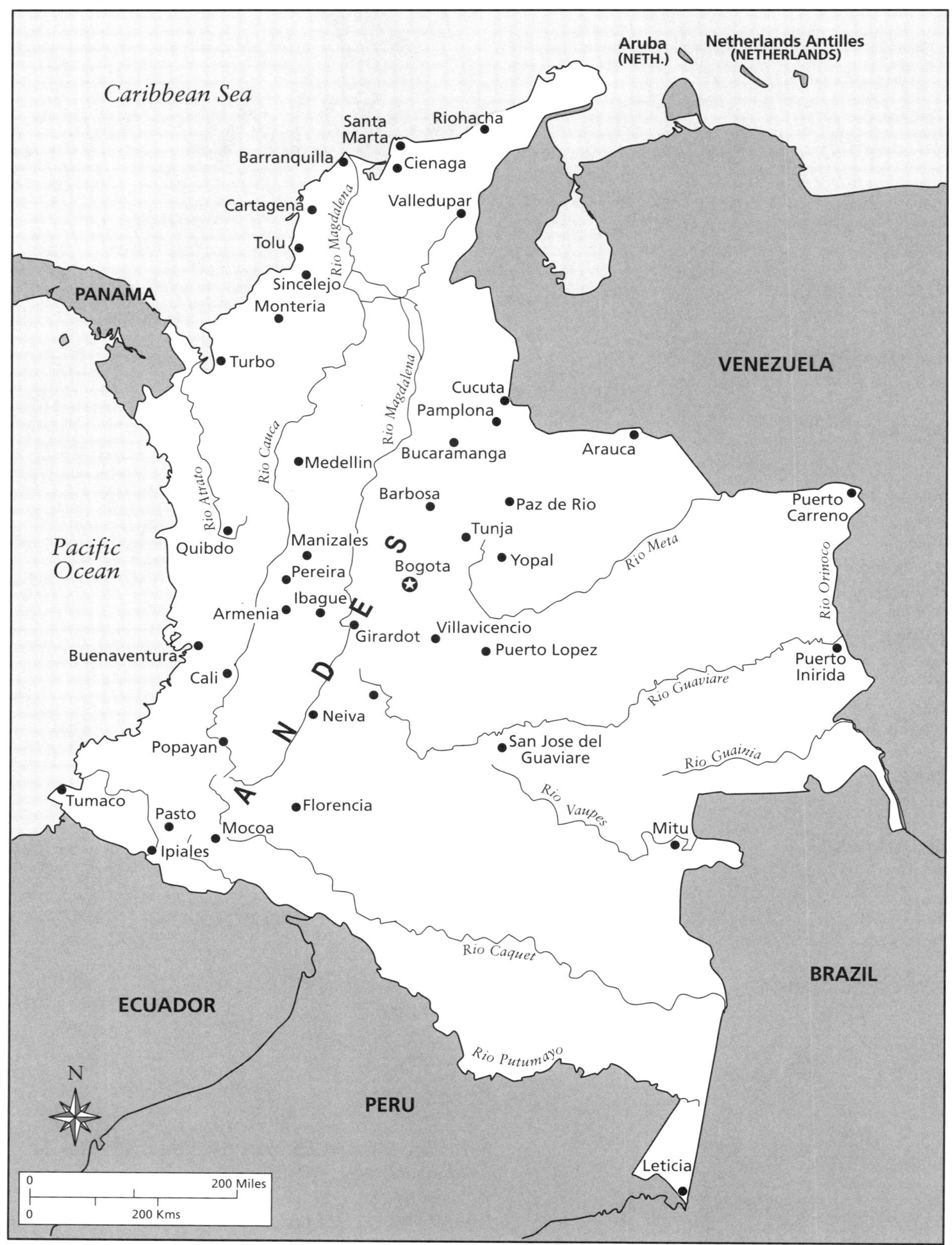

Aruba
(NETH.)
Netherlands Antilles
(NETHERLANDS)
Caribbean Sea
Santa
Marta
Riohacha
Barranquilla
Cienaga
Cartagena
Valledupar
Tolu
Rio Magdalena
Sincelejo
PANAMA
Monteria
Turbo
VENEZUELA
Rio Magdalena
Cucuta
Pamplona
Bucaramanga
Arauca
Rio Cauca
Medellin
Rio Atrato
Barbosa
Paz de Rio
Puerto
Carreno
Tunja
Quibdo
Manizales
Pacific
Ocean
Yopal
Rio Meta
Pereira
Bogota
Ibague
Rio Orinoco
Armenia
Girardot
Villavicencio
Buenaventura
Puerto Lopez
Puerto
Inirida
Cali
Rio Guaviare
Neiva
ANDES
San Jose del
Guaviare
Popayan
Rio Guainia
Tumaco
Rio Vaupes
Florencia
Pasto
Mitu
Mocoa
Ipiales
Rio Caquet
BRAZIL
ECUADOR
Rio Putumayo
N
PERU
Leticia
0
200 Miles
0
200 Kms

(2,900 km; 1,798 mi), Ecuador (590 km; 366 mi), and Panama (225 km; 140 mi). Colombia is involved in a maritime boundary dispute with Venezuela in the Gulf of Venezuela and a territorial dispute with Nicaragua over the Colombian islands of Providencia and San Andrés. Colombia also has a territorial dispute with Honduras over cays in the San Andrés and Providencia archipelago.

The capital of Colombia is Santa Fe de Bogotá with a 1997 estimated population of 6,004,782. Bogotá is one of the most spectacular cities in South America, entirely enclosed by lofty mountain ranges. It occupies about 77 sq km (30 sq mi) in the autonomous Special District, established in 1955. There are 22 other cities with populations of more than 200,000.

Topographically, Colombia is divided into four regions: the central highlands, the Atlantic lowlands, the Pacific lowlands, and eastern Colombia, to the east of the Andes.

Near the Ecuadorean border the Andes Mountains fan out into three distinct ranges, known as cordilleras, which run through the country from the south on a northeasterly axis. The three principal chains are the Cordillera Occidental, the Cordillera Central, and the Cordillera Oriental. The western and central cordilleras run parallel with the Pacific coast. The highest peak of the central system is Nevado del Huila (5,750 m, 18,865 ft). The third chain runs northeastward, bifurcating into an eastern branch, the Sierra de los Andes, and a northern branch, the Sierra Perija, which terminates south of the Guajira Peninsula. The highest point of this range, Sierra Nevada de Cucuy, rises to 5,580 m (18,307 ft) above sea level. This cordillera also contains the Sabana de Bogotá, the massive plateau on which the capital is built. The Atlantic lowlands consist of the plains north of the highlands but connected with them through the Cauca and Magdalena River valleys. The region includes the semiarid Guajira Peninsula and the Sierra Nevada de Santa Marta, an isolated mountain system with peaks over 5,791 m (19,000 ft). The Pacific lowlands consist of jungles and swamps and the low Serranía de Baudó, which is geologically separate from the Andean chain. Adjoining the Panama frontier is the Atrato Swamp, a bottomless muck that has defied engineers trying to build the Pan-American Highway across it. The sparsely populated eastern three-fifths of the country comprise vast llanos, or plains, in the north and selvas, or jungle forests, in the south.

The river system includes the Magdalena with a length of 1,549 km (963 mi), of which 1,300 km (808 mi) are navigable, the Cauca with a length of 1,015 km (631 mi), of which 249 km (155 mi) are navigable, the Caquetá, a tributary of the Amazon with a length of 2,200 km (1,367 mi), the Meta, a tributary of the Orinoco with a length of 1,000 km (621 mi), and the Putumayo, a tributary of the Amazon with a length of 1,800 km (1,119 mi). Shorter rivers include the Guaviare, Baudó, Atrato, San Juan, and Patía. There are a number of lakes in the Atlantic lowlands, such as Ciénaga de Zapotosa, Ciénaga Sapayan, Ciénaga de Oro, Ciénaga de Tadia, and Ciénaga Chilloa.

Geography

Area sq km: 1,141,748 sq mi 440,829
World Rank: 26th
Land Boundaries, km: Brazil 1,643; Ecuador 590; Panama 225; Peru 2,900; Venezuela 2,050
Coastline, km: 2900
Elevation Extremes meters
- Lowest: Pacific Ocean 0
- Highest: Nevado del Huila 5,750

Land Use % Arable land: 4
- Permanent Crops: 1
- Permanent Pastures: 39
- Forest and Woodland: 48

Other: 8

Population of Principal Cities (1997 est.)

Armenia	283,842
Barrancabermeja	180,653
Barranquilla	1,157,826
Bello	304,819
Bucaramanga	508,240
Buenaventura	266,988
Cali	1,985,906
Cartagena	812,595
Cartago	117,166
Ciénaga	144,340
Cúcuta	589,196
Dosquebradas	163,599
Envigado	109,240
Florencia	114,848
Floridablanca	246,834
Ibagué	419,883
Itagui	169,374
Magangue	104,496
Malambo	112,289
Manizales	358,194
Medellín	1,970,691
Montería	327,249
Neiva	305,625
Palmira	256,823
Pasto	362,227
Pereira	434,267
Popayán	218,057
Quibdó	123,102
Riohacha	114,608
Santa Marta	343,038
Santa Fe de Bogotá, D.C.	6,004,782
Sincelejo	213,916
Soacha	266,817
Soledad	264,583
Tuluá	138,124
Tumaco	114,802
Tunja	118,406
Turbo	127,045
Valledupar	296,624
Villavicencio	299,296

CLIMATE AND WEATHER

Colombia is located within a few degrees of the equator, but temperatures and climatic variations are governed by altitude. There are two main seasons, the wet season lasting from March to May and from September to November and the dry season lasting from December to February and from June to August, except in the northern plains where there is one long wet season from May through October.

The country is divided climatically into three zones. The hot zone (tierra caliente) constituting 90 percent of the land area is generally below 915 m (3,000 ft). Here the mean annual temperature is 23.8°C (75°F) to 26.6°C (80°F), the mean maximum is 37.7°C (100°F), and the minimum is 18°C (65°F).

The temperate zone (tierra templada) has elevations between 915 m and 1,980 m (3,000 ft and 6,500 ft) covering about 8 percent of the country, particularly the intermontane valleys. Here the mean annual temperature varies between 18°C (65°F) and 23.9°C (75°F).

The cool zone (tierra fría) comprises regions over 1,980 m (6,500 ft), particularly the plateaus and terraces of the Colombian Andes. Here the temperature varies between 12.7°C and −17°C (55°F and 14°F). The annual mean temperature at the capital, Bogotá, with an elevation of 2,598 m (8,524 ft), is 13.8°C (57°F).

Climate and Weather

Mean Temperature
Hot Zone: 75°F to 80°F
Temperate Zone 65°F to 75°F
Cool Zone 55°F to 1.4°F
Average Rainfall 14 in to 35 in

POPULATION

Population Indicators

Total Population: 1999 38,297,000
World Rank: 30th
Density per sq mi: 86.9 per sq km 33.5
% of annual growth (1994–99): 1.7
Male %: 49.2
Female %: 50.8
Urban %: 70.3
Age Distribution: % 0–14: 33.1
15–29: 30.0
30–44: 20.6
45–59: 9.9
60–74: 5.2
75 and over: 1.3
Population 2020: 50,246,000
Birth Rate per 1,000: 25.9
Death Rate per 1,000: 5.9
Population Doubling Time (years): —
Infant Mortality Rate per 1,000 live births: 26.9
Rate of Natural Increase per 1,000: 20.0
Total Fertility Rate: 2.9
Expectation of Life (years): Males 65.4
Females 73.4
Marriage Rate per 1,000: 2.3
Divorce Rate per 1,000: —
Total Number of Households: 4,772,000
Average Size of Households: 5.4
% of Illegitimate Children: 24.8
Induced Abortions: —
Rate per 100 live births: —

ETHNIC COMPOSITION

Colombia is one of the most Spanish of all South American nations, although persons of pure Spanish descent constitute only 20 percent (the most commonly cited figure) of the population. The proportion of white ancestry is therefore an important measure of the status of mixed groups such as the mestizos, who constitute more than half of the population, and the mulattoes, who constitute 14 percent. Blacks make up 4 percent, Indians 1 percent, and zambos (persons of mixed black and Indian ancestry) 3 percent. Perceptions of ethnicity are determined not only by color but also by geography. Persons residing in Popayán and Antioquía are considered to have a white background, while Chocoano usually connotes a black because of black preponderance in Chocó. The importance of color in Colombian society is reflected in the complex racial nomenclature and the number of words used to classify and describe racial groups.

Spanish values dominate Colombian society and the ideal for the nonwhite groups is to approximate and adopt all possible Spanish traits. Because of their longer exposure to Spanish culture, blacks have been more successfully Hispanized than Indians. Racial minorities have remained without any shared identity or cultural cohesion. Economic disparities between the wealthy and upper-class whites and the poorer blacks and Indians have also tended to institutionalize the notion of white superiority. Perhaps because of this reason mestizos, who exhibit more white characteristics than mulattoes, have found it easier to achieve upward mobility. There are an estimated 60 Indian tribes scattered throughout the country. Some of these tribes have remained very primitive nomadic groups, although all tribes have had some contact with outsiders. Indian affairs are administered by the National Indian Institute.

Ethnic minorities include Jews, Germans, Lebanese, Italians, and North Americans.

LANGUAGES

The official language is Spanish. Colombian Spanish is generally considered to be the purest in Latin America. The Colombian Language Academy has maintained close ties with its counterpart in Spain. There are, however, a number of words and expressions not found elsewhere that give Colombian Spanish a distinctive character. Colombia's diversity is reflected in the fact that some regions use *tú* as the familiar form of address while others use *vos*. Most of the innumerable Indian dialects are dying out although those like Aymara, Arawak, Chilacha, Carib, Quechua, Tupi-Guaraní, and Yurumangi still survive. Missionary work by the Spanish colonizers guaranteed that, unlike in Peru or Bolivia, all but the most isolated highlands or forest populations of Native Americans came to speak Spanish as their primary tongue.

Principal Languages and Their Speakers

Amerindian languages	330,000
Arawakan	40,000
Cariban	20,000
Chibchan	160,000
Other	100,000
English Creole	50,000
Spanish	37,920,000

RELIGIONS

Colombia is considered one of the most strongly Roman Catholic countries in Latin America, not only in the proportion of its population claiming adherence to the faith but also in terms of the depth of conviction of the common believers and the influence of the hierarchy in social and political affairs. More than 92% of Colombians have been baptized in the church, and most Colombians regularly attend Mass, observe holy days, and receive sacraments. The ratio of priests to believers is also one of the highest in Latin America.

The relations between church and state are governed by the Concordat of 1973, which replaced the Concordat of 1887. Unlike the 1887 concordat, the 1973 concordat did not define Roman Catholicism as the official religion but as "the religion of the great majority of the Colombians." It recognized the pope's right to name bishops but removed tax-exempt status for church properties. The concordat also altered the church's role in three major areas. The jurisdiction of the church over so-called mission territories with Indian populations was restricted and educational and social services provided by the church were to be transferred to the state. Mandatory teaching of the catechism in schools and the ecclesiastical right to censor university texts were taken away and the church was expected to conform to state regulations even in its own schools. Lastly, the right of Colombians to contract civil marriages was recognized.

The church's ecclesiastical organization reflects its strength and penetration. The primate is the archbishop of Bogotá who is invariably a cardinal. He presides over eight archdioceses and 27 dioceses. The clergy number over 5,000, almost all of whom are native Colombians serving 1,600 parishes, growing by 30 a year.

Religious minorities include 300,000 Protestants and 12,000 Jews. Protestant membership has grown since 1968, but evangelical churches have not gained the kind of firm foothold that they have planted in some other Latin American countries.

Religious Affiliations

Roman Catholic	35,200,000
Other	3,100,000

HISTORICAL BACKGROUND

There is great uncertainty as to when the first human settlement of South America took place, possibly more than 20,000 years ago. Two waves of Mesoamerican migration, crossing the Isthmus of Panama, occurred around 1500 B.C. and 500 B.C.E. The fourth century B.C. brought a further wave of migration: the Chibcha from Central America, dispersing the Arawaks living along the Caribbean coast. Another tribe from the islands, the Caribs, mounted periodic raids on the Chibcha from the end of the first millennium A.D. onward, forcing them to resettle at higher elevations. At the time of Spanish exploration and conquest, the tribes with the most advanced and influential culture were the Chibcha (or Muisca) and the Tairona.

Colombia, known as New Granada, was under Spanish rule from 1538, as a colony until 1717 and as a vice-royalty until 1819. It was part of the republic of Gran Colombia until 1830, when Venezuela and Ecuador seceded from the united republic.

Colombia has a long liberal, democratic history centered on competition between the Liberal and Conservative Parties. The Liberals were associated with anticlericalism, federalism, and free trade while the Conservatives advocated a strong central government, supported protectionism, and allied themselves with the Roman Catholic Church. Although some governments have been authoritarian, Colombia has experienced dictatorship only five times in its history: 1830–31, 1854, 1884–94, 1904–09, and 1953–57.

Colombia's recent history has been marked by three key elements: the dominance of the two parties, political violence, and the National Front coalition. Disputes between the two parties have often engendered violence. The greatest bloodshed came in the War of a Thousand Days (1899–1902) and La Violencia (1948–58) in which 100,000 and between 100,000 and 200,000, respectively, died. Currently Colombia is plagued by violence from several leftist guerrilla groups and by high levels of criminal violence involving both street criminals and drug lords.

In response to La Violencia and a period of dictatorship under Gustavo Rojas Pinilla from 1953–57, the two parties formed the National Front coalition in which the Liberals and Conservatives alternated the presidency and evenly split the congressional seats and the bureaucracy for 16 years from 1958 to 1974. Since the end of the National Front, the Liberal Party has dominated politics, capturing the presidency in 1974, 1978, 1986, 1990, and 1994. Conservatives regained the highest office in 1998.

Since the late 1970s Colombia has been a battleground between the government and left-wing guerrillas. The guerrillas have failed to dislodge the government, but have caused major national disruption as has the growing power of the drug cartels and the death squads formed to protect the cartels. During the late 1980s, several prominent politicians were kidnapped or assassinated by drug dealers in an effort to stop the government's tough antidrug campaign. In 1989, following the assassination of Liberal Party leader Carlos Galán, President Virgilio Barco Vargas declared a "war" against the drug cartels. One of his most controversial measures was to extradite drug traffickers wanted in the United States. Drug-related violence increased during the 1989–90 presidential campaign, and three presidential candidates were murdered.

Under the adminstration of César Gaviria Trujillo (1990–94), the country developed a new constitution to replace the one that had been serving, with many amendments, since 1886. This, it was somewhat vainly hoped, would diversify political participation away from Liberal/Conservative dominance. The government succeeded in getting several guerrilla groups to lay down arms and form parties, but the two largest, the Colombian Revolutionary Armed Forces (FARC) and the National Liberation Army (ELN), remained in the bush. Colombia's political crisis and instability deepened when the victorious presidential candidate, Ernesto Samper Pizano of the Liberals, was accused of taking cash from the Cali drug cartel and other illegitimate sources to finance his campaign. Despite many calls for his resignation at home and abroad, he served out the duration of his term. During this term, the national economy took a steep turn for the worse, the United States suspended aid and cooperation because of the accusations against Samper, and guerrilla activity increased to the point where many feared for the survival of the state. Right-wing paramilitaries sprang up to combat the guerrillas on their own terms (which all too frequently involved vigilante justice and other human rights abuses), often tacitly working with units of the army.

When Andrés Pastrana Arango came to power in 1998 as the first Conservative president since 1986, he promised a major peace overture, raising the stakes controversially by effectively ceding a tract of land about the size of El Salvador in southern Colombia to the FARC, declaring it a demilitarized zone. The guerrillas, however, were reluctant to be drawn into formal talks. The ELN and the paramilitaries responded by demanding zones of their own and places at the peace conference, but FARC leaders regarded the idea of the paramilitary chief Carlos Castaño sitting as an equal at the negotiating table as a nonstarter. In 2000, Pastrana succeeded in getting his $7.5 billion "Plan Colombia" approved; this included a considerable boost in military capacities, helped by U.S. and European aid that was part of the plan, as well as rural development schemes to try to wean peasants away from growing coca. The ultimate aim was to force the guerrillas into negotiations. But the FARC responded by warning of an escalation in violence in the far south and by mounting cross-border raids, to the consternation of Ecuador, Brazil, and Venezuela.

CONSTITUTION

Colombia, in spite of its internal instability, has a firm tradition of constitutional democracy and has been ruled by elected governments for all but four years (1953–57) of the present century. The nation had 10 constitutions from 1811 until 1886. The constitution of 1886 was amended many times (1910, 1936, 1945, 1957, 1959, and 1968) before giving way to a completely new constitution in 1991.

The new constitution put a brake on the centralizing tendencies the accretion of amendments to the old constitution had produced and attempted to break the dual-party stranglehold on politics. The idea was to open up the political process to new voices and tendencies and perhaps in this way marginalize the leftist guerrilla movements in the countryside and deny them popular legitimacy. This worked better in theory than in practice: the Liberals and Conservatives still dominate politics, and the guerrillas are in a stronger position than ever. Other provisions of the 1991 constitution limited the executive's use of emergency decrees, bolstered the rights of the individual, revamped the judicial system, liberalized criminal procedure, and pruned the legislature. The Chamber of Representatives was shrunk from 199 members to 161, with each department electing at least two representatives. The Senate went from 114 seats to 102, and senators now have a nationwide rather than a departmental constituency. Up to five additional seats in the lower house could be awarded to ethnic minorities, and indigenous peoples soon after seated their first representatives. The changes to the justice system most notably shifted the conduct of trials from a system based on the Napoleonic Code to something more closely resembling U.S. practice and set up a constitutional court for the first time.

Executive power is vested in the president of the republic, who is elected by popular suffrage for a four-year term. He is constitutionally prohibited from seeking reelection for a consecutive term. In addition, the president is the commander in chief of the armed forces and the head of the national police. The country has no vice president, and currently the rules of succession are unclear.

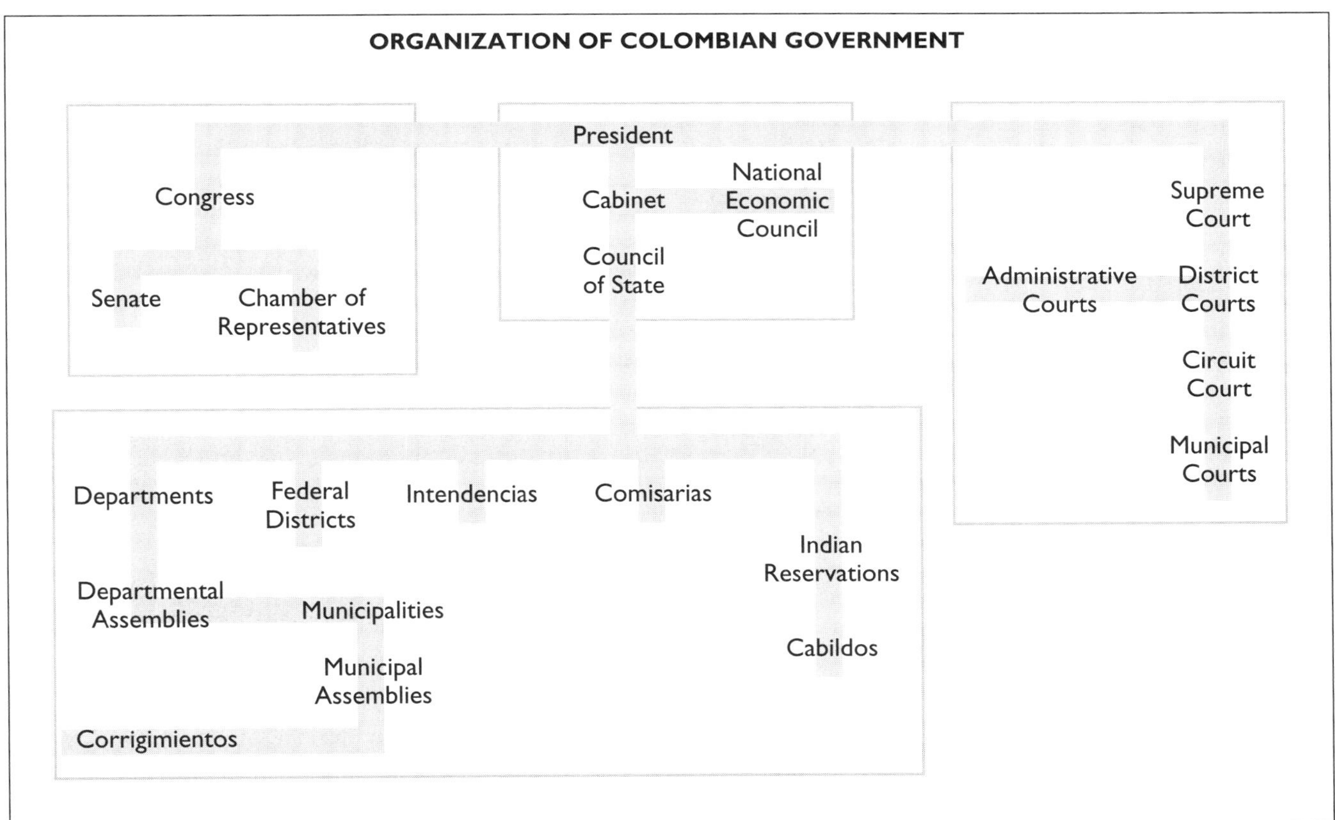

Suffrage is universal, and the voting age was reduced from 21 to 18 in 1977. Women were enfranchised in 1957. There are strict residency requirements for registration as a voter. Elections are held in spring of even-numbered years, municipal and departmental assembly elections alternating with presidential and congressional elections. Voters vote for party lists rather than for individual candidates. Electoral practices are regulated by the Electoral Guarantees Court. Despite the relatively free character of the elections, voter abstention is widespread (up to 70 percent in the early 1990s, as much because of political violence as because of voter apathy).

LOCAL GOVERNMENT

For purposes of local government Colombia is divided into 23 departments, the federal district of Bogotá, four *intendencias*, and five *comisarias*. The *intendencias* and the *comisarias* are together known as national territories.

The departments have directly elected assemblies and, since the new constitution came into effect, elected governors as well. The territories are controlled directly by the central government. Although the territories comprise 46 percent of the land area, they support only 1.9 percent of the population.

Departments are further subdivided into municipalities, which are either administrative and commercial centers, or municipal seats known as *cabaceras* surrounded by rural localities known as *veredas*. The municipalities are administered by *alcaldes*, or mayors, who served as gubernatorial agents until March 1988, when the country's first mayoral elections were held. Municipalities are divided, though not officially, into zones or wards called *corrigimientos*, each headed by an official known as a *corregidor.* The Indian reservations form a separate administrative category. They are administered by their own authorities, known as *cabildos*, which are popularly elected councils.

Local Government

Principal administrative divisions, capitals, area, population

AREA AND POPULATION

Departments	Capitals	area sq mi	area sq km	population 1993 census
Antioquia	Medellín	24,445	63,912	4,919,619
Atlántico	Barranquilla	1,308	3,388	1,837,468
Bolívar	Cartagena	10,030	25,978	1,702,188
Boyacá	Tunja	8,953	23,189	1,315,579
Caldas	Manizales	3,046	7,888	1,030,062
Caquetá	Florencia	34,349	88,965	367,898
Cauca	Popayán	11,316	29,308	1,127,678
César	Valledupar	8,844	22,905	827,219
Chocó	Quibdó	17,965	46,530	406,199
Córdoba	Montería	9,660	25,020	1,275,623

(continued)

Cundinamarca	Santa Fe de Bogotá, D.C.	8,735	22,623	1,875,337
Huila	Neiva	7,680	19,890	843,798
La Guajira	Riohacha	8,049	20,848	433,361
Magdalena	Santa Marta	8,953	23,188	1,127,691
Meta	Villavicencio	33,064	85,635	618,427
Nariño	Pasto	12,845	33,268	1,443,671
Norte de Santander	Cúcuta	8,362	21,658	1,162,474
Orinoguia-Amazonia	—	186,519	483,083	688,805
Quindio	Armenia	712	1,845	495,212
Risaraida	Pereira	1,598	4,140	844,184
San Andrés y Providencia	San Andrés	17	44	61,040
Santander	Bucaramanga	11,790	30,537	1,811,741
Sucre	Sincelejo	4,215	10,917	701,105
Tolima	Ibagué	9,097	23,562	1,286,078
Valle	Cali	8,548	22,140	3,736,090
Capital district				
Santa Fe de Bogotá, D.C.		613	1,587	5,484,244
TOTAL		440,762	1,141,568	37,422,791

PARLIAMENT

The Congress (Congreso) is a bicameral legislature consisting of a Senate and a Chamber of Representatives, each elected for a four-year term coinciding with the presidential term. Members of Congress are elected on a proportional basis, but every department is guaranteed at least two seats in each house. Each house also makes special provision for members appointed from minority groups; the Senate's elected membership of 100 is joined by two members of the indigenous community, and the Chamber's membership, allowing for up to five such appointees, currently numbers 163, of which two are indigenous and two are from other recognized minorities.

Bills are introduced in either chamber by congressmen or by ministers. Most legislation is referred to one of eight standing committees whose approval is necessary for further consideration. Party discipline is strict in both houses, and members tend to vote in blocs. Among the functions of Congress are the election of the presidential designate, election of the members of the Supreme Court, and adoption of amendments to the constitution. Among the powers specifically granted to the Senate are the trial of officials impeached by the Chamber of Representatives and authorization of a declaration of war. The Chamber elects the comptroller general and originates all legislation dealing with taxation.

In the 2002 legislative election, the Liberal Party managed to lose its paper-thin majorities in both the Chamber of Representatives and the Senate.

POLITICAL PARTIES

Colombia has a two-party system dominated by the Liberal and Conservative Parties, two of the oldest political parties in Latin America, dating back to 1848. Despite the intensity of party loyalties, few ideological differences exist between the two, particularly since the formation of the National Front power-sharing agreement in 1957. Both parties follow middle-of-the-road, free-market policies at home and pro–U.S. policies abroad, and both are strongly tied to the elite strata of society. If there is a difference, it is in the Liberal Party's orientation toward urban groups, the commercial and industrial sector, and moderate social and agrarian reform, versus the Conservative Party's orientation toward the rural aristocracy, the Roman Catholic Church, and the military. Even in internal organization the two parties are dominated by their leadership, whose policy decisions the rank and file have no choice but to follow. Ideological labels are also misleading in terms of the membership on whom the parties depend for their support. Labor is allied with the Conservative Party because of its ties with the church.

Since 1957, when the two parties agreed to share power, political dynamics have been characterized by the growth of factions within each party. Local organizations of both the Conservative and Liberal parties are headed by local party bosses whose principal function is to trade votes as power brokers. The system perhaps reached a pinnacle of corruption under the presidency of Ernesto Samper, when not only the president but also a substantial percentage of the legislators were suspected of ties to drug traffickers.

The main challenge to the two-party system in the 1970s came from Alianza Nacional Popular (ANAPO, National Popular Alliance), founded in 1961 by the former dictator Rojas Pinilla. ANAPO's main planks were designed to appeal to the lower classes and constituted a blend of populism, Catholicism, and nationalism. It splintered and lost influence in the late 1970s, and no viable third party took its place in the 1980s, leading to increasing political expression through terrorism and violence. The 1991 constitution was designed in part to bring these groups into the mainstream and was briefly successful in doing so. The Democratic Alliance–April 19 Movement, formed by leaders of the former terrorist group M-19, headed by Antonio Navarro Wolff, won 10 percent of the votes in the 1991 legislative elections. However, it could not build on that success, and it must be considered today as just one of a number of fairly inconsequential minor parties.

The Patriotic Union, formed in May 1985, was purportedly the political arm of the Colombian Revolutionary Armed Forces, but it became increasingly detached from FARC, which continued fighting, and it has suffered severe losses to its leadership through assassination. The Christian Democratic Party has been small and fairly weak for years.

A number of guerrilla groups have appeared on the scene since the 1970s, and two are significant enough to be reckoned with: the National Liberation Army (Ejército de Liberación Nacional, ELN) and the Colombian

Revolutionary Armed Forces (Fuerzas Armadas Revolucionarias de Colombia, FARC). The paramilitary groups that have garnered increasing influence in reaction against the guerrillas have their own political face: the National Restoration Movement.

Political Parties

Liberal Party, 1815
Social Conservative Party, 1849
National Salvation Movement, 1900
Democratic Alliance-April 19 Movement
Patriotic Union, 1985
Christian Democratic Party
Metapolitical Unitarian Movement, 1985
Women for Democracy, 1991
National Restoration Movement, 1989
National Popular Alliance, 1971
Communist Party
Socialist Workers' Party, 1977
Hope, Peace and Liberty, 1991
Movement for Workers' Self-Defense, 1978
Colombia has a number of clandestine and rebel groups including
National Guerrilla Coordination - Simón Bolívar, 1985
National Liberation Army
Colombia Revolutionary Armed Forces
Popular Front of National Liberation

Political Parties: Strength in Parliament Most Recent Elections

Senate (*Senado de la República*). The upper house is presently composed of 102 members, including two appointed to represent indigenous communities; each department is entitled to at least two senators. Following the election of March 10, 2002, the Liberal Party held 28 seats; the Social Conservative Party, 13; others, 61.

Chamber of Representatives (*Cámara de Representantes*). The lower house is presently composed of 161 members elected for a four-year term by proportional representation. Following the election of March 10, 2002, the Liberal Party held 54 seats; the Social Conservative Party, 21; the Coaliclón, 17; others, 69.

LEGAL SYSTEM

The legal system was historically based on Spanish law. It has undergone major modifications as a result of the 1991 constitution. Criminal trials have shifted the burden of proof from the accused to the accuser. Two new offices have been mandated: the general prosecutor to investigate and pursue cases against suspected offenders through the courts and the public defender, charged with monitoring the general prosecutor's work and safeguarding the human rights of ordinary citizens in the legal process. The constitution also mandated creation of a Judicial Council to review judges' professional qualifications and a Constitutional Court.

The Colombian judicature is headed by the Supreme Court. The 24 judges of the Supreme Court are elected by serving members of the court. The term of office is five years and the magistrates may be reelected indefinitely until they attain the age of 65. The president of the court is elected by the members annually. The court enjoys broad powers, including the right to veto decrees and review legislation. Under a constitutional provision known as popular action, any citizen may file a case before the Supreme Court challenging the constitutionality of a law.

On the next lower level, the country is divided into 61 judicial districts, each of which has a superior court of three or more judges elected by members of the Supreme Court. These judges, in turn, elect judges of the lower courts, such as municipal courts and circuit courts. A parallel system of administrative courts also exists headed by the Council of State. There is one administrative court for each department charged with hearing complaints against the government.

The judiciary is overburdened and there are backlogs of up to five years resulting from a morass of red tape. It is also the target of charges of political patronage, extortion, and corruption. Reforms to the civilian penal code in 1993 were thought to be heavily influenced by drug dealers, and a military penal code reform similarly fell short of international expectations that crimes involving human rights violations would be tried in civilian courts. Colombia is trying to do away with courts composed of "faceless" participants—judges, prosecutors, witnesses whose identities are shielded—in security-related cases, which frequently violate due process. There is no capital punishment.

LAW ENFORCEMENT

Law Enforcement

Offenses reported to the police per 100,000: 641
Murder: 81.9
Assault: 110.5
Burglary: —
Automobile Theft: 32.4
Population per Police officer: 420
Death Penalty: Abolished 1910

HUMAN RIGHTS

Colombia is statutorily free and yet everywhere in chains owing to the unrelenting violence of its society. A constitutionally authorized state of siege, which permits the curtailment of some civil and political liberties, was imposed increasingly during the 1970s and 1980s.

The Colombian government justified this and other measures infringing on civil liberties as necessary to contain the terrorism of the drug cartels and the politically inspired violence that threatens the security of the state.

The human rights situation worsened during the late 1980s and 1990s as a result of the government's war against the drug cartels and the continuing guerrilla warfare against the central government. Many of the government's units charged with conducting operations against the drug cartels kidnapped, attacked, or murdered civilians whom they suspected of involvement in drugs. Although torture was illegal under the 1981 penal code, suspects were tortured or disappeared. The drug cartels carried on a systematic campaign of terror against the police, the press, and high government officials. The drug lords were also responsible for terrorist attacks against public facilities and a systematic campaign against judges and public prosecutors. Successive administrations broke the Medellín cartel and jailed the leaders of the Cali cartel; nonetheless, smaller narcotics traffickers continue to function, and the problem remains beyond the control of law enforcement or the military.

The government campaign against leftist guerrillas continued to yield frequent accusations of human rights abuses. Before President Pastrana offered the Colombian Revolutionary Armed Forces (FARC) a "sanctuary" in southern Colombia in an attempt to coax the group into negotiations, the military would raid suspected guerrilla positions without regard for civilian casualties. The guerrillas, in turn, would take hostages in an effort to collect "war taxes" and would murder civilians thought to be spies. Efforts to investigate paramilitary crimes were successful in only a few cases. Human Rights Watch has offered evidence that a number of military units have worked hand in glove with paramilitary forces.

Whereas under the old constitutional regime there was controversy over trying civilians accused of certain crimes in military courts, the present regime is feeling international pressure to try more cases involving human rights abuses by the military in civilian courts. Thus far the army and its intelligence service have largely managed to escape prosecution in the ordinary court system.

The Colombian Constitution specifically proscribes the death penalty. Indemnities have been awarded by the Council of State for wrongful death at the hands of government forces.

The rights of the public to a fair trial and due process are guaranteed by the constitution and generally honored in practice, with some glaring exceptions in the case of special courts in which "faceless" judicial officials have manipulated testimony and violated defendants' rights. These courts were phased out in 1999.

Freedoms of the press, speech, religion, and assembly are constitutionally guaranteed and have been generally respected to the extent that the government is capable of guaranteeing them. Public meetings, marches, and demonstrations are normally held without police interference. But with guerrillas controlling more than 40 percent of the country's territory (and paramilitary groups staking their own claims), and with approximately of 90 percent of violent crimes going unsolved, to call the state's capacities for order and justice severely inadequate is to understate the case.

Prison conditions in Colombia are starkly overcrowded (40 percent beyond capacity). Because of violence, Colombia has one of the world's largest internally displaced populations, and the government has rarely honored its own promises and obligations to assist them in meeting basic needs.

A number of Colombian organizations are involved in monitoring the human rights situation in the country. These include the Permanent Committee for the Defense of Human Rights, the Political Prisoners' Solidarity Committee, and Colombian Commission of Jurists. Colombia was also one of the first nations to ratify the American Convention on Human Rights, the Lima Declaration, and the Riobamba Code of Conduct.

FOREIGN POLICY

Colombia has only a limited diplomatic tradition, and often the country has been too consumed by its internal problems to give much interest to foreign affairs. As the largest Spanish-speaking nation in South America, Colombia naturally aspires to being a regional power among the Andean nations and in the Caribbean. This has at times produced friction with its big neighbor, Venezuela, which has always had similar aspirations, and the two countries nearly came to blows in 1979 over a marine boundary dispute in the Gulf of Venezuela (or Guajira, as Colombians refer to it). However, foreign policy is still primarily governed by economic determinants such as the need to gain expanded markets.

In global affairs Colombia prefers the low-key approach and has usually opted for multilateral initiatives to solve international disputes. This along with a continuing commitment to collective security has led Colombia to follow a generally conservative line on most foreign policy issues. It has shown a readiness to follow the lead of the United States in inter-American affairs. Relations with the United States have always been a central concern. During the 1960s Colombia was the showcase of the Alliance for Progress. The United States for several years "decertified" Colombia as a nation cooperating against the narcotics trade; Colombia responded that the decision to suspend assistance was politically motivated. Colombians have always been critical about Washington's single-minded focus on drug smuggling. But as Colombia's security situation deteriorates, it is more dependent than ever on U.S. assistance. Having mended fences, new president Andrés Pastrana asked the United States (and Europe) for a sizable contribution of military aid to finance a several-billion-dollar campaign against the traffickers. Many Americans are wary of being drawn into Colombia's civil war, yet the aid package is likely to pass in some form.

Although Colombia looks to the United States for leadership in hemispheric economic and security relations, its basic commitment is to its South American neighbors to whom it is bound by historic and cultural ties. Colombia was the prime mover in such regional alliances as the Andean Common Market (now the Andean Community of Nations). In the early 1990s, Colombia joined Mexico and Venezuela in a "Group of Three" to discuss energy and infrastructure issues, and in 1994 the trio signed a 10-year trade liberalization pact. Colombia views this as an intermediate step toward the proposed Free Trade Area of the Americas pact encompassing the entire Western Hemisphere. Beyond trade issues, Colombia was an active supporter of Panama's efforts to win a new treaty with the United States over the Panama Canal.

Colombia joined the United Nations in 1945. It is a member of 14 UN organizations and 34 other international organizations.

DEFENSE

The defense structure is headed by the president as commander in chief. The line of command runs through the minister of war, who is always a senior military officer, to the commanding general of the armed forces and the chief of staff of the armed forces. Military policy is formulated on the advice of the Superior Council of National Defense and the Advisory Council of Military Forces.

Military manpower is provided by compulsory military service under which all males between the ages of 18 and 50 are technically subject to the draft. However, this provision of the law is not strictly enforced, and only a small percentage of those eligible are drafted for a period of two years.

Military Indicators

Total Active Duty Personnel: 146,300
Military Manpower per 1,000: 4.0
Military Expenditures $million: 2,000
- as % of GNP: 2.6
- per capita $: 55
- as % of central government expenditures: 16.2

Arms Imports $million: 60
Arms Exports $million: 0

ECONOMY

Colombia's economy was historically primarily agricultural, with coffee and sugar the largest contributors to the gross domestic product (GDP). Because of wildly fluctuating world market conditions, Colombia has been trying to reduce its dependency on coffee by expanding the manufacturing and mining sectors. The rapid development of oil, coal, and other nontraditional industries has helped the country greatly to reduce its dependence on coffee.

The most significant growth has come in the oil industry, which was insignificant at the start of the 1980s. By the end of the 1990s it had surpassed coffee as the country's most valuable (legal) export. Oil and gas contributed 35 percent of Colombian export earnings in 1996, even though the minerals sector of the economy represented just 5.3 percent of national output at the time. Beyond fossil fuels, Colombia's rivers contain tremendous and largely untapped hydroelectric potential, and the country has large coal deposits, significant gold and nickel reserves, and the vast bulk of the world's extraction of emeralds.

Colombia's diversification into manufacturing has happened at a much slower rate than in the energy sector. The industrial sector constituted 13 percent of GDP in 1970 and 17 percent in 1996. About a quarter of this was food processing, much of which involved the milling of coffee. Other major manufacturing categories were textiles, leather goods, chemicals and pharmaceuticals, car assembly, and electrical engineering products. Manufacturing is concentrated in cities, primarily in the four most populous urban centers.

The telecommunications sector was deregulated in the 1990s, with cellular services growing at a smart pace. This industry represented 2.7 percent of GDP in 1999 and was expected to continue increasing its share. The privatization and deregulation policies pursued by Gaviria and his successors also benefited the financial industry, bringing investment and modernization of services from abroad, mainly Spanish banking firms, though the recession the country entered in 1998 called attention to flaws in the balance sheets of quite a few. The small stock exchanges of Bogotá, Medellín, and Cali also enjoyed unprecedented growth in the years prior to the recession.

Colombia's more open trade policies brought substantially improved access to U.S. and European markets, but the country ran a worsening trade deficit as the 1990s proceeded. Continued dependence on primary product exports left Colombia at the mercy of world markets when the terms of trade for commodities turned downward, as was the case for the greater part of the decade. The trade situation was counterbalanced by a surge in foreign investment—until political instability caused many investors to have second thoughts. The pervasive violence and drug-related corruption that helped bring on the downturn of the late 1990s bears considerable relation to the social inequities of the country: a population that is severely stratified, a widening gap in wealth brought on in part precisely by the policies that revolutionized production, and a workforce largely lacking in education beyond grade-school level. The International Monetary Fund is pressing for budget cuts and tax reforms from the Pastrana administration, but there is considerable opposition from the Liberal opposition in the legislature and the public sector workers directly affected by any cutbacks. Colombia was able to go a long time tolerating incredibly high levels of domestic strife and chaos without serious consequences in terms of growth or debt accumulation before its fortunes turned downward. More than anything, clearly, it now needs a settlement of its conflicts to restore confidence and resume development.

Principal Economic Indicators

Gross National Product $: 87.125 billion
GNP per capita $: 2,180
GNP Average Annual Growth Rate (1990–97) %: 2.6
GNP per capita Average Annual Growth Rate (1990–97) %: 0.7
Origin of Gross Domestic Product %
- Agriculture: 14
- Mining: 4
- Manufacturing: 14
- Construction: 5
- Public Utilities: —
- Transportation and Communications: 8
- Trade: 12
- Financial and Other Services: 34
- Government: 9

Gross Domestic Product by Type of Expenditure %
- Private Consumption: 69
- Government Consumption: 13
- Gross Domestic Investment: 22
- Foreign Trade: Exports: 16
  Imports: −20

% of Income Received by Poorest 20%: 3.6
% of Income Received by Richest 10%: 39.5

Price and earnings indexes (1995 = 100)

	1991	1992	1993	1994	1995	1996	1997
Consumer price index	42.9	54.4	66.8	82.7	100.0	120.2	142.5
Monthly earnings index	—	—	—	—	100.0	—	—

Finance

National Currency: Colombia Peso (Col$)
Exchange Rate: $1 = Col$ 1345.0
Money Supply Stock in National Currency billion: 9,937.3
M1 per capita: 277,000
Central Bank Discount Rate %: 24.9
Total External Debt $million: 15,273
Debt Service Ratio %: 16.1
Balance of Payments $million: −5,888
International Reserves SDRs million: 7,173
Ratio of External Debt to Total Reserves: 1.6
Average Annual Rate of Inflation/Consumer Price Index Growth Rate %: 17.7

Official Development Assistance

ODA $million: 166
- as % of GNP: 0.2
- per capita: $ 4
- Foreign Direct Investment $million: 3,038

Central Government Revenues and Expenditures

Fiscal Year: Calendar Year
Revenues $million: 26,000
Expenditures $million: 30,000
Budget Deficit $million: 4,000
Tax Revenues as % of GDP: 10.1
Highest Tax Bracket %
- Individual: 35
- Corporate: 35

Employment and Labor

Economically Active Population: 9,558,000
Female Participation Rate %: 32.8
Activity Rate %: 34.3
Labor by Sector: %
- Agriculture, Forestry, Fishing: 28.5
- Manufacturing, Mining: 14.5
- Construction: 2.9
- Transportation and Communications: 4.2
- Trade, Hotels, and Restaurants: 14.9
- Finance, Insurance, Real Estate: 3.3
- Public Administration, Defense: —
- Services: 23.6

Unemployment %: 12.2

Agriculture

Agriculture's Share of GDP %: 13
Average Annual Rate of Growth (1965–98) %: 2.7
Number of Farms 000: 1,548
Average Size of Farm ha: 26.3
Number of Tractors per 1,000 hectares: 9.4
Irrigation, % of Farms having: 19
Artificial Fertilizer kg/hectare: 101
Total Farmland as % of land area: 34.7
Livestock: Cattle 000: 28,261
- Sheep 000: 2,416
- Hogs 000: 2,480
- Chickens 000: 85,000

Forests: Production of Roundwood (000 cubic meters): 20,491
Fisheries: Total Catch tons 000: 122.7

Mining

% of GDP: 5.1
Value of Mineral Production $million: 4,045.4

Manufacturing

Value Added $million: 10,846
Industrial Production Growth Rate %: −1.2

Energy

Commercial Energy Production metric tons of oil equivalent 000: 67,624
Commercial Energy Consumption metric tons of oil equivalent 000: 30,481
Commercial Energy Consumption per capita kg: 761
Average Annual Growth Rate 1980–97 %: 0.9
Net Energy Imports % of use: −122
Electricity Installed Capacity kW 000: 10,758
- Production kW-hr million: 45,303

Coal Reserves tons million: 4,539
- Production tons 000: 26,020

Natural Gas Proven Reserves cubic meters billion: 234
Production cubic meters million: 4,437
Crude Petroleum Reserves barrels million: 2,800
Production barrels million: 227
Consumption barrels million: 98
Refinery Capacity barrels per day 000: 249
Pipelines Length km: 4,935

Foreign Trade

Imports $million: 13,863.1
Exports $million: 10,327.8
Export Volume % Annual Growth Rate (1990–97): 4.8
Import Volume % Annual Growth Rate (1990–97): 17.7

Major Trading Partners

	Imports	Exports
European Union %	18.5	25.5
United States %	33.8	34.3
Eastern Europe %	1.3	0.5
Japan %	8.9	3.5
Others %	37.5	36.2

Transportation

Roads Total Length mi: 66,238 km 106,600
Paved %: 12
Automobiles: 1,150,000
Trucks and Buses: 550,000
Persons per vehicle: 21
Railroad; Track Length mi: 2,007 km 3,230
Passenger-mi million: 9.6
Freight-mi million: 166.4
Merchant Marine: No. of Vessels: 101
Total Deadweight Tonnage 000: 403.0
International Cargo Loaded tons 000: 159,084
International Cargo Off-loaded tons 000: 456,636
Airports with Scheduled Flights: 43
Traffic: Passenger-mi million: 2,837
Freight-mi million: 662
Length of Canals mi: 8,900 km 14,300

Tourism

Number of Tourists to 000: 841
Number of Tourists from 000: 1,140
Tourist Receipts $million: 851
Tourist Expenditures $million: 822

Communications

Telephones 000: 3,873
Cost of Local Calls 3 mins: $0.02
Cellular Telephones 000: 275
Fax Machines 000: 100
Personal Computers 000: 630
Internet Hosts per million persons: 58
Mail: Post Offices: 1,655
Pieces of Mail Handled million: 136
Pieces of Mail Handled per person: 3.9

EDUCATION

Schooling is universal, free, and obligatory for five years from the ages of seven to 12, but in practice, 30 percent or more of rural children do not attend.

Schooling lasts 11 years divided into five years of primary school, four years of lower secondary or middle school, and two years of upper secondary school. On the completion of secondary school, students are awarded the *bachillerato* (baccalaureate). There is a high failure, dropout, and grade repetition rate because of the rigidity of the examination system and the low quality of education generally. By 1987, 90 percent of children between the ages of seven and 11 attended primary school, more than doubling enrollment in a single generation. But enrollment rates at secondary schools are far lower, even after increasing sixfold since the early 1960s. In 1998 there were 46,707 primary schools and 8,161 secondary schools.

The academic year runs from February to November. The medium of instruction is Spanish throughout.

The public school system comprises national, departmental, and municipal schools. The private sector is made up of schools run by the Roman Catholic Church and a few other religious organizations, schools run by nonreligious private organizations, and cooperative schools run by communities. All private schools are required to be licensed, must conform to state curricula models, and are subject to supervision by public authorities.

Primary teachers are trained in secondary-level normal schools and secondary school teachers in university institutes of pedagogy. By 1990 about 55 percent of secondary school teachers had university degrees. Unqualified teachers are not nearly as prevalent as in the 1960s, prior to a burst of public investment in education. Nonetheless, teacher training is sorely inadequate to meet growing needs. Schools faced with a shortage of qualified teachers often employ part-time personnel informally known as "taxicab teachers."

Although the national literacy rate is impressive at 91.3 percent (1995), well over the Latin American average, it is much lower in the countryside where even those who have acquired literacy soon lapse into functional illiteracy. In an unusual departure from the norm in Latin America, women have a slightly higher overall rate of literacy than men. Adult education and literacy programs are conducted by a number of organizations, such as the armed forces, business organizations, and religious and welfare institutions.

The primary responsibility for public education is divided between the central government and the departments. About 55 percent of primary-school costs are met by the national Ministry of Education, 22 percent by the departments, and 23 percent from the private-school resources, although the actual proportion varies widely from region to region. The central government has greatly increased financial support for public secondary education. In the past, tuition was charged at the secondary level; even though the government granted scholarships to students in both private and public institutions, the effect was to confine secondary education to the elite, reinforcing social stratification. Since the government assumed primary financial responsibility for secondary schools in 1975, the rate of attendance has greatly increased.

By law the government is required to spend at least 10 percent of its annual budget on education. Total expenditure on education was equivalent to 3.7 percent of GDP in 1994.

Higher education is provided by 20 general public universities, one open university (recently established to expand educational opportunities for Colombians by offering distance learning), one technical university, and universities of education, education technology, and industry. Additionally, there are two public colleges of administration, one school of police studies, one institute of fine art, one polytechnic, and one conservatory. The private sector has 25 secular universities, four Roman Catholic universities, one college of education, and one school of public administration. The mushrooming of higher education, though it has democratized university studies to a limited degree, has come at the expense of quality instruction. The largest and the oldest university is the National University of Bogotá, founded in 1572. Other major universities are the University of Antioquía in Medellín, Universidad Javeriana, Foundation University of Bogotá, Xavier University, Gran Colombia University, and Universidad de los Andes.

Education

Literacy Rate %: 91.3
- Male %: 91.2
- Female %: 91.4

First Level: Primary schools: 46,707
- Teachers: 170,526
- Students: 4,327,507
- Student-Teacher Ratio: 25.4
- Net Enrollment Ratio: 85

Second Level: Secondary Schools: 8,161
- Teachers: 141,484
- Students: 2,879,681
- Student-Teacher Ratio: 20.3
- Net Enrollment Ratio: 50

Vocational Level: Schools: —
- Students: —

Third Level: Institutions: —
- Teachers: 54,164
- Students: 510,649
- Student-Ratio Level: 9.4
- Gross Enrollment Ratio: 17.2
- Students per 100,000: 1,643
- % of Population Age 25 and over with Postsecondary Education: —

Public Expenditure on Education as % of GDP: 3.5

SCIENCE AND TECHNOLOGY

Science and Technology

Scientists and Engineers in R&D per 1 million persons: —
Expenditures in R&D as % of GDP: —
High-Tech Exports $million: 303
Patent Applications by Residents: 87

MEDIA

In 1995 34 daily newspapers were published in Colombia, with a total circulation of 1.5 million. The largest-selling daily is *El Espectador,* one of the most influential newspapers in the Spanish-speaking world, followed by the liberal *El Tiempo.*

Both these papers tend to support the Liberal Party line. Bogotá has three other dailies. Others are published in Barranquilla (three), Bucaramanga (two), Cali (three), Cartagena, Cúcuta (two), Manizales, Medellín (two), Montería, Neiva, Pasto, Pereira (three), Popayán, Santa Marta, Tunja, and Villavicencio. The periodical press numbers more than a thousand titles with a combined circulation of 850,000 copies.

Relations between the press and the state have been characterized by frequent government attempts to restrict a free press, most recently during the presidency of Ernesto Samper. But, generally, freedom of the press has been preserved and abuses have been infrequent. All newspapers are privately owned and function as official or unofficial spokesmen for the various political factions. At least a dozen Colombian presidents have been journalists, and a close alliance exists between the media and the political system. Journalism is of a very high level and newspapers are major organs of political debate. Journalists perform their duties under conditions scarcely imaginable: only Algeria has seen more reporters and editors killed during the 1990s.

The domestic news agencies are Colprensa and CIEP-El País. Foreign news bureaus in Bogotá include AP, UPI, AFP, ANSA, IPS, DPA, Efe, Reuters, and TASS.

Television, introduced in 1954, is administered by the National Institute of Radio and Television (INRAVISION). There are two services, a national service, with three channels (two commercial, one educational) and a network of 17 powerful transmitters and repeater stations, and Telebogotá, an official commercial service that can be received only in Bogotá and two other regional channels. The national service is on the air all the time. Two privately run stations were seeking to start up in 1998.

Media

Daily Newspapers: 46
- Total Circulation 000: 2,200
- Circulation per 1,000: 64

Books Published: —
Magazines: —
Radio Receivers 000: 5,400
per 1,000: 150
Television sets 000: 7,314
per 1,000: 188

MOST IMPORTANT MEDIA:

Press. The following are dailies published at Bogotá, unless otherwise noted: *El Espectador* (215,000), *Ilerista,* Liberal; *El Tiempo* (200,000 daily, 350,000 Sunday); *El Espacio* (165,000), *Turbayista* Liberal; *El Colombiano* (Medellín, 120,000), Conservative; *El País* (Cali, 70,000 daily, 110,000 Sunday), *Ospina-pastranista* Conservative; *La República* (70,000), *El Nuevo Siglo* (68,000), *Alvarista* Conservative; *El Heraldo* (Barranquilla, 65,000); *Occidente* (Cali, 50,000); *El Pueblo* (Cali, 50,000), Liberal; *La Patria* (Manizales, 25,000), Conservative. In August 1988 PC leader Misael Pastrana Borrero launched a new conservative daily, *La Prensa*, at Bogotá to counter the Liberal influence of *El Tiempo* and *El Espectador*.

News agencies. The domestic facility is the National News Agency "Colprensa" (Agencia Nacional de Noticias "Colprensa"); in addition, a number of foreign agencies maintain offices at Bogotá.

Radio and television. The six radio networks, of which only the small Radiodifusora Nacional is publicly owned, service more than 500 stations and some 4.4 million receivers. The country's three national television channels are controlled by the Instituto Nacional de Radio y Televisión, although broadcasting time is distributed among private production companies. There are also four regional channels, while cable service for Bogotá was introduced in 1985.

CULTURE

Cultural Indicators

Public Libraries Number: 974
Volumes: 2,381,000
Registered borrowers: —
Museums Number: 74
Annual Attendance: 1,542,000
Cinema Production of Long Films: —
Number of Cinemas: —
Seating Capacity: —
Annual Attendance million: —
Annual Attendance per capita: —

STATUS OF WOMEN

Colombia's deep traditions of Catholicism tended to restrict the ambitions of women until fairly recent times. In the 1970s and 1980s the country experienced social modernization on a broad scale, even as bouts of violence threatened to unmoor society. The percentage of women working expanded so that by 1985 one-third of the labor force was female. Forty-three percent of women are now in the paid workforce. This has had several effects: the old-time subservience to men was extensively undermined once women experienced a degree of financial independence; for poorer families, which had always been more reliant on female labor, women's earnings were a vital supplement; and the birth rate dropped sharply. Upper-class women have long had the benefit of higher education, and it became customary for them to contribute their energies to social welfare, education, and the arts; some (a larger number than is typical for Latin America) even went far in politics. The Samper administration had a woman foreign minister, María Emma Mejía, and one of Samper's former ambassadors, Noemi Sanín, ran a strong third in the presidential election of 1998. It is still the case, however, that women who achieve are regarded as something of a novelty.

Women have equal civil and property rights by law. Their economic situation, though improving, is inferior; especially in rural areas, they are concentrated in low-productivity, low-income sectors. Although Colombian women are legally entitled to pay equal to that of their male counterparts and are normally paid equal salaries when employed by the government, this is not generally the case in private industry. A growing number are receiving higher education; they currently comprise 40 percent of the university population, allowing them a much wider range of career options.

Colombia is one of the original signatories to the UN Declaration on Population. It is also one of the few Latin American countries to adopt family planning as an official policy and to integrate it into development plans. In 1968 the Colombian Congress enacted legislation supporting planned parenthood and established the Institute of Family Welfare as an official agency. Private efforts in this field have been coordinated since 1985 by the Colombian Family Welfare Association (Asociación Pro-Bienestar de la Familia Colombiana, PROFAMILIA), a member of the International Planned Parenthood Federation. The hierarchy of the Roman Catholic Church has voiced only moderate opposition to these programs.

More than 60 percent of married women of childbearing age use birth control. The fertility rate has dropped steadily since the mid-1960s; overall, women have an average of 2.7 children, though the figure for rural areas is higher.

A divorce law came into force only in the mid-1970s and was valid only for civil marriages, not Catholic ones.

Women

Gender Empowerment Measure: 41
Seats Held in Parliament by Women %: 9.8
Female Administrators and Managers %: 31.0
Female Professional and Technical Workers %: 44.0
Women's Share of Earned Income %: 33
Women in Government %: 25

HEALTH, FOOD, AND NUTRITION

Health

Number of Physicians: 36,551
Number of Dentists: 13,815
Number of Nurses: 46,376
Number of Pharmacists: —
Population per Physician: 914
Number of Hospitals: 947
Hospital Beds per 10,000: 14
Hospital Bed Occupancy Rate: 57.2
Infant Mortality Rate per 1,000 live births: 40
Maternal Mortality Rate per 100,000 live births: 100
Total Health Expenditures as % of GDP: 3.98
Health Expenditures per capita $: 51
HIV Infected % of adults: 0.36
Cigarette Consumption per smoker per year: 1,684
% of Smokers: Male: 35
Female: 19
Access to Safe Water %: 96

Food and Nutrition

Food Supply as % of FAO Requirements: 119
% of Consumption Expenditures on Food: 45.0
Daily Available Calories per capita: 2,758
% of Total Calories derived from:
Cereals: 32.5
Potatoes, cassava: 7.4
Meat, poultry: 6.8
Fish: 0.3
Eggs, milk: 7.7
Fruits, vegetables: 7.6
Fats, oils: 10.8

ENVIRONMENT

Colombia's constitution of 1992 is considered by those knowledgeable about ecology one of the "greenest" ever devised. It has elevated environmental affairs to a standalone ministry and added five new institutes dealing with conservation-related issues. It also redistributed some decision-making powers outward, giving a greater say over nature and resource management to local communities, in particular, Afro-Colombian and indigenous communities. The country has had framework laws on the environment since 1974, earlier than just about any other Latin American state. Enforcement is spotty, however. The government does not exercise control over its entire territory, first of all. It has made a priority of foreign investment to exploit the land's energy potential, particularly in the *llanos* in the eastern portion of the state, but the consequences are habitat destruction as exploration areas are denuded of vegetation and problems of waste disposal, compounded by frequent guerrilla attacks on pipelines, creating oil spills. The new ministry has a deficiency in terms of expert staff to carry out directives. International and local nongovernmental organizations, however, have helped fill in the gaps in order to implement conservation plans in partnership with private industry, and they have assisted in education outreach to change popular attitudes toward the natural world and raise awareness of how certain activities harm the environment.

The primary environmental issues in Colombia today are deforestation, soil contamination by pesticides, and air pollution from vehicular exhaust in cities, Bogotá most of all. Deforestation is claiming between 300,000 and 800,000 hectares a year. The pace of deforestation slowed slightly in the early 1990s; by the middle of the decade, forests still accounted for 46 percent of the country's territory.

The nation has 9.4 million hectares protected as nature reserves, equivalent to 9 percent of its area; of these, 2.5 million hectares are classified as international biosphere reserves. Colombia ranks among the top 10 countries in the UN Environmental Program's "megadiversity" ratings, accounting for an incredible 10 percent of the world's biological diversity. It has more species of birds (1,776) and amphibians (620) than any country on earth.

Environment

Forest Area sq km: 530,000
Average Annual Deforestation sq km: 2,622
Nationally Protected Areas as % of Total Land Area: 9.0
Freshwater Access cubic meters per capita: 26,722
Emissions of Organic Water Pollutants kg per day: 111,139
CO_2 Emissions per capita ton: 1.7

CHRONOLOGY

1944 Discontent with government of Alfonso López Pumarejo leads to violence in Bogotá; Conservative rival Laureano Gómez Castro is imprisoned.

1946 Presidential elections are held; Conservative Mariano Ospina Pérez wins over two Liberal candidates, Gabriel Turbay and leftist Jorge Eliécer Gaitán.

1948 The assassination of Gaitán, Bogotá's mayor, provokes mass riot, known as bogotazo, in which 2,000 are killed; undeclared civil war, called La Violencia, breaks out.

1949 Repression and violence escalates; Ospina Perez fires all Liberal governors; Laureano Gómez elected president on the Conservative ticket in an election boycotted by the opposition.

1952 Colombia relinquishes rights over Monjes Archipelago to Venezuela.

1953 A civilian-military coalition led by General Gustavo Rojas Pinilla deposes Gomez; Rojas is named president.

1954 Violence is renewed as Rojas becomes a virtual dictator.

1957 Rojas reelected by a puppet assembly; arrest of Conservative leader Guillermo León Valencia is followed by the "Days of May" riots and demonstrations; Rojas forced to hand over power to a five-man junta headed by General Gabriel Paris and go into exile; Liberal and Conservative parties issue Declaration of Sitges creating the National Front and agreeing to share power and alternate in presidency.

1958 Alberto Lleras Camargo is elected president unopposed on the Liberal ticket; Colombian Institute of Agrarian Reform created to undertake country's first serious land reform program; Colombia joins Latin American Free Trade Area.

1959 Rojas is tried for illegal use of power and stripped of political rights.

1961 Rojas forms the National Popular Alliance Party (ANAPO).

1962 State of siege is raised; Valencia is elected president.

1965 State of siege is reimposed, following continuing political violence.

1966 Carlos Lleras Restrepo, a Liberal, is elected president.

1969 Colombia joins the Andean Group.

1970 Misael Pastrana Borrero is elected president on a Conservative ticket.

1971 Supporters of the ANAPO form an armed wing known as the Movimiento 19 de Abril (M-19).

1973 A new concordat is signed with the Vatican.

1974 National Front pact relating to the rotation of the presidency ends; Liberal Alfonso López Michelsen is elected president.

1975 López imposes state of siege as guerrilla groups escalate violence in urban and rural areas.

1976 Colombia forgoes further U.S. aid as a demonstration of its own self-sufficiency.

1978 Julio César Turbay Ayala, the Liberal candidate, elected president; Colombia signs eight-nation Amazon Pact.

1980 M-19 guerrillas seize Dominican Republic embassy in Bogotá, taking U.S. ambassador and 24 other diplomatic personnel as hostages; seizure ends with the kidnappers being flown to Cuba.

1982 Belisario Betancur Cuartas, the Conservative candidate, is elected; state of siege lifted once more; amnesty law passed under which 350 rebels are freed.

1984 Justice Minister Rodrigo Lara Bonilla slain; Betancur declares state of siege; two rebel groups sign truce.

1985 M-19 rebels take the Palace of Justice but government troops recapture it; Nevado del Ruiz volcano erupts, killing 25,000; state of economic and social emergency declared.

1986 Liberal candidate Virgilio Barco Vargas elected president; six guerrilla groups form joint front called the Coordinadora Guerrillera Simón Bolívar (CGSB).

1987 Supreme Court declares extradition treaty with the United States unconstitutional.

1988 Attorney general is assassinated; first direct elections to the mayoralities are disrupted by violence and more than 30 candidates killed.

1989 Drug trafficking cartels blamed for the deaths of several leading politicians; Barco reinstates by decree a treaty that allows Colombian drug traffickers to be summarily extradited to the United States; guerrilla groups under the CGSB agree to government's peace initiative; M-19 formally announces that peace treaty has been reached and is formally constituted as a political party.

1990 César Gaviria Trujillo is elected president and in his victory speech vows to bring terrorism to its knees, later issues decree pledging that drug traffickers who surrender to the central government will not be extradited.

1991 More than 50 die in attacks launched by rebels protesting their exclusion from assembly elected to reform Colombia's constitution; Popular Liberation Army (ELP) ends its 23-year war against the government; the new constitution, promising stronger judicial protections for the individual and restricting emergency decree powers of the executive, is ratified.

1992 Strikes by telecommunications workers protesting impending privatization and by those in the electric power industry disrupt economy; Medellín drug cartel kingpin Pablo Escobar escapes from prison.

1993 Police gun down Escobar after attempting for months to negotiate his surrender; his death brings the demise of the Medellín cartel.

1994 "Group of Three" (Mexico, Venezuela, Colombia) sign 10-year trade liberalization pact; Amnesty International calls Colombia one of the world's worst human rights violators; Liberals win elections; new president Ernesto Samper Pizano is shortly afterward accused of taking drug money in his campaign, provoking political crisis.

1996 Congress exonerates Samper in drug scandal; United States removes Colombia from its list of countries cooperating in narcotics control, blocking its access to aid from multilateral lending institutions.

1998 Liberals hold the majority in parliamentary elections, but barely so in each house; Andrés Pastrana Arango wins presidential election for Conservatives, makes bid for talks with Colombian Revolutionary Armed Forces (FARC) by offering to demilitarize 15,000 square miles in Caquetá and Meta departments, essentially ceding territorial control to the guerrillas.

1999 Military opposition to Pastrana's peace strategy leads to resignation of defense minister and more than 200 army officers; United Self-Defense Forces of Colombia (AUC), the leading paramilitary group, demands inclusion in peace negotiations; United States recertifies Colombian cooperation against drug smuggling.

2000 United States offers $1.3 billion, mostly in military aid, to support Pastrana's $7.5 billion "Plan Colombia" to fight drug trafficking and promote legal forms of development.

2002 Right-wing candidate Álvaro Uribe Vélez wins landslide victory in presidential election, marking the first time a winner is chosen in the first round of voting.

BIBLIOGRAPHY

Bushnell, David. *The Making of Modern Colombia: A Nation in Spite of Itself*. Berkeley, Calif., 1993.

Drexler, Robert W. *Colombia and the United Slates: Narcotics Traffic and a Failed Foreign Policy*. Jefferson, N.C., 1997.

Farnsworth-Alvear, Ann. *Dulcinea in the Factory: Myths, Morals, Men and Women in Colombia's Industrial Experiment, 1905–1960*. Durham, N.C., 2000.

Giraldo, Javier. *Colombia: The Genocidal Democracy*. Monroe, Me., 1996.

Human Rights Watch. *Colombia: Killer Networks*. New York, 1996.

Jaramillo, Carlos Felipe. *Liberalization, Crisis, and Change in Colombian Agriculture*. Boulder, Colo., 1998.

OFFICIAL PUBLICATIONS

Colombia. *Colombia estadística* (2 vol.; annual); *XV Censo nacional de población y IV de vivienda* (1985).

CONTACT INFORMATION

Embassy of Colombia
2118 LeRoy Place NW
Washington, D.C. 20008
Phone: (202)387-8338 Fax: (202)232-8643

INTERNET RESOURCES

- National Administration Department of Statistics http://www.dane.gov.co

COMOROS

BASIC FACT SHEET

OFFICIAL NAME:
Federal Islamic Republic of the Comoros (République Fédérale Islamique des Comores)

ABBREVIATION:
CO

CAPITAL:
Moroni

HEAD OF STATE:
President Azali Assoumani (resigned 2002)

HEAD OF GOVERNMENT:
Prime Minister Hamada Madi (from 2000)

NATURE OF GOVERNMENT:
Republic

POPULATION:
563,000 (1999)

AREA:
1,795 sq km (693 sq mi) (excluding the island of Mayotte, which voted in a referendum in 1976 to remain linked with France as an overseas department; however, all figures in this section relating to the period before 1976 include Mayotte unless otherwise indicated). In 1997 the islands of Anjouan and Mohedi declared their independence.

ETHNIC MAJORITY:
Mixed groups of African, Arab, and Malagasy descent

LANGUAGES:
French (official) and Comorian (national)

RELIGIONS:
Islam and Christianity

UNIT OF CURRENCY:
Comoran Franc

NATIONAL FLAG:
Green with a white crescent in the center of the field, its points facing downward; there are four white five-pointed stars placed in a line between the points of the crescent.

NATIONAL EMBLEM:
None

NATIONAL ANTHEM:
"The Flag Is Flying"

NATIONAL HOLIDAYS:
July 6 (Independence Day, National Day); also variable Islamic festivals

DATE OF INDEPENDENCE:
July 20, 1996

DATE OF CONSTITUTION:
October 20, 1996

GEOGRAPHICAL FEATURES

In 1978 the Islamic regime adopted new names for the islands as part of its de-Westernization drive: Njazidja for Grande-Comore; Nzwani for Anjouan; Mwali for Moheli; and Mahore for Mayotte. The old names and spellings are retained in this chapter to avoid confusion.

Comoros is in the northern entrance of the Mozambique Channel, about halfway between the northern tip of Madagascar and the mainland coast of Mozambique. Comoros includes three main islands—Grande-Comore, Anjouan, and Moheli—and several islets, with a total land area of 1,795 sq km (693 sq mi). Grande-Comore, the largest of the islands, comprises 1,148 sq km (443 sq mi); Moheli, 290 sq km (112 sq mi); and Anjouan, 357 sq km (138 sq mi). The archipelago extends 177 km (110 mi) eastsouth-east to west-northwest and 97 km (60 mi) north-northeast to south-southwest. The total length of the coastline is 285 km (177 mi). Comoros also claims de jure sovereignty over the island of Mayotte (374 sq km, 144 sq mi), but the

Comoros

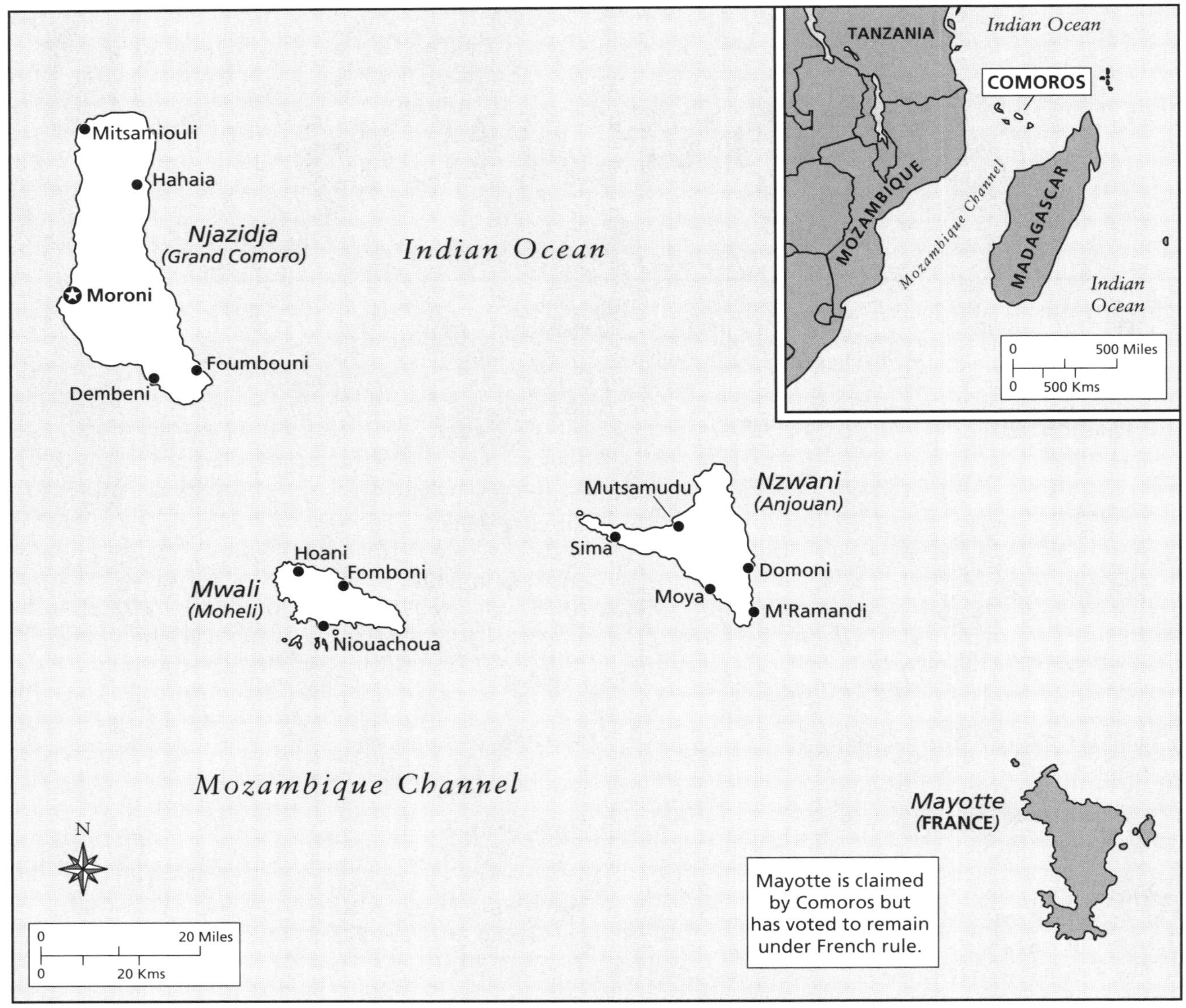

republic's jurisdiction is not accepted by the Moharais, as inhabitants of Mayotte are known, who have voted for union with France as an overseas department.

The Comoros are volcanic in origin, and Mount Kartala on Grande-Comore (2,561 m; 8,402 ft) is an active volcano. The center of Grand-Comore is a desert lava field. The black basalt relief rises 1,200 to 1,600 m (3,950 to 5,250 ft) on Anjouan and 500 to 800 m (1,650 to 2,600 ft) on Moheli. Mayotte has a lagoon fringed with coral reefs.

Geography

Area sq km: 1,795 sq mi 693
World Rank: 175th
Land Boundaries, km: 0
Coastline, km: 340
Elevation Extremes meters
Lowest: Indian Ocean 0
Highest: Mount Kartala 2,360

Land Use % Arable land: 35
Permanent Crops: 10
Permanent Pastures: 7
Forest and Woodland: 18
Other: 30

Population of Principal Cities

Moroni	30,000

CLIMATE AND WEATHER

The islands have a tropical climate, with a dry season from May to October and a wet season from November to April. Temperatures average 28°C (82°F) in the wet season and 20°C (68°F) in the dry season. Rainfall varies between 1,100 and 5,500 mm (43 and 217 in). The prevailing winds are the Indian monsoons from the north in the wet season and the continental southeast winds in the dry season.

Climate and Weather

Mean Temperature 68°F to 82°F
Average Rainfall: 43 in to 217 in

POPULATION

Population Indicators

Total Population: 1999 563,000
World Rank: 163rd
Density per sq mi: 783 per sq km 302.4
% of annual growth (1994–99): 3.1
Male %: 48.5
Female%: 51.5
Urban%: 28.5
Age Distribution: % 0–14: 47.6
15–29: 27.0
30–44: 13.1
45–59: 7.7
60–74: 3.5
75 and over: 1.0
Population 2020: 1,022,000
Birth Rate per 1,000: 45.8
Death Rate per 1,000: 10.3
Population Doubling Time (years): 23
Infant Mortality Rate per 1,000 live births: 75.3
Rate of Natural Increase per 1,000: 35.5
Total Fertility Rate: 6.7
Expectation of Life (years): Males 56.4
Females 61.0
Marriage Rate per 1,000: —
Divorce Rate per 1,000: —
Total Number of Households: —
Average Size of Households: 5.6
% of Illegitimate Children: —
Induced Abortions: —
Rate per 100 live births: —

ETHNIC COMPOSITION

The islands have a mixed population, consisting of persons of African, Arab, and Malagasy descent. The racial composition also shows Malay, Indian, Chinese, and Persian influences. The principal ethnic group, known as the Antalaotra, is of mixed origin.

The original inhabitants of the islands were Idumians from the Red Sea region. During the Middle Ages, Arabs invaded the islands, arriving in successive waves, and set up small sultanates. Because these sultanates were constantly engaged in internecine warfare, the archipelago came to be known as the Islands of the Quarreling Sultanates. The islands were also visited by Indian, Malay, and Chinese traders, adding to the racial variety.

At the time of independence there were nearly 1,500 Europeans, mainly French, living in the archipelago. Most of the French departed following the expropriation of French property in 1976.

LANGUAGES

The national language is Comorian, a hybrid language related to Swahili, with borrowed Arabic words. The official language is French. Both Swahili and Arabic are understood by the majority of the inhabitants.

Principal Languages and Their Speakers

Arabic	
Comorian	423,000
Comorian-French	73,000
Comorian-Malagasy	31,000
Comorian-Arabic	9,000
Comorian-Swahili	3,000
Comorian-French-other	22,000
French	110,000
Other	3,000

RELIGIONS

Islam in its Sunni form is the religion of the vast majority of Comorans. Christianity is the majority religion on the island of Mayotte, and the Christian-Muslim conflict is one of the factors that influenced Mahorais to reject union with Comoros.

According to the constitution, Islam is the "wellspring of the principles and rules that guide the state and its institutions." However, most aspects of freedom of religion and the right to practice openly non-Islamic faiths are guaranteed and respected in practice. There are established churches for Protestants and Catholics. Although Christian missionaries work in local hospitals and schools, they are not allowed to proselytize openly.

Religious Affiliations

Sunni Muslim	559,000
Christian	4,000

HISTORICAL BACKGROUND

The archipelago has served in past centuries as a stepping stone between the African continent and Madagascar, as a southern outpost for Arab traders operating along the East African coast, and as a center of Islamic culture. The name *Comoros* is derived from the Arabic *kamar* or *kumr*, meaning "moon," although this name was first applied by Arab geographers to Madagascar. According to one local legend, King Husain ibn Ali established a settlement on Comoros at the beginning of the 11th century. He undoubtedly found Bantu peoples who apparently migrated to the island before the 14th century. The Bantus were greeted by an earlier group of inhabitants, a Malayo-Indonesian people.

In the 15th and 16th centuries, Shirazi Arabs established a settlement on the northwest coast of Madagascar and on Njazidja and Nzwani. The Shirazi, who divided Njazidja into 11 sultanates and Nzwani into two, extended their rule to Mahoré and Mwali, although the latter in the 19th century came under the control of Malagasy rulers. The Shirazi built mosques and established Islam as the religion of the islands. By the end of the 16th century, the Comoros had become a center of regional trade, exporting rice, ambergris, spices, and slaves to ports in East Africa and the Middle East in exchange for opium, cotton cloth, and other items.

Comoros was exposed to European contacts following visits by Portuguese and British navigators in the 16th century. French rule dates from 1841, when the king of Mayotte was persuaded to cede his island to France. The rulers of the other three main islands followed his example one by one between 1886 and 1909, and in 1912 Les Comores was proclaimed a French colony. In 1914 the islands were joined administratively to Madagascar. As the minor appendage of a larger and culturally different country, Comoros was neglected and remained in precolonial condition until independence. Whatever economic and political reforms were instituted were designed to benefit the French ruling class and foreign companies. The traditional social structure remained undisturbed, and the old ruling class was absorbed into the bureaucracy as minor officials. The economy was entirely dependent on French subsidies, and the country had neither the local resources nor the infrastructure necessary to stand on its own feet.

In 1973, growing demands for self-government resulted in agreement with France to obtain independence in five years. The agreement provided for France to retain responsibility for defense, foreign affairs, and currency during the transition period. In July 1975 the Comoran legislature passed a resolution unilaterally declaring independence. The deputies from Mayotte abstained, and that island remained a French protectorate.

After the declaration of independence, Ahmed Abdallah, leader of the preindependence government and head of the Democratic Union of the Comoros, was designated president. He was deposed in August 1975 in a coup engineered by the Front National Unie (FNU), a coalition of opposition parties. Ali Soilih, a leader of the People's Party who took part in the coup, was elected president by the FNU in January 1976.

Soilih envisaged a socialist revolution as the answer to the country's political and economic problems. He implemented a series of reforms that included a drastic reduction in the bureaucracy, a reconstruction of the administrative structure, and a new system of land distribution. He destroyed old government records and gave considerable authority to popular committees of young people. In an effort to curb the power of Islamic religious leaders, he banned the veil and the fivefold daily prayer. Reforms were accompanied by reports of the government's brutality toward citizens. Unrest grew, and at least three unsuccessful coups were attempted between April 1976 and January 1978.

Soilih was finally ousted in a coup led by French mercenaries in May 1978. He was placed under house arrest and was killed, allegedly while trying to escape. His predecessor, Abdallah, was restored as president.

Abdallah dominated the Comoran government from his return to power in 1978 until his assassination in November 1989. Daunted by reprisals that accompanied the return, political opposition reemerged only in 1982. Unopposed, Abdallah was overwhelmingly reelected to a second term as president in September 1984. A member of the French-based opposition reportedly attempted to get his name on the ballot but was disqualified on technical grounds. There were also unverified charges of electoral fraud during the presidential election, and non-Comoran observers stated that the announced percentage of eligible voters participating conflicted with their own observations of low turnout in some areas. However, most observers of the Comoran political scene believe that Abdallah would have won the election under any circumstances, although with somewhat less than the 99 percent he received.

Following the election, Abdallah gained passage of constitutional amendments abolishing the position of prime minister and reducing the powers of the Federal Assembly. In the 1987 legislative elections all of Abdallah's candidates were declared elected in balloting termed "a grotesque masquerade" by opponents.

During the 1980s there were at least three unsuccessful coups against the regime. Abdallah was assassinated in November 1989 in an attack on his palace by a group of rebels led by disgruntled former army commander Ahmed Muhammad. Said Muhammad Djohar, head of the Supreme Court, became president of the interim government and won election to the office in March 1990.

In 1991 the new president of the Supreme Court led an unsuccessful coup to oust President Said Muhammad Djohar. Thereupon opposition leaders led by Mohamed Taki Abdelkarim met in Paris to plot seizure of the government. In 1992 army officers mounted another coup that was put down, but not before serious clashes with progovernment troops. A period of instability followed with President Djohar naming and firing nine prime ministers as well as members of the Election Commission. In 1995, Colonel Bob Denard who had led an earlier coup in 1978 reappeared and seized President Djohar and established a military committee of transition headed by a little-known army captain, Ayouba Combo. Within a day, French paratroopers landed and quickly rounded up Denard and his mercenaries. Prime Minister Mohamed Caabi el Yachroutu named himself president while a former prime minister, Said Ali Mohamed, set up a rival government. Following French-inspired negotiations, elections were held in 1996 in which Taki won with 64.3 percent of the vote. Antigovernment strikes and riots erupted in 1997 in support of civil servants who had not been paid for years. Faced with open rebellion the president dismissed the governor of Anjouan whereupon the latter declared the independence of Anjouan. The island of Moheli also declared independence. Meanwhile, Anjouan itself faced a civil war by rival factions. In 1998, Taki, wearied by all these troubles, died of a heart attack and was succeeded as president by Tadjidine Ben Said Massonde, a former prime minister. His authority was now limited to Grande-Comore. Within a year he was overthrown by a military coup led by Col. Assoumani Azali.

CONSTITUTION

Under the constitution approved by popular referendum in 1996, Comoros is a federal Islamic republic. The constitutional head of state is the president, elected by universal suffrage for a five-year term; reelection is permitted only once. The president is assisted by an appointed council of ministers, and he appoints a prime minister, as head of government, from the majority party in the assembly. Each island elects a governor and island assembly. The governors enjoy considerable administrative autonomy, and the assemblies have some legislative freedom. The constitution also prescribes the rough division of government revenues between the federation and the individual islands.

Legislative power is vested in a bicameral legislature, consisting of the 42-member Federal Assembly, elected by universal suffrage for four-year terms, and the 15-member Senate, selected by an electoral college for six-year terms.

LOCAL GOVERNMENT

For purposes of local administration, Comoros is divided into three prefectures coterminous with the three main islands and their surrounding islets. These islands are further organized into seven regions and 55 to 60 moudirias, or regional council centers. Moudirias are broken down into bavous (districts), the basic units of local government. District government is conducted by district assemblies, or councils, elected by universal suffrage.

Local Government

Principal administrative divisions, capitals, area, population

AREA AND POPULATION

Islands	Capitals	area sq mi	area sq km	population 1995 estimate
Mwali (Moheili)	Fomboni	112	290	27,600
Nzwani (Anjouan)	Mutsamudu	164	424	211,900
Ngazidja (Grande-Comore)	Moroni	443	1,148	250,500
TOTAL		719	1,862	490,000

PARLIAMENT

The bicameral parliament consists of the 42-member Federal Assembly, elected by universal suffrage for four-year terms, and the 15-member Senate, selected by an electoral college for six-year terms. The Federal Assembly was

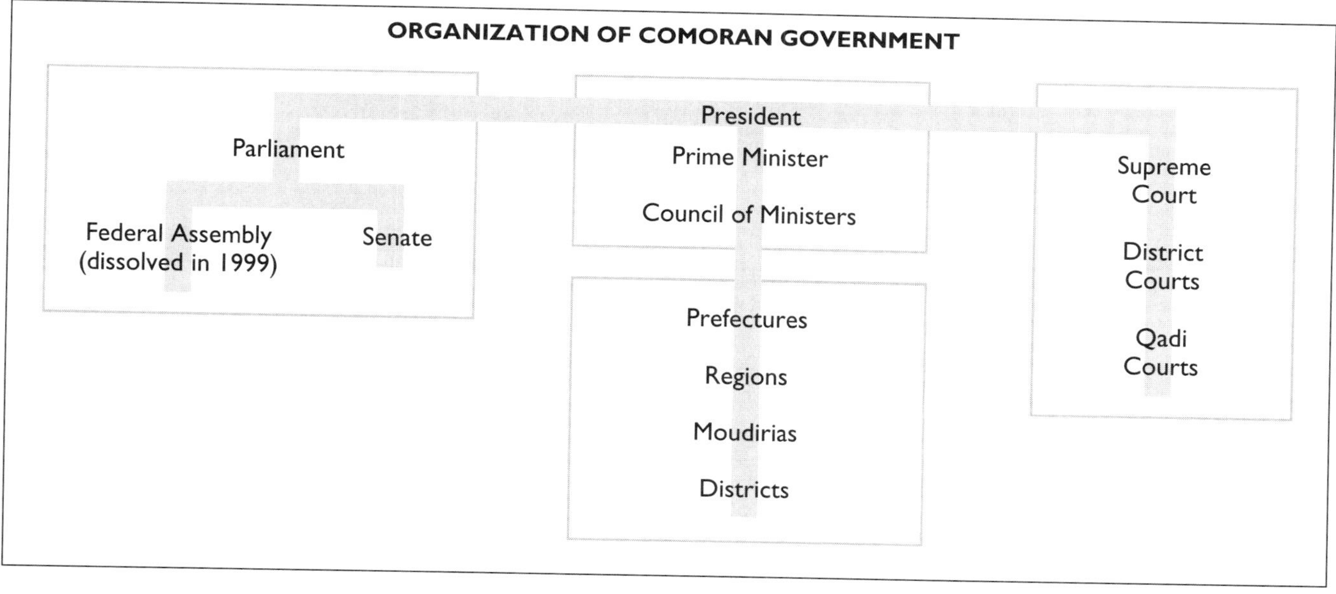

dissolved following the coup of April 30, 1999. Matters covered by federal legislation included defense; mail and telecommunications; external and interisland transportation; civil, penal and industrial law; external trade; federal taxation; long-term economic planning; education; and health.

The council of each island is directly elected for four years. Each electoral ward, of which there may not be fewer than 10 or more than 35 per island, elects one councillor. Each council meets for not more than 15 days at a time, in March and December, and if necessary in extraordinary sessions. The councils are responsible for nonfederal legislation, including local taxation, and must be consulted on federal matters that affect the island, such as economic development.

POLITICAL PARTIES

Until 1989 the only authorized political party was the Union Comorienne pour le Progrès (Udzima). However, with the new constition adopted in 1996, parties that showed a certain amount of electoral strength were permitted to continue in existence and all others were to disband. The largest party in the country is Rassemblement National pour le Developement, which holds nearly 90 percent of the seats in the legislature and supports the current president. The Front National pour la Justice is an Islamic fundamentalist organization that holds three seats in the Federal Assembly. In addition to these two parties, there were more than a dozen political organizations active in Comoros.

Political Parties

Forum for National Recovery, 1994
Movement for Democracy and Progress
Democratic Front of the Comoros
Islands' Fraternity and Unity Party
Forces for Republican Action, 1996
National Rally for Development, 1996
Maecha Bora Party
National Front for Justice
Rally for Democracy and Revival, 1993
Rally for Change and Democracy, 1990
Movement for Renovation and Democratic Action
Comoran Popular Front
Comoran Party for Democracy and Progress
Rally for the Triumph of Democracy, 1993
There are three separatist groups in Anjuan, one of the three islands. They are
Anjouan People's Movement
Organization for the Independence of Anjouan
Democratic Front Party

Political Parties: Strength in Parliament Most Recent Elections

Federal Assembly (Assemblée Federale). Following the two-stage balloting of December 1 and 8, 1996, the seats were distributed as follows: the National Rally for Development, 39 seats; the National Front for Justice, 3; and independents 1. The Assembly was suspended by the military junta which assumed power in April 1999; however, the new leaders pledged to go forward with preparations for legislative elections in 2000.

LEGAL SYSTEM

The judicial system is headed by the Supreme Court in Moroni. Subordinate courts of first instance are in each district or moudiria. There are 16 religious courts, or qadi courts, which apply the Shari'a, or Muslim personal law. Juries are employed in criminal trials.

No information is available on correctional facilities or the penal system.

LAW ENFORCEMENT

Law Enforcement

Offenses reported to the police per 100,000: —
Murder: —
Assault: —
Burglary: —
Automobile Theft: —
Population per Police officer: 960
Death Penalty: Yes, but no execution since 1975

HUMAN RIGHTS

In terms of political and civil rights, Comoros is classified as a partly free country. Feudal rule and the dominance of Islam have long been the two main characteristics of Comoro society. This tradition, reinforced during the French period, survived a brief, brutal rule by Ali Soilih, who strove to modernize the institutions, collectivize society, and reduce the role of Islam. In the 1978 coup that overthrew him, this experiment came to an end. Ahmed Abdallah and his band of French mercenaries put the islands back on their traditional course. They ruled with a far lighter hand but have not shrunk from suppressing opposition and resorting to censorship.

FOREIGN POLICY

Comoran relations with France, the only foreign country with any interest in the troubled islands, have been soured by the issue of Mayotte, which seceded from Comoros in 1975. The OAU has tried to reconcile the warring factions on the islands but with little success.

DEFENSE

The national army, the Forces Armées Comoriènnes, has 700 to 800 soldiers under about 20 French officers.

Military Indicators

Total Active Duty Personnel: —
Military Manpower per 1,000: —
Military Expenditures $: —
as % of GNP: —
per capita $: —
as % of central government expenditures: —

Arms Imports $: 0
Arms Exports $: 0

ECONOMY

Comoros is one of the 49 low-income countries of the world. A UN team reported in 1975 that the islands' economy faced total collapse in the wake of French withdrawal. Comoros has a free-market economy in which the dominant sector is private.

Up-to-date national accounts for Comoros do not exist.

One of the poorest nations of the world, Comoros suffers from several severe problems, including poor transportation, a young and rapidly growing population, few natural resources, and a market too small to support a manufacturing base. The low educational level of the labor force limits productivity. It is heavily dependent on foreign technical assistance.

Principal Economic Indicators

Gross National Product: $209 million
GNP per capita: $400
GNP Average Annual Growth Rate (1990–97)%: −3.1
GNP per capita Average Annual Growth Rate (1990–97)%: −5.7
Origin of Gross Domestic Product %
Agriculture: 39
Mining: —
Manufacturing: 4
Construction: 7
Public Utilities: 1
Transportation and Communications: 4
Trade: 27
Financial Services: —
Other Services: 3
Government: 14
Gross Domestic Product by Type of Expenditure %
Private Consumption: 80
Government Consumption: 22
Gross Domestic Investment: 19
Foreign Trade: Exports: 14
Imports: −35
% of Income Received by Poorest 20%: —
% of Income Received by Richest 10%: —

Price and earnings indexes (1995 = 100)

	1992	1993	1994	1995	1996	1997
Consumer price index	98.2	100.0	125.0	133.9	138.7	137.5
Monthly earnings index	—	100.0	121.0	137.0	—	—

Finance

National Currency: Comoran France (CF)
Exchange Rate: $1 = CF 456.27
Money Supply Stock in National Currency billion: 13,341
M1 per capita: 23,000
Central Bank Discount Rate%: —
Total External Debt $million: 219
Debt Service Ratio%: 3.0

Balance of Payments $million: −18.9
International Reserves SDRs million: —
Ratio of External Debt to Total Reserves: 4.2

Average Annual Rate of Inflation/Consumer Price Index Growth Rate%: 3.5

Official Development Assistance

ODA $: 40
as % of GNP: 17.1
per capita: $ 80
Foreign Direct Investment $million: —

Central Government Revenues and Expenditures

Fiscal Year: Calendar Year

Revenues $million: 55
Expenditures $million: 71
Budget Deficit $: 16 million
Tax Revenues as % of GDP: —
Highest Tax Bracket %
Individual: —
Corporate: —

Employment and Labor

Economically Active Population: 215,000
Female Participation Rate%: 40.0
Activity Rate%: 44.4
Labor by Sector: %
Agriculture, Forestry, Fishing: 79.4
Manufacturing, Mining: 6.5
Construction: —
Transportation and Communications: —
Trade, Hotels, and Restaurants: —
Finance, Insurance, Real Estate: —
Public Administration, Defense: —
Services: 14.1

Unemployment%: 20

Agriculture

Agriculture's Share of GDP %: 39
Average Annual Rate of Growth (1965–98) %: —
Number of Farms 000: —
Average Size of Farm ha: —
Number of Tractors per 1,000 hectares: —
Irrigation, % of Farms having: —
Artificial Fertilizer kg/hectare: —
Total Farmland as % of land area: 44.8
Livestock: Cattle 000: 50
Sheep 000: 20

(continued)

Hogs 000: —
Chickens 000: 440
Forests: Production of Roundwood (000 cubic meters): —
Fisheries: Total Catch tons 000: 13.5

Mining

% of GDP: —
Value of Mineral Production $million: —

Manufacturing

Value Added $million: 9.9
Industrial Production Growth Rate%: −6.5

Energy

Commercial Energy Production metric tons of oil equivalent 000: —
Commercial Energy Consumption metric tons of oil equivalent 000: 18
Commercial Energy Consumption per capita kg: 37
Average Annual Growth Rate 1980–97%: —
Net Energy Imports % of use: 100
Electricity Installed Capacity kW 000: 5
Production kW-hr million: 16
Coal Reserves tons million: —
Production tons 000: —
Natural Gas Proven Reserves cubic meters billion: —
Production cubic meters million: —
Crude Petroleum Reserves barrels million: —
Production barrels million: —
Consumption barrels million: —
Refinery Capacity barrels per day 000: —
Pipelines Length km: —

Foreign Trade

Imports $million: 52.8
Exports $million: 11.4
Export Volume % Annual Growth Rate (1990–97): —
Import Volume % Annual Growth Rate (1990–97): —
Balance of Trade $

Balance of trade (current prices)

	1993	1994	1995	1996	1997
CF000,000	−10.6	−17.2	−19.2	−22.2	−23.6
% of total	46.2%	64.8%	69.4%	82.0%	81.8%

Major Trading Partners

	Imports	Exports
European Union%	40.0	52.5
United States %	—	28.7
Eastern Europe %	1.9	—
Japan %	5.7	—
Others%	52.4	18.8

Transportation

Roads Total Length mi: 544 km 875
Paved %: 76
Automobiles: 7,080
Trucks and Buses: 4,870
Persons per vehicle: 41
Railroad; Track Length mi: — km —
Passenger-mi million: —
Freight-mi million: —
Merchant Marine: No. of Vessels: 6
Total Deadweight Tonnage 000: 3.6
International Cargo Loaded tons 000: 12
International Cargo Off-loaded tons 000: 107
Airports with Scheduled Flights: 2
Traffic: Passenger-mi million: 1.9
Freight-mi million: —
Length of Canals mi: — km —

Tourism

Number of Tourists to 000: —
Number of Tourists from 000: —
Tourist Receipts $million: 8
Tourist Expenditures $million: 6

Communications

Telephones 000: 4.5
Cost of Local Calls 3 mins: $0.01
Cellular Telephones 000: 0.1
Fax Machines 000: —
Personal Computers 000: —
Internet Hosts per million persons: 324
Mail: Post Offices: 36
Pieces of Mail Handled million: 0.9
Pieces of Mail Handled per person: 1.5

EDUCATION

In principle, education is free, universal, and compulsory for eight years, from the ages of seven to 15. Enrollments have risen sharply in recent years, but only 25 percent enter secondary school, even though enrollments doubled at that level between 1970 and 1980.

All children attend Koranic schools until they are able to read (but not necessarily understand) classical Arabic. Schooling lasts 13 years, divided into six years of primary school, four years of middle school, and three years of secondary school. Since independence in 1975, all French teachers have left. Consequently the lycées, or secondary schools, had to be closed in 1975. Primary education, however, continued to function.

The academic year runs from October to July. The medium of instruction is French.

There is a severe shortage of teachers in the school system. Although the student-teacher ratio is high without being unacceptable, variations are considerable among schools. However, 58 percent of the teachers did not have even a junior secondary school certificate (BEPC), and only two held the baccalaureate. The shortage of classrooms has been a problem for a number of years and is met by a double-shift system. The secondary-school system is almost entirely dependent on expatriate teachers, formerly from France and now from other French-speaking countries in Africa.

Little vocational training took place until 1974, when the ILO helped establish a center for artisan training on Anjouan.

Comoros has no institutions of higher education.

Education

Literacy Rate%: 57.3
- Male%: 64.2
- Female%: 50.4

First Level: Primary schools: 275
- Teachers: 1,737
- Students: 77,837
- Student-Teacher Ratio: 43
- Net Enrollment Ratio: 53

Second Level: Secondary Schools: —
- Teachers: 613
- Students: 17,474
- Student-Teacher Ratio: 25.5
- Net Enrollment Ratio: —

Vocational Level: Schools: —
- Students: 163

Third Level: Institutions: —
- Teachers: —
- Students: 400
- Student-Ratio Level: —
- Gross Enrollment Ratio: 0.6
- Students per 100,000: —
- % of Population Age 25 and over with Postsecondary Education: —

Public Expenditure on Education as % of GDP: 3.9

SCIENCE AND TECHNOLOGY

Science and Technology

Scientists and Engineers in R&D per 1 million persons: —
Expenditures in R&D as % of GDP: —
High-Tech Exports $: —
Patent Applications by Residents: —

MEDIA

The press consists of two weekly papers. In the absence of a local daily press, newspapers from Madagascar circulate throughout the islands.

Radio service is provided by the government-owned Radio Comoros, which operated one shortwave station and one FM station and broadcasts in French and Comorian.

There were two libraries.

Media

Daily Newspapers: —
- Total Circulation 000: —
- Circulation per 1,000: —

Books Published: —
Magazines: —
Radio Receivers 000: 61
- per 1,000: 97

Television sets 000: 2
- per 1,000: 5

MOST IMPORTANT MEDIA:

Press. The nation's print media consists of two weeklies, the state-owned, *Al Watwany* (1,500) and the independent *L'Archipel.*

News agencies. The domestic facility is the Agence Comores Press (ACP), located at Moroni.

Radio and television. The government-operated Radio-Comores serviced some 95,000 receivers in 1998. The country's first independent radio station, Radio Tropiques FM, was closed down after one week of transmission in April 1991 and again in July 1993, at which time its director was arrested for "disturbing the peace." The one remaining independent outlet, Udzima's Voix des Iles, was silenced in February 1994, although news bulletins from Radio France Internationale began transmitting via satellite in March. In 1989 the French government provided 5 million francs for construction of the islands' first television station, which in 1998 serviced approximately some 600 sets.

CULTURE

Cultural Indicators

Public Libraries
- Number: —
- Volumes: —
- Registered borrowers: —

Museums:
- Number: —
- Annual Attendance: —

Cinema:
- Production of Long Films: —
- Number of Cinemas: —
- Seating Capacity: —
- Annual Attendance: —
- Annual Attendance per capita: —

STATUS OF WOMEN

Women do not have equal rights in Comoros. While the 1992 constitution recognizes their right to suffrage, women otherwise play a limited role in politics in Comoros. Islamic law prevents most women from owning property. Polygamy is often practiced with a man establishing two or more households. Divorce is relatively easy for men, but the wife retains the family home. While schooling is free and universal, girls are less likely to be enrolled in school than their male counterparts.

Women

Gender Empowerment Measure: —
Seats Held in Parliament by Women %: —
Female Administrators and Managers %: —
Female Professional and Technical Workers %: —
Women's Share of Earned Income %: —
Women in Government %: 3

HEALTH, FOOD, AND NUTRITION

Health

Number of Physicians: 77
Number of Dentists: 6
Number of Nurses: 155
Number of Pharmacists: 6
Population per Physician: 6,600
Number of Hospitals: —
Hospital Beds per 10,000: 25
Hospital Bed Occupancy Rate: —
Infant Mortality Rate per 1,000 live births: 111
Maternal Mortality Rate per 100,000 live births: —
Total Health Expenditures as % of GDP: 5.40
Health Expenditures per capita $: 28
HIV Infected % of adults: —
Cigarette Consumption per smoker per year: —
% of Smokers: Male: —
Female: —
Access to Safe Water %: 48

Food and Nutrition

Food Supply as % of FAO Requirements: 79
% of Consumption Expenditures on Food: 67.3
Daily Available Calories per capita: 1,850
% of Total Calories derived from:
Cereals: 44.3
Potatoes, cassava: 15.4
Meat, poultry: 1.9
Fish: 3.0
Eggs, milk: 1.1
Fruits, vegetables: 8.3
Fats, oils: 9.4

ENVIRONMENT

One of the most densely populated countries with one of the highest birth rates, Comoros faces many environmental challenges, including soil erosion, water quality, deforestation, poor farming techniques, and lack of protected lands. In addition, the major urban areas suffer from poor waste removal and growing air and water pollution. The government of Comoros has identified some of the problems its faces, but is challenged by the lack of resources to effectively address them.

Environment

Forest Area sq km: —
Average Annual Deforestation sq km: —
Nationally Protected Areas as % of Total Land Area: —
Freshwater Access cubic meters per capita: —
Emissions of Organic Water Pollutants kg per day: —
CO_2 Emissions per capita ton: 0.1

CHRONOLOGY

1946 Comoros is granted administrative autonomy as an overseas territory of France.

1961 Comoros achieves internal autonomy under a special statute.

1968 Comoros gains greater internal autonomy.

1973 An agreement for independence within five years is signed in Paris.

1974 In a special referendum, all islands except Mayotte vote for independence; French parliament decides that each island should vote separately on a new constitution.

1975 Chamber of Deputies votes a unilateral declaration of independence and proclaims Republic of the Comoros, with Ahmed Abdallah Abderemane as president. Chamber of Deputies establishes itself as a constituent assembly to draft a constitution.

Abdallah is overthrown in coup led by Ali Soilih, leader of a four-party coalition known as National United Front (NUF).

National Assembly is dissolved.

Armed supporters of Ali Soilih land on Anjouan, arrest Abdallah and his supporters, and crush an Anjouan secessionist movement.

The newly established National Revolutionary Council transfers most of its powers to the 12-member National Executive Council, headed by the president, Prince Said Mohamed Jaffar.

Comoros is admitted to the United Nations.

Ali Soilih and unarmed followers land on Mayotte in an effort to persuade the Mahorais to join the union.

1976 Soilih is elected president, replacing Jaffar.

National Revolutionary Council is reconstituted as the National Institutional Council.

Island of Mayotte rejects union with Comoros in two referendums.

French estates in Comoros are nationalized and French officials are repatriated.

1977 Comoros seeks repatriation of its citizens from Madagascar following racial riots.

1978 President Soilih is ousted in coup led by a French mercenary named Bob Denard and is killed as he tries to flee the country; former president Ahmed Abdallah and former vice president Mohammed Ahmed are installed as coleaders of the new government.

The band of 50 mercenaries, headed by Denard, remains to run vital services, but their presence infuriates other African nations, and Comoros is expelled from the OAU meeting in July.
New constitution is drafted and approved by 99.31 percent of the votes.
Diplomatic relations with France are resumed and the two countries sign agreements on economic and military cooperation.
Abdallah is elected president.
1979 The newly elected Federal Assembly approves formation of a one-party state.
OAU readmits Comoros as the mercenaries leave.
1982 Prime Minister Salim Ben Ali is dismissed and replaced by Ali M'Roudjae.
1983 Anti-Abdallah plot is thwarted in Canberra, Australia, and three plotters are convicted.
1984 Abdallah is reelected for a second six-year term.
The office of prime minister is abolished through a constitutional amendment.
1985 Comoros joins the Indian Ocean Commission.
1987 Legislative elections return the entire slate of candidates presented by Abdallah.
1989 Abdallah is assassinated. Said Muhammad Djohar is named interim president.
1990 Djohar is elected president.
1992 Another new constitution is approved restoring the prime ministership and the country holds its first democratic elections.
1995 Mercenaries under the command of Bob Denard attempt to overthrow Djohar's government.
Djohar is taken prisoner.
French forces suppress the coup attempt and free Djohar, but do not reinstate him as president.
1996 In elections, Mohamed Taki Abdoulkarim is elected president in a contest of 15 candidates.
1997 The OAU must come to the aid of the Comoros to put down an armed insurrection on the island of Anjouan; the rebels sought reunification with France.
1998 In March, President Mohamed Taki Abdulkarim is reelected head of state and M. Ahmed Abdou is elected prime minister; in November, Abdulkarim dies and Tajiddine Ben Said Massounde assumes presidency.
1999 Anjouan representatives refuse to sign an OAU agreement proposing central administration of the three islands; Colonel Assoumani Azali takes control of the government in a bloodless coup.

BIBLIOGRAPHY

Gorse, Jean. *Territoire des Comores.* Paris, 1964.
Newitt, N. *The Comoro Islands.* London, 1985.
Ottenheimer, M., and H. J. Ottenheimer. *Historical Dictionary of the Comoro Islands.* Metuchen, N.J., 1994.
World Bank. *The Comoros: Problems and Prospects of a Small Island Economy.* Washington, D.C., 1979.

OFFICIAL PUBLICATIONS

Comoros. *Comoros—Recent Economic Developments* (IMF Staff Country Report [1996]) *Recensement géneral de la population et de l'habitat 15 September 1980.*

CONTACT INFORMATION

Embassy of Comoros
336 East 45th Street, 2nd Floor
New York, N.Y. 10017
Phone: (212) 349-2030

INTERNET RESOURCES

- Comoro Islands (unofficial)
  http://www.ksu.edu/sasw/comoros/comoros.html

CONGO, DEMOCRATIC REPUBLIC OF THE (FORMERLY ZAÏRE)

BASIC FACT SHEET

OFFICIAL NAME:
Democratic Republic of the Congo (République Démocratique du Congo)

ABBREVIATION:
CG

CAPITAL:
Kinshasa

HEAD OF STATE AND HEAD OF GOVERNMENT:
Joseph Kabila (from 2001)

NATURE OF GOVERNMENT:
One-party dictatorship

POPULATION:
50,481,000 (1999)

AREA:
2,344,932 sq km (905,378 sq mi)

ETHNIC MAJORITY:
Bantu tribes

LANGUAGES:
French (official), Lingala, Kingwana, Kikongo, Tshiluba, Swahili

RELIGIONS:
Roman Catholicism and animism

UNIT OF CURRENCY:
Zaire (Z.)

NATIONAL FLAG:
Light blue with a large yellow five-pointed star in the center and a columnar arrangement of six small yellow five-pointed stars along the hoist side.

NATIONAL EMBLEM:
Light blue with a large yellow five-pointed star in the center and a horizontal arrangement of six small yellow five-pointed stars along the top.

NATIONAL ANTHEM:
"Arise, Congolese, United by Fate"

NATIONAL HOLIDAYS:
National Day (anniversary of the regime, November 24); January 1; January 4 (Martyrs of Independence Day); Easter Monday; May 1 (Labor Day); Ascension Day; Whitmonday; May 20 (Mouvement Populaire de la Révolution Day); June 24 (Zaire Day); June 30 (Independence Day); August 1 (Parents' Day); Assumption Day; All Saints' Day; October 27 (Three Z Day); December 25

DATE OF INDEPENDENCE:
June 30, 1960

DATE OF CONSTITUTION:
June 24, 1967, amended August 1974, revised February 15, 1978, amended April 1990; transitional constitution promulgated in April 1994; in November 1998 a draft constitution was approved, but it has not yet been ratified.

Democratic Republic of the Congo

GEOGRAPHICAL FEATURES

The Democratic Republic of the Congo is a rectangular-shaped inland nation in the south-central part of the African continent, with a narrow strip of land on the northern bank of the Zaïre estuary as the only outlet to the Atlantic. It includes the greater part of the Congo River basin and lies on the equator, with one-third of the country to the north and two-thirds to the south. It is the third-largest nation in Africa, with a land area of 2,344,932 sq km (905,378 sq mi). The length of the coastline is 40 km (25 mi). The greatest distance both north-south and east-west is about 2,250 km (1,400 mi). Congo shares its international border of about 10,030 km (6,235 mi) with nine neighbors: Central African Republic (1,577 km; 980 mi); Sudan (628 km; 390 mi); Uganda (965 km; 599 mi); Rwanda (217 km; 135 mi); Burundi (233 km; 145 mi); Tanzania (459 km; 285 mi); Zambia (1,930 km; 1,198 mi); Angola (2,511 km; 1,559 mi); Cabinda (225 km; 140 mi); and the Republic of Congo (2,410 km; 1496 mi).

The Democratic Republic of the Congo is divided into four physical regions. The vast, low-lying central area is a basin-shaped plateau sloping toward the west and with an average elevation of 400 m (1,310 ft). This area is surrounded by mountainous terraces in the west, plateaus merging into savannas in the south and southeast, and dense grasslands in the northwest, with an elevation in the south of 1,000 to 2,000 m (3,280 to 6,560 ft) and in the north of 600 to 800 m (1,970 to 2,625 ft). High mountain ranges enclose the country in the north, including the Ngoma, Virunga, Ruwenzori, Blue Mountains, Kundelunga, and Marungu, with the altitude rising to 5,000 m (16,400 ft). The coastline of Congo is bordered by a small plain 100 km (62 mi) wide.

The country is almost entirely drained by the 4,505 km (2,800 mi)-long Congo River and its many tributaries. The lower Congo is not navigable, but the upper and middle Congo are navigable for 2,575 km (1,600 mi). The Congo is the world's second-largest river, after the Amazon, in terms of volume of water (339,600 cu m per sec; 12 million cu ft per sec).

Geography

Area sq km: 2,344,932 (905,378 sq mi)
World Rank: 12th
Land Boundaries, km: Angola 2511; Burundi 233; Central African Republic 1,577; Republic of the Congo 2,410; Rwanda 217; Sudan 628; Uganda 965; Zambia 1930; Tanzania 459
Coastline, km: 40
Elevation Extremes meters
- Lowest: Atlantic Ocean 0
- Highest: Margherita Peak 5,110

Land Use % Arable land: 3
- Permanent Crops: 0
- Permanent Pastures: 7
- Forest and Woodland: 77
- Other: 13

Population of Principal Cities (1994 est.)

Boma	135,284
Bukavu	201,569
Butembo	109,406
Goma	109,094
Kalemi	101,309
Kananga	393,030
Kikwit	182,142
Kinshasa	4,655,313
Kisangani	417,517
Kolwezi	417,810
Likasi	299,118
Lubumbashi	851,381
Matadi	172,730
Mbanadaka	169,841
Mbuji-Mayi	806,475
Mwene-Ditu	137,459
Tshikapa	180,860
Uvira	115,590

CLIMATE AND WEATHER

The seasons are reversed north and south of the equator. Both regions have two short wet and two short dry seasons. North of the equator the rainy season lasts from early April to late October and the dry season from early November to March. The hours of daylight remain practically unchanged throughout the year. On the southern plateau—farthest from the equator—there is one long rainy season and one dry season, with a characteristic tropical climate influenced by the trade winds. Eastern Congo and upper Shaba have a mountainous climate, with lower temperatures sometimes falling to 0°C (32°F) at night. The average rainfall for the entire country is about 1,070 mm (42 in), and it falls more or less regularly every year. The central region receives at least 1,520 to 2,030 mm (60 to 80 in) a year, and the rainy season extends to 130 days a year. Storms are violent but seldom last for more than a few hours. At the equator temperatures vary from 15.6°C to 37.8°C (60°F to 100°F), with a mean maximum about 32.2°C (90°F). The hottest month is February. Humidity always is high, ranging upward from 65 percent. Temperatures drop on the edges of the Congo River basin to about 25°C (77°F), with cooler nights.

Climate and Weather

Mean Temperature
On the Equator 90°F to 100°F
Zaire River Basin 77°F
Average Rainfall 42 in
Central Region 60 in to 80 in

POPULATION

Population Indicators

Total Population: 1999 50,481,000
World Rank: 23rd
Density per sq mi: 55.8 (21.5 per sq km)
% of annual growth (1994–99): 3.1
Male %: 49.2
Female %: 50.8
Urban %: 29.1
Age Distribution: %
- 0–14: 47.3
- 15–29: 25.9
- 30–44: 14.1
- 45–59: 8.1
- 60–74: 3.8
- 75 and over: 0.8

Population 2020: 92,852,000
Birth Rate per 1,000: 4,492
Death Rate per 1,000: 13.5
Population Doubling Time (years): 22
Infant Mortality Rate per 1,000 live births: 89.0
Rate of Natural Increase per 1,000: 31.4
Total Fertility Rate: 6.2

Expectation of Life (years): Males 51.3
Females 54.5
Marriage Rate per 1,000: —
Divorce Rate per 1,000: —
Total Number of Households: 1,064,000
Average Size of Households: 5.6
% of Illegitimate Children: —
Induced Abortions: —
Rate per 100 live births: —

ETHNIC COMPOSITION

More than 99 percent of the Congonese are of African descent and the population is divided into more than 200 tribes. No single ethnic group can claim a majority on the national level, but each has its own territory where it is predominant.

Based on cultural and historical criteria, three ethnic zones exist in the Congo: northern and southern savanna, central rain forest, and eastern highlands. Each has its own tribes or tribal clusters.

The most important of the ethnic groups are the Kongo, Luba, Lunda, Mongo, and Zande. None of these groups numbers more than 3 million. The primary feelings of identity among these groups are ethnic rather than national, but the pressure of the events of the independence period has created a rudimentary consciousness of common interests.

The resident alien population numbers roughly 900,000, including Angolans, Sudanese, Zambians, and West Africans. Since 1970 the non-African alien population has declined, and their number is estimated at 50,000, half the preindependence figure. Belgians still constitute the majority, followed by Portuguese, Italians, Greeks, Arabs, Lebanese, Pakistanis, and Indians. Most of them are civil servants, missionaries, traders, teachers, or planters.

LANGUAGES

French is the official language and the medium of instruction in secondary and higher education, but only a small percentage of the population have a working knowledge of it, and efforts to introduce French into the primary schools have failed. Nearly all Congoans speak languages of the Bantu subgroup of the central branch of the Niger-Congo family. The eastern branch of the Niger-Congo family and the central Sudanic family also are represented. The principal language is Bantu, with its 14 clusters of languages spoken by over 17 million people. The Kongo, Luba, Mongo, and Lunda belong to this language family. Zande is the most important of the eastern branch and Moru-Mngbetu of the central Sudanic family. The total number of languages and dialects is estimated at 700.

Principal Languages and Their Speakers

Boa	1,180,000
Chokwe	920,000
English	—
French	3,900,000
Kongo	8,100,000
Kongo (lingua franca)	15,000,000
Lingala (lingua franca)	35,000,000
Luba	9,080,000
Lugbara	810,000
Mongo	6,800,000
Ngala and Bangi	2,920,000
Rundi	1,940,000
Rwanda	5,180,000
Swahili (lingua franca)	25,000,000
Teke	1,380,000
Zande (Azande)	3,080,000
Other	9,080,000

RELIGIONS

It is estimated that about half of the Congoans are, at least nominally, Christians. Of these, three-quarters are Roman Catholic and one-quarter Protestant. Most of the non-Christian population is composed of adherents of traditional religions or syncretic sects. The traditional religions are not formalized but embody some common concepts, such as animism, belief in spirits, and ancestor worship. The syncretic sects are a mixture of Christianity and traditional beliefs centered around new prophets. One of these sects, Kimbanguism, has about 3 million members and in 1969 became the first independent African church to be admitted to the World Council of Churches.

Congo has been the scene of one of the most intense Christian missionary efforts, and both Catholic and Protestant organizations have had a profound impact on the development of the nation, particularly in the fields of education and health.

Religious Affiliations

Religion	Adherents
Roman Catholic	20,700,000
Protestant	15,950,000
African Christian	6,750,000
Traditional beliefs	5,400,000
Muslim	710,000
Other	970,000

HISTORICAL BACKGROUND

Little archaeological evidence exists of the people that inhabited the region that is today the Congo. However, it is known that people have been in the area since the Stone Age. The first and most obvious distinction to be made between the various peoples who first populated the area of Zaire is between the small-scale, segmentary societies of the rain forest zone and the state systems of the savanna. Most of the peoples of the rain forest area were organized into village communities, under the leadership of chiefs or of dominant clans or lineages. Some of these communities were able to absorb or conquer neighboring villages and thus develop into sizable chiefdoms. In specific instances, as among the Mangbetu, these expanding societies provided the basis for a common sense of identity among otherwise unrelated peoples. Elsewhere, however, social fragmentation remained one of the most salient characteristics of the rain forest peoples.

From the history of the southern savanna, the traditional habitat of several large-scale societies with centralized political systems, variously described as kingdoms, empires, and chiefdoms, emerged between 1200 and 1500 A.D. These include the Kongo, Lunda, Luba, and Kuba state systems, all of which shared certain common features, such as a centralized structure of authority identified with a single ruler, more often than not enjoying the attributes of divine kingship.

Therefore, to a far greater extent than many African nations, the Democratic Republic of the Congo is a European/colonial creation that has little antecedent history.

By masterful diplomacy King Leopold II of Belgium induced the Berlin Conference of 1884–85 to recognize his personal claim over the Congo, which officially became a Belgian colony in 1908. Belgian rule was harsh, and development of the colony was driven primarily with a view to economic profit. Belgium failed to prepare the Congo for independence, and consequently bears partial responsibility for the upheavals that followed soon after independence.

Controversy erupted before independence on the issue of federalism versus centralism. Most political organizations, which were ethnically based, favored decentralization; only Patrice Lumumba supported a unitary state. The question was not settled by the time the nation became independent. At independence in 1960 Patrice Lumumba became prime minister and Joseph Kasavubu president. Belgian administrators were to stay to train the new executives, and the army was to remain under Belgian control. Five days after independence, the armed forces mutinied. The appointment of Joseph-Desire Mobutu as chief of staff helped to defuse the rebellion. Nevertheless, a political crisis developed as Belgians fled and Belgian troops took measures to protect Belgian nationals. Katanga and South Kasai Provinces seceded, and Lumumba called in UN troops to intervene.

Disagreements between Kasavubu and Lumumba over the handling of the secession resulted in Lumumba's dismissal. He was subsequently murdered by his enemies in Katanga. Mobutu temporarily took control of the government but returned power to Kasavubu in February 1961. Parliament reconvened in August 1961 with most rival groups forming a government of national unity. Only Moise Tshombe and his secessionist followers refused to join. Their rebellion was finally suppressed in 1963.

In 1964 a new constitution was promulgated that placed greater emphasis on federalism. It created new provinces and established a federalist, presidential system with a bicameral national assembly. Despite the changes, rebellion continued while Tshombe and Kasavubu struggled to assume power. In November 1965 Mobutu intervened and took over the presidency. A new constitution was promulgated in 1967, but the army held power; political activity ended. Mobutu established the Mouvement Populaire de la Révolution (MPR), which became the sole party in the country. He consolidated power in the central government and in an increasingly powerful presidency. He ruled with the assistance of a presidential bureau. The legislature, which was not frequently convened, had little influence. All opposition was suppressed.

The official philosophy of Congo became Mobutism, which was more a personal cult than a strict ideology. Mobutu was publicly referred to as "the guide" and "the father of the nation." Mobutism included a campaign for authenticity and national identity under which colonial place names and Christian names were Africanized by mandate. Much of the thrust of the militant Africanization programs generated by the ideology of Mobutism was blunted by the economic and military failures of the Mobutu regime in the late 1970s. This forced Mobutu to depend more and more on Western powers and generally to retrace his steps toward a more pragmatic stance in political and social matters.

After almost a decade of prosperity, Congo relapsed into near civil war following the invasion of Shaba Province in 1977 and 1978 by the National Front for the Liberation of the Congo. The Mobutu regime was rescued solely by the intervention of French forces, although some assistance was received from a number of other states, such as Uganda, Morocco, Central African Republic, and Saudi Arabia, as well as Belgium.

Opposition to Mobutu's regime again manifested itself in 1984. In January and March a number of bombs exploded in Kinshasa, causing loss of life, and a rebel force occupied the town of Moba, in Shaba Province, for two days in November before it was recaptured by Congoan troops. Congo accused Belgium of harboring the groups responsible for such violent opposition and claimed that the rebels had crossed into Congo from neighboring Tanzania. However, the main opposition groups in Belgium did not acknowledge involvement in the occupation of Moba, suggesting instead that rebellious Congoan troops had been responsible. It was widely believed that the violent opposition in Congo had been orchestrated to disrupt the presidential election, which Mobutu, as the sole candidate, won easily.

Although Mobutu remained entrenched in power as the 1990s began, he was being challenged on a number of fronts. His third seven-year term as president expired in 1991 but he continued to rule without any constitutional sanction, appointing a succession of front men as

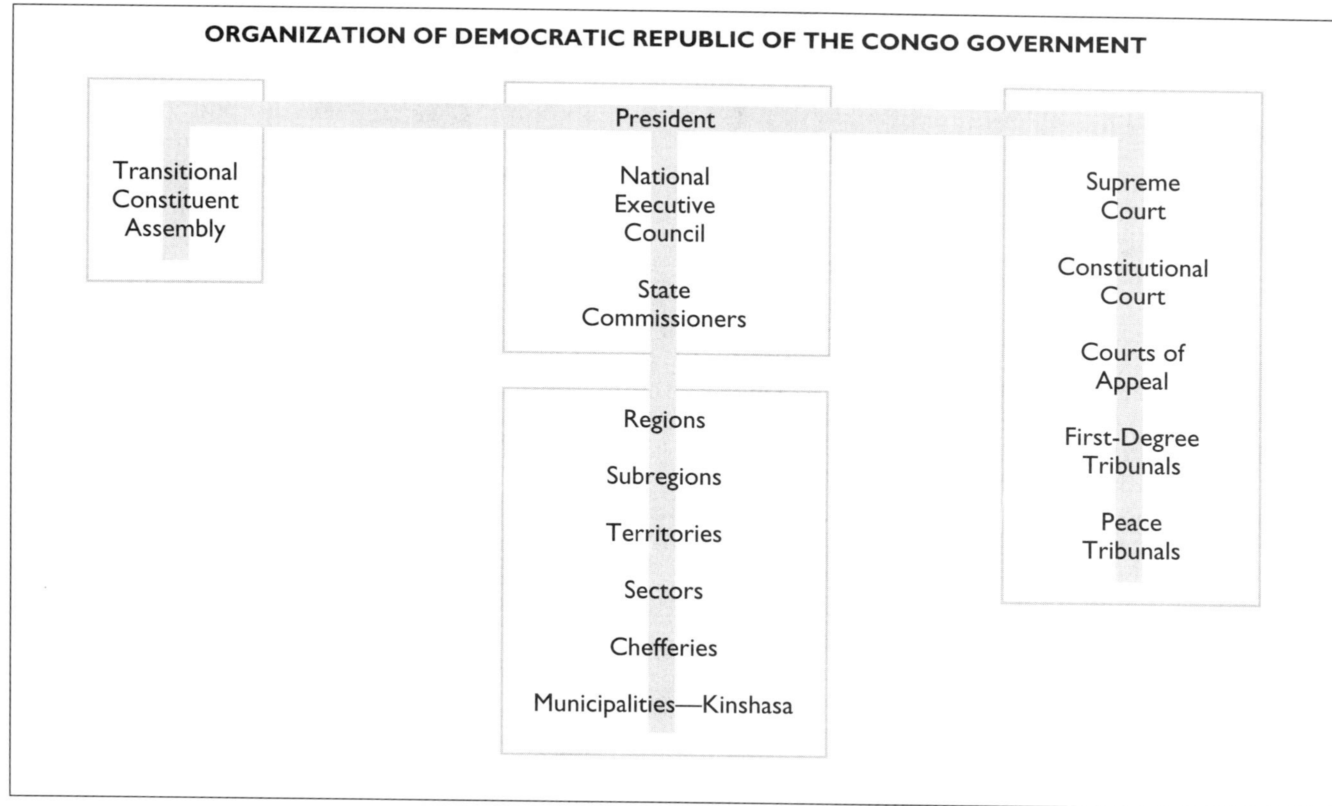

prime ministers and making vague gestures of ending his one-party rule. The struggle between the president and the opposition forces reached an impasse when the country was invaded in 1996 by some 700,000 to 1,000,000 Hutus who soon were opposed by some 400,000 Banyamulenga Tutsis. The Tutsis, organized into an army called Alliance for the Liberation of Congo-Zaïre (AFDL), were led by anti-Mobutu guerrilla leader Laurent Kabila, who easily overran most of eastern Zaïre. Within a year AFDL was before the gates of Kinshasa, having driven the Zaïrean army as well as the Hutus out of the rest of the country. Mobutu fled the country, and, after a murderous rampage by Mobutu loyalists, AFDL forces entered the capital. Kabila named himself president of the renamed Democratic Republic of the Congo. Soon after seizing power, Kabila himself faced a series of civil wars with a number of foreign mercenary armies, including Tutsi, Ugandan, and Angolan, carving up the country. On January 16, 2001, Kabila was assassinated by a disaffected bodyguard. His son, Joseph Kabila, was immediately sworn in as the new president.

CONSTITUTION

Numerous constitutional changes took place during the rule of Mobutu Sese Seko. All were undertaken to further consolidate Mobutu's power. According to the constitution of February 1978, Congo is described as a united, democratic, secular state. The constitution accords equal rights to all citizens and freedom of expression, conscience, and religion. All citizens were declared members of the Mouvement Populaire de la Révolution (MPR) and from the age of 18 would have the right to vote. The MPR, founded in 1967, was established by the constitution as the nation's only political party in 1970.

The head of state is the president who is elected for a seven-year term and who served concurrently as the president of the MPR. He appointed and dismissed the National Executive Council, a cabinet of state commissioners. In addition he presided over the MPR political bureau, the MPR congress, and legislative and judicial councils. He held the power to legislate with the consent of the legislative council and was accountable to the people by means of an annual policy statement. The president was also the commander in chief of the armed forces and gendarmerie.

The legislative body was the National Legislative Council and was composed of people's commissioners in a single chamber. By constitution it was elected by universal and secret suffrage to a five-year term and was chosen from a slate of candidates approved by the MPR.

Mobutu had been making some movement toward a more democratic form of government, including scheduling elections for the legislature in 1997. However, following a successful rebellion led by General Laurent Désiré

Kabila, the new government announced on May 29, 1997, a program of constitutional reform and, in November 1998, a draft constitution were approved by President Kabila and await ratification by national referendum. Under the new constitution, the president is still head of the government and chief of state. In August 2000, Kabila established the Transitional Constituent Assembly, appointing all 300 members.

LOCAL GOVERNMENT

There are 10 regions each with its own regional commissioner and six councillors who are appointed by the president. The regions are subdivided into 41 subregions. The capital city of Kinshasa constitutes a separate unit under a governor and urban commissioners appointed by the president of the republic.

Local Government

Principal administrative divisions, capitals, area, population

AREA AND POPULATION

		area		population 1994
Provinces	**Capitals**	**sq mi**	**sq km**	**estimate**
Bandundu	Bandundu	114,154	295,658	4,907,000
Bas-Congo	Matadi	20,819	53,920	2,578,000
Equateur	Mbandaka	155,712	403,292	4,789,000
Kasai-Occidental	Kananga	59,746	154,742	3,117,000
Kasai-Oriental	Mbuji-Mayi	65,754	170,302	3,778,000
Katanga	Lubumbashi	191,845	496,877	5,602,000
Maniema	Kindu	51,062	132,250	1,048,000
Nord-Kivu	Goma	22,967	59,483	3,546,000
Orientale	Kisangani	194,302	503,239	5,432,000
Sud-Kivu	Bukavu	25,147	65,130	3,093,000
City				
Kinshasa	—	3,848	9,965	4,655,000
Total		905,354	2,344,858	42,545,000

PARLIAMENT

The Transitional Constituent Assembly was established in August 2000 by former president Laurent Kabila. It is a unicameral body of 300 members appointed by Kabila.

POLITICAL PARTIES

President Kabila banned political party activity indefinitely and led the Alliance of Democratic Forces for the Liberation of Congo-Zaïre or AFDL. The sole legal political party until 1991 was the Popular Movement of the Revolution or MPR, which may be replaced by the Union for the Republic or UPR. While the government allowed the formation of other political parties after 1991, since the coup of 1997, it remains the only political party to hold office. President Joseph Kabila lifted the ban on all parties in May 2001. Other parties, however, include: Union for Democracy and Social Progress or UDPS, Congolese Rally for Democracy or RCD, Democratic Social Christian Party or PDSC, Union of Federalists and Independent Republicans or UFERI, and Unified Lumumbast Party or PALU.

Political Parties

Alliance of Democratic Forces for the Liberation of Congo-Zaire, 1996. It consists of three revolutionary groups
- Popular Revolutionary Party, 1967
- National Council of Resistance
- Revolutionary Movement for the Liberation of Congo-Zaire

Popular Movement for Renewal, 1967

Union for the Republic and Democracy. It consists of two former government parties
- Union of Independent Democrats
- Democratic and Social Christian Party, 1991

Political Forces of the Conclave, 1993

Union of Federalists and Independent Republicans, 1990

Sacred Union of the Radical Opposition, 1991
- Union for Democracy and Social Progress, 1980
- Convention of Reformist Nationlists
- Federalist Christian Democracy
- African Socialist Party

Renovated Sacred Union, 1993

Alliance of Republicans for Development and Progress, 1994

Alliance of African Nationalists, 1994

National Christian Democratic Party, 1994

Congo has a number of clandestine groups in exile. They include

Congolese National Movement

Unified Lumumbist Party

Congolese National Liberation Front

Congolese Liberation Party

Active rebel groups control parts of the country. They include

Congolese Rally for Democracy, 1998

Movement for the Liberation of Congo, 1998

Union of Republican Nationalists for Liberation

Mai-Mai Ingelima

Council of Resistance and National Liberation

Political Parties: Strength in Parliament Most Recent Elections

All 300 members of the Transitional Constituent Assembly were appointed by former president Laurent Kabila.

LEGAL SYSTEM

The basis of Congoan law is the Belgian penal code, with certain modifications to provide for African traditions.

The court system consists of the Supreme Court of Justice; three courts of appeal, at Kinshasa, Kisanganí, and Lubumbashi; first-degree tribunals in each region and the city of Kinshasa; district tribunals in each district and city; and peace tribunals in each city and territory. The constitution also provides for a Constitutional Court to rule on the constitutionality of laws. Judges and public prosecutors are appointed by the president of the republic on the advice of the Superior Council of the Magistrate. They cannot be removed but may be transferred.

LAW ENFORCEMENT

Law Enforcement

Offenses reported to the police per 100,000: —
- Murder: —
- Assault: —
- Burglary: —
- Automobile Theft: —
- Population per Police officer: 910

Death Penalty: Yes.

HUMAN RIGHTS

The Kabila government's human rights record remained poor. Citizens do not have the right to change their government peacefully. Security forces were responsible for numerous extrajudicial killings, disappearances, torture, beatings, rape, and other abuses. In general, security forces committed these abuses with impunity, although a special military tribunal tried and executed some security force members for various human rights abuses. Prison conditions remained harsh and life threatening. Security forces increasingly used arbitrary arrest and detention throughout the year. Prolonged pretrial detention remained a problem, and citizens often were denied fair public trials. The special military tribunal tried civilians for political offenses and executed civilians, frequently with total disregard for process protections. The judiciary remained subject to executive influence and continued to suffer from a lack of resources, inefficiency, and corruption. It was largely ineffective as either a deterrent to human rights abuses or a corrective force. Security forces violated citizens' rights to privacy. Forcible conscription of adults and children continued, although children were conscripted to a lesser extent than in the previous year. Government security forces continued to use excessive force and committed violations of international law in the war that started in August 1998. On at least three occasions, government aircraft bombed civilian populated areas in rebel-held territory. Although a large number of private newspapers often published criticism of the government, the government continued to restrict freedom of speech and of the press by harassing and arresting newspaper editors and journalists and seizing individual issues of publications, as well as by continuing to increase its restrictions on private radio broadcasting. The government severely restricted freedom of assembly and association. The government continued to restrict freedom of movement; it required exit visas and imposed curfews even in cities not immediately threatened by the war. The government continued to ban political party activity and used security services to stop political demonstrations, resulting in numerous arrests and detentions. It also harassed and imprisoned members of opposition parties and harassed human rights nongovernmental organizations. Violence against women is a problem and rarely was punished. Female genital mutilation persists among isolated populations in the north. Discrimination against indigenous pygmies and ethnic minorities is a problem. Serious governmental and societal violence and discrimination against members of the Tutsi ethnic minority continued; however, the government protected many Tutsis who were at risk and permitted 1,341 to leave the country. The government arrested labor leaders during public sector strikes and allowed private employers to refuse to recognize unions. Child labor, including use of child soldiers remained a common problem. There were credible reports of beatings, rapes, and extrajudicial killings of Tutsis; however, societal abuses of Tutsis in government-controlled areas were far fewer than in 1998 because by the start of the year surviving Tutsis generally either had left the government-controlled part of the country or were in hiding, places of refuge, or government custody.

There were numerous credible reports that Mai Mai groups fighting on the side of the government committed serious abuses, including many extrajudicial killings and the torture of civilians.

FOREIGN POLICY

During his long rule, Mobutu generally enjoyed the support of Western powers who used him as a pawn in the cold war and also exploited his corrupt administration to secure favorable mining leases. But this support evaporated by the early 1990s. In 1993 the United States, Belgium, and France issued a statement describing Mobutu as the "architect of Zaïre's ruin," and calling for his resignation. The onset of the civil war and the collapse of the Zairean army before the swift march of Kabila-led Tutsi forces, posed a dilemma for Western powers who did not know whether to shore up the tottering and corrupt Mobutu or support an unknown guerrilla leader. When Kabila emerged triumphant most nations of the world immediately recognized him, but the continuing civil anarchy in the country and the involvement of Angolan, Ugandan, and Tutsi militias further complicated the situation. A multinational effort to end the conflict led to the Lusaka Award, which was disregarded by Kabila. The assassination of Kabila has raised the specter that Congo may eventually disintegrate in the face of its internal troubles.

DEFENSE

The defense structure is headed by the president of the republic, who also is the defense minister. Control is exercised through the military high command.

The main source of military manpower is voluntary enlistment, but the government attempts to achieve an ethnic balance through controlled recruitment. According to a year 2000 estimate, about 30,700 males annually reach the military age of 20. The former Zaïrean armed forces disbanded in 1997 and subsequently some 20,000 to 40,000 personnel of the Congo Liberation Army constitute the national armed forces.

Despite heavy military aid and arms transfers from the West, the Congoan army has a poor track record. The armed forces are heavily concentrated on the southern border and in Shaba.

Military Indicators

Total Active Duty Personnel: —
Military Manpower per 1,000: —
Military Expenditures $: 110 million
  as % of GNP: 0.3
  per capita $: 0
  as % of central government expenditures: 3.7

Arms Imports $: 0
Arms Exports $: 0

ECONOMY

The economy of the Democratic Republic of the Congo—a nation endowed with vast potential wealth—has declined drastically since the mid-1980s. The new government instituted a tight fiscal policy that initially curbed inflation and currency depreciation, but these small gains were quickly reversed when the foreign-backed rebellion in the eastern part of the country began in August 1998. The war has dramatically reduced government revenue, and increased external debt. Foreign businesses have curtailed operations due to uncertainty about the outcome of the conflict and because of increased government harassment and restrictions. Poor infrastructure, an uncertain legal framework, corruption, and lack of openness in government economic policy and financial operations remain a brake on investment and growth. A number of IMF and World Bank missions have met with the new government to help it develop a coherent economic plan but associated reforms are on hold.

Principal Economic Indicators

Gross National Product: $5.201 billion
GNP per capita: $110
GNP Average Annual Growth Rate (1990–97) %: −9.6
GNP per capita Average Annual Growth Rate (1990–97) %: −12.8
Origin of Gross Domestic Product %
  Agriculture: 58
  Mining: 5
  Manufacturing: 5
  Construction: 2
  Public Utilities: 2
  Transportation and Communications: 3
  Trade: 16
  Financial Services: 6
  Other Services: 6
  Government: 3
Gross Domestic Product by Type of Expenditure %
  Private Consumption: 86
  Government Consumption: 8
  Gross Domestic Investment: 3
  Foreign Trade: Exports: 13
    Imports: −10
% of Income Received by Poorest 20%: —
% of Income Received by Richest 10%: —

Price and earnings indexes (1995 = 100)

	1993	1994	1995	1996	1997
Consumer price index	0.1	15.6	100.0	758.8	2,090.7
Earnings index	—	—	—	—	—

Finance

National Currency: Zaire (Z)
Exchange Rate: $1 = Z 115,000
Money Supply Stock in National Currency billion: 1.889
M1 per capita: 42,400
Central Bank Discount Rate: —
Total External Debt $: 13.8 billion
Debt Service Ratio %: —

Balance of Payments $: −415 million
International Reserves SDRs: 45 million
Ratio of External Debt to Total Reserves: 64.7

Average Annual Rate of Inflation/Consumer Price Index
  Growth Rate %: NA

Official Development Assistance

ODA: $126 million
  as % of GNP: 2.0
  per capita: $3
  Foreign Direct Investment $: 1 million

Central Government Revenues and Expenditures

Fiscal Year: Calendar Year

Revenues $: 269 million
Expenditures $: 244 million
Budget Surplus $: 2.5 million
Tax Revenues as % of GDP: 5.3
Highest Tax Bracket %
  Individual: 50
  Corporate: —

Employment and Labor

Economically Active Population: 13,848,000
Female Participation Rate %: 35.2
Activity Rate %: 36.1
Labor by Sector: %
  Agriculture, Forestry, Fishing: 65.1
  Manufacturing, Mining: 15.9
  Construction: —
  Transportation and Communications: —

Trade, Hotels, and Restaurants: —
Finance, Insurance, Real Estate: —
Public Administration, Defense: —
Services: 19.0

Unemployment %: NA

Agriculture

Agriculture's Share of GDP %: 58
Average Annual Rate of Growth (1965–98) %: 2.0
Number of Farms 000: 4,480
Average Size of Farm ha: 2.3
Number of Tractors per 1,000 hectares: 0.3
Irrigation, % of Farms having: 0.1
Artificial Fertilizer kg/hectare: 1
Total Cropland as % of Farmland: 70.6
Livestock: Cattle 000: 1,000
Sheep 000: 1,020
Hogs 000: 1,170
Chickens 000: 25,000
Forests: Production of Roundwood (000 cubic meters): 47,189
Fisheries: Total Catch tons: 194,000

Mining

% of GDP: 4.3
Value of Mineral Production $: 226.5 million

Manufacturing

Value Added $: 808 million
Industrial Production Growth Rate %: NA

Energy

Commercial Energy Production metric tons of oil equivalent: 14,364,000
Commercial Energy Consumption metric tons of oil equivalent: 14,539,000
Commercial Energy Consumption per capita kg: 311
Average Annual Growth Rate 1980–97 %: −0.2
Net Energy Imports % of use: 1
Electricity Installed Capacity kW: 118,000
Production kW-hr: 435
Coal Reserves tons: 88 million
Production tons: 95,000
Natural Gas Proven Reserves cubic meters billion: 1
Production cubic meters: —
Crude Petroleum Reserves barrels: 187 million
Production barrels: 11 million
Consumption barrels: 400,000
Refinery Capacity barrels per day: 17,000
Pipelines Length km: 390

Foreign Trade

Imports $: 420 million
Exports $: 506 million
Export Volume % Annual Growth Rate (1990–97): −15.8
Import Volume % Annual Growth Rate (1990–97): −18.3
Balance of Trade $

Balance of trade (current prices)

	1991	1992	1993	1994	1995	1996
U.S. $000,000	+108	+403	+477	+643	+581	+708
% of total	3.4%	18.5%	26.3%	33.8%	25.0%	27.8%

Major Trading Partners

	Imports	Exports
European Union %	57.9	58.7
United States %	4.9	15.7
Eastern Europe %	0.8	4.5
Japan %	2.7	6.5
Others %	33.7	14.6

Transportation

Roads Total Length mi: 95,708 (154,027 km)
Paved %: —
Automobiles: 762,000
Trucks and Buses: 550,000
Persons per vehicle: 33
Railroad; Track Length mi: 3,162 (5,088 km)
Passenger-mi: 360 million
Freight-mi: 1.258 billion
Merchant Marine: No. of Vessels: 27
Total Deadweight Tonnage: 30,700
International Cargo Loaded tons: 2,395,000
International Cargo Off-loaded tons: 1,453,000
Airports with Scheduled Flights: 12
Traffic: Passenger-mi: 135 million
Freight-mi: 29 million
Length of Canals mi: 9,300 (15,000 km)

Tourism

Number of Tourists to: 32,000
Number of Tourists from: —
Tourist Receipts $: 6 million
Tourist Expenditures $: 16 million

Communications

Telephones 000: 36
Cost of Local Calls 3 mins: $0
Cellular Telephones 000: 10
Fax Machines 000: 5
Personal Computers 000:
Internet Hosts per million persons:
Mail: Post Offices: 304
Pieces of Mail Handled: —
Pieces of Mail Handled per person: —

EDUCATION

The state theoretically provides free, universal, and compulsory education for six years, from ages six to 12. Secondary education is not compulsory from ages 12 to 17. Education and literacy among females is greatest among primary age groups with a sharp decline during secondary and university levels of education.

The academic year runs from September to July. The mediums of instruction are Kikongo, Tshiluba, Lingala, or Swahili in the primary grades and French in the secondary and university levels. Schooling consists of 12 years, with six years of primary education divided into three two-year sections: elementary, middle, and terminal. Students are not divided into formal grades at the first level. There also are a few unsubsidized private schools. Over 92 percent of the primary- and secondary-school population attend subsidized schools, over 70 percent of which are run by the Roman Catholic Church.

There is a critical shortage of trained teachers. Less than one-fourth of primary-school teachers have university diplomas. The Compulsory Civic Service was instituted in 1966 to create a pool of trained personnel by making a two-year teaching stint mandatory for all students who received a license after 1966. Education is a high priority for the country and accounts for a substantial portion of the national budget.

All universities in Congo were reorganized and nationalized in 1971 as the National University, with four campuses, at Kisangani, Kananga, Kinshasa, and Lubumbashi.

Education

Literacy Rate %: 77.3
- Male %: 86.6
- Female %: 67.7

First Level: Primary schools: 14,885
- Teachers: 12,105
- Students: 5,417,506
- Student-Teacher Ratio: 44.8
- Net Enrollment Ratio: 61

Second Level: Secondary Schools: 4,276
- Teachers: 59,325
- Students: 640,298
- Student-Teacher Ratio: 22.6
- Net Enrollment Ratio: 23

Vocational Level: Schools: —
- Students: 701,148

Third Level: Institutions: —
- Teachers: —
- Students: 93,266
- Student-Ratio Level: —
- Gross Enrollment Ratio: 2.3
- Students per 100,000: 212
- % of Population Age 25 and over with Postsecondary Education: —

Public Expenditure on Education as % of GDP: —

SCIENCE AND TECHNOLOGY

Science and Technology

Scientists and Engineers in R&D per 1 million persons: —
Expenditures in R&D as % of GDP: —
High-Tech Exports $: —
Patent Applications by Residents: 2

MEDIA

There are nine daily newspapers with a combined circulation of 112,000. There are also more than 12 weekly, monthly, and quarterly periodicals.

The official news agency is Agence Congo Presse (AZAP), based in Kinshasa, with regional correspondents in the Republic of the Congo and a foreign bureau at Brussels. A second agency—Documentation and Information for and about Africa (DIA)—founded by the Catholic Church in 1956, functions as an independent private company.

The state-owned La Voix du Congo operates in Kinshasa and in provincial stations. An international service, the Voice of the Brotherhood, is broadcast from Lubumbashi.

Television was introduced in 1966. There are two stations, one in Kinshasa and the other in Lubumbashi.

Media

Daily Newspapers: 9
- Total Circulation 000: 112
- Circulation per 1,000: 3

Books Published: 64
Magazines: —
Radio Receivers 000: 3,480
- per 1,000: 81

Television sets 000: 1,800
- per 1,000: 41

MOST IMPORTANT MEDIA:

Press. The following are dailies published at Kinshasa, unless otherwise noted: *Solongo* (10,000); *Mjumbe* (Lubumbashi); *Boyoma* (Kisangani); *Le Passeport Africain*, weekly, recommended publication in mid-1994. A number of independent papers, largely critical of the Mobutu regime, commenced publication in 1990. In early 1991 two directors of the evening daily, *Elima*, were detained after printing articles alleging government corruption; in October a bomb blast destroyed the paper's offices, and in November 1993 publication was suspended by the government.

News agencies. The domestic facility is the Congolese Press Agency (CPA); Agence France-Presse, Xinhua, and Reuters also maintain bureaus at Kinshasa.

Radio and television. Radio broadcasting is provided by the government over the national station, La Voix du Congo, and regional stations. Commercial television is provided by the government-operated, commercial Television Congolaise. There were approximately 5.0 million radio and 173,000 television receivers in 1998.

CULTURE

Cultural Indicators

Public Libraries
- Number: —
- Volumes: —
- Registered borrowers: —

Museums
- Number: —
- Annual Attendance: —

Cinema
Production of Long Films: —
Number of Cinemas: —
Seating Capacity: —
Annual Attendance: —
Annual Attendance per capita: —

STATUS OF WOMEN

The role of women in Congolese society is given great emphasis in doctrine of the ruling MPR. Women's rights to own property and participate in the political and economic sectors are protected by law, and a growing number of women work in the professions, government, service, and the universities. Nevertheless, custom, tradition, and existing law continue to constrain women from attaining a position of complete equality in society. Women generally earn less than their male counterparts in the same jobs. In addition, married women must obtain their husband's authorization before opening a bank account, accepting a job, or renting or selling real estate.

Women

Gender Empowerment Measure: —
Seats Held in Parliament by Women %: —
Female Administrators and Managers %: —
Female Professional and Technical Workers %: —
Women's Share of Earned Income %: —
Women in Government %: 2

HEALTH, FOOD, AND NUTRITION

Health

Number of Physicians: 2,469
Number of Dentists: 41
Number of Nurses: 27,601
Number of Pharmacists: 59
Population per Physician: 15,584
Number of Hospitals: 400
Hospital Beds per 10,000: 21
Hospital Bed Occupancy Rate: —
Infant Mortality Rate per 1,000 live births: 131
Maternal Mortality Rate per 100,000 live births: 870
Total Health Expenditures as % of GDP: 2.38
Health Expenditures per capita $: 5
HIV Infected % of adults: 4.35
Cigarette Consumption per smoker per year: —
% of Smokers: Male: —
Female: —
Access to Safe Water %: 25

Food and Nutrition

Food Supply as % of FAO Requirements: 85
% of Consumption Expenditures on Food: 61.7
Daily Available Calories per capita: 1,879
% of Total Calories derived from:
Cereals: 16.6
Potatoes, cassava: 55.3
Meat, poultry: 1.9
Fish: 0.5
Eggs, milk: 0.1
Fruits, vegetables: 7.8
Fats, oils: 6.7

ENVIRONMENT

The Congo's most significant environmental problem is widespread poaching that threatens the viability of a number of species. The country also suffers from growing water pollution and deforestation. Refugees who arrived in mid-1994 were responsible for significant deforestation, soil erosion, and wildlife poaching in the eastern part of the country.

Environment

Forest Area sq km: —
Average Annual Deforestation sq km: —
Nationally Protected Areas as % of Total Land Area: 4.5
Freshwater Access cubic meters per capita: 21,134
Emissions of Organic Water Pollutants kg per day:
CO_2 Emissions per capita ton: 0.1 ton

CHRONOLOGY

1960 Congo gains independence, with Patrice Lumumba of the Mouvement National Congolaise (MNC) as prime minister and Joseph Kasavubu of the Alliance des Bakongo as president; opposed to a centralized rather than federal government, Katanga, the country's richest province, declares independence under Moise Tshombe; Congolese soldiers mutiny; Belgian forces withdraw and Belgian civilians flee the country; at the government's request, the UN Security Council dispatches troops; Lumumba requests Soviet aid; Lumumba and Kasavubu dismiss one another; Albert Kalondji proclaims the independence of South Kasai; Joseph Mobutu, chief of staff of the Congolese National Army (ANC) seizes power; Lumumbists under Antoine Gizenga organize a countergovernment at Stanleyville; Lumumba is arrested.

1961 Lumumba is executed; Joseph Ileo forms a provisional government; a tentative agreement between the Leopoldville government and the secessionist governments of Katanga and Kasai establishes a centralized government; under UN protection, the National Legislative Council reopens and approves a coalition government headed by Cyrille Adoula as prime minister; diplomatic relations with Belgium are reestablished; UN troops move against Katanga.

1962 The Kitona agreement resolves the Katanga secession; the Stanleyville government is dissolved; Gizenga and Kalondji are arrested.

1963 President Kasavubu declares a state of emergency and dissolves the National Legislative Council; Tshombe is appointed prime minister.

1964 A commission headed by Joseph Ileo drafts a constitution; the country's name is changed from the Republic of Congo to the Democratic Republic of Congo (DROC); rebels capture Stanleyville; the Katangan gendarmerie and white mercenaries attack rebel strongholds; rebels under Christophe Gbenye use white hostages to halt government forces; UN forces withdraw.

1965 Prime Minister Tshombe and President Kasavubu engage in a power struggle; General Mobutu seizes power for a second time and names a government of national unity, with Leonard Mulamba as prime minister.

1966 Mobutu abolishes the National Legislative Council and assumes legislative powers; Prime Minister Mulamba is dismissed and one-time prime minister Kimba is executed; another mutiny breaks out in Katanga.

1967 The new constitution is promulgated, naming the Mouvement Populaire de la Révolution (MPR) the country's sole political party; after a plane carrying Tshombe is hijacked over Algeria, mercenaries launch a rebellion in the east; the rebellion collapses and rebels flee to Rwanda; the MPR issues the Manifesto of Nsele.

1969 Patrice Lumumba is declared a national hero.

1970 Running unopposed, Mobutu is elected president in the DROC's first presidential election.

1971 As part of a sweeping program of Africanization, the country is renamed the Republic of Zaire.

1972 A National Executive Council is formed to replace the cabinet.

1973 All foreign-owned firms, plantations, and mining companies are nationalized.

1974 The constitution is revised to make the MPR synonymous with the state.

1976 Congo defaults on foreign loans; currency is devalued.

1977 Guerrillas of the Cuban-backed Congolese National Liberation Front, based in Angola, invade the Zaïrean region of Shaba (formerly called Katanga), straining relations with the Soviet Union; Congo receives aid from Morocco, Sudan, Uganda, and Western nations to fight against the rebels.

1978 Guerrillas of the Congolese National Liberation Front (reportedly backed by Angola, Cuba, and the Soviet Union) invade Shaba again through Zambia and occupy Kolwezi and Mutshalaha; French and Belgian troops launch successful rescue operations.

1979 President Neto of Angola reaches an agreement with Mobutu regarding the creation of a supervisory body to prevent guerrilla operations across the common border.

1983 Amnesty International publishes a report harshly critical of the human rights record in Zaïre; Mobutu grants amnesty to all political exiles who return by June 30; some exiles return, but a strong opposition movement remains in Belgium.

1984 Despite continued resistance against his regime within Zaire, Mobutu is reelected president.

1985 The MPR is restructured, strengthening Mobutu's position; Nguza Karl-I-Bond returns from exile; restrictions on seven members of outlawed UDPS are ended.

1989 Zairean students in Belgium are ordered to return to Zaire by year's end; Mobutu announces termination of two friendship and cooperation treaties between Zaire and Belgium.

1990 In response to growing public discontent, Mobutu vows to end the ban on multiparty politics; nevertheless, the government continues to use violence to suppress political opposition.

1993 Western nations, including France and Belgium, send troops in order to protect their citizens living in Zaire from the growing violence.

1994 Mobutu names as prime minister Kengo Wa Dondo, a proponent of austerity and free-market reforms.

1997 Rebel forces led by General Laurent Kabila take control of the government after more than a year of fighting; Kabila immediately changes the name of the country from Zaire to the Democratic Republic of the Congo; Mobutu flees to Morocco, where he dies of cancer in September.

1998 Anti-Kabila rebel forces attempt to take the capital but are defeated.

2000 Ethnic fighting erupts in the rebel-held east; UN peacekeepers monitor the cease-fire.

2001 Kabila is assassinated in January, and his son Joseph Kabila is named president . . . . Ugandan, Rwandan, and Zimbabwean troops begin withdrawing from the country, and UN troops are deployed in the rebel-held town of Kisangani. In May, President Kabila lifts the ban on all parties that were in operation under former president Mobuto Sese Seko.

2002 Mount Nyiragongo, among Africa's most active volcanoes, erupts, destroying the town of Goma.

BIBLIOGRAPHY

Bobb, F. Scott. *Historical Dictionary of Congo*. Metuchen, N.J., 1988.

Callaghy, Thomas M. *The State-Society Struggle: Zaire in Comparative Perspective*. New York, 1984.

Dembour, Marie-Bénédicte. *Recalling the Belgian Congo*. New York, 2000.
Hochschild, Adam. *King Leopold's Ghost*. Boston, 1998.
Kronston, Gregory. *Zaire to the 1990s: Will Retrenchment Work?* New York, 1986.
Lemarchand, Rene. *Political Awakening in the Belgian Congo*. Westport, Conn., 1982.
O'Ballance, Edgar. *The Congo-Zaire Experience, 1960–98*. New York, 2000.
Schatzberg, Michael C. *Politics and Class in Zaire: Bureaucracy, Business and Beer in Lisala*. New York, 1980.
Vengroff, Richard. *Development Administration at the Local Level: The Case of Zaire*. Syracuse, N.Y., 1983.
Young, Crawford, and Thomas Turner. *The Rise and Decline of the Zairean State*. Madison, Wisc., 1985.

OFFICIAL PUBLICATIONS

Congo, Dem. Rep. of the (Zaire). *Annuaire statistique* (irreg.); *Recensement scientifique de la population du juillet 1984*.

CONTACT INFORMATION

Embassy of Democratic Republic of Congo
1800 West Hampshire Avenue NW
Washington, D.C. 20009
Phone: (202) 234-7690 Fax: (202) 237-0748

INTERNET RESOURCES

- Zaire—A Country Study
  http://lcweb2.loc.gov/frd/cs/zrtoc.html
- Permanent Mission of the Democratic Republic of the Congo to the United Nations
  http://www.un.int/drcongo/

CONGO, REPUBLIC OF THE

BASIC FACT SHEET

OFFICIAL NAME:
Republic of the Congo (République du Congo)

ABBREVIATION:
CF

CAPITAL:
Brazzaville

HEAD OF STATE & GOVERNMENT:
President Denis Sassou-Nguesso (from 1997)

NATURE OF GOVERNMENT:
Republic

POPULATION:
2,717,000 (1999)

AREA:
342,000 sq km (132,046 sq mi)

ETHNIC MAJORITY:
Bakongo, Bateke, Mboshi, and Sangha

LANGUAGES:
French (official), Lingala, and Monokutuba

RELIGIONS:
Christianity and animism

UNIT OF CURRENCY:
Communauté Financière Africaine franc (C.F.A.F.)

NATIONAL FLAG:
Divided diagonally from the lower hoist side by a yellow band; the upper triangle (hoist side) is green and the lower triangle is red, using the popular pan-African colors of Ethiopia.

NATIONAL EMBLEM:
A shield with a red lion bearing a torch of freedom on a green field split by a green wavy bar representing the Zaïre River. The shield is flanked by two elephants standing on a red log draped with a gold ribbon carrying the legend *Unité, Travail, Progrès.* On the crest are seven staves rising from a band inscribed "République du Congo."

NATIONAL ANTHEM:
"On This Day the Sun Rises"

NATIONAL HOLIDAYS:
August 15 (National Day, Independence Day); January 1; May 1 (Labor Day); June 22 (Anniversary of the People's Army); August 13–15 (Anniversary of the Three Glorious Days); December 25; December 31 (Birth of the Parti Congolaise du Travail)

DATE OF INDEPENDENCE:
August 15, 1960 1946

DATE OF CONSTITUTION:
July 8, 1979; draft constitution adopted by transitional parliament in September 2001, approved in a national referendum in January 2, 2002

GEOGRAPHICAL FEATURES

The Republic of the Congo, in West Africa, has an irregularly shaped area of 342,000 sq km (132,046 sq mi), extending 1,006 km (625 mi) north-northeast to south-southwest and 402 km (250 mi) east-southeast to west-northwest. Its total international land boundaries of 4,469 km (2,777 mi) are artificial ones drawn by former colonial powers. The frontier lengths are: Cameroon (520 km; 323 mi); Central African Republic (467 km; 290 mi); the Democratic Republic of the Congo (2,410 km; 1,497 mi); Angola (201 km; 125 mi); and Gabon (1,903 km; 1,181 mi). The length of the Atlantic coastline is 169 km (105 mi).

The country is divided into four topographical regions. The coastal region is a treeless plain stretching for about 161 km (100 mi) along the Atlantic coast and extending for about 64 km (40 mi) inland to the Mayombe

Republic of the Congo

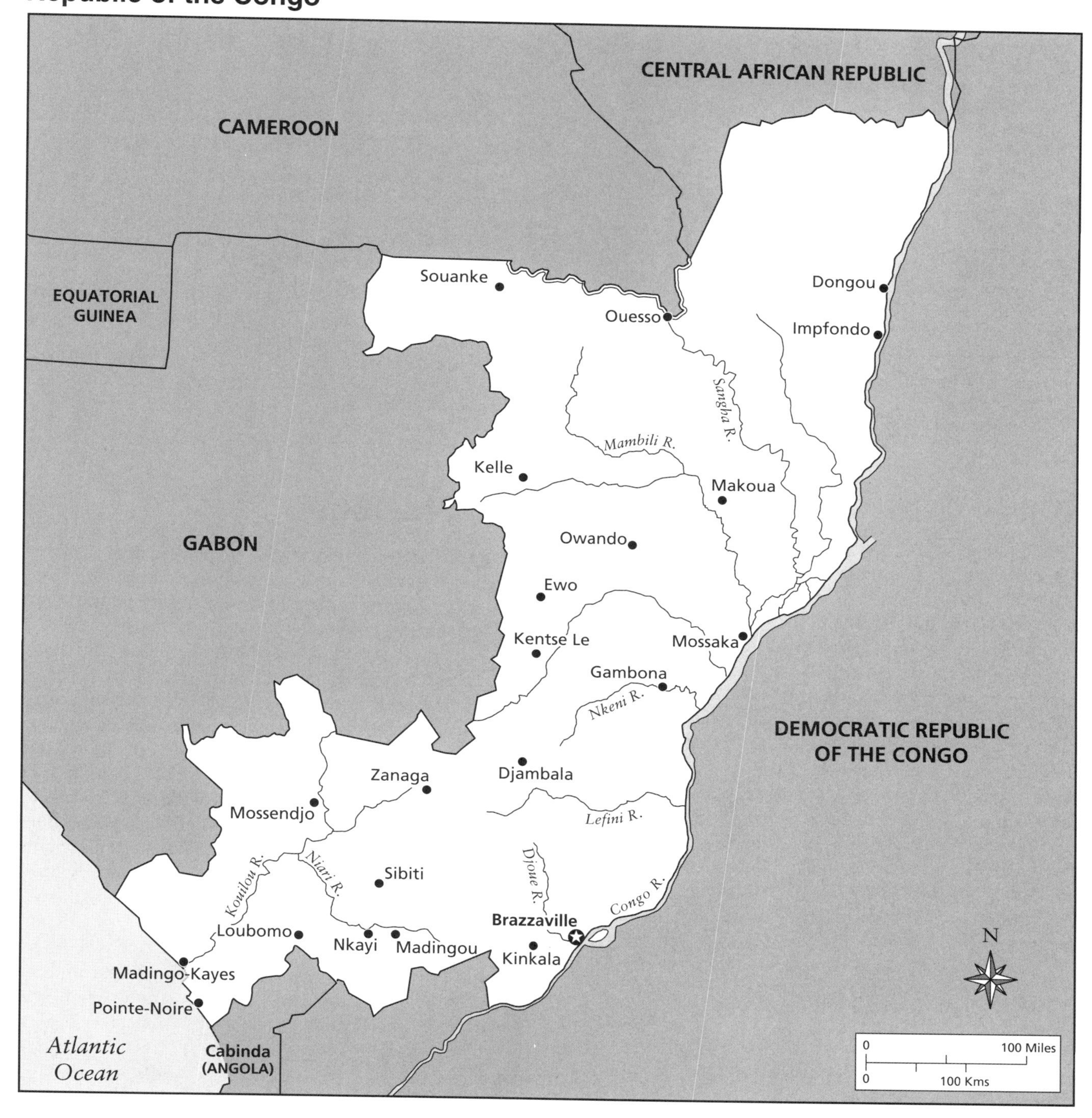

escarpment and to the foothills of the Crystal Mountains. The area is marked by extensive swamps, lakes, and rivers. Inland the sharp ridges of the Mayombe escarpment run parallel to the coast, reaching elevations of 488 m to 610 m (1,600 to 2,000 ft). The Niari Valley, lying between the Chaillu Mountains and the Mayombe Mountains and extending for about 322 km (200 mi) in the south-central area, contains the most fertile soil in the country. The central highlands, known as the Bateke Plateau, form the watershed between the Niari and the Ogowe river systems. Much of this region, encompassing an area of 130,000 sq km (50,000 sq mi), is covered by dense forests. The northeastern section of the country lies within the Zaïre River basin and is composed of largely impassable floodplains in the lower portion and a dry savanna in the upper portion.

Geography

Area sq km: 342,000 (132,046 sq mi)
World Rank: 63rd
Land Boundaries, km: Angola 201; Cameroon 523; Central African Republic 467; Democratic Rep. of the Congo 2410; Gabon 1903
Coastline, km: 169
Elevation Extremes meters
- Lowest: Atlantic Ocean 0
- Highest: Mount Berongou 903

Land Use % Arable land: 0
- Permanent Crops: 0
- Permanent Pastures: 29
- Forest and Woodland: 62
- Other: 9

Population of Principal Cities

Brazzaville	937,579
Pointe-Noire	576,206

CLIMATE AND WEATHER

The Republic of the Congo has a tropical climate characterized by high temperatures, high rainfall, and high humidity, with little seasonal variation. The seasons are reversed north and south of the equator. North of the equator the rainy season lasts from April until late October and the dry season from early November until late March. Temperatures range from 26.6°C to 32°C (80°F to 90°F) on the average, although lower temperatures have been recorded nearer the coast under the influence of the Benguela (Antarctic) current. Humidity is consistently high throughout the year, with average daily readings of 80 percent.

Rainfall varies regionally, with higher precipitation in the north. The annual average is about 1,520 mm (60 in), while parts of the Congo Basin may receive up to twice that amount. Violent winds and squalls are common in the wet season.

Climate and Weather

Mean Temperature 80°F to 90°F
Average Rainfall: 60 in

POPULATION

Population Indicators

Total Population: 1999 2,717,000
World Rank: 134th
Density per sq mi: 20.6 (7.9 per sq km)
% of annual growth (1994–99): 2.3
Male %: 48.7
Female %: 51.3
Urban %: 52.0
Age Distribution: % 0–14: 44.7
- 15–29: 27.2
- 30–44: 13.3
- 45–59: 9.1
- 60–74: 4.6
- 75 and over: 0.7

Population 2020: 3,945,000
Birth Rate per 1,000: 42.5
Death Rate per 1,000: 14.6
Population Doubling Time (years): 32
Infant Mortality Rate per 1,000 live births: 90
Rate of Natural Increase per 1,000: 27.9
Total Fertility Rate: 5.9
Expectation of Life (years): Males 48.6
Females 53.4
Marriage Rate per 1,000: —
Divorce Rate per 1,000: —
Total Number of Households: 326,000
Average Size of Households: 4.7
% of Illegitimate Children: —
Induced Abortions: —
- Rate per 100 live births: —

ETHNIC COMPOSITION

All the Congolese are Bantus except for small, isolated groups of Negrillos and Sudanese immigrants. Of the 15 main ethnic groups, divided into 75 tribes, four stand out. The most important is the Kongo, or Bakongo, whose tribes live in the south, between Brazzaville and the coast, and account for 45 percent of the population. The second ethnic family is the Mboshi, also called Boubangui, who currently inhabit the Cuvette and Likoula regions and constitute about 16 percent of the population. The third important group is the Bateke, or Teke, who live in the plateau country north of Brazzaville and constitute about 20 percent of the population. Finally, the Sanga family of tribes inhabit the northern forest zone, which they share with the Binga, or Babinga, Pygmies, whose ancestors are believed to be the original inhabitants of the land.

There is a great deal of interethnic rivalry, particularly in the political sphere. Intertribal riots are common and, despite misleading labels, political groups are based largely on ethnic loyalties. In the urban areas each ethnic group tends to isolate itself in its own residential quarter.

LANGUAGES

The official language is French, which is used extensively in government and in the schools. Only a small proportion of the African population use French as a working language.

Each ethnic group has its own traditional language. Kikongo is the most widely used local dialect. Two trade languages are used as lingua francas for intertribal communication: Lingala in the north and Monokutuba in the south. All African languages belong to the Bantu family.

Principal Languages and Their Speakers

Bobangi	30,000
French	1,400,000
Kongo	1,400,000
Kola	20,000
Lingala (lingua franca)	—
Maka	50,000
Mbete	130,000
Mboshi	310,000
Monokutuba (lingua franca)	1,600,000
Punu	80,000
Sango	70,000
Teke	470,000
Other	140,000

RELIGIONS

About 65 percent of the Congolese are nominally Christian, with Catholics composing the majority of this group. There is a tiny Muslim community of approximately 2 percent of the population. The remaining 33 percent of the Congolese are either animists or members of unorthodox sects.

In theory, freedom of religion is guaranteed by law. In practice, members of the ruling PCT are prohibited from practicing religion. Jehovah's Witnesses had not been allowed to exercise their right to worship, allegedly because they do not recognize the authority of the state. In February 1978 the government banned all religious groups except Roman Catholics, certain Protestant denominations, Muslims, and followers of regional sects.

Religious Affiliations

Roman Catholic	1,110,000
Traditional beliefs	890,000
Protestant	660,000
Muslim	60,000

HISTORICAL BACKGROUND

The first settlers to the region that is now the Republic of the Congo came 40,000 to 100,000 years ago. The first large-scale societies were formed only 500 to 1,000 years ago. Three kingdoms emerged from the numerous peoples and villages: the Loango on the Atlantic coast, the Kongo in the southwest, and the Tio on the northern plains. Political power was marked by control over the spirit cults and trade.

The first Europeans arrived in 1483 in Kongo. The Portuguese were welcomed to the region. However, this came to an end when the Portuguese began to trade slaves in the early 16th century. The 17th through 19th centuries were marked by an increase in the slave trade from the Republic of the Congo and the continued influence of Western cultures on the country. In order to bring an end to colonial fighting over territory, the Republic of the Congo came under the administration of the French.

From 1910 until 1958, the Republic of the Congo, then known as Moyen-Congo, was an administrative unit of the Federation of French Equatorial Africa, which also included Gabon, Chad (Tchad), and Oubangui-Chari (Central African Republic). Brazzaville was the headquarters of the federation. French colonial rule suffered from lack of well-defined policy. In the aftermath of World War II a series of administrative and social reforms was initiated, providing for increased Congolese participation in the governing process.

Congo has had five governments since independence, all of them unstable and four of them terminated by violence. The army has dominated the government since 1968. Interethnic rivalries have added to the instability, and each regime each has been associated with the ascendancy of a particular tribe and the exclusion of the others.

Congo achieved full independence in August 1958 under a strong, centralized government led by Abbé Fulbert Youlou, a radical former Roman Catholic priest from the south. Youlou's attempts to establish one-party rule resulted in trade union strikes and mass demonstrations that led to his resignation in 1963.

Alphonse Massamba-Débat took over leadership of a provisional government that was formed by the military with the support of the trade unions. Massamba-Débat adopted Marxist-Leninist policy and attempted unsuccessfully to develop a socialist economic system. The communist-inspired Mouvement National de la Révolution (MNR) was made the nation's sole political party, and its role became increasingly important during Massamba-Débat's tenure. His radical approach alienated the army, which staged a successful coup in August 1968. The leader of the coup, Captain Marien Ngouabi, became president and drew up a new constitution, approved in 1969, under which his Parti Congolais du Travail (PCT) became the sole party. The constitution proclaimed the nation The People's Republic of the Congo. The regime called itself marxist but maintained close economic ties with France.

Opposition to one-party rule, particularly in the south, resulted in Ngouabi's assassination in 1977. Former president Massamba-Débat was implicated in the plot and later executed, although his complicity was never proved. The PCT military committee appointed Joachim Yhombi-Opango president. However, his antileft feelings and his failure to deal with a worsening economic crisis led to his resignation in 1979. He was replaced by his chief rival, Col. Denis Sassou-Nguesso. The Military

Council was abolished, and amnesty was given to political exiles. A socialist constitution was approved by referendum. Although nominally Marxist, the government became increasingly liberal and pro-Western in order to placate the right and deal with the country's serious economic problems. Sassou-Nguesso was reelected president in 1984. His position was strengthened at the expense of the prime minister through constitutional amendments approved that year. Ongoing ethnic rivalries and worsening economic problems led to a coup attempt in July 1987, which resulted in the arrest of 20 army officers and the eventual arrest and imprisonment of Yhombi-Opango. Sassou-Nguesso was reelected again for a five-year term in 1989. The Congolese Workers' Party officially dropped its Marxist ideology in 1990.

President Sassou-Nguesso introduced a multiparty system in 1991 and convened an all-party National Conference to chart the future course of the country. The National Conference approved the draft of a new democratic constitution, which dropped "People's" from the country's name, transferred most of the presidential powers to the prime minister, and scheduled a referendum. The referendum, held in 1992, secured a 96 percent approval. At the presidential balloting, Pascal Lissouba of the Pan-African Union for Social Democracy emerged as the winner. Lissouba faced a stormy legislature. Waves of civil unrest paralyzed the country. For a time the military occupied Brazzaville and forced the president to appoint a unity government under Claude Antoine Dacosta as prime minister. Dacosta was followed by Gen. Yhombe-Opango, but the state of armed rebellion continued. Regional and ethnic rivalries continued to fan the flames of discontent as the Lissouba administration sought to end the pro–Sassou-Nguesso northerners' dominance of the military as well as to disarm the numerous militias. In 1996 there was a short-lived mutiny, which was ended only on terms imposed by the rebels. Preparations for the 1997 presidential elections soon escalated into a virtual civil war between the two major contenders, Lissouba and Sassou-Nguesso. With the help of mercenaries and regular troops from Angola, Sassou-Nguesso captured Brazzaville, while Lissouba fled the capital. Sassou-Nguesso named a new broadly representative government, but abolished the post of prime minister. Militias loyal to Lissouba continued to resist throughout 1998 and early 1999. In 1999 the government and militias signed a peace agreement in the Zambian capital, Lusaka, and in 2001 some 15,000 militia gave up their weapons. In September a new constitution was adopted by the transitional parliament.

CONSTITUTION

The constitution of the People's Republic of the Congo, approved by popular referendum in 1979, the country's fifth since gaining independence, was abolished in 1991 at a national conference. It was replaced with a basic law that established a presidency, a bicameral legislature, and a prime ministership. This basic law was adopted in 1992 by referendum. This constitution was suspended in 1997. In September 2001 a draft constitution was adopted by the transitional parliament and was approved in a national referendum on January 2, 2002.

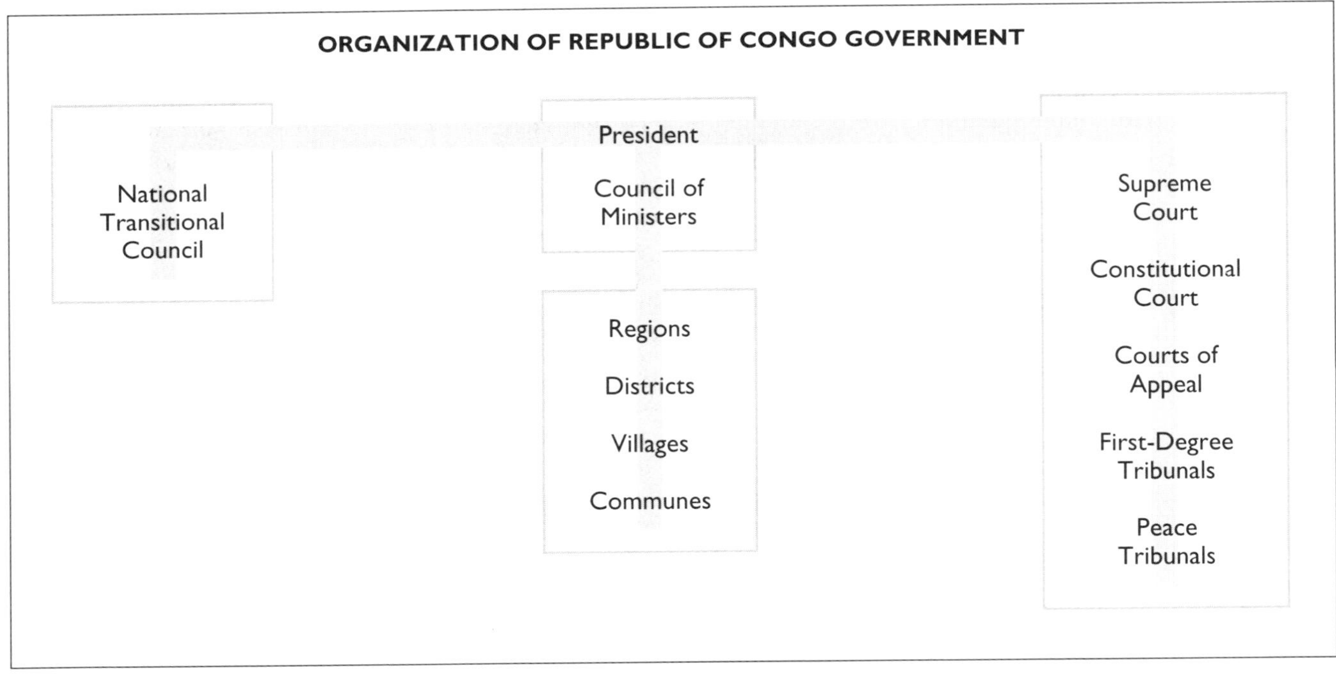

LOCAL GOVERNMENT

In conformity with a 1995 law, the country was divided into 10 regions, which were then divided into 76 districts. In addition to these 76 districts, there are six urban councils.

Local Government

Principal administrative divisions, capitals, area, population

AREA AND POPULATION

Regions	Capitals	area sq mi	sq km	population 1992 estimate
Bouenza	Madingou	4,733	12,258	177,357
Cuvette Est	Owando	28,900	74,850	151,839
Cuvette Ouest	Ewo			
Kouilou	Pointe-Noire	5,270	13,650	89,296
Lékoumou	Sibiti	8,089	20,950	74,420
Likouala	Impfondo	25,500	66,044	70,675
Niari	Loubomo	10,007	25,918	120,077
Plateaux	Djambala	14,826	38,400	119,722
Pool	Kinkala	13,110	33,955	182,671
Sangha	Ouesso	21,542	55,795	35,961
Communes				
Brazzaville	—	39	100	937,579
Loubomo	—	7	18	83,605
Mossendjo	—	2	5	16,405
Nkayi	—	3	8	42,465
Ouesso	—	2	5	16,171
Pointe-Noire	—	17	44	576,206
TOTAL		132,047	342,000	2,694,449

PARLIAMENT

Until 1997 the parliament of the Republic of the Congo was bicameral. The lower house, the National Assembly, consisted of 125 members elected directly from single-member districts for terms of five years. If a candidate did not win a majority of the votes, then a second round of voting was required between the top two finishers. The upper house, the Senate, consists of 60 members who were elected indirectly from local and regional councils for a period of six years. One-third of the Senate was elected every two years. The parliament was suspended in 1997, and in 1999 the unicameral 75-member Transitional Council was established in its place.

POLITICAL PARTIES

The Republic of the Congo is a multiparty state. Among the most important parties is the Congolese Labor Party, which is the party of the president and the former ruling party when the Congo was a one-party state. In addition to the PCT is the Pan-African Union for Social Development, or UPADS, which lost control in a no-confidence vote in 1992. Most of the parties have aligned with other parties to form three major groupings. The first is the Presidential Tendency, which includes the UPADS and other minor parties. The second is the Union for Democratic Renewal, which includes the Congolese Movement for Democracy and the Rally for Democracy and Social Progress. The final group, the United Democratic Forces, consists of the Congolese Labor Party and several minor parties.

Political Parties

- Democratic and Patriotic Forces, 1997, an alliance of
  - Congolese Labor Party, 1969
  - Patriotic Union for National Reconstruction
  - National Union for Democracy and Progress, 1990
- Union for Democratic Renewal, 1992, an alliance of
  - Congolese Movement for Democracy and Integral Development, 1989
  - Rally for Democracy and Social Progress
- Republican Forum for Democracy and National Unity, 1997, an alliance of
  - Pan-African Union for Social Democracy
  - Rally for Democracy and Development, 1990
  - Congolese Party for Reconstruction, 1992
  - Union for Congolese Democracy, 1989
  - Union for Democracy and Social Progress, 1994
- Union of Democratic Forces
- Union for Democracy and the Republic, 1992
- Union for the Republic, 1995
- National Alliance for Democracy, an alliance of
  - Union for Social Progress and Democracy, 1991
  - Alliance for Democracy and the Republic
  - Congolese Association for Development and Solidarity
  - Congolese Liberal Party
  - Forum for Democracy and the Republic
  - Independent Social Republican Party
  - National Convention for Democracy and Development
  - Rally of the Congolese People
  - Republican Democratic Front
  - Union of Congolese Democrats
- Congolese Social Democratic Party, 1990
- Party for Unity, Work and Progress, 1995
- Movement for Congolese Reconciliation, 1996
- Democratic Center, 1993

Political Parties: Strength in Parliament Most Recent Elections

Senate (Sénat). Following balloting on July 26, 1992, the Pan-African Union for Social Democracy held 23 seats; the Congolese Movement for Democracy and Integral Development, 13; the Rally for Democracy and Development, 8; the Rally for Democracy and Social Progress, 5; the Congolese Labor Party, 3; Forces for Change, 1; independents, 7.

National Assembly (Assemblée Nationale). Following the balloting of May-October 1993, the Presidential Tendency was credited with winning 65 seats (the Pan-African Union for Social Democracy, 47; the Rally for Democracy and Development, 6; the Union of Democratic Forces, 3; the Congolese Party for Reconstruction, 2; the Union for Congolese Democracy, 1; the Union for Development and Social Progress, 1; others, 5); the Opposition Coalition, 56 (the Congolese Movement for Democracy and Integral Development, 28; the Congolese Labor Party, 15; the Rally for Democracy and Social Progress, 10; the Union for Democratic Renewal, 2; pro-PCT independent, 1); the Union for Democracy and the Republic, 2; the Patriotic Union for National Renewal, 1; independent, 1. The

(continued)

formation of the Union for the Republic in March 1995 reduced the UPADS representation to 35, without diminishing the Presidential Tendency's majority. However, at by-elections in April 1995 the Opposition Coalition gained 5 additional seats (PCT, 3; MCDDI, 2), thereby technically reducing the government's strength to a plurality of 60.

LEGAL SYSTEM

The legal system is inherited from the French but has been modified by successive regimes. The court system consists of the Supreme Court, the Court of Appeals, the Criminal Court, tribunaux de grande instance (country courts), tribunaux d'instance (magistrates' courts), and labor courts. The Revolutionary Court of Justice, created in 1969, deals with cases involving state security. Its nine judges are appointed by the Central Committee of the PCT. Customary courts were abolished under the constitution of 1973.

The Supreme Court is in practice an arm of the government rather than an independent body.

Whereas the constitution guarantees protection against arbitrary indictment, arrest, and detention, in practice a warrant is not required to make arrests. There is a habeas corpus provision, but in cases involving the security of the state, people arrested can be held without a court hearing. Individuals detained for nonpolitical offenses are entitled to an attorney and are judged by a generally impartial judiciary. By law the right to a fair and public trial exists in all cases.

LAW ENFORCEMENT

Law Enforcement

Offenses reported to the police per 100,000: 32
- Murder: 1.5
- Assault: 4.7
- Burglary: 0.2
- Automobile Theft: 0.2
- Population per Police officer: 870

Death Penalty: Yes, but last execution was in 1982

HUMAN RIGHTS

The government's human rights record was poor, and there continued to be numerous serious abuses. Citizens do not have the right to change their government peacefully. Security forces, which included many undisciplined and poorly cotrolled former members of nongovernmental militias, were responsible for extrajudicial killings, including summary executions; disappearances; rapes; beatings and physical abuse of detainees and the civilian population; arbitrary arrest and detention; and arbitrary searches and widespread looting of private homes. Prison conditions remainded life threatening. The judiciary was overburdened, underfinanced, and subject to corruption and political influence. It was unable to ensure fair and expeditious trials. The government infringed on citizens' privacy rights. The government continued to monopolize domestic broadcast media, although private newspapers circulated freely and were sometimes critical of the authorities. The government permitted opposition political parties and nongovernmental organizations, including human rights organizations, to function, and there was a relatively open dialog on public policy issues. The government sent mixed signals on political participation by opposition figures. While many former cabinet ministers and other officials of the Lissouba government returned to Brazzaville during the year and were permitted to resume political activities, the government also repeatedly stated that the most senior figures—including former President Lissouba and Prime Minister Kolelas—would be subject to trial for war crimes. Security forces restricted freedom of movement within the country. Violence and societal discrimination against women are serious problems, and incidents of rape increased during the renewal of civil unrest. Some minority indigenous San peoples face severe exploitation and are inherited by Bantu patrons. Societal discrimination on the basis of ethnicity remained widespread. Ethnic and regional tensions continued to contribute to large-scale organized civil voilence. Child labor, reportedly including forced labor, persists. Citizens sometimes resorted to vigilante justice, killing those presumed to be criminals.

FOREIGN POLICY

The People's Republic of the Congo, as the Republic of Congo has been known since 1969, withdrew from the French Community in 1973 but remained economically linked to France. Until the 1980s Brazzaville maintained close ties to communist countries and adopted generally a leftist stance on foreign policy issues. The overthrow of the Lissouba government in 1997 reportedly involved a number of foreign powers and Hutu militiamen. The Kabila government in the Democratic Republic of the Congo supported Lissouba while Angola supported the victorious Sassou-Nguesso. In 1998 the European Union declared that Congo had abandoned the rule of law and was in a state of anarchy.

DEFENSE

The defense structure is headed by the president, who also exercises direct control over the Ministry of Defense. The line of command runs through the chief of staff to the general staff on the pattern of the French military structure.

Manpower is provided by voluntary enlistment, although a compulsory military service system is provided for by law. Males between the ages of 15 and 49 are eligible for military service. On release from active duty, servicemen are placed in reserve for 15 years.

Total strength of the armed forces is 10,000.

The combat-worthiness of the Congolese army is limited by the persistence of ethnic conflicts within the units, poor logistics, and total dependence on foreign-supplied material, including combat boots and uniforms. Traditionally the army has largely been recruited from the northern peoples, notably the Mbochi Kouyou, but many of the officers are southerners of the Bakongo tribe. There is no defense production in the country.

Military Indicators

Total Active Duty Personnel: 10,000
Military Manpower per 1,000: 3.9
Military Expenditures $: 48 million
 as % of GNP: 2.9
 per capita $: 19
 as % of central government expenditures: 11.1
Arms Imports $: 10
Arms Exports $: 0

ECONOMY

The economy is a mixture of village agriculture and handicrafts, an industrial sector based largely on oil, support services, and a government characterized by budget problems and overstaffing. Oil has supplanted forestry as the mainstay of the economy, providing a major share of government revenues and exports. In the early 1980s, rapidly rising oil revenues enabled the government to finance large-scale development projects with gross domestic product growth averaging 5 percent annually, one of the highest rates in Africa. Moreover, the government has mortgaged a substantial portion of its oil earnings, contributing to the government's shortage of revenues. The January 12, 1994, devaluation of franc zone currencies by 50 percent resulted in inflation of 61 percent in 1994 but inflation has subsided since. Economic reform efforts continued with the support of international organizations, notably the World Bank and the IMF. The reform program came to a halt in June 1997 when civil war erupted. Denis Sassou-Nguesso, who returned to power when the war ended in October 1997, publicly expressed interest in moving forward on economic reforms and privatization and in renewing cooperation with international financial institutions. However, economic progress was badly hurt by slumping oil prices in 1998, which worsened the Republic of the Congo's budget deficit. A second blow was the resumption of armed conflict in December 1998, which worsened the Republic of the Congo's budget deficit. Even with the IMF's renewed confidence and high world oil prices, Congo is unlikely to realize growth of more than 5 percent in 2001–02. With the country's return to a fragile peace, the IMF approved a $14-million credit in November 2000 to aid postconflict reconstruction.

Principal Economic Indicators

Gross National Product: $1.827 billion
GNP per capita: $670
GNP Average Annual Growth Rate (1990–97) %: −2.9
GNP per capita Average Annual Growth Rate (1990–97) %: −5.7
Origin of Gross Domestic Product %
 Agriculture: 11
 Mining: 33
 Manufacturing: 8
 Construction: 2
 Public Utilities: 1
 Transportation and Communications: 8
 Trade: 12
 Financial Services: 8
 Other Services: 8
 Government: 14
Gross Domestic Product by Type of Expenditure %
 Private Consumption: 55
 Government Consumption: 22
 Gross Domestic Investment: 51
 Foreign Trade: Exports: 64
 Imports: −93
% of Income Received by Poorest 20%: 7
% of Income Received by Richest 10%: 43.5

Price and earning indexes (1995 = 100)

	1991	1992	1993	1994	1995	1996
Consumer price index	109.2	111.3	113.6	170.1	206.5	206.0
Earnings index	—	—	—	—	—	—

Finance

National Currency: CFA Franc (CFAF)
Exchange Rate: $1 = CFAF 608.36
Money Supply Stock in National Currency billion: 1.349
M1 per capita: 52,800
Central Bank Discount Rate %: 7.60
Total External Debt $: 5.3 billion
Debt Service Ratio %: 5.2
Balance of Payments $: −251.9 million
International Reserves SDRs: 83 million
Ratio of External Debt to Total Reserves: 83.3
Average Annual Rate of Inflation/Consumer Price Index
 Growth Rate %: 3

Official Development Assistance

ODA: $65 million
 as % of GNP: 3.9
 per capita: $23
 Foreign Direct Investment $: 4 million

Central Government Revenues and Expenditures

Fiscal Year: Calendar Year

Revenues $: 870 million
Expenditures $: 970 million
Budget Deficit $: 100 million
Tax Revenues as % of GDP: 29.6
Highest Tax Bracket %
Individual: 50
Corporate: 45

Employment and Labor

Economically Active Population: 563,000
Female Participation Rate %: 45.6
Activity Rate %: 29.5
Labor by Sector: %
Agriculture, Forestry, Fishing: 52.2
Manufacturing, Mining: 8.8
Construction: 4.5
Transportation and Communications: 5.1
Trade, Hotels, and Restaurants: 11.8
Finance, Insurance, Real Estate: 0.5
Public Administration, Defense: —
Services: 15.1

Unemployment %: NA

Agriculture

Agriculture's Share of GDP %: 11
Average Annual Rate of Growth (1965–98) %: 2.8
Number of Farms 000: 143
Average Size of Farm ha: 1.4
Number of Tractors per 1,000 hectares: 4.8
Irrigation, % of Farms having: 0.7
Artificial Fertilizer kg/hectare: 3.0
Total Cropland as % of Farmland: 100
Livestock: Cattle 000: 72
Sheep 000: 114
Hogs 000: 44
Chickens 000: 1,800
Forests: Production of Roundwood (000 cubic meters): 4,806
Fisheries: Total Catch tons: 37,000

Mining

% of GDP: 32.8
Value of Mineral Production $: 659.9 million

Manufacturing

Value Added $: 75 million
Industrial Production Growth Rate %: NA

Energy

Commercial Energy Production metric tons of oil equivalent: 13,540,000
Commercial Energy Consumption metric tons of oil equivalent: 1,242,000
Commercial Energy Consumption per capita kg: 459
Average Annual Growth Rate 1980–97 %: −0.8
Net Energy Imports % of use: −990
Electricity Installed Capacity kW: 118,000
Production kW-hr: 435
Coal Reserves tons: —
Production tons: —
Natural Gas Proven Reserves cubic meters: 91 billion
Production cubic meters: 2 million
Crude Petroleum Reserves barrels: 1.506 billion
Production barrels: 74 million
Consumption barrels: 3 million
Refinery Capacity barrels per day: 21,000
Pipelines Length km: 25

Foreign Trade

Imports $: 408.4 million
Exports $: 948.5 million
Export Volume % Annual Growth Rate (1990–97): 9.6
Import Volume % Annual Growth Rate (1990–97): 9.0
Balance of Trade $

Balance of trade (current prices)

	1992	1993	1994	1995	1996	1997
CFAF 000,000	+214.8	+168.6	+192.2	+260.8	+100.0	+448.8
% of total	52.5%	38.6%	22.0%	28.7%	6.7%	29.9%

Major Trading Partners

	Imports	Exports
European Union %	54.0	35.9
United States %	10.0	42.1
Eastern Europe %	0.2	—
Japan %	2.6	0.3
Others %	33.3	21.7

Transportation

Roads Total Length mi: 7,929 (12,760 km)
Paved %: 10
Automobiles: 36,100
Trucks and Buses: 15,600
Persons per vehicle: 48
Railroad; Track Length mi: 494 (795 km)
Passenger-mi: 141 million
Freight-mi: 152 million
Merchant Marine: No. of Vessels: 22
Total Deadweight Tonnage: 10,800
International Cargo Loaded tons: 8,987,000
International Cargo Off-loaded tons: 736,000
Airports with Scheduled Flights: 5
Traffic: Passenger-mi: 139 million
Freight-mi: 10.5 million
Length of Canals mi: 696 (1,120 km)

Tourism

Number of Tourists to: 44,000
Number of Tourists from: —
Tourist Receipts $: 4 million
Tourist Expenditures $: 39 million

Communications

Telephones 000: 21
Cost of Local Calls 3 mins: $0
Cellular Telephones 000: —
Fax Machines 000: 0.1
Personal Computers 000: —

Internet Hosts per million persons: —
Mail: Post Offices: 114
Pieces of Mail Handled: 1.8 million
Pieces of Mail Handled per person: 0.7

EDUCATION

Education is free, compulsory, and universal in theory for children between ages six and 16. The academic year runs from October to June. The medium of instruction in French.

Schooling consists of 13 years, divided into primary, intermediate, and secondary. The primary program is divided into three levels of two years each: preparatory, elementary, and middle. Intermediate and secondary education consist of three types of programs: postprimary training course in practical skills, a seven-year, or long, academic course, and a four-year, or short, general education course. The long course is divided into two cycles, the first cycle including grades six through three (grades being numbered in descending order) and the second cycle of grades two, one, and the finale or terminale class. The curriculum in the secondary grades is almost identical to that used in France, but those in primary grades are adapted to African and Congolese environments.

A national center for adult education was opened in 1965 with UNESCO and UNDP assistance. Under the "Roll Up Your Sleeves" campaign, instructors were required to teach illiterates for two hours a day without pay in the countryside.

Vocational education is provided by 36 technical schools, including a technical lycée at Brazzaville.

All schools are under the Ministry of Education. Policy is formulated by the Higher Council of Education. There are 10 regional directorates, and at every level there are school commissions. An inspectorate is responsible for supervision and standardization

Higher education is provided by Université Nationale de Congo.

Education

Literacy Rate %: 74.9
Male %: 83.1
Female %: 67.2
First Level: Primary schools: 1,612
Teachers: 7,060
Students: 497,305
Students-Teacher Ratio: 70.4
Net Enrollment Ratio: —
Second Level: Secondary Schools: —
Teachers: 5,710
Students: 189,381
Student-Teacher Ratio: 33.2
Net Enrollment Ratio: —

Vocational Level: Schools: —
Students: 25,269

Third Level: Institutions: —
Teachers: 656
Students: 13,806
Student-Ratio Level: 21.0
Gross Enrollment Ratio: 5.3
Students per 100,000: 582
% of Population Age 25 and over with Postsecondary Education: —
Public Expenditure on Education as % of GDP: 5.9

SCIENCE AND TECHNOLOGY

Science and Technology

Scientists and Engineers in R&D per 1 million persons: —
Expenditures in R&D as % of GDP: —
High-Tech Exports $: —
Patent Applications by Residents: —

MEDIA

Congolese press consists of six dailies and 21 periodicals of which the most widely circulated is *La Semaine Africaine* with 8,000 readers. It is a weekly out of Brazzaville that is privately owned by the Catholic Church.

The national news agency is Agence Congolaise d'Information, established in 1962. Foreign press correspondents are required to employ government information services exclusively as the sources of their reports Foreign news bureaus in Brazzaville include Tass and AFP.

The government-owned Radiodiffusion Télévision Nationale Congolaise operates one medium-wave, four shortwave, and five FM transmitters and broadcasts in French, Lingala, and Kikongo under the call sign Voice of the Congolese Revolution. A second service, Radio Brazzaville, operated by the Office de Radiodiffusion Télévision Française, relays broadcasts from Paris.

Television, introduced in 1962, is limited to Brazzaville and its environs. Programs are imported from France. Most are in French, but some are in Lingala and Kikongo.

Media

Daily Newspapers: 6
Total Circulation 000: 19
Circulation per 1,000: 8
Books Published: —
Magazines: 3
Radio Receivers 000: 240
per 1,000: 95
Television sets 000: 42
per 1,000: 17

MOST IMPORTANT MEDIA:

Press. *Mweti* (7,000) is a French-language daily published at Brazzaville; French-language weeklies include *Etumba* (8,000), *La Semaine* (7,000), *Le Stade* (6,500), and *Semaine Africaine*. In September 1996 the government

(continued)

reportedly ordered all private newspapers and magazines closed for allegedly violating a law passed in July requiring all nongovernment publishers to obtain a commercial license.

News agencies. The official news agency is Agence Congolaise d'Information (ACI); Agence France-Presse, Novosti, and TASS are represented at Brazzaville.

Radio and television. Broadcasting is controlled by the state-owned Radiodiffusion-Télévision Congolaise (RTC). La Voix de la Révolution Congolaise offers radio programming in French, English, Portuguese, and a variety of indigenous languages, while Télévision Nationale Congolaise operates one television station. In 1989 France agreed to provide funding for a satellite reception facility. In November 1993 a Radio France Internationale (RFI) correspondent was expelled for having allegedly spread "lies and misinformation" about the postelectoral violence. In April 1999 the government established a new official radio station, Radio Brazzaville. In 1998 approximately 335,000 radio and 25,900 television receivers were in use.

CULTURE

Cultural Indicators

Public Libraries
- Number: 4
- Volumes: 103,000
- Registered borrowers: 27,670

Museums
- Numbers: 10
- Annual Attendance: 113,000

Cinema
- Production of Long Films: —
- Number of Cinemas: 30
- Seating Capacity: 4,400
- Annual Attendance: —
- Annual Attendance per capita: —

STATUS OF WOMEN

Under the constitution, women have the same rights as men in the private, political, and social domains, and for equal work women are entitled to the same social welfare rights as men. There is a disparity, however, between salaries for men and women, and women are relegated to a secondary role in society. Women have played an important role in the government, and most recently one has occupied a high-level position as minister of basic education and literacy. In secondary schools increasing numbers of young women are enrolled in technical courses, and university attendance among women continues to rise.

Women

Gender Empowerment Measure: —
Seats Held in Parliament by Women %: 12
Female Administrators and Managers %: —
Female Professional and Technical Workers %: —
Women's Share of Earned Income %: —
Women in Government %: 4

HEALTH, FOOD, AND NUTRITION

Health

Number of Physicians: 613
Number of Dentists: 35
Number of Nurses: 1,624
Number of Pharmacists: 175
Population per Physicians: 4,028
Number of Hospitals: —
Hospital Beds per 10,000: 33
Hospital Bed Occupancy Rate: —
Infant Mortality Rate per 1,000 live births: 133
Maternal Mortality Rate per 100,000 live births: 890
Total Health Expenditures as % of GDP: 3.99
Health Expenditures per capita $: 50
HIV Infected % of adults: 7.78
Cigarette Consumption per smoker per year: —
% of Smokers: Male: —
Female: —
Access to Safe Water %: 60

Food and Nutrition

Food Supply as % of FAO Requirements: 96
% of Consumption Expenditures on Food: 37
Daily Available Calories per capita: 2,141
% of Total Calories derived from: —
Cereals: 22.3
Potatoes, cassava: 39.3
Meat, poultry: 3.4
Fish: 2.7
Eggs, milk: 1.1
Fruits, vegetables: 7.5
Fats, oils: 11.6

ENVIRONMENT

Some of the major environmental problems facing the Republic of the Congo today include chaotic urbanization, which has led to the accumulation of solid wastes, lack of sanitation facilities and adequate drinking water, pollution, and environmentally related sickness. In addition to the human health factors, deforestation, disappearance of fauna, and erosion of urban and coastal areas are of growing concern.

Environment

Forest Area sq km: 195,000
Average Annual Deforestation sq km: 416
Nationally Protected Areas as % of Total Land Area: 4.5
Freshwater Access cubic meters per capita: 298,963
Emissions of Organic Water Pollutants kg per day: 1,039
CO_2 Emissions per capita ton: 1.9

CHRONOLOGY

1960 The Republic of the Congo becomes an independent republic under President Fulbert Youlou.

1961 Independent Congo's first constitution is approved in a popular referendum.

1963 Youlou resigns office in the wake of mass demonstration and riots; Alphonse Massamba-Débat is named president.
New constitution is promulgated and approved by referendum.
Pascal Lissouba is appointed prime minister.
1964 Mouvement National de la Révolution (MNR) is organized as the sole political party in the Congo, with its youth wing, Jeunesse de Mouvement National de la Révolution (JMNR), as a paramilitary force.
1966 Attempted military coup is suppressed.
Congo joins UDEAC, a customs union with Chad, Gabon, Cameroon, and Central African Republic.
1968 Army seizes power following army-JMNR confrontation; Marien Ngouabi, the army commander in chief, replaces Massamba-Débat as president.
1969 Parti Congolais du Travail (PCT) replaces the MNR as the sole political party of the country; Republic of the Congo is renamed People's Republic of the Congo as the nation continues its leftward course.
1970 Ngouabi promulgates new constitution based on Soviet and East European models.
1971 Student riots erupt in Brazzaville.
In major government reshuffle, Ngouabi dismisses four members of the Political Bureau of the PCT and 50 members of the PCT's Central Committee.
1973 New constitution, independent Congo's fourth, is approved in nationwide referendum; elected National Assembly is revived.
Congo withdraws from French Community.
Henri Lopes is named prime minister.
1975 Political Bureau of the PCT is replaced by the Special Revolutionary General Staff.
Major Louis Sylvain Ngoma forms a new cabinet.
Congolese government nationalizes the oil industry.
1977 President Ngouabi is assassinated by a four-man commando squad.
Joachim Yhombi-Opango assumes the presidency as head of an 11-member military committee.
Constitution is suspended and the National Assembly is dissolved.
Former president Massamba-Débat is executed for plotting assassination. Diplomatic relations are reestablished with the United States.
1979 President Yhombi-Opango steps down and is replaced by Denis Sassou-Nguesso. The constitution of 1973 is readopted and is overwhelmingly approved in a national referendum; the National Assembly is reestablished.
1984 President Sassou-Nguesso is reelected with expanded powers.
Former president Yhombi-Opango is released from prison.
1987 The government suppresses a coup by military officers. Yhombi-Opango is imprisoned for complicity with the rebels.
1988 Discovery of toxic waste dumping into the Congo leads to the dismissal of the minister of environments and scientific research and the minister of information. Amnesty is extended to most political prisoners.
1989 Sassou-Nguesso is reelected to a third term.
1990 The Congolese Workers' Party officially drops its marxist ideology.
1991 Congo officially becomes a multiparty state.
1992 In free presidential elections, Pascal Lissouba defeats Gen. Sassou-Nguesso.
1993 Franc zone currencies are devalued by 50 percent, spurring 61 percent inflation in Congo; bloody fighting erupts between Lissouba government forces and supporters of Sassou-Nguesso over disputed parliamentary elections.
1994 A cease-fire is established between government and opposition forces.
1997 Following outbreak of a civil war, Gen. Sassou-Nguesso proclaims himself president with the support of the military; Lissouba goes into hiding in Burkina Faso.
1998 Warfare resumes in December.
1999 Sassou-Nguesso and Lissouba sign a peace treaty providing for integrated military forces and demilitarized political parties.
2001 Transitional parliament adopts a draft constitution. Some 15,000 militia are disarmed in a cash-for-arms deal.

BIBLIOGRAPHY

Allen, Christopher. *The Congo.* New York, 1989.
Allen, Chris, and Michael Martin. *Benin and the Congo: Politics, Economics and Society.* Boulder, Colo., 1986.
Fegley, Randall. *The Congo.* Oxford, 1993.

OFFICIAL PUBLICATIONS

Congo, Rep. of the. *Annuaire statistique; Recensement général de la population et de l'habitat de 1984.*

CONTACT INFORMATION

Embassy of the Congo
4891 Colorado Avenue NW
Washington, D.C. 20011
Phone: (202) 726-5500 Fax: (202) 726-1860

INTERNET RESOURCES

République du Congo (Official site in French)
http://www.congo-site.cg/

COSTA RICA

BASIC FACT SHEET

OFFICIAL NAME:
The Republic of Costa Rica (República de Costa Rica)

ABBREVIATION:
CR

CAPITAL:
San José

HEAD OF STATE AND GOVERNMENT:
President Abel Pacheco de la Espriella (2002)

NATURE OF GOVERNMENT:
Constitutional democracy

POPULATION:
3,594,000 (1999)

AREA:
50,900 sq km (19,652 sq mi)

ETHNIC MAJORITY:
Europeans and mestizos

LANGUAGE:
Spanish

RELIGION:
Roman Catholicism

UNIT OF CURRENCY:
Colon (¢)

NATIONAL FLAG:
Five horizontal stripes, two stripes at the top and bottom, two white inner stripes, and a wide red center band with the country's coat of arms

NATIONAL EMBLEM:
Three towering volcanic peaks between two seas, the Caribbean Sea in the foreground and the Pacific Ocean in the background. The other elements of the national emblem are two white-sailed black schooners, a representation in yellow of the Meseta Central, an orange sun, five white stars, a white scroll bearing the legend *República de Costa Rica* decorated with myrtle branches, a deep blue ribbon tied like a corona bearing in white letters the legend *América Central*, red and gold ears of corn at the sides and a conquistador's cross at the base.

NATIONAL ANTHEM:
"Noble Native Land, Your Beautiful Flag"

NATIONAL HOLIDAYS:
September 15 (Independence Day); January 1 (New Year's Day); April 11 (Anniversary of the Battle of Rivas); May 1 (Labor Day); July 25 (Anniversary of the Annexation of Guanacaste Province); October 12 (Columbus Day). Also 10 Christian festivals, including Christmas and the Day of St. Joseph, Costa Rica's patron saint.

DATE OF INDEPENDENCE:
September 15, 1821

DATE OF CONSTITUTION:
November 7, 1949

GEOGRAPHICAL FEATURES

Costa Rica is in the Central American isthmus. It occupies an area of 50,900 sq km (19,652 sq mi). It has two coastlines; that on the Caribbean stretches 212 km (132 mi), and that on the Pacific extends 1,016 km (631 mi). Costa Rica shares its international land boundary of 663 km (412 mi) with two countries: Panama (363 km; 226 mi) and Nicaragua (300 km; 186 mi).

Costa Rica has three main topographical regions. The largest is the Central Highlands, which reach elevations of more than 3,657 m (12,000 ft). Nestled in the Central Highlands is the Meseta Central, which consists of two upland basins separated by low volcanic hills.

Costa Rica

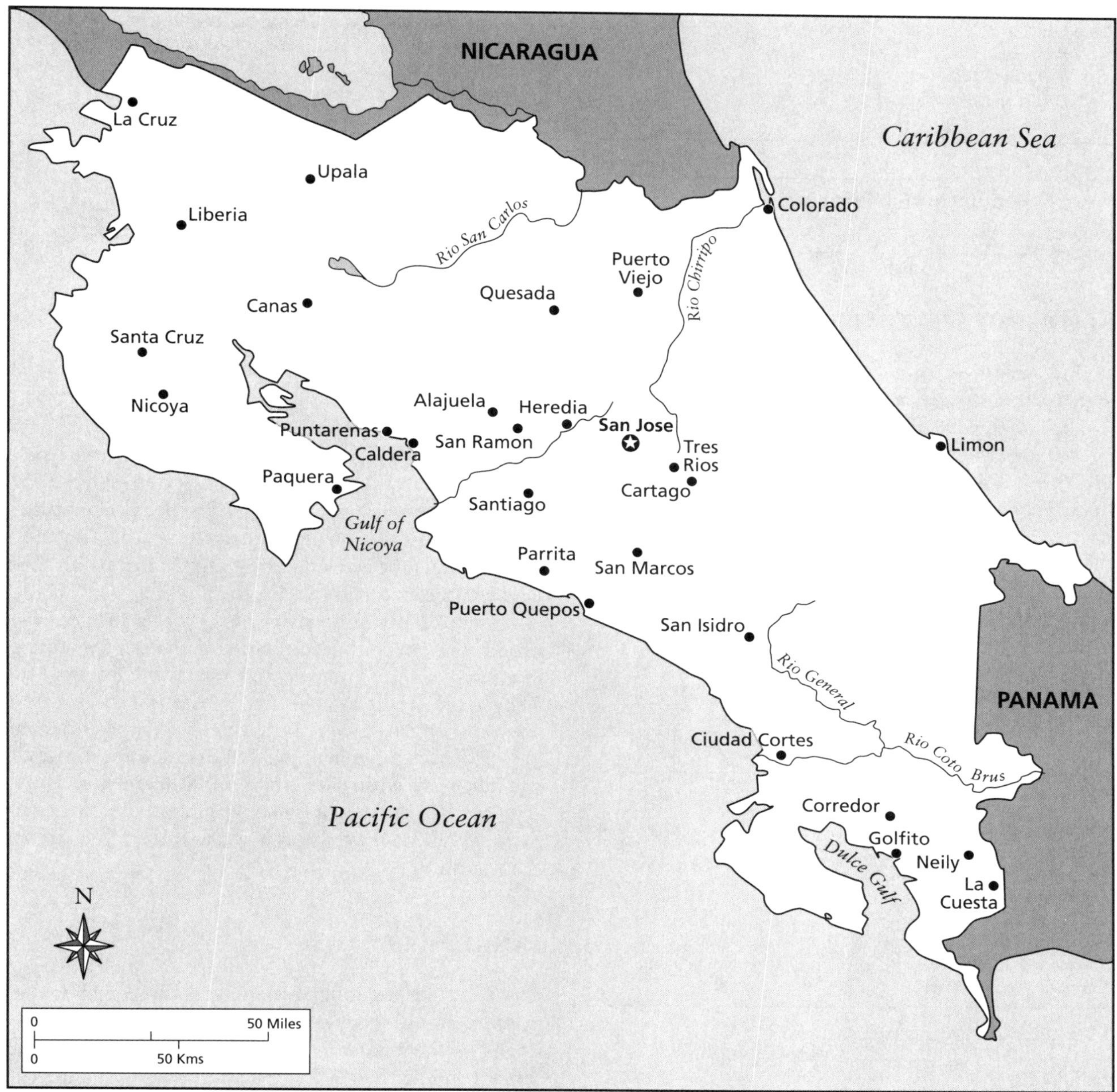

The eastern basin is known as Cartago and the western basin is known as San José. The only other upland valley of importance is the General Valley. It lies to the south of the Cordillera de Talamanca, extending to the Panamanian border. The cordillera has 10 peaks over 2,987 m (9,800 ft), the highest of them being the Chirripó Grande (3,810 m; 12,500 ft), the highest point in the country. The Pacific coastal region consists of the Palmar lowland complex, the Guanacaste Plain, the Cordillera de Guanacaste, the valley of the Tempisque River, and the three peninsulas of Burica, Osa, and Nicoya. The Atlantic coastal plain is low, swampy, and heavily forested.

The country is drained by 18 small rivers, of which the Tempisque River is navigable for 35 km (22 mi), and the San Juan is navigable from its mouth to Lake Nicaragua. The other major rivers are the General, Sixaola, San José, and Grande de Tarcoles.

Geography

Area sq km: 50,900 sq mi 19,652
World Rank: 128th
Land Boundaries, km: Nicaragua 309; Panama 330
Coastline, km: 1,290
Elevation Extremes meters

(continued)

Lowest: Pacific Ocean 0
Highest: Cerro Chirripo 3,810
Land Use % Arable land: 6
Permanent Crops: 5
Permanent Pastures: 46
Forest and Woodland: 31
Other: 12

Population of Principal Cities

San José	329,154

CLIMATE AND WEATHER

Costa Rica has two seasons: a wet season from May through November and a dry season from December to April. The country has three climatic zones: a torrid zone, which includes the two coastal plains up to about 450 m (1,500 ft), with a temperature range of 29.4°C to 32.2°C (85°F to 95°F); a temperate zone, which includes the Meseta Central and other regions between 450 m (1,500 ft) and 1,500 m (5,000 ft), with a temperature range of 23.9° to 26.7° (75°F to 80°F); and a cold zone, comprising areas over 1,524 m (5,000 ft), with a temperature range of 5°C to 15°C (41°F to 59°F). The Pacific coast receives most of its rain between May and October, but on the Caribbean coast the rainfall is less seasonal. The average rainfall is 2,540 mm (100 in).

Climate and Weather

Mean Temperature
Torrid Zone: 85°F to 90°F
Temperate Zone: 75°F to 80°F
Cold Zone 41°F to 59°F
Average Rainfall: 100 in
Pacific Area 28 to 50 in
Central Highlands 70 in
Caribbean Coast 196 in

POPULATION

Population Indicators

Total Population: 1999 3,594,000
World Rank: 125th
Density per sq mi: 182.2 per sq km 70.3
% of annual growth (1994–99): 1.9
Male %: 50
Female %: 50
Urban %: 43.9
Age Distribution: % 0–14: 37.9
15–29: 31.5
30–44: 15.8
45–59: 9.2
60–74: 4.4
75 and over: 1.2
Population 2020: 4,935,000
Birth Rate per 1,000: 23.8
Death Rate per 1,000: 4.2
Population Doubling Time (years): 36
Infant Mortality Rate per 1,000 live births: 13.3
Rate of Natural Increase per 1,000: 19.6
Total Fertility Rate: 2.8
Expectation of Life (years): Males 71.9
Females 77.5
Marriage Rate per 1,000: 7.1
Divorce Rate per 1,000: —
Total Number of Households: 772,000
Average Size of Households: 4.1
% of Illegitimate Children: 46.6
Induced Abortions: —
Rate per 100 live births: —

ETHNIC COMPOSITION

Some 96 percent of the population is white or mestizo, 2 percent is black, 1 percent is Amerindian, and 1 percent Chinese. The European population is descended from the early Spanish settlers. Costa Rica has been called the most homogeneous nation in Central America. The mestizo population is the second-largest ethnic group, but the line between mestizo and white is negligible.

The primary minority group in Costa Rica consists of blacks who are the descendants of slaves. They are concentrated on the Atlantic coast, around Puerto Limón. They retain their attachment to Caribbean culture and seem more British West Indian than Central American.

There are three main Amerindian groups in the country, but none with more than 5,000 members. The government has pursued a policy of integration of the tribes, although efforts have been made to maintain elements of their cultures.

LANGUAGES

Costa Rica has no official language, but Spanish is the national tongue spoken by the vast majority of people. English is the second most common language and is widely spoken among the black population on the Atlantic Coast, although they speak a version of the Jamaican dialect.

Principal Languages and Their Speakers

Chibchan languages	10,000
Bribri	6,000
Cabécar	4,000
Chinese	7,000
English Creole	72,000
Spanish	3,505,000

RELIGIONS

Roman Catholicism is the state religion, but the constitution guarantees religious freedom. The government does provide 1 percent of its budget to support the Catholic Church through the Ministry of Foreign Relations and Worship. There are approximately 40,000 Protestants in the country. Other religious minorities include Chinese Buddhists and Jews.

Religious Affiliations	
Roman Catholic	3,090,000
Other	500,000

HISTORICAL BACKGROUND

Human habitation in Costa Rica can be traced back at least 10,000 years. Between A.D. 1000 and 1400, a civilization emerged near Guayabo that developed pottery techniques that were among the most advanced in Central America. However, when Christopher Columbus landed in 1502, the Spanish found the region sparsely populated.

Following an unsuccessful attempt to colonize the region in 1506, an expedition was dispatched from Panama in 1522. The second effort proved more successful after the discovery of gold, and the leader of this effort, Gil González Dávila, dubbed the land Costa Rica or "rich coast." By the 1560s, disease had decimated most of the native population, and in 1562, Juan Vásquez de Coronado was appointed governor, and he laid the foundation for the eventual complete settlement of Costa Rica. For most of the colonial period, the nation was left in obscurity, although Spain forced the closure of its ports in 1665 in response to piracy.

Costa Rica won its independence from Spain in 1821. Four months later, it was absorbed into the short-lived Mexican empire of Agustín Iturbide. After the fall of Iturbide, Costa Rica became a member of the United Provinces of Central America in 1823. It declared itself a sovereign republic in 1848, and its independence was formally recognized by Spain in 1850.

Costa Rica has had a long history of stable democratic government with only two periods of unrest. The first occurred in 1917 when Federico Tinoco seized the presidency. He was forced to relinquish the office in 1919. In 1948 civil war erupted over the results of the presidential election. The antigovernment forces of the Social Democratic Party (later the National Liberation Party) were successful, and a provisional government headed by José Figueres Ferrer was formed. Figueres abolished the army in 1948. Under his leadership, a new constitution was prepared and democratic elections held.

In 1955, antigovernment forces from Cuba, Nicaragua, Venezuela, Dominican Republic, and Colombia invaded the nation, but with aid from the Organization of American States the invaders were defeated. In 1963, Costa Rica joined the Central American Common Market.

During the Sandinista Revolution in Nicaragua, Costa Rica extended substantial support to the rebels. However, after the overthrow of the Somoza regime, anti-Sandinista contras established bases in Costa Rica. The continued presence of the contras increased tensions between the two nations for the remainder of the decade. Costa Rica turned to international bodies to end the Nicaraguan conflict and, in 1987, President Oscar Arias Sánchez won the Nobel Peace prize for his efforts to bring about peace.

Meanwhile, foreign debt constrained the nation's economy. By 1982, Costa Rica's foreign reserves were exhausted and debt repayment was halted. This led to debt rescheduling the following year. Efforts at structural readjustment led to a massive strike against the government in 1989. The nation's problems were exacerbated in 1990, when an earthquake left 14,000 homeless. In 1991, Costa Rica, Guatemala, El Salvador, Honduras, and Nicaragua agreed to integrate their economies over a six-year period. Economic reforms continued with the election in 1998 of conservative candidate Miguel Ángel Rodríguez.

CONSTITUTION

The constitution of 1949 made Costa Rica a democratic and unitary republic. The government is divided into three branches: executive, legislative, and judicial. An elaborate system of checks and balances assigned by the constitution somewhat limits the power of the presidency, especially by Latin American standards. The legislature can override presidential vetoes, and the Supreme Court has the right of judicial review over legislative and administrative acts. All members of the executive branch are barred from participating in election campaigns.

The executive consists of the president, two vice presidents, and the Consejo de Gobierno (Council of Government). The election process is under the control of the Tribunal Supremo Electoral (TSE, Supreme Electoral Tribunal), an autonomous institution. Elections are held every four years on the first Sunday in February. The president and the two vice presidents must receive at least 40 percent of the vote or a runoff election is held. Deputies to the National Assembly and municipal councils are elected by a system of proportional representation.

LOCAL GOVERNMENT

The principal units of local government are seven provinces. The provinces are divided into 81 counties (*cantones*), which are in turn subdivided into 344 districts (*distritos*). The provinces have no self-government, and governors are appointed by the president. Local authority in each *canton* is vested in the municipal council. The executive officer of the council, the *jefe político*, is

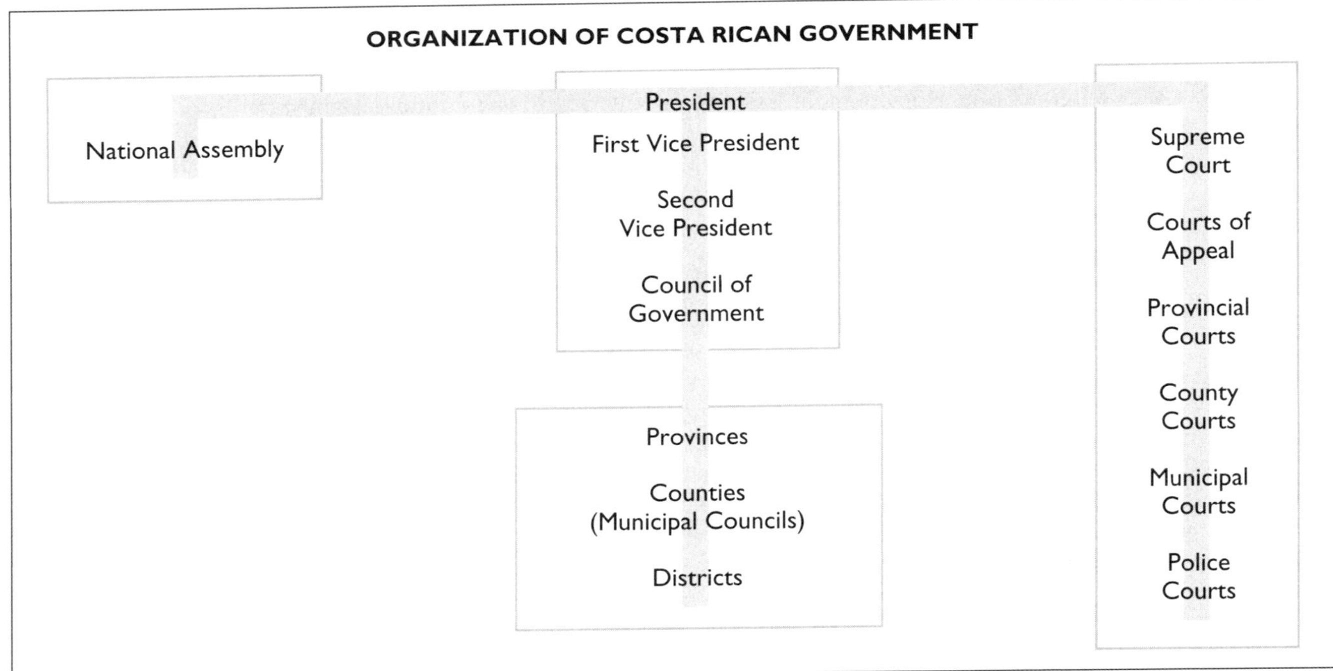

appointed by the president and has veto power over any ordinance passed by the council.

Local Government

Principal administrative divisions, capitals, area, population

Area and population

Provinces	Capitals	area sq mi	area sq km	population 1998 census
Alajuela	Alajuela	3,766	9,753	631,883
Cartago	Cartago	1,207	3,125	395,011
Guanacaste	Liberia	3,915	10,141	277,081
Heredia	Heredia	1,026	2,657	283,371
Limón	Limón	3,548	9,188	272,212
Puntarenas	Puntarenas	4,354	11,277	392,639
San José	San José	1,915	4,959	1,273,504
TOTAL		19,730	51,100	3,525,701

PARLIAMENT

The National Assembly is a unicameral body elected by direct popular vote for a four-year term. Deputies may not be reelected for successive terms. The National Assembly's 57 members are elected according to a system of proportional representation.

The assembly meets in a regular session twice a year, and special sessions may be convened by the president. The legislature wields substantive power, including the right to override a presidential veto by a two-thirds majority. Its functions include the enacting of laws, declaration of war, approval of the national budget, and impeachment of the president.

Suffrage is universal for all citizens over the age of 20 and for all married men and teachers over the age of 18. Voting is compulsory for all citizens under 70.

POLITICAL PARTIES

The ruling political party is the Social Christian Unity Party, a loose alliance of conservative parties, including the Calderonist Republican Party, Christian Democratic Party, and Popular Union Party, plus the former Democratic Renovation Party. The principal opposition party is the National Liberation Party (PLN), founded by former president José Figueres Ferrer in the aftermath of the 1948 revolution. The PLN is the largest and best organized of Costa Rican parties and represents the best of the Latin American Left. It is affiliated with the Socialist International.

Political Parties

Social Christian Unity Party, a loose alliance of conservative parties including
- Calderonist Republican Party, 1976
- Christian Democratic Party, 1962
- Popular Union Party

National Liberation Party, 1948
National Union Party, 1985
National Movement
Popular Vanguard Party, 1931
Democratic Force Party, 1994

Costa Rican People's Party, 1984
Workers' Party
Radical Democratic Party, 1982
National Christian Alliance Party
Costa Rican Econology Party, 1984
General Union Party, 1981
Libertarian Movement Party, 1995

Political Parties: Strength in Parliament Most Recent Elections

Following the election on February 3, 2002, the Social Christian Unity Party held 19 seats; the National Liberation Party, 17; the Citizens' Action Party, 14; the Libertarian Movement Party, 6; the Costa Rica Renewal, 1.

LEGAL SYSTEM

The legal system is headed by the Supreme Court of Justice, composed of 17 justices and one chief justice elected by the National Assembly for eight-year terms. The high court has five chambers and appoints all lower court justices. Subordinate courts are organized at three levels: provincial, cantonical, and district. Directly below the Supreme Court are two civil courts of appeal and two criminal courts of appeal. There is an original criminal court in all seven of the provinces, and 61 municipal courts. The lowest courts are the police courts, which are presided over by magistrates.

LAW ENFORCEMENT

Law Enforcement

Offenses reported to the police per 100,000: 868
- Murder: 5.3
- Assault: 11.1
- Burglary: 232.4
- Automobile Theft: 23.1
- Population per Police officer: 480

Death Penalty: Abolished 1887

HUMAN RIGHTS

Costa Rica is one of the most democratic nations of Central and South America and has a history of tolerance and individual liberty. Habeas corpus is a constitutional right, and arraignment is required within 24 hours of arrest. Freedom of the press, speech, religion, and assembly have never been curtailed or abridged in recent history. The labor movement is weak, but it is free to strike, organize, and bargain collectively. Not only are domestic and foreign travel and emigration unhindered, but Costa Rica also provides asylum for many political refugees.

FOREIGN POLICY

Costa Rica has taken an active role in promoting regional peace and stability. The government has worked to increase trade between Central American states and to attract foreign investment. It has also sought to develop a regional trade organization to stabilize coffee products and to expand the North American Free Trade Area (NAFTA) to Central America. Costa Rica is a member of 14 UN organizations and 29 other international organizations. Instability in Nicaragua has led to heavy immigration from that nation through the 1980s and 1990s, and the Costa Rican government has sought to both limit refugee flows and to gain international aid to deal with the resultant social problems.

DEFENSE

The constitution outlaws a national army. National security functions are provided by the police and the Civil Guard. In 1996, the guard was eliminated as a separate entity and now operates on an equal basis with the rural guard and border patrol. The Civil Guard has a strength of 6,000, and service in the guard is voluntary. A national naval force consists of five patrol boats and an armed tug.

The president is the commander in chief of the guard, but control of the force is through the minister of public safety. A civilian director is in charge of the day-to-day operations of the force. The budget is under control of the minister of government. Most weapons and equipment have been furnished by the United States.

Military Indicators

Total Active Duty Personnel: —
Military Manpower per 1,000: —
Military Expenditures $: 50 million
- as % of GNP: 0.6
- per capita $: 15
- as % of central government expenditures: 2.7

Arms Imports $: 0
Arms Exports $: 0

ECONOMY

Costa Rica has a free-market economy dominated by the private sector. The economy is based on agriculture and manufacturing. The nation's major trade partners include the United States, Germany, and Italy. About one-quarter of the working population is engaged in farming or agriculture. The principal crops are bananas and coffee. Other important crops include sugarcane, rice, and corn. Manufacturing employs some 20 percent of the workforce, mainly in textiles, fertilizers, and construction materials. Fishing is increasingly important along both coasts.

Principal Economic Indicators

Gross National Product: $9.275 billion
GNP per capita: $2,680
GNP Average Annual Growth Rate (1990–97)%: 2.3
GNP per capita Average Annual Growth Rate (1990–97) %: 0.5
Origin of Gross Domestic Product %
  Agriculture: 10
  Mining: —
  Manufacturing: 19
  Construction: 3
  Public Utilities: 4
  Transportation and Communications: 5
  Trade: 20
  Financial Services: 11
  Other Services: 7
  Government: 14
Gross Domestic Product by Type of Expenditure %
  Private Consumption: 60
  Government Consumption: 17
  Gross Domestic Investment: 27
  Foreign Trade: Exports: 39
    Imports: −43
% of Income Received by Poorest 20%: 4
% of Income Received by Richest 10%: 34.1

Price and earnings indexes (1995 = 100)

	1993	1994	1995	1996	1997	1998	1999
Consumer price index	71.5	81.2	100.0	117.5	133.1	148.6	162.9
Earnings index	70.3	82.8	100.0	116.4	—	—	—

Finance

National Currency: Colon (C)
Exchange Rate: $1 = C243.55
Money Supply Stock in National Currency billion: 166.9
M1 per capita: 46,600
Central Bank Discount Rate %: 35
Total External Debt $million: 3.2
Debt Service Ratio %: 10.4

Balance of Payments $million: –254
International Reserves SDRs million: 625
Ratio of External Debt to Total Reserves: 3.0

Average Annual Rate of Inflation/Consumer Price Index
  Growth Rate %: 11.2

Official Development Assistance

ODA: $27 million
  as % of GNP: 0.3
  per capita: $8
  Foreign Direct Investment $million: 559

Central Government Revenues and Expenditures

Fiscal Year: Calendar Year

Revenues $million: 1.1
Expenditures $million: 1.34
Budget Deficit/Surplus $: 240 million
Tax Revenues as % of GDP: 26.3
Highest Tax Bracket %
  Individual: 25
  Corporate: 30

Employment and Labor

Economically Active Population: 1,232,000
Female Participation Rate %: 30.5
Activity Rate %: 36.9
Labor by Sector: %
  Agriculture, Forestry, Fishing: 21.2
  Manufacturing, Mining: 17.7
  Construction: 6.5
  Transportation and Communications: 5.2
  Trade, Hotels, and Restaurants: 19.4
  Finance, Insurance, Real Estate: 4.2
  Public Administration, Defense: —
  Services: 24.2

Unemployment %: 5.7

Agriculture

Agriculture's Share of GDP %: 10
Average Annual Rate of Growth (1965–98) %: 3.2
Number of Farms 000: 82
Average Size of Farm ha: 38.3
Number of Tractors per 1,000 hectares: 24.6
Irrigation, % of Farms having: 44
Artificial Fertilizer kg/hectare: 203
Total Farmland as % of land area: 56.2
Livestock: Cattle 000: 1,527
  Sheep 000: 3
  Hogs 000: 280
  Chickens 000: 17,000
Forests: Production of Roundwood (000 cubic meters): 4,806
Fisheries: Total Catch tons 000: 20.8

Mining

% of GDP: —
Value of Mineral Production $million: 3.8

Manufacturing

Value Added $million: 1,285
Industrial Production Growth Rate %: 10.5

Energy

Commercial Energy Production metric tons of
  oil equivalent 000: 1,157
Commercial Energy Consumption metric tons of
  oil equivalent 000: 2,663
Commercial Energy Consumption per capita kg: 769
Average Annual Growth Rate 1980–97 %: 1.5
Net Energy Imports % of use: 57
Electricity Installed Capacity kW 000: 1,165
  Production kW-hr million: 4,840
Coal Reserves tons million: —
  Production tons 000: —

Natural Gas Proven Reserves cubic meters billion: 23
Production cubic meters million: —
Crude Petroleum Reserves barrels million: —
Production barrels million: —
Consumption barrels million: 4
Refinery Capacity barrels per day 000: 15
Pipelines Length km: 176

Foreign Trade

Imports $million: 3,029.7
Exports $million: 2,217.5
Export Volume % Annual Growth Rate (1990–97): 12.6
Import Volume % Annual Growth Rate (1990–97): 15.8
Balance of Trade $

Balance of trade (current prices)

	1992	1993	1994	1995	1996	1997
U.S. $000,000	−712	−1,012	−931	−682	−761	−1,134
% of total	17.1%	21.3%	18.2%	11.7%	12.2%	16.1%

Major Trading Partners

	Imports	Exports
European Union %	11.3	28.2
United States %	44.3	43.4
Eastern Europe %	0.5	0.2
Japan %	5.5	0.9
Others %	38.3	27.2

Transportation

Roads Total Length mi: 22,121 km 35,600
Paved %: 17
Automobiles: 259,000
Trucks and Buses: 132,940
Persons per vehicle: 8.5
Railroad; Track Length mi: 590 km 950
Passenger-mi million: 3.7
Freight-mi million: 45.8
Merchant Marine: No. of Vessels: 24
Total Deadweight Tonnage 000: 8.4
International Cargo Loaded tons 000: 2,643
International Cargo Off-loaded tons 000: 4,054
Airports with Scheduled Flights: 14
Traffic: Passenger-mi million: 1,135
Freight-mi million: 30.0
Length of Canals mi: 454 km 730

Tourism

Number of Tourists to 000: 943
Number of Tourists from 000: 330
Tourist Receipts $million: 660
Tourist Expenditures $million: 312

Communications

Telephones 000: 557
Cost of Local Calls 3 mins: $0.03
Cellular Telephones 000: 19
Fax Machines 000: 2.2
Personal Computers 000: —
Internet Hosts per million persons: 439
Mail: Post Offices: —
Pieces of Mail Handled million: 28
Pieces of Mail Handled per person: 8.5

EDUCATION

In Costa Rica, education is free, universal, and compulsory for nine years from ages six to 15. The language of instruction is Spanish. Schooling lasts for 11 years, divided into six years of primary school, three years of lower secondary education, and two years of the higher secondary system. Vocational training is provided in three-year industrial schools. The school year runs from March through November.

Education

Literacy Rate %: 94.8
Male %: 94.7
Female %: 95.0
First Level: Primary schools: 3,544
Teachers: 15,806
Students: 508,923
Student-Teacher Ratio: 31.4
Net Enrollment Ratio: 92
Second Level: Secondary Schools: 285
Teachers: —
Students: 207,231
Student-Teacher Ratio: —
Net Enrollment Ratio: 43

Vocational Level: Schools: —
Students: 25,269

Third Level: Institutions: 29
Teachers: —
Students: 79,759
Student-Ratio Level: —
Gross Enrollment Ratio: 31.9
Students per 100,000: 2,919
% of Population Age 25 and over with Postsecondary Education: —

Public Expenditure on Education as % of GDP: 4.5

SCIENCE AND TECHNOLOGY

Science and Technology

Scientists and Engineers in R&D per 1 million persons: 532
Expenditures in R&D as % of GDP: 0.21
High-Tech Exports $: 221 million
Patent Applications by Residents: —

MEDIA

The press is totally free of official control or manipulation, and often criticizes the government openly and vigorously.

Costa Rica has no official news agency. The largest daily newspapers (*La Nación*, *La Prensa Libre*, and *La República*) are published in Spanish. In addition, a bilingual daily, *The Tico Times*, is also widely read. All radio stations are privately owned: 40 are commercial, and five are owned by religious or cultural organizations. There are also five private television services, all based out of San José. There are 11 independent book publishers in the nation.

Media

Daily Newspapers: 5
  Total Circulation 000: 333
  Circulation per 1,000: 102
Books Published: 963
Magazines: —
Radio Receivers 000: 760
  per 1,000: 224
Television sets 000: 750
  per 1,000: 220

MOST IMPORTANT MEDIA:

Press. Except as noted, the following are published daily at San José; *La Nación* (113,00), conservative; *Diario Extra* (100,000), independent; *La República* (60,000), independent; *La Prensa Libre* (50,000), independent; *Eco Católico* (19,000), Catholic weekly; *La Gaceta* (5,200), official government gazette.

News agencies. The regional Agencia Centroamericana de Noticias (ACAN) serves in lieu of a domestic facility. Agence France-Presse, Deutsche Presse-Agentur, Prensa Latina, and Tass maintain offices at San José.

Radio and television. Broadcasting is supervised by the government's Departamento Control Nacional de Radio-Televisión. Television and radio stations are commercial, except for several offering religious or cultural programming. The Sistema de Radio y TV Cultural (SINART) network was organized by the government in 1978 to transmit news and cultural programs, while US-based Cable Network News (CNN) is available by subscription.

CULTURE

Cultural Indicators

Public Libraries:
  Number: 83
  Volumes: 555,000
  Registered borrowers: 501,034
Museums
  Number: 32
  Annual Attendance: 948,000
Cinema
  Production of Long Films: 2
  Number of Cinemas: 39
  Seating Capacity: —
  Annual Attendance: 1.7 million
  Annual Attendance per capita: 0.5

STATUS OF WOMEN

Women make up half of the population in Costa Rica. They outnumber men in some urban areas. Approximately a quarter of the workforce is female, and that number has been growing since the 1960s. Although Costa Rica is a conservative, Catholic nation, the government supports birth control and some 69 percent of women use contraception. There is universal suffrage and women participate in politics, though in a limited fashion; 7 percent of the legislature is female.

Women

Gender Empowerment Measure: 28
Seats Held in Parliament by Women %: 15.8
Female Administrators and Managers %: 23.4
Female Professional and Technical Workers %: 45.4
Women's Share of Earned Income %: 27
Women in Government %: 21

HEALTH, FOOD AND NUTRITION

Health

Number of Physicians: 4,422
Number of Dentists: 1,332
Number of Nurses: 2,600
Number of Pharmacists: 1,254
Population per Physician: 763
Number of Hospitals: 33
Hospital Beds per 10,000: 18
Hospital Bed Occupancy Rate: —
Infant Mortality Rate per 1,000 live births: 14
Maternal Mortality Rate per 100,000 live births: 60
Total Health Expenditures as % of GDP: 6.51
Health Expenditures per capita $: 132
HIV Infected % of adults: 0.55
Cigarette Consumption per smoker per year: —
% of Smokers: Male: 35
  Female: 20
Access to Safe Water %: 100

Food and Nutrition

Food Supply as % of FAO Requirements: 128
% of Consumption Expenditures on Food: 39.1
Daily Available Calories per capita: 2,865
% of Total Calories derived from:
Cereals: 34.4
Potatoes, cassava: 1.3
Meat, poultry: 6.7
Fish: 0.3
Eggs, milk: 9.3
Fruits, vegetables: 5.8
Fats, oils: 13.6

ENVIRONMENT

Partially in response to the economic potential of ecotourism, and partially as a result of the nation's relative economic prosperity, Costa Rica has undertaken widescale efforts to preserve its environment. The government has enacted environmental legislation and encouraged public-private partnerships to maintain existing natural areas and to reclaim agricultural areas for natural habitats. Costa Rica is the only nation in Latin America in which the rate of reforestation exceeds the rate of loss of rain forests. In addition, there are 30 national parks and wildlife refuges, which range from small islands off the coast to the huge and essentially pristine La Amistad International Park on the border with Panama. Some 30 percent of the nation's territory is protected.

Environment

Forest Area sq km: 12
Average Annual Deforestation sq km: 414
Nationally Protected Areas as % of Total Land Area: 13.7
Freshwater Access cubic meters per capita: 27,425
Emissions of Organic Water Pollutants kg per day: 32,301
CO_2 Emissions per capita ton: 1.4

CHRONOLOGY

1948 The bloodiest civil war in Costa Rican history erupts when elections are annulled; the Costa Rican army is disbanded and outlawed; a new National Assembly promulgates new constitution.

1955 Antigovernment forces invade Costa Rica with support from Cuba, Nicaragua, Venezuela, Dominican Republic, and Colombia; Figueres appeals for OAS aid; the invading forces are dispersed.

1963 Costa Rica joins the Central American Common Market.

1979 Costa Rica extends substantial support to the Sandinista revolution in Nicaragua.

1982 Debt repayment is halted as foreign reserves are exhausted.

1983 The presence of Nicaragua contras on Costa Rican territory increases tension between the two neighbors; external debt is rescheduled with the IMF.

1984 Costa Rica seeks hike in military aid. Costa Rica calls on Contadora nations to supervise the Costa Rican–Nicaraguan border.

1985 United Brands sells its banana plantations in the country.

1987 Arias wins Nobel Peace Prize for efforts to end Nicaraguan Civil War.

1989 Trade unions and civic groups strike in protest against the government's policies on structural adjustment.

1990 An earthquake leaves 14,000 homeless.

1991 The presidents of Guatemala, El Salvador, Honduras, Nicaragua, and Costa Rica agree to integrate their countries' economies over a six-year period.

1998 Conservative Miguel Ángel Rodríguez is elected president.

BIBLIOGRAPHY

Honey, Martha. *Hostile Acts: U.S. Policy in Costa Rica in the 1980s.* Gainesville, Fla., 1994.

Leitinger, Ilse, ed. *The Costa Rican Women's Movement: A Reader.* Pittsburgh, Pa., 1997.

Longley, Kyle. *The Sparrow and the Hawk: Costa Rica and the United States during the Rise of José Figueres.* Tuscaloosa, Ala., 1997.

MacDonald, Laura. *Supporting Civil Society: The Political Role of Non-governmental Organizations in Central America.* New York, 1997.

Wilson, Bruce. *Costa Rica: Politics, Economics, and Democracy.* Boulder, Colo., 1998.

Yashar, Deborah. *Demanding Democracy: Reform and Reaction in Costa Rica and Guatemala, 1870s–1950s.* Stanford, Calif., 1997.

OFFICIAL PUBLICATIONS

Costa Rica. *Anuario estadístico: Censo de población 1984; Plan nacional de desarrollo, 1986–90* (2 vol.).

CONTACT INFORMATION

Embassy of Costa Rica
2114 S Street NW
Washington, D.C. 20008
Phone: (202) 234-2945 Fax: (202) 265-4795

INTERNET RESOURCES

- Central Bank of Costa Rica: Economic Indicators
  http://websiec.bccr.fi.cr/indicadores/indice.web

CÔTE D'IVOIRE

BASIC FACT SHEET

OFFICIAL NAME:
République de Côte d'Ivoire (Republic of Ivory Coast)

ABBREVIATION:
IV

CAPITAL:
Yamoussoukro (Abidjan remains the administrative center)

HEAD OF STATE AND HEAD OF GOVERNMENT:
President Laurent Gbagbo (from 2000)

HEAD OF GOVERNMENT:
Prime Minister Affi N'Guessan (from 2000)

NATURE OF GOVERNMENT:
Multiparty parliamentary system.

POPULATION:
15,818,000 (1999)

AREA:
322,463 sq km (124,503 sq mi)

ETHNIC MAJORITY:
Akan, Lagoon, Krou, Mande, Senoufo, and Lobi

LANGUAGE:
French (official)

RELIGIONS:
Animism, Islam, and Christianity

UNIT OF CURRENCY:
Communauté Financière Africaine franc (C.F.A.F.)

NATIONAL FLAG:
Tricolor of orange, white, and green vertical stripes

NATIONAL EMBLEM:
A shield displaying an elephant's head in profile flanked by two palm trees with the rising sun above and a scroll bearing the legend "République de Côte D'Ivoire" beneath

NATIONAL ANTHEM:
"Hail, Hospitable Land of Hope"

NATIONAL HOLIDAYS:
August 7 (Independence Day, National Day); January 1 (New Year's Day); Christian festivals include Assumption, All Saints' Day, Good Friday, Easter Monday, Ascension, Pentecostal Monday, and Christmas; also, variable Islamic festivals are observed

DATE OF INDEPENDENCE:
August 7, 1960

DATE OF CONSTITUTION:
November 3, 1960

GEOGRAPHICAL FEATURES

Côte d'Ivoire, on the southern coast of West Africa, is roughly square in shape, with an area of 124,503 sq mi (322,463 sq km). Its coastline along the Gulf of Guinea extends for 315 mi (507 km). It is also bounded by Liberia and Guinea on the west; Mali and Burkina Faso on the north; and Ghana on the east. The de facto capital is Abidjan (1996 pop., est., 2,500,000); the official capital is Yamoussoukro (1995 est. pop., 110,000).

The coast of Côte d'Ivoire is fringed by a parallel line of sandbars and deep lagoons. Woodlands cover the continental shore and extend 165 mi (265 km) inland from the Gulf of Guinea in the east and west and 60 mi (100 km) in the center. The western part of the country is mountainous. In the north lies a savanna covered with grass and trees. Côte d'Ivoire is drained by four major rivers, which run roughly parallel from north to south. They are the Comoé, the Bandama, the Sassandra, and the Cavally. Each is navigable for only about 30 mi

Côte d'Ivoire

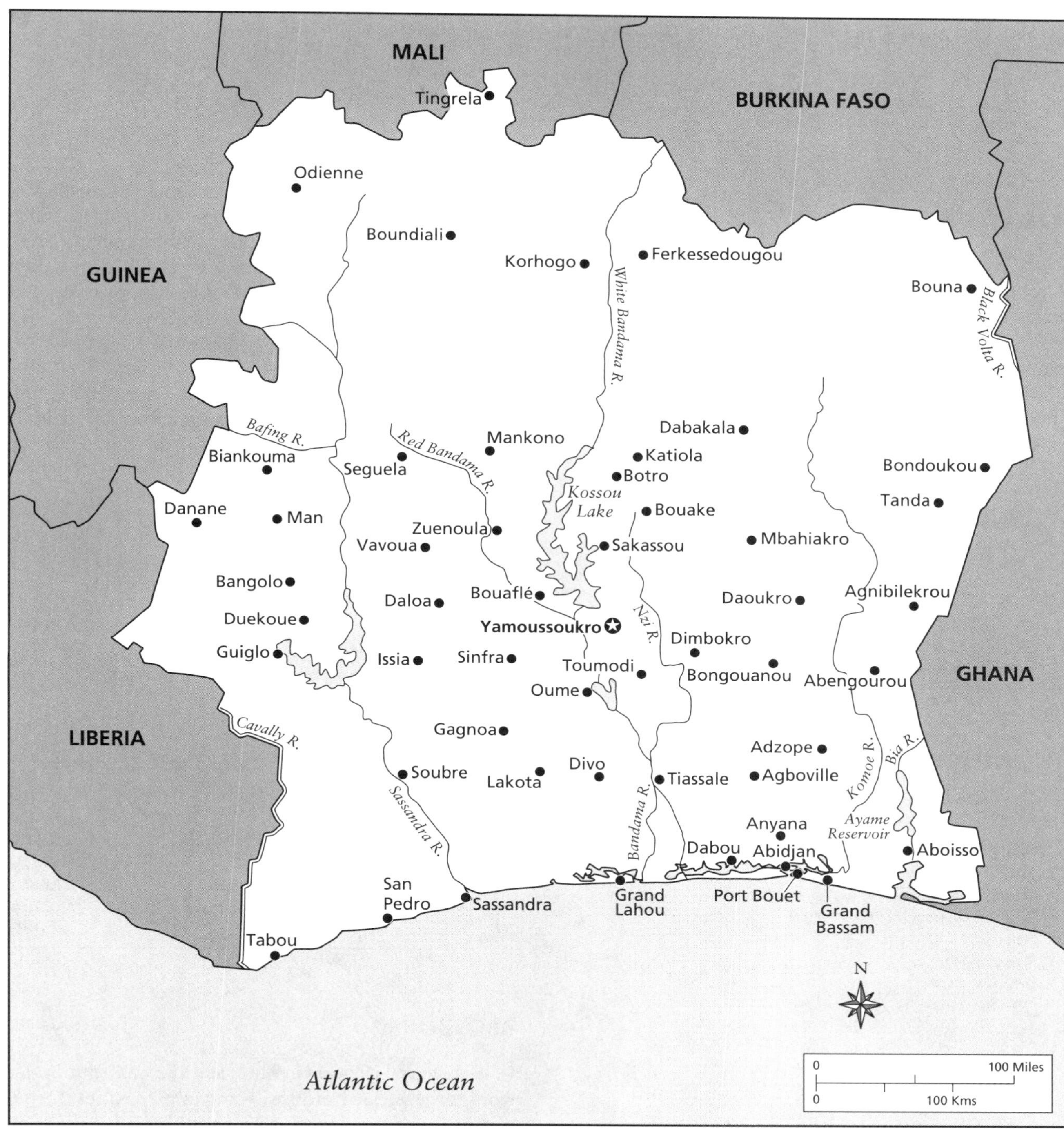

(48 km), except for the Sassandra, which is navigable for about 50 mi (80 km).

Geography

Area sq km: 322,463 sq mi 124,503
World Rank: 68th
Land Boundaries, km: Burkina Faso 584; Ghana 668; Guinea 610; Liberia 716; Mali 532
Coastline, km 515
Elevation Extremes meters
  Lowest: Gulf of Guinea 0
  Highest: Mount Nimba 1,752
Land Use % Arable land: 8
  Permanent Crops: 4
  Permanent Pastures: 41
  Forest and Woodland: 22
  Other: 25

Population of Principal Cities (1995 est.)

Abidjan (de facto; legislative)	2,500,000
Bouaké	330,000
Daloa	123,000
Korhogo	109,445
Yamoussoukro (de jure; administrative)	110,000

CLIMATE AND WEATHER

Côte d'Ivoire has a tropical climate. The average annual temperature is 79°F (26.1°C). Average annual rainfall ranges from 75 in (1905 mm) along the coast to 45 in (1145 mm) in the savanna. The coastal region receives an average annual rainfall of 80 to 230 in (2,030 to 3,040 mm). The prevailing wind systems are the southwestern monsoons and the northeastern Harmattan, a dry, scorching wind from the Sahara.

Climate and Weather

Mean Temperature
Coastal Region 73°F to 80°F
Northern Areas 90°F to 94°F
Average Rainfall 80 in to 120 in
Central Forest Region 53 in to 100 in
Northern Region 20 in

POPULATION

Population Indicators

Total Population: 1999 15,818,000
World Rank: 55th
Density per sq mi: 127.0 per sq km 49.1
% of annual growth (1994–99): 2.9
Male %: 51.1
Female %: 48.9
Urban %: 39
Age Distribution: % 0–14: 46.8
15–29: 27.3
30–44: 15.0
45–59: 7.5
60–74: 2.8
75 and over: 0.6
Population 2020: 25,268,000
Birth Rate per 1,000: 37.2
Death Rate per 1,000: 13.8
Population Doubling Time (years): —
Infant Mortality Rate per 1,000 live births: 86
Rate of Natural Increase per 1,000: 23.4
Total Fertility Rate: 5.1
Expectation of Life (years): Males 50.0
Females 52.2
Marriage Rate per 1,000: —
Divorce Rate per 1,000: —
Total Number of Households: —
Average Size of Households: 5.4
% of Illegitimate Children: —
Induced Abortions: —
Rate per 100 live births: —

ETHNIC COMPOSITION

There are more than 60 ethnic groups in Côte d'Ivoire. No single ethnic group constitutes more than 15 percent of the population, although some are dominant in particular regions. Approximately 44 percent of the population is urban. Côte d'Ivoire does not impose significant restrictions on immigration, and about 20 percent of workers are from neighboring countries. Many of these foreign workers eventually return home after having worked in Côte d'Ivoire for several years. The country also has a significant non-African population, including 100,000 Lebanese, 37,000 French nationals, and many Syrians and Indians.

LANGUAGES

The official language is French, which is the language of the media, education, and government. Approximately 60 African languages are also spoken, among them Agni, Baoulé, Senoufo, and Malinke-Bambara-Dioula.

Principal Languages and Their Speakers

Akan (including Baule and Anyi)	4,750,000
French	7,900,000
Gur ([Voltaic] including Senufo and Lobi)	1,850,000
Kru (including Bete)	1,660,000
Malinke (including Dyula and Bambara)	1,810,000
Southern Mandé (including Dan and Guro)	1,220,000
Other (non-Ivorian population)	4,520,000

RELIGIONS

Côte d'Ivoire is a secular state, and the constitution provides for religious freedom. About 60 percent of the population is Muslim; about 12 percent are Christians; and the rest of the population follows traditional religions. Among Christian churches, the Catholic Church is organized under the metropolitan archdiocese of Abidjan and seven suffragan dioceses. There are numerous Protestant bodies, some of which are essentially cults. These include the Harrist-Methodist Church, founded by an African prophet, William Wade Harris.

In 1990, Pope John Paul II consecrated the Basilica of Our Lady of Peace in Yamoussoukro, the largest Christian church in the world.

Religious Affiliations

Muslim	6,120,000
Roman Catholic	3,280,000
Traditional beliefs	2,690,000
Nonreligious	2,120,000
Protestant	840,000
Other	770,000

HISTORICAL BACKGROUND

The first recorded history of Côte d'Ivoire comes from North African traders who traversed the Sahara, and the first important cities in the region were established to serve commercial interests. Islam was introduced to the region by Arab traders, and it spread rapidly within Côte d'Ivoire after the 11th century. Unification of the country was hindered by the dense rain forests that covered the southern half of the country, and the area that now constitutes Côte d'Ivoire was ruled by different ethnic and religious groups; people lived in small, isolated villages, and their only contact with the larger world was through the traders who passed through. A Muslim state was established in the north in the early 18th century; four other states ruled independently over other parts of the country; independence movements resisted French subjugation and persisted into the late 20th century.

The first French posts were established in Côte d'Ivoire in 1843. In 1893 the territory was formally named Ivory Coast and placed under a French governor. Sixty-five years later, on December 4, 1958, Ivory Coast accepted the new French constitution and opted for the status of an autonomous republic within the French Community. On August 7, 1960, the Republic of Ivory Coast proclaimed its complete independence. It changed its name officially to Côte d'Ivoire in 1985.

Ivory Coast gained independence with hardly a murmur, let alone bloodshed. The peaceful departure of the French was, in part, a reflection of the deep pro-French sentiments of the people. Forty years after independence, Ivory Coast remains the most Francophone of West African states. French economic conservatism—not African nationalism—dominates the country's economic and foreign policies. Both capital and management of industry are largely in the hands of private French citizens. The French educational, administrative, and judicial systems have been retained with little change. A significant portion of Côte d'Ivoire's foreign trade is with France. Daily newspapers from Paris are more widely read than local newspapers in Abidjan. French is the country's sole official language.

Côte d'Ivoire's French connection, which is perhaps the key to its political stability, is determined by two factors. One is the almost mystical Francophilism of the Ivorian leadership. The second is the pragmatic benefit of French association for the country's economic development. Côte d'Ivoire's phenomenal economic progress through the mid-1980s was in no small part due to France's role.

Félix Houphouët-Boigny was the main political leader from the 1940s, when he organized an international political party to fight colonialism. He became president of the autonomous republic in 1959 and remained president until his death in 1993, winning the right to retain his post in the nation's first multiparty presidential election, in October 1990. Houphouët-Boigny's administration was characterized by moderation and a constant search for consensus and dialogue instead of political confrontation. Most potential opposition was defused and their members even absorbed into the ruling party. The government did not show undue concern for its internal security, nor did it enact extraordinary legislation directed against the opposition. Largely as a result of the president's skillful management, until 1990 the stability of the central government was the most striking feature of Côte d'Ivoire.

Political unrest was sporadic and hampered by weak leadership. In 1963 two coup plots were discovered. One was conceived by a young group of radicals and the other by northerners resentful of control of the government by southern Ivorians. The president responded by cutting the size of the army to reduce the chance of intervention by the armed forces, introducing a regional development plan, and setting up more management of businesses by indigenes.

The government has at various times faced charges of corruption. In 1977, to deal with those allegations, Houphouët-Boigny removed ministers from three key departments—Finance, Economic Planning, and Foreign Affairs—and passed legislation designed to prevent high-level corruption. Additional anticorruption measures were approved in 1984, and former housing officials were imprisoned for misconduct.

In the 1980s economic austerity led to more unrest, as well as political liberalization. Strikes and demonstrations, staged mostly by students and professionals, occurred frequently from late 1980 to mid-1983. The longest was held in the spring of 1983 by teachers protesting the withdrawal of free housing rights. The strike was aided by sympathetic doctors. It was ended through a presidential back-to-work edict. A degree of political openness was introduced in 1980 with the first free elections for seats in the National Assembly, which was expanded from 80 to 147 members. More than 600 people ran for office, and only 27 of the previous 80 incumbents were returned to the chamber. The National Assembly was later expanded to 175 members.

Massive protests by students, teachers, farmers, and professionals flared again in 1990 in response to the government's decision to cut salaries and increase taxes. Growing political pressure forced Houphouët-Boigny to legalize opposition parties and run in the country's first contested election since independence. Amid charges of electoral fraud, Houphouët-Boigny won with 85 percent of the vote. The ruling Democratic Party (PDCI) won 165 seats in the 175-member parliament in the nation's first multiparty parliamentary elections. The Ivorian Popular Front (IPI) won nine seats, and the Ivorian Worker's Party won one seat.

On December 7, 1993, President Houphouët-Boigny died. The National Assembly selected its president, Henri Konan Bédié, to succeed him as the nation's president. On October 22, 1995, Bédié won reelection to the presidency, receiving 96 percent of the vote; however, the election was boycotted by the major opposition parties. In 1998, several constitutional changes were approved that strengthened the president's powers, including a provision to lengthen his term of office from five to seven years.

On December 24, 1999, President Bédié was overthrown in a largely nonviolent military coup, and General Robert Guei, a former armed forces chief of staff, was installed as president. It was the country's first coup since Côte d'Ivoire achieved independence in 1960. The new president promised a democratic government and elections. He suspended the constitution, the parliament, and the courts and in their place created a nine-man National Committee of Public Salvation, which was to rule until elections could be held. Guei gave as the reasons for the coup the preceding government's ethnic intolerance and its practice of holding political prisoners.

On July 23–24, 2000, voters approved a new constitution, with more than 86 percent of the votes cast in favor of the new government. The constitution set the qualifications for candidates for president, lowered the voting age from 21 to 18, reduced the presidential term from seven years to five, and eliminated the death penalty. It also granted amnesty to those who had participated in the December coup.

Presidential elections in October were boycotted by the PDCI and Islamic leaders, who were barred from running in the elections. Guei declared himself the winner of the election even though early voting results showed Laurent Gbagbo, the FPI candidate, leading the vote. A popular uprising brought Gbagbo to power. Gbagbo assembled a new government that included FPI and PDCI members but excluded the Rally of Republicans (RDR). Fighting erupted between the mostly Muslim followers of Alassane Ouattara, the leader of the RDR, and the Christian followers of President Gbagbo. The two leaders met in 2001 and pledged to work toward reconciliation; however, a National Reconciliation Forum, set up by Gbagbo in October, was boycotted by General Guei. The UN insisted on reconciliation before resuming aid, and it remains to be seen whether the country, once among the wealthiest in Africa, will be able to regain its economic footing, which it lost in the uncertainty following the coup.

CONSTITUTION

The constitution of 1960 created a secular, democratic, and social republic with a strong president and a National Assembly, whose powers are restricted to specific subjects. All other matters of state are left to the executive and are dealt with by decrees. The executive can also pro-

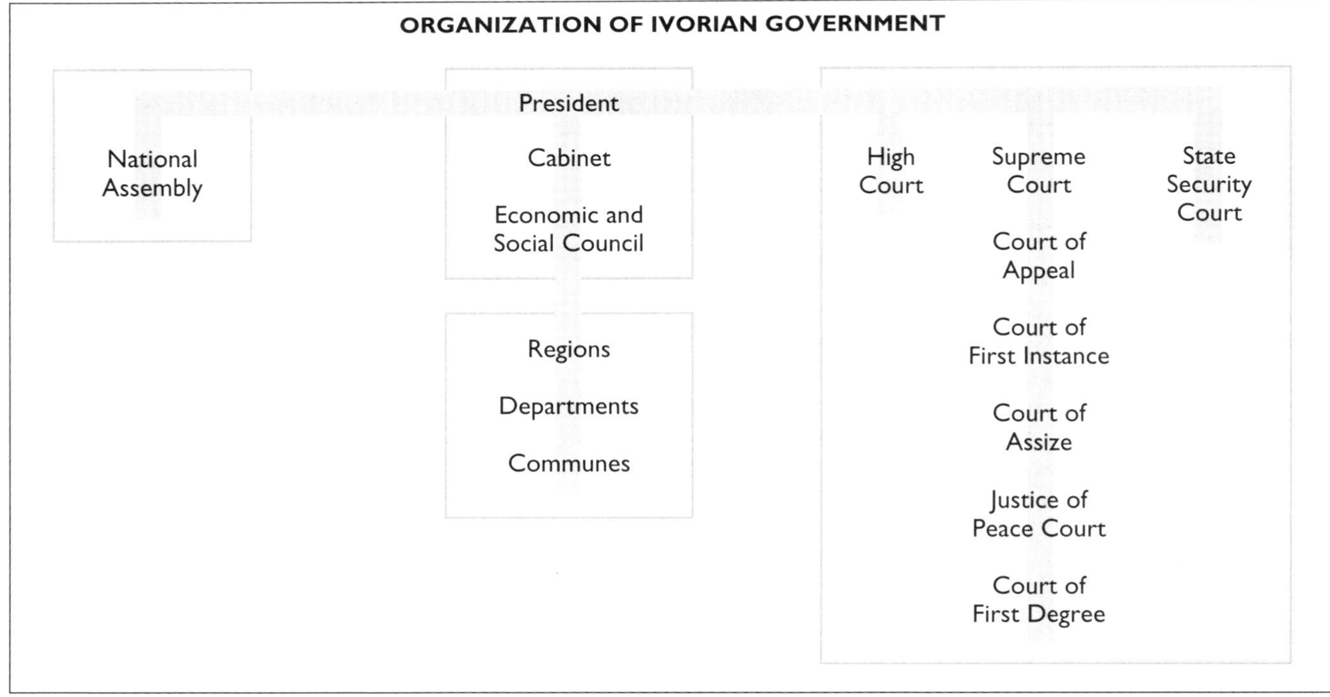

pose legislation. The president is the head of state, head of government, prime minister, commander in chief, and guarantor of judicial independence. He appoints his own cabinet. The constitution also created the Economic and Social Council, which advises the president on bills, ordinances, and decrees and proposes desirable reforms. It also serves as a medium through which public interest groups can make their views known to the government.

Suffrage is universal for all citizens 18 years of age or older. Voters choose a complete slate rather than vote for individuals.

LOCAL GOVERNMENT

Côte d'Ivoire is divided into 16 regions, 50 departments, and 196 communes. Each department is governed by a local council.

Local Government

Principal administrative divisions, area, population

Area and population

Department	area sq km	population 1995 census
Abengourou	5,200	216,058
Abidjan	8,550	2,485,847
Aboisso	6,250	255,895
Adzopé	5,230	237,870
Agboville	3,850	203,493
Agnibilékrou	1,700	84,349
Bangolo	2,060	79,979
Beoumi	2,820	90,327
Biankouma	4,950	98,236
Bondoukou	10,040	174,251
Bongouanou	5,570	224,958
Bouafle	3,980	165,822
Bouake	4,700	450,594
Bouna	21,470	135,813
Boundiali	7,895	127,847
Dabakala	9,670	81,820
Daloa	5,450	359,753
Danane	4,600	222,839
Daoukro	3,610	86,494
Dimbokro	4,920	141,968
Divo	7,920	387,106
Duekoue	2,930	102,168
Ferkessedougou	17,728	172,893
Gagnoa	4,500	276,217
Grand-Lahou	2,280	52,559
Guiglo	11,220	170,321
Issia	3,590	195,663
Katiola	9,420	130,635
Korhogo	12,500	390,229
Lakota	2,730	116,771
Man	4,990	294,724
Mankono	10,660	123,362
M'bahiakro	5,460	102,531
Odienne	20,600	169,764
Oume	2,400	141,268
Sakassou	1,880	59,362
San-Pedro	6,900	170,669
Sassandra	5,190	108,090
Sequela	11,240	121,235
Sinfra	1,690	121,903
Soubre	8,270	310,790
Tabou	5,440	58,147
Tanda	6,490	204,070
Tengreia	2,200	54,847
Tiassaie	3,370	133,708
Touba	8,720	107,886
Toumodi	2,780	80,802
Vavoua	6,160	168,292
Yamoussoukro	6,160	281,442
Zuenoula	2,830	114,027
TOTAL	320,763	10,815,694

PARLIAMENT

Côte d'Ivoire has a unicameral legislature, the National Assembly, a 175-member legislative body whose members are elected by direct and universal suffrage to serve for five-year terms. The Assembly holds two sessions each year, during which it enacts legislation in the two areas of policy under its jurisdiction. The first category comprises nationality, the criminal and judicial systems, taxation, currency, the electoral system, and public administration. The second category includes areas in which the Assembly sets policy; these include defense, education, labor, transportation, and communications.

POLITICAL PARTIES

From the time Côte d'Ivoire became independent in 1960 until recently, the Parti Démocratique de la Côte d'Ivoire (Democratic Party of the Côte d'Ivoire; PDCI) has been the only political party in the nation. This situation evolved as a result of the party's control of the electoral process, rather than of an official prohibition against opposition parties. In 1990, however, under pressure from political opponents, President Houphouët-Boigny allowed other parties to field slates of candidates in the nation's first multiparty elections. In the balloting, the PDCI retained 165 seats in the National Assembly; two opposition parties, the Ivorian Popular Front and the Ivorian Workers' Party, won nine seats and one seat, respectively. Other parties operating in Côte d'Ivoire are Rally of the Republicans and the Ivorian Socialist Party.

Political Parties

Democratic Party, 1946
Union of Social Democrats
Ivorian Workers' Party, 1990
Union of Political Parties for the Presidential Group, 1995, a merger of
    African Federal Party

(continued)

Progressive Movement
National Union for Economic Progress
Party for Unity and Socioeconomic Development
Rally of Forces for the Republic
Republican Front, 1995
Rally of Republicans, 1994
Ivorian Popular Front, 1988
Union of Democratic Forces, an alliance of six parties including Party for Social Progress
Ivorian Popular Front-Renaissance, 1996
Ivorian Socialist Party
Republican Party, 1987
Social-Democrat Party, 1990
Alliance for Social Democracy, 1994
Liberal Party
Ivorian Communist Party, 1990
National Union for Democracy

Political Parties: Strength in Parliament Most Recent Elections

National Assembly (Assemblée Nationale). The chamber contains 225 members elected for five-year terms in single-seat constituencies. At the elections of December 10, 2000, and January 14, 2001, the Ivorian Peoples Front won 96 seats; Democratic Party of Ivory Coast, 94; Rally of the Republicans, 5-boycott; Party of Ivorian Workers, 4; Union of Democrats of Ivory Coast, 1; Movement of Future Forces, 1; nonpartisan, 22, and vacant, 2.

LEGAL SYSTEM

The court system comprises two levels. The Supreme Court, High Court of Justice, and the State Security Court constitute the higher level; the Court of Appeal, the courts of first instance, the courts of assize, the justice of peace courts, and the courts of first degree constitute the lower level. The High Court of Justice, composed of deputies chosen by the National Assembly from among its own members, has the power to impeach the president for high treason.

Although Ivorian law guarantees the right to a fair public trial, this provision is not always honored in rural areas, where justice is administered through traditional institutions. Defendants have the right to legal counsel, and, in theory if not always in practice, attorneys are appointed to represent indigent defendants.

LAW ENFORCEMENT

Law Enforcement

Offenses reported to the police per 100,000: 67
Murder: 2.5
Assault: 73.1
Burglary: 19.5
Automobile Theft: 11.9
Population per Police officer: 4,640
Death Penalty: Yes, but executions are rare.

HUMAN RIGHTS

Côte d'Ivoire is classified as a partly free nation. A strongly Francophile country, it has based its human rights structure on that of France. Citizens enjoy a large measure of free speech and complete freedom of religion. Most news media are government owned and support government policies; however, foreign publications are widely available. In 1994, the Supreme Court of Côte d'Ivoire upheld the three-year prison sentences given two journalists who had been convicted of inciting revolt. That same year, the editor of a weekly progovernment newspaper was sentenced to six months in prison for libeling a government official.

FOREIGN POLICY

Côte d'Ivoire is a staunch ally of France, on which it depends for its economic and military well-being, and it has maintained good relations with the United States and other Western countries. President Bédié was instrumental in achieving a cease-fire between the Sierra Leone government and rebel forces in 1996; the cease-fire was signed in Abidjan.

Côte d'Ivoire supported the U.S. position in the Persian Gulf War in 1991.

DEFENSE

The president is charged with responsibility for the nation's defense. He is assisted by the Ministerial Defense Council and the Military Defense Council. Service commanders report to the Minister of Defense.

Military forces are recruited by conscription. Conscripts' obligation lasts 25 years, of which two are on active duty and the remainder in reserves. Active troop strength in 1996 was 8,900.

Much of the training of the armed forces is done by France.

Military Indicators

Total Active Duty Personnel: 8,900
Military Manpower per 1,000: 0.6
Military Expenditures $: 98 million
as % of GNP: 1.1
per capita $: 7
as % of central government expenditures: 4.2
Arms Imports $: 0
Arms Exports $: 0

ECONOMY

The annual gross domestic product of Côte d'Ivoire (1997 est.) is $25.8 billion, or $1,700 per capita. The basis of the economy is agriculture, and approximately 60 percent of the labor force is employed in that area of the economy. The country's annual budget in 1993 was $3.4 billion. Although the budget is balanced, the nation's economy is slowed by significant foreign debt, which was $16.1 billion (est.) in 1996. The country received a number of loans from the International Monetary Fund during the 1990s and devalued its currency in 1994, which helped the economy rebound from a long slump.

Total exports in 1996 were $4.2 billion, primarily to France and Germany; total imports were $3.2 billion, primarily from France and Nigeria. The rate of inflation in consumer prices, which soared briefly after the devaluation of the currency in 1994, was 3.4 percent in 1997.

Growth was negative in 2000 because of the difficulty of meeting the conditions of international donors, continued low prices of key exports, and postcoup instability. In 2001–02, a moderate rebound in the cocoa market could boost growth back above 3 percent; however, political instability could further impede growth.

The basis of the Ivorian economy is agriculture. The main cash crops are coffee, cocoa, bananas, timber, sugarcane, plantains, cotton, and pineapples. Other crops are raised primarily for domestic consumption; these include rice, corn, millet, yams, cassava, and peanuts. The country is a leading producer of cocoa and coffee. The small manufacturing sector emphasizes the processing of agricultural goods.

The agricultural sector is largely private, although the government does operate some large farms. Land ownership is restricted to Ivorian nationals.

Principal Economic Indicators

Gross National Product: $10.152 billion
GNP per capita: $710
GNP Average Annual Growth Rate (1990–97) %: 0.9
GNP per capita Average Annual Growth Rate (1990–97) %: −2.0
Origin of Gross Domestic Product %
- Agriculture: 31
- Mining: —
- Manufacturing: 18
- Construction: 2
- Public Utilities: 2
- Transportation and Communications: 8
- Trade: 18
- Financial Services: 8
- Other Services: 8
- Government: 10

Gross Domestic Product by Type of Expenditure %
- Private Consumption: 65
- Government Consumption: 13
- Gross Domestic Investment: 12
- Foreign Trade: Exports: 44
- Imports: −33

% of Income Received by Poorest 20%: 6.8
% of Income Received by Richest 10%: 28.5

Price and earnings indexes (1995 = 100)

	1992	1993	1994	1995	1996	1997	1998
Consumer price index	67.9	69.4	87.5	100.0	102.5	108.2	113.3
Minimum earnings index	90.9	90.9	90.9	100.0	—	—	—

Finance

National Currency: CFA Franc (CFAF)
Exchange Rate: $1 = CFAF 608.37
Money Supply Stock in National Currency billion: 944.5
M1 per capita: 63,900
Central Bank Discount Rate %: 5.75
Total External Debt $million: 16,100
Debt Service Ratio %: 16

Balance of Payments $million: 34.6
International Reserves SDRs million: 634
Ratio of External Debt to Total Reserves: 22.4

Average Annual Rate of Inflation/Consumer Price Index Growth Rate %: 3.4

Official Development Assistance

ODA $: 552 million
- as % of GNP: 7.8
- per capita: $55
- Foreign Direct Investment $million: 435

Central Government Revenues and Expenditures

Fiscal Year: Calendar Year

Revenues $million: 2,400
Expenditures $million: 2,700
Budget Deficit $: 300
Tax Revenues as % of GDP: 20.8
Highest Tax Bracket %
- Individual: 10
- Corporate: 35

Employment and Labor

Economically Active Population: 4,263,000
Female Participation Rate %: 32.3
Activity Rate %: 39.4
Labor by Sector: %
- Agriculture, Forestry, Fishing: 61.6
- Manufacturing, Mining: 2.3
- Construction: 2.0
- Transportation and Communications: 2.8
- Trade, Hotels, and Restaurants: 12.4
- Finance, Insurance, Real Estate: —
- Public Administration, Defense: —
- Services: 13.9

Unemployment %: NA

Agriculture

Agriculture's Share of GDP %: 31
Average Annual Rate of Growth (1965–98) %: 2.2
Number of Farms 000: 550
Average Size of Farm ha: 5

(continued)

Number of Tractors per 1,000 hectares: 1.5
Irrigation, % of Farms having: 3
Artificial Fertilizer kg/hectare: 11
Total Farmland as % of land area: 8.6
Livestock: Cattle 000: 1,312
Sheep 000: 1,347
Hogs 000: 271
Chickens 000: 31,059
Forests: Production of Roundwood (000 cubic meters): 14,782
Fisheries: Total Catch tons 000: 74.1

Mining

% of GDP: 0.2
Value of Mineral Production $million: 13.3

Manufacturing

Value Added $million: 1,022
Industrial Production Growth Rate %: 9

Energy

Commercial Energy Production metric tons of oil equivalent 000: 4,908
Commercial Energy Consumption metric tons of oil equivalent 000: 5,597
Commercial Energy Consumption per capita kg: 394
Average Annual Growth Rate 1980–97 %: −0.5
Net Energy Imports % of use: 12
Electricity Installed Capacity kW 000: 1,173
Production kW-hr million: 1,913
Coal Reserves tons million: —
Production tons 000: —
Natural Gas Proven Reserves cubic meters billion: 23
Production cubic meters million: —
Crude Petroleum Reserves barrels million: 100
Production barrels million: 7
Consumption barrels million: 25
Refinery Capacity barrels per day 000: 64
Pipelines Length km: —

Foreign Trade

Imports $million: 2,447
Exports $million: 3,105
Export Volume % Annual Growth Rate (1990–97): 5.5
Import Volume % Annual Growth Rate (1990–97): 6.8
Balance of Trade $

Balance of trade (current prices)

	1992	1993	1994	1995	1996	1997
CFAF 000,000,000	+138.53	+114.2	+457.9	+349.5	+734.8	+813.2
% of total	10.1%	8.7%	17.7%	10.6%	20.3%	20.3%

Major Trading Partners

	Imports	Exports
European Union %	56.0	56.6
United States %	3.9	5.7
Eastern Europe %	0.1	8.0
Japan %	3.8	1.1
Others %	36.2	28.6

Transportation

Roads Total Length mi: 31,168 km 50,160
Paved %: 10
Automobiles: 271,000
Trucks and Buses: 150,000
Persons per vehicle: 34
Railroad; Track Length mi: 405 km 651
Passenger-mi million: 117
Freight-mi million: 182
Merchant Marine: No. of Vessels: 51
Total Deadweight Tonnage 000: 98.6
International Cargo Loaded tons 000: 4,173
International Cargo Off-loaded tons 000: 7,228
Airports with Scheduled Flights: 11
Traffic: Passenger-mi million: 139
Freight-mi million: 10.5
Length of Canals mi: 609 km 980

Tourism

Number of Tourists to 000: 301
Number of Tourists from 000: 5
Tourist Receipts $million: 72
Tourist Expenditures $million: 159

Communications

Telephones 000: 116
Cost of Local Calls 3 mins: $0.11
Cellular Telephones 000: —
Fax Machines 000: —
Personal Computers 000: —
Internet Hosts per million persons: —
Mail: Post Offices: 364
Pieces of Mail Handled million: 46
Pieces of Mail Handled per person: 3.2

EDUCATION

Côte d'Ivoire provides free education to its citizens, and elementary education for children between the ages of seven and 13 is compulsory. There were more than 1.4 million elementary students in the early 1990s, and approximately 293,000 students were attending secondary and vocational schools.

The National University of Côte d'Ivoire, in Abidjan, enrolls approximately 21,000 students; a number of Ivorians attend university abroad. The literacy rate is about 40 percent.

Education

Literacy Rate %: 40.1
Male %: 49.9
Female %: 30.0
First Level: Primary schools: 7,185
Teachers: 36,058
Students: 1,609,929
Student-Teacher Ratio: 44.6
Net Enrollment Ratio: 47

Second Level: Secondary Schools:
- Teachers: 9,505
- Students: 463,810
- Student-Teacher Ratio: 48.8
- Net Enrollment Ratio: —

Vocational Level: Schools: —
- Students: 11,037

Third Level: Institutions: —
- Teachers: —
- Students: 51,215
- Student-Ratio Level: —
- Gross Enrollment Ratio: 4.4
- Students per 100,000: 396
- % of Population Age 25 and over with Postsecondary Education: 8.7

Public Expenditure on Education as % of GDP: 4.7

SCIENCE AND TECHNOLOGY

Science and Technology

Scientists and Engineers in R&D per 1 million persons: —
Expenditures in R&D as % of GDP: —
High-Tech Exports $: 1,564 million
Patent Applications by Residents: —

MEDIA

The Ministry of Information publishes two daily newspapers. In addition, there are many periodicals, all published in French. Newspapers and magazines are also imported from France. Although there is no official press censorship, those who publish material critical of the government or deleterious to public morality are subject to fine, imprisonment, or expulsion.

The official broadcasting organization is Radiodiffusion Télévision Ivorienne. In addition, there are 17 other television stations and 71 AM radio stations.

Côte d'Ivoire comprises seven large cultural/ethnic groups, all of which have many members in neighboring countries as well. In simplest terms, there are four large regional cultural areas in the country: East Atlantic (Akan), West Atlantic (Kru), Voltaic, and Mandé. The existence of these large ethnic groups, each itself comprising other, smaller groups, complicates the ability of the national government to create a strong national identity.

Media

Daily Newspapers: 1
- Total Circulation 000: 90
- Circulation per 1,000: 7.0

Books Published: —
Magazines: —
Radio Receivers 000: 1,600
- per 1,000: 110

Television sets 000: 790
- per 1,000: 59

MOST IMPORTANT MEDIA:

Press. The following are published daily at Abidjan, unless otherwise noted: *Ivoire Dimanche* (75,000), weekly, taken over in 1990 by *Fraternité-Matin* group; *Fraternité-Matin* (61,000), official PDCI organ; *Ivoir Soir* (40,000), PDCI organ launched in 1987 to concentrate on social and cultural events as a complement to *Fraternité-Matin*; *Reveil de l'Afrique Noire* (20,000), commenced publication in late 1986 to serve as a catalyst of francophone African unity; *Le Nouvel Horizon* (15,000), FPI weekly; *Abidjan 7 Jours* (10,000), weekly; *Le Regard* (10,000), independent bimonthly launched in February 1991; *Journal Officiel de la Côte d'Ivoire* (1,000), published weekly by the Ministry of the Interior; *La Voie*, FPI organ; *Fraternité-Hebdo*, weekly PDCI organ; *La Voix d'Afrique*, monhly regional magazine; *Notre Temps*, independent weekly launched in May 1991; *Le Populaire Nouvelle Formule*, independent daily; *Le Renaissance*. In May 1994 *Soir Info*, an evening daily, replaced the short-lived *Bonsoir la Côte d'Ivoire*.

After the arrest of at least eight journalists in the first half of 1994, *Fraternité-Matin* defended the Konan-Bédié administration against charges that the government was seeking to curtail freedom of the press. In November a new press body, the Ivorian Association of Democratic Press (Association de Presse Démocratique Ivoirienne-APDI), was launched to "defend press freedoms at all times."

News agencies. The domestic agency is Agence Ivoirienne de Presse (AIP). Agence France-Presse, ANSA, and Reuters maintain offices at Abidjan.

Radio and television. The government-operated Ivorian Radio (Radiodiffusion Ivoirienne) and Ivorian Television (Télévision Ivoirienne).

CULTURE

Cultural Indicators

Public Libraries
- Number: 1
- Volumes: 25,000
- Registered borrowers: 2,120

Museums
- Number: —
- Annual Attendance: —

Cinema
- Production of Long Films: 2
- Number of Cinemas: 60
- Seating Capacity: 70,000
- Annual Attendance: 7.3 million
- Annual Attendance per capita: 0.6

STATUS OF WOMEN

Long held in a subordinate role, women began to play a more prominent role in Ivorian public life in the late 1980s. As late as the 1960s, women were prohibited from establishing bank accounts in their own names and could not control their own property. Access to divorce was severely limited, and property descended patrilineally (a man's nephews inherited his property, rather than his sons).

In 1973 the government established the Ministry of Women's Affairs to combat discrimination against women, and legislation improved women's legal position. Although women continued to receive unfavorable treatment compared to men, the number of women attending university and entering professional fields previously closed to them has continued to grow.

Women

Gender Empowerment Measure: —
Seats Held in Parliament by Women %: 8.5
Female Administrators and Managers %: —
Female Professional and Technical Workers %: —
Women's Share of Earned Income %: —
Women in Government %: 3

HEALTH, FOOD, AND NUTRITION

Health

Number of Physicians: 2,020
Number of Dentists: 219
Number of Nurses: 3,691
Number of Pharmacists: 135
Population per Physician: 5,931
Number of Hospitals: —
Hospital Beds per 10,000: 8
Hospital Bed Occupancy Rate: —
Infant Mortality Rate per 1,000 live births: 137
Maternal Mortality Rate per 100,000 live births: 810
Total Health Expenditures as % of GDP: 3.35
Health Expenditures per capita $: 28
HIV Infected % of adults: 10.06
Cigarette Consumption per smoker per year:
% of Smokers: Male:
Female:
Access to Safe Water %: 82

Food and Nutrition

Food Supply as % of FAO Requirements: 109
% of Consumption Expenditures on Food: 48.0
Daily Available Calories per capita: 2,517
% of Total Calories derived from:
Cereals: 41.5
Potatoes, cassava: 26.1
Meat, poultry: 2.0
Fish: 1.0
Eggs, milk: 0.8
Fruits, vegetables: 10.0
Fats, oils: 7.4

ENVIRONMENT

Côte d'Ivoire, because it is so heavily dependent on agriculture, has not suffered serious problems of industrial pollution. However, it has in the 1990s instituted measures to reverse the soil depletion caused by overuse of the land and to combat the deforestation that resulted from growth in the nation's timber industry. Modern methods of agriculture are being introduced along with mechanization to replace the labor-intensive practices of the past.

Côte d'Ivoire is a signatory to a number of international environmental protection treaties, including treaties on biodiversity, climate change, hazardous waste, marine dumping, ozone layer protection, and ship pollution.

Environment

Forest Area sq km: 55,000
Average Annual Deforestation sq km: 308
Nationally Protected Areas as % of Total Land Area: 6.3
Freshwater Access cubic meters per capita: 5,362
Emissions of Organic Water Pollutants kg per day: 15,414
CO_2 Emissions per capita ton: 0.9

CHRONOLOGY

1944 Félix Houphouët-Boigny founds the interterritorial African Democratic Rally, the first major political party in Africa.
1948 Protesters demand self-rule in mass demonstrations in Abidjan.
1949 Protests turn to violence.
1950 Houphouët-Boigny changes his approach, cooperating with the French.
1958 Côte d'Ivoire is proclaimed a republic within the French Community.
1959 Côte d'Ivoire forms a customs union in 1959 with Dahomey (Benin), Niger, and Burkina Faso.
1960 Côte d'Ivoire gains independence from France; Felix Houphouët-Boigny becomes president.
1961 The Ivoirian military is nationalized.
1965 Houphouët-Boigny is reelected for a second five-year term.
1969 Some 1,600 unemployed Ivoirians are arrested for demonstrating against proforeign hiring policies for government jobs; in response to demands by the prosocialist Movement of Ivorian Primary and Secondary School Students for government reform of Abidjan University, the government arrests 150 protesters, deports foreign students, and closes the university for two weeks.
1973 A military coup is averted.
1980 Houphouët-Boigny survives an assassination attempt.
1982 Government closes Abidjan University in response to student unrest.
1990 Houphouët-Boigny is reelected for a sixth five-year term.
1993 President Houphouët-Boigny dies and is replaced by Henri Konan Bédié.
1994 Côte d'Ivoire devalues its currency and institutes economic reforms.
1995 President Bédié is reelected to office, receiving 96 percent of the vote.

1996 United Nations Industrial Development Organization, meeting in Abidjan, announces plan to spur industrial development in Africa.

1999 A military coup takes place, and General Robert Guei is installed as president.

2000 Voters approve a new constitution in general elections . . . . Laurent Gbagbo, believed to be the real winner in presidential elections, is proclaimed president after a popular uprising against the perceived rigging of the election forces Guei to flee the country. Fighting erupts between Gbagbo's mainly southern Christian supporters and followers of Alassane Ouattara, who are mostly Muslims from the north.

2001 President Gbagbo and opposition leader Ouattara agree to work toward reconciliation. Calls for presidential and legislative elections are renewed after Ouattara's party gains a majority at local polls. Gbagbo sets up a National Reconciliation Forum that General Guei refuses to attend.

BIBLIOGRAPHY

Harshe, Rajan. *Pervasive Entente: France and the Ivory Coast*. Atlantic Highlands, N.J., 1984.

Mundt, Robert J. *Historical Dictionary of the Ivory Coast*. Metuchen, N.J., 1995.

Rapley, John. *Ivorien Capitalism: African Entrepreneurs in Côte d'Ivoire*. Boulder, Colo., 1993.

Zartman, William, and Christopher L. Delegado. *The Political Economy of the Ivory Coast*. New York, 1984.

OFFICIAL PUBLICATIONS

Côte d'Ivoire. *Côte d'Ivoire—Statistical Annex* (IMF Staff Country Report ([1996]); *Recensement général de la population et de l'habitat 1988*.

CONTACT INFORMATION

Embassy of Côte d'Ivoire
2424 Massachusetts Avenue NW
Washington, D.C. 20008
Phone: (202) 797-0300

INTERNET RESOURCES

- Côte d'Ivoire—A Country Study
  http://lcweb2.loc.gov/frd/cs/citoc.html
  http://www.abs.gov.au

CROATIA

BASIC FACT SHEET

OFFICIAL NAME:
Republic of Croatia (Republika Hrvatska)

ABBREVIATION:
HR

CAPITAL:
Zagreb

HEAD OF STATE:
President Stjepan Mesic (elected 2000)

HEAD OF GOVERNMENT:
Prime Minister Ivica Racan (from 2000)

NATURE OF GOVERNMENT:
Presidential parliamentary democracy

POPULATION:
4,677,000 (1999)

AREA:
56,610 sq km (21,857 sq mi)

MAJOR ETHNIC GROUPS:
Croats, Serbs

LANGUAGES:
Croatian

RELIGIONS:
Roman Catholicism

UNIT OF CURRENCY:
Kuna

NATIONAL FLAG:
Red, white, and blue horizontal bands with Croatian Coat of Arms creed and white checkered.

NATIONAL EMBLEM:
A red-and-white checkered field, with a crown that shows the oldest-known Croatian coat of arms (a golden six-pointed star and a silver crescent on a blue shield) and the coats of arms of the Republic of Dubrovnik (two red bars on a dark blue field), Dalmatia (three yellow lion heads on a light blue shield), Istria (a yellow ibex on a dark blue shield), and Slavonia (a golden six-pointed star and a black marten between the rivers Drava and Sava).

NATIONAL ANTHEM:
"Our Beautiful Homeland"

NATIONAL HOLIDAYS:
Statehood Day (30 May)

DATE OF INDEPENDENCE:
25 June 1991

DATE OF CONSTITUTION:
22 December 1990

GEOGRAPHICAL FEATURES

Croatia is part of Central Europe and has a wishbone shape, with one leg following the Adriatic seacoast and the other roughly parallel leg surrounding Bosnia-Herzegovina. Croatia's northern neighbor is Slovenia; to the northeast lies Hungary; to the east lies Serbia; to the south lies Bosnia-Herzegovina, with the southernmost tip being bordered by Montenegro; and the Adriatic Sea provides the western boundary. It is situated at 45°10′ N, 15°30′ E. The total area is 56,610 sq km with 56,410 sq km (21,824 sq mi) of land and 200 sq km of water. The land area is larger than Denmark and slightly smaller than West Virginia.

The three major geographic areas of Croatia are the Pannonian, the Peri-Pannonian, and the coastal regions. The coastal belt is primarily karst with dry summers. The highest mountains in Croatia are Biokova in Dalmatia, rising 1762 m abruptly from the narrow sea coast, and Dinara, which is 1831 m high. The hills and mountains

Croatia

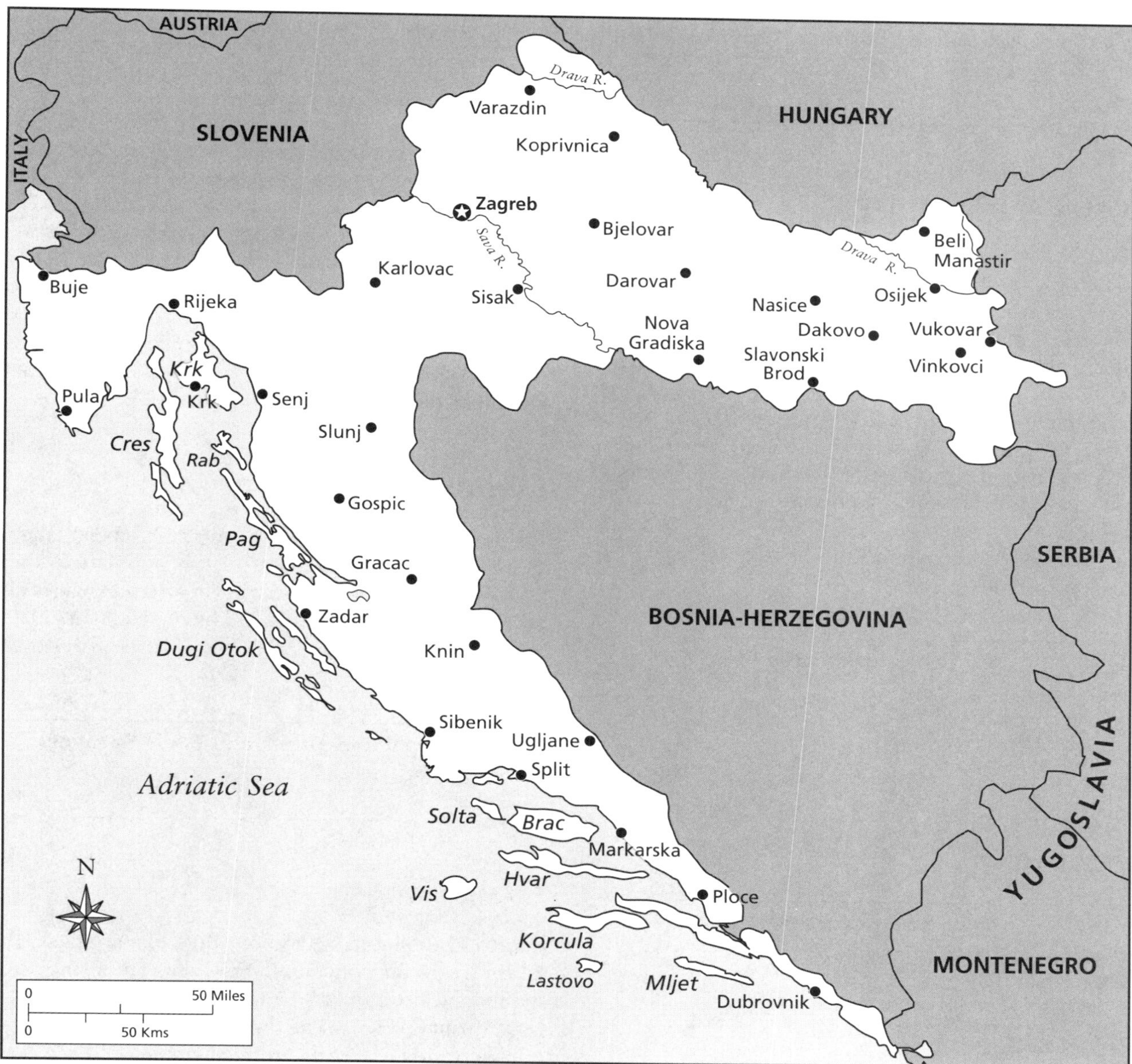

separate Pannonian Croatia from the coastal area. While much of Croatia is above 500 m, there are mainly lowlands in the eastern and northwestern parts of the republic. The lowlands are primarily used to raise livestock and for farming, with forested regions lying in the northwestern hills and valleys.

Much of Croatia's appeal to visitors lies in its 1,185 islands and inlets providing 4,058 km of coastline with 1,777 m of the coastline on the mainland, including several large peninsulas.

Hydrotrade routes utilize the Adriatic Sea as well as the Sava and Darva Rivers. The inland countries of Austria and Hungary transverse Croatia for coastal access.

Geography

Area sq km: 56,610 sq mi 21,857
World Rank: 126th
Land Boundaries, km: Bosnia 932; Hungary 329; Serbia 266; Slovenia 670
Coastline, km: 5,790
Elevation Extremes meters
- Lowest: Adriatic Sea 0
- Highest: Dinara 1,830

Land Use % Arable land: 21
- Permanent Crops: 2
- Permanent Pastures: 20
- Forest and Woodland: 38
- Other: 19

Population of Principal Cities (1991)

Osijek	129,792
Rijeka	167,964
Split	200,459
Zagreb	867,717

CLIMATE AND WEATHER

Croatia has a continental climate in the north and a Mediterranean climate in the central and coastal regions. Croatia's prevailing winds are the bura, jugo, and maestrale. Daily and annual temperature ranges are moderate. The average January temperature in Zagreb is 32°F, 42°F in Dubrovnik, and 37°F in Rijeka. In July the average temperature in Zagreb, Dubrovnik, and Rijeka are 72°F, 83°F, and 82°F, respectively. The Adriatic keeps the coastal region temperate year-round while cold and snow cover the central, mountainous, and northern regions in the winter. Annual precipitation is 35 in, 48 in, and 60.4 in in Zagreb, Dubrovnik, and Rijeka, respectively.

Climate and Weather

Mean Temperature
January 27°F to 37°F
July 61°F to 84°F
Average Rainfall 24.6 in

POPULATION

Population Indicators

Total Population: 1999 4,677,000
World Rank: 115th
Density per sq mi: 214 per sq km 82.6
% of annual growth (1994–99): −0.2
Male %: 48.5
Female %: 51.5
Urban %: 54.3
Age Distribution: % 0–14: 19.4
15–29: 20.7
30–44: 22.7
45–59: 18.3
60–74: 12.9
75 and over: 4.5
Population 2020: 4,469,000
Birth Rate per 1,000: 10.5
Death Rate per 1,000: 10.0
Population Doubling Time (years): —
Infant Mortality Rate per 1,000 live births: 8.9
Rate of Natural Increase per 1,000: −0.1
Total Fertility Rate: 1.5
Expectation of Life (years): Males 68.6
Females 76.0
Marriage Rate per 1,000: 5.3
Divorce Rate per 1,000: 1.0
Total Number of Households: 1,544,000
Average Size of Households: 3.1
% of Illegitimate Children: —
Induced Abortions: —
Rate per 100 live births: —

ETHNIC COMPOSITION

Croatia is one of the most ethnically homogeneous countries in the world, mainly due to the virtual ethnic cleansing conducted during recent wars. As of 1991, Croats constituted 78 percent of the population with Serbs, the next largest ethnic group, constituting 12 percent of the population. Bosnians make up 0.9 percent of the population; Hungarians and Slovenians each account for 0.5 percent of the population, with the remaining 8.1 percent consisting of Roma, Italians, Czechs, Slovaks, Germans, and other minorities.

LANGUAGES

Croatian, a Slavic language, became the official language in 1847. Ninety-six percent of the population speaks Serbo-Croatian. The Serbian and Croatian languages differ by only about 20,000 words and by the fact that Croatian uses Latin letters while Serbian is written with Cyrillic letters.

Principal Languages and Their Speakers

Serbo-Croatian (Croatian)	4,490,000
Other	190,000

RELIGIONS

Roman Catholicism is the norm in Croatia, practiced by 72 percent of the population. Following far behind are the Orthodox Christians with 14.1 percent. There are 1.3 percent Muslim, 0.6 percent Protestant, and 12 percent unknown or other category in the country.

Religious Affiliations

Roman Catholic	3,370,000
Serbian Orthodox	660,000
Sunni Muslim	60,000
Protestant	30,000
Other	560,000

HISTORICAL BACKGROUND

The area now known as Croatia has had a long, tumultuous, and rarely independent history. Greek colonists first populated the Adriatic islands around 400 B.C.E. The Romans began their rule of the eastern Adriatic coast around 100 B.C.E. Croats did not start to arrive until around the year 600. The name Croatia is mentioned for the first time in official documents in 852. Croats point to Tomislav, in 925, as the first Croatian king, who unified the areas of Pannonia and Dalmatia. The last Croatian king, Petar Svacic, died in 1102 and Croatia was subsumed into the Hungarian Kingdom for the next 800 years, with Turkish occupation beginning in 1433. Croatia was ruled as part of the Hungarian Kingdom, including the period the Habsburgs ruled Hungary. The Croatian Assembly voted to accept the Austrian Habsburgs as its ruling dynasty in 1527, ignoring the Hungarian Kingdom's territorial claims, and by 1699 the Turks had largely been driven out of Croatia. Croatia was divided into three territories at this time, with the islands and main coastal areas falling under Venetian rule, mainland Croatia remaining under Habsburg rule, and the Dubrovnik Republic constituting the only independent portion.

By 1815 the brief French rule had been terminated and the former Venetian territory and the Dubrovnik Republic, which had been united with mainland Croatia by Napoléon, were now, like Hungary, under Habsburg rule. In 1848 Croatia expelled the occupying Hungarians while the Hungarians were busy fighting Habsburg domination. All the Croatian provinces were united at this point in history and the Croats aided the Austrians in defeating the Hungarians. As part of Austro-Hungarian punishment for its involvement in World War I, the Treaty of Trianon reallocated the Croatian territory to the artificially created "Kingdom of Serbs, Croats and Slovenes," which was renamed Yugoslavia in 1929.

During World War II Croatian antifascists were led by Josip Broz Tito. Ante Pavelic was the leader of the virtual Nazi puppet state, under the influence of the German and Italian occupation of Yugoslavia. Non-Croats were killed en masse. In 1945 the individual components making up Yugoslavia forced the territory to be renamed the Federative Socialist Republic of Yugoslavia, with Croatia recognized as one of the republics. Forty-five years later, in 1990, Croatia held its first post–World War II multiparty elections and proclaimed Franjo Tudjman its president.

The first decade of Croatian independence (1991–2000) was marked by one of the most violent civil conflicts ever in the region, in which Croatia and Serbia were locked in a bitter struggle to control areas populated by both Serbs and Croats. On June 25, 1991, Croatia declared its independence from Yugoslavia and war with the Serbs of the Yugoslav National Army erupted. Croatia was internationally recognized as an independent nation and joined the United Nations in 1992. In the initial stages of the war a third of Croatian territory had come under Serb control in the 1991–92 fighting. Croatia launched a major military offensive and its troops quickly overran Serb positions in western Slavonia. Serb forces retaliated by shelling Zagreb. In a new offensive Croatian forces overran Serb positions in western Krajina, capturing the capital, Knin, and prompting the mass flight of ethnic Serbs from the region. In the wake of Croatian military successes Croatia was a key participant in the Dayton talks that yielded a Bosnian peace agreement in 1995. Croatia is estimated to have suffered 13,583 deaths (and nearly 40,000 people injured) as well as material damages estimated at $27 billion. Buoyed by military successes the Croatian Democratic Union (HDZ) won the 1995 lower house elections easily. Tudjman died in 1999. The absence of major world figures at his funeral reflected international frustration with Croatia's failure to progress on democratic reforms at home. Vlatko Pavletic served as interim president until elections were held in February 2000, which were won by Stjepan Mesic, leader of the Croatian People's Party. In parliamentary elections held the following January, Tudjman's HDZ was defeated by a center-left coalition of six parties, including the Social Democratic Party and the Social Liberal Party. Ivica Racan of the Social Democratic Party was named prime minister.

CONSTITUTION

Croatia's constitution is dated December 22, 1990. It promotes many basic civil rights and human rights as well as an organizational structure for the government. Croatia has a presidential/parliamentary form of government. The government of the Republic of Croatia consists of a prime minister, deputy prime ministers, ministers, and other members. According to the Croatian constitution, a vote of no confidence in the prime minister or individual government members or the government as a whole requires the approval of at least one-tenth of the House of Representatives. A vote of no confidence in the government may also be requested by the prime minister.

The executive branch consists of the president, who is the head of state. Franjo Tudjman was Croatia's first president upon Croatia's independence from the former Republic of Yugoslavia. Vlatko Pavletic served as acting president after Franjo Tudjman's death in November 1999. Stjepan Mesic was elected in a run-off election on February 7, 2000. Presidential elections are held every five years for a five-year term of office. Croatia has universal suffrage guarantees in its constitution. The prime minister and deputy prime ministers are appointed by the president. The prime minister is subject to a vote of confidence. Croatia's current prime minister is Ivica Racan and the three deputy prime ministers are Goran Granic, Slavko Linic, and Zeljka Antunovic, who were all appointed in 2000.

The legislative branch is composed of a bicameral assembly called the Sabor, which consists of the Zupanijski Dom (House of Counties) and the Zastupnicki Dom (House of Representatives). Five of the House of Counties legislators are presidential appointees with the remaining 63 members elected for four-year terms. The 127 House of Representative members are all elected for four-year terms. A new law passed in October 1999 increased the number of seats from 127 to 151 based on the number of Croatians living outside Croatia. Non-resident

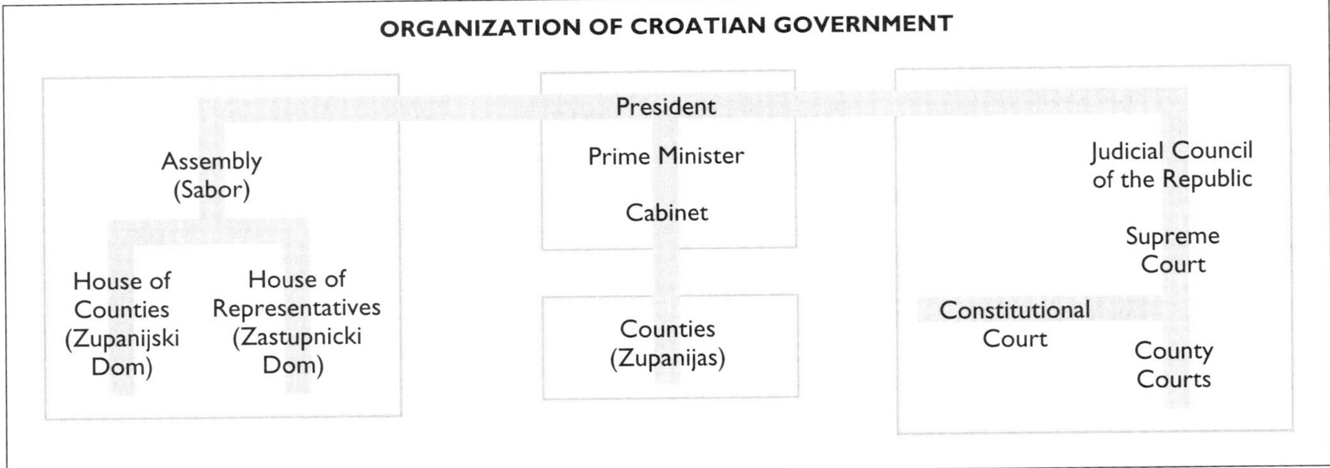

Croatians participating in elections has been highly controversial.

In the judicial branch, the Supreme Court and the Constitutional Court both have judges appointed by the Judicial Council of the Republic for eight-year terms. The Judicial Council is elected by the House of Representatives.

LOCAL GOVERNMENT

Local government exists in the form of municipalities and districts or towns as determined by law. The local self-governments are subordinate to the state administration.

Local administration and self-government territories are called counties. There are 21 administrative counties as well as two self-governing districts, *kotari,* known as Glina and Knin, with these last two being under local Serb control. National minorities with 8 or more percent share in the total population have had the right to self-government in special districts, but as of May 2000 a new constitutional amendment was passed which abolishes this special privilege. Only after a new census is taken will this provision apply.

Although regional and local governments were granted considerable authority by the Croatian constitution over management of their cities, Franco Tudjman's Croatian Democratic Union became more and more autocratic during his tenure from 1990–1999. Fighting the Serbs caused a strengthening of the central government while completely overpowering some local governments with war death tolls, refugee, and other social services problems. This resulted in organizations such as George Soros's Open Society Institute creating facilities like the Croatian Law Center (CLC) in 1994 to promote the rule of law in Croatia through the establishment of legal principles in accord with international standards. The CLC promotes governmental decentralization by helping to revise legislation leading to the reform of local self-government.

Local Government

Principal administrative divisions, capitals, area, population

AREA AND POPULATION

City	Capitals	area sq mi	area sq km	population 1991 census
Zagreb	—	497	1,288	867,717
County				
Bjelovar-Bilogora	Bjelovar	1,019	2,640	144,042
Dubrovnik-Neretva	Dubrovnik	689	1,784	126,329
Istria	Pazin	1,087	2,815	204,346
Karlovac	Karlovac	1,278	3,311	174,105
Kopivnica-Krizevci	Koprimica	688	1,783	129,907
Krapina-Zagorje	Krapina	477	1,235	149,534
Lika-Senj	Gospic	1,447	3,748	71,215
Medimurje	Cakovec	282	730	119,866
Osijek-Baranja	Osijek	1,397	3,619	331,979
Pozenga-Slavonija	Pozega	917	2,374	134,548
Primorje-Gorski Kotar	Rijeka	1,381	3,578	323,130
Sibenik	Sibenik	722	1,871	109,171
Sisak-Moslavina	Sisak	1,976	5,117	287,002
Slavonski Brod-Posavina	Slavonski Brod	782	2,026	174,998
Split-Dalmatia	Split	1,745	4,520	474,019
Varazdin	Varazdin	478	1,238	187,343
Virovitica-Prodravina	Virovitica	798	2,068	104,625
Vukovar-Srijem	Vukovar	943	2,442	231,241
Zadar-Krnin	Zadar	2,453	6,352	272,003
Zagreb	Zagreb	800	2,071	167,145
TOTAL		21,856	56,610	4,784,265

PARLIAMENT

The Croatian parliament, known as the Assembly or the Sabor, consists of the Zupanijski Dom (House of Counties) and the Zastupnicki Dom (House of Representatives or Deputies). The House of Counties consists of 68 members with up to five of these members designated by the president. The remaining members are directly elected by secret ballot with three representatives elected per county. The president becomes a House of Counties member for life at the conclusion of his term in office, unless he expressly renounces this post. The House of Representatives has 151 deputies directly elected by secret ballot.

The representatives of both houses in the Croatian Sabor serve four-year terms. Both houses can be dissolved by majority votes of their members. The president can also dissolve the House of Representatives. Both houses have regular sessions twice each year, first between January 15th and June 30th and then between September 15th and December 15th. Emergency sessions may be called either by the president or a majority of the members of both houses.

The House of Counties proposes bills and the calling of referenda to the House of Representatives. It gives opinions to the House of Representatives on laws and constitutional amendment issues. After the House of Representatives passes a law, the House of Counties may exercise a kind of veto power by returning the law to the House of Representatives, with a substantiated opinion, for fresh consideration and a new vote. The House of Representatives can then only pass the law with a majority vote or a two-thirds vote if the type of law being passed so requires. The House of Representatives amends the constitution, passes laws, adopts state budgets, declares war and peace, decides on national boundary alterations, calls referenda, carries out elections, supervises the government's work, and grants clemency. The chairman of the House of Representatives presides over the Croatian Sabor.

Prior to taking effect, laws are published in Croatia's official gazette, the *Narodine Novine*. Laws are normally promulgated by the president within eight days of passage by the House of Representatives. There must be a justifiable reason to have a different effective date.

The Sabor commissions an ombudsman to protect the constitutional and legal rights of citizens in proceedings before the government and bodies vested with public powers. The House of Representatives elects the ombudsman for an eight-year term.

POLITICAL PARTIES

From the end of World War II to 1990 there was only one authorized political party in Croatia, the Croatian Communist Party, which was designated the League of Communists of Yugoslavia. At the time of the collapse of communism the Croatian Democratic Union (HDZ), led by Franjo Tudjman, won a decisive majority in each of the national assembly chamber. After leading the nation to independence HDZ retained power even after the death of Tudjman in 1999. The principal opposition is the Joint List Bloc formed by a number of smaller parties, including Croatian Peasant Party, Croatian National Party, Croatian Christian Democratic Union, Istrian Democratic Assembly, Croatian Social Liberal Party, and Social Democratic Party. The Joint List Bloc garnered only 18 percent of the popular vote in the 1995 elections.

Political Parties

- Croatian Democratic Union, 1989
- Joint List Bloc, 1995, an alliance of opposition parties including
  - Croatian Peasant Party, 1904
  - Croatian National Party, 1991
  - Croatian Christian Democratic Union, 1992
  - Istrian Democratic Assembly, 1990
  - Croatian Party of Slavonia and Baranja, 1992
- Croatian Social Liberal Party, 1989
- Liberal Party, 1998
- Social Democratic Party, 1937
- Croatian Party of Rights, 1990
- Croatian Independent Democrats, 1994
- Serbian National Party, 1991
- Independent Democratic Serbian Party, 1995
- Alliance of Croatian Coast and Mountains Department, 1990
- Christian Democrats of Meomurje, 1992
- Social Democratic Union, 1992
- Action of the Social Democrats, 1994
- Croatian Party of Rights 1861, 1995
- Croatian Democratic Party, 1989
- Croatian Muslim Democratic Party
- Green Action
- Socialist Workers Party, 1997

Political Parties: Strength in Parliament Most Recent Elections

House of Counties. The most recent elections for three upper house seats per country (for a total of 63 elected members) were held on April 13–15, 1997, and resulted in the following distribution of the elected members: Croatian Democratic Union, 40; Croatian Peasant Party, 9; Croatian Social-Liberal Party, 6; Social Democratic Party of Croatia-Party of Democratic Changes, 4; the Istrian Democratic Assembly, 2; and the Croatian Party of Rights, 2.

House of Representatives. At the elections of January 3, 2000, 151 seats were filled as follows: SDP and HSLS (Social Democratic Party of Croatia, Croatian Social Liberal Party, Primorian-Goranian Union, Slavonian-Baranian Croatian Party), 71 seats; Croatian Democratic Community, 46 seats; United List (Croatian Peasanst's Party, Istrian Democratic Assembly, Liberal Party, Croatian People's Party, Croatian Social Democrat's Action), 25 seats; HSP and HKDU (Croatian Rights Party, Croatian Christian Democratic Union), 5 seats; Serbian National Party, 1 seat; Hungarian Democratic Community of Croatia, 1 seat; nonpartisan representative minorities, 2 seats; and representative Croatians abroad, 6 seats.

LEGAL SYSTEM

The Croatian legal system is based upon civil law, but has some characteristics similar to the American legal system. The Croatian constitution guarantees a presumption of innocence and court trial. Once arrested, persons are entitled to be informed of the charges within the shortest time possible, to be informed of their rights, to assistance of counsel and, like the Fifth Amendment of the United

States Constitution, to not be forced to testify against themselves or to admit guilt. There is also a "double jeopardy" clause preventing someone from being tried twice for the same crime after a sentence has been rendered. The Supreme Court is the highest court of the land. Under the Supreme Court fall the State Judicial Council, the High Commercial Court, the Administrative Court, the Public Prosecutor's Office, the Public Attorney's Office (ombudsman), the Magistrates Court, the County Courts, the Commercial Courts, the County Prosecutors' Offices, and the County Public Attorneys' Offices. Completely separate is the Constitutional Court, which hears cases concerning the legality and constitutionality of elections as well as other constitutional issues.

LAW ENFORCEMENT

Law Enforcement

Offenses reported to the police per 100,000: 1,334
- Murder: 7.4
- Assault: 23.2
- Burglary: 379.8
- Automobile Theft: 20.9
- Population per Police officer: —

Death Penalty: Abolished 1990

HUMAN RIGHTS

Croatia's human rights violations are not new, despite the fact that Croatia adopted the Constitutional Law of Human Rights and Freedoms and the Rights of Ethnic and National Communities or Minorities in December 1991 and amended it in April 1992. This law gives effect to the United Nations treaty obligations on human rights. On November 6, 1992, the United Nations reiterated its concern that since Croatia's declaration of independence, the ongoing territorial disputes had massively violated human rights with significant loss of life, disappearances, summary executions, and torture resulting in the destruction of entire towns and displacement of entire minority populations. The UN also voiced concern over the pervading Croatian military presence, including military members wearing fascist emblems, the constant discrimination and harassment of ethnic Serbs and other minorities within Croatia, and other signs of the ultraright nationalism sweeping through Croatia. In 1998 Croats continued to deny Serbs access to their homes in Croatia, persecuted Serbs and other minorities, and held protest rallies against Serbs. The anti-Serbian protest rally held in Borovo Selo by the ultranationalist Croatian Party of Rights (Hrvatska Stranka Prava, HSP) resulted in a governmental ban on all public demonstrations in eastern Slavonia. In 1998 freedom of the press in Croatia was effectively denied by the lack of an independent newspaper and electronic media and the governmental prosecution of hundreds of newspaper journalists.

The Croatian government's human rights record remained poor in 1999 with serious police brutality issues. The 1999 U.S. *Human Rights Report* critiqued Croatia's national, racial, and ethnic minority situation as follows:

> Constitutionally, ethnic minorities enjoy the same protection as other self-identified ethnic and religious groups. However, in practice a pattern of often open and severe discrimination continues against ethnic Serbs and, at times, other minorities in a wide number of areas, including the administration of justice, employment, housing, and freedom of movement. The Government often maintained a double standard of treatment based on ethnicity. Members of minority groups in principle have equal constitutional protections with Croat citizens, and their ethnic rights are provided for in the preamble to the Constitution.

FOREIGN POLICY

The end of Croatia's so-called Homeland War with Serbia and the death of Tudjman represent the close of an era in Croatian history. With more or less secure borders guaranteed by U.N.–mandated accords, Croatia's goal in foreign relations has changed to gaining international recognition, particularly with Western nations. It has gained admission to the Council of Europe and the Organization for Security and Cooperation in Europe, but the chances of joining either NATO or the European Economic Union (EU) are viewed as more remote. It has a special relationship with the Muslim-dominated Republic of Bosnia and Herzegovina.

DEFENSE

Croatia's military branches include the include Ground Forces, Naval Forces, Air and Air Defense Forces, Frontier Guard, and Home Guard. Males reach military age in Croatia at 19, but there is no conscription.

There are an estimated 1,189,000 males between the ages of 15–49 with 944,000 of them fit for military service. Approximately 34,000 males turn 19 annually. Croatia spends roughly $950,000,000 annually on its military, which is about 5 percent of Croatia's gross domestic product.

Military Indicators

Total Active Duty Personnel: 58,000

Military Manpower per 1,000: 12.1

Military Expenditures $million: 950
- as % of GNP: 5
- per capita $: —
- as % of central government expenditures: —

Arms Imports $: 110
Arms Exports $: 0

ECONOMY

In 1998 Croatia was the second most prosperous area of the former Republic of Yugoslavia. Now Croatia is struggling with economic problems caused by long-term communist mismanagement, infrastructure damage suffered during recent wars, huge displaced populations of refugees, both entering and exiting Croatia, and the dissolution of some Western funding. While the government under Franjo Tudjman partially stabilized some of the economy on a macroeconomic level and normalized creditor relations, privatization is not progressing as rapidly as it should since independence roughly a decade ago. Tudjman's government placed four commercial banks under its control and others are threatened by bankruptcy. In 1997 Croatia's account deficit accounted for about 12 percent of the gross domestic product, with that figure being reduced to 8 percent the following year. The economy emerged from its mild recession in 2000, with tourism the main income generator. Massive unemployment remains a key negative element. Croatia is relying on more Western aid being invested to help restore the economy and, with the election of the first post-Tudjman government, efforts to secure large-scale Western finance have begun.

Principal Economic Indicators

Gross National Product $: 19.343 billion
GNP per capita: $4,060
GNP Average Annual Growth Rate (1990–97) %: 2.7
GNP per capita Average Annual Growth Rate (1990–97) %: 2.7
Origin of Gross Domestic Product %
- Agriculture: 11
- Mining: —
- Manufacturing: 28
- Construction: 2
- Public Utilities: —
- Transportation and Communications: 4
- Trade: 16
- Financial Services: 8
- Other Services: 30
- Government: 30

Gross Domestic Product by Type of Expenditure %
- Private Consumption: 71
- Government Consumption: 27
- Gross Domestic Investment: 3
- Foreign Trade: Exports: 1
- Imports: 1

% of Income Received by Poorest 20%: —
% of Income Received by Richest 10%: —

Price Index (1995 = 100)

	1993	1994	1995	1996	1997	1998	1999
Consumer price index	46.4	96.2	100.0	104.3	108.6	115.6	120.8
Annual earnings index	29	69	100	112	131	147	167

Finance

National Currency: Kuna (HRK)
Exchange Rate: $ 1 = HRK 6.359
Money Supply Stock in National Currency billion: 10,683
M1 per capita: 2,240
Central Bank Discount Rate %: 7.90
Total External Debt $million: 5,904
Debt Service Ratio %: 6.7
Balance of Payments $million: −2342.7
International Reserves SDRs million: —
Ratio of External Debt to Total Reserves: —
Average Annual Rate of Inflation/Consumer Price Index Growth Rate %: 3.7

Official Development Assistance

ODA $million: 39
- as % of GNP: 0.2
- per capita: $9
- Foreign Direct Investment $million: 873

Central Government Revenues and Expenditures

Fiscal Year: Calendar Year
Revenues $million: 5,300
Expenditures $million: 6,300
Budget Deficit $million: 1,000
Tax Revenues as % of GDP: 43.3
Highest Tax Bracket %
- Individual: 35
- Corporate: —

Employment and Labor

Economically Active Population: 2,040,000
Female Participation Rate %: 42.9
Activity Rate %: 45.3
Labor by Sector: %
- Agriculture, Forestry, Fishing: 16.7
- Manufacturing, Mining: 28.0
- Construction: 4.5
- Transportation and Communications: 5.5
- Trade, Hotels, and Restaurants: 10.9
- Finance, Insurance, Real Estate: 2.8
- Public Administration, Defense: 5.1
- Services: 10.0

Unemployment %: 15.9

Agriculture

Agriculture's Share of GDP %: 11
Average Annual Rate of Growth (1965–98) %: —
Number of Farms 000: 569
Average Size of Farm ha: —
Number of Tractors per 1,000 hectares: 3.6
Irrigation, % of Farms having: 0.3
Artificial Fertilizer kg/hectare: —
Total Farmland as % of land area: 57.0
Livestock: Cattle 000: 443
- Sheep 000: 427
- Hogs 000: 1,166
- Chickens 000: 9,959

Forests: Production of Roundwood (000 cubic meters): 33.7
Fisheries: Total Catch tons 000: 21.4

Mining

% of GDP: —
Value of Mineral Production $million: 119.7

Manufacturing

Value Added $million: 5,227
Industrial Production Growth Rate %: 0

Energy

Commercial Energy Production metric tons of oil equivalent 000: 4,011
Commercial Energy Consumption metric tons of oil equivalent 000: 7,650
Commercial Energy Consumption per capita kg: 1,687
Average Annual Growth Rate 1980–97 %: —
Net Energy Imports % of use: 48
Electricity Installed Capacity kW 000: 3,633
Production kW-hr million: 8,863
Coal Reserves tons million: 39
Production tons 000: 108
Natural Gas Proven Reserves cubic meters billion: 22
Production cubic meters million: 1,869
Crude Petroleum Reserves barrels million: 55
Production barrels million: 12
Consumption barrels million: 37
Refinery Capacity barrels per day 000: 294
Pipelines Length km: 690

Foreign Trade

Imports $million: 7,787.8
Exports $million: 4,511.7
Export Volume % Annual Growth Rate (1990–97): —
Import Volume % Annual Growth Rate (1990–97): —

Balance of trade (current prices)

	1993	1994	1995	1996	1997	1998
U.S.						
$ 000,000	−763	−969	−2,877	−3,276	−4,782	−3,837
% of total	8.9%	10.2%	23.7%	26.6%	35.5%	29.7%

Major Trading Partners

	Imports	Exports
European Union %	59.4	51.0
United States %	2.7	2.0
Eastern Europe %	10.5	7.9
Japan %	1.3	—
Others %	20.1	39.0

Transportation

Roads Total Length mi: 16,732 km 26,928
Paved %: 81
Automobiles: 710,910
Trucks and Buses: 77,394
Persons per vehicle: 6.0
Railroad; Track Length mi: 1,676 km 2,699
Passenger-mi million: 598
Freight-mi million: 1,071
Merchant Marine: No. of Vessels: 203
Total Deadweight Tonnage 000: 140.9
International Cargo Loaded tons 000: 3,948
International Cargo Off-loaded tons 000: 7,776
Airports with Scheduled Flights: 5
Traffic: Passenger-mi million: 306
Freight-mi million: 2.4
Length of Canals mi: 468 km 785

Tourism

Number of Tourists to 000: 4,112
Number of Tourists from 000: —
Tourist Receipts $million: 1,584
Tourist Expenditures $million: 771

Communications

Telephones 000: 1,287
Cost of Local Calls 3 mins: $0.03
Cellular Telephones 000: 34
Fax Machines 000: 38
Personal Computers 000: 100
Internet Hosts per million persons: 515
Mail: Post Offices: 1,190
Pieces of Mail Handled million: 262
Pieces of Mail Handled per person: 58

EDUCATION

Croatia is thought to have an excellent educational system. There is universal public education for all children, and the quality is uniform throughout the country, regardless of the urban, suburban, or rural environment. Part of the proof of the success of Croatia's educational system is in its literacy rate of 96 percent. Croatians determine their career paths by their high school selection of either trade school or college preparatory school (*gimnazija*). The trade schools prepare students for technical and practical careers such as nursing, machine construction, and tourism while those in the gimnazija prepare for university. Croatia has universities in Split, Rijeka, Osijek, and Zagreb. Zagreb University was founded in 1669. Croatia also has colleges in Zadar and Pula. Colleges are considered less specialized than universities, and offer degrees in subjects like teaching rather than subjects like languages, law, or medicine. Croatian universities tend to not have attendance-based courses and many Croatian university students work full time, going to their universities to take final examinations (traditionally oral) at the end of each semester.

Education

Literacy Rate %: 96.7
Male %: 98.8
Female %: 94.8
First Level: Primary schools: 1,928
Teachers: 24,194
Students: 431,795

Student-Teacher Ratio: 17.8
Net Enrollment Ratio: 8.2
Second Level: Secondary Schools: 482
Teachers: 15,269
Students: 196,740
Student-Teacher Ratio: 12.9
Net Enrollment Ratio: 66.0
Vocational Level: Schools: 3
Students: 2,660
Third Level: Institutions: 61
Teachers: 5,814
Students: 77,525
Student-Ratio Level: 13.3
Gross Enrollment Ratio: 28.3
Students per 100,000: 1,917
% of Population Age 25 and over with Postsecondary Education: 6.4
Public Expenditure on Education as % of GDP: 5.3

SCIENCE AND TECHNOLOGY

Science and Technology

Scientists and Engineers in R&D per 1 million persons: 1,916
Expenditures in R&D as % of GDP: 1.03
High-Tech Exports $million: 266
Patent Applications by Residents: 273

MEDIA

Croatian media are still subject to state suppression. Tudjman's government forced newspaper workers out of their offices at gunpoint, fined and taxed newspapers out of business, and used other tactics to suppress negative comments about the government. The Croatian government exercises strict controls over the national television and radio stations and four of the five daily newspapers in the country. The government flooded the newspaper market with new newspapers in the hopes that this would financially force the independent papers out of business. These new newspapers have limited appeal and would not survive without government funding.

Media

Daily Newspapers: 6
Total Circulation 000: 2,600
Circulation per 1,000: 575
Books Published: 2,671
Magazines: 352
Radio Receivers 000: 1,100
per 1,000: 230
Television sets 000:1,100
per 1,000: 230

MOST IMPORTANT MEDIA:

Press. The following are dailies published in Serbo-Croat: *Vecernji List* (Evening Paper, Zagreb, 200,000); *Slobodna Dalmacija* (Free Dalmatia, Split, 110,000); *Novi List* (New Paper, Rijeka, 60,000); *Vjesnik* (Courier, Zagreb, 50,000); *Novi Vjesnik* (New Courier, Zagreb, 45,000); *Glas Slavonije* (Slavonia News, Osijek, 25,000); *Glas Istre* (Istrian News, Pula, 18,000).

Radio and television. Croatian Radio-Television (Hrvatska Radiotelevizija) broadcasts in Serbo-Croat over three radio stations and two television channels, while two commercial television channels (OTV and Marjan) also operate. There were approximately 1.3 million radio and 1.2 million TV sets in 1998.

After a long dispute with the government and a demonstration by 100,000 supporters in November 1996, independent Radio 101 received a five-year license in November 1997. Also in November 1997, Radio Vukovar resumed broadcasting in the eastern Slavonian city for the first time since it fell to a Serbian assault six years earlier.

CULTURE

Cultural Indicators

Public Libraries Number: 232
Volumes: 4,606
Registered borrowers: 7,080
Museums Number: 143
Annual Attendance: —
Cinema Production of Long Films: 6
Number of Cinemas: 147
Seating Capacity: —
Annual Attendance: —
Annual Attendance per capita: —

STATUS OF WOMEN

Although the government collects only limited statistics on the problem, informed observers believe that violence against women, including spousal abuse, remains common. One nongovernmental organization (NGO) that operates a hot line and support services for women assessed that spousal abuse continues to be a large and unrecognized problem. Alcohol abuse and poor economic circumstances for veterans of the military conflict are cited as contributing factors. A government commission on equality indicated to NGOs that it would recommend that the government track statistics on violence against women; however, this has not been done.

Amendments to the Penal Code that went into effect in 1998 removed violence perpetrated within the family (except against children) from the categories of crimes to be prosecuted automatically by the state attorney. The victim now must file a request to prosecute, thereby severely curtailing efforts by health care workers and police to act on suspected cases of violence in the home. The Constitutional Court upheld the constitutionality of this procedure. The nonpartisan Parliamentary Women's Caucus promised to seek amendments of these laws but has not yet done so.

Based on anecdotal evidence, it is likely that some women are trafficked for the purpose of forced prostitution.

Sexual harassment is a violation of the penal code section on abuse of position but is not specifically included in the employment law. NGOs reported that in practice, women generally do not resort to the penal code for relief for fear of losing their jobs. In a positive development, the labor union of the Pliva pharmaceutical company signed a collective agreement that specifically forbids sexual harassment.

The law does not discriminate by gender. However, in practice women generally hold lower paying positions in the workforce. Government statistics from previous years showed that, while women constitute roughly 50 percent of the workforce, they occupy few jobs at senior levels, even in areas such as education and administration, where they are a clear majority of the workers. Considerable anecdotal evidence has suggested that women hold by far the preponderance of low-level clerical and shopkeeping positions, as well as primary and secondary school teaching jobs. Women reportedly are often among the first to be fired or laid off. NGOs and labor organizations report a practice in which women received short-term work contracts renewable every three to six months, creating a climate of job insecurity for them. While men occasionally suffer from this practice, it is disproportionately used against women to dissuade them from taking maternity leave. Legislation was passed in 1998 limiting the use of short-term work contracts to a maximum of three years.

While there is no national organization devoted solely to the protection of women's rights, many small, independent groups are active in the capital and larger cities. One of the most active was B.a.B.e. (Be active, Be emancipated).

Women

Gender Empowerment Measure: 30
Seats Held in Parliament by Women %: 16.2
Female Administrators and Managers %: 26
Female Professional and Technical Workers %: 52
Women's Share of Earned Income %: 55
Women in Government %: 19

HEALTH, FOOD, AND NUTRITION

Health

Number of Physicians: 9,138
Number of Dentists: 1,798
Number of Nurses: —
Number of Pharmacists: 1,598
Population per Physician: 524
Number of Hospitals: 84
Hospital Beds per 10,000: 59
Hospital Bed Occupancy Rate: 81.6
Infant Mortality Rate per 1,000 live births: 16
Maternal Mortality Rate per 100,000 live births: —
Total Health Expenditures as % of GDP: —
Health Expenditures per capita $: —
HIV Infected % of adults: 0.01
Cigarette Consumption per smoker per year: —
% of Smokers: Male: —
Female: —
Access to Safe Water %: 96

Food and Nutrition

Food Supply as % of FAO Requirements: 95
% of Consumption Expenditures on Food: 37
Daily Available Calories per capita: 2,413
% of Total Calories derived from:
Cereals: 30.2
Potatoes, cassava: 7.0
Meat, poultry: 5.9
Fish: 0.2
Eggs, milk: 12.0
Fruits, vegetables: 6.8
Fats, oils: 12.8

ENVIRONMENT

Mortality from respiratory diseases is twice as high in large cities as in small ones and it is three times higher in larger cities than it is in rural areas. Air pollution has also damaged the country's forests and nearly one-fourth of the trees are moderately to severely defoliated. Air pollution is compounded by the country's heavy reliance under Tito on brown coal and lignite. Thermal power plants are among the biggest contributors to air and water pollution. As a result the country's monuments are showing signs of irreversible deterioration. Over one-half of the country's soil is subject to erosion because of improper cultivation on steep lands.

Environment

Forest Area sq km: 18,000
Average Annual Deforestation sq km: 0
Nationally Protected Areas as % of Total Land Area: 6.6
Freshwater Access cubic meters per capita: 15,863
Emissions of Organic Water Pollutants kg per day: 50,014
CO_2 Emissions per capita ton: 3.9

CHRONOLOGY

1941 Germany and Italy set up the so-called Independent State of Croatia, run by the Croat Ustase regime of Ante Pavelic; the Ustase begin the expulsion and extermination of Serbs, Jews, Gypsies, and antifascist Croats, killing more than 500,000; the communist Partisans, led by ethnic Croat Josep Broz Tito, organize resistance against the Ustase and their Axis supporters.

1944 Partisan control of Croatian territory, except for the major cities, is nearly complete; Partisans retaliate against anti-Partisan Croats, slaughtering tens of thousands.

1945 Both World War II and the Croatian civil war end; the Yugoslavia Socialist Federation is formed, led by Marshall Tito, consisting of six republics: Croatia, Slovenia, Bosnia-Herzegovina, Serbia, Montenegro, and Macedonia.

1948 Tito breaks relations with the Soviet Union; Tito replaces Croatian-nationalist members of the Croatian Communist Party with centralist officials of his own choosing.

1969 Efforts at decentralization by the Yugoslavian federal government fuel a cultural flowering in Croatia known as the "Croatian Spring," a movement that gained nationalist momentum under the reformist leadership of Miko Tripalo and Savka Dabcevic-Kucar.

1971 Tito responds to calls for greater Croatian autonomy by dismissing and/or imprisoning numerous intellectual and cultural leaders, including Tripalo, Dabcevic-Kucar, and members of the cultural organization Matica Hravatska.

1974 Yugoslavia adopts a new republican constitution but undermines the autonomy nominally granted to Croatia by continuing to exercise centralized control of the Croatian Communist Party.

1980 Tito dies; Yugoslavia's economy takes a turn for the worse.

1985 Yugoslavia's economic crisis hits its nadir, with production and living standards at 1965 levels.

1988 Slobodan Milosevic, the president of Serbia, embarks on a campaign to recentralize Yugoslavia.

1989 Croatia, along with Slovenia, resists centralization and calls for its own multiparty elections.

1990 In the first multiparty national elections since World War II, the Communist Party is defeated by the Croatian Democratic Union (HDZ), a conservative nationalist party led by Franjo Tudjman; President Tudjman's administration begins to purge Serbs from positions of authority, prompting fear among Serbs of a reprise of the ethnic cleansing campaigns of the 1940s.

1991 Serb-dominated Krajina in the southwest secedes from Croatia to join with Serbia; Croatia declares independence; civil war breaks out in Krajina between ethnic Serbs and ethnic Croats; the government of Yugoslavia declares war on Croatia, bombs the cities of Vukovar and Dubrovnik, and occupies about one-third of Croatian territory.

1992 The UN dispatches 14,000 peace-keeping troops to Croatia; the European Community and the United States recognize Croatia's independence; Croatia supports Croats against Serbs and Muslims in the war in Bosnia-Herzegovina; Tudjman is reelected to a five-year term as president of Croatia.

1995 Tudjman, Milosevic, and President Alija Izetbegovic of Bosnia-Herzegovina sign a peace accord in Dayton, Ohio, ending the war in Bosnia-Herzegovina; Croatia reasserts control over Krajina, leading to a mass exodus of Croatian Serbs; the HDZ dominates legislative elections but loses seats.

1997 Tudjman is reelected, but independent election monitors criticize his control over the media and curtailed minority suffrage.

1998 After two years under UN supervision, Eastern Slavonia and Baranja are returned to Croatian control.

1999 Tudjman dies and is succeeded by Vlatko Pavletic as acting president.

2000 Stjepan Mesic, leader of the Croatian People's Party, is elected president, ending HDZ rule.

BIBLIOGRAPHY

Covic, Boze, ed. *Croatia between War and Independence*. Zagreb, Croatia, 1991.

"Croatia." *World Geographical Encyclopedia*. Milan, 1995.

"Croatia." *The CIA World Factbook*. Washington, D.C., 1997.

Gazi, Stephen. *A History of Croatia*. New York, 1993.

Goldstein, Ivo. *Croatia: A History*. London, 1999.

Institute for Social Research. *Croatian Society on the Eve of Transition*. Zagreb, Croatia, 1993.

Tanner, Marcus. *Croatia: A Nation Forged in War*. New Haven, Conn., 1997.

OFFICIAL PUBLICATIONS

Croatia. *Census of Population, Households, Dwellings and Farms 31st March 1991; Statistical Yearbook.*

CONTACT INFORMATION

Embassy of Croatia
2343 Massachusetts Avenue NW
Washington, D.C. 20008
Phone: (202) 588-5899 Fax: (202) 588-8936

INTERNET RESOURCES

- Central Bureau of Statistics
  http://www.dzs.hr/Eng/Default.htm
- Ministry of Foreign Affairs
  http://www.mvp.hr/mvprh-www-eng/home-eng.html

CUBA

BASIC FACT SHEET

OFFICIAL NAME:
Republic of Cuba (República de Cuba)

ABBREVIATION:
CU

CAPITAL:
Havana

HEAD OF STATE & HEAD OF GOVERNMENT:
President of the State Council, Chairman of the Council of Ministers, and First Secretary of the Communist Party of Cuba Fidel Castro Ruz (president from 1976; prime minister from 1959)

NATURE OF GOVERNMENT:
One-party communist dictatorship

POPULATION:
11,159,000 (1999)

AREA:
114,520 sq km (44,216 sq mi)

ETHNIC MAJORITY:
Mulatto

LANGUAGE:
Spanish

RELIGION:
Roman Catholicism

UNIT OF CURRENCY:
Peso

NATIONAL FLAG:
Three blue and two white horizontal stripes on which a red equilateral triangle containing a white five-pointed star is superimposed on the hoist side.

NATIONAL EMBLEM:
A shield flanked by branches of oak and laurel. The upper portion of the shield is a seascape containing a blue green channel between two rocky promontories with a sun on the horizon. Suspended between the two headlands is a key memorializing the designation "Key to the Gulf of Mexico," applied to Cuba by the Spanish monarchs. The lower half of the shield is divided between a blue-and-white-striped design and a royal palm between two conical mountains. The shield is crested by a red wool cap on a liberty pole rising from a fasces of bound rods.

NATIONAL ANTHEM:
"March to the Battle, People of Bayamo"

NATIONAL HOLIDAYS:
May 20 (Independence Day); January 1 (New Year's Day); January 2 (Day of the Revolution); February 24 (Proclamation of Baire); May 1 (Labor Day); July 26 (Attack on Moncada Fort); October 10 (Proclamation of Yara); December 7 (Day of National Mourning); December 24 and 25 (Christmas); also Holy. Thursday and Good Friday

DATE OF INDEPENDENCE:
May 20, 1902

DATE OF CONSTITUTION:
February 14, 1976, amended July 1992

GEOGRAPHICAL FEATURES

The island of Cuba is located on the northern rim of the Caribbean Sea about 150 km (90 mi) south of Key West. It is the largest of the West Indian islands with one-half of the land area of the West Indies. In addition to the main island, the archipelago includes the Isla de la Juventud (formerly the Isle of Pines), near the south coast, in the Gulf of Batabano and some 1,600 coastal cays and islets. The main island, which occupies 94.7 percent of the national territory, extends 1,223 km (760 mi) east to west and 89 km (55 mi) north to south. The remaining territory comprises Isla de la Juventud and numerous small islets and cays. The total coastline stretches 3,235 km (2,010 mi).

Cuba

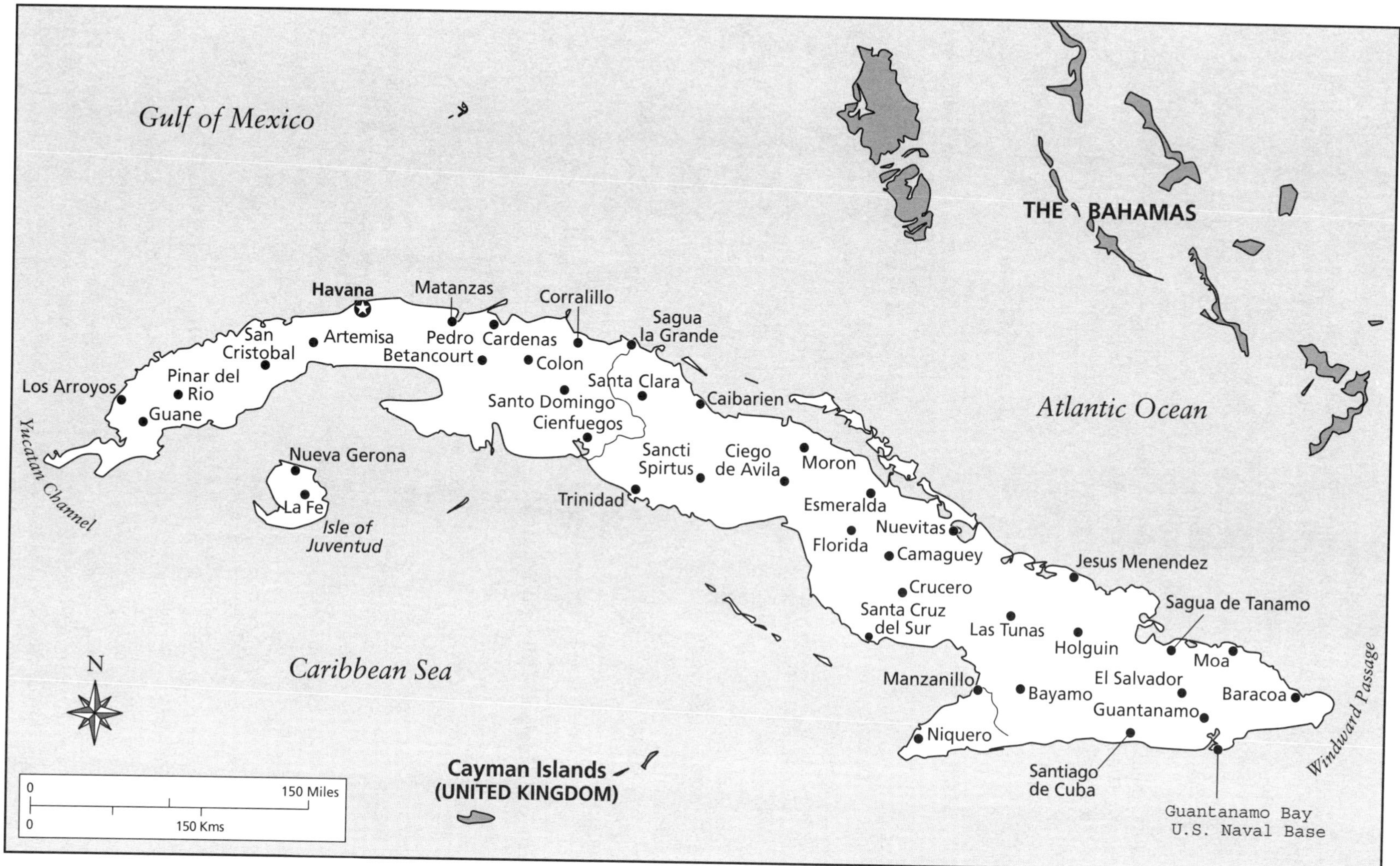

Gulf of Mexico
THE BAHAMAS
Atlantic Ocean
Caribbean Sea
Yucatan Channel
Windward Passage
Havana
Matanzas
Corralillo
Sagua la Grande
San Cristobal
Artemisa
Pedro Betancourt
Cardenas
Colon
Los Arroyos
Pinar del Rio
Guane
Santa Clara
Caibarien
Santo Domingo
Cienfuegos
Nueva Gerona
La Fe
Isle of Juventud
Sancti Spirtus
Ciego de Avila
Moron
Trinidad
Esmeralda
Nuevitas
Florida
Camaguey
Jesus Menendez
Crucero
Santa Cruz del Sur
Las Tunas
Holguin
Sagua de Tanamo
Moa
Manzanillo
Bayamo
El Salvador
Baracoa
Guantanamo
Niquero
Santiago de Cuba
Guantanamo Bay U.S. Naval Base
Cayman Islands (UNITED KINGDOM)
N
0
150 Miles
0
150 Kms

Topographically Cuba consists of flatlands and rolling plains making up two-thirds of the national territory, and three mountain systems making up the remainder. The largest of the mountain ranges is the Sierra Maestra including Cuba's highest peak, Pico Turquino (1,993 m, 6,539 ft), and also minor ranges, such as Sierra Cristal and Cuchillas de Toa. The central mountain system includes the Escambray Mountains, Sierra de Trinidad, and Sierra de Sancti Spíritus. The third mountain system consists of the western highlands, Sierra del Rosario and Sierra de los Organos. The lowlands include valleys, such as the Central Valley, and swamps, such as the Zapata Swamp.

Cuba has more than 200 rivers as well as small streams and arroyos that are dry during the summer. The longest river is the Cauto, which flows into the Gulf of Guacanayabo after flowing about 370 km (230 mi) from the Sierra Maestra.

Geography

Area sq km: 114,520 sq mi 44,216
World Rank: 104th
Land Boundaries, km: US Naval Base Guantanamo 29
Coastline, km: 3,235
Elevation Extremes meters
- Lowest: Caribbean Sea 0
- Highest: Pico Turquino 1,993

Land Use % Arable land: 24
- Permanent Crops: 7
- Permanent Pastures: 27
- Forest and Woodland: 24
- Other: 18

Population of Principal Cities (1994 est.)

Bayamo	137,663
Camagüey	293,961
Cienfuegos	132,038
Guantánamo	207,796
Havana	2,241,000
Holguín	242,085
Las Tunas	126,930
Manzanillo	107,650
Matanzas	123,843
Pinar del Río	128,570
Santa Clara	205,400
Santiago de Cuba	440,084

CLIMATE AND WEATHER

Although situated entirely in the Tropic Zone, the moderating influence of trade winds gives Cuba a temperate, semitropical climate. There are two seasons: the dry one, lasting from November to April, and the wet season, from May through October. The country's moderate rainfall is generally well distributed, but about 75 percent of the precipitation occurs in the wet season when there are heavy downpours of short duration. Pinar del Río receives the most rainfall with the amount diminishing progressively toward the east. Cuba lies in the southern track of maximum frequency of the tropical hurricane belt, and the island experiences at least one hurricane every other year.

Climate and Weather

Mean Temperature 70°F to 81°F
Havana 77°F
Average Rainfall: Mountains 70 in
Lowlands 35 in to 55 in
Easternmost areas 25 in

POPULATION

Population Indicators

Total Population: 1999 11,159,000
World Rank: 66th
Density per sq mi: 260.7 per sq km 100.7
% of annual growth (1994–99): 0.5
Male %: 50.3
Female %: 49.7
Urban %: 74.4
Age Distribution: %
- 0–14: 22.3
- 15–29: 29.4
- 30–44: 31.3
- 45–59: 14.8
- 60–74: 8.4
- 75 and over: 3.9

Population 2020: 11,744,000
Birth Rate per 1,000: 13.5
Death Rate per 1,000: 7.2
Population Doubling Time (years): —
Infant Mortality Rate per 1,000 live births: 8.0
Rate of Natural Increase per 1,000: 6.3
Total Fertility Rate: 1.8
Expectation of Life (years): Males 73.9
Females 77.6
Marriage Rate per 1,000: 17.7
Divorce Rate per 1,000: 6.0
Total Number of Households: 2,860,000
Average Size of Households: 3.7
% of Illegitimate Children: —
Induced Abortions: 124,059
- Rate per 100 live births: 71.3

ETHNIC COMPOSITION

In 1994, the ethnic composition was estimated to be mixed race, 51 percent; white, 37 percent; black, 11 percent; and other (mostly Chinese) 1 percent. Ethnic data is no longer reported in census figures, and these percentages are extrapolated from 1950s data.

The basic racial stock of the mestizo or mulattos (these terms are interchangeable in Cuba, although strictly mestizo refers to a person of Spanish and Native American parentage and mulatto to a person of Spanish and black parentage) and the whites (known as criollos) is Spanish. For over 400 years Spanish immigrants from all regions of Spain, especially Andalusia, formed the dominant social, economic, and political class, imposing Spanish standards on all walks of life. Even mestizos were oriented toward criollo society and upward mobility was associated with white physical and cultural traits.

The blacks are descendants of slaves imported into Cuba from 1517 to 1865 (when the slave trade was officially abolished) from all parts of West Africa but particularly Yoruba (Lucumi) and Calabar (Carabalies), both in what is now Nigeria. The black population, now known as Afro-Cubans, also includes some Haitians and Jamaicans. The African impact on Cuban life is most evident in music, literature, and religious cults.

The two other ethnic minorities are the Chinese (known as amarillos or Orientals) and eastern Mediterranean and German Jews, the former referred to as turcos, because they came from provinces of the Ottoman Empire. Large expatriate communities existed in Havana and the larger cities before the revolution, including Haitian, French, Irish, Japanese, British, Canadians, and Americans. Few of these remained on the island after the revolution. The majority of the inhabitants of Isla de la Juventud once spoke English.

Traditionally, racial origin and ethnicity have been considered important in Cuba, and society was divided along lines of class and color, with the blacks forming the disadvantaged and poorest class. Racial tensions continued to exist as long as the blacks remained in the majority, and there were race riots as late as 1912 when over 3,000 blacks were killed. Interpersonal relations were based on stereotyped perceptions of blacks as lazy, ignorant, and uncouth. There were also fears on the part of whites of absorption by blacks, and these fears were only dispelled in the 1940s through stepped-up immigration of white Europeans. Another positive factor in race relations was the rise in influence of the mestizos who represented the national integration of races. Nationalist Cubans upheld the virtues of mestizos against the upper-class white supremacists, and Castro has declared that all Cubans are mestizo in spirit. After the revolution, Castro tried deliberately to build a fluid and de-ethnicized society by stressing Cubanness and racial blends as opposed to rigid categorization. Increased homogenization also resulted from the fact that most of the refugees from Cuba during this period belonged to the upper-class white communities. Discrimination on the basis of race has been eliminated by law and, to a large extent, moderated in practice. The government's economic and agrarian reforms and the campaign against illiteracy have helped to bridge the gap between the races. However, these efforts have drawn fire from both blacks and whites. The blacks have claimed that the trend is not toward a true integration of races but toward the assimilation of blacks into the white culture, and the whites have resented the loss in jobs and prestige through competition with blacks. Racial inequalities have not been entirely eradicated and still survive not only in interpersonal attitudes and relations but also in more crucial areas of public life. There are few blacks in the higher echelons of government, the Communist Party, or the media.

LANGUAGES

Spanish is the official language, spoken by virtually the entire population. Cuban Spanish has been described as "disfigured Castillian" and is generally spoken with a slurred accent associated with Andalusian speech. The vocabulary includes many words of Indian, African, and English origins. Under Castro all names of public places and institutions have been cubanized, particularly those that were associated with U.S. interests.

Principal Languages and Their Speakers

Spanish	11,159,000

RELIGIONS

Afro-Cuban religions, a blend of native African religions and Roman Catholicism, are widely practiced in Cuba. Officially, Cuba has been an atheist state for most of the Castro era. Prior to the revolution Roman Catholicism was predominant, although permeated by Santería (a native African religion) and rather weak in rural areas. In the early 1960s church and state confronted one another with open hostility, the church seeing the revolutionary government as antireligious and the government seeing the church as a potential source of counterrevolution. In 1962, the government seized and shut down more than 400 Catholic schools, and expelled many clergy. The 1976 constitution proclaimed scientific materialism as the base of the state and education but recognized and guaranteed religious freedom, although with restrictions. By the 1980s both the church and the government had made some concessions and had entered a period of rapprochement. In 1992 the constitution was amended to characterize the state as secular instead of atheist. The Catholic Church is the largest independent institution in Cuba today, but continues to operate under significant pressure. The Cuban government continues to refuse to allow the church to have independent printing press capabilities, to have full access to the media, or to establish institutions, such as local schools.

In November 1996, President Castro invited Pope John Paul II to visit Cuba after agreement was reached allowing the church to carry out its religious activities in preparation for the visit. In 1997 Christmas was officially recognized as a holiday for the first time since 1969 and the following year was permanently reinstated as a national holiday. During the pope's visit, the Cuban government permitted four open-air masses, provided media coverage, and assisted with transportation of the public to the masses. While on the island, January 21–25 1998, Pope John Paul II spoke of broadening the space and freedom of action of the Catholic Church and asked Fidel Castro to grant a prisoner amnesty. The Cuban government responded by freeing at least 300 prisoners, some 70 of which were being held on political charges. Other Cuban religious groups have also benefited from the increased openness toward religion. A small Jewish congregation survives in Havana, Santiago, Camagüey, and other parts of the island.

Religious Affiliations	
Roman Catholic	4,410,000
Other (mostly nonreligious and atheist)	6,750,000

HISTORICAL BACKGROUND

Prior to Christopher Columbus's visit in 1492, Cuba was inhabited by various indigenous groups, who were unable to resist the Spanish invaders. The conquest began in 1511 led by Diego de Velázquez, and Cuba then served as the staging post for expeditions to the rest of the Americas. British and French buccaneers targeted the Spanish fleets regularly during this period. Native population declined rapidly under Spanish rule, through violence and disease, and was replaced with African slaves. In 1762, Cuba was briefly taken by a British force led by George Pocock, but returned to Spanish rule in 1763. While the rest of Latin America sought independence during the early 19th century, Cuba remained in Spanish hands and uprisings were brutally supressed. By 1868, popular unrest spilled over into the Ten Years' War, ended by truce in 1878 with reforms promised by Spain. Failure to deliver on these promises prompted another revolt in 1895, led by José Martí. The United States sympathized with the rebels, and when the USS *Maine* was sunk in Havana harbor the Spanish-American War broke out.

When the war ended, in 1898, the United States established a military government on the island, and although occupation and direct rule ended in 1902, bad feelings developed early between Americans and Cuban patriots and were exacerbated by the reported arrogance and racism of U.S. troops and war correspondents. The United States also imposed humiliating conditions on Cuba as it worked toward independence. These conditions provided that Cuba permit no foreign bases (except those of the United States), lease in perpetuity to the United States the naval base at Guantánamo, accept the acts of the military government as legitimate, omit Isla de la Juventud from national boundaries, and give the United States the right to intervene in Cuba for any of various reasons, including the protection of life, property, and individual liberty. These conditions, known as the Platt Amendment (after U.S. Senator Orville Platt), were in force until they were revoked in 1934. During this period of semi-independence as an American protectorate, U.S. economic hegemony over the island was firmly established. By 1928 U.S. investments in Cuba constituted 17.7 percent of all U.S. investments in Latin America. The United States controlled 75 percent of the sugar crop, public utilities, ranching, and mining. U.S. economic exploitation became the principal target of Cuban nationalists. Anti-Americanism has been the one consistent theme of Cuban history in the 20th century.

During the mid-20th century, Cuban politics was dominated by Fulgencio Batista Zaldívar, who ruled the country directly or indirectly from 1933 to 1944 and from 1952 to 1959. Batista's last years in power were characterized by increasing repression and corruption that generated popular support for his overthrow. Weakened by disaffection from the military and Cuba's large middle class, the regime crumbled and Batista fled the country. A revolutionary movement under the leadership of Fidel Castro Ruz, who had been waging a guerrilla campaign against the central government since 1954, overthrew his regime.

After a brief period of moderation, Castro moved to the left, purportedly adapting Marxist ideas to Latin American conditions. He consolidated power through the use of the Communist Party as the governing vehicle and institued a program of widespread reform that included land reform and the nationalization of all foreign-owned land and businesses. The United States responded by terminating diplomatic relations and sponsoring an invasion of anti-Castro exiles, which was defeated at the Bay of Pigs in April 1961. Castro declared Cuba a communist state in December 1961. The following year, the Organization of American States (OAS) voted to exclude Cuba. Castro's isolation in the Western Hemisphere pushed him into closer relations with the Soviet Union, which offered him massive amounts of military and economic aid. The Soviet Union's placement of missiles in Cuba precipitated a confrontation with the United States in 1962.

In 1965 Castro established the Communist Party of Cuba (PCC) as the sole legal party. A new constitution, establishing Cuba as a socialist state, was adopted in 1976. The first congress of the PCC was held in 1975, establishing a National Assembly, which chose Castro as head of state and government the following year.

During the 1960s and 1970s Castro attempted to export his revolution to other Latin American countries and aid leftist insurgents in several third world countries. Cuban troops were sent to Angola in 1976 and to Ethiopia in 1977. Military aid was sent to the Sandinista government in Nicaragua in 1979. Diplomatic isolation gradually improved during the late 1970s, with the OAS lifting its sanctions in 1975, and relations with the United States improving slightly. In 1979, Cuba hosted the meeting of Non-Aligned Nations, and Castro was elected head of the group for three years.

In 1980, exit restrictions were lifted temporarily and some 125,000 refugees fled to the United States, including large numbers of prisoners and the mentally ill. This placed renewed strain on U.S.–Cuban relations, as did Cuban assistance for the left-wing regimes and rebels in Nicaragua, El Salvador, and Grenada. Despite a meeting with Soviet leader Mikhail Gorbachev in Havana in 1989, Castro rejected the possibility of any Soviet-style political or economic reforms. The collapse of the USSR in the early 1990s hit the Cuban economy hard, as aid and trade subsidies were ended, and an economic crisis in 1993–94 created another wave of refugees to the United States, ending only when the Americans agreed to allow 20,000 Cuban immigrants each year. In 1996 the United States signed the Helms-Burton Act, aimed at tightening the economic embargo by making foreign investors liable to penalties in U.S. courts. At the end of the 20th century, Castro had to outlast his ninth U.S. president, with threats to the revolution growing but by no means certain to cause changes.

CONSTITUTION

Cuba's constitution, first published in 1975 and approved in the same year by the first congress of the Cuban Communist Party, was ratified by a 97.7 percent vote in a special referendum on February 16, 1976, and made effective eight days later on the anniversary of the 1898 war of independence. The constitution replaced the Fundamental Law of the Republic, instituted on February 7, 1959, which modified and largely replaced the constitution of 1940, Cuba's second since independence. Minor modifications to the constitution in 1992 attempted to make foreign investment easier, and also changed the religious nature of the state from atheist to secular.

The constitution established Cuba as a socialist state in which all power belongs to the working people. The state guarantees work, medical care, education, food, clothing, and housing. The Republic of Cuba is defined as part of the world socialist community, which included the USSR. Cuba also states its hopes to establish one large (socialist) community of nations within Latin America and the Caribbean. The state is charged with the direction of the economic life of the nation in accordance with socialist doctrines. The state guarantees freedom of the press, assembly, religion, speech, demonstration, and association within the confines of the law and in accordance with the goals of socialist society. Freedoms, according to the constitution, are dependent on obligations to the society and state and they may not be exercised in opposition to the existence and purposes of the socialist state. The state recognizes the right of small farmers to own, inherit, and sell land and other means of production, but this right again is not unequivocal. In general, the constitution is a Marxist document that marks another stage in the institutionalization of the Cuban revolution.

The president of the Council of State is the head of state and of government. He presides over the Council of State and the Council of Ministers, signs the decree-laws and other resolutions of the Council of State, and commands the Revolutionary Armed Forces. Executive authority is concentrated in two institutions: a Council of State elected from among members of the National Assembly, and a Council of Ministers whose chairman serves as the head of government. The Council of State comprises a president, five vice presidents, a secretary, and 23 other members. It represents the National Assembly between sessions. Among the functions of the council are the calling of special sessions of the National Assembly, setting the date for elections to a new Assembly, issuance of decree-laws between sessions of the National Assembly, mobilization in the event of war, and revocation of acts of the Council of Ministers and executive committees of local organs of people's power that are contrary to the constitution. The Council of Ministers is the highest administrative organ. It is composed of the head of state and government, the first vice president, vice presidents, ministers, and the president of the Central Planning Board. It has an executive committee composed of the president, the first vice president, and vice presidents of the Council of Ministers. The Council of Ministers conducts general administration, prepares the budget, draws up bills, implements laws, issues decrees, prepares development plans, and supervises national security. Policy making is a function of the Council; administration is the function of each ministry.

Outside the Council of Ministers there are powerful state bodies, such as the Central Planning Board (Junta Central de Planificación, JUCEPLAN), the National Institute of Agrarian Reform (Instituto Nacional de Reforma Agraria, INRA), and the National Bank. There are also independent agencies whose chiefs have the rank of ministers but are not members of the Council of Ministers. These agencies include the Cuban Petroleum Institute, Cuban Academy of Sciences, Book Institute, Tobacco Enterprise, and the Cuban Broadcasting Institute. Members of the Council of Ministers and the Council of State are, with few exceptions, drawn from the ranks of Castro's associates during the Sierra Maestra days.

Together with the state, the Cuban Communist Party dominates all aspects of daily life, controlling the means of production and the distribution of goods, as well as internal security, public communication, health, and education. Internal security is under the direction of the Ministry of Interior, which operates border guards and several other police forces, regulates immigration, and maintains a system

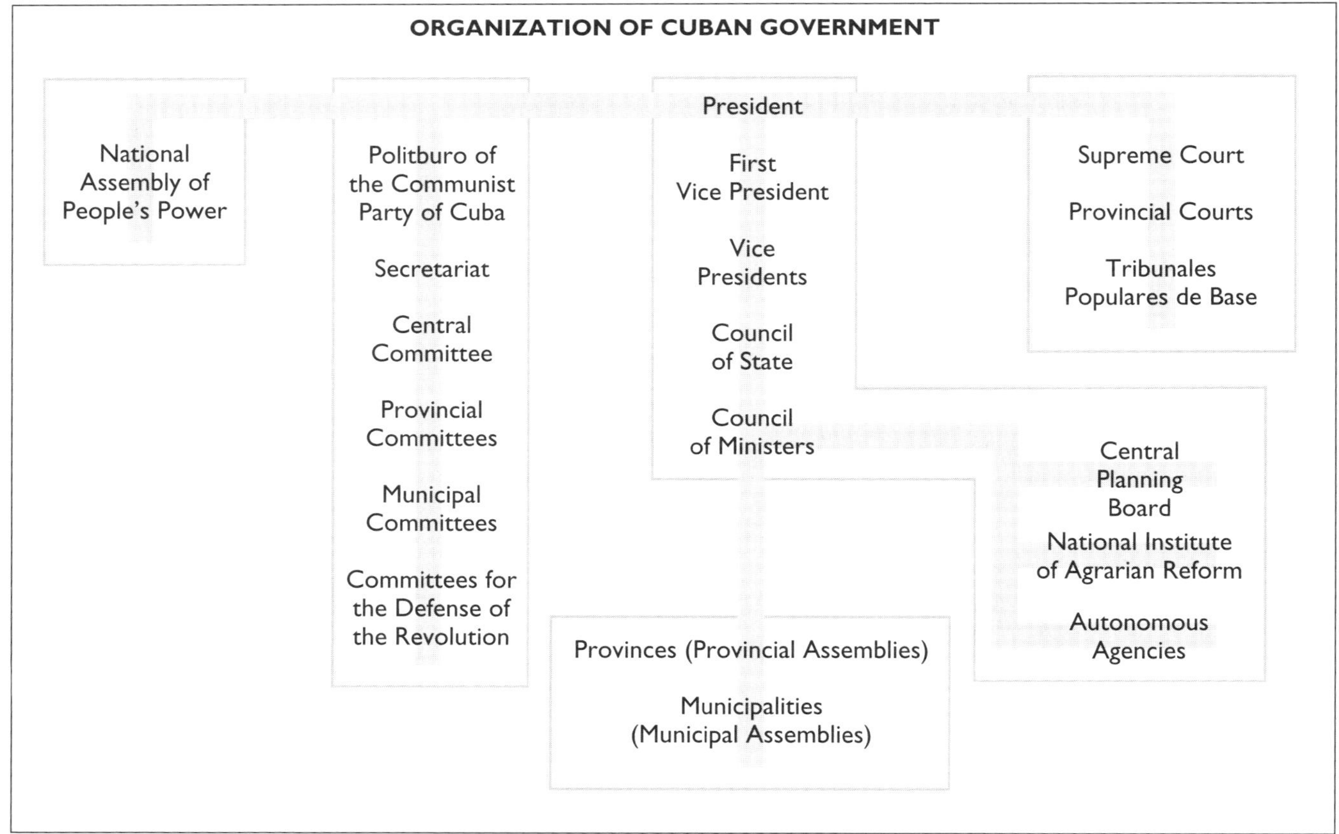

of neighborhood informers and block wardens known as the Committees for the Defense of the Revolution.

Between 1959 and 1976, the Cuban government was a charismatic revolutionary regime based on the preeminence of Fidel Castro as "the Maximum Leader of the Revolution." Administration was enigmatic, paternalist, and personalistic and was further complicated by the overlapping relationships between the "Fidelistas" or followers of Fidel Castro, the Communist Party, the military, and other loci of power. Despite growing emphasis on mass participation, power remains concentrated in the hands of a few selected on the basis of their loyalty to Castro. Although some authority has been dispersed and the government has become more structured, Castro retains control of the executive branch, the legislature, the military, and the Communist Party. Bureaucracy suffers from a lack of clear-cut and well-defined lines of authority and an overemphasis on party loyalty. Decisions are still made at the top, and there is little input from either the bureaucrats or the rank-and-file party members.

Castro's regime has achieved not only a reasonable degree of stability but also respectability. There appears to be no serious threat to the government from within or without. Fidelism has become entrenched as the official ideology of the nation, and the over 50 percent of the population born after the revolution have been so thoroughly indoctrinated in it that they may sustain it even after the original Fidelistas have disappeared from the scene. The older opponents of the revolution are either in prison or in exile. The government has been eminently successful in its mass mobilization programs, in the total destruction of the old order, in the neutralization of the church, and in social and cultural spheres, such as universal literacy and free health care. At least until the economic crises of the 1990s, other achievements included the liberation of women, expansion of child care centers, introduction of one of the most comprehensive social security systems in Latin America, and the clearing of the urban slums that disfigured prerevolutionary Cuba.

LOCAL GOVERNMENT

The local government structure was entirely remodeled under the 1976 constitution. The country is divided into 14 provinces and 169 municipalities, simplifying the original division into six provinces, 55 regions, and 344 municipal administrations.

The 14 provinces are from west to east: Pinar del Río, Habana, Ciudad de la Habana, Matanzas, Villa Clara, Cienfuegos, Sancti Spíritus, Ciego de Ávila, Camagüey, Las Tunas, Holguín, Granma, Santiago de Cuba, and Guantánamo. In addition Isla de la Juventud is defined as a special municipality.

There are popular assemblies at the provincial and municipal level. Members of the local Assemblies of the People's Power are elected for two-and-one-half year terms. The members of municipal assemblies are elected directly, and an executive committee elected from among its own members heads each municipal assembly. The members of these executive committees form provincial assemblies, also headed by provincial executive committees. A commission of Communist Party members and youth and trade union representatives proposes membership in provincial executive committees.

Municipal assemblies are responsible for schools, hospitals, stores, hotels, cinemas, public utilities, and municipal transport. They also elect magistrates to preside over the municipal people's courts. The provincial assemblies regulate intercity transport and provincial trade and elect judges to the provincial courts.

Supplementing and paralleling the local administration apparatus is a mass organization known as the Committees for the Defense of the Revolution (Comités de Defensa de la Revolución, CDR). These neighborhood committees enroll most of the adult population and act as a surveillance organization with over 73,000 local committees.

Local Government

Principal administrative divisions, capitals, area, population

Area and population

Provinces	Capitals	area sq mi	area sq km	population 1998 estimate
Camagüey	Camagüey	6,174	15,990	780,762
Ciego de Avila	Ciego de Avila	2,668	6,910	403,134
Cienfuegos	Cienfuegos	1,613	4,178	391,666
Ciudad de la Habana	—	281	727	2,198,392
Granma	Bayamo	3,232	8,372	824,897
Guantánamo	Guantánamo	2,388	6,186	508,664
Holguín	Holguín	3,591	9,301	1,020,660
La Habana	Havana	2,213	5,731	693,889
Las Tunas	Las Tunas	2,544	6,589	523,810
Matanzas	Matanzas	4,625	11,978	654,516
Pinar del Río	Pinar del Río	4,218	10,925	729,330
Sancti Spíritus	Sancti Spíritus	2,604	6,744	457,921
Santiago de Cuba	Santiago de Cuba	2,382	6,170	1,023,293
Villa Clara	Santa Clara	3,345	8,662	832,356
Special municipality				
Isla de la Juventud	Nueva Gerona	926	2,398	78,818
TOTAL		42,804	110,861	11,122,308

PARLIAMENT

The unicameral National Assembly of People's Power (Asamblea Nacional del Poder Popular) with 510 members is elected for five-year terms by direct universal voting. According to the constitution, the assembly is the supreme state organ. It holds two ordinary sessions per year, and special sessions when requested by one-third of the deputies or by the Council of State.

The functions of the National Assembly include amendment of the constitution, approval of laws, supervision of all organs of state, revocation of unconstitutional decree-laws passed by the Council of State, approval of the state budgets and development plans, ratification of treaties and declaration of war, election of the president, the first vice president, vice presidents, and members of the Council of Ministers, and election of the president, vice president, and other judges of the People's Supreme Court. Under the 1976 constitution, suffrage is universal over age 16.

POLITICAL PARTIES

According to the 1976 constitution, the Communist Party of Cuba is the leading force of society and the state. It is also the only legally recognized party in Cuba. Its structure and polices are those of a traditional Marxist-Leninist party, with adjustments for regional realities. There is no separation between party echelons and public officials, and most national leaders have dual functions in the party and government. The party owes as much loyalty to Fidelism as it does to Marxism-Leninism.

Political Parties

Communist Party. Illegal opposition parties include
Cuban Democratic Convergence, 1991
Party for Human Rights, 1988
Cuban Committee for Human Rights
Cuban Committee for Human Rights and National Reconciliation
Harmony Movement, 1990
Political Rights Defense Association
Cuban Democratic Party

Political Parties: Strength in Parliament Most Recent Elections

National Assembly of People's Power. A direct election was held on January 11, 1998, coincident with replenishment of the provincial assemblies. All 601 candidates approved by the Communist Party of Cuba received the 50 percent favorable vote required for election. (The Assembly had been enlarged from 589 to 601 members for the balloting; however, when the new body convened, its membership was reported to be 595.)

LEGAL SYSTEM

The Cuban legal system is based on Spanish and U.S. law, modified by Marxist jurisprudence. The judiciary, known as the Judicial Power, is headed by the People's Supreme Court. The Supreme Court is charged with transmitting to the rest of the judicial system instructions received from the leadership of the revolution. The judiciary is governed by the Law of the Organization of the Judicial System drafted by the Commission of Judicial Studies of the Central Committee of the Communist Party of Cuba. The law eliminated military tribunals and extended popular participation throughout the judicial system. Lay judges sit along with professional judges in all courts, and are selected for three-year terms of two one-month sessions per year.

The Supreme Court is divided into five chambers after reforms in 1973: criminal, civil and administrative, state security, labor, and military, each chamber being composed of three professional and two lay judges. The National Assembly of People's Power elects all judges. Professional judges are appointed for five-year terms and the chief justice for a seven-year term. Through its governing council, the court proposes laws, issues regulations, and directs the entire court system.

The 14 provincial courts at the next level are divided into three chambers: criminal, civil, and state security. Each chamber has three lay and professional judges, the latter serving five-year terms. Communist Party commissions select judges.

Popular participation in judicial activities is strongest in neighborhood people's courts, known as Tribunales Populares de Base. These courts are composed of worker judges selected by the local Communist Party units and serve on the bench in addition to their regular jobs.

There are two types of correctional institute under the Ministry of Justice: the penitentiary (including maximum-security prisons) and the state work farm. Work farms, or *granjas*, are minimum security prisons intended for prisoners who are being rehabilitated through productive labor.

Conditions in Cuban prisons have been cited by the Inter-American Human Rights Commission, Amnesty International, and the International Commission of Jurists as among the most inhumane in the world. Political prisoners suffer torture, deprivation of food, abuse, and severe psychological pressures.

LAW ENFORCEMENT

Law Enforcement

Offenses reported to the police per 100,000: —
- Murder: —
- Assault: —
- Burglary: —
- Automobile Theft: —
- Population per Police officer: 650

Death Penalty: Yes

HUMAN RIGHTS

In terms of political and civil rights, Cuba is ranked as a country that is not free. Castro's Cuba has had one of the worst human rights records in the Western Hemisphere. Fundamental human rights of expression, association, assembly, movement, and press are severely restricted by Cuban law. The creation of such crimes as "dangerousness," spreading enemy propaganda or unauthorized news, and insulting dead war heroes, provides authorities with the power to imprison or keep under surveillance any individuals considered a threat to the regime, regardless of their criminal activities or intent. Harassment and prosecution of dissidents is common, and the state continues to imprison hundreds of political prisoners, despite signs of an apparent opening following the papal visit in 1998.

Individuals can be held for "illegal exit" if caught exercising their right to leave the country, and those who do so are now banned from returning. Free trials are undermined by the restriction of defense rights, and by the political oversight exercised by the Council of State. Courts frequently ignore those due process rights that do exist under the constitution. Harsh penalties for supporting the U.S. embargo on Cuba were introduced in 1999. Dissidents are frequently arrested and sentenced to considerable prison sentences for "acts against the security of the state" and other offenses. Any organized opposition to the regime is similarly dealt with.

Independent journalism is similarly restricted and persecuted. Journalists are frequently harassed by police, and held in detention as a warning against covering such events as International Human Rights Day. Independent labor unions are banned, and individuals attempting to establish or participate in illegal groups are harassed and detained. To attract foreign investment, Cuba has tightened labor controls and employees' rights. Prison labor is still used for agricultural camps, clothing assembly, and other factories, and prisoners work without pay in severe conditions violating international labor and prison standards.

Opposition is silenced through persistent use of surveillance, phone tapping, and intimidation. Threats of criminal prosecution and house arrests were used in October and November 1999 while Cuba played host to the Ibero-American Summit in Havana. International human rights and humanitarian monitors are routinely denied access to the country. The International Committee of the Red Cross (ICRC) has not been allowed to conduct prison visits since 1989.

Severe conditions exist in Cuba's prisons. Prisoners suffer from malnourishment and overcrowding, and from a lack of appropriate medical attention. Reports of physical and sexual abuse are common and solitary confinement is frequently used for long periods. All detainees are subject to political reeducation sessions—refusal leads to further punishment and mistreatment. Pretrial detainees are often not separated from convicted prisoners, or minors from adults. Complaints or appeals against harsh treatment and poor conditions leads to solitary confinement, restricted visits, or denial of medical treatment. Political prisoners are particularly badly treated, and are not routinely released at the end of their sentences, instead relying on presidential decrees.

Cuba maintains the death penalty for over 100 crimes, and in March 1999 they were expanded to include drug trafficking and corruption of minors. Procedural failings and a lack of judicial independence facilitate miscarriages of justice, and appeals are minimal. Reports of arbitrary disappearance and execution among prisoners were common throughout the 1960s, 1970s, and 1980s, and likely continue to this day. At least 12 prisoners sentenced to death were reportedly executed in 1999.

International reaction to Cuba's lack of regard for human rights has increased slightly in the late 1990s as relations with Havana generally improve and nations seek signs of political relaxation. The United Nations passed a resolution in April 1999 expressing concern for Cuban human rights practices. The European Union has condemned Cuba's continued use of the death penalty. Canada, long voicing its support for ending the trade embargo with Cuba, reassessed its policy in 1999 and suspended programs that did not further the protection of human rights in Cuba. The U.S. government remains committed to the embargo, and uses it to express its concern over the human rights situation in Cuba. In 1999, several U.S. lawmakers visited Castro and urged political and economic reforms, including greater respect for human rights. They were denied access to political prisoners during their visit.

Cuba is the closest model of a Soviet-style totalitarian system in the Western Hemisphere.

FOREIGN POLICY

Due to economic hardship and the end of the cold war, Cuban foreign policy, once one of the most ambitious in Latin America, has been redirected and scaled down. Priorities today are finding new sources of trade, aid and foreign investment, and promoting international opposition to the U.S. trade embargo and the Helms-Burton Act. Cuba maintains relations with over 160 nations and has civilian assistance workers, mainly medical staff, in more than 20 of these. Support for Latin American and African guerrilla movements, including the deployment of over 75,000 troops, seems largely to have been abandoned. In the past, this support, along with Cuba's Marxist-Leninist government and its alignment with the USSR, had contributed to its isolation in the Western Hemisphere, in particular its suspension from the Organization of American States (OAS) in January 1962. Since relaxing its foreign policy, Cuba has reestablished relations with most countries in Latin America and the Caribbean.

In the 1970s and 1980s, Cuba spent millions of dollars exporting revolution to Latin America and Africa. Cuban forces played key roles in Angola, Ethiopia, and Nicaragua and as advisers in the Congo and Mozambique. By the late 1980s, these deployments were ending: Cuban forces left Angola by 1991, Nicaragua after 1990, and Ethiopia around the same period. After the 1992 peace accord in El Salvador, Castro stated that support for guerrillas was no longer central to Cuban foreign policy.

Relations with the United States, viewed by many Cubans as a colonial power due to its involvement in Cuban politics for much of the 20th century, have always dominated foreign policy. Cuba has sought to counteract the effect of U.S. policy by moving closer to the Soviet Union, and since 1990 by seeking wider international support for its trade and investment needs. U.S. policy has focused on maintaining the trade embargo while providing humanitarian assistance for ordinary Cubans, and is heavily criticized by the Cuban government. The Helms-Burton or Libertad Act of 1996 brought further international support for the Cuban position and condemnation of the U.S. approach. Relations with the United States are also affected by alleged Cuban involvement with the drug trade in the Caribbean, and by mass migration from Cuba. A long-running dispute between the two countries has been over the status of the U.S. naval base at Guantanámo Bay in southern Cuba.

Cuba is a founder member of the United Nations, and participates in many of its organizations. Membership in other international organizations includes the International Atomic Energy Agency, the International Labor Organization, Interpol, the World Health Organization, and the Group of 77.

DEFENSE

The president as commander in chief heads the defense structure. The line of command runs through the defense minister (Raúl Castro, brother of Fidel Castro) to the joint general staff. The Revolutionary Army is divided geographically into three field armies: western, central, and eastern. Within these armies there are six independent army corps and independent groups that can function even if the higher echelons are destroyed.

In practice, the Central Committee of the Cuban Communist Party wields military power, which is two-thirds military in composition, and Castro and his brother Raúl deal directly with the commanders. As in other communist armies, the commissar system is an important element in the indoctrination of the armed forces. Communist Party cells work in each formation and unit down to company level.

There are three paramilitary organizations: the Frontier Guards, the Youth Labor Army, and the Defensa Civil, or the territorial militia.

Military manpower is provided by compulsory military service requiring the enlistment of all males between 16 and 49. The term of service is three years. Most of the persons drafted are inducted into the Youth Labor Army rather than the regular forces. All enlisted men and officers undergo indoctrination in Marxism and Cuban socialism.

The FAR is one of the largest armed forces in Latin America, with large numbers of reserves ready for mobilization in 24 to 48 hours. The force is intensely disciplined and loyal to Fidel Castro personally. Until the 1990s, Cuba received the latest military hardware from the USSR, and the army was extremely well equipped. The army leadership, particularly the old-line Fidelistas, is proud of its guerrilla traditions going back to the Sierra Maestra days. FAR is maintained in a state of constant preparedness because the regime has always felt threatened by the United States. FAR's credentials were enhanced by its string of successes in Angola and Ethiopia, where Cuban soldiers showed themselves to be capable of striking hard and fast and of solving logistical transport problems successfully. In the late 1980s and 1990s, Cuba withdrew its forces from overseas in the light of peace agreements in Africa, and the termination of Soviet support. The situation throughout the 1990s has been one of stagnation and decline, although the armed forces still have preferential status in Cuban economy and society. The last Soviet troops based in Cuba were withdrawn by 1993, from a maximum strength of 2,000 plus.

Military Indicators

Total Active Duty Personnel: 53,000
Military Manpower per 1,000: 4.7
Military Expenditures $million: 350
  as % of GNP: 1.6
  per capita $: 32
  as % of central government expenditures: —
Arms Imports $million: 0

Arms Exports $million: 0

ECONOMY

Cuba's economy remains organized on socialist principles of state control. Most of the means of production are owned and operated by the government and about three-quarters of the workforce are employed by the state. Already in stagnation and depression since commodity price slumps in the 1980s, the economy in the 1990s suffered extensively from the collapse of the Soviet Union and the withdrawal of trade and aid subsidies. The government sought to alleviate the crisis by opening up small sectors of the economy to private enterprise, legalizing the dollar, and authorizing self-employment. The measures were aimed at the tourist sector, which by the late 1990s surpassed the sugar industry as the primary source of foreign currency. Significant resources are now being diverted to improving Cuba's tourist infrastructure, and measures such as dollar shops introduced to keep tourist revenues in the country. The sugar industry has suffered from poor management and bad harvests, and is in need of substantial reform. Foreign investment in joint ventures has been actively sought, although United States restrictions on dealings with Cuba have affected investors from most interested nations. There is a widening gap in the economy between those who have access to dollars, or employment which provides such access, and those restricted to dealing in Cuban pesos. Many Cubans are forced to turn to the flourishing black market to secure essentials as well as luxuries, and government crackdowns are limited to organized groups in recognition of the importance of the black market to the survival of the economy. Due to defaults on international debt, Cuba is denied access to funding from international institutions such as the World Bank, and must rely on high-interest rate short-term loans to finance imports such as fuel and food.

Principal Economic Indicators

Gross National Product: $16.9 billion
GNP per capita: $1,540
GNP Average Annual Growth Rate (1990–97) %: —
GNP per capita Average Annual Growth Rate (1990–97) %: —
Origin of Gross Domestic Product %
  Agriculture: —
  Mining: —
  Manufacturing: —
  Construction: —
  Public Utilities: —
  Transportation and Communications: —
  Trade: —
  Financial Services: —
  Other Services: —
  Government: —
Gross Domestic Product by Type of Expenditure %
  Private Consumption: —
  Government Consumption: —
  Gross Domestic Investment: —
  Foreign Trade: Exports: —
    Imports: —
% of Income Received by Poorest 20%: —
% of Income Received by Richest 10%: —

Price and earnings indexes (December 1996 = 100)

	1983	1984	1985	1986	1987	1988	1989
Implicit consumer deflator index	94.9	98.0	100.0	101.4	102.8	103.1	—
Monthly earnings index	95.9	99.0	100.0	100.1	98.1	99.6	100.0

Finance

National Currency: Cuban Peso (Cu$)
Exchange Rate: $1 = Cu$1,000
Money Supply Stock in National Currency billion: —
M1 per capita: —
Central Bank Discount Rate %: —
Total External Debt $million: 30,500
Debt Service Ratio %: —

Balance of Payments $million: —
International Reserves SDRs million: —
Ratio of External Debt to Total Reserves:
Average Annual Rate of Inflation/Consumer Price Index Growth Rate %: —

Official Development Assistance

ODA $million: 46
as % of GNP:
per capita: $7
Foreign Direct Investment $million: 873

Central Government Revenues and Expenditures

Fiscal Year: Calendar Year
Revenues $million: —
Expenditures $million: —
Budget Deficit $million: —
Tax Revenues as % of GDP: —
Highest Tax Bracket %
Individual: —
Corporate: —

Employment and Labor

Economically Active Population: 4,470,000
Female Participation Rate %: 36.1
Activity Rate %: 44.2
Labor by Sector: %
Agriculture, Forestry, Fishing: 22.3
Manufacturing, Mining: 18.9
Construction: 8.8
Transportation and Communications: 7.0
Trade, Hotels, and Restaurants: 6.6
Finance, Insurance, Real Estate: —
Public Administration, Defense: —
Services: 30.7
Unemployment %: 8

Agriculture

Agriculture's Share of GDP %: —
Average Annual Rate of Growth (1965–98) %: —
Number of Farms 000: 1.8
Average Size of Farm ha: 1,047
Number of Tractors per 1,000 hectares: 30.0
Irrigation, % of Farms having: 35
Artificial Fertilizer kg/hectare: 199
Total Farmland as % of land area: 78.3
Livestock: Cattle 000: 4,650
Sheep 000: 310
Hogs 000: 1,500
Chickens 000: 12,000
Forests: Production of Roundwood (000 cubic meters): 3,152
Fisheries: Total Catch tons 000: 87.7

Mining

% of GDP: —
Value of Mineral Production $million: —

Manufacturing

Value Added $million: 5,560
Industrial Production Growth Rate %: 6

Energy

Commercial Energy Production metric tons of oil equivalent 000: 4,011
Commercial Energy Consumption metric tons of oil equivalent 000: 7,650
Commercial Energy Consumption per capita kg: 1,687
Average Annual Growth Rate 1980–97 %: —
Net Energy Imports % of use: 48
Electricity Installed Capacity kW 000: 3,988
Production kW-hr million: 11,189
Coal Reserves tons million: —
Production tons: —
Natural Gas Proven Reserves cubic meters billion: 3
Production cubic meters million: —
Crude Petroleum Reserves barrels million: 100
Production barrels million: 1.0
Consumption barrels million: 40
Refinery Capacity barrels per day 000: 301
Pipelines Length km: —

Foreign Trade

Imports $million: 2,185.0
Exports $million: 3,860.0
Export Volume % Annual Growth Rate (1990–97): −14.4
Import Volume % Annual Growth Rate (1990–97): −8.4

Balance of trade (current prices)

	1991	1992	1993	1994	1995	1996
U.S. $ 000,000	−1,332	−412	−551	−797	−1,166	−1,179
% of total	38.4%	15.1%	19.2%	24.4%	28.3%	24.4%

Major Trading Partners

	Imports	Exports
European Union %	30	11
United States %	—	—
Eastern Europe %	9	75.2
Japan %	1	2.7
Others %	60	10.1

Transportation

Roads Total Length mi: 16,839 km 27,100
Paved %: 56
Automobiles: 20,000
Trucks and Buses: 33,000
Persons per vehicle: 205
Railroad; Track Length mi: 3,033 km 4,881
Passenger-mi million: 1,880
Freight-mi million: 937
Merchant Marine: No. of Vessels: 393
Total Deadweight Tonnage 000: 924.6
International Cargo Loaded tons 000: 8,092
International Cargo Off-loaded tons 000: 15,440
Airports with Scheduled Flights: 14
Traffic: Passenger-mi million: 1,648
Freight-mi million: 31.2
Length of Canals mi: 149 km 240

Tourism

Number of Tourists to 000: 1,390
Number of Tourists from 000: 55
Tourist Receipts $million: 1,100
Tourist Expenditures $million: —

Communications

Telephones 000: 353
Cost of Local Calls 3 mins: $0
Cellular Telephones 000: 1.9
Fax Machines 000: 0.4
Personal Computers 000: —
Internet Hosts per million persons: 0.1
Mail: Post Offices: 1,545
Pieces of Mail Handled million: 28
Pieces of Mail Handled per person: 2.6

EDUCATION

Education is free, universal, and compulsory from the ages of six to 12, with subsequent schooling also free. After the revolution, the eradication of illiteracy was a high priority for the government, and all private schools were nationalized in 1961. During the late 1960s, around 10,000 new classrooms were provided in rural areas, along with traveling libraries and 270,000 teachers who led the literacy campaign. The organization of a network of adult schools followed the campaign, and a parallel system of education began to develop. In the early 1990s, some 917,889 pupils attended primary schools, about 597,997 students were enrolled in secondary schools, and about 314,168 students attended technical schools, teachers colleges, and other schools. The country's higher educational institutions enrolled about 242,434 students.

The education system introduced after the revolution includes general education, 12 or 13 grades preceded by a preschool stage, higher or university education, teacher training education, adult education directed toward the eradication of residual illiteracy and continued study by working people, technical education in parallel with secondary education, language instruction, and specialized education. All levels are free, with supplemental scholarships to cover living expenses and medical assistance. Education receives high priority, and the numbers of students enrolled has increased sharply from prerevolution days. The largest university is the University of Havana, opened in 1728, and others include the University of the Orient, the Universidad Central de la Villas, and the Universidad Ignacio Agramonte.

Education

Literacy Rate %: 95.7
Male %: 96.2
Female %: 95.3
First Level: Primary schools: 9,864
Teachers: 90,565
Students: 1,074,153
Student-Teacher Ratio: 11.9
Net Enrollment Ratio: 99
Second Level: Secondary Schools: 2,175
Teachers: 46,722
Students: 460,438
Student-Teacher Ratio: 9.8
Net Enrollment Ratio: 59

Vocational Level: Schools: 618
Students: 244,253

Third Level: Institutions: 35
Teachers: 22,967
Students: 122,346
Student-Ratio Level: 5.3
Gross Enrollment Ratio: 12.7
Students per 100,000: 1,116
% of Population Age 25 and over with Postsecondary Education: —

Public Expenditure on Education as % of GDP: 6.6

SCIENCE AND TECHNOLOGY

Science and Technology

Scientists and Engineers in R&D per 1 million persons: 1,612
Expenditures in R&D as % of GDP: 0.84
High-Tech Exports $million: —
Patent Applications by Residents: 109

MEDIA

The government is the sole owner of the media and the sole purveyor of the news. The purpose of the media is defined in Leninist terms as political indoctrination and mass mobilization and integration. No criticism of the government is permitted. In 1992 there were 17 daily newspapers, with a total circulation of 1,315,000. The three main newspapers are the Communist Party daily, *Granma*; *Juventud Rebelde*, the paper of the Communist Youth; and *Trabajadores*, published by the Cuban Federation of Workers. Provincial newspapers include the *Tribuna de la Habana* and *Sierra Maestra* in Santiago de Cuba, and they focus on local issues. Magazines include the weekly *Bohemia*, which covers all aspects of the news and is the oldest periodical in Cuba; the monthly *Opina*, aimed at a younger audience, with information on available consumer goods; and *Mujeres*, published by the Federation of Cuban Women. A number of specialized cultural magazines and newspapers also have wide réaderships.

Television was introduced in 1950, and is operated by two national networks, Televisión Cubana and Tele-Rebelde, with 58 broadcast stations in 1998. There are several national radio networks and one international, all of which are administered by the Cuban Institute of Radio and Television. In 1999, there were 150 AM broadcast stations, five FM, and one shortwave. In 1993 there were approximately 2.14 million radios and 2.5 million televisions.

In March 1997, Cable News Network (CNN) became the first American news bureau to operate in Cuba since 1969, following a loosening of restrictions by both the Cuban and U.S. governments. News agencies from elsewhere in the world faced no such restrictions, and those with offices in Cuba include Itar-Tass, BTA, AFP, and Reuters. Prensa Latina, the Cuban news agency, has offices in Moscow, Prague, Sofia, Paris, and Mexico City.

Media

Daily Newspapers: 17
- Total Circulation 000: 1,315
- Circulation per 1,000: 120

Books Published: 932
Magazines: 160
Radio Receivers 000: —
- per 1,000: —

Television sets 000: 2,200
- per 1,000: 200

MOST IMPORTANT MEDIA:

Press. The following are published at Havana, unless otherwise noted: *Granma*, official PCC organ, morning and weekly editions; *Juventud Rebelde*, organ of the Communist Youth; *Los Trabajadores*, labor oriented; *Tribuna de la Habana; Adelante* (Camagüey); *Sierra Maestra* (Santiago de Cuba); *Vanguardia* (Santa Clara). Circulation figures are currently unkown because of severe cutbacks in the availability of newsprint to all papers (including party organs) in late 1990. In addition, it was announced in February 1991 that *Granma* would thenceforth be issued only from Tuesday to Saturday, while *Juventud Rebelde* and *Los Trabajadores* would appear only on Sunday and Monday, respectively.

News agencies. The domestic facilities are the government-controlled Prensa Latina and Agencia de Información Nacional (AIN). A large number of foreign agencies maintain offices at Havana.

Radio and television. Broadcasting is controlled by the Ministry of Communications and Instituto Cubano de Radio y Televisión. There are five national radio networks (classical music, drama, general entertainment, news and sports, 24-hour news) in addition to short-wave service provided by Radio Habana, Cuba; some 50 TV stations operate throughout the country. A Spanish-language TV channel, Multimedia Caribe, began operating in March 1995. There were approximately 4.0 million radio and 3.1 million television receivers in 1998.

CULTURE

Cultural Indicators

Public Libraries Number: 328
- Volumes: 3,911,000
- Registered borrowers: —

Museums Number: 241
- Annual Attendance: 8,159,000

Cinema Production of Long Films: 6
- Number of Cinemas: 903
- Seating Capacity: 187,900
- Annual Attendance: 23.8
- Annual Attendance per capita: 2.2

STATUS OF WOMEN

The position of women in Cuba has been both positively and negatively affected by the 40 years of revolutionary government. Equality, both racially and sexually, was a major goal of the revolution, and women were encouraged to enter into employment and education to participate in creating the socialist society. The government takes a generally liberal position toward contraception and abortion, and birth control clinics provide all adults with access to contraceptives and abortion. Universal access to child care and summer youth camps facilitated employment of working mothers.

Educationally, women have benefited greatly from the expansion in all levels of schooling and technical training, and from this base come many of the other benefits. Many women carry out work in sectors traditionally dominated by men, such as agriculture and livestock raising, as well as running cooperatives and local, regional, and national committees. There are women on the Central Committee of the Communist Party, and in positions as departmental ministers in the government. However, these numbers are limited: there are 20 women and 110 men on the Committee of the Communist Party Political Bureau, and only 5 percent of the Presidents of the Municipal Assemblies of People's Power are women, while for vice presidents the figure is 11 percent.

Women are also still expected to run the home, shouldering the burden of most, if not all, domestic tasks. The economic crisis has worsened the situation, with women the first to be expelled from the productive to informal sectors of the labor market: child care, street vending, even prostitution. The rise in violence in society has also affected women disproportionately, not least through the increase in sexual assault. Shortages of medicines and a decline in health care also affect women with decreased availability of contraception, access to abortion, and reproductive health care.

Women

Gender Empowerment Measure: 25
Seats Held in Parliament by Women %: 22.8
Female Administrators and Managers %: 18.5
Female Professional and Technical Workers %: 47.8
Women's Share of Earned Income %: 31.0
Women in Government %: 8

HEALTH, FOOD, AND NUTRITION

Health

Number of Physicians: 46,860
Number of Dentists: 8,057
Number of Nurses: 73,943
Number of Pharmacists: —

(continued)

Population per Physician: 231
Number of Hospitals: 244
Hospital Beds per 10,000: 65
Hospital Bed Occupancy Rate: —
Infant Mortality Rate per 1,000 live births: 13
Maternal Mortality Rate per 100,000 live births: 95
Total Health Expenditures as % of GDP: —
Health Expenditures per capita $: —
HIV Infected % of adults: 0.02
Cigarette Consumption per smoker per year: 2,566
% of Smokers: Male: 49
Female: 25
Access to Safe Water %: 94

Food and Nutrition

Food Supply as % of FAO Requirements: 99
% of Consumption Expenditures on Food: 26.7
Daily Available Calories per capita: 2,291
% of Total Calories derived from:
Cereals: 36.5
Potatoes, cassava: 5.9
Meat, poultry: 5.3
Fish: 0.6
Eggs, milk: 7.9
Fruits, vegetables: 4.0
Fats, oils: 13.1

ENVIRONMENT

The main problems facing Cuba's environment are: pollution of Havana Bay and other heavily populated areas; deforestation and land pollution; and tourist development. Operating under standard socialist methods of industrialization and economic development, Cuba for many years paid little regard to the environmental damage such a path caused. Recently, with economic crises and a crumbling infrastructure, the level of pollution into such areas as the Havana Bay has increased, as existing safeguards fell. Efforts to increase sugarcane and other agricultural production have also harmed the environment, with large quantities of fertilizers and pesticides entering the ecosystem. The ability of Cuba's limited resources to maintain a program of reforestation means that the area of land cleared each year for fuel, lumber, or farming purposes exceeds the area replanted.

Cuban policymakers have been heavily promoting tourism in an attempt to boost the struggling economy. The development of infrastructure to support and promote tourists, and the simple numbers of tourists themselves, pose a significant new threat to the environment. New beachfront hotels are being constructed in prime habitats for rare species, and attempts by ecologically minded scientists to stop the developments are countered by the pressing need for hard currency. Increased numbers of tourists will further damage the coral reefs around the island, which constitute an ecosystem second in complexity and diversity only to rain forests. The experience of neighboring islands, such as Bermuda and Jamaica, show just how serious the impact of tourism can be, ranging from damage to coral reefs to depletion of water tables.

Cuba is a signatory to several international agreements concerning the environment, including the Antarctic, Biodiversity, Climate Change, Desertification, Endangered Species, Environmental Modification, Hazardous Wastes, Law of the Sea, Marine Dumping, Ozone Layer Protection, and Ship Pollution treaties.

Environment

Forest Area sq km: 18,000
Average Annual Deforestation sq km: 0
Nationally Protected Areas as % of Total Land Area: 6.6
Freshwater Access cubic meters per capita: 3,120
Emissions of Organic Water Pollutants kg per day: 172,973
CO_2 Emissions per capita ton: 2.8

CHRONOLOGY

1933 1959 Fulgencio Batista y Zaldívar takes power.
1934 Platt Amendment revoked.
1952 Batista retakes power in military coup.
1953 Revolt by Fidel Castro quickly subdued.
1956 Castro and rebels land in Cuba and take to the Sierra Maestra, aided by Ernesto "Che" Guevara. Guerrilla war commences.
1959 Batista flees Cuba, and Castro enters Havana.
1960 Cuba is declared a socialist country.
1961 1,500 Cuban exiles, trained and financed by the CIA, invade Cuba at the Bay of Pigs. Castro's forces defeat the invaders.
1962 OAS excludes Cuba. Soviet Union installs long-range missiles in Cuba. United States imposes naval blockade and the two superpowers go "eyeball to eyeball." The Cuban missile crisis is resolved with the Soviet Union removing the missiles and the United States agreeing not to launch further attacks on Cuba.
1965 Communist Party of Cuba established as sole legal party.
1967 Che Guevara killed in Bolivia leading revolutionary group.
1974 OAS votes to normalize relations with Cuba.
1976 Cuban troops help Soviet-backed Angolan government in civil war.
1977 Cuban troops sent to Ethiopia.
1980 100,000 refugees allowed to flee to United States.
1983 U.S. troops invade Grenada and expel Cuban forces.
1988 Cuban forces removed from Angola.
1992 July, Constitution modified to attract foreign investment and to designate the government as secular and not atheist. October, U.S. Congress passes Cuban Democracy Act prohibiting foreign subsidiaries of U.S. companies from trading with Cuba, and tightening travel restrictions.

1993 Last Soviet troops leave Cuba. Sugar harvest falls to a 30-year low.
1994 August: antigovernment demonstrations bring easing of export restrictions, 30,000 Cubans leave for the United States, many on rafts and small boats.
1995 May: 20,000 refugees are admitted to the U.S. base at Guantánamo Bay.
1996 February 24: two planes from the Miami-based anti-Castro group Brothers to the Rescue are shot down over Cuban airspace. A human rights organization, Concilio Cubano, formed in 1995, is persecuted by the government and over 200 members arrested and harassed. Clinton signs the Helms-Burton, or Libertad, Act enacting penalties on foreign companies trading with Cuba who also operate in the United States. November: Castro visits the Vatican and invites the pope to visit Cuba.
1997 In July and September a series of bombings targets tourist hotels in Havana, and are blamed on exile groups. Cable News Network (CNN) is permitted to operate in Cuba. On July 12 there is a ceremonial homecoming for the remains of revolutionary leader Ernesto ("Che") Guevara and six Cuban guerrillas who were killed in Bolivia on Oct. 9, 1967. November: leader of the powerful Miami-based Cuban American National Foundation, Jorge Más Canosa, dies.
1998 January 21–25: Pope John Paul II visits Cuba, and holds mass in Havana. He calls for greater freedom within Cuba, and a lifting of the U.S. embargo.
1999 July: the head of the U.S. Chamber of Commerce, Thomas Donahue, visits Cuba to look at potential business ties, the first such visit for 40 years. In October, George Ryan of Illinois, a Republican, visits Cuba and meets with Castro for seven hours—the first sitting American governor for 40 years to visit the island. November: Castro hosts the Ibero-American Summit in Havana. December: Cuba demands return of Elián González, a refugee who lost his mother and other companions after the boat they were traveling on to Florida sank. Relatives in Miami were caring for the boy, but his father remains in Cuba.
2000 February: the United States demands the withdrawal of a Cuban diplomat linked to a Miami immigration official accused of spying for the Cuban government. April: U.S. federal agents snatch Elián González from his relatives' home in Miami and return him to his father. Castro cancels trade talks with the EU after it condemns Cuba's human rights record. June: U.S. courts uphold the custody rights of Elián's father, and father and son return to Cuba to a rapturous welcome. September: Cuba wins 11 gold medals at the Sydney Olympics.
2002 The United States exports food to Cuba for the first time in more than 40 years to help it cope with the devastation caused by Hurricane Michelle.

BIBLIOGRAPHY

Anderson, John Lee. *Che Guevara: A Revolutionary Life*. New York, 1998.

Bethell, Leslie, ed. *Cuba: A Short History*. Cambridge, Mass., 1993.

Eckstein, Susan Eva. *Back from the Future: Cuba Under Castro*. New Brunswick, N.J., 1995.

Franklin, Jane. *Cuba and the United States: A Chronological History*. Chicago, 1997.

Hatchwell, Emily, and Simon Calder. *Cuba: A Guide to the People, Politics and Culture*. Brooklyn, N.Y., 1999.

Kaplowitz, Donna Rich. *Anatomy of a Failed Embargo: U.S. Sanctions against Cuba*. Boulder, Colo., 1998.

Leonard, Thomas M. *Castro and the Cuban Revolution*. Westport, Conn., 1999.

Perez-Stable, Marifeli. *The Cuban Revolution: Origins, Course, and Legacy*. Oxford, U.K., 1998.

Rosendahl, Mona. *Inside the Revolution: Everyday Life in Socialist Cuba*. Ithaca, N.Y., 1998.

Stanley, David. *Lonely Planet Cuba*. London, 1997.

Suchlicki, Jaime. *Cuba: From Columbus to Castro and Beyond*, 4th ed. Washington D.C., 1997.

Thomas, Hugh. *Cuba or the Pursuit of Freedom*. New York, 1998.

OFFICIAL PUBLICATIONS

Cuba. *Anuario estadístico; Censo de población y viviendas, 1981.*

CONTACT INFORMATION

Cuba, Interest Section
2630 and 2639 16th Street NW
Washington, D.C. 20009
Phone: (202) 797-8518 Fax: (202) 986-7283

INTERNET RESOURCES

- CubaNet http://www.cubanet.org/
- Republica de Cuba: Ministerio de Salud Publica http:/www3.itu.int/missions/Cuba

CYPRUS

BASIC FACT SHEET

OFFICIAL NAME:
Republic of Cyprus (Dimokratia Kyprou)

ABBREVIATION:
CY

CAPITAL:
Nicosia

HEAD OF STATE AND GOVERNMENT:
President Glafkos Ioannou Klirides

NATURE OF GOVERNMENT:
Parliamentary democracy

POPULATION:
856,000 (1999)

AREA:
9,251 sq km (3,572 sq mi)

MAJOR ETHNIC GROUPS:
Greek, Turkish

LANGUAGES:
Greek, Turkish, English

RELIGIONS:
Greek Orthodox, Islam

UNIT OF CURRENCY:
Cypriot pound

NATIONAL FLAG:
Map of Cyprus in gold set above two olive branches in green on a white field.

NATIONAL EMBLEM:
A gracefully shaped gold shield displaying a white dove holding in its bill an olive branch. Surrounding the emblem is a decorative garland made up of large olive branches.

NATIONAL ANTHEM:
"Ethnikos Hymnos" (Hymn to liberty)

NATIONAL HOLIDAYS:
Cyprus Independence Day (August 16); Greek Independence Day (March 25); Greek National Day (October 28); New Year's Day; all major Christian religious days

DATE OF INDEPENDENCE:
August 16, 1960

DATE OF CONSTITUTION:
August 16, 1960

GEOGRAPHICAL FEATURES

The third-largest island in the Mediterranean, Cyprus lies off the southern coast of Turkey and the western shore of Syria, north of Egypt. Including the small island outposts of Cape Andreas, Cyprus has an area of 9,251 sq km (3,572 sq mi), extending 227 km (141 mi) northeast to southwest and 97 km (60 mi) southeast to northwest. The length of the coastline is 538 km (334 mi). The northern part of Cyprus, north of the so-called Attila Line, or Green Line, is under Turkish occupation, with control formally recognized only by Turkey.

The capital is Nicosia, partly under Turkish occupation, with a 1993 population in the Greek sector of 186,000. Other major cities in the Greek sector are Limassol, Larnaca, and Paphos. Famagusta and Kyrenia are the major population centers in the Turkish sector.

The Troodos Mountains cover most of the southern and western portions of the country, and the Kyrenia range extends in a narrow band along the northern coastline. Coastal lowlands surround the island. The highest peak is Mount Olympus (1,951 m; 6,401 ft), in the Troodos range.

The Mesaoria Plain is the agricultural heartland of the country, and in its middle lies Nicosia, the divided capital of the island. A network of rivers rises in the Troodos, most becoming dry courses in summer.

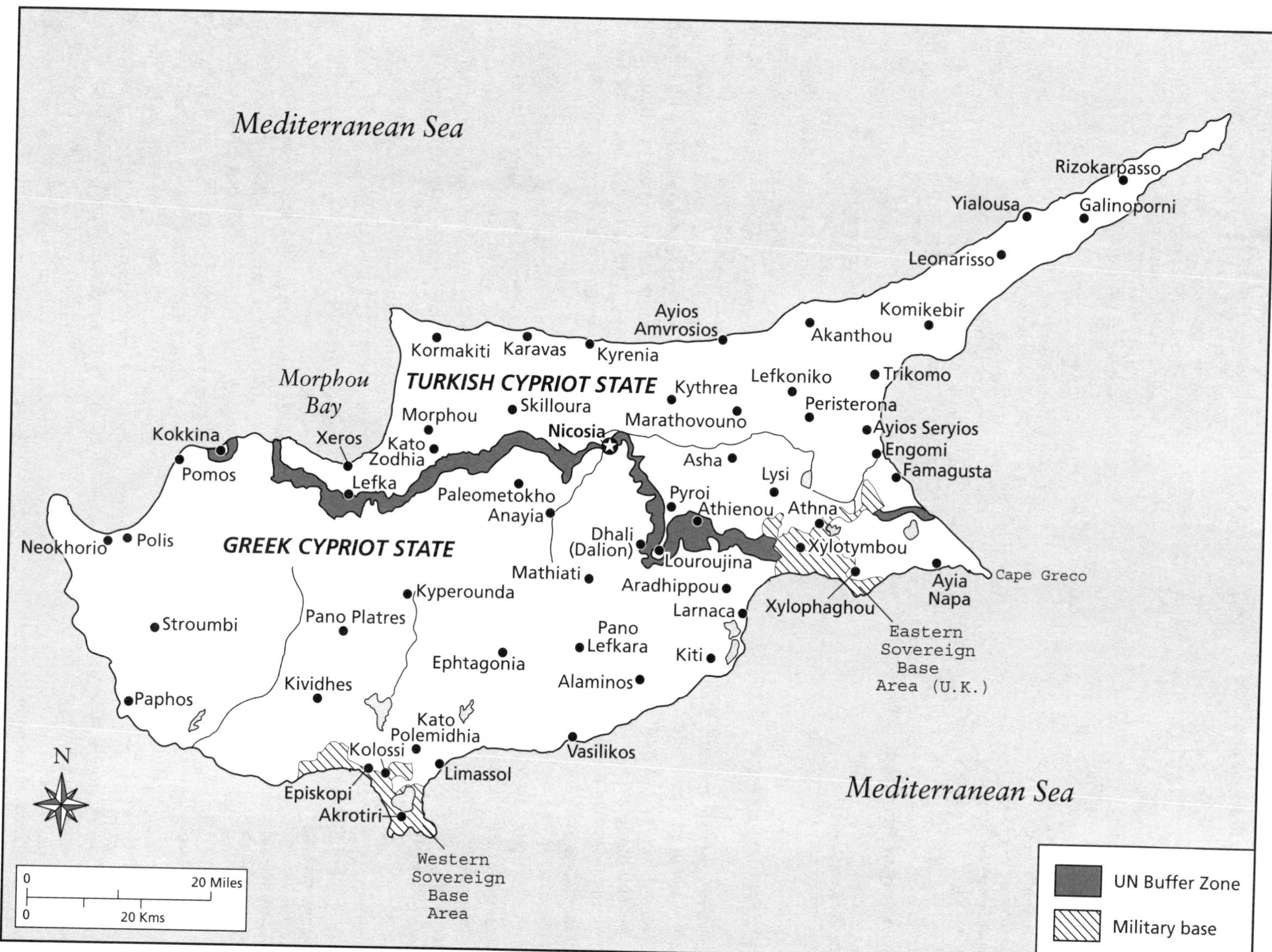
Cyprus
Mediterranean Sea
Rizokarpasso
Yialousa
Galinoporni
Leonarisso
Komikebir
Ayios Amvrosios
Akanthou
Kormakiti
Karavas
Kyrenia
Morphou Bay
TURKISH CYPRIOT STATE
Kythrea
Lefkoniko
Trikomo
Peristerona
Skilloura
Morphou
Marathovouno
Ayios Seryios
Kokkina
Xeros
Nicosia
Kato Zodhia
Engomi
Asha
Pomos
Famagusta
Lefka
Lysi
Paleometokho
Pyroi
Anayia
Athienou
Athna
Neokhorio
Polis
Dhali (Dalion)
GREEK CYPRIOT STATE
Xylotymbou
Louroujina
Mathiati
Ayia Napa
Cape Greco
Kyperounda
Aradhippou
Xylophaghou
Stroumbi
Pano Platres
Larnaca
Pano Lefkara
Eastern Sovereign Base Area (U.K.)
Ephtagonia
Kiti
Kividhes
Alaminos
Paphos
Kato Polemidhia
Kolossi
Vasilikos
N
Limassol
Episkopi
Mediterranean Sea
Akrotiri
Western Sovereign Base Area
0 20 Miles
0 20 Kms
UN Buffer Zone
Military base

Geography

Area sq mi: 3,572 sq km 9,251
World Rank: 164th
Land Boundaries, km: —
Coastline, km: 648
Elevation Extremes meters
Lowest: Mediterranean Sea 0
Highest: Olympus 1,952
Land Use % Arable land: 12
Permanent Crops: 5
Permanent Pastures: 0
Forest and Woodland: 13
Other: 70

Population of Principal Cities (1994 est.)

Limassol	143,400
Nicosia (Lefkosia)	186,400

CLIMATE AND WEATHER

The warm, Mediterranean climate is rather dry, with winter rainfall mainly between November and March. In general, the island experiences mild, wet winters succeeded by hot, dry summers. The higher mountain areas are comparatively cooler and more moist than the rest of the island and receive the highest annual rainfall, up to 1,000 mm (39.4 in.). The least rainfall occurs in the Mesaoria. Droughts are frequent, and sometimes severe. Summer temperatures are high in the lowlands even near the sea and can reach particularly uncomfortable readings in the Mesaoria. The mean annual temperature of the country is 20°C (68°F), and there is a high average of sunshine, even during the winter.

Climate and Weather

Mean Temperature 68°F
Average Rainfall
Mesaoria and Karpasian Peninsula 15.7 in to 17.7 in
Higher Mountains 39.4 in

POPULATION

Population Indicators

Total Population: 1999 856,000
World Rank: 155th
Density per sq mi: 239.6 per sq km 92.5
% of annual growth (1994–99): 1.0
Male %: 49.8
Female %: 50.2
Urban %: 67.7
Age Distribution: % 0–14: 25.4
15–29: 22.0
30–44: 22.3
45–59: 15.4
60–74: 10.2
75 and over: 4.7
Population 2020: 1,067,000
Birth Rate per 1,000: 15.4
Death Rate per 1,000: 7.7
Population Doubling Time (years): —
Infant Mortality Rate per 1,000 live births: 4.9
Rate of Natural Increase per 1,000: 7.7
Total Fertility Rate: 2.1
Expectation of Life (years): Males 75.3
Females 79.8
Marriage Rate per 1,000: 9.6
Divorce Rate per 1,000: —
Total Number of Households: 160,000
Average Size of Households: 3.5
% of Illegitimate Children: 0.4
Induced Abortions: —
Rate per 100 live births: —

ETHNIC COMPOSITION

Cyprus consists not merely of two ethnic groups but of two ethnic nations. Neither group considers themselves as primarily Cypriots; one considers itself Greek and the other Turkish, and the ties that bind them to these larger nationalities have determined the course of Cypriot history in recent years. Paradoxically, this ethnic self-identification is of comparatively recent origin; before the 1800s few in Cyprus called themselves either Greeks or Turks, having been united to those countries only as districts of their empires.

There is a small British minority of a few thousand in the country, dating to British rule and the more recent peacekeeping force involvement in Cyprus. There are a few Latin families in the southern port towns, remnants of the Venetian and Lusignan upper classes of pre-Ottoman times.

LANGUAGES

Three major languages are used in Cyprus: Greek in the Republic of Cyprus, Turkish in the Turkish sector, and English in both. English has become the principal language of the media, commerce, and education.

Cypriot Greek is actually three forms of Greek, all common to mainland Greece as well. The liturgical language of the Orthodox church is *koine,* the lingua franca of the Mediterranean world at the beginning of the Christian era. The standard Greek is known as *demotiki.* The third significant form is known as *katharevousa,* the literary Greek on the Attic model.

Cypriot Turkish is the standard Turkish of modern Turkey, as modified by Atatürk.

Principal Languages and Their Speakers

Greek	630,000
Turkish	190,000
Other	30,000

RELIGIONS

Religion is important in Cyprus primarily because it follows and reinforces ethnic and linguistic identity. The Church of Cyprus is in the Greek Orthodox tradition. It dates back to the introduction of Christianity on the island in A.D. 45, and the autonomy of the church was affirmed by the Byzantine emperor Zeno in the fifth century. The constitution of the Church of Cyprus was drawn up in 1909 and states that the church is governed by the Holy Synod.

Monasteries have always played an important role in the life of the Church of Cyprus, and they are the source of bishops, who are required to be celibate following Orthodox practices. Clergy are generally married, however, and traditionally chosen by their fellow villagers and sent for training before ordination. Religious observances vary widely, but generally Greek Cypriots are more religious than Greek mainlanders.

Other Christian denominations are represented on the island in smaller groups. In the Turkish sector, Islam is the dominant faith (primarily Sunni Muslims), although religion plays a more muted role in the north than in the south and serves more as a political tool.

Religious Affiliations

Greek Orthodox	630,000
Muslim (mostly Sunni)	190,000

HISTORICAL BACKGROUND

One of the oldest cultures in the Mediterranean, Cyprus has long been a crossroads between East and West. Despite many turnovers it has always been closest to Greece, sharing ethnic origins, language, religion, and social mores. Cyprus was the center of a Neolithic settlement as early as 3700 B.C.E. It was famous in the ancient world for its copper (*kyprios* in Greek) and it is believed either that its name is derived from the name of the mineral or, alternatively, that the mineral derived its name from the island. A far outpost of the Hellenic world by the second century B.C., the Greeks were followed soon after by the Phoenicians, and thereafter it was conquered successively by Egyptians, Persians, Greeks under Alexander the Great, Romans, and the Byzantines. Its Christian history began with Paul the Apostle accompanied by Barnabas and Mark the Evangelist in the second half of the first century. Although it underwent a series of Arab invasions in the seventh century, it was spared Arab domination. In 1191 the island was wrested by the English prince Richard I from its Byzantine ruler, Isaac Comnenus, and later sold to the Knights Templar and transferred by that order to Guy de Lusignan. Lusignan lived only two years after assuming control in 1192 but the dynasty that he founded ruled Cyprus as an independent Norman kingdom for more than three centuries. Conquered by Venice in 1489, Cyprus fell to the Turks in 1562.

Ottoman rule ended in 1878 when under a convention with Turkey initiated by Prime Minister Disraeli at the Congress of Berlin, Britain took over the administration of the island. Upon the entry of the Ottoman Empire in World War I on the side of the Central Powers, Cyprus was annexed to the British Crown, and later placed under a governor.

British rule was marred by the *enosis* movement (the agitation for self-determination and reunion with Greece), which erupted into violence on a number of occasions between the two world wars. The agitation for union with Greece gained force after World War II and pitted Greece against Turkey and threatened the unity of NATO of which both were members. As a compromise Greece and Turkey accepted proposals for an independent republic and the formula was accepted by the British government and the Greek ethnarch, Archbishop Makarios III. The settlement provided for a number of instruments defining the island's political status and also guaranteeing the continuation of British military installations. Independence was officially declared on August 16, 1960, with Britain, Greece, and Turkey as guarantor powers.

In 1974, Makarios was overthrown by a military coup led by the Cypriot National Guard. Turkey invaded Cyprus by sea and air on July 20, asserting its right to protect the Turkish Cypriot minority. Turks gained control of 40 percent of the island, and many Greek Cypriots were displaced. The separate Turkish state proclaimed on November 15, 1983, was declared invalid by the UN Security Council (Turkey does not recognize the government of the Republic of Cyprus). The island remains divided today, and except for some escalated tensions in 1996, there has been little movement toward resolution of the stalemate. Efforts at reunification continue under the auspices of the United Nations.

CONSTITUTION

Since 1974, Cyprus has been divided de facto into the government-controlled southern two-thirds of the island, and the Turkish-controlled northern one-third. The government of the Republic of Cyprus continues to be the internationally recognized authority, but in practice its power extends only to the Greek-Cypriot controlled areas.

The Greek-Cypriot constitution went into effect on August 16, 1960, the day Cyprus became independent. It was not subjected to popular referendum, although many of its provisions were modified in 1964. The constitution was drafted by British, Greek, and Turkish experts and it specifically prohibited union with any other country or the partition of the island, and set forth civil and political rights for both ethnic groups. The president of the republic is both head of state and head of government; there is no prime minister. There is technically an office of vice

ORGANIZATION OF CYPRIOT GOVERNMENT

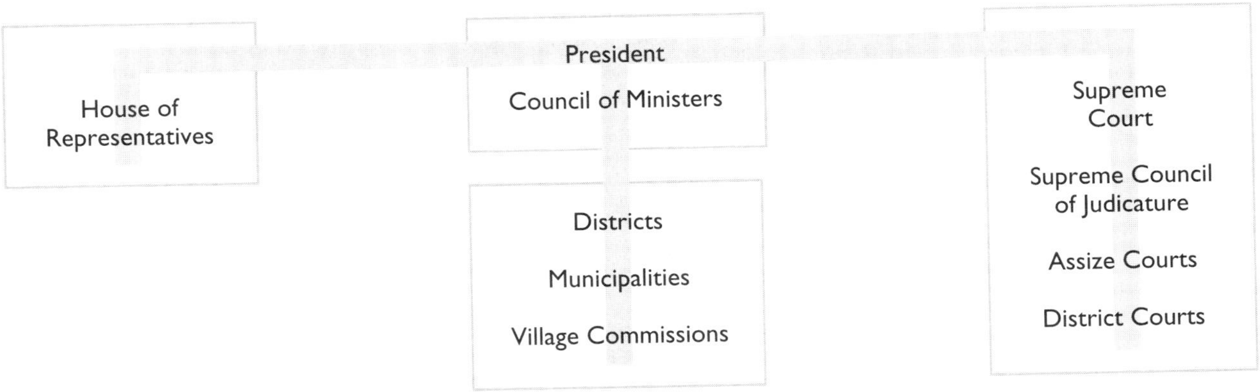

House of Representatives

President

Council of Ministers

Districts

Municipalities

Village Commissions

Supreme Court

Supreme Council of Judicature

Assize Courts

District Courts

president, but no elections have been held for it since 1973. The president is elected by universal suffrage for a five-year term and may be reelected. Executive powers are exercised by the president through the Council of Ministers.

This constitution was breached when the Turkish Cypriots declared an independent Turkish Republic of Northern Cyprus in 1983. In 1985 they adopted their own constitution, which provides for a president, prime minister, and cabinet. The president is elected by universal suffrage for seven-year renewable terms. Executive functions are entrusted to a prime minister and a 10-member cabinet.

LOCAL GOVERNMENT

Cyprus is divided into six administrative districts: Nicosia, Paphos, Larnaca, Limassol, Famagusta, and Kyrenia (the last two in the Turkish sector). Each district is administered by a district officer appointed by the Ministry of the Interior. Mayors and councils for the municipalities are appointed by the central government. Village commissions are also appointed by the Ministry of the Interior, although recent legislation provides for their popular election.

Local Government

Principal administrative divisions, capitals, area, population

AREA AND POPULATION

Districts	Capitals	area sq mi	area sq km	population 1992 estimate
Famagusta	Famagusta	766	1,984	30,798
Kyrenia	Kyrenia	247	640	—
Larnaca	Larnaca	433	1,121	100,242
Limassol	Limassol	538	1,393	173,634
Nicosia	Nicosia	1,049	2,717	244,779
Paphos	Paphos	539	1,396	52,572
TOTAL		3,572	9,251	602,025

PARLIAMENT

The legislative power of the Republic of Cyprus is exercised by the House of Representatives. Electoral law provides for proportional representation from each of six constituencies, and parliamentary seats are then distributed according to the electoral strength of each party. Members are elected by universal suffrage of adults over the age of 18. By a 1985 resolution 56 members are to be elected by the Greek-Cypriot community and 24 by the Turkish-Cypriot community; Turkish-Cypriot members have not attended the House since 1963, but the House has kept those seats vacant in accordance with the constitution.

The House is in quorum when at least one-third of the members are present. Legislation is the first order of business, and bills are referred to appropriate committees. Political parties are represented on committees in proportion to the total number of their seats in the House.

The president of the Republic of Cyprus and the vice president have the right of final veto on any law passed by the House that concerns certain issues of foreign affairs, defense, and security. Other types of legislation may be delayed and returned to the House, but must be promulgated into law if the House reaffirms its decision.

In the Turkish sector the 1985 constitutional declaration has resulted in elections for parliament and a prime minister, although they are not officially recognized outside of the sector.

POLITICAL PARTIES

The political parties in the Republic of Cyprus are the Democratic Rally (right-wing), which advocates a pro-Western and free enterprise policy; the Democratic Party (center-right), a moderate party following the policies of former president Makarios; the Progressive Party of the Working People (left-wing), with a pro-marxist bent; the

Unified Democratic Union of Cyprus (socialist), a small party favoring nonalignment; and the United Democrats (center-left), a moderate group. In the Turkish-Cypriot community, the parties are: National Unity (right), founded by Rauf Denktash; the Democratic Party (center-right), the other main conservative group, usually aligned with the NUP; the Republican Turkish (left); Communal Liberation (center-left); National Revival (center-right), which represents the interests of settlers from mainland Turkey; the Patriotic Unity Movement (left); and the National Justice Party (ultra-nationalist).

Political Parties

Democratic Rally, 1976
Liberal Party, 1986
United Democrats, 1996
New Horizons, 1996
Unified Democratic Union-Socialist Party
Democratic Party, 1976
Progressive Party of the Working People, 1941
Ecologists, 1995

Political Parties: Strength in Parliament Most Recent Elections

House of Representatives. The chamber has 59 members, 56 elected for five-year terms by proportional representation and three representing the Maronite, Roman Catholic, and Goumenian minorities. The Turkish minority is allocated 24 seats. At the elections of May 27, 2001, the Progressive Party of the Working People won 20 seats; Democratic Coalition, 19; Democratic Party, 9; Social Democrats Movement, 4; New Horizons, 1; United Democrats, 1; Fighting Democratic Movement, 1; Ecological and Environmental Movement, 1; and Maronite, Roman Catholic, and Goumenian minorities, 3.

LEGAL SYSTEM

In 1964 the Supreme Constitutional Court and the High Court of Justice were merged into the Supreme Court. The Supreme Council of Judicature performs the judicatory functions of the former High Court. Below the supreme court are the assize courts and the district courts. District courts perform as the courts of first instance for all but the most serious of crimes. Assize courts have an unlimited criminal jurisdiction in the first instance. The Supreme Court hears all criminal appeals but has no original jurisdiction in criminal matters.

Trial procedures are based on English common law. There are no juries, and all trials are public. Punishments allowed by law include death by hanging, life imprisonment, and whipping. However, in practice these harsher punishments are rarely meted out, and pardons and parole procedures have been expanded in recent years.

The basic structure of the Turkish-Cypriot legal system follows that of the Greek Cypriot sector.

LAW ENFORCEMENT

Law Enforcement

Offenses reported to the police per 100,000: 689
- Murder: 1.9
- Assault: 17.7
- Burglary: 203.3
- Automobile Theft: 3.0
- Population per Police officer: 180

Death Penalty: Yes, but only in exceptional circumstances

HUMAN RIGHTS

The Republic of Cyprus generally respects human rights norms and practices. However, human rights groups report continued instances of police brutality. In the Turkish sector, police abuse of the rights of suspects and detainees is considered a problem. Suspects are often not permitted to have their lawyers present when questioned, although this right is provided for under basic Turkish-Cypriot law. Authorities in the sector also exert some restrictions over general freedom of movement.

Violence against women continues to be of concern in both areas, particularly domestic abuse.

FOREIGN POLICY

The government of Cyprus has historically followed a non aligned foreign policy, although it increasingly identifies with the West. It maintains close relations with Greece, and in recent years has expanded its relations with Russia, Israel, and Syria, from which it purchases most of its oil. Cyprus is a member of the United Nations and has signed the General Agreement on Tariffs and Trade (GATT) and the Multilateral Investment Guarantee Agency Agreement (MIGA).

Turkey does not recognize the government of Cyprus. The Republic of Cyprus' 1990 application for full EU membership sparked a protest when Turkey argued that the move required its consent. Negotiations began in 1998 following an EU enlargement summit. In 1999 Turkey was again angered when the Republic of Cyprus announced plans to deploy missiles capable of reaching Turkey's coast.

DEFENSE

The National Guard is the primary defense force in the Cypriot sector, and is responsible to the president of the republic through the minister of the interior and defense. Manpower is supplied through conscription of males when they reach age 18, and recruits serve for 26 months after which they join the reserve. There is very little formal military tradition in Cyprus, and most training is conducted by Greeks from the mainland.

The Turkish Cypriot Security Force is officered by members of the Turkish army on temporary assignment, who are responsible to the president of the Turkish sector.

Besides these indigenous forces there are four other military powers with armed forces on the island: Great Britain, Greece, Turkey, and the UN peacekeeping forces. Britain retains sovereignty over two bases on the southern coast, Akrotiri and Dhekelia. Greece maintains forces under the direction of the Ministry of National Defense in Athens. Turkey is the most powerful military presence on the island and reports to the Ministry of National Defense in Ankara. The UN troops have been present in Cyprus since 1964, and they operate in the buffer zone of the Turkish and Greek Cypriot cease-fire lines.

Military Indicators

Total Active Duty Personnel: 10,000
Military Manpower per 1,000: 13.0
Military Expenditures $million: 495
  as % of GNP: 5.8
  per capita $: 672
  as % of central government expenditures: 17.1

Arms Imports $million: 50
Arms Exports $million: 0

ECONOMY

Cyprus has an open, free-market, service-based economy with some light manufacturing, and is among the most prosperous nations in the Mediterranean region. In the past 20 years, the economy has shifted from agriculture and light manufacturing to a concentration in services and tourism, which contributes 70 percent to the gross domestic product and employs over 60 percent of the labor force.

Principal Economic Indicators

Gross National Product: $10.839 billion
GNP per capita: $14,930
GNP Average Annual Growth Rate (1990–97) %: —
GNP per capita Average Annual Growth Rate (1990–97) %: —
Origin of Gross Domestic Product %
  Agriculture: 5
  Mining: —
  Manufacturing: 13
  Construction: 9
  Public Utilities: 2
  Transportation and Communications: 8
  Trade: 19
  Financial Services: 16
  Other Services: 7
  Government: 13
Gross Domestic Product by Type of Expenditure %
  Private Consumption: 60
  Government Consumption: 17
  Gross Domestic Investment: 24
  Foreign Trade: Exports: 49
    Imports: −49
% of Income Received by Poorest 20%: 7.9
% of Income Received by Richest 10%: —

Finance

National Currency: Cypriot Pound £C
Exchange Rate: $1 = £C 0.5326
Money Supply Stock in National Currency billion: 0.654
M1 per capita: 1,000
Central Bank Discount Rate %: 7.0
Total External Debt $million: 1,560
Debt Service Ratio %: —

Balance of Payments $million: −382.7
International Reserves SDRs million: 911
Ratio of External Debt to Total Reserves: —
Average Annual Rate of Inflation/Consumer Price Index
  Growth Rate %: 3.5

Official Development Assistance

ODA $million: 187
  as % of GNP: —
  per capita: $41
  Foreign Direct Investment $million: —

Central Government Revenues and Expenditures

Fiscal Year: Calendar Year
Revenues $million: 2,900
Expenditures $million: 3,400
Budget Deficit $million: 500
Tax Revenues as % of GDP: —
Highest Tax Bracket %
  Individual: —
  Corporate: —

Employment and Labor

Economically Active Population: 303,000
Female Participation Rate %: 38.6
Activity Rate %: 47.0
Labor by Sector: %
  Agriculture, Forestry, Fishing: 10.1
  Manufacturing, Mining: 15.9
  Construction: 8.7
  Transportation and Communications: 6.2
  Trade, Hotels, and Restaurants: 25.4
  Finance, Insurance, Real Estate: 7.6
  Public Administration, Defense: —
  Services: 21.6

Unemployment %: 3.3

Agriculture

Agriculture's Share of GDP %: 5
Average Annual Rate of Growth (1965–98) %: —
Number of Farms 000: 48
Average Size of Farm ha: 3.8
Number of Tractors per 1,000 hectares: 13.7
Irrigation, % of Farms having: 40

Artificial Fertilizer kg/hectare: 144
Total Farmland as % of land area: 35.6
Livestock: Cattle 000: 61
Sheep 000: 262
Hogs 000: 415
Chickens 000: 3,500
Forests: Production of Roundwood (000 cubic meters): 54
Fisheries: Total Catch tons 000: 3.1

Mining

% of GDP: 0.3
Value of Mineral Production $million: 23.7

Manufacturing

Value Added $million: 899
Industrial Production Growth Rate %: −4

Energy

Commercial Energy Production metric tons of oil equivalent 000: —
Commercial Energy Consumption metric tons of oil equivalent 000: 1,961
Commercial Energy Consumption per capita kg: 2,701
Average Annual Growth Rate 1980–97 %: —
Net Energy Imports % of use: 100
Electricity Installed Capacity kW 000: 699
Production kW-hr million: 2,473
Coal Reserves tons 000: —
Production tons 00: —
Natural Gas Proven Reserves cubic meters million: —
Production cubic meters million: —
Crude Petroleum Reserves barrels million: —
Production barrels million: —
Consumption barrels million: 6
Refinery Capacity barrels per day 000: 26
Pipelines Length km:

Foreign Trade

Imports $million: 3,982.5
Exports $million: 1,391.0
Export Volume % Annual Growth Rate (1990–97): —
Import Volume % Annual Growth Rate (1990–97): —

Major Trading Partners

	Imports	Exports
European Union %	48.6	28.4
United States %	16.8	0.7
Eastern Europe %	5.5	36.3
Japan %	6.0	0.1
Others %	23.1	34.5

Transportation

Roads Total Length mi: 6,307 km 10,150
Paved %: 57
Automobiles: 219,749
Trucks and Buses: 103,852
Persons per vehicle: 2.6
Railroad; Track Length mi: — km —
Passenger-mi million: —
Freight-mi million: —
Merchant Marine: No. of Vessels: 1,416
Total Deadweight Tonnage 000: 36,198.1
International Cargo Loaded tons 000: 2,232
International Cargo Off-loaded tons 000: 5,028
Airports with Scheduled Flights: 2
Traffic: Passenger-mi million: 1,588
Freight-mi million: 26
Length of Canals mi: —

Tourism

Number of Tourists to: —
Number of Tourists from: —
Tourist Receipts $million: 1,783
Tourist Expenditures $million: 293

Communications

Telephones 000: 347
Cost of Local Calls 3 mins: $0
Cellular Telephones 000: 45
Fax Machines 000: 7.0
Personal Computers 000: 30
Internet Hosts per million persons: 532
Mail: Post Offices: 738
Pieces of Mail Handled million: 58
Pieces of Mail Handled per person: 79

EDUCATION

There are two educational systems in the country, given the Greek and Turkish separation. Attendance is nearly 100 percent in both sectors, and the literacy rate of the entire island is fairly high, at 94 percent.

The Republic of Cyprus offers education at the preprimary, primary, secondary, and higher levels. Attendance is compulsory at the primary and secondary levels. Most schooling at this level is free, although there are also private schools. The basic language of instruction is Greek, and English is widely taught as well. Overall standards are high, with continual assessment, and specialization begins at the secondary level in gymnasiums and lyceums. There are no universities in Cyprus, but higher education is provided in six public institutions: the Pedagogical Academy, the Higher Technical Institute, the Forestry College, the School of Nursing and Midwifery, the Hotel and Catering Institute, and the Psychiatric School of Nursing. Some students elect to pursue higher education at universities in Greece.

In the Turkish sector, education became compulsory for children up to ages 15 or 16 in 1975. The language of instruction is Turkish, and textbooks are obtained from the mainland. The curriculum is similar to that of the Greek schools, although there are few provisions for preprimary education. There are no universities in the northern sector, but the Teacher Training College in Kyrenia and the Higher Technical Institute in Famagusta serve the needs of higher education.

Education

Literacy Rate %: 95.2
- Male %: 97.8
- Female %: 92.8

First Level: Primary schools: 383
- Teachers: 3,498
- Students: 64,884
- Student-Teacher Ratio: 18.5
- Net Enrollment Ratio: 96

Second Level: Secondary Schools: 107
- Teachers: 3,832
- Students: 53,738
- Student-Teacher Ratio: 14.0
- Net Enrollment Ratio: 93

Vocational Level: Schools: 11
- Students: 4,066

Third Level: Institutions: 32
- Teachers: 648
- Students: 7,765
- Student-Ratio Level: 12.0
- Gross Enrollment Ratio: 20.6
- Students per 100,000: 1,069
- % of Population Age 25 and over with Postsecondary Education: 17.0

Public Expenditure on Education as % of GDP: 4.4

SCIENCE AND TECHNOLOGY

Science and Technology

Scientists and Engineers in R&D per 1 million persons: —
Expenditures in R&D as % of GDP: —
High-Tech Exports $million: —
Patent Applications by Residents: —

MEDIA

The Republic of Cyprus publishes nine daily newspapers, including the *Cyprus Mail* in English. Most papers represent a particular political viewpoint. In the Turkish sector, five dailies are printed. In addition, both sectors publish weekly editions and periodicals. Private ownership is the norm in both the Greek and Turkish sectors. There is no censorship, but publication permits are required.

The national news agency is the Cyprus News Agency in the Greek sector and the Turk Ajansi Kibris in the Turkish sector. Foreign news agencies are represented in Nicosia. The Cyprus Broadcasting Corporation, a semi-governmental body modeled on the BBC, operates both radio and television services. Turkish radio and television are operated by Bayrak Radio and Television Corporation. In addition, the British Forces Broadcasting Service is in operation.

Media

Daily Newspapers: 14
- Total Circulation 000: 81
- Circulation per 1,000: 110

Books Published: 1,040
Magazines: 37
Radio Receivers 000: 210
- per 1,000: 288

Television sets 000: 105
- per 1,000: 143

MOST IMPORTANT MEDIA:

Press. The following newspapers are published daily at Nicosia in Greek, unless otherwise noted (circulation figures are daily averages for January 1994); *Phileleftheros* (Liberal, 21,886), independent; *Apogevmatini* (Afternoon, 7,291), independent; *Simerini* (Today, 7,290), right-wing; *Haravghi* (Dawn, 6,927), AKEL organ; *Alithia* (Truth, 4,897), right-wing; *Agon* (Struggle, 4,069), right-wing; *Eleftherotypia* (Free Press), centrist; *Cyprus Mail*, independent, in English; *Machi* (Battle), right-wing.

News agencies. A Greek-sector Cyprus News Agency (Kypriakon Praktoreion Eidiseon—KPE) was established in 1976; numerous foreign bureaus maintain offices at Nicosia.

Radio and television. Prior to the 1974 conflict, broadcasting was controlled by the semigovernmental Cyprus Broadcasting Corporation (Radiofonikon Idryma Kyprou—RIK) and the government-owned Radyo Bayrak and Radyo Bayrak Televizyon. At present, radio service in the Greek sector is provided by the RIK, in addition to three private island-wide and 24 local stations. The RIK maintains television service from its station at Mount Olympus, while the RB and the RBT stations broadcast from the Turkish sector. At present, the Greek channel ET-1 is rebroadcast on Cyprus, while radio service is also provided by the BBC East Mediterranean Relay and by the British Forces Broadcasting Service, Cyprus.

CULTURE

Cultural Indicators

Public Libraries Number: 103
- Volumes: 236,000
- Registered borrowers:

Museums Number: 26
- Annual Attendance: 96,000

Cinema Production of Long Films: 1
- Number of Cinemas: 35
- Seating Capacity: 8,400
- Annual Attendance million: 11.3
- Annual Attendance per capita: 1.0

STATUS OF WOMEN

Throughout Cyprus, women generally have the same legal status as men. During the 1990s, laws in both the Greek and Turkish sectors were updated to reflect a broadening of rights for women, particularly concerning marriage, divorce, child custody, and citizenship. In the workforce, legal provisions in both communities require equal pay for men and women performing the same job. This is enforced effectively at the professional level, but women in agricultural and textile positions are still routinely paid less than their male counterparts.

Women face no legal obstacles to their participation in the political process. They are clearly underrepresented in government, but they do hold some cabinet, judicial, and other senior jobs. In the most recently elected House of Representatives, women hold four of the 50 seats.

Domestic abuse continues to be a problem in Cyprus. In the Greek Cypriot community it is an issue receiving increased attention, and in 1994 a law was passed making abuse easier to report and prosecute. To date it has had little effect, largely because of family pressure and the fact that most women are still economically dependent upon their male family members. In the Turkish sector domestic abuse is also estimated to be high, but is less openly discussed and more often considered "family matters" outside of the legal system.

Women

Gender Empowerment Measure: 66
Seats Held in Parliament by Women %: 5.4
Female Administrators and Managers %: 10.2
Female Professional and Technical Workers %: 40.8
Women's Share of Earned Income %: 28.0
Women in Government %: 5

HEALTH, FOOD, AND NUTRITION

Health

Number of Physicians: 1,455
Number of Dentists: 498
Number of Nurses: 2,536
Number of Pharmacists: 423
Population per Physician: 433
Number of Hospitals: 110
Hospital Beds per 10,000: 52
Hospital Bed Occupancy Rate: 75.7
Infant Mortality Rate per 1,000 live births: 9
Maternal Mortality Rate per 100,000 live births: —
Total Health Expenditures as % of GDP: 3.96
Health Expenditures per capita $: 64
HIV Infected % of adults: —
Cigarette Consumption per smoker per year: —
% of Smokers: Male: —
Female: —
Access to Safe Water %: 100

Food and Nutrition

Food Supply as % of FAO Requirements: 150
% of Consumption Expenditures on Food: 22.7
Daily Available Calories per capita: 3,708
% of Total Calories derived from:
Cereals: 24.1
Potatoes, cassava: 2.1
Meat, poultry: 20.6
Fish: 0.8
Eggs, milk: 12.5
Fruits, vegetables: 6.4
Fats, oils: 15.3

ENVIRONMENT

There are two major pressing environmental issues faced by Cyprus: water resource problems (including the lack of reservoirs, seasonal disparity in precipitation, increased salination, water pollution from sewage and industrial wastes, and coastal degradation); and the loss of wildlife and wildlife habitats due to increasing urbanization. Cyprus is party to various international environmental agreements, including those concerned with biodiversity, endangered species, hazardous wastes, nuclear test bans, ozone layer protection, and ship pollution.

Environment

Forest Area sq km: —
Average Annual Deforestation sq km: 0
Nationally Protected Areas as % of Total Land Area: —
FreshWater Access cubic meters per capita: —
Emissions of Organic Water Pollutants kg per day: —
CO_2 Emissions per capita ton: 7.3

CHRONOLOGY

1959 Under the London-Zurich Agreement, guaranteed by the United Kingdom, Greece, and Turkey, Cyprus is granted independence as a republic; Archbishop Makarios III is elected president and Fazil Kucuk vice president.

1960 The constitution of Cyprus takes effect; the first elections to the House of Representatives are held.

1963 Archbishop Makarios issues 13 proposals to amend the constitution in an effort to assure Greek ascendancy in government.

1964 The Cypriot National Guard is formed. The UN peacekeeping force reaches Cyprus.

1967 Kucuk declares the Turkish Provisional Administration.

1968 Makarios is reelected president by an overwhelming majority.

1974 Gen. George Grivas, the Eoka leader, dies. Makarios is overthrown by right-wing National Guard troops, who name Nicos Sampson as head of state; Makarios flees the country. Turkish army invades Cyprus and after heavy fighting occupies the northern third of the country, including the cities of Famagusta and Kyrenia and part of Nicosia. Makarios returns from Greece and is reinstated as president.

1975 The Turkish-held northern sector proclaims itself as the Turkish Federated State of Cyprus, with Rauf Denktash as president.

1977 Makarios dies and is succeeded in office by Spyros Kyprianou, who is elected president.

1983 The northern sector proclaims independence as the Turkish Republic of Northern Cyprus. Kyprianou is reelected president.

1988 George Vassiliou is elected president.

1990 The republic submits a formal application for full EU membership, sparking a storm of debate from the Turkish Cypriot community.

1993 Glafkos Klirides is elected president. Turkish Cypriots hold multiparty parliamentary elections.

1994 The republic begins a five-year development plan, greatly expanding computerization and telecommunications.

1995 TRNC President Rauf Denktash wins reelection.

1996 For the first time since 1974, violent clashes between Greek Cypriot and Turkish Cypriot forces result in the death of two demonstrators and escalated tensions.

1997 The Republic of Cyprus purchases missiles capable of reaching the Turkish coast, evoking threats of retaliation from Turkey. President Klerides and TRNC President Rauf Denktash engage in a series of face-to-face meetings to discuss settlement.

1998 Glafkos Klirides is reelected president by a narrow margin. Accession negotiations begin in March.

1999 The republic's plan to deploy additional missiles again provokes Turkey's ire.

2002 Klirides and Denktash hold their first face-to-face meeting in four years in December. This meeting is followed by a second one, for which Denktash crosses to the south for the first time since the Turkish invasion of 1974.

BIBLIOGRAPHY

Christophorou, Demetrakis. *History of Cyprus*. Nicosia, 1993.

Demetriades, Evros I. (ed.). *Population and Human Resources Development in Cyprus: Research and Policy Issues*. Nicosia, 1992.

Gazioglu, Ahmet C. *Two Equal and Sovereign Peoples: A Documented Background to the Cyprus Problem and the Concept of Partnership*. Lefkosa, 1997.

Katsiaounis, Rolandos. *Labour, Society, and Politics in Cyprus during the Second Half of the Nineteenth Century*. Nicosia, 1996.

Mirbagheri, Farid. *Cyprus and International Peacemaking*. New York, 1998.

Press and Information Office, Republic of Cyprus. *The Cyprus Problem: Historical Review and Latest Developments*. Nicosia, 1993.

Press and Information Office, Republic of Cyprus. *The Republic of Cyprus: An Overview*. Nicosia, 1994.

Press and Information Office, Republic of Cyprus. *Report on the Demographic Structure of the Cypriot Communities*. Nicosia, 1994.

Sonyel, Salahi R. *Cyprus, the Destruction of a Republic*. Cambridgeshire, England, 1997.

Solsten, Eric (ed.). *Cyprus, A Country Study*. Washington, D.C., 1993.

Theophylactou, Demetrios A. *Security, Identity, and Nation Building: Cyprus and the European Union in Comparative Perspective*. Brookfield, Mass., 1995.

Wilson, Rodney. *Cyprus and the International Economy*. New York, 1992.

OFFICIAL PUBLICATIONS

Cyprus. *Census of Industrial Production* (annual); *Census of Population 1992; Economic Report* (annual); *Statistical Abstract* (annual).

CONTACT INFORMATION

Embassy of Cyprus
2211 R Street NW
Washington, D.C. 20008
Phone: (202) 462-5772   Fax: (202) 483-6710

INTERNET RESOURCES

- The Cyprus Government http://www.pio.gov.cy/
- Department of Statistics and Research
  http://www.pio.gov.cy/dsr
  http://www.odci.gov/cia/publications/factbook/geos/cy.html

CZECH REPUBLIC

BASIC FACT SHEET

OFFICIAL NAME:
Czech Republic (Česká Republika)

ABBREVIATION:
CZ

CAPITAL:
Prague

HEAD OF STATE:
President Vaclav Hável (from 1993)

HEAD OF GOVERNMENT:
Prime Minister Milos Zeman (from 1998)

NATURE OF GOVERNMENT:
Parliamentary democracy

POPULATION:
10,290,000 (1999)

AREA:
78,866 sq km (30,450 sq mi)

MAJOR ETHNIC GROUPS:
Czechs and Slovaks

LANGUAGE:
Czech

RELIGIONS:
Roman Catholic, Protestant, Orthodox

UNIT OF CURRENCY:
Koruna

NATIONAL FLAG:
A white stripe over a red stripe with a blue triangle extending from hoist to midpoint

NATIONAL EMBLEM:
The ornate white lion of the royal house of Bohemia. On the lion's shoulder is displayed a small red and blue shield featuring a flaming grenade against a stylized outline of Mount Krivak. The large red shield is of unusual heraldic shape—square at the bottom and triangular at the top.

NATIONAL ANTHEM:
"Kde Domov Muj?" ("Where is My Native Land?")

NATIONAL HOLIDAYS:
May 9 (Anniversary of the Liberation); October 28 (Nationalization Day); December 26 (St. Stephen's Day); Labor Day; New Year's Day; Christmas; Easter Monday

DATE OF INDEPENDENCE:
October 28, 1918

DATE OF CONSTITUTION:
December 16, 1992 (ratified)

GEOGRAPHICAL FEATURES

The Czech Republic is a landlocked nation in the center of Europe, southeast of Germany. Its total area is 78,866 sq km (30,450 sq mi). The nation borders Austria, Poland, Germany, and Slovakia. There are two broad regions: Bohemia in the west, and Moravia in the east. Bohemia consists of rolling plains, hills, and plateaus, surrounded by low mountains. Moravia is much more hilly and mountainous.

Europe's major watershed runs through the Czech Republic and separates the basins of the North, Baltic, and Black Seas. The nation's principal rivers include the Labe (Elbe), Vltava, Morava, Odra (Oder), and Dyje. There are also 455 natural lakes in the republic, including a complex of five limestone lakes of glacial origin in the region of Bohemia. In addition, there are some 21,800 artificial lakes which have been created for farm fishing. The nation also possesses a number of natural springs renowned for their therapeutic value. The warmest of these is the thermal spring at Karlovy Vary with a temperature of 72°C (162°F).

The Czech Republic lies on the borderline of two major mountain systems: the Hercynian and the

Czech Republic

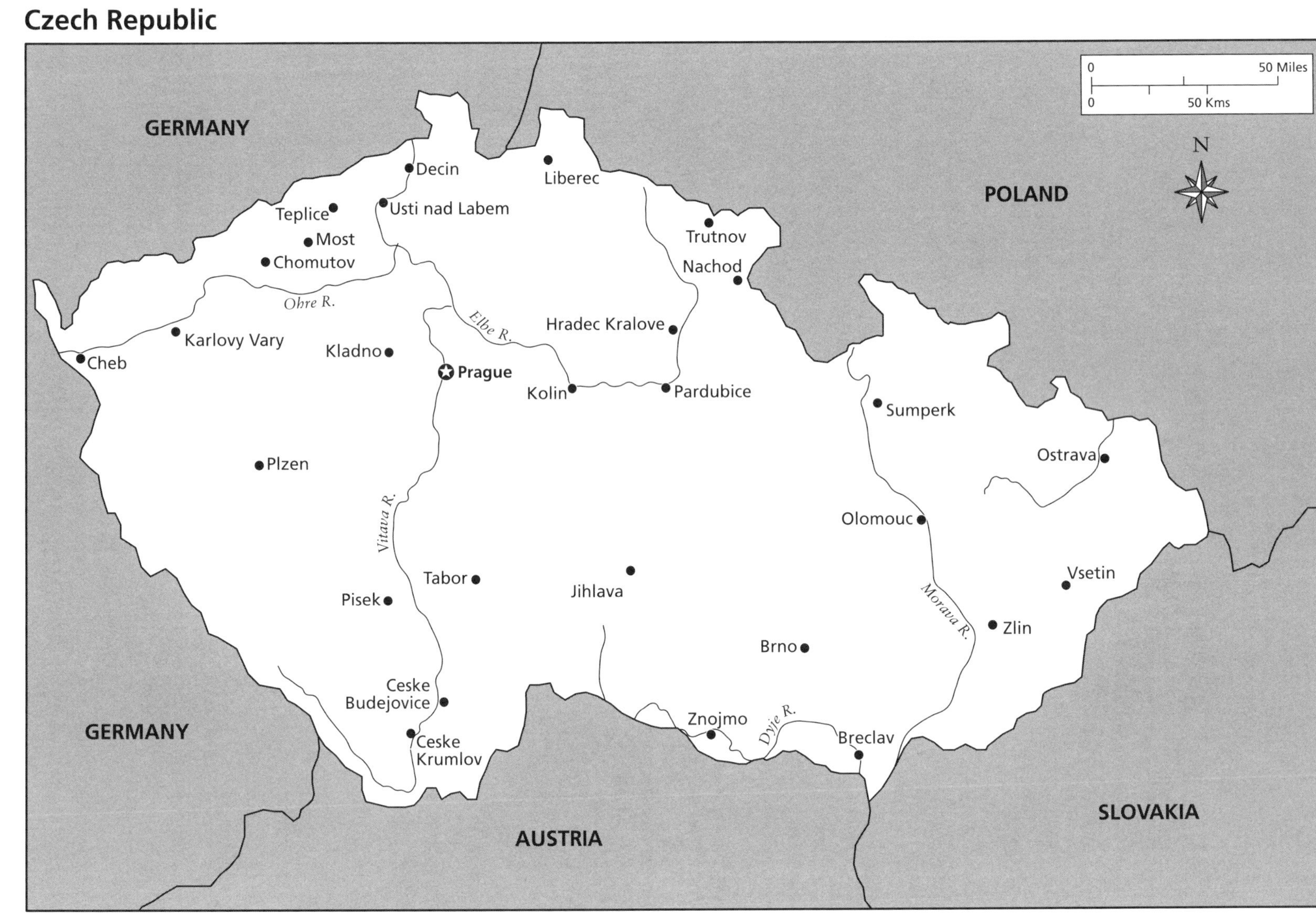

Alpine-Himalayan. The Krkonoše (Giant Mountains) mountain range stretches into Bohemia and creates a natural border with Poland. The range is the highest in the republic. The Hrubý Jesenik (Ash Mountains) are the second tallest mountains in the country and are located in northern Moravia. The third highest range in the Czech Republic is the Šumava (Bohemian Forest). These hilly ranges are known as the Cesky Les. The fourth major mountain range in the nation is the Morava-Silesian Beskydy Mountains, which lie in the eastern part of the Czech Republic and in northern Moravia. They are a frontier range that runs north to south and borders Poland and the Slovak Republic.

The capital is Prague, situated on both sides of the Vltava River, near the center of Bohemia. Although one of the newest national capitals of Europe, it is one of the continent's oldest and most picturesque cities.

Geography

Area sq km: 78,866 sq mi: 30,450
World Rank: 117th
Land Boundaries, km: Austria 362; Germany 646; Poland 658; Slovakia 215
Coastline, km: 0
Elevation Extremes meters
Lowest: Elbe River 115
Highest: Snezka 1,602
Land Use % Arable land: 41
Permanent Crops: 2
Permanent Pastures: 11
Forest and Woodland: 34
Other: 12

Population of Principal Cities (1996 est.)

Brno	388,899
Hradec Králové	100,528
Liberec	100,604
Olomouc	104,845
Ostrava	324,813
Plzen	171,249
Prague	1,209,855

CLIMATE AND WEATHER

The Czech Republic is in Europe's temperate zone, and as such has relatively mild winters and summers, with only moderate precipitation. The mean annual temperature nationwide ranges from 6°C to 10°C (43°F to 50°F), although elevation greatly affects temperature. In the continental eastern regions, temperature variants are greater in the spring than in the fall.

Rainfall is influenced by elevation, the direction of exposure, shelter from winds, and situation on the windward or leeward side of mountains. Generally, rainfall increases toward the east. In the lowlands, precipitation occurs mainly in the summer. The more hilly regions and piedmont areas receive up to 1,372 mm (54 in) of rainfall a year and the mountains up to 1,397 mm (55 in) annually.

Climate and Weather

Mean Temperature 43°F to 50°F
Summer 86°F/Winter 5°F
Average Rainfall 54 in to 55 in
Bohemia 22 in

POPULATION

Population Indicators

Total Population: 1999 10,290,000
World Rank: 72nd
Density per sq mi: 337.9 per sq km: 130.5
% of annual growth (1994–99): −0.1
Male %: 48.5
Female %: 51.5
Urban %: 75.2
Age Distribution: % 0–14: 21.0
15–29: 21.8
30–44: 22.6
45–59: 16.8
60–74: 12.7
75 and over: 5.1
Population 2020: 10,309,000
Birth Rate per 1,000: 8.8
Death Rate per 1,000: 10.9
Population Doubling Time (years): Population is declining
Infant Mortality Rate per 1,000 live births: 6.0
Rate of Natural Increase per 1,000: −2.1
Total Fertility Rate: 1.4
Expectation of Life (years): Males 70
Females 76.9
Marriage Rate per 1,000: 5.6
Divorce Rate per 1,000: 3.2
Total Number of Households: 3,557,000
Average Size of Households: 2.9
% of Illegitimate Children: 15.6
Induced Abortions: 61,590
Rate per 100 live births: 64.1

ETHNIC COMPOSITION

The split between the Czech Republic and Slovakia resulted in the dissolution of a multiethnic state and the emergence of a relatively homogeneous population in the Czech Republic. Ethnic Czechs now make up some 94.4 percent of the total population. Other ethnic groups include Slovaks (3 percent), Poles (0.6 percent), Germans (0.5 percent), Gypsies (0.3 percent), and Hungarians (0.2 percent). There are also a small Jewish and Russian population. Following the 1994 breakup of Czechoslovakia, some 300,000 Slovaks declared themselves Czech citizens.

LANGUAGES

Both Czech and Slovak are spoken in the Czech Republic. Many Czechs speak German as well as English, which has become the most desired foreign language in the universities. During the communist era, Russian was taught in school, but the language is little used today. The major ethnic groups, including the Poles, Germans, and Hungarians, speak their own languages. In addition, the Jews and Gypsies speak the languages of their community for general communication, but use Yiddish or their own languages in private conversation.

Principal Languages and Their Speakers

Bulgarian	3,000
Czech	8,353,000
German	48,000
Greek	3,000
Hungarian	20,000
Moravian	1,324,000
Polish	60,000
Romanian	1,000
Romany	33,000
Russian	5,000
Rutherian	2,000
Silesian	44,000
Slovak	315,000
Ukranian	8,000
Other	70,000

RELIGIONS

Moravia was Christianized in the 9th and tenth centuries by Cyril and Methodius. The Kingdom of Bohemia became Catholic under King Wenceslas. Roman Catholicism is the majority religion, although a deeply persecuted one from 1947 to 1990. Roman Catholics account for 39.2 percent of the population. The Czechoslovak Hussite Church is a reformed Catholic sect that split with Rome after World War I and is the second largest Christian denomination.

Protestants make up only 4.6 percent of the Czech Republic. Lutheranism is the dominant Protestant denomination. Other Protestant churches include the Evangelical Church of the Czech Brethren and the Reformed Christian Church.

Of the 300,000 Jews in Czechoslovakia before World War II, only about 40,000 survived. Due to continued emigration, only about 5,000 to 6,000 remain.

Religious Affiliations

Religion	Adherents
Roman Catholic	4,020,000
Evangelical Church of Czech Brethren	200,000
Czechoslovak Hussite	180,000
Silesian Evangelical	30,000
Eastern Orthodox	20,000
Atheist and nonreligious	4,110,000
Other	1,730,000

HISTORICAL BACKGROUND

The earliest inhabitants of the present-day Czech lands were Celtic tribes who settled in Bohemia as early as 500 B.C. The Celts were displaced by seminomadic German tribes. In the fourth century the Germans began to move westward, and by the fifth century, the region was a Slavic domain. The sixth century witnessed the onslaught of the Avars, a pastoral people speaking a Ural-Altaic language. They were repelled by Samo, who unified the Slavic tribes and in 625 established the Samo Empire, which lasted until 658 as the first Czech polity. Early in the ninth century the Moravian Empire emerged, and German missionaries began to spread Christianity within the empire. The Moravians allied themselves with the Germans, and Moravia was permanently drawn to the West.

The Moravian Empire disintegrated with the Magyar invasions. The Czech tribes broke away and swore allegiance to the Franks, while the Slovaks remained under Magyar rule for successive centuries. The political center of gravity shifted as a result of the demise of the Moravian Empire, and a new empire emerged in Bohemia in the 10th century. This empire was controlled by chiefs of the Cechove, from which Czech is derived. The third ruler of this dynasty was King Wenceslas, who became the national saint. The Bohemian Kingdom eventually became a fiefdom of the Holy Roman Empire. After the royal line came to an end in 1306, a new royal family was started by John of Luxembourg, who was the son of the Holy Roman Emperor.

The reign of the second Luxembourg king, Charles IV (1347–78), is known as the Golden Age of Czech history. During his reign, Prague became an archbishopric, and a supreme court and university were established. Following his election as Holy Roman Emperor in 1355, Prague became the imperial city, and extensive building projects were undertaken, including the Charles Bridge across the Vltava.

In the aftermath of the Golden Age, the Hussite movement emerged and dominated Czech history for the next 100 years. Jan Hus, rector of the University of Prague, rejected the corruption, wealth, and hierarchy of the Roman Catholic Church and espoused the teachings of John Wycliffe. Hus was condemned as a heretic and burned at the stake in 1415. His death sparked generations of religious warfare, pitting Catholics against reformers, and Czechs against Germans. This conflict was exacerbated by dynastic squabbles, which were finally ended in 1526, when Ferdinand united the crowns of St. Stephen and

St. Wenceslas under Austrian control. Austria would rule the Czechs for 392 years, until 1918.

The early years of Austrian rule were marked by efforts to suppress Czech nationalism and the Hussites. On November 8, 1620, the Czechs were decisively defeated at the Battle of White Mountain. From then on, Austrian rule was secure.

Concurrent with this period of Austrian hegemony, the Czech lands were devastated by the Thirty Years War (1618–48) between the Catholic and Protestant powers of Europe. The Treaty of Westphalia (1648) ended the war and incorporated the Bohemian Kingdom into the Habsburg imperial system. German became the official language.

During the Enlightenment period, reforms were enacted that limited the power of the Roman Catholic Church, and Josef II (1780–90) abolished serfdom and, through the Edict of Toleration in 1781, extended religious freedom of worship to Lutherans and Calvinists.

The first half of the 19th century witnessed a rebirth of Czech nationalism. However, the Revolution of 1848 was crushed by the imperial Austrian forces and absolutism was restored under the Habsburg emperor Franz Josef (1848–1916).

The establishment of the Dual Monarchy and the reconfiguration of the empire into the Austro-Hungarian Empire did not bring any concessions to the Czechs. When World War I began, the Czechs intensified their efforts to break away from the empire. Czech and Slovak leaders joined together to establish the Czech National Council and set up centers of resistence in Vienna, Prague, Budapest, and Bratislava. In the fall of 1918, the Allies recognized the council as the government of an independent republic. At the Paris Peace Conference, the Allies approved the establishment of the Czechoslovak Republic, including Bohemia, Moravia, Silesia, Slovakia, and Ruthenia.

Czechoslovakia was founded on October 28, 1918. A new constitution was adopted and a national assembly and president were elected. Czech and Slovak were recognized as the national languages and special protections were granted to minorities. In an effort to defuse potential separatist movements, the national government was highly centralized and provincial assemblies had only nominal powers.

Between 1918 and 1938 Czechoslovakia had relatively stable governments, but there soon emerged a struggle between the national government and the Sudeten Germans. A strong sense of German nationalism among this minority fueled the rise of the Sudeten Nazi Party, which supported Adolf Hitler's pan-Germanism.

After Hitler's annexation of Austria on March 13, 1938, Czechoslovakia became the next target. Hitler wished to use the Sudetenland as a bridgehead for further expansion into Eastern Europe. Neither Great Britain nor France desired war and capitulated to Hitler's demands at the Munich Conference for the swift return of Sudetenland to Germany. The Munich Agreement stripped Czechoslovakia of 38 percent of Bohemia and Moravia. It also yielded 11,882 sq km (4,586 sq mi) to Hungary and part of the region of southern Tesin to Poland. Meanwhile, encouraged by Hitler, both Slovakia and Ruthenia asserted their independence. In November 1938 a new republic was established that consisted of three autonomous units: Bohemia-Moravia, Slovakia, and Carpatho-Ukraine, as sub-Carpathian Ruthenia was renamed. Hitler completed his conquest of the republic on March 15, 1938, when he forced the Czech government to capitulate and become a German protectorate.

German rule was moderate at first, but, following student demonstrations in November 1939, became brutal under the direction of the notorious Reinhard Heydrich, and after his assassination, Gen. Kurt Daluege. A government-in-exile was established in London and Czech and Slovak resistence was active throughout the war.

The postwar settlement resulted in numerous boundary and population changes. Ruthenia was ceded to the Soviet Union. All Sudeten Germans were expelled under harsh conditions. Territory that had been ceded to Poland was returned and the nation engaged in a population exchange with Hungary.

In 1946, a Communist-led coalition government assumed power following elections in which the Communists polled 38 percent of the vote. In 1948, the Communists staged a coup and charged the non-communist political parties with subversion. All non-communists were purged from the government, which began nationalizing private industry. A new constitution was enacted and the provinces of Bohemia, Moravia, and Slovakia were replaced by 19 administrative provinces. Numerous arrests, confiscations, and executions occurred as the Communists sought to enhance their power. There were also restrictions placed on churches and church property was confiscated.

In 1950, the government banned all books published in Czechoslovakia before 1948. That same year all monastic houses were seized and a new criminal code was adopted. A year later, there were mass purges. In 1960, a new constitution was adopted and the nation's name changed to the Czechoslovak Socialist Republic.

However, in 1968, pro-reform Communists gained power and Alexander Dubček was named the first secretary. The so-called Prague Spring initiated a series of reforms, but the Soviet Union responded by organizing an invasion of the nation by its Warsaw Pact allies. Thousands were executed or exiled and Dubček was replaced by Gustav Husak.

The reform spirit remained strong and in 1977 a group of dissidents and reform-minded intellectuals issued Charter 77. These efforts culminated in 1989 when Husak resigned and the "Velvet Revolution" led to the demise of the Communist Party. Playwright Vaclev Hável became president and a noncommunist cabinet took power. The following year, the Communists were defeated in national elections. Hável was reelected president.

In 1992, a leftist government came to power in Slovakia. The new government pressed for a dissolution of Czechoslovakia. The result was the breakup of the nation in the "Velvet Divorce." A new constitution was established. The next year, Hável was elected president of the new Czech Republic.

By 1997, privatization efforts had begun to yield results and the Czech economy reoriented itself to the West more quickly than any of the other former Eastern bloc nations. This aided negotiations with the EU for admittance to the organization. In 1998, Hável was again elected president. The Czech Republic became one of three former Warsaw Pact nations to join NATO in 1999.

CONSTITUTION

The new constitution of the Czech Republic, which became effective following the breakup of Czechoslovakia, detailed the relationship between the executive and legislative branches and established an independent judiciary. It also defined the civil rights of the new nation. Under the constitution the nation is a democratic, unitary republic. There is universal suffrage for those 18 years and older.

The chief executive is the president who is elected by the parliament for a five-year term. The president may serve a maximum of two consecutive terms. The president is the commander in chief of the armed forces, but power is limited to the right to veto bills passed by the legislature, with the exception of constitutional acts. In 1998, Vaclav Hável was reelected president.

The legislature consists of two bodies—the Chamber of Deputies and the Senate. The legislature approves all bills and ratifies international treaties. The government consists of the prime minister, deputy prime minister, and cabinet ministers. The government manages the administration and has legislative initiative for the state budget. Because of the presence of a number of political parties (16 different parties in the 1996 elections), governments are usually coalitions of a number of parties. Management of the state budget and control of state property is the domain of the Supreme Audit Office. The office is an independent controlling agency that also audits the government. Many aspects of the economy are overseen by the Czech National Bank. The president and executives of the bank are appointed by the president. The bank is independent of the cabinet and its main goal is to maintain the stability of the currency.

The judiciary is divided between the Constitutional Court and the Supreme Court. The Constitutional Court consists of 15 judges who are appointed by the president and approved by the Senate. Judges serve for 10 years. The court oversees constitutional issues. The Supreme Court is the highest judicial body in all legal matters, except constitutional matters.

LOCAL GOVERNMENT

The Czech Republic is divided into eight self-governing regions known as kraje. These regions are almost completely sovereign, in that the national government can intervene in local affairs only if there is a violation of national law. Local officeholders are limited to terms of four years. Within the regions, there are more than 6,000

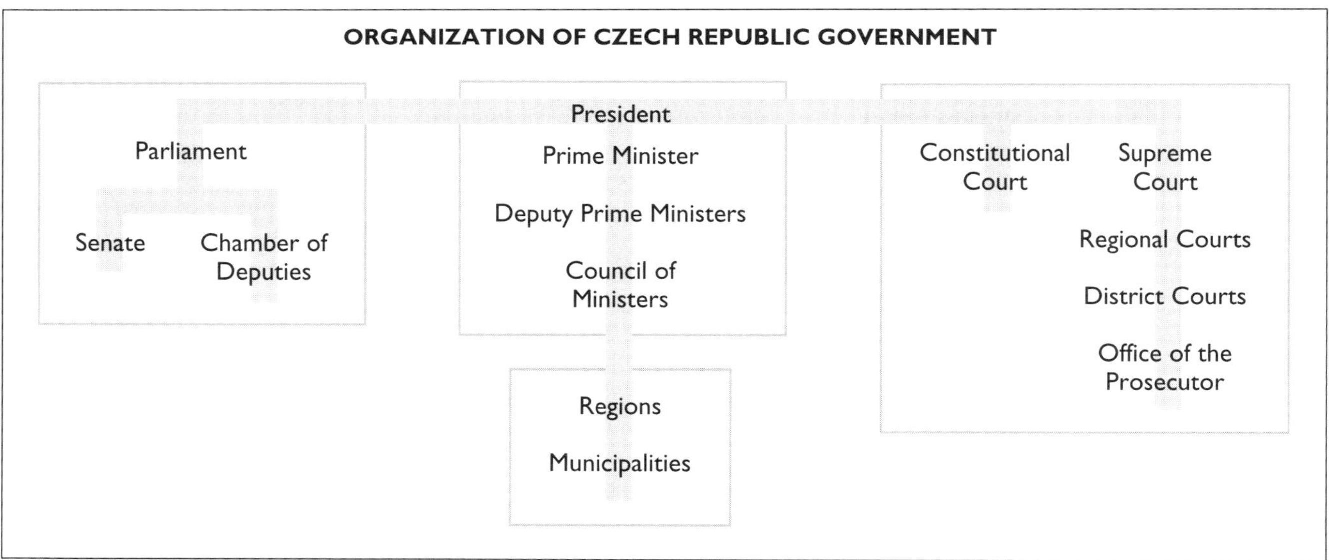

municipal governments. These local governments are also self-governing and highly autonomous.

Local Government

Principal administrative divisions, capitals, area, population

AREA AND POPULATION

Geographic regions	Capitals	area sq mi	area sq km	population 1998 estimate
Jizny Cechy	Ceské Budējovice	4,381	11,346	700,773
Jizni Morava	Brno	5,802	15,028	2,052,832
Severni Cechy	Usti nad Labem	3,011	7,799	1,179,242
Severni Morava	Ostrava	4,273	11,068	1,967,813
Stredni Cechy	Prague	4,253	11,014	1,105,964
Vychodni Cechy	Hiradec Králové	4,340	11,240	1,233,858
Zapadni Cechy	Plzeñ	4,199	10,875	858,188
Capital city				
Prague	—	192	496	1,200,455
TOTAL		30,450	78,866	10,299,125

PARLIAMENT

The Czech parliament is a bicameral legislature. The lower house is the Chamber of Deputies. It is based on a system of proportional representation. Political parties must gain at least 5 percent of the vote in order to obtain seats in the Chamber. Deputies in the Chamber must be at least 21 years old. The lower house consists of 200 representatives who are elected for a four-year term. The Chamber can be dissolved by the president under certain guidelines provided by the constitution. Such a dissolution occurred in 1997 following the collapse of the center-right coalition because of longstanding disputes among the members.

The upper house of the legislature is the Senate. The Senate is made up of 81 senators elected for six-year terms. The minimum age for election to the Senate is 40 years old, and senators are elected by majority vote. Every two years one-third of the Senate is reelected. The Senate cannot be dissolved.

A bill is passed by the Chamber of Deputies and then sent to the senate, which can approve it, veto it, or send it back with amendments. Constitutional amendments and international treaties must be approved by a 60 percent majority.

There is universal suffrage for those 18 years and older.

POLITICAL PARTIES

Assembly for the Republic—Republican Party of Czechoslovakia (SPR-RSE), right-wing, nationalist party.

Czech Social Democratic Party (CSSD), center-left party that was founded in 1878, but banned by the communists in 1948.

Christian Democratic Union-Czechoslovak People's Party (KDU-CSL), conservative, Christian party that is the successor to the Catholic People's Party.

Civic Democratic Party (ODS), center-right party, which supports privatization and strong ties with the West.

Communist Party, leftist party that has splintered into factions including the Communist Party of Bohemia and Moravia (KSCM).

Freedom Union (US), conservative party formed by defectors from the ODS.

Green Party, left of center, environmental party.

Political Parties

Czech Social Democratic Party, 1878
Civic Democratic Party, 1991
Christian and Democratic Union, 1918
Freedom Union, 1998
Civic Democratic Alliance, 1989
Democratic Union, 1994
Communist of Bohemia and Moravia, 1990
Association for the Republic-Czech Republican Party, 1990
Democratic Left Party, 1993
Left Bloc Party, 1993
Party of Czechoslovak Communists
Free Democrats-Liberal National Social Party, 1995
Civic National Movement, 1996
Green Party, 1989
Patriotic Republican Party, 1995
Bohemian-Moravian Center Union, 1990
Pensioners for Life Securities

Political Parties: Strength in Parliament Most Recent Elections

Chamber of Representatives. Following balloting on June 19–20, 1998, the seats were distributed as follows: Czech Social Democratic Party, 74; Civic Democratic Party, 63; Communist Party of Bohemia and Moravia, 24; Christian and Democratic Union-Czech People's Party, 20; Freedom Union 19.

Senate. Following the balloting of November 12 and 19, 2000, for 27 seats, the results were as follows: Coalition of Four (Christian and Democratic Union-Czechoslovak People's Party, Freedom Union, Civic Democratic Alliance, Democratic Union), 17 seats; Civic Democratic Party, 8; Czech Social Democratic Party, 1; and nonpartisan, 1.

LEGAL SYSTEM

Civil law is based on Austro-Hungarian codes, and there has been an effort to bring the nation's legal system into line with the obligations of the Organization on Security and Cooperation in Europe (OSCE) by eliminating the vestiges of Marxist-Leninist legal theory. The judiciary is an independent branch of the government. It is divided into two broad courts, the Constitutional Court and the Supreme Court. The Constitutional Court consists of 15 judges who are appointed by the president and approved by the Senate. Judges serve for 10 years. The court oversees constitutional issues. The Supreme Court is the highest judicial body in all legal matters, except constitutional matters. It has three councils, one each for civil, penal, and military cases.

There is a system of upper courts, which are located in the capitals of the various regions. In addition, each district has a lower court known as a district court and made up of three judges, one professional and two judges chosen by the community.

LAW ENFORCEMENT

Law Enforcement

Offenses reported to the police per 100,000: 1,911
- Murder: 2.0
- Assault: 89.4
- Burglary: 621.5
- Automobile Theft: 95.7
- Population per Police officer: 640

Death Penalty: Abolished 1990

HUMAN RIGHTS

Human and civil rights are guaranteed by the Bill of Fundamental Rights and Freedoms. Czechs enjoy freedom of speech, religion, and press.

Following the breakup of Czechoslovakia, the Czech Republic enacted a restrictive citizenship law that limited the number of residents who could become citizens. Those former Czechoslovakians who did not become Czech citizens were not permitted to vote, serve in the government, or participate in the privatization programs. In addition, citizenship had to be established before persons could petition for redress of past official actions or the wrongful confiscation of property. Amendments added in 1996 made it possible for those with criminal records to gain citizenship.

Certain minority groups within the Czech Republic face varying forms of discrimination. The Gypsy or Roma population remains the target of the most significant discrimination.

FOREIGN POLICY

Since 1989, Czech foreign policy has been characterized by a pro-Western orientation. Successive governments have worked to join Western governmental organizations. The main goals were membership in the European Union (EU) and NATO. An agreement between the Czech Republic and the EU was signed in 1992 that covered various aspects of trade liberalization.

In its efforts to join NATO, the Czech Republic became a member of the Partnership for Peace (PfP) program, which was perceived as a precursor to full membership in the alliance. As a PfP member, the Czechs participated in NATO peacekeeping operations in Bosnia. In December 1997, the nation was invited to join the alliance. It formally joined NATO in March 1999.

Czech foreign policy has also promoted regional cooperation. In 1992, the Czech Republic, Hungary, and Poland signed a free trade agreement known as the Central European Free Trade Area (CEFTA). This initiative called for the elimination of trade restrictions among member-states and the eventual removal of trade barriers between CEFTA and the EU. CEFTA was also seen as a means to promote individual entry into the EU by demonstrating the capability to remove trade restrictions and encourage free trade.

DEFENSE

Since the end of the cold war, the Czech military has adopted a number of Western-style reforms to strengthen civilian control of the armed forces and has cut personnel by some 25,000. The president is the commander in chief of the military. The government also initiated a variety of cooperative programs with Western militaries, including joining the PfP. The goal of these efforts was Czech entry into NATO, which occurred in 1999.

Military Indicators

Total Active Duty Personnel: 44,000
Military Manpower per 1,000: 4.3
Military Expenditures: $3,118 million
- as % of GNP: 1.8
- per capita: $596
- as % of central government expenditures: 4.1

Arms Imports: $0
Arms Exports: $120

ECONOMY

The Czech Republic was initially regarded as the most prosperous and advanced of the postcommunist Central European states. However, a series of problems undercut the country's transformation. The economy of the Czech Republic is marked by a continuing decline in industrial production and a trade deficit. The major exports of the country are machinery and manufactured goods, and a third of the workers remain in the industrial sector. Mining is also a major industry and coal provides the nation's major energy source. The service industry employs the majority of workers. The major trading partners of the nation are the European Union states and Slovakia.

The economy grew about 2.5 percent in 2000 and should achieve somewhat higher growth in 2001. Growth is led by exports to the EU, especially Germany, and foreign investment, while domestic demand is reviving. Uncomfortably high fiscal and current account deficits could be future problems. Unemployment is down to 8.7 percent as job creation continues in the rebounding economy; inflation is up to 3.8 percent but still moderate. The EU put the Czech Republic just behind Poland and Hungary in preparations for accession, which will give further impetus and direction to structural reform.

Principal Economic Indicators

Gross National Product: $53.952 billion
GNP per capita: $5,240
GNP Average Annual Growth Rate (1990–97): −0.3
GNP per capita Average Annual Growth Rate (1990–97): −0.2
Origin of Gross Domestic Product %
- Agriculture: 5
- Mining: —
- Manufacturing: 28
- Construction: 4
- Public Utilities: 6
- Transportation and Communications: 6
- Trade: 8
- Financial Services: 29
- Other Services: 29
- Government: 29

Gross Domestic Product by Type of Expenditure %
- Private Consumption: 58
- Government Consumption: 22
- Gross Domestic Investment: 20
- Foreign Trade: Exports: 52
  Imports: −53
- % of Income Received by Poorest 20%: 10.5
- % of Income Received by Richest 10%: 23.5

Price and earnings indexes (1995 = 100)

	1993	1994	1995	1996	1997	1998
Consumer price index	83.3	91.7	100.0	198.8	118.0	130.6
Annual earnings index	71.2	84.4	100.0	118.4	130.9	143.0

Finance

National Currency: Koruna (Ka)
Exchange Rate: $1 = Ka 35.357
Money Supply Stock in National Currency billion: 451.6
M1 per capita: 43,800
Central Bank Discount Rate %: 6.0
Total External Debt $million: 20,700
Debt Service Ratio %: 10.5
Balance of Payments $million: −3,271
International Reserves SDRs million: 8,659
Ratio of External Debt to Total Reserves: 0.7
Average Annual Rate of Inflation/Consumer Price Index Growth Rate %: 10

Official Development Assistance

ODA: $447 million
- as % of GNP: 0.8
- per capita $: 43
- Foreign Direct Investment $million: 2,554

Central Government Revenues and Expenditures

Fiscal Year: Calendar Year
Revenues $million: 1,420
Expenditures $million: 1,460
Budget Deficit: $460 million
Tax Revenues as % of GDP: 31.6
Highest Tax Bracket %
- Individual: 40
- Corporate: 35

Employment and Labor

Economically Active Population: 5,283,000
Female Participation Rate %: 46.2
Activity Rate %: 51.1
Labor by Sector: %
- Agriculture, Forestry, Fishing: 6.5
- Manufacturing, Mining: 32.8
- Construction: 9.1
- Transportation and Communications: 7.5
- Trade, Hotels, and Restaurants: 15.8
- Finance, Insurance, Real Estate: 6.7
- Public Administration, Defense: 5.2
- Services: 15.6

Unemployment %: 5

Agriculture

Agriculture's Share of GDP %: 5
Average Annual Rate of Growth (1965–98) %: —
Number of Farms 000: 26.9
Average Size of Farm ha: —
Number of Tractors per 1,000 hectares: 21.1
Irrigation, % of Farms having: 0.8
Artificial Fertilizer kg/hectare: 97
Total Farmland as % of land area: 55.4
Livestock: Cattle 000: 1,690
- Sheep 000: 94
- Hogs 000: 3,995
- Chickens 000: 27,846

Forests: Production of Roundwood (000 cubic meters): 12,906
Fisheries: Total Catch tons 000: 21.8

Mining

% of GDP: —
Value of Mineral Production $million: 1,050.3

Manufacturing

Value Added $million: 9,896
Industrial Production Growth Rate %: 6.9

Energy

Commercial Energy Production metric tons of oil equivalent 000: 31,539
Commercial Energy Consumption metric tons of oil equivalent 000: 40,576
Commercial Energy Consumption per capita kg: 3,938
Average Annual Growth Rate 1980–97 %: – 1.5
Net Energy Imports % of use: 22
Electricity Installed Capacity kW 000: 13,652
  Production kW-hr million: 60,647
Coal Reserves tons million: 5,142
  Production tons 000: 70,947
Natural Gas Proven Reserves cubic meters billion: 4
  Production cubic meters million: 290
Crude Petroleum reserves barrels million: 6
  Production barrels million: 0.7
  Consumption barrels million: 43
  Refinery Capacity barrels per day 000: 187
Pipelines Length km: —

Foreign Trade

Imports $million: 20,915
Exports $million: 17,099
Export Volume % Annual Growth Rate (1990–97): —
Import Volume % Annual Growth Rate (1990–97): —
Balance of Trade $

Balance of trade (current prices)

	1993	1994	1995	1996	1997	1998
U.S.						
$000,000	–4,483	–35,146	–94,733	–240,148	–139,688	–76,319
% of total	0.5%	3.6%	7.7%	18.0%	8.8%	4.3%

Major Trading Partners

	Imports	Exports
European Union %	56.4	55.2
United States %	3.7	1.8
Eastern Europe %	27.3	30.0
Japan %	1.7	0.5
Others %	10.9	12.5

Transportation

Roads Total Length mi: 77,528 km: 124,770
Paved %: 13
Automobiles: 3,113,476
Trucks and Buses: 204,238
Persons per vehicle: 3.1
Railroad; Track Length mi: 5,860 km: 9,430
Passenger-mi million: 4,985
Freight-mi million: 17,439
Merchant Marine: No. of Vessels: 22
  Total Deadweight Tonnage 000: 446.2
  International Cargo Loaded tons 000: —
  International Cargo Off-loaded tons 000: —
Airports with Scheduled Flights: 2
Traffic: Passenger-mi million: 1,469
  Freight-mi million: 16.0
Length of Canals mi: 295 km: 475

Tourism

Number of Tourists to 000: 16,325
Number of Tourists from 000: —
Tourist Receipts $million: 2,875
Tourist Expenditures $million: 1,630

Communications

Telephones 000: 2,444
Cost of Local Calls 3 mins: $0
Cellular Telephones 000: 49
Fax Machines 000: 74
Personal Computers 000: 550
Internet Hosts per million persons: 2,115
Mail: Post Offices: 3,511
  Pieces of Mail Handled million: 729
  Pieces of Mail Handled per person: 71

EDUCATION

Many children attend preschool and kindergarten in the Czech Republic, but formal education begins at age six. Children remain in school for nine years after which they can choose between vocational or apprenticeship schools and secondary schools (high schools). Entrance into universities is determined by a student's score on the "maturita" (school exit) exam. Universities are quite competitive and students are now expected to help pay for their college education. The largest and most prestigious university is Charles University in Prague, which was founded in 1348. There are also an increasing number of private schools.

Education

Literacy Rate %: 100
  Male %: 100
  Female %: 100
First Level: Primary schools: 4,212
  Teachers: 63,019
  Students: 1,004,565
  Student-Teacher Ratio: 15.9
  Net Enrollment Ratio: 9.8
Second Level: Secondary Schools: 361
  Teachers: 10,903
  Students: 133,093
  Student-Teacher Ratio: 12.2
  Net Enrollment Ratio: 88
Vocational Level: Schools: 832
  Students: 229,909
Third Level: Institutions: 23
  Teachers: 12,892
  Students: 139,774
  Student-Ratio Level: 10.8
  Gross Enrollment Ratio: 20.8
  Students per 100,000: 1,741
  % of Population Age 25 and over with Postsecondary Education: 8.5
Public Expenditure on Education as % of GDP: 6.1

SCIENCE AND TECHNOLOGY

Science and Technology

Scientists and Engineers in R&D per 1 million persons: 1,222
Expenditures in R&D as % of GDP: 1.20
High-Tech Exports $: 1,981 million
Patent Applications by Residents: 601

MEDIA

The end of communist rule in 1989 resulted in the establishment of numerous new journals and media outlets. By 1996, there were approximately 1,168 journals and periodicals published in the republic. In addition, there were 90 daily newspapers. The largest is *Mladá Fronta Dnes* with a circulation of 381,000. The newspaper was a youth paper under the communist regime, but it is now a modern, Western-style daily.

The Czech Republic has a dual public-private broadcasting system. Czech Radio and Czech Television are state owned. Licenses have been granted for 70 independent radio stations and 52 television stations. The two main independent television broadcasting companies are Nova and Prima. Overall, there are 150 radio stations and 118 television stations.

Media

Daily Newspapers: 23
Total Circulation 000: 2,259
Circulation per 1,000: 219
Books Published: 9,309
Magazines: 1,168
Radio Receivers 000: 9,100
per 1,000: 884
Television sets 000: 4,200
per 1,000: 406

MOST IMPORTANT MEDIA:

Press. The following dailies are published in Czech at Prague, unless otherwise noted: *Mladá Fronta Dnes* (Youth Front Today, 381,000), former organ of the Socialist Union of Youth; *Právo* (Justice, 360,000), former KSCM organ (called *Rudé Právo* until September 1995), now independent; *Blesk* (Lightning, 354,000), Swiss-owned independent; *Svobodné Slovo* (Free Word, 163,000), CSS organ; *Hospodárské Noviny* (Economic News, 157,000), business paper; *Vecernik Praha* (Evening Prague, 112,000); *Nová Svoboda* (New Freedoms, Ostrava, 100,000); *Lidové Noviny* (People's News, 100,000), independent, *Haló Noviny* (Hello News), new KSCM organ.

News agencies. The state-owned domestic service is the Czech News Agency (Ceská Tisková Kancelár-CTK, or Ceteka). Numerous foreign agencies also maintain bureaus at Prague.

Radio and television. The former federal broadcasting structures ended on January 1, 1993, when the state-funded Czech Radio (Ceský Rozhlas) and Czech Television (Ceska Televize) assumed full responsibility within the Czech Republic. The strict government control of the communist era had ended in 1991, when the supervision of broadcasting was transferred to independent authorities approved by the respective parliaments. In March 1991 the republics were authorized to license independent radio and television stations, with the first independent TV outlet, Nova Television, being launched at Prague in 1994 (and gaining a two-thirds audience share by 1995), followed by Premiera (subsequently renamed Prima).

CULTURE

Cultural Indicators

Public Libraries
Number: 9,453
Volumes: 56,577,000
Registered borrowers: 2,908,221
Museums
Number: 676
Annual Attendance: 17,666,000
Cinema
Production of Long Films: 22
Number of Cinemas: 940
Seating Capacity: 330,000
Annual Attendance: 9.3 million
Annual Attendance per capita: 0.9

STATUS OF WOMEN

The nation has universal suffrage for all citizens over 18 years of age and women are given the same civil rights as men. However, there is no government agency to oversee enforcement of equal rights, and discrimination occurs in both the home and society in general. Politics also continues to be dominated by men, although the newer independent parties have placed women in leadership positions.

Women

Gender Empowerment Measure: 24
Seats Held in Parliament by Women %: 13.9
Female Administrators and Managers %: 26.7
Female Professional and Technical Workers %: 55.4
Women's Share of Earned Income %: 39
Women in Government %: 1

HEALTH, FOOD, AND NUTRITION

Health

Number of Physicians: 32,195
Number of Dentists: 6,267
Number of Nurses: —
Number of Pharmacists: 4,032
Population per Physician: 321
Number of Hospitals: 299
Hospital Beds per 10,000: 89
Hospital Bed Occupancy Rate: 79.0
Infant Mortality Rate per 1,000 live births: 10
Maternal Mortality Rate per 100,000 live births: 15
Total Health Expenditures as % of GDP: 5.94
Health Expenditures per capita $: 169

(continued)

HIV Infected % of adults: 0.04
Cigarette Consumption per smoker per year: 3,187
% of Smokers: Male: 43
Female: 31
Access to Safe Water % 100

Food and Nutrition

Food Supply as % of FAO Requirements: 129
% of Consumption Expenditures on Food: 26.7
Daily Available Calories per capita: 3,175
% of Total Calories derived from:
Cereals: 26.7
Potatoes, cassava: 4.7
Meat, poultry: 11.7
Fish: 0.4
Eggs, milk: 10.6
Fruits, vegetables: 4.3
Fats, oils: 19.4

ENVIRONMENT

There are 1,246 protected areas or national parks in the Czech Republic. The largest of these areas is the Krkonose National Park. The major environmental concerns of the nation involve lasting damage from industrial output during the post–World War II era. The use of coal and other fossil fuels has led to significant levels of acid rain, which have damaged forests. In addition, industrial runoff from mining and manufacturing has led to air and water pollution in areas of northwest Bohemia and northern Moravia, especially around Ostrava.

Environment

Forest Area sq km: 26,000
Average Annual Deforestation sq km: −2
Nationally Protected Areas as % of Total Land Area: 15.8
Freshwater Access cubic meters per capita: 1,554
Emissions of Organic Water Pollutants kg per day: 162,615
CO_2 Emissions per capita ton: 12.3

CHRONOLOGY

1945 The post–World War II peace settlements result in the expulsion of Sudeten Germans, Hungarians, and territorial losses to Russia and the acquisition of land from Poland.
1946 After elections in which they received 38 percent of the vote, the Communists establish a coalition government.
1948 A Communist coup results in the purge of all non-Communists from the government and numerous arrests and executions; the government begins to nationalize private land and industry.
1949 Council for Mutual Economic Assistance (CMEA) is formed; government places restrictions on churches and confiscates church property; thousands are arrested in purges.
1950 Government bans all books published in Czechoslovakia before 1948; most monastic houses are confiscated; new criminal code is passed.
1951 In mass purges, members of Central Committee are arrested, tried, and executed.
1960 New constitution is promulgated; the official name of the state is changed to Czechoslovak Socialist Republic.
1968 Pro-reform Communists gain power; Alexander Dubček named first secretary; the "Prague Spring" initiates a series of reforms, which end the more ruthless aspects of the Communist regime; in response, the Soviet Union organizes an invasion of Czechoslovakia by its Warsaw Pact allies. Thousands are arrested, executed, or exiled. Dubček is replaced by Gustav Husak.
1977 A group of dissidents and intellectuals issues Charter 77.
1989 Husak resigns and the Communists give up power in what is known as the "Velvet Revolution;" human rights activist and playwright Vaclev Hável becomes president, and a new, noncommunist controlled cabinet is sworn in.
1990 In general elections, the Communists are soundly defeated and Hável's party, Civic Forum, captures 170 seats in the National Assembly, compared to the 47 of the Communists; Hável is reelected president.
1992 Czechoslovakia dissolves into two nations, the Czech Republic and Slovakia in the so-called Velvet Divorce; a new constitution is established.
1993 Hável is elected president of the Czech Republic.
1997 Privatization efforts yield significant results and the Czech economy reorients itself to the West faster than any of the other former Soviet satellites; the nation enters into the Accession Partnership agreement as negotiations with the EU proceed for admission to the union.
1998 Hável is reelected president.
1999 The Czech Republic is one of three former Warsaw Pact nations to join the organization's cold war nemesis, the North Atlantic Treaty Organization (NATO).

BIBLIOGRAPHY

Dedek, Oldrich. *The Break-up of Czechoslovakia: An In-depth Economic Analysis*. Aldershot, England, 1996.
Klaus, Vaclav. *Renaissance: The Rebirth of Liberty in the Heart of Europe*. Washington, D.C., 1997.
Krejci, Oskar. *Czechoslovak National Interests*. New York, 1996.
OECD. *Regional Problems and Policies in the Czech Republic and the Slovak Republic*. Paris, 1996.

Price Waterhouse. *Doing Business in the Czech Republic*. New York, 1995.

Sutherlin, John. *The Greening of Central Europe: Sustainable Development and Environmental Policy in Poland and the Czech Republic*. Lanham, Md., 1999.

Svejnar, Jan, ed. *The Czech Republic and Economic Transition in Eastern Europe*. San Diego, 1995.

OFFICIAL PUBLICATIONS

Czech Republic. *Statistická rocenka Ceské Republiky* (Statistical Yearbook of the Czech Republic).

CONTACT INFORMATION

Embassy of Czech Republic
3900 Spring of Freedom Street NW
Washington, D.C. 20008
Phone: (202) 274-9100 Fax: (202) 966-8540

INTERNET RESOURCES

- Czech Statistical Office
  http://infox.éunet.cz/csu/csu_e.html

DENMARK

BASIC FACT SHEET

OFFICIAL NAME:
Kingdom of Denmark (Kongeriget Danmark)

ABBREVIATION:
DE

CAPITAL:
Copenhagen

HEAD OF STATE:
Queen Margrethe II (from 1972)

HEAD OF GOVERNMENT:
Prime Minister Anders Fogh Rasmussen

NATURE OF GOVERNMENT:
Parliamentary democracy

POPULATION:
5,316,000 (1999)

AREA:
43,076 sq km (16,627 sq mi) (excluding Greenland and the Faeroe Islands)

ETHNIC MAJORITY:
Scandinavian

LANGUAGE:
Danish

RELIGION:
Protestant

UNIT OF CURRENCY:
Krone

NATIONAL FLAG:
The Dannebrog or "Danish cloth," the oldest national symbol in continuous use in the Western world; a white cross, off-center toward the hoist, on a field of red

NATIONAL EMBLEM:
Denmark has a simple state emblem—three lions on a gold shield with nine red hearts—and a much older royal arms. In the royal arms three shields are imposed upon one another. The "Heart Shield" contains the ancestral arms of the ruling family, two red bars on gold (Oldenburg) and a gold cross on blue (Delmenhorst). On the medium shield are devices against red backgrounds representing duchies absorbed by the realm: a silver nettle shield (Holstein), a silver swan (Stormarn), a mounted knight in gold armor (Ditmarsh), and a gold horsehead (Lauenburg). The chief escutcheon is quartered by a large Dannebrog cross. One quadrant bears the 12th-century royal state emblem. In another, two blue lions on gold signify Schleswig. Below the arm of the silver cross, four devices in blue appear on one side, displaying three gold crowns commemorating the union of Denmark, Norway, and Sweden in 1397, and three silver figures representing Danish dependencies: a falcon for Iceland, a ram for the Faeroe Islands, and a polar bear for Greenland. A blue lion on a gold background surrounded by red hearts mark the royal title as the ruler of the ancient tribe of the Wends; underneath is a gold wivern, a fabled winged creature with a dragon's head, representing dominion over the Goths. Two Norse giants stand beside the arms. Gold chains of Danish orders circle the shield with pendants dangling. A red ermine-lined gold-fringed cape topped with a bejeweled royal crown frame the ornate emblem.

NATIONAL ANTHEM:
"Kong Kristian Stod Ved Hojen Mast" (King Christian stood by the lofty mast) and "Der er et Yndigt Land" (There is a lovely land)

NATIONAL HOLIDAYS:
Constitution Day, June 5; birthday of the queen, April 16; all major Christian festivals

DATE OF INDEPENDENCE:
800

DATE OF CONSTITUTION:
June 5, 1953

Denmark

Streymoy
Torshavn
FAEROE ISLANDS
0 25 Miles
0 25 Kms
N
Skagerrak
Skagen
Hirtshals
Hjorring
Frederikshavn
SWEDEN
Læso
Thisted
Logstor Bredning
Lim Fjord
Alborg
Kattegat
Anholt
Skive
Viborg
Randers
Holstebro
Grena
JUTLAND
Silkeborg
Ringkobing
Herning
Arhus
Ringkobing Fjord
Skjern
Øresund
Helsingor
L. Arreso
Horsens
Hillerod
Ise Fjord
Samso
Vejle
Varde
Fredericia
Odense Fjord
Kalundborg
Holbaek
Copenhagen
Esbjerg
Kolding
Roskilde
Fano
Zealand
Amager
Odense
Ringsted
Soro
Great Bælt
Haderslev
Fyn
Naestved
Faborg
Svendborg
Baltic Sea
Abenra
Als
Vordingborg
Sondeborg
Mon
Aero
Nakskov
Falster
Langeland
Lolland
Nykobing
Bornholm
North Sea
Roune
GERMANY

GEOGRAPHICAL FEATURES

Located in southern Scandinavia, the Kingdom of Denmark consists of Denmark proper, the Faeroe Islands, and Greenland. Denmark itself comprises the peninsula of Jutland (Jylland) and some 406 islands with a total land area of 43,076 sq km (16,627 sq mi) extending 402 km (250 mi) north to south and 354 km (220 mi) east to west. The only land boundary, with Germany, is 68 km (42 mi) long. The country is surrounded by water on the other three sides: the Skaggerak on the north; the Kattegat, the Øresund, and the Baltic Sea on the east; and the North Sea on the west. The total length of the coastline is 7,403 km (4,600 mi). There are no border or other territorial disputes.

The precise size of Denmark proper is subject to constant variation owing to marine erosion and deposit and reclamation work. Not included in the land area are inlets or fjords directly connected with the sea. The country's 406 islands (of which only 97 are inhabited) account for more than one-third of the land area. The largest are Zealand (Sjaelland, 7,015 sq km; 2,709 sq mi), Fünen (Fyn, 2,984 sq km; 1,152 sq mi), Lolland (1,234 sq km; 480 sq mi), Bornholm (588 sq km; 227 sq mi), and Falster (514 sq km; 198 sq mi).

The capital is Copenhagen (København), on the island of Zealand (Sjaelland) and the adjoining island of Amager on the western shore of the Øresund.

Denmark is a low-lying country, with its highest point, Yding Skovhoj in East Jutland, only 173 m (568 ft) above sea level. The surface relief is characterized by glacial moraine deposits, which form undulating plains with gently rolling hills interspersed with lakes. The largest lake is Arreso (40.6 sq km; 15.7 sq mi). Between the hills are extensive level outwash plains of the meltwater formed from stratified sand and gravel outside the ice limit. These heathland plains are the site of the country's densest settlements.

The boundary line between the sandy West Jutland and the loam plains of East and North Denmark is the most important geographical dividing line in the country. West of the line is a region of scattered farms; to the east, villages and towns.

Valleys furrow the moraine landscape. The East Jutland inlets were created by the intruding sea in the lowest part of the valleys, to which glacial erosion also contributed. The inlets form natural harbors, making maritime activities easy means of livelihood. The Gudenâ River, the longest river in Denmark (158 km; 98 mi), follows the intersecting valley systems.

Flat sand and gravel tracts make up one-tenth of the total land area, particularly prevalent in the northern part of the country, such as in the Limfjorden area. These low-lying regions are often swampy. Along the coast of South Jutland, where there is a strong tidal variation, there are salt marshes. Dune landscapes form an almost unbroken belt along the entire coast of Jutland.

Denmark is in the north temperate zone, where the natural type of vegetation is the deciduous forest, but as it borders on the coniferous belt, spruce and fir thrive in plantations. About 11 percent of the land area is forest. Beech, oak, elm, and lime thrive in a few locations. Natural plant communities also include dune vegetation and heathland plants, which occur chiefly on the sandy heaths of West Jutland.

Greenland, the largest island in the world, has a total land area of 2,173,600 sq km (840,000 sq mi). Of this area, 1,833,900 sq km (708,100 sq mi) lie under its icecap. The greatest north-to-south distance is 2,670 km (1,660 mi), and the greatest east-to-west distance is 1,290 km (800 mi). The coastline runs 39,090 km (24,289 mi).

Greenland is mountainous, with lofty fringes, the highest point of which is Gunnbjorns Fjaeld, 7,700 m (12,140 ft). The average thickness of the ice field is 1,515 m (4,971 ft).

The Faeroe Islands are in the Atlantic, northwest of Denmark. The Faeroes' 19 islands, of which 18 are inhabited, cover an area of 1,399 sq km (540 sq mi). The islands range 120 km (70 mi) north to south and 79 km (49 mi) northeast to southwest.

The Faeroe landscape is characterized by a stratified series of basalt sheets, with intervening thinner layers of solidified volcanic ash (tufa). The highest peak is Slaettaretindur (882 m; 2,894 ft) on Østerø.

Geography

Area sq km: 43,076 sq mi 16,627
World Rank: 133rd
Land Boundaries, km: Germany 68
Coastline, km: 7,314
Elevation Extremes meters
- Lowest: Lammeljord −7m
- Highest: Yding Shovhoj 173

Land Use % Arable land: 60
- Permanent Crops: 0
- Permanent Pastures: 5
- Forest and Woodland: 10
- Other: 25

Population of Principal Cities (1996 est.; MU)

City	Population
Alborg	159,980
Arhus	279,759
Copenhagen	1,362,264
Odense	183,564

CLIMATE AND WEATHER

Denmark lies on the northwestern fringe of continental Europe, where the Gulf Stream brings warmth to the northern regions. The westerly winds temper the winter climate. The mean temperature in the coldest month is

12°C (22°F) higher than the average for Denmark's latitude. The waters of the Baltic isolate Denmark from the continental climate of Eastern Europe. However, in exceptional winters, when ice closes the Baltic, cold air streams from the east can spread over the country, causing hard winters. The lowest temperature ever recorded in Denmark was −31°C (−23.8°F).

Conversely, easterly air streams during periods of high pressure in summer may hold off the westerly sea winds. The sun then shines for a longer period and there is a heat wave. The highest temperature ever recorded was 35.8°C (96.4°F).

Generally, however, the climate is in the intermediate range. The mean temperature of the coldest month, February, is −0.4°C (about 31°F); that of the warmest, July, 16.6°C (61.5°F), but there are great variations from the normal, especially in winter. The number of annual frost days ranges from 70 on the coasts to 120 in the interior.

The weather is very changeable. As the fronts swing over the Danish region throughout the year, the weather is constantly changing. Westerly winds predominate, especially in gales. Gale damage is most common in West Jutland, particularly in spring.

The mean annual precipitation is 60 cm (23.6 in), ranging from about 80 cm (31.3 in) in southwest Jutland to about 40 cm (15.8 in) in the area of the Storebaelt (Great Belt). The number of days with precipitation fluctuates between 120 and 200. Snow falls from January through March, six to nine days a month. Rain is heaviest during August and October and lightest during the spring and winter months.

Climate and Weather

Mean temperature
February 31°F
July 61.5°F
Average Rainfall 23.6 in
Jutland 31.3 in
Great Belt 15.8 in

POPULATION

Population Indicators

Total Population: 1999 5,316,000
World Rank: 105th
Density per sq mi: 319.5 per sq km 123.4
% of annual growth (1994–99): 0.4
Male %: 49.4
Female %: 50.6
Urban %: 85.1
Age Distribution: % 0–14: 17.5
15–29: 20.8
30–44: 22.0
45–59: 19.9
60–74: 12.7
75 and over: 7.0
Population 2020: 5,527,000
Birth Rate per 1,000: 12.9
Death Rate per 1,000: 11.6
Population Doubling Time (years): —
Infant Mortality Rate per 1,000 live births: 5.7
Rate of Natural Increase per 1,000: 1.3
Total Fertility Rate: 1.8
Expectation of Life (years): Males 72.6
Females 77.8
Marriage Rate per 1,000: 6.5
Divorce Rate per 1,000: 2.4
Total Number of Households: 2,027,000
Average Size of Households: 2.2
% of Illegitimate Children: 46.5
Induced Abortions: 17,598
Rate per 100 live births: 25.2

ETHNIC COMPOSITION

Denmark was traditionally one of the most ethnically homogeneous nations in the world. Recent decades have seen an influx of guest workers and asylum seekers, particularly from Turkey, the Middle East, and South Asia. Racially, there is no special Danish type. The present population is based on a racial mixture of the New Stone Age and various groups that have immigrated since. The Nordic group is, nevertheless, more prominent, being characterized by blond, curling hair and blue eyes.

The only non-Scandinavian minority other than recent immigrant arrivals is a German community in South Jutland numbering about 40,000, or less than 0.8 percent of the population.

The population of Greenland is partly Eskimo but consists chiefly of Greenlanders, a Mongoloid-Caucasian mixture of Eskimos and Danes.

LANGUAGES

The official language is Danish, a branch of the East Scandinavian group of the Gothonic (Germanic-Teutonic) family of languages derived from Primitive Norse. In about the 12th century, Danish began to evolve separately from Swedish. With Christianity came the Latin script. Another cultural influence was German, which filtered through the Hanseatic merchants and brought in its wake hundreds of new words for products and merchandise and also abstract words.

The period of early modern Danish (1500–1700) saw the written language become fixed in more or less the form it has today. Until 1700, the written and spoken languages varied considerably, and dialects dominated spoken Danish. However, with the growing centralization of the kingdom, a standard spoken language began to take shape, called Rigsmalet. From the end of the 17th century, Romance loan words began to be adopted, such as musical and banking terms from Italian, cooking and fashion words from French, and scientific terminology from classical languages. Maritime words also were adopted from Dutch. More recently, Danish has borrowed heavily from English.

Danish is spoken by about 5.3 million people, 5 million of them in metropolitan Denmark itself, with much smaller clusters in Germany, Norway, Greenland, and the New World. Faeroe Island inhabitants speak a distinct language, Faeroese.

Principal Languages and Their Speakers

Arabic	37,000
Danish	4,968,000
English	18,000
German	25,000
Iranian languages	12,000
Norwegian	14,000
South Slavic languages	38,000
Swedish	14,000
Turkish	45,000
Other	145,000

RELIGIONS

The national church (*folkekirken*) of Denmark, under paragraph 4 of the constitution, is Evangelical Lutheran.

Christianity was introduced in 826 by the Benedictine monk Ansgar, from northern France. But it was not nationally adopted until about 960, when, according to the Saxon chronicler Widukind, the monk Poppo converted King Harald Bluetooth after miraculously carrying a red-hot iron in his hands. The story of the Danish church in the Middle Ages reflects the continental struggle between the crown and the church. From about 1520 a reform movement gathered strength and resulted in the smooth adoption of Lutheranism in 1536 under the leadership of Johan Bugenhagen, Peder Palladius, and Hans Tausen. From 1660 the Lutheran State Church was headed by the king, ruling as an absolute monarch.

Religious life in the 19th century was influenced by three outstanding personalities: Bishop J. P. Mynster, Søren Kierkegaard, and N. F. S. Grundtvig, who renewed the hymn tradition.

As absolutism gave way to constitutionalism in 1849, religious freedom was introduced. The state supports the church as a national institution and as part of the Danish heritage. Financially, the church is maintained by a state tax, which is levied on church members along with an ordinary income tax. In addition, the state extends grants for the maintenance of old churches as national monuments. At the same time all other religious groups enjoy full freedom of association and worship.

Spiritually, the Danish church has no single authority. Clergy are trained in the theological faculties of the universities of Copenhagen and Aarhus. Numbers of new ordinations have been steadily declining in recent years. To make up for the lag, laymen and laywomen are being ordained in more numbers.

The Danish Church Abroad was founded in 1919 to care for Danish communities outside the kingdom, the largest of which is in South Schleswig. Although weekly church attendance is estimated at less than 5 percent of the population, the national church exercises a strong influence on many aspects of social and cultural life.

The vast majority of Danes (86.6 percent in 1997) belong, at least nominally, to the established church. Other Protestant sects (Danish Baptists, Methodists, Seventh-Day Adventists, Pentecostals, Reformed Church, Anglicans, and Mormons), as well as Russian Orthodox, number no more than a few thousand each. The German minority has its own independent Lutheran churches, in addition to parishes within the main Danish church.

The Roman Catholic Church has maintained a presence in Denmark since 1849. Most of the 33,000 Catholics live in or around Copenhagen. Some 25 percent of the Catholics are descendants of immigrant Slavs. The majority of the guest workers of the 1970s are Muslims, creating a Muslim community currently estimated at 84,000. There are about 3,400 Jews and small concentrations of Baha'is and Buddhists.

Religious Affiliations

Evangelical Lutheran	4,600,000
Other	720,000

HISTORICAL BACKGROUND

Little is known of Denmark's early history. Harald Bluetooth (d. 985), the first Christian king of Denmark, conquered Norway, and his son Sweyn conquered England. Under Canute (1018–35) Norway, England, and Denmark were united, but shortly after his death the union with England came to an end and Norway seceded. Danish hegemony was reestablished over Norway and Sweden by the Union of Kalmar in 1397. In 1523 Sweden broke free, but the union with Norway remained until 1814. The Reformation was established in Denmark during the reign of Christian III (1534–59). A series of wars with Sweden resulted in the loss of southern Sweden as well as Danish control of the Øresund. Meanwhile, under Frederick III (1648–70) and Christian V (1670–99), absolute monarchy was reestablished and remained in force until 1849. Denmark was on the losing side in the Napoleonic Wars and as a result lost Norway by the Peace of Kiel (1814). Within the next half-century Denmark had lost to Prussia her southern provinces of Schleswig, Holstein, and Lauenburg. North Schleswig was returned to Denmark through a plebiscite after World War I. The Virgin Islands were ceded to the United States in 1917. A democratic constitution was introduced in 1849 and a revised one adopted in 1915. Denmark was invaded by the Germans in 1940 and served as a springboard for the invasion of Norway.

Greenland, discovered by Eric the Red, entered a formal union with Denmark in 1397. However, Denmark exercised no actual sovereignty until Hans Egede reached the island in 1721. Iceland came under Danish control along with Norway in 1381 and remained so after Norway was separated from Denmark in 1814.

Iceland became an independent republic in 1944, and Denmark recognized its independence the following year, when World War II ended. In 1948 the Faeroe Islands were granted home rule, and Greenland won the same status in 1979. When NATO was formed in 1949, Denmark became a charter member of the alliance. However, it remained outside of the European Economic Community until 1973, and even after its admission, the Danish populace remained vigilant against undue encroachment by Brussels on national sovereignty.

Denmark has had many short-lived and unstable coalition governments since the 1950s. The period from 1975 to 1982 was dominated by Social Democratic prime minister Anker Jørgensen, who led a succession of governments and grappled with an increasingly unfavorable economic climate that featured swelling unemployment and budget deficits. The tough decisions needed in such circumstances caused the government's support to collapse in September 1982, and fresh elections brought in a coalition headed by a Conservative, Poul Schlüter.

Schlüter managed to navigate the shoals of unsteady support in the Folketing for a decade. During that time, he shepherded the European Community's Single European Treaty (removing trade barriers between member states) through a referendum (1987), but voters rejected the more sweeping Treaty on European Union (Maastricht Treaty) in 1992. Opposition parties also were able to force through the Folketing a measure obligating the government to inform visiting foreign warships that nuclear weapons were banned in Denmark, creating friction with NATO allies. Each of these crises was resolved: the NATO dispute through the use of diplomatically ambiguous language; the rejection of Maastricht by creating several exemptions from the treaty's obligations to reassure Danes that national prerogatives would not be overridden. The treaty was ratified in May 1993. By then, Schlüter had been compelled to resign (January 1993) owing to a cabinet scandal involving the handling of refugee visas. The Social Democrats reclaimed the prime minister's seat for their leader, Poul Nyrup Rasmussen, who has held on through periods of minority government and narrow coalition majorities in parliament. In the late 1990s, the sharp rise of the anti-immigrant People's Party reflected popular discomfort that Denmark was becoming a more multicultural society and led to national debate about the need for and treatment of refugees and immigrant labor.

In 2000, the Danes rejected adoption of the euro as their national currency by 53 percent. In parliamentary elections held in November 2001, the center-right Liberal Party became Denmark's majority political party. It then formed a coalition government with the Conservative People's Party, and Anders Fogh Rasmussen was named prime minister.

CONSTITUTION

Denmark is one of the oldest monarchies in Europe, completing its first millennium in 1985. On the adoption of the nation's first written constitution, in 1849, absolute monarchy gave way to representative democracy. The so-called June Constitution (Junigrundloven) established three seminal principles: Judicial authority should reside in independent courts; legislative authority should rest jointly with king and parliament; and executive authority should be vested in the king, but he would not perform any act of state except on the authority of a minister.

The June Constitution was for its time one of the most liberal in Europe. The two chambers of the Folketing were elected under universal suffrage by all independent men over 30. But it was not until 1901 that King Christian IX signed "the change of system" (*systemskifte*) and appointed a ministry based on the majority only in the lower chamber. This principle was written into the constitution in 1953.

A constitutional amendment in 1915 gave women and servants the vote.

After World War II, a new constitution was spearheaded by the Social Democrats and Radical Liberals and became law on June 5, 1953. It abolished the upper chamber. The voting age was reduced from 25 to 23. Later amendments, confirmed by referendums, further reduced it, ultimately to 18. To safeguard minorities, a provision was included for referendums on parliamentary bills when demanded by one-third of the members. Together with the new constitution, the new Act of Succession was passed, permitting female succession to the throne. It was under this act that Queen Margrethe II succeeded her father, King Frederik IX, as head of state in 1972.

The executive is the cabinet, headed by the prime minister, who is the head of government. Ministers are the administrative heads of their respective ministries. Cabinet decisions are based on consensus, not vote.

All government bills and administrative measures come before the Council of State (Statsradet), which consists of the cabinet under the presidency of the monarch. In addition to Folketing bills, the Council of State also ratifies international treaties and agreements and reprieves certain long-term prison sentences.

Since the turn of the century, no Danish government has commanded a majority in the Folketing. Governments

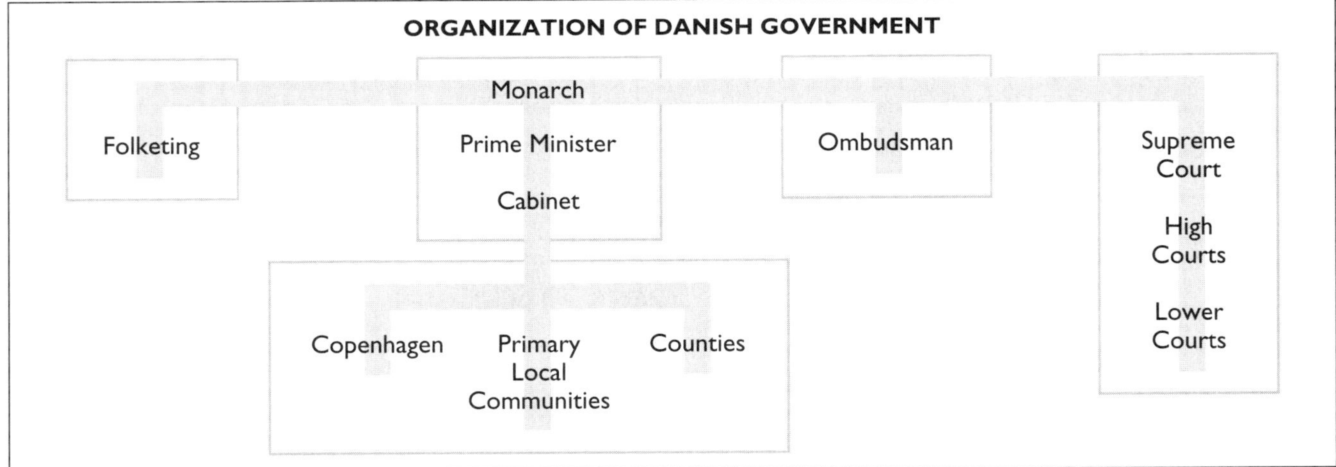

as a rule are minority governments made up of a number of parties.

The constitution of 1953, following a Swedish precedent, provided that the Folketing appoint one or two persons as ombudsman, and this office was established in 1955. The ombudsman is directed to see that no one in public service pursues unlawful activities, makes arbitrary or unjust decisions, or is guilty of error or neglect.

Up to 1953 Greenland was governed as a colony. The 1953 constitution accorded it the status of a fully integrated part of the Kingdom of Denmark. Greenland sends two members to the Folketing. Greenland affairs are the responsibility of the minister for Greenland, while local affairs are handled in part by a democratically elected Provincial Council (Landsradet) and in part by a Danish governor (landshovding). The two correspond to the Danish County Council and county prefect, respectively. Special legislation applies to Greenland in certain areas.

The Faeroe Islands were a Danish county until 1948, when self-government was introduced. The democratically elected assembly (Lagting) has legislative powers in all local affairs. The local government (Landsstyre) handles all local affairs. The Danish government is represented on the islands by a commissioner (rigsombudsmand). Recently there has been a groundswell in the Faeroes for greater local sovereignty.

LOCAL GOVERNMENT

Danish local government was thoroughly reorganized in 1970. Local government boundaries in many cases had been untouched for more than 800 years. Previously, the country was divided into 89 boroughs (*kobstaeder*) and 23 county authorities (*amstkommuner*), the latter being subdivided into more than 1,500 urban and rural districts (*sogne kommuner*). The distinction between urban and rural boroughs was abolished, the number of primary local governments (*primaerkommuner*) was reduced to 277, and the number of county authorities was reduced to 14. The primary local governments are chosen by the Elected Council (Kommunalbestyrelse) chaired by a mayor or *borgmester*. The reform did not affect the national capital, which continues to be governed by the elected City Council (borgerrepraesentation) of 55 members and an executive consisting of a chief burgomaster (*overborgmester*), five burgomasters (*borgmester*), and five aldermen (*radmaend*).

Counties are governed by the elected County Council (*Amtsiad*) chaired by the county mayor (*amtsborgmester*). Central government functions at county level are discharged by a prefect as chairman of a special council consisting of four members appointed by the County Council.

Greenland is divided administratively into the subprovinces (*landsdele*) of West Greenland, East Greenland, and North Greenland. There are 16 provincial districts (*tandsradaskredse*), each of which elects one member of the Greenland Provincial Council by direct vote every four years. The 159 habitations are grouped into 19 local districts (*kommuner*), each with a local council (*kommunalbestyrelse*) varying in size.

The Faeroe Islands are divided into seven regions (*sysler*), each under a sheriff (*sysselmand*), who constitutes the local authority with some judicial functions. There are 50 local districts with 120 settlements (*bygder*), some with as few as 30 inhabitants.

Local Government

Principal administrative divisions, capitals, area, population

AREA AND POPULATION

		area		population 1997
Counties	**Capitals**	**sq mi**	**sq km**	**estimate**
Arhus	Arhus	1,761	4,561	628,725
Bornholm	Ronne	227	588	45,018
Frederiksborg	Hillerod	520	1,347	356,854
Fyn	Odense	1,346	3,486	471,422

Kobenhavn	—	203	526	609,123
Nordjyliand	Alborg	2,383	6,173	492,155
Ribe	Ribe	1,209	3,132	223,335
Ringkobing	Ringkobing	1,874	4,853	271,483
Roskilde	Roskilde	344	891	226,683
Sonderjylland	Abenra	1,520	3,938	253,639
Storstrom	Nykobing Falster	1,312	3,398	257,776
Vestsjaelland	Soro	1,152	2,984	290,793
Viborg	Viborg	1,592	4,122	232,630
Municipalities				
Copenhagen (Kobenhavn)	—	34	88	483,658
Frederiksberg	—	3	9	89,230
TOTAL		16,639	43,094	5,275,121

PARLIAMENT

The Danish electoral system is one of the most complex in the world. It has undergone few changes in the past 60 years. The older parties have sought to raise the 2% threshold limit for seats distributed by proportional representation to reduce the proliferation of new parties, while the smaller ones have called for the elimination of the threshold rule altogether. While the proportional system has added to the instability of Danish governments, Danes cherish this principle as making their democracy more democratic.

Suffrage is equal and universal for all adults over 18. The 175 seats (excluding those of Greenland and the Faeroe Islands) in the national legislature, the unicameral Folketing, are distributed in advance among the three election areas (*amrader*) into which the country is divided—metropolitan Copenhagen, the islands, and Jutland—and these are subdivided into 14 county constituencies and three metropolitan constituencies in Copenhagen. A total of 135 representatives are elected in 17 districts, with 40 additional seats divided among those parties that have secured at least 2 percent of the vote but whose district representation does not accord with their overall strength. There also are two representatives each from Greenland and the Faeroe Islands.

The distribution is mostly determined by population totals and density, subject to constant adjustment. Normal voter turnout ranges from 80 percent to 90 percent, with invalid or blank votes less than 0.6 percent.

Danish elections are dominated by political parties. Only a few people run as independents, and only one independent candidate was elected in recent years. Typically, 12 to 13 parties put up candidates in the elections. Parties already represented in the Folketing are automatically entitled to nominate candidates and participate in the election campaign, which is partly financed by public funds. Parties that are new or not represented are accorded these privileges only if they collect signatures totaling 1/175th of the votes cast in the previous election. There are no by-elections, as vacancies are filled by candidates of the same party who have received the next-largest number of votes. Party strength in the Folketing thus remains fixed from one election to the next unless a member breaks away from a party.

Much of the work of parliament is done in 19 standing committees, whose competence corresponds to those of the ministries. There also are committees on standing orders, proof of elections, scientific research, and other issues of concern.

Under the constitution, no taxes may be levied until the finance bill or interim measures have been approved by the Folketing. Similarly, no expenditures may be incurred without such authority. However, because the finance bill is drafted some months before the fiscal year, it is impossible to foresee income or expenditures. Consequently, the practice has developed whereby the government requests the Folketing's Finance Committee (Finansudvalget) to approve unforeseen items. This practice makes this committee one of the most powerful parliamentary organs.

With the abolition of the upper chamber, the Landsting, in 1953, provision was made in the constitution for holding referendums. Within three working days of the passage of a bill, one-third of the Folketing members may apply to the speaker for a referendum to be held on the proposed measure. The prime minister is responsible for initiating the referendum, which must take place not earlier than 12 and not later than 18 working days after he has announced it. The bill is annulled if it is opposed by a majority of the Folketing electors and at least 30 percent of those entitled to vote. Certain types of bills, such as money bills, are excluded from this provision. The first referendum took place in 1963.

POLITICAL PARTIES

The four "old" parties in Danish politics are the Social Democrat, the Radical Liberal, the Liberal, and the Conservative People's parties covering the ideological spectrum from left to right. They also have dominated government coalitions during most of the 20th century. The Justice Party, Center Democrats, and the Christian People's Party have been coopted into coalitions mainly as supporting parties. The 1973 elections marked an end to this quadrumvirate. The Communist Party, the Left Socialists (who split from the Socialist People's Party), and the Justice Party (unrepresented in the Folketing since 1960) were returned to the Folketing, and, in addition, three new parties gained representation for the first time: the Center Democrats, the Christian People's Party, and the Progress Party, all at the expense of the traditional parties. This fragmentation has meant more power-sharing and greater instability, a process that continued well into the 1990s, even though there were Social Democrat–led governments throughout most of the 1970s and again after 1993, while Conservative People's–led coalitions dominated from 1982 to 1993.

The Liberal Party (Venstre, Danmarks Liberale Parti, V) is the oldest Danish political party, founded in 1870 in opposition to the ruling conservative elite. It spearheaded the struggle against the monarchy to secure the principle of parliamentary government. It hews to classic liberal positions in its platform, upholding individual freedoms in a pluralistic society. In its economic policy it stands for a free-market economy with a strong private sector, deregulation, and restraints on trade union power. It advocates trimming social welfare provisions in the interest of budgetary stringency. In foreign policy it is pro-NATO and pro-EU and advocates closer Nordic cooperation.

The Social Democrats (Socialdemocratiet, SD) were founded in 1871 as a marxist party. In its early years it concentrated on trade union organization and won its first parliamentary seat in 1884. From 1920 it began to attract voters from outside the ranks of labor and became the largest political party in the Folketing in 1924—a position it has maintained since, although it has never won an outright majority. The Social Democrats laid the foundations of the modern Danish welfare state while in office with the Radical Liberals from 1929 to 1943. Party ideology has long shed its marxist tenets and may best be described as democratic socialism, supporting full-employment policies and an extensive array of welfare-state benefits. In foreign policy it is slightly left of center, supporting NATO and the EU while opposing the more federalist aspects of European unity.

The Conservative People's Party (Det Konservative Folkeparti, KF) was formed in 1876 as the United Right, a group of landowners and upper-class supporters of monarchical rule. It regrouped to form the KF in 1915. When in alliance with the Liberals from 1950 to 1953, it carried out a major reform of the constitution. The KF is a pro–free enterprise group that advocates low taxes, low wages, and low inflation. It supports both NATO and the EU more strongly than other parties do. The KF has adopted some of the classic Liberal stances on domestic freedoms.

The Radical Liberals (Det Radicale Venstre, RV) split from the Liberals in 1905. Wedged between socialists and nonsocialists, the RV has had a moderating influence on both. In foreign policy the RV's policies are more in line with those of the socialists, opposing excessive military expenditures.

The Center Democrats (Centrum-Demokraterne, CD) are a splinter party that broke away from the Social Democrats in 1973 in protest against the latter's drift to the left.

The Progress Party (Fremskridtspartiet, FP) was founded in 1972 as a populist movement protesting excessive taxation and "paper-shuffling bureaucracy." In the 1973 elections the FP gained 16 percent of the vote to become the second largest party in the Folketing, but its support sharply declined afterward, reviving briefly in the late 1980s before it fractured in 1994 and hived off the Danish People's Party, which has similar positions but is better organized and has captured most of the protest vote.

Other Danish parties include the Socialist People's Party, the Christian People's Party, the Danish Communist Party, the Justice Party (also called the Single Tax Party), and the Left Socialists.

Political Parties

Social Democratic Party 1871
Radical Liberal Party 1905
Center Democrats 1973
Conservative People's Party 1916
Liberal Party 1870
Progress Party 1972
Danish People's Party 1995
Socialist People's Party, 1958
Red-Green Unity List 1989, a coalition of left-wing parties
- Left Socialist Party 1967
- Communist Party 1919

Christian People's Party 1970
Justice Party 1919

Political Parties: Strength in Parliament Most Recent Elections

In the most recent elections of November 18, 2001, for 179 seats, the Left Liberal Party of Denmark won 56 seats; Social Democracy in Denmark, 52; Danish People's Party, 22; Conservative People's Party, 16; Socialist People's Party, 12; Radical Left-Social Liberal Party, 9; Unity List-The Red Greens, 4; Christian People's Party, 4; Party for People's Government, 1; People's Party, 1; Forward, 1; and Eskimo Community, 1.

LEGAL SYSTEM

Denmark has a civil law system that goes back to about 1200. After the introduction of absolute rule in 1660, the king decreed in 1683 a general code applicable to the whole country, the Danish Code of Christian V.

The text of the Danish Code has never been altered, nor did new laws appear as amendments in the initial period after 1683. All legislation since then has been in the form of separate statutes. Few of the provisions of the Danish Code are still in force. But no attempt has been made to codify the mass of legislation in a comprehensive code, so it may be said that Denmark does not possess a general civil code.

Judges are constitutionally independent, although appointed by the Crown on the recommendation of the minister of justice. Judges can be dismissed only by the Special Court of Indictment.

The highest court is the Supreme Court (Hojesteret), with 19 judges, which also functions as a court of appeals. The court usually sits in two divisions of at least five judges each. All matters not specifically assigned to a lower court fall within the purview of one of the two high courts (Landsretter) under the Supreme Court, the eastern wing sitting in Copenhagen with jurisdiction over the islands and the western sitting in Viborg with jurisdiction over Jutland. On the next level are the lower courts (Underret), of which there are 84. Each lower court has only one judge, except in Copenhagen and Aarhus.

There is a special high court for Greenland. There are also special courts, such as the Tax Tribunal, the Maritime and Commercial Court, and the Labor Court.

LAW ENFORCEMENT

Law Enforcement

Offenses reported to the police per 100,000: 10,525
- Murder: 4.9
- Assault: 190.1
- Burglary: 2,046.3
- Automobile Theft: 663.3
- Population per Police officer: 600

Death Penalty: Abolished 1978

HUMAN RIGHTS

Human rights are well protected in Denmark and enforced by the office of the ombudsman. Arrested persons must be brought before a judge within 24 hours of detention. In serious crimes, the accused is placed in solitary confinement. All trials are public except in divorce and paternity trials, or rape and child molestation cases. The rights of aliens are protected by the 1983 Alien Act, and Danish media have engaged in public education campaigns to prevent the rise of racism toward immigrants and refugees from Asia, North Africa, and the Middle East. Natives of Greenland and the Faeroe Islands enjoy all the rights and privileges of Danish citizens.

In 1987 the Human Rights Center, mandated by the Folketing, was established with state funding to conduct research and provide information on a broad range of human rights issues. The Equal Rights Council deals with sex discrimination. Women hold strong representation in both the cabinet and the Folketing. The rights of homosexuals are safeguarded by the state; Denmark became the first country to recognize same-sex civil marriages in 1989.

If anything, human rights groups occasionally criticize Denmark for being too tolerant, in the sense of allowing neo-Nazi groups space to operate. However, in 1995 the Danish National Socialist Movement was prevented from starting its own radio station.

FOREIGN POLICY

Danish foreign policy is thoroughly pro-Western and is based on close links with four organizations: the United Nations, NATO, the Nordic Council, and the European Union.

Although committed to collective security, Denmark has consistently resisted pressures by NATO to increase defense spending. In 1984, the Social Democrats and their allies secured legislation making Denmark the first NATO nation to withdraw completely from missile deployment. In 1988 there was great controversy over NATO's policy of not declaring which ships carried nuclear weapons; many Danes on the left wanted to ban all such ships from Danish ports, but a compromise was worked out. Danish troops have participated in NATO peacekeeping operations in Kosovo and elsewhere.

Denmark was admitted to the European Community (now the EU) in 1973, but Greenland withdrew from membership in 1985. Copenhagen has always, with an eye to popular suspicion of Brussels, guarded its sovereignty more tightly against EU supranational encroachment than most members. It demonstrated this in 1992, when a referendum went against the EU's Maastricht Treaty on closer integration, forcing the government to renegotiate some of its terms regarding common defense, policing, citizenship, and currency. Denmark opted not to participate in Europe's Economic and Monetary Union; the Social Democratic-led government promised to hold off deciding the matter until after elections in 2002. But recent strain on the Danish krone has caused it to have second thoughts and to schedule another referendum on joining EMU for autumn 2000. Denmark did join the EU Schengen Agreement on freeing internal border controls.

Denmark places great emphasis on relations with developing countries and is one of the few nations to meet the U.N. goal of contributing 0.7% of gross domestic product (GDP) as developmental assistance. As a member of the Nordic Council, Denmark maintains close relations with the other members of the council—Norway, Iceland, Sweden, and Finland. In 1982 Denmark joined Norway and Sweden in resuming diplomatic relations with the Vatican, ending a four-century rupture.

DEFENSE

The sovereign is the constitutional head of the armed services. The operational command is vested in the Ministry of Defense. Denmark has a unified defense ministry and a single defense command. The chief of defense, the head of the Defense Command, is a serving officer whose deputy is the chief of the defense staff. Both are members of the Defense Council, along with the chiefs of the army, navy, and air force and the commander of the Danish operational forces.

Conscription is authorized by the constitution. The period of service is nine months in peacetime. The right of conscientious objection is recognized, and about 15 percent of eligible Danes invoke the right annually. Defense legislation is extensive and includes the Acts of 1950, 1960, 1969, and 1973 and the Royal Decree of 1952, amended in 1961.

Defense personnel are trained at specialized schools: artillery personnel at the Army Fire Support School at Varde, West Jutland, and infantry personnel at the Army Combat School at Oxboel, West Jutland. Regular officers are trained at the Defense College, Copenhagen, a triservice institution that also is the staff college.

The army is organized into supply troops, signal corps, engineers, artillery, army aviation, infantry, and armored troops. The latter include old regiments of infantry and cavalry. Operationally, the kingdom is divided into the Western Land Command, the Eastern Land Command, and the Bornholm Region. The Eastern Land Command has two standing force brigades; the Western Land Command, three. For territorial defense Denmark is divided into seven regions: three in Jutland, one in Fünen, two in Zealand, and one in Bornholm.

Although a member of NATO, Denmark does not permit the stationing of foreign troops on its soil (except in Greenland, where it has allowed the United States to shoulder most of the responsibility for the island's defense) or NATO troop exercises in Bornholm. Denmark does not allow the stationing of nuclear weapons on its territory, but it will tacitly allow nuclear-armed NATO ships in port.

The principal naval bases are at Copenhagen, Kørsør, and Frederikshavn. The navy is charged with guard duties off the Faeroe Islands and Greenland. The air force consists of a tactical air command.

Military Indicators

Total Active Duty Personnel: 32,900
Military Manpower per 1,000: 6.2
Military Expenditures $million: 3,118
as % of GNP: 1.8
per capita $: 596
as % of central government expenditures: 4.1

Arms Imports $: 80
Arms Exports $: 20

ECONOMY

The Danish economy today is characterized by very high rates of taxation, high levels of government spending (equivalent to 56 percent of GDP in 1998, up from 25 percent in 1960), but only a modest degree of public ownership of industry. The service sector, especially public services, is correspondingly high, accounting for 72 percent of the workforce and 63 percent of GDP (not counting financial services) in 1998. Private services have grown vigorously in the 1990s, primarily in retailing, hotels and restaurants, and commerce- and business-related services and communications. The state has liberalized the telecommunication sector bit by bit since consolidating all companies into a single, state-owned firm, Teledanmark—now private—in 1991.

The finance system (commercial banks, mortgage lenders, insurance companies, pension funds) has been consolidating and increasingly trying to compete on a Europe-wide scale. The Copenhagen Stock Exchange joined with its Stockholm counterpart to create Nordic Exchanges, NOREX, in 1999. The financial sector occupied 2.6 percent of the labor force in 1998 and generated 6.4 percent of gross domestic product.

Manufacturing jobs were 17 percent of the total in 1998, and manufacturing activity accounted for just 18.2 percent of GDP. Over the years since the 1960s, Denmark has lost footwear, textile, and clothing-related jobs to lower-wage countries while the chemical and pharmaceutical industries have increased employment. The food processing industry remains important, given Denmark's prominence in dairying and meat production. All told, the country has lost about 20 percent of the industrial employment it had in the mid-1960s. Even the declining sectors have demonstrated impressive productivity improvements, and the country has managed to retain many of the high-skill jobs associated with manufacturing, such as design and marketing, even as factory jobs move "offshore." The Danish industrial landscape is still predominantly one of small and mid-sized concerns, with many firms still controlled by individual families. Construction provided employment for about 6 percent of the workforce in 1998 and was responsible for 5.3 percent of national output; the building industry is cyclical in nature and does not export its services.

Denmark currently extracts enough oil and gas from its North Sea wells to take care of its own energy needs. It has also been active in seeking out nonpolluting sources of power, such as wind farms, and renewable energy sources provided 10 percent of the country's electricity in 1998. The fossil fuel and electricity industries, state owned, were allowed private investment in 1998 for the first time to stimulate competition.

Denmark emerged from World War II with most of its economy intact, although considerably depleted. The devaluation of the krone in 1949 helped to boost exports, while the Marshall Plan helped to stimulate the weaker sectors. At the beginning of the 1950s Danish exports were primarily farm products. As a result, the farmers favored liberalization of trade and removal of import restrictions. Industry, however, was more protectionist. Faced with growing competition from abroad, Danish industry nonetheless surged in the 1950s, increasing production, employment, and share of exports. By the end of the 1950s Denmark had established itself as a significant industrial exporter, helping to swing the balance of payments into Denmark's favor.

The year 1973 was a watershed in Danish economic history. In that year, Denmark joined the Common Market, along with Great Britain, and the first oil crisis hit. During 1973–75 inflation climbed by 20 percent annually; unemployment was at an all-time high; and the balance of payments deficit increased from Kr3 billion in 1975 to Kr12 billion in 1976, equal to 5 percent of the GDP. The problem was exacerbated by the second oil crisis, of 1978–80. Government efforts to keep the lid on inflation and improve the balance of payments produced unpleasant side effects: lower wages, higher interest rates, high unemployment, deteriorating public finances, and higher taxes.

The Schlüter government passed a tax reform in 1986, and subsequent changes in the tax code took place under its successor in 1994 and 1998. While lowering top marginal rates was certainly one aim, the net effect has been to draw more earnings into the revenue system through greater transparency, fewer loopholes, and a broader tax base, and this has created a more equitable income distribution. Another emphasis has been a shift toward "green" taxation based on resource consumption, adoption of energy efficient technologies, and reduced emission of greenhouse gases.

A series of conservative-leaning governments in the 1980s and early 1990s also attempted to put the brakes on the growth of public spending and public-sector employment and prepare the ground for the heightened competition that would come with the signing of the Single European Act removing many of the European Community's internal trade barriers and protections. The government retains control over postal services, public transportation, and, for the most part, utilities, and of course the welfare state continues to provide generous health, education, pension, and unemployment benefits, and other transfer payments. With revenues on the increase, though, the socialist team that took the reins of power from 1993 managed to turn around the nation's string of deficits to record a slight budgetary surplus in 1998, even as unemployment fell sharply, to about 5 percent from 10.1 percent when Rasmussen became prime minister, and government expenditure as a percentage of GDP fell off from 64.2 percent to 55.8 percent over the same time period.

Denmark has always been very trade dependent, with imports and exports each equivalent to about one-third of GDP. Manufactures make up 76 percent of exports, and agricultural products 15 percent. Most of the country's exports (leading sectors: machines and instruments, chemicals and pharmaceuticals, textiles, clothing, and furniture) go to other EU countries (68 percent), with Germany the largest single export market. The country ran current account deficits steadily for almost three decades until 1990; since then it has had a surplus. Although Denmark meets the criteria for participating in the European Union's Economic and Monetary Union, phase three, popular sentiment has been running against giving monetary sovereignty to Brussels, and in 2000, 53 percent of the population rejected adoption of the euro as the national currency.

Danish growth and investment have been slightly below average for industrial countries over the period since 1960. Savings rates have been correspondingly lower as well, and this has caused Denmark to slip down the rankings of income by country (now 10th in income per capita in Europe as measured by purchasing power parity), but it has taken steps to enhance savings and capital formation through the tax code, and it remains one of the world's most prosperous nations.

Principal Economic Indicators

Gross National Product: $184.347 billion
GNP per capita: $34,890
GNP Average Annual Growth Rate (1990–97) %: 2.5
GNP per capita Average Annual Growth Rate (1990–97) %: 2.1
Origin of Gross Domestic Product %
- Agriculture: 4
- Mining: 1
- Manufacturing: 19
- Construction: 5
- Public Utilities: 2
- Transportation and Communications: 10
- Trade: 14
- Financial Services: 19
- Other Services: 5
- Government: 22

Gross Domestic Product by Type of Expenditure %
- Private Consumption: 54
- Government Consumption: 26
- Gross Domestic Investment: 15
- Foreign Trade: Exports: 35
- Imports: −29

% of Income Received by Poorest 20%: 3.5
% of Income Received by Richest 10%: 25.6

Price and earnings indexes (1995 = 100)

	1992	1993	1994	1995	1996	1997	1998
Consumer price index	94.9	96.0	98.0	100.0	102.1	104.4	106.3
Hourly earnings index	90.6	92.7	96.7	100.0	—	—	—

Finance

National Currency: Danish Krone (DKr)
Exchange Rate: $1 = Dkr 6.916
Money Supply Stock in National Currency billion: 325.5
M1 per capita: 61,700
Central Bank Discount Rate %: 2.75
Total External Debt $million: —
Debt Service Ratio %: —

Balance of Payments $million: 921
International Reserves SDRs million: 11,301
Ratio of External Debt to Total Reserves: —

Average Annual Rate of Inflation/Consumer Price Index Growth Rate %: 2.2

Official Development Assistance

Donor ODA $million: 1,704
- as % of GNP: 0.92
- per capita: $320.5
- Foreign Direct Investment $million: 6,373

Central Government Revenues and Expenditures

Fiscal Year: Calendar Year
Revenues $million: 62,100
Expenditures $million: 66,400
Budget Deficit $million: 4,300
Tax Revenues as % of GDP: —
Highest Tax Bracket %
- Individual: 59
- Corporate: 32

Employment and Labor

Economically Active Population: 2,812,000
Female Participation Rate %: 45.3
Activity Rate%: 53.4
Labor by Sector: %
- Agriculture, Forestry, Fishing: 4.4
- Manufacturing, Mining: 20.7
- Construction: 6.2
- Transportation and Communications: 7.0
- Trade, Hotels, and Restaurants: 16.8
- Finance, Insurance, Real Estate: 10.0
- Public Administration, Defense: 6.0
- Services: 28.5

Unemployment %: 7.9

Agriculture

Agriculture's Share of GDP %: 4
Average Annual Rate of Growth (1965–98) %: 2.3
Number of Farms 000: 68.8
Average Size of Farm ha: 35.9
Number of Tractors per 1,000 hectares: 61.8
Irrigation, % of Farms having: 19
Artificial Fertilizer kg/hectare: 255
Total Farmland as % of land area: 64.2
Livestock: Cattle 000: 1,974
Sheep 000: 142
Hogs 000: 12,004
Chickens 000: 18,156
Forests: Production of Roundwood (000 cubic meters): 2,288
Fisheries: Total Catch tons 000: 1,886.9

Mining

% of GDP: 0.9
Value of Mineral Production $million: 1,289.7

Manufacturing

Value Added $million: 26,633
Industrial Production Growth Rate %: 1.3

Energy

Commercial Energy Production metric tons of oil equivalent 000: 20,274
Commercial Energy Consumption metric tons of oil equivalent 000: 21,107
Commercial Energy Consumption per capita kg: 3,994
Average Annual Growth Rate 1980–97 %: 0.8
Net Energy Imports % of use: 4
Electricity Installed Capacity kW 000: 11,144
Production kW-hr million: 36,790
Coal Reserves tons million: —
Production tons:
Natural Gas Proven Reserves cubic meters billion: 10.9
Production cubic meters million: 4,936
Crude Petroleum Reserves barrels million: 957
Production barrels million: 75
Consumption barrels million: 74
Refinery Capacity barrels per day 000: 189
Pipelines Length km: 688

Foreign Trade

Imports $million: 41,626.4
Exports $million: 47,221.8
Export Volume % Annual Growth Rate (1990–97): 5.6
Import Volume % Annual Growth Rate (1990–97): 6.3

Balance of trade (current prices)

	1993	1994	1995	1996	1997	1998
DKr 000,000	+43,077	+41,596	+29,500	+31,206	+25,293	+13,776
% of total	9.1%	8.5%	5.9%	5.8%	4.2%	2.2%

Major Trading Partners

	Imports	Exports
European Union %	68.7	59.9
United States %	4.7	3.7
Eastern Europe %	3.7	4.3
Japan %	2.7	3.5
Others %	20.3	28.6

Transportation

Roads Total Length mi: 44,378 km 71,420
Paved %: 100
Automobiles: 288,464
Trucks and Buses: 335,690
Persons per vehicle:
Railroad; Track Length mi: 1,780 km 2,865
Passenger-mi million: 3,004
Freight-mi million: 1,360
Merchant Marine: No. of Vessels: 456
Total Deadweight Tonnage 000: 7,589.1
International Cargo Loaded tons 000: 20,284
International Cargo Off-loaded tons 000: 37,314
Airports with Scheduled Flights: 13
Traffic: Passenger-mi million: 3,340
Freight-mi million: 117
Length of Canals mi: 259 km 417

Tourism

Number of Tourists to 000: 2,073
Number of Tourists from 000: 4,972
Tourist Receipts $million: 3,672
Tourist Expenditures $million: 4,280

Communications

Telephones 000: 3,203
Cost of Local Calls 3 mins: $0.13

Cellular Telephones 000: 822
Fax Machines 000: 250
Personal Computers 000: 1,416
Internet Hosts per million persons: 9,670
Mail: Post Offices: 64
Pieces of Mail Handled: 1,828
Pieces of Mail Handled per person: 350

EDUCATION

The earliest Danish schools were established from the 10th to the 12th centuries. The University of Copenhagen was established in 1479 through a papal bull of Sixtus IV. In 1536 the state took over the grammar schools from the Catholic Church, and the history of national education may be said to begin from that date. From the 15th to the 19th centuries the most decisive influence on education was the national Lutheran Church. The state, for its part, acknowledged its obligation to provide the physical facilities for such schooling. In 1689 a high commission reorganized the entire school system, requiring townships to pay for primary schools, maintain evening classes for adults, and make school attendance compulsory for children between ages seven and 14. It also created the first normal schools.

The Enlightenment and the rise of the merchant class, who needed a more practical type of school, led to dissatisfaction with the church's role in education. The Free School Movement sought to emphasize freedom of choice in education. These schools had no entrance or leaving examinations, instruction was confined to the lectures, and the curriculum was unstructured.

Section 76 of the Danish constitution specifies that education shall be compulsory. In 1976 a new education act came into effect. It introduced nine years of comprehensive primary and lower secondary education for all, a noncompulsory 10th year, and an optional preschool year. There is a noncompulsory leaving examination after ninth grade (taken by 90–95 percent of students), and a similar advanced leaving examination after 10th grade (about 85 percent sit for this). About one-quarter of Danish youths go no further than the basic course of education. A refinement in 1994 aimed to tailor instruction more individually to students' needs and talents.

Danish education is characterized by a rich variety of options for the schoolgoer. Although compulsory education begins at age seven, most children attend one of four types of preschools: *vuggestuer* (day nurseries) for children up to three; *bornehaver* (kindergartens) for three- to six-year-olds; *bornehaveklasser* (preschool classes) for five- to six-year-olds; and *integrerede institutioner* (integrated schools).

Education at the upper secondary level is divided into four main types: general upper secondary education (Gymnasium), which prepares students over a three-year course for higher education; Hojere Forbeledelseseksamen (HF, the two-year higher preparatory examination course); the Hojere handelseksamen (HHX, the higher commercial examination, a three-year course of study); and Hojere Teknisk Eksamen (HHX, the higher technical examination course, a three-year vocational and educational program). Each of these courses leads to an examination that governs admission to higher education. There are separate schools that provide an apprenticeship-type vocational training course that prepares students for work in trade and industry.

There are about 80 residential folk high schools. For the 14-to-18 age groups there are continuation schools (*efterskoler*) and youth schools (*ungdomskoler*). The former have the flavor of folk high schools and teach young people practical subjects for a year beyond their compulsory schooling. Youth schools are designed for school-leavers who lack particular aptitudes. The agricultural *landbrugsskoler* accept students for agricultural training.

About 12 percent of all Danish students are educated privately. All private schools are entitled to receive state subsidies that in principle match what is spent to educate pupils in municipal schools, minus the fees charged to parents of private school students, provided they meet a minimum enrollment standard and their instructional standards are comparable to those of the state schools.

For centuries the country's only university was the University of Copenhagen, which celebrated its 500th anniversary in 1979. The second was established at Aarhus in 1928. Odense followed in 1964, Roskilde in 1972, and Aalborg in 1974. Aalborg is a congeries of schools and colleges. Roskilde is an experimental university based on student participation and innovative instruction. On the whole, universities are fairly autonomous, with the general control of the Ministry of Education limited to examinations, degrees, enrollment, and staffing.

The country has recently restructured its university setup to match the model used in the English-speaking world.

Aside from the traditional universities, there are institutions to provide short-cycle nonuniversity higher education in technical, commercial, and agricultural disciplines and medium-cycle nonuniversity education in a wide range of fields. The specialized universities are the Technical University (engineering), the Royal Danish School of Pharmacy, the Royal Danish Veterinary and Agricultural University (all of these were founded in the 19th century), the Royal Danish School of Educational Studies, and three business schools (Copenhagen, Aarhus, South Jutland).

Education is a state responsibility, shared by the central government, counties, and municipalities. Primary and lower secondary schools are under local government control, while gymnasia and HF courses are run by the counties.

General adult education is offered on a nonformal basis to all who are over 18 years of age. There is also vocational training tailored to specific job market requirements and open education presented at vocational schools and universities. All three types of adult education together enrolled 59,000 in 1995.

The overall education budget in 1997 was 83.7 billion Danish kroner, representing 13.1 percent of public spending.

Education

Literacy Rate %: 100
- Male %: 100
- Female%: 100

First Level: Primary schools: 2,536
- Teachers: 58,500
- Students: 605,798
- Student-Teacher Ratio: 10.4
- Net Enrollment Ratio: 99

Second Level: Secondary Schools: 153
- Teachers: 11,000
- Students: 75,793
- Student-Teacher Ratio: 6.8
- Net Enrollment Ratio: 86

Vocational Level: Schools: 237
- Students: 188,417

Third Level: Institutions: 158
- Teachers: 8,000
- Students: 155,661
- Student-Ratio Level: 19.5
- Gross Enrollment Ratio: 45.0
- Students per 100,000: 3,261
- % of Population age 25 and over with Post-secondary Education: 18.9

Public Expenditure on Education as % of GDP: 8.3

SCIENCE AND TECHNOLOGY

Science and Technology

Scientists and Engineers in R&D per 1 million persons: 3,259
Expenditures in R&D as % of GDP: 1.95
High-Tech Exports $million: 5,479
Patent Applications by Residents: 2,658

MEDIA

The Danish press dates back to 1666, when the first Danish paper, *Den Danske Mercurius*, was published by the Crown as an official bulletin. Press censorship existed until 1849, but since then the Danish press has been one of the freest. Article 77 of the Constitutional Act also bans any kind of censorship. Even military information can be published unless the government prohibits it.

Four papers founded in the 18th century still publish today: *Berlingske Tidende* (1749, Copenhagen), *Stiftstidende* (1767, Aalborg), *Stiftstidende* (1772, Fyens), and *Stiftstidende* (1794, Aarhus).

There is no truly national press. Most of the dailies are concentrated in Copenhagen, which claims about half of the total daily newspaper circulation. Although the number of newspapers has been falling, circulation has remained stable enough to make per capita circulation one of the world's highest. The typical newspaper avoids sensationalism; the nearest approaches to it are found in the midday tabloids *BT* and *Ekstra Bladet*, representing respectively the Conservative and Radical Liberal party lines.

Ownership of the Danish press has traditionally been in the hands of local private families or limited-liability companies. But since 1945 there has been increasing concentration of ownership in the hands of a few publishing houses or chains. Some 25 percent of total circulation of all dailies plus two large weeklies, numerous district papers, a book publishing business, and a printshop are controlled by the Berlingske Group. Another large newspaper chain is owned by the Berg Group, which publishes six dailies.

Special interest and political party affiliations are other old traditions in the Danish press. Only the Communist *Land og Folk* is directly owned by a party, but beginning in 1849, newspapers began to be tied to, or strongly espouse, various parties. The rivalry among political party papers has continued to the present day. In Copenhagen, for example, *Berlingske Tidende* is the Conservative voice while *Politiken* supports the Radical Liberals and *Det Fri Aktuelt* supports the Social Democrats. The national Lutheran Church is represented by *Kristeligt Dagblad*. The church also runs a news bureau called Kristeligt Pressebureau. With the weakening of the political press in recent years, the independents have grown stronger.

The country's most influential newspapers are *Berlingske Tidende, Det Fri Aktuelt*, and *Politiken*, and the first is well regarded abroad. Among serious newspapers, *Information* has a place of its own. Among provincial papers, *Jyllands Posten* is the best known.

Denmark's besk known weekly magazine is *Billed Bladet*, with a circulation of 280,000. It is followed by the family magazine *Familie Journalen* (366,600), *Idenyt Hus Og Have* (1,300,000), *Se Og Har* (315,000) *TV Bladet* (280,000), *Samvirke* (685,000), *Hjemmet* (244,000), *Helse-Familiens Laegeblad* (355,000), and the children's magazine *Anders & Co.* (142,000).

The national news agency is the Ritzaus Bureau, cooperatively owned by the Danish press. It has a working relationship with multinational agencies such as Reuters, AFP, and DPA, which have bureaus in Denmark.

Broadcasting used to be a monopoly of the Danish State Television and Radio Service (Danmarks Radio), which began operating in 1925. Although technically under the Ministry of Cultural Affairs, it is an independent institution governed by the Radio Council of 27 members elected by the Folketing. About half of the telecasts are imports. Revenues are derived solely from licenses, as there is no advertising. In 1986 the Folketing allowed private broadcasting for the first time, starting with independent local radio stations. The first commercial television channel started up in 1988, and a satellite channel first began beaming programs to viewers in 1991. Denmark had about 5.6 million radio receivers and around half as many television sets in 1993. Faeroese Radio and Greenland Radio are independent. Greenland Television is cable only.

Denmark has numerous publishing houses, spread throughout the country but concentrated in Copenhagen.

Media

Daily Newspapers: 51
Total Circulation 000: 1,610
Circulation per 1,000: 308
Books Published: 11,973
Magazines: 205
Radio Receivers 000: 5,200
per 1,000: 988
Television sets 000: 2,200
per 1,000: 536

MOST IMPORTANT MEDIA:

Press. The following newspapers are published at Copenhagen, unless otherwise noted (circulation figures for first half of 1994); *Ekstra Bladet* (177,000 weekdays, 193,000 Sunday), independent Conservative; *Politiken* (153,000 weekdays, 205,000 Sunday), independent Radical Liberal; *Morgenavisen Jyllands-Posten* (Viby, 152,000 weekdays, 249,000 Sunday), independent; *Berlingske Tidende* (134,000 weekdays, 197,000 Sunday), independent Conservative; *Jydske Vestkysten* (Esbjerg, 95,000 weekdays, 109,000 Sunday); *Alborg Stiftstidende* (Alborg, 72,000 weekdays, 92,000 Sunday), independent; *Fyens Stiftstidende* (Odense, 66,000 weekdays, 98,000 Sunday), independent; *Aarhus Stiftstidende* (Aarhus, 62,000 weekdays, 83,000 Sunday), independent; *Det Fri Aktuelt* (43,000 daily), Social Democratic.

News agency. The domestic agency, owned by the Danish newspapers, is Ritzaus Bureau; numerous foreign bureaus also maintain offices at Copenhagen.

Radio and television. Radio and television stations have traditionally been controlled by the government-owned, noncommercial Danish State Radio and Television Service (Danmarks Radio). The monopoly was terminated by the Folketing in 1986, which sanctioned the immediate establishment of independent local radio broadcasting, with a nationwide commercial television channel commencing operation in late 1988, followed by a satellite television station in 1991.

CULTURE

Cultural Indicators

Public Libraries Number: 250
Volumes: 34,685,000
Registered borrowers: —
Museums Number: 280
Annual Attendance: 8,548,000
Cinema Production of Long Films: 12
Number of Cinemas: 315
Seating Capacity: 50,000
Annual Attendance: 9.6
Annual Attendance per capita: 1.7

STATUS OF WOMEN

In perhaps no other part of the world do women enjoy the degree of equality that Scandinavia affords, and Denmark places itself firmly in the Scandinavian tradition. A 1997 survey of European women found more Danish women (two-thirds) saying they were "very satisfied" with their lives than those of any other country. Even here, however, women earn significantly less than men, in spite of laws mandating equal pay going back to 1973. "Women's work" remains concentrated in poorly compensated occupations like teaching, clerical work, and other low-skilled or unskilled services. Many married women are in the work force (more than 80 percent), but quite a few of these work part time. Still, with more women today graduating with advanced degrees, higher-paying fields such as science, engineering, and management are open to women as never before. Women represented about 45 percent of the paid labor force in 1998.

Women were granted the vote in 1915 and won the right to run for office at the same time. They typically hold between 20 and 30 percent of seats in the Folketing, and from the late 1940s onward there has been at least one female minister in every cabinet formed. After a 1921 law passed, women were guaranteed equal opportunity in and access to official positions, excepting only the clergy and the military, and even these exceptions eventually fell by the wayside. Military training became an option for women in 1971. The Nordic countries have since 1974 cooperated to advance the equal rights agenda in tandem.

Family planning is integrated into the national health service, with service delivery delegated to county level. Abortion is available on request for the first trimester and is covered by national insurance. The country's social policies consciously steer toward equalization of opportunity through family allowances, special aid for single mothers, public provision of day care, and the like. Divorce became no-fault in 1970, and the divorce rate is high. Ever more prevalent are consensual unions, though, favored by a substantial proportion of the population (only in Sweden is the frequency of unmarried couples cohabiting higher).

Women

Gender Empowerment Measure: 3
Seats Held in Parliament by Women %: 33.0
Female Administrators and Managers %: 19.2
Female Professional and Technical Workers %: 46.8
Women's Share of Earned Income %: 42.0
Women in Government %: 19

HEALTH, FOOD, AND NUTRITION

Health

Number of Physicians: 14,497
Number of Dentists: 5,088
Number of Nurses: 63,841
Number of Pharmacists: —
Population per Physician: 358
Number of Hospitals: 163
Hospital Beds per 10,000: 35
Hospital Bed Occupancy Rate: 80.4
Infant Mortality Rate per 1,000 live births: 8
Maternal Mortality Rate per 100,000 live births: 9
Total Health Expenditures as % of GDP: 6.30
Health Expenditures per capita $: 1,588
HIV Infected % of adults: 0.12
Cigarette Consumption per smoker per year: 2,532
% of Smokers: Male: 37
Female: 37
Access to Safe Water %: 100

Food and Nutrition

Food Supply as % of FAO Requirements: 138
% of Consumption Expenditures on Food: 17.9
Daily Available Calories per capita: 3,704
% of Total Calories Derived From:
Cereals: 21.7
Potatoes, cassava: 3.2
Meat, poultry: 22.5
Fish: 2.1
Eggs, milk: 9.1
Fruits, vegetables: 3.8
Fats, oils: 15.4

ENVIRONMENT

The importance Denmark places on the environment is underscored by the decision of the European Environment Agency to situate its headquarters in Copenhagen. The nation's own environment ministry dates to 1971; in 1994 it was consolidated with the ministry of energy into one. The revamped ministry has worked to realign the tax system to put a price on resource consumption. Denmark has had a carbon dioxide emissions tax since 1993, with a part of the proceeds earmarked for energy conservation programs and research and development to increase efficiencies in energy supply. With nuclear energy widely unpopular in Scandinavia these days, the government has worked to develop windpower and biogas facilities drawing on fertilizer and slaughterhouse wastes.

Denmark's Forest Act prevents most woodlands from being plowed under for agricultural, commercial, or residential activity, but it fails to protect old-growth forests from being harvested for timber. The Worldwide Fund for Nature has assessed the country's forests as "eroded" from a standpoint of genetic diversity and in poor health.

The Environmental Protection Agency requires impact statements before permitting new industrial plants or expansions to get under way. Similarly, government-sponsored projects and transportation investments have to be vetted by the agency for possible ecological effects. The National Environmental Research Institute monitors the nation's soil and air quality, purity of streams, lakes, and fjords, and ecology of the countryside, and it gives policy advice. Denmark's special concerns are smog and particulates from vehicle emissions, nitrogen and phosphorus contamination of the North Sea and surface freshwater from fertilizer runoff, and contamination caused by animal wastes. Marine pollution is one area where the government has cooperated with both nongovernmental groups and other Nordic nations.

Flooding threatens certain parts of the coastline (parts of Jutland and the south shore of Lolland Island), and these have a series of dikes to keep the seas at bay.

Environment

Forest Area sq km: 4,000
Average Annual Deforestation sq km: 0
Nationally Protected Areas as % of Total Land Area: 32.3
Freshwater Access cubic meters per capita: 2,460
Emissions of Organic Water Pollutants kg per day: 91,815
CO_2 Emissions per capita ton: 10.7

CHRONOLOGY

1945 Denmark is liberated from German occupation; Vilhelm Buhl takes office at head of coalition government
1948 Faeroe Islands granted home rule.
1949 Denmark joins NATO.
1953 New constitution promulgated along with new Act of Succession permitting female succession to throne; Greenland integrated into the Kingdom of Denmark.
1955 Parliament approves appointment of a national ombudsman on Swedish model.
1958 Education Act passed incorporating far-reaching reforms.
1960 Agricultural Commission initiates reform of land tenure.
1962 Helsinki Agreement on Nordic Cooperation is signed, with Denmark as a founding member.
1966 Odense University founded.
1968 Radical Liberal/Conservative/Liberal governing coalition courts controversy by attempting to outlaw pornography.
1970 Local government reform reduces number of local administrative units and rationalizes their finances.
1971 Helsinki Agreement is revised.
1972 King Frederik IX dies; his daughter succeeds to the throne as Queen Margrethe II; Roskilde Uni-

versity founded; New Primary Education Act is passed.

1973 Denmark joins European Community; abortion legalized.

1975 Social Democrat Anker Jørgensen returns to office, remains in power until 1982 as head of four cabinets.

1976 Social Assistance Act is passed; government razes "Free City" zone of counterculturists in Copenhagen.

1982 Jørgensen quits; Poul Schlüter heads a Conservative/Liberal coalition; Greenland decides in referendum to leave EEC, becomes overseas territory in association with Community in 1985.

1984 General election confirms Schlüter in power with fresh coalition of center-right parties.

1986 Folketing fails to approve EC's Single European Act for harmonizing trade; Schlüter gains approval of it through referendum.

1988 Controversy stirred by proposal to ban NATO warships that might be carrying nuclear warheads from Danish ports; compromise allows NATO to continue with its policy of secrecy.

1989 Denmark is first nation to allow same-sex civil marriages.

1990 Increase in popularity of antitax, anti-immigrant Progress Party; ruling coalition responds by putting cuts in social welfare on agenda.

1992 Referendum rejects Maastricht Treaty on European Union after it has gained Folketing approval; negotiations allow Denmark to opt out of European plans for a common defense, common citizenship, border controls, and common currency; longest suspension bridge in Europe is completed to link Zealand with Jutland.

1993 Scandal over an immigration case causes resignation of Schlüter and formation of a Social Democrat–led government under Poul Nyrup Rasmussen; fresh referendum approves Maastricht Treaty with the opt-out provisions.

1994 Parliamentary elections confirm Rasmussen team in office with a coalition of Social Democrats, Social Liberals, and Center Democrats.

1995 Danish National Socialist (neo-Nazi) Movement is barred from launching radio station.

1998 Referendum backs Treaty of Amsterdam designed to further integration of European Union; Denmark endorses EU Schengen Agreement allowing for "borderless" community by participants but defers decision on joining Economic and Monetary Union; new governing bloc in Faeroe Islands seeks greater degree of sovereignty.

1999 Danes reject adoption of the euro as their national currency by 53 percent.

2001 The Liberal Party wins a majority of seats in parliamentary elections and forms a minority government with the Conservative People's Party. Anders Fogh Rasmussen becomes prime minister.

BIBLIOGRAPHY

Andersen, T. M., et al., eds. *Macroeconomic Perspectives on the Danish Economy.* London, 1999.

Cave, W., and P. Himmelstrup. *The Welfare Society in Transition: Problems and Prospects of the Welfare Model.* Copenhagen, 1994.

Dahl, ed. *Danish Law in a European Perspective.* Holmes Beach, Fla., 1996.

Fisher, Peter, trans. *Saxo Grammaticus: The History of the Danes.* Rochester, N.Y., 1998.

Hasselbalch, Ole, and Per Jacobsen, eds. *Labour Law and Industrial Relations in Denmark.* Cambridge, Mass., 1999.

Hibbs, Douglas. *Solidarity or Egoism: The Economics of Sociotropic and Egocentric Influences on Political Behavior: Denmark in International and Theoretical Perspective.* Aarhus, 1993.

Holbraad, Carsten. *Danish Neutrality: A Study in the Foreign Policy of a Small State.* Oxford, 1991.

Kjaergaard, Thorkild. *The Danish Revolution, 1500–1800: An Ecohistorical Interpretation.* Cambridge, 1994.

Lyck, Lise, ed. *Denmark and EC Membership Evaluated.* New York, 1992.

Nannestad, Peter. *Danish Design or British Disease? Danish Economic Crisis Policy in Comparative Perspective.* Aarhus, 1992.

Organization for Economic Cooperation and Development. *Denmark, 1995–96.* Paris, 1996.

Thomas, Alastair H., and Stewart P. Oakley. *Historical Dictionary of Denmark.* Lanham, Md., 1998.

OFFICIAL PUBLICATIONS

Denmark. *Folke-og boligtaellingen, 1981* (Population and Housing Census); *Statisk arbog* (Statistical Yearbook).

CONTACT INFORMATION

Embassy of Denmark
3200 Whitehaven Street NW
Washington, D.C. 20008
Phone: (202) 234-4300 Fax: (202) 328-1470

INTERNET RESOURCES

- Statistics Denmark
  http://www2.dst.dk/internet/startuk.htm

DJIBOUTI

BASIC FACT SHEET

OFFICIAL NAME:
Republic of Djibouti (Jumhuriyah Djibouti) (formerly French Territory of the Afars and the Issas)

ABBREVIATION:
DJ

CAPITAL:
Djibouti

HEAD OF STATE:
President Ismail Omar Guelleh (from 1999)

HEAD OF GOVERNMENT:
Prime Minister Deleíta Mohamed Dileita (from 2000)

NATURE OF GOVERNMENT:
Parliamentary democracy

POPULATION:
669,000 (1999)

AREA:
23,000 sq km (8,880 sq mi)

ETHNIC MAJORITY:
Issas (Somalis) and Afars (Danakils)

LANGUAGES:
French (official); Somali, and Afar (lingua francas)

RELIGION:
Islam

UNIT OF CURRENCY:
Djibouti franc (D.F.)

NATIONAL FLAG:
Blue and green horizontal stripes on the fly and white stripe on the hoist with a five-point star

NATIONAL EMBLEM:
None

NATIONAL ANTHEM:
"Arise with Strength"

NATIONAL HOLIDAYS:
June 27 (Independence Day, National Day); also variable Islamic festivals

DATE OF INDEPENDENCE:
June 27, 1977

DATE OF CONSTITUTION:
September 4, 1992

GEOGRAPHICAL FEATURES

Djibouti (formerly known as French Somaliland and later as the French Territory of the Afars and the Issas) is in northeastern Africa and occupies an area of 23,000 sq km (8,880 sq mi). The coastline on the Gulf of Den and the Gulf of Tadjoura runs 314 km (196 mi).

Djibouti shares its total international land boundary of 517 km (320 mi) with three countries: Ethiopia (337 km; 209 mi), Eritrea (113 km 70 mi), and Somalia (58 km; 36 mi).

The entire country is mostly a sand and stone desert broken in places by lava streams and salt lakes. The three principal geographic regions are the coastal plain, less than 200 m (650 ft) in elevation; the mountains backing the plains with lofty peaks, such as Moussa Ali (2,101 m; 6,694 ft); and behind the mountains, the plateau rising from 300 to 1,500 m (1,000 to 5,000 ft). The coastline is deeply indented by the Gulf of Tadjoura, which is 45 km (28 mi) across at its entrance and penetrates 58 km (36 mi) inland.

Djibouti

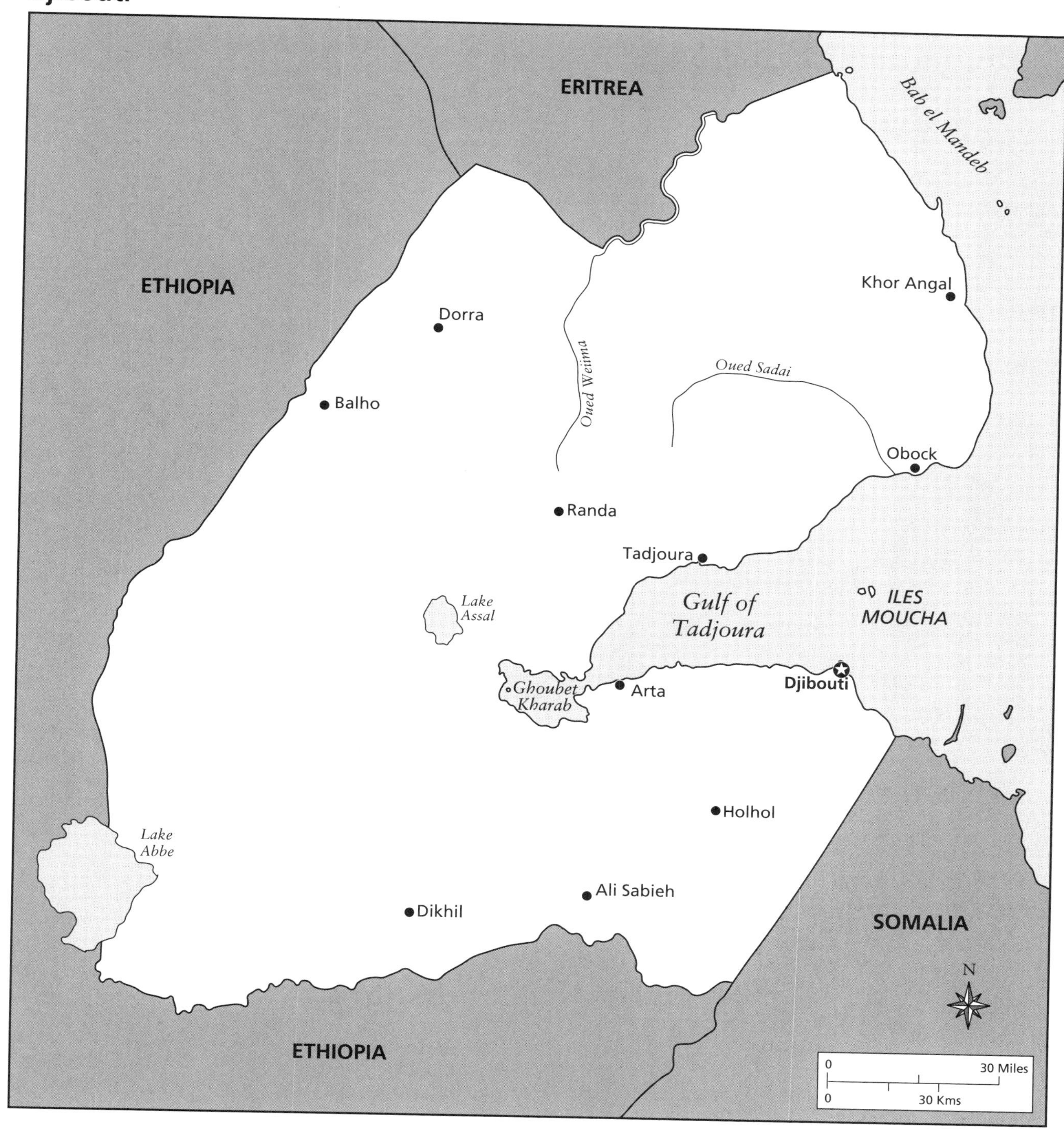

Few streams flow above the surface except following rains. The drainage is partly eastward to the coast and partly inland to Lake Assal and Lake Abbe.

Geography

Area sq km: 23,000 sq mi 8,880
World Rank: 149th
Land Boundaries, km: Eritrea 113; Ethiopia 337; Somalia 58
Coastline, km 314
Elevation Extremes meters
Lowest: Asal −155
Highest: Moussa'ali 2,028
Land Use % Arable land: —
Permanent Crops: —
Permanent Pastures: 9
Forest and Woodland: 0
Other: 81

Population of Principal Cities	
Djibouti	383,000

CLIMATE AND WEATHER

The climate is torrid and dry. There are two seasons: a hot summer from May to October and a relatively cool season from November to April. In the summer temperatures in Djibouti reach 40°C (104°F) on most days, with occasional readings of 45°C (113°F). The rainfall is sparse and erratic, with a national average of 127 mm (5 in) annually.

Climate and Weather

Mean Temperature 85°F to 104°F
Average Rainfall 5 in

POPULATION

Population Indicators

Total Population: 1999 669,000
World Rank: 159th
Density per sq mi: 74.7 per sq km 28.8
% of annual growth (1994–99): 2.7
Male %: 51.9
Female %: 48.1
Urban %: 82.8
Age Distribution: % 0–14: 39.4
15–29: 32.9
30–44: 16.9
45–59: 7.4
60–74: 2.8
75 and over: 0.6
Population 2020: 1,045,000
Birth Rate per 1,000: 38.6
Death Rate per 1,000: 15.0
Population Doubling Time (years): 32
Infant Mortality Rate per 1,000 live births: 106.0
Rate of Natural Increase per 1,000: 23.6
Total Fertility Rate: 5.4
Expectation of Life (years): Males 48.7
Females 52.0
Marriage Rate per 1,000: 6.7
Divorce Rate per 1,000: 1.9
Total Number of Households: —
Average Size of Households: 5.6
% of Illegitimate Children: 3.2
Induced Abortions: —
Rate per 100 live births: —

ETHNIC COMPOSITION

The indigenous population is divided almost equally between two Hamitic groups: the Somalis (also known as Issas or Ishak) and the Afars (also known as Danakils). The Issas live in the south and the Afars in the north and west. By recent estimates the former numbered about 220,000 and the latter about 134,000.

Djibouti's foreign community makes up an estimated 10 percent of the population. Arabs and French make up the majority; other foreigners include Greeks, Indians, and Italians.

LANGUAGES

The official language is French, but both Somali and Afar are used as lingua francas. Arabic also is spoken extensively on the coast. Neither Afar nor Somali has a script, although attempts are being made to devise a Somali script.

Principal Languages and Their Speakers	
Afar	230,000
Arabic	70,000
French	100,000
Somali	290,000
Gadaboursi	—
Issa	—
Issaq	—
Other	70,000

RELIGIONS

Islam is the religion of virtually the entire native population. There is a Roman Catholic bishopric in Djibouti with about 7,500 communicants, mostly French. Djibouti also has Protestant and Greek Orthodox churches.

Religious Affiliations	
Sunni Muslim	650,000
Christian	19,000

HISTORICAL BACKGROUND

The region that makes up modern day Djibouti was once grazing lands used by several tribes including the Afars of Ethiopia and the Issas of Somalia. By A.D. 825, the tribes that settled there had converted to Islam. For more than seven centuries the region was under the control of Arab traders who were replaced in the 16th century by sultans from the Afar tribe. With both the British and French vying for control of the region, Djibouti (formerly known as French Somaliland) was under French rule from 1859 to 1977. At the time of independence it was France's last overseas territory on the African mainland. One of the most inhospitable and arid regions in the world, Djibouti's only attraction to its French rulers lay in the port of Djibouti, which was, until the closure of the Suez Canal,

France's third largest port. The only major French presence outside the capital was the rail link to Ethiopia owned by the Compagnie du Chemin de Fer Franco-Ethiopien. The French departure was peaceful, and current relations between France and Djibouti are good.

Djibouti's political stability is balanced precariously on the relations between its two major communities—Afars (of Ethiopian origin) and Issas (of Somali origin)—as well as the military inclinations of its two neighbors, Somalia and Ethiopia. The politically dominant Issas supported independence, while the Afars wanted continued connection to France. Preindependence fighting between the two communities was marked by bombing, kidnappings, and terrorism by the Somalis. After independence, the Afars were more actively involved in acts of violence. At independence, Hassan Gouled Aptidon, leader of the Ligue Populaire Africaine pour l'Indépendence (LPAI), became president. He chose Ahmed Dini, an Afar, to be prime minister in a cabinet in which Issas dominated almost two to one.

Racial riots led to the resignation of Dini in 1977 and the appointment of a special Commission of Afars. The president agreed to its demands for more Afar representation in the civil service and the military. In February 1978, a new cabinet was announced with Abdullah Kamil, an Afar and head of the Commission of Afars, as prime minister. That same year there was yet another reshuffle, with Kamil being replaced by Barkat Gourad Hamadou, who launched a policy of rapid detribalization. Since independence, all prime ministers have been Afars, yet charges of Issa domination persist.

In 1981 President Gouled was reelected for a six-year term in a single-man race. That same year, a constitutional amendment established a single-party state, with the Rassemblement Populaire pour le Progrès (RPP), which had replaced the LPAI, as sole legal party. The opposition went underground.

Gouled achieved a measure of stability during the 1980s and was reelected unopposed in 1987. Nevertheless, ethnic tensions remained and seemed to increase during the last years of the decade.

In 1990 the two main underground groups opposed to President Gouled met in Brussels and decided to form a common front. The Democratic Front for the Liberation of Djibouti, supported mainly by the Afars, and the National Djibouti Movement for the Installation of Democracy, supported mainly by the Issas, joined forces under the name of the Union of the Democratic Movement. In late 1991, Afar rebels sought to take control of the traditional northern territory. Civil war erupted and the fighting lasted nearly four months. The government agreed to concessions including a new constitution in 1992 and a peace accord in 1994.

Entering the 1997 general elections, there was renewed conflict between Afar separatists and the Issas-dominated government. Hassan Gouled used force this time to cruch the rebels and after the election also crushed the Isaak-Somali rebels who sought their own republic of Somaliland. In 2000, Ismael Omar Guelleh, who helped Gouled defeat the Isaak-Somalis, became president of Djibouti and sought to strengthen its ties with France. In February, he signed a peace agreement with the rebels, finally putting an end to the civil war.

CONSTITUTION

Djibouti held a constitutional referendum in 1992 in which the single political party rule of the country ended. The referendum (approved by 96.6 percent of the voters) authorizes the formation of up to four political parties, which must maintain ethnic balances. The nation has a presidential form of government, with a prime minister and cabinet drawn from the Chamber of Deputies. The president is the head of state and is elected by universal suffrage for six years.

Legislative power is in the hands of a 65-member Chamber of Deputies. The judicial system is based on Islamic law.

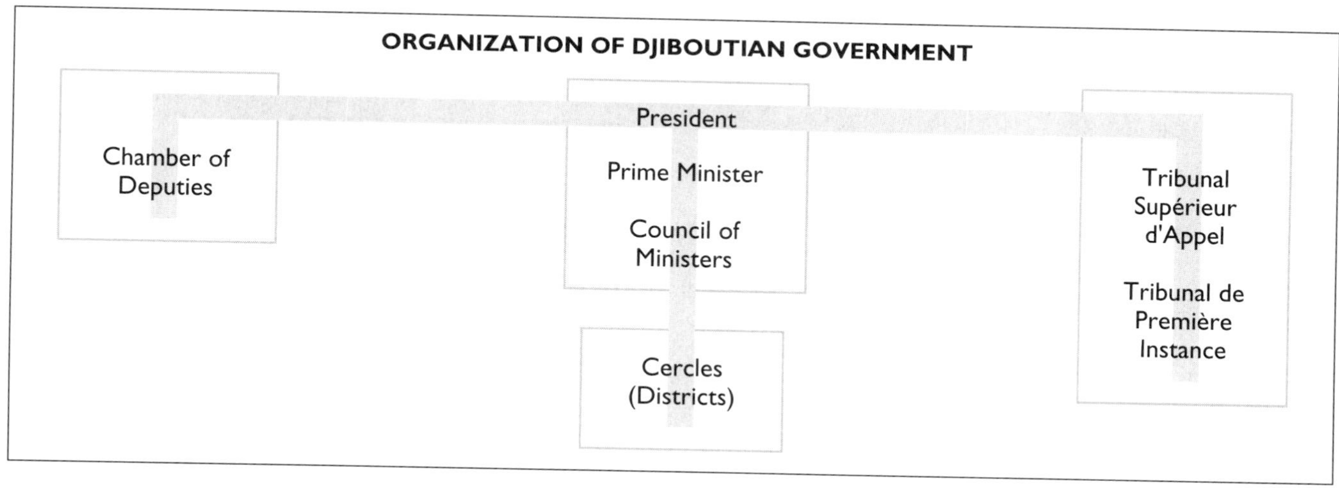

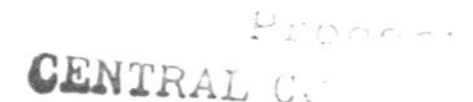

LOCAL GOVERNMENT

For purposes of local administration Djibouti is divided into five *cercles*, or administrative areas: Djibouti, Dikhil, Ali-Sabieh, Tadjourah, and Obock.

Local Government

Principal administrative divisions, capitals, area, population

AREA AND POPULATION

Districts	Capitals	area sq mi	area sq km	population 1982 estimate
Ali Sabih (Ali-Sabieh)	Ali Sabih	925	2,400	15,000
Dikhil	Dikhil	2,775	7,200	30,000
Djibouti	Djibouti	225	600	200,000
Obock	Obock	2,200	5,700	15,000
Tadjoura (Tadjourah)	Tadjoura	2,825	7,300	30,000
TOTAL		8,950	23,200	335,000

PARLIAMENT

The national legislature is the Chamber of Deputies, a 65-member unicameral body. Members are elected for five-year terms by universal suffrage from a list presented by the only legal party, Popular Rally for Progress. The list of candidates is claimed to reflect the traditional balance between different ethnic groups. In the 1987 election, all candidates were elected unopposed.

POLITICAL PARTIES

The constitutional reforms enacted in 1992 limited the number of political parties to four, though there are a number of banned organizations in operation. The four recognized parties are: Front Pour la Restauration de l'Unité et de la Démocratie (FRUD, Front for the Restoration of Unity and Democracy) which was founded in 1991 as the merger of militant Afar groups that sought ethnic representation in the government and engaged in armed conflict in order to advance its cause; Parti National Démocratique (PND, National Democratic Party) is a centrist party that seeks democratic reforms; the Parti du Renouveau Démocratique (PRD, Party of Democratic Renewal), which was founded in 1992, seeks the formation of a parliamentary system of democracy; and the Rassemblement Populaire pour le Progrès (RPP, Popular Rally for Progress) was the only legal party in the country from 1979 to 1992.

Political Parties

- Popular Rally for Progress, 1979
- United Opposition Front 1992, a coalition of Afar groups including
  - Action for Revision of Order in Djibouti, 1991
  - Front for the Restoration of Unity and Democracy, 1991
  - Djibouti Patriotic Resistance Front
  - Djibouti Democratic Union, 1992
  - Group for the Democracy of the Republic, 1996
  - National Democratic Party, 1992
  - Democratic Union for Djiboutian Justice and Equality, 1988
  - Democratic Movement of Djiboutian Youth, 1991
  - Front for the Liberation of the Somali Coast
  - Djibouti People's Party, 1981
  - Movement for Unity and Democracy, 1990
  - Party of Democratic Renewal, 1992
  - Afar Masses Organization, 1993
  - Contrist and Democratic Reforms Party, 1993

Political Parties: Strength in Parliament Most Recent Elections

The **Chamber of Deputies** (Chambre des Députés) is a unicameral body of 65 members elected for five-year terms. Prior to 1992 there was no alternative to a single list presented by the Popular Rally for Progress. Under the system of limited pluralism approved in September 1992 a total of four parties may compete for Chamber seats. At balloting on December 19, 1997, the Popular Rally for Progress and a faction of the Front for the Restoration of Unity and Democracy teamed to capture all 65 seats (54 and 11, respectively), easily outpacing two contenders.

LEGAL SYSTEM

The judicial system consists of two types of courts: Tribunal de Première Instance, which hears only civil cases; and Tribunal Supérieur d'Appel, which hears criminal cases. Cases involving Muslim personal law and customary law are heard by the qadi and by tribunals of the first and second degree. The judiciary has remained largely independent of military and executive pressures. However, there were several allegations in 1984 of corruption within the judiciary, including one that individuals could arrange favorable judgments in commercial disputes by bribery.

LAW ENFORCEMENT

Law Enforcement

Offenses reported to the police per 100,000: 402
- Murder: 4.4
- Assault: 12.4
- Burglary: 40.0
- Automobile Theft: 16.0
- Population per Police officer: —

Death Penalty: Yes, but no executions since 1977

HUMAN RIGHTS

The government's human rights record continues to be poor. Citizens have not yet been allowed to exercise the right to change their government. Despite multiparty elections, there has been no change in government since independence in 1977. Members of the security forces committed at least one extrajudicial killing. There are credible reports that some members of the security forces beat and otherwise abuse, and at times torture, detainees and sexually assault female inmates. There are credible reports that soldiers rape women in rural districts. Prison conditions are harsh. The government continues to harass, intimidate, and imprison political opponents and union leaders and to arrest and detain persons arbitrarily. It also infringes on citizens' privacy rights.

The government at times restricts freedom of speech and the press. Police occasionally jail or intimidate journalists. The government has limited freedom of assembly and restricted freedom of association. The government discourages proselytizing. There are some limits on freedom of movement. Discrimination against women persists, and the practice of female genital mutilation (FGM) continues to be widespread. Discrimination on the basis of ethnic background persists. The government imposes some limits on unions and their leaders, and there are reports of instances of forced labor.

FOREIGN POLICY

Djibouti is in one of the most vulnerable regions in Africa, and is faced with three hostile neighbors, particularly Somalia. Its population is mixed containing both Ethiopian-oriented Afars and Somali-oriented Issas. Somalia has long viewed Djibouti as part of Greater Somalia while Ethiopia, without an outlet to the sea, has coveted the country's fine port. The Somali civil war ignited the ethnic tensions in the country resulting in a deterioration of the relations between the two countries. A territorial dispute with Eritrea flared in 1996 leading to a severance of diplomatic relations. The country's security depends on a French garrison of 4,500 troops and France remains the guarantor of Djibouti's independence.

DEFENSE

The total strength of the armed forces is 9,600 (including 1,500 gendarmerie). The defense structure is headed by the president.

The army is deployed along the Somali and Ethiopian borders. The armed forces are almost entirely Issa in membership. Afar demands for parity have been resisted by the Issa-dominated government and continue to plague efforts toward intertribal harmony.

Military Indicators

Total Active Duty Personnel: 9,600
Military Manpower per 1,000: 15.4
Military Expenditures $: 22 million
- as % of GNP: 4.5
- per capita $: 52
- as % of central government expenditures: 13.9

Arms Imports $: 0
Arms Exports $: 0

ECONOMY

The economy is based on service activities connected with the country's strategic location and status as a free-trade zone in northeast Africa. Two-thirds of the inhabitants live in the capital city, the remainder being mostly nomadic herders. Scanty rainfall limits crop production to fruits and vegetables, and most food must be imported. Djibouti provides services as both a transit port for the region and an international transshipment and refueling center. It has few natural resources and little industry. The nation is, therefore, heavily dependent on foreign assistance to help support its balance of payments and to finance development projects. An unemployment rate of 40 percent to 50 percent continues to be a major problem. Inflation is not a concern, however, because of the fixed tie of the franc to the U.S. dollar. Per capita consumption dropped an estimated 35 percent over the last seven years because of recession, civil war, and a high population growth rate (including immigrants and refugees). Also, renewed fighting between Ethiopia and Eritrea has disturbed normal external channels of commerce. Faced with a multitude of economic difficulties, the government has fallen in arrears on long-term external debt and has been struggling to meet the stipulations of foreign aid donors.

Principal Economic Indicators

Gross National Product: $500 million
GNP per capita: $780
GNP Average Annual Growth Rate (1990–97) %: —
GNP per capita Average Annual Growth Rate (1990–97) %: —
Origin of Gross Domestic Product %
- Agriculture: 3
- Mining: —
- Manufacturing: 5
- Construction: 5
- Public Utilities: 8
- Transportation and Communications: 15
- Trade: 15
- Financial Services: 9
- Other Services: 4
- Government: 23

Gross Domestic Product by Type of Expenditure %
- Private Consumption: 71
- Government Consumption: 38
- Gross Domestic Investment: 12
- Foreign Trade: Exports: 47
- Imports: −67

% of Income Received by Poorest 20%: —
% of Income Received by Richest 10%: —

Price and earnings indexes (1995 = 100)

	1990	1991	1992	1993	1994	1995	1996
Consumer price index	100.0	106.8	110.4	115.3	122.8	128.8	134.2
Earnings index	—	—	—	—	—	—	—

Finance

National Currency: Djiboutian Franc (DF)
Exchange Rate: $1 = DF 177.721
Money Supply Stock in National Currency billion: 35,925
M1 per capita: 58,600
Central Bank Discount Rate %: —
Total External Debt $million: 276
Debt Service Ratio %: 2.8

Balance of Payments $million: −18.9
International Reserves SDRs million: 52
Ratio of External Debt to Total Reserves: 3

Average Annual Rate of Inflation/Consumer Price Index
Growth Rate %: 3

Official Development Assistance

ODA $: 97 million
as % of GNP: —
per capita: $ 153
Foreign Direct Investment $million: —

Central Government Revenues and Expenditures

Fiscal Year: Calendar Year
Revenues $million: 156
Expenditures $million: 175
Budget Deficit $: 19 million
Tax Revenues as % of GDP: —
Highest Tax Bracket %
Individual: —
Corporate: —

Employment and Labor

Economically Active Population: 282,000
Female Participation Rate %: 40.8
Activity Rate %: 61.5
Labor by Sector: %
Agriculture, Forestry, Fishing: 75.2
Manufacturing, Mining: 11.0
Construction: —
Transportation and Communications: —
Trade, Hotels, and Restaurants: —
Finance, Insurance, Real Estate: —
Public Administration, Defense: —
Services: 13.8

Unemployment %: 50

Agriculture

Agriculture's Share of GDP %: 3
Average Annual Rate of Growth (1965–98) %: —
Number of Farms 000: 1.2
Average Size of Farm ha: 0.4
Number of Tractors per 1,000 hectares: —
Irrigation, % of Farms having: —
Artificial Fertilizer kg/hectare: —
Total Farmland as % of land area: 0.5
Livestock: Cattle 000: 190
Sheep 000: 470
Hogs 000: —
Chickens 000: —
Forests: Production of Roundwood (000 cubic meters): —
Fisheries: Total Catch tons 000: 0.3

Mining

% of GDP: —
Value of Mineral Production $million: —

Manufacturing

Value Added $million: 23
Industrial Production Growth Rate %: 3

Energy

Commercial Energy Production metric tons of
oil equivalent 000: —
Commercial Energy Consumption metric tons of
oil equivalent 000: 548
Commercial Energy Consumption per capita kg: 909
Average Annual Growth Rate 1980–97 %: —
Net Energy Imports % of use: 100
Electricity Installed Capacity kW 000: 85
Production kW-hr million: 184
Coal Reserves tons million: —
Production tons 000: —
Natural Gas Proven Reserves cubic meters billion: —
Production cubic meters million: —
Crude Petroleum Reserves barrels million: —
Production barrels million: —
Consumption barrels million: —
Refinery Capacity barrels per day 000: —
Pipelines Length km: —

Foreign Trade

Imports $million: 214.4
Exports $million: 17.3
Export Volume % Annual Growth Rate (1990–97): —
Import Volume % Annual Growth Rate (1990–97): —
Balance of Trade $

Balance of trade (current prices)

	1992	1993	1994	1995	1996	1997
U.S.						
$ 000,000	−205.9	−183.9	−180.7	−167.4	−160.9	−160.6
% of total	65.9%	56.4%	61.6%	69.0%	67.0%	65.3%

Major Trading Partners

	Imports	Exports
European Union %	46.6	62.6
United States %	3.7	0.8
Eastern Europe %	0.7	0.0
Japan %	7.2	0.9
Others %	41.8	35.7

Transportation

Roads Total Length mi: 1.796 km 2,890
Paved %: 13
Automobiles: 8,550
Trucks and Buses: 1,870
Persons per vehicle: 56
Railroad; Track Length mi: 66 km 106
Passenger-mi million: 173
Freight-mi million: 187
Merchant Marine: No. of Vessels: 10
Total Deadweight Tonnage 000: 4.1
International Cargo Loaded tons 000: 414
International Cargo Off-loaded tons 000: 958
Airports with Scheduled Flights: 1
Traffic: Passenger-mi million: 42
Freight-mi million: 4
Length of Canals mi: —

Tourism

Number of Tourists to 000: —
Number of Tourists from 000: —
Tourist Receipts $million: 13
Tourist Expenditures $million: 7

Communications

Telephones 000: 7.6
Cost of Local Calls 3 mins: $0
Cellular Telephones 000: —
Fax Machines 000: 0.1
Personal Computers 000: 1.0
Internet Hosts per million persons: 10
Mail: Post Offices: 10
Pieces of Mail Handled million: 16
Pieces of Mail Handled per person: 281

EDUCATION

Djibouti has not yet introduced compulsory, universal, and free education. Schooling lasts 13 years, divided into six years of primary school, four years of middle school, and three years of secondary school. The academic year runs from September to May. The medium of instruction is French. There is a general lack of qualified teachers and funding for facilities. France sends aid; it has also sent teachers, helped coordinate policy, and sponsored a teacher-training center.

Education

Literacy Rate %: 46.2
Male %: 60.3
Female %: 32.7
First Level: Primary schools: 81
Teachers: 1,005
Students: 33,960
Student-Teacher Ratio: —
Net Enrollment Ratio: 32

Second Level: Secondary Schools: 26
Teachers: 628
Students: 11,628
Student-Teacher Ratio: —
Net Enrollment Ratio: —

Vocational Level: Schools: —
Students: —

Third Level: Institutions: 1
Teachers: 13
Students: 130
Student-Ratio Level: —
Gross Enrollment Ratio: 0.2
Students per 100,000: 22
% of Population Age 25 and over with Postsecondary Education: —

Public Expenditure on Education as % of GDP: 3.8

SCIENCE AND TECHNOLOGY

Science and Technology

Scientists and Engineers in R&D per 1 million persons: —
Expenditures in R&D as % of GDP: —
High-Tech Exports $: —
Patent Applications by Residents: —

MEDIA

No daily newspapers are published in the country. Three nondaily newspapers are published (all in French) in Djibouti. Two of these are official publications. Book publishing does not exist.

The official radio and television service, Radiodiffusion-Télévision de Djibouti (RTD), operates one shortwave and two medium-wave transmitters and one television station. Radio programs are broadcast in French, Afar, Issa, and Arabic. The television station, with one transmitter, reaches 80 percent of the population.

There are two public libraries. The Public Library of Djibouti has 11,000 volumes.

Media

Daily Newspapers: —
Total Circulation 000: —
Circulation per 1,000: —
Books Published: —
Magazines: 7
Radio Receivers 000: 35
per 1,000: 61
Television sets 000: 42
per 1,000: 73

MOST IMPORTANT MEDIA:

Press. The pro-government *La Nation de Djibouti* (4,000) appears weekly, while *Carrefour Africain* (500), a Roman Catholic publication, is issued twice monthly.

(continued)

News agencies. The domestic facility is Agence Djiboutienne de Presse (ADP). In addition, Agence France-Presse maintains an office at Djibouti.

Radio and television. Radiodiffusion-Télévision de Djibouti transmitted in French, Afar, and Arabic.

CULTURE

Cultural Indicators

Public Libraries
- Number: —
- Volumes: —
- Registered borrowers: —

Museums
- Number: —
- Annual Attendance: —

Cinema
- Production of Long Films: —
- Number of Cinemas: —
- Seating Capacity: —
- Annual Attendance: —
- Annual Attendance per capita: —

STATUS OF WOMEN

Women legally possess full civil rights, but in practice, due to custom and traditional societal discrimination in education, they play a secondary role in public life and have fewer employment opportunities than men. Few women work in managerial and professional positions; women largely are confined to trade and secretarial fields. Customary law, which is based on Islamic Shari'a law, discriminates against women in such areas as inheritance, divorce, and travel.

Women

Gender Empowerment Measure: —
Seats Held in Parliament by Women %: 0
Female Administrators and Managers %: —
Female Professional and Technical Workers %: —
Women's Share of Earned Income %: —
Women in Government %: 1

HEALTH, FOOD, AND NUTRITION

Health

Number of Physicians: 97
Number of Dentists: 10
Number of Nurses: —
Number of Pharmacists: 14
Population per Physician: 5,258
Number of Hospitals: 8
Hospital Beds per 10,000: 27
Hospital Bed Occupancy Rate: —
Infant Mortality Rate per 1,000 live births: 164
Maternal Mortality Rate per 100,000 live births: —
Total Health Expenditures as % of GDP: —
Health Expenditures per capita $: —
HIV Infected % of adults: 0.6
Cigarette Consumption per smoker per year: —
% of Smokers: Male: —
Female: —
Access to Safe Water %: 90

Food and Nutrition

Food Supply as % of FAO Requirements: 79
% of Consumption Expenditures on Food: 50.3
Daily Available Calories per capita: 1,831
% of Total Calories derived from:
Cereals: 48.6
Potatoes, cassava: 0.3
Meat, poultry: 5.1
Fish: 0.2
Eggs, milk: 6.0
Fruits, Vegetables: 1.8
Fats, oils: 15.7

ENVIRONMENT

A desert climate is Djibouti's greatest environmental problem as the desert continues to encroach. Also of concern is the lack of potable water for the country's growing population.

Environment

Forest Area sq km: —
Average Annual Deforestation sq km: —
Nationally Protected Areas as % of Total Land Area: —
Freshwater Access cubic meters per capita: —
Emissions of Organic Water Pollutants kg per day: —
CO_2 Emissions per capita ton: 0.6

CHRONOLOGY

1946 French Somaliland becomes a French overseas territory.
1957 The territory is granted limited autonomy.
1958 The first territorial assembly is elected.
1967 The territory, now renamed Territory of the Afars and the Issas, is granted a semi-autonomous executive headed by a president and a council of eight members, elected by a Chamber of Deputies.
1968 Ali Arif Bourhan, Afar leader, is elected president, and his party gains 26 of 32 seats in the Chamber of Deputies.
1973 The territory reaffirms ties with France.
1975 France announces decision to grant full and unlimited autonomy to the territory, but with French military presence; Somali-inspired violence erupts against the decision.
1976 Ali Arif resigns the presidency.

1977 The Territory of the Afars and the Issas gains independence under the name of Djibouti.
Issa leader Hassan Aptidon is elected as the nation's first president; Aptidon names the first cabinet, with Ahmed Dini Ahmed as prime minister.
Djibouti joins the United Nations, OAU, and Arab League; Ahmed Dini Ahmed resigns along with four cabinet members following Afar-Issa strife.
1978 Foreign Minister Abdallah Muhammad Kamil is named prime minister but later is replaced by Barkat Gourad Hamadou, another Afar.
1979 Afar guerillas attack military barracks with Ethiopian help. President Gouled announces formation of a new political party, Popular Rally for Progress (Rassemblement Populaire pour le Progrès, RPP). Landlocked East African nations initial agreements to airlift goods to Djibouti for transshipment through the Suez Canal.
1981 Djibouti is declared a free port.
The constitutional law is approved.
1982 In new elections to the Chamber of Deputies, RPP wins all seats, with a reported 91 percent of the eligible voters approving the party's single list.
Legislation is enacted making RPP the country's only legal political party.
1983 Refugees from Ethiopia cross into Djibouti.
1987 Gouled is reelected unopposed.
1989 Somali refugees escaping their country's civil war flee to neighboring Djibouti.
1990 The two main underground opposition groups form a common front, the Union of the Democratic Movement.
1992 A new constitution is approved that allows up to four political parties.
RPP wins all of the seats in the assembly.
1994 Rebels in the northern part of the country who make up the Front for the Restoration of Unity and Democracy (FRUD) join the ruling party in a coalition government.
1997 In parliamentary elections, the RPP-FRUD coalition wins all 65 seats.
Hassan Gourad Aptidon celebrates 20 years as president of Djibouti.
1998 Barkat Gourad Hamadou begins his 20th year as prime minister.
1999 Ismael Omar Gelleh is elected president.
2000 The government and the radical faction of FRUD sign a peace agreement, putting an end to the civil war. Soon thereafter, Ahmed Dini, former prime minister and leader of the radical faction of FRUD, returns to Djibouti after nine years in exile.
2001 Dilleita Mohammed Dilleita becomes prime minister.

BIBLIOGRAPHY

Koburger, Charles W. *Naval Strategy East of Suez: The Role of Djibouti*. Westport, Conn., 1992.

Lewis, I. M. *People of the Horn of Africa*. London, 1969.

Thompson, Virginia, and Richard Adloff. *Djibouti and the Horn of Africa*. London, 1968.

Vevan, Robert S. *Djibouti: Pawn of the Horn of Africa*. Metuchen, N.J., 1995.

OFFICIAL PUBLICATIONS

Annuaire Statistique de Djibouti

CONTACT INFORMATION

Embassy of Djibouti
1156 15th Street NW, Suite 515
Washington, D.C. 20005
Phone: (202) 331-0270 Fax: (202) 331-0302

INTERNET RESOURCES

- Ambassade de la République de Djibouti en France (French-language site of Djibouti embassy in France) http://www.amb-djibouti.org/

DOMINICA

BASIC FACT SHEET

OFFICIAL NAME:
Commonwealth of Dominica

ABBREVIATION:
DQ

CAPITAL:
Roseau

HEAD OF STATE:
President Vernon Shaw (from 1998)

HEAD OF GOVERNMENT:
Prime Minister Pierre Charles

NATURE OF GOVERNMENT:
Parliamentary democracy

POPULATION:
77,000

AREA:
752 sq km (291 sq mi)

ETHNIC MAJORITY:
African Black

LANGUAGES:
English, French patois

RELIGION:
Christianity

UNIT OF CURRENCY:
East Caribbean dollar (E.C. $)

NATIONAL FLAG:
Three crosses—of yellow, black, and white, and representing the Trinity—span the flag and are centered in a field of green. Ten green, five-pointed stars, representing the 10 parishes of Dominica, are within a red disk representing socialism at the center of the flag and surround a green parrot at the disk's center.

NATIONAL EMBLEM:
A shield with four quarters—the first showing a coconut tree, the second a crapaud, the third a Carib canoe, and the fourth a banana tree—is crested by a silver and azure wreath mounted by a lion passant guardant; on either side is a beaked Sisseron parrot; and on a scroll underneath is the Creole motto *Apré Bondie C'est la Ter* (After God we love the soil).

NATIONAL ANTHEM:
"Isle of Beauty, Isle of Splendor"

NATIONAL HOLIDAYS:
November 3 and 4 (National Days); May 5 (Labor Day); May 26 (Whitmonday); July 2 (Caricom Day); August 4 (August Bank Holiday); December 25 and 26 (Christmas); January 1 (New Year's Day); March 1 and 2 (Carnival); Easter

DATE OF INDEPENDENCE:
November 3, 1978

DATE OF CONSTITUTION:
November 3, 1978

GEOGRAPHICAL FEATURES

The largest of the Windward Islands, Dominica is at the northern end of the Windward chain of the Lesser Antilles, between Guadeloupe and Martinique. Dominica is roughly rectangular in shape, 47 km (29 mi) long and 26 km (16 mi) wide, with a total land area of 752 sq km (291 sq mi). The total length of the coastline is 148 km (92 mi). The island is dominated by a high mountain range running like a spine with lateral spurs on either side. The highest peak is Morne Diablotin (1,446 m; 4,747 ft). None of the many rivers is navigable, but they give limited access to the interior.

Dominica

DOMINICAN REP.
Puerto Rico (U.S.)
British Virgin Islands (U.K.)
Virgin Islands (U.S.)
Anguilla (U.K.)
ST. KITTS AND NEVIS
ANTIGUA AND BARBUDA
Montserrat (U.K.)
Guadeloupe (Fr.)
DOMINICA
Caribbean Sea
Martinique (Fr.)
ST. LUCIA
Aruba (NETH.)
Netherlands Antilles (NETH.)
ST. VINCENT AND THE GRENADINES
BARBADOS
GRENADA
VENEZUELA
0 150 Miles
0 150 Kms
TRINIDAD AND TOBAGO
Cape Capuchin
Vieille Case
Calibishie
Portsmouth
Glanvillia
Prince Rupert Bay
Wesley
Toulaman R.
Marigot
Salibia
Coulihaut
Morne Raquette
Castle Bruce
Salisbury
Atlantic Ocean
St. Joseph
Layou R.
Pont Casse
Rosalie
Mahaut
Massacre
Laudat
La Plaine
Caribbean Sea
Roseau
Roseau R.
Pointe Michel
N
Berekua
Grand Bay
Soufrière
Scotts Head
0 6 Miles
0 6 Kms

Geography

Area sq km: 752 sq mi 291
World Rank: 183rd
Land Boundaries, km: 0
Coastline, km 148
Elevation Extremes meters
  Lowest: Caribbean Sea 0
  Highest: Morne Diablatins 1,147
Land Use % Arable land: 9
  Permanent Crops: 13
  Permanent Pastures: 3
  Forest and Woodland: 67
  Other: 8

Population of Principal Cities

Roseau	15,853

CLIMATE AND WEATHER

The climate is tropical, with extremes of heat and humidity tempered by constant sea breezes, which sometimes reach hurricane force during the hurricane season from July to September. The temperature range is 21.1°C to 32.2°C (70°F to 90°F). Rainfall varies, with the eastern coast receiving 5,000 to 7,600 mm (200 to 300 in), whereas the drier western coast receives 1,000 to 1,800 mm (40 to 72 in). The wettest season is normally June to October, although January sometimes has more rain.

Climate and Weather

Mean Temperature 70°F to 90°F
Average Rainfall:
East Coast 200 in to 300 in
West Coast 40 in to 72 in

POPULATION

Population Indicators

Total Population: 1999 77,000
World Rank: 199th
Density per sq mi: 265.5 per sq km 102.7
% of annual growth (1994–99): 0.9
Male %: 49.8
Female %: 50.2
Urban %:
Age Distribution: % 0–14: 33.3
  15–29: 28.3
  30–44: 16.3
  45–59: 9.7
  60–74: 11.8
  75 and over: 11.8
Population 2020: 93,000
Birth Rate per 1,000: 18.4
Death Rate per 1,000: 5.3
Population Doubling Time (years): 63
Infant Mortality Rate per 1,000 live births: 9.6
Rate of Natural Increase per 1,000: 13.1
Total Fertility Rate: 1.9
Expectation of Life (years): Males 74.5
  Females 80.4
Marriage Rate per 1,000: 3.3
Divorce Rate per 1,000: 0.4
Total Number of Households: 19,000
Average Size of Households: 3.6
% of Illegitimate Children: —
Induced Abortions: —
  Rate per 100 live births: —

ETHNIC COMPOSITION

Most of the inhabitants are descended from West African slaves imported as plantation laborers in the 17th and 18th centuries. The island was once occupied by the Arawaks, who were exterminated by the Caribs, a warrior tribe. Only some 1,200 members of this tribe survive, at the Carib Reserve at Salybia.

LANGUAGES

English is the official language, but most of the people speak a French patois of uncertain origin.

Principal Languages and Their Speakers

English	—
English Creole	77,000
French Creole	69,000

RELIGIONS

Roman Catholics constitute about 70 percent of the population, but there are long-established Anglican and Methodist Churches. The 1979 "Dread Act" bans the Rastafarian sect, but this law is not enforced.

Religious Affiliations

Roman Catholic	54,000
Protestant	13,000
Other	10,000

HISTORICAL BACKGROUND

Originally inhabited by first the Arawaks and then the Carib Indians, they named the island Wai'tukubuli, or 'Tall Is Her Body'. The Kalinago or "Island Caribs" had paddled northward up the chain of the Antilles, and the Arawakan-speaking Igneri are thought to have settled in Dominica around 400 C.E.

The first known Europeans to sight the island were led by Christopher Columbus, who sailed past on a Sunday in 1493 (hence the name Dominica). Dominica was claimed by both France and England in the 17th century, but in 1748 it was stipulated that the island should be left in the hands of the Caribs. In 1763 Dominica was assigned to Great Britain under the Treaty of Paris, but was captured by the French in 1778, then restored to Great Britain in 1783. In 1795 the French made an abortive attempt to seize the island, and burned the capital in a later attempt in 1805. Finally the French were induced to abandon their claims on payment of 8,000 pounds. Dominica joined the Federation of the West Indies as an independent member in 1958 and remained so until the dissolution of the federation in 1962. In 1967 Dominica became one of the West Indies Associated States, with full autonomy in internal affairs. Following a decision in 1975 by the Associated States to seek independence, Dominica became an independent republic within the Commonwealth in 1978.

At independence, Patrick Roland John, leader of the Dominica Labour Party (DLP), became prime minister. In 1979 John was forced to step down as a result of unrest following government attempts to introduce legislation restricting trade unions and the press. James Oliver Seraphine was designated his successor. Both John and Seraphine were denied reelection in the general elections of July 1980. The Dominica Freedom Party (DFP) won decisively, and its leader, Mary Eugenia Charles, became the first woman to become a prime minister in the Caribbean.

Security issues dominated Charles's first years in office. In January 1981 the government disarmed the Defense Force because of reported trading of weapons for marijuana. Later that year it instituted a state of emergency following two coup attempts by John's supporters. John was implicated in the plots and imprisoned. He was initially tried and acquitted on the charges, but in 1985 he was retried and sentenced to 12 years' imprisonment.

In January 1985 the DLP joined ranks with two other opposition parties—the Dominica Liberation Movement and the United Dominica Labour Party—to form the Labour Party of Dominica (LDP). In the July 1985 general elections, the DFP was returned to power, winning 15 of the 21 seats in the House of Assembly. By 1987 the DFP had gained two more seats in the House of Assembly, with the remaining four belonging to the LPD.

In the May 1990 general elections, Charles and the DFP were returned for a third five-year term, but with a sharply reduced majority. The DFP retained only 11 seats in the House of Assembly, the LPD won four, and the two-year-old Dominica United Worker's Party (DUWP) won six. Prime Minister Mary Eugenia Charles stepped down in 1995 in favor of Brian Alleyne. In 1995 the United Workers Party was swept into power with Edison James as the new prime minister. Five years later, the LPD won 10 seats in the House of Assembly and Roosevelt Douglas became prime minister. Shortly thereafter, Douglas die unexpectedly and Pierre Charles became prime minister.

CONSTITUTION

Under the constitution that came into effect on independence, Dominica is a sovereign democratic republic with an elected president and a parliamentary form of government. The president is elected by the House of Assembly for a term of five years and may not hold office for more than two terms. A presidential candidate is nominated jointly by the prime minister and the leader of the opposition, and automatically elected upon such nomination. In case of disagreement the choice is made by secret ballot in the House of Assembly. Executive authority is vested in the president, the head of state, who appoints as prime minister that member of the House of Assembly who commands the support of the majority of other elected members. Other ministers, who together with the prime minister constitute the cabinet, are appointed on

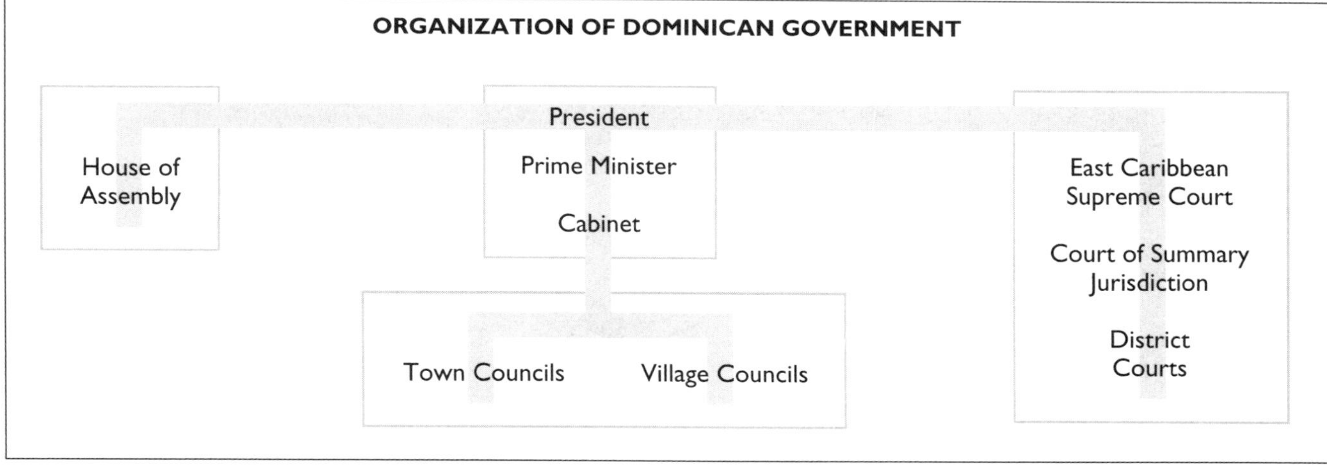

the advice of the prime minister, who is head of government. Not more than three ministers may be chosen from among appointed senators. The president can remove a prime minister from office if a resolution of no confidence is passed by the House of Assembly and the prime minister does not either resign within three days or advise the president to dissolve the House of Assembly.

LOCAL GOVERNMENT

The administration of the towns of Roseau and Portsmouth is entrusted to town councils, each of which consists of five elected and three nominated members. The main source of income is property taxation. The councils have to submit their annual estimates of revenue and expenditures to the governor-general for approval. The remainder of the island is divided into 25 rural districts administered by a council that is partly elected and partly appointed.

Local Government

Principal administrative divisions, area, population

Area and Population

	area		population 1991
Parishes	**sq mi**	**sq km**	**estimate**
St. Andrew	69.3	179.6	11,106
St. David	49.0	126.8	6,977
St. George	20.7	53.5	20,365
St. John	22.5	58.5	4,990
St. Joseph	46.4	120.1	6,183
St. Luke	4.3	11.1	1,552
St. Mark	3.8	9.9	1,943
St. Patrick	32.6	84.4	8,929
St. Paul	26.0	67.4	7,495
St. Peter	10.7	27.7	1,643
TOTAL	285.3	739.0	71,183

PARLIAMENT

The unicameral House of Assembly consists of 21 elected representatives and nine senators. Depending on the wishes of the House of Assembly, the latter may be elected or appointed by the president: five on the advice of the prime minister, and four on the advice of the leader of the opposition. The life of the House of Assembly is five years, and it can amend the constitution. The leader of the opposition is appointed by the president and wields considerable influence.

Every citizen over age 18 is eligible to vote.

POLITICAL PARTIES

There are three major political parties in Dominica. Dominica United Workers' Party is currently the largest, holding 11 of the 21 seats in the House. The Dominica Freedom Party holds five seats and the left-wing party founded in 1985, Labour Party of Dominica, holds five also.

Political Parties

United Workers Party, 1988
Labor Party, 1985
Dominica Freedom Party

Political Parties: Strength in Parliament Most Recent Elections

House of Assembly. The chamber has 32 members, 21 elected for five-year terms in single-seat constituencies, nine appointed senators, the Speaker, and one ex-officio. At the elections of January 31, 2000, the United Workers' Party won 9 seats; Dominica Labour Party, 10; Dominica Freedom Party, 2; and appointed senators, Speaker, and ex-officio, 11.

LEGAL SYSTEM

The legal system is based on English common law and statute law and is administered by the East Caribbean Supreme Court, consisting of the Court of Appeal and the High Court. One of the six puisne judges of the High Court is resident in Dominica and presides over the Court of Summary Jurisdiction. Four magistrates or district courts deal with summary offenses and civil offenses involving not more than $500. The attorney general is the principal legal adviser to the government as well as the director of public prosecutions.

The island's only prison is Goodwill Prison at Roseau, with accommodations for 84 men and 16 women.

LAW ENFORCEMENT

Law Enforcement

Offenses reported to the police per 100,000: 1,956
- Murder: 4.2
- Assault: 25.2
- Burglary: 1,078.1
- Automobile Theft: 33.6
- Population per Police officer: 300

Death Penalty: Yes

HUMAN RIGHTS

In terms of civil and political rights Dominica is a free country. The government generally respects human rights. The principal human rights problems are the occasional use of excessive force by the police, poor prison conditions, societal violence against women and children, and discrimination against indigenous Carib Indians.

FOREIGN POLICY

Dominica is a member of the Commonwealth, OAS, and the United Nations, and its diplomatic contacts outside of these groupings are negligible. It maintains only a token presence in Washington, and the United States, likewise, has no immediate representation in Roseau. However, it receives and is dependent on U.S. foreign aid and it generally sides with the United States on regional issues.

DEFENSE

The Dominican defense force was officially disbanded in April 1981. There is no ministry of defense.

Military Indicators

Total Active Duty Personnel: —
Military Manpower per 1,000: —
Military Expenditures $million: —
- as % of GNP: —
- per capita $: —
- as % of central government expenditures: —

Arms Imports $million: —
Arms Exports $million: —

ECONOMY

Dominica is one of the lower-middle-income countries of the world, with a free-market economy in which the private sector is dominant.

The economy is dependent on agriculture, primarily the production of bananas, coconuts, citrus fruits, and root crops. A small manufacturing sector is based on soap and garment industries. Despite its location, Dominica is not a major tourist destination; the industry remains undeveloped because of rocky beaches and lack of transportation facilities.

Principal Economic Indicators

Gross National Product: $225 million
GNP per capita: $3,040
GNP Average Annual Growth Rate (1990–97) %: 0.7
GNP per capita Average Annual Growth Rate (1990–97) %: 0.4
Origin of Gross Domestic Product %
- Agriculture: 17
- Mining: 1
- Manufacturing: 6
- Construction: 7
- Public Utilities: 4
- Transportation and Communications: 15
- Trade: 12
- Financial Services: 12
- Other Services: 1
- Government: 16

Gross Domestic Product by Type of Expenditure %
- Private Consumption: 21
- Government Consumption: 23
- Gross Domestic Investment: 24
- Foreign Trade: Exports: 17
- Imports: 17

% of Income Received by Poorest 20%: —
% of Income Received by Richest 10%: —

Price and earnings indexes (1995 = 100)

	1992	1993	1994	1995	1996	1997	1998
Consumer price index	97.2	98.7	98.7	100.0	101.7	104.2	105.2
Earnings index	—	—	—	—	—	—	—

Finance

National Currency: East Caribbean Dollar (EC$)
Exchange Rate: $1 = EC$ 2.7
Money Supply Stock in National Currency billion: 0.097
MI per capita: 1,310
Central Bank Discount Rate %: 6.4
Total External Debt $million: 110
Debt Service Ratio %: 7.0

Balance of Payments $million: −38.7
International Reserves SDRs: 18
Ratio of External Debt to Total Reserves: 3.8

Average Annual Rate of Inflation/Consumer Price Index Growth Rate %: 1.7

Official Development Assistance

ODA $million: 43
- as % of GNP: 19.8
- per capita: $589
- Foreign Direct Investment $million:

Central Government Revenues and Expenditures

Fiscal Year: 1 July–30 June
Revenues $million: 77
Expenditures $million: 78
Budget Deficit $million: 1
Tax Revenues as % of GDP: —
Highest Tax Bracket %
- Individual: —
- Corporate: —

Employment and Labor

Economically Active Population: 26,400
Female Participation Rate %: 34.5
Activity Rate %: 38
Labor by Sector: %
- Agriculture, Forestry, Fishing: 27.9
- Manufacturing, Mining: 8.8
- Construction: 10.7
- Transportation and Communications: 4.6
- Trade, Hotels, and Restaurants: 13.9
- Finance, Insurance, Real Estate: 3.1
- Public Administration, Defense: 5.8
- Services: 13.1

Unemployment %: 15

Agriculture

Agriculture's Share of GDP %: 17
Average Annual Rate of Growth (1965–98) %: —
Number of Farms 000: 10.1
Average Size of Farm ha: 2.5
Number of Tractors per 1,000 hectares: 12.9
Irrigation, % of Farms having: —
Artificial Fertilizer kg/hectare: 259
Total Farmland as % of land area: 30.7
Livestock: Cattle 000: 13
Sheep 000: 8
Hogs 000: 5
Chickens 000: 190
Forests: Production of Roundwood (000 cubic meters): —
Fisheries: Total Catch tons: 0.9

Mining

% of GDP: 0.7
Value of Mineral Production $million: 1.5

Manufacturing

Value Added $million: 13
Industrial Production Growth Rate %: −0.4

Energy

Commercial Energy Production metric tons of oil equivalent 000: —
Commercial Energy Consumption metric tons of oil equivalent 000: 21
Commercial Energy Consumption per capita kg: 290
Average Annual Growth Rate 1980–97 %: —
Net Energy Imports % of use: 71
Electricity Installed Capacity kW: 8
Production kW-hr million: 37
Coal Reserves tons million: —
Production tons 000: —
Natural Gas Proven Reserves cubic meters billion: —
Production cubic meters million: —
Crude Petroleum Reserves barrels million: —
Production barrels million: —
Consumption barrels million: —
Refinery Capacity barrels per day 000: —
Pipelines Length km: —

Foreign Trade

Imports $million: 109.6
Exports $million: 54.2
Export Volume % Annual Growth Rate (1990–97): —
Import Volume % Annual Growth Rate (1990–97): —

Balance of trade (current prices)

	1992	1993	1994	1995	1996	1997
EC						
$ 000,000	−140.3	−123.6	−137.3	−199.3	−216.1	−193.3
% of total	32.7%	32.3%	35.8%	46.4%	44.5%	40.3%

Major Trading Partners

	Imports	Exports
European Union %	21.2	61.2
United States %	31.4	5.2
Eastern Europe %	0.3	—
Japan %	5.6	—
Others %	41.5	33.6

Transportation

Roads Total Length mi: 475 km 765
Paved %: 50
Automobiles: 2,770
Trucks and Buses: 2,839
Persons per vehicle: 13
Railroad; Track Length mi: —
Passenger-mi million: —
Freight-mi million: —
Merchant Marine: No. of Vessels: 7
Total Deadweight Tonnage 000: 3.2
International Cargo Loaded tons 000: 103
International Cargo Off-loaded tons 000: 181
Airports with Scheduled Flights: 2
Traffic: Passenger-mi million: —
Freight-mi million: —
Length of Canals mi: —

Tourism

Number of Tourists to: —
Number of Tourists from: —
Tourist Receipts $million: 33
Tourist Expenditures $million: 5

Communications

Telephones 000: 18
Cost of Local Calls 3 mins: $0
Cellular Telephones 000: —
Fax Machines 000: 0.3
Personal Computers 000: —
Internet Hosts per million persons: 521
Mail: Post Offices: 131
Pieces of Mail Handled million: 2.9
Pieces of Mail Handled per person: 4.2

EDUCATION

Education is free and compulsory for 10 years, from ages five to 15. Schooling lasts for 14 years, divided into seven years of primary school, five years of secondary school, and two years of postsecondary courses.

The medium of education is English throughout. The school year runs from September to July.

Teacher training is provided by the Teacher Training Institute at Roseau.

Higher education is provided by a branch of the University of the West Indies.

Administrative responsibility for education rests with the Board of Education, headed by a chief education officer. No information is available on public expenditures on education.

Education

Literacy Rate %: 90.6
- Male %: —
- Female %: —

First Level: Primary schools: 64
- Teachers: 641
- Students: 12,627
- Student-Teacher Ratio: 29.8
- Net Enrollment Ratio:

Second Level: Secondary Schools: 13
- Teachers: —
- Students: 6,493
- Student-Teacher Ratio: —
- Net Enrollment Ratio: —

Vocational Level: Schools: —
- Students: —

Third Level: Institutions: 2
- Teachers: 34
- Students: 484
- Student-Ratio Level: 14.2
- Gross Enrollment Ratio: —
- Students per 100,000: —
- % of Population Age 25 and over with Postsecondary Education: —

Public Expenditure on Education as % of GDP: 5.5

SCIENCE AND TECHNOLOGY

Science and Technology

Scientists and Engineers in R&D per 1 million persons: —
Expenditures in R&D as % of GDP: —
High-Tech Exports $million: —
Patent Applications by Residents: —

MEDIA

Three nondaily newspapers are published in the capital, the *Official Gazette* (biweekly) and the *New Chronicle* (weekly), with a combined circulation of over 5,000.

The press is vigorous, and its attack on government corruption was a major factor in the success of the opposition Dominica Freedom Party in 1980. However, the government announced in December 1980 that it was moving against persons involved in the publication of unregistered newspapers.

There is no national news agency, but Reuters' Caribbean service is received by the media.

There is a small book publishing industry, with an average annual output of 20 titles.

Radio Dominica, founded in 1971, is a partly government-owned and partly commercial station operated by the Dominica Broadcasting Corporation. It broadcasts in both English and French patois daily. There are two television stations and commercial cable service available.

Media

Daily Newspapers: 0
- Total Circulation 000: —
- Circulation per 1,000: —

Books Published: —
Magazines: —
Radio Receivers 000: 65
- per 1,000: 875

Television sets 000: 10
- per 1,000: 141

MOST IMPORTANT MEDIA:

Press. The following are published at Roseau: *The Tropical Star* (3,000); *New Chronicle* (2,500), independent weekly; *Official Gazette* (550), weekly.

Radio and television. The government-operated Dominica Broadcasting Corporation (DBC) provides radio service in English and French patois; two independent subscription services, Marpin Television and Video One, offer cable programs from the United States.

CULTURE

Cultural Indicators

Public Libraries Number:
- Volumes: —
- Registered borrowers: —

Museums Number: —
- Annual Attendance: —

Cinema Production of Long Films:
- Number of Cinemas: —
- Seating Capacity: —
- Annual Attendance: —
- Annual Attendance per capita: —

STATUS OF WOMEN

Beyond the general protection of the constitution, women do not benefit from any specific civil rights legislation. There is little open discrimination against women, yet sexual harassment and domestic violence cases are common. Property ownership continues to be deeded to "heads of households," who are usually males. When the male head of household dies without a will, the wife cannot inherit the property or sell it, although she can live in it and pass it to her children. The Dominica National Council of Women, a nongovernmental organization

(NGO), has developed local adult education and small business training programs for women.

Women

Gender Empowerment Measure: —
Seats Held in Parliament by Women %: 18.8
Female Administrators and Managers %: 36
Female Professional and Technical Workers %: 57
Women's Share of Earned Income %: —
Women in Government %: 31

HEALTH, FOOD, AND NUTRITION

Health

Number of Physicians: 23
Number of Dentists: 6
Number of Nurses: 265
Number of Pharmacists: 27
Population per Physician: 3,200
Number of Hospitals: 53
Hospital Beds per 10,000: 25
Hospital Bed Occupancy Rate: 94.6
Infant Mortality Rate per 1,000 live births: 21
Maternal Mortality Rate per 100,000 live births: —
Total Health Expenditures as % of GDP: 8.06
Health Expenditures per capita $: 192
HIV Infected % of adults: —
Cigarette Consumption per smoker per year: —
% of Smokers: Male: —
Female: —
Access to Safe Water %: 77

Food and Nutrition

Food Supply as % of FAO Requirements: 125
% of Consumption Expenditures on Food: 43.1
Daily Available Calories per capita: 3,032
% of Total Calories derived from:
Cereals: 27.2
Potatoes, cassava: 7.8
Meat, poultry: 9.9
Fish: 1.6
Eggs, milk: 9.1
Fruits, vegetables: 9.8
Fats, oils: 8.6

ENVIRONMENT

The island of Dominica has made a conscious effort to protect its lush tropical resources, in large measure to protect its growing tourist industry. The government has been working for many years to ensure that the country continues to be one of the most beautiful and pristine nations in the world while at the same time allowing for economic development.

Environment

Forest Area sq km: —
Average Annual Deforestation sq km: —
Nationally Protected Areas as % of Total Land Area: —
Freshwater Access cubic meters per capita: —
Emissions of Organic Water Pollutants kg per day: —
CO_2 Emissions per capita ton: 1.1

CHRONOLOGY

1978 Dominica achieves full independence within the Commonwealth with Patrick Roland John as prime minister and incumbent governor Sir Louis Cools-Lartique as head of state.
Fred E. Degazon, Speaker of the House of Assembly, is elected and sworn in as president.

1979 Following a general strike, President Degazon retires, and his successor, Sir Louis Cools-Lartique, resigns after only 24 hours in office; Jenner Armor is named interim president and James Oliver Seraphine interim prime minister pending general elections.

1980 In general elections the opposition Dominica Freedom Party wins 17 of the 21 elective seats in the House of Assembly; the party's leader, Mary Eugenia Charles, is appointed prime minister, with Aurelius Marie as president.
Hurricane David and Hurricane Allen hit the island and virtually wipe out the plantations and fishing industry.

1983 As a member of the Organization of East Caribbean States, Dominica takes part in the U.S.–led invasion of Grenada.

1985 The Dominica Labour Party joins with the Dominica Liberation Movement and the United Dominica Labour Party to form the Labour Party of Dominica. The Dominica Freedom Party wins the general elections.

1989 Hurricane Hugo causes severe damage to the island and its banana industry.

1990 Charles is reelected prime minister; the Dominica Freedom Party wins 11 seats in the House of Assembly, the Labour Party of Dominica wins four, and the Dominica United Worker's Party wins six.

1992 The government begins a policy that grants citizenship to foreigners who invest in the Dominican economy.

1993 Sir Crispin Anselm Sorhaindo is elected president in October.

1995 After 15 years in office, Prime Minister Charles resigns.
The Dominica United Worker's Party wins 11 of 21 seats in the House of Assembly; its leader, Edison James, becomes prime minister.
Hurricane Luis devastates Dominica's banana crop.

1998 Vernon Lorden Shaw of the United Worker's Party is elected president.

2000 In January popular elections, the Labour Party of Dominica wins 10 seats, making Roosevelt Douglas prime minister; in October, Douglas unexpectedly dies.

Pierre Charles becomes prime minister.

BIBLIOGRAPHY

Atwood, Thomas. *History of the Island of Dominica.* Totowa, N.J., 1971.

Evans, P. C. H. *Dominica.* London, 1989.

Honeychurch, L. *The Dominica Story.* London, 1995.

Myers, Robert A., ed. *Dominica.* Oxford, U.K., 1987.

Trouillot, Michel-Rolph. *Peasants and Capital: Dominica in the World Economy.* Baltimore, Md., 1988.

———*Dominica: Priorities and Prospects for Development.* Washington, D.C., 1985.

OFFICIAL PUBLICATIONS

Dominica. *Dominica—Recent Economic Developments* (IMF Staff Country Report [1997]); *Population and Housing Census 1991; Statistical Digest* (irreg).

CONTACT INFORMATION

Embassy of Dominica
3216 New Mexico Avenue NW
Washington, D.C. 20016
Phone: (202) 364-6781 Fax: (202) 364-6791

INTERNET RESOURCES

- Dominica (official web site)
http://www.dominica.dm/index.htm

DOMINICAN REPUBLIC

BASIC FACT SHEET

OFFICIAL NAME:
Dominican Republic (República Dominicana)

ABBREVIATION:
DRMG

CAPITAL:
Santo Domingo

HEAD OF STATE AND HEAD OF GOVERNMENT:
President Rafael Hipólito Mejía Domínguez (from 2000)

NATURE OF GOVERNMENT:
Parliamentary democracy

POPULATION:
8,130,000 (1999)

AREA:
48,734 sq km (18,816 sq mi)

ETHNIC MAJORITY:
Mulatto

LANGUAGES:
Spanish

RELIGIONS:
Roman Catholicism

UNIT OF CURRENCY:
Dominican Republic peso (R.D. $)

NATIONAL FLAG:
A white cross superimposed on a field of four rectangles with the upper left and lower right in blue, and the upper right and lower left in red. At the center of the cross is the national emblem.

NATIONAL EMBLEM:
A shield divided by a white cross into alternating blue and red quarters. In the foreground is a white bible opened to the first chapter of the Gospel of St. John resting on six national flags in saltire, three to a side. Above the bible is a gold pulpit cross and above the shield, on a blue riband, is the national motto, God, Country, and Liberty (*Dios, Patria, Libertad*). The shield is flanked by green branches of laurel and palm tied at the bottom with a white, red, and blue ribbon. On a red scroll at the base is the country's name in black letters.

NATIONAL ANTHEM:
"Dominicans, Let Us Raise Our Song."

NATIONAL HOLIDAYS:
January 1 (New Year's Day); January 21 (Altagracia Day); January 26 (Duarte Day); February 27 (Independence Day, National Day); April 14 (Pan American Day); May 1 (Labor Day); July 16 (Foundation of Sociedad la Trinitaria); August 15 (Crowning of Our Lady of Altagracia); August 16 (Restoration of Independence); September 24 (Day of Our Lady of Las Mercedes); October 12 (Columbus Day); October 24 (United Nations Day); Christian festivals include All Saints' Day, Immaculate Conception, Good Friday, Ascension, Corpus Christi, Epiphany, St. Joseph's Day, Day of Sts. Peter and Paul, and Christmas.

DATE OF INDEPENDENCE:
February 27, 1844

DATE OF CONSTITUTION:
November 28, 1966

GEOGRAPHICAL FEATURES

The Dominican Republic occupies the eastern two-thirds of the island of Hispaniola and includes the islands of Beata, Catalina, Saona, Alto Velo, and Catalinita in the Caribbean Sea, with a total land area of 48,734 sq km (18,816 sq mi). The country extends 386 km (240 mi) east to west and 261 km (162 mi) north to south. The coastline on the Atlantic Ocean and the Caribbean Sea stretches 602 km (374 mi). The Dominican Republic shares its total international boundary of 290 km (180 mi) with Haiti.

Dominican Republic

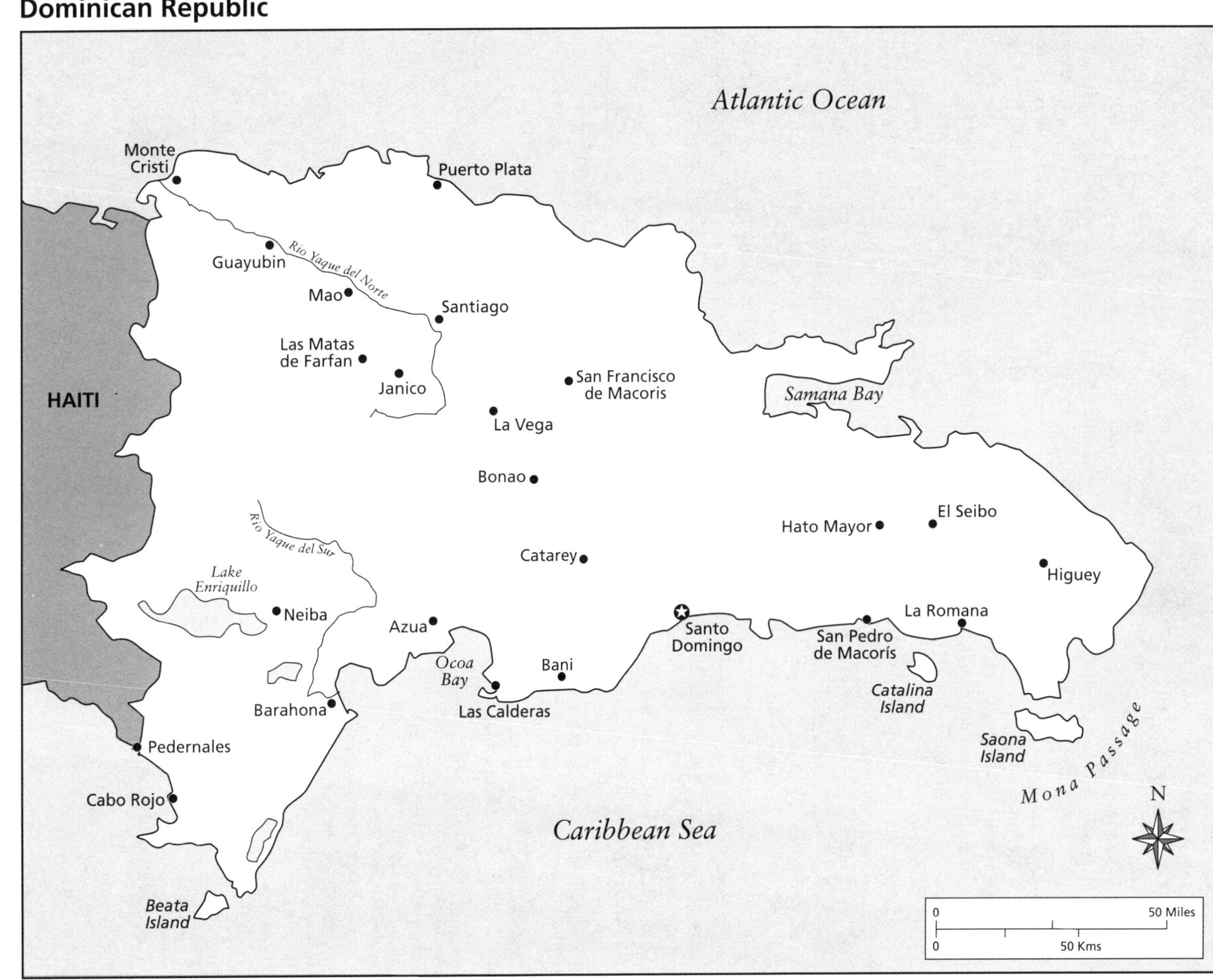

The capital is Santo Domingo, founded in 1493, the oldest European settlement in the New World and the site of the oldest cathedral and the oldest university in the Western Hemisphere. With a 1998 population of 1,555,656 Santo Domingo has more than 50 percent of all the urban population.

The Dominican Republic is divided geographically into more than 20 regions, but the main topographical divisions are the highlands and the lowlands. The highlands consist of four parallel mountain ranges—the Cordillera Central, Cordillera Septentrional, Sierra de Neiba, and Sierra de Baoruco (Bahoruco)—in the west and the Cordillera Oriental in the east. The Cordillera Central, which divides the country into two parts, contains Pico Duarte, the highest peak in the West Indies, with an elevation of 3,175 m (10,417 ft). The lowlands consist of long parallel valleys lying for the most part in a northwest-to-southeast direction. The most extensive of these valleys, the Cibao, is drained on its western flank by the Yaque del Norte, the country's longest river, and on its eastern flank by the Yuna River. The San Juan Valley is drained by a tributary of the Artibonito River and by the Yaque del Sur and its tributary, the San Juan. The Caribbean coastal plain is drained by the Ozama River and the Macorís River. All these rivers are for the most part shallow and subject to seasonal changes in flow. Both the Ozama and the Macorís are navigable for short distances.

Geography

Area sq km: 48,734 sq mi 18,816
World Rank: 130th
Land Boundaries, km: Haiti 275
Coastline, km 1,288
Elevation Extremes meters
- Lowest: Lago Enriquillo −46
- Highest: Pico Duarte 3,175

Land Use % Arable land: 21
- Permanent Crops: 9
- Permanent Pastures: 43
- Forest and Woodland: 12
- Other: 15

Population of Principal Cities (1993)

City	Population
La Romana	132,834
San Francisco de Macorís	129,943
San Pedro de Macorís	123,987
Santiago	364,859
Santo Domingo	1,555,656

CLIMATE AND WEATHER

The country has a tropical maritime climate, but the heat of the tropics is moderated by the ocean currents and year-round trade winds, as well as by the general elevation. The temperature averages between 22.2°C (72°F) and 28.3°C (83°F). It rarely falls below 15.6°C (60°F) or rises above 32.2°C (90°F). The coastal plain has an annual mean temperature of 25.5°C (78°F), but the Cordillera Central has a more temperate climate with a mean of 20°C (68°F). Frosts are common at higher elevations.

The rainy season extends from May to November, with the maximum precipitation in the late spring and fall. In general, rainfall is heaviest in the north and east and diminishes toward the rain-shadow regions of the south and west. The highest precipitation recorded in the country is 2,790 mm (110 in) on the northeastern slopes of the Cordillera Oriental. The Samaná Peninsula, La Vega, El Seibo, and the Puerto Plata region receive moderately heavy rainfall, although Santiago de los Caballeros, Monte Cristi, and the Neiba Valley receive scant rains. Nationwide the mean rainfall is between 1,390 mm and 1,520 mm (55 in to 60 in).

The Dominican Republic is exposed to Caribbean hurricanes from June through November, although it lies out of the two tracks of maximum intensity, which pass to the east and west.

Climate and Weather

Mean Temperature 72°F to 83°F
Coastal Plain 78°F
Central Cordillera 68°F
Average Rainfall 55 in to 60 in

POPULATION

Population Indicators

Total Population: 1999 8,130,000
World Rank: 86th
Density per sq mi: 432.6 per sq km 167.0
% of annual growth (1994–99): 1.7
Male %: 48.7
Female %: 51.3
Urban %: 56.0
Age Distribution: %
- 0–14: 36.5
- 15–29: 29.5
- 30–44: 16.4
- 45–59: 9.6
- 60–74: 4.8
- 75 and over: 1.2

Population 2020: 11,085,000
Birth Rate per 1,000: 23.5
Death Rate per 1,000: 5.7
Population Doubling Time (years): 34
Infant Mortality Rate per 1,000 live births: 47.7
Rate of Natural Increase per 1,000: 17.8
Total Fertility Rate: 2.7
Expectation of Life (years): Males 66.9
Females 71.3

Marriage Rate per 1,000: 3.6
Divorce Rate per 1,000: —
Total Number of Households: 1,804,000
Average Size of Households: 3.9
% of Illegitimate Children: 67.2
Induced Abortions: 562
Rate per 100 live births: 0.5

ETHNIC COMPOSITION

Mulattoes, considered as a separate race in official censuses, form the largest group in the Dominican Republic, accounting for 73 percent of the population, followed by whites accounting for 16 percent and blacks for 11 percent.

Haitians constitute the bulk of the black population; a smaller portion of blacks is made up of descendants of former American slaves who immigrated to Haiti in the 19th century. The white population includes those of pure Spanish descent, Lebanese, and German Jews. The heaviest concentration of whites is in Santiago de los Caballeros because only those of pure Spanish blood were once allowed to settle there. Other ethnic groups include Chinese, Japanese (a small colony of Japanese farms the Constanza Valley), and other Asians.

Although race is an important determinant of social status, there is no overt racial discrimination in the Dominican Republic other than a general prejudice against Haitians. Mulattoes have dominated the government and the armed forces since the rise of Trujillo, himself a mulatto of middle-class origin.

LANGUAGES

Spanish is the official language, spoken by about 98 percent of the people. The remaining 2 percent speak Haitian Creole, especially along the Haitian border.

The use of English is growing, and the Dominican vocabulary includes many American words as a result of cultural connections with the United States.

Principal Languages and Their Speakers

French (Haitian) Creole	160,000
Spanish	7,970,000

RELIGIONS

By the Concordat of 1954, Roman Catholicism is the state religion of the Dominican Republic. More than 90 percent of the population consider themselves Catholics, at least nominally.

Religious minorities include Protestants, Haitian vodun (voodoo) cultists, Baha'is, and Jews. Religious freedom for these communities is protected by law.

Religious Affiliations

Roman Catholic	6,650,000
Protestant	520,000
Other	960,000

HISTORICAL BACKGROUND

The first inhabitants of the island of Hispaniola were a branch of the Arawak nation known as Taino. The people were largely wiped out within a century of Spanish colonization, but vestiges of their language, culture, and agricultural practices survive. European settlement began with the first voyage of Columbus in 1492–93. After the Spaniards claimed most of Central and South America, though, they neglected their Caribbean colonies, allowing the French to seize and settle the western half of Hispaniola in the late 17th century. Misgovernance by Spain in the restoration period following the Napoleonic wars led the colony of Santo Domingo to proclaim its independence in 1821, but a year later the new country was invaded and occupied by Haitians led by President Jean-Pierre Boyer. The Haitians abolished slavery; nonetheless, their overlordship was deeply resented. The Dominican Republic achieved independence from Haiti in 1844, under Juan Pablo Duarte.

The period from 1844 to 1864 was dominated by two strongmen: Pedro Santana and Buenaventura Báez. Both tried repeatedly to make the Dominican Republic a protectorate of a foreign power to guard against incursions from Haiti; this led to reannexation by Spain in 1861. But popular revolt put an end to Spanish rule in 1865. The departure of the Spanish left groups in several regions and factions contesting power; chaos prevailed until the late 1870s. The 1880s and 1890s saw the country ruled over by Ulíses Heureaux, first as president, then as dictator, growing gradually more despotic and extravagant until his assassination in 1899. Another era of prolonged instability followed with rival factions taking up arms; this culminated in the assassination of President Ramón Cáceres in 1911. A military coup in 1916 prompted direct intervention by U.S. Marines, who remained until 1924, when a civilian government led by Horacio Vásquez assumed control.

Rafael Leonidas Trujillo, a marine-trained sergeant, overthrew Vásquez in 1930 and began a three-decades-long dictatorship in which he ruled at times directly (1930–38; 1942–52) and at other times through surrogates, including his own brother and his protégé, Joaquín Balaguer. Trujillo expanded industry and public works and liquidated the country's debt; he also set up state monopolies over all main economic activities, which enriched his family and associates. But no form of popular representation was permitted, and power was maintained through blackmail, torture, and murder. In 1937 the regime slaughtered between 10,000 and 20,000 Haitian immigrants in a retaliatory strike against Haiti's uncovering Dominican covert agents in Port-au-Prince. In 1960, Trujillo's agents tried to assassinate Venezuelan president Rómulo Betancourt, leading the United States to downgrade its relations with Santo Domingo.

Trujillo's assassination in 1961 ushered in another period of political turmoil. Left-of-center democrat Juan Bosch Gaviño won the 1962 presidential election, the country's first free elections since the 1920s, but was overthrown by a military coup in 1963 and replaced by a three-man civilian junta. The junta, in turn, was overthrown by Bosch supporters in 1965. A civil war ensued, during which U.S. troops briefly intervened to prevent the pro-Bosch forces from regaining control. The war ended inconclusively, with an agreement to hold new elections. Balaguer, candidate of the conservative Partido Reformista Social Cristiano (PRSC), won the 1966 election, defeating Bosch, candidate of the left-wing Partido Revolucionario Dominicano (PRD). The political situation remained volatile, however, with both the left and the right mounting unsuccessful coups.

The period from 1966 to 1996 was the era of Balaguer, who served as president for all except an interlude from 1978 to 1986 when the PRD won two elections. Balaguer's early rule witnessed rapid growth, though many did not share in the prosperity, and persecution of political opponents. Under PRD president Antonio Guzmán Fernández there was considerable political liberalization that included replacement of military officers not inclined to support civilian rule. Guzmán's economic reform efforts were hampered by opposition control of the Senate; rising oil prices and declining sugar prices forced him to implement unpopular belt-tightening measures. Guzmán committed suicide just before his term ended in 1982, for reasons that remain unclear. His successor, Salvador Jorge Blanco, could not cope with low export prices for sugar, rising inflation, diminished U.S. aid, hurricanes, and growing corruption. In 1985 there were violent confrontations between protesters and police over price rises for staple goods and austerity measures demanded by the IMF in return for loans. The aged Balaguer's return to power was characterized by profligate spending on public works and grandiose prestige projects as well as Machiavellian machinations to retain political control.

The 1996 election was a three-way contest that saw the PRSC candidate eliminated in the first round of voting, leading Balaguer to throw his party's support behind the centrist Partido de la Liberación Dominicana (PLD) candidate and ultimate victor, Leonel Fernández Reyna. Fernández was praised for ending the country's relative isolation and improving relations with other Caribbean countries, but he was also attacked for tolerating continued administrative corruption and for failing to translate renewed economic growth into alleviation of poverty. As a result, the presidential election of 2000 was won by Hipólito Mejía, the PRD candidate.

CONSTITUTION AND GOVERNMENT

The present constitution of the Dominican Republic, promulgated in 1966 and reformed in 1994, is the nation's 25th. All these constitutions guaranteed the rights of cit-

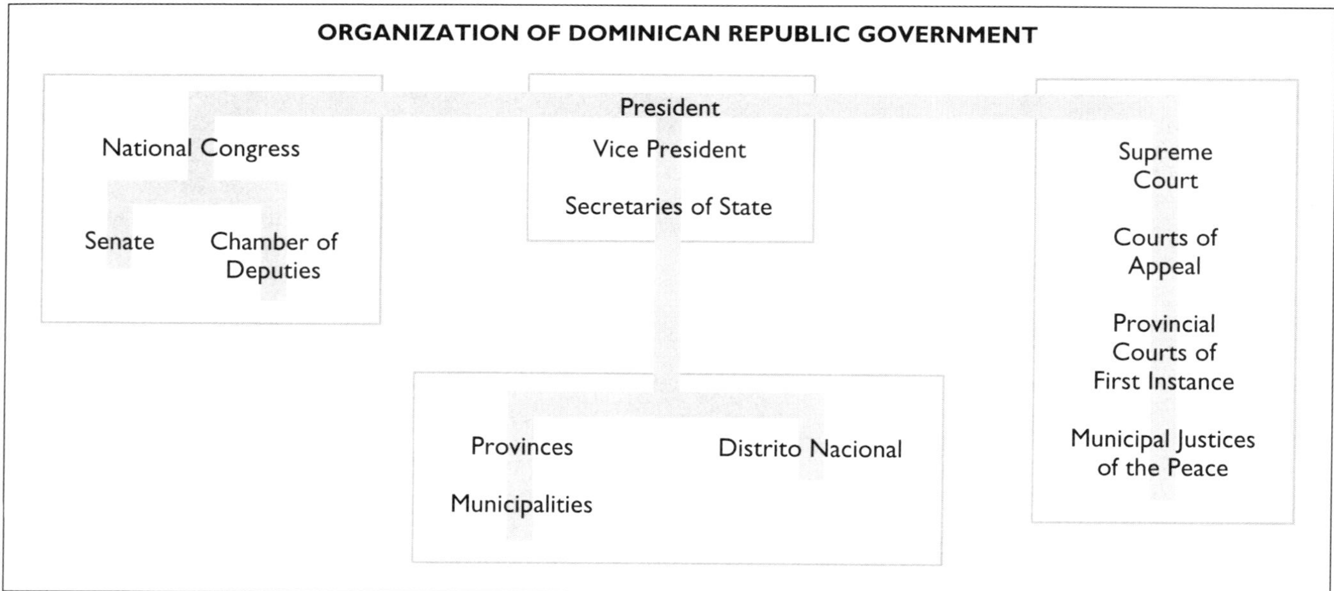

izens and set up governments based on fine checks and balances, yet few of their provisions were ever observed in practice.

The constitution of 1966 set up a civil, republican, democratic, and representative government. Among the many freedoms that it guarantees are the right to own private property, freedom of worship, freedom of speech, freedom of association, freedom of movement, and the right to strike. It also charges the state to provide free, universal, and compulsory education, redistribute land and eliminate the large estates (known as *latifundios*), introduce Social Security services, and promote family life.

Executive authority is vested in the president, elected to four-year terms by direct popular vote. A vice president is elected on the same ticket. The president is the head of the public administration and the supreme chief of the armed forces. The president also appoints cabinet ministers called secretaries of state. Since 1994, no president is allowed to serve consecutive terms.

Legislative power is vested in a bicameral legislature. The highest court is the Supreme Court.

Suffrage is universal and required by law for all citizens over the age of 18 and all who are or have been married, even if they are not yet 18.

LOCAL GOVERNMENT

The country is divided for the purposes of local government into 29 provinces, each headed by a governor, and the Distrito Nacional.

The provinces are subdivided into 154 municipalities and municipal districts. The Distrito Nacional is governed as a municipality. Each municipality is governed by a mayor assisted by a municipal council, consisting of no fewer than five members. Both the mayors and the members of the municipal council are popularly elected for four-year terms. There are also 868 rural townships directly administered by the central government.

Local governments have only the slightest of revenue-raising capabilities, and their budgets have been kept meager by the central government; moreover, the state has recently privatized a number of basic local administrative responsibilities such as water, sanitation, and transport.

Local Government

Principal administrative divisions, area, population

AREA AND POPULATION

Provinces	area sq mi	population 1993 preliminary census
Azua	2,532	194,209
Baoruco	1,283	101,742
Barahona	1,739	157,772
Dajabón	1,021	63,995
Duarte	1,605	272,277
El Seibo	1,786	94,244
Espaillat	838	197,617
Hato Mayor	1,329	76,761
Independencia	2,008	38,185
La Altagracia	3,010	112,396
Elia Pina	1,424	59,321
La Romana	654	158,132
La Vega	2,286	335,140
María Trinidad Sánchez	1,271	122,165
Monsenõr Nouel	992	144,327
Monte Cristi	1,925	94,429
Monte Plata	2,633	162,630
Pedernales	2,077	16,975
Peravia	1,648	199,661
Puerto Plaza	1,857	255,061
Salcedo	440	99,965
Samaná	854	73,094
San Cristóbal	1,265	409,381
San Juan	3,571	247,029
San Pedro de Macorís	1,255	212,886
Sánchez Ramirez	1,196	158,218
Santiago	2,836	690,548
Santiago Rodríguez	1,112	60,015
Santo Domingo	1,401	2,134,779
Valverde	823	146,087
TOTAL	48,671	7,089,041

PARLIAMENT

The National Congress (Congreso Nacional) consists of a 30-member Senate (Senado) and a 149-member Chamber of Deputies (Cámara de Diputados). Members of the Congress are elected for four-year terms.

Both houses normally meet each year on February 27 and August 16 for sessions of 90 days, extendable for a period of 60 days. Bills may be introduced by the president of the republic, senators, deputies, the Supreme Court (in judicial matters), and the Central Electoral Board (in electoral matters) and must be approved by both chambers before being submitted to the president. A presidential veto may be overridden by a two-thirds vote in both chambers.

The Congress has broad legislative powers and is empowered to approve or reject treaties, levy taxes and approve expenditures, regulate the national debt, and grant authorization to the president to leave the country for more than 15 days. It can proclaim a state of siege or national emergency.

POLITICAL PARTIES

Since the end of the 1965 civil war Dominican politics has been dominated by the Christian Social Reformist Party (Partido Reformista Social Cristiano, PRSC), a conservative party that draws its support mainly from the church, the peasantry, and the middle class.

In 1978 the Dominican Revolutionary Party (Partido Revolucionario Dominicano, PRD), having moderated its political philosophy, won the presidency for the first time, promising greater personal liberties along with a more populist (and less U.S.–oriented) economic program. The party's founder, Juan Bosch, broke away in 1974 to start a new party, the Dominican Liberation Party (Partido de la Liberación Dominicana, PLD).

The PLD later metamorphosed into a centrist party, and in 1996 its presidential candidate, Leonel Fernández, won; however, it remained distinctly a minority in Congress.

There are also a dozen or so minor parties. The Dominican Communist Party was outlawed from 1962 until 1977.

Political Parties

National Patriotic Front, 1996
Dominican Liberation Party, 1974
Social Christian Reformist Party, 1963
Dominican Revolutionary Party, 1939
Independent Revolutionary Party, 1990
Quisqueyan Democratic Party, 1965
Alliance for Democracy, 1992
Democratic Integration Movement, 1970
Movement of National Conciliation, 1968
Revolutionary Social Christian Party
Dominican Communist Party, 1977
Dominican Popular Movement, 1965

Political Parties: Strength in Parliament Most Recent Elections

Senate (Senado). Following the election of May 16, 2002, the Dominican Revolutionary Party held 24 seats; the Dominican Liberation Party, 3; and the Social Christian Reformist Party, 3.

President: Amable Aristy Castro.

Chamber of Deputies (Cámara de Diputados). As a result of the election of May 16, 2002, the Dominican Revolutionary Party held 83 seats; the Dominican Liberation Party, 49; and the Social Christian Reformist Party, 17.

LEGAL SYSTEM

The legal system is based on French civil codes. The Dominican judicature is headed by the Supreme Court of Justice, consisting of at least nine justices appointed by the National Judicial Council (whose own membership is nominated jointly by the three leading parties) and an attorney general appointed by the executive. The Supreme Court has the power to rule on constitutional questions and has jurisdiction in all cases involving the president, vice president, cabinet members, members of Congress, and members of the judiciary.

Immediately below the Supreme Court are five courts of appeal. Each court of appeal has five judges, including the president.

Judges are independent of the executive branch. Their terms of office correspond to that of the president and other elected officials.

Each of the 29 provinces and the Distrito Nacional form judicial districts with courts of first instances. These judicial districts are further divided into municipal districts, each with one or more local justices of the peace. Judges of the lower courts are appointed by the Supreme Court and are subject to the high court's discipline.

The national penitentiary is La Victoria in Santo Domingo. There are some 20 other prisons, of which the largest are located at La Vega, Puerto Plata, San Francisco de Macorís, Moca, San Juan, San Cristóbal, and Barahona. There is no provision for capital punishment in the Dominican legal system.

LAW ENFORCEMENT

Law Enforcement

Offenses reported to the police per 100,000: 946
- Murder: 11.9
- Assault: 30.8
- Burglary: 154
- Automobile Theft: 24.8
- Population per Police officer: 580

Death Penalty: Abolished 1966

HUMAN RIGHTS

The Dominican Republic has made great strides toward political freedom since the assassination of the dictator Trujillo, the civil war of 1965, and the period of instability that followed. The peaceful transfer of power in 1978, the first to occur from one civilian party to another in this century, was a landmark in this process of democratization. Dominicans now enjoy the broad range of human rights guaranteed in the 1966 constitution, aside from significant but episodic lapses.

The country's biggest human rights problem remains mistreatment of and racism toward Haitian immigrants. Illegals have virtually no legal recourse against deportation, and even those legally present are routinely discriminated against in employment and other areas of life; on some plantations the working conditions of Haitians approach indentured servitude. Women also suffer from domestic violence—a serious problem throughout the country—sexual harassment and abuse, and circumscribed economic opportunities.

There are problems of extrajudicial killings by uniformed personnel—at times by the military or civil defense forces but mainly by the police—abuse of suspects, and arbitrary detention.

Trials are fair and open, and court-appointed lawyers are assigned free of charge for the indigent. No special political or security courts exist, and civilians may not be tried in a military court. A residence may not be searched without due process, and this means in the presence of a prosecutor or assistant prosecutor.

Unions are generally allowed political space to organize, with the notable exception of the free-trade zones, an issue international human rights groups have called attention to.

Many political exiles returned after the 1979 amnesty, but a ban remained in effect for certain members of the Trujillo family. Political parties are allowed to exist and campaign freely. However, parties that do not register with the Central Electoral Board are considered illegal.

FOREIGN POLICY

Much recent Dominican diplomacy has been oriented toward facilitating trade and tourism. Concerns that the North American Free Trade Agreement signed in 1993 would cause the United States to shift a considerable portion of investments in manufacturing from the Dominican Republic to Mexico led the Dominican government to support the eventual expansion of NAFTA into a Free Trade Area of the Americas.

In 1997, President Fernández signed a free trade pact with five Central American countries. The following year, he upgraded relations with Cuba to consular level. Since the departure of Balaguer, relations with Haiti have improved, though tensions remain over border issues, illegal immigration, and treatment of Haitians in the Dominican Republic. The United States and the Dominican Republic have a number of perennial bilateral issues, namely, investment and trade, particularly terms of access to the U.S. market for Dominican exports; the transshipment of illicit drugs from Colombia to the United States by way of the Dominican Republic, which has become a vexing concern for both sides; and the Dominican government's ongoing interest in the welfare of its expatriate community in the New York area and elsewhere.

The Dominican Republic joined the United Nations in 1945. It is a member of 16 UN organizations and various other international organizations, including the Organization of American States, the Ibero-American Community of Nations, and the Africa-Caribbean-Pacific (also known as the Lomé Convention) group of the European Union.

DEFENSE

The defense structure is headed by the president of the republic as supreme commander. The line of command runs through the secretary of state for the armed forces and the deputy secretaries of state for the army, navy, and air force to the chief of staff and general staff of each branch.

Military manpower is provided through voluntary service, though the constitution states that each Dominican has the duty to provide whatever civil or military service the state requires.

The total strength of the armed forces is 24,500.

Annual military expenditures in 1997 (estimated) totaled \$87 million, representing 1.5% of gross domestic product (GDP).

The armed forces of the Dominican Republic have only limited offensive capability and are designed to provide primarily symbolic protection. Most of the hardware is supplied by the United States, which intervened twice in the 20th century.

Military Indicators

Total Active Duty Personnel: 24,500
Military Manpower per 1,000: 3.1
Military Expenditures $million: 122
as % of GNP: 1.1
per capita $: 16
as % of central government expenditures: 6.8

Arms Imports $million: 10
Arms Exports $million: 0

ECONOMY

With sugar and other commodity export (coffee, cocoa, tobacco) prices in a slump through most of the 1980s and early 1990s, the Dominican Republic resolved to diversify its economic base. The promotion of special export processing free-trade zones helped boost the manufacturing sector to 17% of GDP by 1996, eclipsing agriculture (including fishing, livestock, and forestry, 12.9 percent of GDP) in value though not in number of jobs. Tourism became the country's leading source of foreign exchange by the mid-1990s; with 35,750 hotel rooms, the Dominican Republic has the most of any Caribbean country. Mining has become relatively less important.

In 1991 an agreement with the International Monetary Fund and a debt rescheduling deal with the "Paris Club" of creditor nations helped bring about macroeconomic stability, but overspending on public works continued to feed inflation. The growth of the free trade zones and tourism reduced the state's share of the economy, as those industries are largely tax exempt.

Under President Fernández the country enjoyed several years of healthy growth, yet important constraints remain: the ongoing, severe "brain drain" to the United States (somewhat offset by the remittances sent back home), a poor education system, lack of retraining for those whose jobs are lost as a result of more open trade, the inefficiencies of the state-owned electricity industry, and the limits on the willingness of the United States to absorb the country's textile exports. In December 2000, the new Mejía administration passed broad tax legislation, which it hoped would provide enough revenue to offset rising oil prices and to service foreign debt.

Principal Economic Indicators

Gross National Product: $14.148 billion
GNP per capita: $1,750
GNP Average Annual Growth Rate (1990–97)%: 3.5
GNP per capita Average Annual Growth Rate (1990–97)%: 1.6
Origin of Gross Domestic Product%
- Agriculture: 13
- Mining: 2
- Manufacturing: 18
- Construction: 9
- Public Utilities: 2
- Transportation and Communications: 10
- Trade: 18
- Financial Services: 10
- Other Services: 8
- Government: 9

Gross Domestic Product by Type of Expenditure %
- Private Consumption: 75
- Government Consumption: 5
- Gross Domestic Investment: 23
- Foreign Trade: Exports: 24
  Imports: −27

% of Income Received by Poorest 20%: 4.2
% of Income Received by Richest 10%: 39.6

Price and earnings indexes (1995 = 100)

	1992	1993	1994	1995	1996	1997	1998
Consumer price index	78.0	82.1	88.9	100.0	105.4	114.1	230.2
Earnings index	72.2	83.3	83.3	100.0	—	—	—

Finance

National Currency: Suere (S/)
Exchange Rate: $1 = S/4,498
Money Supply Stock in National Currency billion: 20.884
M1 per capita: 2,760
Central Bank Discount Rate %: 17.3
Total External Debt $million: 12,500
Debt Service Ratio %: 4.9
Balance of Payments $million: −163
International Reserves SDRs: 263
Ratio of External Debt to Total Reserves: 9.7
Average Annual Rate of Inflation/Consumer Price Index Growth Rate %: 31

Official Development Assistance

ODA $million: 153
- as % of GNP: 0.8
- per capita: $15
- Foreign Direct Investment $million: 691

Central Government Revenues and Expenditures

Fiscal Year: Calendar Year
Revenues $million: 3,600
Expenditures $million: 3,600
Budget Deficit $million: 0
Tax Revenues as % of GDP: 15.5
Highest Tax Bracket %
- Individual: 25
- Corporate: 25

Employment and Labor

Economically Active Population: 1,915,000
Female Participation Rate %: 28.9
Activity Rate %: 33.9
Labor by Sector: %
- Agriculture, Forestry, Fishing: 22.0
- Manufacturing, Mining: 12.7
- Construction: 4.3
- Transportation and Communications: 2.1
- Trade, Hotels, and Restaurants: 10.0
- Finance, Insurance, Real Estate: 1.2
- Public Administration, Defense: —
- Services: 18.9

Unemployment %: 6.9

Agriculture

Agriculture's Share of GDP %: 13
Average Annual Rate of Growth (1965–98) %: 3.0
Number of Farms 000: 385
Average Size of Farm ha: 6.3
Number of Tractors per 1,000 hectares: 2.4
Irrigation, % of Farms having: 25
Artificial Fertilizer kg/hectare: 50
Total Farmland as % of land area: 49.8
Livestock: Cattle 000: 2,528
- Sheep 000: 135
- Hogs 000: 960
- Chickens 000: 37,698

Forests: Production of Roundwood (000 cubic meters): 982
Fisheries: Total Catch tons: 25.9

Mining

% of GDP: 2.8
Value of Mineral Production $million: 126

Manufacturing

Value Added $million: 1,298
Industrial Production Growth Rate %: 2.4

Energy

Commercial Energy Production metric tons of oil equivalent 000: 1,423
Commercial Energy Consumption metric tons of oil equivalent 000: 5,453
Commercial Energy Consumption per capita kg: 673
Average Annual Growth Rate 1980–97%: 0.2
Net Energy Imports % of use: 74
Electricity Installed Capacity kW: 1,450
- Production kW-hr million: 6,506

Coal Reserves tons million: —
- Production tons 000: —

Natural Gas Proven Reserves cubic meters billion: —
- Production cubic meters million: —

Crude Petroleum Reserves barrels million: —
- Production barrels million: —
- Consumption barrels million: 15
- Refinery Capacity barrels per day 000: 50

Pipelines Length km: 104

Foreign Trade

Imports $million: 2,626.4
Exports $million: 2,007.8
Export Volume % Annual Growth Rate (1990–97): 1.6
Import Volume % Annual Growth Rate (1990–97): 8.4

Balance of trade (current prices)

	1992	1993	1994	1995	1996	1997
U.S. $000,000	−1,613	−1,607	−1,620	−2,020	−2,390	−2,701
% of total	58.9%	61.1%	56.0%	56.9%	59.5%	60.5%

Major Trading Partners

	Imports	Exports
European Union %	2.0	8.6
United States %	37.4	83.6
Eastern Europe %	—	—
Japan %	1.5	0.8
Others %	59.1	6.9

Transportation

Roads Total Length mi: 7,643 km 12,300
Paved %: 49
Automobiles: 209,000
Trucks and Buses: 141,400
Persons per vehicle: 21
Railroad; Track Length mi: 1,083 km 1,743
Passenger-mi million: —
Freight-mi million: —
Merchant Marine: No. of Vessels: 28
Total Deadweight Tonnage 000: 10.4
International Cargo Loaded tons 000: 2,550
International Cargo Off-loaded tons 000: 4,182
Airports with Scheduled Flights: 7
Traffic: Passenger-mi million: 145
Freight-mi million: 1.7
Length of Canals mi: —

Tourism

Number of Tourists to: 2,309
Number of Tourists from 000: 354
Tourist Receipts $million: 1,604
Tourist Expenditures $million: 85

Communications

Telephones 000: 569
Cost of Local Calls 3 mins: $0
Cellular Telephones 000: 33
Fax Machines 000: 2.5
Personal Computers 000: —
Internet Hosts per million persons: 18
Mail: Post Offices: 215
Pieces of Mail Handled million: 9.8
Pieces of Mail Handled per person: 1.3

EDUCATION

Education is free, universal, and compulsory for eight years from the ages of six to 14. Schooling lasts for 12 years divided into six years of primary school, two years of lower secondary, and four years of upper secondary school. A significant percentage of rural schools do not contain all six primary grades. Secondary education is divided into a two-year cycle for all students and a four-year upper-secondary cycle for preparing students for university entrance. On completion of secondary school, students receive the baccalaureate *(bachillerato)*. Academic standards are low, and grade repetitions and dropouts are common.

The medium of instruction is Spanish, but both Portuguese and English are offered as second languages in secondary schools.

Private school enrollment is increasing at a faster pace than public school enrollment. Nearly all of the private schools are located in urban centers, and most are church operated.

Formerly compulsory under Trujillo, adult education became voluntary and was expanded beyond literacy programs to include vocational training and teacher training.

Agricultural education is provided in four agricultural schools, industrial education in polytechnic institutes and schools of arts and crafts, and business and commercial education in private commercial schools.

The national educational system is directed by the Ministry of Education and the National Council for Education, and the cost of public education is borne by the central government.

Higher education is provided by eight universities and various other institutions such as the Institute of Higher Studies and the Higher Institute of Agriculture. The universities enrolled 73,461 students in 1998, of which close to 60 percent were women.

Education

Literacy Rate %: 82.1
Male %: 82.0
Female %: 82.2
First Level: Primary schools: 4,001
Teachers: 42,135
Students: 1,462,722
Student-Teacher Ratio: 34.7
Net Enrollment Ratio: 81
Second Level: Secondary Schools: —
Teachers: 10,757
Students: 240,441
Student-Teacher Ratio: 22.4
Net Enrollment Ratio: 22
Vocational Level: Schools: —
Students: 22,975
Third Level: Institutions: 7
Teachers: 5,091
Students: 73,461
Student-Ratio Level: 14.4
Gross Enrollment Ratio: —
Students per 100,000: —
% of Population age 25 and over with Postsecondary Education: —
Public Expenditure on Education as % of GDP: 1.9

SCIENCE AND TECHNOLOGY

Science and Technology

Scientists and Engineers in R&D per 1 million persons: —
Expenditures in R&D as % of GDP: —
High-Tech Exports $million: 2
Patent Applications by Residents: —

MEDIA

Eleven daily newspapers are published in the Dominican Republic, the largest of which is *Listín Diario*, with a circulation of 55,000. Thirty-nine non daily newspapers are also published. The periodical press consists of more than two hundred titles.

The press is reasonably free of political controls. However, there is still a certain amount of press self-censorship, particularly concerning issues that affect the interests of the media companies owning the papers.

There is no national news agency. UPI, EFE, ANSA, and IPS have permanent bureaus in Santo Domingo.

There are 15 book publishers that publish only in Spanish. The Dominican Republic adheres to the Buenos Aires Copyright Convention.

There are around 140 commercially operated radio stations. Nine stations are operated by Radio Televisión Dominicana, which is government-owned.

Television, introduced in 1952, now covers 90 percent of the population. There are eight television channels, of which one is government owned.

Media

Daily Newspapers: 11
  Total Circulation 000: 264
  Circulation per 1,000: 35
Books Published: —
Magazines:
Radio Receivers 000: 1,180
  per 1,000: 154
Television sets 000: 680
  per 1,000: 87

MOST IMPORTANT MEDIA:

Press. The following privately owned newspapers are published at Santo Domingo, unless otherwise noted: *Listín Diario* (55,000), moderate independent; *Ultima Hora* (50,000); *El Nacional* (45,000), leftist nationalist; *El Caribe* (29,000), moderate nationalist; *La Noticia* (18,000); *La Información* (Santiago de los Caballeros), 15,000.

News agencies. There is no domestic facility; several foreign agencies maintain bureaus at Santo Domingo.

Radio and television. Broadcasting is supervised by the Dirección General de Telecomunicaciones. There are over 140 radio stations as well as seven commercial television networks, two of which also offer educational programming.

CULTURE

Cultural Indicators

Public Libraries Number: —
  Volumes: —
  Registered borrowers: —
Museums Number: —
  Annual Attendance: —
Cinema Production of Long Films: —
  Number of Cinemas: —
  Seating Capacity: —
  Annual Attendance million: —
  Annual Attendance per capita: —

STATUS OF WOMEN

Although sexual discrimination is prohibited by law, women have not traditionally shared equal social and economic status with men. Women made considerable economic progress in the 1980s and 1990s, however. The employment rate for women, once the lowest in Latin America, has grown at more than double the rate for men. Industrial processing jobs in the free trade zones in particular have opened up new opportunities for women in apparel and electronics assembly; some 70 percent of workers in these zones are female. However, with labor organizing actively discouraged in the free trade zones, hours are long, conditions substandard, and wages average 20 percent below the legal minimum for the country.

Divorce is easily attainable by either party, and women can hold property in their own names apart from their husbands. Among urban households, around one-quarter are headed by women. Women now represent well more than half of all university students; finding ways to keep these highly educated women productively engaged in the country rather than abroad remains a challenge.

Women are participating increasingly in nongovernmental organizations, cooperatives, and community-based organizations to get around barriers that have largely excluded them from traditional politics.

Domestic violence, sexual harassment, and sexual exploitation are persistent and large-scale problems in the Dominican Republic. The government has an Office of Women's Rights to help women assert their legal rights and combat spousal abuse. But there are no shelters for battered women. Prostitution and trafficking in women and girls are rife, and HIV infections are increasing.

Women

Gender Empowerment Measure: 58
Seats Held in Parliament by Women %: 10
Female Administrators and Managers %: 21.2
Female Professional and Technical Workers %: 49.5
Women's Share of Earned Income %: 24
Women in Government %: 12

HEALTH, FOOD, AND NUTRITION

Health

Number of Physicians: 11,130
Number of Dentists: 1,898
Number of Nurses: 6,035
Number of Pharmacists: 115
Population per Physician: 671
Number of Hospitals: 723
Hospital Beds per 10,000: 12
Hospital Bed Occupancy Rate: —
Infant Mortality Rate per 1,000 live births: 46
Maternal Mortality Rate per 100,000 live births: 110
Total Health Expenditures as % of GDP: 3.72
Health Expenditures per capita $: 38
HIV Infected % of adults: 1.89
Cigarette Consumption per smoker per year: 1,303
% of Smokers: Male: 66
Female: 14
Access to Safe Water %: 79

Food and Nutrition

Food Supply as % of FAO Requirements: 103
% of Consumption Expenditures on Food: 46
Daily Available Calories per capita: 2,323
% of Total Calories Derived From:
Cereals: 31.4
Potatoes, cassava: 3.2
Meat, poultry: 7.3
Fish: 0.7
Eggs, milk: 6.4
Fruits, vegetables: 10.2
Fats, oils: 16.0

ENVIRONMENT

Owing to its variety of microclimates, the country's biodiversity is impressive; one can pass from deserts of giant cactus to mountain pine forests to palm-fringed shores and sugarcane plantations. Endangered species that figure prominently are the *jutias*, the country's only indigenous mammal (a rodent), and the *cotorra*, a parrot.

Deforestation has been the Dominican Republic's most serious environmental problem. Despite the government's ban, tree cutting goes on throughout rural areas as the poor, having no access to gas or electricity, collect fuelwood for cooking. Only about 13 percent of the land remains covered by forest and woodland. The stripping of trees has caused extensive erosion in many areas and more destructive flooding following tropical storms, damaging not only soil quality but also marine reefs and the aquatic life they support due to runoff.

Tourism development, particularly on the country's northern coast, brings pollution and disturbs habitat, posing a threat to maritime and plant life.

Environment

Forest Area sq km: 16,000
Average Annual Deforestation sq km: 264
Nationally Protected Areas as % of Total Land Area: 25.2
Freshwater Access cubic meters per capita: 2,467
Emissions of Organic Water Pollutants kg per day: 54,935
CO_2 Emissions per capita ton: 1.6

CHRONOLOGY

1930 Rafael Leonidas Trujillo overthrows Horacio Vásquez and begins a three-decade-long dictatorship.

1937 Following Haiti's discovery of Dominican spies on its soil, Trujillo orders slaughter of 10,000 to 20,000 Haitian immigrants.

1947 Trujillo outlaws Dominican Communist Party.

1959 Invasion attempted by dissident Dominicans supported by Fidel Castro of Cuba fails.

1960 Agents of Trujillo injure Venezuelan president Rómulo Betancourt in assassination attempt.

1961 Trujillo assassinated; Joaquín Balaguer, already serving as president, continues in office.

1962 Juan Bosch of leftist Dominican Revolutionary Party (PRD) elected president.

1963 Bosch overthrown in military coup; new regime led by Donald Reid Cabral.

1965 Uprising by Bosch supporters succeeds temporarily; civil war ensues with rightist military officers; United States intervenes decisively in support of rightists.

1966 Balaguer, leading right-wing Reformist Party, wins election.

1978 PRD wins power under Silvestre Antonio Guzmán Fernández.

1982 Guzmán commits suicide; PRD retains presidency as Salvador Jorge Blanco is elected.

1985 Strikes and violence against government and IMF-imposed austerity measures.

1986 Balaguer returned to presidency at head of Christian Social Reformist Party (PRSC).

1988–89 Further violent protests against high prices of staples and utilities.

1990 Balaguer reelected by slim margin over Bosch; government initiates, then relaxes (after a general strike leads to the death of 12 people) austerity program aimed at securing an IMF agreement.

1991 Balaguer government rounds up and deports thousands of Haitian workers in response to international concern about near-serfdom on sugar plantations; IMF standby loan agreement and debt rescheduling agreement with the "Paris Club" of nations are both signed.

1992 Country commemorates 500th anniversary of Columbus's arrival with the dedication of a monumental mausoleum to the explorer and a giant lighthouse in the shape of a cross.

1994 Balaguer wins sixth term as president amid widespread fraud charges and a campaign branding his chief opponent, José Francisco Peña Gómez, a "Haitian"; Balaguer accedes to certain constitutional changes, including a law barring presidents from succeeding themselves.

1996 Leonel Fernández Reyna elected president with barely 51% of vote in runoff.

1997 Partial privatization of certain state-owned companies signed into law by President Fernández.

1998 Fernández government criticized for poor preparedness and slow response in the wake of severe damage done by Hurricane Georges.

2000 Hipólito Mejía of PRD elected president.

BIBLIOGRAPHY

Atkins, G. Pope. *The Dominican Republic and the United States: From Imperialism to Transnationalism.* Athens, Ga., 1997.

Griffith, Ivelaw L., and Betty N. Sedoc-Dahlberg, eds. *Democracy and Human Rights in the Caribbean.* Boulder, Colo., 1997.

Haggerty, Richard A. *Dominican Republic and Haiti: A Country Study.* Washington, D.C., 1991.

Hartlyn, Jonathan. *The Struggle for Democratic Politics in the Dominican Republic.* Chapel Hill, N.C., 1998.

Howard, David. *The Dominican Republic in Focus: A Guide to the People, Politics and Culture.* Northampton, Mass., 1998.

Pons, Frank M. *The Dominican Republic: A National History.* New Rochelle, N.Y., 1994.

Safa, Helen I. *The Myth of the Male Breadwinner: Women and Industrialization in the Caribbean.* Boulder, Colo., 1995.

OFFICIAL PUBLICATIONS

Dominican Republic. *Cifras dominicanas* (irreg.); *VI Censo nacional de población y vivienda, 1981.*

CONTACT INFORMATION

Embassy of Dominican Republic
1715 22nd Street NW
Washington, DC 20008
Phone: (202) 332-6280 Fax: (202) 265-8057

INTERNET RESOURCES

- Banco Central de la República Dominicana
  http://www.bancentral.gov.do/
- Oficina Nacional de Estadística
  http://www.estadistica.gov.do/

ECUADOR

BASIC FACT SHEET

OFFICIAL NAME:
Republic of Ecuador (República del Ecuador

ABBREVIATION:
EC

CAPITAL:
Quito

HEAD OF STATE & HEAD OF GOVERNMENT:
President Gustavo Noboa Bejarano (from 2000)

NATURE OF GOVERNMENT:
Constitutional democracy

POPULATION:
12,411,000 (1999)

AREA:
270,670 sq km (104,505 sq mi)

ETHNIC MAJORITY:
Mestizos and Indians

LANGUAGES:
Spanish (official) and Quechua

RELIGION:
Roman Catholicism

UNIT OF CURRENCY:
U.S. dollar

NATIONAL FLAG:
Tricolor, with the top yellow stripe being equal to the combined width of the blue center stripe and the red lower stripe with the coat of arms superimposed at the center

NATIONAL EMBLEM:
An oval shield on which Mt. Chimborazo is shown against a light blue sky; a river flows down the mountain slopes to the deep blue waters in the foreground, sailing on which is a steamboat, with the caduceus, the symbol of Mercury, the god of commerce, as the mast; above the mountain is a white band with a golden Mayan sun and four zodiac signs; the shield is crested by the condor of the Andes, flanked by a panoply of flags on either side and branches of laurel joined at the base by the Roman fasces.

NATIONAL ANTHEM:
"Hail, O Fatherland"

NATIONAL HOLIDAYS:
January 1 (New Year's Day); May 1 (Labor Day); May 24 (Battle of Pichincha); July 24 (Birth of Simón Bolívar); August 10 (Independence of Quito); October 9 (Independence of Guayaquil); October 12 (Discovery of America); November 3 (Independence of Cuenca); December 6 (Foundation of Quito); Christian festivals include Christmas, All Souls' Day, All Saints' Day, Good Friday and Easter Sunday.

DATE OF INDEPENDENCE:
May 24, 1822

DATE OF CONSTITUTION:
August 10, 1998

GEOGRAPHICAL FEATURES

Ecuador straddles the equator on the northwest coast of South America, occupying an area of 270,670 sq km (104,505 sq mi), extending 714 km (444 mi) north to south and 658 km (409 mi) east to west. The length of the Pacific coastline is 2,237 km (1,390 mi). The national territory includes the Galápagos Islands, an archipelago scattered over 59,570 sq km (23,000 sq mi) of ocean with a total land area of 7,770 sq km (3,000 sq mi).

Ecuador shares its total land boundary of 2,010 km (1,249 mi) with Colombia (590 km, 366 mi) and Peru (1,420 km, 881 mi).

The Andes split the country into three distinct topographical regions: the Costa, or coastal plain; Sierra, or highlands; and Oriente, or Amazon region.

Ecuador

The Costa makes up 16.5 percent of the national territory and forms a rich agricultural belt stretching from the Pacific to the Sierra. Its width varies from 25 km (15 mi) to 200 km (125 mi).

The Sierra, constituting 24.3 percent of the national territory, is a plateau 2,500 m (8,200 ft) to 3,000 m (9,850 ft) above sea level between two parallel spines of the Andes, the Cordillera Occidental and the Cordillera Central. The Sierra is studded with 22 massive volcanoes, the highest of which are Chimborazo (6,271 m, 20,574 ft) and Cotopaxi (5,896 m, 19,344 ft). The Sierra is subject to occasional severe earthquakes and landslides.

The Oriente, constituting 57.4 percent of the national territory, is a flat and gently undulating expanse of rain forest east of the Andes.

The Costa is drained by the Guayas, Esmeraldas, Daule, and Vinces Rivers. The rivers of the Oriente, such as the Pastaza, Paute, Nape, and Zamora, eventually flow into the Atlantic through the Amazon.

Geography

Area sq km: 270,670 sq mi 104,505
World Rank: 74th
Land Boundaries, km: Colombia 590; Peru 1,420
Coastline, km: 2,237
Elevation Extremes meters
Lowest: Pacific Ocean 0
Highest: Chimborazo 6,267
Land Use % Arable land: 6
Permanent Crops: 5
Permanent Pastures: 18
Forest and Woodland: 56
Other: 15

Population of Principal Cities (1997 est.)

Ambato	160,302
Cuenca	255,028
Durán	135,675
Esmeraldas	117,722
Guayaquil	1,973,880
Ibarra	119,243
Loja	117,365
Machala	197,350
Manta	156,981
Milagro	119,371
Portoviejo	167,956
Quevedo	120,640
Quito	1,487,513
Riobamba	117,270
Santo Domingo	183,219

CLIMATE AND WEATHER

Ecuador has a tropical climate in the Costa and the Oriente, where monthly temperatures average 26.7°C (80°F). There are two seasons: a hot, rainy period from January to May and a cool, dry season the rest of the year.

In the Sierra, the annual mean temperature varies between 10°C (50°F) to 15.6°C (60°F). There is virtually no seasonal change, and days and nights are of equal duration throughout the year. However, temperatures may vary by as much as 22.2°C (40°F) in a single day.

Rainfall is heavy throughout the Amazon Basin and in the Costa, but scanty in the Andean plateau. Precipitation ranges from 355.6 mm (14 in) at Ancon on the dry Santa Elena Peninsula to 1,143.0 mm (45 in) in Guayaquil, 1,473.2 mm (58 in) in Quito, 2,540 mm (100 in) on the lower Andean slopes and 5,080 mm (200 in) in the Oriente.

The prevailing winds blow from the east across the Amazon Basin and from the west across the warm Equatorial Current in the rainy season and the cold Humboldt Current in the dry season.

Climate and Weather

Mean Temperature
Costa 80°F
Sierra 50°F to 60°F
Quito 55°F
Average Rainfall
Santa Elena Peninsula 14 in
Guayaquil 45 in
Quito 58 in
Lower Andean Slopes 100 in
Oriente 200 in

POPULATION

Population Indicators

Total Population: 1999 12,411,000
World Rank: 62nd
Density per sq mi: 118.2 per sq km 45.6
% of annual growth (1994–99): 2.0
Male %: 49.7
Female %: 50.3
Urban %: 38.8
Age Distribution: % 0–14: 38.8
15–29: 28.5
30–44: 17.3
45–59: 9.0
60–74: 4.7
75 and over: 1.7
Population 2020: 16,904,000
Birth Rate per 1,000: 15.8
Death Rate per 1,000: 4.4
Population Doubling Time (years): —
Infant Mortality Rate per 1,000 live births: 30.5
Rate of Natural Increase per 1,000: 11.4
Total Fertility Rate: 11.4
Expectation of Life (years): Males 67.5
Females 72.6
Marriage Rate per 1,000: 6.4
Divorce Rate per 1,000: 0.6
Total Number of Households: —
Average Size of Households: 4.1
% of Illegitimate Children: 32.1
Induced Abortions: —
Rate per 100 live births: —

ETHNIC COMPOSITION

Ecuador does not include ethnicity in its census. Unofficial data ranks mestizos as Ecuador's majority group, with 45 percent, followed by Indians at 40 percent, whites at 10 percent, and blacks at 5 percent.

There are as many as 700 separate Indian groups. In the Sierra, the most distinctive are the Otavalos, the Salasacas, and the Saraguros. There are only two groups of unassimilated Indians on the Costa, the Colorados and the

Cayapas. The three most primitive tribes live in the Oriente: the Jívaros, Aucas, and Yumbos. The Amazon basin is also the home of the Zaparos, Cofán, and other tribes.

Blacks occupy a slightly higher social position than the Indians but lower than that of the mestizos. The percentage of unmixed blacks is small.

The largest alien ethnic group are Lebanese, who are concentrated in Guayaquil. The most famous members of this group are former presidents Mahuad and Jamil Abdalá Bucaram. Chinese are found throughout Ecuador but are centered primarily on the coast in the town of Quevedo. Small expatriate English, Irish, French, and German communities are found in the major cities.

LANGUAGES

Spanish is spoken by about 93 percent of the population. Almost all Indians speak Quechua, the Ecuadorian variant of Quechua. In the western Costa, the Cayapa and Colorado languages are still spoken. The most widespread Indian language in the Oriente is Jívaro. Zaparo, Tetete, Cofán, Aushiria, and Siona are also spoken.

Principal Languages and Their Speakers

Quechuan (and other Amerindian languages)	870,000
Spanish	11,540,000

RELIGIONS

Ecuador has no state religion, but 92 percent of the population are at least nominally Roman Catholic. The constitution guarantees freedom of worship.

The Catholic Church in Ecuador takes bold stands on social issues, advocating tax and land reforms and, in some cases, family planning and rejection of the capitalist order.

Non-Catholic religious groups account for 2 percent of the population. They include Protestants, who maintain about 12 schools. Jews number about 2,000. Indians in the Oriente profess tribal religions, but little information is available about these religions.

Religious Affiliations

Religion	Number
Roman Catholic	11,480,000
Other	930,000

HISTORICAL BACKGROUND

Pre-Hispanic Ecuador was inhabited by a number of diverse Indian tribes. By 1000 these groups formed a loose confederation called the Kingdom of Quito, which became a part of the Inca Empire just before the arrival of the Spaniards. The Inca armies under Huayna Capac (r. 1493–1525) conquered Quito and made it a major administrative and military outpost. Before he died, Capac divided his empire between his eldest son, Atahualpa, born to a Quito princess, and his legitimate heir, Huascar. War broke out between Atahualpa and Huascar in which the latter was defeated and slain in the Battle of Cajamarca.

The first Spanish conquistador to sight Ecuador was Bartolomé Ruiz, Francisco Pizarro's pilot in 1526, who was on his way to Peru. His first landing place was Esmeraldas, so named from the emeralds obtained by the Spaniards from the Indians. Arriving in Cajamarca in 1532 Pizarro invited Atahualpa to a meeting and then had him assassinated. One of Pizarro's lieutenants, Sebastián de Benalcazar, found the old Indian capital of Quito left in ashes by the retreating Incas and on that site founded in 1534 San Francisco de Quito. He became the first Spanish governor of Quito. In 1542 the Spanish Crown promulgated the so-called New Laws in an attempt to impose its authority. Opposition from the conquistadores to the New Laws led to the assassination of the Spanish viceroy as well the governor, Gonzalo Pizarro. The Audiencia of Quito, as Ecuador was known before the War of Independence, was established by royal decree in 1563. The 16th and 17th centuries were relatively quiet periods in Ecuadorian history. But by the beginning of the early 18th century the Spanish monarchy fell into a state of increasing weakness. The firm grip that had been maintained on colonial economic life was relaxed.

The struggle for independence took place in two phases. The first was precipitated by the Napoleonic invasion of Spain in 1808. A governing junta was established, composed of criollos, under the leadership of the president of the Audiencia. A congress in 1811 declared complete independence and established the state of Quito. Opposed by the Viceroyalty of Peru and the rest of the Audiencia, the junta launched a military offensive against the Spanish forces in which they were crushed in 1812. The second phase of the independence movement was launched in Guayaquil where another rebel junta was formed. It sought the help of leaders of the independence movement in other parts of the continent, especially the Venezuelan Simón Bolívar and his lieutenant Antonio José de Sucre in the north and the Argentine José de San Martin in the south. At the decisive Battle of Pichincha in 1822 the rebel forces won a great victory, thus ending the Spanish era.

The rebel leaders met in Guayaquil in 1822 to consider the future of the liberated provinces. For the next eight years, Ecuador was part of Gran Colombia, which included Venezuela, Colombia, Panama, and Ecuador. When this union collapsed in 1830, the Republic of Ecuador was established with Juan José Flores as its first president. Flores dominated Ecuadorian politics for the first 15 years of independence. Flores was ousted after a popular uprising, which produced bloody street fighting.

Although a civilian rule was established, the influence of the military was paramount during the next 15 years in which the chief figure was General José María Urbina. Between 1845 and 1860 Ecuador experienced a new period of political turbulence. The country was ruled by 11 presidents or juntas, in most cases members of the Liberals Party; there were frequent civil wars and three constitutions. General García Moreno, a pro-Catholic conservative, seized power during this anarchy and retained it for the next 15 years. Under his authoritarian rule, conservatism and the Conservative Party reached new heights and church-state relations were closer than they have ever been since.

The conservative era lasted until 1895 when the Revolution of 1895 brought the Liberal Flavio Eloy Alfaro to power. He and his liberal successors reversed Moreno's policies. Church and state were separated and freedoms of the press and worship were established. Eloy Alfaro was overthrown in 1911 by a military uprising. His successor, General Leonidas Plaza Gutierrez, who had served as president once before from 1901 to 1905, faced a deepening economic crisis, which led to his ouster by a junta in 1925. The junta named Isidore Ayora as president, but pressured by the deteriorating economic climate and opposition from the military, he was forced to resign in 1931.

The 1930s were a period of anarchy in Ecuador. But it marked the rise of one of Ecuador's stormy petrels, José María Velasco Ibarra, who, with a large following among the lower classes, was president five times (1934–35, 1944–47, 1952–56, 1960–61, and 1968–72). The border dispute between Ecuador and Peru came to a head in 1942 when Peru invaded Ecuador's Southern and Oriente Provinces. The Rio Protocol awarded to Peru the greater part of the Amazon territory claimed by Ecuador. During his second term as president, Velasco Ibarra formally suspended the 1945 Liberal constitution and promulgated a new constitution in 1946 that granted more power to the president. This marked the end of the Liberal era in Ecuadorian politics. The election of Galo Plaza Lasso in 1948 ushered in a period of relative stability. He was the first chief executive since 1924 to complete his term of office. He was followed by a series of interrupted presidencies punctuated by juntas. Velasco's three terms as well as the term of his 1961 successor, Carlos Julio Arosemena Monroy, ended prematurely in coups.

In 1972 the military under Gen. Guillermo Rodríguez Lara canceled the election and restored the Liberal constitution of 1945. The junta ruled until 1979 when Jaime Roldós Aguilera was elected president. Roldós was killed in a plane crash in 1981 and was succeeded by his Christian Democratic vice president, Osvaldo Hurtado Larrea. The conservative Léon Febres Cordero won the 1984 presidential election. In the 1988 presidential election Borja Cevallos of the Democratic Left won a comfortable majority. In 1992 Sixto Durán-Ballén Córdovez of the Republican Unity Party swept the polls by winning 19 of the 21 provinces. In 1996 the populist Abdalá Bucaram achieved his long-time goal of becoming president. But his administration was cut short in 1997 when the Chamber of Representatives ousted him for "mental incapacity," and designated its presiding officer Fabián Alarçon Rivera as his successor. In 1998 Jamil Mahuad Witt of Popular Democracy, a Christian Democrat, secured 51.3 percent of the vote to become president. Mahuad settled the long-standing border dispute (dating from the 16th century) involving a 125,000 sq mi tract of land between the Putumayo and Marañón Rivers with Peru. The agreement awarded the disputed territory to Peru, but control (although not sovereignty) of the town of Tiwintzá and a corridor from the border was assigned to Ecuador, which was also granted free navigation rights along the Amazon and the right to establish two port facilities within Peruvian territory.

In response to a faltering economy, Mahuad announced austerity measures in 1997, which were met with strikes and public protest. In 1999, the government defaulted on external loans. Seeking to stabilize the economy, Mahuad announced his plan to replace the national currency with the U.S. dollar. In January 2000, he was forced from power by the army and indigenous protesters, and Vice President Gustavo Noboa Bejarano became president. Noboa adopted the U.S. dollar as Ecuador's national currency in March 2000.

CONSTITUTION

Under its 18th constitution, passed in 1998, Ecuador has a president, who acts as head of state and head of government, and a 121-member unicameral legislature, known as the National Chamber of Representatives.

The president appoints the cabinet, provincial governors, and diplomatic representatives, and directs international relations. He can declare a state of emergency upon notice to the Chamber. The president serves a four-year term and is ineligible for reelection.

Voting is by free, secret, direct ballot for all Ecuadorians 18 years and older, and compulsory for literate Ecuadorians under age 65.

The constitution of 1998 establishes the autonomy of the Central Bank in setting monetary policy, mandates that the state maintain economic balances, and eliminates state monopoly over strategic areas of the economy.

LOCAL GOVERNMENT

Ecuador is divided into 21 provinces, each administered by a governor appointed by the president. Provinces are subdivided into 115 cantons or municipalities. A canton is administered by a *jefe político*, or political chief, appointed by the president. Cantons are subdivided into *parroquias* (parishes), each administered by a *teniente político*, a political lieutenant.

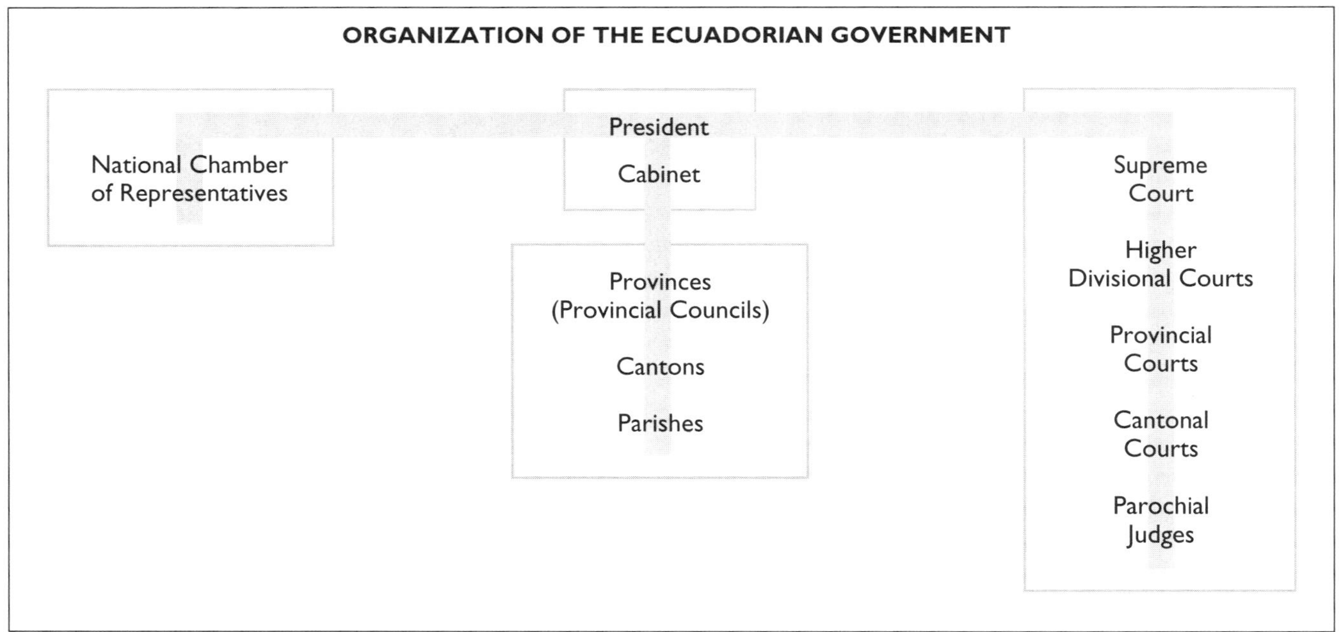

Local Government

Principal administrative divisions, capitals, area, population

Area and population

Regions / Provinces	Capitals	area sq mi	area sq km	population 1997 estimate
Amazónica				
Morona-Santiago	Macas	13,100	33,930	131,845
Napo	Tena	9,918	25,690	146,319
Pastaza	Puyo	11,496	29,774	57,339
Sucumbíos	Nueva Loja	7,076	18,327	128,512
Zamora-Chinchipe	Zamora	8,923	23,111	94,339
Costa				
El Oro	Machala	2,259	5,850	524,466
Esmeraldas	Esmeraldas	5,884	15,239	389,967
Guayas	Guayaquil	7,916	20,503	3,201,672
Los Ríos	Babahoyo	2,770	71,759	630,303
Manabí	Portoviejo	7,289	18,879	1,211,064
Insular				
Galápagos	Puerto Baquerizo Moreno	3,093	8,010	14,713
Sierra				
Azuay	Cuenca	3,137	8,125	597,798
Bolívar	Guaranda	1,521	3,940	178,706
Cañar	Azogues	1,205	3,122	210,340
Carchi	Tulcan	1,392	3,605	160,983
Chimborazo	Riobamba	2,536	6,569	412,836
Cotopaxi	Latacunga	2,344	6,072	299,443
Imbabura	Ibarra	1,760	4,559	316,793
Loja	Loja	4,257	11,026	418,292
Pichincha	Quito	4,987	12,915	2,295,739
Tungurahua	Ambato	1,288	3,335	428,116
TOTAL		105,037	272,045	11,936,858

PARLIAMENT

Legislative power is vested in the National Chamber of Representatives, whose 121 members are elected for four-year terms from lists of candidates drawn up by legally recognized parties. Representatives are eligible for reelection.

The National Chamber ratifies treaties, elects members of the Superior and Supreme Courts, and appoints the comptroller general, the attorney general, and the superintendent of banks. Congress can override the president's amendment of a bill and may reconsider a rejected bill after one year. It can request a referendum and revoke a state of emergency.

POLITICAL PARTIES

Political parties include the following:

Social Christian Party (Partido Social Cristiano, PSC) Moderate center-right, with main strength in the Costa.

Conservative Party (Partido Conservativo Ecuatoriano, PCE) Far right-wing, centered in Quito.

Democratic Left (Izquierda Democrática, ID) Socialist center-left, strong among government workers and professionals in the Sierra.

Popular Democracy (Democracia Popular, DP) Progressive, Christian-democratic; strong in Quito.

Radical Alfarista Front (Frente Radical Alfarista, FRA) Socialist, populist left-of-center; main strength is in the Costa.

Roldosist Party (Partido Roldosista Ecuatoriano, PRE) Populist centrist; strong in the Costa.

Concentration of Popular Forces (Concentración de Fuerzas Populares, CFP) Populist left-of-center; strong in Costa.

Pachakutik–New Country (Pachakutik–Nueva Patria, P-NP) Far left populist, represents indigenist movement; strong in northern and central Sierra.

Political Parties

Democratic Party, 1981
People, Change and Democracy
Nationalist Revolutionary Party
Republican Party, 1988
There are a number of guerrilla groups of which the most active is
Elroy Alfaro Popular Armed Forces- Alfaro Lives
Social Christian Party, 1951
Ecuadorian Roldosist Party, 1982
Popular Democracy, 1977
New Country Movement, 1997
Democratic Popular Movement
Democratic Left
Alfarist Radical Front, 1978
Ecuadorian Popular Revolutionary Action, 1958
Independent Movement for an Authentic Republic, 1996
Concentration of Popular Forces, 1946
Radical Liberal Party, 1895
Ecuadorian Conservative Party, 1855
Left Broad Front, a coalition of six parties of which the most important is
Ecuadorian Communist Party

Political Parties: Strength in Parliament Most Recent Elections

The current legislature is a unicameral **National Congress** (Congreso Nacional) of 121 popularly elected members serving five-year terms. Following the most recent election on May 31, 1998, the Popular Democracy held 35 seats; the Social Christian Party, 26; the Ecuadorian Roldosist Party, 25; the Democratic Left, 17; the Pachakutik Plurinational United Movement-New Country, 6; the Alfarist Radical Front, 3; the Democratic Popular Movement, 2; the Ecuadorian Conservative Party, 2; others, 5.

LEGAL SYSTEM

In 1861 Ecuador adopted the Civil Code of Chile, which is based on the Napoleonic and Spanish codes.

The judiciary consists of a Supreme Court of Justice, higher divisional courts, provincial courts, cantonal courts, and parochial judges.

The Supreme Court consists of 15 judges and two prosecutors, elected by Congress for six-year terms. The president of the court is elected annually by the membership. The court usually sits in five chambers of three judges each.

Preventive detention is illegal, and the criminal code forbids isolated confinement for more than 24 hours. Mayors and municipal council presidents are constitutionally empowered to grant bail and habeas corpus.

Defendants have the right to counsel, to face their accusers, to refrain from testifying against themselves, and to appeal their sentences to intermediate courts and to the Supreme Court.

Judges play a central role in investigations as well as in deciding guilt or innocence. There is no trial by jury. Legal investigations as well as prosecutions are carried out by the attorney general, solicitor general, and provincial prosecutors, who defend state interests in criminal and civil cases.

Military courts are empowered to try only those cases involving acts against military installations and infractions of military regulations.

The correctional system is operated by the National Directorate of Prisons under the Ministry of Government. The two largest institutions are the García Moreno prison in Quito and the Penitenciario del Litoral in Guayaquil.

LAW ENFORCEMENT

Law Enforcement

Offenses reported to the police per 100,000: 466
Murder: 10.5
Assault: 32.9
Burglary: 94.4
Automobile Theft: 36.5
Population per Police officer: 260
Death Penalty: Abolished 1906

HUMAN RIGHTS

In terms of civil and political rights, Ecuador is ranked as a free country. There are no political prisoners, and preventive detention is not practiced. Political and security courts do not exist.

However, the U.S. State Department reports find extensive human rights abuses stemming from corruption in the legal and judicial systems. Persons are subject to arbitrary arrest and, unless they pay bribes, may wait years before being tried. More than half the prisoners in jail have not been formally sentenced.

The constitution guarantees freedom of speech and freedom of expression. There are no restrictions on normal trade union activities.

FOREIGN POLICY

The border dispute with Peru has been Ecuador's principal foreign policy issue. Ecuador asserted that the Río Protocol, which set a border between Ecuador and Peru following full-scale war in 1942, does not accurately describe the area of the Upper Cenepa River valley in the Cordillera, rendering demarcation "inexecutable."

In January–February 1995, soldiers fought an intense but localized war in the disputed territory. Peace was brokered by the four guarantors of the Río Protocol (Argentina, Brazil, Chile, and the United States), and in March 1999 presidents Mahuad of Ecuador and Fujimori of Peru signed a treaty demarcating a definitive boundary.

The United States and Ecuador maintain close ties, cooperating to combat narcotics trafficking, build trade and investment, and foster Ecuador's economic development. Ecuador is a signatory to the United Nations and the Organization of American States. It belongs to the Rio Group, the Latin American Integration Association, and the Andean Pact.

DEFENSE

The defense structure is headed by the president who acts as commander in chief and is advised by the National Defense Council. The line of command runs from the president through the minister of national defense to the joint command of the armed forces and the commanders of the three services. In 1996, total active duty personnel numbered 57,000, 87.6 percent in the army, 7.2 percent in the navy, and 5.2 percent in the air force. The country is divided into six military zones (Quito, Guayaquil, Cuenca, Machala, and Loja, and a sixth zone comprising the Oriente), the three naval districts (Guayaquil, Quito, and the Oriente) and two air force districts (Quito and Guayaquil). All three services are independent.

Military manpower is provided by a compulsory one-year conscription law under which all able-bodied men are liable for service at the age of 20. In February 1999 President Jamil Mahaud announced that he would cut the draft by 60 percent and reassign one-quarter of the army to the police force. Domestic terrorism is a smaller problem in Ecuador than it is in Peru and Colombia, but the security of the northern frontier area against drug traffickers and insurgent Colombian groups is a continuing concern.

Military Indicators

Total Active Duty Personnel: 57,100
Military Manpower per 1,000: 4.8
Military Expenditures $million: 611
- as % of GNP: 3.7
- per capita $: 54
- as % of central government expenditures: 18.3

Arms Imports $million: 260
Arms Exports $million: —

ECONOMY

Ecuador is ranked as a lower middle-income country with a mixed public-private economy.

The country's economy is heavily dependent on petroleum exports and moves in lockstep with the price of oil in the world market. Fluctuations in other key exports, such as bananas, coffee, cocoa, and shrimp also exert a substantial domestic impact.

Economic growth has been uneven in recent years due to the on-again, off-again application of fiscal stabilization reforms. In 1996 Abdalá Bucaram proposed a schedule for privatizing some government-owned industries, but popular discontent led to his dismissal in February 1997. Confronting an economy racked by mismanagement, damage from El Niño, and low world oil prices, President Jamil Mahuad announced a fiscal austerity package in January 1999 that also provoked violent protests. The beginning of 1999 saw the banking sector collapse, which helped precipitate an unprecedented default on external loans later that year. Continued economic instability drove a 70 percent depreciation of the currency throughout 1999, which eventually led the government to adopt the U.S. dollar as the national currency in 2000. Shortly thereafter, the IMF approved $2 billion in aid for Ecuador.

Ecuador has established free-trade areas with Colombia, Chile, and within the Andean Community, and it belongs to the World Trade Organization (WTO) and Asociación Latinoamericana de Integración (ALADI).

Principal Economic Indicators

Gross National Product $: 18.785 billion
GNP per capita $: 1,570
GNP Average Annual Growth Rate (1990–97) %: 0.9
GNP per capita Average Annual Growth Rate (1990–97) %: −1.3
Origin of Gross Domestic Product %
- Agriculture: 17
- Mining: 15
- Manufacturing: 15
- Construction: 3
- Public Utilities: 1
- Transportation and Communications: 9
- Trade: 15
- Financial Services: 12
- Other Services: 6
- Government: 7

Gross Domestic Product by Type of Expenditure %
- Private Consumption: 69
- Government Consumption: 9
- Gross Domestic Investment: 19
- Foreign Trade: Exports: 21
- Imports: −24

% of Income Received by Poorest 20%: 5.4
% of Income Received by Richest 10%: 37.6

Price and earnings indexes (1995 = 100)

	1992	1993	1994	1995	1996	1997	1998
Consumer price index	44.0	63.9	81.4	100.0	124.4	162.5	221.1
Hourly earnings index	187.5	206.3	218.8	—	—	—	—

Finance

National Currency: Sucre (S/)
Exchange Rate: $1 = S/4,498.0
Money Supply Stock in National Currency billion: 5,439.5
M1 per capita: 453,000
Central Bank Discount Rate %: 64.74

Total External Debt $million: 12,500
Debt Service Ratio %: 28.1

Balance of Payments $million: −74.3
International Reserves SDRs million: 1,662
Ratio of External Debt to Total Reserves: 7.3
Average Annual Rate of Inflation/Consumer Price Index Growth Rate %: 31

Official Development Assistance

ODA $million: 176
as % of GNP: 1.0
per capita $: 14
Foreign Direct Investment $million: 831

Central Government Revenues and Expenditures

Fiscal Year: Calendar Year
Revenues $million: 3,600
Expenditures $million: 0
Budget Deficit $million: —
Tax Revenues as % of GDP: —
Highest Tax Bracket %
Individual: —
Corporate: —

Employment and Labor

Economically Active Population: 3,360,000
Female Participation Rate %: 26.4
Activity Rate %: 34.8
Labor by Sector: %
Agriculture, Forestry, Fishing: 30.8
Manufacturing, Mining: 12.0
Construction: 5.9
Transportation and Communications: 3.9
Trade, Hotels, and Restaurants: 14.2
Finance, Insurance, Real Estate: 2.4
Public Administration, Defense: —
Services: 24.9
Unemployment %: 6.9

Agriculture

Agriculture's Share of GDP%: 17
Average Annual Rate of Growth (1965–98) %: 3.5
Number of Farms 000: 517
Average Size of Farm ha: 15.4
Number of Tractors per 1,000 hectares: 5.5
Irrigation, % of Farms having: 34
Artificial Fertilizer kg/hectare: 29
Total Farmland as % of land area: 30.5
Livestock: Cattle 000: 5,329
Sheep 000: 2,056
Hogs 000: 2,795
Chickens 000: 64,736
Forests: Production of Roundwood (000 cubic meters): 10,361
Fisheries: Total Catch tons 000: 339.9

Mining

% of GDP: 10.5
Value of Mineral Production $million: 1,883.6

Manufacturing

Value Added $million: 3,095
Industrial Production Growth Rate %: 2.4

Energy

Commercial Energy Production metric tons of oil equivalent 000: 22,792
Commercial Energy Consumption metric tons of oil equivalent 000: 8,513
Commercial Energy Consumption per capita kg: 713
Average Annual Growth Rate 1980–97 %: 0.3
Net Energy Imports % of use: 16.8
Electricity Installed Capacity kW 000: 2,539
Production kW-hr million: 8,349
Coal Reserves tons million: 24
Production tons 000: —
Natural Gas Proven Reserves cubic meters billion: 105
Production cubic meters million: 102
Crude Petroleum Reserves barrels million: 2,115
Production barrels million: 141
Consumption barrels million: 53
Refinery Capacity barrels per day 000: 148
Pipelines Length km: 2,158

Foreign Trade

Imports $million: 4,195.2
Exports $million: 4,361.5
Export Volume % Annual Growth Rate (1990–97): 10.2
Import Volume % Annual Growth Rate (1990–97): 10.1

Balance of trade (current prices)

U.S.	1993	1994	1995	1996	1997	1998
$000,000	+680.7	+508.9	+532.4	+1,510.5	+709.5	+809.8
% of total	13.3%	7.3%	6.6%	18.3%	7.3%	8.8%

Major Trading Partners

	Imports	Exports
European Union %	15.3	19.3
United States %	30.7	42.5
Eastern Europe %	0.4	2.7
Japan %	8.6	2.7
Others %	44.9	32.7

Transportation

Roads Total Length mi: 26,785 km 43,106
Paved %: 18
Automobiles: 395,000
Trucks and Buses: 58,650
Persons per vehicle: 25
Railroad; Track Length mi: 600 km 966
Passenger-mi million: 17
Freight-mi million: 6
Merchant Marine: No. of Vessels: 154
Total Deadweight Tonnage 000: 504.1
International Cargo Loaded tons 000: 11,783
International Cargo Off-loaded tons 000: 1,958

(continued)

Airports with Scheduled Flights: 14
Traffic: Passenger-mi million: 876
Freight-mi million: 111
Length of Canals mi: 932 km 1,500

Tourism

Number of Tourists to 000: 511
Number of Tourists from 000: 330
Tourist Receipts $million: 255
Tourist Expenditures $million: 235

Communications

Telephones 000: 748
Cost of Local Calls 3 mins: $0.01
Cellular Telephones 000: 50
Fax Machines 000: 30
Personal Computers 000: 45
Internet Hosts per million persons: 44
Mail: Post Offices: 267
Pieces of Mail Handled million: 18
Pieces of Mail Handled per person: 1.6

EDUCATION

Education is free, universal, and compulsory for eight years from the ages of six to 14. Schooling lasts for 12 years, divided into six years of primary school, three years of middle school, and three years of secondary school. Special programs have been developed to make primary educational facilities accessible to rural youths, an estimated 15 percent of whom are illiterate.

The academic year runs from October to July in the Sierra and from April or May to January in the Costa. The medium of instruction is Spanish, although Quechua and other indigenous languages are sometimes used.

Private schools account for 22 percent of secondary school enrollment and 18 percent of primary school enrollment and are judged to be better than public schools. Private schools also account for more than half of the enrollment of technical schools. The Catholic Church runs about 800 schools, Protestant denominations about 12.

Public schools are run by the state or by the municipalities; in the latter case they are under the direction of the mayors or the municipal councils. Municipalities are obligated to allocate 30 percent of their budgets to education, although the actual figure rarely reaches 18 percent.

Ecuador has 20 universities (16 state and four private) and three technical colleges. Chief among the public universities are the Central University (the country's oldest), University of Cuenca, University of Loja, University of Guayaquil, and the Technical University of Portoviejo. The largest private universities are Catholic University of Quito, Catholic University of Guayaquil, and the Lay University Vicente Rocafuerte.

Education

Literacy Rate %: 90.1
Male %: 92.0
Female %: 88.2
First Level: Primary schools: —
Teachers: 63,647
Students: 1,986,753
Student-Teacher Ratio: 31.4
Net Enrollment Ratio: 92
Second Level: Secondary Schools: —
Teachers: 62,630
Students: 813,557
Student-Teacher Ratio: 13.0
Net Enrollment Ratio: —
Vocational Level: Schools: —
Students: —
Third Level: Institutions: —
Teachers: 12,856
Students: 206,541
Student-Ratio Level: 16.1
Gross Enrollment Ratio: 20.0
Students per 100,000: 2,012
% of Population Age 25 and over with Postsecondary Education: 12.7
Public Expenditure on Education as % of GDP: 3.4

SCIENCE AND TECHNOLOGY

Science and Technology

Scientists and Engineers in R&D per 1 million persons: 146
Expenditures in R&D as % of GDP: 0.02
High-Tech Exports $million: 20
Patent Applications by Residents: 8

MEDIA

Ecuador's press is free and vigorous. Ownership of the media is broad-based, although foreign investment in broadcast organs is restricted.

The four dailies of Quito and six dailies of Guayaquil account for the bulk of newspaper circulation and readership. Foreign news bureaus represented include UPI, Reuters, Agencia EFE, AP, DPA, and ANSA.

There are eight major book publishers, with a modest annual output. Ecuador adheres to the Universal Copyright and Buenos Aires conventions.

Ecuador boasts 324 commercial radio stations, 14 of which are on the air for 24 hours. All stations are required by law to broadcast 15 minutes of adult education programs daily.

Television, introduced in 1959, now reaches more than 1 million inhabitants in five cities through 16 stations.

Media

Daily Newspapers: 24
Total Circulation 000: 808
Circulation per 1,000: 72
Books Published: 11
Magazines: 199
Radio Receivers 000: 3,240
per 1,000: 277
Television sets 000: 1,700
per 1,000: 148

MOST IMPORTANT MEDIA:

Press. The following are daily newspapers published at Guayaquil, unless otherwise noted: *El Universo* (175,000 daily, 290,000 Sunday), independent Conservative; *El Comercio* (Quito, 132,000), independent Conservative; *Ultimas Noticias* (Quito, 90,000), evening counterpart of *El Comercio; Hoy* (Quito, 55,000), center-left; *El Tiempo* (Quito, 35,000), independent Conservative; *El Telégrafo* (45,000 daily, 55,000 Sunday), Liberal; *Expreso* (30,000), center-right; *La Razón* (28,000), Liberal.

News agencies. There is no domestic facility. A number of foreign agencies maintain bureaus at either Quito or Guayaquil.

Radio and television. Broadcasting is supervised by the nongovernmental Asociación Ecuatoriana de Radiodifusion (AER) and the Instituto Ecuatoriano de Telecomunicaciones (Ietel). Of the more than 300 radio stations (the most numerous, on a per capita basis, in Latin America), about two dozen are facilities of the religious La Voz de los Andes. There are 14 television stations, most of which are commercial.

CULTURE

Cultural Indicators

Public Libraries Number: —
Volumes: —
Registered borrowers: —
Museums Number: —
Annual Attendance: —
Cinema Production of Long Films: 1
Number of Cinemas: 134
Seating Capacity: 75,300
Annual Attendance million: 6.8
Annual Attendance per capita: 0.6

STATUS OF WOMEN

Ecuador was the first country in Latin America to grant women suffrage (in 1929) and its constitution establishes complete legal equality for both sexes.

Because of the economic need to maintain more than one income per household, women are entering the workforce earlier and staying longer. Women filled three of 16 cabinet positions in 1999 and one party, the Independent Movement for an Authentic Republic (MIRA), is headed by a woman, Rosalia Arteaga Serrano, who served as Ecuador's interim president in 1997 (February 9–11) and first female vice president.

The Center for Women's Action, a nongovernmental organization, organizes and educates women about discriminatory labor practices, family law, and domestic violence. Largely due to its efforts, Ecuador in 1995 passed the Law against Violence Affecting Women and Children, which criminalized spousal abuse and created family courts. Some communities have established their own centers to counsel abused women, and the government began to address this question seriously with the formation of the Comisaria de la Mujer, or Women's Bureau, in 1994.

Abortion is illegal. Family-planning support is provided by the Ministry of Health, most universities, and two private organizations, Asociación pro Familia Ecuadoriana (APROFE) and the Ecuadorian Center of Family Education.

Women

Gender Empowerment Measure: 69
Seats Held in Parliament by Women %: 3.7
Female Administrators and Managers %: 27.5
Female Professional and Technical Workers %: 46.6
Women's Share of Earned Income %: 19
Women in Government %: 10

HEALTH, FOOD, AND NUTRITION

Health

Number of Physicians: 12,149
Number of Dentists: 1,524
Number of Nurses: 4,215
Number of Pharmacists: 906
Population per Physician: 904
Number of Hospitals: 429
Hospital Beds per 10,000: 16
Hospital Bed Occupancy Rate: 57.5
Infant Mortality Rate per 1,000 live births: 57
Maternal Mortality Rate per 100,000 live births: 150
Total Health Expenditures as % of GDP: 4.14
Health Expenditures per capita $: 44
HIV Infected % of adults: 0.28
Cigarette Consumption per smoker per year: —
% of Smokers: Male: —
Female: —
Access to Safe Water %: 70

Food and Nutrition

Food Supply as % of FAO Requirements: 106
% of Consumption Expenditures on Food: 36.1
Daily Available Calories per capita: 3,327
% of Total Calories derived from:
Cereals: 66.3
Potatoes, cassava: 1.6
Meat, poultry: 2.4
Fish: 0.4
Eggs, milk: 1.8
Fruits, vegetables: 6.2
Fats, oils: 7.7

ENVIRONMENT

Ecuador's constitution states that all citizens have the right to live in a pure environment. Yet Ecuador is under siege from a host of ecological stresses, including rapid urbanization and large-scale petroleum exploration and processing in the Oriente. In 1996, the Ministry of Environment was created to systematize ecological management and concentrate efforts to protect Ecuador's natural resources. Other efforts to confront ecological problems have been undertaken by groups representing peasant and indigenous communities and organizations such as Fundación Natura, specializing in education in schools, and Ecociencia, primarily concerned with research.

Much domestic and international attention has been focused on the exploitation of the Oriente by the petroleum industry. In November 1993 five Amazon Indian tribes filed suit against Texaco to claim compensation totaling U.S. $1.5 billion for the company's spilling some 17 million barrels of oil in its 25 years of operations in the region.

Ecuador has ratified the Biodiversity Convention, the Climatic Changes Treaty, and the Forest Declaration, and abides by the principles of the Rio Declaration. The Law of Forestry and Conservation of Natural Areas and Wildlife of 1981 established the national patrimony of natural areas and created 17 protected areas, including the Galápagos.

Environment

Forest Area sq km: 111,000
Average Annual Deforestation sq km: 1,890
Nationally Protected Areas as % of Total Land Area: 43.1
Freshwater Access cubic meters per capita: 26,305
Emissions of Organic Water Pollutants kg per day: 25,297
CO_2 Emissions per capita ton: 2.1

CHRONOLOGY

1945 Ecuador becomes a charter member of the United Nations; a new constitution is promulgated in December.

1947 President José Maria Velasco Ibarra is deposed in a military coup whose leaders are in turn ousted by counterrevolutionaries; a provisional government is established.

1948 Galo Plaza Lasso wins presidential elections; Ecuador becomes a charter member of the Organization of American States (OAS).

1952 Former president Velasco is elected president.

1956 Conservative candidate Camilo Ponce Enríquez wins a narrow victory.

1960 Velasco is returned to the presidency by a wide margin.

1961 President Velasco signs the Alliance for Progress, a 10-year economic treaty with the United States; Velasco is forced to resign and Vice President Carlos Arosemena Monroy is sworn in as president.

1963 Arosemena is ousted and replaced by a military junta; the junta initiates liberal economic and social programs, including land reform.

1966 Violent demonstrations erupt across the country; the opposition forces the junta out of power; Otto Arosemena Gomez is named president.

1967 A new constitution is promulgated.

1968 Velasco is elected to the presidency a fifth time.

1970 Velasco assumes dictatorial powers.

1972 The military ousts Velasco and coup leader General Guillermo Rodríguez Lara assumes the office of president; Rodríguez's government announces a five-year economic plan emphasizing agriculture, housing, and industry; Ecuador begins exporting petroleum.

1976 Admiral Alfredo Poveda Burbano takes over government leadership at the head of a three-man junta.

1978 Jaime Roldós Aguilera is elected president.

1979 Roldós is sworn in; the new constitution takes effect; clashes with Peru erupt over the ongoing border dispute.

1981 International arbitration resolves the border conflict; President Roldós dies in a plane crash and Vice President Osvaldo Hurtado Larrea is sworn in as president.

1983 Floods devastate Ecuador.

1984 Léon Febres Cordero Rivadeneira of the conservative Social Christian Party is elected president.

1986 World oil prices continue to decline, depressing Ecuador's economy; the Social Christian Party loses seats in legislative elections.

1987 President Cordero is captured and beaten in one of several unsuccessful military uprisings; a major earthquake causes widespread damage; its fiscal crisis deepening, Ecuador indefinitely suspends payments on foreign debt, which exceeds $9 billion.

1988 Democratic Left candidate Rodrigo Borja Cevallos is elected president.

1992 Sixto Durán-Ballén Córdovez assumes the presidency.

1993 In the nation's worst-ever natural disaster, a landslide in Azuay province kills several hundred and causes more than $100 million in damage; a wave of strikes protests President Ballén's privatization scheme.

1994 In midterm elections, Social Christians gain a majority in Congress; massive roadblocks by Indian groups impede the government's plans to reclaim communal lands.

1995 Crossfire in the Cenepa frontier escalates into war with Peru; Vice President Alberto Dahik, accused of peculation of reserve funds, flees to Costa Rica.

1996 Abdalá Bucaram Ortíz of the Roldosist party becomes president, and Rosalía Arteaga Serrano, an independent, becomes the first woman vice president.

1997 About 2 million workers participate in a general strike in February; days later, as 10,000 mostly indigenous protesters lay siege to the capitol building, Congress dismisses Bucaram for "mental incapacity"; Vice President Arteaga proclaims herself president but steps aside when Congress elects Fabian Alarcón interim president; in July Congress votes to dismiss the entire Supreme Court; the El Niño weather pattern damages crops and leaves over 20,000 people homeless; numerous Ecuadorian banks collapse in the wake of the Asian fiscal crisis.

1998 Jamil Mahuad Witt of the Popular Democracy Party wins the presidency; a new constitution is promulgated; in October President Mahuad and President Alberto Fujimori of Peru sign a treaty accepting border limits along a 78-km line of disputed territory.

1999 Annual inflation reaches 60 percent; banks close for five days; Ecuador defers payments on $6 billion in debt.

2000 In January 10,000 protesters march on Quito to demand the resignation of President Mahuad, and 1,500 protesters take over the capitol building; a military junta briefly takes power in a coup; in the face of opposition from the United States, United Nations, and the OAS, the junta relinquishes control, and Vice President Gustavo Noboa Bejarano is sworn in as president; the World Trade Organization allows Ecuador to impose $200 million in economic sanctions on the European Union over the banana trade dispute; President Noboa replaces the sucre with the U.S. dollar as the official national currency; the International Monetary Fund approves $2 billion in aid for Ecuador.

BIBLIOGRAPHY

BOOKS

Conaghan, Catherine M. *Unsettling Statecraft: Democracy and Neoliberalism in the Central Andes.* Pittsburgh, 1994.

Hamilton, Sarah. *The Two-Headed Household: Gender & Rural Development in the Ecuadorean Andes.* Pittsburgh, 1998.

Hidrobo Estrada, Jorge. *Power & Industrialization in Ecuador.* Boulder, Colo., 1992.

Isaacs, Anita. *The Politics of Military Rule & Transition in Ecuador, 1972–92.* Pittsburgh, 1993.

Kelly, Robert C. *Ecuador.* Houston, 1998.

Marcela, Gabriel. *Security Cooperation: Resolving the Ecuador-Peru Conflict.* Miami, 1999.

OECD. *Political Feasibility of Adjustment in Ecuador and Venezuela.* Washington, D.C., 1994.

Pineo, Ronn F. *Social & Economic Reform in Ecuador.* Gainesville, Fla., 1996.

Radcliffe, Sarah. *Remaking the Nation: Place, Identity and Politics in Latin America.* New York, 1996.

Rappaport, Joanne. *Cumbe Reborn: An Andean Ethnography of History.* Chicago, 1994.

Tokman, Victor E. *Regulation and the Informal Economy: Microenterprises in Chile, Ecuador, and Jamaica.* Boulder, Colo., 1996.

FILM

Amazon, The Invisible People. Color film, 60 min. Vanguard Films.

Ecuador and the Galápagos Islands. Color film, 21 min. International Video.

Edge of Survival. Color film, 90 min. Wharton International Films.

The Icemen of Chimborazo. Color film, 90 min. Guayasamin.

Nomads of the Rain Forest. Color video, 50 min. University of California-Berkeley.

OFFICIAL PUBLICATIONS

Ecuador. *Série estadística* (quinquennial); *Censo de población (V) y de vivienda (IV) 1990.*

Accountant General. *Government Accounts and Fund Accounts.*

Central Bank. *Annual Report, Daily Statements.*

Customs Department. *Customs Revenue Reports.*

National Budget Office. *Statements of Financial & Cash Positions.*

National Institute for Statistics and Index: *Monthly and Trimestral Statements.*

CONTACT INFORMATION

Embassy of Ecuador
2535 15th Street NW
Washington, D.C. 20009
Phone: (202) 234-7200 Fax: (202) 667-3482

INTERNET RESOURCES

- Instituto Nacional de Estadística y Censos (in Spanish) http://www4.inec.gov.ec/master.htm
- Banco Central del Ecuador http://www.bce.fin.ec

EGYPT

BASIC FACT SHEET

OFFICIAL NAME:
Arab Republic of Egypt (Jum-hūrīyah Misr al-Arabīya)

ABBREVIATION:
EY

CAPITAL:
Cairo

HEAD OF STATE:
President Muhammad Hosni Mubarak (from 1981)

HEAD OF GOVERNMENT:
Prime Minister Atif Muhammad Ubaid (from 1999)

NATURE OF GOVERNMENT:
Modified democracy

POPULATION:
64,560,000 (1999)

AREA:
1,001,449 sq km (386,660 sq mi)

ETHNIC MAJORITY:
Arab

LANGUAGE:
Arabic

RELIGION:
Islam (official)

UNIT OF CURRENCY:
Egyptian pound (£E.)

NATIONAL FLAG:
Tricolor of three equal horizontal stripes—red, white and black—with the national emblem in the central white stripe

NATIONAL EMBLEM:
A sylized, upright eagle, gold and white in color, facing forward with wings partly raised and its beak turned to its own right. On its chest the stripes of the flag are vertically displayed and in its claws is a scroll with the words in Arabic script, "Arab Republic of Egypt."

NATIONAL ANTHEM:
"To Thee, to Thee, My Country, I Give My Love and My Heart."

NATIONAL HOLIDAYS:
July 23 (National Day; Revolution Day), June 8 (Evacuation Day); December 27 (Victory Day); also variable Islamic festivals and the Coptic festival Sham-al-Nasim. The Nile Food Festival, June 17, is an unofficial holiday.

DATE OF INDEPENDENCE:
February 28, 1922

DATE OF CONSTITUTION:
September 11, 1971

GEOGRAPHICAL FEATURES

Egypt is at the northeastern corner of Africa and forms a rough quadrangle covering 386,660 sq mi (1,101,449 sq km) and extending 976 mi (1,571 km) southeast to northwest and 743 mi (1,196 km) northeast to southwest. It is bordered on the south by Sudan and on the east by Libya.

The capital is Cairo, one of the world's largest cities, with a metropolitan population of 9,690,000 (1996 est.). The other major urban centers are Alexandria (3,584,000), Giza (3,700,100), Shubra el-Khemia (1,204,000), and Port Said (460,000).

The country is divided into two regions: Lower Egypt, or Wagh al-Bahari; and Upper Egypt, or al-Said. Lower Egypt is the broad, alluvial Nile Delta, while Upper Egypt is a tableland rising to 1,500 ft (457 m).

The two main topographical divisions are the Western Desert and the Eastern Desert. The Western Desert, which covers 68 percent of the land area, is an arid region covered by vast, rolling plains of sand and large depressions, many of which lie below sea level. The Eastern Desert,

Egypt

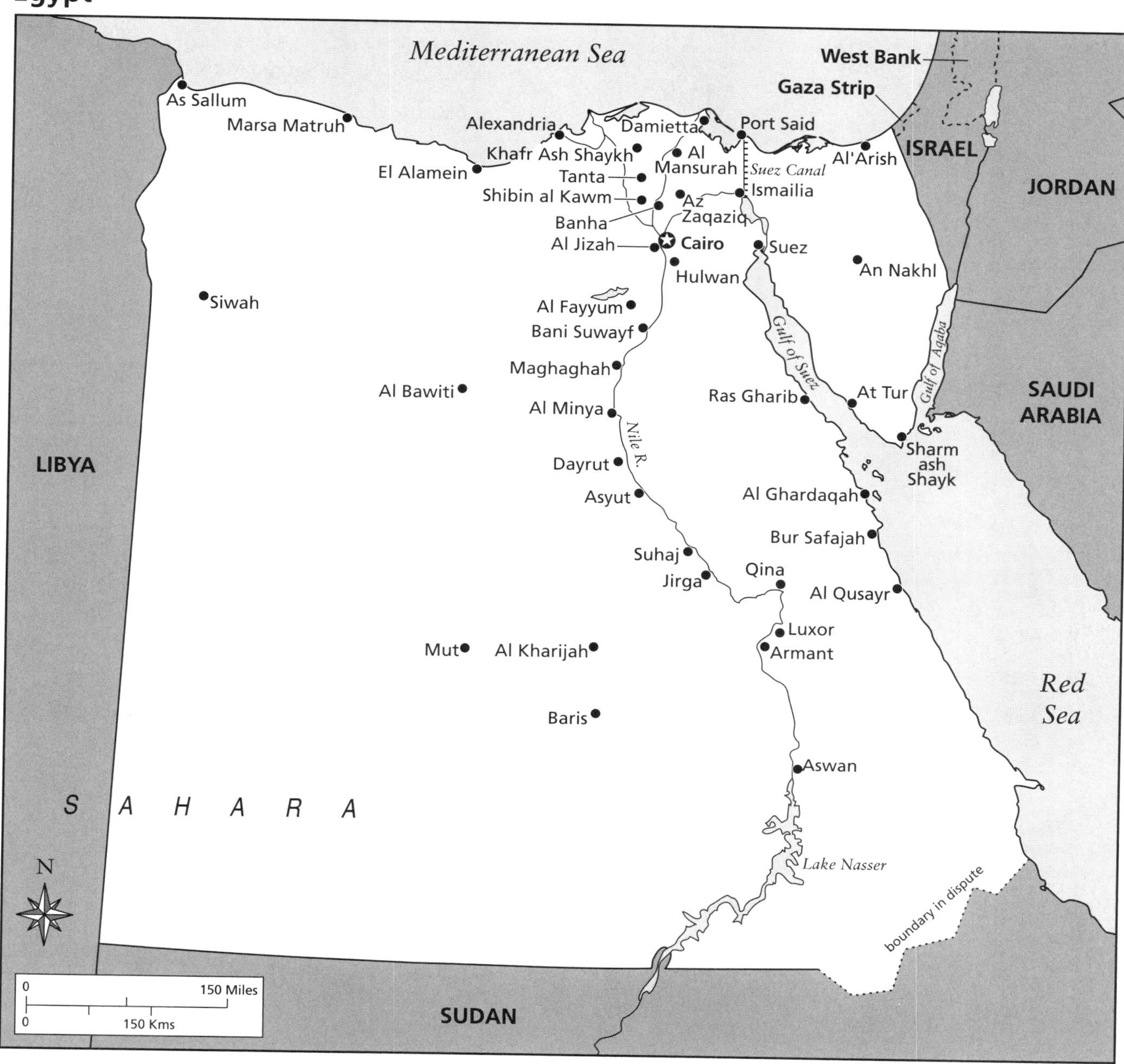

also called the Arabian Desert, is an elevated plateau broken by deep valleys that covers 22 percent of the land area. Human settlements are limited to the Nile River valley and Nile Delta, which cover 4 percent of the land area.

The Nile River is not only the longest river in Africa but also is the lifeline of Egypt. It flows through Egypt for nearly 1,000 m (1,609 km) after entering the country at Wadi Halfa. Throughout the length of Egypt there are no significant tributaries entering the Nile. The annual flooding of the Nile has governed for centuries the agricultural life of the country. The day traditionally celebrated for the entry of the floodwaters is June 17. The water then continuously rises until, at full flood in September, 17.6 billion cu ft (500 million cu m) of water flows by Cairo daily. At Cairo the Nile spreads out over a broad estuary to form a fertile delta of 8,494 sq mi (22,000 sq km), through which flow the two main distributary branches: the eastern Damietta and the western Rosetta. These are supplemented by a network of irrigation canals and four main shallow lakes. Below Aswan is a region of cascades known as the first cataract, which serves as a barrier to upstream navigation and isolates Egypt from Sudan.

The largest lake is the man-made Lake Nasser, a reservoir behind the Aswan High Dam.

Geography

Area sq km: 1,001,449 sq mi 386,660
World Rank: 30th
Land Boundaries, km: Gaza Strip 11; Israel 255; Libya 1,150; Sudan 1,273
Coastline, km 2,450
Elevation Extremes meters
Lowest: Qathara Depression −133
Highest: Mount Catherine 2,629
Land Use % Arable land: 2
Permanent Crops: 0
Permanent Pastures: 0
Forest and Woodland: 0
Other: 98

Population of Principal Cities (1992 est.)

Alexandria	3,700,000
Aswan	220,000
Asyūt	321,000
Banhā	136,000
Bani Suywaf	179,000
Bur Sa'id (Port Said)	460,000
Cairo	9,900,000
Damanhur	222,000
al-Fayyum	250,000
Hulwan (Helwan)	352,300
Al-Isma ilyah	255,000
Al-Jizah (Giza)	2,144,000
Kafr ad-Dawwar	226,000
Kafr ash-Shaykh	102,910
Al-Mahallah al-Kubra	408,000
Al-Mansurah	371,000
Al-Minyā	208,000
Qina	141,000
Sawhaj	156,000
Shibin al-Kawm	158,000
Shubra al-Khaymah	834,000
As-Suways (Suez)	388,000
Tanja	380,000
Al-Uqsur (Luxor)	155,000
Az-Zapaziq	287,000

CLIMATE AND WEATHER

Egypt has a warm, arid climate with two seasons: a cool winter from November to April and a hot summer from May to October. Prevailing northerly winds temper the climate along the Mediterranean coast, where temperatures in the summer rarely exceed 91°F (33°C). The interior has a true desert climate, with temperatures usually rising to 100°F to 110°F (38°C to 43°C). The desert temperatures are subject to wide variations. During the winter there may be occasional cold spells, and light frosts and light snow are not unknown.

Rainfall is almost entirely limited to the coastal area, where it averages 8 in (200 mm) a year. Cairo receives 1 in (25 mm) a year. In the interior it may rain only once in several years.

The climate is made oppressive in early summer by the dust-laden *khamsin*, a sandstorm from the south that blows intermittently and may continue for days, with accompanying winds up to 90 mph (145 kph).

Climate & Weather

Mean Temperature
Cairo January 45°F to 85°F
Cairo July 71°F to 96°F
Interior 100°F to 110°F
Average Rainfall: Coastal Areas 8 in
Cairo 1 in
Interior: 0 in

POPULATION

Population Indicators

Total Population: 1999 64,560,000
World Rank: 15th
Density per sq mi: 167.6 per sq km 64.7
% of annual growth (1994–99): 2.1
Male %: 51.2
Female %: 48.8
Urban %: 44.6
Age Distribution: % 0–14: 36.9
15–29: 28.3
30–44: 18.4
45–59: 10.6
60–74: 4.9
75 and over: 0.9
Population 2020: 88,701,000
Birth Rate per 1,000: 27.8
Death Rate per 1,000: 8.6
Population Doubling Time (years): 37
Infant Mortality Rate per 1,000 live births: 71.0
Rate of Natural Increase per 1,000: 19.2
Total Fertility Rate: 3.5
Expectation of Life (years): Males 65.4
Females 69.5
Marriage Rate per 1,000: 83
Divorce Rate per 1,000: —
Total Number of Households: 9,733,000
Average Size of Households: 4.9
% of Illegitimate Children: 0.0
Induced Abortions: —
Rate per 100 live births: —

ETHNIC COMPOSITION

Egypt has remained ethnically homogeneous, with native Egyptians constituting over 90 percent of the population. This distinct ethnicity has been one of the strengths of the Egyptian nation.

The major ethnic minorities, who form about 10 percent of the population, are Bedouin Arabs, Nubians, Greeks, Italians, and Maltese, though none of these communities are numerically significant. Of these, the

Bedouins and Nubians are being progressively assimilated into the native population.

LANGUAGES

Arabic is the official language and the language universally spoken by Egyptians. Though the government officially favors modern Arabic, colloquial Arabic in its Egyptian form is widely used in the media and in many universities. The most important minority languages are Coptic and Nubian. Coptic, the ancient language of pharaonic Egypt, ceased to be a spoken language after the Arab invasion of the seventh century, but it survives in the liturgy of the Copts. A few thousand Berber tribespeople speak Berber, while the Arabic-speaking Nubians still retain Nubian as their mother tongue.

Both the English and French languages declined during the Nasser era (1954–70) when all Western influences became anathema. However, both English and French have remained popular, particularly among educated Egyptians.

Principal Languages and Their Speakers

Arabic	63,790,000
Other	770,000

RELIGIONS

Islam in its Sunni form is the official religion of Egypt and the religion of approximately 89 percent of the population. The power of Islam in Egypt is symbolized by the mosque and the University of al-Azhar, considered the oldest existing university and the most influential center of Islamic learning. Because of Islam's hold on the people, the government often seeks to enlist the aid of religion in furthering its programs and exercises considerable control over religious affairs. Public expressions of piety and participation in Friday communal prayers by public leaders are accepted means of eliciting popular support. However, presidents Nasser, Sadat, and Mubarak found themselves opposed by the fundamentalist Muslim Brotherhood, which continues to be the most serious threat to the regime.

The largest religious minority is the Coptic Christian community, constituting about 4 percent of the population. The Copts are descendants of ancient Egyptians who were Christianized in the early centuries of the Christian era. In the fifth century the Coptic Church seceded from the main body of orthodoxy at Constantinople and joined the Monophysite faith. The position of Coptic Christians in Egyptian society has become more difficult in recent decades. The Copts charge with justification that they are persecuted by Muslim extremists bent on exterminating all non-Muslims in the Arab world. President Mubarak has publicly emphasized the full equality of Copts and other religious minorities with Muslims. The government also has made clear that Egypt, its Islamic character notwithstanding, remains a secular state governed by civil law based on the Napoleonic Code. Nevertheless, the Copts consider themselves victims of discrimination as well as overt persecution. As evidence they cite that all top civil service posts are held by Muslims, as are nearly all senior diplomatic positions and heads of universities.

Religious Affiliations

Sunni Muslim	57,460,000
Coptic Orthodox	6,460,000
Protestant	640,000

HISTORICAL BACKGROUND

Egypt has the oldest recorded history of any country outside China and India. It was ruled from around 3400 B.C. by many dynasties of pharaohs who presided over a great civilization and erected majestic monuments. As the power of the pharaohs waned, the country was periodically conquered by invaders, including the Assyrians and the Persians. In 332 B.C. Alexander the Great of Macedonia invaded Egypt and established the dynasty of the Ptolemies who ruled Egypt from 323 B.C. to 30 B.C. The best known ruler of this dynasty was Queen Cleopatra who was defeated along with her lover Mark Antony at the Battle of Actium in 31 B.C. by Octavius, later Emperor Augustus. Egypt became fully Christian around the third century. After the official division of the Roman Empire under Constantine II around 340, Egypt became part of the Eastern Empire, or Byzantium. In 639–42, Muslim hordes from Arabia conquered Egypt and during the next several centuries completely Arabized and Islamized it.

The British, who came in 1882 and departed in 1922, were the last of many foreign rulers. The British were never really interested in colonizing Egypt but only in securing their passage through the Suez. British control was nominal and indirect, though it remained until the end of World War II, with a true ending not written until Britain's debacle in the Suez invasion of 1956. French legal and educational traditions proved more durable in Egypt than those of Britain, and Western culture is even now filtered into Egypt through the medium of French.

Egypt's modern history began with a military coup in July 1952, which toppled King Farouk. The revolt of young officers was led by Maj. Gen. Muhammad Nagib. Farouk officially abdicated in June 1953. A republic was established under Col. Gamal Abdel Nasser, who was made prime minister in 1954 and president in June 1956. Nasser heralded Arab nationalism and unity as well as ardent opposition to Israel. Internally, he fostered social and economic change and strove to end British influence.

Unable to obtain satisfactory assistance from the West, in 1955 Nasser accepted military and other forms of aid from the Soviet Union. The next year Egypt nationalized the Suez Canal. As a result, Britain, France, and Israel invaded Egypt in October but withdrew under pressure from the superpowers and the United Nations. On February 1, 1958, Egypt and Syria formed the United Arab Republic (UAR) under Nasser's leadership, although Syria reasserted its independence in 1961.

Egypt suffered heavy losses in the Six-Day War with Israel in June 1967, including the occupation by Israel of the Sinai Peninsula. This defeat led to greater Egyptian reliance on the Soviet Union and the overhaul of both state machinery and the ruling Arab Socialist Union Party.

The death of Nasser in September 1970 was a turning point in recent Egyptian history. Power was transferred to Vice President Anwar al-Sadat, who eventually made peace with Israel and moved Egypt into the Western orbit. Yet, Sadat was forced to reach for Soviet aid in preparation for renewed warfare with Israel. Egypt and Syria fought Israel for 18 days in October 1973. After initial Egyptian advances, Israel was gaining ground when U.S. secretary of state Henry Kissinger arranged a cease-fire. Forces on both sides were disengaged east of the Suez Canal. Sadat was designated for a second six-year term as president in 1976, and the following year made a dramatic visit to Jerusalem seeking a settlement with Israel.

In March 1979, Egypt's new peace cabinet approved the peace treaty with Israel, which called for gradual return of the Sinai Peninsula to Egypt and which also was ratified in a public referendum. By 1981 Egypt relied heavily on the United States for military and economic support. In September 1981, facing growing domestic unrest, the government jailed about 1,000 dissidents, including Muslim fundamentalists, journalists, and Nasserites. On October 6, 1981, Sadat was assassinated by Muslim militants. The People's Assembly immediately nominated Vice President Muhammad Hosni Mubarak as Egypt's new president.

The years following 1981 were marked by growing domestic instability due to economic problems and the emerging strength of Muslim fundamentalism. Despite these challenges, Mubarak remained firmly in control. Egypt also reestablished relations with other Arab states following its isolation and condemnation over the treaty with Israel. Mubarak's diplomatic skill led to the return of the Sinai Peninsula to Egypt in 1982. President Mubarak was reelected to a second term as president in October 1987 and to a third term in 1993.

Egypt's new ties with the United States were strengthened during the Persian Gulf War in 1991. Although Mubarak first tried to bring about an Arab diplomatic solution, he later sent 40,000 Egyptian troops as part of a multinational force led by the United States in defense of Saudi Arabia.

In the 1990s, several Muslim extremist groups carried out bombings and attacks on tourists to weaken the Mubarak government, seeking a government and society in Egypt ruled strictly according to Islamic doctrine. Mubarak himself narrowly escaped assassination by Muslim fundamentalists during a visit to Ethiopia in 1995. Egyptian security forces carried out raids against Islamic militants, but the challenge of Muslim fundamentalism remained.

In 1996 Kamal Ahmed al-Ganzouri was named prime minister and he launched what was widely perceived as economic liberalization. His new cabinet emphasized Egypt's role as an advocate for stability and peace in the Middle East. In 2000 Mubarak again tried to broker peace between Israel and the Palestinians, but escalating violence toward the end of the year found him espousing increasingly hostile positions toward Israel. In 2001 he condemned U.S. air raids against Iraq. Later that year, Mubarak supported the U.S. campaign against terrorism that was prompted by terrorist attacks in New York City and Washington, D.C., on September 11, 2001.

CONSTITUTION

Egypt's government is based on the constitution of 1971, which proclaims Egypt as an Arab republic with a democratic and socialist system derived from the country's historical heritage and the spirit of Islam. The constitution provides for a strong executive. Executive authority is vested in the president, the head of state, who is nominated by at least one-third of the members of the People's Assembly, approved by at least two-thirds, and elected by popular referendum. The president serves a six-year term, but may be reelected for subsequent terms. The president may take emergency measures in the interests of the state and can call a national referendum on "matters of supreme interest." The president also appoints the prime minister and other ministers.

The Council of Ministers, described as "the government" in the constitution, is the supreme executive organ of the state. It consists of the prime minister, the head of government, deputy prime ministers, ministers, and deputy ministers. The principle of ministerial responsibility to the legislature is constitutionally established, and the assembly may pass a no-confidence vote against the prime minister.

After President Sadat's assassination in October 1981, a state of emergency was proclaimed. It was extended by presidential decree in successive years, and renewed by President Mubarak in 1992. Under these emergency laws designed to combat civil unrest and terrorism, certain constitutional safeguards that protect civil and political liberties can be suspended.

LOCAL GOVERNMENT

Local government consists of three levels of jurisdiction: governorates, towns, and villages. In 1999 there were

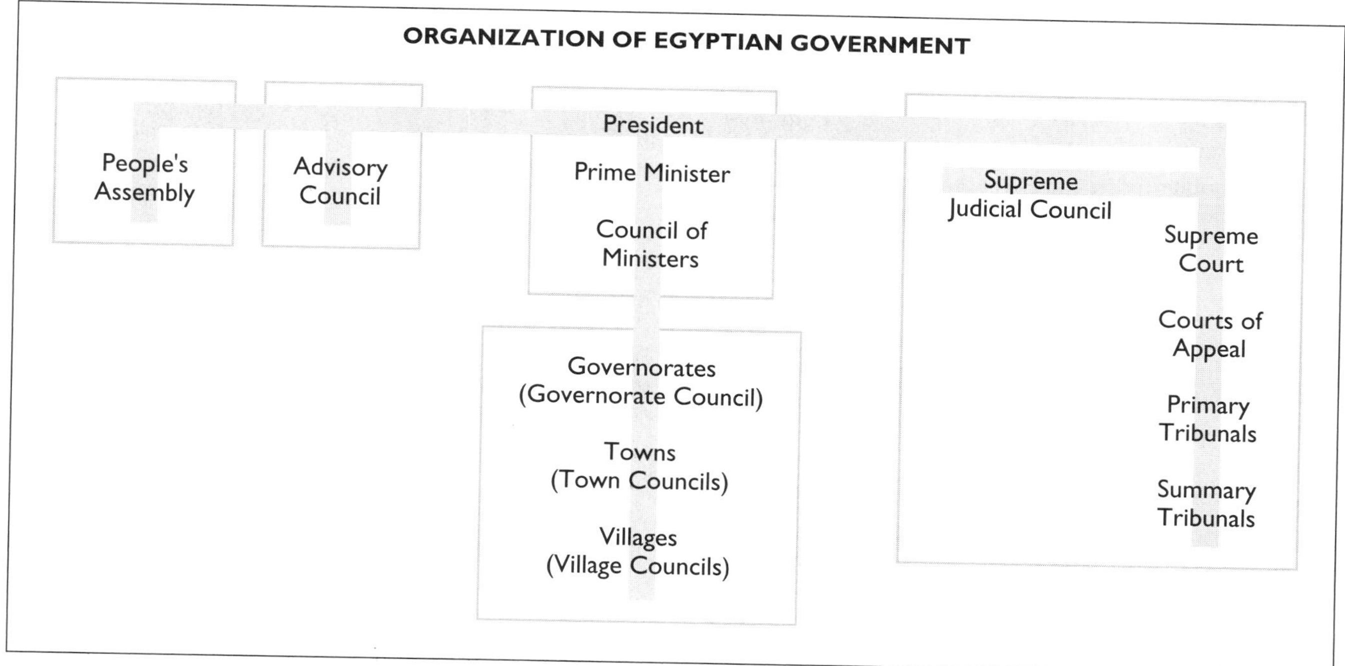

26 governorates: Ad-Daqahliyah, Al-Bahr al-Ahmar, Al-Buhayrah, Al-Gharbiyah, Al-Iskandariyah, Al-Jizah, Al Minufiyah, Al Minya, Al Qahirah, Al-Qalyubiyah, Al-Wadi al-Jadid, Ash-Sharqiyah, As-Suways (Suez), Aswan, Asyut, Bani Suwayf, Bur Sa'id. Dumyat, Janub Sina', Kafr ash Shaykh, Matruh, Qina, Shamal Sina', and Suhaj.

Each governorate is administered by a governor, who is both the chief regional executive and the representative of the central government. Local self-government consists of governorate councils, town councils, and village councils. An appointed chief executive is the head of the council at every level. All councils also are subject to national executive guidance and control. Local councils are composed of three types of members: nominated members (usually technical or professional persons), elected members chosen and designated by the National Democratic Party, and ex officio members assigned by appropriate ministries. All elected and nominated members have terms of four years. The financial resources of the local councils include local property and land taxes, subsidies from the central government, and revenues from a joint fund.

Local Government

Principal administrative divisions, capitals, area, population

Area and population

Regions Governorates	Capitals	area sq mi	sq km	population 1996 estimates
Frontier				
Al-Bahr al-Ahmar	Al-Ghurdaqah	78,643	203,685	155,695
Janub Sina	At-Tur	12,796	33,140	54,495
Matruh	Marsa Matruh	81,897	212,112	211,866
Shamal Sina	Al-Arish	10,646	27,574	252,750
Al-Wadi al-Jadid	Al-Kharijah	145,369	378,505	141,737
Lower Egypt				
Al-Buhayrah	Damanhur	3,911	10,130	3,981,209
Ad-Daqahliyah	Al-Mansurah	1,340	3,471	4,223,655
Dumyat	Dumyat	227	589	914,614
Al-Gharbiyah	Tanja	750	1,942	3,404,827
Al-Isma iliyah (Ismailla)	—	557	1,442	715,009
Kafr ash-Shaykh	Kafr ash-Shaykh	1,327	3,437	2,222,290
Al-Minufiyah	Shibin al-Kawm	592	1,532	2,758,499
Al-Qalyubiyah	Banha	387	1,001	3,302,860
Ash-Shanqiyah	Az-Zaqaziq	1,614	4,180	4,287,848
Upper Egypt				
Aswan	Aswan	262	679	973,671
Asyūt	Asyut	600	1,553	2,802,185
Bani Suwayt	Bani Suwayt	510	1,322	1,860,180
Al-Fayyum	Al-Fayyum	705	1,827	1,989,881
Al-Jizah	Al-Jizah	32,878	85,153	4,779,865
Al-Minya	Al-Minya	873	2,262	3,308,875
Quina	Quina	715	1,851	2,441,420
Sawhaj	Sawhaj	597	1,547	3,125,000
Urban				
Bur Sa'id (Port Said)	—	28	72	469,533
Al-Iskandariyah (Alexandria)	—	1,034	2,679	3,328,196
Al-Qahirah (Cairo)	—	83	214	6,789,497
Al-Uqsur (Luxor)	—	2	2	360,503
As-Suways (Suez)	—	6,888	17,840	417,610
TOTAL		385,229	997,739	59,274,400

PARLIAMENT

The national legislative is called the People's Assembly (Majlis al-Shaa'ab), a unicameral body elected for five-year terms. It consists of 454 members, 444 elected by popular vote and 10 members appointed by the president. The legislative powers are circumscribed by the fact that the president has the right to rule by decree and to veto a bill passed by the Assembly. The Assembly functions primarily as a policy-approving rather than as a policy-initiating body.

Under the constitution of 1971, suffrage is universal over age 18. Voting is specified as a national duty, and failure to vote entails a fine. Presidential elections occur every six years, in the form of a plebiscite of approval in which only one candidate is presented to the electorate. The president also appoints the prime minister and other ministers. There is also the Advisory Council, or Majlis al-Shura, which serves only in a consultative role. Its 264 members serve for six-year terms; 176 are elected by popular vote, 88 are appointed by the president.

POLITICAL PARTIES

Egypt has been a virtual one-party state since the 1952 revolution and has become increasingly intolerant of opposition under the Mubarak administration. The ruling party is the National Democratic Party (NDP), founded by President Sadat in 1978. Few of the opposition parties have significant legislative representation and most of them have no legal standing either. Opposition parties generally tend to boycott elections because of electoral laws and practices designed to work against them. There are a number of clandestine Muslim fundamentalist groups working outside the political system. The most important of these groups is the Muslim Brotherhood.

Political Parties

National Democratic Party, 1978
New Wafd Party, 1978
Socialist Labor Party, 1978
Liberal Socialist Party, 1976
National Progressive Unionist Party, 1976
National Party
Party of Social and Democratic Construction
Green Party, 1990
There are a number of illegal Muslim fundamentalist terrorist groups including
- Muslim Brotherhood, 1928
- Holy War
- Islamic Group
- Egypt's Revolution

Political Parties: Strength in Parliament Most Recent Elections

After elections to the current Assembly held October 18, October 29, and November 8, 2000, the distribution of seats (1995 results in parentheses) was as follows: the National Democratic Party (NDP), 388 (317); the New Wafd Party 7 (6); the National Progressive Unionist Party 6 (5); the Liberal Socialist Party 1 (1); the Nasserist Party, 3 (1); and independents, 37 (114). Ten members were appointed by the president and two seats are currently vacant.

LEGAL SYSTEM

The legal system of Egypt is based on Islamic law, the Napoleonic Code, and English common law. Religious courts were abolished in 1956 and the entire court system was secularized and unified.

Courts are divided into four levels of jurisdiction. There are summary tribunals in each district, primary tribunals in each governorate, six courts of appeal, and the Supreme Court of Appeals at Cairo, with a chief justice, four deputy justices, and 36 justices. The Supreme Judicial Council guarantees the independence and integrity of the courts and supervises the whole judicial system.

Arrested persons have the right of habeas corpus, and there is a system of bail. Constitutional and legal safeguards of due process in the arrest and pretrial custody stages are generally observed. Arrests occur openly and with warrants, and the accused are brought before an independent judiciary. Exceptions to these procedures have sometimes occurred during the state of emergency laws enacted in the 1980s and 1990s following President Sadat's assassination.

Egyptian law provides for public trial and equal treatment before the law. Persons accused of espionage, plotting to overthrow the government, or similar crimes, however, are tried in state security courts, often in closed proceedings. Defendants are permitted to be present during these proceedings and are represented by lawyers conducting an active defense.

Under President Mubarak the judiciary enjoys a relatively large measure of independence.

Article 2 of the constitution states that Islamic jurisprudence is the principal source of law. However, application of Islamic law is limited to the so-called family status courts, which have jurisdiction over such matters as divorce and inheritance for Muslims.

LAW ENFORCEMENT

Law Enforcement

Offenses reported to the police per 100,000: 3,693
- Murder: 1.6
- Assault: 0.7
- Burglary: —
- Automobile Theft: 3.1
- Population per Police officer: 580

Death Penalty: Yes

HUMAN RIGHTS

Egypt is a republic with a strong authoritarian presidency, and the country's political and economic structures have been shaped largely by the ideological bent of the president. President Mubarak tended to use his power and influence with caution. However, he extended in 1994 the state of emergency decreed following Sadat's assassination in 1981 in order to counter "the regrettable terrorist acts in the country, including the attacks on tourists, assassination of officials, bombing of banks, and the treacherous killing of innocent civilians, police officers, and police commanders." The most significant political opposition to Mubarak's regime has been the powerful Muslim Brotherhood, which he allowed to engage in limited political activity in his first two terms but moved against more aggressively in the latter 1990s.

The goal of extremist Muslim groups' terrorist campaigns is the establishment of a fundamentalist Islamic state in Egypt. During the 1990s, Egyptian security forces and terrorist groups continued violent exchanges, and the government's crackdown against terrorism restricted many basic rights.

FOREIGN POLICY

Egypt has strengthened its ties with the Arab world, at the same time forging a closer relationship with the West, particularly the United States. Egypt was readmitted to the Arab League in 1989 and league headquarters returned to Cairo from Tunis. Mubarak served as head of the Organization of African Unity (OAU) in 1989 and 1993, consolidating his country's position in that key group. Egypt also took a prominent role in the Persian Gulf War of 1991, firmly supporting the United States by sending 40,000 Egyptian troops against Iraq, the second-largest army in the coalition forces.

Egypt continued to play a leading role in Middle East affairs during the 1990s, working actively in the peace process negotiations. It supported the 1994 Jordan–Israel peace treaty and other initiatives. Mubarak met with Israeli leaders and worked with the United States to improve relationships between the countries of the Middle East.

DEFENSE

Egypt's defense structure is headed by the president of the republic, who also is the military governor-general and supreme commander. In addition, the president presides over the National Defense Council, the senior policy body of the government in military affairs. Under the president are the minister of war and a deputy commander in chief, who also functions as the chief of staff and the commander of the army.

Military manpower is provided by compulsory conscription of adult males between the ages of 18 and 30 for up to 36 months of service. The total strength of the armed forces in the early 1990s was about 430,000. Egypt's defense spending was $3.28 billion, or about 8.2 percent of the country's gross domestic product (GDP).

Military Indicators

Total Active Duty Personnel: 450,000
Military Manpower per 1,000: 7.2
Military Expenditures $: 2.653 billion
as % of GNP: 5.7
per capita $: 43
as % of central government expenditures: 13.7

Arms Imports $: 1,900 million
Arms Exports $: 0

ECONOMY

Egypt's economy is one of state capitalism, with increasing emphasis on the private sector. Agriculture remains the largest sector of the economy, involving 30.5 percent of Egypt's labor force, though it accounts for only 15 percent of the country's GDP. Industry, including manufacturing, mining, construction, and power, is the second largest sector and accounts for 31 percent of GDP.

By the late 1980s Egypt faced serious population pressure on its limited resources. Only 5.2 percent of its land is arable, the birth rate of 27.8 per 1,000 is among the highest in the world, and Egypt must import three-fifths of its food. The collapse of world oil prices in the 1980s and the cost of the Persian Gulf War posed a crisis for the Egyptian economy as its balance of payments deficit expanded rapidly.

To meet the economic crisis, Egypt began large-scale economic reforms, with the support of the International Monetary Fund (IMF). By the mid-1990s, the government had reduced budget deficits, curtailed inflation, ended many government subsidies, and built up foreign reserves. New business legislation marked the government's new policy toward privatizing industry and liberalizing trade and investment. This shift toward a more market-oriented economy has brought increased foreign investment.

The massacre of tourists at Luxor in 1997 by Muslim extremists marked a setback given tourism's key role in the economy. However, government action to counter terrorism and insure public safety led to a revival of foreign visitors within a short period.

By mid-1998, however, the pace of structural reform slackened, and lower combined hard-currency earnings resulted in pressure on the Egyptian pound and sporadic U.S. dollar shortages. Monetary pressures have since eased, with the 1999–2000 higher oil prices, a rebound in tourism, and a series of minidevaluations of the pound. The development of a gas export market is a major plus factor in future growth. In 2001, the attacks of September 11 in New York City and Washington, D.C., and the ensuing war in Afghanistan dealt a heavy blow to Egypt's tourist industry.

Principal Economic Indicators

Gross National Product: $72.164 billion
GNP per capita: $1,200
GNP Average Annual Growth Rate (1990–97)%: 2.8
GNP per capita Average Annual Growth Rate (1990–97)%: 0.8
Origin of Gross Domestic Product %
- Agriculture: 15
- Mining: —
- Manufacturing: 25
- Construction: 5
- Public Utilities: 2
- Transportation and Communications: 10
- Trade: 17
- Financial Services: 5
- Other Services: 7
- Government: 7

Gross Domestic Product by Type of Expenditure %
- Private Consumption: 75
- Government Consumption: 10
- Gross Domestic Investment: 20
- Foreign Trade: Exports: 23
  Imports: −28

% of Income Received by Poorest 20%: 8.7
% of Income Received by Richest 10%: 26.7

Price and earnings indexes (1995 = 100)

	1992	1993	1994	1995	1996	1997	1998
Consumer price index	71.3	79.9	86.4	100.0	108.3	112.8	114.4
Earnings index	72.7	86.4	93.2	100.0	—	—	—

Finance

National Currency: Egyptian Pound (£E)
Exchange Rate: $1 = £E 3.4
Money Supply Stock in National Currency billion: 44,521
M1 per capita: 720
Central Bank Discount Rate %: 12.00
Total External Debt $million: 30,500
Debt Service Ratio %: 7.3

Balance of Payments $million: −711
International Reserves SDRs million: 13,260
Ratio of External Debt to Total Reserves: 1.9

Average Annual Rate of Inflation/Consumer Price Index
Growth Rate %: 4.9

Official Development Assistance

ODA $: 1.713 billion
- as % of GNP: 2.2
- per capita: $ 31
- Foreign Direct Investment $million: 1,076

Central Government Revenues and Expenditures

Fiscal Year: 1 July–30 June
Revenues $million: 19,200
Expenditures $million: 19,800
Budget Deficit $: 600 million
Tax Revenues as % of GDP: 16.6
Highest Tax Bracket %
- Individual: 32
- Corporate: 40

Employment and Labor

Economically Active Population: 17,572,000
Female Participation Rate %: 23.0
Activity Rate %: 30.4
Labor by Sector: %
- Agriculture, Forestry, Fishing: 30.5
- Manufacturing, Mining: 12.9
- Construction: 5.9
- Transportation and Communications: 4.8
- Trade, Hotels, and Restaurants: 9.0
- Finance, Insurance, Real Estate: 1.7
- Public Administration, Defense: —
- Services: 22.3

Unemployment %: 9.4

Agriculture

Agriculture's Share of GDP %: 15
Average Annual Rate of Growth (1965–98)%: 2.8
Number of Farms 000: 3,896
Average Size of Farm ha: 0.7
Number of Tractors per 1,000 hectares: 25.1
Irrigation, % of Farms having: 112
Artificial Fertilizer kg/hectare: 384
Total Farmland as % of land area: 5.2
Livestock: Cattle 000: 3,022
- Sheep 000: 4,300
- Hogs 000: 29
- Chickens 000: 86,000

Forests: Production of Roundwood (000 cubic meters): 2,698
Fisheries: Total Catch tons 000: 305.7

Mining

% of GDP: 9.8
Value of Mineral Production $million: 5,151.3

Manufacturing

Value Added $million: 5,486
Industrial Production Growth Rate %:

Energy

Commercial Energy Production metric tons of oil equivalent 000: 57,997
Commercial Energy Consumption metric tons of oil equivalent 000: 39,581
Commercial Energy Consumption per capita kg: 656
Average Annual Growth Rate 1980–97%: 2.5
Net Energy Imports % of use: −47
Electricity Installed Capacity kW 000: 16,015
- Production kW-hr million: 48,664

Coal Reserves tons million: 53
- Production tons 000: —

Natural Gas Proven Reserves cubic meters billion: 576
- Production cubic meters million: 12,333

Crude Petroleum Reserves barrels million: 3,696
Production barrels million: 337
Consumption barrels million: 192
Refinery Capacity barrels per day 000: 546
Pipelines Length km: 1,767

Foreign Trade

Imports $million: 11,739.0
Exports $million: 3,441.1
Export Volume % Annual Growth Rate (1990–97): 0.7
Import Volume % Annual Growth Rate (1990–97): 5.1
Balance of Trade $

Balance of trade (current prices)

	1992	1993	1994	1995	1996	1997
U.S.						
$ 000,000	−5,242	−5,959	−6,271	−8,314	−9,505	−9,293
% of total	46.2%	56.9%	49.2%	54.6%	57.3%	54.2%

Major Trading Partners

	Imports	Exports
European Union %	38.9	45.8
United States %	18.8	15.2
Eastern Europe %	7.1	2.7
Japan %	2.7	1.3
Others %	32.5	35.0

Transportation

Roads Total Length mi: 36,000 km 58,000
Paved %: 78
Automobiles: 1,280,000
Trucks and Buses: 423,300
Persons per vehicle: 35
Railroad; Track Length mi: 2,989 km 4,810
Passenger-mi million: 29,821
Freight-mi million: 1,600
Merchant Marine: No. of Vessels: 444
Total Deadweight Tonnage 000: 1,685.2
International Cargo Loaded tons 000: 14,808
International Cargo Off-loaded tons 000: 22,860
Airports with Scheduled Flights: 11
Traffic: Passenger-mi million: 5,432
Freight-mi million: 136
Length of Canals mi: 2,175 km 3,500

Tourism

Number of Tourists to 000: 3,213
Number of Tourists from 000: 2,921
Tourist Receipts $million: 2,800
Tourist Expenditures $million: 1,278

Communications

Telephones 000: 2,716
Cost of Local Calls 3 mins: $0
Cellular Telephones 000: 14
Fax Machines 000: 3.5
Personal Computers 000: 235
Internet Hosts per million persons: 10
Mail: Post Offices: 7,197
Pieces of Mail Handled million: 309
Pieces of Mail Handled per person: 5.2

EDUCATION

Education is, in principle, universal, free, and compulsory for five years between the ages of six and 13. Schooling consists of six years of primary school, three years of preparatory school, and three years of secondary school. Higher education is provided by state universities and technical colleges. Al-Azhar University, founded in 970 at Cairo, enrolls about 90,000 students.

Education

Literacy Rate %: 51.4
Male %: 63.6
Female %: 38.8
First Level: Primary schools: 16,188
Teachers: 302,916
Students: 7,470,437
Student-Teacher Ratio: 24.7
Net Enrollment Ratio: 89
Second Level: Secondary Schools: 7,307
Teachers: 235,313
Students: 4,242,245
Student-Teacher Ratio: 24.7
Net Enrollment Ratio: 65

Vocational Level: Schools: 1,351
Students: 1,900,406

Third Level: Institutions: 125
Teachers: 38,828
Students: 696,988
Student-Ratio Level: —
Gross Enrollment Ratio: 18.1
Students per 100,000: 1,674
% of Population Age 25 and over with Postsecondary Education: 4.6

Public Expenditure on Education as % of GDP: 5.6

SCIENCE AND TECHNOLOGY

Science and Technology

Scientists and Engineers in R&D per 1 million persons: 459
Expenditures in R&D as % of GDP: 0.22
High-Tech Exports $: 2 million
Patent Applications by Residents: 504

MEDIA

The media are entirely state controlled. Nevertheless, Cairo is the largest publishing center in the Middle East and the media capital of the Arab world. *Al-Ahram* is the country's leading newspaper.

Media

Daily Newspapers: 17
Total Circulation 000: 3,949
Circulation per 1,000: 64
Books Published: 3,108
Magazines: 266
Radio Receivers 000: 16,450
per 1,000: 265
Television sets 000: 7,400
per 1,000: 126

MOST IMPORTANT MEDIA:

Press. The following are Cairo dailies published in Arabic, unless otherwise noted: *al-Ahram* (1,000,000 daily, 1,200,000 Friday), semiofficial; *al-Akhbar* (800,000), Saturday edition published as *Akhbar al-Yawm* (1,100,000); *al-Jumhuriyah* (650,000), semi-official; *al-Misaa*; *Le Journal d'Egypte* (72,000), in French; *Egyptian Gazette* (36,000), in English; *Le Progrès Egyptien* (22,000), in French; *al-Hayat; al-Destour*, independent weekly; and *al-Usbu*, independent "nationalist" weekly. Party organs include the Socialist Labor weekly *al-Shaab* (50,000); the Liberal Socialist weekly *al-Akrar*; the National Progressive Unionist weekly *al-Ahali; al-Wafd*, NWP daily; *Shabab Beladi*, NDP weekly; and *The Greens* (*al-Khudr*).

News agencies. The domestic agency is the Middle East News Agency—MENA (Wakalat al-Anba ash-Sharq al-Awsat). In addition, numerous foreign bureaus maintain offices at Cairo.

Radio and television. The Egyptian Radio and Television Union (ERTU) operates numerous radio stations broadcasting in Arabic and other languages, and some three dozen television stations transmitting in two programs. Commercial radio service is offered by Middle East Radio (Idha'at ash-Sharq al-Awsat).

The first Egyptian communications satellite was launched by the European Space Agency in 1998; some 80 channels were expected to be broadcast regionally by the satellite, known as "Nilesat," under the control of the ERTU.

CULTURE

Cultural Indicators

Public Libraries
Number: 352
Volumes: 3,782,000
Registered borrowers: —
Museums
Number: 34
Annual Attendance: 2,076,000
Cinema
Production of Long Films: 72
Number of Cinemas: 138
Seating Capacity: 106,000
Annual Attendance: 12.9 million
Annual Attendance per capita: 0.2

STATUS OF WOMEN

By law and in many respects in practice, women are granted equality. Women work outside the home and serve in the military. They are represented in the professions, including medicine, law, and education, and they serve in the People's Assembly and the cabinet. Labor laws guarantee women equal pay for equal work in the public sector, and women constitute 17 percent of business owners. Women are free to travel internally and abroad, though a married woman must have her husband's permission to obtain a passport. In general, social pressures and the resurgent Islamic fundamentalist trend restrict women's rights in many ways. Moreover, in rural areas, prevailing cultural values curtail many freedoms and women often occupy a subordinate role in society there.

Women

Gender Empowerment Measure: 88
Seats Held in Parliament by Women %: 2.0
Female Administrators and Managers %: 11.5
Female Professional and Technical Workers %: 29.5
Women's Share of Earned Income %: 25
Women in Government %: 2

HEALTH, FOOD, AND NUTRITION

Health

Number of Physicians: 129,000
Number of Dentists: 15,150
Number of Nurses: —
Number of Pharmacists: 34,700
Population per Physician: 472
Number of Hospitals: 6,418
Hospital Beds per 10,000: 19
Hospital Bed Occupancy Rate: —
Infant Mortality Rate per 1,000 live births: 70
Maternal Mortality Rate per 100,000 live births: 170
Total Health Expenditures as % of GDP: 2.61
Health Expenditures per capita $:28
HIV Infected % of adults: 0.03
Cigarette Consumption per smoker per year: —
% of Smokers: Male: —
Female: —
Access to Safe Water %: 84

Food and Nutrition

Food Supply as % of FAO Requirements: 133
% of Consumption Expenditures on Food: 50.2
Daily Available Calories per capita: 3,327
% of Total Calories derived from:
Cereals: 66.3
Potatoes, cassava: 1.6
Meat, poultry: 2.4
Fish: 0.4
Eggs, milk: 1.8
Fruits, vegetables: 6.2
Fats, oils: 7.7

ENVIRONMENT

Although Egypt has passed laws to protect its unique ecosystems, plants, and animals, environmental issues are secondary to the needs of a growing population and pressure for increased food production. Irrigating farmland has caused increasing soil salinization, estimated to affect 28 percent of all agricultural areas. In addition, urban sprawl and windblown sand continue to remove arable soil from use.

Water pollution is a growing environmental threat, brought about by runoff of salinized drainage water from irrigated areas, the use of farm pesticides, and lack of adequate sewage disposal. Industrial and mining wastes also contribute to the problem. Oil pollution from off-shore oil rigs and pipelines and coastal shipping is a significant threat to Egypt's coral reefs, fisheries, and tourist beaches.

Environment

Forest Area sq km: 0
Average Annual Deforestation sq km: 0
Nationally Protected Areas as % of Total Land Area: 0.8
Freshwater Access cubic meters per capita: 949
Emissions of Organic Water Pollutants kg per day: 34,168
CO_2 Emissions per capita ton: 1.7

CHRONOLOGY

1946 British troops withdraw except from the Suez Canal Zone.
1952 Farouk is overthrown by the army in a bloodless coup and is exiled.
1953 Egypt is declared a republic under General Neguib as president.
1956 Neguib is replaced by General Gamal Abdel Nasser. Nasser announces nationalization of the Suez Canal. France, Britain, and Israel attack Egypt but are forced to withdraw following U.S. intervention.
1958 Egypt and Syria agree to a short-lived union as the United Arab Republic.
1967 Six-Day War with Israel ends in Arab defeat and Israeli occupation of Sinai and Gaza Strip.
1970 Nasser dies and is succeeded as president by Anwar Sadat.
1973 In the Yom Kippur War, Egypt attempts unsuccessfully to retake territory lost to Israel in Six-Day War.
1978–79 Camp David talks under the mediation of U.S. President Jimmy Carter results in historic peace treaty with Israel, which is immediately denounced by the Arab League. Egypt is expelled from the Arab League.
1981 Sadat is assassinated by Islamic Fundamentalists. Hosni Mubarak, vice president, assumes presidency.
1987 Mubarak is reelected president.
1989 Egypt rejoins the Arab League.
1993 Mubarak is reelected president.
1995 Mubarak is the target of an assassination attempt in Addis Ababa, Ethiopia.
1997 Fifty-eight tourists are killed by gunmen, allegedly from Egypt's Islamic Group, in front of the Temple of Hatshepsut near Luxor.
1999 Mubarak begins his fourth term in office.
2000 The High Court brings to a legal end the common practice of men preventing their wives from traveling abroad. Egypt, Lebanon, and Syria sign an agreement to build a gas pipeline that will transport Egyptian natural gas to Tripoli, Lebanon, and Syria. Another pipeline would carry gas to Turkey and on to European markets. Mubarak recalls Egypt's ambassador to Israel in protest of the deaths of Palestinians at the hands of Israeli police.

BIBLIOGRAPHY

Elkhafif, Mahmoud A. T. *The Egyptian Economy.* New York, 1996.
Juman, Salwas, Salwas Gomma, and Mostafa K. Tolba. *Environmental Policy-Making in Egypt.* Gainseville, Fla. 1997.
Mayfield, James B. *Local Government in Egypt.* Cairo, 1996.
Tripp, Charles, and Roger Owen. *Egypt under Mubarak.* London, 1990.
Vatikiotis, P. J. *The History of Modern Egypt.* Baltimore, Md., 1991.

OFFICIAL PUBLICATIONS

Egypt. *Population, Housing, and Establishment Census, 1986; Statistical Yearbook.*

CONTACT INFORMATION

Embassy of Egypt
3521 International Court NW
Washington, D.C. 20008
Phone: (202) 895-5400 Fax: (202) 244-4319

INTERNET RESOURCES

- Egypt State Information Service http://www.sis.gov.eg
- Egypt's Information Highway http://www.idc.gov.eg.

EL SALVADOR

BASIC FACT SHEET

OFFICIAL NAME:
Republic of El Salvador (República de El Salvador)

ABBREVIATION:
ES

CAPITAL:
San Salvador

HEAD OF STATE & HEAD OF GOVERNMENT:
President Francisco Guillermo Flores Pérez (from 1999)

NATURE OF GOVERNMENT:
Partial democracy

POPULATION:
5,839,000

AREA:
20,935 sq km (8,124 sq mi)

ETHNIC MAJORITY:
Mestizos

LANGUAGES:
Spanish

RELIGIONS:
Roman Catholicism

UNIT OF CURRENCY:
Colón (C.)

NATIONAL FLAG:
Tricolor consisting of a white stripe between two horizontal blue stripes. The national emblem appears in the center of the while stripe.

NATIONAL EMBLEM:
An equilateral triangle in which a red Phrygian liberty cap, crowned by a radiant rainbow, rises from a range of five volcanic peaks bathed by two oceans. A golden nimbus around the cap carries the date 15 September 1821, the date of independence. The triangle is superimposed on a panoply of five national flags, two on either side and one at the apex. The emblem is framed in a circular laurel wreath of seven clusters on each side, both sides ending at the topmost lateral flags, and in an outer ring of golden letters bearing the name of the republic: República de El Salvador en la América Central. Beneath the triangle is the national motto: Dios, Union, Libertad (God, Union, Liberty).

NATIONAL ANTHEM:
"Let Us Proudly Hail the Fatherland."

NATIONAL HOLIDAYS:
September 15 (National Day, Independence Day); January 1 (New Year's Day); May 1 (Labor Day); October 12 (Day of the Race); November 5 (First Call for Independence); December 31 (New Year's Eve); Christian festivals include Holy Week, Christmas, All Souls' Day, and Feast of El Salvador del Mundo.

DATE OF INDEPENDENCE:
September 15, 1821

DATE OF CONSTITUTION:
December 6, 1983

GEOGRAPHICAL FEATURES

El Salvador is the smallest mainland nation in the Western Hemisphere and the only Central American country with no Caribbean coast. It has an area of 21,041 sq km (8,124 sq mi). El Salvador shares its international border of 538 km (334 mi) with two countries: Honduras, 342 km (212 mi) and Guatemala, 203 km (126 mi). The border with Guatemala was established in 1938. The border with Honduras has never been demarcated or surveyed.

In 1992, the International Court of Justice settled the boundary dispute between Honduras and El Salvador, but the border is not yet marked. El Salvador, Honduras, and Nicaragua must still resolve a dispute regarding several islands and maritime rights in the Gulf of Fonseca.

The topography is very mountainous, and the country is also known as the "Land of Volcanoes." Earth-

El Salvador

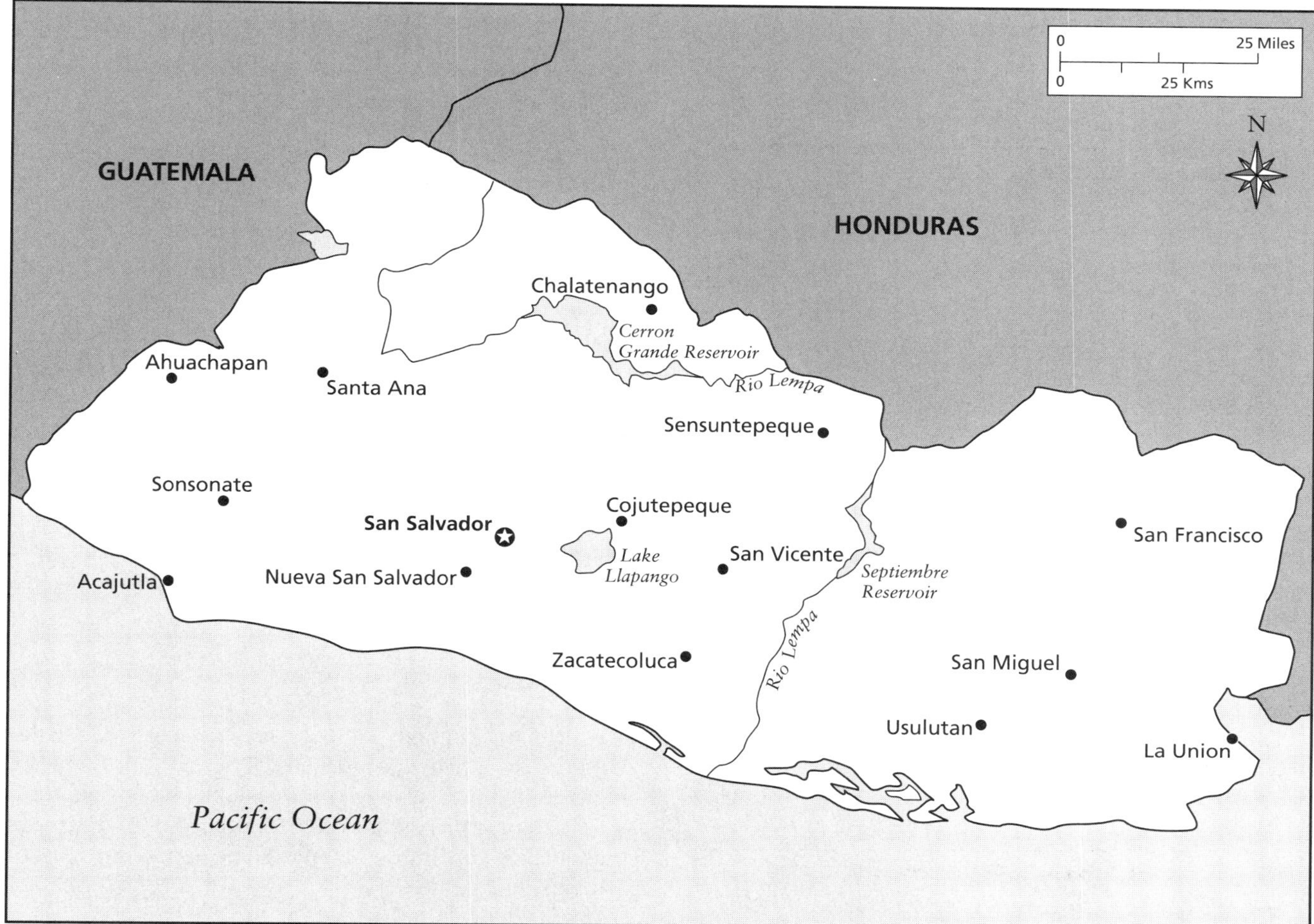

quakes are common, the last severe one occurring in 1986. It has a Pacific coastline of 307 km and a plateau region in the central part of the country. San Salvador, the capital, is divided by two east to west mountain ranges, the Coastal Range and the Cordillera Apeneca, and the country consists of three topographical regions: the southern coastal plain, the northern lowlands, and the central highlands plateau. The southern coastal plain is a narrow, relatively flat belt extending the length of the country from the Guatemalan border to the Gulf of Fonseca. El Salvador also includes the islands of Meanguera, Conehaguita, Martin Perez, Punta Zacate, and Meanguerita. The northern lowlands are formed by the valley of the Lempa River and the Sierra Madre. The central plateau, which runs between the two mountain ranges, is interspersed with mountains and volcanoes, the largest of which is Lamatepec, or Santa Ana (2,385 m, 7,825 ft). Other volcanoes include San Vicente, or Chichoutepec; San Miguel, or Chaparrastique; San Salvador; and Izalco, which is known as the lighthouse of the Pacific because of its brilliant flares visible for hundreds of miles at sea.

El Salvador is located in a very unstable geological zone and is subject to frequent earthquakes. San Salvador was completely destroyed by an earthquake in 1854 and was struck again in 1919, 1965, and 1986, causing destruction and loss of life.

Nearly 150 rivers flow across the country into the Pacific Ocean, but none of them is navigable except the Lempa (260 km, 162 mi). There are three lakes, all noted for their scenic beauty and popular with tourists: Lake Guija, near the Guatemalan border; Lake Coatepeque; and Lake Llopango, near San Salvador. The latter is in the crater of an old volcano.

Geography

Area sq km: 21,041 sq mi 8,124
World Rank: 151st
Land Boundaries, km: Guatemala 203; Honduras 342
Coastline, km: 307
Elevation Extremes meters
 Lowest: Pacific Ocean 0
 Highest: Cerro El Pital 2,730

(continued)

Land Use % Arable land: 27
Permanent Crops: 8
Permanent Pastures: 29
Forest and Woodland: 5
Other: 31

Population of Principal Cities (1992; MU)

Apopa	100,763
Delgado	104,790
Mejicanos	145,000
Nueva San Salvador	116,575
San Miguel	182,817
San Salvador	422,570
Santa Ana	202,337
Soyapango	251,811

CLIMATE AND WEATHER

El Salvador is located just within the tropic of Cancer, at 14° north of the equator. The climate is warm rather than hot, and nights are cool, except on the coastal plain. There are two distinct seasons: a dry season, from November to April, and a rainy season, from May to November. The annual average temperature ranges from 18°C to 32°C. During the rainy season, rainfall averages 260 mm a month. Although it is not prone to hurricanes, in 1998 Hurricane Mitch damaged parts of the country.

Climate and Weather

Mean Temperature 64°F to 90°F
Average Rainfall 10 in

POPULATION

Population Indicators

Total Population: 1999 5,839,000
World Rank: 99th
Density per sq mi: 718.7 per sq km 277.5
% of annual growth (1994–99): 1.6
Male %: 48.6
Female %: 51.4
Urban %: 50.4
Age Distribution: % 0–14: 38.7
15–29: 28.7
30–44: 16.0
45–59: 9.2
60–74: 5.4
75 and over: 1.9
Population 2020: 7,852,000
Birth Rate per 1,000: 38.6
Death Rate per 1,000: 15.0
Population Doubling Time (years): 34
Infant Mortality Rate per 1,000 live births: 106.0
Rate of Natural Increase per 1,000: 23.6
Total Fertility Rate: 5.4
Expectation of Life (years): Males 48.7
Females 52.0
Marriage Rate per 1,000: 4.3
Divorce Rate per 1,000: 0.5
Total Number of Households: —
Average Size of Households: 5.6
% of Illegitimate Children: 3.2
Induced Abortions: —
Rate per 100 live births: —

ETHNIC COMPOSITION

El Salvador's population consists of 94 percent mestizo, or mixed indigenous and European ancestry, 5 percent indigenous ancestry, and 1 percent European ancestry. The two major indigenous groups are from the Pipil, a Nahuatl-speaking Toltec people from Mexico, who arrived during the 11th century, and the Lenca, who are believed to be an offshoot of the early Mayans. Most European ancestry derives from the Spanish conquerors who came during the 16th through the 18th centuries.

LANGUAGES

The official language is Spanish, which is spoken by virtually the entire population. The only indigenous language believed to remain is Kekchi, which also exists in Guatemala and southern Belize. The indigenous languages of the Pipil (Nahuatl) and Lenca are nearly extinct.

Principal Languages and Their Speakers

Spanish	5,839,000

RELIGIONS

Approximately 78 percent of the population is Roman Catholic. The patron of the country is El Salvador del Mundo (The Savior of the World), whose fiesta in August is a national holiday. Protestant churches have grown significantly since 1992 (when the signing of the peace accords encouraged more missionary efforts from abroad), and now account for 17 percent of the population. The Catholic Church has been an active voice for social justice, and many members of the clergy were killed during El Salvador's civil war for their outspoken views on key issues, such as agrarian reform.

Religious Affiliations

Roman Catholic	4,570,000
Protestant	1,000,000
Other	270,000

HISTORICAL BACKGROUND

The land that is now El Salvador was home to early indigenous cultures. The Olmec culture, which was situated near present-day Chalchuapa, is believed to have existed around 2000 B.C., and other cultures from around 3000 B.C. The Mayan culture was prominent in the area, and archaeological ruins in present-day Joya de Cerén show evidence of a large civilization at about A.D. 600. The Payu culture, centered around present-day Tazumal, flourished from about A.D. 300–1200, especially after the descent and disappearance of the Mayan culture, around 900.

At the time of Spanish arrival, the Pipil culture (descended from the Toltecs and Aztecs) was dominant in the area. Don Pedro de Alvarado arrived at the Port of Acajutla in 1524, and present-day San Salvador was founded in 1525. The Spanish controlled the area soon thereafter. It remained under Spanish rule as part of New Spain until the 19th century. El Salvador gained its independence from Spain in 1821, which was 10 years after Father José Matías Delgado made the first call for national independence from his church pulpit at La Merced. In 1824, El Salvador joined the United Provinces of Central America, remaining in that federation until 1841.

Abolition of communal land in the 1880s placed about 75 percent of the lands, and 90 percent of wealth, in the hands of the infamous 14 families. This set the stage for a ruling class of wealthy landowners, influencing much of Salvadoran politics and constituting a major factor in the civil war of the late 20th century.

During the 1930s, demand for social change grew. In 1932 the army, led by Gen. Maximiliano Hernández Martínez, crushed a popular insurrection, murdering over 30,000 civilians. His highly autocratic and repressive regime lasted until 1944, when he was ousted following a general strike. The army continued to control politics through a series of civilian and military juntas. None of the governments were able to improve conditions for the majority of Salvadorans, who lived in extreme poverty. As El Salvador became more crowded, Salvadorans moved into the border area with Honduras. This small safety valve was eliminated when war broke out with Honduras in 1969 following a soccer match in San Salvador. While the government became more oppressive, and paramilitary groups and death squads become more prominent, U.S. military support for the country grew.

Disillusionment with the government's inability to initiate social reform led to the formation of guerrilla groups in the 1970s. In 1979 a group of army officers overthrew the government of Gen. Carlos Humberto Romero. José Napoléon Duarte, a member of the junta, was sworn in as president in December 1980. The junta was unable to control violence by guerrilla groups or sections of the army and right-wing death squads, frequently hired by landowners to suppress opposition. Archbishop Oscar Romero was killed while saying mass in 1980, which incited further armed rebellion, led by the Farabundo Martí National Liberation Movement (FMLN). By December 1981, over 300,000 Salvadorans were refugees, and large areas of some northern provinces were almost completely depopulated. U.S. support continued, even while many Americans protested U.S. involvement in El Salvador, and the American government continued to deny that any American soldiers were stationed in El Salvador. (Over 30 American casualties laid to rest in 1986 disprove that denial.)

Discussions in 1987 led to an agreement on forming a committee to negotiate a cease-fire and amnesty for the rebels, but following the murder of the president of the Human Rights Commission, the guerrillas withdrew from the talks. In 1989, Alfredo Cristiani won election. Violence continued, however, highlighted by the murder by military forces of six Jesuits that same year. In April 1990, the United Nations began mediation between the government and FMLN. On January 16, 1992, a cease-fire took effect. In 1994, National Republican Alliance (ARENA) member Dr. Armando Calderón Sol was elected president. While representing a conservative agenda, ARENA has, as it has stayed in power, learned to balance its conservative views with the pressing needs of most Salvadorans. The land transfer program, which was agreed to in the cease-fire, has been carried out, but other poverty-related problems remain, although quality of life is improving. The country is still recuperating from 12 years of civil war and rebuilding a gutted infrastructure. In March 1999, Francisco Flores, also of the ARENA party, became president of El Salvador.

CONSTITUTION

El Salvador has had numerous constitutions since independence, of which the last, promulgated in 1983 and amended since then, is still in force. It establishes a republican, democratic, and representative form of government. Executive power is vested in the president, who is elected for a five-year term and is ineligible for reelection. The president is also commander in chief of the armed forces and appoints cabinet ministers.

LOCAL GOVERNMENT

El Salvador is divided into 14 departments, which are further divided into 39 districts and 262 municipalities. Departments are run by a governor who is appointed by the president. Municipalities are run by municipal councils, composed of a mayor, legal representative, and from two to 12 councilmen, who are elected for four-year terms.

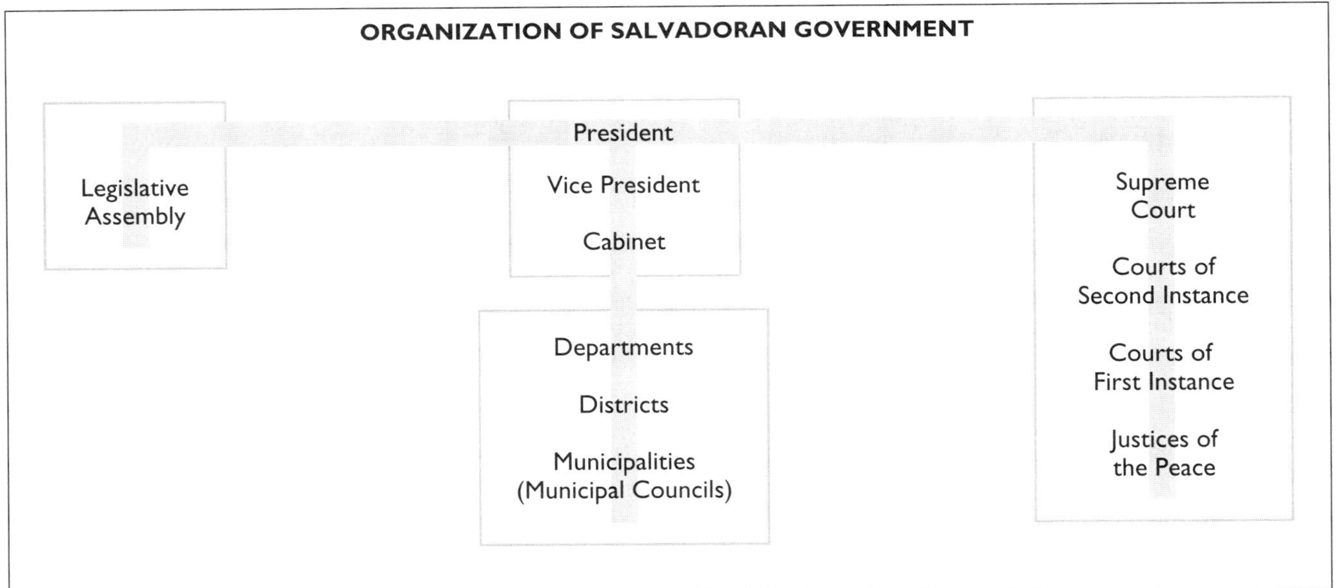

Local Government

Principal administrative divisions, capitals, area, population

AREA AND POPULATION

Departments	Capitals	area sq mi	area sq km	population 1992 census
Ahuachapán	Ahuachapán	479	1,240	261,168
Cabañas	Sensuntepeque	426	1,104	138,426
Chalatenango	Chalatenango	779	2,017	177,320
Cuscatlán	Cojutepeque	292	756	178,502
La Libertad	Nueva San Salvador	638	1,653	513,866
La Paz	Zacatecoluca	473	1,224	245,915
La Unión	La Unión	801	2,074	255,565
Morazan	San Francisco	559	1,447	160,146
San Miguel	San Miguel	802	2,077	403,411
San Salvador	San Salvador	342	886	1,512,125
San Vicente	San Vicente	457	1,184	143,003
Santa Ana	Santa Ana	781	2,023	458,587
Sonsonate	Sonsonate	473	1,225	360,183
Usulután	Usulután	822	2,130	310,362
TOTAL		8,124	21,041	5,118,599

PARLIAMENT

The parliament is called the Legislative Assembly (Asamblea Legislativa), whose 84 members are elected for three-year terms by popular vote. It meets twice a year, beginning June 1 and December 1. Additional sessions may be called by the president or the Permanent Committee of the Assembly. The Permanent Committee also conducts business in between legislative sessions.

POLITICAL PARTIES

Major Salvadoran Political Parties (1999):

National Republican Alliance (ARENA)—Conservative political group; it is the political party of the current president.

Farabundo Martí National Liberation Front (FMLN)—Former guerrilla organization that now has a voice in the political process; in 1999 presidential elections, they received the second largest number of votes.

Christian Democratic Party (PDC)—Centrist political party, heavily influenced by the writings of Pope Leo XIII, Pope John XXIII, and philosopher Jacques Maritain. José Napoleón Duarte Fuentes became a member and, later, secretary general of the party.

Political Parties

National Republican Alliance
Christian Democratic Party
Christian Social Union, 1997
National Conciliation Party, 1961
United Democratic Center, 1998, a coalition consisting of
  Democratic Convergence, 1987
  Democratic Party, 1995
Farabundo Marti National Liberation Front, 1980
New Treaty United People
Democratic Republican League, 1999
Liberal Democratic Party, 1994
Free People
National Action Party

Political Parties: Strength in Parliament Most Recent Elections

Formerly a 60-member body, the **Legislative Assembly** (*Asamblea Legislativa*), currently consists of 84 legislators, 64 elected from multimember constituencies and 20 by proportional representation, serving three-year terms. At the most recent election of March 12, 2000, the Nationalist Republican Alliance won 29 seats; the Farabundo Martí National Liberation Front, 31; the National Conciliation Party, 13; the Christian Democratic Party, 6; the United Democratic Center, 3; and the National Action Party, 2.

LEGAL SYSTEM

Salvadoran law is based on Spanish law, influenced by Roman law and the Napoleonic Code, and modified by recent political changes. The legal system is headed by the Supreme Court. Below the Supreme Court are eight courts of second instance, composed of two magistrates and two substitutes each. On the third level are courts of first instance, located in each departmental capital and other major cities and towns. The lowest courts are justices of the peace, located in all towns. There are also special courts, such as the "peace courts," which often rule on crimes committed during El Salvador's civil war.

LAW ENFORCEMENT

Law Enforcement

Offenses reported to the police per 100,000: —
- Murder: —
- Assault: —
- Burglary: —
- Automobile Theft: —
- Population per Police officer: 100

Death Penalty: Only for exceptional crimes; last execution in 1973

HUMAN RIGHTS

El Salvador's constitution guarantees freedom of speech, movement, assembly, and religion. In meeting the terms of the cease-fire, the government has reduced the military by over 70 percent. It has also removed policing duties from the military and turned them over to a civilian police force. The former rebels have been integrated into political life (as the party known as FMLN), and they received almost 30 percent of the vote in the 1999 presidential elections. Problems still exist in the use of excessive force by police in some instances. Violence against women and homosexuals is still widespread. Domestic violence is still a largely unresolved issue, exacerbated by machismo attitudes and at times contributed to by ultra-orthodox church doctrine. Homosexual prostitutes especially are at extremely high risk of violence, while gay nightclubs often have difficulty remaining open, both because of the nightclubs' tendency to be a target of right-wing/homophobic groups and their patrons' need to be anonymous for personal safety reasons. The Supreme Court stepped up efforts in 1998 to discipline judges for incompetence and corruption. However, those who have fought for human rights have often become the targets of violence themselves.

FOREIGN POLICY

The ending of the civil war has also brought about a more peaceful foreign policy. Relations with Honduras have been more civil, and there is a more concerted effort to maintain good relations with all other Central American countries.

El Salvador maintains something of a love/hate relationship with the United States. Although it maintains good relations, and does extensive trade with the United States, many Salvadorans still resent U.S. involvement in the civil war. Many Salvadorans now live in the United States and Canada as a result of the civil war, sending home an estimated US$1 billion in aid (in the form of money, clothing, and other items) annually.

Beyond the Western Hemisphere, El Salvador has welcomed investment in the country in order to help it rebuild. The European Union has put more focus on Central America in general, and El Salvador in particular, in 1999 and 2000.

DEFENSE

Males between 18 and 30 years of age are conscripted. Those who do not serve full-time perform 18 months' military service by participating in weekly training sessions. Defense spending accounts for about 1 percent of the gross domestic product.

Military Indicators

Total Active Duty Personnel: 28,400
Military Manpower per 1,000: 5.0
Military Expenditures $million: 10.1
- as % of GNP: 1.1
- per capita $: 18
- as % of central government expenditures: 7.4

Arms Imports $million: 20
Arms Exports $million: 0

ECONOMY

El Salvador is one of the lower-middle-income countries of the world, but its once thriving economy was devastated by civil war in the 1980s as well as a series of earthquakes. In 1998 the government emphasized conservative economic and fiscal policies to promote foreign investment. Inflation fell to an unprecedented low of 2 percent. Exports reached a record level and were the main engine of growth. Productivity in other sectors remained weaker, however. For the last few years El Salvador has experienced sizable deficits in both its trade and fiscal accounts. The trade deficit has been offset by remittances from the large number of Salvadorans living abroad and from external aid. The three earthquakes in 2000 and 2001 have caused havoc in the economy, and it may take a decade for the nation to recover. The government has stepped up its privatization efforts, targeting the state telephone company as well as pension funds.

Principal Economic Indicators

Gross National Product: $10.704 billion
GNP per capita: $1,810
GNP Average Annual Growth Rate (1990–97)%: 3.5
GNP per capita Average Annual Growth Rate (1990–97) %: 1.4
Origin of Gross Domestic Product %
- Agriculture: 14
- Mining: —
- Manufacturing: 21
- Construction: 4
- Public Utilities: 1
- Transportation and Communications: 18
- Trade: 17
- Financial Services: 12
- Other Services: 18
- Government: 6

Gross Domestic Product by Type of Expenditure %
- Private Consumption: 87
- Government Consumption: 8
- Gross Domestic Investment: 20
- Foreign Trade: Exports: 20
  Imports: −35

% of Income Received by Poorest 20%: 5.5
% of Income Received by Richest 10%: 29.5

Price and earnings indexes (1995 = 100)

	1993	1994	1995	1996	1997	1998	1999
Consumer price index	82.2	90.9	100.0	109.8	114.7	117.6	117.9
Earnings index	77.8	90.1	100.0	109.0	—	—	—

Finance

National Currency: Colon (C)
Exchange Rate: $1 = C 8.755
Money Supply Stock in National Currency billion: 9.898
M1 per capita: 1,760
Central Bank Discount Rate %: 7.74
Total External Debt $million: 2,600
Debt Service Ratio %: 5.9

Balance of Payments $million: 95.9
International Reserves SDRs million: 744
Ratio of External Debt to Total Reserves: 2.6
Average Annual Rate of Inflation/Consumer Price Index Growth Rate %: 2

Official Development Assistance

ODA $million: 763
- as % of GNP: 7.128
- per capita: $130.6
- Foreign Direct Investment $million: 12

Central Government Revenues and Expenditures

Fiscal Year: Calendar Year

Revenues $million: 1,750
Expenditures $million: 1,820
Budget Deficit $million: 70
Tax Revenues as % of GDP: —
Highest Tax Bracket %
- Individual: 30
- Corporate: 25

Employment and Labor

Economically Active Population: 2,136,000
Female Participation Rate %: 37.1
Activity Rate %: 39.1
Labor by Sector: %
- Agriculture, Forestry, Fishing: 27.4
- Manufacturing, Mining: 19.3
- Construction: 6.9
- Transportation and Communications: 4.0
- Trade, Hotels, and Restaurants: 19.4
- Finance, Insurance, Real Estate: 1.3
- Public Administration, Defense: —
- Services: 20.2

Unemployment %: 7.7

Agriculture

Agriculture's Share of GDP%: 14
Average Annual Rate of Growth (1965–98) %: 0.6
Number of Farms 000: 271
Average Size of Farm ha: 5.4
Number of Tractors per 1,000 hectares: 6.1
Irrigation, % of Farms having: 21
Artificial Fertilizer kg/hectare: 106
Total Farmland as % of land area: 64.7
Livestock: Cattle 000: 457
- Sheep 000: 5
- Hogs 000: 314
- Chickens 000: 7,980

Forests: Production of Roundwood (000 cubic meters): 6,804
Fisheries: Total Catch tons: 13.1

Mining

% of GDP: 0.4
Value of Mineral Production $million: 40.3

Manufacturing

Value Added $million: 521
Industrial Production Growth Rate %: 7.0

Energy

Commercial Energy Production metric tons of oil equivalent 000: 2,649
Commercial Energy Consumption metric tons of oil equivalent 000: 4,095
Commercial Energy Consumption per capita kg: 691
Average Annual Growth Rate 1980–97%: 1.1
Net Energy Imports % of use: 35

Electricity Installed Capacity kW 000: 751
Production kW-hr million: 3,405
Coal Reserves tons million: —
Production tons 000: —
Natural Gas Proven Reserves cubic meters billion: —
Production cubic meters million: —
Crude Petroleum Reserves barrels million: —
Production barrels million: —
Consumption barrels million: 5
Refinery Capacity barrels per day 000: 21
Pipelines Length km: —

Foreign Trade

Imports $million: 2,261.8
Exports $million: 8,12.7
Export Volume % Annual Growth Rate (1990–97): 2.2
Import Volume % Annual Growth Rate (1990–97): 10.9
Balance of Trade $

Balance of trade (current prices)

	1993	1994	1995	1996	1997	1998
U.S.						
$ 000,000	−1,180.5	−1,448.9	−1,855.3	−1,646.5	−1,614.3	−1,849.6
% of total	44.6%	47.1%	48.2%	44.6%	37.3%	42.3%

Major Trading Partners

	Imports	Exports
European Union %	10.6	25.0
United States %	41.5	22.6
Eastern Europe %	0.5	—
Japan %	6.3	0.8
Others %	41.1	51.6

Transportation

Roads Total Length mi: 7,655 km 12,320
Paved %: 14
Automobiles: 102,000
Trucks and Buses: 159,700
Persons per vehicle: 21
Railroad; Track Length mi: 349 km 562
Passenger-mi million: 3.4
Freight-mi million: 20.3
Merchant Marine: No. of Vessels: 15
Total Deadweight Tonnage 000: —
International Cargo Loaded tons 000: 221
International Cargo Off-loaded tons 000: 1,023
Airports with Scheduled Flights: 1
Traffic: Passenger-mi million: 1,229
Freight-mi million: 9.8
Length of Canals mi: —

Tourism

Number of Tourists to 000: 542
Number of Tourists from 000: 868
Tourist Receipts $million: 75
Tourist Expenditures $million: 72

Communications

Telephones 000: 255
Cost of Local Calls 3 mins: $0.06
Cellular Telephones 000: 14
Fax Machines 000: —
Personal Computers 000: —
Internet Hosts per million persons: 4.3
Mail: Post Offices: 237
Pieces of Mail Handled million: 21
Pieces of Mail Handled per person: 3.6

EDUCATION

Education is free, and lasts for 12 years, although many students have traditionally dropped out after primary school. The system has been plagued with high non-attendance and dropout rates, but this situation is improving. In 1999, El Salvador reached a literacy rate of 84 percent, considerably higher than its Central American neighbors, and in 1996, 94 percent of children attended primary school.

Education

Literacy Rate %: 74.1
Male %: 77.4
Female %: 71.3
First Level: Primary schools: 3,961
Teachers: 26,259
Students: 1,042,256
Student-Teacher Ratio: 39.7
Net Enrollment Ratio: 79.0
Second Level: Secondary Schools: —
Teachers: —
Students: 29,257
Student-Teacher Ratio: —
Net Enrollment Ratio: 21

Vocational Level: Schools: 13
Students: 88,588

Third Level: Institutions: —
Teachers: 4,643
Students: 77,359
Student-Ratio Level: 16.7
Gross Enrollment Ratio: 17.7
Students per 100,000: 2,031
% of Population Age 25 and over with Postsecondary Education: 6.3

Public Expenditure on Education as % of GDP: 2.2

SCIENCE AND TECHNOLOGY

Science and Technology

Scientists and Engineers in R&D per 1 million persons: 20
Expenditures in R&D as % of GDP: —
High-Tech Exports $million: 45
Patent Applications by Residents: 3

MEDIA

The Salvadoran media are generally controlled by right-wing and business interests. The following newspapers are published daily in San Salvador: *El Diario de Hoy, La Prensa Gráfica, El Mundo*, and *La Noticia*. *Diario Oficial* is government owned. There is no domestic news agency. The media rely primarily on the state-run National Information Center and the regional Central American News Agency. Virtually all of the licensed radio stations are commercial with the exception of the government-owned Radio Nacional de El Salvador.

Media

Daily Newspapers: 6
- Total Circulation 000: 284
- Circulation per 1,000: 53

Books Published: —
Magazines: —
Radio Receivers 000: 2,080
- per 1,000: 373

Television sets 000: 1,300
- per 1,000: 241

Most Important Media:

Press. The following newspapers are published daily at San Salvador, unless otherwise noted: *El Diario de Hoy* (103,000 daily, 86,000 Sunday), ultraconservative; *La Prensa Gráfica* (64,000 daily, 109,000 Sunday), conservative; *El Mundo* (58,000 daily, 63,000 Sunday); *La Noticia* (25,000); *Diario Oficial* (2,100), government owned. The plant of the formerly conservative *Diario Latino*, which was sold to a workers' group in May 1989 and subsequently accused of being a mouthpiece of the FMLN, was destroyed by fire in February 1991, but the paper succeeded in resuming publication on a limited basis shortly thereafter.

News agencies. There is no domestic facility, the media relying primarily on the government's National Information Center (Centro de Información Nacional—CIN) and the regional Central American News Agency (Agencia Centroamericana de Noticias—ACAN).

Radio and television. Broadcasting is supervised by the official Administración Nacional de Telecomunicaciones (Antel). Virtually all of the licensed radio stations are commercial, one exception being the government-operated Radio Nacional de El Salvador. Two of San Salvador's six television channels feature educational programming and are government operated.

CULTURE

Cultural Indicators

Public Libraries Number: —
- Volumes: —
- Registered borrowers: —

Museums Number: 20
- Annual Attendance: 1,333,000

Cinema Production of Long Films: —
- Number of Cinemas: —
- Seating Capacity: —
- Annual Attendance: —
- Annual Attendance per capita: —

STATUS OF WOMEN

Although women have the right to vote, they are not as prevalent in high-ranking corporate and government positions, and earn considerably less than their male counterparts. Domestic and other types of violence against women are widespread.

Women

Gender Empowerment Measure: 34
Seats Held in Parliament by Women %: 15.5
Female Administrators and Managers %: 25.7
Female Professional and Technical Workers %: 44.1
Women's Share of Earned Income %: 34.0
Women in Government %: 18

HEALTH, FOOD, AND NUTRITION

Health

Number of Physicians: 4,525
Number of Dentists: 1,182
Number of Nurses: 5,094
Number of Pharmacists: —
Population per Physician: 1,219
Number of Hospitals: 78
Hospital Beds per 10,000: 17
Hospital Bed Occupancy Rate: 54.9
Infant Mortality Rate per 1,000 live births: 64
Maternal Mortality Rate per 100,000 live births: 300
Total Health Expenditures as % of GDP: 5.86
Health Expenditures per capita $: 58
HIV Infected % of adults: 0.58
Cigarette Consumption per smoker per year: —
% of Smokers: Male: 38
Female: 12
Access to Safe Water %: 62

Food and Nutrition

Food Supply as % of FAO Requirements: 113
% of Consumption Expenditures on Food: 37.0
Daily Available Calories per capita: 2,577
% of Total Calories derived from:
Cereals: 55.9
Potatoes, cassava: 2.0
Meat, poultry: 2.7
Fish: 0.2
Eggs, milk: 6.0
Fruits, vegetables: 5.2
Fats, oils: 7.7

ENVIRONMENT

El Salvador's two main environmental problems are overuse of land (due to its population density) and pollution from manufacturing and energy production. The government has made great strides to ensure that as much as possible of the remaining rain forest in the country is not developed.

Environment

Forest Area sq km: 1,000
Average Annual Deforestation sq km: 38
Nationally Protected Areas as % of Total Land Area: 0.5
Freshwater Access cubic meters per capita: 3,197
Emissions of Organic Water Pollutants kg per day: 16,385
CO_2 Emissions per capita ton: 0.7

CHRONOLOGY

1943 Maxmiliano Hernández Martínez raises the export tax, garnering widespread criticism from landed families.

1944 An attempted coup to oust Martínez fails; national strikes and civil unrest result; Martínez resigns.

1945 January elections are corrupted to ensure the election of President Salvador Castaneda Castro.

1948 Castaneda is ousted from power by the Juventud Militar (Military Youth); a junta, led by Maj. Oscar Osorio, takes over the country's rule.

1960 Lieutenant Colonel José Maria Lemus is overthrown; a military junta, led by Lieutenant Colonel Julio Adalberto Rivera, takes over; the PDC (Christian Democratic Party) is formed.

1961 A right-wing military faction overthrows the junta but retains Rivera as leader.

1962 Rivera is elected president, buoyed by the Partido de la Conciliación National; the PCN continues to support national leaders and directly or indirectly rule the country.

1964 In a revised electoral process, the PDC wins many assembly and mayoral seats, including José Napoleón Duarte Fuentes, who becomes mayor of San Salvador.

1967 The leftist PAR party is accused of communism and suppressed; PCN candidate Colonel Fidel Sánchez Hernández becomes president.

1969 Honduras evicts Salvadoran people from Honduran border lands, spurring violent clashes between Salvadorans the Honduran military; tension explodes into war after a soccer match in San Salvador between the two countries.

1972 Colonel Molina of the PCN suspends vote counting and has the assembly declare him president; Duarte, the apparent winner, is tracked down, arrested, beaten, and exiled.

1976 Molina attempts land reform but capitulates to the demands of the landed elite; death squads appear in large numbers, targeting Fuerzas Populares de Liberación "Farabundo Martí" (FPL) members and Catholic clergy of the Christian Base Communities.

1977 PCN candidate Carlos Humberto Romero is elected president in a corrupt election; hundreds of protesters are killed in postelection clashes.

1979 As violence sweeps the nation, Romero is deposed in an army-led coup; a state of siege is imposed; the new military, calling itself the Revolutionary Government Junta, invites two prominent Social Democratic civilians to join it.

1980 Another military coup establishes a new junta, which includes two Christian Democrats, Morales and Dada; the Revolutionary Coordinator of the Masses, a coalition of reform groups, calls for open insurrection; protests in January and February are violently put down by police and dozens are killed; Archbishop Oscar Arnulfo Romero y Galdamez, one of the most respected figures in the country and an outspoken critic of the government, is murdered while saying mass; Dada resigns from the junta and is replaced by Duarte.

1981 Leftist guerrillas launch a "final offensive"; an electoral law is passed calling for a legislative assembly; Mexico and France recognize FDR-FMLN guerrillas as a legitimate political force.

1982 Five right-wing parties win 60 percent of the vote in national elections and form the Government of National Unity with Alvaro Magana Borja as interim president; delegates sign the Pact of Apaneca, a peace treaty.

1983 An antigovernment army faction stages a mutiny at Sensuntepeque; Marianela García Villas, president of the Human Rights Commission, is assassinated; the Assembly ratifies a new constitution.

1984 Rebels and the army engage in numerous clashes; the PDC's José Napoleón Duarte wins presidential elections.

1985 Mexico resumes diplomatic ties with the Duarte regime; Duarte's daughter is kidnapped and released in exchange for captive guerrillas.

1986 In August, government-rebel peace talks take place in Lima, Peru; in October, a severe earthquake causes extensive damage to San Salvador, killing 1,500 people and injuring more than 10,000.

1987 El Salvador is one of five Central American nations that sign a preliminary peace agreement calling for regional cease-fires; Herbert Anaya Sanabria, president of the Human Rights Commission, is murdered.

1989 National Republican Alliance (ARENA) candidate Alfredo Cristiani Burkard wins the March presidential election; following the breakdown of peace talks between the government and leftist rebels, Farabundo Martí National Liberation Front (FMLN) launches a major offensive in November.

1990 Cristiani suspends relations with Nicaragua over the issue of Sandinistas supplying arms to the

FMLN; soldiers stand trial on charges of murder and terrorism in the 1989 slaying of six Jesuits.

1992 A UN-mediated cease-fire takes effect on January 16, ending the civil war in which an estimated 75,000 to 150,000 were killed; FMLN becomes an opposition party.

1994 ARENA member Dr. Armando Calderón Sol is elected president.

1997 In March elections, FMLN wins elections in six of the 14 departments.

1998 Hurricane Mitch strikes El Salvador and other Central American countries.

1999 ARENA candidate Francisco Flores becomes president of El Salvador.

2001 Massive earthquakes kill 1,200 people and destroy tens of thousands of homes

BIBLIOGRAPHY

Booth, John A., and Thomas M. Walker. *Understanding Central America*, Boulder, Colo., 1993.

Haggerty, Richard A., ed. *El Salvador: A Country Study*. Washington, D.C., 1988.

OFFICIAL PUBLICATIONS

El Salvador. *Censos nacionales: V censo de población y IV de vivienda (1992); El Salvador en cifras* (annual); *Indicadores económicos y sociales* (annual); *Plan de desarrollo económico y social 1989–1994.*

CONTACT INFORMATION

Embassy of El Salvador
2308 California Street, NW
Washington, D.C. 20008
Phone: (202) 265-9671

INTERNET RESOURCES

- Banco Central de Reserva de El Salvador
  http://www.bcr.gob.sv/

EQUATORIAL GUINEA

BASIC FACT SHEET

OFFICIAL NAME:
Republic of Equatorial Guinea (República de Guinea Ecuatorial)

ABBREVIATION:
EG

CAPITAL:
Malabo (formerly Santa Isabel)

HEAD OF STATE:
President Teodoro Obiang Nguema Mbasogo (from 1979)

HEAD OF GOVERNMENT:
Prime Minister Cándido Muatetema Rivas

NATURE OF GOVERNMENT:
Emerging democracy

POPULATION:
466,000 (1999)

AREA:
27,972 sq km (10,800 sq mi)

ETHNIC MAJORITY:
Fang

LANGUAGES:
Spanish (official), Fang (vernacular)

RELIGION:
Roman Catholicism

UNIT OF CURRENCY:
Coopération Financière en Afrique Centrale franc (C.F.A.F.)

NATIONAL FLAG:
Tricolor of green, white, and red horizontal stripes with a blue triangle on the hoist side and the national emblem in the center of the white stripe

NATIONAL EMBLEM:
A "God Tree" with six stars over it and the national motto—*Unidad, Paz, Justicia* (Unity, Peace, Justice)—beneath it

NATIONAL ANTHEM:
"Let's Walk Through the Arbor of Our Immense Happiness"

NATIONAL HOLIDAYS:
March 5 (Independence Day, National Day); January 1 (New Year's Day); Christian festivals, including Epiphany, Good Friday, Good Saturday, Easter, Day of St. Joseph the Worker, Ascension Day, Corpus Christi, Assumption Day, All Saints' Day, and Christmas

DATE OF INDEPENDENCE:
March 5, 1968

DATE OF CONSTITUTION:
November 17, 1991, amended January 1995

GEOGRAPHICAL FEATURES

Equatorial Guinea is on the western coast of West-central Africa and consists of a mainland province and five islands: Bioko (formerly Macias Nguema Biyogo and Fernando Po), Pagalu (formerly Annabon), Elobey Grande, Elobey Chico, and Corisco. Bioko is 32 km (20 mi) from the coast of Cameroon, and Pagalu is about 350 km (220 mi) from mainland Gabon. Corisco and the Elobey Islands are off the southwestern coast of Bioko and close to the Gabonese coast. The total land area is 27,972 sq km (10,799 sq mi), of which mainland Río Muni along with Corisco and the Elobey Islands cover 25,952 sq km (10,020 sq mi) and Bioko and Pagalu cover 2,020 sq km (780 sq mi). Río Muni extends 248 km (154 mi) east-northeast to west-southwest and 167 km (104 mi) south-southeast to north-northwest. Bioko extends 74 km (46 mi) northeast to southwest and 37 km (23 mi) southeast to northwest. The Río Muni coastline is 167 km (104 mi) long, and the Bioko coastline totals 174 km (108 mi).

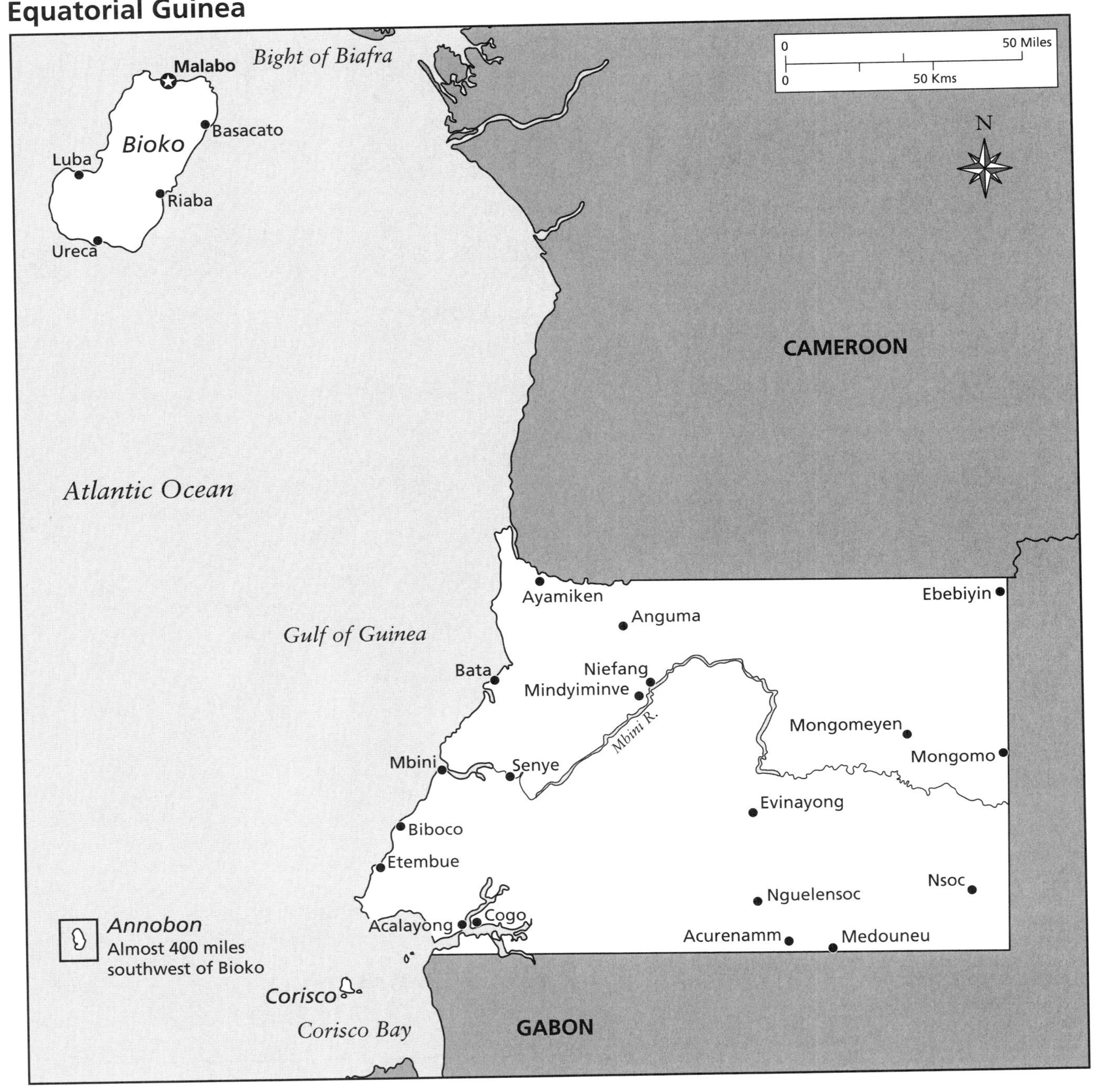

Bioko is the largest island in the Gulf of Guinea and has two large volcanic formations separated by a valley that bisects the island. The coastline is high and rugged in the south but lower and more accessible in the north. In the north of the island is Mount Malano (3,007 m; 9,865 ft). In the center is Pico de Moka, with an alpine environment. In the south is Gran Caldera. Río Muni on the African mainland is a jungle enclave with a coastal plain rising steeply toward the Gabon border. In the interior the plain gives way to a succession of valleys separated by low hills and spurs of the Crystal Mountains. The highest peaks are Monte Chocolate (1,100 m; 3,609 ft); the Piedra de Mzas, Monte Mitra, and Monte Chime, rising to 1,200 m (3,937 ft). Corisco, covering 15 sq km (6 sq mi) and Elobey Grande and Elobey Chico each about 2.5 sq km (1 sq mi) are volcanic islands.

Geography

Area sq km: 27,972 (10,800 sq mi)
World Rank: 144th
Land Boundaries, km: Cameroon 189; Gabon 350
Coastline, km 296
Elevation Extremes meters
Lowest: Atlantic Ocean 0
Highest: Mount Malabo 3,008
Land Use % Arable land: 5
Permanent Crops: 4
Permanent Pastures: 4
Forest and Woodland: 46
Other: 41

Population of Principal Cities

Malabo	58,040

CLIMATE AND WEATHER

Equatorial Guinea has an equatorial climate, with average temperatures at Malabo exceeding 25°C (77°F) and average annual rainfall exceeding 2,000 mm (78 in). Wet and dry seasons alternate; from June to August Río Muni is dry and from December to February it is wet, whereas the reverse is true in Bioko. March to May and September to December are transitional months.

Annual rainfall varies from 1,930 mm (76 in) at Malabo to 10,973 mm (432 in) at Ureka, Bioko. Rain falls almost daily on Pagalu Island. Malabo has an inhospitable climate, with average temperatures reaching 33.4°C (92°F), but in the southern Moka Plateau the average temperature is 20.6°C (69°F). On mainland Río Muni the average temperature range is 15°C to 21.6°C (59°F to 71°F).

Tornadoes and violent windstorms are frequent occurrences in the country.

Climate and Weather

Mean Temperature
Malabo 77°F
Mainland 59°F to 71°F
Rainfall
Malabo 76 in
Ureka, Bioko 432 in

POPULATION

Population Indicators

Total Population: 1999 466,000
World Rank: 164th
Density per sq mi: 43
% of annual growth (1994–99): 2.6
Male %: 49.9
Female %: 50.1
Urban %:
Age Distribution: % 0–14: 41.7
15–29: 25.1
30–44: 15.7
45–59: 11.2
60–74: 5.3
75 and over: 1.0
Population 2020: 783,000
Birth Rate per 1,000: 40.8
Death Rate per 1,000: 16.2
Population Doubling Time (years): 27
Infant Mortality Rate per 1,000 live births: 107.0
Rate of Natural Increase per 1,000: 24.6
Total Fertility Rate: 5.5
Expectation of Life (years): Males 48.4
Females 51.6
Marriage Rate per 1,000: —
Divorce Rate per 1,000: —
Total Number of Households: —
Average Size of Households: 4.5
% of Illegitimate Children: —
Induced Abortions: —
Rate per 100 live births: —

ETHNIC COMPOSITION

The ethnic composition of Equatorial Guinea is notable for its complexity and variety. The dominant group is the Fang (also known as Fon and, in Spanish, Pamue), who make up 80 percent to 90 percent of the population of Río Muni. Earlier settlers, such as the Kombe, Balengue, Bujebas, and Bengas, have been pushed toward the coast by Fang expansion. All Río Munians are of Bantu stock, as are the Bubi, who were the original inhabitants of Bioko. The Bubi are now estimated to number 15,000 but they are outnumbered by Fang migrants from the mainland and by a few thousand Fernandinos, descendants of slaves liberated by the British navy in the 19th century.

Until recently the majority of the inhabitants of Bioko were Hausa, Ibo, Ibibo, and Efik contract workers on the plantations. Their numbers have been depleted by repatriation and voluntary emigration.

LANGUAGES

Spanish is the official language of the republic and the effective cultural and administrative medium of communication, although it is spoken by only 4 percent to 5 percent of the population. British sway over Bioko in the first half of the 19th century is reflected in the use of pidgin English (known locally as Pichinglis) as a lingua franca. Fang is the main vernacular and the only indigenous language with a national status. A rare pidgin form of Bantu speech known as fa d'Ambo survives as an isolated language found on Pagalu.

Principal Languages and Their Speakers	
Bubi	40,000
Fang	390,000
French	—
Krio (English Creole)	—
Spanish	—
Other	30,000

RELIGIONS

At least 90 percent of the population is believed to be nominally affiliated with the Roman Catholic Church. There are influential Protestant groups in Río Muni and the islands. Church and state entered on a collision course in 1973, and Spanish priests and nuns of the Immaculate Conception were expelled from the country. Most Catholic schools were either closed or placed under the control of the single political party, Partido Unico Nacional de Trabajadores (PUNT, United National Workers' Party). All Catholic priests and nuns were arrested as the official campaign against the church intensified. Churches were closed and used to store agricultural produce. Macias Nguema Biyogo, described as a militant atheist, dropped his Christian name Francisco in 1975 to rid himself of Christian "trappings." President Obiang ordered the reopening of all Catholic churches following the 1979 coup.

Religious Affiliations	
Roman Catholic	430,000
Other	30,000

HISTORICAL BACKGROUND

During the 12th and 13th centuries, the Bantu people moved to what is today Equatorial Guinea. The land was already inhabited by Pygmies and Ndowe people. In the end, however, the warlike Fang people dominated the region. Eventually, the region came under the influence of the Portuguese as the Fang were forced inland to avoid being part of the growing slave trade.

Equatorial Guinea was under the rule of Portugal from 1494 to 1778, Spain from 1778 to 1781, Great Britain from 1781 to 1843, and Spain from 1858 to 1968. From 1904 the country was ruled by the Spanish through an institution known as *patronato de indígenas* (patronage of the natives), under which the natives were classified as legal minors and *encomendado* (entrusted) to the Claretian missionaries. Natives were not allowed to dispose of their land freely or transact any business involving more than 2,000 pesetas. They were subjected to a system of forced labor by contract. They were represented in courts by the Curadoria, the Spanish legal representative of minors. In 1938 the colony was redesignated Spanish Territories of the Gulf of Guinea, and educated natives were permitted to claim Spanish citizenship as *emanicipados*. Spanish Guinea became a province of Spain in 1959, and in 1964 Río Muni and Fernando Po (Bioko) were created as two provinces under an autonomous regional government. Full independence was granted in 1968. Power passed into the hands of a militantly anti-Western and anti-Christian Fang group led by Macias Nguema Biyogo who became the nation's first president. The following year Macias seized emergency powers during an international crisis and subsequently instituted a highly centralized, single-party state. The constitution adopted in 1973 gave the president virtually unlimited powers. During his 11-year rule Macias turned his country into the "Auschwitz of Africa." Throwing off all constitutional and civilized restraints he cut off his country from all contact with the outside world (except for a few hundred Cuban military advisers). As the economy disintegrated he embarked on an orgy of mass executions and religious persecution that claimed thousands of lives.

In 1979 Macias was overthrown in a coup led by his nephew, Teodoro Obiang Nguema Mbasogo, who assumed the presidency of a Supreme Military Council. (Macias was subsequently arrested; put on trial; found guilty of treason, genocide, embezzlement, and violation of human rights; and executed by a firing squad.) In 1982 President Obiang Nguema was appointed president for another seven years immediately prior to the publication of a new constitution providing for the eventual return to civilian government.

President Obiang has proved himself to be one of the most durable of African dictators and also one of the most brutal. Although widely condemned both at home and abroad for his brutal suppression of human rights, he has managed to keep himself in power through rigging elections on the one hand and by imprisoning, torturing, and intimidating his opponents. Political parties were banned following Obiang's coup, and legislative elections were held in 1983 and 1988 that returned unopposed candidates nominated by the president. Obiang announced the formation of a government party, the Democratic Party of Equatorial Guinea, in 1987 as a step toward democratization and the possible legalization of other groups. However, no other parties have been permitted, and opponents are repressed. The Obiang regime survived four coup attempts in 1981, 1983, 1986, and 1988, mainly with the help of the 500-man Moroccan mercenary palace guard. A new constitution was approved in 1991, and multiparty elections took place in November 1993 but were internationally condemned as undemocratic. In the 1996 elections, Obiang claimed victory with 99.6 percent of the votes. International monitors called this election and the legislative elections held in 1999 a sham. The next presidential elections are scheduled for 2003, and so far one exiled opposition leader, Florentino Ecomo Nsogo, head of the Party of Reconstruction and Social Well-Being, has returned home in response to an appeal by Obiang for parties to register in the election.

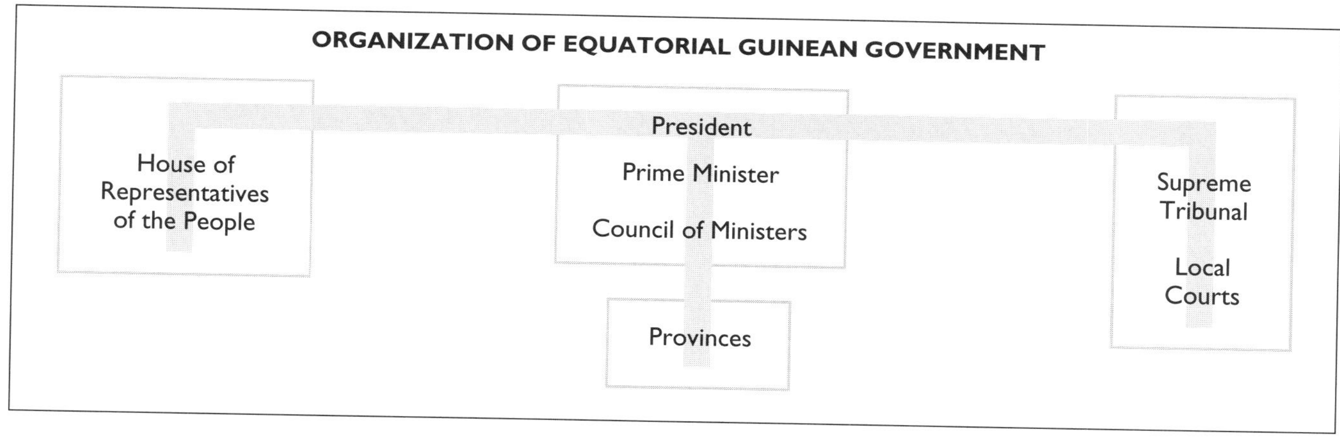

CONSTITUTION

The current constitution, approved by referendum in 1982, provides for a president who is head of state, head of government, and commander in chief. He is empowered to appoint and dismiss ministers and to determine and direct national policy. Obiang was appointed president for a seven-year term just prior to the adoption of the constitution. At the end of the period, under the constitution, the president was to be elected for a seven-year term by universal suffrage. The constitution also provides for a State Council of 11 members (including the chairman of the House of Representatives, the president of the Supreme Tribunal, and the minister of defense), which also acts as an electoral college. The national legislature is the House of Representatives, which is elected for a term of five years; its members must be 45 to 60 years of age. It sits twice a year, in March and September, for two-month sessions. The National Council for Social and Economic Development serves the administration in an advisory capacity. The constitution was modified in 1991 allowing for multiple political parties.

LOCAL GOVERNMENT

For purposes of local administration Equatorial Guinea is divided into six provinces, four mainland and two insular. Each province is subdivided into two to seven districts, administered by local councils. Regional and provincial administrations were abolished in 1973.

Local Government

Principal administrative divisions, capitals, area, population

AREA AND POPULATION

Regions / Provinces	Capitals	area sq mi	area sq km	population 1987 estimate
Insular		785	2,034	70,280
Annobon	Palè	7	17	2,360
Bioko Norte	Malabo	300	776	2,360
Bioko Sur	Luba	479	1,241	11,320
Continental		10,045	26,017	259,950
Centro-Sur	Evinayong	3,834	9,931	55,970
Kie-Ntem	Ebebiyin	1,552	3,943	74,050
Litoral	Bata	2,573	6,665	75,640
Wele-Nzas	Mongomo	2,115	5,478	54,290
TOTAL		10,831	28,051	330,230

PARLIAMENT

Under the constitution the national legislature is the House of Representatives, an 80-member unicameral assembly whose members must be 45 to 60 years of age and are popularly elected for five-year terms. It sits twice a year, in March and September, for two-month sessions.

POLITICAL PARTIES

While in theory (and to some extent in practice) Equatorial Guinea is a multiparty state, the country is ruled by its president and his party, Democratic Party for Equatorial Guinea or PDGE, which holds 68 of the 80 seats in parliament. Other parties with at least one seat include the Convergence Party for Social Democracy or CPDS, the Democratic Social Union or UDS, and the Liberal Democratic Convention or CLD. Additionally there are more than a dozen political parties that have no representation in the national assembly.

Political Parties

Democratic Party, 1987
Liberal Democratic Convention, 1992
Social Democratic Union, 1992
Progress Party, 1983
Popular Union, 1992
Convergence for Social Democracy, 1984
- Democratic Movement for the Liberation of Equatorial Guinea, 1981
- African Socialist Party

Socialist Party
Social Democratic Party, 1992
Republican Democratic Forces, 1997

(continued)

Social Democratic and Popular Convention
Social Democratic Coalition Party, 1993
Opposition Coordination of Equatorial Guinea
- Union for Democracy and Social Development
- Party of Reunification

Coordinating Board of Opposition Democratic Forces, 1983
- National Alliance for the Restoration of Democracy, 1974
- Movement for the Liberation and Future of Equatorial Guinea
- Liberation Front of Equatorial Guinea
- Democratic Reform

Revolutionary Command Council of Socialist Guinean Patriots and Cadres, 1981

Political Parties: Strength in Parliament Most Recent Elections

Party	Seats
Democratic Party	75
Popular Union	4
Convergence for a Social Democracy	1

LEGAL SYSTEM

The judicial system is headed by the Supreme Tribunal at Malabo, which hears appeals from civil and military courts in the administrative divisions. All judges are appointed by the president and serve at his pleasure.

The current court system is a combination of traditional, civil, and military justice, which often operates in an ad hoc manner for lack of established procedures and experienced judicial personnel. Most trials are speedy. In cases of petty theft or civil dispute, all parties are brought before the judge, who listens, questions, and then most often sets a fine to be paid by one party or the other. Fines also may be levied in lieu of imprisonment in cases against the state.

LAW ENFORCEMENT

Law Enforcement

Offenses reported to the police per 100,000:
- Murder:
- Assault:
- Burglary:
- Automobile Theft:
- Population per Police officer: 190

Death Penalty: Yes.

HUMAN RIGHTS

In terms of civil and political rights Equatorial Guinea is classified as a country that is not free. The regime of dictator Macias Nguema Biyogo was so repressive and brutal that any regime must appear civilized in comparison. The government of Teodoro Obiang Nguema Mbasogo has concentrated all its efforts on undoing the harm done by the former dictator. As part of its program for national reconstruction, the new government established a legal frame of reference and is building up new legal institutions and procedures. The government has stated that because of the destruction of the country's economy and social services under Macias it may be years before the country enjoys political and civil rights.

FOREIGN POLICY

Because of continuing Spanish opposition to the Obiang regime, diplomatic relations between Spain and Equatorial Guinea were suspended in 1997. France is the only country still maintaining reciprocal diplomatic relations with Equatorial Guinea, which is the only non-Francophone member of UDEAC, the Central African Customs and Economic Union. As the only Spanish-speaking African country, Equatorial Guinea is anxious to develop links with Latin America and has been accorded permanent observer status with OAS.

DEFENSE

The defense structure is headed by the president, who is the commander in chief of the Guardia Nacional. Little is known of the armed forces except that in the past, they had been trained by Cuban and Chinese personnel. The total strength of the Guardia Nacional is estimated at 1,400 with 2,000 additional paramilitary personnel. The country spends less than 1 percent of gross domestic product (GDP) on the military (1998).

Military Indicators

Total Active Duty Personnel: 1,300
Military Manpower per 1,000: 3
Military Expenditures $: 2 million
- as % of GNP: 1.6
- per capita $: 6
- as % of central government expenditures: 21.0

Arms Imports $: 0
Arms Exports $: 0

ECONOMY

The discovery and exploitation of large oil reserves have contributed to dramatic economic growth in recent years. Forestry, farming, and fishing are also major components of GDP. Subsistence farming predominates. Although preindependence Equatorial Guinea counted on cocoa production for hard currency earnings, the deterioration of the rural economy under successive brutal regimes has diminished potential for agriculture-led growth. A number of aid programs sponsored by the World Bank and the IMF have been cut off since 1993 because of the government's gross corruption and mismanagement. Businesses, for the most part, are owned by government officials and their family members. Undeveloped natural resources include titanium, iron ore, manganese, uranium, and alluvial gold. The country responded favorably to the devaluation of the CFA franc in January 1994. Boosts in production, along with high world oil prices, stimulated growth in 2000, with oil accounting for 90 percent of greatly increased exports.

Principal Economic Indicators

Gross National Product: $444 million
GNP per capita: $1,060
GNP Average Annual Growth Rate (1990–97)%: 12.1
GNP per capita Average Annual Growth Rate (1990–97)%: 9.6
Origin of Gross Domestic Product %
- Agriculture: 47
- Mining: —
- Manufacturing: 21
- Construction: 5
- Public Utilities: 3
- Transportation and Communications: 2
- Trade: 9
- Financial Services: 2
- Other Services: 3
- Government: 5

Gross Domestic Product by Type of Expenditure %
- Private Consumption: 59
- Government Consumption: 16
- Gross Domestic Investment: 25
- Foreign Trade: Exports: 55
- Imports: −55
- % of Income Received by Poorest 20%: —
- % of Income Received by Richest 10%: —

Price and earnings indexes (1995 = 100)

	1987	1988	1989	1990	1991	1992	1993
Consumer price index	92.3	93.4	98.9	100.0	96.8	89.9	93.5
Earnings index	—	—	—	—	—	—	—

Finance

National Currency: CFA Franc (CFAF)
Exchange Rate: $1 = CFAF 608.36
Money Supply Stock in National Currency billion: 9.5
M1 per capita: 22,300
Central Bank Discount Rate %: 7.60
Total External Debt $million: 254
Debt Service Ratio %: 0.5

Balance of Payments $million: −268.1
International Reserves SDRs million: —
Ratio of External Debt to Total Reserves: —

Average Annual Rate of Inflation/Consumer Price Index Growth Rate %: 6

Official Development Assistance

ODA: $—
- as % of GNP: —
- per capita: $—
- Foreign Direct Investment $million: —

Central Government Revenues and Expenditures

Fiscal Year: 1 April–31 March

Revenues $million: 47
Expenditures $million: 43
Budget Surplus $: 4 million
Tax Revenues as % of GDP: —
Highest Tax Bracket %
- Individual: —
- Corporate: —

Employment and Labor

Economically Active Population: 103,000
Female Participation Rate %: 35.7
Activity Rate %: 39.2
Labor by Sector: %
- Agriculture, Forestry, Fishing: 57.9
- Manufacturing, Mining: 1.8
- Construction: 1.9
- Transportation and Communications: 1.7
- Trade, Hotels, and Restaurants: 3.0
- Finance, Insurance, Real Estate: 0.4
- Public Administration, Defense: —
- Services: 8.2

Unemployment %: —

Agriculture

Agriculture's Share of GDP %: 47
Average Annual Rate of Growth (1965–98) %: —
Number of Farms 000: —
Average Size of Farm ha: —
Number of Tractors per 1,000 hectares: 0.8
Irrigation, % of Farms having: —
Artificial Fertilizer kg/hectare: —
Total Cropland as % of Farmland: —
Livestock: Cattle 000: 5
- Sheep 000: 6
- Hogs 000: 5
- Chickens 000: 245

Forests: Production of Roundwood (000 cubic meters): 811
Fisheries: Total Catch tons 000: 3,700

Mining

% of GDP: 20.2
Value of Mineral Production $million: 26

Manufacturing

Value Added $million: 1.9
Industrial Production Growth Rate %: 7.4

Energy

Commercial Energy Production metric tons of oil equivalent 000: —
Commercial Energy Consumption metric tons of oil equivalent 000: —
Commercial Energy Consumption per capita kg: —
Average Annual Growth Rate 1980–97 %: —
Net Energy Imports % of use: —

(continued)

Electricity Installed Capacity kW 000: 5,000
Production kW-hr million: 20
Coal Reserves tons million: —
Production tons 000: —
Natural Gas Proven Reserves cubic meters billion: 37
Production cubic meters million: —
Crude Petroleum Reserves barrels million: 12
Production barrels million: 3
Consumption barrels million: 10,000
Refinery Capacity barrels per day 000: —
Pipelines Length km: —

Foreign Trade

Imports $million: 61.6
Exports $million: 61.7
Export Volume % Annual Growth Rate (1990–97): —
Import Volume % Annual Growth Rate (1990–97): —
Balance of Trade $

Balance of trade (current prices)

	1990	1991	1992	1993	1994	1995
CFAF 000,000,000	−8.5	−15.5	−2.8	0.0	+17.1	+5.2
% of total	29.7%	43.7%	9.3%	0.0%	31.0%	6.4%

Major Trading Partners

	Imports	Exports
European Union %	31.5	47.2
United States %	39.9	—
Eastern Europe %	—	—
Japan %	0.3	—
Others %	28.3	52.8

Transportation

Roads Total Length mi: 1,667 (2,682 km)
Paved %: 19
Automobiles: 6,500
Trucks and Buses: 4,000
Persons per vehicle: 37
Railroad; Track Length mi: —
Passenger-mi million: —
Freight-mi million: —
Merchant Marine: No. of Vessels: 3
Total Deadweight Tonnage 000: 6,700
International Cargo Loaded tons 000: 110,000
International Cargo Off-loaded tons 000: 64,000
Airports with Scheduled Flights: 1
Traffic: Passenger-mi million: 4
Freight-mi million: 700,000
Length of Canals mi: —

Tourism

Number of Tourists to: —
Number of Tourists from: —
Tourist Receipts $million: 2
Tourist Expenditures $million: —

Communications

Telephones 000: 2.5
Cost of Local Calls 3 mins: $0
Cellular Telephones: —
Fax Machines 000: 0.1
Personal Computers: —
Internet Hosts per million persons: —
Mail: Post Offices: 23
Pieces of Mail Handled million: —
Pieces of Mail Handled per person: —

EDUCATION

Education is, in principle, free, universal, and compulsory for eight years, from ages six to 14.

Schooling is a 12- or 14-year program and consists of six or eight years of first-level education, four years of middle-level education, and two years of second-level education.

The academic year runs from October to June. The medium of instruction is Spanish.

There is a teacher training school at Malabo and a normal school at Bata. Adult literacy rates are reported to have increased from 20 percent in 1978 to 78 percent in 1998–99.

Two higher educational centers (at Malabo and Bata) are administered by the Spanish Universidad Nacional de Educacion a Distancia.

Education

Literacy Rate %: 78.5
Male %: 89.6
Female %: 68.1
First Level: Primary schools: 781
Teachers: 1,381
Students: 75,751
Student-Teacher Ratio: 54.9
Net Enrollment Ratio: —
Second Level: Secondary Schools: —
Teachers: 466
Students: 14,511
Student-Teacher Ratio: 31.1
Net Enrollment Ratio: —

Vocational Level: Schools: —
Students: 2,105

Third Level: Institutions: —
Teachers: 58
Students: 578
Student-Ratio Level: 10.0
Gross Enrollment Ratio: —
Students per 100,000: 164
% of Population Age 25 and over with Postsecondary Education: —

Public Expenditure on Education as % of GDP: 1.8

SCIENCE AND TECHNOLOGY

Science and Technology

Scientists and Engineers in R&D per 1 million persons: —
Expenditures in R&D as % of GDP: —
High-Tech Exports $: —
Patent Applications by Residents: —

MEDIA

Equatorial Guinea has one daily newspaper with a circulation of about 2,000. Equatorial Guinea has no national news agency. Neither does it have a book publishing industry.

Equatorial Guinea has three radio stations: Africa 2000 broadcasts cultural and sports programs in Spanish; Radio Ecuatorial Bata broadcasts programs in Spanish, French, and vernacular languages; and Radio Santa Isabel offers programs in Spanish, French, Fang, Bubi, Annobones, and Combe. All three stations are owned by the government. There is one television station in the nation.

Media

Daily Newspapers: 1
Total Circulation 000: 2
Circulation per 1,000: 4.3
Books Published: —
Magazines: —
Radio Receivers 000: 200
per 1,000: 488
Television sets 000: 37
per 1,000: 92

Most Important Media:

Press. The following are published irregularly at Malabo: *Ebano* (1,000), in Spanish; *Poto Poto* (Bata), in Spanish and Fang; *Unidad de la Guinea Ecuatorial.* In January 1994 the weekly *El Sol* became the first private newspaper to be recognized by the government.

News agency. The only facility currently operating at Malabo is Spain's Agencia EFE.

Radio and television. Radio Nacional de Guinea Ecuatorial (RNGE) broadcasts over two stations at Malabo and one at Bata in Spanish and vernacular languages. The government's Television Nacional transmits over one channel at Malabo.

CULTURE

Cultural Indicators

Public Libraries
Number: —
Volumes: —
Registered borrowers: —
Museums
Number: —
Annual Attendance: —
Cinema
Production of Long Films: —
Number of Cinemas: —
Seating Capacity: —
Annual Attendance: —
Annual Attendance per capita: —

STATUS OF WOMEN

The law states that both sexes, and all tribal groups, are equal and entitled to the same rights and privileges. For a variety of reasons, women are accorded a lower status than men are and have a correspondingly lower status and influence in the society and government. Men often take several wives, but women are never permitted multiple husbands. Social tradition and the fact that women produce most of the basic food items keep most women engaged in agriculture or domestic work. Five times as many males as females enter secondary school, and eight times as many graduate at this level. Because of the severe need for skilled people of all types, however, women can have professional careers and do hold important jobs in the health sector and in other socially oriented ministries.

Women

Gender Empowerment Measure: 5.0
Seats Held in Parliament by Women %: —
Female Administrators and Managers %: —
Female Professional and Technical Workers %: —
Women's Share of Earned Income %: —
Women in Government %: 4.9

HEALTH, FOOD, AND NUTRITION

Health

Number of Physicians: 99
Number of Dentists: —
Number of Nurses: 154
Number of Pharmacists: —
Population per Physician: 3,532
Number of Hospitals: —
Hospital Beds per 10,000: 29
Hospital Bed Occupancy Rate: —
Infant Mortality Rate per 1,000 live births: 167
Maternal Mortality Rate per 100,000 live births: —
Total Health Expenditures as % of GDP: 7.60
Health Expenditures per capita $: 28
HIV Infected % of adults: —
Cigarette Consumption per smoker per year: —
% of Smokers: Male: —
Female: —
Access to Safe Water %: 95

Food and Nutrition

Food Supply as % of FAO Requirements:
% of Consumption Expenditures on Food: 62.0
Daily Available Calories per capita: —
% of Total Calories derived from: —
Cereals: —
Potatoes, cassava: —
Meat, poultry: —
Fish: —
Eggs, milk: —
Fruits, vegetables: —
Fats, oils: —

ENVIRONMENT

One legacy of colonial Spanish rule was the preservation of much of Equatorial Guinea's biodiversity. Spanish rule helped preserve rain forests and animal life that otherwise might have been destroyed by too rapid development. However, since the end of colonial rule, the country's resources have been poorly managed and are now threatened. The country suffers from problems common to developing countries, including deforestation, shortages of potable water, and contamination of water resources. While the government has adopted a number of plans to curb deforestation and protect the biodiversity of the country, little has actually been achieved. With a stagnant economy and growing demand for agricultural land to feed a booming population, the exploitation of natural resources as a source of money and food is likely to continue.

Environment

Forest Area sq km: —
Average Annual Deforestation sq km: —
Nationally Protected Areas as % of Total Land Area: —
Freshwater Access cubic meters per capita: 69,541
Emissions of Organic Water Pollutants kg per day: —
CO_2 Emissions per capita ton: 0.3

CHRONOLOGY

1968 Equatorial Guinea formally proclaims its independence with Macias Nguema Biyogo as president and Atanasio Ndong as foreign minister.

1969 New agreements covering economic and educational programs are signed with Spain.
Conflict erupts between Fang and Bubis on Fernando Po Island (Bioko).
Relations with Spain are strained as ethnic strife widens.
Spanish troops withdraw from the country, and Spanish civilians are repatriated.
Foreign Minister Ndong is accused of fomenting unrest and is arrested and reportedly killed; mass purge of Macias Nguema Biyogo's political enemies follows.

1970 PUNT is formed and declared the sole legal political party in the country.

1972 Macias Nguema Biyogo is proclaimed president for life.
New agreement is signed with Spain.

1973 PUNT's Third Party Congress approves new constitution, and provincial autonomy is abolished.
Under a program of Africanizing geographical names, Fernando Po is renamed Macias Nguema Biyogo, Santa Isabel is renamed Malabo, Annabon is renamed Pagalu, and Rio Benito River is renamed Mbini.

1974 Government launches a campaign of terror, causing nearly 100,000 citizens to seek asylum in neighboring countries.
In a parallel campaign against the Catholic Church, Spanish bishops and nuns are expelled, Catholic schools and churches are closed, African nuns and priests are arrested, and Equatorial Guineans are compelled by decree to drop their Christian names.
A minor dispute with Gabon is resolved as Gabon withdraws claim.

1975 The ekuele is introduced as the national currency, replacing the Guinean peseta.
Nigerian government charges Equatorial Guinea with inhuman treatment of Nigerian workers; Nigerian workers are evacuated.

1976 United States suspends diplomatic relations with Equatorial Guinea.

1979 President Macias is overthrown in a coup led by his nephew Teodoros Obiang Mguema Mbasogo, who sets up the Supreme Military Council with himself as president; Macias is arrested, tried on a number of charges, including treason, embezzlement, genocide, and other atrocities, found guilty, and shot by a firing squad. King Juan Carlos of Spain visits the country and receives a warm welcome, signifying the pro-Spanish and pro-Western tilt of the new regime.
Relations with the United States are restored.

1980 Fishing accord with the Soviet Union is revoked.

1982 Obiang Nguema Mbasogo is appointed president for a second term of seven years.
New constitution is approved by 95 percent of the voters.
Cristino Seriche Bioko is named prime minister.

1983 Equatorial Guinea joins the Customs and Economic Union of Central Africa and the Central African Economic Community.

1985 Equatorial Guinea adopts the CFA franc as its national currency.

1987 Obiang announces the formation of a government party, the Partido Democrático de Guinea Ecuatorial.

1989 Obiang is elected president in a contest in which he is the only candidate.

1990 Amnesty International accuses Equato-Guinean authorities of torturing political prisoners.
1992 A 1991 law allowing for a multiparty democracy goes into effect.
1996 President Nguema Mbasogo is reelected with 99 percent of the votes cast.
1999 Legislative elections dominated by the ruling Democratic Party of Equatorial Guinea are widely condemned as fraudulent.

BIBLIOGRAPHY

Fegley, Randall. *Equatorial Guinea: An African Tragedy*. New York, 1989.

Linger-Goumaz, Max. *Historical Dictionary of Equatorial Guinea*. Lantham, Md., 2000.

OFFICIAL PUBLICATIONS

Equatorial Guinea. *Censos Nacionales, I de Poblacion y I de Vivienda—4 al 17 de Julio de 1983*; *Equatorial Guinea—Background Appendices* and *Recent Economic Developments* (IMF Staff Country Reports [1995 and 1996]); *Guinea en cifras* (irreg.).

CONTACT INFORMATION

Embassy of Equatorial Guinea
1511 K Street NW, Suite 405
Washington, D.C. 20005
Phone: (202) 393-0525 Fax: (202) 393-0348

INTERNET RESOURCES

- Official Home Page of the Republic of Equatorial Guinea http://www.equatorialguinea.org

ERITREA

BASIC FACT SHEET

OFFICIAL NAME:
State of Eritrea (Hagere Ertra)

ABBREVIATION:
ER

CAPITAL:
Asmara

HEAD OF STATE & HEAD OF GOVERNMENT:
President Issayas Aferworki (from 1993)

NATURE OF GOVERNMENT:
Emerging democracy

POPULATION:
3,985,000

AREA:
121,144 sq km (46,774 sq mi)

MAJOR ETHNIC GROUP:
Tigrinya (50%); Tigre and Kunama (40%)

LANGUAGES:
Afar, Amharic Arabic, Tigre, Kunama, Tigrinya

RELIGIONS:
Muslim, Christian

UNIT OF CURRENCY:
Nakfa

NATIONAL FLAG:
Red isosceles triangle (based on the hoist side) dividing the flag into two right triangles; the upper triangle is green, the lower one is blue; a gold wreath encircling a gold olive branch is centered on the hoist side of the red triangle

NATIONAL ANTHEM:
"Eritrea, Eritrea, Eritrea"

NATIONAL HOLIDAYS:
National Day, May 24

DATE OF INDEPENDENCE:
May 24, 1993

DATE OF CONSTITUTION:
May 23, 1997

GEOGRAPHICAL FEATURES

Eritrea, a relatively new country, is located in the northern part of the Horn of Africa with its eastern section bordering the Red Sea. Its size is 121,144 sq km (46,774 sq mi). On the western border lies Sudan, while to the south and southeast Eritrea borders Ethiopia and Djibouti, respectively. The country's geographical features provide a rich diversity of topography and climate within short distances of each other. The geographical features can be classified into four categories.

The first category is the Kebesa Plateau of central Eritrea, at 6000–8,000 ft (1,829–2,438 m) above sea level. It features an elevated plain dotted with hills. Deep canyons, valleys, and fertile plains also mark the plateau. On the eastern part of the plateau, the area is covered with shrub, juniper, and olive trees. The Hazemo Plains, a flat and fertile agricultural land, spreads to the south in the Akele Guzai districts with ancient villages, archaeological sites, monasteries, and wildernesses of eclectric mix. Here also is found Eritrea's highest mountain, Eimba Soira, a towering edifice with foreboding majesty. On the northern section of the plateau, the terrain breaks into an uneven descent of fertile valleys and rises to high mountains and intermediate plateaus called *roras*. The vegetation contains some wooded areas on the eastern slopes of the plateau known as *bahri*, with lush scenery in the summer. Some of the main rivers emptying their waters into the Red Sea include Komaile, Haddas, and Algede. About 30 miles west of Asmara, the terrain breaks into a steep descent to the Barka lowlands. The Mereb and Anseba Rivers originate from the Kebessa Plateau and drain their waters into

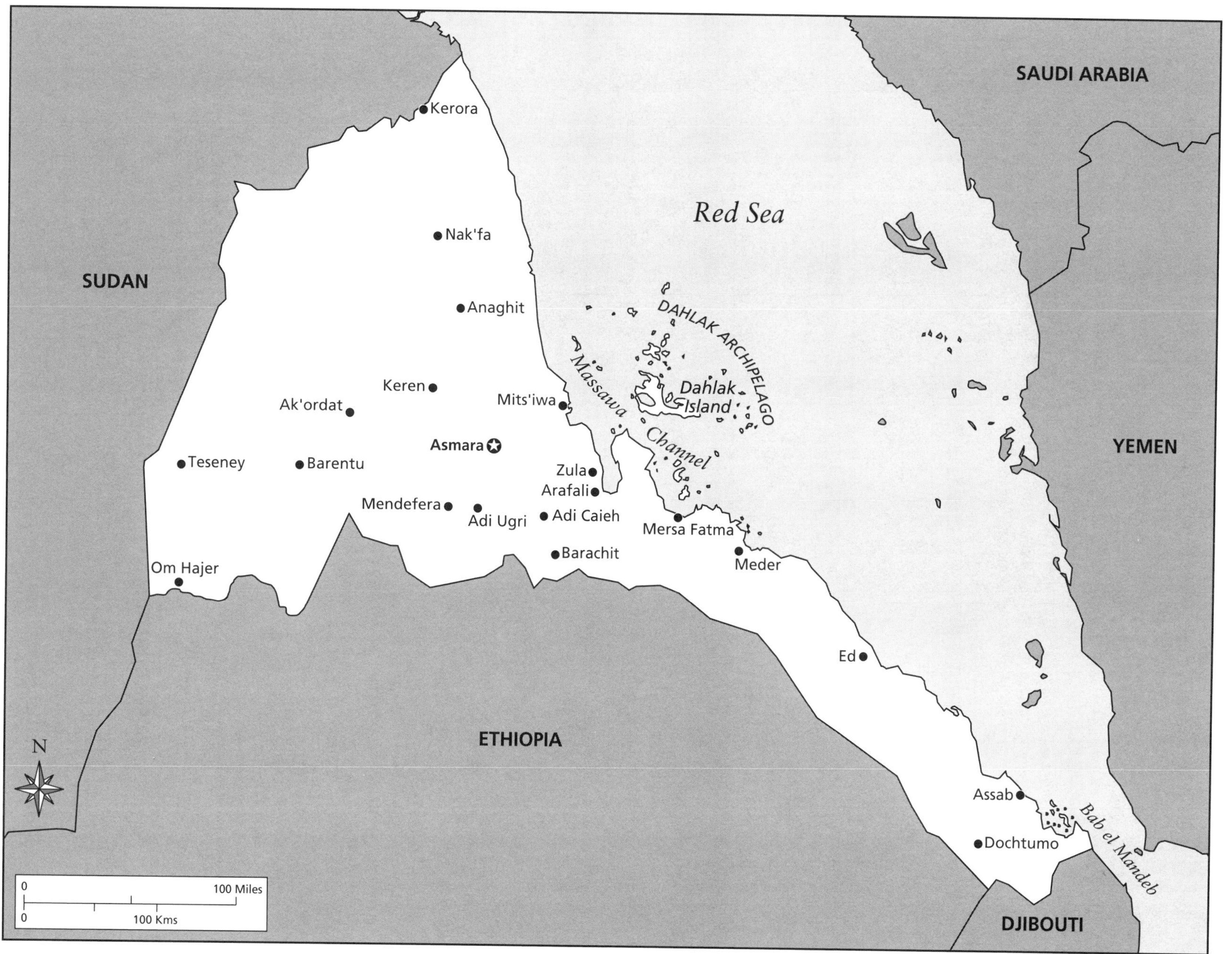
Eritrea
SAUDI ARABIA
Red Sea
SUDAN
YEMEN
DAHLAK ARCHIPELAGO
Dahlak Island
Massawa Channel
Kerora
Nak'fa
Anaghit
Keren
Ak'ordat
Mits'iwa
Asmara
Teseney
Barentu
Zula
Arafali
Mendefera
Adi Ugri
Adi Caieh
Mersa Fatma
Barachit
Meder
Om Hajer
Ed
ETHIOPIA
N
Assab
Bab el Mandeb
Dochtumo
0
100 Miles
0
100 Kms
DJIBOUTI

the Barka plains and Sudan. The MayBella River, which originates from the center of Asmara, is one of the major tributaries of the Mereb. The Nefhee River originates just outside Asmara and is important for cultivation on the Gergar and Mensura Plains in the upper Barka.

The breadbasket of Eritrea is the Barka lowland at an elevation between 3,000 and 5,000 ft. It is a mixture of desert plains, arid prairies, palm trees, and fertile soil in the Gash valley where wild animals such as lions, elephants, and a host of assorted game are abundant. The cities of Barentu, Tessenei, Tecombia, and Ali Ghider are important trading centers supporting the dynamic agricultural activity that was resurrected in the postliberation period of the 1990s. Some 70 miles due south, at the edge where the lowlands touch the highlands, is the spectacular Laito Canyon.

The Red Sea Plains on the eastern seaboard, at an elevation of between 1,000 and 3,000 ft, contain a strip of sandy soil running north to south paralleling the Red Sea itself. In the north the region is sandy, covered with sparse grass and shrubs. On the southern seacoast lies the Dankel (Danakil) Depression, featuring inhospitable terrain consisting of dark volcanic soil with extremely hot temperatures the year round.

The northern highlands feature bare and stark mountains with intervals of fertile valleys at 6000 to 8000 ft above sea level. The rivers Lebka, Laba, and Falat originate from this area and drain their waters into the Red Sea. The small towns of Nakfa, Af Abet, Karora, and SheEb are closely identified with Eritrea's struggle for independence as military bases and sites of Eritrean wars of liberation.

Geography

Area sq km: 121,144 sq mi 46,774
World Rank: 99th
Land Boundaries, km: Djibouti 113; Ethiopia 912; Sudan 605
Coastline, km: 2,234
Elevation Extremes meters
- Lowest: Kobar Sink −75
- Highest: Soira 3,013

Land Use % Arable land: 12
- Permanent Crops: 1
- Permanent Pastures: 48
- Forest and Woodland: 20
- Other: 19

Population of Principal Cities

Asmara	431,000

CLIMATE AND WEATHER

Eritrea's seasons are classified into annual quarters as KewEy (fall), Ayet (winter), Hagay/Tsidiaya (autumn), and Keremty (summer). These seasons correspond to seasonal rains for planting and harvesting crops. Traditionally, the year starts on September 1, when the annual Udet, a type of harvest festivity, is celebrated.

On the Kebessa Plateau, the climate is moderate with a year round temperature of 60–65°F (16–19°C) around Asmara, the capital city. The northern plateau shares an identical climate to the Kebessa. The vast stretch of the seacoast, north to south, is hot and humid. Massawa, with an average temperature of 77°F (25°C), and Assab, slightly higher at 78°F (26°C), are the main coastal cites. In July the temperature for Massawa and Assab averages 95°F (35°C). Annual precipitation for Massawa is 7.6 in. For Assab, the rainfall rarely comes above 1.2 in. The rainfall in the south and west is similar to the western slopes resulting in the lush forests and grasslands that support animals such as lions and elephants.

Climate and Weather

Temperature Range
Summer 90°F to 120°F
Winter 76°F to 82°
Average Rainfall 5.6 in

POPULATION

Population Indicators

Total Population: 1999 3,985,000
World Rank: 118th
Density per sq mi: 85.2 per sq km: 32.9
% of annual growth (1994–99): 3.7
Male %: 49.9
Female %: 50.1
Urban %: 15.1
Age Distribution: %
- 0–14: 46.1
- 15–29: 23.0
- 30–44: 15.9
- 45–59: 8.9
- 60–74: 4.4
- 75 and over: 1.6

Population 2020: 7,471,000
Birth Rate per 1,000: 39.8
Death Rate per 1,000: 14.7
Population Doubling Time (years): 23
Infant Mortality Rate per 1,000 live births: 98.0
Rate of Natural Increase per 1,000: 25.1
Total Fertility Rate: 5.3
Expectation of Life (years): Males 49.1
Females 52.1
Marriage Rate per 1,000: 6.8
Divorce Rate per 1,000: —
Total Number of Households: —
Average Size of Households: —
% of Illegitimate Children: —
Induced Abortions: —
- Rate per 100 live births: —

ETHNIC COMPOSITION

Eritrea's population is composed of four major ethnic groups. The first group is the Nilotic extract consisting of the Baza/Kunama, Mogolo, and Nara, who speak Hamitic languages. They rely on sedentary agriculture, herding, and hunting. They occupy the southwestern part of the country along the Gash and Setit River banks. The Baza are considered the earliest inhabitants of this area.

The second group is the Baja and the Beniamir. They occupy the northwestern and northern stretch of the Barka and Anseba Rivers, extending as far north as the Nakfa and Karora districts. They both use the Tigre and Hidareb languages. Their ancestry is variously attributed to Beja from southern Egypt. There are also claims that they belong to the Sabean or Himyaritic from South Arabia.

On the southeastern seacoasts are found the third ethnic group, the Saho/Asawrta and Afar peoples both of Hamitic origin and languages. They both share a nomadic life of harsh existence in an inhospitable physical environment. The Afar make their nomadic tours in the Danakil areas. The Sahos migrate to the western lowlands from their habitat in the southeastern part of the Kebessa Plateau.

The fourth, and dominant, ethnic group, the Tigrignia-speaking population, is located at the Kebessa Plateau. They identify themselves as Agaazian, which means "onward marching warriors." The Arabs changed the nomenclature to Habash, meaning of mixed blood/race. The spoken language by the Agaazian people was Ge'ez, a Semitic language from which Tigre and Tigrignia were derived. They share a common heritage and ancestry with the Aksumite Kingdom of Tigray, in Ethiopia. The manner of their arrival in Eritrea is traced to South Arabia from where they crossed the Red Sea and settled on the plateau. They intermingled with the local inhabitants to form the Habasha community, who have since dominated political and cultural life in the highlands of modern Eritrea and northern Ethiopia.

LANGUAGES

Principal Languages and Their Speakers

Cushitic languages	
Afar	170,000
Bilin	120,000
Hadareb (Beja)	150,000
Saho	120,000
Nilotic languages	
Kunama	110,000
Nara	80,000
Semitic languages	
Arabic (Rashaida)	10,000
Tigre	1,260,000
Tigrinya	1,950,000

RELIGIONS

The Eritrean population is evenly divided between Muslims and Christians. Christianity entered Eritrea and Ethiopia at the same time in the fourth century C.E. when Syrian missionaries from Tyre succeeded in converting the Aksumite ruler, King Ezana, to Christianity. In the 15th century, the first rift on doctrinal matters emerged between the Eritrean and the Ethiopian Churches. The theological rift led to protracted civil wars involving the northern and the southern churches. Gradually the violence subsided as the church in general lost its evangelical zeal and focused on administrative issues. Meanwhile, the church's relation with Alexandria, Egypt, continued until the 1940s when the Ethiopian Church declared its autonomy from Alexandria. The war with Ethiopia in 1998 has caused some politicization of the Eritrean Coptic Orthodox Church. In late 1998 the church separated itself from the Ethiopian diocese and established its own synod.

Islam was introduced in Eritrea sometime in the seventh century A.D. when the followers of the prophet Muhammad sought refuge in the region from their Jewish persecutors in Arabia. It gained its ascendance when the Arabs overran Egypt, seriously crippling Egyptian and Nubian Christianity. Islamic warriors and merchants, mixing commerce with religious fervor, pushed southward to northeastern Sudan and penetrated the northern and western lowlands of Eritrea. Islamic mosques replaced churches and monasteries. On the seacoast, they occupied the Eritrean islands of Dahlak off Massawa and marched on the eastern highlands. From there, they edged upward to western and northern Eritrea in the mid-19th century.

Catholicism and Protestantism arrived late in the 1840s. Their evangelizing mission was thwarted due to the xenophobic impulses of the Coptic Orthodox Church. Today, the Eritrean government has enforced rights of worship on an equal basis and the dominance once enjoyed by the Coptic Orthodox Church is severely curtailed.

Religious Affiliations

Muslim	2,760,000
Eritrean Orthodox	1,220,000

HISTORICAL BACKGROUND

Paleontologists have identified areas in Eritrea, as well as some on the Denakil Depression in Ethiopia, as sites of the origin of the human species. Whereas the Eritrean plateau was an integral part of the Aksumite Kingdom, which flourished from the fourth century B.C. until the sixth century A.D., the lowlands were independent principalities and dominions as far as eastern Sudan on the west and Massawa on the eastern part of the Eritrean coast.

However, the modern history of Eritrea is strongly affected by colonialism. From the 16th century the area was occupied by the Ottoman Turks. In the 17th century, the Funj Kingdom of Sinar, modern Sudan, controlled the Gash-Barka lowlands and attempted to subjugate the

Beniamir and Beja population. After the decline of the Funj, Egypt ruled over much of Eritrea from 1819 to 1886. Egyptian influence over Eritrean territories was precarious and costly. It gave way to European colonialism in the 19th century.

With the opening of the Suez Canal, the Red Sea became an important waterway for trade and commerce. The opening of the canal and its impact on the Red Sea also coincided with the colonial scramble for Africa. Gradually Italy took initial steps in acquiring a foothold on the Red Sea coast. In 1869 an Italian company, in the name of the Italian government, bought the port of Assab from the local chief. Very quickly, Italian rulers invested energy and resources to develop Eritrea as an extension of Italy itself, and on January 1, 1890, Eritrea was declared Italy's first colony in Africa. Eritrea's political identity was to be forged anew through the political instruments that Italian colonialism brought to bear from 1890 to 1940, and in the 10 years of British military administration, 1941–51.

Italy mixed a brutal policy of racism with industrial ingenuity to rule Eritrea. The colony, with its ideal Mediterranean climate and sufficient space for immigration, was a valuable asset for Italy. To facilitate effective exploitation of the colony, Italian engineers built roads, railways, and tunnels, and developed agriculture making Eritrea an extension of the Italian model. However, in order to prevent local rebellion by the Eritrean peoples, the colonial rulers strictly enforced official segregation in all areas of life. When Italy joined the Axis during World War II, it unwittingly initiated its own demise as a colonial power in Eritrea. Britain targeted Italy as a threat to its interests in East Africa. In successive battles waged between 1939 and 1941, British forces crushed the Italian Fascists and dislodged them first from Eritrea and then from Ethiopia.

Between 1941 and 1951, Eritrea, still under colonial status, was administered by Britain as an occupied enemy territory. The British found in Eritrean society that, under Italian colonialism, Eritreans endured horrendous oppression. Eritreans yearned for freedom from Italian colonialism, but they also were too alienated to be united with Ethiopia. Ethiopia's failure to contest the territory during Italian colonialism and its willingness to quickly renounce its claim to Eritrea reinforced Eritrean alienation from Ethiopia. During the Italian rule of their land, Eritreans solidified their sense of separate identity based on their colonial experiences.

The British Military Administration (BMA) was mandated by the United Nations to see Eritrea through a transitional phase either to independence or to a political union with Ethiopia. The BMA ruled Eritrea as an occupied "enemy territory." As a result of Italy's belligerence during World War II, Britain decided to expropriate those economic resources established by Italy in Eritrea. With respect to industrial and economic capital, what the Italians built in Eritrea, the British uprooted and destroyed.

However, on matters of political development, the British embarked on a liberal democratic restructuring of Eritrean politics. They expanded the educational sector, allowed for freedom of expression through free speech, and permitted freedom of assembly through political parties and labor unions.

When the British mandate over Eritrea ended in 1951, the United Nations decided to federate Eritrea with Ethiopia for 10 years after which the Eritreans would be given a chance for self-determination—either for union with Ethiopia or independence. Federation allowed Eritrea to have its own parliament with complete control of domestic affairs. Eritrea's seaports, its currency, and its foreign affairs were delegated to the Ethiopian emperor, Haile Selassie. In 1961, Haile Selassie arbitrarily dissolved the Eritrean parliament over the objection of its independent-minded parliamentarians. He declared Eritrea an Ethiopian province in 1962. The same year, an independence movement calling itself Mahber ShowAte (a company of seven) was formed as a clandestine movement for the liberation of Eritrea. Mahber ShowAte evolved into the Eritrean Liberation Movements (ELM) later to be known as the Eritrean Liberation Front (ELF) with declared goals of armed insurrection against the Ethiopian rulers.

The ELF demonstrated formidable military skills against the Ethiopian army. However, its political capacity lagged behind its military successes. As it evolved in military strength and organizational complexity, its key figures in the leadership failed to ameliorate simmering ethnic and religious conflicts. A splinter group, under the leadership of Issaias Afewerki, calling itself the Eritrean Peoples Liberation Front (EPLF), was formed in 1970.

EPLF took a stand against internal dissension imposing rigid military discipline combined with economic and political development in the areas it controlled. It thoroughly politicized the populace as a base of support for its military operations against the Ethiopians. Meanwhile, ELF was sidetracked from its military mission against the Ethiopians and waged war against the EPLF. A civil war pitting the two liberation fronts erupted and continued between 1970 and 1980. In 1980, ELF forces were defeated and fled to Sudan, where they were disarmed by the Sudanese and allowed to live there as refugees.

Between 1980 and 1991, the EPLF faced successive military campaigns by Ethiopian troops equipped with Soviet weapons and military advisers from East Germany, Cuba, and South Yemen. After prolonged guerrilla attacks and ambushes, the Ethiopian army and its advisers were exhausted. Finally in 1987, EPLF forces demolished a third of the Ethiopian army in the Battle of Af Abet. In 1990, EPLF liberated the port of Massawa and was poised to take over Asmara. The liberation war ended on May 24, 1991, when the EPLF liberated all of Eritrea.

On May 25, 1991, guerrilla forces lead by the Ethiopian Peoples Revolutionary Democratic Front (EPRDF) marched into Addis Ababa and replaced the military regime that had ruled Ethiopia since 1974. The EPLF and the EPRDF, having agreed to cooperate in solving Ethiopian and Eritrean disagreements, peacefully subscribed to a two-year waiting period before formally declaring Eritrean independence. At the end of the two years, Eritrea would conduct a referendum under international supervision for Eritreans to vote for independence or a federal union with Ethiopia. In 1993, the referendum was conducted. Eritreans overwhelmingly voted for Eritrean independence. On May 24, 1993, the country was declared a free and independent state. Ethiopia, Sudan, the United States, and the Organization of African Unity (OAU) extended recognition of Eritrea's independence.

After 30 years of liberation struggle, Eritrea focused on the task of reconstruction and rehabilitation. The government of Eritrea adopted a policy of self-reliance vowing to use its manpower to carry out economic development. However, disagreements over contested borders with Yemen and Ethiopia led to open military clashes. The war with Yemen broke out in 1995 and was quickly settled by international arbitration. The dispute with Ethiopia proved to be more lasting.

In 1997, Eritrea abandoned the Ethiopian currency, the birr, as legal tender, and issued its own currency, the nakfa. Tensions on both sides of the border grew fast, as economic transactions became sources of conflict as a result of the new instruments of trade, the nafa and the birr. The tension grew into a crisis when, early in 1997, Ethiopian militias destroyed border towns inhabited by Eritreans in the Badime district. Both countries established a border commission to deal with the crisis. Before the commission could begin its task, a border skirmish in June 1998 involving Eritrean regulars and Ethiopian militias grew into an open war when Ethiopia declared war on Eritrea. After two years of bloody war that claimed thousands of lives on both sides, and the displacement of a third of Eritrean civilians, the two countries signed an Agreement of Cessation of Hostilities on June 18, 2000. In December, Eritrea and Ethiopia signed a peace agreement that formally ended the war and established a commission to demarcate their border. By mid-2001, both Ethiopia and Eritrea had completed their troop withdrawal from the border zone. The United Nations continued to monitor the peace process.

CONSTITUTION

The government of the State of Eritrea started as a "provisional" government until the inauguration of the constitution. Since the referendum of 1993, the government had operated informally, lacking the ground rules established on constitutional provisions. Its organizational and operational directives were announced on May 19, 1993, in Proclamation No. 37/1993. In February 1994, the EPLF was disbanded and replaced by the Peoples Front for Democracy and Justice (PFDJ). The PFDJ divided the country into governorates and subgovernorates to be administered by officials handpicked from the ranks of the PFDJ and with experiences in EPLF political and military history.

The current governing body is the National Assembly consisting of 75 members of the PFDJ and 75 elected from the provinces by popular vote. The president is the head of the Assembly and head of the State Council or cabinet. As a "transitional" regime, the government enjoyed enormous popularity among the people. However, the tentative nature of its structure handicaps the regime and prevents it from claiming formal legitimacy.

The constitution was written in 1996 and submitted to the National Assembly. After a lengthy debate, the National Assembly accepted the constitution in 1997. On May 23, 1997, the Constituent Assembly, consisting of Eritreans from abroad and from the newly reconstituted electoral districts, ratified the Eritrean constitution.

The constitution emphasizes individual rights and liberties with particular attention to women's suffrage. Female soldiers made up more than 35 percent of both the Eritrean guerrilla forces before independence and the defense forces after independence. Voting age is set at 18 years. A parliamentary election scheduled to take place in 1998 to inaugurate the Eritrean Republic did not occur due to the eruption of war with Ethiopia in the spring of 1998.

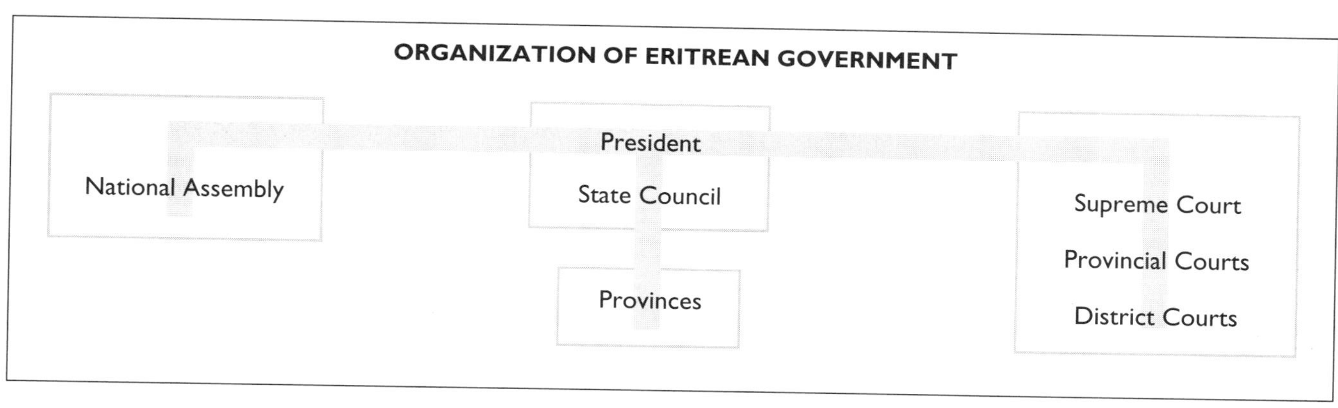

LOCAL GOVERNMENT

Local government and administration resembles the ward system of city politics in Western societies like the United States, the difference being that there is a high level of authoritarian discipline and accountability strictly enforced by the PFDJ on provincial and local councils.

The PFDJ directs electoral activities and grass-roots recruitment of candidates arguing that the population needs electoral education. Locally elected governing councils govern villages, towns, and cities. However, there is visible influence of the PFDJ in nominating and electing council members and village administrators as there is in the determination of district and province governors. The PFDJ has not shied away from exhibiting paternalistic authoritarianism throughout Eritrea, claiming that authority is indispensable for steady political and economic development.

Local Government

Principal administrative divisions, capitals, area, population

AREA AND POPULATION

		area		population 1997
Regions	**Capitals**	**sq mi**	**sq km**	**estimate**
Debub-Keih-Bahri	Asseb (Aseb)	10,660	27,600	—
Semien-Keih-Bahri	Massawa (Mitsiwa)	10,730	27,800	—
Anseba	Keren	8,960	23,200	—
Gash-Barka	Barentu	12,820	33,200	—
Debub	Mendefera	3,090	8,000	—
Maekel	Asmara (Asmera)	500	1,300	—
TOTAL		46,770	121,100	3,590,000

PARLIAMENT

In May 1997 the new constitution, after an extensive national debate, was adopted by a 527-member Constituent Assembly. Out of this body, a new National Assembly was impaneled consisting of 75 members of the PFDJ, 60 appointed from the Constituent Assembly, and 15 representing Eritreans living abroad. The election slated for 1998 to formally establish an Eritrean Republic has been postponed due to the outbreak of hostilities with Ethiopia.

POLITICAL PARTIES

The only existing party in Eritrea is the Peoples Front for Democracy and Justice (PFDJ). The constitution envisions a multiparty system based on secular party programs and platforms. Parties based on religious or ethnic affiliations are forbidden by the constitution. The government has recently announced that plans are underway to conduct elections based on specific election rules. The announcement anticipates spontaneous party formation of autonomous groups outside the party in government, the PFDJ.

Political Parties

People's Front for Democracy and Justice
Eritrea Liberation Front-includes numerous factions

THE LEGAL SYSTEM

The constitution, temporarily inactive due to the emergency situations as a result of the war with Ethiopia, provides for an independent court. However, the government has used it as an ad hoc tool to activate the legal process. The judiciary branch consists of 29 district courts, 10 provincial courts, and the Supreme Court. District courts have mandates to try civil, criminal, and tort cases. Provincial courts serve as appellate courts and review the procedural and constitutional standards used at the lower court level. The Supreme Court is the court of last resort that reviews the appellate courts' decisions and calls for their standing or reversal.

LAW ENFORCEMENT

Law Enforcement

Offenses reported to the police per 100,000: —
- Murder: —
- Assault: —
- Burglary: —
- Automobile Theft: —
- Population per Police officer: —

Death Penalty: Yes.

HUMAN RIGHTS

The written constitution guarantees personal and civil liberties with provisions for due process of law. There are explicit guarantees for the free exercise of religion, assembly, and the press. Universal suffrage for those 18 years and over is guaranteed, and women enjoy equal rights in inheritance, property ownership, marriages, and child rearing. Due to the delay in the implementation of the constitution resulting from the war with Ethiopia in 1998, the government's credibility in abiding by the constitutional provisions has not yet been tested.

Amnesty International, in its 1998 and 1999 reports, has declared some political prisoners were detained in violation of their human rights and due process. The government has countered by claiming that the detainees belonged to elements within the Eritrean Liberation Front (ELF) who were engaged in attempts at violent overthrow of the government and in the murder of innocent civilians.

FOREIGN POLICY

Eritrea is a member of the Organization of African Unity (OAU) and the Intergovernmental Agency for Democracy and Development (IGADD). Eritrea and Ethiopia, erstwhile good friends, waged war beginning in May 1998. After a bitter war lasting two years, the United Nations and the OAU brokered the Cessation of Hostilities Agreement in July 2000. Relations with Sudan, Yemen, and Djibouti are cordial. In general, Eritrea, which hitherto has been cool to the notion of joining the Arab League, has expressed interest since the outbreak of war with Ethiopia, but the Arab League has not expressed enthusiasm in courting Eritrea. Relations with the European Union and the West in general are cordial.

DEFENSE

The armed forces consist of the army, militia ground forces, navy, and air force. Armament expenditure is a closely guarded secret, though it is estimated to approach 30 percent of the gross domestic product (GDP). In 1995, the government demobilized 45 percent of the armed forces only to recall them in 1998 with the outbreak of war with Ethiopia.

Military Indicators

Total Active Duty Personnel: —
Military Manpower per 1,000: —
Military Expenditures $million: —
- as % of GNP: —
- per capita: $—
- as % of central government expenditures: —

Arms Imports: $0
Arms Exports: $0

ECONOMY

The capital base left by the Italians at the end of World War II was squandered when the British dismantled the factories, stripped the harbors, and destroyed government buildings. The Ethiopians repeated the plunder when they took down cable highways, telecommunication poles, and industrial machinery during the independence drive. Thirty years of armed struggle has also ravaged the roads, bridges, and overall infrastructure, leaving the country poor and bankrupt. The recent state of war placed a serious impediment to the country's meager income from remittances from Eritreans overseas. Today, Eritrea subsists on rudimentary peasant farming complemented by the service sector. Agricultural contribution to the GDP is estimated at about 18 percent. The service sector contributes the bulk of the GDP at about 60 percent. Industry suffers from outmoded tools, lack of spare parts, and lack of input materials. Its contribution to the GDP is about 19 percent. Since independence, the government has encouraged private investment and the development of fisheries, but it has not registered significant results.

Principal Economic Indicators

Gross National Product: $852 million
GNP per capita: $230
GNP Average Annual Growth Rate (1990–97) %: 2.9
GNP per capita Average Annual Growth Rate (1990–97): 0.3
Origin of Gross Domestic Product %
- Agriculture: 18
- Mining: —
- Manufacturing: 12
- Construction: 4
- Public Utilities: 1
- Transportation and Communications: 13
- Trade: 28
- Financial Services: 4
- Other Services: 3
- Government: 10

Gross Domestic Product by Type of Expenditure %
- Private Consumption: —
- Government Consumption: —
- Gross Domestic Investment: —
- Foreign Trade: Exports: —
- Imports: —

% of Income Received by Poorest 20%: —
% of Income Received by Richest 10%: —

Price and earnings indexes

	1991	1992	1993	1994	1995
Consumer price index	91.9	100.0	119.2	127.4	141.3
Earnings index	—	—	—	—	—

Finance

National Currency: Nakfa
Exchange Rate: $1 = Nakfa 7.2
Money Supply Stock in National Currency billion: —
M1 per capita: —
Central Bank Discount Rate %: —
Total External Debt $million: 162
Debt Service Ratio %: 0.1

Balance of Payments $million: 4.9
International Reserves SDRs million: —
Ratio of External Debt to Total Reserves: —
Average Annual Rate of Inflation/Consumer Price Index Growth Rate %: 4

Official Development Assistance

ODA $million: 158
- as % of GNP: 20.6
- per capita $: 41
- Foreign Direct Investment $million: 0

Central Government Revenues and Expenditures

Fiscal Year: Calendar Year
Revenues $million: 226
Expenditures $million: 453
Budget Deficit $million: 227
Tax Revenues as % of GDP: —
Highest Tax Bracket %
Individual: —
Corporate: —

Employment and Labor

Economically Active Population: 647,000
Female Participation Rate %:
Activity Rate %:
Labor by Sector: %
Agriculture, Forestry, Fishing: 2.6
Manufacturing, Mining: 49.5
Construction: 10.5
Transportation and Communications: 12.7
Trade, Hotels, and Restaurants: 2.4
Finance, Insurance, Real Estate: 1.6
Public Administration, Defense: 20.3
Services: 20.3
Unemployment %: —

Agriculture

Agriculture's Share of GDP %: 18
Average Annual Rate of Growth (1965–98) %: —
Number of Farms 000: —
Average Size of Farm ha: —
Number of Tractors per 1,000 hectares: 19
Irrigation, % of Farms having: 6
Artificial Fertilizer kg/hectare: —
Total Farmland as % of land area: 3.6
Livestock: Cattle 000: 1,320
Sheep 000: 1,530
Hogs 000: —
Chickens 000: 4,300
Forests: Production of Roundwood (000 cubic meters): —
Fisheries: Total Catch tons 000: 3.0

Mining

% of GDP: 0.1
Value of Mineral Production $million: 0.3

Manufacturing

Value Added $million: 58
Industrial Production Growth Rate %: —

Energy

Commercial Energy Production metric tons of oil equivalent 000: —
Commercial Energy Consumption metric tons of oil equivalent 000: —
Commercial Energy Consumption per capita kg: —
Average Annual Growth Rate 1980–97%: —
Net Energy Imports % of use: —
Electricity Installed Capacity kW 000: —
Production kW-hr million: —
Coal Reserves tons million: —
Production tons 000: —
Natural Gas Proven Reserves cubic meters billion: —
Production cubic meters million: —
Crude Petroleum reserves barrels million: —
Production barrels million: —
Consumption barrels million: —
Refinery Capacity barrels per day 000: —
Pipelines Length km: —

Foreign Trade

Imports $million: 423.6
Exports $million: 66.0
Export Volume % Annual Growth Rate (1990–97): —
Import Volume % Annual Growth Rate (1990–97): —
Balance of Trade $

Balance of trade (current prices)

	1992	1993	1994	1995
U.S. $000,000	−263.0	−239.0	−331.0	−323.0
% of total	89.8%	76.8%	71.9%	66.6%

Major Trading Partners

	Imports	Exports
European Union %	27.2	2.7
United States %	5.9	—
Eastern Europe %	—	—
Japan %	—	—
Others %	66.9	97.3

Transportation

Roads Total Length mi: 2,442 km: 3,930
Paved %: 21
Automobiles: 5,350
Trucks and Buses: —
Persons per vehicle: —
Railroad; Track Length mi: —
Passenger-mi million: —
Freight-mi million: —
Merchant Marine: No. of Vessels: —
Total Deadweight Tonnage 000: —
International Cargo Loaded tons 000: —
International Cargo Off-loaded tons 000: —
Airports with Scheduled Flights: 2
Traffic: Passenger-mi million: —
Freight-mi million: —
Length of Canals mi: —

Tourism

Number of Tourists to 000: 188
Number of Tourists from 000: —
Tourist Receipts $million: —
Tourist Expenditures $million: —

Communications

Telephones 000: 17
Cost of Local Calls 3 mins: $0
Cellular Telephones 000: —
Fax Machines 000: 0.8
Personal Computers 000: —
Internet Hosts per million persons: —
Mail: Post Offices: 35
Pieces of Mail Handled million: 1.8
Pieces of Mail Handled per person: 0.5

EDUCATION

The educational system inherited from the Ethiopian system has been overhauled and completely restructured. The fundamental organizational structure remains the same in that there are elementary, secondary, and tertiary levels, but the emphasis on goals and objectives has drastically changed. The curriculum for higher education emphasizes technical, vocational, and scientific education with complementary focus on business and public administration. There is only one center of higher learning, the University of Asmara. In theory, education is provided free at all levels. Villages have been mobilized to take responsibility for building common elementary schools. The schools are located at strategic locations in the rural areas to serve several villages. Most funds for building school facilities are derived from local contributions with the government contributing about 15 percent of the cost. The government is responsible for providing teachers to the common schools.

Education

Literacy Rate %: 20
Male %: —
Female %: —
First Level: Primary schools: 537
Teachers: 5,828
Students: 241,725
Student-Teacher Ratio: 41.5
Net Enrollment Ratio: 31
Second Level: Secondary Schools: 86
Teachers: 2,031
Students: 78,902
Student-Teacher Ratio: 38.8
Net Enrollment Ratio: 15

Vocational Level: Schools: 4
Students: 1,246

Third Level: Institutions: 1
Teachers: 144
Students: 2,032
Student-Ratio Level: 14.1
Gross Enrollment Ratio: 1.1
Students per 100,000: 102
% of Population Age 25 and over with Postsecondary Education: —

Public Expenditure on Education as % of GDP: 1.9

SCIENCE AND TECHNOLOGY

Science and Technology

Scientists and Engineers in R&D per 1 million persons: —
Expenditures in R&D as % of GDP: —
High-Tech Exports $million: —
Patent Applications by Residents: —

MEDIA

The government's role in the media is dominant. There are a few start-up private newspapers and publications, but all media of press and the airwaves are under total government control. The Peoples Party for Democracy and Justice (PFDJ) controls the workings of the Eritrean News Agency (ERINA), the daily *Haddas Eritrea* and the weekly *Eritrean Profile*. Dimtsi Hafash, the official Eritrean Radio Station, started during the war of liberation and has continued its operation under the control of PFDJ after independence.

The film and theater industry is at its infancy. There is eagerness and enthusiasm to demonstrate unique Eritrean cultural content in literature, film, and theater, but the level of creativity and development is seriously impaired by the absence of cultural organizations to shepherd the process.

Media

Daily Newspapers:
Total Circulation 000: —
Circulation per 1,000: —
Books Published: 106
Magazines: —
Radio Receivers 000: —
per 1,000: —
Television sets 000: 22
per 1,000: 6.0

MOST IMPORTANT MEDIA:

Press. The principal press organ is *Hadas Eritrea* (New Eritrea, 25,000), published biweekly in Tigrigna and Arabic; there is also an English weekly, *Eritrea Profile*.

Radio and television. The Eritrean national radio service is Voice of the Masses (Dimtsi Hafash), broadcasting in Afar, Amharic, Arab, Kunama, Tigre, and Tigrigna. Eri-TV, broadcasting from Asmara and Assab, can be received in about 90 percent of the country.

CULTURE

Cultural Indicators

Public Libraries Number: —
Volumes: —
Registered borrowers: —
Museums Number: —
Annual Attendance: —

(continued)

Cinema Production of Long Films: —
Number of Cinemas: —
Seating Capacity: —
Annual Attendance: —
Annual Attendance per capita: —

STATUS OF WOMEN

The role of women in all sectors of society is highly visible. During the armed struggle, women made up 35 percent of the Eritrean Defense Forces. The government encourages women's rights with a heightened zeal making sure there is proportional and fair recruitment of women in education, employment, promotion, and the military services. Recently, however, the role of women in the military services has been reduced.

Women

Gender Empowerment Measure: 58
Seats Held in Parliament by Women %: 14.7
Female Administrators and Managers %: 17
Female Professional and Technical Workers%: 30
Women's Share of Earned Income %: 52
Women in Government %: 7.8

HEALTH, FOOD, AND NUTRITION

Health

Number of Physicians: 68
Number of Dentists: —
Number of Nurses: 488
Number of Pharmacists: —
Population per Physician: 46,200
Number of Hospitals: 10
Hospital Beds per 10,000: 9
Hospital Bed Occupancy Rate: —
Infant Mortality Rate per 1,000 live births: 146
Maternal Mortality Rate per 100,000 live births: 140
Total Health Expenditures as % of GDP: —
Health Expenditures per capita $: —
HIV Infected % of adults: 3.17
Cigarette Consumption per smoker per year: —
% of Smokers: Male: —
Female: —
Access to Safe Water % —

Food and Nutrition

Food Supply as % of FAO Requirements: —
% of Consumption Expenditures on Food: —
Daily Available Calories per capita: —
% of Total Calories derived from:
Cereals: —
Potatoes, cassava: —
Meat, poultry: —
Fish: —
Eggs, milk: —
Fruits, vegetables: —
Fats, oils: —

ENVIRONMENT

In recent years, drought has caused massive destruction of the ecosystem of the country. The result has been massive deforestation, overgrazing, and topsoil erosion. Since 1991, the government, under the banner of "every raindrop must be caught," has conducted environmental rejuvenation programs with appreciable results.

Environment

Forest Area sq km: 3,000
Average Annual Deforestation sq km: 0
Nationally Protected Areas as % of Total Land Area: 5
Freshwater Access cubic meters per capita: 2,269
Emissions of Organic Water Pollutants kg per day: 22,175
CO_2 Emissions per capita ton: —

CHRONOLOGY

1941 Britain wrests Eritrea from Italy and rules over the country as an occupied enemy territory under a UN mandate.
1950 United Nations calls for Eritrean federation with Ethiopia.
1952 Eritrea federated with Ethiopia for a period of 10 years after which complete union or independence to be determined by Eritrean referendum.
1961 The Eritrean Liberation Front (ELF) launches armed resistance against Ethiopian subversion of the federal provisions.
1962 Emperor Haile Selassie of Ethiopia arbitrarily dissolves the Eritrean parliament and declares Eritrea an Ethiopian province.
1970 Eritrean nationals within the ELF split and form the Eritrean Peoples Liberation Front (EPLF).
1974 Emperor Haile Selassie overthrown in a military coup to be replaced by the Derg, whose hard stand on Eritrea escalates the war, precluding a mediated settlement.
1988 In the Battle of AfAbet, Ethiopian troops suffer a serious defeat in which EPLF fighters demolish a third of the Ethiopian army.
1991 EPLF liberates Eritrea on May 24.
1992 Eritrea conducts a national referendum for independence or union with Ethiopia. Outcome confirms overwhelming vote for independence.
1993 Eritrea declares its independence on April 24.
1997 Eritrea issues its own currency, abandoning its use of the Ethiopian birr.
1998 War breaks out between Eritrea and Ethiopia.

2000 Eritrea and Ethiopia sign a peace agreement.
2001 Ethiopia and Eritrea complete their troop withdrawal from the border zone; the United Nations continues to monitor the peace process.

BIBLIOGRAPHY

Alamin Mohammed Said. *Sewra Eritrea.* Lawrenceville, N.J.,1994.

Amanuel Mihreteab. "Reintegrating Ex-Fighters in Post—Conflict Eritrea: Problems and Prospects." *Review of Eritrean Studies* 3 (1999): 27–82.

Gurdon, Charles. *The Horn of Africa.* New York, 1994.

Rosen, Richard A., and Bereket Habte Selassie."The Eritrean Constitutional Process." *Journal of Eritrean Studies* 3 (1999): 139–179.

Wriggins, Howard. *Dynamics of Regional Politics: 4 Systems on the Indian Ocean Rim.* New York, 1992.

OFFICIAL PUBLICATIONS

Eritrea. *Eritrea—Recent Economic Developments* (IMF Staff Country Report [1996]); *Ethiopia and Eritrea: A Documentary Study* (1993).

CONTACT INFORMATION

Embassy of Eritrea
1708 New Hampshire Avenue NW
Washington, D.C. 20009
Phone: (202) 319-1991 Fax: (202) 319-1304

INTERNET RESOURCES

- Government of Eritrea
  http://www.NetAfrica.org/eritrea/

ESTONIA

BASIC FACT SHEET

OFFICIAL NAME:
Republic of Estonia (Eesti Vabariik)

ABBREVIATION:
EN

CAPITAL:
Tallinn

HEAD OF STATE:
President Arnold Rüütel

HEAD OF GOVERNMENT:
Prime Minister Mart Laar (from 1999)

NATURE OF GOVERNMENT:
Emerging democracy

POPULATION:
1,439,000 (1999)

AREA:
45,227 sq km (17,462 sq mi)

MAJOR ETHNIC GROUPS:
Estonian, Russian

LANGUAGES:
Estonian, Russian

RELIGIONS:
Evangelical Lutheran, Estonian Orthodox, Russian Orthodox

UNIT OF CURRENCY:
Estonian Kroon

NATIONAL FLAG:
Three equal horizontal bands of blue (top), black, and white

NATIONAL EMBLEM:
The coat of arms consists of three blue lions with silver eyes and red tongues facing left on a golden baroque shield. Except for the top, the shield is surrounded by a garland of two intertwined golden oak branches.

NATIONAL ANTHEM:
"My Native Land, My Joy"

NATIONAL HOLIDAYS:
February 24 (Independence Day)

DATE OF INDEPENDENCE:
September 6, 1991

DATE OF CONSTITUTION:
June 28, 1992

GEOGRAPHIC FEATURES

Estonia is located in northeastern Europe and borders both the Baltic Sea and the Gulf of Finland. The nation also borders Russia and Latvia. There is an ongoing border dispute with Russia over some 2,000 sq km (772 sq mi) in the Narva and Pechory regions of Russia, which Estonia claims on the basis of the 1920 Peace Treaty of Tartu. Along with Latvia and Lithuania, Estonia is one of the countries collectively known as the Baltic states. Its total area is 45,226 sq km (17,462 sq mi), although only 43,211 sq km (16,684 sq mi) are land. Some 5 percent of Estonian territory is water. There are nearly 1,200 lakes in the nation. The principal lakes are Lake Peipus, which partially lies in Russia, and Lake Võrtjärv. The longest rivers in the country are the Pärnu, the Kasari, and the Emajõgi. In total, there are over 7,000 rivers, streams, and drainage canals. Estonian territory includes 1,521 islands in the Baltic Sea, the largest of which are Saaremaa at 2,922 sq km (1,128 sq mi) and Hiimuaa at 1,023 sq km (395 sq mi).

The maritime location exerts a significant influence on the nation. It has 3,794 km (2,371 mi) of coastline, but its land border extends only 633 km (396 mi). The coast

Estonia

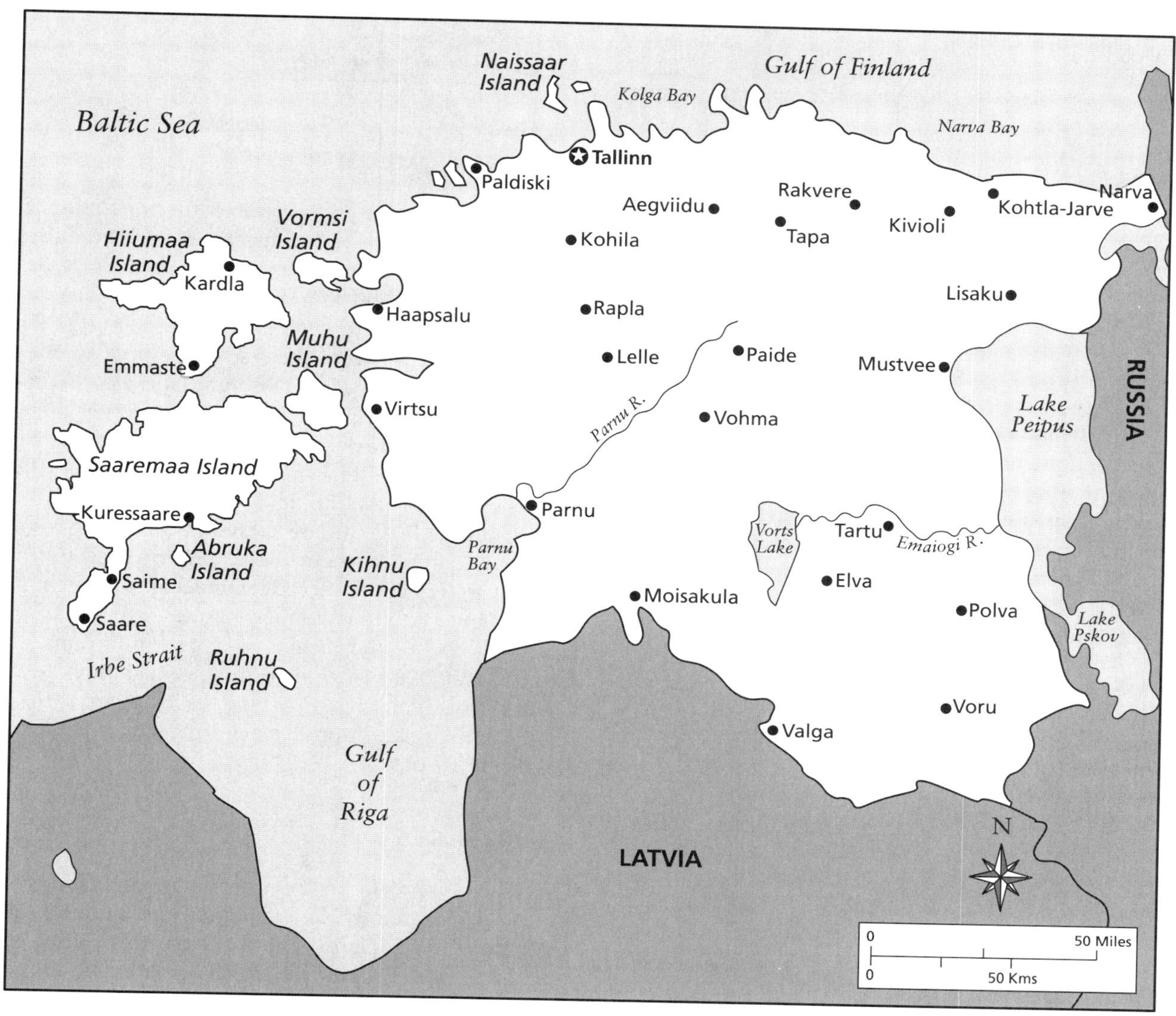

varies from limestone cliffs to sandy beaches in the west. The water of the Baltic Sea is brackish, but contains abundant quantities of some fish species. Because of the distance from the Atlantic Ocean, tides have little variation.

Estonia is comparatively flat and two-thirds of the country is less than 50 m (163 ft) above sea level. Most of the terrain consists of marshy lowlands and floods are common in the spring. The nation is rich in wetlands with over 165,000 marshes. The highest point in both the nation and the Baltic region as a whole is Suur Munamägi ("Great Egg Hill"), which rises 318 m (1,043 ft). Much of the western mainland of the nation has emerged as the result of the gradual uplifting of Europe: the northwestern areas are rising at a rate of 2.5 mm per year. The central regions of Estonia are marked by the Pandivere Upland, which at its highest point rises 166 m (544 ft) above sea level. There is also a broad, flat limestone plateau that forms a coastal cliff along the south of the Gulf of Finland.

Tallinn is the nation's capital and largest city. Almost one-third of the population lives in Tallinn. Other major cities include Tartu and Narva. Some 47.6 percent of Estonian territory remains forested woodlands.

Geography

Area sq km: 45,227 sq mi 17,462
World Rank: 132nd
Land Boundaries, km: Lativa 339; Russia 294
Coastline, km: 3,794
Elevation Extremes meters
  Lowest: Baltic Sea 0
  Highest: Suur Munamägi 318
Land Use % Arable land: 22
  Permanent Crops: 0
  Permanent Pastures: 11
  Forest and Woodland: 31
  Other: 36

Population of Principal Cities (1996 est.)

Tallinn	427,500
Tartu	103,400

CLIMATE AND WEATHER

Although a northern country, the influence of the Gulf Stream keeps the climate relatively mild. The maritime influences dominate the nation's weather. There are moderate winters and cool summers. The warmest month is July and the average temperature during the month ranges from 16 to 18°C (60° to 64°F). February is the coldest month with temperatures as low as −3.5°C (−38°F). Areas of Estonia are so far north that in the winter they receive daylight for a maximum of six hours per day. However, in the summer, the north coast receives over 18 hours of sunshine. From December onward for approximately 100 days, most of the nation is permanently covered in snow. Average precipitation is 550–650 mm (21–26 in) with rainfall heaviest at the end of the summer and lightest during the spring.

Climate and Weather

Mean Temperature
West 42.8°F
East 36°F to 40°F
Average Rainfall 21 in to 26 in

POPULATION

Population Indicators

Total Population: 1999 1,439,000
World Rank: 147th
Density per sq mi: 82.4 per sq km 31.8
% of annual growth (1994–99): −0.8
Male %: 46.9
Female %: 53.1
Urban %: 71.6
Age Distribution: % 0–14: 22.2
15–29: 21.4
30–44: 21.0
45–59: 18.5
60–74: 11.7
75 and over: 5.1
Population 2020: 1,299,000
Birth Rate per 1,000: 9.0
Death Rate per 1,000: 12.9
Population Doubling Time (years): —
Infant Mortality Rate per 1,000 live births: 10.5
Rate of Natural Increase per 1,000: −3.9
Total Fertility Rate: 1.3
Expectation of Life (years): Males 67.5
Females 72.6
Marriage Rate per 1,000: 4.9
Divorce Rate per 1,000: 3.7
Total Number of Households: —
Average Size of Households: 4.1
% of Illegitimate Children: 32.1
Induced Abortions: —
Rate per 100 live births: —

ETHNIC COMPOSITION

Estonians constitute 65.1 percent of the population, which makes Estonia the most homogeneous of the Baltic states. Estonians are descended from the Finno-Ugric peoples and have ethnic and linguistic ties to the Finns and the Hungarians. The Setu people of southeastern Estonia are ethnically distinct from the rest of the population. They number approximately 13,000 and speak a distinct dialect. The largest minority group in the nation is the Russians, who make up some 28.7 percent of the population. In addition, there are small groups of Ukrainians, Belarusians, and Finns.

Under a 1993 law on ethnicity, all minority groups with populations more than 3,000 have a right to cultural autonomy. However, the government has pursued a policy designed to integrate these groups into the larger society through education and social programs. Some 80,000–100,000 nonethnic Estonians, including Russians, Jews, Finns, Poles, Gypsies, and so forth, are recognized as Estonian through proficiency in language and because of historical ties.

LANGUAGES

Estonian is the official language. Estonian belongs to the Finno-Ugric family of languages spoken in Finland, Hungary, and Lapland. There are several dialects of Estonian, however, and some groups, such as the Setu, speak very distinct forms of the language. In addition, Russian and Ukrainian are widely spoken among minority groups. English and Russian are widely spoken and understood as second languages.

Principal Languages and Their Speakers

Belarusian	20,000
Estonian	940,000
Finnish	10,000
Russian	400,000
Ukrainian	40,000
Other	30,000

RELIGIONS

Christianity is the dominant religion in Estonia. There is no state church and the constitution guarantees freedom of religion, conscience, and thought. Lutheranism is the main Christian denomination among native Estonians with over 200,000 active church members in 166 congregations, organized into 12 deaneries. The Estonian Orthodox Church is the next most popular church, with about 280,000 members. There is a growing number of other churches including Baptist, Seventh-Day Adventist, Pentecostalist, and Roman Catholic. Religious activities are regulated by the Ministry of Internal Affairs in accordance with the Churches and Congregations Act (1993).

Religious Affiliations

Estonian Orthodox	280,000
Evangelical Lutheran	200,000
Other	960,000

HISTORICAL BACKGROUND

In 3000 B.C.E., the first Finno-Ugarian settlements were established in Estonia. Between 1030 and 1050, Tartu and Tallinn were founded. Beginning in the 12th century Germanic knights invaded Estonia, and efforts were made to convert the native peoples to Christianity. In 1219, Danish king Valdemar II conquered northern Estonia, including Tallinn. In 1248, Tallinn became part of the German Hanseatic League. In the 1300s, an Estonian uprising prompted the Danes to sell the remainder of Estonia to the Germans, and feudalism and serfdom were established in the nation by the German Livonian Order (a branch of the Teutonic Order).

The Reformation swept through Estonia in the 1520s. The Livonian War led to the collapse of the Livonian Order and Estonia was split with the northern half under Swedish control while the southern territories came under Polish-Lithuanian rule. In 1629, the Altmark armistice left Sweden in control of the Estonian mainland and northern Latvia. In 1645, the Swedes also took control of Saaremaa. While under Swedish control, Estonia became a Protestant country.

Russia gained control of Estonia as a result of the Great Nordic War (1700–21). However, the Estonian provinces retained a special status within the Russian Empire. In was not until 1819 that feudalism and serfdom were abolished in Estonia.

In the 1860s, there was an awakening of Estonian nationalism, but the Russification efforts of Czar Alexander III resulted in Russian being designated the official language, and efforts were made to convert the population to Orthodox Christianity. Nonetheless, groups such as Noor Eesti (Young Estonia) continued to work toward Estonian independence.

In 1918, Estonia declared its independence and launched a war of liberation against both the Soviets and German occupation forces. On February 2, 1920, the Tartu-Dorpat Treaty granted Estonia full independence. The 1919 constitution was promulgated and Estonia became a parliamentary democracy. The nation oriented itself toward the West, and by the 1930s, the standard of living of Estonia equaled that of most Western nations. In 1939, the Molotov-Ribbentrop Pact divided Europe between Adolf Hitler and Josef Stalin and Estonia was placed in the Soviet sphere of influence. The Soviets occupied Estonia in 1940 and annexed the nation as part of the greater Soviet Union. Prominent Estonians were executed or sent to Siberia (some 11,000 in all). In response the Estonians began an armed resistence movement against the Russians and welcomed the German invasion of 1941. However, the German occupation proved just as harsh. The Soviets reoccupied Estonia in 1944 and annexed some 1,946 sq km (751 sq mi) of territory to the Russian federation. Resistence to Russian rule continued and some 15,000 Estonians were killed in the fighting against the occupying forces. In an effort to suppress the rebellion and prevent flight from the nation, the Soviets closed the coastline to native Estonians, and in 1949 began the collectivization of agriculture.

After Stalin's death, those Estonians who were exiled to labor camps were allowed to return, beginning in 1956. However, tensions between the Estonians and the Soviets continued and by the 1960s, there were widespread protests against the occupation. These protests were given impetus by the "Letter of Forty," which culminated in a protest movement led by intellectuals and students in 1979–80 against Russification.

Popular resistence reemerged in the 1980s. In 1988, the "Singing Revolution," which was marked by mass protests characterized by singing, led to the reintroduction of the Estonian flag. These events prompted the Estonian Supreme Soviet to assert Estonian sovereignty. Estonia was spared the harsh military crackdown imposed on the other Baltic republics in their struggles for independence, and in 1991 it declared independence in the wake of the failed coup against Soviet leader Mikhail Gorbachev.

Following the promulgation of a new constitution in 1992, and subsequent elections, Estonia became a member of the Council of Europe, NATO's Partnership for Peace Program, and an associate member of the Western European Union. The last Russian troops withdrew from the nation in 1994, and in 1998, Estonia began accession discussions with the European Union.

In 1992, Lennart Meri became president, and Mart Laar, a member of the reform-minded Fatherland Union, became prime minister. After 1995 parliamentary elections, a coalition of center-left parties formed the government, and Meri was reelected president in 1996. The Estonian Coalition Party won a majority of votes in 1999 parliamentary elections; however, Laar formed a governing coalition of center-right parties and became prime minister a second time.

CONSTITUTION

Estonia is a parliamentary democracy. The head of state is the president. One must be a minimum of 40 years old to

run for the office. The president is chosen every five years by the parliament. In the election, if no single candidate gains a two-thirds majority, there is a runoff election in which the president is chosen by an electoral assembly made up of the parliament and members of local governments (for a total of 374 members). In order to nominate a presidential candidate a party must have at least one-fifth of the seats in parliament. The head of the government is the prime minister, who is appointed by the president and confirmed by the parliament. The president also appoints the Council of Ministers or government, which also must be confirmed by the parliament. The parliament (Riigikogu) is a unicameral chamber made up of 101 deputies who serve for four-year terms.

The voting age is 18, and suffrage is universal. In addition, resident noncitizens are allowed to vote in local elections.

LOCAL GOVERNMENT

The Local Government Organization Act of 1993 establishes the functions and organization of the subnational branches of governments. Estonian local government is divided into two levels: counties and municipalities or rural towns. There are 15 administrative divisions or counties in Estonia. In addition, there are 254 towns and municipalities that have a high degree of local control over issues such as taxation and administration. Localities also have control over their budgets. Two-thirds of the local governments represent communities with populations of less than 3,000. Local government is usually made up of a council (volikogu) whose members are elected for three-year terms. The executive of the council is the government (valitsus), which is headed by a mayor elected for a three-year term. In most areas, noncitizen residents are allowed to vote in local elections.

Local Government

Principal administrative divisions, capitals, area, population

Area and population

Counties	Capitals	area sq mi	sq km	population 1998 estimate
Harju	Tallinn	1,673	4,333	538,149
Hiiu	Kāardia	395	1,023	11,862
Ida-Viru	Johvi	1,299	3,364	197,530
Jārva	Paide	1,013	2,623	43,368
Jōgeva	Jōgeva	1,005	2,604	41,622
Lāāne	Haapsalu	920	2,383	31,949
Lāāne-Viru	Rakvere	1,337	3,464	76,144
Pārnu	Pārnu	1,856	4,806	100,457
Polva	Polva	836	2,165	35,956
Rapla	Rapla	1,151	2,980	40,153
Saare	Kuressaare	1,128	2,922	40,202
Tartu	Tartu	1,193	3,090	151,301
Valga	Valga	790	2,047	38,985
Vijandi	Vijandi	1,386	3,589	62,782
Voru	Voru	890	2,305	43,384
TOTAL		17,462	45,227	1,453,844

PARLIAMENT

The Riigikogu is a unicameral body with 101 members who are elected by direct popular vote to serve every four years. The duties of the Riigikogu include considering legislation and overseeing the executive branch. In addition to passing legislation and controlling the budget, the Riigikogu appoints the chairman of the National Court, the president of the Bank of Estonia, the legal chancellor, and the commander in chief of the defense forces. The body also must approve international treaties and any government loans.

POLITICAL PARTIES

Center Party—centrist party.
Coalition Party—coalition of four conservative parties that emphasizes the free market and decentralization of government.
Moderates—coalition of two center-left parties
Progressive Party—center-right party formed by defectors from the Center Party.
Right-Wingers—conservative party.
Russian Party of Estonia—promotes the interests of the Russian minority in Estonia.
Union Pro Patria or Fatherland League—conservative party.
(There are also a number of minor parties).

Political Parties

Fatherland Union, 1995
Estonian Reform Party, 1994
Moderates, 1990
Estonian Center Party, 1991
Estonian Rural People's Party, 1994
Estonian Coalition Party, 1991
Estonian Rural Union, 1991
Estonian Pensioners' and Families' League
Estonian United People's Party
Estonian Democratic Labor Party, 1992
Farmers' Assembly, 1992
Progress Party, 1996
Estonian Blue Party
Russian Party of Estonia
Estonian Christian People's Party

Political Parties: Strength in Parliament Most Recent Elections

Unicameral **Parliament** (Riigikogu) of 101 members. At the most recent election of March 7, 1999, the Estonian Center Party won 28 seats; the Fatherland Union, 18; the Estonian Reform Party, 18; the Moderates, 17; the Estonian Coalition Party, 7; the Estonian Rural People's Party, 7; and the United People's Party, 6.

LEGAL SYSTEM

The Estonian legal system is based on civil law. The court system is divided into three levels. At the local level there are city, county, and administrative courts. Next, there are circuit courts that have appellate functions. The highest legal body is the Supreme Court.

The Supreme Court has administrative, civil, and criminal chambers. Each chamber has a chairman who oversees the caseload and conduct of cases. The chairman may also call upon members of other chambers to participate in cases. The Appeals Selection Committee, made up of members of each of the chambers, decides which appeals will be heard. Constitutional questions are examined by the Constitutional Review Chamber, whose members are elected by the Supreme Court. Members of the chamber may not serve more than two five-year terms.

Judges at all levels are appointed by the parliament and serve for life. They may be removed from office only by a court judgment. In addition, they are not allowed to hold any other elected or appointed position.

The Estonian constitution forbids the establishment of emergency or summary courts.

LAW ENFORCEMENT

Law Enforcement

Offenses reported to the police per 100,000: 2,383
- Murder: 24.3
- Assault: 29.3
- Burglary: 1,160.7
- Automobile Theft: 169.1
- Population per Police officer: —

Death Penalty: Yes.

HUMAN RIGHTS

Universal suffrage is guaranteed by the constitution. In addition, Estonian law does not allow discrimination on the basis of race, nationality, gender, occupation, religion, or culture. The Estonian government has worked to preserve the rights of ethnic minorities in the nation. The National Minorities Cultural Autonomy Act of 1993 grants minority groups with at least 3,000 members special status and the right to establish local authorities in order to preserve cultural, religious, or linguistic identity.

FOREIGN POLICY

Since independence from the Soviet Union in 1991, Estonia has pursued closer ties with the West in both the economic and defense spheres. In the initial period after independence, Estonia worked to quicken the pace of the Soviet troop withdrawal, which was not completed until 1994. Estonia also sought to resolve border disputes with Russia including that over territory in the Russian areas of Narva and Pechory. Although a technical border agreement was reached in 1996, the accord has not been ratified. Along with its other neighbors, Estonia has sought entry into NATO, and in 1994 the republic entered the alliance's Partnership for Peace program. The nation has supported broad, collective security initiatives among the Baltic nations and regional integration in general. Estonia is a member of the Baltic Assembly and the Baltic Council of Ministers and belongs to the Baltic free-trade area. Estonia has also sought entry into the EU. In 1998, formal accession talks began between the EU and Estonia.

DEFENSE

The Estonian military numbers 5,000. The commander in chief is the president of the republic. The nation has conscription for all males age 18. The length of service is one year. The armed forces are divided between an army, air force, and navy. The army has three battalions, and the navy consists of nine patrol and coastal defense vessels (several of these vessels were actually donated to Estonia by Germany and Denmark). There is also a special company of troops, which is used for peacekeeping missions under the auspices of the Baltic Peacekeeping Battalion (BALTBAT), that participates in missions of international organizations such as NATO or the UN. Estonia has contributed troops to peacekeeping missions in the former Yugoslavia. In addition, there is the Kaitseliit, a volunteer paramilitary force that numbers 8,500. The unit serves as an auxiliary force for civil defense and emergency response. The Ministry of the Interior has some 2,000 border patrol troops under its command, and these include a small maritime force that functions as a coast guard.

As a small country bordering Russia, Estonia has attempted to enhance its security by integration with the West, including participation in NATO through the Partnership for Peace program and the Western European Union as an observer. Under a 1996 decree, the Estonian military is working to make its weapons, organization, and tactics compatible with NATO standards in anticipation of NATO membership.

Military Indicators

Total Active Duty Personnel: 3,500
Military Manpower per 1,000: 2.4
Military Expenditures $million: 118
- as % of GNP: 1.1
- per capita $: 80
- as % of central government expenditures: 2.9

Arms Imports $million: 5
Arms Exports $million: 0

ECONOMY

After independence, Estonia embarked on extensive efforts to foster free and open trade and orient its economy toward the West. The nation also pursued disciplined fiscal and monetary policies that contained inflation and unemployment. For instance, Estonia tied its currency to the German deutsche mark at a fixed rate of 8 to 1. Estonia was among the first of the East European states to enter into formal accession talks with the EU in 1998. Service industries make up the bulk of the nation's economy, although manufacturing and forest products are also significant. Industry and construction employ the largest number of Estonians among the major industries. The major manufacturing sectors are oil shale, shipbuilding, chemical products, textiles, electronics, and transportation. The nation's main exports are textiles, food products, machinery, and metals. Its most significant imports include machinery, food products, minerals, textiles, and metals. Estonia's main trade partners are Finland, Russia, Sweden, Germany, and Latvia.

Principal Economic Indicators

Gross National Product: $4.899 billion
GNP per capita: $3,360
GNP Average Annual Growth Rate (1990–97) %: −2.8
GNP per capita Average Annual Growth Rate (1990–97) %: −1.7
Origin of Gross Domestic Product %
- Agriculture: 9
- Mining: 2
- Manufacturing: 17
- Construction: 5
- Public Utilities: 3
- Transportation and Communications: 9
- Trade: 19
- Financial Services: 8
- Other Services: 8
- Government: 4

Gross Domestic Product by Type of Expenditure %
- Private Consumption: 59
- Government Consumption: 23
- Gross Domestic Investment: 29
- Foreign Trade: Exports: 80
- Imports: −91

% of Income Received by Poorest 20%: 6.6
% of Income Received by Richest 10%: 31.3

Price and earnings indexes

	1993	1994	1995	1996	1997	1998
Consumer price index	−1,206	−4,584	−8,061	−13,748	−20,948	−20,945
Earnings index	5.4%	11.9%	16.1%	21.8%	20.5%	19.2%

Finance

National Currency: Estonian Kroon [EEK]
Exchange Rate: $1 = EEK 14.527
Money Supply Stock in National Currency billion: 10.786
M1 per capita: 7,310
Central Bank Discount Rate %: 4.3
Total External Debt $million: 270
Debt Service Ratio %: 0.5

Balance of Payments $million: −561.9
International Reserves SDRs million: 447
Ratio of External Debt to Total Reserves: 0.3
Average Annual Rate of Inflation/Consumer Price Index Growth Rate %: 11.2

Official Development Assistance

Donor ODA $million: 147
- as % of GNP: 1.8
- per capita: $62
- Foreign Direct Investment $million: 581

Central Government Revenues and Expenditures

Fiscal Year: Calendar Year
Revenues $million: 1,700
Expenditures $million: 1,800

Budget Deficit $million: 100
Tax Revenues as % of GDP: 29.9
Highest Tax Bracket %
Individual: 26
Corporate: 26

Employment and Labor

Economically Active Population: 730,000
Female Participation Rate %: 47.6
Activity Rate %: 48.9
Labor by Sector: %
Agriculture, Forestry, Fishing: 12.9
Manufacturing, Mining: 25.5
Construction: 7.5
Transportation and Communications: 8.8
Trade, Hotels, and Restaurants: 16.0
Finance, Insurance, Real Estate: 5.5
Public Administration, Defense: 5.3
Services: 17.4
Unemployment %: 3.6

Agriculture

Agriculture's Share of GDP %: 9
Average Annual Rate of Growth (1965–98) %: —
Number of Farms 000: 10.4
Average Size of Farm ha: —
Number of Tractors per 1,000 hectares: 13.3
Irrigation, % of Farms having: —
Artificial Fertilizer kg/hectare: —
Total Cropland as % of Farmland: 22.7
Livestock: Cattle 000: 312
Sheep 000: 34
Hogs 000: 329
Chickens 000: 2,700
Forests: Production of Roundwood (000 cubic meters): 3,730
Fisheries: Total Catch tons: 124.1

Mining

% of GDP: 1.6
Value of Mineral Production $million: 58.3

Manufacturing

Value Added $million: 1,254
Industrial Production Growth Rate %: 3.0

Energy

Commercial Energy Production metric tons of oil equivalent 000: 3,788
Commercial Energy Consumption metric tons of oil equivalent 000: 5,556
Commercial Energy Consumption per capita kg: 3,811
Average Annual Growth Rate 1980–97 %: −0.9
Net Energy Imports % of use: 32
Electricity Installed Capacity kW 000: 3,287
Production kW-hr million: 7,607
Coal Reserves tons million: —
Production tons 000: 13,310
Natural Gas Proven Reserves cubic meters billion: —
Production cubic meters million: —
Crude Petroleum Reserves barrels million: —
Production barrels million: —
Consumption barrels million: —
Refinery Capacity barrels per day 000: —
Pipelines Length km: —

Foreign Trade

Imports $million: 3,197.2
Exports $million: 2,074.1
Export Volume % Annual Growth Rate (1990–97): —
Import Volume % Annual Growth Rate (1990–97): —
Balance of Trade $

Balance of trade (current prices)

	1994	1995	1996	1997	1998	1999
U.S.						
$000,000	77.7	100.0	123.1	136.1	150.5	156.3
% of total	73.0	100.0	125.7	150.5	—	—

Major Trading Partners

	Imports	Exports
European Union %	64.8	51.1
United States %	2.3	2.2
Eastern Europe %	21.7	39.3
Japan %	2.0	0.7
Others %	9.2	6.6

Transportation

Roads Total Length mi: 9,316 km 14,992
Paved %: 54
Automobiles: 383,444
Trucks and Buses: 72,607
Persons per vehicle: 3.3
Railroad; Track Length mi: 636 km 1,024
Passenger-mi million: 262
Freight-mi million: 2,634
Merchant Marine: No. of Vessels: 234
Total Deadweight Tonnage 000: 680.4
International Cargo Loaded tons 000: 11,460
International Cargo Off-loaded tons 000: 3,996
Airports with Scheduled Flights: 3
Traffic: Passenger-mi million: 67
Freight-mi million: 0.4
Length of Canals mi: 311 km 500

Tourism

Number of Tourists to 000: 825
Number of Tourists from 000: 1,659
Tourist Receipts $million: 353
Tourist Expenditures $million: 90

Communications

Telephones 000: 412
Cost of Local Calls 3 mins: $0.07
Cellular Telephones 000: 31

(continued)

Fax Machines 000: 13
Personal Computers 000: 10
Internet Hosts per million persons: 2,782
Mail: Post Offices: 582
Pieces of Mail Handled million: 49
Pieces of Mail Handled per person: 32

EDUCATION

Estonia has 741 comprehensive schools that provide elementary and secondary education: 602 Estonian language; 103 Russian language; and 37 bilingual. In addition, there are 22 institutions that provide postsecondary education (13 of these are private) and 105 vocational schools (12 of which are private). There are 10 universities, including four private colleges.

Education

Literacy Rate %: 99.7
Male %: 99.9
Female %: 99.6
First Level: Primary schools: 741
Teachers: 15,453
Students: 218,600
Student-Teacher Ratio: 14.1
Net Enrollment Ratio: 94
Second Level: Secondary Schools: —
Teachers: —
Students: —
Student-Teacher Ratio: —
Net Enrollment Ratio: 77
Vocational Level: Schools: 84
Students: 27,806
Third Level: Institutions: 22
Teachers: —
Students: 23,169
Student-Ratio Level: —
Gross Enrollment Ratio: 38.1
Students per 100,000: 2,670
% of Population Age 25 and over with Postsecondary Education: 13.7
Public Expenditure on Education as % of GDP: 6.9

SCIENCE AND TECHNOLOGY

Science and Technology

Scientists and Engineers in R&D per 1 million persons: 2,017
Expenditures in R&D as % of GDP: 0.57
High-Tech Exports $million: 173
Patent Applications by Residents: 18

MEDIA

Before independence, the Estonian press was controlled by the Communist Party. One of the first private papers to be created was *Eesti Ekspress*, a general interest and entertainment weekly with a circulation of about 40,000. The first private daily was *Postimees*, which is the top-selling daily with a circulation of 74,000. In 1997 there were seven national dailies, two of which are published in Russian. There are also 18 weeklies (six published in Russian) and 22 regional papers (four published in Russian). Total newspaper circulation is 661,000.

The first private licences for television stations were issued in 1992. Estonia now has one public and three private television channels. In 1993, Estonia stopped transmission of Russian broadcasts from Moscow and St. Petersburg, but Estonian public television (Eesti Televisioon) airs Russian-language programs and news.

Eesti Raadio is the nation's public radio station and it broadcasts on four different channels (including a Russian-language channel). In addition, there are 33 private radio stations.

Media

Daily Newspapers: 7
Total Circulation 000: 373
Circulation per 1,000: 242
Books Published: 2,291
Magazines: 470
Radio Receivers 000: —
per 1,000: —
Television sets 000: 610
per 1,000: 411

MOST IMPORTANT MEDIA:

Press. The following are Estonian-language dailies published at Tallinn unless otherwise noted (circulation figures for February 1994); *Postimees* (Postman, 74,000), leading Tartu paper; *Rahva Hää* (Voice of the People, 64,400), government organ; *Maaleht* (Land, 62,000), rural weekly; *Eesti Ekspress* (Estonian Express, 40,000), weekly; *Päevaleht* (Daily, 31,000); *Õhtuleht* (Evening Gazette, 26,800); *Molodyozh Estoniya* (Estonia, 17,000), in Russian; *Hommikuleht* (morning paper, 14,500); *The Baltic Independent* (7,200), English-language weekly.

News agencies. The Estonian Telegraph Agency (Eesti Teadate Agentuur-ETA) coordinates its services with Latvian and Lithuanian agencies. The Baltic News Service (BNS) began operations in 1991.

Radio and television. Estonian Radio (Eesti Raadio) broadcasts in Estonian, Russian, Swedish, Finnish, English, Esperanto, Ukrainian, and Belarusan; Estonian Television (Eesti Televisson) transmits over four channels in Estonian and Russian. Estonian Commercial Television (Eesti Reklaamitelevisioon) began broadcasting in 1992.

CULTURE

Cultural Indicators

Public Libraries Number: —
Volumes: —
Registered borrowers: —

Museums Number: —
Annual Attendance: —
Cinema Production of Long Films: 3
Number of Cinemas: 220
Seating Capacity: —
Annual Attendance:
Annual Attendance per capita: 0.7

STATUS OF WOMEN

The constitution of Estonia guarantees equal protection under the law. However, women continue to face disparities in opportunity in the economic and political spheres.

Women

Gender Empowerment Measure: 47
Seats Held in Parliament by Women %: 10.9
Female Administrators and Managers %: 37.4
Female Professional and Technical Workers %: 67.5
Women's Share of Earned Income %: 42
Women in Government %: 10

HEALTH, FOOD, AND NUTRITION

Health

Number of Physicians: 4,680
Number of Dentists: 820
Number of Nurses: 7,302
Number of Pharmacists: 930
Population per Physician: 319
Number of Hospitals: 107
Hospital Beds per 10,000: 84
Hospital Bed Occupancy Rate: 83.7
Infant Mortality Rate per 1,000 live births: 19
Maternal Mortality Rate per 100,000 live births: 41
Total Health Expenditures as % of GDP: 3.62
Health Expenditures per capita $: 228
HIV Infected % of adults: 0.01
Cigarette Consumption per smoker per year: 1,819
% of Smokers: Male: 52
Female: 24
Access to Safe Water %: —

Food and Nutrition

Food Supply as % of FAO Requirements: —
% of Consumption Expenditures on Food: 41.0
Daily Available Calories per capita: —
% of Total Calories derived from:
Cereals: —
Potatoes, cassava: —
Meat, poultry: —
Fish: —
Eggs, milk: —
Fruits, vegetables: —
Fats, oils: —

ENVIRONMENT

Power plants in the northeast of Estonia have heavily polluted the region by burning oil shale. Hence the air has contained large concentrations of sulfur dioxide, which produces significant acid rain. In addition, there is profound pollution and contamination of soil and groundwater with petroleum and chemicals at the former Soviet military installations. Soil and groundwater contamination is also present as the result of agricultural use of the land. These areas and many small lakes are polluted by organic waste from livestock and fertilizer runoff. Finally, many coastal areas are polluted by industrial discharge.

Environment

Forest Area sq km: 20,000
Average Annual Deforestation sq km: −196
Nationally Protected Areas as % of Total Land Area: 12.1
Freshwater Access cubic meters per capita: 8,829
Emissions of Organic Water Pollutants kg per day: —
CO_2 Emissions per capita ton: 11.2

CHRONOLOGY

1918	Estonia declares independence from Russia and engages in an armed struggle against both German and Russian forces.
1920	The Tartu-Dorpat Treaty recognizes Estonian independence.
1939	The Molotov-Ribbentrop Pact places Estonia in Soviet sphere of influence.
1940	Soviets invade Estonia.
1941	German occupation of Estonia.
1944	Soviet reoccupation of Estonia and the annexation of Estonian territory; Estonian resistence to Soviet rule leads to massive deportations and the deaths of some 15,000 Estonians.
1949	The forced collectivization of agriculture begins.
1956	Those surviving Estonians who were deported to Siberia begin to return.
1968	First open, mass protests against Soviet occupation since the end of World War II.
1979–80	"The Letter of Forty," a protest by intellectuals against continuing efforts at Russification of the country; mass student protests.
1988	"The Singing Revolution": mass demonstrations by 300,000 Estonians in Tallinn, marked by singing; reintroduction of the Estonian flag; establishment of popular resistence organizations; the Estonian Supreme Soviet declares the nation "sovereign."
1989	Estonian reestablished as an official language.

1990 The Congress of Estonia is organized in an effort to assert independence from the Soviet Union; Estonia is spared the harsh military crackdown imposed on Latvia and Lithuania.
1991 After the failed coup against Soviet leader Mikhail Gorbachev, Estonia declares its independence; on September 6, Estonian independence is recognized by Moscow.
1992 The Republic of Estonia is reestablished and elections are held that place conservatives in power; a new constitution is promulgated.
1993 Estonia becomes a member of the Council of Europe and enters into a trade agreement with the EU; along with Latvia and Lithuania, the republic creates a Baltic free-trade zone.
1994 The last Russian troops leave Estonia; the republic joins NATO's Partnership for Peace program, and becomes an associate member of the Western European Union.
1998 Estonia begins accession talks with the European Union.
1999 Mart Laar forms a center-right coalition government.

BIBLIOGRAPHY

Bergquist, William, and Berrne Weiss. *Freedom!: Narratives of Change in Hungary and Estonia.* San Francisco, 1994.

Commission on Security and Cooperation in Europe. *Human Rights and Democratization in Estonia.* Washington, D.C., 1993.

Knudsen, Olav F. *Stability and Security in the Baltic Sea Region: Russian, Nordic, and European Aspects.* London, 1999.

Laar, Mart. *War in the Woods: Estonia's Struggle for Survival, 1944–1956.* Washington, D.C., 1992.

OECD. *Review of Agricultural Policies: Estonia.* Paris, 1996.

Odling-Smee, John. *Estonia.* Washington, D.C., 1992.

Shen, Raphael. *Restructuring the Baltic Economies: Disengaging Fifty Years of Integration With the USSR.* Westport, Conn., 1994.

Taagepera, Rein. *Estonia: Return to Independence.* Boulder, Colo., 1993.

OFFICIAL PUBLICATIONS

Estonia. *Eesti Statistika Aastaraamat* (Estonia Statistical Yearbook); *Estonian Human Development Report* (annual).

CONTACT INFORMATION

Embassy of Estonia
2131 Massachusetts Avenue NW
Washington, D.C. 20008
Phone: (202) 588-0101 Fax: (202) 588-0108

INTERNET RESOURCES

- Bank of Estonia. Statistical Datasheets
  http://www.ee/epbe/datasheet/index.html
- Statistical Office of Estonia
  http://www.stat.ee/wwwstat/eng_stat/

ETHIOPIA

BASIC FACT SHEET

OFFICIAL NAME:
Federal Democratic Republic of Ethiopia (Ityopia Federalawi Demokrasiyawi Repeblik)

ABBREVIATION:
ET

CAPITAL:
Addis Ababa

HEAD OF STATE:
President Girma Wolde-Giyorgiz

HEAD OF GOVERNMENT:
Prime Minister Meles Zenawi (from 1995)

NATURE OF GOVERNMENT:
Republic

POPULATION:
59,680,000 (1999)

AREA:
1,133,882 sq km (437,794 sq mi)

ETHNIC MAJORITY:
Amhara, Tigrai, and Galla

LANGUAGES:
Amharic (official); also Arabic, Tigrinya, Tigre, and Guraginya

RELIGIONS:
Christianity, Islam, and animism

UNIT OF CURRENCY:
Birr (E.B.)

NATIONAL FLAG:
Tricolor of green, yellow, and red horizontal stripes with a yellow pentagram and single yellow rays emanating from the angles between the points on a light blue disk centered on the three bands.

NATIONAL EMBLEM:
A circle within a wreath. Within the circle are a star with 14 points, a cogwheel, and a plow

NATIONAL ANTHEM:
"Ityopia, Ityopia, Kidemi"

NATIONAL HOLIDAYS:
September 12 (National Day, National Revolution Day); September 11 (Ethiopian New Year's Day and Reunion of Eritrea with Ethiopia); March (Commemoration of the Battle of Adawa of 1896); April 6 (Victory Day); May 1 (Labor Day); Christian festivals include Maskal, or the Feast of the Finding of the True Cross; Christmas; Timkat or Epiphany; and Good Friday according to the Copitc calendar; also variable Muslim festivals

DATE OF INDEPENDENCE:
Ethiopia is one of oldest independent countries in the world and was under foreign rule—Italian military occupation—for only six years, from 1935 to 1941.

DATE OF CONSTITUTION:
August 22, 1998 (effective)

GEOGRAPHICAL FEATURES

Ethiopia, in the Horn of Africa, has an area of 1,133,882 sq km (437,794 sq mi), extending 1,639 km (1,018 mi) east to west and 1,155 km north to south. Ethiopia is land locked with no coastlines.

Ethiopia borders Djibouti and Somalia on the east, Eritrea on the north, Kenya on the south, and Sudan on the west.

The Abyssinian plateau is the highest elevation in Africa. Swift rivers and tributaries forming some of the most spectacular gorges, river valleys, and low-lying plains dissect the whole country. At the highest summit in the Northern Mountains, northeast of the famous Lake Tana, the elevation soars to 4,620 m (15,153 ft). The Ethiopian plateau, which makes up two-thirds of the country, consists of two topographical regions: the high plateau bisected by the Great Rift Valley to the west, and

Ethiopia

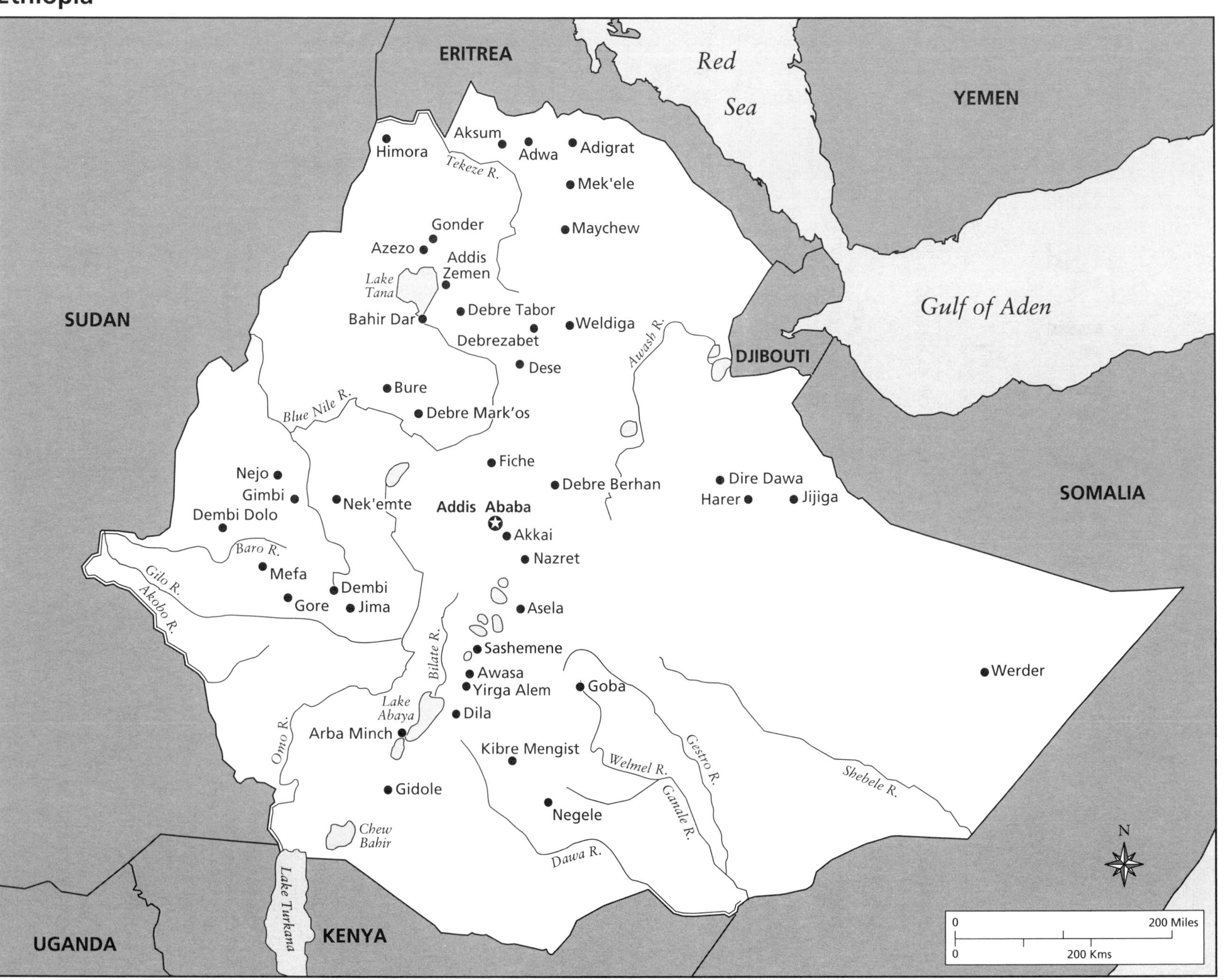
ERITREA
Red
Sea
YEMEN
Gulf of Aden
DJIBOUTI
SOMALIA
SUDAN
UGANDA
KENYA
Lake Turkana
Himora
Aksum
Adwa
Adigrat
Tekeze R.
Mek'ele
Gonder
Maychew
Azezo
Addis
Zemen
Lake
Tana
Bahir Dar
Debre Tabor
Weldiga
Debrezabet
Awash R.
Dese
Bure
Blue Nile R.
Debre Mark'os
Fiche
Nejo
Gimbi
Nek'emte
Debre Berhan
Dire Dawa
Harer
Jijiga
Dembi Dolo
Addis Ababa
Akkai
Baro R.
Nazret
Mefa
Gilo R.
Dembi
Akobo R.
Gore
Jima
Asela
Sashemene
Bilate R.
Awasa
Yirga Alem
Goba
Werder
Lake
Abaya
Dila
Arba Minch
Omo R.
Kibre Mengist
Welmel R.
Gestro R.
Shebele R.
Gidole
Ganale R.
Negele
Chew
Bahir
Dawa R.
N
0
200 Miles
0
200 Kms

the lower Somali Plateau to the east. The high plateau or central plateau is marked by a number of mountain ranges, such as the Cercher, Aranna, and Chelalo. Toward the southeast lies the Somali Plateau, a flat, arid, and sparsely populated semi-desert. The southern half of Ethiopia is bisected by the Great Rift Valley, which runs in a northeast-to-southwest direction. Its floor, 40 to 60 km (25 to 37 mi) in width, is occupied by a number of lakes, such as Zwai, Langano, Abiata, Shala, Awasa, Abaya, and Chamo. To the north the Great Rift is marked by the Danakil Depression, a large triangular region of the Afar Plains. The Danakil Depression, extending northeast beyond the borders with Eritrea, is believed to be the hottest place on earth.

Numerous rivers originate in the highlands and flow outward in many directions through the deep gorges. Because of the westward slope of the highlands, many of the larger rivers are tributaries of the Nile. Of these, the largest are the Abbai (Blue Nile), the Tekeze in the north, and the Baro in the south, which account for half of the outflow of water from the country. The Blue Nile has its source in Lake Tana. Lake Tana is the country's largest lake, in the west-central section of the plateau. The lake contains islands on which ancient churches and church relics of classical significance can be found. A total of 32 km (20 mi) downstream the river drops through the Tisisat (Smoke of Fire) falls. The Baro River drains the southern plateau, which is navigable up to Gambela, the Akobo, and the Gilo. Together they form the headwaters of the Sobat River in Sudan. The only river west of the Great Rift Valley that is not part of the Nile system is the Omo, which drains southward into Lake Rudolph and is known in its upper course as the Gibbie. There also are a number of closed river basins of which the largest, the Awash, flows through the Afar Plains into Lake Abe. The Wabi Shebele and Genale (Juba in Somalia) river systems drain the highlands of the southeast.

Geography

Area sq km: 1,133,882 sq mi 437,794
World Rank: 27th
Land Boundaries, km: Djibouti 337; Eritrea 912; Kenya 830; Somalia 1,626; Sudan 1,606
Coastline, km: 0
Elevation Extremes meters
- Lowest: Denakil 125
- Highest: Ras Dashen Terara 4,620

Land Use % Arable land: 12
- Permanent Crops: 1
- Permanent Pastures: 40
- Forest and Woodland: 25
- Other: 22

Population of Principal Cities (1994)

Addis Ababa	2,112,737
Dire Dawa	164,851
Gonder	112,249
Harer	131,139
Nazret	127,842

CLIMATE AND WEATHER

Ethiopia has three climatic zones: a cool, or *dega*, zone, consisting of the central parts of the western and eastern sections of the high plateaus and the area around Harer, with terrain generally above 2,400 m (7,900 ft) in elevation; a temperate, or *weina dega*, zone, comprising portions of the high plateau between 1,500 and 2,400 m (4,900 and 7,900 ft); and the hot, or *kolla*, zone, encompassing an area with an altitude of less than 1,500 m (5,000 ft) and including the eastern Ogaden, the Blue Nile, and Tekeze valleys and the Kenayan and Sudanese border regions. In the cool zone the hottest months are March to May, and temperatures range from 15.6°C (60°F) to near freezing. Near the mountaintops snow falls in winter and alpine conditions prevail. In the temperate zone temperatures range from 15.6° to 29.4°C (60° to 85°F).

There are two distinct seasons: the rainy season, or *kremt*, lasting from mid-June to mid-September; and the dry season, or *bega*, lasting from mid-September to mid-June. The main rainy season is preceded by a period of sporadic rains, known as the *balg*, during April and May. Rains are heaviest in the southwest, near Gore, where they reach 2,640 mm (104 in) a year. Average annual precipitation over the central plateau is 1,200 mm (48 in).

The prevailing wind system is the southwesterly monsoon in the rainy season and the northeasterly wind from the Eritrean seacoasts in the dry season.

Climate and Weather

Mean Temperature
Cool Zone 60°F to freezing
Temperate Zone 60°F to 85°F
Hot Zone High 140°F
Average Rainfall
Addis Ababa 48 in
Asmara 16 in
Gore 104 in
Danakil Depression 4 in

POPULATION

Population Indicators

Total Population: 1999 59,680,000
World Rank: 19th
Density per sq mi: 136.3 per sq km 52.6
% of annual growth (1994–99): 2.4
Male %: 50
Female %: 50
Urban %: 9.9

(continued)

Age Distribution: % 0–14: 46.6
15–29: 22.7
30–44: 15.6
45–59: 8.9
60–74: 4.5
75 and over: 1.7
Population 2020: 89,943,000
Birth Rate per 1,000: 48.2
Death Rate per 1,000: 16.2
Population Doubling Time (years): —
Infant Mortality Rate per 1,000 live births: 107.0
Rate of Natural Increase per 1,000: 32.0
Total Fertility Rate: 7.0
Expectation of Life (years): Males 48.4
Females 51.6
Marriage Rate per 1,000: —
Divorce Rate per 1,000: —
Total Number of Households: 4.5
Average Size of Households: —
% of Illegitimate Children: —
Induced Abortions: —
Rate per 100 live births: —

ETHNIC COMPOSITION

The great Ethiopianist Carlo Contii Rossini described Ethiopia as an "ethnic museum." His description is apt given that Ethiopia comprises more than 70 ethnic groups distinguished by separate origins, physical appearance, culture, religions, and languages.

There are at least 100 minor ethnic groups, which include the Falasha, or Ethiopian Jews, who live in the Semien Mountains and around Lake Tana. The Nilotic tribes along the Sudan border, and the Agew of the central plateau are some of the ancient ethnic groups. Although they constitute about a third of the Ethiopian population, the Amharas and the closely related Tigrayans dominate the country politically, culturally, and linguistically. The largest ethnic group, estimated to constitute over 38 percent of the Ethiopian population, is the Oromos. In the last two decades, the rise of a nationalist political consciousness among the Oromos has led to the quest for independent statehood for Oromoia. The Amharas and the Tigrayans are Semete and speak two distinct Semetic languages. They occupy the highland provinces that form the historical and geographical core of Ethiopia. With the exception of the Shankella, the vast majority of the populations of Ethiopian peoples are part of the Afroasiatic race.

Whereas previous governments attempted to assimilate the various ethnic groups through policies of Amharization, the current regime in Addis Ababa has divided the country along ethnic lines. The regime argues that organizing the country along ethnic lines will help those ethnic groups that were neglected under the Amharization assimilation programs of previous regimes. The Amharas, whose domination of the political system was challenged by the decentralization of ethnic groups, have rejected the program and openly protested its implementation. In the northern areas, the process of Amharization has advanced significantly, resulting in the complete Amharization of a significant number of Falashas and Tigrayans in Gonder. The constitution of 1955 recognized the existence of different population groups and provided safeguards of their identities. However, it did not regard Ethiopia as a pluralistic and open state.

LANGUAGES

More than 70 languages and 200 dialects are spoken in Ethiopia, but only six are spoken by a large number of people. The six languages commonly used in the country are: Amharic, Oromoffa, Somali, Guragie, Agaw, and Danakil. Amharic is the official language of Ethiopia proper, and Oromoffa is regaining some popularity among the Oromo people. Amharic uses the Ge'ez script while Oromoffa uses the Latin script. At least half of the population speaks Amharic, but the country has more speakers of Cushitic than of Semitic languages. As a consequence of the large number of languages, many Ethiopians are bilingual and even trilingual. Only the Shankellas speak languages belonging to the Nilo-Saharan family.

Ge'ez, or Ethiopic, is considered a sacred language as well as the language of philosophy and literature and is usually referred to as Lesana Ge'ez/AgAzeeyan (the tongue of the free). It is no longer spoken, but its syllabary is used in writing Amharic and Tigrinya. Ge'ez is the liturgical language of the Ethiopian Orthodox Church and until the 19th century was the exclusive language of literature. Amharic, called the language of the king (Lessane Nigus), is the national language, the lingua franca, and the language of instruction at the primary level and in administration.

At the turn of the 20th century, French was the language of instruction in secondary schools. Italian was also used for a brief period in the 1930s mainly in the civil service sector. Both French and Italian were eclipsed by the popularity of English when it became the language of instruction of secondary and higher education as well as employed in the civil services.

Principal Languages and Their Speakers

Amharic	17,930,000
Gurage	2,800,000
Oromo (Oromita)	18,510,000
Sidamo	1,910,000
Somali	2,420,000
Tigrinya	4,290,000
Walaita	1,650,000
Other	10,180,000

RELIGIONS

Until 1975 the Ethiopian Orthodox Church was the state church of Ethiopia with status equal to the state's. The Ethiopian Orthodox Church, associated with the Coptic Church of Egypt, is one of the oldest Christian churches in the world, having been established in the fourth century, when the Ethiopian king Ezana was converted by the Syrian missionary Freminatious. Until 1959 the Ethiopian Church was subordinate to the Church of Alexandria and was administered through an abuna, or metropolitan, who always was an Egyptian Copt. In 1959, under pressure from the emperor, the Ethiopian Church became autocephalous under its own patriarch. Members of the clergy are numerous, and it is estimated that one in every five Ethiopians belongs to an ecclesiastical order. The church's influence has declined in recent years, facing stiff competition from Islam and Protestantism. The resurgence of Islam, compounded by Middle Eastern funds for building mosques and Islamic schools, has eclipsed the remarkable dominion the Orthodox Church had in Ethiopia.

The estimated population of Christians is about 42 percent. For administrative purposes the church is divided into 10 dioceses. The number of churches is estimated at over 20,000.

Other religions, particularly Western Protestant evangelical denominations, have unrestricted access to proselytize and participate in welfare delivery activities. Missionaries and aid workers affiliated with the Protestant, Catholic, and Muslim faiths, and the Orthodox Church itself, are allowed to proselytize and engage in charitable services.

Although it does not possess the same monolithic unity as the Ethiopian Orthodox Church, Islam is followed by an estimated 30 percent of the population, and its adherents are spread over more ethnic groups and geographical regions. In the lowland regions of the west and south, traditional animist religions persist. The number of animists is estimated at 15 percent of the population. But certain animist beliefs and practices pervade much of the popular religions of Christians and Muslims.

The Falasha, also known as Beta Israel (House of Israel) or Black Jews, follow a primitive form of Judaism built on the Torah, which includes not only the Pentateuch but also the Old Testament. They also observe all the major Jewish holidays. Most of them live in Semien, south of Gondar.

Religious Affiliations

Ethiopian Orthodox	20,380,000
Other Christian	4,920,000
Muslim (mostly Sunni)	17,960,000
Traditional beliefs	7,280,000
Other	9,140,000

HISTORICAL BACKGROUND

One of the oldest nations in the world, Ethiopia was one of the most stable countries in Africa until the overthrow of Emperor Haile Selassie in 1974. In its classical sense, the country's name is associated with an ancient empire known as Ethiopia ruled by a biblical queen called Sheba. Classical Ethiopia extended its realm as far as southern Egypt and covered the whole length of East Africa and beyond, including the island of Madagascar, South Arabia, and parts of southwestern India. It was replaced in the first century A.D. by a much weaker realm covering only the Ethiopian plateau and part of southern Arabia. With the advent of the Persian Empire and its subsequent rule over Asia Minor in the seventh century, Ethiopia's rule declined. Sometime between A.D. 300–400, Christianity entered Ethiopia.

Ethiopian legend tells of the Queen of Sheba visiting King Solomon. During her long stay, the queen conceived a son who was then born on her way to her capital of Aksum, in northern Ethiopia. All Ethiopian emperors claimed royal lineage to King Solomon through the Queen's son, whom she named Menelik I.

In the fourth century A.D., two kings, Abraha and Asbaha, declared Christianity as a state religion. Some two centuries later, in the sixth century, the Persians invaded southern Arabia and Asia Minor, and reduced the empire to its African base in northern Ethiopia. Islamic conquest in the seventh century further deprived the empire of its northern territories in eastern Sudan and caused it to shrink to the territory encompassed by northern Ethiopia today. The empire remained docile and isolated until the 16th century when Portuguese explorers, curious about its geographical features and religious traditions, made extensive studies of the country. The Portuguese visit was propitious, because it coincided with a massive Islamic invasion under the leadership of Ahmad Ibn Ibrahim Gran, supported by the Ottoman Empire at his base in southeastern Ethiopia. Christopher da Gama and a contingent of 400 Portuguese soldiers fought against Gran and restored the tattered empire. In the 17th and 18th centuries, the Ethiopian kingdom disintegrated due to internal strife. In 1855, Emperor Tewodros reunited the country and restored central authority. He distinguished himself as a unifier of the empire, but his rule was also marked by wonton violence directed against all sectors of society. In 1867, he detained a group of British and European visitors. Britain sent an expeditionary force to release the hostages. In the ensuing battle at Magdala, Tewodros's capital, his forces were defeated and he committed suicide in 1868.

Emperor Yohannes (1872–89) succeeded Tewodros and kept the country united. He confronted persistent Muslim and European invasions until his death in 1889 in the battle of Mettemma with a resurgent Muslim sect from Sudan. Menelik II, who showed adroit diplomatic and military skills, succeeded Yohannes. Menelik is recognized for his victory over the Italians in the Battle of Adawa in 1896. When he died in 1913, his daughter Zawditu ruled as an empress, but was overshadowed by her regent successor, Tafari Makonnen, later to be known as Emperor Haile Selassie.

Haile Selassie's rule lasted for 44 years with the exception of a five-year interval (1936–41) during which the country was under Italian control. In his long years in power, the emperor expanded educational opportunities and modernized the armed forces and the civil service. He also instituted a series of government reforms, such as granting a constitution and establishing a cabinet and parliament. Yet, real power remained firmly in his hands. Despite his reforms, the country remained feudal, with a coterie among the noble class amassing disproportionate wealth at the expense of the vast peasant class.

During the 1960s support for his regime crumbled. Discontent increased after an abortive 1960 coup, and secessionist movements were established in several provinces, particularly Eritrea. In 1974 a wave of strikes broke out in response to Haile Selassie's autocratic rule as well as deteriorating economic conditions and the government's failure to prevent the death of over 200,000 people in the 1972–74 famine. Haile Selassie was deposed in a military coup in September 1974; a Provisional Military Administrative Council (PMAC) composed of junior officers took power.

In December 1974 Ethiopia was declared a socialist state. The government nationalized foreign interests and began a program of land reform. In 1977 Col. Mengistu Haile Mariam became head of government as the chairman of the PMAC. Besieged by political opponents on the left and confronted with secession demands by Eritrea, he ruthlessly eliminated his opponents and aggressively fought the secessionists. Taking advantage of the situation, Somalia invaded the Ogaden in July 1977. With the aid of Cuba, the Soviet Union, and South Yemen, which had been Somalia's allies, Ethiopia forced Somalia out of the area by March 1978. However, sporadic fighting continued until 1988.

Mengistu conducted eight military offensives accompanied by Soviet supplied MiGs, tanks, and military advisers against the Eritreans. The Eritreans, under the leadership of the Eritrean Peoples Liberation Front (EPLF), mobilized strong resistance and, in 1989 at the Battle of AfAbet, destroyed one-third of the Ethiopian army. The Tigray Peoples Liberation Front (TPLF), the Oromo Liberation Front (OLF), and the Ethiopian Peoples Revolutionary Democratic Front (EPRDF) coordinated their military offense with that of the EPLF and assaulted the Ethiopian army in the provinces south of Eritrea. By 1988 Mengistu was forced to admit that much of Eritrea was in EPLF's hands. By the end of 1989, the military balance had shifted against the Mengistu regime. The EPLF in Eritrea and the EPRDF in Ethiopia escalated the war forcing the Ethiopian army to retreat to the vicinity of Addis Ababa. On May 28, 1991, the Ethiopian Civil War came to an end when the EPRDF took possession of Addis Ababa and announced a coalition government. Mengistu had resigned on May 21, fleeing the capital to seek refuge in Zimbabwe.

Meanwhile, the Eritrean People's Liberation Front gained control of the Eritrean capital of Asmara and announced the formation of a provisional government to administer Eritrea until a referendum could be held on the issue of independence.

A multiparty conference in Addis Ababa adopted a national charter providing guarantees for human rights. It also elected an 87-member Council of Representatives whose chairman, Meles Zenawi, became de facto interim president. In accordance with the National Charter's promise of self-determination for ethnic groups, the country was divided into 14 regional administrations, which would have autonomy in matters of regional law and internal affairs. Nevertheless, the transitional government found itself locked into a struggle with the Oromos and the Eritreans. Hostilities between the Oromo Liberation Front (OLF) and EPRDF continued in various parts of the country for two years until the former joined the government. Meanwhile, Eritrea proclaimed its independence in 1993. The severe famine that began in the early 1980s continued through the early 1990s. By 1992 more than 13.5 million people were affected by the drought and a further 1.4 million were affected by internal conflicts. More than 200 people were dying of starvation every week in the southeast. In 1995 Ethiopia was formally proclaimed a federal democratic republic with a titular federal president. Negaso Gidada was elected president and Meles Zenawi was named to the far more powerful office of prime minister.

When Eritrea became independent from Ethiopia, the common border had not been precisely defined, and in 1998, clashes broke out between Ethiopia and Eritrea, each accusing the other of seizing territory. By 1999, the dispute had developed into a full-scale war, and tens of thousands of soldiers died before a peace agreement was signed in December 2000. By mid-2001, Ethiopian and Eritrean troops had withdrawn from the border region, and the United Nations was monitoring the peace process. Meles was reelected prime minister in October 2000.

CONSTITUTION

The constitution of 1995 establishes a three-branch government. The legislative body is composed of the House of Peoples' Representatives and the House of the Federation. The House of People's Representatives is elected by a plurality from electoral districts within the kilils for five-year terms. State assemblies appoint members to the House of Federation.

The executive branch includes the president of the republic as head of state, and the prime minister as head of

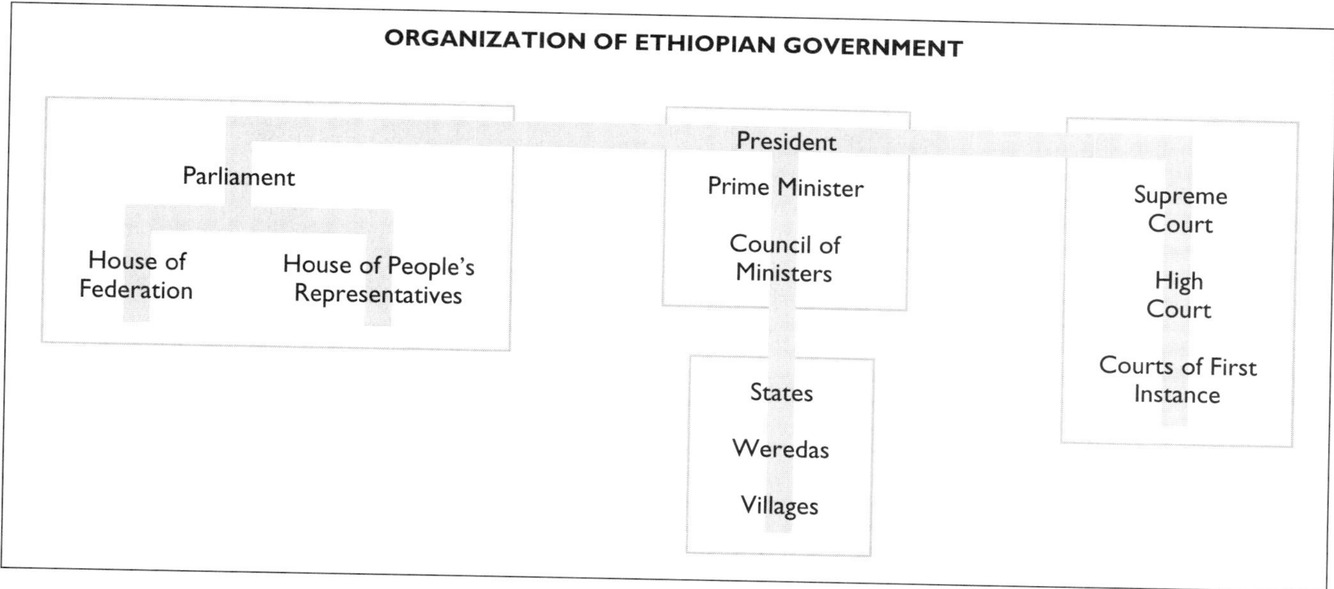

government. The head of state exercises ceremonial functions with little or no effect on policy deliberations. The prime minister, by contrast, wields enormous powers of cabinet appointments. He is also the commander in chief of the armed forces. The constitution as it stands in its 1995 form accommodates the political goals of the EPRDF, which is itself dominated by the Tigray People's Liberation Front (TPLF). Critics argue that most cabinet appointments and policy deliberations are driven by the TPLF.

LOCAL GOVERNMENT

In June 1991 town meetings were held throughout the country in which "Peace and Stability Commissions" were selected by local citizens to act as de facto local governments. These commissions were slated to administer local affairs until after a transitional national government was established and a new constitution was written and ratified. Subsequently the commissions were used to expedite the snap election of June 1991. Under the directives given in the 1991 Transitional Charter (Part I, Article 2), local governments were defined as components of the local government. Each unit of government was recognized as an extension of the autonomous regional states (*kilil*) each delegated with a mandate to "preserve its identity and have it respected, promote its culture, and history and use and develop its language." The constitution of 1995 reiterated the same clause.

The organization of authority, as stated in Article 46, No. 2, in the new constitution, takes into consideration ethnolinguistic differences, and "settlement patterns" and attempts to address them by drawing borderlines for the purpose of creating the member states of the federal system. At the apex of authority is the federal government. It is composed of nine states (*kilil*) and two cities (Addis Ababa and Harer) with chartered status. A collection of *weredas* inhabited by peoples of similar language and ethnic affiliations make a state. Similarly a collection of villages are designated as *weredas*. The smallest unit of local government is the village. The equivalent of a village in an urban setting is the *kebele*. There are approximately 32,000 *kebeles*, and 600 *weredas* in Ethiopia constituting the nine *kilils* and two chartered cities.

The administrative practices of local governments are eclectic and decidedly autonomous mainly due to the experimental nature of the *kilil* system that is still resented by a large segment of the population. In all aspects of local government, the traditional patterns of local and city administration, especially the mayoral (*kentiba*) hierarchy of city governance, is apparent in towns and cities.

Local Government

Principal administrative divisions, area, population

AREA AND POPULATION

Regions	area sq mi	area sq km	population 1994 estimate
Addis Ababa	—	—	2,112,737
Affar	—	—	1,106,383
Amhara	—	—	13,834,297
Benishangul-Gumuz	—	—	460,459
Dire Dawa	—	—	251,864
Gambela	—	—	181,862
Hariai	—	—	131,139
Oromiya	—	—	18,732,525
Southern Nations, Nationalities and Peoples	—	—	10,377,028
Tigray	—	—	3,136,267
TOTAL	437,794	1,133,882	—

PARLIAMENT

The tradition of parliamentary government in Ethiopia started in 1955 when Haile Selassie reformed the 1931 constitution to expedite modernization. After the overthrow of Haile Selassie in 1974, the succeeding marxist regime abrogated the 1955 constitution. In 1987 the Workers Party of Ethiopia, an ideologue marxist party created in 1984 and controlled by the then dictator Mengistu Haile Mariam, introduced the Peoples Democratic Republic of Ethiopia (PDRE) under a new constitution. A parliament known by its Amharic name as the Shengo, comprising 835 members from electoral districts representing 80,000 inhabitants of rural areas and 15,000 residents of urban areas, was seated. The Shengo proved ineffective as a representational body, because the personality of Mengistu Haile Mariam overshadowed and undercut parliamentary functions. With the overthrow of Mariam in 1991, the PRDE was replaced by the new Federal Democratic Republic of Ethiopia (FDRE), introduced by the EPRDF in 1995.

In 1995 the EPRDF introduced a new constitution ratified by a Constituent Assembly. The new constitution created the Federal Democratic Republic of Ethiopia, comprising nine states and the cities of Addis Ababa and Harer as autonomous constituencies. The head of state is the president of the republic while the head of government is the prime minister.

The nine states were districted into electoral ethnic constituencies to ensure parliamentary representation of all ethnic groups and nationalities. Voting age is 18 years or older. Parliament comprises two chambers. The lower house, or House of People's Representatives, consists of 547 seats, and the upper house, the House of the Federation, consists of 110 representatives. The assemblies of the federal states elect the upper house—the Council of Federation. The term of service is five years. In May 2000, 50 parties and 500 independent candidates contested for elections to the council. Those affiliated with the EPRDF scored an overwhelming electoral victory, guaranteeing Meles Zenawi, the EPRDF's leader, another term in office.

POLITICAL PARTIES

Political representation in Ethiopia is virtually nonexistent save for the new experiment the EPRDF launched in 1991. Even then, the prospects for organized political parties with a credible degree of autonomy and freedom is very precarious. Whatever parties and organized participation there are today in Ethiopia are strictly under the control and countenance of the EPRDF. The EPRDF itself is composed of a coalition of 18 smaller ethnic-based organizations all of which, are subordinated to and under virtual control of the dominant party, the Tigray Peoples Liberation Front (TPLF).

Political awareness is extremely limited among the masses. Ethiopia's high birth rate and vast geography combined with minuscule investment in the development of human capital have resulted in a low level of literacy. Lack of exposure to the practice of establishing organizations that would articulate the political ideas, beliefs, and values of organized groups with a mature sense of political judgment and would hold political elites responsible for the successes or failures of a party agenda and platform have never been allowed to flourish.

In its attempt to introduce pluralism, the TPLF leadership encouraged the creation of various ethnic groups and organized them for political representation. Among those groups that initially subscribed to the TPLF's overtures, the most praminent was the Oromo Liberation Front (OLF). The OLF represented the largest single ethnic group in Ethiopia. By contrast, the TPLF represented the smallest ethnic group, the northern province of Tigray. The tension created by the inequalities of power among the affiliated ethnic coalitions was bound to create political friction, which spilled over into regional crisis. The first crisis started in the snap elections of 1992 when some of the ethnic organizations, particularly the OLF and the All Amhara Peoples Organization (AAPO), refused to participate claiming that they deserved to play larger roles in the exercise of political power. They refused to accept TPLF's institutional domination and boycotted the election. Subsequently, the OLF withdrew from the governing coalition and resorted to armed struggle. It called for Oromo self-determination, the outcome of which would be either federation or complete independence.

The AAPO also withdrew from the government, but before it could organize armed resistance, TPLF cadres overpowered the leadership. Its leader, Asrat Woldeyes, was taken to jail where he developed persistent illnesses leading to his release and subsequent death in the United States where he went for medical treatment. His fate generated bitter anger among his ethnic constituency, the Amharas. They accused the TPLF of having prolonged his detention unnecessarily and causing his premature death. The Ogaden Liberation Front and the Western Somali Liberation Front participated in the elections of 1992 and 1995. Their influence has since been overshadowed by EPRDF's policy of exclusive exercise of power leading to diminished political efficacy and sporadic rebellion in their constituent region, the Ogaden territory. Subsequent developments promoting the democratic evolution of party activity from that of a controlled and contrived posture to a genuine representation of an articulate ideology have produced little progress.

Political Parties

Ethiopian People's Revolutionary Democratic Front, 1988
Tigre People's Liberation Front, 1975
Amhara National Democratic Movement, 1980

Oromo People's Democratic Organization, 1990
Southern Ethiopia People's Democratic Organization
Afar Liberation Front, 1975
Afar People's Democratic Organization, 1992
Oromo Liberation Front
Alliance for the Liberation of the Oromos, Somalis and Afars, 1997
Somali Abo Liberation Front
Western Somalia Liberation Front, 1975
Ethiopian Democratic Union
All-Amhara People's Organization
Coalition of Ethiopian Democratic Forces, 1991
Ethiopian People's Revolutionary Party, 1997
Ethiopian People's Democratic Alliance, 1982
Ethiopian Movement for Democracy, Peace and Unity, 1990
Ethiopian National Democratic Party, 1994
Afar Revolutionary Democratic Union Front, 1991
Afar National Democratic Movement, 1995
Oromo People's Liberation Front, 1992
Ogaden National Liberation Front, 1986
Islamic Union
Tigrean Alliance for National Democracy, 1995

Political Parties: Strength in Parliament Most Recent Elections

Council of People's Representatives. The chamber has 527 members elected to five-year terms in single-seat constituencies. In the elections of May 14 and August 31, 2000, the Oromo People's Democratic Organization won 177 seats; Amhara National Democratic Movement, 134; Tigray People's Liberation Front, 38; Walayta, Gamo, Gofa Dawro Konta People's Democratic Organization, 27; Solami People's Democratic Party, 19; Ethiopian People's Revolutionary Democratic Front, 19; Sidama People's Democratic Organization, 18; Gurage Nationalities Democratic Movement, 15; Kafa Shaka People's Democratic Organization, 10; Afar National Democratic Party, 8; Gedeyo People's Revolutionary Democratic Front, 7; Benishangul Gumuz People's Democratic Unity Front, 6; Bench Madji People's Democratic Unity Front, 5; Kembata Alabaa and Tembaro, 4; Gambela People's Democratic Front, 3; South Ethiopia People's Democratic Front, 3; South Ethiopia People's Democratic Union, 2; Ethiopians' Democratic Unity Party, 2; Argoba People's Democratic Movement, 1; All Ambara People's Organization, 1; Oromo Liberation Unity Front, 1; Oromo National Congress, 1; Silte People's Democratic Unity Party, 1; Yem People's Democratic Unity Party, 1; Hadiya National Democratic Organization, 1; Kore Nationality Democratic Organization, 1; Burgi People's Democratic Union, 1; and nonpartisans, 12.

LEGAL SYSTEM

The judiciary branch is stipulated by the 1995 constitution as constituting the third branch of government. The court system consists of the Federal Supreme Court, the Federal High Court, and the courts of first instance (original jurisdiction). There is an overlap of judicial functions between the federal and the state courts. The courts of first instance and the Federal High Court serve simultaneously as courts of original jurisdiction and supreme courts for the federal states. The federal courts have sole jurisdiction of judicial review with respect to state cases.

LAW ENFORCEMENT

Law Enforcement

Offenses reported to the police per 100,000: 263
- Murder: 16.4
- Assault: 49.9
- Burglary: 6.3
- Automobile Theft: 2.3
- Population per Police officer: 1,100

Death Penalty: Yes

HUMAN RIGHTS

Under the Haile Selassie monarchic state and the marxist dictatorship that replaced it, Ethiopia experienced widespread violations, of human rights. The 1991 government brought about a substantial change in the freedom of movement, which was under tight control during the communist era. However, the division of the country along ethnic lines compromised that freedom. The new administrative laws extend freedom of movement, but residence and employment in a particular province is largely restricted to the dominant ethnic group within that province.

Human rights violations under the current EPRDF regime are also regarded as dismal. The level of brutality against the defenseless and the disregard for the rights of civilian prisoners and prisoners of conscience by successive Ethiopian regimes was uniformly repudiated by independent observers such as Africa Watch and Amnesty International. All these regimes have been engaged constantly in suppressing revolts of insurgent groups and border conflicts with Somalia, Sudan, and Eritrea. They also share the same patterns of conducting arbitrary arrests, torture, and summary executions.

Part of Ethiopia's war strategy, under the EPRDF, involved mass expulsion of Eritreans and Ethiopians of Eritrean blood and dumping them in a no-man's land at the Eritrean border. According to Eritrean official data, close to 70,000 civilians were stripped of their possessions and their citizenship in contravention of the 1995 Ethiopian constitution and were deported to Eritrea. The deportees included women, children, senior citizens, hospital patients, and children whose parents were deported separately.

FOREIGN POLICY

The liberation and subsequent independence of Eritrea introduced a new dilemma for Ethiopia. The loss of Eritrean ports rendered Ethiopia land-locked and dependent on Eritrea and Djibouti for access to the sea. Even though Eritrea pledged free access to the sea to Ethiopian goods, gradually tension between the two countries escalated into deeper misunderstandings on matters of port administration, maintenance, and management.

Ethiopia gradually shifted its primary port activity to Djibouti. When Eritrea abandoned the Ethiopian bir as its legal tender and introduced its own currency, the nakfa, Ethiopia refused to accept the Eritrean currency and demanded trade transactions between the two countries to be conducted on the basis of letters of credit backed by hard currency, specifically the American dollar. Relations between the two countries soured and deteriorated resulting in open warfare in May 1997 in the Badime War. When Ethiopian border police started dismantling border posts and uprooting Eritrean farmers from their villages and farms, Eritrea responded by occupying the Badime plains on the western border connecting the two countries. Between May 1997 and February 2000, the two countries clashed in intermittent wars involving the deployment of an estimated half a million troops. The United Nations, the Organization of African Unity (OAU), and the European Union have since attempted to mediate a reconciliation between the two countries. During the 35th Ordinary Session of the Assembly of the Heads of States of the OAU held in Algiers, Algeria, on July 12–14, 1999, the OAU endorsed the Framework Agreement and the Modalities for resolving the border war between the two countries. Both subscribed to the documents initially, but later Ethiopia balked at accepting the Technical Agreement for Implementation of the Framework Agreement and Modalities. Repeated mediation by the United States, the European Union, and the OAU have so far failed to produce any reconciliation as Ethiopia has upped the ante by demanding that Eritrea renounce any border claims that it may have. Eritrea has refused to do so, adamantly stating that to abandon territories it considered legally belonging to it would amount to renouncing its won sovereignty and supremacy over its own borders.

Following up the diplomatic failures, Ethiopia carried out new waves of attacks on Eritrean positions in May 2000. Eritrean troops were driven away from their defensive positions at the border and deep into Eritrean territory. Ethiopia's gain in the military offensive resulted in both countries agreeing to new terms of cease-fire. On June 18, 2000, both countries signed the Agreement on Cessation of Hostilities. On July 31, 2000, the UN Security Council authorized the creation of the UN Mission in Ethiopia and Eritrea (UNMEE). The mandates of UNMEE include monitoring the cessation of hostilities, troop redeployment, and implementation of a UN observer force of about 4,200 to be stationed inside Eritrean territory until the borders are eventually demarcated.

Relations with Sudan deteriorated after 1994 when Sudan was singled out as supporting terrorists espousing an Islamic mission to destabilize the Horn of Africa. Ethiopia, along with Eritrea and Uganda, sought help from the United States to confront Islamic terrorists inspired and supported by Sudan. Relations with Sudan remained irreconcilable until the closing weeks of 1999. In early 2000, the two countries drew closer in view of Ethiopia's attempt to isolate its new enemy, Eritrea. In March 2000, Ethiopia and Sudan concluded agreements for peaceful resolution of conflicts, border security, and use of Sudanese ports for Ethiopian imports and exports.

In general, Ethiopia's foreign policy, as it enters the 21st century, is driven by Ethiopia's determined hostility to Eritrea. In order to isolate Eritrea, Ethiopia has made overtures to erstwhile suspicious neighbors, including Sudan, Yemen, Egypt, Libya, and the Arab world in general. Its diplomatic pronouncements carry a conciliatory tone to Middle Eastern countries as part of an effort to dispell their disapproval of Ethiopia's traditional alliance with Israel. Because Addis Ababa, Ethiopia's capital, serves as the headquarters for the Organization of African Unity, Ethiopia is well regarded by sub-Saharan African countries.

DEFENSE

Currently, the armed forces are variously estimated at over 500,000 strong. Universal conscription is enforced for all males over the age of 17. The current regime, like the Derg before it, has recruited boys as young as 13 at the height of its war with Eritrea.

In 1998, a border war with Eritrea broke out. The war induced the Ethiopian government to resort to an extensive shopping spree for rebuilding its air and ground forces. Most of the equipment bought between 1998 and 2000 came from Russia. Israel, Bulgaria, Ukraine, and Turkey are emerging as major arms suppliers for the Ethiopian armed forces. In the spring of 1999, North Korean armament specialists arrived in the country, reportedly to expand the armament industry, which was established in the 1980s by the Derg. This military expenditure stands in stark contrast to the dearth of social expenditures in the face of widespread poverty over the past decades.

Military Indicators

Total Active Duty Personnel: —
Military Manpower per 1,000: —
Military Expenditures $million: 118
- as % of GNP: 2.2
- per capita $: 2
- as % of central government expenditures: 9.2

Arms Imports $million: 0
Arms Exports $million: 0

ECONOMY

The combined effect of persistent drought, protracted wars, natural disasters, and misguided economic policies of the Derg have made Ethiopia dependent on food aid from donor countries. Overall economic growth has declined since 1985 and by 1998/99 the GDP growth was flat. Given the population annual growth rate of

3.8 percent, per capita income was continuously declining in the 1990s.

In order to rehabilitate the economy, the Transitional Government of Ethiopia (TGE) pledged that it would adapt liberal free-market policies by singling out agriculture as a primary engine of growth and development. Traditionally, the Ethiopian economy has been heavily dominated by subsistence agriculture with poor or non-existent provisions for environmental control, soil erosion, deforestation, and pest control.

Whatever agricultural capital exists today or in the past is limited to a few government enterprises, which possess expensive agricultural equipment and trained personnel but have made little impact in ameliorating the perpetual food crisis in Ethiopia. Ethiopian food crises tend to be of apocalyptic proportions since the 1890s when the famine of 1889 wiped out scores of villages in northern Ethiopia. Ever since, there has never been a decade of full agricultural employment, production, and distribution in Ethiopia to feed the booming population. Ethiopia is as heavily dependent on foreign food aid at the beginning of the 21st century as it was at the beginning of the 20th century.

Principal Economic Indicators

Gross National Product $: 6.507 billion
GNP per capita $: 110
GNP Average Annual Growth Rate (1990–97) %: 2.2
GNP per capita Average Annual Growth Rate (1990–97) %: 0.0
Origin of Gross Domestic Product %
- Agriculture: 54
- Mining: —
- Manufacturing: 8
- Construction: 3
- Public Utilities: 1
- Transportation and Communications: 5
- Trade: 10
- Financial Services: 8
- Other Services: 4
- Government: 7

Gross Domestic Product by Type of Expenditure %
- Private Consumption: 74
- Government Consumption: 11
- Gross Domestic Investment: 15
- Foreign Trade: Exports: 12
  Imports: 22

% of Income Received by Poorest 20%: 8.6
% of Income Received by Richest 10%: 27.5

Balance of trade (current prices)

	1990	1991	1992	1993	1994	1995
Br 000,000	−1,271.6	−433.1	−1,360.5	−2,325.1	−2,708.3	−4,449.6
% of total	50.8%	55.5%	60.3%	53.9%	39.6%	46.1%

Finance

National Currency: Birr (Br)
Exchange Rate: $1 = Br 6.9530
Money Supply Stock in National Currency billion:
M1 per capita:
Central Bank Discount Rate %:
Total External Debt $million: 5,200
Debt Service Ratio %:
Balance of Payments $million: −23
International Reserves SDRs million:
Ratio of External Debt to Total Reserves:
Average Annual Rate of Inflation/Consumer Price Index Growth Rate %: 0

Official Development Assistance

Donor ODA $million: 648
- as % of GNP: 10.0
- per capita $ 11
- Foreign Direct Investment $million: 4

Central Government Revenues and Expenditures

Fiscal Year:
Revenues $million: 1,000
Expenditures $million: 1,480
Budget Deficit $million: 480
Tax Revenues as % of GDP: —
Highest Tax Bracket %
- Individual: —
- Corporate: —

Employment and Labor

Economically Active Population: 24,606,000
Female Participation Rate %: 41.1
Activity Rate %: 43.3
Labor by Sector: %
- Agriculture, Forestry, Fishing: 87.8
- Manufacturing, Mining: 1.7
- Construction: 0.2
- Transportation and Communications: 0.4
- Trade, Hotels, and Restaurants: 3.8
- Finance, Insurance, Real Estate: 0.1
- Public Administration, Defense: —
- Services: 5.1

Unemployment %: —

Agriculture

Agriculture's Share of GDP %: 54
Average Annual Rate of Growth (1965–98)%: 1.9
Number of Farms 000: 6,092
Average Size of Farm ha: 1.3
Number of Tractors per 1,000 hectares: 0.3
Irrigation, % of Farms having: 2.0
Artificial Fertilizer kg/hectare: 7.0
Total Farmland as % of land area: 6.4
Livestock: Cattle 000: 29,900
- Sheep 000: 21,850
- Hogs 000: 23
- Chickens 000: 55,000

Forests: Production of Roundwood (000 cubic meters): 47,337
Fisheries: Total Catch tons 000: 5.3

Mining

% of GDP: 0.3
Value of Mineral Production $million: 13.9

Manufacturing

Value Added $million: 529
Industrial Production Growth Rate %: —

Energy

Commercial Energy Production metric tons of oil equivalent 000: 16,316
Commercial Energy Consumption metric tons of oil equivalent 000: 17,131
Commercial Energy Consumption per capita kg: 287
Average Annual Growth Rate 1980–97%: −0.1
Net Energy Imports % of use: 5
Electricity Installed Capacity kW 000: 464
Production kW-hr million: 1,328
Coal Reserves tons million: 11
Production tons 000: —
Natural Gas Proven Reserves cubic meters billion: 25
Production cubic meters million: —
Crude Petroleum Reserves barrels million: 0.4
Production barrels million: —
Consumption barrels million: 6
Refinery Capacity barrels per day 000: —
Pipelines Lenght km: —

Foreign Trade

Imports $million: 771.6
Exports $million: 201.7
Export Volume % Annual Growth Rate (1990–97): 7.7
Import Volume % Annual Growth Rate (1990–97): 1.2

Price index (1995 = 100)

	1992	1993	1994	1995	1996	1997
Consumer price index	81.6	84.5	90.9	100.0	94.6	91.4

Major Trading Partners

	Imports	Exports
European Union %	39.3	41.6
United States %	9.5	9.2
Eastern European %	—	0.3
Japan %	4.1	19.0
Others %	47.2	29.9

Transportation

Roads Total Length mi: 17, 622 km 28,360
Paved %: 15
Automobiles: 45,559
Trucks and Buses: 20,462
Persons per vehicle: 842
Railroad; Track Length mi: 486 km 782
Passenger-mi million: 172
Freight-mi million: 86
Merchant Marine: No. of Vessels: 27
Total Deadweight Tonnage 000: 84.3
International Cargo Loaded tons 000: 592
International Cargo Off-loaded tons 000: 3,120
Airports with Scheduled Flights: 31
Traffic: Passenger-mi million: 1,142
Freight-mi million: 77
Length of Canals mi: —

Tourism

Number of Tourists to 000: 91
Number of Tourists from 000: 140
Tourist Receipts $million: 36
Tourist Expenditures $million: 25

Communications

Telephones 000: 143
Cost of Local Calls 3 mins: $0.03
Cellular Telephones 000: —
Fax Machines 000: 1.4
Personal Computers 000: —
Internet Hosts per million persons: —
Mail: Post Offices: 570
Pieces of Mail Handled million: 29
Pieces of Mail Handled per person: 0.5

EDUCATION

Traditionally, education was under the complete control of the Ethiopian Orthodox Church. By 1974, the church no longer played any role in educational life. Education is neither compulsory nor universal by law, but public education is free from the primary to the college level. There is a considerable difference between urban and rural school enrollment rates. Nearly 65 percent of urban children of school age attend school, whereas the percentage of rural children is only 4 percent.

The rural figure is bound to decline further as the provision of educational opportunities for Ethiopian children has failed to keep up with the phenomenal increase in the country's birthrate.

Schooling consists of 12 years, divided into six years of primary school, two years of middle school, and four years of secondary school. National examinations are held at the conclusion of the eighth and 12th grades, and secondary education is concluded with the Ethiopian School Leaving Certificate. Dropout rates are high, averaging between 68 and 70 percent in the primary cycle. Less than 50 percent of first-grade enrollees complete public school. The curricula are based on European, particularly British and French, models. The alien character of the curricula is reinforced by the lack of locally written texts and the absence of qualified indigenous teachers.

The academic year runs from September to June. The medium of instruction, which was formerly Amharic at the primary level, has been replaced by ethnic and local languages. It is too early to judge whether language segmentation will contribute to or hinder learning.

There are two institutions of higher learning: the Addis Ababa University and the Mekele University. Total enrolment approaches 20,000. College and university education suffers from uncertainty and interruptions as the government makes use of students for various campaigns, such as literacy drives in the countryside, or national emergency measures, such as service in the armed forces.

Education

Literacy Rate %: 35.5
  Male %: 45.5
  Female %: 25.3
First Level: Primary schools: 9,276
  Teachers: 83,113
  Students: 2,722,192
  Student-Teacher Ratio: 32.8
  Net Enrollment Ratio: 24.0
Second Level: Secondary Schools: —
  Teachers: 22,779
  Students: 747,142
  Student-Teacher Ratio: 32.8
  Net Enrollment Ratio: —

Vocational Level: Schools: —
  Students: 9,103

Third Level: Institutions: —
  Teachers: 1,937
  Students: 32,671
  Student-Ratio Level: 16.9
  Gross Enrollment Ratio: 0.7
  Students per 100,000: 60
  % of Population Age 25 and over with Postsecondary Education: —

Public Expenditure on Education as % of GDP: 4.7

SCIENCE AND TECHNOLOGY

Science and Technology

Scientists and Engineers in R&D per 1 million persons: —
Expenditures in R&D as % of GDP: —
High-Tech Exports $million: —
Patent Applications by Residents: 4

MEDIA

The Ethiopian News Agency (ENA), founded in 1942, served continuously as a news gathering and disseminating organ of government until it was restructured in 1994 as a semi-private agency with a stated purpose of expanding press freedom. The major impact of the 1994 reform was the expansion of media conglomerates owned and operated by political parties affiliated with the ruling party, TPLF/EPRDF. Among the media organizations that enjoy particular favor in the governing centers are the Walta Information Center, with extensive holdings in the print, electronic, and broadcasting media, and Radio Fana.

Theoretically, the government allows press freedom. The current press laws make a point of insuring free expression for the media, but at the same time place heavy burdens on journalists for disseminating inaccurate or "defamatory" information. The condition placed on journalists was cited by the Committee to Protect Journalists (CPJ), a nonprofit and independent organization, as a "draconian" law. The head of the Ethiopian Free Press Journalist's Association (EFJA) defected in 1999, citing persecution. CPJ and other human rights organizations accuse the government of employing extra-judicial treatment against journalists and independent publishers of newspapers and magazines.

Media

Daily Newspapers: 4
  Total Circulation 000: 81
  Circulation per 1,000; 10
Books Published: —
Magazines: —
Radio Receivers 000: 9,000
  per 1,000: 167
Television sets 000: 250
  per 1,000: 4.2

MOST IMPORTANT MEDIA:

Press. Except as noted, the following are Amharic-language dailies published at Addis Ababa: *Addis Zemen* (41,000); *Ethiopian Herald* (37,000), in English; *Yezareitu Itiopia* (30,000), weekly.

News agencies. The domestic facility is the Ethiopian News Agency (Itiopia Zena Agelgilot-Izea); a number of foreign bureaus maintain offices at Addis Ababa.

Radio and television. The Voice of Ethiopia (Itiopia Demts Beherawi-Naw) broadcasts locally and internationally in Amharic, English, Arabic, and a number of other languages. Ethiopian Television (Itiopia Television) has been broadcasting under government auspices since 1964.

CULTURE

Cultural Indicators

Public Libraries Number: 4
  Volumes: 124,000
  Registered borrowers: 11,680
Museums Number: 1
  Annual Attendance: 6,000
Cinema Production of Long Films: 1
  Number of Cinemas: —
  Seating Capacity: —
  Annual Attendance million: —
  Annual Attendance per capita: —

STATUS OF WOMEN

A 1982 UNICEF study concluded that Ethiopian women are among the most disadvantaged sectors of the population, citing cultural and traditional biases, marriages imposed at a very young age, the hard and time-consuming labor of rural women, and inadequate employment opportunities and decent wages for urban women. Village leadership is male, and all clergy are male. Female circumcision is practiced in the northern parts of the country, although the government has stated its opposition to this practice. The government's token efforts to improve conditions for women have had minimal effect.

Women

Gender Empowerment Measure: —
Seats Held in Parliament by Women %: 7.8
Female Administrators and Managers %: —
Female Professional and Technical Workers %: —
Women's Share of Earned Income %: —
Women in Government %: 11

HEALTH, FOOD, AND NUTRITION

Health

Number of Physicians: 1,466
Number of Dentists: —
Number of Nurses: 3,496
Number of Pharmacists: 364
Population per Physician: 30,195
Number of Hospitals: 86
Hospital Beds per 10,000: 3
Hospital Bed Occupancy Rate: —
Infant Mortality Rate per 1,000 live births: 170
Maternal Mortality Rate per 100,000 live births: 1,400
Total Health Expenditures as % of GDP: 3.80
Health Expenditures per capita $: 4
HIV Infected % of adults: 9.31
Cigarette Consumption per smoker per year: —
% of Smokers: Male: —
Female: —
Access to Safe Water %: 27

Food and Nutrition

Food Supply as % of FAO Requirements: —
% of Consumption Expenditures on Food: 49.0
Daily Available Calories per capita: —
% of Total Calories derived from:
Cereals: —
Potatoes, cassava: —
Meat, poultry: —
Fish: —
Eggs, milk: —
Fruits, vegetables: —
Fats, oils: —

ENVIRONMENT

The Ethiopian highland plateau, as the highest elevation in Africa, contains several rivers and streams that dissect the ground surface and wash out topsoil, rendering agricultural enterprise unproductive. The Blue Nile, originating from Lake Tana in the heart of Ethiopia, accumulates massive floods with rich soil contents that serve to benefit Sudanese and Egyptian farmers. Even if Nile waters were to be harnessed by Ethiopia, the level of capital development for the utilization of water is at a primitive state. There exists no supplemental infrastructure, such as agricultural equipment, pest control, animal husbandry, and sophisticated skills that would complement the availability of Nile waters.

Ethiopia is endowed with a suitable environment for agricultural and recreational industry. However, deforestation and drought combined with incessant wars have degraded the topography. The forest fires that hit at the heart of Ethiopia's virgin forests in February to March 2000 have consumed 70,000-hectares, including ancient trees and rare animals unique to Ethiopia. In view of the fact that only 2 percent of Ethiopia's forests remain due to clear cutting for lumber and fuel, the damage caused by the fires is expected to have a lasting impact on the remaining forests.

There is a low level of industrialization in Ethiopia. As a result, industrial waste and pollution are minimal except in the cities where smog from congested streets creates unacceptable levels of pollution. The capital city, Addis Ababa, like many other Ethiopian cities, suffers from poor sanitation. Local authorities tolerate disorderly urban development by allowing the construction of squalid cardboard houses in the business districts and in the vicinity of government offices.

Environment

Forest Area sq km: 136,000
Average Annual Deforestation sq km: 624
Nationally Protected Areas as % of Total Land Area: 5.5
Freshwater Access cubic meters per capita: 1,795
Emissions of Organic Water Pollutants kg per day: 19,390
CO_2 Emissions per capita ton: 0.1

CHRONOLOGY

1941 British and Ethiopian forces return Emperor Haile Selassie to the throne after an Italian occupation of Ethiopia.
1947 After an Allied treaty with Italy regarding disposition of the former Italian colonies of Eritrea, Italian Somaliland, and Libya, the UN General Assembly votes for the federation of Eritrea with Ethiopia, to be completed by September 1952.
1955 Haile Selassie issues a revised constitution giving limited powers to the parliament.
1960 Members of the imperial guard stage an unsuccessful coup.
1963 Haile Selassie founds the Organization of African Unity at Addis Ababa; a long-standing border dispute between Ethiopia and the Somali Republic erupts into armed warfare.
1964 A truce between Ethiopia and the Somali Republic establishes a demilitarized zone along the border.
1965 Ethiopia accuses Sudan of abetting an Eritrean independence movement.
1967 7,000 Eritreans flee to Sudan to escape Ethiopian military reprisals against secessionists.
1970 Ethiopia lays siege to regions of Eritrea in a failed attempt to end the guerrilla warfare.

1972 A severe drought lasting through 1975 strikes northern Ethiopia.

1974 Soldiers led by Major Mengistu Haile Mariam oust the emperor and institute socialist reforms under a Provisional Military Administrative Council known as the Derg.

1975 Mengistu begins a program of land reform, abolishes the monarchy, and declares Ethiopia a republic.

1977 Critics of the military regime, led by Ethiopian People's Revolutionary Party (EPRP), launch the "White Terror," a campaign of urban guerrilla warfare; the government responds with its own "Red Terror" campaign, arming Ethiopians loyal to the Derg, who kill an estimated 100,000 people suspected of being enemies of the government. The United States withdraws its support for the government.

1978 Mengistu secures support from the USSR and Cuba and wins back territories lost to the revolutionaries.

1984 A northern drought lasting until 1986 plunges the country into famine and 1 million die of starvation; the government attempts forced resettlement of 600,000 northerners to the south.

1987 Mengistu proclaims a new, Soviet-style constitution with popular elections and renames the country the People's Democratic Republic of Ethiopia, but power remains in the hands of the Derg, who elect Mengistu president; the Eritrean People's Liberation Front (EPLF) and the Tigray People's Liberation Front (TPLF) again stage armed resistance.

1989 Having lost the support of the USSR, the Ethiopian national assembly conducts peace talks with the EPLF and the Ethiopian People's Revolutionary Democratic Front (EPRDF), a coalition of opposition groups led by the TPLF.

1990 EPLF forces capture the strategic Eritrean port city of Massawa; EPRDF forces overtake Ethiopia's capital, Addis Ababa.

1991 The EPRDF overthrows Mengistu's government and establishes the Transitional Government of Ethiopia.

1992 Ethiopia's first snap elections are conducted to facilitate redistricting and redrawing of electoral lines along ethnic and language affiliations.

1994 The Constituent Assembly is elected to implement ratification of a new constitution.

1995 A new constitution is promulgated and the Federal Democratic Republic of Ethiopia announced with Negasso Gidada as head of state and Meles Zenawi as prime minister.

1997 War breaks out between Eritrea and Ethiopia over the Badime Triangle, a disputed territory in southwestern Eritrea.

2000 The EPRDF party wins an overwhelming victory in national elections; under supervision of UN troops, Ethiopia and Eritrea sign a peace agreement in December.
Haile Selassie is buried in the Trinity Cathedral of Addis Ababa.

2002 Ethiopian and Eritrean troops withdraw from the border region.

BIBLIOGRAPHY

African-American Institute. *An Evaluation of the June 21, 1992, Elections in Ethiopia.* Washington, D.C., 1992.

Doornbos, Martine, Cliff Lionel, et al. *Beyond Conflict in the Horn: The Prospects for Peace, Recovery, & Development in Ethiopia, Somalia, Sudan & Eritrea.* Trenton, N.J., 1992.

Fassil Nahum. *Constitution For a Nation of Nations: The Ethiopian Prospect.* Trenton, N.J., 1997.

Erlich, Haggai. *Ras Alula and the Scramble for Africa: A Political Biography: Ethiopia & Eritrea 1875–1897.* Trenton, N.J., 1996.

Phillipson, David W. *Ancient Ethiopia: Akum: Its Antecedents and Successors.* London, 1994.

Ruth Iyob. *The Eritrean Struggle for Independence, Domination, Resistance, Nationalism, 1941–1993.* Cambridge, 1995.

Sorenson, John. *Imagining Ethiopia: Struggles for History and Identity in the Horn of Africa.* New Brunswick, N.J., 1993.

OFFICIAL PUBLICATIONS

Ethiopia. *Ethiopia 1984 Population and Housing Census; Ethiopia Statistical Abstract* (annual).

CONTACT INFORMATION

Embassy of Ethiopia
2134 Kalorama Road NW
Washington, D.C. 20008
Phone: (202) 234-2281 Fax: (202) 328-7950

INTERNET RESOURCES

- Ethiopia on the Web:
  http://www.ethiopians.com/
- Addis Abaha Chamber of Commerce
  http://www.addischamber.com

FIJI

BASIC FACT SHEET

OFFICIAL NAME:
Republic of the Fiji Islands

ABBREVIATION:
FJ

CAPITAL:
Suva

HEAD OF STATE:
President Ratu Josefa Iloilo (from 2000)

HEAD OF GOVERNMENT:
Prime Minister Laisenia Qarase (from 2000)

NATURE OF GOVERNMENT:
Republic

POPULATION:
813,000 (1999)

AREA:
18,272 sq km (7,055 sq mi)

ETHNIC MAJORITY:
Indian and Fijian

LANGUAGES:
English (official), Fijian, Hindustani

RELIGIONS:
Christianity and Hinduism

UNIT OF CURRENCY:
Fijian dollar (F. $)

NATIONAL FLAG:
A blue field with the Union Jack in top left corner and the Fijian coat of arms on the fly. The coat of arms shows a gold, imperial lion carrying a coconut in its forepaw, a flying dove carrying an olive branch, stalks of sugarcane, bananas, and a coconut palm.

NATIONAL EMBLEM:
The Fijian coat of arms flanked on either side by a Fijian warrior and hunter with an outrigger canoe on the top. Beneath is the legend *Rere Vak a na Kalow Ka Doka na Tui* (Fear God and Honor the King).

NATIONAL ANTHEM:
"God Save the Queen:

NATIONAL HOLIDAYS:
October 10 (Independence Day, National Day); January 1 (New Year's Day). Variable holidays include the Queen's Birthday, Prince Charles's Birthday, Christian festivals (Good Friday, Christmas, and Boxing Day), Hindu festivals (Dipavali), and Islamic Festivals (Muhammad's Birthday)

DATE OF INDEPENDENCE:
October 10, 1970

DATE OF CONSTITUTION:
July 25, 1990; amended July 25, 1997

GEOGRAPHICAL FEATURES

Fiji, in the South Pacific, is about 2,735 km (1,700 mi) northeast of Sydney, 1,769 km (1,100 mi) north of Auckland, and 4,466 km (2,776 mi) southwest of Honolulu. The country consists of over 822 islands stretched over a total area of 647,497 sq km (250,000 sq mi). The total land area, including the island of Rotuma, which is geographically separate from the main archipelago, is 18,272 sq km (7,055 sq mi). Only 105 of the islands are inhabited; over 500 are islets, and some are mere rocks a few meters in circumference. The largest islands are Vanua Levu, with 5,535 sq km (2,137 sq mi) and Viti Levu, with 10,386 sq km (4,010 sq mi). The total coastline stretches 1,129 km (700 mi).

Fiji's larger islands are mountainous and of volcanic origin, often rising precipitously from the shore. On the southeastern windward sides the islands are covered with dense tropical forests. The highest elevation is Mt. Victoria (1,323 mi; 4,341 ft); there are 28 other peaks over 900 m (3,000 ft). Most islands are surrounded by coral reefs.

Fiji

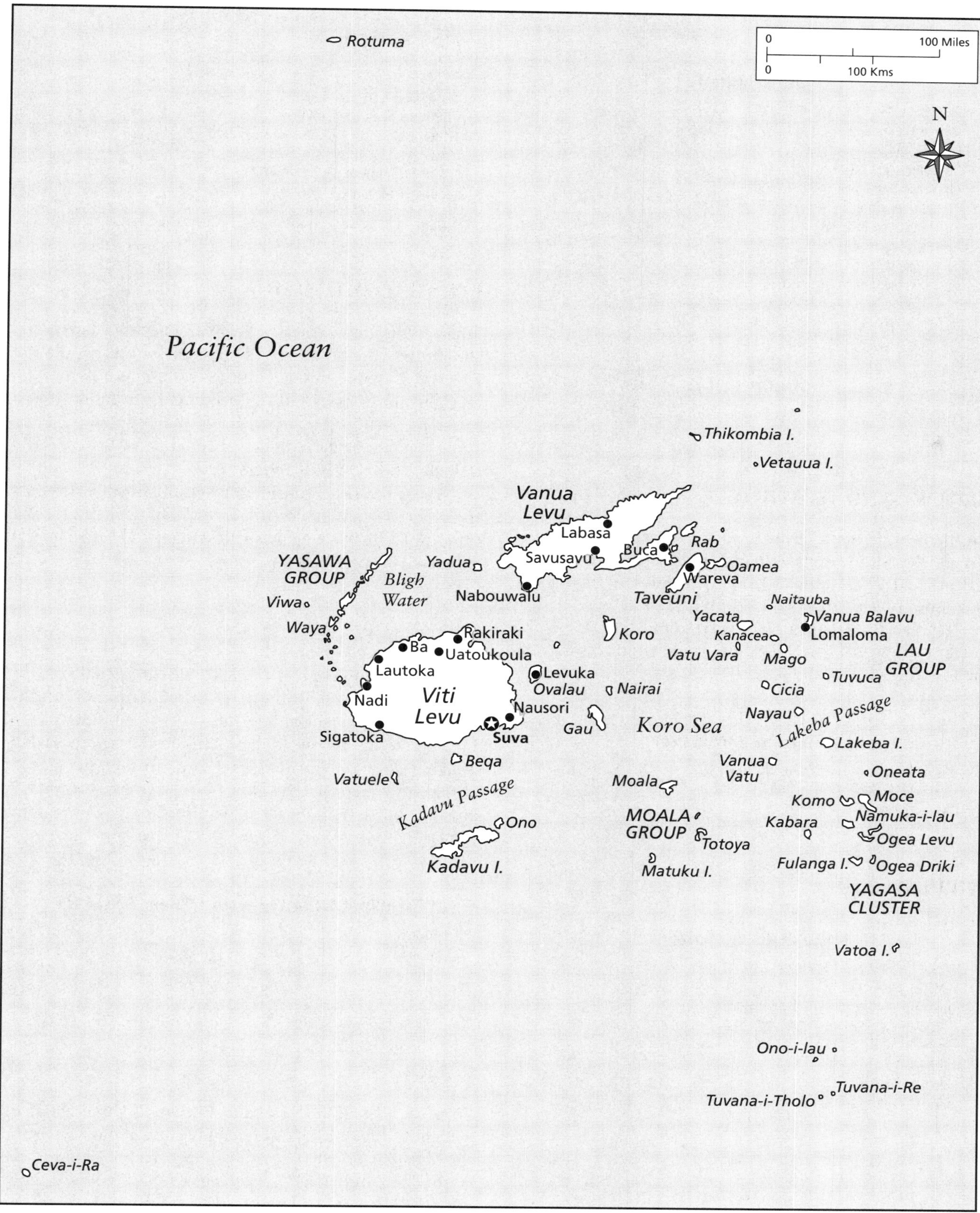

Rotuma
0
100 Miles
0
100 Kms
N
Pacific Ocean
Thikombia I.
Vetauua I.
Vanua
Levu
Labasa
Savusavu
Buca
Rab
Oamea
Wareva
Taveuni
YASAWA
GROUP
Bligh
Water
Yadua
Nabouwalu
Viwa
Waya
Naitauba
Yacata
Vanua Balavu
Lomaloma
Kanacea
Rakiraki
Ba
Uatoukoula
Koro
Vatu Vara
Mago
LAU
GROUP
Lautoka
Levuka
Ovalau
Nairai
Tuvuca
Cicia
Nadi
Viti
Levu
Nausori
Nayau
Sigatoka
Suva
Gau
Koro Sea
Lakeba Passage
Lakeba I.
Beqa
Vanua
Vatu
Oneata
Vatuele
Moala
Komo
Moce
Kadavu Passage
Ono
MOALA
GROUP
Totoya
Kabara
Namuka-i-lau
Ogea Levu
Kadavu I.
Matuku I.
Fulanga I.
Ogea Driki
YAGASA
CLUSTER
Vatoa I.
Ono-i-lau
Tuvana-i-Re
Tuvana-i-Tholo
Ceva-i-Ra

The major river is the Rewa on Viti Levu, which is navigable by small boats for 113 km (70 mi).

Geography

Area sq km: 18,272 sq mi 7,055
World Rank: 155th
Land Boundaries, Km: 0
Coastline, km 1,129
Elevation Extremes meters
Lowest: Pacific Ocean 0
Highest: Tomaniri 1,324
Land Use % Arable land: 10
Permanent Crops: 4
Permanent Pastures: 10
Forest and Woodland: 65
Other: 11

Population of Principal Cities

Suva	167,421

CLIMATE AND WEATHER

On the leeward sides of the islands there are two seasons: wet and dry. Mean annual rainfall ranges between 1,780 mm (70 in) and 2,030 mm (80 in), with Suva receiving the maximum precipitation of 3,120 mm (123 in).

Temperatures at sea level vary from 15.6°C to 32°C to (60°F to 90°F). The prevailing trade winds blow from the east for most of the year.

Climate and Weather

Mean Temperature 60°F to 90°F
Average Rainfall: 70 in to 80 in
Suva: 123 in

POPULATION

Population Indicators

Total Population: 1999 813,000
World Rank: 156th
Density per sq mi: 115.2 per sq km 44.5
% of annual growth (1994–99): 1.3
Male %: 50.8
Female %: 49.2
Urban %: 46.4
Age Distribution: % 0–14: 38.2
15–29: 29.5
30–44: 17.8
45–59: 9.6
60–74: 3.8
75 and over: 0.8
Population 2020: 1,037,000
Birth Rate per 1,000: 22.7
Death Rate per 1,000: 4.6
Population Doubling Time (years): 42
Infant Mortality Rate Per 1,000 live births: 20.0
Rate of Natural Increase per 1,000: 18.7
Total Fertility Rate: 2.8
Expectation of Life (years): Males 70.0
Females 75.0
Marriage Rate per 1,000: 9.6
Divorce Rate per 1,000: —
Total Number of Households: 97,000
Average Size of Households: 6.0
% of Illegitimate Children: 17.3
Induced Abortions: —
Rate per 100 live births: —

ETHNIC COMPOSITION

Fijians, who are ethnically Melanesian with a Polynesian admixture, constitute only 43 percent of the population, whereas Indians, descendants of immigrants who were brought to Fiji as indentured laborers from India, constitute a majority, with 51 percent of the population.

There are small colonies of Americans, Britons, Australians, and New Zealanders.

There has been considerable ethnic hostility between Indians, who suffer economic and political discrimination, and Fijians, who wish to preserve the Melanesian character of the country.

LANGUAGES

The official language is English, which virtually all literate Fijians speak, although both Fijian and Hindustani are used in parliament and in the administration. Fijian belongs to the Malayo-Polynesian group of languages. The spoken dialect is Bau throughout the archipelago except on Rotuma Island, where Rotuman is spoken. Most Indians retain Hindustani as their lingua franca.

Principal Languages and Their Speakers

English	170,000
Fijian	413,000
Hindustani	355,000
Other	45,000

RELIGIONS

Virtually all native Fijians are Christian, while about 80 percent of Fijian Indians are Hindus and about 15 percent are Muslims. Of the Christians, 85 percent belong to the Methodist Church and 12 percent to the Roman Catholic Church. There is a Roman Catholic archbishopric and an Anglican bishopric in Suva. The Methodist Church is organized under a president.

Religious Affiliations	
Christian (mostly Methodist and Roman Catholic)	430,000
Hindu	310,000
Muslim	64,000
Other	9,000

HISTORICAL BACKGROUND

The first settlers of the Fiji islands were Lapita who arrived around 1500 B.C. Twenty-five hundred years later, Polynesians invaded from Tonga and Samoa, engaging the Melanesians in large-scale wars. Intermarriage and time helped merge the two ethnic groups together.

In 1643, the first known European to sight the Fijian islands was Abel Tasman. His description of the dangerous reefs and his account of cannibalism kept Europeans away until 1774. In that year, James Cook stopped at Vatoa. In 1789, Captain William Bligh stopped under the duress of mutineers on the HMS *Bounty*.

The 1800s saw an increase in interaction between Fijian society and Westerners as traders used it as a port seeking sandalwood and bêche-de-mer (succulent sea cucumbers prized in Asia). The traders fueled interclan warfare by swapping goods for guns and metal tools. Stories of cannibalism also grew as most shipwrecked Westerners were eaten. One notable exception was Charles Savage, a Swede, who served as an interpreter and diplomat between warring chiefs.

Early missionary attempts also failed to civilize the Fijians. In 1867, the reverand Thomas Baker was eaten (his shoes are on exhibit at the Fiji Museum). However, Westerners refused to leave the islands alone as they became more important as a Pacific trading post. One such post, Levuka, was razed in 1847 in order to restore peace.

Interaction with Westerners was growing and slowly the Fijis were becoming more Western and open. Cakobau, the self-proclaimed King of Fiji, attempted to form a Western-style government in 1871, but it collapsed after just two years. After that, Fiji was under British rule from 1874, when a convention of chiefs ceded Fiji unconditionally to the United Kingdom, to 1970, when it became a fully independent dominion within the Commonwealth. British rule was marked by the pacification of the countryside, the spread of plantation agriculture, and the introduction of Indian indentured labor. At the same time many traditional institutions, such as communal ownership of land, were maintained intact.

The British introduced a new constitution in 1966 that gave Fiji a ministerial form of government with a predominantly elected Legislative Council. The electoral system was based on a complex combination of communal rolls and cross-voting, reflecting traditional ethnic tensions between Fijians and Indians. In 1967 Ratu Kamisese Mara, head of the Alliance Party, became the chief minister. Fiji achieved independence within the Commonwealth in 1970. At independence, Mara became prime minister.

Fiji's political history has been dominated by ethnic tension between the Fijians, who were a minority but maintained political power, and Indians, who were discriminated against in politics and in land tenure. In 1977 Mara's Alliance Party lost the legislative election to the National Federation Party (NFP), traditionally supported by the Indians. The NFP was unable to form a government, and the AP was returned to power that same year with the largest majority it had ever achieved. In light of the continuing ethnic tensions and the development of the Fijian Nationalist Party that ran on a "Fiji for the Fijians" program, Mara suggested forming a government of national unity in 1980. The suggestion received little attention as disagreements continued between the AP and NFP over Indian demands for reformed land tenure. In 1982, in an election dominated by race, the AP retained power but saw its majority dramatically reduced.

A coalition of the NFP and the Fiji Labor Party (FLP), which had been formed in 1985 with the idea of promoting more effective parliamentary opposition and establishing more extensive government social services, won the general election of April 1987. The new government, led by Timoci Bavadra, was the first in Fijian history to have a majority of Indian ministers. This government was overthrown in May by a military coup under the leadership of Sitiveni Rabuka, who wished to preserve Fijian political domination. In an effort to end the political crisis, Bavadra and Mara agreed to form a bipartisan government, but before it could be established, Rabuka staged another coup. He assumed the position of head of state, announced the establishment of a republic, and appointed a temporary Council of Ministers whose members were primarily Fijian. Rabuka resigned at the end of the year and was replaced by Ratu Sir Penaia Ganilau, the former governor-general. Mara was reappointed prime minister, and Rabuka became home minister.

Fiji returned to civilian rule after 1990 when General Rabuka stepped down as home affairs minister and later resigned his commission and became head of the recently organized Fijian Political Party (SVT). In 1992 the SVT won an overwhelming majority in parliament and Rabuka formed a government of national unity with the support of the Indians. In 1997, a new constitution was passed replacing the 1988 ethnically discriminatory constitution. It provided for the continued Melanesian domination of the Senate, but opened the door to possible Indian control of the House. Following the adoption of the new constitution, Fiji was readmitted to the Commonwealth. In new elections in 2000, Indians managed to obtain legislative majority and the leader of the Indian-dominated Fijian Labour Party, Mahendra Lal Chaudhry, was elected prime minister. However, during a legislative meeting, Fijian nationalists stormed the building and held the prime minister and a number of his colleagues hostage. All hostages were released in July, and the Great Council of Chiefs appointed Fijian Ratu Josefa Iloilo president. The leader of the insurrection, George Speight, was arrested and charged with treason. In 2001, the Fiji High Court ruled the current government illegal, and new elections were held in August that brought the Fijian United Party to power. Its leader, Laisenia Qarase, was named prime minister.

CONSTITUTION

In 1998 a new constitution was promulgated by the president after the Great Council of Chiefs had approved the draft. Under its terms, executive authority is vested in a president who is appointed by the Great Council of Chiefs, who hold their position based upon lineage. The president serves for five years and selects a prime minister to lead the cabinet. The prime minister, who must be a Fijian by ethnicity, selects the remaining members of the cabinet.

The legislature is a bicameral system in which the upper house consists of 32 members who are appointed by the president upon recommendations made by the Council of Chiefs, the cabinet, and the opposition. The House of Representatives consists of 71 members elected by all citizens over the age of 21. The seats are allocated along racial lines with 23 for ethnic Fijians, 19 for Indians, 3 for other races, and the remaining 25 open to all. The legislative session may last as long as five years.

The judiciary consists of the High Court and the Supreme Court, which are the final arbiters of the constitution.

LOCAL GOVERNMENT

For purposes of local administration, Fiji is divided into four administrative divisions, each headed by a division commissioner, assisted by district officers. In addition, eight main urban areas are governed by local authorities. Suva has a city council, Lautoka a town council, and six other main urban areas are administered by township boards. Some members of urban councils are appointed, but the majority of members are elected.

The Fijian community is under a separate administration, known as the Fijian Administration, headed by the Fijian Affairs Board. The Fijian Administration comprises 14 *yasanas* (communal provinces), each with its own partially appointed and partially elected council. Each council has an elected majority and has powers to make bylaws and draw up its own budget. Members are elected for two-year terms, and the council elects a chairperson from among its own members. At the apex of the Fijian Administration is the Great Council of Chiefs, presided over by the minister of Fijian affairs and rural development. The Great Council of Chiefs consists of 22 Fijian members of the House of Representatives, 30 representatives elected by the provincial councils, and 15 representatives nominated by the government.

Local Government

Principal administrative divisions, capitals, area, population

AREA AND POPULATION

Divisions Provinces	Capitals	area sq mi	area sq km	population 1996 estimate
Central	Suva			
Naitasiri	—	643	1,666	126,641
Namosi	—	220	570	5,742

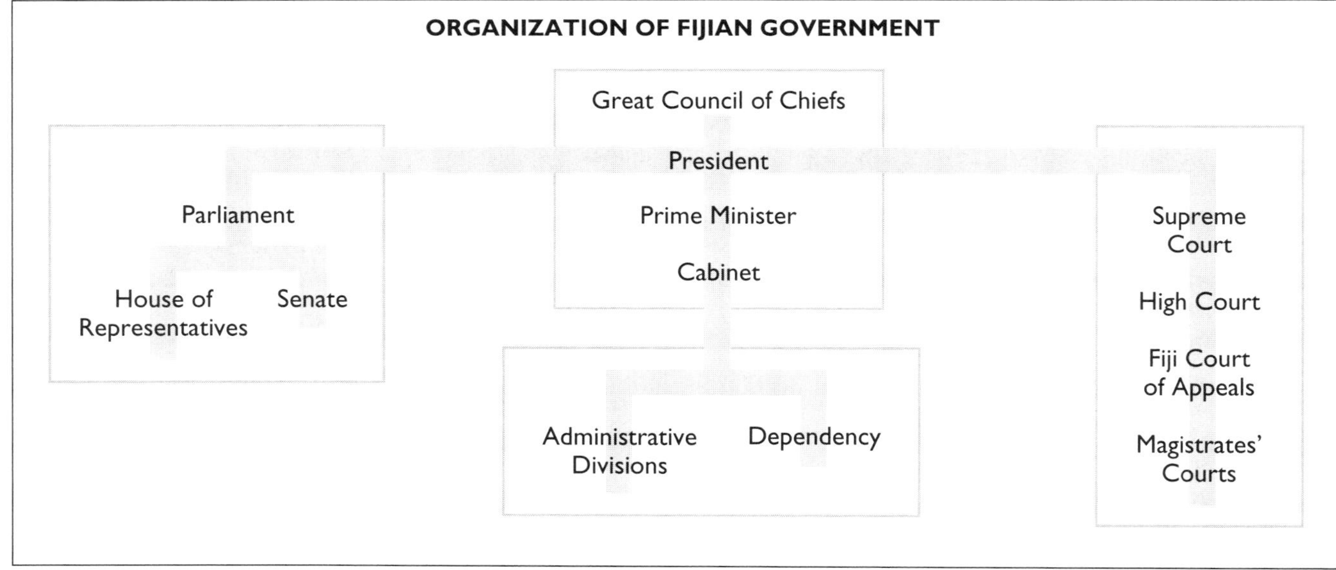

Rewa	—	105	272	101,547
Serua	—	320	830	15,461
Tailevu	—	369	955	48,216
Eastern	Levuka			
Kadavu	—	185	478	9,535
Lau	—	188	487	12,211
Lomaiviti	—	159	411	16,214
Rotuma	—	18	46	2,810
Northern	Labasa			
Bua	—	532	1,379	14,988
Cakaudrove	—	1,087	2,816	44,321
Macuata	—	774	2,004	80,207
Western	Lautoka			
Ba	—	1,017	2,634	212,197
Nadroga-Navosa	—	921	2,385	54,083
Ra	—	518	1,341	30,904
TOTAL	—	7,055	18,272	775,077

PARLIAMENT

The parliament consists of two houses. The Senate (upper house) has 32 members who are appointed by the president based upon recommendations of the Great Council of Chiefs (14 seats), the prime minister (9 seats), and the opposition (8 seats). The House of Representatives (lower house) consists of 71 members. The majority of the seats are reserved for specific ethnic groups with 23 for Fijians, 19 for Indians, 3 for others, and the remaining 25 open to any race. The session may last no longer than five years.

POLITICAL PARTIES

There are more than 15 active political parties in the Fijis. However, the largest and strongest of them are: Soqosoqo ni Vakavulewa ni Taukei (SVT), which defends the right of native Fijians to control politics in the country, and National Federation Party, formed in 1960 with the merger of several smaller organizations, which advocates a multiracial politics, though it is largely Indian. In addition to these two large parties, the Fijian Association Party is a multiracial faction of the SVT and the Fiji Labour Party is a strong Indian party.

Political Parties

Fijian Political Party, 1991
United General Party, 1998
Fiji Labour Party, 1985
Fijian Association Party, 1995
Party of National Unity, 1998
National Federation Party, 1963
Christian Democratic Alliance
Christian Fellowship Party, 1998
Nationalist Vanua Takolavo Party, 1974
Fiji Indian Congress Party, 1991
Western United Front, 1981
Fijian Conservative Party, 1989
Taukei Solidarity Movement, 1987
Fiji Indian Liberal Party, 1991
Fiji Muslim League

Political Parties: Strength in Parliament Most Recent Elections

House of Representatives (Vale). The chamber has 71 members elected for five-year terms in single-seat constituencies. There are 23 seats reserved for Fijians, 19 for Indians, 3 for general voters, 1 for Rotuman Islanders, and 25 open to all races. In the voting of August 25, September 2, and September 19, 2001, the Fiji Labour Party won 27 seats; United Fiji Party, 32; National Federation Party, 1; Conservative Alliance Party, 6; New Labour Unity Party, 2; United General Party, 1; and nonpartisans, 2.

LEGAL SYSTEM

The judiciary is completely independent of the legislative and executive branches of government. The judicial power of the state is vested in the High Court, the Court of Appeal, and the Supreme Court and in such other courts as are created by law. The final appellate court of the state is the Supreme Court. The High Court consists of the chief justice and a number of puisne judges not less than 10. It has unlimited original jurisdiction to hear and determine any civil or criminal proceedings under any law and such other original jurisdiction as is conferred on it under the constitution.

The Court of Appeal consists of a judge, other than the chief justice, also appointed as president of the Court of Appeal, such other judges as are appointed as justices of appeal, and the puisne judges of the High Court. This court has jurisdiction to hear and determine appeals from all judgments of the High Court, and has such other jurisdiction as is conferred by law.

LAW ENFORCEMENT

Law Enforcement

Offenses reported to the police per 100,000: 2,518
- Murder: 11.5
- Assault: 51.3
- Burglary: 463.7
- Automobile Theft: 51.7
- Population per Police Officer: 407

Death Penalty: Yes, for exceptional crimes. Last execution in 1965.

HUMAN RIGHTS

Fiji has successfully maintained the legal, political, and human rights traditions of its former British rulers. In constitutional practice, there are safeguards that ensure freedom from torture; respect for the integrity of the person and the home; right to a fair and open public trial; freedom from arbitrary arrest and imprisonment; and equal treatment before the law irrespective of race, creed, or sex.

FOREIGN POLICY

Fiji's military coups have had an adverse effect on its foreign relations. It was expelled from the Commonwealth in 1987 but readmitted after a few months. In 1999 the appointment of the first Indian prime minister led to a siege of the parliament by Fijian extremists. This led to further ostracism of Fiji by the international community.

DEFENSE

Until 1970 the defense of Fiji was the responsibility of the United Kingdom, and even today there is only a small regular force supplemented by a territorial force and a reserve. In 1989, the total strength of the armed forces was 3,700 men, 3,200 in the army and 500 in the navy. There is a reserve of 5,000. The armed forces are overwhelmingly Fijian in membership, as is the national police force. The command structure of these forces is not clearly established.

Military Indicators

Total Active Duty Personnel: 3,600
Military Manpower per 1,000: 4.6
Military Expenditures $million: 32
as % of GNP: 1.7
per capita $: 42
as % of central government expenditures: 6

Arms Imports $million: 20
Arms Exports $million: —

ECONOMY

Fiji, endowed with forest, mineral, and fish resources, is one of the most developed of the Pacific island economies, though still with a large subsistence sector. Sugar exports and a growing tourist industry are the major sources of foreign exchange. Sugar processing makes up one-third of industrial activity. Roughly 300,000 tourists visit each year, including thousands of Americans following the start of regularly scheduled nonstop air service from Los Angeles. Fiji's growth slowed in 1997 because the sugar industry suffered from low world prices and rent disputes between farmers and landowners. Drought in 1998 further damaged the industry, but its recovery in 1999 contributed to robust GDP growth. Long-term problems include low investment and uncertain property rights. The political turmoil in Fiji has had a severe impact, with the economy shrinking by 8 percent in 1999 and more than 7,000 people losing their jobs. The interim government's 2001 budget is an attempt to attract foreign investment and restart economic activity. The government's ability to manage the budget and fulfill predictions of 4 percent growth for 2001 will depend on a return to stability, a regaining of investor confidence, and the absence of international sanctions (which could cripple Fiji's sugar and textile industry).

Principal Economic Indicators

Gross National Product: $2.007 billion
GNP per capita: $2,460
GNP Average Annual Growth Rate (1990–97) %: 0.4
GNP per capita Average Annual Growth Rate (1990–97)%: –1.1
Origin of Gross Domestic Product %
Agriculture: 22
Mining: —
Manufacturing: 12
Construction: 3
Public Utilities: 1
Transportation and Communications: 15
Trade: 21
Financial Services: 12
Other Services: 16
Government: 16
Gross Domestic Product by Type of Expenditure %
Private Consumption: 67
Government Consumption: 20
Gross Domestic Investment: 15
Foreign Trade: Exports: 56
Imports: –59
% of Income Received by Poorest 20%:
% of Income Received by Richest 10%:

Price and earnings indexes (1995 = 100)

	1992	1993	1994	1995	1996	1997	1998
Consumer price index	92.5	97.3	97.9	100.0	103.1	106.5	112.6
Earnings index	—	—	—	—	—	—	—

Finance

National Currency: Fijian Dollar (F$)
Exchange Rate: $1 = F$ 1.9064
Money Supply Stock in National Currency billion: 0.456
M1 per capita: 590
Central Bank Discount Rate %: 2.50
Total External Debt $million: 338
Debt Service Ratio%: 1.8

Balance of Payments $million: 4.2
International Reserves SDRs $million: 257
Ratio of External Debt to Total Reserves: 0.5
Average Annual Rate of Inflation/Consumer Price Index Growth Rate %: 3

Official Development Assistance

ODA $million: 45
as % of GNP: 2.4
per capita: $58
Foreign Direct Investment $million: —

Central Government Revenues and Expenditures

Fiscal Year: Calendar Year
Revenues $million: 540.65
Expenditures $million: 742.65
Budget Deficit $million: 202

Tax Revenues as % of GDP: 21
Highest Tax Bracket %
Individual: —
Corporate: —

Employment and Labor

Economically Active Population: 241,000
Female Participation Rate %: 21.2
Activity Rate %: 33.7
Labor by Sector: %
Agriculture, Forestry, Fishing: 44.1
Manufacturing, Mining: 9.0
Construction: 4.9
Transportation and Communications: 5.5
Trade, Hotels, and Restaurants: 10.8
Finance, Insurance, Real Estate: 2.5
Public Administration, Defense: —
Services: 15.2
Unemployment %: 6

Agriculture

Agriculture's Share of GDP %: 22
Average Annual Rate of Growth (1965–98) %:
Number of Farms 000: 95
Average Size of Farm ha: 4.2
Number of Tractors per 1,000 hectares: 88.7
Irrigation, % of Farms having: 3
Artificial Fertilizer kg/hectare: 210
Total Farmland as % of land area: 42.6
Livestock: Cattle 000: 360
Sheep 000: 7
Hogs 000: 145
Chickens 000: 4,300
Forests: Production of Roundwood (000 cubic meters): 598
Fisheries: Total Catch tons 000: 32.0

Mining

% of GDP: 0.2
Value of Mineral Production $million: 1.7

Manufacturing

Value Added $million: 156
Industrial Production Growth Rate %: 2.9

Energy

Commercial Energy Production metric tons of oil equivalent 000: —
Commercial Energy Consumption metric tons of oil equivalent 000: 404
Commercial Energy Consumption per capita kg: 527
Average Annual Growth Rate 1980–97 %: —
Net Energy Imports % of use: 76
Electricity Installed Capacity kW 000: 200
Production kW-hr million: 544
Coal Reserves tons million : —
Production tons: —
Natural Gas Proven Reserves cubic meters billion: —
Production cubic meters million: —
Crude Petroleum Reserves barrels million: —
Production barrels million: —
Consumption barrels million: —
Refinery Capacity barrels per day: —
Pipelines Length km: —

Foreign Trade

Imports $million: 830.5
Exports $million: 544.5
Export Volume % Annual Growth Rate (1990–97): —
Import Volume % Annual Growth Rate (1990–97): —

Balance of trade (current prices)

F$	1992	1993	1994	1995	1996	1997
000,000	−275.23	−521.42	−409.36	−454.45	−225.26	−334.16
% of total	20.9%	30.7%	20.4%	22.9%	10.9%	16.8%

Major Trading Partners

	Imports	Exports
European Union %	3.9	20.3
United States %	14.8	17.9
Eastern Europe %	0.1	—
Japan %	8.0	6.8
Others %	79.3	55.0

Transportation

Roads Total Length mi: 3,200 km 5,100
Paved %: 20
Automobiles: 49,712
Trucks and Buses: 33,928
Persons per vehicle: 9.4
Railroad; Track Length mi: 370 km 595
Passenger-mi million: —
Freight-mi million: —
Merchant Marine: No. of Vessels: 64
Total Deadweight Tonnage 000: 60.4
International Cargo Loaded tons 000: 568
International Cargo Off-loaded tons 000: 625
Airports with Scheduled Flights: 13
Traffic: Passenger-mi million: 742
Freight-mi million: 51.6
Length of Canals mi: 126 km 203

Tourism

Number of Tourists to: —
Number of Tourists from : —
Tourist Receipts $million: 312
Tourist Expenditures $million: 55

Communications

Telephones 000: 65
Cost of Local Calls 3 mins: $0
Cellular Telephones 000: 2.2
Fax Machines 000: 3.0
Personal Computers: —
Internet Hosts per million persons: 66

(continued)

Mail: Post Offices: 261
Pieces of Mail Handled million: 24
Pieces of Mail Handled per person: 31

EDUCATION

Education is free for the first eight years but not compulsory. State subsidies are available in secondary and tertiary education in cases of hardship.

Schooling consists of 12 years, divided into six years of primary school and six years of secondary school. The curriculum is of British origin, and courses culminate in British school certificates. The academic year runs from January to December. The medium of instruction is English, but Fijian is taught in all schools.

Of the over 700 schools, only a very small portion are controlled by the government; the rest are run by Christian missions or other private organizations.

Higher education is provided by Fiji's only university, the University of the South Pacific at Suva.

Education

Literacy Rate %: 91.6
Male %: 93.8
Female %: 89.3
First Level: Primary Schools: 693
Teachers: 4,644
Students: 145,630
Student-Teacher Ratio: 31.4
Net Enrollment Ratio: 99
Second Level: Secondary Schools: 142
Teachers: 3,045
Students: 60,237
Student-Teacher-Ratio: 19.8
Net Enrollment Ratio: —

Vocational Level: Schools: 45
Students: 7,283

Third Level: Institutions: —
Teachers: 277
Students: 7,908
Student-Ratio Level: 28.5
Gross Enrollment Ratio: 11.9
Students per 100,000: 757
% of Population Age 25 and over with Postsecondary Education: 4.5

Public Expenditure on Education as % GDP: 5.4

SCIENCE AND TECHNOLOGY

Science and Technology

Scientists and Engineers in R&D per 1 million persons: —
Expenditures in R&D as % of GDP: —
High-Tech Exports $million: —
Patent Applications by Residents: —

MEDIA

Two dailies are published in English at Suva. In addition, five nondailies and periodicals are published in English, three in Fijian, and three in Hindi. All but one are published in Suva.

There is no national news agency, but the government public relations office supplies news to the media.

Fiji has a modest book publishing industry, with at least four active full-time publishers. Fiji adheres to the Berne and Universal Copyright conventions.

The official broadcasting organization, the Fiji Broadcasting Commission (FBC), operates 10 medium-wave transmitters and FM transmitters at Suva and Lautoka. The domestic service is on the air for 110 hours in English, 54-1/2 hours in Hindi, and 38 hours in Fijian. The content of all broadcasts is subject to government control.

Most of the films shown in the country are of U.S. or Indian origin.

The largest libraries are the Suva Public Library, the University of the South Pacific Library, and the Western Regional Library at Lautoka.

There is one museum with annual attendance of over 40,000.

Media

Daily Newspapers: 1
Total Circulation 000: 35
Circulation per 1,000: 45
Books Published: 401
Magazines:
Radio Receivers 000: 450
per 1,000: 574
Television sets 000: 70
per 1,000: 89

MOST IMPORTANT MEDIA:

Press. The first three of the following papers (plus the influential *Pacific Islands Monthly*) are owned by the international media tycoon Rupert Murdoch; all are published at Suva; *The Fiji Times* (27,000), founded in 1869, in English; *Nai Lalakai*, (18,000), Fijian weekly; *Shanti Dut* (8,000), Hindi weekly; *Fiji Republic Gazette,* government weekly in English. The *Times* and the *Fiji Sun* were suspended in the wake of the May 1987 coup, which both had criticized; subsequently the *Sun* formally ceased publication. In 1989 the *Fiji Post*, a government-controlled English-language paper launched in 1987, began publishing as a daily (estimated print run December 1994: 10,000).

Radio and television. The Fiji Broadcasting Commission operates one FM and three AM radio stations broadcasting in English, Fijian, and Hindustani. Communications Fiji Ltd. currently broadcasts in English and Hindi from two FM outlets.

CULTURE

Cultural Indicators

Public Libraries Number: —
Volumes: —
Registered borrowers: —

Museums Number: —
Annual Attendance: —
Cinema Production of Long Films:
Number of Cinemas: —
Seating Capacity: —
Annual Attendance: —
Annual Attendance per capita: —

STATUS OF WOMEN

Few women hold high-level economic or political positions. There is a growing awareness among women of both the Fijian and Indian communities of their right to participate more actively in social and political endeavors outside their homes. Women in the rural areas continue to fill the traditional roles of village life. Tribal inheritance usually is based on a patriarchal system. Women can and do, however, inherit status as chiefs; Fiji's third-highest-ranking chief is a woman.

Official policy favors reduction of population growth and supports family planning. Fiji is among the countries participating in the World Fertility Survey. The private Family Planning Association, founded in 1962, plays an active role in distribution of contraceptives and monitoring of birth control programs. In 1982 a total of 33.4 percent of married women of childbearing age were believed to use family-planning services.

Women

Gender Empowerment Measure: 78
Seats Held in Parliament by Women %: 5.8
Female Administrators and Managers %: 9.6
Female Professional and Technical Workers %: 44.7
Women's Share of Earned Income %: 22
Women in Government %: 10

HEALTH, FOOD, AND NUTRITION

Health

Number of Physicians: 426
Number of Dentists: 40
Number of Nurses: 1,631
Number of Pharmacists: —
Population per Physician: 1,829
Number of Hospitals: 25
Hospital Beds per 10,000: 22
Hospital Bed Occupancy Rate: —
Infant Mortality Rate per 1,000 live births: 23
Maternal Mortality Rate per 100,000 live births: —
Total Health Expenditures as % of GDP: 3.76
Health Expenditures per capita $: 70
HIV Infected % of adults: —
Cigarette Consumption per smoker per year: —
% of Smokers: Male: —
Female: —
Access to Safe Water %: 77

Food and Nutrition

Food Supply as % of FAO Requirements: 135
% of Consumption Expenditures on Food: 34.7
Daily Available Calories per capita: 3,078
% of Total Calories derived from:
Cereals: 38.1
Potatoes, cassava: 5.6
Meat, poultry: 8.8
Fish: 2.0
Eggs, milk: 3.9
Fruits, Vegetables: 1.7
Fats, oils: 17.2

ENVIRONMENT

As an idyllic Pacific island, with few manufacturing industries, it might be expected that Fiji is free from many of the environmental problems to which mainland nations are subject. The two main islands have a rich ecosystem. But Fiji's natural beauty and marine attractions are in themselves the cause of some of its pollution. Coral sand extraction, oil and gas exploration, sewage and waste disposal, and overfishing pose a serious threat to the marine environment. Toxic waste, sewage, and air pollution persist in urban areas, while widespread use of pesticides, fertilizer runoff, and slumping and salination of groundwater contribute to pollution in rural areas. Inadequate farming practices on sloped land and poorly managed logging operations cause soil erosion. Soil transported into coastal ecosystems smothers coral reefs, chokes mangroves, and reduces the local fish population. Since 1969 there has been a more than 40 percent reduction in Fiji's forest resources, primarily as a result of logging. The loss of forest cover is particularly threatening to the highly diverse native flora as well as to the few species of wildlife. In many places the landscape is barren.

Environment

Forest Area sq km: 8,350
Average Annual Deforestation sq km: —
Nationally Protected Areas as % of Total Land Area: —
Freshwater Access cubic meters per capita: 34,732
Emissions of Organic Water Pollutants kg per day: —
CO_2 Emissions per capita ton: 1.0

CHRONOLOGY

1943 Fiji is occupied by Allied forces waging the Solomon Islands campaign; Fijian Indians, offered far less money than their ethnically European and Fijian counterparts, decline to work for the war effort.

1962 The Fijian Legislative council is reconstituted. The franchise is extended to women.

1966 Fiji is granted internal self-government.

1970 Fiji becomes a sovereign and independent state within the Commonwealth with Ratu Sir Kamisese K. T. Mara as prime minister.

1972 In elections to the House of Representatives, Sir Kamisese's Alliance Party wins 33 of 52 seats.

1973 Ratu Sir George Cakobau is named governor-general, succeeding Sir Robert Foster.

1974 The Fijian dollar's link with sterling is severed.

1977 In elections to the House of Representatives, the Alliance Party improves its majority by capturing 35 seats.

1978 The Emperor Gold Mining Company, the nation's fourth largest employer, lays off 1,000 employees.

1982 In elections to the House of Representatives, the ruling Alliance Party loses eight seats, but maintains a majority.

1983 Governor-General George Cakobau dies and is succeeded by Penaia Ganilau.

1985 The Fiji Labour Party is founded by leaders of the Fiji Trades Union Congress.

1987 In the April elections, the ruling Alliance Party is defeated by a coalition of the National Federation Party (NFP) and the Fiji Labour Party (FLP). Ct. Col. Sitiveni Rabuka leads a military coup that overthrows the government. On September 22, Timoci Bavadra of the FLP and Ratu Sir Kamisese Mara of the AP agree to form an interim bipartisan government. Three days later, Rabuka stages a successful second coup. Rabuka revokes the constitution and declares Fiji a republic.

1988 A new draft constitution ensuring key government positions for ethnic Fijians is proposed by the interim government.

1990 Rabuka resigns from the cabinet; Mara agrees to remain as prime minister of the interim government; the new constitution is promulgated by decree of the president; the NFP and FLP claim they will boycott any elections held under the new charter.

1994 Mara is once again reelected prime minister of a coalition government that guarantees a majority of the seats for ethnic Fijians.

1997 Fiji rejoins the Commonwealth.

1998 A new constitution is established creating an ethnic balance between native Fijians, Indians, and other groups.

1999 In the May elections, the FLP defeats Rabuka's Fijian Political Party and Mahendra Chaudhry, an ethnic Indian, becomes prime minister.

2000 In May, George Speight leads Fijian ethnic nationalists, who take hostage Prime Minister Mahendra Chaudhry (an ethnic Indian) and 26 others in an attempt to roll back Fiji's efforts at creating a multiethnic society; in July, the military storms the rebel stronghold and releases the hostages, and the Great Council of Chiefs appoints Ratu Josefa Iloilo president. Speight and 369 of his supporters are arrested and charged with treason.

2001 The Fiji High Court rules that the current military-backed government is illegal. Parliamentary elections in August bring the Fijian United Party to power. Its leader, Laisenia Qarase, is named prime minister.

BIBLIOGRAPHY

Bain, Kenneth. *Treason at 10: Fiji at the Crossroads*. London, 1989.

Brown, Stanley. *Men from Under the Sky: The Arrival of Westerners in Fiji*. Rutland, Vt., 1973.

France, Peter. *Charter of the Land: Custom and Colonization in Fiji*. New York, 1969.

Kelly, John Dunham, and Martha Kaplan. *Represented Communities: Fiji and World Decolonization*. Chicago, 2001.

Macnaught, Timothy. *The Fijian Colonial Experience*. Canberra, 1984.

Norton, Robert. *Race and Politics in Fiji*. New York, 1978.

Nayacakalou, R. R. *Leadership in Fiji*. New York, 1976.

Sutherland, W. *Beyond the Politics of Race*. Sydney, 1992.

OFFICIAL PUBLICATIONS

Fiji. *Annual Employment Survey; Census of Industries* (annual); *Current Economic Statistics* (quarterly); *1986 Census of the Population*.

CONTACT INFORMATION

Embassy of Fiji
2233 Wisconsin Avenue NW, Suite 240
Washington, D.C. 20007
Phone: (202)337-8320 Fax: (202)337-1996

INTERNET RESOURCES

- Fiji Government Online
  http://ww.fiji.gov.fj/core/home/html

FINLAND

BASIC FACT SHEET

OFFICIAL NAME:
Republic of Finland (Suomen Tasavalta)

ABBREVIATION:
FI

CAPITAL:
Helsinki

HEAD OF STATE:
President Tarja Halonen (from 2000)

HEAD OF GOVERNMENT:
Prime Minister Paavo Lipponen (from 1995)

NATURE OF GOVERNMENT:
Parliamentary democracy

POPULATION:
5,167,000 (1999)

AREA:
337,030 sq km (130,119 sq mi)

ETHNIC COMPOSITION:
Finns

LANGUAGES:
Finnish and Swedish

RELIGION:
Evangelical Lutheran

UNIT OF CURRENCY:
Euro

NATIONAL FLAG:
An ultramarine cross with an extended right horizontal on a white background. The Aland Islands have, in addition, a provincial flag.

NATIONAL EMBLEM:
A crowned gold lion on a red shield. The rampant lion brandishes a silver sword in its mailed right forepaw and tramples on a Russian scimitar. Nine silver roses are placed around the central figure, one for each of the ancient provinces from which Finland was formed.

NATIONAL ANTHEM:
"Maammelaulu" (in Swedish, "Vartland"; Our motherland)

NATIONAL HOLIDAYS:
Independence Day (December 6); New Year's Day; Labor Day; all major Christian festivals

DATE OF INDEPENDENCE:
December 6, 1917

DATE OF CONSTITUTION:
March 1, 2000

GEOGRAPHICAL FEATURES

Finland is a far northen country on the European continent with one-third of its territory above the Arctic Circle. Its coastline on the Gulf of Finland, the Baltic Sea, and the Gulf of Bothnia is deeply indented and studded with islands. The capital is Helsinki, on a peninsula on the Gulf of Finland west of the estuary of the Vantaanjoki. It was founded in 1550 by Gustavus Vasa about four miles north of its present site, to which it was transferred when the old site was destroyed by fire in 1640. It became the capital in 1812. There are at least 15 other cities with a population of over 40,000.

The Finnish landscape is characterized by a rather asymmetric distribution of hills and plains with higher elevations to the north. More than half of eastern Finland is hilly with the land gently sloping toward the southwest. Paralleling the coast of the Gulf of Bothnia is a belt of plains. The separation between these plains and the hills is rather sharp in the north compared to the southwest. The surface of the land has been scoured and gouged in recent geological times by glaciers that have left thin

Finland

0
100 Miles
0
100 Kms
N
NORWAY
SWEDEN
RUSSIA
L. Inari
Ivalo
Lokan Reservoir
Torne R.
Sodankyla
Ounas R.
Rovaniemi
Tornio
Kemi
Pudasjarvi
Oulu
Hailuoto
Oulu R.
Raahe
Paltamo
Kajaani
L. Oulu
Kuhmo
Pyha R.
Kokkola
Gulf of Bothnia
Vallgrund
Vaasa
Lapuan R.
L. Pielinen
Lieksa
Kuopio
Joensuu
Varkaus
Jyväskylä
Lake Näsi
Mikkeli
Pori
Nokia
Tampere
Imatra
Rauma
Hämeenlinna
Lahti
Lake Saimaa
Lake Ladoga
Kouvola
ALAND ISLANDS
Turku
Kotka
Vantaa
Maarianhamina
Kimito
Espoo
Helsinki
Gulf of Finland

deposits of gravel, sand, and clay. The resulting formations can be seen most clearly in the shape of complex features such as the Salpausselka ridges and of numerous eskers running north to west and south to east. Another reminder of the Ice Age is the fact that Finland is still emerging from the sea so that its area grows by 7 sq km (2.7 sq mi) annually and the land rises 1 ft to 3 ft every 100 years.

The entire Finnish coast is paralleled by an island zone that reaches its greatest breadth and complexity in the southwest. Finland's offshore islands are numbered by the tens of thousands—the Åland Archipelago alone has nearly 7,000. The Åland and Turku archipelagoes are rich in flora and fauna and abound in fish.

Finland's coastal zone is known appropriately as the golden horseshoe. It is dominated by the two cities of Helsinki and Turku (Abo), the former capital of the country, situated on the mouth of the Aurajoki. The developed coastal zone extends northward from Turku through the so-called Vakka Suomi and on to the Kokemaki River, which drains the lakes of Häme to the port of Pori. Eastward the coastal plain extends to the Russian border. Ostrobothnia (Pohjanmaa to the Finns) also has its coastal zone. It is a land of little relief but of many rivers. Its southern coastal plains, the broadest in Finland, are traversed by a series of parallel flowing rivers, such as Oulujoki, Finland's most impressive river, Ijoki, Simojoki, Kemijoki, and Tornionjoki.

Lakes cover a greater part of southern Finland. In relation to its size Finland has more lakes than any other country. There are 55,000 small lakes and 19 large lakes, including the artificial reservoirs of Lokka and Portipahtta. The largest, Lake Saimaa, is the fifth largest lake in Europe. The lakes are dominated by long, sinuous esker ridges clad in lofy pines and flanked by sandy beaches. Such ridges as Punkaharju, Pyynikki, and Pulkkila are nationally renowned.

The eastern part of Finland is Karelia, part of which was ceded to the Soviet Union by the Armistice of 1944 and the Peace Treaty of 1947. It is dominated by the Saimaa Canal.

Nearly half of Finland's land area is the North Country, or *Nordkalotten* (*Pohjoiskalotti* in Finnish), the land of the Lapps. The timber line passes through it. Below and above the tree line, North Country has extensive swamps, and about a third of the area is covered with bogland. The North Country is intersected by some of the country's longest rivers, such as the Kemi, Muonio, and Tornio. Many of these rivers empty into the freshwater Bothnian Gulf, but some, such as the Paatsjoki and Tenojoki, drain into the Arctic and others have carved dramatic gorges through to Russian Karelia.

Geography

Area sq km: 337,030 sq mi 130,119
World Rank: 64th
Land Boundaries, km: Norway 729; Russia 1,313; Sweden 586
Coastline, km: 1,126
Elevation Extremes meters
  Lowest: Baltic Sea 0
  Highest: Haltia tunturi 1,328
Land Use % Arable land: 8
  Permanent Crops: —
  Permanent Pastures: 0
  Forest and Woodland: 76
  Other: 16

Population of Principal Cities (1997 est.; MU)

Espoo	196,260
Helesinki	532,053
Oulu	111,556
Tampere	166,026
Turku	168,778

CLIMATE AND WEATHER

The Finnish climate is considerably warmer than the country's location close to the Arctic Circle might seem to warrant. Temperatures are ameliorated by the Baltic Sea and the west winds that bring air currents from the Atlantic warmed by the Gulf Stream. In contrast, winds from the Eurasian continent bring cold spells in winter and heat waves in summer. Winter is the longest season. Its short dark days are made up for by the long, light nights of summer. In most of Lapland, the darkless summer, when the sun does not go below the horizon, lasts more than 70 days. The snow cover lasts for more than 90 days in the southwest and up to 250 days in the north.

Climate and Weather

Mean Temperature
Summer 55°F to 68°F
Winter 9°F to 27°F
Average Rainfall
South 24 in to 28 in
North 20 in to 24 in

POPULATION

Population Indicators

Total Population: 1999 5,167,000
World Rank: 106th
Density per sq mi: 30.6 per sq km 15.3
% of annual growth (1994–99): 0.3
Male %: 48.5
Female %: 51.5
Urban %: 79.7
Age Distribution: % 10–14: 19.3
  15–29: 20.5
  30–44: 24.6
  45–59: 17.1
  60–74: 12.9
  75 and over: 5.7

(continued)

Population 2020: 5,110,000
Birth Rate per 1,000: 11.8
Death Rate per 1,000: 9.6
Population Doubling Time (years): —
Infant Mortality Rate per 1,000 live births: 3.9
Rate of Natural Increase per 1,000: 2.2
Total Fertility Rate: 1.7
Expectation of Life (years): Males 72.8
Females 80.2
Marriage Rate per 1,000: 4.6
Divorce Rate per 1,000: 2.6
Total Number of Households: 2,270,000
Average Size of Households: 2.2
% of Illegitimate Children: 33.1
Induced Abortions: 10,013
Rate per 100 live births: 15.4

ETHNIC COMPOSITION

The overwhelming majority of the population is Finnish. National minorities include the Swedish-Finns, whose language enjoys an official status on a par with Finnish, as well as the Sami (Lapps) and the Romani (Gypsies). The Swedish-speaking minority makes up less than 6 percent of the population, down from some 14 percent in the late 19th century. It traces its origins to the Swedish colonists between the 12th and the 19th centuries, when Finland was under varying degrees of Swedish rule. The Swedish culture is strongest in the autonomous Åland (Ahvenanmaa) Islands, where Swedish is the primary language, and around Turku, but it blends with Finnish culture around Helsinki.

The number of Sami is estimated at more than 6,000. Generally, Sami are divided into two groups: mountain Sami, who are reindeer herders, and forest Sami, who are farmers and fishermen. Younger Sami are giving up their traditional lifestyles and adopting Finnish customs and lifestyles. The constitution recognizes the Sami as an indigenous people and guarantees that minority groups such as the Sami and Romani have the right to maintain their language and culture.

Romani seem to have first appeared in the region of Finland in the 16th century. At the end of the 20th century they numbered several thousand, living primarily in or near the urban areas of southern Finland.

Some 85,000 foreign nationals, among them Russians, Estonians, and Swedes, were residents of Finland in 1999, up from 21,000 at the beginning of 1990. Among the foreigners were several thousand refugees from such countries as Somalia, Vietnam, and Iraq.

LANGUAGES

Principal Languages and Their Speakers

Estonian	9,000
Finnish	4,792,000
Russian	20,000
Sami (Lapp)	2,000
Swedish	295,000
Other	49,000

RELIGIONS

The central fact of Finnish religious life is the dominance of Lutheranism. In 1997 approximately 85 percent of the population was registered with a parish of the Evangelical Lutheran Church. Both the Eastern and Western branches of Christianity reached Finland by the 12th century. Finland was largely pagan before the crusade by Eric IX of Sweden in 1155.

The Evangelical Lutheran Church is divided into eight dioceses, including one Swedish-speaking diocese, and some 80 deaneries. There are approximately 600 parishes, which range in size from a few hundred members to tens of thousands.

The status of the church is defined by the constitution and the Ecclesiastical Law and may be described as a "special relationship." The government consults the Church Assembly on issues touching on such "mixed matters" as marriage, divorce, oaths, the care of the poor, and religious instruction. The state, in turn, has a voice in church administration, particularly regarding such matters as whether new dioceses and parishes should be founded and whether new churches should be built. The church and state also cooperate on other programs. The church keeps records of births, marriages, and deaths of all members and cares for most of the country's cemeteries. Roughly half of Finnish children aged four to six make use of daycare facilities provided by the church. On its side, the state pays the salaries of the theological faculty of the National University and provides chaplains and religious instructors for the army, navy, prisons, and hospitals. The second-largest church is the Finnish Orthodox Church, with nearly 60,000 members in 1999, divided among 25 parishes. There are three dioceses: Karelia, Helsinki, and Oulu. Like the Evangelical Lutheran Church, the Finnish Orthodox Church has enjoyed special status as a national church. Its chief source of revenue is the church tax.

The Roman Catholic Church was entered on the register of religious groups in 1929. The diocese of Helsinki still has a relatively small membership, a little over 7,000 in 1999, and just seven parishes.

Among other religious communities in Finland, the Pentecostals are almost as numerous as the Orthodox. Smaller groups include the Finnish Evangelical Free Church, Seventh-Day Adventists, Baptists, Methodists, Jehovah's Witnesses, Mormons, and Jews. By the late 1990s the proportion of the population unaffiliated with any church exceeded 12 percent, up from 2.7 percent in 1950.

Up to the end of the 19th century, Finns had to be members of either the Lutheran or Orthodox church. With independence, the state adopted a more neutral stance toward religion. Complete freedom of religion was guaranteed by the Freedom of Religion Act of 1923. Schools provide religious instruction, but this is in accord with the beliefs of the majority of the students at the school, and students who do not belong to any denomination may study other philosophies of life.

Religious Affiliations

Evangelical Lutheran	4,420,000
Other	750,000

HISTORICAL BACKGROUND

The ancestors of modern day Finns were a Mongoloid people who reached Finland in the early centuries of the Christian era. The region fell under the control of the Swedes following several religious crusades, the first in 1154. By 1293 Swedish rule extended as far as Karelia. Finland shared Swedish history for the next six centuries. In Finland proper, Swedish became the official language while Finnish continued to be spoken by the peasantry, but both Swedes and Finns shared a common faith, first Catholic and then Lutheran. After Sweden's military defeat in 1808–09, Finland was transferred to Russia. Alexander I granted Finland a privileged autonomous status as a grand duchy, and the Finns never revolted, unlike the Poles, and succeeded in retaining a large measure of autonomy. The czor respected the Lutheran religion and never imposed the Russian language on the Finns. During the era of conservative reaction (1809–62), a liberal nationalist movement emerged.

During World War I, Finland took advantage of the Russian Revolution to declare independence on December 6, 1917. A short civil war ensued (January 28–May 10, 1918) in which the Finnish war hero, Karl Mannerheim, beat off both Germany and the Russian Bolsheviks. In 1919 Finland became a democratic and parliamentary republic. During the next 20 years, following the settlement of disputes with Sweden over the Åland Islands and with the Soviet Union over East Karelia, Finland made considerable economic and social progress as a nation. However, at the beginning of World War II, the Soviet Union demanded territorial concessions from Finland, and when they were rejected, invaded the country in 1939. A large area, including the Karelian Isthmus, Vijpuri, and the northwest shore of Lake Ladoga, were ceded to Russia in the peace treaty of 1940. After the German attack on Russia in 1941, the Finns took part in the campaign on the side of the Axis powers. With German defeat, Finland was forced to sign an armistice under which it ceded Petsamo and agreed to lease Porkkala headland to Russia as a military base. It also undertook to pay reparations.

A new Treaty of Friendship and Mutual Assistance was signed with the Soviet Union in 1948. Finnish politics from World War II to 1994 were marked by a remarkably stable presidency under three Finnish statesmen: J. K. Passikivi (1946–56), Urho K. Kekkonen (1956–81), and Mauno Koivisto (1981–94) and a volatile parliamentary system marked by short-lived coalition governments based on shifting alliances. Most have been center-left administrations dominated by the Social Democratic Party, especially under the premiershjp of Kalevi Sorsa between 1972 and 1987. In 1995 Finland joined the European Union. In May 1998, Finland agreed to replace its national currency with a new single European currency, and the euro was adopted in 2002. In February 2000, Tarja Halonen of the Social Democratic Party became Finland's first female president.

CONSTITUTION

A new constitution took effect in Finland on March 1, 2000. It consolidated and updated the previously existing body of constitutional law, which consisted of four separate constitutional acts dating from early in the 20th century plus numerous amendments. Much of Finland's earlier constitutional history was linked to that of Sweden and Russia.

Of the four fundamental laws at the basis of the former constitutional legislation, the most important were the Constitution Act of 1919 and the Parliament Act of 1928, which derived from the Parliament Act of 1906. This 1906 legislation, adopted during the period of Russian rule, established one of the most modern forms of representative government in Europe: it replaced the previous Diet comprising four estates with the unicameral Eduskunta, a legislature of 200 members elected on the basis of proportional representation and universal suffrage.

The new constitution that came into force in 2000 by and large preserved the fundamental principles of the previous constitutional legislation but strengthened the parliamentary features of the Finnish system of government. The individual rights of citizens are guaranteed in chapter 2 of the constitution, which declares that everyone is equal before the law. These rights encompass freedom of movement, speech, religion, and association, and freedom from arbitrary arrest. The right to vote in national elections and referendums is guaranteed to all Finnish citizens who are at least 18 years old. The chapter also mandates protection of the right to privacy, the right to receive a basic education, and the right to gainful employment and to social security. While confirming that Finnish and Swedish are the national languages, it requires that the rights of the Sami, Romani, "and other groups" to maintain their languages and cultures be protected. Chapter 2 also imposes on everyone a responsibility for protection of the environment.

The primary responsibility for ensuring that legislative proposals do not violate the constitution rests on the Eduskunta, with its Constitutional Law Committee playing a leading role. There are two ways in which the constitution may be amended. Under the normal procedure, a

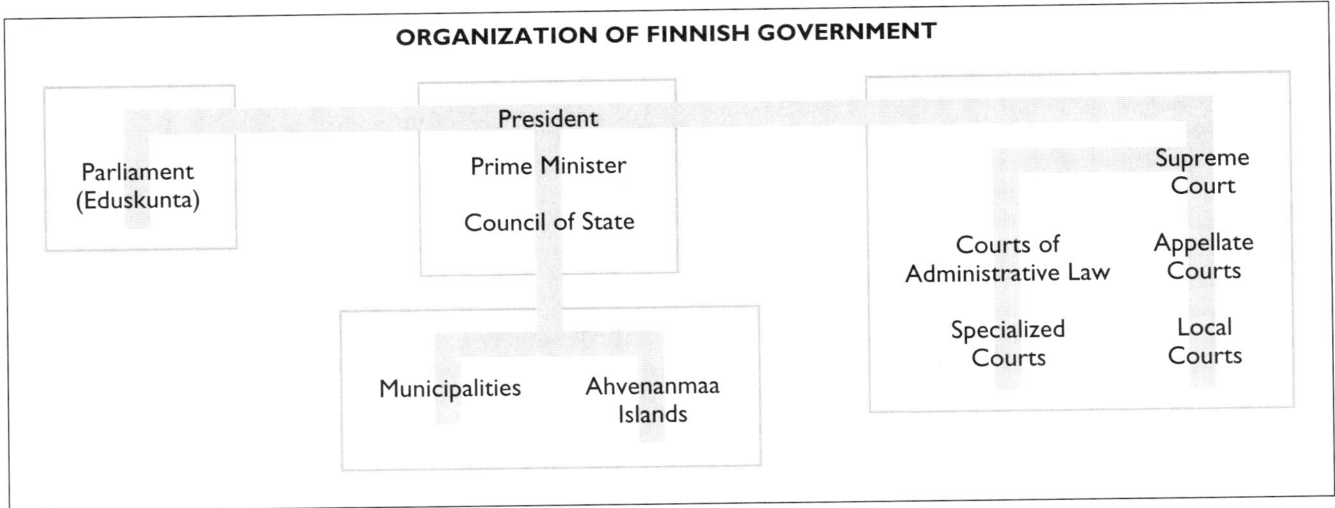

proposal must first be approved by the Eduskunta and left in abeyance, by a simple majority, until the first parliamentary session after the next general election. At that time it may be adopted if it has not been materially altered and receives at least two-thirds of the votes cast. The other procedure is more rapid, to permit timely responses to emergency situations. Under this procedure, the Eduskunta must declare the constitutional proposal urgent, by a five-sixths majority. The proposal can then be adopted, without abeyance, if it receives a two-thirds majority.

The constitution spells out the separation of powers among the governmental branches, guaranteeing legislative authority to the Eduskunta, which also makes decisions on state finances. Executive power is vested in the president and in the Council of State, or government, that is, the prime minister and the other ministers. Judicial authority is granted to independent courts of law, with the highest courts being the Supreme Court and the Supreme Administrative Court.

The president is elected by direct vote for a term of six years and may serve no more than two consecutive terms. Impeachment of the president, on grounds of treason or an offense against humanity, requires a three-fourths vote in the Eduskunta. Traditionally the president has no party ties while in office.

The powers of the Finnish presidency are more circumscribed than they were decades ago. Nonetheless, the president wields substantial authority as commander in chief of the armed forces and as head of state, and the president continues to direct foreign policy (although the constitution now specifies that this be done "in cooperation with the Council of State"). The president appoints the prime minister (upon election by the Eduskunta) and cabinet ministers (upon nomination by the prime minister). The president, the Council of State, and ministries may issue decrees in accordance with the authority granted them in the constitution or by law, but principles involving the rights and obligations of private individuals and other matters of a legislative nature are governed by parliamentary acts.

Upon proposal by the prime minister, the president can dissolve the Eduskunta and can dismiss the Council of State or a minister. (Dismissal is also possible if the Council of State ceases to enjoy the confidence of the Eduskunta.) The powers of the president also include the appointment of department heads and judges and the issuance of pardons. The chancellor of justice, who monitors the actions of officials and others performing public duties to make sure they are in accordance with the law, is appointed by the president and is attached to the Council of State but has no vote. Although the president is the supreme commander of the armed forces, command may be transferred to another Finnish citizen upon recommendation by the Council of State. This was the case when President Kyosti Kallio named Marshal Carl Gustav von Mannerheim commander in chief in 1939 at the outset of the Winter War.

Most legislative initiatives in the Eduskunta are proposed by the government, although individual members of the Eduskunta also have the right to submit bills. The State Council's responsibility to the Eduskunta is expressed largely through interpellations by 20 or more representatives addressed to the government or an individual minister, with a response required in a plenary session of the Eduskunta within 15 days. There also is a question hour, introduced in 1966, when members may cross-examine ministers once a week.

By the year 2000, Finland had had 67 governments since its 1917 declaration of independence. Some lasted just a few months, and one, the third cabinet of Julio Vennola in 1931, held office for less than a month. The longest-serving government was the first administration of Paavo Lipponen, which took office in 1995 and lasted 1,464 days.

LOCAL GOVERNMENT

The main units of local administration are the municipalities, which carry the primary responsibility for providing citizens with education, health, social welfare, and other basic services. Finland has been divided into six provinces since 1997, when nine of the previous 12 provinces were combined into three in an effort to streamline the administration and improve efficiency. The provincial administrations monitor the provision of services by the municipalities, provide regional commands for police and rescue services and the like, and carry responsibility for inspections and certain licenses. The provincial governors are appointed by the president. As of 1999, Finland was divided into 15 electoral districts for parliamentary elections. Under the Local Government Act of 1995 the only official form of local government is the municipality, although a particular municipality may be called a town or city. Municipalities vary enormously in land area and population size. The highest administrative organ of a municipality is the Local Council, elected every four years. This body names the Local Executive Board, which oversees the management of local government functions in accordance with the council's decisions. The board's executive officer is the municipal manager. Vocational colleges, hospitals, and other operations that may be too large and expensive for individual municipalities, especially smaller ones, to deal with may be handled by intermunicipal corporations, of which there are a few hundred in Finland.

At the beginning of 1999, Finland had a total of 452 municipalities, 67 of which were urban municipalities, 70 semiurban municipalities, and 315 rural municipalities. Citizens of other countries residing permanently in Finland are permitted to vote in municipal elections.

The Swedish-speaking Åland Islands (Ahvenanmaa) constitute a separate province and a separate electoral district, and have a semiautonomous status under law. The power of the governor in this province is nominal and subordinate to that of the Lagting (Parliament), whose 30 members are elected every four years. The Lagting elects the Executive Board, with five to seven members. The speaker of the Lagting is the highest official in the province, ranking above the chairman of the Executive Board. The Lagting has legislative authority applicable to the province. In addition, it has special taxing and budgetary powers beyond those pertaining to other regions, including the right to levy an increment on state income revenues. Also, treaties between Finland and other countries that affect Åland cannot come into effect in the province without the Lagting's consent.

Local Government

Principal administrative divisions, capitals, area, population

AREA AND POPULATION

Provinces	Capitals	area sq mi	area sq km	population 1999 estimate
Åland (Ahvenanmaa)	Mariehamn (Maarianhamina)	599	1,552	25,625
Eleia-suomi	Hāmeenlinna	13,273	34,378	2,052,897
Ita-Suomi	Mikkeli	23,444	60,720	599,246
Lānsi-Suomi	Turku	31,265	80,976	1,832,407
Lappi	Rovaniemi	38,203	98,946	196,647
Oulu	Oulu	23,773	61,572	452,824
TOTAL		130,559	338,145	5,159,646

PARLIAMENT

The national legislature is the unicameral Eduskunta (Riksdag in Swedish) of 200 members, elected by universal suffrage in a proportional representation system known as the d'Hondt method. A party receives seats in the Eduskunta in proportion to the number of votes received by that party in each electoral district. The period between elections cannot exceed four years. While the Eduskunta is in session, the president has the right to dissolve it, upon the recommendation of the prime minister and after having consulted the parliamentary groups. The Eduskunta ordinarily is in session almost year-round, except in the summer and on state holidays. Parliamentary activity tends to take place along party lines. When a new government is formed, it must immediately present a statement of its program to the Eduskunta for a show of confidence.

At the outset of each session the Eduskunta chooses from among its members a speaker, whose duties include chairing plenary sessions of the Eduskunta. Also chosen are two deputy speakers, who, together with the speaker and the heads of the select committees, constitute the Speaker's Council, which directs the Eduskunta's work. The Eduskunta appoints a parliamentary ombudsman and two deputy ombudsmen, who are expected to be prominent jurists. The ombudsman oversees the courts, public officials, and other individuals performing public duties to make sure they obey the law, fulfill their responsibilities, and maintain fundamental and human rights.

Committee work undergirds all legislative activity; generally, the committees' makeup reflects the relative strengths of the various parties. Ministers, the speaker, and deputy speakers are not permitted to be committee members.

The so-called Grand Committee, with 25 regular members (plus 13 alternates), once was most important for playing a sort of supervisory role, making up for Finland's lack of an upper house. The Grand Committee is now the main committee responsible for studying EU matters on behalf of the plenary session.

The ultimate forum is the plenary session, in which party groups are seated from the speaker's left to the speaker's right in ideological order. The agenda is prepared by the speaker, who is not allowed to take part in debates or vote in plenary sessions. Legislative proposals must ordinarily be considered in plenary session in two readings. Discussion precedes vote, and no time limit is placed on speeches, interjections, or replies; indeed, members of the Eduskunta enjoy broader freedom to speak on all matters under consideration than is found in the parliaments of many other countries. This right is protected in the constitution.

Matters considered by the Eduskunta may be in the form of bills submitted by the government or legislative, budgetary, or petitionary initiatives put forward by members. After a piece of legislation is approved by the Eduskunta, it is submitted to the president for ratification. If the president does not ratify it, the measure is returned to the Eduskunta for reconsideration; if readopted without material changes, the measure becomes law without ratification. In addition to its legislative function, the Eduskunta supervises the governmental administration, maintaining oversight over financial management and budget compliance with the assistance of the independent State Audit Office.

In general, all Finnish citizens who have reached the age of 18 have the right to vote. For general elections the country is divided into at least a dozen electoral districts, with seats varying in number based on the number of citizens residing in the district. The semiautonomous Åland (Ahvenanmaa) Islands are guaranteed their own constituency, with one representative. As of the year 2000, Finland had 15 electoral districts, including the one for Åland.

POLITICAL PARTIES

Finnish Center Party	Once known as the Agrarian League, still has a strong rural base of support
Finnish Christian League	Substantial support among revivalists
Finnish Social Democratic Party	Socialist
Green League	Enviromentalist
Left-Wing Alliance	Communist, Marxist
National Coalition Party	Conservative
Swedish People's Party	Swedish speakers
Young-Finns	Neoliberal

Political Parties

Finnish Social Democratic Party, 1899
National Coalition, 1918
Left-wing Alliance, 1990
Swedish People's Party, 1906
Finnish Center, 1906
Liberal People's Party, 1965
True Finns Party, 1956
Finnish Christian Union, 1958
Reform Group, 1997
Alliance for Free Finland
Ecological Party, 1990
Communist Party, 1994
Patriotic National Alliance, 1993

Political Parties: Strength in Parliament Most Recent Elections

The **Parliament** (Eduskunta/Riksdagen) is a unicameral body of 200 members. Following the election of March 21, 1999, the seat distribution was as follows: Finnish Social Democratic Party, 51; Finnish Center, 48; National Coalition, 46; Left-Wing Alliance, 20; Swedish People's Party, 12; Green Union, 11; Finnish Christian Union, 10; True Finns Party, 1; Reform Group, 1.

LEGAL SYSTEM

There are three types of courts: the general courts, a parallel system of courts of administrative law, and the special courts. Tenured judges are appointed by the president. The president also appoints the prosecutor-general (who heads the prosecution service), the chancellor of justice, and the deputy chancellor of justice. The Eduskunta appoints the parliamentary ombudsman and two deputies. The chancellor of justice and the parliamentary ombudsman safeguard the legal rights of citizens and the legality of state actions.

The general courts handle both civil and penal cases and exist in three tiers: the local courts, appellate courts, and Supreme Court. In penal cases and in some civil cases the local court usually consists of a chairman and three lay members, with each having a vote. Less important cases may be dealt with by the chairman alone. Appeals of decisions by the local courts are handled by six appellate courts, located in Helsinki, Turku, Vaasa, Kuopio, Kouvola, and Rovaniemi. Each appellate court consists of a president and several councillors. The highest court is the Supreme Court, which accepts appeals of important cases from the appellate courts and also some special courts. It consists of a president and approximately 20 justices, with five justices constituting a quorum.

The system of administrative courts, headed by the Supreme Administrative Court in Helsinki, was established in the 20th century. A network of eight regional administrative courts serve as general courts for administrative matters. Most of the appeals handled by the regional administrative courts deal with tax issues. The courts also hear legal disputes between local and central government organs or private individuals and the government, as well as cases involving civil liberties, such as the confinement of a drug addict or a mentally ill person. Like the Supreme Court, the Supreme Administrative Court consists of a president and about 20 justices, with five required for a quorum.

Among the various special courts is the Court of Impeachment, which tries ministers, justices of the Supreme Court and the Supreme Administrative Court, as well as the chancellor of justice and the parliamentary ombudsman when arraigned for illegal acts in the exercise of their official functions. This court also tries the president if the chief of state is charged with treason or an offense against humanity. The Swedish General Code of 1734 is still basic law in Finland, although only some articles and the general framework remain in force. The court system has undergone reform, and much of the code has been revised, since 1734.

The Finnish prison population has been dropping for decades, primarily because of a decline in convictions for crimes against property. Meanwhile, prisoners convicted of drug-related crimes or crimes of violence and/or robbery have increased slightly in recent years.

LAW ENFORCEMENT

Law Enforcement

Offenses reported to the police per 100,000: 14,799
- Murder: 0.6
- Assault: 40.0
- Burglary: 1,934.9
- Automobile Theft: 53.2
- Population per Police officer: 640

Death Penalty: Abolished 1972.

HUMAN RIGHTS

Finland has experienced no major violations of human rights in recent years. The constitution asserts that human dignity and the rights and freedoms of individuals shall be inviolable, although temporary exceptions to the guarantee of basic rights are allowed in such serious situations as an armed attack on Finland. The importance of the rule of law is underlined in the constitution. Everyone, it declares, shall be equal before the law. Discrimination on such grounds as "sex, age, origin, language, religion, convictions, opinions, state of health, disability" is barred "unless there is an acceptable reason for the same." Among the rights guaranteed to all in the constitution are freedom of association and the right to hold meetings and demonstrations without a permit. The constitution prohibits the deportation or extradition of foreigners in cases where they face a risk of a "death sentence, torture or other treatment violating human dignity." The chancellor of justice and the parliamentary ombudsman are responsible for supervising the implementation of human rights in public life. The ombudsman for aliens monitors discrimination against foreigners. The Council for Equality and the equality ombudsman oversee the progress of equal rights.

In 1999, Amnesty International accused Finland of imprisoning people for their conscientious beliefs under the Military Service Act, which came into effect the previous year. The law reduced the length of military service, but the alternative civilian service required for conscientious objectors remained as long as 395 days, more than twice the time served by half of the conscripts under the new measure; the penalty for refusing alternative service was imprisonment. Amnesty International argued that the length of alternative civilian service was punitive and violated international principles on conscientious objection.

FOREIGN POLICY

The constitution declares that Finland will take part "in international cooperation for the protection of peace and human rights and for the development of society." The president, "in cooperation with the State Council," is responsible for the direction of Finland's foreign policy, which is implemented by the Foreign Ministry. The government, however, is required to keep the Eduskunta, in particular the Eduskunta's Committee for Foreign Affairs and its Grand Committee (regarding European Union matters), informed of developments concerning foreign and security policy. Decisions on war and peace are made by the president with the consent of the Eduskunta.

Having lost two wars with the Soviet Union in 1939–44, Finland was constrained in the ensuing decades to maintain a modus vivendi with its powerful neighbor. It founded its foreign policy on the principles of neutrality and friendship with Moscow, as well as on that of support for Nordic cooperation. In 1992, shortly after the collapse of the Soviet Union, Finland signed a new treaty with Russia, the Soviet Union's successor, that lacked the military obligations imposed in the old, superseded Soviet-Finnish agreement.

The Soviet Union had been Finland's chief trading partner, however, and the new Russia floundered economically, creating severe stresses in the Finnish economy. Finland sought to energize its trade relations with the West. Finland applied in 1992 to join the European Union (EU), although the Finnish public was divided over the merits of EU membership. But EU membership won the endorsement of some 57 percent of the voters in a 1994 referendum and was subsequently approved by the Eduskunta. To allay concern that Finland would lose its neutrality, the Finnish leadership announced that the country would not move to gain admission into NATO. (Finland has cooperated with NATO's Partnership for Peace program, however.)

After officially becoming a member of the EU on January 1, 1995, Finland joined in the movement toward Economic and Monetary Union, adopting the new EU currency, the euro, in 1999 along with most of the other member states. Finnish policy has tended to support increased economic integration of the EU member countries, as distinguished from their political integration, for which Finland has shown less enthusiasm. Finland, not neglecting its traditional regional interests, pushed the EU to adopt a "northern dimension" policy aimed at promoting partnership with Russia and other countries in the vicinity of the Baltic and Barents seas in such fields as energy, the environment, and economic management. To promote democracy and regional stability, Finland has supported expansion of the EU to include additional countries in Central and Eastern Europe. Finland, along with other Nordic countries, has built close ties with Estonia, Latvia, and Lithuania.

Finland has for decades supported the central role of the United Nations in international peacekeeping operations and has taken an active role in them, although Finnish law imposes restrictions on participation in peace enforcement, that is, the use of military force to push warring parties to a peace settlement. Finland has also assisted in peacekeeping operations under the leadership of other organizations, such as the NATO-led IFOR operation in Bosnia in the late 1990s.

Finland pursues its foreign policy objective of promoting human rights largely by working through the EU. Finnish aid to developing countries is delivered both via bilateral programs and through participation in EU assistance programs.

DEFENSE

The terms of the Treaty of Paris signed with the Allied Powers after World War II in 1947 imposed certain restrictions on the Finnish army. It limited the size of the armed forces to 34,400 men, the air force to 3,000 men and 60 combat aircraft, and the navy to 4,500 men with ships totaling 10,000 tons. The treaty also prohibited bombers, submarines, and missiles, as well as nuclear weapons, but in a 1963 agreement Finland was allowed to acquire certain classes of defensive missiles.

The constitution requires every Finn to take part or at least assist in national defense. It vests supreme command of the armed forces in the president of the republic, who may, however, entrust this duty to another person, upon the proposal of the Council of State. The decision to mobilize the armed forces is made by the president, again upon a proposal by the Council of State. The chief military planning and coordinating body is the Defense Council, consisting of the prime minister, the ministers of defense, foreign affairs, interior, finance, trade and industry, along with other ministers the president may name as members, as well as the chief of defense and the chief of the general staff.

The armed forces consist of three military commands (western, eastern, and northern), as well as the air force and the navy, which are separate services with their own commanders in chief and headquarters.

Every Finnish male becomes liable for compulsory military service at the beginning of the year in which he turns 17 and remains on call until the end of the year he turns 60. Military service typically lasts 180, 270, or 362 days, depending on rank and skills. After this obligatory service, conscripts enter the reserves and are subject to periodic refresher training.

Finnish participants in international peacekeeping operations are not permitted to total more than 2,000 at any given time. They are operationally subordinate to the organization carrying out the operation, such as the United Nations or the Organization for Security and Cooperation in Europe. However, they sign a contract with the Finnish government, and the Defense Forces help with peacekeeper training and readiness. Finland in the late 1960s became the first country to set up a separate peacekeeper training program. Between 1956 and 1999, more than 35,000 Finns served in United Nations peacekeeping missions worldwide. Almost all Nordic military observers are trained at an instruction center in Niinisalo; since 1984, trainees have also included officers from NATO members, the Baltic nations, Asia, and South America.

Military Indicators

Total Active Duty Personnel: 31,000
Military Manpower per 1,000: 6.0
Military Expenditures $million: 2,381
- as % of GNP: 2
- per capita $: 467
- as % of central government expenditures: 5.1

Arms Imports $million: 30
Arms Exports $million: 0

ECONOMY

During the 20th century Finland developed from a primarily agrarian possession of the Russian Empire, with industrial activity rooted largely in the abundant Finnish forests, into a member nation of the European Union (EU), with an advanced industrial economy occupying a prominent role in the information and telecommunications revolution transpiring at century's end.

The early 1990s were marked by severe recession, in part a reflection of economic disruption in the former Soviet Union, which had long been a key trade partner. By mid-decade, however, Finland was again registering substantial growth in gross domestic product (GDP) (4.8 percent a year in 1995–98, compared to 2.4 percent for the EU as a whole), although continuing high levels of unemployment (hovering around 10 percent at the end of the 1990s) remained a concern. The increased investment and sharpened competitive pressures attendant on Finland's entry into the EU in 1995 assisted the recovery from recession. Pursuing a policy of economic integration into the EU's Economic and Monetary Union, Finland was among the 11 member countries that launched the euro currency in 1999. Growth in 2001 will be bolstered by strong private consumption yet may be one or two points lower than in 2000, largely because of a weakening in export demand.

The importance of foreign trade in the Finnish economy is reflected in the fact that the export of goods represents almost a third of GDP. By the end of the 1990s the electronics industry, along with metal and engineering products, contributed roughly half of Finland's export revenue. Nearly a third, however, still came from wood, paper, and other forest products. In 1998 the European Union accounted, in terms of value, for more than half of Finnish exports and approximately three-fifths of imports.

Information technology products made up a fifth of total exports in 1998. Finnish economic policy in recent years has encouraged research and development (R&D), notably in the information technology sector. In 1998 the amount invested in R&D represented about 3 percent of the GDP. Two-thirds of this spending came in the private sector. By early 1999, Finland had 60 mobile phone subscriptions for every 100 inhabitants, and over three-quarters of all households had a mobile phone. More than two-fifths of households had at least one personal computer. Finland's level of Internet connectivity was among the highest in the world, with over 110 Internet connections for every 1,000 inhabitants. By 1998, according to the Finnish Bankers' Association, more than four-fifths of all customer transactions took place by computer without the use of paper documents.

The Finnish economy has a small mining sector, producing such metals as chromium, mercury, zinc, silver, copper, and nickel. Because of the country's northern location, the relatively large distances between some of its cities, and its relatively large amount of energy-intensive industry, per capita energy consumption in Finland is among the highest in the world. Since Finland lacks deposits of coal, oil, and natural gas, it must rely heavily on imported energy sources. In 1998, coal, oil, and natural gas accounted for about half of all energy consumption. Nuclear power represented nearly a fifth of consumption, as did wood fuel.

Principal Economic Indicators

Gross National Product: $127.398 billion
GNP per capita $: 24,790
GNP Average Annual Growth Rate (1990–97) %: 0.9
GNP per capita Average Annual Growth Rate (1990–97) %: 0.5
Origin of Gross: Domestic Product %
- Agriculture: 5
- Mining: —
- Manufacturing: 25
- Construction: 5
- Public Utilities: 3
- Transportation and Communications: 9
- Trade: 11
- Financial Services: 19
- Other Services: 3
- Government: 20

Gross Domestic Product by Type of Expenditure %
- Private Consumption: 56
- Government Consumption: 22
- Gross Domestic Investment: 15
- Foreign Trade: Exports: 36
- Imports: −29

% of Income Received by Poorest 20%: 3.7
% of Income Received by Richest 10%: 26.9

Price and earnings indexes (1995 = 100)

	1993	1994	1995	1996	1997	1998	1999
Consumer price index	98.0	99.0	100.0	100.6	101.8	103.2	104.4
Earnings index	93.7	95.5	100.0	103.9	106.0	—	—

Finance

National Currency: Euro (Formerly markka FMK)
Exchange Rate: $1 = FMK 5.4948
Money Supply Stock in National Currency billion: 204.834
M1 per capita: 39,900
Central Bank Discount Rate %: 3.50
Total External Debt $ million: 30,000
Debt Service Ratio %: —

Balance of Payments $million: 6,664
International Reserves SDRs million: 7,470
Ratio of External Debt to Total Reserves: —
Average Annual Rate of Inflation/Consumer Price Index Growth Rate %: 1.2

Official Development Assistance

Donor ODA $million: 355
- as % of GNP: 0.27
- per capita $: 68
- Foreign Direct Investment $million: 12,029

Central Government Revenues and Expenditures

Fiscal Year: Calendar Year
Revenues $million: 33,000
Expenditures $million: 40,000
Budget Deficit $million: 7,000
Tax Revenues as % of GDP: 28.1
Highest Tax Bracket %
- Individual: 38
- Corporate: 28

Employment and Labor

Economically Active Population: 2,521,000
Female Participation Rate %: 47.0
Activity Rate %: 49.4
Labor by Sector: %
- Agriculture, Forestry, Fishing: 7.0
- Manufacturing, Mining: 20.5
- Construction: 6.9
- Transportation and Communications: 7.0
- Trade, Hotels, and Restaurants: 14.0
- Finance, Insurance, Real Estate: 7.9
- Public Administration, Defense: —
- Services: 33.0

Unemployment %: 14.6

Agriculture

Agriculture's Share of GDP%: 5
Average Annual Rate of Growth (1965–98) %: 0.2
Number of Farms 000: 170
Average Size of Farm ha: 12.8
Number of Tractors per 1,000 hectares: 88.7
Irrigation, % of Farms having: 3
Artificial Fertilizer kg/hectare: 210
Total Farmland as % of land area: 42.6
Livestock: Cattle 000: 20,389
Sheep 000: 10,305
Hogs 000: 15,430
Chickens 000: 238,067
Forests: Production of Roundwood (000 cubic meters): 50,217
Fisheries: Total Catch tons: 167.2

Mining

% of GDP: 0.3
Value of Mineral Production $million: 424.1

Manufacturing

Value Added $million: 20,972
Industrial Production Growth Rate %: 7.4

Energy

Commercial Energy Production metric tons of oil equivalent 000: 15,059
Commercial Energy Consumption metric tons of oil equivalent 000: 33,075
Commercial Energy Consumption per capita kg: 6,435
Average Annual Growth Rate 1980–97 %: 1.2
Net Energy Imports % of use: 54
Electricity Installed Capacity kW 000: 14,427
Production kW-hr million: 63,885
Coal Reserves tons million: —
Production tons 000: —
Natural Gas Proven Reserves cubic meters billion: —
Production cubic meters million: —
Crude Petroleum Reserves barrels million: —
Production barrels million: —
Consumption barrels million: 63
Refinery Capacity barrels per day 000: 200
Pipelines Length km: —

Foreign Trade

Imports $million: 30,904.9
Exports $million: 40,556.5
Export Volume % Annual Growth Rate (1990–97): 9.3
Import Volume % Annual Growth Rate (1990–97): 4.3
Balance of Trade $

Balance of trade (current prices)

	1993	1994	1995	1996	1997	1998
U.S.						
$000,000	+30,949	+33,552	+49,952	+42,170	+51,845	+56,918
% of total	12.4%	12.2%	16.9%	13.6%	13.9%	14.2%

Major Trading Partners

	Imports	Exports
European Union %	58.5	52.7
United States %	7.3	7.9
Eastern Europe %	10.2	12.8
Japan %	5.2	2.6
Others %	18.8	24.1

Transportation

Roads Total Length mi: 48,294 km 77,722
Paved %: 63
Automobiles: 1,900,855
Trucks and Buses: 260,115
Persons per vehicle: 2.4
Railroad; Track Length mi: 3,641 km 5,859
Passenger-mi million: 1,626
Freight-mi million: 6,551
Merchant Marine: No. of Vessels: 263
Total Deadweight Tonnage 000: 989.3
International Cargo Loaded tons 000: 33,336
International Cargo Off-loaded tons 000: 36,948
Airports with Scheduled Flights: 24
Traffic: Passenger-mi million: 6,654
Freight-mi million: 165.3
Length of Canals mi: 4,148 km 6,675

Tourism

Number of Tourists to 000: 1,858
Number of Tourists from 000: 4,743
Tourist Receipts $million: 1,716
Tourist Expenditures $million: 2,383

Communications

Telephones 000: 2,796
Cost of Local Calls 3 mins: $0.12
Cellular Telephones 000: 1,018
Fax Machines 000: 132
Personal Computers 000: 930
Internet Hosts per million persons: 42,229
Mail: Post Offices: 1,791
Pieces of Mail Handled million: 1,143
Pieces of Mail Handled per person: 224

EDUCATION

The constitution guarantees to everyone the right to a basic education free of charge and mandates that all shall have an "equal opportunity to receive other educational services in accordance with their ability and special needs, as well as the opportunity to develop themselves without being prevented by economic hardship." Compulsory basic education is provided to all children between ages seven and 16. After 16, education is voluntary, with students spending two to four years, or more, at an upper secondary school or at a vocational school.

An act of 1872 removed secondary schools from ecclesiastical control and placed them under civil authority. It also grouped them under three types: *lyceer* (lycea), *realskoler*, and higher schools for girls. The *lyceer* offered both a four-year course leading to the technical high school and an eight-year course leading to the university.

A hallmark of these reforms was the principle of comprehensiveness, which means that all children attend the same basic school and follow the same curriculum. Under the Basic Education Act, which took effect in 1999, either of Finland's two official languages, Finnish and Swedish, may be used in teaching. Instruction can also occur in Sami or Romani, and in sign language. Special groups or schools may be set up to teach students in a language that is not their mother tongue.

Education is free of charge for degree candidates at the some 20 universities and institutions of higher education in Finland (whose students total more than 130,000, slightly over half of them women), as well as at the over 30 polytechnics. Students entering a university may study for a bachelor's degree, which can take three or four years. But most individuals are admitted to programs leading to a master's degree, which can take five to six years to complete. Those who wish to continue their studies may seek a doctorate. In many fields, however, they may first take an optional predoctoral licentiate's degree; this typically requires about two years of full-time study.

The financial costs of education are borne by both the state (which funds two-thirds of public education expenditures) and the municipalities (one-third). As it is the right and duty of every citizen to be educated, all municipalities are required by law to provide education of equal standard irrespective of financial capacity.

Education

Literacy Rate %: 100
- Male %: 100
- Female %: 100

First Level: Primary schools: 4,474
- Teachers: —
- Students: 588,162
- Student-Teacher Ratio: —
- Net Enrollment Ratio: 99

Second Level: Secondary Schools: 477
- Teachers: —
- Students: 134,851
- Student-Teacher Ratio: —
- Net Enrollment Ratio: 93

Vocational Level: Schools: 520
- Students: 192,200

Third Level: Institutions: 21
- Teachers: 7,790
- Students: 133,359
- Student-Ratio Level: 16.4
- Gross Enrollment Ratio: 66.9
- Students per 100,000: 4,033
- % of Population Age 25 and over with Postsecondary Education: 18.3

Public Expenditure on Education as % of GDP: 7.6

SCIENCE AND TECHNOLOGY

Science and Technology

Scientists and Engineers in R&D per 1 million persons: 2,799
Expenditures in R&D as % of GDP: 2.78
High-Tech Exports $million: 8,124
Patent Applications by Residents: 4,061

MEDIA

In 1997, Finland was estimated to have the highest per capita density of Internet connections in the world. Finland's total newspaper circulation per capita ranked second in Europe in 1999 and third in the world. The total number of registered periodicals exceeded 2,500, and their overall circulation was 18 million.

The volume of book publishing is enormous, with an annual output in 1998 of more than 12,000 titles, most of them in Finnish. The production of titles per 10,000 inhabitants ranked among the highest in Europe. The annual output of Swedish-language titles numbers in the hundreds. Finland has a well-developed network of libraries. As of the late 1990s, book borrowers amounted to roughly half the population, and most libraries provided access to the Internet.

As of the late 1990s the Finnish mass media were dominated by three major corporations: Sanoma-WSOY, Alma Media Oy, and the state-owned, noncommercial Finnish Broadcasting Company, YLE. National television programming is broadcast on four channels: two public-service channels and two commercial channels supported by advertising. YLE broadcasts nationally (including Swedish-language programming) on TV 1 and TV 2. The two companies with commercial TV broadcasting licenses, MTV Oy and Oy Ruutunelonen Ab, broadcast on the MTV3 channel and channel Nelonen, respectively. In the late 1990s Finland had five nationwide radio stations, four public service and one commercial. There were approximately 60 local radio stations, including about a dozen commercial stations in the Helsinki area.

Media

Daily Newspapers: 53
- Total Circulation 000: 2,368
- Circulation per 1,000: 464

Books Published: 12,539
Magazines: 5,711
Radio Receivers 000: 4,950
- per 1,000: 966

Television sets 000: 2,650
- per 1,000: 519

MOST IMPORTANT MEDIA:

Press. The following are dailies published at Helsinki in Finnish, unless otherwise indicated (circulation figures for 1994); *Helsingin Sanomat*

(continued)

(476,163), independent; *Ilta-Sanomat* (212,854), independent; *Aamulehti* (Tampere, 135,184), National Coalition; *Turun Sanomat* (Turku, 119,004), independent; *Maaseudun Tulevaisuus* (110,951, triweekly); *Iltalehti* (105,059), independent; *Kaleva* (Oulu, 95,118), independent; *Savon Sanomat* (Kuopio, 77,012), Center Party; *Hufvudstadsbladet* (60,405 daily, 62,771 Sunday), in Swedish, independent.

News agencies. The Finnish News Agency (Oy Suomen Tietotoimisto-STT/Finska Notisbyran Ab-FNB) is a major independent facility covering the entire country; most leading international bureaus also maintain offices at Helsinki.

Radio and television. Broadcasting is largely controlled by the state-owned Finnish Broadcasting Company (Oy Yleisradio Ab), which offers radio programming in both Finnish and Swedish, and services two television channels; there is one commercial television channel, MTV3, in addition to the offerings of local TV outlets.

CULTURE

A prominent feature of Finnish cultural life is the hundreds of festivals held around the country, including theatrical and musical presentations, among them the well-known Savonlinna Opera Festival. Artistic and cultural activities such as theater, dance, cinema, and music benefit from regular state subsidies, which helps explain why there are almost 60 permanent theaters in such a small country. Tickets consequently are relatively inexpensive, and it is said that virtually every other Finn attends the theater at least once a year. National theatrical arts institutions of note include the National Opera, the National Theater, the TTT Theater in Tampere, and the Svenska Teatern (Swedish Theater) in Helsinki. Film production has been averaging about a dozen or so movies annually in recent years.

Finland has a rich musical tradition. Roughly 40,000 Finns belong to a professional or amateur music association, and choirs are especially popular. The country has some 30 subsidized symphony and chamber orchestras, drawing a million people a year, a large figure for a country with a total population of some five million.

Several ministries provide support to cultural activities, but most funding comes from local authorities and from the Ministry of Education, which is the state body with the chief responsibility for promoting and developing culture. The ministry oversees the Arts Council of Finland, which includes the Central Arts Council, a provider of project grants, as well as nine separate councils that allocate artist grants. There also exist more than a dozen regional arts councils that promote both professional and amateur arts.

Cultural Indicators

Public Libraries Number: 461
- Volumes: 31,700,000
- Registered borrowers: 2,084,354

Museums Number: 572
- Annual Attendance: 2,897,000

Cinema Production of Long Films: 8
- Number of Cinemas: 330
- Seating Capacity: 58,400
- Annual Attendance: 5.3
- Annual Attendance per capita: 1.0

STATUS OF WOMEN

In 1906, Finland, while still a part of the Russian Empire, became the first country in Europe to grant women the right to vote and the first in the world to permit them to run for office. Almost 10 percent of the members elected to the first Eduskunta (Parliament) the following year were women. Despite this promising beginning, the picture of women's rights in Finland over the ensuing years was mixed, with slow progress toward full equality. The first female government minister in Finland took office in 1926. Four years later the Marriage Act freed wives from the guardianship of their husbands and granted them the right to their own property. But it was not until 1988 that women were permitted to enter the clergy of the Evangelical Lutheran Church. It was not until 1994 that a woman became speaker of the Eduskunta, and it was not until 2000 that a woman was elected president.

At the end of the 20th century there were nearly as many women as men in the workforce. Of the 200 members elected to the Eduskunta in 1999, 74, or 37%, were women, one of the highest proportions in the world. Eight women received portfolios in the government that was formed after the 1999 elections: minister for foreign affairs, minister of education, minister at the Ministry of Finance, minister of cultural affairs, minister of social affairs and health, minister at the Ministry of Social Affairs and Health, minister of the environment, and minister of labor. Yet women's average pay was only four-fifths that of men's. Women were still not equally represented in politics and the workplace. In the governmental apparatus, just a fifth of parliamentary committees were chaired by women, and most provincial governors were men, as were most municipal managers and municipal council chairpersons. In the educational sphere, students' choices of fields of study continued to reflect sex distinctions, with men tending to prefer engineering, manufacturing, construction, and agriculture programs, and women, health, welfare, education, services, and humanities.

Still, movement toward full equality between the sexes quickened in recent decades, and this in part reflected a strengthening of legal requirements for equality. The constitution now explicitly stipulates, "Equality of the sexes is promoted in societal activity and working life, especially in the determination of pay and the other terms of employment." This mandate was spelled out in the Act on Equality Between Women and Men, which came into effect at the beginning of 1987 and was aimed at improving the status of women and preventing discrimination on the basis of sex, particularly in the workplace. It required the authorities and employers to promote equality and mandated that men and women be provided with equal opportunities for education and professional development, and implementation is monitored by the office of equality ombudsman. The law was amended in 1992 to prohibit discrimination on the basis of pregnancy and parenthood. An amendment adopted in 1995 required that each sex account for at least 40 percent of the members of government committees, advisory boards and similar bodies, and municipal bodies (but not municipal councils).

Women

Gender Empowerment Measure: 5
Seats Held in Parliament by Women %: 33.5
Female Administrators and Managers %: 25.3
Female Professional and Technical Workers %: 62.5
Women's Share of Earned Income %: 42
Women in Government %: 16

HEALTH, FOOD, AND NUTRITION

Health

Number of Physicians: 13,771
Number of Dentists: 4,696
Number of Nurses: 131,829
Number of Pharmacists: 584
Population per Physician: 371
Number of Hospitals: 380
Hospital Beds per 10,000: 98
Hospital Bed Occupancy Rate: 70.9
Infant Mortality Rate per 1,000 live births: 6
Maternal Mortality Rate per 100,000 live births: 11
Total Health Expenditures as % of GDP: 7.82
Health Expenditures per capita $: 2,046
HIV Infected % of adults: 0.02
Cigarette Consumption per smoker per year: 2,906
% of Smokers: Male: 27
Female: 19
Access to Safe Water %: 100

Food and Nutrition

Food Supply as % of FAO Requirements: 112
% of Consumption Expenditures on Food: 22.5
Daily Available Calories per capita: 3,022
% of Total Calories derived from:
Cereals: 21.2
Potatoes, cassava: 4.3
Meat, poultry: 16.4
Fish: 2.1
Eggs, milk: 16.1
Fruits, vegetables: 4.1
Fats, oils: 14.2

ENVIRONMENT

Finland is heavily forested, and the country has taken active measures to protect and conserve its natural wealth. The Nature Conservation Act of 1923 led to the establishment of Finland's first national parks in 1938. By the end of the 1990s, Finland had 32 national parks, occupying 7,400 sq km (about 2,900 sq mi), or about half of the country's total protected area.

Important environmental legislation was enacted in the 1970s and 1980s. In the 1990s Finnish environmental law was adapted to the requirements of European Union regulations, and a policy statement on the environment was added to the constitution. The Nature Conservation Act of 1996 focused efforts on preserving natural diversity through the protection of varied habitats and native species.

The Ministry of the Environment has jurisdiction over the regulation and protection of the environment. Other agencies playing a role in Finnish environmental policy include the Ministry of Agriculture and Forestry, the Finnish Forest and Park Service, the Finnish Environment Institute (a research center), and several regional environment centers.

The chief concerns faced by Finnish environmentalists in recent years include air pollution from industrial emissions, acid rain produced by power plant emissions, pollution of water by industrial wastes and agricultural chemicals, and the threat posed to wildlife by the loss of habitats. The 1995–99 environmental program for Finnish agriculture placed limits on the use of fertilizers to help reduce the leaching of phosphorus and nitrogen from farms into waterways. Chemical pesticides have also been the target of restrictions.

Environment

Forest Area sq km: 200,000
Average Annual Deforestation sq km: 166
Nationally Protected Areas as % of Total Land Area: 60
Freshwater Access cubic meters per capita: 21,347
Emissions of Organic Water Pollutants kg per day: 92,275
CO_2 Emissions per capita ton: 11.5

CHRONOLOGY

1946 Marshall Carl Gustav von Mannerheim retires as president; Prime Minister Julio Paasikivi is named president, and Mauno Pekkala becomes prime minister.
1948 Agreement of Friendship, Cooperation, and Mutual Assistance is signed with the Soviet Union; Finland cedes part of eastern Karelia to Soviet Union and agrees to pay war reparations. Karl Fagerholm forms first Social Democratic ministry.
1950 Urho Kekkonen heads Agrarian League government.
1953 Sakari Tuomioja heads no-party government.
1954 Ralf Törngren of Swedish People's Party heads brief government, followed by Urho Kekkonen, who becomes prime minister for the second time.

1955 Finland joins the United Nations and the Nordic Council.
1956 Karl Faggerholm heads his second government; Urho Kekkonen is president.
1957 Vaino Sukselainen heads the government, followed by Rainer von Fieandt.
1958 Raino Kuuskoski forms a no-party government but yields to Karl Fagerholm's third government.
1959 Vaino Sukselainen forms his second government.
1961 Martti Miettunen forms his first government. Finland joins the European Free Trade Association.
1962 Ahti Karjalainen forms his first government.
1963 Reino Lehto forms a no-party government.
1964 Johannes Virolainen forms a Center Party government.
1966 Rafael Paasio heads a Finnish Social Democratic government.
1968 Mauno Koivisto heads a Finnish Social Democratic government.
1970 Teuvo Aura heads a brief no-party government but is replaced by Ahti Karjalainen's second government.
1971 Teuvo Aura heads his second no-party government.
1972 Rafael Paasio heads a brief Social Democratic government but yeilds to Kalevi Sorsa of the same party.
1975 Keijo Liinamaa heads a brief government but is replaced by Martti Miettunen's second government. Finland hosts the Conference on Security and Cooperation in Europe.
1977 Kalevi Sorsa heads his second government.
1979 Mauno Koivisto heads his second government.
1981 Urho Kekkonen dies. Mauno Koivisto is elected president.
1982 Kalevi Sorsa heads his third government. Manno Koivisto becomes president.
1987 Finland's first conservative-led government takes office under Harri Holkeri as prime minister.
1991 Esko Aho of the Center Party forms a center-right coalition government.
1994 Martti Ahtisaari is elected president.
1995 Finland becomes a member of the European Union. Social Democrat Paavo Lipponen forms a coalition government.
1999 Paavo Lipponen forms his second coalition government.
2000 Social Democratic Party–member Tarja Halonen becomes Finland's first female president.
2002 The euro replaces the local markka.

BIBLIOGRAPHY

Alho, Olli, ed. *Finland: A Cultural Encyclopedia*. Helsinki, 1997.

Jakobson, Max. *Finland in the New Europe*. Westport, Conn., 1998.

Jussila, Osmo, Seppo Hentila, and Jukka Nevakivi. Translated by Eva-Kaisa Arter. *From Grand Duchy to a Modern State: A Political History of Finland since 1809*. Carbondale, Ill., 2000.

Keränen, Marja, editor. *Gender and Politics in Finland*. Aldershot, England, 1992.

Schoolfield, George C., ed. *A History of Finland's Literature*. Lincoln, Neb., 1998.

Schoolfield, George C. *Helsinki of the Czars: Finland's Capital: 1808–1918*. Columbia, S.C., 1996.

Singleton, Fred, and Anthony F. Upton. *A Short History of Finland*. Cambridge, 1998.

Sreen, J. E. O., compiler. *Finland*. World Bibliographical Series, vol. 31. Oxford, 1997.

Tiilikainen, Teija. *Europe and Finland: Defining the Political Identity of Finland in Western Europe*. Aldershot, England, 1998.

OFFICIAL PUBLICATIONS

Finland. *Annual Statistics of Agriculture; Economic Survey* (annual); *Population Census 1990; Statistical Yearbook of Finland.*

CONTACT INFORMATION

Embassy of Finland
3301 Massachusetts Avenue NW
Washington, D.C. 20008
Phone: (202) 298-5800 Fax: (202) 298-6030

INTERNET RESOURCES

- Embassy of Finland (Washington, D.C.) http://www.finland.org/facts.html
- Statistics Finland http://www.stat.fi/index_en.html

FRANCE

BASIC FACT SHEET

OFFICIAL NAME:
French Republic (République Française)

ABBREVIATION:
FR

CAPITAL:
Paris

HEAD OF STATE:
President Jacques Chirac (from 1995)

HEAD OF GOVERNMENT:
Interim Prime Minister Jean-Pierre Raffarin (from 2002)

NATURE OF GOVERNMENT:
Parliamentary democracy

POPULATION:
59,087,000 (1999)

AREA:
549,183 sq km (212,040 sq mi)

MAJOR ETHNIC GROUPS:
Celtic and Latin

LANGUAGE:
French

RELIGION:
Roman Catholicism

UNIT OF CURRENCY:
Euro

NATIONAL FLAG:
Tricolor of blue, white, and red vertical stripes

NATIONAL EMBLEM:
France does not have an official coat of arms. The unofficial emblem consists of a dark blue oval disk displaying the golden-bound rods and axe of the Roman fasces. Golden oak and olive branches surround the figure. A gold brand with blue letters carries the national motto, *Liberté, Égalité, Fraternité*. Framing the design is the massive gold collar of the Legion of Honor, with the blue, gold, and white grand cross of the order suspended below.

NATIONAL ANTHEM:
"La Marseillaise"

NATIONAL HOLIDAYS:
Bastille Day (July 14); World War II Armistice Day (May 8); World War I Armistice Day (November 11); New Year's Day; Labor Day; all major Christian festivals

DATE OF INDEPENDENCE:
August 843

DATE OF CONSTITUTION:
October 4, 1958

GEOGRAPHICAL FEATURES

France is the largest country in Western Europe, with an area (including the island of Corsica) of 549,183 sq km (212,040 sq mi). It extends 962 km (598 mi) north to south and 950 km (560 mi) east to west. Its total boundary length of 7,660 km (4,759 mi) is shared with seven countries: Belgium, Luxembourg, Germany, Switzerland, Italy, Andorra, and Spain. France's maritime boundaries lie along the Mediterranean Sea (1,700 km; 1,056 mi); the Bay of Biscay and the Atlantic Ocean, including islands (1,800 km; 1,118 mi); and the North Sea and English Channel (1,220 km; 758 mi).

The capital is Paris, on both banks of the Seine River shortly below its junction with the Marne River. It is the largest city in France and the third-largest city in Europe. Paris is not only the administrative and political capital but also the country's intellectual and artistic center.

Shaped in the form of a hexagon, France is distinguished topographically by clear-cut features and divisions. The present landscape is dominated by four Hercynian massifs, composed of granite, sandstone, or

France

North Sea
NETHERLANDS
ENGLAND
GERMANY
Strait of Dover
Dunkerque
Calais
Lille
BELGIUM
English Channel
Dieppe
Amiens
Somme R.
LUXEMBOURG
Cherbourg
Le Havre
Rouen
Beauvais
Reims
Verdun
Metz
St. Lo
Caen
Seine R.
Chalons-sur-Marne
Paris
Versailles
Granville
St. Malo
Nancy
Brest
Marne R.
Strasbourg
St. Briouc
Troyes
Rhine R.
Rennes
Le Mans
Lorient
Orleans
Mulhouse
Vannes
Auxerre
Saone R.
Angers
St. Nazaire
Nantes
Tours
Dijon
Besancon
Loire R.
Vierzon
Bourges
SWITZERLAND
Poitiers
Montlucon
Niort
Vichy
La Rochelle
Annecy
Limoges
Clermont Ferrand
Lyon
Bay of Biscay
Chambery
St. Etienne
ALPS
ITALY
Grenoble
Bordeaux
Romans-sur-Isere
Garonne R.
Rhone R.
MONACO
Nimes
Gulf of Gascogne
Aix-en-Provence
Nice
Bayonne
Toulouse
Montpellier
Cannes
Marseille
Beziers
Pau
Tarbes
Toulon
Gulf of Lion
Lourdes
Carcassonne
PYRENEES
Perpignan
ANDORRA
Bastia
N
SPAIN
Corsica
Ajaccio
Mediterranean Sea
0
100 Miles
0
100 Kms

shale. Between the massifs lie undulating floors of sedimentary formation linked to each other by a series of lowland corridors. Beyond these, to the southeast and southwest, rise the high walls of mountain ranges—the Jura, the Alps, and the Pyrenees—that form the frontiers of France.

Of the Hercynian massifs, the first, the Ardennes Plateau, occupying 1,295 sq km (500 sq mi), is the western tip of a block that is part of the Middle Rhine uplands of Germany and has an elevation of 456 m (1,500 ft). The Vosges, in the south, rises to rounded granite summits more than 1,219 m (4,000 ft) high. The Ardennes and the Vosges enclose the Paris Basin on its eastern side, separating it from the Alsace Plain. The Armorican Massif, which protects the Paris Basin to the west, covers 64,767 sq km (25,000 sq mi) and thrusts out into the Atlantic in two rocky promontories, Brittany and the Cotentin Peninsula. Its hills run east to west in a series of ridges that seldom exceed 366 m (1,200 ft). Finally, there is the Central Massif that covers 77,720 sq km (30,000 sq mi) and whose summit rises to 1,524 m (5,000 ft) or more.

The Pyrenees, whose uplift occurred before that of the Alps, form a barrier that rises more than 3,034 m (10,000 ft) and more or less seals off the border with Spain. From their foothills stretches eastward to the Alps the southern fringe of France—the coastal plain between the Central Massif and the sea. The plains are broken by chains of low hills.

The French Alps represent only a small area of the mountain chain; nonetheless, they occupy 38,860 sq km (15,000 sq mi) of French territory and include the highest peak in Europe, Mont Blanc (4,810 m; 15,782 ft). The Jura Mountains rise to 1,524 m (5,000 ft) along the border, completing the line of natural fortification.

The drainage system of France is based on five major rivers: the Seine, Loire, Garonne, Rhône, and Rhine. The Nord is the terminal point of the lowlands bordering the English Channel, including coastal Flanders and the Walloon areas. The Paris Basin is the cradle of France. At the center of the basin lies Paris, the heart of French culture and history. The basin includes the Île-de-France, parts of Orleans, Upper Normandy, and Picardy. The east region comprises Lorraine, the Vosges Mountains, and Alsace, including the French Rhineland. Burgundy and the Upper Rhine encompass the corridor between Alsace and central France. A series of ridges project north and northeast from the Central Massif, increasing in elevation toward the south and reaching more than 914 m (3,000 ft) in the star-shaped cluster of the mountains of Beaujolais. South of Dijon is the Alps region with its Mediterranean influences. The area is enclosed on the east by the Alps, which are represented by the massifs of Belledone and Pelvoux, the latter rising to over 3,657 m (12,000 ft).

The Mediterranean region lies on the border with Spain and Italy and consists of Languedoc and Provence. Marseilles and Toulon provide gateways to the Mediterranean and the island of Corsica exhibits the same features as Provence although separated by 161 km (100 mi) of water. The island rises 1,676 m (5,500 ft) and possesses a coastal strip only on its eastern side. Languedoc, on the western bank of the Rhône, is rocky and mountainous. Aquitaine covers the basins of the Garonne and the Adour. The center is occupied by the wide Garonne Plain and the region is bordered on the west by the Bay of Biscay. The Central Massif is a triangular area from which many of the nations' rivers flow. Although called central, it is situated almost entirely in the southern half of the country, and its outer edge is less than 80 km (50 mi) from the Mediterranean. While the massif divides northern and southern France, the Loire Valley and the Atlantic region reunite them. This area makes up the central section of the Atlantic seaboard between the Loire and the Gironde. Amorica comprises Brittany and Lower Normandy. Eastern Lower Normandy is geologically part of the Paris Basin, but southwest of Caen the region is hilly and therefore known as the "Norman Switzerland." Extending far out into the English Channel is the Cotentin Peninsula, at the tip of which lies Cherbourg. To the south of Normandy is Celtic Brittany, stronghold of the Bretons. Brittany remains one of the few provinces of France where the rural areas are still overpopulated.

Geography

Area sq km: 549,183 sq mi 212,040
World Rank: 49th
Land Boundaries, km: Andorra 60; Belgium 620; Germany 451; Italy 488; Luxembourg 73; Monaco 4.4; Spain 623; Switzerland 573
Coastline, km: 3,427
Elevation Extremes meters
- Lowest: Rhone River Delta –2
- Highest: Mont Blanc 4,807

Land Use % Arable land: 33
- Permanent Crops: 2
- Permanent Pastures: 20
- Forest and Woodland: 27
- Other: 18

Population of Principal Cities (1990)

Aix-en-Provence	126,854
Amiens	136,234
Angers	146,163
Besancon	119,194
Bordeaux	213,274
Boulogne-Billancourt	101,971
Brest	153,099
Caen	115,624
Clermont-Ferrand	140,167
Dijon	151,636
Grenoble	153,973
Le Havre	197,219
Le Mans	148,465
Lille	178,301
Limoges	136,407

(continued)

Lyon	422,444
Marseille	807,726
Metz	123,920
Montpellier	210,866
Mulhouse	109,905
Nancy	102,410
Nantes	252,029
Nice	345,674
Nimes	133,607
Orléans	107,965
Paris	2,175,200
Perpignan	108,049
Reims	185,164
Rennes	203,533
Rouen	105,470
Saint-Étienne	201,569
Strasbourg	255,937
Toulon	170,167
Toulouse	365,933
Tours	133,403
Villeurbanne	119,848

CLIMATE AND WEATHER

The three main divisions of European climate,—maritime, continental, and Mediterranean—are all found in France. The Atlantic influence brings the country the benefits of the warm waters of the North Atlantic drift. The seasons are marked by mild onsets, frequent fine rain or drizzle, and westerly winds. The continental climate covers eastern France. Its features are a wide seasonal range of temperatures, with cold winters; 80 to 100 days of frost; long periods of snow cover; warm summers with thundershowers; and calm autumns. The Mediterranean influence extends only a short distance northward from the coast. It is characterized by absence of clouds; high evaporation rates; infrequent, but heavy, rains between seasons; and strong winds of which the cold Mistral blowing in from the north is best known.

France receives an average of 450 billion cu m (15,891 trillion cu ft) of precipitation every year as either rain or snow. Coastal areas receive the most in autumn and winter, while inland areas receive the maximum amounts in summer and autumn. The amount of snowfall varies with elevation. The amount of snowfall may rise as high as 47 m (154 ft) on the summit of Mont Blanc.

In the summer southern France's temperature will average 21°C (70°F) and the north's 18°C (65°F). In winter, the extreme southern regions average temperature is 6°C (42°F), but the rest of the nation has temperatures close to freezing.

Climate and Weather

Mean Temperature
Paris 50°F
Nice 57°F
Average Rainfall
Paris and Marseille 22 in
Bordeaux and Lyon 35 in
Brittany and the northern coast 44 in

POPULATION

Population Indicators

Total Population: 1999 59,087,000
World Rank: 21st
Density per sq mi: 281.3 per sq km 108.6
% of annual growth (1994–99): 0.4
Male %: 48.7
Female %: 51.3
Urban %: 74.0
Age Distribution: % 0–14: 19.1
15–29: 22.6
30–44: 22.8
45–59: 15.6
60–74: 12.8
75 and over: 7.1
Population 2020: 58,908,000
Birth Rate per 1,000: 12.6
Death Rate per 1,000: 9.2
Population Doubling Time (years): —
Infant Mortality Rate per 1,000 live births: 4.9
Rate of Natural Increase per 1,000: 3.4
Total Fertility Rate: 1.7
Expectation of Life (years): Males 73.7
Females 81.8
Marriage Rate per 1,000: 4.8
Divorce Rate per 1,000: 1.9
Total Number of Households: 20,899,000
Average Size of Households: 2.6
% of Illegitimate Children: 36.1
Induced Abortions: 162,902
Rate per 100 live births: 21.5

ETHNIC COMPOSITION

Until France acquired a sizable minority community in the 20th century, it was an ethnically homogeneous country with all of its inhabitants of Celtic and Roman stock.

Recent estimates put the number of foreigners living and working in France at about 5 million, or about 9 percent of the population. Of these 1.6 million, have become naturalized French citizens. As part of its perceived imperial obligations, France opened its doors to migration from its colonial and former colonial possessions. The largest numbers came from Algeria, Morocco, Tunisia, French Indochina, and France's West African colonies. In addition, labor shortages in the 1950s and 1960s led the nation to encourage non-European immigration. By the 1970s, efforts were initiated to stem the flow of immigrants. Successive laws were passed to tighten immigration. The major minority groups in France include the Basques, Arab North Africans, West Africans, and Indochinese. The increase in the number of non-European aliens has led to anti-immigrant sentiment and the rise of right-wing, anti-immigrant parties, as well as ethnic violence in some urban areas.

LANGUAGES

French is the official and national language spoken by virtually everyone within French borders. It is also an official language in Francophone Africa and in French dependencies and territories overseas. While it has lost its preeminence in international diplomacy since World War II, it remains a popular third language. There are a number of regional dialects within the nation that are rapidly disappearing. These include Provençal, Breton, Alsatian, Corsican, Catalan, Basque, and Flemish. The influx of English words into the French language has led to a hybrid dialect known as Franglais. This has become a major concern for Francophiles and efforts have been taken to discourage the use of Franglais and promote the French language.

Principal Languages and Their Speakers

Arabic	1,500,000
English	90,000
French	55,330,000
Basque	80,000
Breton	500,000
Catalan (Rousillonais)	260,000
Corsican	260,000
Dutch (Flemish)	90,000
German (Alsatian)	1,510,000
Occitan	920,000
Italian	260,000
Polish	50,000
Portuguese	680,000
Spanish	230,000
Turkish	210,000
Other	750,000

RELIGIONS

France was Christianized by the second century and a strong Christian community had been established in Lyons by 150. The mass baptism of the Frankish king Clovis with his warriors in 496 established the Christian faith as the national creed. The Roman Catholic Church dominated society throughout the Middle Ages, and France was part of the schism that resulted in two rival popes, at Avignon and Rome. France was less affected by the Reformation than many other nations of Europe, but the movement led to the establishment of some 2,000 Protestant Huguenot churches. Religious conflict was widespread until the Edict of Nantes granted some degree of religious freedom in 1598. The revocation of the edict by Louis XIV in 1685 led to a new wave of persecution and the exile of thousands of non-Catholics. Protestants remained a persecuted minority until the French Revolution. Church-state relations were not resolved until the constitution of 1905, which reaffirmed the secular nature of the government. The principal of secularity is not absolute and the government has some control over the appointment of clergy. Also, all clergy are considered civil servants and receive their pay from the state.

Roman Catholics still make up some 90 percent of the population, although their number has been in decline since World War II. Protestants make up some 2 percent of the population and Jews 1 percent. Most Protestants live in Alsace and the Rhône Valley and are members of the Lutheran Church. Although it makes up only about 2 percent of the religious population, Islam is the fastest growing religion in France, thanks to the recent waves of immigrants from North Africa. This has led to conflict over the wearing of religious garb in public and especially in the otherwise secular school systems.

Religious Affiliations

Roman Catholic	45,040,000
Nonreligious	6,290,000
Muslim	3,250,000
Atheist	2,010,000
Protestant	1,090,000
Jewish	610,00
Other	800,000

HISTORICAL BACKGROUND

Little is known of the present territory of France before its conquest by Julius Caesar in 58–51 B.C. The land was inhabited by a Celtic tribe known as the Gauls. Roman rule lasted for five centuries. Roads and cities were built and Latin superceded the Celtic language. Early in the fifth century, Teutonic invaders, including the Visigoths, the Burgundians, and the Franks, conquered regions of Gaul.

The first ruler who took upon himself the title of King of the Franks was Clovis, who in 486 routed the forces of the last Roman governors and established an empire that extended into western Germany. A century of warfare and anarchy followed his death and was brought to an end by Charles Martel, who defeated the Saracens at Tours in 732 and prevented an Islamic invasion of Western Europe, and Charlemange (768–814), who was crowned emperor of the West by the pope in 800. After his death, Charlemagne's Carolingian Empire broke apart. However, his brother's grandson Hugh Capet (987–96) established the royal line that would rule France for the next 800 years.

By the ninth century, feudalism was well-established in France and the Capetians had only nominal hegemony over their territories. Some areas, such as the Duchy of Brittany, were practically independent kingdoms. For several centuries, the kings of France would have to fight to retain power over these feudal holdings, as well as battle the English. By the 12th century, the English controlled Normandy, Brittany, Anjou, and Aquitaine. However, as the power of the French kings expanded, that of the feudal lords and the English waned. The reign of Philip the Fair marked the apogee of the early Capetian power. His emissaries arrested Pope Boniface VIII and removed the seat of the papacy to Avignon, where the popes resided until 1378.

Philip the Fair had no heirs and the throne passed to his nephew, Philip VI, who became the first of the Valois kings. Philip's claim to the throne was challenged by Edward III of England and resulted in the Hundred Years War (1337 to 1453). Although the English won most of the early battles, led by Joan of Arc and Bertrand Du Guesclin the French were able to ultimately defeat them during the reign of Charles VII, and by his death in 1461, the English had been driven from most of France.

Following the expulsion of the English, the French kings were able to consolidate their power and subjugate the feudal lords. Meanwhile, the rise of Protestantism led to a new civil conflict between the Protestant, or Huguenot, groups and the established Catholics. In 1572, thousands of Protestants were slaughtered in the Saint Bartholomew's Day Massacre. However, following the death of Henry III, the Protestant Henry of Navarre ascended the throne as the first ruler of the House of Bourbon. Although he converted to Catholicism in order to consolidate his power, in 1598, he signed the Edict of Nantes, which guaranteed religious freedom for Huguenots. Henry restored peace and stability and embarked upon a course of geographical exploration in the New World.

His successor, Louis XIII, demolished the power of the Protestants at home and the Habsburgs abroad through the Thirty Years' War. He was succeeded by his son Louis XIV who established France as the dominant power on the Continent. Louis reigned for 54 years and transformed France into a centralized absolute monarchy. Known as the Sun King, Louis built the great palace at Versailles and his reign was the golden age of French culture. The French Enlightenment produced such luminaries as Voltaire, Jean-Jacques Rousseau, and Diderot, but it also produced a class that questioned the absolutism of the monarchy.

The signal for the fall of the ancien régime was the summoning of the Estates General in 1789 by Louis XVI in an effort to impose new taxes in order to restore the treasury. Meeting separately, the third estate, the Commons, proclaimed itself the National Assembly and overcame royal opposition. This initiated the French Revolution. In 1791, the National Assembly forced Louis to accept a new constitution. Austria declared war on France in an effort to restore the monarchy and in response the First French Republic was declared. Louis was tried and executed for treason. France then underwent the "Reign of Terror" as radicals, known as Jacobins, sought to eradicate all vestiges of the aristocracy. Although the revolution was launched with the goals of liberty and equality, France soon reverted to totalitarianism.

In 1799, Napoleon Bonaparte established a consulate with himself as first consul. After a series of military victories, Napoleon had himself crowned emperor in 1804. Although he was able to conquer most of Europe, with the notable exception of Great Britain, the emperor's ill-fated invasion of Russia and insurgencies in Spain and Portugal led to his downfall. By 1814, the Allied powers had conquered Paris and restored the Bourbon monarchy. Napoleon was forced into exile, only to return in an attempt to reclaim the throne. Allied forces under the Duke of Wellington defeated Napoleon at the Battle of Waterloo in 1815, and the former emperor was forced into exile on the island of St. Helena.

From 1815 until 1848, France was ruled by three kings, the last of whom was Louis-Philippe of the House of Orleans who attempted to rule as a citizen-king. After the fall of Louis-Philippe, the Second Republic was established with Louis Napoleon, nephew of Napoleon I, as its president. Louis engineered a coup in 1852 and proclaimed himself Napoleon III. His reign was known as the Second Empire (1852–1871). He embarked on an aggressive foreign policy that led to conflict with Prussia and his ultimate defeat in the Franco-Prussian War (1870–71). As a result of the war, France lost Alsace and Lorraine and Napoleon III was overthrown. A new government, the Third Republic, was established.

The republic's constitution, adopted in 1875, granted freedoms of press, speech, and religion, and established a weak presidency and a strong national legislature. Much of World War I (1914–18) was fought on French soil, and although the nation was devastated by the conflict, it was able to regain Alsace and Lorraine. The postwar years were marked by economic depression, political instability, and social unrest. France was unable to counter German aggression following the rise of Adolf Hitler, and when the German dictator invaded Poland in 1939, France joined with Great Britain in declaring war.

At the onset of the war, French military strategy relied on the supposedly impregnable Maginot Line of fortresses between France and Germany. However, the German army was able to easily defeat French forces and Marshall Philippe Petain, an aged hero of World War I, hastily formed a government and sued for peace. With the exception of a small zone near Vichy, France was placed under German control and the Third Republic ended. Opposition to the Germans coalesced around the underground resistence within France and the Free French Forces of General Charles de Gaulle. In the wake of the liberation of Paris in 1944, de Gaulle formed a provisional government. In 1946 the Fourth Republic was proclaimed under a new constitution, which unfortunately reproduced most of the weaknesses of the Third Republic.

In 1953, de Gaulle retired from public life as the nation struggled through a series of weak and rapidly changing governments. A year later France was defeated at the Battle of Dien Bien Phu, and was forced to withdraw from its colonies in Indochina.

France was one of the forces behind the drive for economic and political integration in Europe and in 1957 was one of the founding members of the European Economic Community, which in 1965 became the European Community. However, disagreements with the United States led to the withdrawal of France from NATO's integrated command structure in 1966.

In response to a military insurrection in Algeria in 1958, de Gaulle was invited to form a government. He proposed a new constitution, which, after its adoption, established the Fifth Republic. Algeria was granted independence in 1962. As president, de Gaulle endeavored to maintain the status of France as a great power in an era of declining national resources. In 1968, there were widespread student protests, but de Gaulle was reelected president. However, the following year, he resigned after voters rejected his proposed constitutional amendments. He was replaced by Georges Pompidou. De Gaulle died in 1970.

After Pompidou died in office in 1974, he was replaced by Valéry Giscard d'Estaing, who served until 1981. The election of François Mitterrand marked the end of two decades of rule by the conservative Gaullist parties. Mitterrand's tenure as president was marked by severe economic crises, and by deepening integration into the European Union. In 1985, French special forces sank the Greenpeace ship *The Rainbow Warrior* in Auckland, New Zealand, creating a diplomatic crisis. After his reelection in 1988, Mitterrand presided over the nation as it faced the reunification of Germany and fought alongside the United States and Great Britain in the Persian Gulf War.

The election of Jacques Chirac in 1995 returned the Gaullists to power. Chirac adopted a much more conciliatory approach toward the United States. He also continued on the path of integration, and, in 1999, France was one of the first nations to join the European Monetary Union (EMU). Chirac was reelected in May 2002 in a landslide victory against far-right National Front leader Jean-Marie Le Pen.

CONSTITUTION

The Fifth Republic is governed by the constitution passed on September 28, 1958. It replaced the constitution of the Fourth Republic under which France had notoriously unstable governments. The new constitution was very much the work of one man, Charles de Gaulle, and one event, the Algerian crisis. The constitution replaces the old weak central government with a strong executive, which suited De Gaulle's style. It encompasses the concept of stewardship by which the president does not hold authority strictly as the servant of the people, because his power embodies the historical fact of French statehood, the grandeur of the nation, and the totality of its existence. Hence, the president must be sufficiently removed from politics to make decisions that are in the best interests of the nation, but which may run counter to public opinion. The constitution of the Fifth Republic is unique in French history in both the power it delegates to the executive and the power it retracts from the legislature. Under its terms, the president can dismiss parliament, call for early elections, and issue decrees that carry the weight of law.

Under the constitution, the president is head of state, commander in chief of the military, and presiding officer of the Council of Ministers. The French president's power is broadly divided into three sectors: a "reserved" sector involving foreign affairs and security matters in which the head of state is directly involved; a "delegated" area in which technical matters are assigned to bureaucrats; and a "supervisory" part in which the president intervenes only when necessary.

Presidents are elected through either an absolute majority on the first ballot, or, failing that, a second runoff ballot cast 14 days later in which only a simple majority is needed. In the runoff election, only the top two candidates from the first election may run. There is no limit to the number of seven-year terms a president may serve.

The office of the prime minister has been described alternatively as that of a power broker, a vice president, and a chief of staff. The position has five major tasks: 1) to initiate policy; 2) to coordinate the government's activities; 3) to provide a liaison between the government and the legislature; 4) to maintain a governing coalition or party; and 5) to resolve conflicts between the government and the legislature. Normally the president and prime minister have a close working relationship, but matters become strained when the two figures are from different political parties, a situation known as "cohabitation."

Although responsible to the legislature, the government is not a part of it. When a government is chosen, its members must resign from the legislature if they are members. However, the government does have supremacy over the conduct of legislative business. For instance, if the two houses of the parliament are unable to agree on an act, the government may intervene to secure a compromise.

Two other bodies play a monitory role in the Fifth Republic: the Council of State and the Constitutional Council. The Council of State is a remnant of the prerevolutionary Conseil du Roi. Although it is not mentioned in the constitution, it has an administrative function to advise the

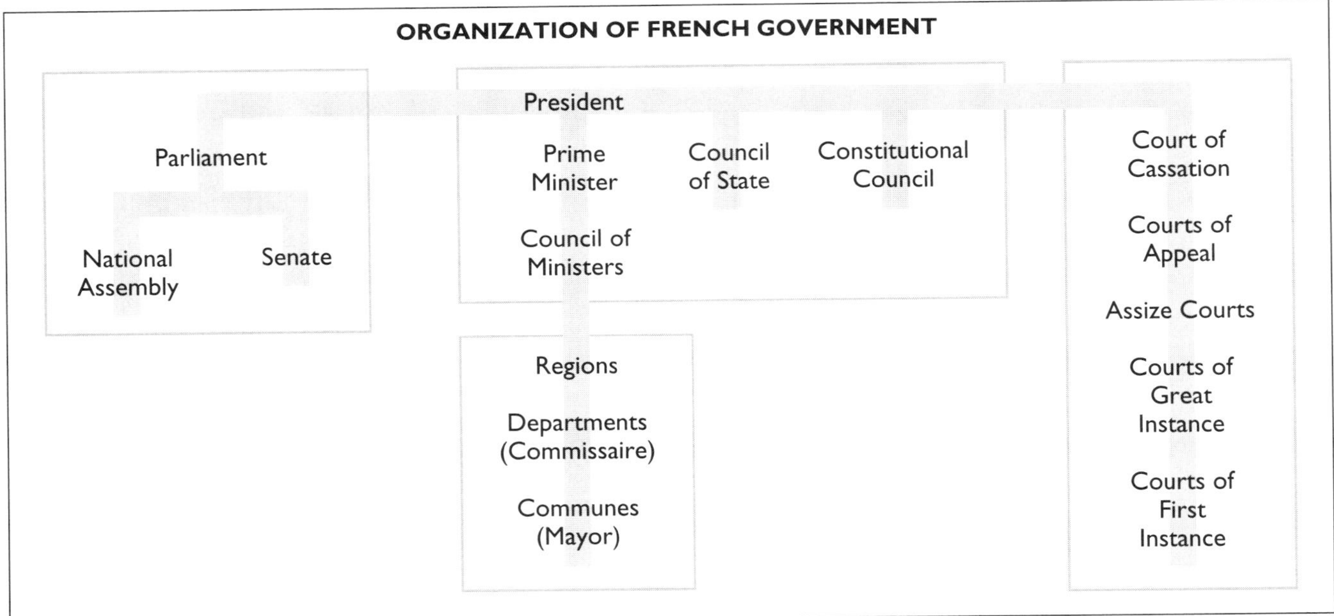

government on all legislation, and it provides constitutional interpretations. The Constitutional Council advises the president, cabinet, and legislature on matters of law. This council further supervises elections.

LOCAL GOVERNMENT

With 36,034 communes, France has more units of local government than any of the other members of the European Union, but only 2 percent of these communes have a population of over 2,000, while 90 percent have fewer than 10,000. These territorial divisions do not reflect demographic or economic realities, but rather traditional boundaries.

The lowest level of local government is the commune, dating from 1789 and based on the parish system of the old regime. At the next level are 96 departments. Above the departments are 22 regions. Successive governments have tried to limit and reduce the number of governments, but to no avail.

National power over the localities is exercised by the Ministry of the Interior and the Council of State. Local governments are funded by a complex and intricate system of finance by which localities receive loans and subsidies and aid for particular joint projects, such as urban integration, from Paris.

In local politics, the mayor has substantial power, and the municipal council is weak and has limited powers. This trend is reinforced by the fact that many mayors also hold national positions in parliament or government. Municipalities with populations over 100,000 enjoy a special privileged status and have more autonomy than smaller communities. They have greater control over issues of finance, planning, and zoning.

Local Government

Principal administrative divisions, capitals, area, population

AREA AND POPULATION

Regions / Departments	Capitals	area sq mi	area sq km	population 1997 estimate
Alsace				
Bas-Rhin	Strasbourg	1,836	4,755	1,005,650
Haut-Rhin	Colmar	1,361	3,525	702,428
Aquitaine				
Dordogne	Périgueux	3,498	9,060	389,173
Gironde	Bordeaux	3,861	10,000	1,276,969
Landes	Mont-de-Marsan	3,569	9,243	319,940
Lot-et-Garonne	Agen	2,070	5,361	303,132
Pyrénées-Atlantiques	Pau	2,952	7,645	595,327
Auvergne				
Allier	Moulins	2,834	7,340	350,490
Cantal	Aurillac	2,211	5,726	154,108
Haute-Loire	Le Puy	1,922	4,977	207,165
Puy-de-Dome	Clermont-Ferrand	3,077	7,970	603,102
Basse-Normandie				
Calvados	Caen	2,142	5,548	639,571
Manche	Saint-Lô	2,293	5,938	485,348
Orne	Alençon	2,356	6,103	293,822
Bourgogne				
Côte-d'Or	Dijon	3,383	8,763	510,841
Nièvre	Nevers	2,632	6,817	229,195
Saône-et-Loire	Mâcon	3,311	8,575	551,460
Yonne	Auxerre	2,868	7,427	333,373

Bretagne				
Côtes-du-Nord	Saint-Brieuc	2,656	6,878	537,332
Finistère	Quimper	2,600	6,733	845,283
Ille-et-Vilaine	Rennes	2,616	6,775	849,682
Morbihan	Vannes	2,634	6,823	637,772
Centre				
Cher	Bourges	2,793	7,235	320,309
Eure-et-Loir	Chartres	2,270	5,880	413,218
Indre	Châteauroux	2,622	6,791	233,445
Indre-et-Loir	Tours	2,366	6,127	550,494
Loir-et-Cher	Blois	2,449	6,343	314,158
Loiret	Orléans	2,616	6,775	616,587
Champagne-Ardenne				
Ardennes	Charleville-Mézières	2,019	5229	290,868
Aube	Troyes	2,318	6,004	293,283
Haute-Marne	Chaumont	2,398	6,211	198,736
Corse				
Corse-du-Sud	Ajaccio	1,550	4,014	124,970
Haute-Corse	Bastia	1,802	4,666	135,814
Franche-Comté				
Doubs	Besançon	2,021	5,234	496,200
Haute-Saône	Vesoul	2,070	5,360	229,812
Jura	Lons-le-Saunier	1,930	4,999	252,845
Territoire de Belfort	Belfort	235	609	137,667
Haute-Normandie				
Eure	Évreux	2,332	6,040	540,854
Seine-Maritime	Rouen	2,424	6,278	1,242,167
Ile-de-France				
Essone	Évry	696	1,804	1,155,425
Hauts-de-Seine	Nanterre	68	176	1,411,595
Paris	Paris	40	105	2,125,350
Seine-et-Marne	Melun	2,284	5,915	1,199,548
Seine-Saint-Denis	Bobigny	91	236	1,407,628
Val-de-Marne	Créteil	59	245	1,240,197
Val-d'Oise	Pontoise	481	1,246	1,120,756
Yvelines	Versailles	882	2,284	1,380,943
Languedoc-Rousillon				
Aude	Carcassone	2,370	6,139	307,566
Gard	Nîmes	2,260	5,853	613,798
Hérault	Montpellier	2,356	6,101	879,577
Lozère	Mende	1,995	5,167	73,046
Pyrénées-Orientales	Perpignan	1,589	4,116	381,650
Limousin				
Corrèze	Tulle	2,261	5,857	235,410
Creuse	Guéret	2,149	5,565	125,915
Haute-Vienne	Limoges	2,131	5,520	355,893
Lorraine				
Meurthe-et-Moselle	Nancy	2,024	5,241	715,377
Meuse	Bar-le-Duc	2,400	6,216	193,394
Moselle	Metz	2,400	6,216	1,017,597
Vosges	Épinal	2,268	5,874	385,158
Midi-Pyrénées				
Ariège	Foix	1,888	4,890	136,633
Aveyron	Rodez	3,373	8,736	265,563
Gers	Auch	2,416	6,257	171,865
Haute-Garonne	Toulouse	2,436	6,309	1,010,442
Haute-Pyrénées	Tarbes	1,724	4,464	233,074
Lot	Cahors	2,014	5,217	157,375
Tarn	Albi	2,223	5,758	342,062
Tarn-et-Garonne	Montauban	1,435	3,718	205,721
Nord-Pas-de-Calais				
Nord	Lille	2,217	5,742	2,563,107
Pas-de-Calais	Arras	2,576	6,671	1,440,966
Pays de la Loire				
Loire-Atlantique	Nantes	2,631	6,815	1,100,686
Maine-et Loire	Angers	2,767	7,166	726,245
Mayenne	Laval	1,998	5,175	283,275
Sarthe	Le Mans	2,396	6,206	523,961
Vendee	La Roche-sur-Yon	2,595	6,720	530,505
Picardie				
Aisne	Laon	2,845	7,369	539,215
Oise	Beauvals	2,263	5,860	772,363
Somme	Amiens	2,382	6,170	554,406
Poitou-Charentes				
Charente	Angoulême	2,300	5,956	340,382
Charente-Maritime	La Rochelle	2,650	6,864	545,951
Deux-Sèvres	Niort	2,316	5,999	346,721
Vienne	Poitiers	2,699	6,990	393,354
Provence-Alpes-Côte d'Azur				
Alpes-de-Haute-Provence	Digne	2,674	6,925	140,792
Alpes-Maritimes	Nice	1,660	4,299	1,018,772
Bouches-du-Rhône	Marseille	1,964	5,087	1,806,207
Hautes-Alpes	Gap	2,142	5,549	120,940
Var	Toulon	2,306	5,973	885,042
Vaucluse	Avignon	1,377	3,567	494,920
Rhône-Alpes				
Ain	Bourg-en-Bresse	2,225	5,762	508,913
Ardèche	Privas	2,135	5,529	285,238
Drôme	Valence	2,521	6,530	429,906
Haute-Savoie	Annecy	1,694	4,388	630,156
Isère	Grenoble	2,869	7,431	1,080,127
Loire	Saint-Étienne	1,846	4,781	748,138
Rhône	Lyon	1,254	3,249	1,573,459
Savoie	Chambéry	2,327	6,028	371,264
TOTAL		210,026	543,965	58,374,853

PARLIAMENT

In the Fifth Republic, the parliament is a bicameral body made up of the Assemblée Nationale (National Assembly) and the Sénat (Senate). The Assembly consists of 577 seats, and the Senate 321. The National Assembly is the lower house, but maintains a slight edge in legislative power. If there is disagreement between the two houses and the disagreement persists for more than two formal readings, and if a joint committee convened to resolve the dispute fails, the National Assembly can rule definitively.

The constitution gives the parliament the power to force the government to resign and to declare war. The parliament also has sole legislative power. Members of either house also enjoy parliamentary immunity and legal action can only be taken after they have left office or if their immunity is stripped by the legislature.

Parliament meets for two short sessions during the year. The first begins on October 2, lasts 80 days, and is mainly concerned with budgetary matters. The second session begins on April 2 and is principally involved with legislation. Special sessions may be convened by the president, prime minister, or a majority of parliament.

On the opening of the October session, each chamber elects its *bureau*, which provides leadership for the session. In the National Assembly, the *bureau* consists of a president, six vice presidents, 12 secretaries, and three *questeurs*. In the Senate, there is a president, four vice-presidents, eight secretaries, and three *questeurs*. The presidents do not have the stature of their counterparts in the United States or Great Britain. The secretaries supervise records and tally votes, and the *questeurs* are responsible for financial and administrative matters. The *bureau* is responsible for the conduct of business, including quorum and discipline.

Bills may be introduced in either house, although finance bills must be submitted to the Assembly. All bills must go through the appropriate committees. There are six standing committees. Four are specialized committees consisting of a maximum of 61 members each, dealing with defense, foreign affairs, finance, law, and administration. The remaining two committees, consisting of a maximum of 121 members each, deal with economic affairs and cultural and social affairs.

Members of the National Assembly are elected for five-year terms with all seats being filled at the same time through direct majoritarian election. Senators are elected for nine-year terms and one-third of the body stands for re-election every three years. They are elected by local electoral colleges composed of mayors, municipal and departmental councillors, and deputies of the department. There are also 12 senators who represent French citizens living overseas and who are nominated by an official advisory committee.

POLITICAL PARTIES

The Greens, left-wing, environmental party (founded in 1984).
National Front (Front National, FN), right-wing, anti-immigrant party (founded in 1972).
Parti Communiste Français (French Communist Party, PCF), left-wing, communist party (founded in 1920).
Parti Radical (Radical Party), right-wing, conservative party.
Parti Républicain (Republican Party, PR), moderate conservative party.
Parti Socialiste Français (French Socialist Party, PSF), center-left party (founded in 1905).
Rassemblement pour la République (Rally for the French Republic, RPR), right-wing, orthodox Gaullist party (founded in 1976).
Union pour la Démocratie Français (Union for French Democracy, UDF), coalition of four centrist parties, allied with the Parti Radical.
There are also a number of minor and regional parties.

Political Parties

Socialist Party, 1905
French Communist Party, 1920
Left Radical Party, 1973
The Greens, 1984
Citizens' Movement, 1993
Rally for the Republic, 1976
Union for French Democracy, 1978, a coalition of right-wing parties
- Democratic Force, 1995
- Radical Party
- Popular Party for French Democracy, 1995

Liberal Democracy, 1977
National Front, 1972
Reformers' Movement, 1992
Ecology Generation, 1992
Red and Green Alternative, 1989
Workers' Struggle
The Right, 1998
National Center of Independents and Peasants
Movement for France, 1994
Federation for a New Solidarity, 1995
Bonapartist Party, 1993

Political Parties: Strength in Parliament Most Recent Elections

Senate (Sénat). The most recent elections were held on September 23, 2001. The distribution of seats from that balloting were as follows: Rally for the Republic, 83; Socialist Party, 68; Centrist Union, 37; Republicans and Independents, 35; Democratic and European Social Rally, 16; Communist, Republican and Citizen, 16; and unattached, 5.

National Assembly (Assemblée Nationale). The French Assembly presently consists of 577 deputies elected by two-round majority voting in single member districts for five-year terms (subject to dissolution). The most recent election, held on May 25 and June 1, 1997, resulted in a total of 319 seats for parties of the Left and 257 seats for parties of the Right, distributed as follows: Socialist Party, 241; Rally for the Republic, 134; Union for French Democracy, 108; French Communist Party, 38; other leftist, 21; other rightist, 14; Radical Socialist Party, 12; The Greens, 7; National Front, 1; independent 1. New elections take place in June 2002.

LEGAL SYSTEM

The distinctive characteristic of the French judicial system is its division into two jurisdictions: the civil and criminal, and the administrative. Civil cases are heard in 454 courts of first instance, or in cases of substantial sums, in courts of great instance, which also have an appellate function. Criminal law is dispensed in one of three sets of courts, depending on the gravity of the offense. Police courts function in almost all localities and deal with minor infractions. More serious matters are brought before correctional courts. Finally, major felonies and crimes are tried at periodic settings of the assize courts, which have three judges and nine jurors (the other courts do not utilize juries). French judges are career civil servants.

French law allows only one appeal in civil and criminal cases. In civil cases, the appeals go to one of 27 regional appeals courts. Criminal cases also go to an appeals court, but there is no effective appeal possible from an assize court. The highest court of the land is the Court of Cassation, which has one criminal and five civil chambers. The entire judiciary is overseen by the Superior Council of the Judiciary, which reports to the president and government.

The administrative court system is much simpler than the civil and criminal and involves those cases of abuse of official power or civil servants failing to perform their duties and therefore harming private interests. The highest administrative tribunal is the Council of State, which hears appeals from the administrative tribunals.

LAW ENFORCEMENT

Law Enforcement

Offenses reported to the police per 100,000: 6,733
- Murder: 4.7
- Assault: 98.8
- Burglary: 812.6
- Automobile Theft: 667.0
- Population per Police officer: 630

Death Penalty: Abolished 1981

HUMAN RIGHTS

Although France does not have a bill of rights, all political and civil liberties are secured by legal guarantees. Two institutions serve as watchdogs of these rights: the Constitutional Council and the Council of State. Both of these institutions investigate and condemn illegal administrative encroachments on individual freedom. Freedom from invasion of privacy is guaranteed by law and respected in practice. The search of a private residence requires a search warrant, except under special circumstances such as drug cases. There is no direct equivalent of habeas corpus in the French legal system although there is a limit of two days before a suspect is transferred to a magistrate for investigation.

The promotion of human rights is also a tenet of French foreign policy. There is a secretary of state for human rights to oversee policy in this regard. The major problem for French authorities in the realm of human rights has been terrorism. The government has granted the power to summarily expel foreigners suspected of terrorism without legal proceedings.

FOREIGN POLICY

De Gaulle established the main principles of French policy that continue to underlie French foreign policy. De Gaulle attempted to reassert France's position as a global power, all the while maintaining a high degree of autonomy. As a result, France developed and maintained independent military capabilities, including nuclear weapons. France refused to sign the nuclear test-ban and nonproliferation treaties, preferring to establish its own *force de frappe*. Paris also endeavored to utilize the institutional framework of the West to augment its rank in the world. France accepted the economic provisions of the Treaty of Rome, but resisted efforts at political integration on a supranational level and twice vetoed British entry into the European Community. Although a founding member of NATO, France withdrew its military forces from the alliance and refused use of its territory for Allied military actions. In economic, as well as military relations, de Gaulle assailed U.S. primacy and asserted French autonomy on issues such as recognition of China, U.S. involvement in Vietnam, and condemnation of Israel.

Although the basic premises of Gaullist foreign policy have never been formally repudiated, successive presidents have retreated from its more extreme positions. The anti-U.S. and anti-British tenor of French policy were reversed and France was brought into closer alignment with the Western alliance. In the process, French foreign policy has become less visionary and more pragmatic.

The election of the socialist president François Mitterrand in 1981 aroused great hopes of a break with the policies of the previous three presidents. However, Mitterrand continued the Gaullist tradition, but modified it to conform to changing global circumstances. Mitterrand reaffirmed his commitment to the established Gaullist line of autonomous national membership in the Atlantic alliance. He then went further than his predecessors and supported a buildup of NATO missiles in Europe. France also supported U.S. actions in other international areas. Mitterrand also managed to both open ties with Israel and restore Franco-Arab relations after the opening.

Within the EC Mitterrand continued the close relations between France and Germany. In 1987, the two nations held bilateral military exercises and later announced the creation of the Franco-German Brigade, a joint military force that was in turn expanded to the Eurocorps, a multilateral military force. France worked to develop an autonomous military arm for the EU and supported increased economic and political integration.

French relations with the developing world have been uneven as the nation's pursuit of nuclear tests in the South Pacific during the tenure of Mitterrand and his successor, Jacques Chirac, angered many nations in the region. In addition, the 1985 government-sponsored sabotage of the Greenpeace ship *The Rainbow Warrior* led to the resignation of the French head of the secret service and the minister of defense. In addition, French support for the military regime in Algeria has soured relations with some Arab states and led to terrorist acts on French soil. Conversely, even as France granted independence to its colonies, it was able to maintain close ties with many of its former possessions, especially in Africa. The Francophone states of Africa have close economic, cultural, and military ties with France. For instance, France aided Chad in repulsing Libyan invaders in 1987. Relations with Iran were initiated under Mitterrand, over objections by the United States.

Under Chirac, France has drawn closer to the United States as the president has sought to maintain French influence in light of diminishing resources and power. Hence, Chirac ordered the reintegration of France into NATO as a means to maintain French influence as NATO expanded and took on new missions. Chirac also supported increased integration in the European Union, including monetary union in order to preserve influence against a reunified Germany.

DEFENSE

The French army claims to be the oldest national army in the world and has a long history marked by both great military victories and innovations and ignominious failures. The constitution of 1958 clearly establishes the primacy of the president in defense matters. He is the commander in chief of the armed forces and oversees governmental committees on national defense.

Conscription was long a hallmark of the French military, but was done away with under President Chirac in an effort to both cut costs and improve the professionalism of the military. In the post–cold war era, successive governments have dramatically cut military expenditures in an effort to meet the criteria necessary for European Monetary Union. Nonetheless, the French maintain a large standing military force of 409,000 divided between the army, navy, and air force.

French military commitments run along two lines. The first is the defense of Western Europe. During the cold war, in spite of the fact that France was not an integrated member of NATO, security policy centered around defense against a Soviet attack. The backbone of this policy was, and continues to be, close military cooperation with Germany. Although Chirac reintegrated France into NATO, present French security policy continues to support the development of an autonomous European Security and Defense Identity (ESDI), which would lessen European reliance on the United States. The second main tenet of French security policy is the defense of national interests around the world. France has bilateral defense agreements with 11 of its former colonies in Africa and with a number of states in the Middle East. Paris has honored these treaties on several occasions by deploying troops to aid these nations.

The French policy of autonomy led governments to maintain a large defense-industrial complex to both supply the national military forces and export weapons systems around the world. France continues to spend more money on research and development, as a percentage of gross domestic product (GDP), on new weapons than any other nation except the United States. Also, French forces almost exclusively use domestically produced weapons, aircraft, and ships. In addition, France developed and deployed its own nuclear weapons (outside of the framework of NATO). The *force du frappe* (the French nuclear force) consists of submarine-launched nuclear missiles, air-dropped weapons, and land-based ballistic missiles.

Military Indicators

Total Active Duty Personnel: 380,800
Military Manpower per 1,000: 6.5
Military Expenditures $: 47.770 billion
- as % of GNP: 3.1
- per capita $: 826
- as % of central government expenditures: 6.6

Arms Imports $million: $150
Arms Exports $million: $2,200

ECONOMY

France maintains a mixed economy that includes a growing services sector, a shrinking but diversified manufacturing base, and a significant agricultural complex. Services now account for the majority of the nation's GDP, but industrial products provide the main export earnings. Major French industries include, steel, machinery, chemicals, automobiles, aircraft, electronics, textiles, and tourism. Major exports include manufactured equipment, chemicals, automobiles, textiles and clothing, foodstuffs, and other agricultural products. Imports consist mainly of oil, machinery, chemicals, and iron and steel products. The nation's primary trading partners are Germany, Italy, Great Britain, Spain, Belgium, and the United States.

More so than in any of the other industrialized nations, the French government maintains substantial influence in the economy and owns majority stakes in key industries such as railways, electricity, aircraft manufacturing, and telecommunications. Efforts to privatize these industries have been proceeding slowly, and are often met with resistence by the public. Through the 1980s and 1990s, the French economy has been plagued by persistently high unemployment (above 10 percent), and efforts to create new jobs are centered on a reduction of the workweek to 35 hours. France entered the European Monetary Union (EMU) in January of 1999, and the strict fiscal requirements for admittance have forced successive governments to curtail spending on programs to stimulate the economy and to raise taxes. However, governments have also avoided deep cuts in the nation's generous social welfare system or the widespread governmental bureaucracy. French agriculture also remains highly protected from market forces. The nation is also one of the world's largest commercial fishing powers.

Principal Economic Indicators

Gross National Product $: 1.541630 trillion
GNP per capita $: 26,300
GNP Average Annual Growth Rate (1990–97) %: 1.0
GNP per capita Average Annual Growth Rate (1990–97) %: 0.5
Origin of Gross Domestic Product %
- Agriculture: 3
- Mining: 1
- Manufacturing: 20
- Construction: 5
- Public Utilities: 3
- Transportation and Communications: 6
- Trade: 14
- Financial Services: 6
- Other Services: 18
- Government: 19

Gross Domestic Product by Type of Expenditure %
- Private Consumption: 56
- Government Consumption: 22
- Gross Domestic Investment: 15
- Foreign Trade: Exports: 36
- Imports: −29

% of Income Received by Poorest 20%: 5.6
% of Income Received by Richest 10%: 26.1

Price and earnings indexes (1995 = 100)

	1992	1993	1994	1995	1996	1997	1998
Consumer price index	94.7	96.6	98.3	100.0	102.0	103.2	103.9
Earnings index	93.4	96.3	99.2	100.0	101.9	104.7	107.6

Finance

National Currency: Euro (Formerly French franc [F])
Exchange Rate: $1 = F 6.0836
Money Supply Stock in National Currency billion: 1,811
M1 per capita: 31,000
Central Bank Discount Rate %: 3
Total External Debt $million: 117,600
Debt Service Ratio %: —

Balance of Payments $million: 39,470
International Reserves SDRs million: 23,732
Ratio of External Debt to Total Reserves: —

Average Annual Rate of Inflation/Consumer Price Index Growth Rate %: 2

Official Development Assistance

Donor ODA $million: 7.915
- as % of GNP: 0.5
- per capita $ 13,415
- Foreign Direct Investment $million: 27,998

Central Government Revenues and Expenditures

Fiscal Year: Calendar Year

Revenues $million: 222,000
Expenditures $million: 265,000
Budget Deficit $million: 43 billion
Tax Revenues as % of GDP: 39.2
Highest Tax Bracket %
- Individual: 33
- Corporate: —

Employment and Labor

Economically Active Population: 25,871,000
Female Participation Rate %: 44.9
Activity Rate %: 44.8
Labor by Sector: %
- Agriculture, Forestry, Fishing: 4.1
- Manufacturing, Mining: 17.4
- Construction: 5.7
- Transportation and Communications: 5.5
- Trade, Hotels, and Restaurants: 14.6
- Finance, Insurance, Real Estate: 9.2
- Public Administration, Defense: —
- Services: 30.3

Unemployment %: 12.4

Agriculture

Agriculture's Share of GDP %: 3
Average Annual Rate of Growth (1965–98) %: 1.7
Number of Farms 000: 735
Average Size of Farm ha: 24.6
Number of Tractors per 1,000 hectares: 78.6
Irrigation, % of Farms having: 8
Artificial Fertilizer kg/hectare: 319
Total Farmland as % of land area: 54.7
Livestock: Cattle 000: 20,389
- Sheep 000: 10,305
- Hogs 000: 15,430
- Chickens 000: 238,067

Forests: Production of Roundwood (000 cubic meters): 46,345
Fisheries: Total Catch tons 000: 838.3

Mining

% of GDP: 0.8
Value of Mineral Production $million: 11,521

Manufacturing

Value Added $million: 254,935
Industrial Production Growth Rate %: 4

Energy

Commercial Energy Production metric tons of oil equivalent 000: 127,843
Commercial Energy Consumption metric tons of oil equivalent 000: 247,534

(continued)

Commercial Energy Consumption per capita kg: 4,224
Average Annual Growth Rate 1980–97%: 1.5
Net Energy Imports % of use: 48
Electricity Installed Capacity kW 000: 107,611
Production kW-hr million: 493,177
Coal Reserves tons million: 139
Production tons 000: 9,045
Natural Gas Proven Reserves cubic meters billion: 19
Production cubic meters million: 3,395
Crude Petroleum Reserves barrels million: 117
Production barrels million: 16
Consumption barrels million: 585
Refinery Capacity barrels per day 000: 1,786
Pipelines Length km: 7,546

Foreign Trade

Imports $million: 273,387.4
Exports $million: 284,045.7
Export Volume % Annual Growth Rate (1990–97): 5.5
Import Volume % Annual Growth Rate (1990–97): 4.6

Balance of trade (current prices)

	1993	1994	1995	1996	1997	1998
F 000,000,000	+89.5	+50.7	+62.7	+85.7	+170.4	+160.1
% of total	3.9%	2.0%	2.2%	3.0%	5.3%	4.6%

Major Trading Partners

	Imports	Exports
European Union %	63.9	63.5
United States %	7.8	5.9
Eastern Europe %	2.4	2.2
Japan %	3.5	2.0
Others %	22.4	26.5

Transportation

Roads Total Length mi: 504,987 km 812,700
Paved %: 92
Automobiles: 25,100,000
Trucks and Buses: 5,005,000
Persons per vehicle: 1.9
Railroad; Track Length mi: 19,847 km 31,940
Passenger-mi million: 34,467
Freight-mi million: 32,466
Merchant Marine: No. of Vessels: 729
Total Deadweight Tonnage 000: 4,981.0
International Cargo Loaded tons 000: 55,296
International Cargo Off-loaded tons 000: 177,696
Airports with Scheduled Flights: 61
Traffic: Passenger-mi million: 41,942
Freight-mi million: 7,740
Length of Canals mi: 9,278 km 14,932

Tourism

Number of Tourists to 000: 70,000
Number of Tourists from 000: 18,077
Tourist Receipts $million: 27,527
Tourist Expenditures $million: 16,328

Communications

Telephones 000: 32,400
Cost of Local Calls 3 mins: $0.13
Cellular Telephones 000: 1,379
Fax Machines 000: 1,900
Personal Computers 000: 7,800
Internet Hosts per million persons: 2,604
Mail: Post Offices: 16,919
Pieces of Mail Handled million: 24,391
Pieces of Mail Handled per person: 419

EDUCATION

France has a rich educational history beginning with Charlemange and the founding of the University of Paris in the 12th century. For the next six centuries, education was controlled by the Catholic Church. The Revolution led to the dismantlement of the church schools and Napoleon established lycées, divided the nation into academies, and consolidated higher education. The present school system was established in 1975 and reformed in 1983.

The school year runs from the end of September to the end of June, with short holidays. Education is compulsory between the ages of six and 16. Preprimary education is not compulsory, but it is free and nearly universal. Elementary education involves grades one through five and secondary education begins at grade six and ends at grade 12. At the end of grade nine students choose between two tracks: one which prepares them for the university, the other for vocational fields. Education in France is highly centralized and the bureaucracy is the largest of the French government.

Most French universities date back to the Renaissance. The earliest was the University of Paris, founded in 1150. Higher education in France is free and involves the traditional university, two-year technical colleges, and prestigious *grandes écoles* that offer postgraduate work. French university students have a long tradition of protest and activism. This has made governments unwilling to undertake significant reforms of the educational system.

Education

Literacy Rate %: 98.8
Male %: 98.9
Female %: 98.7
First Level: Primary schools: 41,244
Teachers: 301,699
Students: 4,012,600
Student-Teacher Ratio: —
Net Enrollment Ratio: 99
Second Level: Secondary Schools: 11,212
Teachers: 454,000
Students: 5,737,458
Student-Teacher Ratio: 12.6
Net Enrollment Ratio: 92

Vocational Level: Schools: —
Students: —

Third Level: Institutions: 1,062
Teachers: 52,663
Students: 2,107,600
Student-Ratio Level: —
Gross Enrollment Ratio: 49.6
Students per 100,000: 3,617
% of Population Age 25 and over with Postsecondary Education: 11.4

Public Expenditure on Education as % of GDP: 5.9

SCIENCE AND TECHNOLOGY

Science and Technology

Scientists and Engineers in R&D per 1 million persons: 2,659
Expenditures in R&D as % of GDP: 2.25
High-Tech Exports $million: 54,183
Patent Applications by Residents: 18,669

MEDIA

The first French newspaper was published in 1631, and the nation has a long history of a free and vocal press (with the notable exception of the Vichy period). Formal freedom of the press was first established with the constitution of 1789. The most influential French daily is *Le Monde*, which is widely read by cultural and political elites. There are 90 large dailies in France, most of which are owned by 10 conglomerates. In addition, there are 522 weeklies and 200 periodicals that are international in nature but are edited in France. Journalism is heavily organized and union members account for some 60 percent of all French journalists. Strikes are common, but usually involve local issues and are quickly resolved. In addition, most publications are subsidized by the government, with the average subsidy amounting to 12 percent.

There are approximately 800 FM and 41 AM radio stations in France, although private advertising on the radio was only legalized in 1987, and the state heavily regulates the industry. There are two state-run television stations, and an increasing number of private stations. Government regulation of the content of these stations has increased the popularity of satellite stations, which bring in programming from around the world. The main purpose of government regulation in the broadcast media is not direct censorship but the promotion of French culture and language.

As in many nations, French culture can be divided between high culture (art, literature, music) and low culture, which encompasses both traditional forms of culture as well as popular culture. In the post–World War II era, France began to lose its dominance as the center for world culture. Other major cities, including London, Rome, and New York, have developed well-established cultural outlets. In addition, the advent of cinema and modern forms of music have transferred the center of popular culture to the United States. In response, the French government has enacted legislation to protect its film and television industry from outside competition. Paris remains the center for such fields as fashion and design.

Media

Daily Newspapers: 118
Total Circulation 000: 13,685
Circulation per 1,000: 237
Books Published: 45,311
Magazines: 2,672
Radio Receivers 000: 50,000
per 1,000: 862
Television sets 000: 33,600
per 1,000: 579

MOST IMPORTANT MEDIA:

Press. The following newspapers are published daily at Paris, unless otherwise noted (circulation figures for 1994); *Quest-France* (Rennes, national circulation, 44 editions, 770,000); *Le Parisien* (419,000), popular morning independent with Gaullist management but some communist readership; *Le Figaro* (377,000), founded 1826, leading morning independent and standard-bearer of the liberal bourgeoisie; *La Montagne-Centre-France* (Clermont-Ferrand, 356,000 combining former *La Montagne, Populaire du Centre, Journal du Centre*), independent; *La Voix du Nord* (Lille, 348,000); *Sud-Ouest* (Bordeaux, 347,000); *Le Monde* (345,000), independent evening paper with international readership and weekly edition in English, left-of-center; *L'Equipe* (329,000); *Le Progrès* (Lyon, 291,000); *L'Est Republicain* (Nancy, 288,000); *Le Dauphiné Libere* (Grenoble, 286,000), leading provincial; *La Nouvelle Republique du Centre-Ouest* (Tours, 262,000); *Nice-Matin* (Nice, 246,500); *La Dépêche du Midi* (Toulouse, 223,500), radical management; *France-Soir* (192,000), leading evening paper, right-wing orientation; *Le Républicain Lorrain* (Metz, 192,000); *International Herald Tribune* (191,300), American, absorbed European edition of *New York Times* in 1967; *Libération* (166,000), politically independent, but culturally leftist; *Le Provencal* (Marseilles, 155,000), largest southeastern daily, Socialist; *Les Echos* (118,000), financial and economic; *La Tribune Desfosses* (100,000), financial; *La Croix-L'Evenement* (93,000), liberal Catholic, popular with left-wing intelligentsia; *L'Humanité* (70,000), communist.

News agencies. The principal French news agency is the semiofficial French Press Agency (Agence France-Presse—AFP), founded in 1835, which operates in most countries and many overseas territories in French, English, and Spanish; other agencies include Agence Centrale Parisienne de Presse (ACP) and Agence Republicaine d'Information (ARI). The leading foreign news agencies also maintain bureaus in France's principal cities.

Radio and television. Until 1972 the government-owned French Radio and Television Organization (Office de Radiodiffusion et Télévision Française—ORTF) held a monopoly of both domestic and international services. Granted fiscal and administrative autonomy under the Ministry of Education in 1959, the ORTF was reorganized in May 1972 following a scandal involving clandestine advertising. In July 1974 legislation was enacted breaking up the ORTF in favor of seven state-financed but independent companies. In 1982 the regulatory function was taken over by a single nine-member committee, which was in turn replaced by a 13-member National Commission of Communication and Franchises (Commission Nationale de la Communication et des Libertates—CNCL) in 1986. In 1989 the Socialist government discarded the CNCL, which had come to be viewed as a vehicle of government control over broadcasting, in favor of a Higher Audiovisual Council (Conseil Supérier de l'Audiovisuel—CSA), one-third of whose nine members are named by the president of the republic, the Senate, and the National Assembly, respectively. At present there are five "public service" (partially state-administered) terrestrial, cable, or satellite television channels (France 2, France 3, TV5 Europe, Arte, La Cinquième) and nine commercial channels (including TF1, Canal Plus, and Metropole 6). There are also four major public service radio stations (France Inter, Radio France, FIP, and France Info), plus some 1,800 commercial stations, of which only eight transmit nationally. There were approximately 53.0 million radio and 43.7 million television receivers in 1998.

CULTURE

Cultural Indicators

Public Libraries Number: 1,141
- Volumes: 64,379,000
- Registered borrowers: 6,094,000

Museums Number: —
- Annual Attendance: —

Cinema Production of Long Films: 141
- Number of Cinemas: 4,365
- Seating Capacity: 919,200
- Annual Attendance million: 130.1
- Annual Attendance per capita: 2.2

STATUS OF WOMEN

Women enjoy full civil rights in France, including universal suffrage. The penal code prohibits spousal abuse and law enforcement authorities vigorously enforce this law. In 1998 the Ministry of Interior reported 7,828 cases of rape and 12,809 instances of other criminal sexual assault. Numerous private and public organizations assist abused women. Prostitution is legal in France but pimping is not. A government agency, the Central Office on the Treatment of Human Beings, deals with trafficking in women and prostitution. In theory women receive wages equal to men for comparable work, but in practice they do not. In the 5,000 largest French firms, the average difference in salary between men and women is 27 percent. The law prohibits sex-based job discrimination and sexual harassment in the workplace. But the scope of the law is narrow and the fines and compensatory damages are modest. The Women's Bureau in the Ministry of Social Affairs and Employment is responsible for the promotion of women's rights.

Women

Gender Empowerment Measure: 31.0
Seats Held in Parliament by Women %: 9.0
Female Administrators and Managers %: 9.4
Female Professional and Technical Workers %: 41.4
Women's Share of Earned Income %: 39.0
Women in Government %: 9

HEALTH, FOOD, AND NUTRITION

Health

Number of Physicians: 160,235
Number of Dentists: 39,284
Number of Nurses: 330,943
Number of Pharmacists: 53,085
Population per Physician: 361
Number of Hospitals: 3,810
Hospital Beds per 10,000: 118
Hospital Bed Occupancy Rate: —
Infant Mortality Rate per 1,000 live births: 9
Maternal Mortality Rate per 100,000 live births: 15
Total Health Expenditures as % of GDP: 9.40
Health Expenditures per capita $: 1,869
HIV Infected % of adults: 0.37
Cigarette Consumption per smoker per year: 3,088
% of Smokers: Male: 40
Female: 27
Access to Safe Water %: 100

Food and Nutrition

Food Supply as % of FAO Requirements: 142
% of Consumption Expenditures on Food: 17.4
Daily Available Calories per capita: 3,588
% of Total Calories derived from:
Cereals: 23.7
Potatoes, cassava: 3.6
Meat, poultry: 15.9
Fish: 1.1
Eggs, milk: 12.7
Fruits, vegetables: 5.3
Fats, oils: 19.4

ENVIRONMENT

The environmental movement in France has not gained the popularity or support that it has in other nations. Nonetheless, environmental parties were able to gain nine seats in parliament in the 1998 elections. The most controversial environmental issue in France involves nuclear energy. In an effort to lessen dependency on imported oil, the French government aggressively built nuclear power plants. Nuclear waste and the potential for accidents have now diminished the popularity of the plants. In addition, the French were roundly criticized for their decision to conduct nuclear tests in the South Pacific.

Environment

Forest Area sq km: 150,000
Average Annual Deforestation sq km: −1,608
Nationally Protected Areas as % of Total Land Area: 10.7
Freshwater Access cubic meters per capita: 3,246
Emissions of Organic Water Pollutants kg per day: 585,382
CO_2 Emissions per capita ton: 6.2

CHRONOLOGY

1944 Liberation of France from German control.
1946 The Fourth Republic is established.
1953 De Gaulle retires from public life.
1954 France is defeated by the Viet Minh in the Battle of Dien Bien Phu and is forced to evacuate Vietnam.
1957 France signs the Treaty of Rome, establishing the European Economic Community.
1958 In response to a military insurrection in Algeria, de Gaulle is invited to form a government to resolve the crisis; he proposes a new presidential-type constitution which leads to the formation of the Fifth Republic with de Gaulle as the first president.
1962 Algeria is granted full independence.
1965 France signs the Brussels Treaty, which establishes the EC.
1966 France withdraws from NATO.
1968 Student riots spark mass protests; De Gaulle is reelected president.
1969 De Gaulle resigns following voter rejection of his constitutional amendments in a referendum; Georges Pompidou is elected president.
1970 De Gaulle dies.
1974 Pompidou dies, Valéry Giscard d'Estaing is elected president.
1981 Socialist François Mitterrand is elected over Giscard d'Estaing.
1984 Socialists abandon plans to establish unified secular education.
1985 French special forces sink the Greenpeace ship *The Rainbow Warrior* in Auckland, New Zealand, creating a diplomatic crisis.
1988 Mitterrand is reelected president.
1991 France joins the coalition against Saddam Hussein.
1995 Gaullist Jacques Chirac is elected president.
1999 France joins European Monetary Union.
2002 The euro replaces the franc as the national currency. Chirac is reelected president in a landslide victory against right-wing National Front leader Jean-Marie Le Pen.

BIBLIOGRAPHY

Brubacker, Rogers. *Citizenship and Nationhood in France and Germany*. Cambridge, Mass., 1992.
Fenby, Jonathon. *France on the Brink*. New York, 1999.
Flynn, Gregory, ed. *Remaking the Hexagon: The New France in the New Europe*. Boulder, Colo., 1995.
Gordon, Philip H. *France, Germany and the Western Alliance*. Boulder, Colo., 1995.
Grant, Robert. *The Changing Franco-American Security Relationship*. Arlington, Va., 1993.
Howorth, Jolyon, et al., ed. *De Gaulle to Mitterrand: Presidential Power in France*. New York, 1994.
Kramer, Steven. *Does France Still Count?* Washington, D.C., 1994.
MacMaster, Neil. *Colonial Migrants and Racism : Algerians in France, 1900–62*. New York, 1997.
Shennan, Andrew. *De Gaulle*. New York, 1993.

OFFICIAL PUBLICATIONS

France. *Annuaire statistique de la France; Données sociales* (triennial); *Recensement général de la population de 1990; Tableaux de l'economie française* (annual).

CONTACT INFORMATION

Embassy of France
4101 Reservoir Road NW
Washington, D.C. 20007
Phone: (202) 944-6000 Fax: (202) 944-6166

INTERNET RESOURCES

- Economie de Statistique
  http://www.insee.fr/vf/produits/pub/ecostat/index.htm

GABON

BASIC FACT SHEET

OFFICIAL NAME:
Gabonese Republic (République Gabonaise)

ABBREVIATION:
GO

CAPITAL:
Libreville

HEAD OF STATE:
President Omar Bongo (from 1967)

HEAD OF GOVERNMENT:
Prime Minister Jean-François Ntoutoume-Emane (from 1999)

NATURE OF GOVERNMENT:
Multiparty democracy

POPULATION:
1,226,000

AREA:
267,667 sq km (103,346 sq mi)

ETHNIC MAJORITY:
Fang, Eshira, Mbede, and Okande

LANGUAGES:
French (official), Fang (vernacular)

RELIGIONS:
Christianity and animism

UNIT OF CURRENCY:
Communauté Financiére Africaine franc (C.F.A.F.)

NATIONAL FLAG:
Tricolor of green, golden yellow, and royal blue horizontal stripes

NATIONAL EMBLEM:
Two black panthers balanced on the spreading roots of a yellow okoume tree grasp a shield with their forepaws. The shield is divided horizontally into two sections: the larger, bottom section shows a fully rigged black schooner flying the national flag; the smaller, top segment shows three flat ornamental disks. The Latin motto *Uniti Progrediemur* (United We Shall Go Forward) appears just below the spreading branches of the okoume tree, and the French motto *Union, Travail, Justice* (Union, Work, Justice) appears above its roots.

NATIONAL ANTHEM:
"United in Concord and Brotherhood Awake Gabon, Dawn is at Hand"

NATIONAL HOLIDAYS:
March 12 (National Day, Renovation Day); January 1 (New Year's Day); May 1 (Labor Day); May 25 (African Freedom Day); August 17 (Independence Day). Christian festivals include Assumption, Easter Monday, All Saints' Day, Christmas, and Pentecost Monday

DATE OF INDEPENDENCE:
August 17, 1960

DATE OF CONSTITUTION:
March 14, 1991

GEOGRAPHICAL FEATURES

Gabon is situated on the western coast of Africa, straddling the equator, with an area of 267,667 sq km (103,346 sq mi). The greatest distance north-northeast to south-southwest is 717 km (446 mi) and east-southeast to west-northwest is 644 km (400 mi). The Atlantic coastline is 739 km (459 mi) long.

Gabon's total international land boundary of 2,344 km (1,457 mi) is shared with three countries: Cameroon (302 km; 188 mi); Republic of Congo (1,656 km; 1,029 mi); and Equatorial Guinea (386 km; 240 mi).

The low-lying coastal plain is narrow in the north (29 km; 18 mi) and south, but broader in the estuary region of Ogooué. South of the Ogooué are numerous lagoons, such as N'Dogo, M'Goze, and M'Komi, along the

Gabon

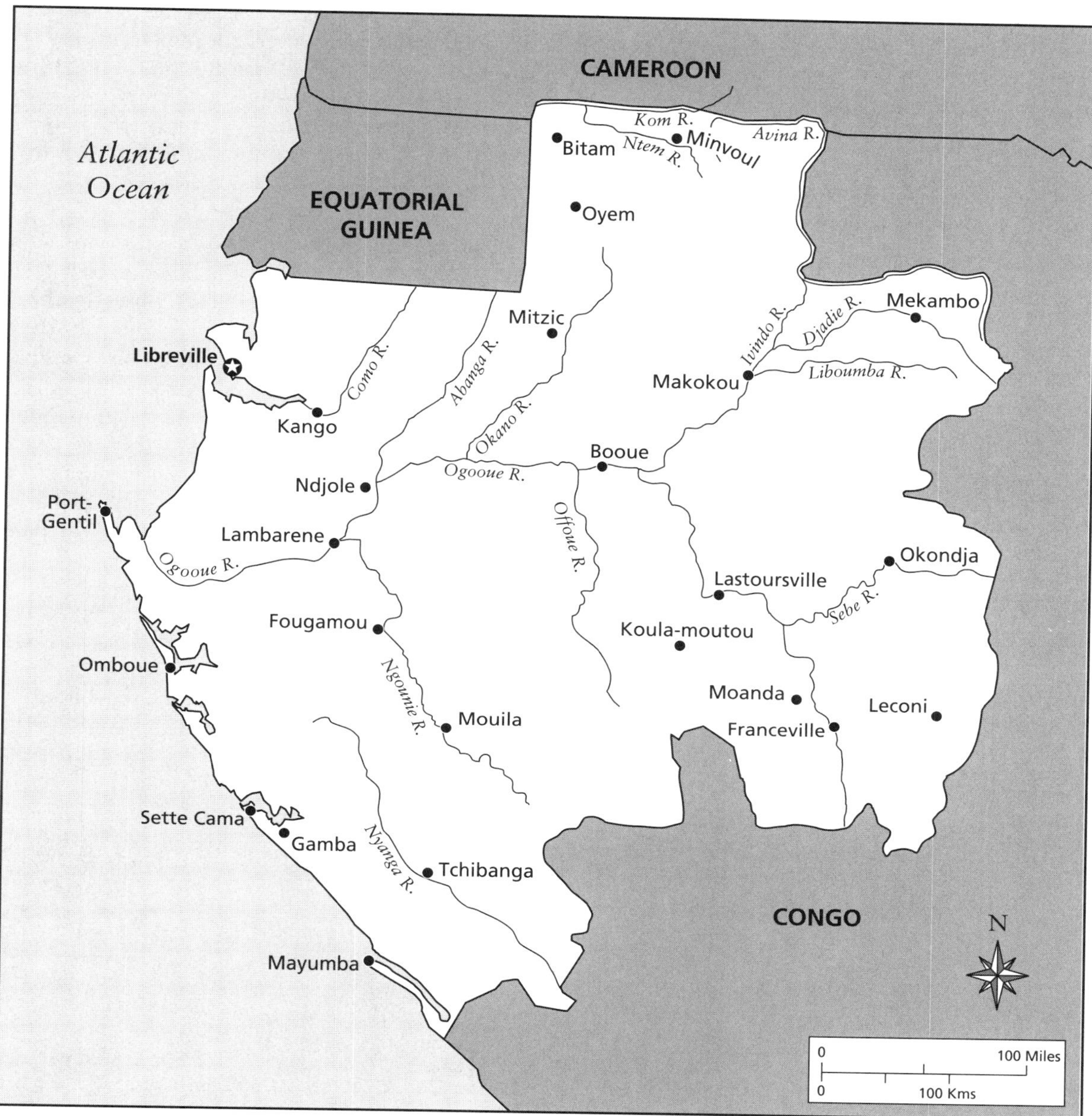

coastline. The interior relief is more complex, though nowhere dramatic. In the north the Crystal Mountains enclose the valleys of the Woleu and N'Tem rivers and the Ivindo Basin. In southern Gabon the coastal plain is dominated by granitic hills. Between N'Gounie and the Ogooué the Chaillus Massif rises to 915 m (3,000 ft). The highest point in Gabon is Mount Iboundji (1,575 m; 5,167 ft).

Geography

Area sq km: 267,667 (103,346 sq mi)
World Rank: 76th
Land Boundaries, km: Cameroon 298; Congo-Brazzaville 1,903; Equatorial Guinea 350
Coastline, km: 885
Elevation Extremes meters
- Lowest: Atlantic Ocean 0
- Highest: Mount Iboundji 1,575

Land Use % Arable land: 1
- Permanent Crops: 1
- Permanent Pastures: 18
- Forest and Woodland: 77
- Other: 3

Population of Principal Cities

Libreville	362,386

CLIMATE AND WEATHER

The climate is equatorial, with abundant rain in the rainy season, small variations in temperature, and a hot and dry summer. From June to September there is virtually no rain, and there is only occasional rain in December and January. Rainfall is very heavy during the rest of the year, averaging 2,540 mm (100 in) a year at Libreville. Farther north of the coast the average annual rainfall rises to 3,810 mm (150 in). Being on the equator, the country enjoys a uniform temperature throughout the year, varying only slightly from the average mean of 26.6°C (80°F). The cold Benguela Current lowers the coastal temperatures.

Climate and Weather

Mean Temperature 80°F
Average Rainfall: 100 in to 150 in

POPULATION

Population Indicators

Total Population: 1999 1,226,000
World Rank: 151st
Density per sq mi: 11.9 (4.6 sq km)
% of annual growth (1994–99): 1.5
Male %: 49.3
Female %: 50.7
Urban %: 73.2
Age Distribution: % 0–14: 33.8
15–29: 23.7
30–44: 17.10
45–59: 17.4
60–74: 6.9
75 and over: 1.2
Population 2020: 1,675,000
Birth Rate per 1,000: 37.6
Death Rate per 1,000: 14.3
Population Doubling Time (years): 48
Infant Mortality Rate per 1,000 live births: 85.0
Rate of Natural Increase per 1,000: 23.3
Total Fertility Rate: 5.4
Expectation of Life (years): Males 53.8
Females 57.2
Marriage Rate per 1,000: —
Divorce Rate per 1,000: —
Total Number of Households: 136,000
Average Size of Households: 4.0
% of Illegitimate Children: —
Induced Abortions: —
Rate per 100 live births: —

ETHNIC COMPOSITION

Excluding the Pygmies, who are the original inhabitants of the country, Gabonese belong to 40 Bantu tribes divided into four tribal groupings: Fang, Eshira, Mbede, and Okande. The largest tribal group is the Fang, who came from the north, perhaps Cameroon, and settled in the middle Ogooué and its estuary in the 19th century. The peoples of the Myene language group—Mpongwe, Orungu, Galoa, and Nkomi—occupy the lower Ogooué and the coast. The Mitshogo-Okande group occupy the center. The Jumba and the Inenga also live along the lower Ogooué. The Kota, known for their carved wood figures, occupy the northeast. Other groups include the Duma, Kanda, Seke, Mbee, and Bongom or Bakele. There are only approximately 3,000 Pygmies in the population. Ethnic distinctions are less sharply drawn and ethnicity is less divisive in Gabon than elsewhere in Africa.

Gabon has a large expatriate population, estimated at over 100,000, of whom 30,000 are French. There are more French in Gabon today than there were in colonial times. One of the most famous of these expatriates was Dr. Albert Schweitzer, whose hospital at Lambaréné is a national landmark.

LANGUAGES

French is the official language of the republic. Fang is the main vernacular, spoken primarily in northern Gabon. Other vernaculars include Myene, Bateke, Bapounou/Eschira, and Bandjabi.

Principal Languages and Their Speakers

Fang	440,000
French	1,000,000
Kota	40,000
Mbete	170,000
Mpongwe (Myene)	180,000
Punu, Sira, Nzebi	210,000
Teke	20,000
Other	170,000

RELIGIONS

Gabon is the most Christian of the Francophone states in Africa and often is called the "Bastion of the Cross of Africa." About 60 percent of the population are Christians, with Roman Catholics composing 70 percent of the Christian population. The Roman Catholic Church has over 250,000 members, with 36 missions, 100 priests, and 251 schools under the archbishop of Libreville. The Christian and Missionary Alliance devotes its activities to the south of the country, while Eglise Evangélique de Gabon is active throughout the country and runs four colleges, 66 primary schools, and two hospitals. The number of Muslims in the country is estimated at 3,000.

Religious Affiliations

Roman Catholic	610,000
Traditional beliefs	230,000
Protestant	220,000
Other	170,000

HISTORICAL BACKGROUND

Sometime between the 16th and 18th centuries, the Pygmies, the original inhabitants of the region, and Bantu-speaking people, who arrived around the first century C.E., were displaced by the Fang who migrated south from Cameroon and Equatorial Guinea. The first westerners were Portuguese who arrived in 1472. While the Portuguese focused their efforts on Bioke and São Tomé, British, Dutch, and French traders stopped in order to obtain slaves, ivory, and precious tropical woods. By 1849 the capital, Libreville, was established as a settlement for freed slaves.

Gabon was under French rule from 1890, when it became formally a part of French Congo. It was separated into an administrative region in 1903 and was reorganized as part of French Equatorial Africa in 1910. Gabon became independent along with other units of French Equatorial Africa in 1960. It allied itself with other moderate states that preferred to retain political, economic, and cultural ties with France.

At independence, Gabon was led by Leon M'Ba, the conservative, pro-French head of the Bloc Démocratique Gabonais (BDG). The opposition centered around the Union Démocratique et Sociale Gabonaise (UDSG) led by Jean-Hilaire Aubame. The two parties, which were evenly matched in support, agreed on a joint slate for elections in 1961, following the adoption of a new constitution. M'Ba won the election with 99.6% of the votes cast. He became the nation's first president, and Aubame was appointed minister of foreign affairs.

M'Ba attempted to merge the two parties, but when the UDSG resisted, its members, including Aubame, were forced to resign from the government. Aubame led a coup that deposed M'Ba in 1964. However, M'Ba was reinstated with the help of the French military, and Aubame was imprisoned. The BDG won the majority of seats in the 1964 elections, with the remainder going to a reorganized UDSG.

President M'Ba died in 1967 and was succeeded by Vice President Albert-Bernard (later Omar) Bongo. The following year, Bongo announced the restructuring of the BDG into a broad-based political grouping, the Parti Démocratique Gabonais (PDG), and declared Gabon a one-party state.

During the 1970s, the country remained a politically stable state. Discontent with the existing one-party system was limited because of high living standards—Gabon had the highest per capita incomes in black Africa—and economic growth. Beginning in 1981, banned opposition groups began to emerge and call for a multiparty system. Bongo resisted reform, insisting that democratic debate was permitted within the PDG. Bongo survived a coup attempt in 1985, but poor economic conditions in the late 1980s due to a decline in the world oil market led to social unrest. Acceding to popular demands, Bongo consented to multiple parties in 1990. He appointed a new prime minister, Csimir Oye-Mba, who named six opposition figures to his cabinet.

In national elections held in 1993 and 1998 Omar Bongo easily won reelection although his opponents charged that the elections were tainted by massive fraud. A qualified multiparty system was introduced in 1991. Constitutional amendments approved by the legislature in 1997 lengthened the presidential term from five to seven years and empowered the president to name both the prime minister and a vice president. The president has managed to successfully divide the opposition while creating token democratic institutions like the National Democracy Council.

CONSTITUTION

The legal basis of the Gabonese government is the constitution of 1991, which was adopted by referendum in July 1995. The constitution established a presidential form of government, in which the president is elected for a seven-year term (renewable only once) by direct universal suffrage. The head of the government is the prime minister, who appoints the council of ministers. The bicameral legislature consists of the National Assembly and the Senate. The 120 members of the National Assembly and the 91 members of the Senate are directly elected for terms of five years. The judiciary includes the Supreme Court, High Court of Justice, Court of Appeal, Superior Council of Magistracy, and other lesser courts.

LOCAL GOVERNMENT

For purposes of regional administration, Gabon is divided into nine provinces, each administered by a governor. These provinces are divided into 37 prefectures (departments), headed by presidentially appointed prefects. There are eight subprefectures led by subprefects. These officers answer to the central government directly. The system of regions, districts, and administrative control posts was supplanted by the present system in 1975.

Only towns and cities have popular representative institutions. Libreville and Port-Gentil have popularly

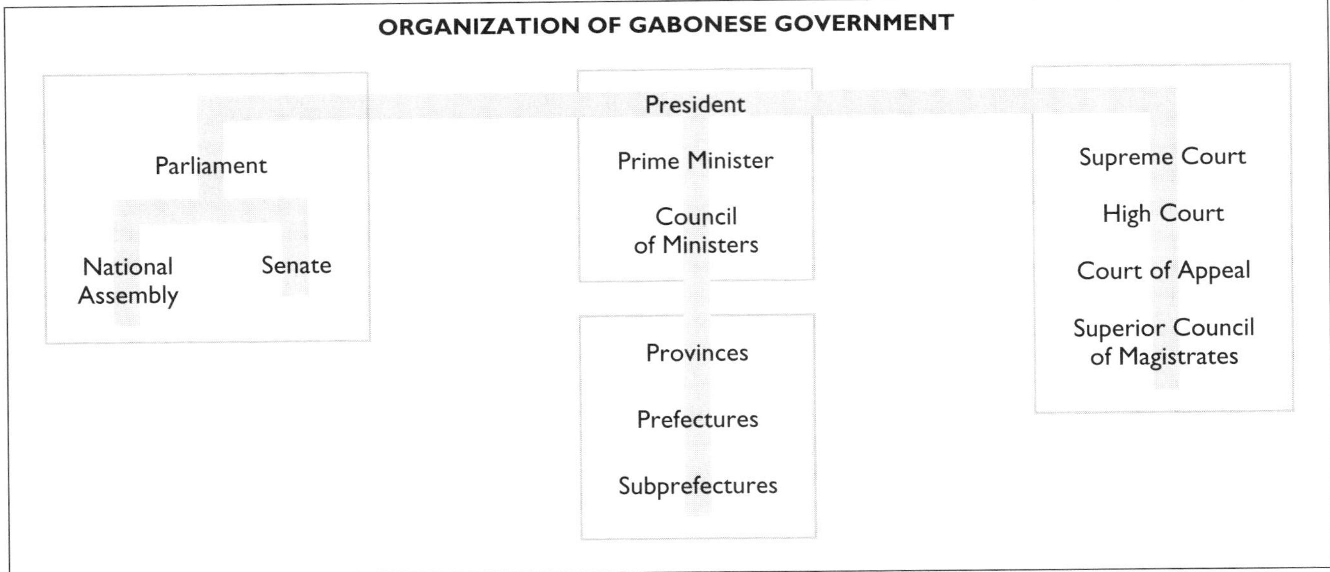

elected mayors and municipal councils. Four towns—Oyem, Bitam, Mouila, and Lambaréné—have communal administrations that are partly elected and partly appointed.

Local Government

Principal administrative divisions, capitals, area, population

Area and Population

		area		population 1983
Provinces	**Capitals**	**sq mi**	**sq km**	**estimate**
Estuaire	Libreville	8,008	20,740	463,187
Haut-Ogooué	Franceville	14,111	36,547	104,301
Moyen-Ogooué	Lambaréné	7,156	18,535	42,316
Ngounie	Mouila	14,575	37,750	77,781
Nyanga	Tchibanga	8,218	21,285	39,430
Ogooué-Ivindo	Makokou	17,790	46,075	48,862
Ogooué-Lolo	Koulamoutou	9,799	25,380	43,915
Ogooué-Maritime	Port-Gentil	8,838	22,890	97,913
Woleu-Ntem	Oyem	14,851	38,465	97,271
TOTAL		103,347	267,667	1,014,976

PARLIAMENT

The bicameral national legislature consists of the National Assembly (Assemblée Nationale) and the Senate (Sénat). The 120 members of the National Assembly and the 91 members of the Senate are directly elected for five-year terms by universal suffrage. The national legislature normally holds two sessions a year. It may be dissolved or prorogued for up to 18 months by the president. New elections must be held within 20 to 40 days of its dissolution. Legislation may be initiated by the president or members of the national legislature. The national legislature may override a president's veto by a two-thirds vote.

Suffrage is universal over age 21.

POLITICAL PARTIES

Gabon is a multiparty state that is largely ruled by the successor party to the one party that ruled the country. The main party is the Gabonese Democratic Party, which succeeded the Gabon Democratic Bloc. Other minor parties include the National Rally of Woodcutters or Bûcherons RNB whose leader Fr. Pual M'ba Abesole won 27 percent of the vote in the 1993 presidential election, the People's Unity Party or PUP, the Circle of Liberal Reformers or CLR, and the Gabonese Party for Progress or PGP.

Political Parties

Gabonese Democratic Party, 1968
Rally for Democracy and Progress
Democratic and Republican Alliance
Movement of Friends of Bongo, 1994
African Forum for Reconstruction, 1992
National Rally of Woodcutters, 1991
Social Democratic Party, 1991
Gabonese Progress Party
Circle of Liberal Reformers, 1992
Movement for National Recovery
Rally of Gauls, 1994
Independent Republicans' Party, 1995
Democratic and Social Union, 1996
Union of Gabonese People
Movement for Democracy, Development and National Reconciliation, 1996

Political Parties: Strength in Parliament Most Recent Elections

Senate (Sénat). Created by a constitutional amendment in 1994, the Senate is a 91-member body elected by members of municipal councils and departmental assemblies. First-ever balloting to fill the body was held on January 26 and February 9, 1997, after which the seats were distributed as follows: the Gabonese Democratic Party, 53; the National Rally of Woodcutters (RNB), 20; the Gabonese Progress Party, 4; the Democratic and Republican Alliance, 3; the Rally for Democracy and Progress and the Circle of Liberal Reformers, 1 each; and independents, 9. At additional elections in November 1997 the RNB, the Union of the Gabonese People, and the People's Unity Party each won a single seat, with the results of a fourth seat being unavailable. It was unclear what effect the most recent balloting had on the overall distribution of seats.

National Assembly (Assemblée Nationale). The sole legislative organ prior to 1997, the National Assembly is a 120-seat body whose members are elected for five-year terms. Following the most recent balloting on December 15 and 29, 1996, and January 12, 1997, the Assembly seats were distributed as follows (1990 figures are in parenthesis): the ruling Gabonese Democratic Party (PDG), 82 (63); the National Rally of Woodcutters (RNB), 12 (20); the Gabonese Progress Party (PGP), 8 (18); the Circle of Liberal Reformers, 3 (0); the Gabonese Socialist Union, 2 (4); 1 each for the African Forum for Reconstruction (0), the Circle for Renovation and Progress (1), the Congress for Democracy and Justice (0), the Democratic and Republican Alliance (0), the Union of Gabonese People (4), the National Rectification Movement—Originals (7), and the Rally for Democracy and Progress (0); and independents, 6. At by-elections on August 10, 1997, the PDG won 3 seats while the RNB and the PGP each secured a seat. One independent was also elected.

LEGAL SYSTEM

The judicial system is headed by the Supreme Court, with four chambers: constitutional, judicial, administrative, and accounts. Immediately below the Supreme Court are three superior courts: the High Court, whose judges are appointed by and from the deputies of the National Assembly; the Court de Sûreté de l'Etat, with 12 members; and the Court of Appeal. Subordinate courts, tribunaux de grande instance (county courts of the first instance), are in Libreville, Port-Gentil, Lamberéné, Mouila, Oyem, Franceville, and Kolamoutou. Appeals from these courts may be heard by the courts of second instance.

LAW ENFORCEMENT

Law Enforcement

Offenses reported to the police per 100,000: 114
- Murder: 1.4
- Assault: 17.9
- Burglary: 2.3
- Automobile Theft: 7.5
- Population per Police officer: 1,290

Death Penalty: Yes.

HUMAN RIGHTS

In terms of political and civil rights, Gabon is ranked as a country that is not free. Human rights are tightly restricted. Gabonese law enforcement officials use beatings in conjunction with interrogation regularly. Central Prison, the government's primary prison, deprives prisoners of proper living conditions, medical facilities, and sufficient food. Amnesty International has reported numerous instances in which criminals and illegal aliens have been beaten and tortured. Law enforcement officials defy legal constraints against arbitrary detention, detaining persons without charge under the constitutional specification prohibiting "acts against the Chief of State." Search warrants are optional, and ransacking of detainee homes is permissible.

Before 1990, freedom of speech was restricted. Criticism of the president and advocacy of multiparty systems were prohibited. All outdoor meetings must be approved or organized by the ruling party. Jehovah's Witnesses and several small syncretistic sects have been banned from practicing. The right of workers to strike is severely restricted under recently imposed regulations as well as a curfew.

FOREIGN POLICY

Gabon is heavily dependent on French support, yet nevertheless resents French dominance in the country's affairs. In 1995 relations between the two countries were temporarily broken off, but were restored quickly. Relations with neighboring countries are often strained as a result of a large number of illegal immigrants from Benin, Cameroon, Congo, and Equatorial Guinea. Nevertheless, Gabon actively participates in the Economic Community of Central African States and holds close relations with Congo, whose president, Denis Sassou-Nguesso, is President Bongo's father-in-law.

DEFENSE

Gabon has virtually no military capability of its own. Defense is based on a series of mutual defense and military assistance agreements with France. France continues to supply arms, equipment, and instructor-advisers. Annual French assistance is in the range of $800,000.

Military Indicators

Total Active Duty Personnel: 4,700
Military Manpower per 1,000: 39
Military Expenditures $: 104 million
- as % of GNP: 2.6
- per capita $: 90
- as % of central government expenditures: 9.6

Arms Imports $: 0
Arms Exports $: 0

ECONOMY

Gabon enjoys a per capita income four times that of most nations of sub-Saharan Africa. This has supported a sharp decline in extreme poverty; yet, because of high income inequality a large proportion of the population remains poor. Gabon depended on timber and manganese until oil was discovered offshore in the early 1970s. The oil sector now accounts for 50 percent of gross domestic product (GDP). Gabon continues to face fluctuating prices for its oil, timber, manganese, and uranium exports. Despite the abundance of natural wealth, the economy is hobbled by poor fiscal management. In 1992, the fiscal deficit widened to 2.4 percent of GDP, and Gabon failed to settle arrears on its bilateral debt, leading to a cancellation of rescheduling agreements with official and private creditors. Devaluation of its currency by 50 percent on January 12, 1994, sparked a one-time inflationary surge, to 35 percent; the rate dropped to 6 percent in 1996. The IMF provided a one-year standby arrangement in 1994–95 and a three-year Enhanced Financing Facility (EFF) at near commercial rates beginning in late 1995. Those agreements mandate progress in privatization and fiscal discipline. France provided additional financial support in January 1997 after Gabon had met IMF targets for mid-1996. In 1997, an IMF mission to Gabon criticized the government for overspending on off-budget items, overborrowing from the central bank, and slipping on its schedule for privatization and administrative reform. The rebound of oil prices in 1999–2000 helped growth, but drops in production hampered Gabon from fully realizing potential gains. An expected decline in oil output may lead to a contraction in GDP in 2001–2002.

Principal Economic Indicators

Gross National Product: $4.752 billion
GNP per capita: $4,120
GNP Average Annual Growth Rate (1990–97) %: −0.1
GNP per capita Average Annual Growth Rate (1990–97) %: −2.7
Origin of Gross Domestic Product %
- Agriculture: 9
- Mining: 45
- Manufacturing: 5
- Construction: 4
- Public Utilities: 2
- Transportation and Communications: 5
- Trade: 7
- Financial Services: 1
- Other Services: 10
- Government: 11

Gross Domestic Product by Type of Expenditure %
- Private Consumption: 31
- Government Consumption: 17
- Gross Domestic Investment: 27
- Foreign Trade: Exports: 65
- Imports: −40

% of Income Received by Poorest 20%: 3.3
% of Income Received by Richest 10%: 54.4

Price and earnings indexes (1995 = 100)

	1990	1991	1992	1993
Consumer price index	100.0	105.4	89.9	93.5
Earnings index	—	—	—	—

Finance

National Currency: CFA Franc (CFAF)
Exchange Rate: $1 = CFAF 608.36
Money Supply Stock in National Currency billion: 219.1
M1 per capita: 188,000
Central Bank Discount Rate %: 7.6
Total External Debt $: 3.9 billion
Debt Service Ratio %: 7.6

Balance of Payments $million: 237.1
International Reserves SDRs million: 105
Ratio of External Debt to Total Reserves: 12.3

Average Annual Rate of Inflation/Consumer Price Index Growth Rate %: 6.2

Official Development Assistance

ODA $ million: 45
- as % of GNP: 0.9
- per capita: $38
- Foreign Direct Investment $million: −50

Central Government Revenues and Expenditures

Fiscal Year: Calendar Year

Revenues $: 1.5 billion
Expenditures $: 1.3 billion
Budget Surplus $: 200 million
Tax Revenues as % of GDP: —
Highest Tax Bracket %
- Individual: 55
- Corporate: 40

Employment and Labor

Economically Active Population: 504,000
Female Participation Rate %: 36.9
Activity Rate %: 43.9
Labor by Sector: %
- Agriculture, Forestry, Fishing: 67.1
- Manufacturing, Mining: 14.1
- Construction: —
- Transportation and Communications: —
- Trade, Hotels, and Restaurants: —
- Finance, Insurance, Real Estate: —
- Public Administration, Defense: —
- Services: 18.8

Unemployment %: 10–14

Agriculture

Agriculture's Share of GDP %: 9
Average Annual Rate of Growth (1965–98) %: −0.4
Number of Farms 000: 71
Average Size of Farm ha: 1.0
Number of Tractors per 1,000 hectares: 5.1

Irrigation, % of Farms having: 1.0
Artificial Fertilizer kg/hectare: 3.0
Total Cropland as % of Farmland: —
Livestock: Cattle 000: 39
Sheep 000: 173
Hogs 000: 208
Chickens 000: 2,700
Forests: Production of Roundwood (000 cubic meters): 4,882
Fisheries: Total Catch tons: 24,400

Mining

% of GDP: 37.4
Value of Mineral Production $million: 1.214 billion

Manufacturing

Value Added $million: 174
Industrial Production Growth Rate %: 2.3

Energy

Commercial Energy Production metric tons of oil equivalent: 19,786,000
Commercial Energy Consumption metric tons of oil equivalent: 1,635,000
Commercial Energy Consumption per capita kg: 1,419
Average Annual Growth Rate 1980–97 %: −3.7
Net Energy Imports % of use: −1,110
Electricity Installed Capacity kW: 310,000
Production kW-hr million: 940
Coal Reserves tons million: —
Production tons: —
Natural Gas Proven Reserves cubic meters billion: 14
Production cubic meters million: 102
Crude Petroleum Reserves barrels: 1.340 billion
Production barrels million: 135
Consumption barrels million: 7
Refinery Capacity barrels per day: 17,000
Pipelines Length km: 284

Foreign Trade

Imports $million: 680.8
Exports $million: 1.040.9
Export Volume % Annual Growth Rate (1990–97): 6.3
Import Volume % Annual Growth Rate (1990–97): 2.6
Balance of Trade $

Balance of trade (current prices)

	1991	1992	1993	1994	1995	1996
CFAF 000,000	+386,100	+362,800	+419,400	+882,000	+870,800	1,095,800
% of total	44.3%	43.6%	46.7%	50.6%	49.3%	52.5%

Major Trading Partners

	Imports	Exports
European Union %	67.6	49.4
United States %	11.8	6.5
Eastern Europe %	0.3	—
Japan %	5.3	8.0
Others %	15.0	36.1

Transportation

Roads Total Length mi: 4,743 (7,633 km)
Paved %: 8
Automobiles: 23,800
Trucks and Buses: 15,700
Persons per vehicle: 29
Railroad; Track Length mi: 415 (668 km)
Passenger-mi million: 21
Freight-mi million: 126
Merchant Marine: No. of Vessels: 29
Total Deadweight Tonnage: 30,200
International Cargo Loaded tons: 12,828,000
International Cargo Off-loaded tons: 212,000
Airports with Scheduled Flights: 23
Traffic: Passenger-mi million: 354
Freight-mi million: 56
Length of Canals mi: 994 (1,600 km)

Tourism

Number of Tourists to 000: 192
Number of Tourists from 000: —
Tourist Receipts $million: 4
Tourist Expenditures $million: 112

Communications

Telephones 000: 32
Cost of Local Calls 3 mins: $0
Cellular Telephones 000: 4
Fax Machines 000: 0.4
Personal Computers 000: 6
Internet Hosts per million persons: —
Mail: Post Offices: 90
Pieces of Mail Handled million: 5.7
Pieces of Mail Handled per person: 4.3

EDUCATION

Education is free, universal, and compulsory, in principle, for 10 years, from ages six to 16. Schooling consists of six years of primary school, four years of middle school, and three years of secondary school, leading to the baccalauréat. The curricula are based on French models, and Gabonization is being introduced only gradually.

The academic year runs from September to June. The medium of instruction is French throughout the school system.

Teachers are trained at six teacher-training institutions.

Private schools are fully integrated with the school system and account for 46 percent of the enrollment at the primary level. Approximately 70 percent of higher secondary teachers are foreigners.

Technical training is provided in 12 technical schools. Higher education is provided by the Université Omar Bongo.

Education

Literacy Rate %: 63.2
  Male %: 73.7
  Female %: 53.3
First Level: Primary schools: 1,105
  Teachers: 4,709
  Students: 247,018
  Student-Teacher Ratio: 52.5
  Net Enrollment Ratio: —
Second Level: Secondary Schools: —
  Teachers: 1,897
  Students: 56,457
  Student-Teacher Ratio: 29.8
  Net Enrollment Ratio: —

Vocational Level: Schools: —
  Students: 9,261

Third Level: Institutions: 2
  Teachers: 299
  Students: 3,000
  Student-Ratio Level: 10.0
  Gross Enrollment Ratio: —
  Students per 100,000: 449
  % of Population Age 25 and over with Postsecondary Education: —

Public Expenditure on Education as % of GDP: 3.2

SCIENCE AND TECHNOLOGY

Science and Technology

Scientists and Engineers in R&D per 1 million persons: 234
Expenditures in R&D as % of GDP: —
High-Tech Exports $: 17 million
Patent Applications by Residents: —

MEDIA

An information bulletin, *Gabon-Matin*, is issued daily in French by the Ministry of Information, with a circulation of 18,000. The government also owns 75 percent of the daily *L'Union*, which has a circulation of 15,000. The national news agency is the Agence Gabonaise de Presse, founded in 1961.

The official broadcasting organization is Radiodiffusion Télévision Gabonaise (RTG), with stations at Libreville, Franceville, Oyem, and Port-Gentil. The national network broadcasts 24 hours a day on shortwave and medium wave bands in French and local languages. A 100-kw shortwave transmitter at Libreville covers the whole country, but it is supplemented by relay stations throughout Gabon. A French-built international radio station, Africa No. 1, the most powerful on the continent, was opened at Moyabi in February 1981. It is a 35 percent state-controlled international commercial radio station, broadcasting in French and English.

RTG operates a television service, with two main 50-kw transmitters at Libreville and Port-Gentil, supplemented in 1972 by two 2-kw transmitters. Coverage now extends inland as far as Kango and Lambaréné. Programs are transmitted by satellite to other African countries. Color television broadcasts began in 1975.

Media

Daily Newspapers: 1
  Total Circulation 000: 20
  Circulation per 1,000: 16
Books Published: —
Magazines: —
Radio Receivers 000: 155
  per 1,000: 119
Television sets 000: 100
  per 1,000: 76

MOST IMPORTANT MEDIA:

Press. The following are published at Libreville: *L'Union* (35,000), government daily; *Gabon-Matin* (18,000), published daily by the Agence Gabonaise de Presse; *La Relance*, weekly PDG organ; *Gabon d'Aujourd'hui*, published weekly by the Ministry of Communications.

News agency. The domestic facility is the Agence Gabonaise de Presse (AGP).

Radio and television. The government-controlled Radiodiffusion-Télévision Gabonaise broadcasts national and regional radio programs in French and local languages, plus educational television programming from Libreville and Port-Gentil. There is also a private channel, Télé-Africa, that broadcasts in French.

CULTURE

Cultural Indicators

Libraries
  Number: 20
  Volumes: —
  Registered borrowers: —
Museums
  Number: —
  Annual Attendance: —
Cinema
  Production of Long Films: —
  Number of Cinemas: —
  Seating Capacity: —
  Annual Attendance: —
  Annual Attendance per capita: —

STATUS OF WOMEN

In recent years women have begun to play an increasing role in the economic, political, and cultural life of the country, particularly in urban areas. The government and the ruling RDG have become more sensitized to women's issues. Newly created government and party institutions are actively promoting women's rights. The Ministry of Women's Affairs in 1984 commanded additional resources, including creation of a national commission for the promotion of women. The ministry's action program still is largely in the planning stage, although an effort is under way to determine women's needs and aspirations in the traditional agricultural sector. The party's women's union is active in organizing women's cultural presentations throughout the country.

Women

Gender Empowerment Measure: —
Seats Held in Parliament by Women %: 10.9
Female Administrators and Managers %: —
Female Professional and Technical Workers %: —
Women's Share of Earned Income %: —
Women in Government %: 6

HEALTH, FOOD, AND NUTRITION

Health

Number of Physicians: 448
Number of Dentists: 32
Number of Nurses: 759
Number of Pharmacists: 71
Population per Physician: 2,504
Number of Hospitals: 27
Hospital Beds per 10,000: 51
Hospital Bed Occupancy Rate: —
Infant Mortality Rate per 1,000 live births: 190
Maternal Mortality Rate per 100,000 live births: 1,100
Total Health Expenditures as % of GDP: 7.53
Health Expenditures per capita $: 22
HIV Infected % of adults: 4.25
Cigarette Consumption per smoker per year: 174
% of Smokers: Male: —
Female: —
Access to Safe Water %: 61

Food and Nutrition

Food Supply as % of FAO Requirements: 91
% of Consumption Expenditures on Food: 54.7
Daily Available Calories per capita: 2,511
% of Total Calories derived from:
Cereals: 26
Potatoes, cassava: 20.3
Meat, poultry: 8.2
Fish: 2.7
Eggs, milk: 2.1
Fruits, vegetables: 16.3
Fats, oils: 7.6

ENVIRONMENT

Gabon is blessed with an abundance of natural resources and biodiversity. In the early 1990s, nearly 85 percent of the land was covered with lush rain forests, of which 35 percent had never been exploited. Its high standard of living (the highest in sub-Saharan Africa) is largely due to the exploitation of its oil reserves. The use of oil has protected other natural resources such as forests. However, with worldwide oil prices falling, there is growing pressure to expand Gabon's economy and to exploit its other natural resources, especially timber. Increased logging threatens Gabon's forests.

Environment

Forest Area sq km: 179,000
Average Annual Deforestation sq km: 910
Nationally Protected Areas as % of Total Land Area: 2.8
Freshwater Access cubic meters per capita: 138,942
Emissions of Organic Water Pollutants kg per day: 1,886
CO_2 Emissions per capita ton: 3.3

CHRONOLOGY

1960 Gabon is formally proclaimed an independent nation, with Leon M'Ba as prime minister.

1961 M'Ba is elected president and heads a government of national union with his opponent, Jean-Hilaire Aubame, as foreign minister.

1963 Aubame is relieved of his foreign affairs portfolio.

1964 Aubame leads a successful coup; French troops, responding to M'Ba's appeal, intervene and restore him to office; Aubame is sentenced to 10 years in prison.
In new elections M'Ba's party, the Gabon Democratic Bloc, wins 31 seats to 16 seats for the opposition Gabonese Democratic and Social Union.

1965 Dr. Albert Schweitzer dies at Lambaréné.

1967 M'Ba is reelected president but dies within months; Vice President Albert-Bernard (later Omar) Bongo succeeds to the presidency.

1968 Parti Démocratique Gabonais (PDG) is proclaimed the sole legal political party in the country.

1969 Gabon recognizes dissident Biafra in Nigerian civil war.

1972 Equatorial Guinea accuses Gabon of invading its islands; Gabon withdraws claims and the issue is settled.

1973 Bongo is reelected president.

1975 Leon Mebiame is named prime minister.

1978 Beninese workers are expelled.
At the Franco-African summit Bongo asks for an African joint force.

1979 As sole candidate in national presidential election, Bongo is reelected for a second seven-year term.

1980 In national municipal and legislative elections independents are permitted to run against official candidates.

1981 Over 10,000 Cameroonians are expelled following a Douala, Cameroon, riot against a soccer team from Gabon.

1982 Members of the opposition Mouvement de Redressment National (MORENA) are arrested for "insulting the president" and sentenced to harsh prison terms. Action provokes strong reaction from Paris.

1983 The Owenda-to-Booué section of the Trans-Gabonais Railway is opened by French and Gabonese presidents.
1984 France agrees to supply Gabon with a 300-mw nuclear power plant, the first in black-ruled Africa.
1986 Chernobyl accident in USSR causes the cancellation of nuclear power plant. MORENA political prisoners are freed.
1990 After much social unrest and increasing pressure from disgruntled workers, President Bongo legalizes opposition and names Casimir Oye-Mba prime minister.
In the country's first multiparty election, Bongo's PDG wins 65 seats in the legislature while opposition parties take the remaining 55.
1991 The government promulgates a new constitution.
1993 Omar Bongo is reelected president, a post held since 1967.
1995 The constitution, which has been in effect since 1991, is approved by referendum.
1996 An Ebola outbreak kills 13 in a remote Gabon village; in legislative elections PDG wins 89 of 120 seats in the Assemblée Nationale and 53 of 91 Senate seats.
1998 Bongo is reelected, gaining two-thirds of the vote.
2001 Outbreak of deadly Ebola virus occurs in December.

BIBLIOGRAPHY

Aicardi de Saint-Paul, Marc. *Gabon: The Development of a Nation*. New York, 1989.

Barnes, James F. *Gabon: Beyond the Colonial Legacy*. Boulder, Colo., 1992.

Gardinier, David E. *Historical Dictionary of Gabon*. 2nd ed. Metuchen, N.J., 1994.

OFFICIAL PUBLICATIONS

Gabon. *Gabon: Poste d'Expansion Economique à Libreville* (1995); *Situation economique, financière et sociale de la République Gabonaise* (annual).

CONTACT INFORMATION

Embassy of Gabon
2034 20th Street NW, Suite 200
Washington, D.C. 20009
Phone: (202) 797-1000 Fax: (202) 332-0668

INTERNET RESOURCES

- Gabon: The Country Fact Book
  http://www.gabon-net.com/english/facts.html

THE GAMBIA

BASIC FACT SHEET

OFFICIAL NAME:
Republic of The Gambia

ABBREVIATION:
GM

CAPITAL:
Banjul (formerly Bathurst)

HEAD OF STATE AND GOVERNMENT:
President Yayah Jammeh (from 1994)

NATURE OF GOVERNMENT:
Republic

POPULATION:
1,336,000 (1999)

AREA:
11,570 sq km (4,467 sq mi)

ETHNIC MAJORITIES:
Mandingo and Fula

LANGUAGES:
English (official), Wolof, and Mandinka

RELIGIONS:
Islam and Christianity

UNIT OF CURRENCY:
Dalasi (D.)

NATIONAL FLAG:
Tricolor of red, blue, and green horizontal stripes divided by narrow white stripes

NATIONAL EMBLEM:
Two heraldic lions holding a blue shield displaying a Mandingo hoe and a Locar ax with a scroll beneath. At the crest of the design is a blue knight's helmet and a green oil palm and peanuts sprouting from a mound. On the scroll is the national motto: "Progress, Peace, Prosperity."

NATIONAL ANTHEM:
"For The Gambia, Our Homeland"

NATIONAL HOLIDAYS:
February 18 (Independence Day, National Day); January 1 (New Year's Day); April 24 (Republic Day); August 15 (Queen's Birthday); Christian festivals include Christmas, Boxing Day, Good Friday, and Easter Monday; variable Islamic festivals also are celebrated.

DATE OF INDEPENDENCE:
February 18, 1965

DATE OF CONSTITUTION:
April 24, 1970; rewritten and approved by national referendum on August 8, 1996

GEOGRAPHICAL FEATURES

The Gambia is on the western coast of Africa along both banks of the Gambia River, with a total land area of 11,570 sq km (4,467 sq mi). The greatest distance east to west is 470 km (292 mi), while the greatest distance north to south is only 47 km (29 mi). The country's Atlantic coastline is 71 km (44 mi) long.

The Gambia is virtually an enclave within Senegal, with which it shares its entire international border of 740 km (459 mi).

Most of The Gambia is low-lying, but generally it is divided into three regions on the basis of topographical features: the valley floor, built up of alluvium with areas known as Bango Faros; a dissected plateau edge consisting of sandy and often precipitous hills alternating with broad valleys; and a sandstone plateau that extends, in places, across the border into Senegal.

The Gambia River is one of the finest waterways in western Africa and is navigable as far as Kuntaur, 240 km (150 mi) upstream, by seagoing vessels and as far as Koina by vessels of shallow draft. Thick mangrove swamps border the lower reaches of the river, and behind these mangroves are the "flats," which are submerged completely during the wet season. Near Banjul the river is 4.8 km (3 mi) wide.

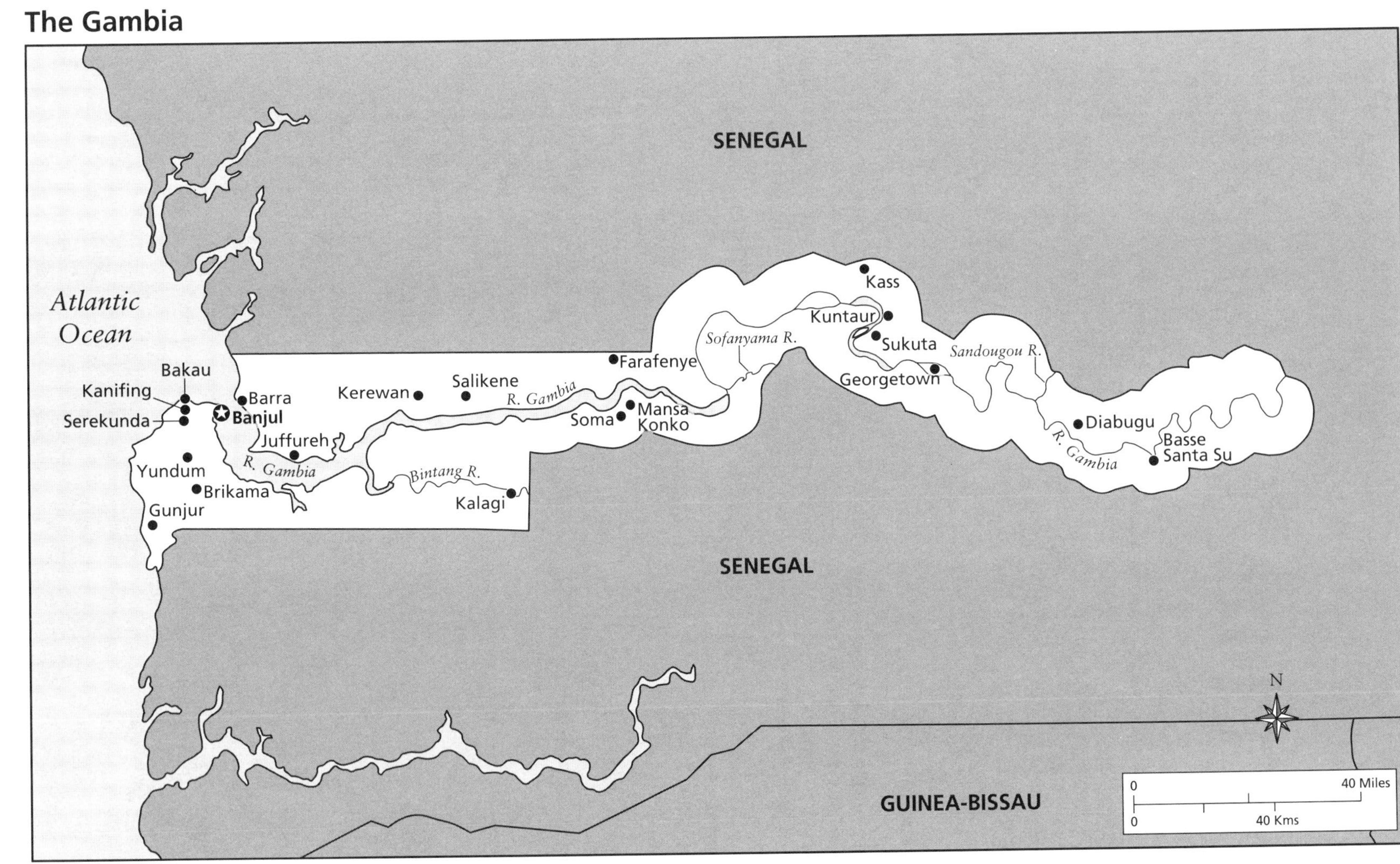
The Gambia
SENEGAL
Atlantic Ocean
Bakau
Kanifing
Serekunda
Banjul
Barra
Kerewan
Salikene
R. Gambia
Farafenye
Sofanyama R.
Kass
Kuntaur
Sukuta
Sandougou R.
Georgetown
Juffureh
R. Gambia
Yundum
Brikama
Gunjur
Bintang R.
Kalagi
Soma
Mansa Konko
Diabugu
R. Gambia
Basse Santa Su
SENEGAL
N
GUINEA-BISSAU
0
40 Miles
0
40 Kms

Geography

Area sq km: 11,570 (4,467 sq mi)
World Rank: 162nd
Land Boundaries, km: Senegal 740
Coastline, km: 80
Elevation Extremes meters
  Lowest: Atlantic Ocean 0
  Highest: 53
Land Use % Arable land: 18
  Permanent Crops: 0
  Permanent Pastures: 9
  Forest and Woodland: 28
  Other: 45

Population of Principal Cities

Banjul	42,407
Serekunda	102,600

CLIMATE AND WEATHER

The climate is subtropical, with a hot and wet season from June to October alternating with a cooler dry season from November to April. Average annual rainfall is about 1,016 mm (40 in), concentrated in the rainy season, with August being the wettest month. Near the coast the summer temperatures vary between 18°C and 32°C (65°F and 90°F), but inland the range is greater, from 10°C to 40°C (50°F to 105°F). From November to April cooler weather prevails, with temperatures as low as 7°C (45°F) in Banjul and surrounding areas. The dry season, however, is plagued by the dusty Harmattan wind blowing from the Sahara. Floods are common in the wet season but not destructive. Receding floodwaters leave swamps, where rice is cultivated.

Climate and Weather

Mean Temperature
Summer Coastal Region 65°F to 90°F
Summer Inland 50°F to 105°F
Winter 45°F
Average Rainfall 40 in

POPULATION

Population Indicators

Total Population: 1999 1,336,000
World Rank: 148th
Density per sq mi: 323.7 (125 per sq km)
% of annual growth (1994–99): 3.6
Male %: 50.1
Female %: 49.9
Urban %: 36.7
Age Distribution: % 0–14: 43.8
  15–29: 27.7
  30–44: 15.1
  45–59: 6.8
  60–74: 3.5
  75 and over: 1.4
Population 2020: 2,399,000
Birth Rate per 1,000: 39.9
Death Rate per 1,000: 17.4
Population Doubling Time (years): 23
Infant Mortality Rate per 1,000 live births: 122
Rate of Natural Increase per 1,000: 22.5
Total Fertility Rate: 5.2
Expectation of Life (years): Males 45.4
  Females 48.7
Marriage Rate per 1,000: —
Divorce Rate per 1,000: —
Total Number of Households: —
Average Size of Households: 8.7
% of Illegitimate Children: —
Induced Abortions: —
  Rate per 100 live births: —

ETHNIC COMPOSITION

Despite its small size, the population of The Gambia is characterized by great diversity; no ethnic group commands an absolute numerical majority.

The Mandingo are the most westerly extension of the Manding group of people, who include the Bambara, Dyula, and Kuranko. The Fula, Fulani, Peul, and Fulbe are found in great numbers from Cameroon and Sudan to the Atlantic coast. The Jola are related to the Serer, with whom they maintain a close relationship. The Serahuli are a mixture of Mandingo, Berber, and Fulbe.

The Mandingo are found throughout the country, and make up about 34 percent of the population. The Fula are concentrated in the east, the Wolof in the west, and the Serahuli in the easternmost region. Two other important communities are the Aku, who are numerous in the capital, and the Diola, who live in the west.

LANGUAGES

The official language of The Gambia is English, although less than 2 percent of the population speak it. Wolof and Mandinka are used as lingua francas and as trade languages. The more Islamized inhabitants speak Arabic.

Principal Languages and Their Speakers

Language	Speakers
English	—
Gambians	
Aku (Krio)	8,000
Atlantic languages	
Diola (Jola)	123,000
Fula (Fulani)	216,000
Manjak	21,000
Serer	32,000
Wolof	168,000

(continued)

Mande languages	
Bambara	10,000
Malinke	455,000
Soninke	102,000
Other	184,000
non-Gambians	184,000

RELIGIONS

The constitution does not specify a state religion, but more than 95 percent of Gambians are Sunni Muslims. Though Islam was introduced in the 12th century, it was not until the Soninke-Marabout wars of the mid-1850s that most of the population was converted to Islam. Of the major tribes, the Mandingo, Fula, and Serahuli are almost entirely Muslim.

Christians are estimated to constitute less than 10% of the population, concentrated in the capital. The most influential Christian tribe is the Aku, who until recently dominated the government and commerce. There is a Roman Catholic bishopric at Banjul.

Most of the Jola tribesmen follow traditional African religions.

Religious Affiliations

Muslim	1,270,000
Other	70,000

HISTORICAL BACKGROUND

Beginning in the 13th century, the region that is now The Gambia was settled by the Wolof, Mandingo, and Fulani, all of them Islamicized peoples from Mali. European exploration began with the discovery of the Gambia River by Portuguese navigators in 1555. The first English merchants arrived here in 1587. The Royal Africa Company acquired a charter in 1687 and established a small fort on James Island, a small island in the river estuary. After suffering losses as a result of attacks by the French, the company was divested of its charter in 1750. From 1765 to 1783 the fort and the nearby settlement were part of the British colony of Senegambia, with the capital at St. Louis. In 1779 the French captured and destroyed Fort James, and in 1783 the greater part of the colony was handed to the French, excluding the small enclave that is now The Gambia.

The Gambia was under British rule from 1816, when Capt. Alexander Grant entered into a treaty with the chief of Kombo for the cession of Banjul Island, to 1963, when The Gambia attained full self-government. British power in The Gambia was never seriously challenged by internal or external forces. Most Gambians were exhausted by the half century of wars that preceded British arrival and welcomed Pax Britannica. The British system of indirect rule also left unchanged the political and social systems that had existed prior to the 19th century. British cultural penetration was limited to Bathurst (now Banjul). British economic and financial administration was characterized by conservatism; the British Colonial Office expected all territories to live within their budgets, and reserves normally were not used for development. British contributions to the development of political institutions were more lasting. The Gambia is one of the few states in Africa to have remained faithful to the basic concepts of Westminster-type parliamentary democracy. The British departure was peaceful, and there is no significant anticolonial sentiment in the country. The Gambia remains a member of the Commonwealth, and current relations with Britain are cordial.

The Gambia gained full independence in 1965 and became a republic in 1970. Sir Dawda Jawara, a Mandingo, and his People's Progressive Party have been in power continually since independence. The national unity that characterized the first years of independence broke down during the 1970s with growing resentment over the power of the Mandingo and Jawara's failure to deal with government corruption and demands for confederation with Senegal. In July 1981, when President Jawara was in London to attend the wedding of Prince Charles, the field force took over Banjul. The uprising was quelled, however, with the help of Senegalese troops dispatched under the terms of a 1965 mutual defense and security treaty.

Senegal and The Gambia in February 1982 announced plans for the creation of the Senegambian Confederation. The process of confederation continued during the mid-1980s. Tariff barriers were harmonized and transportation links improved. Important steps were taken to implement protocols on defense and security. The Gambia gendarmerie was organized on the Senegalese model and was trained and initially commanded by a Senegalese officer. The Gambian army also was trained by Senegalese. Despite the movement toward economic union, the two states continued to function as separate entities, and the confederation was formally dissolved in 1989 after Senegal unilaterally withdrew the troops it had stationed in The Gambia in the wake of the 1981 coup.

Following the breakup of the Senegambia Confederation, the Jawara government was overthrown in 1994 in a bloodless coup led by army officers who installed Lt Yayah Jammeh as chairman of a five-member Armed Forces Provisional Ruling Council. Three days later the council named a 15-member government composed equally of military and civilian members. In 1995 Jammeh named a constitutional commission charged with drafting a constitutional document for the holding of multiparty elections. The regime survived many abortive coups until 1996 when Jammeh was elected to a five-year presidential term as the candidate for the newly formed Alliance for Patriotic Reorientation and Construction (APRC). In the 1997 legislative elections APRC won 33 of the 45 contested seats giving the ruling party the necessary two-thirds majority necessary to

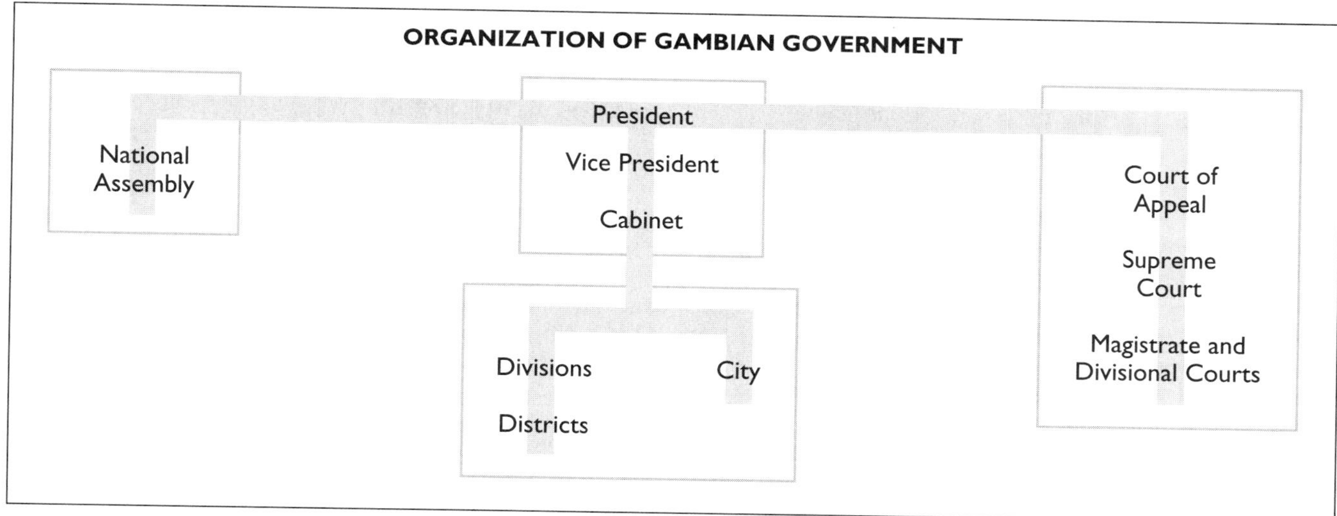

make constitutional changes. In 2001, Jammeh was reelected president in elections that were called fair and democratic by international observers.

CONSTITUTION

The constitutional basis of the Gambian government is the constitution of 1970, which established a republican and presidential form of government. Under the constitution, executive power is vested in the president who is both head of state and head of government, and who is elected directly for a five-year term. He designates a vice president (who is required to belong to the same party as the president), who exercises the functions of a prime minister and leader of government business in the parliament. The president also appoints the cabinet and the principal civil servants.

Legislative power is in the hands of a unicameral parliament, which is elected for a five-year term. The Supreme Court is the highest in the land. There is also a Court of Appeal and various subordinate courts and Islamic courts.

A referendum in 1996 changed the parliament to a National Assembly and increased the membership to 45 directly elected members and four nominated members. The ban on political parties was also lifted.

LOCAL GOVERNMENT

For purposes of regional administration, The Gambia is divided into five divisions and one city, each headed by a commissioner appointed by the president. The divisions are subdivided into 35 districts administered by chiefs with the help of village mayors and councillors. The districts also are grouped into seven area councils, each with an elected majority. Each council has its treasury and is responsible for local government services. Banjul is a separate region with its own city council.

Local Government

Principal administrative divisions, capitals, area, population

AREA AND POPULATION

Divisions	Capitals	area sq mi	area sq km	population 1993 estimate
Kombo St. Mary	Kanifling	29	76	228,214
Lower River	Mansakonko	625	1,618	65,146
MacCarthy Island	Kuntaur/Geor getown	1,117	2,894	156,021
North Bank	Kerewan	871	2,256	156,462
Upper River	Basse	799	2,069	155,059
Western	Birkama	681	1,764	23,917
City				
Banjul	—	5	12	42,326
TOTAL		4,127	10,689	1,038,145

PARLIAMENT

The national legislature is the National Assembly, a unicameral body consisting of 50 members who serve for a five-year term. Forty-five are elected by universal suffrage; four are appointed members. The attorney general sits ex officio.

Among African countries, The Gambia is noted for its fair and free elections. Suffrage is universal over age 18.

POLITICAL PARTIES

Although the Gambia is a multiparty state, the Alliance for Patriotic Reorientation and Construction or APRC controls 33 of the 45 elected seats. The APRC is the political party of Yayah Jammeh who seized power in 1994. Additional parties represented in the national assembly include the United Democratic Party or UDP, the National Reconciliation Party or NRP, and the People's Democratic Organization for Independence and Socialism or PDOIS. The government banned several political parties in 1996, including the People's Progressive Party or PPP, which is headed by former president Dawda K. Jawara (in exile), and the National Convention Party or NCP, which is headed by former vice president Sheriff Dibba.

Political Parties

Alliance for Patriotic Reorientation and Construction, 1996
United Democratic Party, 1996
People's Progressive Party, 1967
National Convention Party, 1975
Gambia People's Party, 1985
People's Democratic Organization for Independence and Socialism, 1986
National Reconstruction Party, 1996
People's Democratic Party, 1991
Movement for Justice in Africa-The Gambia, 1979
Gambia Socialist Revolutionary Party

Political Parties: Strength in Parliament Most Recent Elections

Of the National Assembly's 53 members, 48 are elected to serve five-year terms and four members are appointed. In the most recent elections of January 17, 2002, the Alliance for Patriotic Reorientation and Construction (APRC) captured 45 seats, the People's Democratic Organisation for Independence and Socialism, 3. Thirty-three APRC candidates were elected unopposed. The elections were boycotted by the centrist United Democratic Party.

LEGAL SYSTEM

The judicial system is based on English common law as modified by the legislative enactments of the Gambian National Assembly. Under a Muslim Law Recognition Ordinance, a Muslim court exercises jurisdiction in cases between, or exclusively affecting, Muslims.

Three kinds of law operate in The Gambia: general, Shari'a, and customary law. Shari'a law, governing certain aspects of social interaction of rural Muslims, is observed, even in the capital of Banjul, in marriage, inheritance, divorce, land tenure and utilization, local government, and all other civil and social relations originating in the traditional religious and ethnic situation of the country. General law, based on English statutes and modified to suit the Gambian context, governs criminal cases and trials and most organized business practices. If there were a conflict between general and Shari'a law, general law would prevail. Trial procedures in general law are carefully regulated to insure protection of the rights of the accused.

The court system is headed by the Court of Appeal and the Supreme Court. The Court of Appeal consists of a president, justices of appeal, and judges of the Supreme Court ex officio. The Supreme Court consists of a chief justice and a lower judge. It has unlimited jurisdiction but is subject to the appellate power of the Court of Appeal. The subordinate courts are known as magistrate and divisional courts. These are courts of summary jurisdiction presided over by a magistrate or, in his absence, by two or more lay justices of the peace. In 1974 a system of traveling magistrates was introduced to speed up administration of justice in rural areas. In some areas chiefs retain power to dispense justice according to customary law.

LAW ENFORCEMENT

Law Enforcement

Offenses reported to the police per 100,000: 89
- Murder: 0.4
- Assault: 10.6
- Burglary: 5.6
- Automobile Theft: —
- Population per Police officer: 3,310

Death Penalty: Yes, but last execution was in 1981

HUMAN RIGHTS

In terms of civil and political rights, The Gambia is classified as a free country. The Gambia is a multiparty, functioning democracy in which human rights are guaranteed by the constitution and observed in practice. Constitutional provisions against torture, cruel and inhuman punishment, disappearances, and arbitrary arrests and imprisonments are strictly enforced. The judiciary is independent of the executive and, since there are no armed forces, military courts do not exist. The legal system, modeled on that of the United Kingdom, ensures a fair and open trial for all defendants.

Censorship is nonexistent. Opposition viewpoints are discussed openly both in the print media and on the radio. Although The Gambia is more than 95 percent Muslim, there is no discrimination against non-Muslim minorities. One of the few multiparty states in Africa, The Gambia provides full freedom, both in law and in practice, to form and promote political groups of any persuasion and to contest elections under any label. In 1980 The Gambia hosted the 37-nation OAU Conference on Human and People's Rights.

FOREIGN POLICY

The Gambia's closest external relations have been with two countries: Senegal, which borders The Gambia on three sides, and the United Kingdom, its former colonial master and source of much of its foreign aid. For some time in the early 1980s The Gambia was a partner in the Confederation of Senegambia, but relations between the two countries rapidly deteriorated after the dissolution of the union in 1989. Since 1998 The Gambia has taken an active role in the civil unrest in Guinea-Bissau.

DEFENSE

A defense agreement made in 1965 with Senegal provides for a joint defense committee with a permanent secretariat. Military training may be provided by the United Kingdom and Senegal, if requested by The Gambia. Following the 1981 coup, the government reorganized the field force into a national gendarmerie in which service is voluntary. The gendarmerie is trained by Senegal. Total armed forces number 800.

Military Indicators

Total Active Duty Personnel: 800
Military Manpower per 1,000: 0.6
Military Expenditures $: 15 million
- as % of GNP: 4.6
- per capita $: 13
- as % of central government expenditures: 16.2

Arms Imports $: 0
Arms Exports $: 0

ECONOMY

The Gambia has no important mineral or other natural resources and has a limited agricultural base. About 75 percent of the population depends on crops and livestock for its livelihood. Small-scale manufacturing activity features the processing of peanuts, fish, and hides. Reexport trade normally constitutes a major segment of economic activity, but the 50 percent devaluation of the CFA franc in January 1994 made Senegalese goods more competitive and hurt the reexport trade. The Gambia has benefited from a rebound in tourism after its decline in response to the military's takeover in July 1994. Short-run economic progress remains highly dependent on sustained bilateral and multilateral aid and on responsible government economic management as forwarded by IMF technical help and advice. Annual gross domestic product growth is estimated at 4.9 percent in 2000.

Principal Economic Indicators

Gross National Product: $407 million
GNP per capita: $340
GNP Average Annual Growth Rate (1990–97) %: −0.6
GNP per capita Average Annual Growth Rate (1990–97) %: −4.2
Origin of Gross Domestic Product %
- Agriculture: 21
- Mining: —
- Manufacturing: 6
- Construction: 4
- Public Utilities: 1
- Transportation and Communications: 18
- Trade: 17
- Financial Services: 6
- Other Services: 4
- Government: 11

Gross Domestic Product by Type of Expenditure %
- Private Consumption: 79
- Government Consumption: 18
- Gross Domestic Investment: 16
- Foreign Trade: Exports: 44
  Imports: −57

% of Income Received by Poorest 20%: —
% of Income Received by Richest 10%: —

Price and earnings indexes (1995 = 100)

	1992	1993	1994	1995	1996	1997	1998
Consumer price index	86.3	91.9	93.5	100.0	101.1	103.9	105.1
Earnings index	—	—	—	—	—	—	—

Finance

National Currency: Dalasi (D)
Exchange Rate: $1 =D 10,513
Money Supply Stock in National Currency: 453 million
M1 per capita: 370
Central Bank Discount Rate %: 12.0
Total External Debt $million: 426
Debt Service Ratio %: 8.3

Balance of Payments $million: −23.6
International Reserves SDRs million: 74
Ratio of External Debt to Total Reserves: 3.6

Average Annual Rate of Inflation/Consumer Price Index Growth Rate %: 2.2

Official Development Assistance

ODA: $70.8
- as % of GNP: 9.3
- per capita: $31
- Foreign Direct Investment $million: 13

Central Government Revenues and Expenditures

Fiscal Year: 1 July–30 June

Revenues $million: 88.6
Expenditures $million: 98.2
Budget Deficit $: 9.6 million
Tax Revenues as % of GDP: —
Highest Tax Bracket %
- Individual: —
- Corporate: —

Employment and Labor

Economically Active Population: 326,000
Female Participation Rate %: 46.3
Activity Rate %: 47.3

(continued)

Labor by Sector: %
- Agriculture, Forestry, Fishing: 73.7
- Manufacturing, Mining: 2.9
- Construction: 1.3
- Transportation and Communications: 2.5
- Trade, Hotels, and Restaurants: 5.1
- Finance, Insurance, Real Estate: 1.4
- Public Administration, Defense: 2.5
- Services: 2.9

Unemployment %: NA

Agriculture

Agriculture's Share of GDP %: 21
Average Annual Rate of Growth (1965–98) %: 1.8
Number of Farms 000: —
Average Size of Farm ha: —
Number of Tractors per 1,000 hectares: 0.3
Irrigation, % of Farms having: 1
Artificial Fertilizer kg/hectare: 11
Total Cropland as % of Farmland: 100
Livestock: Cattle 000: 1,027
Sheep 000: 543
Hogs 000: 330
Chickens 000: 13,500
Forests: Production of Roundwood (000 cubic meters): 1,221
Fisheries: Total Catch tons 000: 22,300

Mining

% of GDP: —
Value of Mineral Production $million: —

Manufacturing

Value Added $million: 22
Industrial Production Growth Rate %: NA

Energy

Commercial Energy Production metric tons of oil equivalent 000: —
Commercial Energy Consumption metric tons of oil equivalent 000: —
Commercial Energy Consumption per capita kg: —
Average Annual Growth Rate 1980–97 %: —
Net Energy Imports % of use: —
Electricity Installed Capacity kW 000: 29
Production kW-hr million: 74
Coal Reserves tons million: —
Production tons 000: —
Natural Gas Proven Reserves cubic meters billion: —
Production cubic meters million: —
Crude Petroleum Reserves barrels million: —
Production barrels million: —
Consumption barrels million: —
Refinery Capacity barrels per day 000: —
Pipelines Length km: —

Foreign Trade

Imports $million: 141.3
Exports $million: 21.5
Export Volume % Annual Growth Rate (1990–97): −18.5
Import Volume % Annual Growth Rate (1990–97): −0.8
Balance of Trade $

Balance of trade (current prices)

	1994	1995	1996	1997	1998
CFAF 000,000	−1,695.0	−1,586.0	−2,318.5	−1,624.0	−2,319.4
% of total	71.5%	83.5%	84.7%	84.4%	80.2%

Major Trading Partners

	Imports	Exports
European Union %	47.3	57.1
United States %	5.2	3.6
Eastern Europe %	0.7	—
Japan %	3.5	—
Others %	43.3	39.4

Transportation

Roads Total Length mi: 1,640 (2,640 km)
Paved %: 35
Automobiles: 7,950
Trucks and Buses: 8,240
Persons per vehicle: 72
Railroad; Track Length mi: —
Passenger-mi million: —
Freight-mi million: —
Merchant Marine: No. of Vessels: 11
Total Deadweight Tonnage 000: 2
International Cargo Loaded tons 000: 185
International Cargo Off-loaded tons 000: 240
Airports with Scheduled Flights: 1
Traffic: Passenger-mi million: 31
Freight-mi million: 3
Length of Canals mi: 250 (400 km)

Tourism

Number of Tourists to 000: 91
Number of Tourists from 000: —
Tourist Receipts $million: 23
Tourist Expenditures $million: 16

Communications

Telephones 000: 19
Cost of Local Calls 3 mins: $0
Cellular Telephones 000: 1.4
Fax Machines 000: 1.0
Personal Computers 000: —
Internet Hosts per million persons: —
Mail: Post Offices: —
Pieces of Mail Handled million: —
Pieces of Mail Handled per person: —

EDUCATION

The Gambia has not yet introduced universal, free, and compulsory education.

Primary education lasts for seven years and is followed by a junior secondary cycle of four or five years and a senior secondary cycle of two years. Secondary education culminates in the "advanced" level examination of the West African Examination Council.

The academic year runs from September to July. The medium of instruction is English throughout.

Private and missionary schools are integrated within the school system. Private schools account for 16 percent of primary school enlistment. Vocational training is provided at Banjul and Sapu.

Primary and secondary education policies and programs are coordinated by the Ministry of Education. For purposes of educational administration, the country is divided into two regions.

The Gambia has no university, and Gambians who wish to pursue higher studies have to go abroad. However, the Gambia College at Brikama offers postsecondary courses in teacher training, agriculture, and health.

According to 1998 estimates, only 39 percent of the population can read or write by the age of 15. The number is 53 percent for males and 25 percent for females.

Education

Literacy Rate %: 38.6
- Male %: 52.8
- Female %: 24.9

First Level: Primary schools: 250
- Teachers: 3,158
- Students: 105,471
- Student-Teacher Ratio: 33.4
- Net Enrollment Ratio: 55

Second Level: Secondary Schools: 32
- Teachers: 1,126
- Students: 27,120
- Student-Teacher Ratio: 24.1
- Net Enrollment Ratio: 18

Vocational Level: Schools: —
- Students: —

Third Level: Institutions: —
- Teachers: 155
- Students: 1,591
- Student-Ratio Level: 10.3
- Gross Enrollment Ratio: 1.7
- Students per 100,000: 148
- % of Population Age 25 and over with Postsecondary Education: —

Public Expenditure on Education as % of GDP: 5.5

SCIENCE AND TECHNOLOGY

Science and Technology

Scientists and Engineers in R&D per 1 million persons: —
Expenditures in R&D as % of GDP: —
High-Tech Exports $: —
Patent Applications by Residents: —

MEDIA

There is one daily newspaper in the country; six nondaily newspapers are published, of which the *Gambia News Bulletin*, published three times a week by the government information office, enjoys the widest circulation. Six periodicals also are published, with a total circulation of 4,000.

Gambia News Agency, located in Banjul, is the country's national news agency.

Radio Gambia, the official broadcasting service operates one shortwave transmitter and one FM transmitter. There are four private commercial radio stations and three community ones. Television service began in 1995.

Media

Daily Newspapers: 1
- Total Circulation 000: 2
- Circulation per 1,000: 2

Books Published: 21
Magazines: 10
Radio Receivers 000: 150
- per 1,000: 125

Television sets 000: —
- per 1,000: —

MOST IMPORTANT MEDIA:

Press. The following are English-language publications issued at Banjul: *The Gambia Daily*, state owned; *The Gambia Weekly* (500), published by the Government Information Office; *The Gambia Times*, PPP fortnightly; *The Nation*, fortnightly; *The Daily Observer*, registered in 1992; *The Worker*, thrice-weekly organ of the Gambia Labour Congress; *The Gambia Onward*, thrice-weekly. *Newsmonth*, an independent weekly, commenced publication in April 1993.

News agency. The domestic facility is the Gambia News Agency (Gamna).

Radio and television. Radio broadcasting to the country's estimated 206,000 sets is provided by Radio Syd, a commercial outlet, and by the government-owned Radio Gambia, which relays BBC news and carries programs in English and local languages. The nation's first television station began broadcasting in January 1996, service having previously been available only via transmissions from Senegal.

CULTURE

Cultural Indicators

Libraries
- Number: 5
- Volumes: —
- Registered borrowers: —

Museums
- Number: —
- Annual Attendance: —

Cinema
- Production of Long Films: —
- Number of Cinemas: —
- Seating Capacity: —
- Annual Attendance: —
- Annual Attendance per capita: —

STATUS OF WOMEN

Education of women is increasingly accepted, and women participate in the professions and in political life. Marriages still are often arranged, but there is increasing freedom of personal choice. Family planning, focused on the health and welfare of mother and child, remains controversial but is gaining acceptance. The Women's Bureau in the Office of the President actively promotes debate on women's issues.

Women

Gender Empowerment Measure: 94
Seats Held in Parliament by Women %: 2.0
Female Administrators and Managers %: 15.5
Female Professional and Technical Workers %: 23.7
Women's Share of Earned Income %: 38
Women in Government %: 7

HEALTH, FOOD, AND NUTRITION

Health

Number of Physicians: 61
Number of Dentists: —
Number of Nurses: 430
Number of Pharmacists: —
Population per Physician: 14,536
Number of Hospitals: 13
Hospital Beds per 10,000: 7
Hospital Bed Occupancy Rate: —
Infant Mortality Rate per 1,000 live births: 190
Maternal Mortality Rate per 100,000 live births: 1,100
Total Health Expenditures as % of GDP: 7.53
Health Expenditures per capita $: 22
HIV Infected % of adults: 4.25
Cigarette Consumption per smoker per year: —
% of Smokers: Male: —
Female: —
Access to Safe Water %: 61

Food and Nutrition

Food Supply as % of FAO Requirements: 91
% of Consumption Expenditures on Food: 58.0
Daily Available Calories per capita: 2,157
% of Total Calories derived from:
Cereals: 53.5
Potatoes, cassava: 0.8
Meat, poultry: 1.4
Fish: 1.6
Eggs, milk: 1.5
Fruits, vegetables: 1.3
Fats, oils: 13.0

ENVIRONMENT

Like many developing African nations, The Gambia suffers from environmental problems that have to do with supporting the population. The land is being deforested both for fuel and for the creation of agricultural lands. However, the land also is becoming more desert-like as the farming methods and deforestation rob the land of essential nutrients. The country also has a large number of water-borne diseases that routinely infect the population.

Environment

Forest Area sq km: 1,000
Average Annual Deforestation sq km: 8
Nationally Protected Areas as % of Total Land Area: 2.0
Freshwater Access cubic meters per capita: 6,579
Emissions of Organic Water Pollutants kg per day: 832
CO_2 Emissions per capita ton: 0.2

CHRONOLOGY

1965 The Gambia attains full independence within the Commonwealth, with Sir David (later Dawda) Jawara as prime minister.
Proposal to establish a republic is defeated in a referendum by a narrow margin.

1967 The Muslim Congress Party merges with the ruling People's Progressive Party (PPP).

1968 Sherif Sisay, on being expelled from the PPP, forms a rival political party, the Progressive People's Alliance.

1970 Republic status is approved by voters in a second referendum.
The Gambia becomes a republic with Sir Dawda Jawara as first president.

1971 The dalasi is introduced as The Gambia's national currency.

1972 In national elections the ruling PPP wins 28 of 32 seats in House of Representatives; President Jawara is reelected.

1973 The capital, Bathurst, is renamed Banjul.
President Jawara visits Senegal.

1975 Two new opposition parties are founded: the National Convention Party and the National Liberation Party.

1976 President Senghor of Senegal visits Banjul; new cooperation agreements are signed between the two countries, including one that establishes the Gambia Basin Development Organization.

1977 In election to the House of Representatives the ruling PPP gains 28 of 35 seats.

1979 The PPP holds its first congress in 16 years.
President Jawara announces formation of the National Planning Commission.

1981 Members of the field force unit of the police force stage a coup and seize Banjul while President Jawara is in London.
Senegalese forces help quell the revolt under a 1965 mutual defense and security treaty.

A state of emergency is declared, and over 1,000 people are killed.

1982 The Confederation of Senegambia comes into being, with Jawara as vice president of the new federation.

Jawara's PPP wins 35 seats in elections to the House of Representatives.

1987 Jawara is reelected president. His People's Progressive Party retains its overwhelming majority in the House of Representatives, capturing 31 seats. The opposition National Convention Party wins five.

1989 The Senegambian Confederation is officially dissolved.

1991 Gambia and Senegal sign a bilateral agreement of friendship and cooperation.

1994 A military junta seizes power under Lieutenant Yayah Jammeh.

1996 Jammeh is elected president of the country over three other candidates.

1997 In national elections, the Alliance for Patriotic Reorientation and Construction gains 33 of the National Assembly's 45 elected seats.

2001 Jammeh is reelected president.

BIBLIOGRAPHY

Gailey, Harry A. *Historical Dictionary of The Gambia*. Metuchen, N.J., 1987.

Gamble, David P. *The Gambia*. Santa Barbara, Calif., 1988.

Hughes, A., and Perfect D. Hughes. *Political History of The Gambia, 1816–1992*. Farnborough, England, 1993.

OFFICIAL PUBLICATIONS

Gambia, The. *Statistical Abstract* (annual?); *The Gambia—Recent Economic Developments* (IMF Staff Country Report [1995]).

CONTACT INFORMATION

Embassy of The Gambia
1155 15th Street NW, Suite 1000
Washington, D.C. 20005
Phone: (202)785-1399 Fax: (202)785-1430

INTERNET RESOURCES

- Official WWW Site of The Republic of The Gambia http://www.Gambia.com

GEORGIA

BASIC FACT SHEET

OFFICIAL NAME:
Georgia (Sakartvelo)

ABBREVIATION:
GG

CAPITAL:
Tbilisi

HEAD OF STATE AND GOVERNMENT:
President Eduard Amrosiyewich Georgi Shevardnadze (from 1992)

NATURE OF GOVERNMENT:
Emerging democracy

POPULATION:
5,449,000

AREA:
69,492 sq km (26,831 sq mi)

MAJOR ETHNIC GROUPS:
Georgian (70%), Armenian (8%), Russian (6.3);

LANGUAGES:
Georgian 71%, Russian 9%, Armenian 7%

RELIGION:
Russia and Georgian Orthodox 75%, Muslim 11%, Armenian Apostolic 8%

UNIT OF CURRENCY:
Lavi

NATIONAL EMBLEM:

NATIONAL FLAG:
Maroon field with small rectangle in upper hoist side corner; rectangle divided horizontally with black on top, white below.

NATIONAL ANTHEM:
"Praise Be to the Heavenly Bestower of Blessings"

NATIONAL HOLIDAYS:
Independence Day May 26

DATE OF INDEPENDENCE:
April 9, 1991

DATE OF CONSTITUTION:
October 17, 1995

GEOGRAPHIC FEATURES

Georgia is situated in the southwest Caucasus on the northern periphery of the subtropical zone, between 41°07′ and 43°35′ north latitudes and 40°05′ and 46°44′ west longitudes. Georgia borders Turkey and Armenia to the south, the Russia to the north, Azerbaijan to the east, and the Black Sea to the west. The length of its borders totals 1,499 km (907 mi), 313 km (195 mi) of which is a coastline. Georgia covers 59,492 sq km (26,831 sq mi). Its area exceeds that of such countries as the Netherlands, Belgium, Switzerland, Denmark, and Israel.

Georgia is a mountainous country. Land below 1,967 ft occupies only 31 percent of the total area; 44 percent of its territory lies between 1,967 ft and 5,900 ft, and 25 percent above 5,900 ft. Mountainous areas are located mainly along the northern and southern borders. The highest mountains are: Shkhara, 5,067 m (16,625 ft); Janga, 5,059 m (16,598 ft); Mkinvartsveri (Kazbek), 5,048 m (16,562 ft); Shota Rustaveli, 4,866 m (15,965 ft); Tetnuldi, 4,858 m (15,939 ft); and Ushba, 4,700 m (15,420 ft).

Georgia is divided into three major geographical zones: the northern highlands-Caucasus (*Kavkasioni* in Georgian), the intermountain lowlands, and the uplands

Georgia

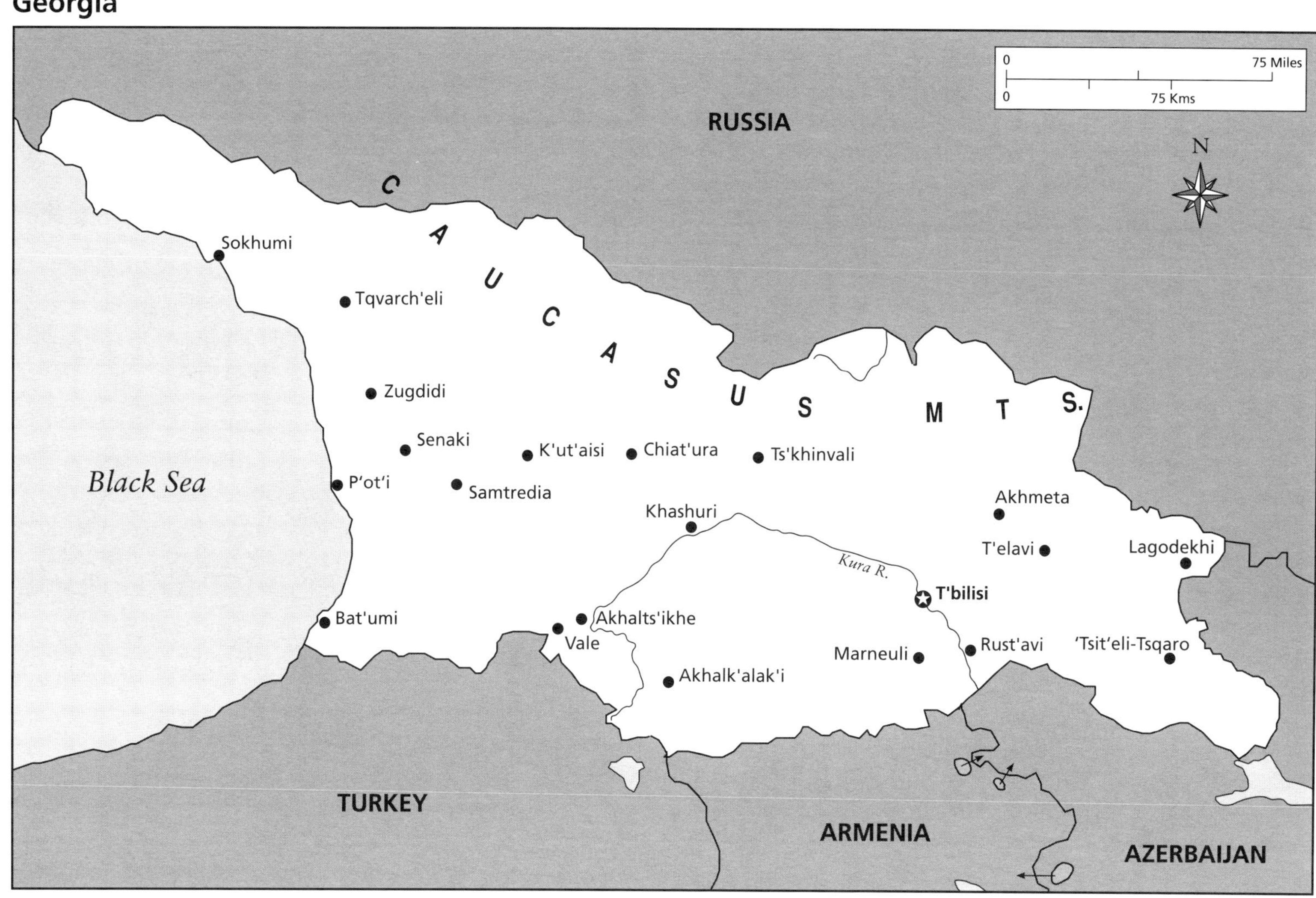
0
75 Miles
0
75 Kms
RUSSIA
N
CAUCASUS MTS.
Sokhumi
Tqvarch'eli
Zugdidi
Senaki
K'ut'aisi
Chiat'ura
Ts'khinvali
Black Sea
P'ot'i
Samtredia
Akhmeta
Khashuri
T'elavi
Lagodekhi
Kura R.
T'bilisi
Bat'umi
Akhalts'ikhe
Vale
Rust'avi
'Tsit'eli-Tsqaro
Marneuli
Akhalk'alak'i
TURKEY
ARMENIA
AZERBAIJAN

of southern Georgia. Kavkasioni and the southern upland are joined by the Likhi Range, which divides Georgia into western and eastern parts.

The main topographal unit of the Kavkasioni highlands is the main range of the Caucasus (average heights are 9,843 ft–11,483 ft above sea level). Caucasus ranges have steep slopes and are separated by deep river basins.

Intermountain lowland covers two-fifths of Georgian territory. The lowland is narrowest in its central part and widens out to the east and the west. The intermountain lowland consists of two major units: on the east, Iveria lowland consisting of the Shida Kartli Plain, the Alazani Plain, and the Bri Plateau, and on the west, the Kolkheti lowland made up of the Kolkheti lowland itself, the Imereti Plain, and premountain hills.

The highest summit of the southern upland, Mt. Didi Abuli, reaches 10,844 ft (average heights—6,562 ft). The southern upland comprises the Meskheti-Trialeti, Dmanisi, and Gomareti volcanic plateaus and Arsiani, Meskheti, Shavsheti, Trialeti, Samsari, and other minor ranges, which are dissected by canyon-like river gorges.

The hydrological network is not equally distributed in Georgia. In comparison to the eastern part of the country, the western part is highly saturated with river basins. The rivers of Georgia belong to the basins of the Black and Caspian Seas. The Mtkvari River, the longest at 1,364 km (847 mi) with its numerous tributaries, belongs to the Caspian basin. The Black Sea basin rivers include the Rioni (327 km; 203 mi), Enguri (213 km; 132 mi), and others. The largest lake is Lake Paravani (37.5 sq km; 14.4 sq mi), the deepest, Lake Ritsa (116 m; 448 ft) and Lake Amtkeli (72–122 m; 286–400 ft). Both are impounded lakes.

Geography

Area sq km: 69,492 sq mi 26,831
World Rank: 121st
Land Boundaries, km: Armenia 164; Azerbaijan 322; Russia 723; Turkey 252
Coastline, km 310
Elevation Extremes meters
- Lowest: Black Sea 0
- Highest: Mkinvartsveri 5,048

Land Use % Arable land: 9
- Permanent Crops: 4
- Permanent Pastures: 25
- Forest and Woodland: 34
- Other: 28

Population of Principal Cities (1994 est.)

City	Population
Bat'umi (Batumi)	137,100
K'ut'aisi (Kutaisi)	240,600
Rust'avi (Rustavi)	155,500
Sukhumi	112,000
T'bilisi (Tbilisi)	1,253,100

CLIMATE AND WEATHER

Georgian climate varies markedly. The relatively small territory is covered by different climatic zones, which are determined by distance from the Black Sea and altitude. Climatic zones range from the humid subtropical to the glacial. Georgia's climate is affected by subtropical influences from the west. The main range of the Caucasus protects Georgia from the cold northern winds. Likhi Range serves as the dividing line between western and eastern Georgia. In western Georgia, the dominant subtropical climate features high humidity and heavy precipitation (average is 1,600 mm). The midwinter average temperature is 8°C and the midsummer average is 22°C. Eastern Georgia has a more continental, moderately humid subtropical climate, with a considerably lower level of precipitation (average is 600 mm). Average temperature in summer is 20°–24°C, in winter 2°–4°C.

High climate zonality is typical for the mountainous areas. Alpine and highland regions have distinct microclimates. Alpine conditions start at 2,100 m.

Glaciers are found only on the main range of the Caucasus (688 sq km) and occupy 508 sq km. The regular snow line begins at 2,800 m.

Climate and Weather

Mean Temperature
- July 73.8°F
- January 27.3°F

Average Rainfall 20 in

POPULATION

Population Indicators

Total Population: 1999 5,449,000
World Rank: 101st
Density per sq mi: 203.1 per sq km 73.4
% of annual growth (1994–99): 0.1
Male %: 47.2
Female %: 52.8
Urban %: 55.7
Age Distribution: %
- 0–14: 24.8
- 15–29: 24.1
- 30–44: 19.2
- 45–59: 17.5
- 60–74: 10.8
- 75 and over: 3.6

Population 2020: 5,178,000
Birth Rate per 1,000: 9.9
Death Rate per 1,000: 6.4
Population Doubling Time (years): —
Infant Mortality Rate per 1,000 live births: 17.4
Rate of Natural Increase per 1,000: 3.5
Total Fertility Rate: 2.2
Expectation of Life (years): Males 68.9
Females 76.5

Marriage Rate per 1,000: 4.9
Divorce Rate per 1,000: —
Total Number of Households: 1,244,000
Average Size of Households: 4.1
% of Illegitimate Children: 17.7
Induced Abortions: 68,883
Rate per 100 live births: 75.6

ETHNIC COMPOSITION

Out of 5.06 million inhabitants, Georgian ethnicity constitutes 70 percent. More than 80 other nationalities make up the balance, including Armenians (8.1 percent), Russians (6.3 percent), Azeris (5.7 percent), Ossetes (3 percent), Greeks (1.9 percent), Abkhazians (1.8 percent), Jews (0.5 percent), and others (2.6 percent).

The ancestors of today's ethnic Georgians were mentioned in Assyrian records about 3,000 years ago. Although Georgians are divided into a dozen distinctive regional groups, they are all highly conscious of Georgian common traditions and cultures. The Georgians constitute an absolute majority in West Georgia (81.4% of total population). Abkhazians mainly reside in the northwest, Greeks, in the central part of the country, Azeris and Armenians, in the south, and Jews, Kurds, and Slavs in larger urban centers.

The exact ethnic makeup and origin of Abkhazians is a debated political issue. Most scholars trace their ancestry back at least two millennia in Georgia and consider them Georgians by origin. Present-day Abkhazians have been a minority within Abkhazia, forming less then 20 percent of the population. There is an Autonomous Region of South Ossetes created by the Bolsheviks in 1922 as part of a divide-and-rule policy in Georgia.

LANGUAGES

The Georgian language is the state language of the country. The Georgian alphabet is among 14 existing throughout the world. Georgian script is an independent, unique system, conveying the sound composition of Georgian speech and forming the written and printed symbols of the national Georgian language. It belongs to the Kartvelian group of Ibero-Caucasian languages. It has 33 letters (5 vowels and 28 consonants) and uses the original script, which has only been slightly modernized.

Most people in urban areas can speak Russian. Ethnic minorities speak their native language in addition to Russian and Georgian. After Russian, English is the most widely spoken foreign language, followed by German, French, and Turkish. The Ossetes speak an Iranian language.

Principal Languages and Their Speakers

Abkhaz	90,000
Armenian	370,000
Azerbaijani (Azeri)	300,000
Georgian (Kartuli)	3,900,000
Ossetian	130,000
Russian	480,000
Other	170,000

RELIGIONS

One-third of the population belongs to the Georgian Orthodox Church, 3 percent to the Russian Orthodox Church, and approximately 5.7 percent of the population belongs to the Armenian Apostolic Church; about 1 to 2 percent of the population belongs to the Roman Catholic faith. About 11 percent of the total population are adherents of is Islam. Jews represent 0.5 percent of the population and mainly live in urban areas.

The Orthodox Church of Georgia traces its foundation to the time of Constantine the Great. Georgia adopted Christianity in 337. In the fifth century (around 466–68) the Georgian Church gained autocephaly and in the 11th century the Georgian Patriarchate was formed. The liturgy is celebrated in Georgian.

Religious Affiliations

Georgian Orthodox	2,000,000
Sunni Muslim	600,000
Armenian Apostolic (Orthodox)	310,000
Russian Orthodox	150,000
Other (mostly nonreligious)	2,390,000

HISTORICAL BACKGROUND

It has been a very long time since humans arrived in Georgia. Near the town of Dmanisi, a human skull dated 1.8 million years old was found. Archaeological evidence attests that there was a flourishing Neolithic culture in the fifth and fourth centuries B.C. in the territory of modern Georgia. The western region was known as Colkhida and eastern Georgia was known as Iberia. In about the fourth century B.C. Georgia was united into a single kingdom with Mtskheta as its capital.

In the fifth century the capital of Georgia moved to Tbilisi. Until the seventh century control over Georgia was contested by the Persian and Byzantine empires. The region was conquered by the Arabs in the seventh century and by the Turkish Seljuks in the 11th century. However, in the 11th century, unified Georgia with its capital in Kutaisi was one of the major powers in the region.

King David IV the Builder (1089–1125), one of the greatest Georgian kings, expelled the Turks in the early 12th century and reunited Georgia as a kingdom. During the reign of Queen Tamar (1184–1213) the Georgian kingdom reached the apex of its political might. This was the era of great architectural projects and flourishing literature, including the great epic poem "The Knight in the Tiger's Skin" dedicated to Queen Tamar by Shota Rustaveli.

Georgian domination in the Caucasus was crushed by the Mongol invaders in the 12th century, which led to the breakup of Georgia into individual principalities. Thereafter Georgia was divided into spheres of influence between Ottoman Turkey and Safavid fran until the 18th century. In the 18th century Vakhtang VI compiled *Kartlis Tskhovreba* (History of Georgia). A Georgian kingdom was proclaimed in the mid-18th century. The Russian czar absolved the last Georgian king in 1801 and Georgia became a part of the Russian Empire.

In 1918 Georgia became an independent republic. However, in 1921 a Soviet regime was installed by the Red Army. In 1922 it became one of the four republics constituting the newly formed USSR. In 1924, after an attempted uprising led by Georgian Mensheviks, more then 5,000 patriots were executed. Georgia had to pass through the ordeal of industrialization and collectivization, suffering severely during the depression of the 1930s and repression of 1937–38. Three hundred thousand Georgian soldiers fell in World War II.

The struggle for independence assumed the form of a widespread national liberation movement and brought victory to Georgians in late 1989. In 1990, multiparty elections were held and, on April 9, a new national parliament declared the independence of Georgia. The well-know dissident Zviad Gamsakhurdia was elected the first president of independent Georgia. Although earlier a victim of totalitarianism, he showed neither a desire nor an ability to maintain a dialogue with the growing opposition.

On December 11, 1990, in reaction to a declaration by Ossetian separatists to secede from Georgia and join with Russia, the Supreme Council of Georgia abolished the Autonomous Region as a political and administrative unit. Fights broke out between Georgians and Ossetians and did not abate until a peacekeeping force comprising Russians, Georgians, and Ossetians was deployed.

In the winter of 1991–92, a military rebellion by the opposition forced Gamsakhurdia to leave Georgia. Unable to cope with many international, economic, and other domestic problems, the rebel Military Council formed a State Council inviting Eduard Shevardnadze, the former USSR minister of foreign affairs, to Georgia. In October 1992 a new Georgian parliament and head of state, Eduard Shevardnadze, were elected.

After Georgian independence, Abkhazian separatists tried to make Abkhazia a part of Russia. Heavy fighting between Georgian troops and Abkhazian separatists started after the central authorities sent troops to protect supply routes in August 1992. The Abkhazian side received support form Russia and as a result more than 250,000 Georgian refugees were expelled by October 1993. In the same month, the Georgian government was forced to seek Russian military help and joined the Commonwealth of Independent States (CIS). In 1994 Abkhazian separatists agreed to a UN peacekeeping force, which consisted of a Russian contingent.

In 1995 Shevardnadze survived a bomb attack, and he was reelected president with 76.8 percent of the vote. A new constitution was promulgated in the same year. The rebel district of Abkhazia conducted elections to its own assembly in 1996, which Georgia declared invalid. At Georgia's request, the CIS imposed sanctions on the

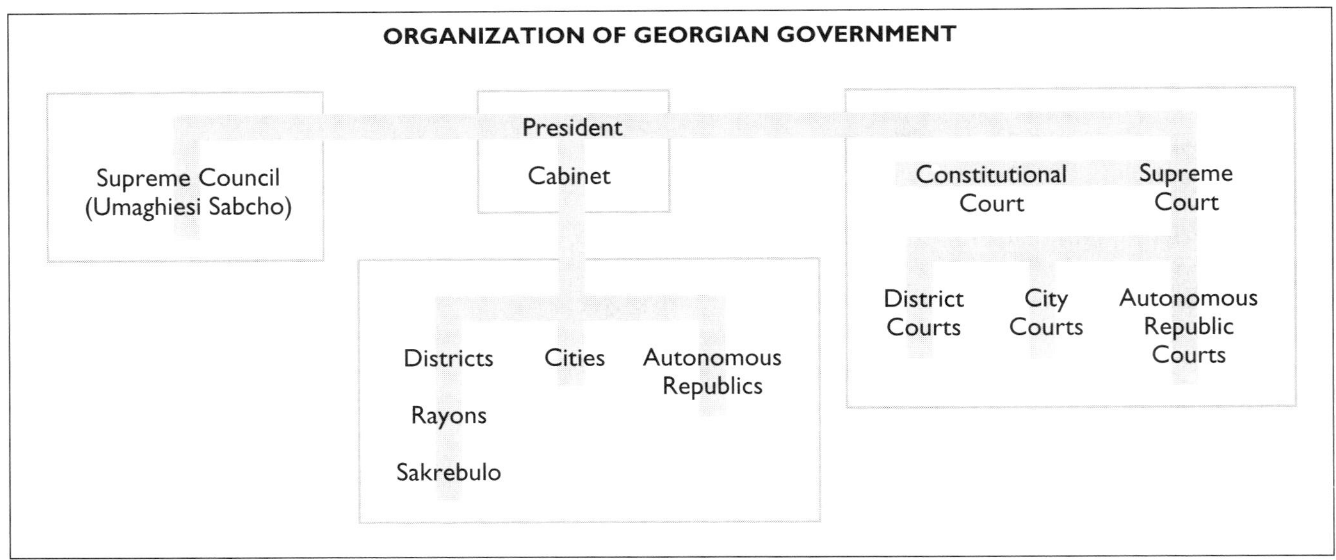

district to force Abkhazia to rejoin Georgia. Brokered by Moscow, a new accord was reached with south Ossetian representatives in 1996. Despite this accord south Ossetians held a direct presidential election. In 1998 Shevardnadze survived a second assassination attempt. He was reelected president in April 2000.

CONSTITUTION

On August 24, 1995 the parliament of Georgia adopted the new constitution. Separation of powers is declared in the constitution as the basic principle of organization. According to the constitution, a publicly elected president directly governs the executive branch and possesses other important powers, but he is not authorized to dismiss the parliament. The president is simultaneously the head of state and the head of executive authority; the state minister is a part of the government who directs the president's office and is entrusted by the president to fulfil his separate tasks. The parliament independently exercises the legislative functions and supervises executive bodies.

LOCAL GOVERNMENT

The administrative division of Georgia is organized on three levels. At the regional level the country is divided into 12 territories: two Autonomous Republics (AR)—Abkhazia and Ajara—which have constitutions, the city of Tbilisi, and 10 districts. The local government at the regional level is a branch of the national government, except for the ARs. The president appoints district governors, who liaise with the local authorities within the regions.

The Ajara AR is governed by its Supreme Council, which elects a chairman among its members. The Abkhazia AR has unilaterally seceded from Georgia and its authorities are not recognized.

The local government of the second, rayon, level (53 rayons and seven towns) is twofold, comprising a district governor, a presidential appointee who represents the national government and is in charge of the executive branch, and a rayon council, a publicly elected body.

At the third level, each rayon is split into *sakrebulo* (1,031), which are administered by directly elected councils.

Local Government

Principal administrative divisions, capitals, area, population

AREA AND POPULATION

Autonomous republics	Capitals	area sq mi	area sq km	population 1993 estimate
Abkhazia	Sokhumi (Sukhumi)	3,343	8,660	516,600
Ajaria	Bat'umi	1,120	2,900	386,700
Districts				
Guria	—	785	2,033	160,800
Imereti	—	2,452	6,349	788,900
Kakheti	—	4,717	12,217	464,000
Kvemo Kartli	—	2,615	6,772	601,500
Racha-Lechkumi	—	1,245	3,224	45,400
Samegrelo	—	1,697	4,395	418,100
Samtskhe-Javakheti	—	2,017	5,224	198,800
Shida Kartli	—	3,043	7,882	485,900
Svaneti	—	1,694	4,389	23,200
Tianeti	—	1,569	4,063	43,800
City				
T'bilisi	—	534	1,384	1,271,800
TOTAL		26,831	69,493	5,405,400

PARLIAMENT

Georgia has a single-chamber parliament consisting of 235 members. The members of the parliament are elected by proportional (150 deputies) and plurality-majority (85 deputies) electoral systems. A party must gain more than 7 percent of votes in order to be seated in the parliament. The last parliamentary elections were held in October 1999 and only three parties could get more than 7 percent of nationwide votes. Those were: Citizens Union of Georgia, a left-center party (132 seats); Bloc "Agordzineba" (Revival), a coalition of six parties, societies, and movements (Socialist party, Agordzineba, Monarchists, etc) (58 seats); and Bloc "Industry Will Save Georgia," a centrist party (15 seats).

POLITICAL PARTIES

There are more than 60 parties and up to 10 blocs registered in Georgia. Although they represent different political platforms, most of them are small and lack well-developed party organization.

Political Parties

- Citizens' Union of Georgia, 1993
- Socialist Party of Georgia, 1995
- National Democratic Party, 1988
- All-Georgian Union of Revival, 1992
- Union of Georgian Traditionalists
- United Republican Party, 1995
- Progress Bloc, a coalition of
    - Democratic Union, 1991
    - Political Association of Georgian Proprietors, 1995
    - Political Union of Young Democrats, 1994
    - Political Union of Tanadgoma, 1995
- Bloc Reformers' Union of Georgia-National Concord, a coalition of
    - Reformers' Union, 1993
    - Georgian Citizens' Political Association, 1995
    - Sportsmen's Union, 1994
- Union for a Law-Governed State, 1995
- All-Georgian Political Organization-Lemi, 1989

(continued)

National Patriotic Movement for Georgia's Salvation, 1997
United Communist Party, 1994
National Liberation Front, 1993
Georgian Social Democratic Party, 1893
Christian Democratic Union
Democratic Georgia Union
Georgian Conservative Monarchists' Party, 1989
Unity Bloc
Agrarian Party, 1994
National Independence Party 1988
People's Socialist Party, 1995

Political Parties: Strength in Parliament Most Recent Elections

Parliament. The chamber contains 235 seats. At the elections of October 13 and November 14, 1999, the Citizens' Union of Georgia won 130 seats; All-Georgian Union for Revival, 64; Industry Will Save Georgia, 15; Georgian Labor Party, 2; nonpartisans, 16; and Abkhazian delegates, 12.

LEGAL SYSTEM

The legal system of Georgia is based on the civil law system. The president represents the executive branch and the parliament has legislative power. Judicial branches are represented by the Supreme Court, the Constitutional Court, the Council of Justice, the supreme courts of the ARs, courts of appeal, circuit courts, and regional and city (districts or town) courts.

The Supreme Court of Georgia is the Highest Cassation Court. The Supreme Court supervises general courts.

The Constitutional Court of Georgia rules on whether the laws and decisions adopted by state and local administrations abide by the constitution.

The Council of Justice, an advising body, chooses and appoints judges for the first level of general courts—the regional and city courts. Circuit courts are comprised of several bodies that rule on issues in criminal law, civil law, etc. The courts of appeal comprise the courts of appeal of Georgia and the Supreme Courts of Ajaria and Abkhazia. The courts of appeal are second-instance courts, which consider decision made by the courts of the first instance.

LAW ENFORCEMENT

Law Enforcement

Offenses reported to the police per 100,000: 325
- Murder: 10.7
- Assault: 107.8
- Burglary: 40.7
- Automobile Theft: 1.5
- Population per Police officer: —

Death Penalty: Yes

HUMAN RIGHTS

The constitution of Georgia sets up legal, organizational and institutional guarantees for human rights and freedoms in the country. Its second chapter contains the list of universally acknowledged rights and freedoms.

Georgia joined several conventions protecting human rights—the International Covenant on Economic, Social and Cultural Rights; the International Covenant on Civil and Political Rights and the Optional Protocol to the International Bill of Human Rights; the International Conventions on the Rights of Children and the Elimination of All Forms of Discrimination against Women; and the Convention against Torture and Other Cruel and Inhuman or Degrading Treatment or Punishment.

Amnesty International (1998) lists the major human rights abuses in Georgia as torture and ill treatment of prisoners, poor prison conditions, and weak trial standards.

FOREIGN POLICY

Given its geographical proximity and historical relationship with Russia and as a member of the CIS, Georgia plays a key role in regional and current international affairs. Georgia joined Partnership for Peace in 1994 to secure limited military cooperation with NATO. In 1999 Georgia joined the Council of Europe and was accepted into the World Trade Organization. Acceptance must be ratified by the parliament. Georgian embassies operate in 20 countries.

DEFENSE

Military Indicators

Total Active Duty Personnel: —
Military Manpower per 1,000: —
Military Expenditures $million: 194
- as % of GNP: 2.4
- per capita $: 37
- as % of central government expenditures: 2.4

Arms Imports $million: 10
Arms Exports $million: 0

ECONOMY

Georgia's economy has traditionally revolved around Black Sea tourism, cultivation of citrus fruits, tea, and grapes, mining of manganese and copper, and output of a small industrial sector producing wine, metals, machinery, chemicals, and textiles. The country imports the bulk of its energy needs. Its only sizable internal energy resource is hydropower. Despite the civil war, the economy has made substantial gains, increasing gross domestic product growth and slashing inflation. Georgia still suffers from energy shortages. The Caspian oil pipeline through Georgia has spurred greater Western investment in the economy. The short-term economic picture, however, is clouded by a growing trade deficit, corruption, and political uncertainties.

Principal Economic Indicators

Gross National Product $: 4.656 billion
GNP per capita $: 860
GNP Average Annual Growth Rate (1990–97) %: −14.9
GNP per capita Average Annual Growth Rate (1990–97) %: −14.8
Origin of Gross Domestic Product %
- Agriculture: 32
- Mining: —
- Manufacturing: 13
- Construction: 4
- Public Utilities: —
- Transportation and Communications: 11
- Trade: 11
- Financial Services: 11
- Other Services and Government: 13

Gross Domestic Product by Type of Expenditure %
- Private Consumption: 89
- Government Consumption: 9
- Gross Domestic Investment: 32
- Foreign Trade: Exports: 36
  Imports: −66

% of Income Received by Poorest 20%: —
% of Income Received by Richest 10%: —

Price and earnings indexes (1995 = 100)

	1992	1993	1994	1995	1996	1997
Consumer price index	0.02	0.24	38.1	100.0	139.4	149.5
Monthly earnings index	0.01	0.18	39.5	100.0	231.4	361.8

Finance

National Currency: Lari
Exchange Rate: $1 =Lari 1.32
Money Supply Stock in National Currency billion:
M1 per capita:
Central Bank Discount Rate %:
Total External Debt $million: 1,300
Debt Service Ratio %: 5.6

Balance of Payments $million: −534.7
International Reserves SDRs million:
Ratio of External Debt to Total Reserves:
Average Annual Rate of Inflation/Consumer Price Index Growth Rate%: 7.1

Official Development Assistance

ODA $million: 162
- as % of GNP: 3.1
- per capita $ 30
- Foreign Direct Investment $million: 50

Central Government Revenues and Expenditures

Fiscal Year: Calendar Year
Revenues $million: 441
Expenditures $million: 606
Budget Deficit $million: 165
Tax Revenues as % of GDP: 4.6
Highest Tax Bracket %
- Individual: —
- Corporate: —

Employment and Labor

Economically Active Population: 1,920,000
Female Participation Rate %: —
Activity Rate %: 35.7
Labor by Sector: %
- Agriculture, Forestry, Fishing: 5.2
- Manufacturing, Mining: 9.8
- Construction: 6.5
- Transportation and Communications: 5.6
- Trade, Hotels, and Restaurants: 6.1
- Finance, Insurance, Real Estate: 1.0
- Public Administration, Defense: 2.6
- Services: 24.9

Unemployment %: 16

Agriculture

Agriculture's Share of GDP %: 29
Average Annual Rate of Growth (1965–98) %: —
Number of Farms 000: 17
Average Size of Farm ha: —
Number of Tractors per 1,000 hectares: 22.9
Irrigation, % of Farms having: 59
Artificial Fertilizer kg/hectare: —
Total Farmland as % of land area: 43.2
Livestock: Cattle 000: 1,027
- Sheep 000: 543
- Hogs 000: 330
- Chickens 000: 13,500

Forests: Production of Roundwood (000 cubic meters): —
Fisheries: Total Catch tons 000: 35

Mining

% of GDP: —
Value of Mineral Production $million: —

Manufacturing

Value Added $million: 150
Industrial Production Growth Rate %: 8.1

Energy

Commercial Energy Production metric tons of oil equivalent 000: 694
Commercial Energy Consumption metric tons of oil equivalent 000: 2,295

(continued)

Commercial Energy Consumption per capita kg: 423
Average Annual Growth Rate 1980–97 %: −6.5
Net Energy Imports % of use: 70
Electricity Installed Capacity kW 000: 4,558
Production kW-hr million: 6,800
Coal Reserves tons million: —
Production tons 000: 40
Natural Gas Proven Reserves cubic meters billion: —
Production cubic meters million: 45
Crude Petroleum Reserves barrels million: —
Production barrels million: 3.0
Consumption barrels million: 3
Refinery Capacity barrels per day 000: 106
Pipelines Length km: 670

Foreign Trade

Imports $million: 379.0
Exports $million: 154.4
Export Volume % Annual Growth Rate (1990–97): —
Import Volume % Annual Growth Rate (1990–97): —
Balance of Trade $

Balance of trade (current prices)

	1992	1993	1994	1995	1996	1997
U.S. $000,000	+19	−448	−365	−339	−351	−484
% of total	14.1%	32.9%	32.4%	32.8%	29.6%	34.3%

Major Trading Partners

	Imports	Exports
European Union %	13.4	5.6
United States %	4.7	0.4
Eastern Europe %	30.0	39.4
Japan %	0.2	0.1
Others %	51.6	54.5

Transportation

Roads Total Length mi: 13,049 km 21,000
Paved %: 94
Automobiles: 441,828
Trucks and Buses: 50,220
Persons per vehicle: 11
Railroad; Track Length mi: 983 km 1,583
Passenger-mi million: 792
Freight-mi million: 705
Merchant Marine: No of Vessels: 54
Total Deadweight Tonnage 000: 1,108
International Cargo Loaded tons 000: —
International Cargo Off-loaded tons 000: —
Airports with Scheduled Flights: 1
Traffic: Passenger-mi million: 3,291
Freight-mi million: —
Length of Canals mi: —

Tourism

Number of Tourists to 000: 317
Number of Tourists from 000: 433
Tourist Receipts $million: —
Tourist Expenditures $million: —

Communications

Telephones 000: 554
Cost of Local Calls 3 mins: $0
Cellular Telephones 000: 0.2
Fax Machines 000: 0.5
Personal Computers 000: —
Internet Hosts per million persons: 11
Mail: Post Offices: —
Pieces of Mail Handled million: 1,025
Pieces of Mail Handled per person: 188

EDUCATION

Obtaining a good education is a high priority for Georgians, and almost the entire population can read and write; the literacy rate is 99 percent.

In 1997, there were up to 900,000 pupils attending primary and secondary schools, 56,000 in vocational schools, and 43,000 in technical secondary school. The larger ethnic minorities have their own schools and Russians, Armenians, Azeris, Abkhazians, and Ossetians use their native languages for instruction. By the beginning of the 1997–98 academic year about 32,000 schools of general education were functioning in the country.

There are 21 state-run institutions of higher education and up to 130 private schools, including 12 and 83, respectively, situated in Tbilisi. The oldest and the most prestigious is Tbilisi State University.

Education

Literacy Rate %: 99.5
Male %: 99.7
Female %: 99.4
First Level: Primary schools: 3,378
Teachers: —
Students: 815,000
Student-Teacher Ratio: —
Net Enrollment Ratio: 82
Second Level: Secondary Schools: —
Teachers: —
Students: —
Student-Teacher Ratio: —
Net Enrollment Ratio: 71

Vocational Level: Schools: —
Students: 29,300

Third Level: Institutions: 19
Teachers: —
Students: 93,000
Student-Ratio Level: —
Gross Enrollment Ratio: 38.1
Students per 100,000: 2,845
% of Population Age 25 and over with Postsecondary Education: —

Public Expenditure on Education as % of GDP: 5.2

SCIENCE AND TECHNOLOGY

Science and Technology

Scientists and Engineers in R&D per 1 million persons: —
Expenditures in R&D as % of GDP: —
High-Tech Exports $million: —
Patent Applications by Residents: 265

MEDIA

The constitution and the 1991 press law provide for freedom of the press, and new laws further support this freedom; however, although the independent press was increasingly active, the government constrained some press freedoms. According to journalists, security and law enforcement authorities attempted to intimidate the press through public comments and private admonitions. The recent Administrative Code contains a freedom of information section that provides for public access to government meetings and documents. Journalists lacked effective legal protection, a circumstance that hindered investigative journalism. The Civil Code and other legislation make it a crime to insult the honor and dignity of an individual, and place the burden of proof on the accused.

Some 200 independent newspapers are in circulation. The press increasingly serves as a check on government, frequently criticizing the performance of high-level officials. Increasingly, independent newspapers have been replacing the government-controlled press as the population's source of information; the leading independent daily newspaper, *Alia*, has a national circulation nearly 20 percent higher than the government-controlled daily. However, observers report that this seems to be mostly a Tbilisi-based phenomenon and that independent newspapers continue to struggle in the provinces. Several newspapers are serious and reputable sources of information. High printing costs and general poverty, especially in the countryside, limit the circulation of most newspapers to a few hundred or a few thousand. The government finances and controls one newspaper (which also appears in Russian-, Azeri-, and Armenian-language versions) and a radio and television network with a national audience; they reflect official viewpoints.

Media

Daily Newspapers: 12
Total Circulation 000: —
Circulation per 1,000: —
Books Published: 314
Magazines: —
Radio Receivers 000: —
per 1,000: —
Television sets 000: 1,200
per 1,000: 220

Most Important Media:

Press. The following are published at Tbilisi in Georgian, unless otherwise noted: *Akhalgazrda Iverieli* (Young Iberian), triweekly; *Alia Sakhartveldon* (Alia from Georgia), daily; *Georgian Times*, in English; *Mamuli* (Native Land), Rustaveli Society fortnightly; *Respublika* (Republic), government weekly; *Sakartvelos Respublika* (Republic of Georgia), government daily; *Tavisupali Sakartvelo* (Free Georgia), former Round Table-Free Georgia organ; *Vestnik Gruzil* (Georgian Herald), government daily, in Russian. The pro-Gamsakhurdia *Iberia Spectr* was suspended in September 1993 for publishing material "offensive to the nation and insulting to the government."

News agencies. The domestic facility is the Georgian Information Agency (Sakinform), headquartered at Tbilisi.

Radio and television. Radio Tbilisi broadcasts in Georgian, Russian, and a number of regional languages; Tbilisi Television broadcasts in Georgian and Russian.

CULTURE

Cultural Indicators

Public Libraries Number: —
Volumes: —
Registered borrowers: —
Museums Number: —
Annual Attendance: —
Cinema Production of Long Films: —
Number of Cinemas: —
Seating Capacity: —
Annual Attendance million: —
Annual Attendance per capita: —

STATUS OF WOMEN

Georgians believe that there is a strong tradition of respect toward women in Georgian society that leads to socially defined roles for women.

Most women care for the household and children, as well as work outside the home. Following the transition to the market economy, women have become more successful at work than men have and in the majority of families women are the principal breadwinners.

Women still play a secondary role in politics, but there are a few female ministers in Georgia. Currently, the minister of environment and the minister of trade and foreign economic affairs are women. There are 16 female members of parliament.

Women

Gender Empowerment Measure: 73
Seats Held in Parliament by Women %: 6.9
Female Administrators and Managers %: 18.3
Female Professional and Technical Workers %: 41.8
Women's Share of Earned Income %: 39
Women in Government %: 3

HEALTH, FOOD, AND NUTRITION

Health

Number of Physicians: 29,900
Number of Dentists: —
Number of Nurses: 64,100
Number of Pharmacists: —
Population per Physician: 182
Number of Hospitals: 422
Hospital Beds per 10,000: 105
Hospital Bed Occupancy Rate: —
Infant Mortality Rate per 1,000 live births: 21
Maternal Mortality Rate per 100,000 live births: 33
Total Health Expenditures as % of GDP: 4.45
Health Expenditures per capita $: 152
HIV Infected % of adults: 0.01
Cigarette Consumption per smoker per year: —
% of Smokers: Male: —
Female: —
Access to Safe Water %: —

Food and Nutrition

Food Supply as % of FAO Requirements: —
% of Consumption Expenditures on Food: 38.3
Daily Available Calories per capita: —
% of Total Calories derived from:
Cereals: —
Potatoes, cassava: —
Meat, poultry: —
Fish: —
Eggs, milk: —
Fruits, vegetables: —
Fats, oils: —

ENVIRONMENT

With the assistance of the World Bank, Georgia has prepared a National Environmental Action Plan (NEAP) that has strengthened overall institutional capacity and environmental institutions and encouraged integration of environmental concerns in economic and sectoral policies.

Despite this institutional framework, current major environmental issues include deforestation; erosion; air pollution, particularly in Rustavi; heavy pollution of the Mtkvari River and the Black Sea; inadequate supplies of potable water; soil pollution from toxic chemicals; and inadequate hazardous and solid waste management.

Environment

Forest Area sq km: 30,000
Average Annual Deforestation sq km: 0
Nationally Protected Areas as % of Total Land Area: 2.7
Freshwater Access cubic meters per capita: 11,632
Emissions of Organic Water Pollutants kg per day: 84,601
CO_2 Emissions per capita ton: 0.5

CHRONOLOGY

1940s Two million Meshketians are deported from south Georgia to Siberia on Joseph Stalin's orders.

1953 Stalin dies; Nikita Khrushchev becomes first secretary of the Communist Party of the Soviet Union and begins a process of de-Stalinization throughout the Soviet Union.

1972 Eduard Shevardnadze becomes the first secretary of the Communist Party of Georgia.

1977 Zviad Gamsakhurdia forms the Initiative Group for the Defense of Human Rights.

1985 Mikhail Gorbachev becomes leader of the Soviet Union and initiates policies of *glasnost* (openness) and *perestroika* (restructuring), which inadvertently fuel the nationalistic sentiment of Georgia.

1989 The Georgia Supreme Soviet declares Georgian the official state language; secessionist Abkhazian and Ossetian nationalists demand autonomy for their regions, provoking violent demonstrations.

1990 In Georgia's first multiparty elections, the Round Table–Free Georgia coalition, a collection of pro-independence parties led by Gamsakhurdia, wins a majority of seats in the Georgia Supreme Soviet.

1991 On April 9, the Georgia Supreme Soviet formally declares Georgia's independence from the Soviet Union; in May Gamsakhurdia is elected Georgia's first president; Georgia declines to join the new Commonwealth of Independent States (CIS); violent clashes between Gamsakhurdia supporters and Shevardnadze supporters escalate into a full-scale civil war; Gamsakhurdia declares a state of emergency in Tbilisi and orders the arrest of opposition leaders.

1992 With military and Russian backing, Gamsakhurdia is ousted in January; the presidency is abolished and Shevardnadze is named acting chairman of the State Council, the new national legislature; elections confirm Shevardnadze as chairman of the State Council; Abkhazia reinstates its 1925 constitution; a mostly Russian peacekeeping force enforces a cease-fire between Ossetians and Georgians.

1993 Pro-Gamsakhurdia forces are suppressed; Gamsakhurdia dies in exile; Abkhazi separatists repel Georgian forces and over 200,000 ethnic Georgians flee Abkhazia; Georgia joins CIS.

1994 Georgia agrees to permit Russia to continue operating three military bases in Georgia in exchange for military supplies and training; the United Nations brokers a cease-fire between the government of Georgia and Abkhazi separatists and dispatches a Russian peacekeeping force of

2,500; Abkhazia adopts a new constitution declaring independence; by the year's end, 30,000 refugees reportedly have returned to their homes in Abkhazia.

1995 Shevardnadze survives an assassination attempt; a privatization program is launched; Georgia adopts a new constitution reinstating the office of president, and Shevardnadze is named president; President Shevardnadze is reelected in November with over 70 percent of the vote, and his party, the Citizens' Union of Georgia, wins the most seats in parliament.

1996 CIS imposes economic sanctions on Abkhazia at Georgia's request.

1997 Shevardnadze denounces Russia's importation of Abkhazian fruit; more than 1,700 prisoners are granted amnesty and released.

1998 Shevardnadze survives a second assassination attempt; Russia agrees to allow Georgia joint control of military airbases in Georgia; four UN military observers are taken hostage by Abkhazian separatists; Georgia and Turkey agree to build a major oil pipeline across Georgia; more than 30,000 ethnic Georgians flee Abkhazia after renewed fighting breaks out in May; the United Nations brokers a cease-fire.

1999 Georgia is admitted to the Council of Europe; Pope John Paul II visits Georgia; the Citizens' Union of Georgia again dominates legislative elections.

2000 Shevardnadze is reelected president, receiving nearly 80 percent of the vote.

BIBLIOGRAPHY

Braund, David. *Georgia in Antiquity: A History of Colchis and Transcaucasian Iberia, 550 BC-AD 562*. New York, 1994.

Curtis, Glenn E. (ed.), *Armenia, Azerbaijan, and Georgia: Country Studies*. Washington, D.C, 1995.

Rosen, Roger. *Georgia: A Sovereign State in the Caucasus*. Hong Kong, 1999.

Suny, Ronald Grigor. *The Making of the Georgian Nation*. Stanford, Calif., 1988.

OFFICIAL PUBLICATIONS

Georgia. *Georgia—Recent Economic Developments* (IMF Staff Country Report [1997])

CONTACT INFORMATION

Embassy of Georgia
1511 K Street NW, Suite 424
Washington, D.C. 20005
Phone: (202)393-5959 Fax: (202)393-6060

INTERNET RESOURCES

- UNDP Human Development Report Georgia 1998 http://www.undp.org.ge/frset1.htm
- Embassy of Georgia in the United States of America http://www.georgiaemb.org
- Parliament of Georgia http://server.parliament.ge

GERMANY

BASIC FACT SHEET

OFFICIAL NAME:
Federal Republic of Germany (Bundesrepublik Deutschland)

ABBREVIATION:
FRG

CAPITAL:
Berlin

HEAD OF STATE:
President Johannes Rau (from 1999)

HEAD OF GOVERNMENT:
Chancellor Gerhard Schöder (from 1998)

NATURE OF GOVERNMENT:
Parliamentary democracy

POPULATION:
82,100,000

AREA:
357,002 sq km (137,847 sq mi)

ETHNIC GROUP:
German

LANGUAGE:
German

RELIGIONS:
Roman Catholic and Protestant

UNIT OF CURRENCY:
Euro

NATIONAL FLAG:
Tricolor of black, red, and gold horizontal stripes

NATIONAL EMBLEM:
Sylized black eagle displayed with red beak and claws against a dark gold shield

NATIONAL ANTHEM:
No official national anthem, but "Deutschlandlied" is used widely, especially its third verse

NATIONAL HOLIDAYS:
German Unity Day, June 17; Repentance Day, Wednesday before the third Sunday in November; New Year's Day; Labor Day; all major Christian festivals

DATE OF INDEPENDENCE:
September 21, 1949

DATE OF CONSTITUTION:
September 21, 1949

GEOGRAPHICAL FEATURES

On October 3, 1990, the unification of communist East Germany with democratic West Germany increased the new nation's land area. The country grew overnight by 30 percent with the accession of the eastern lands. From the Western German perspective, the increase was from 248,577 sq km (95,976 sq mi) to 357,002 sq km (137,847 mi), making it about the size of the state of Montana in the United States.

Germany now extends 877 km (548 mi) from north to south and 640 km (400 mi) from east to west. These extremities include the cities of List in the north, Oberstdorf in the south, Deschka in the east, and Selfkant in the west.

Germany has an extraordinary variety of landscapes. From north to south, it is divided into five regions with different topographical features: the North German Plain (northern lowlands), Central Upland Range, Terrace Region (scarp lands), alpine foothills, and Bavarian Alps.

Germany

DENMARK
Baltic Sea
North Sea
Flensburg
Kiel
Rostock
Lubeck
Cuxhaven
Wilhelmshaven
Hamburg
Schwerin
Emden
Bremerhaven
Oldenburg
Bremen
Elbe R.
Oder R.
NETHERLANDS
POLAND
Weser R.
Meppen
Lingen
Brandenburg
Hannover
Wolfsburg
Berlin
Potsdam
Osnabruck
Braunschweig
Munster
Bielefeld
Hameln
Magdeburg
Hamm
Cottbus
Essen
Dortmund
Duisberg
Ruhr R.
Elbe R.
Halle
Leipzig
Kassel
Weser R.
Dusseldorf
Monchen-
gladbach
Dresden
Cologne
Weimar
Bonn
Siegen
Erfurt
Jena
Gera
Chemnitz
Aachen
Rhine R.
Zwickau
Lahn R.
BELGIUM
Koblenz
Frankfurt
am Main
Bayreuth
Wiesbaden
Hanau
CZECH REPUBLIC
Main R.
Mainz
Darmstadt
LUX.
Trier
Moselle R.
Bamberg
Wurzburg
Mannheim
Kaiserslautern
Heidelberg
Nurnberg
Saarbrucken
Heilbronn
Regensburg
Karlsruhe
Deggendorf
Stuttgart
Danube R.
Passau
FRANCE
Rhine R.
Ulm
Dachau
Augsburg
Munich
AUSTRIA
Freiburg
Lake
Constance
Oberammergau
N
Friedrichshafen
Garmisch-
Partenkirchen
SWITZERLAND
LIECHTENSTEIN
0
100 Miles
0
100 Kms

The greater part of the country drains into the North Sea via the Rhine, Ems, Weser, and Elbe Rivers. A small area north and northeast of Hamburg drains into the Baltic Sea. Moreover, a large area in the southeast lies in the Danube River basin, which eventually empties into the Black Sea from Romania. The divide between the watersheds of the Danube and Rhine basins winds around Baden-Württemberg and Bavaria, most of which drains into the former. A small area north of the Bodensee, however, drains into the Rhine.

Geography

Area sq km: 357,002 sq mi 137,847
World Rank: 62nd
Land Boundaries, km: Austria 784; Belgium 167; Czech Republic 646; Denmark 68; France 451; Luxembourg 138; Netherlands 577; Poland 456; Switzerland 334
Coastline, km 2,389
Elevation Extremes meters
Lowest: Freepsum Lake −2
Highest: Zugspitze 2,962
Land Use % Arable land: 33
Permanent Crops: 1
Permanent Pastures: 15
Forest and Woodland: 31
Other: 20

Population of Principal Cities (1996 est.)

Aachen	247,923
Augsburg	259,699
Bergisch Gladbach	105,478
Berlin	3,471,418
Bielefeld	324,066
Bochum	400,395
Bonn	291,431
Bottrop	120,642
Braunschweig	252,544
Bremen	549,357
Bremerhaven	130,400
Chemnitz	266,737
Cologne (Köln)	965,697
Cottbus	123,214
Darmstadt	138,980
Dortmund	598,840
Dresden	469,110
Duisburg	535,250
Düsseldorf	571,030
Erfurt	211,108
Erlangen	101,406
Essen	614,861
Frankfurt am Main	650,055
Freiburg im Breisgau	199,273
Fürth	108,418
Gelsenkirchen	291,164
Gera	123,555
Göttingen	126,253
Hagen	212,003
Halle	282,784
Hamburg	1,707,901
Hamm	183,408
Hannover	523,147
Heidelberg	138,781
Heilbronn	121,509
Herne	179,897
Hildesheim	106,101
Ingolstadt	111,979
Jena	101,061
Kaiserslautern	102,002
Karlsruhe	275,690
Kassel	201,573
Kiel	246,033
Koblenz	109,219
Krefeld	249,606
Leipzig	470,778
Leverkusen	162,252
Lübeck	216,986
Ludwigshafen	167,369
Magdeburg	257,656
Mainz	183,720
Mannheim	311,292
Moers	107,095
Monchengladbach	266,702
Mulheim an der Ruhr	176,530
Munich (München)	1,236,370
Münster	265,061
Neuss	148,796
Nuremberg	492,425
Oberhausen	224,397
Offenbach am Main	116,533
Oldenburg	151,382
Osnabrück	168,618
Paderborn	133,717
Pforzheim	118,763
Potsdam	136,619
Recklinghausen	127,216
Regensburg	125,836
Remscheid	122,260
Reutlingen	108,565
Rostock	227,535
Saarbrücken	187,032
Salzgitter	117,713
Schwerin	114,688
Siegen	111,398
Solingen	165,735
Stuttgart	585,604
Ulm	115,721
Wiesbaden	267,122
Witten	104,754
Wolfsburg	126,331
Wuppertal	381,884
Würzburg	127,295
Zwickau	102,563

CLIMATE AND WEATHER

Germany is situated in a climatic zone where westerly winds and a maritime climate from the Atlantic Ocean prevail over most of the country most of the year. Sharp changes in temperature are rare, and there is precipitation all year round. Maritime influences are predominant in the northwest along the coast. Continental conditions and greater temperature extremes between day and night and between summer and winter occur increasingly inland. The continental high-pressure center with easterly wind flows sometimes influences the eastern regions of the country, making for colder winters and warmer summers in that area. In addition to the maritime and continental climates to which most of Germany is exposed, the Alpine regions in the extreme south and, to a lesser degree, a few of the upland sections of the central and western areas have a mountain climate in which temperatures decrease with higher elevations and precipitation increases when moisture-laden air is forced to lift over higher terrain. Variable local winds develop as high and irregular terrain deflects prevailing winds.

Climate and Weather

Mean Temperature 48°F
South January 28°F
July 67°F
North January 35°F
July 61°F to 64°F
Berlin January 34°F
July 64°F
Dresden January 32°F
July 66°F
Higher Mountains January 21°F
Average Rainfal 24 in to 31 in
Northern Mountains 79 in
Mainz 16 in
Herz Mountains 58 in

POPULATION

Population Indicators

Total Population: 1999 82,100,000
World Rank: 12th
Density per sq mi: 495.6 per sq km 230.0
% of annual growth (1994–99): 0.2
Male %: 48
Female %: 52
Urban %: 85.3
Age Distribution: % 0–14: 14.6
15–29: 24.0
30–44: 20.1
45–59: 20.6
60–74: 13.6
75 and over: 7.2
Population 2020: 77,984,000
Birth Rate per 1,000: 9.3
Death Rate per 1,000: 10.7
Population Doubling Time (years): —
Infant Mortality Rate per 1,000 live births: 5.6
Rate of Natural Increase per 1,000: −1.4
Total Fertility Rate: 1.3
Expectation of Life (years): Males 72.5
Females 79.0
Marriage Rate per 1,000: 5.2
Divorce Rate per 1,000: 2.0
Total Number of Households: 36,230,000
Average Size of Households: 2.2
% of Illegitimate Children: 13.4
Induced Abortions: 103,586
Rate per 100 live births: 13.5

ETHNIC COMPOSITION

The German nation grew out of a number of tribes. There were Franks, Saxons, Bavarians, and Swabians before there were Germans. The differences among them are still felt today. Strong group loyalties complement and counterbalance German national consciousness and often vie with it as a focus of a citizens' self-identity. These include Bavarians, Swabians, and Franks, who reside in the south; Rhinelanders, Palatinans, and Hessians in the center; Westphalians, Lower Saxons, and Schleswig-Holsteiners in the north; and Thuringians, Brandenburgers, and other Germans in the eastern states.

Until the early 1970s, Germany was one of the most ethnically homogeneous nations in Europe. The extensive and systematic Nazi extermination of those deemed as "non-Teutonic" and the post–World War II resettlement of East European Germans into the former West Germany intensified the strengthening of this ethnic homogeneity. Only a fraction of the pre–World War II Jewish population and an even smaller group of Gypsies exists. In the mid-1980s, an estimated 35,000 Jews from the 530,000 of Weimar Germany remained. Two-thirds of them married non-Jews, resulting in a loosening of the traditional barriers. Presently, the Jewish population is around 70,000. Similarly, estimates of the Gypsy (Sinti Romany) population range from 30,000 to 50,000, compared to a prewar population of 500,000. Moreover, Germany has committed itself to the cultivation of the Sorbian minority, which faced annihilation under the authoritarian dictatorships of the 20th century. The Sorbs descend from the Slavic tribes of the sixth century and are located in the eastern states.

Over the past 40 years, three streams of migration brought droves of foreigners to Germany. Individuals immigrating to Germany typically have come from southern and eastern Europe. Others have traveled from more remote locations. The common thread among them was the search for a better life. Reasons for the influx include employment, repatriation, and asylum. The first wave consisted of foreign workers, the second of refugees, and the third of people from the freed East Bloc. In the late 1950s and early 1960s, Germany sought the labor of Italians as "guest workers." The country soon extended this category to include Greeks and Spaniards, and then Portuguese, Yugoslavs, and Turks. It has received refugees over the years from countries in turmoil (e.g., Afghanistan, Pakistan, and Vietnam). This includes 2.5 million German repatriates from the former East bloc, especially the former Soviet Union, who have been coming to Germany since 1987. All three waves presented a new and unsettling experience. In the past, Germans experienced *emigration* rather than *immigration*. They had never been confronted with large numbers of foreigners living and working with them nor confronted with the task of supporting them. In many ways, these influxes changed the social landscape of Germany permanently. By 1980, Turks and other non-Europeans made up nearly 40 percent of the immigrant group. Today, 9 percent of the population consists of foreigners, 3 percent of which are Turks.

LANGUAGES

German is one of the large groups of Indo-European languages, and, within that, one of the Germanic languages. It is related to Danish, Norwegian, Swedish, Dutch, Flemish, and English. The nation's official language is German. It is spoken on radio and television, used in the press, and taught in the schools. Many people in different parts of the country, however, speak regional dialects, used in informal situations. German is the mother tongue of nearly 100 million people in the world today. It is spoken as the official language of Austria and Liechtenstein and is one of the official languages of Switzerland. Some people along the borders in South Tyrol of northern Italy, parts of Belgium, the French Alsace, and Luxembourg also use German as their native language. German minorities in Poland, Romania, and countries of the former Soviet Union have partly retained German as their native language as well.

Standard German, known as High German (Hochdeutsch), is used in the national media and in education. However, Germany has a rich linguistic culture of dialects. For instance, the average German speaks his own dialect, depending on birthplace (e.g., Bavaria, Berlin, Hamburg, Hesse, Saxony, or Thuringia).

Although less important than English or French in international transactions, German is a favored language in most educational systems.

Principal Languages and Their Speakers

German	74,960,000
Greek	360,000
Italian	610,000
Polish	280,000
South Slavic languages	1,180,000
Turkish	2,110,000
Kurdish	400,000
Other	2,580,000

RELIGIONS

The experience of Nazi interference in church affairs persuaded Roman Catholic and Protestant clergy that safeguards were essential for church autonomy. Beyond accepting freedom of conscience, the Basic Law (Grundgesetz) of 1949 adopted Weimar's formulation of church-state relations that provided for church autonomy in religious matters. The German preamble, thus, states: "The German people...conscious of their responsibility before God and man. . . ." The constitution guarantees a free church in a free state. It states that no state church exists. There are no politico-religious ties between the German state and German church administrations. Churches are independent of state control.

However, separation between church and state is not total. Unlike the United States, German society has created a working partnership between church and state. This relationship is subject to the Basic Law and governed by agreements. The situation is manifest in the involvement of the churches in education, social services, and the military. The state, for instance, finances part of the cost of certain church establishments (e.g., kindergartens and schools). The churches, also, are empowered to levy taxes on their members, which as a rule are collected by the state against reimbursement of costs. Moreover, the clergy are trained mainly at state universities, and the churches have a say in appointments to chairs of theology. In addition, the social and charitable commitment of the churches remains an integral function of public life in Germany.

Despite the maintenance of church membership by most Germans and the absence of major friction between church and state, secular attitudes are becoming evident in public life. Increasing numbers have severed their formal ties with organized religion.

Religious Affiliations

Affiliation	Members
Protestant (mostly Evangelical Lutheran)	35,140,000
Roman Catholic	27,850,000
Muslim	1,750,000
Other (mostly nonreligious)	17,360,000

HISTORICAL BACKGROUND

Germanic tribes first appeared in European history in the first century B.C., when the Cimbri and Teutons clashed with Roman legions in Gaul and on the Alps. Later, as the Roman Empire began to disintegrate, the Alemanni, Burgundians, Franks, Lombards, Ostrogoths, and Visigoths settled in the region between the Rhine and the Elbe rivers. However, it was not until Charlemagne (768–814) that the Germans acquired a political unity.

After Charlemagne's death, his empire soon fell apart. In the course of various inheritance divisions, a western and an eastern realm developed, with the eastern realm being called Deutschland (the land of Deutsch speakers). Germany's western frontier was fixed relatively early and has remained fairly stable. But the eastern frontier was pushed eastward for hundreds of years until it contracted in the 20th century.

The transition from the East Franconian to German Reich usually is dated from 911, when Conrad I was elected the first German king. The official title was first Frankish king. It later became the Roman king while the name of his realm was first Roman Empire, and later Holy Roman Empire, to which the words "of the German Nation" were added. It was an electoral monarchy that later became dynastic. Otto I, the greatest of his dynasty, united Germany and Italy and was crowned first Holy Roman Emperor in 962. His successors were engaged in constant struggles within Germany as well as with the papacy, and it was not until the new Salian dynasty that a new upswing occurred. Under Henry III (1039–56), German power reached its zenith, only to decline once again. In 1138, a century of rule by the Staufer began the Hohenstaufen dynasty. Its most brilliant ruler was Frederick I "Barbarossa" (1115–90), who led the empire into a golden age. Under his successors, the empire broke up. With the end of Hohenstaufen rule in 1268, the temporal princes became sovereign land dukes. Germany did not again become a true national state until the 19th century.

The Habsburgs took power in the 13th century under Rudolf I (1273–91). The Golden Bull or the Imperial Constitution issued by Charles IV in 1356 regulated the election of the German king by seven electors privileged with special rights. These sovereign electors and their towns gradually gained in power and influence. The towns linked into leagues, the most important of which, the Hanseatic League, became the leading Baltic power in the 14th century. The power of the emperors was curtailed and increasingly eroded by capitulations, which they negotiated at their elections with the various princes. The empire was further weakened in the 16th century by the Reformation, which led to the division of Germany into two camps. In 1522–23, the Reich knights rose in revolt, and, in 1525, the Peasants' Revolt erupted, the first revolutionary movement in German history. The dukes profited most from the Reformation when they were given the right to dictate the religion of their subjects by the Treaty of Augsburg of 1555. This treaty failed to end the conflict between the faiths, although four-fifths of the country had become Protestant. In the following decades, the Catholic Church was able to recapture many areas. A local conflict in Bohemia triggered the Thirty Years' War (1618–48), which widened into Europe's worst and perhaps last major religious conflict. The war devastated and depopulated much of Germany. In 1648, the Treaty of Westphalia ceded territories to France and Sweden and ultimately confirmed the withdrawal of Switzerland and the Netherlands from the Reich.

In the 18th century, Prussia became the premier German state, especially through the military brilliance of Frederick II (the Great, 1740–86). During the French Revolution and the Napoleonic wars, German nationalism resurfaced and triumphed briefly in the Frankfurt Parliament of 1848. The following decades witnessed the rise of Prussia under its autocratic prime minister, Otto von Bismarck. After a series of successful wars (1864–71) with Denmark, Austria, and France, Bismarck brought about the union of German states (excluding Austria) that formed the Second Reich. In 1871, Wilhelm I was proclaimed the German emperor in the Versailles Hall of Mirrors. This signaled the eclipse of France and the rise of Germany as a European superpower. Bismarck avoided further wars by creating an elaborate alliance network. With the advent of Wilhelm II as German emperor and the dismissal of Bismarck, the delicate international equilibrium was disturbed after 1890. Under Wilhelm II, Germany undertook a collision course with the other major imperial powers, leading to World War I, in which it suffered an ignominious defeat. Both the military and the monarchy collapsed. Wilhelm II abdicated and fled the country. Germany became a republic in 1918.

The new state, known as the Weimar Republic, confronted anarchic conditions. The Social Democratic Party, which as the majority party was charged with the transition to the new political order, left the political structure of the Second Reich untouched. The armed forces remained under the command of the imperial officer corps, while the reactionary bureaucracy entrenched themselves in the administration. In 1925, Field Marshal Paul von Hindenburg was elected president. Bedeviled by inflation, the Ruhr occupation by France, and left-wing and Nazi coups, the Weimar Republic's final deathblow came with the world economic crisis of 1929.

The Weimar Republic not only died unmourned, but it also begat a monster in Adolf Hitler. On January 30, 1933, Hitler became Reich chancellor. The 12 years that followed were among the blackest in German history. It witnessed one of the most brutal dictatorships, the virtual annihilation of European Jewry, and the bloodiest war in military annals. The Third Reich was consumed in the ashes of a vast Götterdämmerung, which pales in comparison to all other historical disasters. Most of Germany lay in ruins and under the heels of occupying powers. Germany's future looked bleak. In 1945 Germany was divided by the victorious Allies into four occupation zones controlled by the Soviet Union, United States, United Kingdom, and France. In 1949, pending a peace

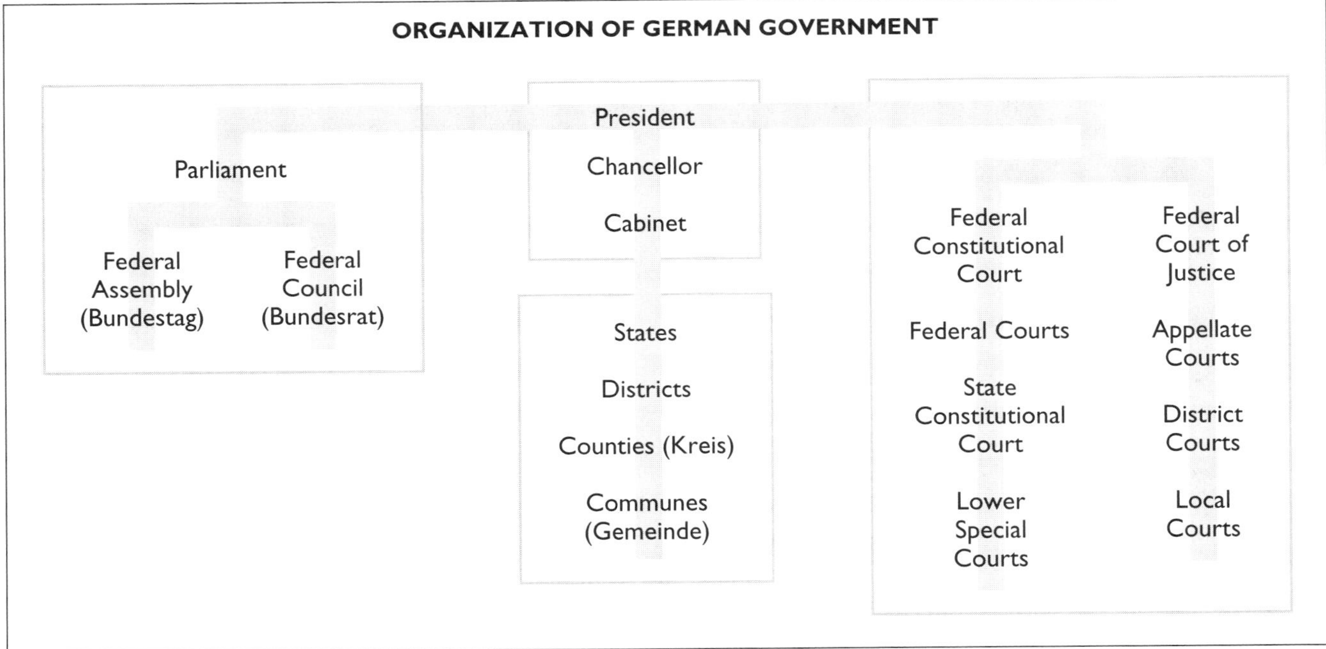

settlement, the U.S., British, and French zones were consolidated into West Germany (the Federal Republic of Germany [FRG]) and the Soviet Zone into East Germany (German Democratic Republic [GDR]). Former German territories in the East (including East Prussia) were ceded to Poland and the Soviet Union. The city of Berlin, inside the Soviet Zone, was likewise divided into four zones under the four occupying powers. Eight districts in Berlin were united with the GDR and 12 districts with the FRG. For the first 20 years of its existence the FRG was under the rule of Christian Democrats led by Konrad Adenauer, Ludwig Erhard, and Kurt-George Kiesinger. There was a major shift in 1969 when the Social Democratic Party swept into power under Willy Brandt. The Socialists remained in power until 1982 when the Christian Democrats were returned to power under Helmut Kohl as chancellor. Kohl remained in power until 1998, presiding over the reunion of East Germany and West Germany in 1990. Germany took a lead in the formation of the European Union and has remained one of its strongest supporters. In 1998 Kohl suffered a stunning defeat at the hands of a resurgent Socialist-led coalition under Gerhard Schröder.

CONSTITUTION

The German constitution is the Basic Law (Grundgesetz) and was enacted on May 22, 1949, for the former West German state. It was viewed as a temporary constitution until Germany was reunited. With a unified Germany, the Basic Law serves both regions of the once divided nation. The authors of the Basic Law used the Weimar Constitution of 1919 and the post–World War II constitutions of the various states as models. The framers determined to avoid the weak, multiparty democracy of the Weimar Republic and the authoritarianism of the Third Reich. Although amended some 30 times in its first 32 years, the Basic Law has functioned successfully, giving Germany its longest period of democracy in modern times, including a successive transition in the postunification era.

Articles 1 through 19 enumerate the basic rights that apply to all citizens. They include equality before the law; freedom of speech, assembly, the press, and worship; freedom from prejudice based on race, sex, religion, or ideology; and the right of conscientious objection to military service. Article 18 provides a caveat to these rights and sanctions their forfeiture in the case of those who abuse them.

The majority of the 146 articles of the Basic Law outline the makeup and functions of the various governmental bodies as well as the careful system of checks and balances that governs their interactions. Other major areas that are addressed by the Basic Law are the distribution of power between the federal government and the various state governments; the administration of federal laws; government finance; and administration during emergencies. Economic matters are largely ignored, although Article 14 does guarantee property and the rights of inheritance and restricts expropriation to cases involving the public weal.

The system of federalism established in the Basic Law follows a tradition dating to the founding of the Second

Reich in 1871. The Federal Republic is a community of states, each having its own constitution and administrative structures. Sovereignty is vested in the federation. The Basic Law divides authority between the federation and the states, thus constitutionally guaranteeing a mutual dependence and an ongoing important role for the states.

The federal government can legislate only in areas specifically prescribed by the Basic Law. Areas that come under the exclusive administrative and legislative jurisdiction of the federal government including foreign affairs, defense, citizenship, currency, rail and air transportation, and postal services. Areas of concurrent legislation relating to the economy and ecology also have increasingly come under federal jurisdiction. By virtue of their omission from the enumerated exclusive or concurrent federal powers, a large number of matters, including education, culture, church affairs, police, media, and local government are left primarily to the jurisdiction of the states. The states also retain considerable powers of taxation.

The Federal Constitutional Court is vital to the preservation of German federalism. The Bundesrat (Federal Council, upper house of parliament), representing state interests, elects its judges. Its jurisdiction extends to cases involving differences or incompatibilities between federal and state laws, or between federal and state rights and duties as well as interstate disputes. Thus, this house of parliament is the guardian of German federalism.

Amendments to the Basic Law require the affirmative vote of two-thirds of the members of the two federal legislative bodies—the Bundestag (Federal Assembly, lower house of parliament) and Bundesrat.

Within the dual executive created by the Basic Law, the president, as head of state, clearly is subordinate to the federal chancellor, the head of government. The president's functions are largely formal or ceremonial.

The federal chancellor and his cabinet ministers are collectively known as the federal government. The chancellor controls the composition of the cabinet. Although ministers are given considerable freedom of action, only the chancellor is responsible to the Bundestag for government policies. The Bundestag may not censure cabinet ministers. The chancellor controls the federal bureaucracy, the distribution of public funds, and the implementation of legislation. He may veto budgetary appropriations not to his liking. In wartime, the chancellor assumes supreme command over the armed forces from the minister of defense. The number of ministers is left to the discretion of the chancellor. As a rule, German cabinets are highly stable. Nearly all ministers rise and fall with the chancellor, and resignations for political reasons are rare, even though the realities of coalition governments generate occasional public differences.

LOCAL GOVERNMENT

Germany consists of 16 states. These include Baden-Württemberg, Bayern (Bavaria), Berlin, Brandenburg, Bremen, Hamburg, Hessen (Hesse), Niedersachsen (Lower Saxony), Mecklenburg-Vorpommern (Mecklenburg-West Pomerania), Nordrhein-Westfalen (North Rhine-Westphalia), Rheinland-Pfalz (Rhineland-Palatinate), Saarland, Sachsen (Saxony), Sachsen-Anhalt (Saxony-Anhalt), Schleswig-Holstein, and Thüringen (Thuringia). The Basic Law requires that the "constitutional order in the states . . . conforms to the principles of republican, democratic, and social government based on the rule of law." With this exception, the states are free to form any type of governmental structure. Most states are governed by a cabinet led by a minister-president and have a unicameral legislative body known as the Landtag. The relationship between the legislature and the executive duplicates the system at the federal level. Legislatures are popularly elected, normally for a four-year term of office. The Council of Elders (Altestenrat) manages the affairs of the Landtag. The Landtag elects the chief executive (*Ministerpräsident*) who, in turn, appoints the members of his cabinet. State cabinets (*Staatsregierung*) contain eight to 10 ministers.

There are three levels of local government under the states. The largest states are divided into districts (*Regierungbezirke*), each headed by a district president (*Regierungspräsidenten*), who is subordinate to the state's minister of the interior. There are no separate legislative or judicial agencies at this level. The next fundamental units of local government are the counties (*Kreise*; singular, *Kreis*), administered by a Landrat, *Kreisrat*, or *Oberkreisdirektor*. The legislative body at this level is the Kreistag. The third level of local government is the *Gemeinde*, which may apply to a town, village, or city. *Gemeinden*, also, contain elected councils, which, in turn, elect an executive *Bürgermeister* (mayor).

Local Government

Principal administrative divisions, capitals, area, population.

AREA AND POPULATION

States Administrative districts	Capitals	area sq mi	 sq km	population 1996 estimate
Baden-Württemberg	Stuttgart	13,804	35,752	10,344,000
Freiburg	Freiburg	3,613	9,357	2,093,000
Karlsruhe	Karlsruhe	2,671	6,919	2,648,400
Stuttgart	Stuttgart	4,076	10,558	3,871,900
Tübingen	Tübingen	3,443	8,918	1,730,700
Bayern	Munich	27,240	70,551	12,014,700
Mittelfranken	Ansbach	2,798	7,246	1,670,400
Niederbayern	Landshut	3,988	10,330	1,147,200
Oberbayern	Munich	6,768	17,530	3,985,200
Oberfranken	Bayreuth	2,792	7,230	1,111,000

(continued)

Oberpfalz	Regensburg	3,741	9,690	1,056,200
Schwaben	Augsburg	3,859	9,994	1,724,600
Unterfranken	Würzburg	3,294	8,532	1,320,100
Berlin	—	344	891	3,467,300
Brandenburg	Potsdam	11,381	29,476	2,545,500
Bremen	Bremen	156	404	678,700
Hamburg	Hamburg	292	755	1,708,500
Hessen	Wiesbaden	8,152	21,114	6,016,300
Darmstadt	Darmstadt	2,874	7,445	8,688,800
Giessen	Giessen	2,078	5,381	1,057,200
Kassel	Kassel	3,200	8,289	1,270,300
Mecklenburg-Vorpommern	Schwerin	8,946	23,170	1,820,600
Niedersachsen	Hannover	18,383	47,612	7,795,100
Braunschweig	Braunschweig	3,126	8,097	1,678,500
Hannover	Hannover	3,493	9,046	2,142,100
Lüneburg	Lüneburg	5,986	15,505	1,607,900
Weser-Ems	Oldenburg	5,778	14,965	2,366,600
Nordrhein-Westfalen	Düsseldorf	13,158	34,078	17,908,500
Arnsberg	Arnsberg	3,090	8,002	3,825,400
Delmold	Delmold	2,517	6,518	2,018,300
Düsseldorf	Düsseldorf	2,042	5,289	5,287,000
Köln	Köln	2,844	7,365	4,199,300
Münster	Münster	2,665	6,903	2,578,500
Rheinland-Pfalz	Mainz	7,662	19,846	3,983,300
Koblenz	Koblenz	3,117	8,072	1,492,400
Rheinhessen-Pfalz	Mainz	2,646	6,852	1,985,200
Trier	Trier	1,901	4,923	505,700
Saarland	Saarbrücken	992	2,570	1,083,100
Sachsen	Dresden	7,109	18,413	4,557,200
Chemnitz	—	2,354	6,097	1,687,100
Dresden	—	3,062	7,930	1,759,400
Leipzig	—	1,693	4,836	1,110,700
Sachsen-Anhalt	Magdeburg	7,895	20,447	2,731,500
Dessau	Dessau	1,652	4,280	571,800
Halle	Halle/Saale	1,710	4,430	905,900
Mageburg	Magdeburg	4,532	11,738	1,253,800
Schleswig-Holstein	Kiel	6,089	15,770	2,730,600
Thüringen	Erfurt	6,244	16,171	2,496,700
TOTAL		137,846	357,021	81,881,600

PARLIAMENT

The federal legislature consists of two chambers: the Bundestag and Bundesrat (the lower and upper chambers). The Bundestag is the only popularly elected organ at the federal level and is by far the more important of the two legislative chambers. Its members are elected every four years. The size of the Bundestag has gradually increased, from 402 in 1949 to 669 in 2000.

The key organizing agents of the Bundestag are the caucuses (Fraktionen), parliamentary groups of the political parties. Deputies belonging to the same party constitute a single caucus provided there are 15 party members in the house. Technically, although not constitutionally, the Bundestag is composed of caucuses and not individual deputies. Only caucuses may initiate legislative proposals. Debate time and representation in the standing committees are determined in accordance with the relative strength of the caucus. Even independent delegates have visiting rights with the caucuses. The importance of the caucuses in organizing the work of the chamber also extends to the relationship between the leadership of the parties and individual deputies. Party discipline and hence party voting are high—about 85 percent to 90 percent of all votes are straight party votes, with deputies following the caucus leadership or the results of a caucus vote. Free votes, where the party gives no binding instructions to its deputies, are rare. A deputy who cannot support a party line may leave a caucus and join another without having to run for election again.

The daily agenda of the chamber is determined by the Council of Elders (Ältestenrat), in essence a steering committee, composed of the Bundestag president, who is himself a member of the largest caucus, three vice presidents, and 12 to 15 representatives of all the caucuses. The Ältestenrat schedules debates, allots time to each party, and assigns committee chairmanships to each in proportion to its parliamentary strength. A second executive body in the Bundestag is the Präsidium, consisting of the president and the vice presidents, which is responsible for overall administration and personnel recruitment.

Parliamentary committees are more important in Germany than in Great Britain or France but less so than in the United States. Functional standing committees (*Ausschüsse*) number approximately 19 and have 17 to 29 members. Sometimes opposition parties have a share of committee chairmanships. The committees cannot pigeonhole or reject bills but must examine them carefully, take testimony, and propose amendments, if necessary, to the whole house.

POLITICAL PARTIES

Since the first general election held in unified Germany in 1990, six parties have emerged in prominence in the Bundestag: the Christian Democratic Union (CDU), Christian Social Union (CSU), Free Democratic Party (FDP), Social Democratic Party of Germany (SPD), Party for Democratic Socialism (PDS), and Alliance '90/The Greens. The SPD, CDU, CSU, and FDP were formed in the western states between 1945 and 1947. In the five decades since their establishment, these four parties have undergone significant changes. At the federal level, they have all formed coalitions with one another once or been in opposition. Today, they all see themselves as "popular" parties representing a cross section of German society. As a result of unification, other parties in the unified Germany are new and small. Although the Green Party (Die Grünen) existed in the former West Germany since 1979, it joined forces with Alliance '90 (Bündnis 90) in 1993 so that both could contend at the national political level. The Party for Democratic Socialism (Partei für demokratischen Sozialismus, PDS) is the successor to the former Socialist Unity Party of Germany (Sozialistische Einheitspartei Deutschlands, SED), the communist party that ruled in the former GDR. In the 1998 election, it cleared the 5 percent hurdle due largely to the support of voters in the former GDR, thus acquiring parliamentary group status. As of 1998, the membership numbers of these parties were as follows: SPD 775,400; CDU 625,800; CSU 178,900; FDP 68,000; Alliance '90/The Greens 50,200; and PDS 95,000.

Political Parties

Social Democratic Party, 1945
Alliance '90/The Greens, 1980
Christian Democratic Union, 1945
Christian Social Union
Free Democratic Party
Party of Democratic Socialism, 1946
The Republicans, 1983
National Democratic Party, 1964
German Social Union, 1990
German People's Union, 1987
German Communist Party, 1968
Instead Party, 1993
League of Free Citizens, 1994
The Greys, 1989
Democratic Party, 1995

Political Parties: Strength in Parliament Most Recent Elections

Federal Assembly (Bundestag). The 672-member lower chamber is the world's largest democratically elected legislative body. Deputies are chosen for four-year terms (subject to dissolution) by direct popular vote under a complicated electoral system combining direct and proportional representation. The election of September 27, 1998, yielded the following distribution of seats: Social Democratic Party of Germany, 298; Christian Democrats, 245 (Christian Democratic Union, 198; Christian Social Union, 47); Alliance '90/The Greens, 47; Free Democratic Party, 43; Party of Democratic Socialism, 36.

LEGAL SYSTEM

Germans are a very law conscious and court-minded people. There is hardly any area of human relations untouched by some rule, order, or regulation, whether it be the nighttime working hours of bakers or the time when parents should keep their children quiet. Germans are more inclined to settle their disputes through legal means than through informal negotiations and bargaining. Further, the judicial process is relatively speedy and inexpensive. On a per capita basis there are nine times as many judges in Germany as in the United States, and over half of all lawyers are either judges or in the civil service. Thus, the complexity of law affects the social, political, and economic arenas as well.

German law is an amalgam of two streams of influence: Roman legal codes introduced by Italian jurists in the Middle Ages and the Napoleonic Code enforced in the Rhineland during the French occupation in the 19th century. After the founding of the Second Reich in 1871, a process of legal revision began that was completed only toward the turn of the century. These codes form the basis of a unified legal system and are the same in all states, even in such matters as bankruptcy, divorce, criminal offenses, and extradition. The codified character of German law also means that, unlike Anglo-American law, there is no judge-made or common law. The German judge may not set precedents and thus make law but must be a neutral administrator only, fitting particular cases to the existing body of law. Although neutral in theory, the German judge is not, according to the rules of procedure, a disinterested referee of court proceedings but an active inquisitor, trying to appraise the facts and determining their legal relevance.

The Basic Law guarantees the rights of defendants. A suspect cannot be forced to talk to the police. If statements were made under duress, they may be retracted later during a court trial. Suspects may not be subjected to physical abuse, torture, drugs, deceit, or hypnosis. Only the minimum force necessary for arrest is authorized. A suspect must be brought before a judge no later than the day following arrest, and the judge must issue a warrant of arrest specifying the reasons for detention, or else release the suspect.

There is no separate system of federal and state courts. With the exception of the national high courts of appeal, all regular tribunals are state courts. Although national law outlines the basic organization of the judiciary, it is established and administered by state statutes. The other significant characteristics of the court structure are its collegial nature and the extensive system of specialized courts. Regular courts, both civil and criminal, are organized on four levels: local, district, appellate, and federal. The 670 local courts (*Amtsgerichte*) are in small and medium-sized towns and usually are staffed by a single judge, who may be assisted by two lay judges in criminal cases. These courts also perform some administrative functions, such as in bankruptcy. At the next level are the district courts (*Landsgerichte*), each consisting of separate chambers of three to five judges. At the third level are the appellate courts (*Oberlandesgerichte*), which take cases only on appeal, except for cases involving treason and anticonstitutional activity. In Germany, appeals involve both reexamination of the facts in a case and its procedural and legal aspects. These courts also are divided into panels of three to five judges. At the apex is the Federal Court of Justice at Karlsruhe, which has 132 judges divided into 20 panels or senates. It holds no original jurisdiction. There are five kinds of special courts, most under state control: administrative courts, social courts, labor courts, financial courts, and the single Federal Patents Court in Munich. The highest level of each kind of court falls under the authority of the federal government. The final type of court is the constitutional court. There are several constitutional courts that function in several of the different states. All of them are administratively independent and financially autonomous. Judges of the Federal Constitutional Court may be removed only upon a motion from the court itself.

LAW ENFORCEMENT

Law Enforcement

Offenses reported to the police per 100,000: 8,038
- Murder: 4.6
- Assault: 108.2
- Burglary: 1,927.1
- Automobile Theft: 260.1
- Population per Police officer: —

Death Penalty: Abolished

HUMAN RIGHTS

Unlike the United States or the United Kingdom, Germany does not have a strong civil libertarian tradition. German legal and political theory for the most part has emphasized the duties of the individual vis-à-vis the state rather than state responsibilities toward the protection of individual liberties.

Evidence suggests that the rule of law applies less to lower-status, disadvantaged groups than to the "establishment." There is no German version of the American Civil Liberties Union and no culturally ingrained sympathy for the underdog. The German humanistic tradition is, above all, abstract and philosophical, not pragmatic.

Further, the legal system itself has a strong upper-class flavor. The bottom half of society is estranged from the courts not only because of these class differences but also because of the pedantic legalese and jargon in which legal procedures and principles are couched. Bureaucratic red tape, often a mask for inefficiency and lack of compassion, also deters the less fortunate from even seeking justice. Nevertheless, there has been remarkable progress in this direction in the past 40 years. The Basic Law is as strong a bulwark of freedom as can be found in any country. Virtually all the classic liberties are specified and guaranteed, including academic freedom, privacy of mail and telephone, freedom from censorship, and the right to refuse military service. Finally, in an extraordinary departure from German constitutional tradition, Article 20 declares that "all Germans shall have the right to resist any person or persons seeking to abolish the constitutional order, should no other remedy be possible." Major controversies involving alleged violations of these basic liberties have occurred only infrequently.

The mushrooming of terrorist and deviant groups, both indigenous and foreign, in the 1970s placed a strain on the evolution of human rights. Much of the domestic violence associated with the notorious Red Army Faction has been contained, although there have been sporadic incidents involving U.S. army personnel stationed in the former West Germany, some of them racially motivated attacks on U.S. black soldiers. Efforts to curb Middle Eastern violence have been less successful because of retaliations against German citizens in Lebanon. In its 1986 report, Amnesty International expressed concern over the length of pretrial detention spent in isolation by persons detained on suspicion of terrorism.

FOREIGN POLICY

Since 1989, international conditions have changed the framework of German foreign policy. Germany is reunified and sovereign in its foreign policy, and its security situation has improved greatly. Previously inconceivable forms of cooperation are now possible in the whole of Europe and the world. German foreign policy is, thus, oriented toward maintaining peace and prosperity, promoting democracy, and developing respect for human rights the world over. It includes the further development of the European Union (EU) as a unit capable of action in all areas of global policy; the safeguarding of peace, democracy, and prosperity in Europe to be achieved through EU enlargement; the strengthening of pan-European cooperation within the Organization for Security and Cooperation in Europe; the further development of the Atlantic Alliance and transatlantic cooperation with the United States; the strengthening of international organizations (e.g., the UN) and a more active role for Germany in these organizations; the promotion of human rights; the further development of relations based on equal partnership with the regions bordering the EU (e.g., the Mediterranean and Middle East); and the preservation of a habitable world for future generations.

Ever since its founding in 1949, the Federal Republic of Germany has been one of the main advocates of European unification. Its founders recognized that European unification would strengthen Europe's position in the world and serve to promote peace, freedom, and prosperity on the continent. Through the process of European integration, a transparent system of close mutual consultation and cooperation has been created that aims to peacefully reconcile the interests of all. With the Single European Act of 1986, the Maastricht Treaty on European Union of 1992, and the Treaty of Amsterdam of 1997, Germany has taken further steps with other European states toward unification. The Maastricht Treaty laid the foundations for economic and monetary union, the third and final stage of which began upon the introduction of a common currency, the euro, on January 1, 1999. Europe has, thus, become the world's second largest single-currency area. Since the entry into force of the Maastricht Treaty, the EU has had a Common Foreign and Security Policy (CFSP) and a common policy in the fields of justice and domestic affairs as well. The preconditions have been created for the development of the EU into a truly comprehensive political union of which Germany has been an integral part since 1952.

DEFENSE

In 1955, 10 years after the end of World War II, the Bundestag authorized the formation of the Bundeswehr (federal armed forces), composed initially of volunteers. Legislation on compulsory military service was promulgated in 1956. By the end of that year, the force numbered 65,000, including 10,000 volunteers from the Federal Border Force (Bundesgrenzschutz or BGS), almost all of whom were World War II veterans. The reappearance of a German armed force, bitterly opposed by sections of the West German populace, had become a reality as a direct result of the cold war. During this time and throughout the remainder of the cold war era, the former East Germany became an integral part of the Warsaw Pact coalition of communist nations led by the former Soviet Union, which was aligned against the NATO coalition of democratic nations led by the United States. Occupation forces from the superpowers remained in Germany until the early 1990s when they gradually disbanded as a result of the Two Plus Four Agreements, which facilitated German unification.

The Basic Law said almost nothing of the status of the army since none existed at the time of its formulation in 1949 and none was envisaged. It did not, however, prohibit the raising of an army (as it did waging an aggressive war), so the federal government found no serious impediment to its creation of one in 1956. Thus, by implication, the sole mission of the Bundeswehr is defense.

Military Indicators

Total Active Duty Personnel: 347,100
Military Manpower per 1,000: 4.2
Military Expenditures $million: 41,160
- as % of GNP: 1.9
- per capita $: 496
- as % of central government expenditures: 5.0

Arms Imports $million: 310
Arms Exports $million: 1,200

ECONOMY

Germany is one of the major industrial countries of the developed world. In 1999, its gross domestic product (GDP), the value of all finished goods produced and services rendered annually, totaled a record DM 3,871.6 billion in the western region of the country. Growth rose to 3 percent in 2000, largely due to recovering global demand; newly passed business and income tax cuts are expected to keep growth strong in 2001. After price adjustments, GDP has doubled in the past 30 years and increased fivefold over 45 years. Germany is the third largest nation in terms of overall economic performance and holds second place with regard to world trade. It is a member of the "G7" group, comprising the seven leading Western industrial countries. The members hold a summit meeting every year at which they coordinate their economic and financial policies at the level of the heads of state or of government.

After the fall of communism, the new Germany experienced economic difficulties throughout the 1990s. The former western regions had to shoulder the burden of high taxes to fund improvements in infrastructure, the environment, and industry in the eastern states. In addition, many eastern enterprises collapsed in the face of western competition. Since 1995, the German unemployment rate has remained high, ranging from 9.5 percent to 11.5 percent. The figures have been much higher in the eastern regions and lower in the western states. Still, Germany remains a powerhouse in the world economy.

Other challenges, also, confront united Germany at the beginning of the 21st century. Being a world industrial leader and the world's second largest trading nation, Germany is deeply integrated into the global economy and extremely dependent on foreign trade, perhaps more so than other countries. However, like other industrial countries, Germany faces the complicated task of adapting its economy to the conditions created by globalization, while at the same time reducing high levels of unemployment, which has been a trend afflicting many European nations throughout the latter part of the preceding century. In addition, Germany must overcome the economic and social divisions still existing between its eastern and western regions since unification. This task remains the major national challenge. Moreover, the extensive process of democratic reform in Eastern Europe and the states of the former Soviet Union continues to place a heavy burden on Germany. Issues of migration, economic aid, technical assistance, and the environment multiply the strain on the already pressed German economy.

Principal Economic Indicators

Gross National Product $: 2.320 trillion
GNP per capita $: 28,280
GNP Average Annual Growth Rate (1990–97) %: 0.7
GNP per capita Average Annual Growth Rate (1990–97) %: 0.2
Origin of Gross Domestic Product %
- Agriculture: 1
- Mining: 2
- Manufacturing: 23
- Construction: 5
- Public Utilities: —
- Transportation and Communications: 5
- Trade: 8
- Financial Services: 13
- Other Services: 19
- Government: 9

Gross Domestic Product by Type of Expenditure %
- Private Consumption: 57
- Government Consumption: 19
- Gross Domestic Investment: 23
- Foreign Trade: Exports: 23
- Imports: −22

(continued)

% of Income Received by Poorest 20%: 7.0
% of Income Received by Richest 10%: 24.4

Price and earnings indexes (1995 = 100)

	1992	1993	1994	1995	1996	1997	1998
Consumer price index	91.5	95.6	98.2	100.0	101.5	103.3	104.3
Hourly earnings index	—	—	—	—	—	—	—

Finance

National Currency: Euro (formerly Deutsche Mark [DM])
Exchange Rate: $1 = DM 1.8167
Money Supply Stock in National Currency billion: 879.8
M1 per capita: 10,700
Central Bank Discount Rate % : 2.5
Total External Debt $million: —
Debt Service Ratio %: —

Balance of Payments $million: −1,520
International Reserves SDRs million: 61,518
Ratio of External Debt to Total Reserves: —
Average Annual Rate of Inflation/Consumer Price Index
Growth Rate %: 1.8

Official Development Assistance

Donor ODA $million: 9,000
as % of GNP: 0.3
per capita $ 109.6
Foreign Direct Investment $million: 18,712

Central Government Revenues and Expenditures

Fiscal Year: Calender Year
Revenues $million: 755,000
Expenditures $million: 832,100
Budget Deficit $million: 26.5
Tax Revenues as % of GDP: —
Highest Tax Bracket %
Individual: 53
Corporate: 30

Employment and Labor

Economically Active Population: 40,083,000
Female Participation Rate %: 42.8
Activity Rate %: 49.1
Labor by Sector: %
Agriculture, Forestry, Fishing: 3.3
Manufacturing, Mining: 27.3
Construction: 9.4
Transportation and Communications: 5.5
Trade, Hotels, and Restaurants: 17.3
Finance, Insurance, Real Estate: 9.2
Public Administration, Defense: 8.4
Services: 19.0
Unemployment %: 12

Agriculture

Agriculture's Share of GDP %: 1
Average Annual Rate of Growth (1965–98)%: —
Number of Farms 000: 581
Average Size of Farm ha: 28.0
Number of Tractors per 1,000 hectares: 110.1
Irrigation, % of Farms having: 4
Artificial Fertilizer kg/hectare: 384
Total Farmland as % of land area: 49.7
Livestock: Cattle 000: 15,277
Sheep 000: 2,302
Hogs 000: 24,795
Chickens 000: 102,731
Forests: Production of Roundwood (000 cubic meters): 38,970
Fisheries: Total Catch tons 000: 270.8

Mining

% of GDP:
Value of Mineral Production $million: 11,803.2

Manufacturing

Value Added $million: 596,225
Industrial Production Growth Rate %: 3

Energy

Commercial Energy Production metric tons of
oil equivalent 000: 139,734
Commercial Energy Consumption metric tons of
oil equivalent 000: 347,272
Commercial Energy Consumption per capita kg: 4,231
Average Annual Growth Rate 1980–97 %: −0.5
Net Energy Imports % of use: 60
Electricity Installed Capacity kW 000: 115,428
Production kW-hr million: 534,902
Coal Reserves tons million: 67,300
Production tons 000: 251,615
Natural Gas Proven Reserves cubic meters billion: 329
Production cubic meters million: 18,998
Crude Petroleum Reserves barrels million: 365
Production barrels million: 21
Consumption barrels million: 745
Refinery Capacity barrels per day 000: 2,108
Pipelines Length km: 7,590

Foreign Trade

Imports $million: 443,223.8
Exports $million: 508,508.5
Export Volume % Annual Growth Rate (1990–97): 3.0
Import Volume % Annual Growth Rate (1990–97): 1.8

Balance of trade (current prices)

	1993	1994	1995	1996	1997	1998
DM 000,000,000	+75.81	+88.73	+103.40	+117.35	+137.35	+148.66
% of total	6.4%	6.8%	7.4%	8.0%	8.4%	8.4%

Major Trading Partners

	Imports	Exports
European Union %	54.7	57.1
United State %	7.1	7.5
Eastern Europe %	8.3	7.4
Japan %	5.5	2.6
Others %	24.4	25.5

Transportation

Roads Total Length mi: 404,325 km 650,700
Paved %: 99
Automobiles: 40,499,442
Trucks and Buses: 2,336,760
Persons per vehicle: 1.9
Railroad; Track Length mi: 54,994 km 88,504
Passenger-mi million: 39,830
Freight-mi million: 45,649
Merchant Marine: No of Vessels: 1,375
Total Deadweight Tonnage 000: 6,832.3
International Cargo Loaded tons 000: 71,028
International Cargo Off-loaded tons 000: 128,448
Airports with Scheduled Flights: 40
Traffic: Passenger-mi million: 39,409
Freight-mi million: 8,611
Length of Canals mi: 4,586 km 7,541

Tourism

Number of Tourists to 000: 16,511
Number of Tourists from 000: 82,975
Tourist Receipts $million: 16,221
Tourist Expenditures $million: 50,675

Communications

Telephones 000: 40,400
Cost of Local Calls 3 mins: $0.12
Cellular Telephones 000: 3,750
Fax Machines 000: 1,447
Personal Computers 000: 13,500
Internet Hosts per million persons: 5,794
Mail: Post Offices: 17,172
Pieces of Mail Handled million: 19,963
Pieces of Mail Handled per person: 244

EDUCATION

Formal compulsory education begins at age six and extends for nine years. Thereafter, it is partly compulsory (there are no penalties if pupils drop out) for an additional three years. There is virtually 100 percent enrollment at the primary level. Within the three-tier secondary educational tradition, most pupils attend Gymnasium. The Gesamtschule, a comprehensive school of recent origin, is growing in popularity; about 9 percent of Germany's 14-years-olds were enrolled in the integrated Gesamtschule in 1993. Females are well represented at most levels of education. Nowadays, they represent roughly 43 percent of all students attending institutions of higher education and are well represented at teachers' colleges and art schools.

Less than 1 percent of primary students and 4 percent of secondary-school students attend private schools.

In current terminology Germans refer to preschool programs as the elementary stage (Elementarstufe) and to the first four years of school as the primary stage (Primarstufe). Preschool programs are voluntary and usually not part of the formal school system. Primary school (Grundschule) includes grades one through four. The primary school offers 23 to 27 class hours of instruction per week, half of it devoted to German and mathematics. At the end of the fourth year the child and his or her parents must make a decision regarding secondary education. In the 1970s a so-called orientation phase was introduced in all states, designed to extend the period of decision and to make the transition to the appropriate secondary school easier.

There are four types of general secondary education, together known as continuation schools: the Hauptschule, the Realschule, the Gymnasium, and the Gesamtschule. The Hauptschule is referred to as the secondary modern or short-course school and the Realschule as the intermediate school. The Gymnasium is called the grammar school or the senior high school. The Gesamtschule offers an all-inclusive curriculum for students from ages six through 19, who are allowed to take whatever courses they choose. Some of the Gesamtschulen are all-day schools, unlike the Gymnasien, which have classes only part of the day but have extensive homework assignments.

The Hauptschule is the main type of secondary school, covering grades five through nine. It is characterized by a high intake from lower social groups and children of foreign workers, and it caters to less academically gifted children. Recently, advanced courses (Aufbauzüge) have been offered from grades eight through 10 to enable pupils to enter academic secondary school in the 11th grade. The Realschule comprises grades five through 10 or seven through 10, concluding at age 16 with the intermediate certificate (Realschulabschlusszeugnis), often called middle maturity (mittlere Reife). There is a parallel continuation (Aufbau) type of school for those who transfer from the Hauptschule. The Realschule offers between 30 and 34 class hours weekly and is a popular choice among the lower middle class, craft workers, and industrial workers because it offers a safe passage to white-collar jobs in middle management without undergoing the rigors of the Gymnasium.

The Gymnasium extends for nine years, from grades five through 13, and is the most academic and prestigious branch of the secondary-school system. The upper secondary school culminates in the Abitur, which is internally set.

There is an alternative route to university education, consisting either of a part-time evening school called Abendgymnasium, or an institution called Studienkolleg, meant primarily for foreigners.

There are well over 100 institutions of higher education in Germany, including specialized institutions such as the Medical University in Hannover, the army universities in Hamburg and Munich, and the Sports University in Cologne. The majority of the institutions fall into three groups: the traditional-type university (Universität); technical universities (Technische Hochschulen); and the comprehensive universities (Gesamthochschulen), combining multiple institutions.

Higher education is tuition-free and admits students from both the Gymnasium and the so-called second-route institutions. The basic right of the holder of an Abitur to enroll at any university in the Federal Republic has been sharply curtailed in recent years by a rapid increase in the number of qualified applicants and the lack of facilities. Thus, admissions in almost all fields are curtailed by *numerus clausus* restrictions. To assist academically qualified students to find places in higher education, a central registry was established in Hamburg in 1971. This registry was replaced in 1973 by a mandatory federal selection process involving all student applications in those fields in which the number of applications exceeds available seats.

In 1998, the Fourth Act to Reform the Framework Act for Higher Education instituted a fundamental overhaul of the higher education system. Through deregulation, a stronger performance orientation, and creation of incentives to excel, it aimed to encourage competition and differentiation, thereby ensuring the international competitiveness of Germany's higher education institutions in the 21st century.

Education

Literacy Rate %: 100
- Male %: 100
- Female %: 100

First Level: Primary schools: 17,910
- Teachers: 199,623
- Students: 3,634,342
- Student-Teacher Ratio: 18.2
- Net Enrollment Ratio: 100

Second Level: Secondary Schools: 17,711
- Teachers: 402,472
- Students: 5,822,242
- Student-Teacher Ratio: 14
- Net Enrollment Ratio: 88

Vocational Level: Schools: 9,245
- Students: 2,435,753

Third Level: Institutions: 335
- Teachers: 152,401
- Students: 1,838,456
- Student-Ratio Level: 12.1
- Gross Enrollment Ratio: 42.7
- Students per 100,000: 2,635
- % of Population Age 25 and over with Postsecondary Education: 19.9

Public Expenditure on Education as % of GDP: 4.7

SCIENCE AND TECHNOLOGY

Science and Technology

Scientists and Engineers in R&D per 1 million persons: 2,831
Expenditures in R&D as % of GDP: 2.41
High-Tech Exports $million: 63,698
Patent Applications by Residents: 62,052

MEDIA

According to the International Press Institute in Vienna, Germany is one of the few countries where the state respects the strong position of a free press. Article 5 of the Basic Law establishes formal guarantees for freedom of opinion, freedom of the press, and rights to accessible information sources. There is no censorship. The state cannot restrict, abridge, or even indirectly interfere with this freedom. Legislators, however, have written two basic restraints into the law. The first provides for lifting constitutional protection in cases of subversion. The second requires the press to observe the general laws protecting personal honor and general propriety. The ultimate judge of the legality of the specific applications of these restraints is the Federal Constitutional Court. The court has enlarged the application of the law to cover not only publication but also the technical processes of production, transportation, and sales. In other words, the law guarantees not only freedom of the press as a theoretical adjunct of freedom of speech and expression, but also independence of the press as an intellectual and business institution. Presently, there are nearly 1,200 accredited correspondents in Bonn and Berlin. They are members of the Federal Press Conference or the Foreign Press Association, both of which are entirely independent of the authorities. Thus, the press is on a par with other national institutions with clearly defined legal status and functions for its well-lobbied membership.

Media

Daily Newspapers: 411
- Total Circulation 000: 25,757
- Circulation per 1,000: 317

Books Published: 70,643
Magazines: 9,010
Radio Receivers 000: 150,000
- per 1,000: 1,875

Television sets 000: 45,000
- per 1,000: 550

MOST IMPORTANT MEDIA:

Press. Newspapers are numerous and widely read, and many of the principal dailies have national as well as local readerships. There are some very large publishing concerns, notably the Axel Springer group, which accounts for some 40 percent of the daily newspaper circulation and is Europe's largest publishing conglomerate. In the eastern Länder (whose press organs are identified by asterisks in the listing below), most papers were transferred from party to private control in 1990. The circulation figures for the following newspapers are for mid-1994: *Bild-Zeitung* (Hamburg and seven other cities, 4,126,000), sensationalist Springer tabloid; *Westdeutsche Allgemeine Zeitung* (Essen, 1,188,000); *Hannoverische Allgemeine Zeitung* (Hanover, 562,000); *Freie Presse* (Chemnitz, 522,000), former PDS organ; *Mitteldeutsche Zeitung* (Halle, 438,000), formerly *Freiheit; Sächsische Zeitung* (Dresden, 426,000); *Thüringer Allgemeine* (Erfurt, 401,000), formerly *Das Volk; Rheinische Post* (Dusseldorf, 400,000); *Süddeutsche Zeitung* (Munich, 400,000), center-left; *Express* (Cologne, 397,000); *Frankfurter Allgemeine Zeitung* (Frankfurt-am-Main, 395,000); *Leipziger Volkszeitung* (Leipzig, 380,500), former PDS organ; *Augsburger Allgemeine* (Augsburg, 368,000); *Südwest Presse* (Ulm, 362,500); *Nürnberger Nachrichten*

(Nuremberg, 347,000); *Magdeburger Volksstimme* (Magdeburg, 342,500), former PDS organ; *BZ* (Berlin, 311,000), Springer group; *Hamburger Abendblatt* (Hamburg, 310,000), Springer group; *Neue Osnabrücker Zeitung* (Osnabrück, 309,000); *Kölner Stadt Anzeiger* (Cologne, 281,000); *Hessische/Niedersachsische Allgemeine* (Kassel, 280,000); *Berliner Zeitung* (Berlin, 270,000), independent; *Die Rheinpfalz* (Ludwigshafen, 247,000); *Rhein-Zeitung* (Koblenz, 242,500); *Abendzeitung/8-Uhr-Blatt* (Munich, 231,500); *Ruhr-Nachrichten* (Dortmund, 220,500); *Berliner Morgenpost* (Berlin, 192,500), Springer group.

News agencies. There are two principal facilities: the German Press Agency (Deutsche Presse-Agentur—DPA), which supplies newspapers and broadcasting stations throughout the Federal Republic, while also transmitting news overseas in German, English, French, Spanish, and Arabic, and the General German News Service (Allgemeiner Deutscher Nachrichtendienst—AND), which was launched in 1946 as the official East German agency and reorganized in 1990.

Radio and television. Terrestrial noncable broadcasting networks are independent, nonprofit, public corporations chartered by the Länder governments. The coordinating body is the Association of Public Law Broadcasting Organizations of the Federal Republic of Germany (Arbeitsgemeinschaft der Offentlich-rechtlichen Rundfunkanstalten der Bundesrepublik Deutschland—ARD). There are three national terrestrial television channels, the first provided by ARD affiliates, the second by Zweites Deutsches Fernsehen (ZDF), and the third (a cultural and educational service) by several of the regional authorities. There are also numerous cable and satellite channels, 50 percent of German households (the highest number in Europe) being wired for cable television. In early 1994 a new state-supported cultural service, Deutschland Radio, was launched to promote a sense of community between eastern and western Germans. As of October 1993 there were 282 private radio and TV stations as contrasted with 261 in 1991.

CULTURE

Cultural Indicators

Public Libraries Number: 20,448
- Volumes: 140,108
- Registered borrowers: 11,463,127

Museums Number: 2,709
- Annual Attendance: 90,448,000

Cinema Production of Long Films: 63
- Number of Cinemas: 3,861
- Seating Capacity: 730,000
- Annual Attendance million: 124.5
- Annual Attendance per capita: 1.5

STATUS OF WOMEN

Germany's Basic Law confers equal rights to men and women. Women's groups, however, feel that women remain excluded from the same opportunities as men. They believe the actual practice of equal treatment remains more of a wish than a reality regarding employment, family, and politics, even though women are in the majority by more than two million. Under pressure from the German Women's Council—a women's lobby representing 52 associations with 11 million members—governmental officials have broadened the constitutional and statutory foundations for establishing equality among the sexes.

German society has only gradually applied the principle of equality in politics, law, and education. In 1919, women finally obtained the right to vote and stand for election. Since then, the number of politically active women has increased steadily, though it remains smaller than that of men. Most political parties have introduced quotas to increase the number of female representatives on executive committees. The percentage of female members in the German Bundestag rose from 8.4 percent in 1980 to 30.6 percent in 2001. Also, each federal government since 1961 has included at least one woman. Presently, five of the 15 federal ministers are women. Moreover, all state governments have ministers or commissioners for women's affairs, and nearly 1,500 municipalities have created "equality posts" for women.

Legislative change developed slowly, also. In 1958, the Act on Equal Rights for Men and Women introduced equal rights for women within the institution of marriage based on a division of roles ("housewife marriage model") and matrimonial property. Twenty years later, in 1977, the First Act to Reform the Marriage and Family Law eliminated the traditional marriage model. It legislated the partnership principle by ensuring equal rights for women in marriage and divorce. Further reform developed in 1994 with the Act to Amend the Law Relating to Family Names. It ensured the equality of men and women regarding the right to the use of a name. The law accords no unilateral preference to the man's family name. In addition, rape within the institution of marriage became a punishable offense in 1997.

Educational opportunities for females have improved greatly in Germany. More than half of the secondary students obtaining university entrance qualifications and over 43 percent of all students in higher education are women. The number of women completing a course in vocational training has increased sharply since the 1950s. With more education and equality, over 55 percent of the women in Germany between the ages of 15 and 65 have employment. Despite such success, women's groups still complain of discrimination. Women, they argue, tend to lose their jobs faster than men, find new ones less quickly, receive fewer apprenticeships, and receive lower wages than their male counterparts. By law, however, women can assert their claim of "equal pay for equal work" in court.

Women

Gender Empowerment Measure: 8
Seats Held in Parliament by Women %: 25.5
Female Administrators and Managers %: 25.8
Female Professional and Technical Workers %: 49.0
Women's Share of Earned Income %: 35
Women in Government %: 7

HEALTH, FOOD, AND NUTRITION

Health

Number of Physicians: 273,880
Number of Dentists: 60,616
Number of Nurses: 708,000
Number of Pharmacists: 44,696
Population per Physician: 298
Number of Hospitals: 2,354
Hospital Beds per 10,000: 77
Hospital Bed Occupancy Rate: 82.8
Infant Mortality Rate per 1,000 live births: 7
Maternal Mortality Rate per 100,000 live births: 22
Total Health Expenditures as % of GDP: 8.73
Health Expenditures per capita $: 1,511
HIV Infected % of adults: 0.08
Cigarette Consumption per smoker per year: 3,927
% of Smokers: Male: 73
Female: 22
Access to Safe Water %: 100

Food and Nutrition

Food Supply as % of FAO Requirements: 123
% of Consumption Expenditures on Food: 19
Daily Available Calories per capita: 3,265
% of Total Calories derived from:
Cereals: 20.9
Potatoes, cassava: 4.2
Meat, poultry: 11.3
Fish: 0.9
Eggs, milk: 10.4
Fruits, vegetables: 5.7
Fats, oils: 22.1`

ENVIRONMENT

The Federal Republic's environmental policy includes several areas of ecological concern to German society, which remains a world leader in this domain. Issues regarding water and air quality, noise reduction, energy use, and conservation of nature and resources find themselves affected by politics, economics, and industry.

As in other industrial countries, pollution emissions from factories, automobiles, heating systems, and power stations affect the atmosphere in Germany. Damage to forests provides clear evidence of this. In 1996, 37 percent of tree stocks were slightly damaged and 20 percent distinctly damaged by air pollution. Human health, the soil, lakes, rivers, buildings, and art monuments, also, are at risk. Germany, therefore, introduced a comprehensive clean-air program to check pollution sources through the use of filters, scrubbers, and catalytic converters. As a result, sulfur-dioxide emissions from industrial firing installations and power stations in the western states fell by more than 85 percent between 1980 and 1994, and nitrogen oxide emissions decreased by 65 percent.

Regarding water quality, tougher legislation and greater vision have achieved major improvements in protecting rivers, lakes, and seas. Policies on the discharge of wastewater as well as the public and private construction of new sewage treatment facilities have stemmed organic pollution of surface waters. In the 1970s, polluted rivers like the Rhine and Main had suffered major declines in the diversity of species. Today, because of new political thinking, they have nearly as many species as in the 1920s. Despite such improvements, many rivers and lakes, especially in the eastern states, need further cleaning.

As with air and water, soil now enjoys protection as an environmental medium. The federal government's Soil Protection Concept of 1985 formulated standards for the protection of this environmental medium for the very first time. Moreover, the Federal Soil Conservation Act of 1998 created the prerequisites for effective soil protection.

As a developed nation, Germany is dependent on a secure energy supply. This fact along with environmental concerns make it a hot topic. The discussion of the advantages and disadvantages of using fossil fuels (e.g., coal, oil, gas), renewable energy sources (e.g., solar, water, and wind power), or nuclear power for the generation of electricity is more than a verbal boxing match over appropriate energy sources. At issue are problems with implications for Germany, if not the world, such as the stability of the earth's climate and Germany's attractiveness as a location for business and industry. Germany, therefore, will devote top priority to developing renewable energy sources and energy conservation while it discontinues its reliance on nuclear energy, which is seen as wasteful and ecologically harmful.

Germany's attitude toward waste disposal represents a departure from traditional measures. It focuses on the concept of recycling so that raw materials and resources are effectively conserved and low-waste products are developed. The principle of product responsibility was legally established for the first time through the Packaging Ordinance, which obligates manufacturers and distributors of packaging materials to take back their products after use and recycle them. In 1992, businesses and industries joined to create the private sector Duales System Deutschland ("Green Dot"), which has assumed the job of collecting used packaging materials from consumers and recycling usable materials. The cost is included in the price of the product.

In an effort to combat the effects of radiation on humans, products, and the environment, Germany instituted several stringent laws. The Act on the Peaceful Utilization of Atomic Energy and the Protection against its Hazards (Atomic Energy Act), the Radiation Protection Ordinance, and the X-Ray Ordinance regulate the safe handling of ionizing rays. The guiding principle is to minimize radiation exposure as much as possible. After the reactor accident in Chernobyl, Germany adopted the Act on the Precautionary Protection of the Population against

Radiation Exposure. It created a nationwide early-warning system. This monitoring network supplies daily data on the presence of radioactivity in the environment in Germany at any time.

Environment

Forest Area sq km: 107,000
Average Annual Deforestation sq km: 0
Nationally Protected Areas as % of Total Land Area: 27.0
Freshwater Access cubic meters per capita: 2,169
Emissions of Organic Water Pollutants kg per day: 811,315
CO_2 Emissions per capita ton: 10.5

CHRONOLOGY

1949 The Federal Republic of Germany is born and enacts a new constitution called the Basic Law. The Deutsche Mark replaces the Reichsmark as the national currency. Economic Affairs Minister Ludwig Erhard lifts all price controls. Theodor Heuss is elected president, and Konrad Adenauer enters his first term as federal chancellor.

1951 Revision of the occupation statute grants the Federal Republic limited autonomy in foreign relations.

1954 The Treaty of Paris is signed between the occupying powers and the Federal Republic.

1955 The Hallstein Doctrine proclaims West Germany the sole representative of the German people and prohibits diplomatic relations with countries recognizing East Germany. Western occupation formally ends as West Germany enters NATO and is accepted as a sovereign state.

1956 The Bundestag accepts remilitarization and the creation of the Bundeswehr.

1957 West Germany joins the European Community (EC); the Saar joins West Germany.

1958 Soviets and East Germans close off land access to West Berlin; for the next three years the Allies airlift people and materials to the besieged city.

1959 Heinrich Lübke is elected second president of West Germany.

1961 East Germany constructs the Berlin Wall, sealing off East Berlin's inhabitants from contact with the West.

1963 West Germany signs a treaty of friendship with France. Following the *Der Spiegel* Affair which led to the dismissal of Defense Minister Franz Josef Strauss, Adenauer steps down and is succeeded as chancellor by Ludwig Erhard.

1966 Diplomatic relations are established with Romania, contrary to the Hallstein Doctrine. Ludwig Erhard yields chancellorship to Kurt-Georg Kiesinger, who enters into a Grand Coalition with the SPD and FDP.

1969 Following the CDU electoral reversal, the SPD and FDP join in a coalition government. Gustav Heinemann is elected West Germany's third president. Willy Brandt becomes chancellor.

1970 Brandt launches *Ostpolitik* treaties with East Germany and the Soviet Union, legitimizing the existing German boundaries.

1971 Four-power agreement is signed on Berlin.

1972 Munich Olympics is marred by terrorist kidnappings of Israeli athletes. Treaty on the Basis of Relations is signed with East Germany.

1973 West Germany and Czechoslovakia sign a peace treaty.

1974 Following a spy scandal, Brandt resigns and is succeeded by Helmut Schmidt of the SPD as chancellor. Walter Scheel is elected West Germany's fourth president.

1977 In a daring rescue operation, West German police free captives held by hijackers of a Lufthansa plane in Mogadishu, Somalia.

1979 Karl Carstens is elected West Germany's fifth president.

1982 The FDP leaves Schimdt's coalition government and joins with the CDU to form a new government, under Helmut Kohl.

1983 The CDU/FDP coalition is returned to power with a large majority in national elections.

1984 Richard von Weizsäcker is elected West Germany's sixth president.

1987 In national elections, the CDU suffers significant losses, but Kohl retains the chancellorship.

1989 The Berlin Wall is torn down in the wake of the collapse of the Honecker regime.

1990 East Germany and West Germany begin discussions on reunification, a process culminating with the monetary and political union of the two states. The German electorate chooses Helmut Kohl to be the first chancellor of a united Germany.

1991 Richard von Weizsäcker becomes the first Bundespräsident (federal president) of a united Germany and Germany's sixth overall. The first elected Bundestag of the unified Germany convenes and passes legislation making Berlin the new capital by 2000.

1992 With 2 million guest workers already, Germany accepts 450,000 asylum seekers, of which 27 percent come from the former Yugoslavia. This represents a 70 percent increase from the year before. The government registers nearly 2,500 attacks by right-wing extremists against foreigners.

1993 Germany becomes the final nation to ratify the Maastricht Treaty on the EU. It tightens asylum restrictions, which immediately decreases the number of asylum applications.

1994 National elections return the CDU/FDP coalition to power with a slim majority, allowing Chancellor

Kohl to return for his second term in the unified Germany and fourth overall. Russian and Allied troops complete their final withdrawal from Berlin. The German High Court rules that German military participation in UN peacekeeping missions outside of NATO is constitutional, thus removing a major impediment to Germany's bid for a permanent seat on the UN Security Council.

1995 Roman Herzog is elected as united Germany's second president and Germany's seventh overall. German courts charge seven former East German party officials with manslaughter, making them partly responsible in the "shoot-to-kill" orders issued to border guards.

1996 After five years, the Bundesrat finally resolves to follow the Bundestag to Berlin. Mounting financial strains from German unification and EU integration raise the unemployment rate to 11 percent, making it the highest level since World War II. Under protest from unions and the SPD, Chancellor Kohl announces a plan to reduce welfare benefits in order to bring the German economy into line with the strict criteria for EU monetary union set for 1999.

1997 The German unemployment rate rises to 13 percent, forcing 5 million people out of work, exacerbating Germany's ability to meet EU monetary qualifications. Germany and the Czech Republic sign treaties of joint apology for misdeeds executed during WW II.

1998 The SPD and Bündnis '90/Die Grünen win in the national elections making Gerhard Schröder united Germany's second chancellor and Germany's seventh overall.

1999 Johannes Rau is elected as united Germany's second president and Germany's eighth overall. Former chancellor Helmut Kohl and others are accused of a campaign finance scandal.

2000 Germany and the nuclear industry come to a social consensus regarding the phasing-out of nuclear energy by 2032. Kohl is forced to resign as the CDU's honorary chairman.

2002 Germany adopts the euro as its national currency.

BIBLIOGRAPHY

Berg-Schlosser, Dirk, and Ralf Rytleewski. *Political Culture in Germany.* New York, 1993.

Berghahn, Volker Rolf. *Modern Germany: Society, Economy and Politics in the Twentieth Century.* New York, 1987.

Beyme, Klaus von. *The Political System of the Federal Republic of Germany*. New York, 1983.

Burdick, Charles. *Contemporary Germany: Politics and Culture.* Boulder, Colo., 1984.

Carr, William A. *A History of Germany, 1815–1985.* London, 1991.

Childs, David. *Germany in the Twentieth Century.* New York, 1991.

Gortemaker, Manfred. *Unifying Germany, 1989–90.* New York, 1994.

Gutjahr, Lothar. *German Foreign and Defense Policy after Unification.* New York, 1994.

Huellshoff, Michael G., Andrei S. Markovits, and Simon Reich. *From Bundesrepublik to Deutschland: German Politics after Unification.* Ann Arbor, Mich., 1993.

James, Harold. *German Identity, 1770–1990.* New York, 1989.

Koch, Hanndjoachim. *A Constitutional History of Germany in the Nineteenth and Twentieth Centuries.* New York, 1984.

McAdams, A. James. *Germany Divided: From the Wall to Reunification.* Princeton, N.J., 1993.

Smith, Gordon. *Developments in German Politics.* Durham, N.C., 1992.

Turner, Henry Ashby, Jr. *The Two Germanies since 1945.* New Haven, Conn., 1987.

OFFICIAL PUBLICATIONS

Germany. *Statistisches Jahrbuch für die Bundesrepublik Deutschland; Volkszahlung vom 25. Mai 1987* (Census of Population).

CONTACT INFORMATION

Embassy of Germany
4645 Reservoir Road NW
Washington, D.C. 20007
Phone: (202) 298-8141 Fax: (202) 298-4249

INTERNET RESOURCES

- Federal Statistical Office of Germany
  http://www.statistik-bund.de/e_home.htm

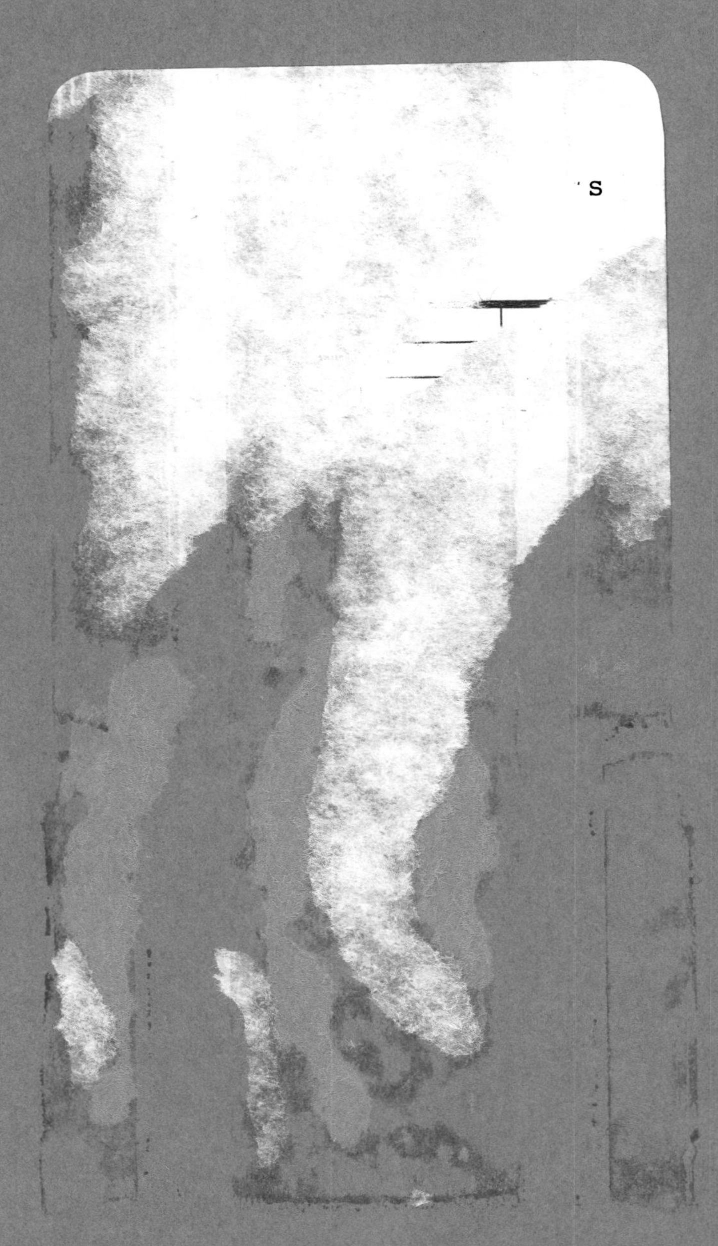